D1329659

The Series of Republished
Articles on Economics
VOLUME XII

Readings in

WELFARE

Selected by a Committee of

The American Economic Association

*The participation of the American Economic Association
in the presentation of this series consists in the
appointment of a committee to determine the subjects
of the volumes and of special committees to select
the articles for each volume.*

ECONOMICS

Selection Committee for This Volume

KENNETH J. ARROW
TIBOR SCITOVSKY

1969

Published for the Association by
RICHARD D. IRWIN, INC., HOMEWOOD, ILLINOIS
Irwin-Dorsey Limited, Nobleton, Ontario

First Printing, January, 1969

Library of Congress Catalog Card No. 68—30847

Printed in the United States of America

Table of contents

v

General introduction

If economics can be described, as it often has been, as the theory of choice, of entrepreneurs' and consumers' choices and their implications, then welfare economics is the theory of how and by what criteria economists and policy-makers make or ought to make their choices between alternative policies and between good and bad institutions. To the superficial observer, modern economics in its beginnings may have seemed like uncritical admiration of the work of the invisible hand of competition and a mere endorsement of the philosophy of laissez faire. Thoughtful economists, however, have always shown great critical discernment and attention to detail, hailing some, deploring other, consequences of competition, exercising choice, advocating policies, and so practicing welfare economics.

Recently, welfare economics has greatly increased in importance. The increased rigor of modern economics has affected this branch of the discipline most profoundly. Economists want to know exactly what they are after, what is the meaning, the limitations, and the importance of economic efficiency and economic progress. Moreover, the economist's better understanding of the nature of economic processes, his growing desire to control and influence factors once considered God-given or outside the realm of rational calculation, the growth of the public sector, and our ever-greater reliance on policy have also contributed to rendering this branch of economics increasingly important. It was not too long ago that the American Economic Association first considered publishing a volume of readings on welfare economics but decided against it for lack of interest and material. Today this is one of the fattest volumes in the series and we were hard put to avoid making it fatter still. This same trend is expressed also in terms of the revealed preference of the profession—the subclass " Welfare Economics " in the *Index of Economic Journals* has grown from one column in the first volume to nine columns in the last (sixth) volume that itself is only twice as large.

In the selection of articles for this volume we were guided by a multiplicity of aims. We had originally hoped to cover all the topics considered important and properly belonging to welfare economics, to include all the papers that made significant advances in their time, to reprint or translate contributions especially difficult to find in translation, and to present the theory in its most up-to-date form. These perhaps overambitious aims had to be severely compromised in the end, owing mainly to limitations of space but also to the

1

difficulty of including excerpts from books and to the fortunate circumstance that several of the French papers originally selected have since appeared in excellent translation in a volume edited by J. R. Nelson, *Marginal Cost Pricing in Practice*.[1] We were least willing to sacrifice breadth of coverage; for its sake some of the most distinguished names of welfare economics could not be represented in this volume.

Part I, *Foundations*, contains the articles that deal with the basic concepts, problems, approaches, and limitations of welfare economics, and one that tries to extend its scope. They may serve as an introduction to what welfare economics is about and what it can accomplish, as well as a warning about what it is not. This latter is not as negative as it sounds; it merely indicates the direction in which the subject might or ought to expand. In the sciences, systematization, the laying of foundations, usually comes after much of the superstructure is already standing, and economics is no exception.

The next three parts deal with what are known as the limitations and failures of the competitive market economy. Modern economics developed more or less as the rationalization of the laissez-faire economy, hence its preoccupation with the private sector and the operation of the market in the private sector. The present great importance of the public sector of the economy dates back only to World War II; and even more recent is the theoretical exploration of its problems: decision making in the public sector, the aggregation of individual preferences relating to collective or indivisible goods, and the problem of collective choice in general. This new branch of welfare economics constitutes Part II under the heading *Political Aspects of Welfare Economics*. It is the nature of the choice and its method of resolution that are political; the issues themselves are economic as well as political.

The next part, *Social versus Private Costs and Benefits*, deals with a problem of the private sector: the failure of market prices properly to reflect social costs and benefits, and of market decisions based on such prices to result in efficient allocation even under ideal competitive conditions. The first and most important exploration of the causes and nature of such failure is contained, of course, in Pigou's *Economics of Welfare*.[2] We assembled merely some of the improvements and advances made since Pigou's work.

Part IV deals with another cause of the failure of competitive market decisions to be the best decisions—*Increasing Returns*. These, whether because of indivisibilities or anything else, can lead to wrong market decisions, not because the rule of marginal-cost pricing is misleading but because it can be unfeasible or unprofitable. Since this was among the earliest problems of welfare economics, it is fitting that the earliest article included in the present volume should be under this heading; it is equally fitting that this should be a French article, because France is the country where the public sector and public policy for the public welfare were never lost sight of.

---

[1] (Englewood Cliffs, N. J.: Prentice-Hall, 1964.)
[2] (4th ed.; London: Macmillan, 1952.)

Part V, *The Measurement of Welfare*, contains once again modern developments, considering that interest in measurement is of recent vintage. The "new" welfare economics of the 1930's is included here by virtue of its attempt to develop a measure for comparing alternative states, and so are attempts to measure nonmonetary costs and benefits, welfare losses due to imperfection, and changes in real income. Measurement has both contributed to and been called for by the modern economist's realistic acceptance of an imperfect world with its less-than-optimal economic organization. Measurement of the loss, or at least of the order of magnitude of the loss, owing to suboptimality must have contributed to its intellectual acceptance; and if the economist is to be something more than a preacher of optimality and market perfection, his policy recommendation in an imperfect, suboptimal world must mostly be based on the measurement of its costs and hoped-for gains.

Part VI, *Taxes and Prices*, contains the papers that appraise alternatives in an imperfect world, seek the least objectionable of equally odious measures, deal with the second best where the first best is unattainable, and discuss the problems of public enterprise in a mixed economy. It is here that welfare economics comes closest to descending from its ivory tower and making itself useful for the practical conduct of practical affairs.

The final part, *Investment and Growth*, contains applications of the welfare criterion partly to the dynamic problems of resource allocation over time, partly to the special problems of resource allocation within the investment sector.

We are aware, as welfare economists especially are aware, of the impossibility of pleasing everybody with our choice of papers and topics. An early request to a group of colleagues for advice about what to include brought not only great help, which we gratefully acknowledge, but it also disclosed individual preferences far too divergent to aggregate into a transitive social preference ordering. The final choice is necessarily ours, but we want to express our regret for our inability to include sections on income distribution, socialist economics, and such newly emerging topics as the economics of education and medical care. In view of the availability of the *Index of Economic Journals*, we decided to follow the example R. A. Gordon and L. R. Klein set in their A.E.A. *Readings in Business Cycles* by not including a bibliography. It is true that the *Index* contains only English-language articles, but the contribution of foreign-language papers to welfare economics did not seem to us important enough to justify a separate bibliography. Besides, a good select bibliography for the 1939–59 period has recently been published as part of E. J. Mishan's excellent "A Survey of Welfare Economics, 1939–1959."[3]

---

[3] In *Surveys of Economic Theory* (London: Macmillan) and (New York: St. Martin's, 1965), Vol. I, pp. 154–222.

Part I
FOUNDATIONS

The papers assembled in this part fall into two categories—abstract, technical contributions to the concepts, methods, and analytic approach of welfare ecomonics, and commonsense warnings that the framework of the subject as well as the economist's customary universe of discourse are too narrow and leave out much that contributes the most to man's welfare, even to his economic welfare. In language, approach, and level of abstraction the two sets of papers could hardly be more different; yet they belong together because the former explain what welfare economics is and the latter what it is not, but what, perhaps, it ought to be. Welfare economics is a growing subject, and in what direction it should grow and what topics and issues it should encompass are among its fundamental questions.

The modern emphasis on rigor, on the careful definition of concepts and clarification of their nature and limitations, is nowhere more evident than in the first set of papers in this part. Bergson's paper contains the first complete and rigorous statement of the conditions of the welfare optimum and the definition of a social welfare function. It also contains a useful and generous summary of previous work in the field.

Lange's paper remains, after more than 25 years, the most elegant and compact statement of the necessary conditions for optimal resource allocation under various alternative definitions of optimality. However, mathematical limitations restrict the generality of Lange's exposition; thus, there is no place for corner equilibria (in which some goods may not be produced at all so that marginal rates of substitution for the producer need not equal the corresponding marginal rates for the consumer). Also, Lange did not explain carefully the distinction between necessary and sufficient conditions. Under the postwar influence of the development of nonlinear programming, these deficiencies were remedied by several authors. Debreu's paper gives the most general results, at least for an economy without increasing returns; use is made of advanced mathematical tools.

Harsanyi has linked up Bergson's concept of a social welfare function with

5

the modern theory of choice under uncertainty. Daniel Bernoulli[1] had, as long ago as 1738, advanced the hypothesis that rational behavior under uncertainty could be described as the maximization of the mathematical expectation of utility. Frank Ramsey,[2] in 1926 (published in 1931) and, independently, John von Neumann and Oskar Morgenstern,[3] in 1944, had shown that if rational behavior under uncertainty were regarded as characterized by certain reasonable-sounding axioms, then Bernoulli's hypothesis could be deduced as a theorem. Harsanyi has shown that if both society and its members are regarded as rational in this sense and if social welfare is simply some function of individual utilities, then it can be demonstrated that social welfare must in fact be a sum of individual utilities.

Any economic system in the modern world is necessarily complex; in particular, information about the different parts of the economy is necessarily dispersed. In the debates about the possibility of socialism in the 1920's and 1930's, several writers, particularly Friedrich von Hayek, stressed the problems raised for central planning by the need for information and the costs of acquiring it. The most careful and rigorous statement of the problem and some studies of decentralized mechanisms for achieving optimal allocation with minimal informational demands are to be found in Hurwicz's paper in this section.

In the second category of papers, Radomysler and Hicks stress the narrowness of traditional welfare economics and warn against the aridity into which it might too easily fall. Hicks argues that our increasing affluence renders wealth relatively unimportant; de Jouvenel discusses the other things that increasing affluence is rendering relatively more important, dealing with many interesting issues neglected when economic progress is defined and measured by too simple a yardstick. In the past, the major achievement of welfare economics has been to provide a rigorous framework for what seemed too vague and elusive and to create a measuring rod for what was thought nonmeasurable. This paper is a welcome reminder that we have a long way to go yet in that direction, and that the things measured are not, by that fact alone, more important than those we have not yet succeeded in measuring.

---

[1] "Specimen theoriae novae de mensura sortis," *Commentarii Academiae Scientiarum Imperiales Petropolitanae* 5 (1738), 175–92. English translation by L. Sommer, "Exposition of a New Theory on the Measurement of Risk," *Econometrica* 12(1954), 23–36.

[2] "Truth and Probability," pp. 156–98, in F. P. Ramsey, *The Foundations of Mathematics and Other Logical Essays* (London: K. Paul, Trench, Trubner, and Co., 1931).

[3] *Theory of Games and Economic Behavior* (Princeton, N. J.: Princeton University Press, 1944).

A reformulation of certain aspects of welfare economics[*]

ABRAM BERGSON

The object of this paper is to state in a precise form the value judgments required for the derivation of the conditions of maximum economic welfare which have been advanced in the studies of the Cambridge economists,[1] Pareto and Barone, and Mr. Lerner.[2] Such a formulation, I hope, will clarify certain aspects of the contribution of these writers and at the same time provide a basis for a more precise understanding of the principles of welfare.

I shall develop my analysis under a set of assumptions which in certain respects differ from those introduced in the welfare studies. It will be assumed throughout the discussion that the amounts of all the factors of production, other than labor, are fixed and, for convenience, nondepreciating. While a variable capital supply is included in some of the welfare studies, this is not a well-developed part of the analysis, and for present purposes it will be desirable to confine to the simpler case the discussion of the evaluations required,[3] I shall assume, also, that the variables involved in the analysis—the

[*] *Quarterly Journal of Economics*, 52 (1938): pp. 310–34. Chapter 1 in *Essays in Normative Economics* (Cambridge, Mass.: Harvard University Press, 1966), pp. 3–26. Slightly edited from original published version in the *Quarterly Journal of Economics*, February, 1938. Reprinted by courtesy of the author and Harvard University Press.

[1] I use this caption to designate those economists whose names are directly attached to the Cambridge School—Marshall, Professor Pigou, Mr. Kahn—as well as others, such as Edgeworth, whose welfare analysis is in all essentials the same as that of the Cambridge group. But in the course of my discussion I shall refer mainly to the studies of the first group of economists. This will ease my task considerably, and, I believe, will involve no loss of generality.

[2] The studies referred to are Alfred Marshall, *Principles of Economics* (all references to the third—London, 1895—edition); A. C. Pigou, *Economics of Welfare* (all references to the fourth—London, 1932—edition); R. F. Kahn, "Notes on Ideal Output," *Economic Journal*, March 1935; Vilfredo Pareto, *Cours d'Economie Politique* (all references to the Lausanne—1897—edition); Enrico Barone, "The Ministry of Production in a Socialist State" (translated from the Italian article of the same title in *Giornale degli Economisti*, 1908; the translation appearing in F. A. von Hayek, ed., *Collectivist Economic Planning*, London, 1935); and A. P. Lerner, "The Concept of Monopoly and the Measurement of Monopoly Power," *Review of Economic Studies*, June 1934, and A. P. Lerner, "Economic Theory and Socialist Economy," *Review of Economic Studies*, October 1934.

[3] On a simple model, similar to that of Barone, the analysis may be extended to the case of a variable capital supply.

amounts of the various commodities consumed and services performed—are infinitesimally divisible. This assumption will be interpreted more strictly than is usually done; otherwise it is the postulate of the welfare writers, and its introduction here will involve no significant departure from their analyses. Finally, I shall assume that there are only two kinds of consumers' goods, two kinds of labor, and two factors of production other than labor in the community, and that each commodity is produced, with labor and the other factors, in a single production unit. This assumption is introduced only to simplify the notation employed. The discussion will apply, with no modification, to the many-commodity, many-factor, and many-production unit case.[4]

THE MAXIMUM CONDITIONS IN GENERAL

Among the elements affecting the welfare of the community during any given period of time are the amounts of each of the factors of production, other than labor, employed in the different production units, the amounts of the various commodities consumed, the amounts of the different kinds of work done, and the production unit for which this work is performed by each individual in the community during that period of time. If we use A and B to denote the two kinds of labor; C and D to denote the two factors of production other than labor; and X and Y to denote the two consumers' goods; we may express this relationship in the form

$$W = W(x_1, y_1, a_1^x, b_1^x, a_1^y, b_1^y, \ldots,$$
$$x_n, y_n, a_n^x, b_n^x, a_n^y, b_n^y, C^x, D^x, C^y, D^y, r, s, t, \ldots). \quad (1)$$

Here C^x and D^x are the amounts of the nonlabor factors of production C and D employed in the production unit producing the consumers' good X; C^y and D^y are the amounts of these factors employed in the production unit producing the consumers' good Y; x_i and y_i are the amounts of X and Y consumed by the ith individual; and a_i^x, b_i^x, a_i^y, and b_i^y are the amounts of each kind of work performed by him for each production unit during the given period of time.[5] The symbols $r, s, t, \ldots$, denote elements other than the amounts of commodities, the amounts of work of each type, and the amounts of the nonlabor factors in each of the production units—elements affecting the welfare of the community.

Some of the elements $r, s, t, \ldots$, may affect welfare, not only directly, but indirectly through their effect on (say) the amounts of X and Y produced with any given amount of resources—for example, the effects of a change in

---

[4] The assumption that each commodity is produced in one production unit, it is true, excludes an element of "external economies" from the analysis. But in the present essay I am interested only in the maximum conditions for the community's welfare, and not in the departures from the maximum under a given institutional setup. To the extent that in the many-production unit case there are external economies, these will require no modification in the maximum conditions I shall present, for these conditions relate only to marginal *social* value productivities.

[5] I am assuming that an individual's labor time may be divided among the different types of work in any desired proportions.

the weather. On the other hand, it is conceivable that variations in the amounts of commodities, the amounts of work of each type, and the amounts of non-labor factors in each of the production units also will have a direct and indirect effect on welfare; as, for instance, a sufficient diminution of x_i and y_i may be accompanied by an overturn of the government. But, for relatively small changes in these variables, other elements in welfare, I believe, will not be significantly affected. To the extent that this is so, a partial analysis is feasible.

I shall designate the function,

$$E = E(x_1, y_1, a_1^x, b_1^x, a_1^y, b_1^y, \ldots,$$
$$x_n, y_n, a_n^x, b_n^x, a_n^y, b_n^y, C^x, D^x, C^y, D^y), \tag{2}$$

which is obtained by taking $r, s, t, \ldots$, in (1) as given, the Economic Welfare Function.[6]

Let us write the amounts of X and Y produced respectively by the X and Y production units as functions,

$$X = X(A^x, B^x, C^x, D^x); \qquad Y = Y(A^y, B^y, C^y, D^y), \tag{3}$$

where A^x and B^x are the amounts of the two kinds of labor and C^x and D^x are the amounts of the other two factors of production employed in the X production unit; and A^y, B^y, C^y, D^y are defined similarly for the Y production unit.

If we assume that E varies continuously with $x_1, y_1, \ldots$, we may write as a general condition for a position of maximum economic welfare that, subject to the limitations of the given technique of production and the given amounts of resources,

$$dE = 0. \tag{4}$$

Equation (4) requires that in the neighborhood of the maximum position any small adjustment will leave the welfare of the community unchanged. By use of (3) and (4) it is possible immediately to state in general terms the conditions for a maximum welfare.[7]

One group of maximum conditions relates to the consumption and supply of services by each individual in the community. They require that the marginal welfare of each commodity and the marginal economic diswelfare of each type of work be the same with respect to each individual in the community.[8] If we denote the marginal economic welfare of commodity X with

---

[6] It should be emphasized that in (2) other factors affecting welfare are taken as given. I do *not* assume that economic welfare is an independent element which may be added to other welfare to get total welfare.

[7] The conditions I shall develop in this section are a group of necessary conditions for a maximum. They are also the conditions for any critical point, and are sufficient in number to determine the location of such a point (or points) if there is one. Below, pp. 22ff, I consider the problem of determining whether a given critical point is a maximum or not.

[8] This rather awkward terminology is adopted instead of, say, the phrase "marginal economic welfare *of* the *i*th individual" in order to include the possibility that an increment of X or Y given to the *i*th individual will affect the welfare of others.

respect to the ith individual, $\partial E/\partial x_i$, and of Y, $\partial E/\partial y_i$, the first group of these conditions requires that, for all i, and for some p, q, and ω,

$$\frac{\partial E}{\partial x_i} = \omega p \tag{5}$$

and

$$\frac{\partial E}{\partial y_i} = \omega q. \tag{6}$$

Similarly, if we denote the marginal economic diswelfare of the various types of work with respect to the ith individual $\partial E/\partial a_i^x$, $\partial E/\partial b_i^x$, $\partial E/\partial a_i^y$, $\partial E/\partial b_i^y$, the second group of these conditions requires that, for all i and for some g^x, h^x, g^y, h^y, and for the ω already chosen,

$$-\frac{\partial E}{\partial a_i^x} = \omega g^x, \tag{7}$$

$$-\frac{\partial E}{\partial a_i^y} = \omega g^y, \tag{8}$$

$$-\frac{\partial E}{\partial b_i^x} = \omega h^x, \tag{9}$$

$$-\frac{\partial E}{\partial b_i^y} = \omega h^y. \tag{10}$$

The minus signs and the multiplicative factor ω are inserted in these equations for convenience.

The remaining maximum conditions relate to production. They require that the economic welfare of the consumers' goods produced by a marginal increment of each type of work should equal the negative of the diswelfare of that increment of work, and that the increment of economic welfare due to the shift of a marginal unit of factors C and D from one production unit to another should equal the negative of the diswelfare caused by this adjustment. Using the notation $\partial X/\partial A^x$ for the marginal productivity of A^x, and a similar notation for the other marginal productivities, we may write these conditions in the form

$$p \frac{\partial X}{\partial A^x} = g^x, \tag{11}$$

$$q \frac{\partial Y}{\partial A^y} = g^y, \tag{12}$$

$$p \frac{\partial X}{\partial B^x} = h^x, \tag{13}$$

$$q \frac{\partial Y}{\partial B^y} = h^y, \tag{14}$$

and

$$\omega \left(p \frac{\partial X}{\partial C^x} - q \frac{\partial Y}{\partial C^y} \right) = - \left(\frac{\partial E}{\partial C^x} - \frac{\partial E}{\partial C^y} \right), \tag{15}$$

$$\omega \left(p \frac{\partial X}{\partial D^x} - q \frac{\partial Y}{\partial D^y} \right) = - \left(\frac{\partial E}{\partial D^x} - \frac{\partial E}{\partial D^y} \right). \tag{16}$$

In equations (11) through (14), ω, which was present in all terms, has been divided out.[9] The derivatives on the right-hand sides of (15) and (16) indicate the effect on welfare of an adjustment in C or D for which all other elements— x^i, y^i, etc.—in welfare are constant. Such an effect would arise, for example, through a positive or negative evaluation of the relative amounts and kinds of "factory smoke" emitted in the two production units for varying amounts of one or the other factors employed in each unit.

It will be convenient to designate p the *price* of X; q the *price* of Y; and g^x, g^y, h^x, h^y, the *wages*, respectively, of the types of work A^x, A^y, B^x, B^y. Equations (5) and (6) thus require that the marginal economic welfare per "dollar's worth" of each commodity, $\partial E/\partial x_i \cdot 1/p$ and $\partial E/\partial y_i \cdot 1/q$, be the same for each commodity and for all individuals in the community. Similarly, equations (7) through (10) require that the marginal economic diswelfare per "dollar's worth" of each kind of work be the same with respect to each kind of work and each individual in the community; equations (11) through (14) require that the wages of each type of labor should equal the marginal value productivity of that type of labor,[10] and with an analogous interpretation, equations (15) and (16) require that the marginal value productivity equal the cost due to a shift in C or D from one use to another.

MAXIMUM CONDITIONS IN DIFFERENT ANALYSES

The maximum conditions just presented are the general conditions for a position of maximum economic welfare for any Economic Welfare Function. The maximum conditions presented in the welfare studies relate to a particular family of welfare functions. Their derivation thus requires the introduction of restrictions on the shape of the Economic Welfare Function presented here. Three groups of value propositions suffice for this purpose.

I shall designate the various maximum conditions derived by the names

---

[9] Strictly speaking, this procedure assumes a value proposition, which we shall introduce later, to the effect that ω is unequal to zero.

[10] In the present essay it will be understood that all value productivities are *social* value productivities. Compare n. 4 above.

of those writers, or groups of writers, who have been especially responsible for their elucidation. For reasons which will appear I have altered somewhat the content of the conditions, and there are differences in the analyses of the various writers which must also be noted. The latter differences will be pointed out in this section and in the one following.

The Lerner Conditions. The First Group of Value Propositions: *a shift in a unit of any factor of production, other than labor, from one production unit to another would leave economic welfare unchanged, provided the amounts of all the other elements in welfare were constant.*

The First Group of Value Propositions enables us to state certain of the maximum conditions in terms of the production functions alone. From these evaluations the right-hand side of (15) and of (16) must equal zero. To refer again to the example mentioned above, the net effect on the community's welfare of the "factory smoke" arising from a shift of the nonlabor factors from one use to another is taken as zero. The two equations thus may be written

$$p\frac{\partial X}{\partial C^x} = q\frac{\partial Y}{\partial C^y}, \tag{17}$$

$$p\frac{\partial X}{\partial D^x} = q\frac{\partial Y}{\partial D^y}, \tag{18}$$

and they now impose the condition that the marginal value productivity of factors other than labor be the same in every use.

Equations (17) and (18) still contain the variables p and q, which involve derivatives of the Economic Welfare Function. If we combine (17) and (18), however, we have two equations,

$$\frac{q}{p} = \frac{\partial X}{\partial C^x} \bigg/ \frac{\partial Y}{\partial C^y} = \frac{\partial X}{\partial D^x} \bigg/ \frac{\partial Y}{\partial D^y}, \tag{19}$$

the second of which involves only the derivatives of the production functions. It requires that in the maximum position the ratio of the marginal productivity of a factor in one use to its marginal productivity in any other use be the same for all factors of production, other than labor. The first equation of (19) requires that all these ratios equal the price ratio.

The significance of (19) for the determination of maximum welfare may be expressed in the following manner: whatever the relative evaluations of commodity X and commodity Y, that is, in Barone's terminology, whatever their ratio of equivalence, (19) requires that in the maximum position, given that one factor C is so distributed that a small shift from one production unit to another would alter the amounts of X and Y in such a manner as to leave welfare unchanged—that is, given that C is so distributed that $(\partial X/\partial C^x)/(\partial Y/\partial C^y)$ equals the ratio of equivalence of the two commodities, then the

other factors in order to be so distributed must have a ratio of marginal productivities equal to $(\partial X/\partial C^x)/(\partial Y/\partial C^y)$.

The condition (19) can also be interpreted in another manner, which, however, does not bring out as directly the significance of the condition for a
position of maximum *welfare*. The equality of the marginal productivity ratios
implies that there is no possible further adjustment for which the amount of
one commodity will be increased without that of another being reduced. A
shift in one factor from X to Y can at best be just compensated by a shift of
another from Y to X, if (19) is satisfied.[11]

The Pareto-Barone-Cambridge Conditions. The Fundamental Value Propositions of Individual Preference: *if the amounts of the various commodities
and types of work were constant for all individuals in the community except any
ith individual, and if the ith individual consumed the various commodities and
performed the various types of work in combinations which were indifferent to
him, economic welfare would be constant.*

The First Group of Value Propositions, which were set forth previously,
imply that under the assumption that the amounts of the factors of production
other than labor are constant, the Economic Welfare Function may be
written as

$$E = E(x_1, y_1, a_1^x, b_1^x, a_1^y, b_1^y, \ldots, x_n, y_n, a_n^x, b_n^x, a_n^y, b_n^y). \qquad (20)$$

For from these propositions a shift in C or D from one production unit to
another would have no effect on welfare, if all the other elements were constant. The Fundamental Value Propositions require that E be some function
of the form

$$E = E[(S^1(x_1, y_1, a_1^x, b_1^x, a_1^y, b_1^y), \ldots,$$
$$S^n(x_n, y_n, a_n^x, b_n^x, a_n^y, b_n^y)], \qquad (21)$$

where the function

$$S^i = S^i(x_i, y_i, a_i^x, b_i^x, a_i^y, b_i^y) \qquad (22)$$

---

[11] Mr. Lerner, as far as I am aware, is the only economist to present (17) and (18) in the
form of (19), his interpretation being the second of the two alternatives I have noted. In
the studies of Pareto, Barone, and Marshall the conditions (17) and (18) are presented with
the price ratios already equated to the individual marginal rates of substitution (see below).
In the studies of Professor Pigou and Mr. Kahn the procedure is the same as that of Pareto,
Barone, and Marshall, except that Pigou and Kahn include in their analysis the possibility of
departures from (17) and (18) due to aspects such as "factory smoke."

Mr. Lerner advances the conditions (19) for all factors of production, labor as well as
nonlabor (*Review of Economic Studies*, October 1934, p. 57). On the face of the matter this
formulation is inconsistent with Mr. Lerner's own advocacy of the supremacy of individual
tastes in the sphere of consumption, and I have therefore taken the liberty to modify his
conditions accordingly. The other economists also do not allow in their analysis for individual preferences as between employment in different units, as distinct from different kinds of
labor.

expresses the loci of combinations of commodities consumed and work performed which are indifferent to the ith individual.

The Fundamental Value Propositions enable us to restate all the consumption and labor supply conditions in terms of the individual indifference functions, S^i. The conditions must be expressed, however, relatively to some one of them, say (5). Thus consider the equation

$$\frac{\partial E}{\partial x_i} \bigg/ \frac{\partial E}{\partial y_i} = \frac{p}{q}, \tag{23}$$

obtained from (5) and (6) by division. Using the Fundamental Value Propositions,

$$\frac{\partial E}{\partial x_i} \bigg/ \frac{\partial E}{dy_i} = \frac{\partial E}{\partial S^i}\frac{\partial S^i}{\partial x_i} \bigg/ \frac{\partial E}{\partial S^i}\frac{\partial S^i}{\partial y_i} = \frac{\partial S^i}{\partial x_i} \bigg/ \frac{\partial S^i}{\partial y_i}. \tag{24}$$

The last ratio in (24) represents the slope of the indifference locus of the ith individual or, in the Hicks and Allen terminology, the marginal rate of substitution of commodity Y for commodity X.[12] Thus (23) requires that the marginal rate of substitution of the two commodities be the same for all individuals. By successively combining (5) with equations (7) through (10), a similar result is obtained with respect to the other elements of welfare.

All the production conditions may now be stated in terms of the indifference functions and the production functions. For equations (11) through (14), the statement that the wage of each type of work should equal its marginal value productivity may be interpreted to mean that the marginal product of a given type of work employed in producing a given commodity should equal the marginal rate of substitution of that commodity for that type of work. In the same manner, conditions (19) not only require that the ratios of marginal productivities of the various factors other than labor be equal, but that these ratios should equal the marginal rate of substitution of the two commodities.

The Fundamental Value Propositions thus require that, whatever the ratios of equivalence between the various commodities and types of work, given that the types of work performed and commodities consumed by one individual are so fixed that for any small adjustment among them economic welfare is unchanged—that is, given that the marginal rates of substitution and marginal productivities for this individual equal the respective ratios of equivalence—then for all other individuals to be similarly situated, their marginal rates of substitution must be the same as those of this individual.

---

[12] See J. R. Hicks and R. G. D. Allen, "A Reconsideration of the Theory of Value," *Economica*, February 1934.

Under our implicit assumption of homogeneous factors, the respective marginal productivities, of course, must in any case be equal for all individuals.

Again, the Fundamental Value Propositions may be interpreted also to mean that in the maximum position it is impossible to improve the situation of any one individual without rendering another worse off.[13]

The Cambridge Conditions. Let us designate

$$m_i = px_i + qy_i - g^x a_i^x - h^x b_i^x - g^y a_i^y - h^y b_i^y, \tag{25}$$

the Share of the ith individual. In (25), p, q, etc., are taken proportional to the respective marginal rates of substitution of individuals. Thus m^i is defined, aside from a proportionality factor. The sum of m^i for the community as a whole is equal to the difference between the total wages and the total value of consumers' goods in the community.

The Propositions of Equal Shares: *If the Shares of any ith and kth individuals were equal, and if the prices and wage rates were fixed, the transfer of a small amount of the Share of i to k would leave welfare unchanged.*

The Propositions of Equal Shares enable us to state in terms of the distribution of Shares the remaining condition (5) to which we related consumption and labor supply conditions in order to reformulate them in terms of individual indifference functions (above, p. 13). According to the Propositions of Equal Shares, if the Shares of i and k are equal, then for the given price-wage situation,

$$dE = \frac{\partial E}{\partial m_i} dm_i + \frac{\partial E}{\partial m_k} dm_k = 0, \tag{26}$$

for $dm_i = -dm_k$. Equation (26) is equivalent to the condition imposed by (5), that the marginal economic welfare per " dollar's worth " of X is the same for

---

[13] The Pareto-Barone-Cambridge Conditions are developed by Marshall in the *Principles* (pp. 413–15, 526–27; Appendix XIV), but the derivation of the production conditions is based upon the very simple illustrative assumption of a producer-consumer expending his capital and labor in such a manner as to maximize his utility. Under more general assumptions the conditions are developed, without the utility calculus used by Marshall, by Pareto (*Cours*, I, pp. 20ff, II, pp. 90ff.) and Barone (" Ministry of Production "), and with the utility calculus, by Professor Pigou (*Economics of Welfare*, particularly pp. 131–43) and Mr. Kahn (*Economic Journal*, March 1935). All of these writers either develop the consumption conditions independently of their formulation of the production conditions (Marshall, Pareto) or assume the consumption conditions *ab initio* (Barone, Pigou, Kahn); and, as we shall indicate, the interpretations vary. Mr. Lerner in his study in the *Review of Economic Studies*, June 1934, presents all the conditions together and interprets them most lucidly in the second of the two senses I have pointed out.

As I have noted elsewhere (n. 11), none of these writers includes in his analysis individual preferences between production units. Also, Professor Pigou and Mr. Kahn include the possiblity of departures from (19), and perhaps from (11), (12), (13), (14), for the direct effects on welfare of shifts of the factors of production from one use to another.

i and k.[14] Thus, if the Shares of all individuals are equal, the condition (5) is satisfied.[15]

The three groups of value propositions are not only sufficient for the derivation of the maximum conditions presented in the welfare studies; they are necessary for this procedure. For it is possible, and I shall leave the development of the argument to the reader, to deduce from the maximum conditions presented the restriction imposed upon the Economic Welfare Function by the value judgments introduced.

But it should be noted that the particular value judgments I have stated are not necessary to the welfare analysis. They are essential only for the establishment of a particular group of maximum conditions. If the production functions and individual indifference functions are known, they provide

---

[14] The proof is as follows:

$$\frac{\partial E}{\partial m_i} = \frac{\partial E}{\partial x_i}\frac{\partial x_i}{\partial m_i} + \frac{\partial E}{\partial y_i}\frac{\partial y_i}{\partial m_i} + \frac{\partial E}{\partial a_i^x}\frac{\partial a_i^x}{\partial m_i} + \frac{\partial E}{\partial b_i^x}\frac{\partial b_i^x}{\partial m_i} + \frac{\partial E}{\partial a_i^y}\frac{\partial a_i^y}{\partial m_i} + \frac{\partial E}{\partial b_i^y}\frac{\partial b_i^y}{\partial m_i}.$$

By (25),

$$1 = p\frac{\partial x_i}{\partial m_i} + q\frac{\partial y_i}{\partial m_i} - g^x\frac{\partial a_i^x}{\partial m_i} - h^x\frac{\partial b_i^x}{\partial m_i} - g^y\frac{\partial a_i^y}{\partial m_i} - h^y\frac{\partial b_i^y}{\partial m_i}.$$

Using this equation, (23), and other similar equations,

$$\frac{\partial E}{\partial m_i} = \frac{\partial E}{\partial x_i}\cdot\frac{1}{p}.$$

[15] Among the welfare studies the Cambridge Conditions are the distinctive characteristic of the writings of the members of the Cambridge School. They are advanced in the works of all the Cambridge economists and in none of the other welfare studies we have considered. But certain qualifications must be noted.

The Cambridge economists require an equal distribution of incomes ($px_i + qy_i$) rather than of Shares, as the condition for equality of the marginal economic welfare per "dollar" for all individuals (with qualifications which we shall note directly, cf. Kahn, *Economic Journal*, March 1935, pp. 1–2; Pigou, *Economics of Welfare*, pp. 82 ff.; Marshall, *Principles*, p. 795). If it is assumed that the amounts of the various types of labor performed by each individual in the community are given, this condition is of course the same as ours. But otherwise for a requirement of equal incomes there is unlikely to be any position which satisfies all the conditions for a maximum. For it would be necessary that in the neighborhood of the maximum position the marginal productivity and marginal diswelfare of each type of work be zero.

The condition of equal incomes is not necessarily inconsistent with the other postulates. There might be some indifference functions and production functions such that all the maximum conditions are satisfied. But it may be noted here, in general, as a minimum requirement, that the various conditions must be consistent with each other. Compare Lange, *Review of Economic Studies*, October 1936, pp. 64–65, and Lerner, *Review of Economic Studies*, October 1936, p. 73.

For convenience I have presented the Cambridge Conditions in a rather simple form. In a more elaborate exposition of the conditions advanced by the Cambridge economists I should have to introduce—and on *a priori* grounds I believe it desirable to introduce—modifications in the distribution of Shares for changes in the price-wage situation which might affect different individuals differently—some moving to a more preferable position, and others to a less preferable one—and for other special differences between individuals. See the reference to the distribution of *wealth* in Marshall, pp. 527, 595, and to the distribution of the *Dividend* in Pigou, p. 89; but see also the reference to the distribution of *money incomes*, in Kahn, pp. 1–2.

sufficient information concerning the Economic Welfare Function for the determination of the maximum position, if it exists.[16] In general, any set of value propositions which is sufficient for the evaluation of all alternatives may be introduced, and for each of these sets of propositions there corresponds a maximum position. The number of sets is infinite, and in any particular case the selection of one of them must be determined by its compatibility with the values prevailing in the community the welfare of which is being studied. For only if the welfare principles are based upon prevailing values can they be relevant to the activity of the community in question. But the determination of prevailing values for a given community, while I regard it as both a proper and necessary task for the economist, and of the same general character as the investigation of the indifference functions for individuals, is a project which I shall not undertake here. For the present I do not attempt more than the presentation of the values current in economic literature in a form for which empirical investigation is feasible.[17]

DIFFERENT ANALYSES FURTHER CONSIDERED

The formulation I have used to derive the maximum conditions of economic welfare differs in several respects from that of the welfare studies. It will be desirable to review briefly the relevant points of the various expositions and the departures of the present essay from them. I shall continue to use the set of assumptions stated on pages 7 and 8.

In the Cambridge analysis,[18] the welfare of the community, stated symbolically,[19] is an aggregate of the form,[20]

$$E = \sum U^i(x_i, y_i, a_i^x, b_i^x, a_i^y, b_i^y),\tag{27}$$

---

[16] See n. 7 above.

[17] This conception of the basis for the welfare principles should meet Lionel Robbins' requirement that the economist take the values of the community as data. But insofar as I urge that the economist also *study* these data it represents perhaps a more positive attitude than might be inferred as desirable from his essays. See *The Nature and Significance of Economics* (London, 1932), particularly chap. vi. Whether the approach will prove a fruitful one remains to be seen.

It may be noted that though Professor Robbins is averse to the study of indifference curves (pp. 96ff.), his own analysis requires an assumption that a movement of labor from one use to another is indifferent to the laborer and that a shift of other factors of production is indifferent to the community. Without these assumptions, for which I can see no *a priori* justification, his whole discussion of alternative *indifferent* uses, and his references to the most adequate satisfaction of demand from a given amount of means are without basis.

[18] The passages in the Cambridge studies which are particularly informative as to the Cambridge concept of welfare are Marshall, pp. 80ff; 200ff., 527, 804; Pigou, pp. 10–11, 87, 97; Kahn, pp. 1, 2, 19; and also F. Y. Edgeworth, *Papers Relating to Political Economy*, II (London, 1925), p. 102 (from the *Economic Journal*, 1897).

[19] Aside from Marshall's appendices, the exposition of Marshall, Professor Pigou, and Mr. Kahn is nonmathematical, but the few relationships we discuss here may be presented most conveniently in a mathematical form. This will also facilitate comparison with the studies of Pareto and Barone.

[20] In the analyses of Professor Pigou and Mr. Kahn some modification of (27) would be introduced to take care of the direct effects (as in the case of " factory smoke ") on aggregate welfare of shifts of factors of production from one use to another.

In this expression U^i is some function of the indifference function, S^i, and measures the satisfactions derived by the ith individual from x_i, y_i, a_i^x, b_i^x, a_i^y, b_i^y. If individual temperaments are about the same—that is, if individuals are capable of equal satisfactions—the marginal utilities or derivatives of the utility functions of different individuals, it is assumed, will be equal for an equal distribution of Shares.[21]

It is possible to derive all the maximum conditions, in specific terms, from the equation

$$\sum dU^i = 0. \tag{28}$$

The technique used by the Cambridge economists is less direct and varies in certain respects. For our present purposes these procedural differences are of little special interest, but it will facilitate our discussion of the analysis of Pareto and Barone if we append the following notes.

Marshall develops the Pareto-Barone-Cambridge consumption and labor supply conditions separately from the rest of his analysis.[22] These conditions are that for some price-wage situation, p, q, g^x, h^x, g^y, h^y, and for all i,

$$w^i = \frac{U_1^i}{p} = \frac{U_2^i}{q} = \frac{-U_3^i}{g^x} = \frac{-U_4^i}{h^x} = \frac{-U_5^i}{g^y} = \frac{-U_6^i}{h^y}. \tag{29}$$

In (29), w^i is the marginal utility of money to the ith individual and U_1^i, U_2^i, U_3^i, etc., are the marginal utilities of the various commodities and disutilities of the various types of work. In Marshall's exposition it is shown that, for any given amounts of X, Y, A^x, B^x, A^y, B^y, if the conditions (29) are not satisfied, some U^i can be increased without any other being decreased. Thus for (28) to hold, (29) must be satisfied. Professor Pigou and Mr. Kahn do not develop the conditions (29), but assume them *ab initio* in their analysis.

If the conditions (29) are satisfied, (28) may be written in the form

$$\sum w^i \Delta_i = 0, \tag{30}$$

where

$$\Delta_i = p \, dx_i + q \, dy_i - g^x \, da_i^x - h^x \, db_i^x - g^y \, da_i^y - h^y \, db_i^y. \tag{31}$$

The remaining conditions again may be derived from (30). However, in Mr. Kahn's reformulation of Professor Pigou's analysis,[23] it is assumed also that the Shares are distributed equally, and the remaining conditions are developed from the requirement that

$$\sum \Delta_i = 0. \tag{32}$$

---

[21] With the qualifications of n. 15 above.
[22] See the references in n. 13 above.
[23] *Economic Journal*, March 1935.

The summation in (32), with certain qualifications, is Professor Pigou's index of the National Dividend.[24] The procedures of Professor Pigou and Marshall differ from this, but the variations need not be elaborated here.[25]

Pareto and Barone also assume initially that conditions (29) are satisfied, but Pareto, like Marshall, shows in an early section of his work that, otherwise, it is possible to increase the *ophélimité* of some individuals without that of any others being decreased.[26] To develop the remaining conditions, aside from the Cambridge Conditions, Pareto expressedly avoids the use of (28) on the ground that "nous ne pouvons ni comparer ni sommer celles-ci [dU^1, dU^2, etc.], car nous ignorons le rapport des unités en lesquelles elles sont exprimées."[27] Instead Pareto proceeds directly to (32) and deduces the maximum conditions for production from it. In this, evidently for the same reason, Barone follows.[28] Neither Pareto nor Barone introduces the Cambridge Conditions into his analysis. Pareto merely assumes that the shares are distributed "suivant la règle qu'il plaira d'adopter," or in a "manière convenable,"[29] and Barone that they are distributed according to some "ethical criteria."[30]

The basis for developing production conditions directly from (32), for Pareto, is that this equation will assure that if the quantities of products "étaient convenablement distribuées, il en resulterait un maximum d'ophélimité pour chaque individu dont se compose la société."[31]

Barone adopts the requirement that the sum be zero because, in his words,

this means that every other series of equivalents different from that which accords with this definition would make that sum negative. That is to say, either it causes a decline in the welfare of all, or if some decline while others are raised, the gain of the latter is less than the loss of the former (so that even taking all their gain from those who gained in the change, reducing them to their former position, to give it completely to those who lost, the latter would always remain in a worse position than their preceding one without the situation of others being improved).[32]

Mr. Lerner, in the first of his two studies on welfare, advances as a criterion for a maximum position the condition that it should be impossible in this position to increase the welfare of one individual without decreasing that of another. From this criterion he develops graphically various maximum conditions. Like Pareto and Barone, he does not introduce the Cambridge Conditions into his analysis but, as he indicates, ignores the problem of

---

[24] Professor Pigou's index does not include cost elements; it relates to large adjustments —whence the problem of backward and forward comparisons; and it is expressed as a percentage of the total value product at the initial position. See *Economics of Welfare*, chap. vi.

[25] But see pp. 20–25, below.

[26] *Cours*, I, pp. 20ff.

[27] *Ibid.*, II, p. 93.

[28] See Barone, p. 246.

[29] *Cours*, II, pp. 91, 93, 94.

[30] Barone, p. 265.

[31] *Cours*, II, pp. 93, 94.

[32] Barone, p. 271.

distribution.[33] In his later paper Mr. Lerner presents our first group of maximum conditions (p. 12), on the basis of the criterion for a maximum that it should be impossible to increase the production of one commodity without decreasing that of another.[34]

In my opinion the utility calculus introduced by the Cambridge economists is not a useful tool for welfare economies. The approach does not provide an alternative to the introduction of value judgments. First of all, the comparison of the utilities of different individuals must involve an evaluation of the relative economic positions of these individuals. No extension of the methods of measuring utilities will dispense with the necessity for the introduction of value propositions to give these utilities a common dimension. Secondly, the evaluation of the different commodities cannot be avoided, even though this evaluation may consist only in a decision to accept the evaluations of the individual members of the community. And, finally, whether the direct effects on aggregate utility of a shift of factors of production from one use to another are given a zero value, as in Marshall's analysis, or a significant one, as in the analyses of Professor Pigou and Mr. Kahn,[35] alternatives are involved, and accordingly value judgments must be introduced.

While the utility calculus does not dispense with value judgments, the manner in which these value judgments are introduced is a misleading one. Statements as to the aggregative character of total welfare, or as to the equality of marginal utilities when there is an equal distribution of Shares, provided temperaments are about the same, do have the ring of *factual* propositions, and are likely to obscure the evaluations implied. The note by Mr. Kahn, in reference to his own formulation of the maximum conditions for economic welfare, that "many will share Mr. Dobb's suspicion 'that to strive after such a maximum is very much like looking in a dark room for a black hat which may be entirely subjective after all'"[36] is not one to reassure the reader as to the nature of the welfare principles derived in this manner. To the extent that the utility calculus does conceal the role of value judgments in the derivation of welfare principles, the criticism directed against the Cambridge procedure by Professor Robbins and others[37] is not without justification.

The approach, it must also be noted, requires a group of value propositions additional to those I have presented. So far as the Cambridge economists require that the economic welfare of the community be an *aggregate* of individual welfares, value judgments must be introduced to the effect that each individual contributes independently to the total welfare. These value propositions, which imply the complete measurability of the Economic Welfare

---

[33] *Review of Economic Studies*, June 1934.

[34] *Review of Economic Studies*, October 1934.

[35] See p. 8, and n. 20 above.

[36] *Economic Journal*, March 1935, p. 2n.

[37] Robbins, *The Nature and Significance of Economic Science*; C. Sutton, "The Relation between Economic Theory and Economic Policy," *Economic Journal*, March 1937.

Function aside from an arbitrary origin and a scalar constant, are not necessary for the derivation of the maximum conditions, and accordingly are not essential to the analysis.[38]

The derivation of conditions of maximum economic welfare without the summation of individual utilities, by Pareto, Barone, and Mr. Lerner, is a stride forward from the Cambridge formulation. Pareto's exposition of the basis for the procedure is somewhat ambiguous. Properly stated, the argument for developing production conditions directly from (32) is the same as that used in developing consumption conditions. The increment Δ_i in (31) indicates the preference direction of the ith individual.[39] If Δ_i is positive, the ith individual moves to a preferable position. The condition that $\sum \Delta_i$ be equal to zero does not assure that the *ophélimité* of each individual be a maximum, but that it be impossible to improve the position of one individual without making that of another worse. This, disregarding the misleading comparison of losses and gains, is the interpretation of Barone, and it is also the condition for a maximum used by Mr. Lerner.

But in avoiding the addition of utilities, Pareto, Barone, and Mr. Lerner also exclude the Cambridge Conditions from their analyses. None of the writers indicates his reasons for the exclusion, and I believe it has not proved an advantageous one. The first two groups of value propositions are introduced in the studies of Pareto and Barone by the use of, and in the argument as to the use of, (32) as a basis for deriving maximum conditions, and in the analysis of Mr. Lerner by the criteria adopted for a maximum. In this respect the formulations differ little from that of the Cambridge economists. With the accompanying statements by Pareto and Barone that *the distribution of Shares* is decided on the basis of some " ethical criteria " or " rule," or with the complete exclusion of the problem by Mr. Lerner, this approach is not more conducive to an apprehension of the value content of the first two groups of maximum conditions. In the case of Mr. Lerner's study a misinterpretation does in fact appear. For in his analysis, the first group of maximum conditions are advanced as objective in a sense which clearly implies that they require no value judgments for their derivation.[40]

Further, it must be emphasized, though the point is surely an obvious one, that unless the Cambridge Conditions, or a modified form of these conditions, are introduced there is no reason in general why it is more preferable to have the other conditions satisfied than otherwise. Placing $\sum \Delta_i$ equal to zero does not assure that there are no other positions for which welfare is greater, but only that there are no other positions for which the welfare of one individual

---

[38] Lange's discussion of utility determinateness (O. Lange, " On the Determinateness of the Utility Function," *Review of Economic Studies*, June 1934) errs insofar as it implies that welfare economics requires the summation of the independently measurable utilities of individuals, that is, his second utility posutulate.

[39] R. G. D. Allen, " The Foundation of a Mathematical Theory of Exchange," *Economica* May 1932.

[40] *Review of Economic Studies*, October 1934, p. 57.

is greater without that of another being less. In general, if conditions regarding distribution are not satisfied, it is just as likely as not that any position for which $\sum \varDelta_i$ does not equal zero will be *more* desirable than any position for which it does equal zero.

In the Pareto-Barone analysis, though not in that of Mr. Lerner, there is reason to believe that, in a general form, maximum conditions regarding distribution are assumed to be satisfied. While the distribution of Shares is not specified, it is consistent with some "ethical criteria," or "rule." Whatever the rule is, it should follow that in the maximum position the marginal economic welfare "per dollar" with respect to all individuals is the same. Otherwise, in the light of that rule, some other distribution would be preferable. If this interpretation is correct, the special exposition used by Pareto and Barone to support their derivation of maximum conditions is inappropriate. In (32) it is true that each dollar does not express the same amount of utility in the Cambridge sense, since the value propositions of independence are not introduced. But each dollar does express the same amount of welfare. The argument used to place (32) equal to zero is thus not the Pareto-Barone one, but that if it were unequal to zero, a further adjustment increasing the summation would be possible, and this would directly increase welfare, *regardless* of whether the position of some individuals were improved and that of others worsened by the change.[41]

EVALUATION OF A CHANGE IN WELFARE

I have noted elsewhere that the conditions for a maximum welfare which are presented on pages 7–16 are the conditions for any critical point. They are sufficient to inform us whether or not we are at the top or bottom of a hill, or at the top with respect to one variable, and the bottom with respect to another. The requirement for a *maximum* position is that it be possible to reach the position from any neighboring point by a series of positive adjustments. For the determination of such a position, it is necessary to know the sign $(+, -, 0)$ of any increment of welfare.

In the welfare studies the sign of dE is specified only for limited groups of adjustments. It will be of interest to note these conditions, and the value judgments required, though I shall not review again the formulations of the various writers.

i) If we assume that all the conditions for a critical point are satisfied, except those relating to the distribution of the factors of production between different uses, one additional group of value judgments gives us sufficient information concerning the shape of the Economic Welfare Function to determine the sign of an increment of welfare. These value propositions are: *if all individuals except any* ith *individual remain in positions which are indifferent to them, and if the* ith *individual moves to a position which is preferable to him,*

---

[41] This argument is more fully developed in the section following.

economic welfare increases. If we denote a more preferable position by a positive movement of S^i, these value propositions require that

$$\frac{\partial E}{\partial S^i} > 0, \tag{33}$$

for any i. Let us write from (21)

$$dE = \sum \frac{\partial E}{\partial x_i} dx_i + \frac{\partial E}{\partial y_i} dy_i + \frac{\partial E}{\partial a_i^x} da_i^x + \frac{\partial E}{\partial b_i^x} db_i^x$$

$$+ \frac{\partial E}{\partial a_i^y} da_i^y + \frac{\partial E}{\partial b_i^y} db_i^y. \tag{34}$$

Using equations (5) through (10), and the notation of (31),

$$dE = \omega \sum \Delta_i. \tag{35}$$

By (33) and the equations (5) through (10), ω must have the same sign as the price-wage rates in Δ_i. We shall take this sign as positive. Thus if the Shares are distributed equally, and if the prices and wage rates are proportionate to the marginal rates of substitution of the different kinds of commodities and types of work, economic welfare has the sign of Professor Pigou's index of the National Dividend. It will be increased by any adjustment which results in the movement of factors of production to a position of higher marginal value productivity.

   ii) If the assumption that the Cambridge Conditions are satisfied is relaxed, (35) may be written in the form

$$dE = \sum \omega^i \Delta_i \tag{36}$$

where ω^i is the marginal economic welfare per dollar with respect to the ith individual. Using the evaluation in (33) it follows that, for any adjustment for which no Δ_i decreases and some Δ_i increases, economic welfare will increase.

   iii) Continuing to use the assumptions of (ii), let us write

$$\lambda_{ik} = \frac{\omega_i}{\omega^k}, \tag{37}$$

and

$$dE = \omega^k \sum \lambda_{ik} \Delta_i. \tag{38}$$

   Let us introduce the value propositions: *for a given price-wage situation, and any i and k, if the Share of i is greater than that of k, a decrease in the Share of k would have to be accompanied by a larger increase in the Share of i, for economic welfare to remain unchanged.* Since it can be shown that if the Share of the ith individual increases by dm_i a concomitant decrease, $-\lambda_{ik} dm_i$, in the share of the kth will leave economic welfare unchanged,[42] these value propositions require that λ_{ik} be less than unity. It follows that, for any given adjustment, if $\sum \Delta_i$ is positive, and if Δ_i does not vary with λ_{ik}, or if it decreases with λ_{ik}, economic welfare will increase. In other words, if the change in the National Dividend is not counteracted by a change in its distribution, the welfare of the community will be increased, even if some Δ_i increase and others decrease.

The adjustments in (i) are those considered by Mr. Kahn; in (ii) by Pareto, Barone, and Mr. Lerner; and in (iii) by Marshall and Professor Pigou. As Professor Pigou has pointed out,[43] the sign of an increment of welfare for some adjustments is left undetermined in his analysis. To determine the sign of dE for all adjustments, all the λ's would have to be evaluated and a similar group of value judgments for the case where prices and wages are not proportional to the marginal rates of substitution would have to be introduced. On *a priori* grounds there is no reason why more information should not be obtained, since the comparison involved in evaluating the λ's is the same as that required for the Value Propositions of Equal Shares. For some additional and fairly rough evaluations, the range of adjustments included can be extended considerably, though an element of uncertainty is involved. Two such approximations, perhaps, are of sufficient interest to note, though they are not introduced in the welfare studies.

iv) The assumptions of (ii) are retained. Let us suppose that with respect to some individual, say the kth,

$$\sum \lambda_{ik} = N, \tag{39}$$

the sum being taken for all i. Thus ω^k is the average ω. If we write

$$\alpha_i = \lambda_{ik} - 1, \qquad \beta_i = \Delta_i - \frac{\sum \Delta_i}{N}, \tag{40}$$

then

$$dE = \omega^k (\sum \alpha_i \beta_i + \sum \Delta_i). \tag{41}$$

The first term in the brackets may be regarded as an index of the distribution of the National Dividend. It follows immediately from (41) that (*a*) if Δ_i is positively correlated with λ_{ik}, dE will be positive for an increase in the Dividend and conversely (*b*) if the coefficient of variation of the ω's is less than one hundred percent; that is, if the standard deviation of λ_{ik} is less than unity, and if the coefficient of variation of Δ_i is also less than one hundred per-

---

[42] This relationship follows immediately from the equations

$$dE = \frac{\partial E}{\partial m_i} dm_i + \frac{\partial E}{\partial m_k} dm_k = \omega^i dm_i + \omega^k dm_k.$$

[43] *Economics of Welfare*, p. 645.

cent, dE will have the sign of the index of the Dividend *regardless* of changes in its distribution.[44]

To determine precisely whether the conditions enumerated are satisfied would, of course, require a complete evaluation of the λ's. But the following rough evaluations would be sufficient to assure the likelihood of the results. For (*a*), it must be possible to say that " on the average " the change in distribution does not affect the " poor " more than the " rich," or vice versa. For (*b*) it is necessary to conceive of an individual or group of individuals who are, on the whole, in an average position from the point of view of welfare and to determine whether, for a given position, ω^i " on the average " is likely to be somewhat less than twice the marginal economic welfare per "dollar" for the average individuals, that is, less than twice ω^k. (This should be stated in terms of the average shift in Shares for which welfare remains unchanged.) If it is determined that such a position is occupied, it would be likely that if tastes did not vary greatly—that is, if the relative variation of Δ_i were not very large—dE would increase for an increase in the Dividend. Since, however, the relative variation of Δ_i would ordinarily become excessively large as $\sum\Delta_i$ approached zero, it would be highly uncertain, for adjustments close to the maximum, whether or not an unfavorable change in distribution would obliterate the change in the Dividend.

---

[44] From (41),

$$dE = \omega^k(Nr_{\lambda\Delta\sigma_\lambda\sigma_\Delta} + \sum\Delta)$$
$$= \omega^k(Nr_{\lambda\Delta\sigma_\lambda\sigma_\Delta}/\sum\Delta + 1)\sum\Delta$$

The proposition (*a*) follows immediately, and (*b*) is based on the fact that $r_{\lambda\Delta}$ must be less than unity.

The foundations of welfare economics*

OSCAR LANGE

1. Welfare economics is concerned with the conditions which determine the total economic welfare of a community. In the traditional theory the total welfare of a community was conceived as the *sum* of the welfares (utilities) of all constituent individuals. The problem of maximization of total welfare thus involved the weighing against each other the losses of utility and gains of utility of different individuals. This implies *interpersonal* comparability of utility, as is seen in the dictum about the marginal utility of a dollar for the poor man and for the rich man. Such implication, however, is open to epistemological criticism on the ground of lack of operational significance. In consequence a restatement of the principles of welfare economics is in progress[1] which tries to dispense with the interpersonal comparability of utility. Such restatement, however, implies a restriction of the field of welfare economics. This paper intends to give a precise statement of the basic assumptions and propositions of welfare economics and to discuss their operational significance.

2. In order to dispense with interpersonal comparability of utility the total welfare of a community has to be defined not as the sum of the utilities of the individuals (a scalar quantity) but as a *vector*. The utilities of the individuals are the components of this vector. Let there be θ individuals in the community and let $u^{(i)}$ be the utility of the ith individual. Total welfare is then the vector

$$u = (u^{(1)}, u^{(2)} \cdots, u^{(\theta)}). \tag{2.1}$$

* *Econometrica*, 10(1942): 215–28. Reprinted by courtesy of *Econometrica*.

[1] Some of the recent literature: A. P. Lerner, "The Concept of Monopoly and the Measurement of Monopoly Power," *Review of Economic Studies*, June, 1934; A. Burk, "A Reformulation of Certain Aspects of Welfare Economics," *Quarterly Journal of Economics*, February, 1938; H. Hotelling, "The General Welfare in Relation to Problems of Taxation and of Railway and Utility Rates," *Econometrica*, July, 1938; L. Robbins, "Interpersonal Comparisons of Utility," *Economic Journal*, December, 1938; N. Kaldor, "Welfare Propositions and Interpersonal Comparisons of Utility," *Economic Journal*, September, 1939; J. R. Hicks, "The Foundations of Welfare Economics," *Economic Journal*, December, 1939; T. de Scitovszky, "A Note on Welfare Propositions in Economics," *Review of Economic Studies*, November, 1941.

It is convenient for our purpose to order vectors on the basis of the following definition: a vector is said to be greater than another vector when at least one of its components is greater than the corresponding component of the other vector, and none is less.[2] Thus a vector increases when at least one of its components increases and none decreases. According to the definition adopted, a *maximum* of total welfare occurs when conditions cannot be changed so as to increase the vector u, i.e., when it is impossible to increase the utility of any person without decreasing that of others.[3] We have, therefore, $u = $ max when

$$u^{(i)} = \text{max} \qquad (i = 1, 2, \cdots, \theta) \tag{2.2}$$

subject to

$$u^{(j)} = \text{const} \qquad (j = 1, 2, \cdots, i-1, i+1, \cdots, \theta). \tag{2.3}$$

3. Let the utility of each individual be a function of the commodities in his possession. Denoting by $x_1^{(i)}, x_2^{(i)}, \cdots, x_n^i$ the quantities of n commodities in the possession of the ith individual, his utility is $u^{(i)} = u^{(i)}(x_1^{(i)}, x_2^{(i)}, \cdots, x_n^{(i)})$. Denote further by

$$X_r = \sum_{i=1}^{\theta} x_r^{(i)}$$

the total amount of the rth commodity in the community. These amounts are not constant but subject to technological transformation, the possibilities of which are circumscribed by a transformation function $F(X_1, X_2, \cdots, X_n) = 0$. Our problem is to maximize total welfare subject to the constraint of the transformation function.

We thus have the following maximum problem:

$$u^{(i)}(x_1^{(i)}, x_2^{(i)}, \cdots, x_n^{(i)}) = \text{max} \qquad (i = 1, 2, \cdots, \theta)$$

subject to the side relations

$$u^{(j)}(x_1^{(j)}, x_2^{(j)}, \cdots, x_n^{(j)}) = \text{const} \qquad (j = 1, 2, \cdots, i-1, i+1, \cdots, \theta), \tag{3.1}$$

$$X_r = \sum_{i=1}^{\theta} x_r^{(i)} \qquad (r = 1, 2, \cdots, n), \tag{3.2}$$

$$F(X_1, X_2, \cdots, X_n) = 0. \tag{3.3}$$

---

[2] The ordering of vectors according to this definition must be distinguished from the ordering of vectors according to their length (defined as usual). When a vector is greater than another in the above sense then its length is also greater than the length of the other vector, but the reverse does not hold true. According to our definition the vectors form a partially ordered system which does not have the "chain" property: given u and v, either $u \geqq v$ or $v \geqq u$.

[3] In the language of the theory of partially ordered systems a maximum of total welfare is a "maximal" element of the set of admissible vectors u. Cf. Garrett Birkhoff, *Lattice Theory*, American Mathematical Society, Colloquium Publications, Vol. XXV, 1940, p. 8. The set of admissible vectors is given by the conditions (3.2) and (3.3) in the text.

This is equivalent to maximizing the expression

$$\sum_{i=1}^{\theta} \lambda_i u^{(i)}(x_1^{(i)}, x_2^{(i)}, \cdots, x_n^{(i)}) + \sum_{r=1}^{n} v_r \left(\sum_{i=1}^{\theta} x_r^{(i)} - X_r \right)$$

$$+ vF(X_1, X_2, \cdots, X_n), \qquad (3.4)$$

where the λ's and the v's are Lagrange multipliers and $\lambda_i \equiv 1$ successively for $i = 1, 2, \cdots, \theta$. The result obtained is the same for each i.

The first-order maximum conditions yield, after elimination of the Lagrange multipliers, the $(n-1)\theta$ equations[4]

$$\frac{u_r^{(i)}}{u_s^{(i)}} = \frac{F_r}{F_s} \qquad (r \text{ and } s = 1, 2, \cdots, n; i = 1, 2, \cdots, \theta), \qquad (3.5)$$

which together with the equations (3.1) and (3.3) serve to determine the $n\theta$ quantities $x_r^{(i)}$. The equations (3.5) can also be written in the form

$$\frac{\partial x_s^{(i)}}{\partial x_r^{(i)}} = \frac{\partial X_s}{\partial X_r} \qquad (r \text{ and } s = 1, 2, \cdots, n; i = 1, 2, \cdots, \theta). \qquad (3.6)$$

The latter form shows clearly the economic interpretation and the operational significance of our maximum conditions. The left-hand side of (3.6) is the marginal rate of substitution of two commodities (the amounts of the remaining commodities being kept constant) which leaves the individual's utility unaffected. The right-hand side is the marginal rate of technological transformation of the two commodities. Thus each individual's marginal rate of substitution of any two commodities must be equal to the marginal rate of transformation of these commodities. Both rates can be determined empirically, the second from the technological conditions of transformation, the first by offering each individual choices between different "bundles" of commodities and adjusting the "bundles" so as to make his choice indifferent.

The derivation of (3.5) or (3.6) does not imply interpersonal comparability of utility. This can be seen also in the following way. From (3.5) we have

$$\frac{u_r^{(i)}}{u_r^{(j)}} = \frac{u_s^{(i)}}{u_s^{(j)}} (r \text{ and } s = 1, 2, \cdots, n; i \text{ and } j = 1, 2, \cdots, \theta; j \neq i). \qquad (3.7)$$

Each side is the ratio of the marginal utilities of different individuals. The numerical value of these ratios is *indeterminate*.

This treatment of the maximum total welfare problem does not imply the

---

[4] The subscripts stand for partial derivatives. Thus, e.g.,

$$u_r^{(i)} = \frac{\partial u^{(i)}}{\partial x_r^{(i)}} \qquad \text{and} \qquad F_r = \frac{\partial F}{\partial X_r}.$$

measurability of the individuals' utility either. The equations (3.5)–(3.7) are invariant with regard to any positive transformation $\phi^{(i)}(u^{(i)})$ (where $\phi^{(i)} > 0$)[5] of the utility functions of the individuals. Only the *projective* properties of these functions are used. This implies only ordering, not measurement, of each individual's utility.

The equations (3.5) or (3.6) contain *in nuce* most theorems of welfare economics,[6] e.g., all the propositions in Pigou's *Economics of Welfare*. The only theorems not contained in these equations are those which relate to the optimum distribution of incomes. This limitation and the problem of how it can be overcome in a way which is operationally significant will be the subjects of the remaining part of this paper.

4. The solution given by (3.5) or (3.6) contains arbitrary parameters, namely the constants of the right-hand side of (3.1). These parameters express the level at which the utilities of all the other individuals are held constant while the utility of the *i*th individual is being maximized. Thus our solution is *relative* to the values chosen for these parameters. It gives, for instance, the conditions under which the poor man's utility cannot be increased any more without diminishing the rich man's utility (or vice versa), but the level at which the rich man's utility is held constant is arbitrary. Obviously, the poor man's utility corresponding to a situation of maximum total welfare will be different when the level of the rich man's utility is chosen differently.

In an exchange economy the constants on the right-hand side of (3.1) are uniquely related to the money incomes of the respective individuals. This follows from the maximization of the individuals' utility. Let $u^{(i)}(x_1^{(i)}, x_2^{(i)}, \cdots, x_n^{(i)}) = $ max, subject to

$$\sum_{r=1}^{n} p_r x_r^{(i)} = M^{(i)}.$$

where $M^{(i)}$ is the individual's income and the p's are the prices of the commodities. The value of $u_{\max}^{(i)}$ depends on $M^{(i)}$ and on the p's as parameters. The p's can be determined from equations which express the equality of demand and supply of each commodity, but $M^{(i)}$ remains arbitrary.[7] Thus the problem of determining the constants on the right-hand side of (3.1) reduces, in an exchange economy, to that of determining the distribution of

---

[5] In fact, they are invariant with respect to any transformation such that $\phi^{(i)\prime} \neq 0$. But the second-order maximum conditions admit only positive transformations. Negative transformations would change the maximum into a minimum.

[6] For a somewhat fuller treatment of this point see the Appendix.

[7] The $M^{(i)}$ must, however, satisfy the relation

$$\sum_{i=1}^{\theta} M^{(i)} = \sum_{r=1}^{n} p_r X_r,$$

which follows from (3.2) and from the budget equations

$$\sum_{r=1}^{n} p_r x_r^{(i)} = M^{(i)}.$$

incomes. The conditions of maximum total welfare expressed in (3.5) or (3.6) leave this distribution arbitrary.

5. In order to arrive at the optimum determination of the constants on the right-hand side of (3.1) it does not suffice to maximize the vector u. We must be able to choose between different vectors u which cannot be ordered in the way defined above.[8] This can be done in two ways. One is to weigh against each other the gains of utility and the losses of utility of different individuals. This need not, however, imply the acceptance of the traditional definition of total welfare as the sum of the utilities of the individuals. The weighting can be based, instead, upon a *social valuation* of the importance of the individuals, the subject exercising the valuation being an agency of the organized community (e.g., Congress).[9] The other way is to establish *directly* a social valuation of the distribution of commodities or incomes between the individuals, without reference to the individuals' utilities. In the first case the optimum distribution of incomes (and of commodities) is determined by a social valuation of the individuals' utilities. In the second case the utilities of the individuals appear as a more or less accidental by-product of the direct social valuation of the distribution of incomes (or of commodities).

In both cases the social valuation can be expressed in the form of a *scalar function of the vector u*, i.e., $W(u)$, except that in one case the community (or rather its agency) chooses the most preferred vector u and adjusts the distribution of incomes and of commodities among the individuals so as to obtain the desired vector, while in the other case it chooses the most preferred distribution of incomes (or commodities) directly and the vector u adjusts itself to this choice. We shall call the function W the *social value function*.

It is convenient to give names to the different derivatives of this function. We shall call them *marginal social significances*. Let $W_i = \partial W/\partial u^{(i)}$ and call it the marginal social significance of the ith individual. As $u^{(i)} = u^{(i)}(x_1^{(i)}, x_2^{(i)}, \ldots, x_n^{(i)})$, we can form the derivative $\partial W/\partial x_r^{(i)}$. It will be called the marginal social significance of the rth commodity in the hands of the ith individual. In the preceding section it was shown that in an exchange economy a unique relation exists between $u^{(i)}$ and the individual's money income $M^{(i)}$. Hence we can form $\partial W/\partial M^{(i)}$, which will be called the marginal social significance of the ith individual's income.

Between these derivatives there are the relations

$$\frac{\partial W}{\partial x_r^{(i)}} = W_i u_r^{(i)}, \tag{5.1}$$

$$\frac{\partial W}{\partial M^{(i)}} = W_i \mu_i \quad \text{where} \quad \mu_i = \frac{\partial u^{(i)}}{\partial M^{(i)}}; \tag{5.2}$$

---

[8] I.e., we need now the "chain" property mentioned in footnote 2 above.

[9] In a democratically organized community these agencies will have to reflect the valuations of the majority.

μ_i is called the marginal utility of income.[10] We have also

$$\frac{\partial W}{\partial x_r^{(i)}} = \frac{\partial W}{\partial M^{(i)}} \frac{\partial M^{(i)}}{\partial x_r^{(i)}}.$$

But

$$M^{(i)} = \sum_{r=1}^{n} p_r x_r^{(i)}$$

(*vide* Section 4) and $\partial M^{(i)}/\partial x_r^{(i)} = p_r$. Consequently, we have the relation

$$\frac{\partial W}{\partial x^{(i)}} = \frac{\partial W}{\partial M^{(i)}} p_r \tag{5.3}$$

Our problem is now to maximize W subject to the side relations (3.2) and (3.3). This leads to the maximizing of the following expression

$$W(u^{(1)}, u^{(2)} \cdots, u^{(\theta)}) + \sum_{r=1}^{n} v_r \left(\sum_{i=1}^{\theta} x_r^{(i)} - X_r \right) + vF(X_1, X_2, \cdots, X_n) \tag{5.4}$$

where the v's are Lagrange multipliers.

Eliminating the Lagrange multipliers, we obtain the first-order maximum conditions

$$\frac{\partial W}{\partial x_r^{(i)}} \div \frac{\partial W}{dx_s^{(j)}} = \frac{F_r}{F_s}$$

$$(r \text{ and } s = 1, 2, \cdots, n; i \text{ and } j = 1, 2, \cdots, \theta . \tag{5.5}$$

For $j = i$ and $s \neq r$ these equations become, taking account of (5.1),

$$\frac{u_r^{(i)}}{u_s^{(i)}} = \frac{F_r}{F_s}; \tag{5.6}$$

---

[10] μ_i is also the Lagrange multiplier used in maximizing $u^{(i)}$ subject to $M^{(i)} = \text{const.}$ The first-order maximum conditions are in this case (omitting the superscript i in order to simplify the notation) $u_r = \mu p_r (r = 1, 2, \cdots, n)$. Write

$$\partial u/\partial M = \sum_{r=1}^{n} u_r \, \partial x_r/\partial M.$$

It can be shown (cf. J. R. Hicks, *Value and Capital*, Oxford University Press, 1939, p. 308) that

$$\frac{\partial x_r}{\partial M} = \frac{\mu U_r}{U},$$

where

$$U = \begin{vmatrix} 0 & u_1 & \cdots & u_n \\ u_1 & u_{11} & \cdots & u_{1n} \\ \cdots & \cdots & \cdots & \cdots \\ u_n & u_{n1} & \cdots & u_{nn} \end{vmatrix}$$

and U_r is the cofactor of the element u_r in the first row. Thus we get

$$\frac{\partial u}{\partial M} = \mu \sum_{r=1}^{n} \frac{u_r U_r}{U} = \mu.$$

for $j \neq i$ and $s = r$ they turn into

$$\frac{\partial W}{\partial x_r^{(i)}} = \frac{\partial W}{\partial x_r^{(j)}}. \tag{5.7}$$

The conditions (5.6) are identical with (3.5) and have the same economic interpretation. Their operational significance has already been established. The equations (5.7) state that each commodity must have the same marginal social significance in the hands of each individual. The operational significance of this condition requires further inquiry.

6. In virtue of (5.1)–(5.3) the equation (5.7) can be written in the following alternative forms

$$\frac{\partial W}{\partial M^{(i)}} = \frac{\partial W}{\partial M^{(j)}}, \tag{6.1}$$

$$W_i u_r^{(i)} = W_j u_r^{(j)}, \tag{6.2}$$

$$W_i \mu_i = W_j \mu_j. \tag{6.3}$$

Equation (6.1) states that the marginal social significance of each individual's income must be the same. According to (6.2) the weighted marginal utility of each commodity, and according to (6.3) the weighted marginal utility of income, must be the same for each individual, the marginal social significance of the individual serving as weight.

The operational significance of the maximum conditions obtained depends on which of the two types of social valuation is used. When the communal agency makes its valuation directly in terms of the distribution of commodities or incomes among the individuals, the equations (5.7) and (6.1) can be used. They have, in this case, an immediate operational significance. The communal agency need not bother about the individuals' utilities and it considers W as a direct function of the x's or of the M's, i.e., as being in the form $W(x_1^{(1)}, \cdots, x_n^{(1)}; \cdots; x_1^{(\theta)}, \cdots, x_n^{(\theta)})$ or $W(M^{(1)}, \cdots, M^{(\theta)})$. A direct valuation in terms of the distribution of commodities is in practice a very complicated affair. It requires a separate evaluation of the marginal social significance of each commodity in the hands of each individual. Therefore, it is rarely fully practiced, except in times of emergency, e.g., during war, when practice comes pretty close to it. A direct valuation in terms of the distribution of incomes does not present the same technical obstacles. It requires only an evaluation of the marginal social significance of each individual's income. This can be done by means of one or a few simple principles and is actually practiced, for instance, in framing income-tax legislation.

When the social valuation is made in terms of weighting the individuals' utilities the equations (6.2) and (6.3) have to be used. This requires a knowledge of the marginal utilities of the different individuals. There exists no operational procedure by which such a knowledge can be gained. To that extent (6.2) and (6.3) lack operational significance. This, however, does not make them completely meaningless. It is possible to form certain a priori hypotheses about the relationships between individuals' marginal utilities and to investigate what consequences in terms of the distribution of incomes or of commodities follow. Thus it is possible to control the valuations made directly in terms of incomes or commodities in the light of these hypotheses.

The most interesting of such hypotheses is the hypothesis that the function $\mu_i(M^{(i)})$, which expresses the marginal utility of income, is the same for each individual. In this case (6.3) becomes

$$W_i\mu(M^{(i)}) = W_j\mu(M^{(j)}) \qquad (i \text{ and } j = 1, 2, \cdots, \theta), \tag{6.4}$$

where μ is written without subscript because the function is the same for all individuals. Let us also assume that the community adopts an equalitarian social ideal; i.e., the marginal social significance of each individual is the same. Then $W_i = W_j$ for all i's and j's and we obtain from (6.4)

$$M^{(i)} = M^{(j)} \qquad (i \text{ and } j = 1, 2, \cdots, \theta). \tag{6.5}$$

Each individual has to get the same income.[11]

In this way it is possible to check up the consistency of the social valuation with the professed ideal of an economic society which, like ours, claims to attach to each individual the same marginal social significance. Upon the hypothesis that the marginal-utility-of-income function is the same for all individuals the inequalities in the distribution of incomes are inconsistent with the equalitarian ideal professed. In a similar way the actual distribution of incomes (or of commodities) can be checked up with regard to other hypotheses made and with regard to other social valuations of the individuals' utilities.

7. It is seen from (5.5) that the maximum conditions are invariant under a transformation $\phi(W)$ of the social-value function, where $\phi' > 0$[12]. Thus only the projective properties of W are used. Only the ordering, not the measurement, of the social valuations is involved.

The utilities of the individuals need not be measurable either. Let us subject the utility functions of the individuals to the transformation $\phi^{(i)}(u^{(i)})$, where $\phi^{(i)} > 0$[13] and $i = 1, 2, \cdots, \theta$. We obtain, instead of (6.2),

$$\frac{\partial W}{\partial \phi^{(i)}} \phi^{(i)} = \frac{\partial W}{\partial \phi^{(j)}} \phi_r^{(j)}. \tag{7.1}$$

---

[11] This does not imply that each individual's *money earnings* must be the same. Among the goods $x_r^{(i)}$ there are included leisure, safety, and attractiveness of the different occupations, social prestige, etc., and prices have to be assigned to them. If an individual prefers, for the reasons indicated, an occupation in which he earns less money than he could earn in some other one, he can be considered as purchasing certain goods associated with the occupation he chooses and as paying a price for them. Thus differences in money earnings which correspond to the individuals' preferences for the various occupations are not in contradiction with the equality of incomes discussed in the text. This takes care of the question of incentives. Cf. on this subject the present writer's essay, *On the Economic Theory of Socialism*, Minneapolis, University of Minnesota Press, 1938, pp. 101–2.

[12] Cf. footnote 5 above.

[13] Cf. footnote 5 above.

This can be written

$$\frac{\partial W}{\partial \phi^{(i)}} \phi^{(i)'} u_r^{(i)} = \frac{\partial W}{\partial \phi^{(j)}} \phi^{(j)'} u_r^{(j)}, \tag{7.2}$$

whence

$$\frac{\partial W}{\partial u^{(i)}} u_r^{(i)} = \frac{\partial W}{\partial u^{(j)}} u_r^{(j)}, \tag{7.3}$$

which is identical with (6.2). In a similar way it can be shown that (6.3) is invariant under the transformation $\phi^{(i)}$.

8. Let us restate our conclusions. The propositions of welfare economics can be divided into two parts. One part is based on maximizing the vector u and is concerned with conditions which permit increasing the utility of one individual without diminishing the utility of anybody else. It comprises all propositions of welfare economics except those which relate to the optimum distribution of incomes. These propositions are all operationally significant. The other part requires the setting up of a social-value function $W(u)$ which is maximized. The maximum conditions thus obtained may be expressed either directly in terms of the commodities and incomes allowed to different individuals or in terms of the marginal utilities of the individuals. In the first case propositions of immediate operational significance are obtained but each individual's utility is determined quasi-accidentally as a by-product of the valuations made in terms of commodities or incomes. In the other case the optimum distribution of incomes must be derived from certain a priori hypotheses concerning the functions expressing the marginal utility of incomes of the different individuals. Although these hypotheses have no direct operational significance, they lead to definite conclusions as to the appropriate distribution of incomes. They may, therefore, be used as check-ups of a distribution of incomes established by direct valuation.

Neither the social valuations nor the utilities of the individuals need be measurable; it is sufficient that they can be ordered.

APPENDIX

In order to simplify the exposition the transformation function introduced at the beginning of Section 3 is assumed to refer to the whole economy. This is a strong oversimplification of reality, admissible only under special circumstances. Actually the technological transformation of commodities is performed by individuals ("firms"; even in a socialist society there would be separate productive establishments) and each individual is confronted with a transformation function of his own. Only when the transformation functions of the individuals are all the same can they be combined in a unique way into a transformation function for the economy as a whole. Otherwise the conditions of transformation in the economy as a whole depend on how the transformation of commodities is distributed among the individuals (i.e., the relation between total "outputs" and total "inputs" depends on how much "output" and "input" is done by each individual). Thus in order to give a better picture of an actual economic system we must assume each individual to be confronted with a separate transformation function.

Denote by $f^{(i)}(y_1^{(i)}, y_2^{(i)}, \cdots, y_n^{(i)}) = 0$ the transformation function of the ith individual, where $y_r^{(i)}$ is the quantity of the rth commodity he transforms. Denote, as before, by $x_r^{(i)}$ the quantity of the rth commodity which the ith individual possesses. The amount of a commodity which an individual possesses need not be equal to the amount he obtains or gives up through transformation, for he may acquire commodities or get rid of them by means other than technological transformation (e.g., by exchange or gift). But for the economy as a whole these amounts are equal. We have, therefore

$$\sum_{i=1}^{\theta} x_r^{(i)} = \sum_{i=1}^{\theta} y_r^{(i)}$$

for $r = 1, 2, \cdots, n$.

In place of the maximum problem in Section 3 we now have

$$u^{(i)}(x_1^{(i)}, x_2^{(i)}, \cdots, x_n^{(i)}) = \max \qquad (i = 1, 2, \cdots, \theta),$$

subject to the side relations

$$u^{(j)}(x_1^{(j)}, x_2^{(j)}, \cdots, x_n^{(j)}) = \text{const} \qquad (j = 1, 2, \cdots, i-1, i+1, \cdots, \theta), \qquad (1)$$

$$f^{(i)}(y_1^{(i)}, y_2^{(i)}, \cdots, y_n^{(i)}) = 0 \qquad (i = 1, 2, \cdots, \theta), \qquad (2)$$

$$\sum_{i=1}^{\theta} x_r^{(i)} = \sum_{i=1}^{\theta} y_r^{(i)} \qquad (r = 1, 2, \cdots, n). \qquad (3)$$

This leads to the expression

$$\sum_{i=1}^{\theta} \lambda_i u^{(i)} + \sum_{i=1}^{\theta} \gamma_i f^{(i)} + \sum_{r=1}^{\theta} v_r \left(\sum_{i=1}^{\theta} x_r^{(i)} - \sum_{i=1}^{\theta} y_r^{(i)} \right), \qquad (4)$$

where the Greek letters stand for Lagrange multipliers and $\lambda_i \equiv 1$ successively for $i = 1, 2, \cdots, \theta$.

Eliminating the Lagrange multipliers, we arrive at the first-order maximum conditions

$$\frac{u_r^{(i)}}{u_s^{(i)}} = \frac{f_r^{(j)}}{f_s^{(j)}} \qquad (r \text{ and } s = 1, 2, \cdots, n; \ i \text{ and } j = 1, 2, \cdots, \theta), \qquad (5)$$

which take the place of (3.5) in the text.

The propositions usually found in the literature on welfare economics are special cases of the conditions (5). We obtain from (5)

$$\frac{f_r^{(i)}}{f_s^{(i)}} = \frac{f_r^{(j)}}{f_s^{(j)}} \qquad (6)$$

$$\frac{u_r^{(i)}}{u_s^{(i)}} = \frac{u_r^{(j)}}{u_s^{(j)}} \qquad (i \neq j) \qquad (7)$$

The relation (6) states that the marginal rate of transformation of any two commodities must be the same for each individual (i.e., "firm").[14] If the commodities are both factors, this means that the ratio of their marginal productivities (in terms of any given product) must be the same in each firm of the economy. If they are both products, the ratio of their marginal factor cost (in terms of any given factor) must be the same in all firms. If one is a factor and the other a product, the marginal productivity of the factor in terms of that product must be the same in each firm.[15] These are all theorems well-known in welfare economics. The relation (7) indicates the well-known theorem that the marginal rate of substitution of any two commodities must be the same for each individual. With these relations in mind, we see that, according to (5), any individual's marginal rate of substitution of two commodities has to be equal to the ratio of the marginal factor costs of these commodities in any firm of the economy. The last is the most widely known theorem of welfare economics.

---

[14] The relation (6) can be interpreted as the condition of maximum total physical output. In a similar way as total welfare was defined as the vector u, total physical output can be defined as the vector $X = (X_1, X_2, \cdots, X_n)$, where

$$X_s = \sum_{i=1}^{\theta} x_s^{(i)} = \sum_{i=1}^{\theta} y_s^{(i)}$$

We have then the problem

$$X_r = \max \qquad\qquad (r = 1, 2, \cdots, n)$$

subject to the side relations

$$X_s = \text{const} \qquad (s = 1, 2, \cdots, r-1, r+1, \cdots, n), \qquad (i)$$

$$X_s = \sum_{i=1}^{\theta} y_s^{(i)} \qquad\qquad (s = 1, 2, \cdots, n), \qquad (ii)$$

$$f^{(i)}(y_1^{(i)}, y_2^{(i)}, \cdots, y_n^{(i)}) = 0 \qquad (i = 1, 2, \cdots, o), \qquad (iii)$$

which leads to the conditions (6). The maximum total output is determined purely by the technological transformation possibilities without any reference to utility. Since the relation (6) is part of any maximum-welfare conditions, whether involving the social-value function W or only the vector u, the maximization of total physical output may be considered as the most narrow type of a concept of maximum total welfare. It is concerned only with the possibility of increasing the output of some commodities without diminishing the output of any other commodity, regardless of who is to get the commodities (cf. Lerner, *op. cit.*, p. 57). We may thus consider the problem of maximum total welfare in three stages (instead of in two, as in the text): (1) maximizing the vector X, (2) maximizing the vector u, (3) maximizing the scalar function W. The maximum conditions in each stage include the maximum conditions of the preceding one.

[15] This condition implies the absence of unemployment. An unemployed factor can be considered as being employed by an "industry" or "firm" where its marginal productivity is nil. Any shift of the factor to an industry or firm where its marginal productivity is positive increases total physical output (as defined in the preceding footnote). The distinction between two types of propositions of welfare economics, one dealing with the allocation of resources and the other dealing with the degree of utilization of resources, which has been recently proposed by Mr. Scitovszky (*op. cit.*, p. 77), while useful pedagogically, is unnecessary from the analytic point of view. All propositions of welfare economics concerned with the degree of utilization of resources can be treated as allocational propositions.

It was assumed here that each commodity appears as a variable both in the utility functions and in the transformation functions. This need not be the case, however. It may appear only in the utility functions as, for instance, a " gift of nature " which is not produced. Then the relation (7) still applies to it, but the other relations do not. Or, what is of greater practical importance, it may appear in the transformation functions without appearing in the utility functions; i.e., it is a factor of production which has no direct utility. In this case the relation (6) alone applies to it.

Through proper interpretation the relation (5), or (6) and (7) which are derived from it, can be taken as giving the dynamic conditions of maximum total welfare over a period of time. For this purpose we consider the period over which total welfare is maximized as being divided into a finite number of discrete intervals (e.g., " days " or " weeks "); the first of these intervals constitutes the " present," the other ones are in the future.[16] The same physical good in different time intervals is considered to constitute different commodities. The utility functions $u^{(i)}(x_1^{(i)}, x_2^{(i)}, \cdots, x_n^{(i)})$ and the transformation functions $f^{(i)}(y_1^{(i)}, y_2^{(i)}, \cdots, y_n^{(i)}) = 0$ are taken as covering the whole period of time over which total welfare is maximized. These functions thus contain among their variables commodities in different future time intervals as well as commodities in the " present." The relations (5)–(7) refer then to intertemporal as well as intratemporal substitution and transformation. Condition (5) states, among other things, that the intertemporal marginal rates of substitution must be equal to the corresponding intertemporal marginal rates of transformation.

Thus the condition (5) implicitly determines the rate of capital accumulation which maximizes total welfare over time. The result is pretty much along the lines of the traditional theory. The intertemporal marginal rate of substitution is the marginal rate of time preference [which, according to (7), for any given commodity must be the same for each individual] and the intertemporal marginal rate of transformation is the marginal productivity of waiting [which, according to (6), for any given commodity must be the same for each firm] of the traditional theory.[17] The two must be equal when total welfare is maximized over time. It should be noticed, however, that though for any given commodity and any given two time intervals these rates are the same for each individual (and firm), they need not be the same for different commodities or different pairs of time intervals. We have a separate rate of time preference and of (equal to the former) marginal productivity of waiting for each

---

[16] Cf., for instance, Hicks, *Value and Capital*, Oxford University Press, 1939, pp. 122–27.

[17] Speaking more precisely, the marginal rate of time preference and the marginal productivity of waiting differ by unity from the marginal rate of intertemporal substitution or transformation, respectively. The marginal rate of time preference is usually defined as $u_r^{(i)}/u_s^{(i)} - 1$. Cf. R. G. D. Allen, *Mathematical Analysis for Economists*, London, Macmillan and Co., 1938, p. 344. Correspondingly, the marginal productivity of waiting may be defined as $f_r^{(i)}/f_s^{(i)} - 1$. The subscripts r and s refer here to different time intervals.

commodity[18] and for each pair of time intervals. Nor need the time preference and the marginal productivity of waiting be necessarily positive.[19]

Our treatment can be generalized further by assuming that the transformation function of each individual (or firm) depends also on the quantities transformed by other individuals (or firms) in the economy. Taking the most general case, the transformation functions are then of the form $f^{(i)}(y_1^{(1)}, \cdots, y_n^{(1)}; \cdots; y_1^{(\theta)}, \cdots, y_n^{(\theta)}) = 0$. The maximum conditions (5) become

$$\frac{u_r^{(i)}}{u_s^{(i)}} = \frac{f_r^{(j)} + \sum_{k \neq j} f_r^{(k)}}{f_s^{(j)} + \sum_{k \neq j} f_s^{(k)}}. \tag{8}$$

The terms under the summation signs represent "external economies" and "external diseconomies," which play such a distinguished role in the analysis of Professor Pigou.

---

[18] Using the terminology of Mr. Keynes, *The General Theory of Employment, Money and Interest*, New York: Harcourt Brace Co., 1937, p. 223, we obtain a system of optimum (from the social point of view) "own rates" of interest.

[19] The proposition made in the traditional treatment of the theory of interest that under conditions of zero capital accumulation these rates are positive rests on empirical assumption, not on theoretical deduction. The empirical assumption is either that the marginal rate of time preference is positive under these conditions and determines a positive value of the marginal productivity of waiting (time-preference theory of interest, or conversely, that the latter is positive and determines a positive value of the first (marginal-productivity theory of interest). Whether any of these assumptions (and which one) is true is an empirical, not a theoretical, question.

Valuation equilibrium and Pareto optimum*†

GERARD DEBREU

For an economic system with given technological and resource limitations, individual needs and tastes, a valuation equilibrium with respect to a set of prices is a state where no consumer can make himself better off without spending more, and no producer can make a larger profit; a Pareto optimum is a state where no consumer can be made better off without making another consumer worse off. Theorem 1 gives conditions under which a valuation equilibrium is a Pareto optimum. Theorem 2, in conjunction with the Remark, gives conditions under which a Pareto optimum is a valuation equilibrium. The contents of both theorems (in particular that of the first one) are old beliefs in economics. Arrow[1] and Debreu[2] have recently treated this question with techniques permitting proofs. A synthesis of their papers is made here. Their assumptions are weakened in several respects; in particular, their results are extended from finite dimensional to general linear spaces. This extension yields as a possible immediate application a solution of the problem of infinite time horizon (see sec. 6). Its main interest, however, may be that by forcing one to a greater generality it brings out with greater clarity and simplicity the basic concepts of the analysis and its logical structure. Not a single simplification of the proofs would indeed be brought about by restriction to the finite dimensional case.

As far as possible the mathematical structure of the theory has been dissociated from the economic interpretation, to be found in brackets.

* *Proceedings of the National Academy of Sciences*, 40(1954): pp. 588–92. Reprinted by courtesy of the author and The National Academy of Sciences.

† Based on Cowles Commission Discussion Paper, Economics, No. 2067 (January, 1953). Communicated by John von Neumann, May 6, 1954. This article has been prepared under contract Nonr-358(01), NR 047–006 between the Office of Naval Research and the Cowles Commission for Research in Economics.

I am grateful to E. Malinvaud, staff members and guests of the Cowles Commission, in particular I. N. Herstein, L. Hurwicz, T. C. Koopmans, and R. Radner for their comments.

[1] K. J. Arrow, "An Extension of the Basic Theorems of Classical Welfare Economics," *Proceedings of the Second Berkeley Symposium* (Berkeley: University of California Press, 1951), pp. 507–532.

[2] G. Debreu, "The Coefficient of Resource Utilization," *Econometrica*, 19, 273–92, 1951.

1. The economic system. Let L be a linear space (on the reals R)[3] The economic system can be described as follows:

The ith consumer ($i = 1, \ldots, m$) chooses a point x_i [his consumption] in a given subset X_i [his consumption-set] of L. [x_i completely describes the quantities of commodities he actually consumes, to be thought of as positive, and the quantities of the various types of labor he produces, to be thought of as negative. X_i is determined by constraints of the following types: quantities of commodities consumed (labor produced) must be nonnegative (nonpositive), and, moreover, they must enable the individual to survive.] There is on X_i a complete ordering, denoted by

$$\underset{i}{\leqq}$$

[corresponding to the preferences of that consumer].[4] x_i^0 is a saturation point of X_i, if, for all $x_i \in X_i$, one has

$$x_i \underset{i}{\leqq} x_i^0.$$

The jth producer ($j = 1, \ldots, n$) chooses a point y_j [his production] in a given subset Y_j [his production-set] of L. [y_j is a complete description of all his outputs, to be thought of as positive, and his inputs, to be thought of as negative. Y_j is determined by technological limitations.]

Denote

$$x = \sum_i x_i, \; y = \sum_j y_j;$$

they are constrained to satisfy the equality $x - y = \zeta$, where ζ is a given point of L. [ζ corresponds to the exogenous resources available (including all capital existing at the initial date). $x - y$ is the *net* consumption of all consumers and all producers together. It must clearly equal ζ.][5]

---

[3] A real linear space L is a set where the addition of two elements ($x + y$) and the multiplication of a real number by an element (tx) are defined and satisfy the eight axioms:
1. For all x, y, z in L, $(x + y) + z = x + (y + z)$.
2. There is an element $0 \in L$ such that for every $x \in L$, $x + 0 = x$.
3. For every $x \in L$, there is an $x' \in L$ such that $x + x' = 0$.
4. For all x, y in L, $x + y = y + x$. For all x, y in L, t, t' in R,
5. $t(x + y) = tx + ty$,
6. $(t + t')x = tx + t'x$,
7. $t(t'x) = (tt')x$,
8. $1x = x$.

[4] An order is a reflexive and transitive binary relation (generally denoted by $\leqq$). $x \sim x'$ means $x \leqq x'$ and $x' \leqq x$, while $x < x'$ means $x \leqq x'$ and not $x' \leqq x$. The order is complete (as opposed to partial) if for any x, x' one has $x \leqq x'$ and/or $x' \leqq x$.

One may object to completeness of the preference ordering as well as to its transitivity. The reader must therefore note that, with slight modifications of the definitions and the assumptions, Theorems 1 and 2 can easily be proved for *arbitrary* binary relations on the X_i.

[5] Usually the net consumption is only constrained to be at most equal to the available resources. But this implies that any surplus can be freely disposed of. Such an assumption on the technology should be made explicit (see sec. 6) while requiring at the same time $x - y = \zeta$.

A $(m + n)$-tuple $[(x_i), (y_j)]$, one x_i for each i, one y_j for each j, is called a state of the economy. [It is a complete description of the activity of every consumer and every producer.] A state $[(x_i), (y_j)]$ is called attainable if $x_i \in X_i$ for all i, $y_j \in Y_j$ for all j, $x - y = \zeta$.

2. *Valuation equilibrium.* $v(z)$ will denote a (real-valued) linear form on L.[6] [It gives the value of the commodity-point z. When L is suitably specialized, this value can be represented by the inner product $p \cdot z$, where p is the price system.] A state $[(x_i^0), (y_i^0)]$ is a valuation equilibrium with respect to $v(z)$ if:

$$[(x_i^0), (y_j^0)] \text{ is attainable.} \tag{2.1}$$

$$\text{For every } i \text{ "} x_i \in X_i, v(x_i) \leqq v(x_i^0) \text{" implies "} x_i \underset{i}{\leqq} x_i^0 \text{".} \tag{2.2}$$

[Best satisfaction of preferences subject to a budget constraint.]

$$\text{For every } j \text{ "} y_j \in Y_j \text{" implies "} v(y_j) \leqq v(y_j^0) \text{".} \tag{2.3}$$

[Maximization of profit subject to technological constraints.]

3. *Pareto optimum.* The set $X_1 \times \ldots \times X_m$ of m-tuples (x_i), for each i, is (partially) ordered as follows: $(x_i') \geqq (x_i)$ if and only if

$$x_i' \underset{i}{\geqq} x_i \text{ for all } i.$$

A state $[(x_i^0), (y_j^0)]$ is a Pareto optimum if:

$$[(x_i^0), (y_j^0)] \text{ is attainable.} \tag{3.1}$$

$$\text{There is no attainable state } [(x_i), (y_j)] \text{ for which } (x_i) > (x_i^0). \tag{3.2}$$

[It is impossible to make one consumer better off without making another one worse off.]

4. *A valuation equilibrium is a Pareto optimum.* The following assumptions will be made:

I. *For every i, X_i is convex.*

II. *For every*

$$i, \text{"} x_i' \in X_i, x_i'' \in X_i, x_i' \underset{i}{<} x_i'' \text{"}$$

implies "$x_i' \underset{i}{<} (1 - t)x_i' + tx_i''$ for all t, $0 < t < 1$".

These two axioms on the convexity of the consumption-sets and the convexity of preferences have been used by Arrow and Debreu[7] in a different context.

THEOREM 1. *Under assumptions I and II, every valuation equilibrium $[(x_i^0), (y_j^0)]$, where no x_i^0 is a saturation point, is a Pareto optimum.*

---

[6] For all x, y, $v(x + y) = v(x) + v(y)$. For all t, x, $v(tx) = tv(x)$. $v(z)$ is said to be trivial if it vanishes everywhere.

[7] K. J. Arrow, and G. Debreu, "Existence of an Equilibrium for a Competitive Economy," *Econometrica*, 1954.

Proof:

$$\text{``}x_i \in X_i \text{ and } x_i \underset{i}{>} x_i^0 \text{'' implies ``}v(x_i) > v(x_i^0).\text{''} \qquad (4.1)$$

This is a trivial consequence of definition (2.2).

$$\text{``}x_i \in X_i \text{ and } x_i \underset{i}{\sim} x_i^0 \text{'' implies ``}v(x_i) \geqq v(x_i^0).\text{''} \qquad (4.2)$$

Since x_i^0 is not a saturation point, there is $x_i' \in X_i$, such that

$$x_i' \underset{i}{>} x_i^0, \text{ hence } x_i' \underset{i}{>} x_i.$$

Consider $x_i(t) = (1 - t)x_i + tx_i'$. By assumption II, for all $t, 0 < t < 1$,

$$x_i(t) \underset{i}{>} x_i, \text{ hence } x_i(t) \underset{i}{>} x_i^0,$$

so (by [4.1]) $v(x_i^0) < v(x_i(t)) = (1 - t)\,v(x_i) + tv(x_i')$. Let t tend to zero; in the limit $v(x_i^0) \leqq v(x_i)$.

To complete the proof we consider a state $[(x_i), (y_j)]$, where $x_i \in X_i$ for all i, $y_j \in Y_j$ for all j, and show that if $(x_i) > (x_i^0)$, the state is not attainable; i.e., $x - y \neq \zeta$.

$(x_i) > (x_i^0)$ means that for all

$$i, x_i \underset{i}{\geqq} x_i^0, \text{ and for some } i', x_{i'} \underset{i'}{>} x_{i'}^0;$$

so by (4.1) and (4.2)

$$\sum_i v(x_i) > \sum_i v(x_i^0);$$

i.e., $v(x) > v(x^0)$. On the other hand, (2.3) implies $v(y) \leqq v(y^0)$, so $v(x) - v(y) > v(x^0) - v(y^0)$. Since $x^0 - y^0 = \zeta$, $v(x - y) > v(\zeta)$, which rules out $x - y = \zeta$.

5. *A Pareto optimum is a valuation equilibrium.* In this section L is a topological linear space.[8] Let x_i', x_i'' be points of X_i; we define $I(x_i', x_i'') = \{t \mid [(1 - t)x_i' + tx_i''] \in X_i\}$. When X_i is convex, $I(x_i', x_i'')$ is a real interval with possibly one or two end-points excluded. In addition to assumptions I and II, three further assumptions are needed here.

III. *For every i, x_i, x_i', x_i'' in X_i the sets*

$$\{t \in I(x_i', x_i'') \mid (1 - t)x_i' + tx_i'' \underset{i}{\geqq} x_i\}$$

and

$$\{t \in I(x_i', x_i'') \mid (1 - t)x_i' + tx_i'' \underset{i}{\leqq} x_i\}$$

are closed in $I(x_i', x_i'')$.

---

[8] A topological linear space is a linear space with a topology such that the functions $(x, y) \to x + y$ from $L \times L$ to L and $(t, x) \to tx$ from $R \times L$ to L are continuous. For definition of a topology, of the topology on a product, of a continuous function see N. Bourbaki, *Eléments de mathematique* (Paris: Hermann, et Cie, 1940), Part I, Book 3, chap. i. For the representation of continuous linear forms on L see S. Banach, *Théorie des opérations linéaires* (Warsaw, 1932), in particular, chap. iv, sec. 4.

This weak axiom of continuity for preferences has been introduced by Herstein and Milnor[9] in another context. We define

$$Y = \sum_j Y_j \text{ (the set of all } y = \sum_j y_j, \text{ where } y_j \in Y_j \text{ for all } j).$$

IV. *Y is convex.* [The assumption that the aggregate production-set is convex is strictly weaker than the assumption that the individual production-sets Y_j are all convex.]

V. *L is finite dimensional and/or Y has an interior point.* [The assumption that *Y* has an interior point will be shown in section 6 to be implied by free disposal of commodities.]

THEOREM 2. *Under assumptions I–V, with every Pareto optimum $[(x_i^0),$ $(y_j^0)]$, where some x_i^0 is not a saturation point, is associated a (nontrivial) continuous linear form $v(z)$ on L such that:*

$$\text{For every } i \text{ "} x_i \in X_i, \; x_i \underset{i}{\geq} x_i^0 \text{" implies "} v(x_i) \geq v(x_i^0). \text{"} \tag{5.1}$$

$$\text{For every } j \text{ "} y_j \in Y_j \text{" implies "} v(y_j) \leq v(y_j^0). \text{"} \tag{5.2}$$

Proof: From assumptions I, II, and III follows:

$$a) \text{ "} x_i', x_i'' \text{ in } X_i, \; x_i' \underset{i}{\leq} x_i'' \text{"}$$

implies " *for all t,*

$$0 \leq t \leq 1, \; x_i' \underset{i}{\leq} [(1 - t)x_i' + tx_i''] \in X_i. \text{"}$$

By assumption III, the set

$$\{t \in I(x_i', x_i'') | (1 - t)x_i' + tx_i'' \underset{i}{<} x_i'\}$$

is open in $I(x_i', x_i'')$. Its intersection with the interval]0, 1[(end-points excluded) is open. We wish to show that this intersection is empty. If it were not, it would contain two numbers $t_1 < t_2$. Take the corresponding points x_i^1, x_i^2. Then

$$x_i^1 \underset{i}{<} x_i' \underset{i}{\leq} x_i''.$$

By assumption II,

$$x_i^1 \underset{i}{<} x_i'' \text{ gives } x_i^1 \underset{i}{<} x_i^2.$$

$$\overline{\quad : \quad : \quad : \quad : \quad}$$
$$x_i' \quad x_i^1 \quad x_i^2 \quad x_i''$$

Similarly,

$$x_i^2 \underset{i}{<} x_i' \text{ gives } x_i^2 \underset{i}{<} x_i^1, \text{ a contradiction.}$$

[9] I. N. Herstein and J. Milnor, "An Axiomatic Approach to Measurable Utility," *Econometrica*, 21, 291–297, 1953.

As an immediate consequence of (a), for all i, the sets

$$X_{i(x_i^0)} = \{x_i \in X_i \mid x_i \underset{i}{\geqq} x_i^0\}$$

and

$$\mathring{X}_{i(x_i^0)}^0 = \{x_i \in X_i \mid x_i \underset{i}{>} x_i^0\}$$

are convex.

Let i' be a value of i for which x_i^0 is not a saturation point, and consider the set

$$Z = \mathring{X}_{i'(x_{i'}^0)} + \sum_{i \neq i'} X_{i(x_i^0)} - \sum_j Y_j.$$

$\zeta \notin Z$, this is the definition of a Pareto optimum $[(x_i^0), (y_j^0)]$. Z is convex as it is the sum of convex sets. If

$$Y = \sum_j Y_j$$

has an interior point, Z also has one. The Hahn-Banach theorem[10] can therefore be applied to Z and ζ. There is a (nontrivial) continuous linear form $v(z)$ on L such that $v(z) \geqq v(\zeta)$ for all $z \in Z$, i.e., since

$$\xi = \sum_i x_i^0 - \sum_j y_j^0, \qquad v[\sum_i (x_i - x_i^0) - \sum_j (y_j - y_j^0)] \geqq 0$$

for all $x_{i'} \in \mathring{X}_{i'(x_{i'}^0)}$, $x_i \in X_{i(x_i^0)}$ (for $i \neq i'$), $y_j \in Y_j$ (for all j).

In this statement $\mathring{X}_{i'(x_{i'}^0)}$ can be replaced by $X_{i'(x_{i'}^0)}$, for every

$$x_{i'} \in X_{i'}, \, x_{i'} \underset{i'}{\sim} x_{i'}^0,$$

can be exhibited, as in the proof of (4.2), as a limit of points belonging to $\mathring{X}_{i'(x_{i'}^0)}$. Therefore,

b) $\sum_i v(x_i - x_i^0) + \sum_j v(y_j^0 - y_j) \geqq 0$ for all $x_i \in X_i(x_i^0)$, $y_j \in Y_j$.

By making all but one of the x_i, y_j equal to the corresponding x_i^0, y_j^0, one proves that for the remaining term in (b) $v(x_i - x_i^0) \geqq 0$ for all $x_i \in X_i(x_i^0)$ (or $v(y_j^0 - y_j) \geqq 0$ for all $y_j \in Y_j$) which is precisely the statement of Theorem 2.

(5.2) is identical to (2.3), but (5.1) does not necessarily imply (2.2), and Theorem 2 does not quite correspond to the title of this section. The following Remark, due to Arrow[11] in its essence, tries to fill this gap:

REMARK. *Under assumptions I and III, if there is, for every i, an $x_i' \in X_i$ such that $v(x_i') < v(x_i^0)$, then (5.1) implies (2.2).*

---

[10] In a real topological linear space, if Z is a convex set with interior points, ζ a point which does not belong to Z, there is a closed hyperplane through ζ, bounding for Z. (See for example, N. Bourbaki, *Eléments de mathématique* [Paris: Hermann et Cie, 1953], Part I, Book 5, chap. ii, in particular, sec. 3.)

[11] Arrow, *op. cit.*, Lemma 5.

Consider an $x_i \in X_i$, $v(x_i) \leq v(x_i^0)$. Let $x_i(t) = (1 - t) x_i + tx_i'$. For all t, $0 < t < 1$, $v(x_i(t)) < v(x_i^0)$ and thus, by (5.1),

$$x_i(t) \underset{i}{<} x_i^0$$

The set

$$\{t \in I(x_i, x_i') \,|\, (1 - t)x_i + tx_i' \underset{i}{\leq} x_i^0\}$$

contains the interval $]0, 1[$; since it is closed in $I(x_i, x_i')$ (by assumption III), it contains 0, i.e.,

$$x_i \underset{i}{\leq} x_i^0.$$

[The condition that there is $x_i' \in X_i$ such that $v(x_i') < v(x_i^0)$ means that the consumer does not have such a low $v(x_i^0)$ that with any lower value he could not survive.]

6. *The free disposal assumption.*   An example will show the economic justification of assumption V when L is not finite dimensional. Suppose that there is an infinite sequence of commodities [because, for example, economic activity takes place at an infinite sequence of dates, a case studied by Malinvaud[12] with different techniques]. The space L will be the set of infinite sequences of real numbers (z_h) such that Sup $|z_h| < +\infty$. L is normed by $\|z\| = $ Sup $|z_h|$.

The assumption of free disposal for the technology means that if $y \in Y$ and $y_h' \leq y_h$ for all h, then $y' \in Y$ [if an input-output combination is possible, so is one where some outputs are smaller or some inputs larger; it is implied that a surplus can be freely disposed of]. With this assumption, if Y is not empty, it clearly has an interior point: select a number $\rho > 0$ and a point $y \in Y$; consider y' defined by $y_h' = y_h - \rho$ for all h. The sphere of center y', radius ρ, is contained in Y.

Other examples of linear spaces in economics are provided by the case where there is a finite number l of commodities, and time and/or location is a continuous variable. The activity of an economic agent is then described by the l rates of flow of the commodities as functions of time and/or location. The space L is the set of l-tuples of functions of the continuous variable.

In any case, if L is properly chosen, the existence of an interior point for Y will follow from the free disposal assumption. Then application of Theorem 2 will give a continuous linear form $v(z)$.

---

[12] E. Malinvaud, "Capital Accumulation and Efficient Allocation of Resources," *Econometrica*, 21, 233–68, 1953.

Cardinal welfare, individualistic ethics, and interpersonal comparisons of utility*†

JOHN C. HARSANYI

I

The naïve concept of social welfare as a sum of intuitively measurable and comparable individual cardinal utilities has been found unable to withstand the methodological criticism of the Pareto school. Professor Bergson[1] has therefore recommended its replacement by the more general concept of a social welfare function, defined as an arbitrary mathematical function of economic (and other social) variables, of a form freely chosen according to one's personal ethical (or political) value judgments. Of course, in this terminology everybody will have a social welfare function of his own, different from that of everybody else, except to the extent to which different individuals' value judgments happen to coincide with one another. Actually, owing to the prevalence of individualistic value judgments in our society, it has been generally agreed that a social welfare function should be an increasing function of the utilities of individuals: if a certain situation, X, is preferred by an individual to another situation, Y, and if none of the other individuals prefer Y to X, then X should be regarded as socially preferable to Y. But no other restriction is to be imposed on the mathematical form of a social welfare function.

Recently, however, Professor Fleming[2] has shown that if one accepts one further fairly weak and plausible ethical postulate, one finds one's social

* *Journal of Political Economy*, 63(1955): pp. 309–21. Reprinted by courtesy of the author and the *Journal of Political Economy*.

† I am indebted to my colleagues at the University of Queensland, Messrs. R. W. Lane and G. Price, for helpful comments. Of course, the responsibility for shortcomings of this paper and for the opinions expressed in it is entirely mine.

1 A. Bergson (Burk), "A Reformulation of Certain Aspects of Welfare Economics," *Quarterly Journal of Economics*, LII (February, 1938), 310–34, and "Socialist Economics", in *A Survey of Contemporary Economics*, ed. H. S. Ellis (Philadelphia, 1949), esp. pp. 412–20.

2 J. M. Fleming, "A Cardinal Concept of Welfare," *Quarterly Journal of Economics*, LXVI (August, 1952), 366–84. For a different approach to the same problem see L. Goodman and H. Markowitz, "Social Welfare Functions Based on Individual Rankings," *American Journal of Sociology*, Vol. LVIII (November, 1952).

welfare function to be at once restricted to a rather narrow class of mathematical functions so as to be expressible (after appropriate monotone transformation of the social welfare and individual utility indexes if necessary) as the weighted sum of the individuals' utilities. This does not mean, of course, a return to the doctrine that the existence of an additive cardinal utility function is intuitively self-evident. The existence of such a function becomes, rather, the consequence of the ethical postulates adopted and is wholly dependent on these postulates. Still, Fleming's results do in a sense involve an unexpected revival of some views of the pre-Pareto period.

In this paper I propose, first of all, to examine the precise ethical meaning of Fleming's crucial postulate and to show that it expresses an *individualistic* value judgment going definitely beyond the generally adopted individualistic postulate mentioned earlier, though it represents, as I shall argue, a value judgment perfectly acceptable according to common ethical standards (Sec. II). I shall also attempt to show that, if both social and individual preferences are assumed to satisfy the von Neumann–Morgenstern–Marschak axioms about choices between uncertain prospects, even a much weaker ethical postulate than Fleming's suffices to establish an additive cardinal social welfare function (Sec. III). In effect, it will be submitted that a mere logical analysis of what we mean by value judgments concerning social welfare and by social welfare functions leads, without any additional ethical postulates, to a social welfare function of this mathematical form (Sec. IV). Finally, I shall turn to the problem of interpersonal comparisons of utility, which gains new interest by the revival of an additive cardinal welfare concept, and shall examine what logical basis, if any, there is for such comparisons (Sec. V).

II

Fleming expresses his ethical postulates in terms of two alternative conceptual frameworks: one in terms of an "*ideal utilitarianism*" of G. E. Moore's type, the other in terms of a *preference* terminology more familiar to economists. Though he evidently sets greater store by the first approach, I shall adopt the second, which seems to be freer of unnecessary metaphysical commitments. I have also taken the liberty of rephrasing his postulates to some extent.

Postulate A (*asymmetry of social preference*) If "from a social standpoint"[3] situation X is preferred to situation Y, then Y is not preferred to X.

Postulate B (*transitivity of social preference*). If from a social standpoint X is preferred to Y, and Y to Z, then X is preferred to Z.

---

[3] Of course, when I speak of preferences "from a social standpoint," often abbreviated to "social" preferences and the like, I always mean preferences based on a given individual's value judgments concerning "social welfare." The foregoing postulates are meant to impose restrictions on *any* individual's value judgments of this kind, and thus represent, as it were, value judgments of the second order, that is, value judgments concerning value judgments. Later I shall discuss the concept of "preferences from a social standpoint" at some length and introduce the distinctive term "ethical preferences" to describe them (in Sec. IV). But at this stage I do not want to prejudge the issue by using this terminology.

Postulate C (transitivity of social indifference). If from a social standpoint neither of X and Y is preferred to the other, and again neither of Y and Z is preferred to the other, then likewise neither of X and Z is preferred to the other.

These three postulates are meant to insure that "social preference" establishes a *complete ordering* among the possible social situations, from which the existence of a social welfare function (at least of an ordinal type) at once follows. (Actually, two postulates would have suffices if, in the postulates, "weak" preference, which does not exclude the possibility of indifference, had been used instead of "strong" preference.)

Postulate D (positive relation of social preferences to individual preferences). If a given individual i prefers situation X to situation Y, and none of the other individuals prefers Y to X, then X is preferred to Y from a social standpoint.

As already mentioned Postulate D expresses a generally accepted individualistic value judgment.

Finally, Fleming's Postulate E states essentially that on issues on which two individuals' interests (preferences) conflict, all other individuals' interests being unaffected, social preferences should depend exclusively on comparing the relative social importance of the interests at stake of each of the two individuals concerned. In other words, it requires that the distribution of utilities between each pair of individuals should be judged separately on its own merits, independently of how utilities (or income) are distributed among the other members of the community.

Postulate E (independent evaluation of the utility distribution[4] between each pair of individuals). (1) There are at least three individuals. (2) Suppose that individual i is indifferent between situations X and X' and also between situations Y and Y' but prefers situations X and X' to situations Y and Y'. Suppose, further, that individual j is also indifferent between X and X' and between Y and Y', but (unlike individual i) prefers Y and Y' to X and X'. Suppose also that all other individuals are indifferent between X and Y, and likewise between X' and Y'.[5] Then social preferences should always go in the same way between X and Y as they do between X' and Y' (that is, if from a social standpoint X is preferred to Y, then X' should also be preferred to Y'; if from a social standpoint X and Y are regarded as indifferent, the same should be true of X' and Y'; and if from a social standpoint Y is preferred to X, then Y' should also be preferred to X').

Postulate E is a natural extension of the individualistic value judgment expressed by Postulate D. Postulate D already implies that if the choice

---

[4] The more general term "utility distribution" is used instead of the term "income distribution," since the utility enjoyed by each individual will, in general, depend not only on his own income but also, owing to external economies and diseconomies of consumption, on other people's incomes.

[5] It is not assumed, however, that the other individuals are (like i and j) indifferent between X and X' and between Y and Y'. In effect, were this restrictive assumption inserted into Postulate E, this latter would completely lose the status of an independent postulate and would become a mere corollary of Postulate D.

between two situations X and Y happens to affect the interests of the individuals i and j only, without affecting the interests of anybody else, social choice must depend exclusively on i's and j's interests—provided that i's and j's interests *agree* in this matter. Postulate E now adds that in the assumed case social choice must depend exclusively on i's and j's interests (and on weighing these two interests one against the other in terms of a consistent ethical standard), even if i's and j's interests are in *conflict*. Thus both postulates make social choice dependent solely on the *individual* interests directly affected.[6] They leave no room for the separate interests of a superindividual state or of impersonal cultural values[7] (except for the ideals of equity incorporated in the ethical postulates themselves).

At first sight, Postulate E may look inconsistent with the widespread habit of judging the "fairness" or "unfairness" of the distribution of income between two individuals, not only on the basis of these two people's personal conditions and needs, but also on the basis of comparing their incomes with the incomes of the other members of their respective social groups. Thus people's judgments on the income distribution between a given worker and his employer will also depend on the current earnings of other similar workers and employers. But the conflict with Postulate E is more apparent than real. In a society with important external economies and diseconomies of consumption, where the utility of a given income depends not only on its absolute size but also on its relation to other people's incomes, it is not inconsistent with Postulate E that, in judging the income distribution between two individuals, other people's incomes should also be taken into account. An income distribution between a given worker and a given employer, which in the original situation seemed perfectly "fair" in terms of a given ethical standard, may require adjustment in the worker's favor once wages have generally gone up, since the worsening of this worker's position relative to that of his fellows must have reduced him to a lower level of utility.

Postulate E requires that the distribution of *utility* between two individuals (once the utility levels of the two individuals are given) should always be judged independently of how utility and income are distributed among other

---

[6] In view of consumers' notorious "irrationality," some people may feel that these postulates go too far in accepting the consumers' sovereignty doctrine. These people may reinterpret the terms in the postulates referring to individual preferences as denoting, not certain individuals' actual preferences, but rather their "true" preferences, that is, the preferences they *would* manifest under "ideal conditions," in possession of perfect information, and acting with perfect logic and care. With some ingenuity it should not be too difficult to give even some sort of "operational" meaning to these ideal conditions, or to some approximation of them, acceptable for practical purposes. (Or, alternatively, these terms may be reinterpreted as referring even to the preferences that these individuals *ought* to exhibit in terms of a given ethical standard. The latter interpretation would, of course, deprive the postulates of most of their individualistic meaning.)

[7] These postulates do not exclude, however, the possibility that such consideration may influence the relative weights given to different individuals' utilities within the additive social welfare function. Even by means of additional postulates, this could be excluded only to the extent to which the comparison of individual utilities can be put on an objective basis independent of individual value judgments (see Sec. V).

members of the society. In the absence of external economies and diseconomies of consumption, this would necessarily also mean judging the distribution of *income* between two individuals independently of the incomes of others. In the presence of such economies and diseconomies, however, when the utility level of any person depends not only on his own income but also on other persons' incomes, it is not inconsistent with Postulate E that our value judgment on the distribution of income between two individuals should be influenced by the income distribution in the rest of the society—insofar as the income distribution in the rest of the society affects the utility levels of these two individuals themselves and consequently the distribution of utility between them. Postulate E demands only that, once these effects have been allowed for, the distribution of income in the rest of the society must not have any further influence on our value judgment.

III

In accordance with prevalent usage in welfare economics, Fleming's postulates refer to social or individual preferences between *sure prospects* only. However, it seems desirable to have both sorts of preferences defined for choices between *uncertain prospects* as well. More often than not, we have to choose in practice between social policies that promise given definite results only with larger or smaller probabilities. On the other hand, if we subscribe to some sort of individualistic ethics, we should like to make social attitude toward uncertainty somehow dependent on individual attitudes toward it (at least if the latter do not manifest too patent and too great an inconsistency and irrationality).

Since we admit the possibility of external economies and diseconomies of consumption, both social and individual prospects will, in general, specify the amounts of different commodities consumed and the stocks of different goods held by all individuals at different future dates (up to the time horizon adopted), together with their respective probabilities.

As the von Neumann–Morgenstern axioms[8] or the Marschak postulates[9]

---

[8] See J. von Neumann and O. Morgenstern, *Theory of Games and Economic Behavior* (2d ed.; Princeton, 1947), pp. 641 ff.

[9] J. Marschak, "Rational Behavior, Uncertain Prospects, and Measurable Utility," *Econometrica*, XVIII (1950), 111–41, esp. 116–21. Marschak's postulates can be summarized as follows. *Postulate I (complete ordering)*: The relation of preference establishes a complete ordering among all prospects. *Postulate II(continuity)*: If prospect P is preferred to prospect R, while prospect Q has an intermediate position between them (being preferred to R but less preferred than P), then there exists a mixture of P and R, with appropriate probabilities, such as to be exactly indifferent to Q. *Postulate III' (sufficient number of nonindifferent prospects)*: There are at least four mutually nonindifferent prospects. *Postulate IV (equivalence of mixture of equivalent prospects)*: If prospects Q and Q' are indifferent, then, for any prospect P, a given mixture of P and Q is indifferent to a similar mixture of P and Q' (that is, to a mixture of P and Q' which has the same probabilities for the corresponding constituent prospects).

Postulate I is needed to establish the existence of even an *ordinal* utility (or welfare) function, while the other three postulates are required to establish the existence of a *cardinal* utility (or welfare) function. But, as Postulates II and III are almost trivial, Postulate IV may be regarded as being decisive for cardinality as against mere ordinality.

equivalent to them (which latter I shall adopt) are essential requirements for rational behavior, it is natural enough to demand that both social and individual preferences[10] should satisfy them. This gives us:

Postulate a. Social preferences satisfy Marschak's Postulates I, II, III', and IV.

Postulate b. Individual preferences satisfy the same four postulates.

In addition, we need a postulate to secure the dependence of social preferences on individual preferences.

Postulate c. If two prospects P and Q are indifferent from the standpoint of every individual, they are also indifferent from a social standpoint.

Postulate c once more represents, of course, an individualistic value judgment—though a very weak one, comparable to Fleming's Postulate D rather than to his Postulate E.

I propose to show that Postulate c suffices to establish that the cardinal social welfare function defined by Postulate a can be obtained as a weighted sum of the cardinal individual utility functions defined by Postulate b (on the understanding that the zero point of the social welfare function is appropriately chosen).

Theorem I. There exists a social welfare function such that its actuarial value is maximized by choices conformable to the social preferences given. This social welfare function is unique up to linear transformation.

Theorem II. For each individual there exists a utility function such that its actuarial value is maximized by choices conformable to the individual's preferences. This utility function is unique up to linear transformation.

Both theorems follow from Marschak's argument.

Let W denote a social welfare function satisfying Theorem I and U_i denote a utility function of the i'th individual, satisfying Theorem II. Moreover, let W be chosen so that $W = 0$ if for all the n individuals $U_1 = U_2 = \ldots = U_n = 0$.

Theorem III. W is a single-valued function of $U_1, U_2, \ldots, U_n$. This follows, in view of Theorems I and II, from Postulate c.

Theorem IV. W is a homogeneous function of the first order of $U_1, U_2, \ldots, U_n$.

Proof. We want to show that, if the individual utilities $U_1 = u_1$; $U_2 = u_2$; $\ldots$; $U_n = u_n$ correspond to the social welfare $W = w$, then the individual utilities $U_1 = k \cdot u_1$; $U_2 = k \cdot u_2$; $\ldots$; $U_n = k \cdot u_n$ correspond to the social welfare $W = k \cdot w$.

This will be shown first for the case where $0 \leq k \leq 1$. Suppose that prospect O represents $U_1 = U_2 = \ldots = U_n = 0$ for the different individuals and

---

[10] There are reasons to believe that, in actuality, individual preferences between uncertain prospects do not always satisfy these postulates of rational behavior (for example, owing to a certain "love of danger"; see Marschak, *op. cit.*, pp. 137–41). In this case we may fall back again upon the preferences each individual *would* manifest under "ideal conditions" (see n. 4).

consequently represents $W = 0$ for society, while prospect P represents $U_1 = u_1$; $U_2 = u_2; \ldots; U_n = u_n$ for the former and $W = w$ for the latter. Moreover, let Q be the mixed prospect of obtaining either prospect O (with the probability $1 - p$) or prospect P (with the probability p). Then, obviously, Q will represent $U_1 = p \cdot u_1$; $U_2 = p \cdot u_2$; $\ldots$; $U_n = p \cdot u_n$ for the individuals and $W = p \cdot w$ for society. Now, if we write $k = p$, a comparison between the values of the variables belonging to prospect P and those belonging to prospect Q will, in view of Theorem III, establish the desired result for the case where $0 \leq k \leq 1$ (p, being a probability, cannot be <0 or >1).

Next let us consider the case where $k < 0$. Let us choose prospect R so that prospect O becomes equivalent to the mixed prospect of obtaining either prospect R (with the probability p) or prospect P (with the probability $1 - p$). A little calculation will show that in this case prospect R will represent $U_1 = (1 - 1/p) \cdot u_1$; $U_2 = (1 - 1/p) \cdot u_2$; $\ldots$; $U_n = (1 - 1/p) \cdot u_n$ for the different individuals and $W = (1 - 1/p) \cdot U_n$ for society. If we now write $k = 1 - 1/p$, a comparison between the variables belonging to R and those belonging to P will establish the desired result for the case $k < 0$ (by an appropriate choice of the probability p, we can make k equal to any negative number).

Finally, the case where $k > 1$ can be taken care of by finding a prospect S such that prospect P becomes equivalent to the mixed prospect of obtaining either S (with a probability p) or O (with a probability $1 - p$). Then this prospect S will be connected with the values $U_1 = 1/p \cdot u_1$; $U_2 = 1/p \cdot u_2$; $\ldots$; $U_n = 1/p \cdot u_n$ and $W = 1/p \cdot w$. If we now write $k = 1/p$ we obtain the desired result for the case where $k > 1$ (by an appropriate choice of p we can make k equal to any number >1).

Theorem V. W is a weighted sum of the individual utilities, of the form

$$W = \sum a_i \cdot U_i,$$

where a_i stands for the value that W takes when $U_i = 1$ and $U_j = 0$ for all $j \neq i$.

Proof. Let S_i be a prospect representing the utility U_i to the ith individual and the utility zero to all other individuals. Then, according to Theorem IV, for S_i we have $W = a_i \cdot U_i$.

Let T be the mixed prospect of obtaining either S_1 or S_2 or $\ldots S_n$, each with probability $1/n$. Then T will represent the individual utilities U_1/n, $U_2/n, \ldots, U_n/n$ and the social welfare

$$W = \frac{1}{n} \cdot \sum a_i \cdot U_i.$$

In view of Theorem IV, this directly implies that if the individual utility functions take the values $U_1, U_2, \ldots, U_n$, respectively, the social welfare function has the value

$$W = \sum a_i \cdot U_i,$$

as desired.[11]

IV

In the pre-Pareto conceptual framework, the distinction between social welfare and individual utilities was free of ambiguity. Individual utilities were assumed to be directly given by introspection, and social welfare was simply their sum. In the modern approach, however, the distinction is far less clear. On the one hand, our social welfare concept has come logically nearer to an individual utility concept. Social welfare is no longer regarded as an objective quantity, the same for all, by necessity. Rather, each individual is supposed to have a social welfare function of his own, expressing his own individual values—in the same way as each individual has a utility function of his own, expressing his own individual taste. On the other hand, our individual utility concept has come logically nearer to a social welfare concept. Owing to a greater awareness of the importance of external economies and diseconomies of consumption in our society, each individual's utility function is now regarded as dependent not only on this particular individual's economic (and noneconomic) conditions but also on the economic (and other) conditions of all other individuals in the community—in the same way as a social welfare function is dependent on the personal conditions of all individuals.

At the same time, we cannot allow the distinction between an individual's social welfare function and his utility function to be blurred if we want (as most of us do, I think) to uphold the principle that a social welfare function ought to be based not on the utility function (subjective preferences) of *one* particular individual only (namely, the individual whose value judgments are expressed in this welfare function), but rather on the utility functions (subjective preferences) of *all* individuals, representing a kind of "fair compromise" among them.[12] Even if both an individual's social welfare function and his utility function in a sense express his own individual preferences, they must express preferences of different sorts: the former must express what this individual prefers (or, rather, would prefer) on the basis of impersonal social considerations alone, and the latter must express what he actually prefers, whether on the basis of his personal interests or on any other basis. The former may be called his "ethical" preferences, the latter his "subjective" preferences. Only his "subjective" preferences (which define his utility function) will

---

[11] If we want a formal guaranty that no individual's utility can be given a negative weight in the social welfare function, we must add one more postulate (for instance, Postulate D of Sec. II).

[12] This principle is essentially identical with Professor Arrow's "nondictatorship" postulate in his *Social Choice and Individual Values* (New York, 1951), p. 30 (see also n. 11).

express his preferences in the full sense of the word as they actually are, showing an egoistic attitude in the case of an egoist and an altruistic attitude in the case of an altruist. His "ethical" preferences (which define his social welfare function) will, on the other hand, express what can in only a qualified sense be called his "preferences": they will, by definition, express what he prefers only in those possibly rare moments when he forces a special impartial and impersonal attitude upon himself.[13]

In effect, the ethical postulates proposed in Sections II and III—namely, Postulates D, E, and c—can be regarded as simply an implicit definition of what sort of "impartial" or "impersonal" attitude is required to underlie "ethical" preferences: these postulates essentially serve to exclude nonethical subjective preferences from social welfare functions. But this aim may also be secured more directly by explicitly defining the impartial and impersonal attitude demanded.

I have argued elsewhere[14] that an individual's preferences satisfy this requirement of impersonality if they indicate what social situation he would choose if he did not know what his personal position would be in the new situation chosen (and in any of its alternatives) but rather had an equal *chance* of obtaining any of the social positions[15] existing in this situation, from the highest down to the lowest. Of course, it is immaterial whether this individual does not in fact know how his choice would affect his personal interests or merely disregards this knowledge for a moment when he is making his choice. As I have tried to show,[16] in either case an impersonal choice (preference) of this kind can in a technical sense be regarded as a choice between "uncertain" prospects.

---

[13] Mr. Little's objection to Arrow's nondictatorship postulate (see Little's review article in the *Journal of Political Economy*, LX [October, 1952], esp. 426–31) loses its force, once the distinction between "ethical" and "subjective" preferences is noted. It does, then, make sense that an individual should morally *disapprove* (in terms of his "ethical" preferences) of an unequal income distribution which benefits him financially, and should still *prefer* it (in terms of his "subjective" preferences) to a more egalitarian one or should even *fight* for it—behavior morally regrettable but certainly not logically inconceivable.

Arrow's distinction between an individual's "tastes" (which order social situations only according to their effects on his own consumption) and his "values" (which take account also of external economies and diseconomies of consumption and of ethical considerations, in ordering social situations) does not meet the difficulty, since it does not explain how an individual can without inconsistency accept a social welfare function conflicting with his own "values." This can be understood only if his social welfare functions represents preferences of another sort than his "values" do. (Of course, in my terminology Arrow's "values" fall in the class of "subjective" preferences and not in the class of "ethical" preferences, as is easily seen from the way in which he defines them.)

[14] See my "Cardinal Utility in Welfare Economics and in the Theory of Risk-taking," *Journal of Political Economy*, LXI (October, 1953), 434–35.

[15] Or, rather, if he had an equal chance of being "put in the place of" any individual member of the society, with regard not only to his objective social (and economic) conditions, but also to his subjective attitudes and tastes. In other words, he ought to judge the utility of another individual's position not in terms of his own attitudes and tastes but rather in terms of the attitudes and tastes of the individual actually holding this position.

[16] *Op. cit.*

This implies, however, without any additional ethical postulates that an individual's impersonal preferences, if they are rational, must satisfy Marschak's axioms and consequently must define a cardinal social welfare function equal to the arithmetical mean[17] of the utilities of all individuals in the society (since the arithmetical mean of all individual utilities gives the actuarial value of his uncertain prospect, defined by an equal probability of being put in the place of any individual in the situation chosen).

More exactly, if the former individual has any objective criterion for comparing his fellows' utilities with one another and with his own (see Sec. V), his social welfare function will represent the unweighted mean of these utilities, while in the absence of such an objective criterion it will, in general, represent their weighted mean, with arbitrary weights depending only on his personal value judgments. In the former case, social welfare will in a sense be an objective quantity, whereas in the latter case, it will contain an important subjective element; but even in this latter case it will be something very different from the utility function of the individual concerned.[18]

V

There is no doubt about the fact that people do make, or at least attempt to make, interpersonal comparisons of utility, both in the sense of comparing different persons' total satisfaction and in the sense of comparing increments or decrements in different persons' satisfaction.[19] The problem is only what logical basis, if any, there is for such comparisons.

In general, we have two indicators of the utility that *other* people attach to different situations: their preferences as revealed by their actual choices, and their (verbal or nonverbal) expressions of satisfaction or dissatisfaction in each situation. But while the use of these indicators for comparing the utilities that a *given* person ascribes to different situations is relatively free of difficulty, their use for comparing the utility that *different* persons ascribe to each situation entails a special problem. In actual fact, this problem has two rather different aspects, one purely metaphysical and one psychological, which have not, however, always been sufficiently kept apart.

---

[17] Obviously, the (unweighted or weighted) *mean* of the individual utilities defines the same social welfare function as their *sum* (weighted by the same relative weights), except for an irrelevant proportionality constant.

[18] The concept of ethical preferences used in this section implies, of course, an ethical theory different from the now prevalent subjective attitude theory, since it makes a person's ethical judgments the expression, not of his subjective attitudes in general, but rather of certain special unbiased impersonal attitudes only. For a philosophical argument in favor of such an ethical theory, see my "Ethics in Terms of Hypothetical Imperatives," *Mind*, N.S., LXVI (July, 1958) 305–16. (see also the references there quoted in the footnote on p. 309.)

[19] See I. M. D. Little, *A Critique of Welfare Economics* (Oxford, 1950), chap. iv. I have nothing to add to Little's conclusion on the *possibility* of interpersonal comparisons of utility. I only want to supplement his argument by an analysis of the *logical basis* of such comparisons. I shall deal with the problem of comparisons between total utilities only, neglecting the problem of comparisons between differences in utility, since the social welfare functions discussed in the previous sections contain only total utilities of individuals.

The *metaphysical* problem would be present even if we tried to compare the utilities enjoyed by different persons with identical preferences and with identical expressive reactions to any situation. Even in this case, it would not be inconveivable that such persons should have different susceptibilities to satisfaction and should attach different utilities to identical situations, for, in principle, identical preferences may well correspond to different absolute levels of utility (as long as the ordinal properties of all persons' utility functions are the same[20]), and identical expressive reactions may well indicate different mental states with different people. At the same time, under these conditions this logical possibility of different susceptibilities to satisfaction would hardly be more than a metaphysical curiosity. If two objects or human beings show similar behavior in *all* their relevant aspects open to observation, the assumption of some unobservable hidden difference between them must be regarded as a completely gratuitous hypothesis and one contrary to sound scientific method.[21] (This principle may be called the "principle of unwarranted differentiation.") In the last analysis, it is on the basis of this principle that we ascribe mental states to other human beings at all: the denial of this principle would at once lead us to solipsism.[22] Thus in the case of persons with similar preferences and expressive reactions we are fully entitled to assume that they derive the same utilities from similar situations.

In the real world, of course, different people's preferences and their expressive reactions to similar situations may be rather different, and this does represent a very real difficulty in comparing the utilities enjoyed by different people—a difficulty in addition to the metaphysical difficulty just discussed and independent of it. I shall refer to it as the *psychological* difficulty since it is essentially a question of how psychological differences between people in the widest sense (for example, differences in consumption habits, cultural background, social status, and sex and other biological conditions, as well as purely psychological differences, inborn or acquired) affect the satisfaction that people derive from each situation. The problem in general takes the following form. If one individual prefers situation X to situation Y, while another prefers Y to X, is this so because the former individual attaches a *higher* utility to situation X, or because he attaches a *lower* utility to situation Y, than does the latter—or is this perhaps the result of both these factors at the same time? And, again, if in a given situation one individual gives more forcible signs of satisfaction or dissatisfaction than another, is this so because

---

[20] Even identical preferences among uncertain prospects (satisfying the Marschak axioms) are compatible with different absolute levels of utility, since they do not uniquely determine the zero points and the scales of the corresponding cardinal utility functions.

[21] By making a somewhat free use of Professor Carnap's distinction, we may say that the assumption of different susceptibilities of satisfaction in this case, even though it would not be against the canons of *deductive* logic, would most definitely be against the canons of *inductive* logic.

[22] See Little, *A Critique of Welfare Economics*, pp. 56–57.

the former feels more intense satisfaction or dissatisfaction, or only because he is inclined to give stronger expression to his feelings?

This psychological difficulty is accessible to direct empirical solution to the extent to which these psychological differences between people are capable of change, and it is therefore possible for some individuals to make direct comparisons between the satisfactions open to one human type and those open to another. [23] Of course, many psychological variables are not capable of change or are capable of change only in some directions but not in others. For instance, a number of inborn mental or biological characteristics cannot be changed at all, and though the cultural patterns and attitudes of an individual born and educated in one social group can be considerably changed by transplanting him to another, usually they cannot be completely assimilated to the cultural patterns and attitudes of the second group. Thus it may easily happen that, if we want to compare the satisfactions of two different classes of human beings, we cannot find any individual whose personal experiences would cover the satisfactions of both these classes.

Interpersonal comparisons of utility made in everyday life seem, however, to be based on a different principle (which is, of course, seldom formulated explicitly). If two individuals have opposite preferences between two situations, we usually try to find out the psychological differences responsible for this disagreement and, on the basis of our general knowledge of human psychology, try to judge to what extent these psychological differences are likely to increase or decrease their satisfaction derived from each situation. For example, if one individual is ready at a given wage rate to supply more labor than another, we tend in general to explain this mainly by his having a lower disutility for labor if his physique is much more robust than that of the other individual and if there is no ascertainable difference between the two individuals' economic needs; we tend to explain it mainly by his having a higher utility for income (consumption goods) if the two individuals' physiques are similar and if the former evidently has much greater economic needs (for example, a larger family to support).

Undoubtedly, both these methods of tackling what we have called the "psychological difficulty" are subject to rather large margins of error.[24] In general, the greater the psychological, biological, cultural, and social differences between two people, the greater the margin of error attached to comparisons between their utility.

Particular uncertainty is connected with the second method since it depends on our general knowledge of psychological laws, which is still in a

---

[23] On the reliability of comparisons between the utility of different situations before a change in one's "taste" (taken in the broadest sense) and after it, see the first two sections of my "Welfare Economics of Variable Tastes," *Review of Economic Studies*, XXI, (1953–54), 204–8.

[24] Though perhaps it would not be too difficult to reduce these margins quite considerably (for example, by using appropriate statistical techniques) should there be a need for more precise results.

largely unsatisfactory state.[25] What is more, all our knowledge about the psychological laws of satisfaction is ultimately derived from observing how changes in different (psychological and other) variables affect the satisfactions an individual obtains from various situations. We therefore have no direct empirical evidence on how people's satisfactions are affected by the variables that, for any particular individual, are *not* capable of change. Thus we can, in general, judge the influence of these " unchangeable " variables only on the basis of the correlations found between these and the " changeable " variables, whose influence we can observe directly. For instance, let us take sex as an example of " unchangeable " variables (disregarding the few instances of sex change) and abstractive ability as an example of " changeable " variables. We tend to assume that the average man finds greater satisfaction than the average woman does in solving mathematical puzzles *because*, allegedly, men in general have greater abstractive ability than women. But this reasoning depends on the implicit assumption that differences in the " unchangeable " variables, if unaccompanied by differences in the " changeable " variables, are in themselves immaterial. For example, we must assume that men and women equal in abstractive ability (and the other relevant characeristics) would tend to find the same satisfaction in working on mathematical problems.

Of course, the assumption that the " unchangeable " variables in themselves have no influence is *ex hypothesi* not open to direct empirical check. It can be justified only by the a priori principle that, when one variable is alleged to have a certain influence on another, the burden of proof lies on those who claim the existence of such an influence.[26] Thus the second method of interpersonal utility comparison rests in an important sense on empirical evidence more direct[27] than that underlying the first method. On the other hand, the second method has the advantage of also being applicable in those cases where no one individual can possibly have wide enough personal experience to make direct utility comparisons in terms of the first method.

---

[25] Going back to our example, for instance, the disutility of labor and the utility of income are unlikely to be actually independent variables (as I have tacitly assumed), though it may not always be clear in which way their mutual influence actually goes. In any case, income is enjoyed in a different way, depending on the ease with which it has been earned, and labor is put up with in a different spirit, depending on the strength of one's need for additional income.

[26] This principle may be called the " principle of unwarranted correlation " and is again a principle of inductive logic, closely related to the principle of unwarranted differentiation referred to earlier.

[27] There is also another reason for which conclusions dependent on the principle of unwarranted correlation have somewhat less cogency than conclusions dependent only on the principle of unwarranted differentiation. The former principle refers to the case where two individuals differ in a certain variable X (in our example, in sex) but where there is no special evidence that they differ also in a certain other variable Y (in susceptibility to satisfaction). The latter principle, on the other hand, refers to the case where there is no ascertainable difference at all between the two individuals in any observable variable whatever, not even in X (in sex). Now, though the assumption that these two individuals differ in Y (in susceptibility to satisfaction) would be a gratuitous hypothesis in either case, obviously it would be a less unnatural hypothesis in the first case (where there is some observed difference between the two individuals) than in the second case (where there is none).

In any case, it should now be sufficiently clear that interpersonal comparisons of utility are not value judgments based on some ethical or political postulates but rather are factual propositions based on certain principles of inductive logic.

At the same time, Professor Robbins[28] is clearly right when he maintains that propositions which purport to be interpersonal comparisons of utility often contain a purely *conventional* element based on ethical or political value judgments. For instance, the assumption that different individuals have the same susceptibility to satisfaction often expresses only the egalitarian value judgment that all individuals should be treated equally rather than a belief in a factual psychological equality between them. Or, again, different people's total satisfaction is often compared on the tacit understanding that the gratification of wants regarded as "immoral" in terms of a certain ethical standard shall not count. But in order to avoid confusion, such propositions based on ethical or political restrictive postulates must be clearly distinguished from interpersonal comparisons of utility without a conventional element of this kind.

It must also be admitted that the use of conventional postulates based on personal value judgments may sometimes be due not to our free choice but rather to our lack of the factual information needed to give our interpersonal utility comparisons a more objective basis. In effect, if we do not know anything about the relative urgency of different persons' economic needs and still have to make a decision, we can hardly avoid acting on the basis of personal guesses more or less dependent on our own value judgments.

On the other hand, if the information needed is available, individualistic ethics consistently requires the use, in the social welfare function, of individual utilities not subjected to restrictive postulates. The imposition of restrictive ethical or political conventions on the individual utility functions would necessarily qualify our individualism, since it would decrease the dependence of our social welfare function on the actual preferences and actual susceptibilities to satisfaction, of the individual members of the society, putting in its place a dependence on our own ethical or political value judgments (see nn. 4 and 5).

To sum up, the more complete our factual information and the more completely individualistic our ethics, the more the different individuals' social welfare functions will converge toward the same objective quantity, namely, the unweighted sum (or rather the unweighted arithmetic mean) of all individual utilities. This follows both from (either of two alternative sets of) ethical postulates based on commonly accepted individualistic ethical value judgments and from the mere logical analysis of the concept of a social welfare

---

[28] See L. Robbins, "Robertson on Utility and Scope," *Economica*, N.S., XX(1953), 99–111, esp. 109; see also his *An Essay on the Nature and Significance of Economic Science* (2d ed.; London, 1948), chap. vi; and his "Interpersonal Comparisons of Utility," *Economic Journal*, XLIII (December, 1938), 635–41,

function. The latter interpretation also removes certain difficulties connected with the concept of a social welfare function, which have been brought out by Little's criticism of certain of Arrow's conclusions.

Of course, the practical need for reaching decisions on public policy will require us to formulate social welfare functions—explicitly or implicitly— even if we lack the factual information needed for placing interpersonal comparisons of utility on an objective basis. But even in this case, granting the proposed ethical postulates (or the proposed interpretation of the concept of a social welfare function), our social welfare function must take the form of a weighted sum (weighted mean) of all individual utility functions, with more or less arbitrary weights chosen according to our own value judgments.

There is here an interesting analogy with the theory of statistical decisions (and, in general, the theory of choosing among alternative hypotheses). In the same way as in the latter, it has been shown[29] that a rational man (whose choices satisfy certain simple postulates of rationality) must act *as if* he ascribed numerical subjective probabilities to all alternative hypotheses, even if his factual information is insufficient to do this on an objective basis—so in welfare economics we have also found that a rational man (whose choices satisfy certain simple postulates of rationality and impartiality) must likewise act *as if* he made quantitative interpersonal comparisons of utility, even if his factual information is insufficient to do this on an objective basis.

Thus if we accept individualistic ethics and set public policy the task of satisfying the preferences of the individual members of the society (deciding between conflicting preferences of different individuals according to certain standards of impartial equity), our social welfare function will always tend to take the form of a sum (or mean) of individual utilities; but whether the weights given to these individual utilities have an objective basis or not will depend wholly on the extent of our factual (psychological) information.

---

[29] See Marschak's discussion of what he calls "Ramsey's norm," in his paper on "Probability in the Social Sciences," in *Mathematical Thinking in the Social Sciences*, ed. P. F. Lazarsfeld (Glencoe, Ill., 1954), Sec. I, esp. pp. 179–87; also reprinted as No. 82 of "Cowles Commission Papers" (N.S.).

For a survey of earlier literature see K. J. Arrow, "Alternative Approaches to the Theory of Choice in Risk-taking Situations," *Econometrica*, XIX (October, 1951), 404–37, esp. 431–32, and the references there quoted.

Optimality and informational efficiency in resource allocation processes[*]

LEONID HURWICZ

1. INTRODUCTION

This paper is primarily devoted to a study of the (static) optimality properties (e.g., Pareto-optimality of the equilibria) of certain resource allocation
mechanisms. It is shown that one such mechanism (the "greed process") is
optimal in a class of economic environments much broader than the class for
which perfect competition is optimal. More specifically, the greed process has
the desired optimality properties for all environments from which so-called
external economies or diseconomies are absent: unlike perfect competition,
the greed process does not presuppose the absence of indivisible goods, of
discontinuities, or of increasing returns. However, the greed process lacks
the dynamic (stability) properties known to hold for perfect competition,
at least in certain special cases.

That the greed process does have certain optimality properties would be
of little interest were it not for the fact that it belongs to a class of *informationally decentralized* processes and hence shares with perfect competition a
feature that has been extolled as one of the main virtues of the classical
market mechanism. Still, just because it is designed to cover a broader class
of environments, the greed process calls for more information (is informationally less efficient) than the competitive mechanism. To illustrate this, a variant

[*] In K. J. Arrow, S. Karlin, and P. Suppes (eds.), *Mathematical Methods in the Social
Sciences, 1959.* (Stanford: Stanford University Press, 1960): Chapter 3, pp. 27–46. Corrected
by the author. Reprinted by courtesy of the author and Stanford University Press.

This paper is dedicated to Jacob Marschak on the occasion of his sixtieth birthday.

In an earlier version of a part of this paper (5), I expressed my indebtedness for stimulation and comments to a number of colleagues from the Cowles Commission and the University of Minnesota. I am particularly grateful to Kenneth J. Arrow and Hirofumi Uzawa for
valuable suggestions resulting in the simplification of some of the proofs.

The paper is partly based on work done during my tenure of a fellowship at the Center
for Advanced Study in the Behavioral Sciences; its completion was facilitated by grants
(at the University of Minnesota and Stanford University) from the Office of Naval Research
(Tasks NR–042–200 and NR–047–004) and (at Stanford University) from the Rockefeller
Foundation.

of the latter (called " quasi-competitive ") is constructed and is shown to have the desired optimality properties when the environment satisfies the usual divisibility and convexity assumptions, while requiring less information than does the greed process.

Even apart from its dynamic defects, the greed process is completely impractical because it calls for behavior on the part of the economic units that is in conflict with their self-interest. But it must be remembered that this weakness is shared by the competitive mechanism unless, roughly speaking, the environment is *atomistic* (i.e., all units are infinitesimal compared with the whole economy).

In a broader perspective, these findings suggest the possibility of a more systematic study of resource allocation mechanisms. In such a study, unlike in the more traditional approach, the mechanism becomes the unknown of the problem, rather than a datum.[1] Of course, to make the problem meaningful, we must define some domain of variation for this unknown. For instance, in the present paper, this domain is given as a certain class of difference equation systems ("adjustment processes"), but other choices could easily be made. The members of such a domain can then be appraised in terms of their various "performance chacteristics" and, in particular, of their (static and dynamic) optimality properties, their informational efficiency, and the compatibility of their postulated behavior with self-interest (or other motivational variables).

One naturally finds that better performance can be obtained at the expense of coverage with respect to the nature of the economic environment, and vice versa. Thus the perfectly competitive mechanism, high on the scale of informational efficiency, has the other performance characteristics (optimality properties and incentive compatibility) for the rather narrow class of atomistic environments possessing the various divisibility and convexity properties and free from external (dis-)economies. But a conflict with self-interest may arise if the environment is nonatomistic, and the optimality properties may fail when the convexity conditions are not satisfied. The greed process, on the other hand, scores relatively well (although less well than the perfectly competitive process) on the informational scale and is shown to have the static optimality properties, even without atomicity, divisibility, or convexity, for environments from which external (dis-)economies are absent, i.e., for a fairly broad class of environments; however, the greed process has poor dynamic characteristics and is in obvious conflict with individual self-interest.

These facts suggest a host of questions. For instance, for the class of environments free of external (dis-)economies, are there mechanisms whose performance characteristics are strictly better than those of the greed process, say with regard to either dynamic stability or informational efficiency, or compatibility with self-interest? Or, on the other hand, how much can we broaden the class of permissible environments and still expect to find mech-

---

[1] The work of J. Marschak and R. Radner [eg., (6), (9)] is carried on in this spirit. See also T. Marschak (7).

anisms whose performance is at least as good as that of the greed process (i.e., informationally decentralized mechanisms possessing the static optimality properties)? So far, only fragmentary answers are available, indicating that the possibilities either of improving performance for the given classes of environments, or of broadening the coverage of environments without loss of performance, are rather limited.

Thus the choice of a resource allocation mechanism must be made with reference to the class of environments to be covered and in the light of some comparative valuation of the different dimensions of the performance characteristics. Given these data (environment class and performance valuation), the choice becomes a standard problem in optimization. But even when these data are either nonexistent or extremely vague (as they typically are in practice), a systematic analysis of the interrelationship between the environment coverage and the performance characteristics of a resource allocation mechanism should be of interest to those concerned with problems of economic organization, the comparative analysis of economic systems,[2] and the study of various institutional aspects of the economic system, whether it be a nation, a firm, or a government agency. Since the economist is at times called upon to express opinions on policy matters before the institutional framework is selected (e.g., within a firm or a young country), the matter is not altogether academic.

2. THE ECONOMIC ENVIRONMENT AND RESOURCE FLOWS

The economic environment

We distinguish between the economic *environment*, to be considered as given, and the resource allocation mechanism (*adjustment process*), regarded as a variable (unknown) of the problem. There is, of course, some arbitrariness with respect to classifying certain aspects of the economic system under one of these two headings.

The economic environment is described with the help of the following notation and terminology:

$I = \{1, 2, \cdots, n\}$: the set of economic units (households, plants, government agencies, etc.);

$\mathscr{X}$: the commodity space (algebraically, an additive group);

0_x: the identity element of addition in $\mathscr{X}$ (i.e., $x + 0_x = x$);

$\mathscr{X}^{(n)} = \mathscr{X} \times \mathscr{X} \times \cdots \times \mathscr{X}$ (n times): the n-fold Cartesian product of $\mathscr{X}$;

X: the admissible consumption (holdings) set;[3] $X \subseteq \mathscr{X}^{(n)}$; the elements of X are called (admissible) *distributions*;

X^i: the ith projection of X;

---

[2] The relationship of the present work to the Hotelling-Lange-Lerner theory of marginal cost pricing and the socialist "competitive solution" will be discussed elsewhere.

[3] For instance, it is often postulated that $X = (X^+)^{(n)}$ = the n-fold Cartesian product of the nonnegative orthant X^+ of $\mathscr{X}$.

w_0^i: the initial resource endowment of the ith unit; $w_0^i \in X^i \subseteq \mathcal{X}$;

$w_0 = (w_0^1, w_0^2, \ldots, w_0^n) \in X$;

R^i (also written as $\geq_i$):[4] the preference relation of the ith unit (R^i is a transitive, reflexive, connected relation on X);

$R = (R^1, R^2, \ldots, R^n)$;

Z: the *feasible* production set; $Z \subseteq \mathcal{X}^{(n)}$;

Z^i: the ith projection of Z;

$e = (I, \mathcal{X}; X, w_0, R, Z)$: the economic environment;

$e^i = (X^i, w_0^i, R^i, Z^i)$: the "characteristic" of the ith unit.

Resource-flow matrices

We find it convenient here to use the device of treating production in a manner formally analogous to exchange. To this end we introduce a fictitious unit ("nature"), referred to as the 0th unit. Now for $r, s = 0, 1, \ldots, n$, the expression $a_{rs} \in \mathcal{X}$ will represent the net flow of goods from unit s to unit r, with goods received by r counted as positive and goods given up by r as negative. Hence a_{s0} represents the input-output vector[5] of the sth economic unit, with output counted as positive, input as negative. From the definition, since a_{rs} represents *net* flow, it is natural to impose the skew-symmetry condition $a_{rs} + a_{sr} = 0_x$ $(r, s = 0, 1, \ldots, n)$.

An $(n + 1) \times (n + 1)$ matrix a with entries from $\mathcal{X}$, satisfying the skew-symmetry relation, i.e.,

$$a = \begin{pmatrix} a_{00} & a_{01} & \cdots & a_{0n} \\ a_{10} & a_{11} & \cdots & a_{1n} \\ \vdots & \vdots & & \vdots \\ a_{n0} & a_{n1} & \cdots & a_{nn} \end{pmatrix}, \text{ where } a_{rs} \in \mathcal{X}, a_{rs} + a_{sr} = 0_x,$$

is called a *resource-flow matrix* (of order n). The set of all resource-flow matrices of order n is denoted by $\mathcal{A}$.

Given a resource-flow matrix a (of order n), we write

$$a_{\cdot 0} = (a_{10}, a_{20}, \ldots, a_{n0}), \qquad \sigma^i(a) = \sum_{s=0}^{n} a_{is},$$

$$\sigma(a) = [\sigma^1(a), \sigma^2(a), \cdots, \sigma^n(a)],$$

so that $a_{\cdot 0} \in \mathcal{X}^{(n)}$, $\sigma^i(a) \in \mathcal{X}$, and $\sigma(a) \in \mathcal{X}^{(n)}$.

Clearly, if w_0 was the resource endowment n-tuple before the resource flow represented by a occurred, the then resource endowment n-tuple after the flow is given by $w_0 + \sigma(a)$. The n-tuple $a_{\cdot 0}$ represents the production activities of the n units.

---

[4] For $w' \in \mathcal{X}$, $w'' \in \mathcal{X}$, we write $w' >_i w''$ to mean $w' \geq_i w''$ but not $w'' \geq_i w'$; $w' \sim_i w''$ means $w' \geq_i w''$ and $w'' \geq_i w'$.

[5] Even though $\mathcal{X}$ need not be a vector space (linear system) in the algebraic sense of the term, we find it convenient to call the elements of $\mathcal{X}$ vectors.

DEFINITION 1. *A resource-flow matrix $a \in \mathscr{A}$ is said to be* possible *(in e) if it is* admissible *(i.e., $w_0 + \sigma(a) \in X$) and* feasible *(i.e., $a._0 \in Z$).*

DEFINITION 2.
a) *We write $a' \geq_i a''$ if and only if $w_0 + \sigma(a') \geq_i w_0 + \sigma(a'')$.*
b) a' *is said to be* Pareto-superior *to (in e) a'' if $a' \geq_i a''$ for all $i \in I$ and $a' >_k a''$ for some $k \in I$.*
c) a *is said to be* Pareto-optimal *(in e) if* (c_1), a *is possible (in e), and,* (c_2) *no possible a' is Pareto-superior (in e) to a.*
d) *We write $\hat{A}_e = \{a \in \mathscr{A} : \hat{a}$ is Pareto-optimal in $e\}$; $\hat{w} \in \mathscr{X}^{(n)}$ is said to be* Pareto-optimal *(in e) if $\hat{w} = w_0 + \sigma(\hat{a})$ for some $\hat{a} \in \hat{A}_e$.*

3. ADJUSTMENT PROCESS

Given a set ("language") $\mathscr{M}$, n functions ("response rules") f^i ($i = 1$, $2, \ldots, n$), and an "outcome rule" ϕ, we define an ("abstract") adjustment process as $\pi \equiv (f, \phi, \mathscr{M})$, where $f = (f^1, f^2, \ldots, f^n)$. The "response rules" determine the nature of the difference equation system

$$m_{t+1}^i = f^i(m_t^1, m_t^2, \ldots, m_t^n; e) \qquad (i = 1, 2, \ldots, n), \tag{1}$$

where $m_\tau^i \in \mathscr{M}$ represents the message formed by the ith unit at time τ. This equation system may be written more compactly as

$$m_{t+1} = f(m_t; e), \tag{2}$$

with $m_\tau = (m_\tau^1, m_\tau^2, \ldots, m_\tau^n) \in \mathscr{M}^{(n)}$. ($\mathscr{M}^{(n)} = \mathscr{M} \times \mathscr{M} \times \cdots \times \mathscr{M} = $ the n-fold Cartesian product of $\mathscr{M}$.)

The *process is in equilibrium at* $\overline{m} = (\overline{m}^1, m^2, \ldots, \overline{m}^n) \in \mathscr{M}^{(n)}$ if

$$\overline{m} = f(\overline{m}; e). \tag{3}$$

We write $\overline{M}_{e,f} = \{\overline{m} \in \mathscr{M}^{(n)} : \overline{m} = f(\overline{m}; e)\}$, and the elements of this set are called the *equilibrium values* of the process.

With each equilibrium value $\overline{m}$ of the process the outcome rule ϕ (a function not depending on e) associates a (possibly empty) *outcome* set $\overline{A}$ of resource-flow matrices; i.e.,

$$\overline{A} = \phi(\overline{m}), \qquad \overline{m} \in \overline{M}_{e,f}, \qquad \overline{A} \subseteq \mathscr{A}. \tag{4}$$

The elements of $\overline{A}$ are called *solutions.*

Given an adjustment process $\pi = (f, \phi, \mathscr{M})$ and an environment e, we write

$$\overline{A}_{e,\pi} = \bigcup_{\overline{m} \in M_{e,f}} \phi(\overline{m}),$$

i.e., the union of outcomes.

DEFINITION 3. *An adjustment process $\pi = (f, \phi, \mathscr{M})$ is said to be:*
a) decisive *(in e), if [6] $\hat{A}_e \neq \phi$ implies $\overline{A}_{e,\pi} = \phi$, i.e., if, when there are*

---

[6] The symbol $\emptyset$ denotes the empty set.

Pareto-optimal resource flows, there are also solutions;

b) essentially single-valued (*in e*), if $\bar{m} \in \overline{M}_{e,f}$, $\bar{a}' \in \phi(\bar{m})$, $\bar{a}'' \in \phi(\bar{m})$ imply $\bar{a}' \sim_i \bar{a}''$ for each $i \in I$, *i.e., if two solutions contained in the same outcome must be indifferent to all units*;

c) nonwasteful (*in e*), if $\overline{A}_{e,\pi} \subseteqq \hat{A}_e$, *i.e., if every solution is Pareto-optimal*;

d) unbiased (*in e*), if, given the environment $e = (I, \mathcal{X}; X, w_0, R, Z)$ and any optimal $\hat{a} \in \hat{A}_e$, there exists a distribution $w_0^* \in X$ and an optimal $\hat{a}^* \in \hat{A}_e$ such that

$$\sum_{i \in I} w_0^{*i} = \sum_{i \in I} w_0^i, \qquad w_0^* + \sigma(\hat{a}^*) = w_0 + \sigma(\hat{a}),$$

$$\hat{a}^*_{\cdot 0} = \hat{a}_{\cdot 0}, \qquad \hat{a}^* \in \overline{A}_{e^*,\pi},$$

where[7] $e^* = (I, \mathcal{X}; X, w_0^*, R, Z)$; *roughly speaking, this means that any optimal resource distribution can be reached as a solution of the given adjustment process following, if necessary, a redistribution of the initially available resource endowment*;

e) Pareto-satisfactory (*in e*), *if it is essentially single-valued, unbiased, and nonwasteful* (*in e*).

REMARK A. Each of the preceding properties is static in character, since only the equilibrium properties of the process are involved.

REMARK B. Under the classical assumptions of divisibility (of goods), convexity, continuity, etc., perfect competition has each of the preceding properties. Essential single-valuedness is evident. Decisiveness follows from the existence theorems,[8] while unbiasedness and nonwastefulness are the chief concerns of ("classical") welfare economics.[9]

It is well-known that under monopoly (especially of the nondiscriminating variety) nonoptimal solutions may occur; hence such processes are not Pareto-satisfactory.

DEFINITION 4. *An adjustment process is said to be* external *if the ith response function depends on the environment e only through the ith characteristic e^i, i.e., if, for each $i \in I$ and each $m \in \mathcal{M}^{(n)}$, $e^{*i} = e^{**i}$ implies $f^i(m; e^*) = f^i(m; e^{**})$.*

REMARK C. If the process is external, we may write the response function as $f^i(m; e^i)$.

REMARK D. Externality is used in Definition 10 below as part of the concept of informational decentralization. Under externality, an economic unit, apart from the messages received, needs no information concerning (for example) the characteristics of the other units. Externality is among the informational features of the market mechanism stressed by Hayek (4).

---

[7] We sometimes refer to e^* as a *translate* of e.

[8] E.g., Arrow and Debreu (2), McKenzie (8).

[9] See Arrow [1, Theorem 5 (nonwastefulness), Theorem 4 (unbiasedness)] and Debreu [3, Theorem 1 (nonwastefulness), Theorem 2 (unbiasedness)].

4. DECOMPOSABLE ENVIRONMENTS

Since an external process uses no properties of the environment except the n characteristics, it is intuitively clear that the process is not likely to be Pareto-satisfactory in environments whose Pareto-optimal sets are not determined by the various projections. Thus it is natural to focus the study of informationally decentralized processes on a class of environments free of external (dis-)economies; such environments will be called decomposable.[10] Formally, we have

DEFINITION 5. *An economic environment e is said to be* decomposable *if*:
a) the units are independent with regard to admissibility, i.e., $X = X^1 \times X^2 \times \cdots \times X^n$;
b) the units are technologically independent;[11] *i.e.*, $Z = Z^1 \times Z^2 \times \cdots \times Z^n$;
c) each unit is selfish (individualistic);[12] *i.e., for each* $i \in I$*, given the admissible distributions* w^*, w^{**}, $w^{*)}$, $w^{**)}$, *with their* ith *components denoted respectively by* w^{*i}, w^{**i}, $w^{*)i}$, $w^{**)i}$, *we have* $w^{*)} \geqq_i w^{**)}$ *if* $w^* \geqq_i w^{**}$, $w^{*i} = w^{*)i}$, $w^{**i} = w^{**)i}$.
(If the ith *is selfish, we write* $w^{*i} \geqq_i w^{**i}$ *to mean* $w^* \geqq_i w^{**}$.)

5. INFORMATIONALLY DECENTRALIZED ADJUSTMENT PROCESSES

We start by defining the "concrete"[13] adjustment process as a special class of what we have called ("abstract") adjustment processes, obtained by imposing the following two conditions; (a) the "language" $\mathcal{M}$ consists of sets of resource-flow matrices, i.e.,[14]

$$\mathcal{M} \subseteq \{A : A \subseteq \mathcal{A}\} \equiv 2^{\mathcal{A}},$$

and (b) the outcome is determined by consensus in the sense that

$$\phi(\overline{m}^1, \overline{m}^2, \ldots, \overline{m}^n) \equiv \phi(\overline{A}^1, \overline{A}^2, \ldots, \overline{A}^n) = \bigcap_{i \in I} \overline{A}^i.$$

The equations of a concrete process may, therefore, be written as

$$A^i_{t+1} = f^i(A^1_t, A^2_t, \ldots, A^n_t; e) \qquad (i = 1, 2, \ldots, n),$$

or $A_{t+1} = f(A_t; e)$, where $A_\tau = (A^1_\tau, A^2_\tau, \ldots, A^n_\tau)$. The equilibrium condition

---

[10] A term suggested by Jacob Marschak.
[11] This is slightly stronger than the more familiar *additivity* condition (with $\sum Z^i$ denoting the algebraic sum, not union):

$$\left\{ x \in \mathcal{X} : x = \sum_{i \in I} z^i \text{ for some } (z^1, z^2, \ldots, z^n) \in Z \right\} = \sum_{i \in I} Z_i.$$

[12] In the sense that it cares only about its own share (component) of a distribution.
[13] The adjective "concrete" is usually omitted where the context makes the nature of the process clear.
[14] The expression $2^{\mathcal{A}}$ denotes the power set of $\mathcal{A}$.

then becomes $\bar{A} = f(\bar{A}; e)$, where $\bar{A} = (\bar{A}^1, \bar{A}^2, \ldots, \bar{A}^n)$, and the *outcome* is given by

$$\bar{A} = \bigcap_{i \in I} \bar{A}^i.$$

Note that a concrete adjustment process is completely specified by $(\mathcal{M}, f)$, where $\mathcal{M} \subseteq 2^{\mathcal{A}}$ and $f = (f^1, f^i, \ldots, f^n)$, with $f^i(\cdot, e)$ a function on $\mathcal{M}^{(n)}$ into $\mathcal{M}$.

We may think of A_τ^i as a collection of alternative plans a_τ^i formulated by the ith unit at time τ. At one extreme, A_τ^i might be a one-element set, or even empty; at the other, it might be that $A_\tau^i = \mathcal{A}$. In a completely centrally planned economy, with $i = 1$ representing the planning agency, a one-element $A_\tau^1 = \{a^1\}$ might represent the flow of goods prescribed by the central plan. If the other units $(j = 2, 3, \ldots, n)$ had no say whatever in determining the direction of flow, this could be represented by specifying $A_\tau^j = \mathcal{A}$ for each j. In such a case, of course, the "consensus" solution is obtained at a^1.

We are here primarily interested in processes whose informational properties correspond to the intuitive concept of decentralization, e.g., to the sort of decentralization implied by the assertion that the (perfectly competitive) market mechanism is informationally decentralized.

There are those who would simply identify (informational) decentralization with the market and price mechanisms, but this seems too narrow a viewpoint.

The basic idea inherent in the intuitive concept of decentralization seems to be that each unit is permitted to concern itself only with the effects of its actions (or the actions of others) on itself and that it has no direct information about the internal structure of the other units. The latter property has already been introduced under the name of externality (Definition 4 above). The former will now be stated. To begin with, if the ith unit formulates a plan $a = (a_{rs})$, it is permitted to specify only properties of a that determine the actions, (production, exchange) to be undertaken by i; this amounts to specifying, in a, the entities $\sum_{j \in I} a_{ij}$ and a_{i0}, i.e., the ordered pair $s \equiv (d, z)$, where $d \equiv d^i(a) = \sum_{j \in I} a_{ij}$, and $z \equiv z^i(a) = a_{i0}$. Since in our model the ith unit must express itself by selecting a set $A \subseteq \mathcal{A}$, the requirement that i be entitled to only specify $\sum_{j \in I} a_{ij}$ and a_{i0} can be formalized by stating that the process must be *self-relevant* in the sense of:

DEFINITION 6. *A set A of resource-flow matrices is said to be i-relevant if, given $a' \in \mathcal{A}$ and $a'' \in \mathcal{A}$, with $\sum_{j \in I} a_{ij}'' = \sum_{j \in I} a_{ij}'$ and $a_{i0}'' = a_{i0}'$, $a' \in A$ if and only if $a'' \in A$. An adjustment process in which, for each $i \in I$, the ith unit uses only i-relevant messages is called* self-relevant.

Let A be self-relevant for i. Then it may be partitioned into subsets of the form

$$A_s \equiv A_{(d, z)} = \{a \in \mathcal{A} : \sum_{j \in I} a_{ij} = d, a_{i0} = z\},$$

where $s \equiv (d, z)$ is a point of $\mathcal{X} \times \mathcal{X}$. Hence we have

$$A = \bigcup_{s \in S} A_s,$$

where S is some subset of $\mathcal{X} \times \mathcal{X}$; thus it is seen that there is a one-to-one correspondence between self-relevant A's and the S sets. This enables us to write such processes in the form

$$S_{t+1}^i = f^i(S_t^1, S_t^2, \ldots, S_t^n; e) \qquad (i = 1, 2, \ldots, n),$$

where $S_\tau^i \subseteq \mathcal{X} \times \mathcal{X}$ is the image of a self-relevant $A_\tau^i \subseteq \mathcal{A}$, and consists of elements written as (d_τ^i, z_τ^i), $d_\tau^i \in \mathcal{X}$, $z_\tau^i \in \mathcal{X}$, with d_τ^i representing the exchange activities and z_τ^i the production activities of the ith unit.

We refer to S_τ^i as the *plan* of the ith unit at time τ, and its members s_τ^i as its (alternative) *simple plans*. An n-tuple

$$s = [s^1, s^2, \ldots, s^n] \qquad (s^i = (d^i, z^i), i \in I)$$

of simple plans is called a *program*.

If the program s were to be put in operation, the ith unit would be engaging in production activities yielding an input-output vector z^i, and in exchange activities from which it would emerge with a net increment in holdings given by d^i. Clearly, in a closed economy, this could be done only if the program is *consistent*, i.e., if $\sum_{i \in I} d^i = 0_x$.

A self-relevant process is *in equilibrium at* $\bar{S} = (\bar{S}^1, \bar{S}^2, \ldots, \bar{S}^n)$ if

$$\bar{S}^i = f^i(\bar{S}^1, \bar{S}^2, \ldots, \bar{S}^n; e) \qquad (i = 1, 2, \ldots, n).$$

DEFINITION 7. *If the process is in equilibrium at* $(\bar{S}^1, \bar{S}^2, \ldots, \bar{S}^n)$, *a program* $\bar{s} = [\bar{s}^1, \bar{s}^2, \ldots, \bar{s}^n]$ *is called a* solution (program), *provided* $\bar{s}^i \in \bar{S}^i$ *for each* $i \in I$ *and* $\bar{s}$ *is consistent, i.e., provided* $\sum_{i \in I} \bar{d}^i = 0_x$ *and* $\bar{s}^i = (\bar{d}^i, z^i)$.

For a program to be *possible*, it must, of course, be consistent, and furthermore, the conditions of admissibility and feasibility must be satisfied.

DEFINITION 8.[15] *A program* $s = [s^1, s^2, \ldots, s^n]$, *where* $s^i = (d^i, z^i)$, $i \in I$, *is called* achievable *if it is both* feasible [*i.e.*, $(z^1, z^2, \ldots, z^n) \in Z$] *and* admissible [*i.e.*, $(w_0^1 + d^1 + z^1, w_0^2 + d^2 + z^2, \ldots, w_0^n + d^n + z^n) \in X$]. *A program* s *is called* possible *if it is achievable and consistent (i.e.,* $\sum_{i \in I} d^i = 0_x$). *A program* $s*$ *is said to be* Pareto-superior *to* $s**$ *if* $w_0^i + d^{*i} + z^{*i} + \geq_i w_0^i + d^{**i} + z^{**i}$ *for each* $i \in I$ *and* $w_0^k + d^{*k} + z^{*k} >_k w_0^k + d^{**k} + z^{**k}$ *for some* $k \in I$. *A program* s *is said to be* Pareto-optimal *if it is possible and if no possible* s' *is Pareto-superior to* s.

Given the plans $S^1, S^2, \ldots, S^{i-1}, S^{i+1}, \ldots, S^n$, one can form $(n-1)$-tuples of the form

$$(s^1, s^2, \ldots, s^{i-1}, s^{i+1} \ldots, s^n) \equiv s^{)i(}, \text{ where } s^k = (d^k, z^k),$$

---

[15] All concepts are relative to an environment e.

with $s^k \in S^k$, $k \in)i($.[16] As far as the ith unit is concerned, if $s^{)i(}$ were to be put into effect, consistency would require that $d^i = -\sum_{k \in)i(} d^k$. Hence the set of all d^i compatible with the plans S^1, S^2, ..., S^{i-1}, S^{i+1}, ..., S^n is given by

$$\{x \in \mathscr{X} : x = -\sum_{k \in)i(} d^k, (d^k, z^k) \in S^k \text{ for some } z^k\} = -\sum_{k \in)i(} D(S^k),$$

where $D(S) = \{d \in \mathscr{X} : (d, z) \in S \text{ for some } z \in \mathscr{X}\}$; i.e., $D(S)$ is the "*trade projection*" of S. Thus it is clearly in the spirit of informational decentralization to require the ith response rule f^i to depend on the S^k, where $k \in)i($, through $\sum_{k \in)i(} D(S^k)$ only.[17] We introduce:

DEFINITION 9. *A self-relevant adjustment process*

$$S^i_{t+1} = f^i(S^1_t, S^2_t, \ldots, S^n_t; e) \qquad (i = 1, 2, \ldots, n)$$

is called aggregative *if, for each* $i \in I$,

$$f^i(S^{*1}, S^{*2}, \ldots, S^{*n}; e) = f^i(S^{**1}, S^{**2}, \ldots, S^{**n}; e)$$

whenever $\sum_{k \in)i(} D(S^{*k}) = \sum_{k \in)i(} D(S^{**k})$.

We now have all the concepts needed to formulate:

DEFINITION 10. *A (concrete) adjustment process is said to be* informationally decentralized *if it is external, self-relevant, and aggregative.*

Hence an informationally decentralized process can be written in the form

$$S^i_{t+1} = f^i\left(S^i_t, \sum_{k \in)i(} D(S^k_t); e^i\right) \qquad (i = 1, 2, \ldots, n). \tag{5}$$

Of particular interest are *impersonal* processes in which the response rule is the same for all units. This can be expressed formally by:

DEFINITION 11. *An informationally decentralized process f is said to be* impersonal *if for any* $S \subseteqq \mathscr{X} \times \mathscr{X}$, $D \subseteqq \mathscr{X}$, *and* $e^i = e^j$, *we have* $f^i(S, D; e^i) = f^j(S, D; e^j)$.

Such a process may be written as

$$S^i_{t+1} = f^*\left(S^i_t, \sum_{k \in)i(} D(S^k_t); e^i\right) \qquad (i = 1, 2, \ldots, n).$$

6. THE "GREED PROCESS"

Intuitively, it is fairly clear that there is no informationally decentralized process that is Pareto-satisfactory for all conceivable economic environments, and there are examples to confirm this. But even within the class of decomposable environments the existence of such a process may not be self-evident. The purpose of the present section is to show that there does exist an infor-

---

[16] We write $)i(= \{1, 2, \ldots, i-1, i+1, \ldots, n\} = I \sim \{i\}$, $\sim$ here representing the set-theoretic difference.

[17] A somewhat milder condition on f^i, of interest in some contexts, is that f^i be symmetric in S^1, S^2, ..., S^{i-1}, S^{i+1}, ..., S^n. Such symmetry creates *anonymity* for units other than i in their offers to i,

mationally decentralized process [viz. the "greed process" defined by (6) below] that is Pareto-satisfactory for all decomposable environments.

The basic idea of this process is that the response S_{t+1}^i of the ith unit at time $t + 1$ consists of all the (simple) i-achievable[18] plans s_{t+1}^i that are at least as desirable for i as any (simple) i-achievable plan consistent with the aggregate trade projection of the other units' plans at time t. Because S_{t+1}^i consists of plans no less desirable that the best previously offered by others, the process has been labeled the "greed process."

Formally the *greed process* is defined by the following relations[19,20] [which are clearly a special case of (5) and hence informationally decentralized]:

$$S_{t+1}^i = \{s_{t+1}^i \in \mathscr{S}^i : s_{t+1}^i \geqq_i s^{*i} \quad \text{for all } s^{*i} \in S_t^{*i}\},$$

where

$$S_t^{*i} = \left\{s^{*i} = (d^{*i}, z^{*i}) \in \mathscr{S}^i : d^{*i} \in - \sum_{j \in)i(} D(S_t^j)\right\} \qquad (6)$$

and

$$D(S) = \{d \in \mathscr{H} : (d, z) \in S \quad \text{for some } z \in \mathscr{H}\}.$$

At equilibrium therefore

$$\bar{S}^i = \{\bar{s}^i \in \mathscr{S}^i : \bar{s}^i \geqq_i s^{*i} \quad \text{for all } s^{*i} \in \bar{S}^{*i}\},$$

where

$$\bar{S}^{*i} = \left\{s^{*i} = (d^{*i}, z^{*i}) \in \mathscr{S}^i : d^* \in - \sum_{j \in)i(} D(\bar{S}^j)\right\} \qquad (7)$$

and

$$D(\bar{S}^j) = \{\bar{d} \in \mathscr{X} : (\bar{d}, \bar{z}) \in S^j \quad \text{for some } \bar{z} \in \mathscr{X}\}.$$

Pareto-Satisfactoriness of the Greed Process in Decomposable Environments

It is seen from (7) that the greed process is essentially single-valued in the sense of Definition 3(b). To prove Pareto-satisfactoriness, therefore, we must show that it is nonwasteful and unbiased, provided the environment is decomposable.[21]

---

[18] A plan $s = (d, z)$ is called i-achievable if $w_0^i + d + z \in X^i$ and $z \in Z^i$. The set of all i-achievable (simple) plans is denoted by $\mathscr{S}^i$. In a decomposable environment, a program $s = [s^1, s^2, \ldots, s^n]$ is achievable if it is i-achievable for each $i \in I$; hence it is possible if it is consistent and i-achievable for each $i \in I$.

[19] We write $s \geqq_i s^*$, $s = (d, z)$, $s^* = (d^*, z^*)$ if and only if $w_0^i + d + z \geqq_i w_0^i + d^* + z^*$. $\mathscr{S}^i$ is defined in footnote 18.

[20] It may be helpful to give an equivalent but more detailed formulation of the greed process: $S_{t+1}^i = \{s_{t+1}^i = (d_{t+1}^i, z_{t+1}^i) : w_0^i + d_{t+1}^i + z_{t+1}^i \in X^i; \ z_{t+1}^i \in Z^i; \ w_0^i + d_{t+1}^i + z_{t+1}^i \geqq_i w_0^i - \sum_{k \in)i(} d_t^k + z^{*i}$ whenever $w_0^i - \sum_{k \in)i(} d_t^k + z^{*i} \in x^i$ and $z^{*i} \in Z^i$; and for some $z_t^k [k \in)i(]$, $(d_t^k, z_t^k) \in S_t^k$ for each $k \in)i(\}$.

[21] The greed process is also decisive and impersonal in the sense of Definitions 3(a) and 11.

THEOREM 1. *The greed process is nonwasteful in a decomposable environment.*

PROOF. It must be shown that every solution program is Pareto-optimal. Suppose not. Then there exists a nonoptimal solution program $\bar{s} = [\bar{s}^1, \bar{s}^2, \ldots, \bar{s}^n]$. By Definition 7, $\bar{s}$ is consistent; (7) states that $\bar{s}^i$ is i-achievable for each $i \in I$. Hence (see footnote 18), $\bar{s}$ is possible.[22] Therefore, there must exist a possible program $\tilde{s} = [\tilde{s}^1, \tilde{s}^2, \ldots, \tilde{s}^n]$ that is Pareto-superior to $\bar{s}$; i.e.,

$$\tilde{s}^i \geq_i \bar{s}^i \quad \text{for all } i \in I, \tag{8}$$

and, say,

$$\tilde{s}^1 >_1 \bar{s}^1. \tag{9}$$

Using (7), (8), and the fact that $\tilde{s}^i$ is i-achievable (since $\tilde{s}$ is possible), we have

$$\tilde{s}^i \in \bar{S}^i \text{ for all } i \in I. \tag{10}$$

Furthermore, since $\tilde{s}$ is consistent,

$$\tilde{\tilde{s}}^1 \equiv \left(- \sum_{k \in)i(} \tilde{d}^k, \tilde{z}^1 \right) = (\tilde{d}^1, \tilde{z}^1) \equiv \tilde{s}^1, \tag{11}$$

so that $\tilde{\tilde{s}}^1$ is i-achievable. Hence, by (7) and (10), $\bar{s}^1 \geq_1 \tilde{\tilde{s}}^1$, which, in view of (11), contradicts (9).

THEOREM 2. *The greed process is unbiased in a decomposable environment.*

PROOF. Let $\hat{s} = [\hat{s}^1, \hat{s}^2, \ldots, \hat{s}^n]$, where $\hat{s}^j = (\hat{d}^j, \hat{z}^j)$ is a Pareto-optimal program. We wish to show that it is a solution program. To this end, suppose that at the time t_0, the ith individual ($i \in I$) adopts the plan S_0^i defined by

$$S_0^i = \{s_0^i = (d_0^i, z_0^i) \in \mathscr{S}^i : s_0^i \geq_i \hat{s}^i\}. \tag{12}$$

According to the rules of the greed process (6), the plan S_1^i of the ith unit at time $t_0 + 1$ will then be

$$S_1^i = \{s_1^i = (d_1^i, z_1^i) \in \mathscr{S}^i : s_1^i \geq_i s^{*i} \quad \text{for all } s^{*i} \in S_0^{*i}\},$$

where

$$S_0^{*i} = \left\{ s^{*i} = (d^{*i}, z^{*i}) \in \mathscr{S}^i : d^{*i} \in - \sum_{j \in)i(} D(S_0^j) \right\} \tag{13}$$

and

$$D(S_0^j) = \{d \in \mathscr{X} : (d, z) \in S_0^j \text{ for some } z \in \mathscr{X}\}.$$

Now if we can show that

$$S_1^i = S_0^i \text{ for each } i \in I, \tag{14}$$

it will follow that the process is in equilibrium at $(S_0^1, S_0^2, \ldots, S_0^n)$. But then $\hat{s}$ is a solution program since (by its Pareto-optimality) it is consistent and,

---

[22] It is at this point that use is made of the assumption of technological independence.

by (12), $\hat{s}^i \in S_0^i$ for each $i \in I$. It therefore remains only to establish (14), which is accomplished by showing that

$$S_1^i \subseteqq S_0^i \quad \text{for each } i \in I \tag{15}$$

and

$$S_0^i \subseteqq S_1^i \quad \text{for each } i \in I. \tag{16}$$

To prove (15), it is sufficient to show that, for any $s_1^i \in S_1^i$, we have $s^i \geqq {}_i\hat{s}^i$ By (13), this will be so, provided $\hat{s}^i \in S^{*i}$. Since $\hat{s}^i$ is i-achievable (by Pareto-optimality), it is enough to show that $\hat{d}^i \in -\sum_{j \in)i(} D(S_0^j)$, which is true since $\hat{d}^i = -\sum_{j \in)i(} \hat{d}^j$ (by consistency due to Pareto-optimality) and $\hat{d}^j \in D(S_0^j)$ for all j. Hence (15) holds.

Now suppose (16) false. Then for some $i \in I$ and some $s_0^i \in S_0^i$, the requirements of (13) are violated. That is, there exists a consistent program $\tilde{s} = [\tilde{s}^1, \tilde{s}^2, \ldots, \tilde{s}^n]$, with $\tilde{s}^j = (\tilde{d}^j, \tilde{z}^j)$, such that $\tilde{s}^k \in S_0^k$ for all $k \in)i($, $\tilde{s}^i = (-\sum_{k \in)i(} \tilde{d}^k, \tilde{z}^i)$ is i-achievable, and the strict preference inequality $\tilde{s}^i > {}_i s_0^i$ is satisfied. Then, since $s_0^i \geqq {}_i \hat{s}^i$ holds by (12), it follows that

$$\tilde{s}^i > {}_i \hat{s}^i. \tag{17}$$

On the other hand, since (by the construction above) $\tilde{s}^k \in S_0^k$ for all $k \in)i($, we have from (12)

$$\tilde{s}^k \geqq {}_k \hat{s}^k \quad \text{for all } k \in)i(. \tag{18}$$

Now $\tilde{s}$ is possible since it is consistent, $\tilde{s}^j$ is j-achievable for each $j \in I$, and the environment is decomposable. In view of (17) and (18), $\tilde{s}$ is Pareto-superior to the Pareto-optimal program $\tilde{s}$, which yields a contradiction.

7. THE "QUASI-COMPETITIVE" PROCESS

It is natural to raise the question whether one could not find an information-ally decentralized process that is Pareto-satisfactory[23] for all decomposable environments but (in some well-defined sense) simpler than the greed process. This question is not yet completely resolved. But it is of interest to see that a "simpler" process with the desired properties may be found if we are willing to restrict ourselves to a narrower class of "convex" Euclidean environments.[24] This "simpler" process is closely related to the competitive process (especially with respect to equilibrium properties) and is therefore labeled "quasi-competitive." This process is obtained from the greed process in the following manner. Whenever a certain trade d^* is compatible with the "offers" made to i by the other units, i responds (according the to rules of the greed process) as if all nonnegative scalar multiples λd^* ($\lambda \geqq 0$) had also been offered to it.[25]

---

[23] And preferably also decisive and impersonal.
[24] See Definition 12.
[25] Provided, of course, that $\lambda d^* \in \mathscr{X}$. When $\mathscr{X}$ is a vector space (as we shall assume), this condition is always satisfied.

This seems to be in the spirit of the general concept of perfect competition, although it differs from the currently more usual interpretations.[26] Formally, the *quasi-competitive process* is defined,[27] for each $i \in I$, by[28]

$$S_{t+1}^i = \{s_{t+1}^i \in \mathscr{S}^i : s_{t+1}^i \geqq_i \lambda s^{*i} \quad \text{for all } s^{*i} \in S_t^{*i} \text{ and all } \lambda \geqq 0\}, \qquad (19)$$

with S^{*i} defined as in (6); at equilibrium, therefore, for each $i \in I$,

$$\bar{S}^i = \{\bar{s}^i \in \mathscr{S}^i : \bar{s}^i \geqq_i \lambda s^{*i} \quad \text{for all } s^{*i} \in \bar{S}^i \text{ and all } \lambda \geqq 0\}, \qquad (20)$$

with $\bar{S}_t^{*i}$ defined as in (7).

The relationship of the greed and quasi-competitive processes can be made evident as follows. Write the greed process as

$$S_{t+1}^i = g\left[\sum_{j \in)i(} D(S_t^j); e^i\right] \qquad (i = 1, 2, \ldots, n).$$

The the quasi-competitive process may be written as

$$S_{t+1}^i = g\left[\lambda \sum_{j \in)i(} D(S_t^j); e^i\right] \qquad (i = 1, 2, \ldots, n).$$

In the preceding formulas, g is the specific function characterizing the greed response and λD denotes the set $\{\lambda d : d \in D, \lambda \geqq 0\}$, i.e., a cone through D with vertex at 0_x. More explicitly, for any $D^* \subseteqq \mathscr{X}$ and any "characteristic" ϵ, we have

$$g(D^*; \epsilon) = \{(d, z) \in \mathscr{S}_\epsilon : w_0 + d + z \geqq w_0 - d^* + z^*,$$

$$\text{provided } d^* \in D^* \text{ and } (-d^*, z^*) \in \mathscr{S}_\epsilon\},$$

with $\mathscr{S}_\epsilon = \{(d, z) : w_0 + d + z \in X', z \in Z'\}$, $\epsilon = (X', w_0, \geqq, Z')$, $X' \subseteqq \mathscr{X}$, $w_0 \in \mathscr{X}, Z' \subseteqq \mathscr{X}$.

We refer to the quasi-competitive process as *informationally more efficient* than the greed process in the sense that, for a given e^i, the response in the latter is based on the knowledge of the set $D_t \equiv \sum_{j \in)i(} D(S_t^j)$, while for the quasi-competitive response it is sufficient to know the smallest cone λD_t through D_t.[29]

---

[26] Geometrically, in the quasi-competitive process each unit maximizes over the admissible part of the smallest *cone* (with vertex at 0_x) containing the others' offers, while in the usual interpretation of the competitive mechanism there is maximization over the admissible part of the smallest *closed half-space* containing the others' offers and 0_x.

Unlike the process in the usual dynamic models of perfect competition, the quasi-competitive process does not presuppose the existence of a common price vector for the whole market while the adjustments are taking place (i.e., away from equilibrium). However, if the customary assumptions are made (strictly convex and "smooth" indifference surfaces), the cones of the quasi-competitive process turn out to be (nonclosed) half-spaces (plus the vertex) and, *at equilibrium*, a unique price vector prevailing in the whole market may be defined.

(For an illustrative example of the difference between the two processes, see Remark E. In this case, the cone through S_0^2, apart from the vertex A, is an open half-space.)

[27] With $\mathscr{X}$ assumed to be a vector space ("perfect divisibility" of commodities).

[28] $\mathscr{S}^i$ is defined in footnote 18.

[29] A more rigorous formulation of the informational efficiency concept is found in Section 9.

In what follows, we shall show that the quasi-competitive process is non-wasteful for every decomposable environment (Theorem 3) and that it is unbiased for every "convex" environment (Theorem 4). Since essential single-valuedness is evident, it follows that the quasi-competitive process is Pareto-satisfactory. As to other properties, the quasi-competitive process is clearly impersonal (Definition 11). Its decisiveness, expressed in Definition 3(a), could be established, in a manner analogous to the existence of competitive equilibrium, but (as with competitive equilibrium) one would have to make additional restrictions on the nature of the environment.

8. PARETO-SATISFACTORINESS OF THE QUASI-COMPETITIVE PROCESS IN CONVEX ENVIRONMENTS

The quasi-competitive process is seen to be essentially single-valued. An examination of the proof of Theorem 1 above shows that, without any additional assumptions on the environment (in particular, without using any convexity properties), the proof goes through *a fortiori* since $\lambda = 1$ is among the values for which the inequality $s^i \geqq_i \lambda s^{*i}$ must hold. Hence we have:

THEOREM 3. *The quasi-competitive process is nonwasteful for every decomposable environment.*

The counterpart of Theorem 2, on the other hand, does not hold without additional assumptions. We find it convenient to introduce:

DEFINITION 12. *A decomposable environment is called* convex *if*:
a) $\mathscr{X}$ *(the commodity space) is a (real) vector space*;
b) *for each* $i \in I$, *the sets* X^i *and* Z^i *are convex*;
c) *for each* $i \in I$, *and for each* $x^* \in X^i$, *the contour set* $\{x \in X^i : x \geqq_i x^*\}$ *is convex*;
d) *("steepness") from* $x' >_i x''$ *and* $1 \geqq \alpha > 0$, *it follows that* $\alpha x' + (1 - \alpha)x'' >_i x''$.

REMARK E. Property (c) in Definition 12 corresponds to the condition of quasi-concavity of the utility indicator. Property (d), together with continuity of the utility indicator, implies (c). The properties (a)–(d) of Definition 12 are essentially those usually assumed in welfare economics in connection with competitive equilibrium. They are in some respects slightly weaker than those made by Debreu in (3), except that he merely assumes $\sum_{i \in I} Z^i$, rather than each Z^i, to be convex. One should bear in mind, however, that "quasi-competitive" equilibrium is different from competitive equilibrium. For instance, in a situation such as that depicted by Arrow (1, Fig. 3), there is no competitive equilibrium but there does exist a quasi-competitive equilibrium. This may be seen with the help of the Edgeworth box diagram (p. 76). In Figure 1, the holdings of unit 1 increase upwards and to the right, and those of unit 2 downwards and to the left. AB is an indifference curve for unit 1, whose contour set S_0^1, corresponding to the point A, consists of all points on and to the right of AB and on and above AE (as indicated by the

Figure 1.

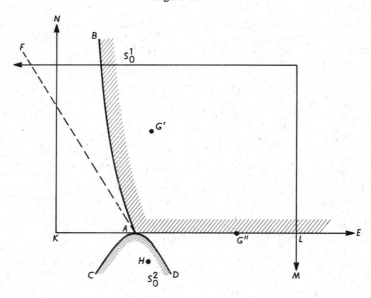

line-shading); thus, for instance, unit 1 prefers G' and G'' to A. CAD is an indifference curve for unit 2, whose contour set S_0^2, corresponding to the point A, consists of points on or below CAD (as indicated by the dot-shading); thus, for instance, unit 2 prefers H to A. Now, with vertex at A, the admissible part $C(S_0^1)$ of the cone through S_0^1 consists of A and all points on and above KE but to the right of AF and KN, while the admissible part $C(S_0^2)$ of the cone through S_2^0 consists of A and all points on or to the left of LM but below KL. Hence A is the best (in fact, the only admissible) point for unit 1 from among points of $C(S_0^2)$, and also the best for unit 2 from among points of $C(S_0^1)$; hence quasi-competitive equilibrium prevails at A.

On the other hand, there is no competitive equilibrium at A: a negatively inclined price line through A would encourage unit 2 to move away from A to the interior of S_0^2, while a horizontal price line through A would encourage unit 1 to move away from A toward E.

THEOREM 4. *The quasi-competitive process is unbiased for every convex environment.*

PROOF. In view of Definition 3(d), it is enough to consider any "translate" of the given environment[30]. Hence, without loss of generality, we may take a Pareto-optimal program $\hat{s} = [\hat{s}^1, \hat{s}^2, \ldots, \hat{s}^n]$, where $\hat{s}^j = (\hat{d}^j, \hat{z}^j)$, such that

$$\hat{d}^j = 0_x \quad \text{for all } j \in I, \tag{21}$$

---

[30] See footnote 7 for definition of the translate.

and the theorem will be proved if it is shown that such a program is a solution of the quasi-competitive process.

As in the proof of Theorem 2, we define the sets

$$S_0^i = \{s_0^i = (d_0^i, z_0^i) \in \mathscr{S}^i : s_0^i \geqq_i \hat{s}^i\} \tag{22}$$

and

$$S_1^i = \{s_1^i = (d_1^i, z_1^i) \in \mathscr{S}^i : s^i \geqq_i \lambda s^{*i} \quad \text{for all } s^{*i} \in S_0^{*i}, \lambda \geqq 0\}, \tag{23}$$

with S_0^{*i} defined as in (13).

It must again be shown that

$$S_1^i \subseteqq S_0^i \quad \text{for each } i \in I \tag{24}$$

and

$$S_0^i \subseteqq S_1^i \quad \text{for each } i \in I. \tag{25}$$

Since the inequality in (23) holds for $\lambda = 1$, (24) follows by the argument used to establish (15) in the proof of Theorem 2.

It remains to establish (25). Suppose (25) is false. Then, for some $i \in I$ and $s_0^i \in S_0^i$, we have $s_0^i \notin S_1^i$. Since $s_0^i \in \mathscr{S}^i$, there must exist a program $\tilde{s} = [\tilde{s}^1, \tilde{s}^2, \ldots, \tilde{s}^n]$, with $\tilde{s}^j = (\tilde{d}^j, \tilde{z}^j)$, and some $0 \leqq \lambda < \infty$ such that

$$\tilde{s}^i \in \mathscr{S}^i, \qquad \tilde{d}^i = -\lambda \sum_{k \in)i(} \tilde{d}^k, \qquad \tilde{s}^k \in S_0^k \text{ for } k \in)i(, \text{ and } \tilde{s}^i >_i s_0^i. \tag{26}$$

To show that this supposition leads to a contradiction, we find it convenient to consider first the case $\lambda \geqq 1$, and then the case $0 \leqq \lambda < 1$.

Case 1: $\lambda \geqq 1$. We define a program $\tilde{\tilde{s}} = [\tilde{\tilde{s}}^1, \tilde{\tilde{s}}^2, \ldots, \tilde{\tilde{s}}^n]$ by the conditions

$$\tilde{\tilde{s}}^i = \left(1 - \frac{1}{\lambda}\right)\hat{s}^i + \frac{1}{\lambda}\tilde{s}^i, \qquad \tilde{\tilde{s}}^k = \tilde{s}^k \quad \text{for each } k \in)i(.$$

Then

$$\sum_{j \in I} \tilde{\tilde{d}}^j = \tilde{\tilde{d}}^i + \sum_{k \in)i(} \tilde{\tilde{d}}^k = \frac{1}{\lambda}\tilde{d}^i + \sum_{k \in)i(} \tilde{d}^k$$

$$= \frac{1}{\lambda}\left(-\lambda \sum_{k \in)i(} \tilde{d}^k\right) + \sum_{k \in)i(} \tilde{d}^k = 0_x,$$

so that $\tilde{\tilde{s}}$ is consistent.

Also, in view of the convexity of X^i,

$$\tilde{\tilde{w}}^i \equiv w_0^i + \tilde{\tilde{d}}^i + \tilde{\tilde{z}}^i = \left(1 - \frac{1}{\lambda}\right)\hat{w}^i + \frac{1}{\lambda}\tilde{w}^i \in X^i,$$

since both $\hat{w}^i \equiv w_0^i + \hat{d}^i + \hat{z}^i \in X^i$ and $\tilde{w}^i \equiv w_0^i + \tilde{d}^i + \tilde{z}^i \in X^i$. Similarly,

$$\tilde{\tilde{z}}^i = \left(1 - \frac{1}{\lambda}\right)\hat{z}^i + \frac{1}{\lambda}\tilde{z}^i \in Z^i,$$

because of the convexity of Z^i.

Hence, $\tilde{s}^i \in \mathscr{S}^i$. On the other hand, for each $k \in)i($, we have $\tilde{s}^k \in \mathscr{S}^k$ by construction, since $\tilde{s}^k = \hat{s}^k \in S_0^k \subseteq \mathscr{S}^k$. Thus it has been shown that $\tilde{s}^j \in \mathscr{S}^j$ for each $j \in I$ and also that $\tilde{s}$ is consistent, which (in a decomposable environment) means that $\tilde{s}$ is possible.

Now, since $\tilde{w}^i$ is a convex mixture of $\hat{w}^i$ and $\tilde{w}^i$, both of which belong to the convex contour set $\{x : x \geq_i \hat{w}^i\}$, it follows that $\tilde{w}^i \geq_i \hat{w}^i$; i.e., equivalently, $\tilde{s}^i \geq_i \hat{s}^i$. Also, for each $k \in)i($, we have $\tilde{s}^k \geq_k \hat{s}^k$, since $\tilde{s}^k = \hat{s}^k \in S_0^k$. Hence $\tilde{s}^j \geq_j \hat{s}^j$ for each $j \in I$. But $\tilde{s}$ is possible and $\hat{s}$ Pareto-optimal. Hence it must be that $\tilde{s}^j \sim_j \hat{s}^j$ for each $j \in I$; in particular, $\tilde{s}^i \sim_i \hat{s}^i$, i.e., equivalently, $\tilde{w}^i \sim_i \hat{w}^i$.

On the other hand, $\tilde{s}^i >_i s_0^i \geq_i \hat{s}^i$, so that $\tilde{w}^i >_i \hat{w}^i$. It then follows from the "steepness" assumption [Definition 12(d)] that $\tilde{w}^i >_i \hat{w}^i$, since $\tilde{w}^i$ is a convex mixture of $\hat{w}^i$ and $\tilde{w}^i$. This contradiction completes the proof for the case $\lambda \geq 1$.

Case 2: $0 \leq \lambda < 1$. For this case, define $s^* = [s^{*1}, s^{*2}, \ldots, s^{*n}]$ by $s^{*k} = (1 - \lambda)\hat{s}^k + \lambda\tilde{s}^k$ for each $k \in)i($ and $s^{*i} = \tilde{s}^i$, with $\tilde{s}$ given by (26) above.

By the convexity assumption, for each $k \in)i($ we have $s^{*k} \in \mathscr{S}^k$ and $s^{*k} \geq_k \hat{s}^k$. On the other hand, since $\tilde{d}^k = 0_x$ by hypothesis, (26) yields

$$d^{*i} = \tilde{d}^i = -\lambda \sum_{k \in)i(} \tilde{d}^k = -\lambda \sum_{k \in)i(} \left(\frac{1}{\lambda} d^{*k}\right) = -\sum_{k \in)i(} d^{*k}.$$

Thus we see that s^* has all the properties given in (26) for $\tilde{s}$, with $\lambda = 1$. Thus Case 2 ($0 \leq \lambda < 1$) has been reduced to Case 1 ($\lambda \geq 1$), which has already been disposed of. This completes the proof of the theorem.

9. INFORMATIONAL EFFICIENCY

It was noted in Section 7 that in "convex" Euclidean environments the quasi-competitive process is informationally more efficient than the greed process. In the present section, we given a more rigorous definition of the concept and a proof of the statement.

Consider an adjustment process $\pi = (f, \phi, \mathscr{M})$. The ith response function f^i has as its domain the set $\mathscr{M}^{(n)} \times E$, where E is a class of economic environments. Define, for any economic environment e, the function f_e^i on $\mathscr{M}^{(n)}$, given by $f_e^i(m) = f^i(m; e)$ for all $m \in \mathscr{M}^{(n)}$. Now, for a given class E, the family of functions $f_e^i(e \in E, i \in I)$ induces a partitioning $\mathscr{P}_{f, E}$ on the space $\mathscr{M}^{(n)}$, with $m', m'' \in \mathscr{M}^{(n)}$ belonging to the same equivalence class if, for each $i \in I$, we have $f_e^i(m') = f_e^i(m'')$ for all $e \in E$. We adopt:

DEFINITION 13. *The adjustment process $\pi^* = (f^*, \phi, M)$ is said to be informationally at least as efficient as $\pi^{**} = (f^{**}, \phi, \mathscr{M})$ over the class of environments E if the partitioning $\mathscr{P}_{f^{**}, E}$ is no less fine than the partitioning $\mathscr{P}_{f^*, E}$. That is, $f^{**i}(m'; e) = f^{**i}(m''; e)$ for all $e \in E$, and each $i \in I$ implies $f^{*i}(m'; e) = f^{*i}(m''; e)$ for all $e \in E$ and each $i \in I$, given any $m', m'' \in \mathscr{M}^{(n)}$.*[31]

---

[31] In other contexts, other partitionings induced by f (in particular, that on E) serve as a natural basis for alternative concepts of informational efficiency.

If π^* is informationally at least as efficient over E as π^{**}, while π^{**} is not (or is) informationally at least as efficient over E as π^{**}, we say that π^* is informationally more efficient over E than π^{**} (as efficient over E as π^{**}).

We shall now show that the quasi-competitive process is informationally more efficient over the class of (Euclidean space) convex environments than the greed process.

We recall that the ith response function for the greed function is of the form $g(D, \epsilon)$, where $D \subseteq \mathscr{X}$ and $\epsilon = e^i$ is an individual "characteristic," while the quasi-competitive process has a response function of the form $g(\lambda D, \epsilon)$, where $\lambda D = \{x \in \mathscr{X} : x = \lambda d, \lambda \geq 0, d \in D\}$, and g is the function defined in Section 7. Since the two processes are certainly not informationally equally efficient, it will suffice to show that if, for some $D', D'' \subseteq \mathscr{X}$, we have $g(D', \epsilon) = g(D'', \epsilon)$ for all convex characteristics ϵ, then $g(\lambda D', \epsilon) = g(\lambda D'', \epsilon)$ for all convex characteristics ϵ.

Since, obviously, $g(\lambda D', \epsilon) = g(\lambda D'', \epsilon)$ if $\lambda D' = \lambda D''$, it is enough to consider the case $\lambda D' \neq \lambda D''$. It will therefore suffice to show that, given D' and D'' such that $\lambda D' \neq \lambda D''$, there exists a convex characteristic ϵ_0 such that $g(D', \epsilon_0) \neq g(D'', \epsilon_0)$. Without loss of generality we confine ourselves to the case of pure trade so that ϵ_0 is given by the admissible set $X_0 \subseteq \mathscr{X}$, initial holdings $\omega_0 \in \mathscr{X}$, and a preference relation ρ_0.

Write $X_0^* = X_0 - \omega_0$ and

$$X' = g(D', \epsilon_0) = \{x \in X_0^* : x \geq d' \quad \text{for every } d' \in D' \cap X_0^*\},$$

with similar definition for X''. (The inequality $x \geq d'$ is in the sense of ρ_0.)

Thus we must find such values ρ_0 (together with X_0 and ω_0) that, given any D' and D'' such that $\lambda D' \neq \lambda D''$, it follows that $X' \neq X''$.

Without loss of generality, we may now assume that there is an element $d_0 \in D''$ such that $d_0 \neq 0_x$ and $\lambda d_0 \notin D'$ for all $\lambda \geq 0$, for otherwise (taking into account the possibility of interchanging the labels D' and D'') it would follow that $\lambda D' = \lambda D''$.

Now suppose we can find a "convex" ordering ρ_0 (in the sense of Definition 12) and $x_0 \in X_0^*$ such that (for $d' \in X_0^*$) $d_0 > x_0 \geq d'$ for all $d' \in D'$ (with inequalities in the sense of ρ_0). Then $x_0 \in X'$, but $x_0 \notin X''$, and the proof is complete. To define the required ordering ρ_0, we find it convenient to rotate the axes in such a way that each point x can be written in the form $x = (y, z)$, where z is scalar, $d_0 = (0_y, \delta_0)$, and we may take $\delta_0 > 0$ since $d_0 \neq 0_x$.

We shall pick an ordering ρ_0 (related to the lexicographic ordering) defined by what follows. Given $x' = (y', z')$ and $x'' = (y'', z'')$,

a) $x' > x''$ (i.e., x' is strictly preferred to x'' in the sense of ρ_0) if and only if $\|y'\| < \|y''\|$, or $\|y'\| = \|y''\|$ and $z' > z''$;

b) $x' \sim x''$ (i.e., x' is indifferent to x'' in the sense of ρ_0) if and only if $\|y'\| = \|y''\|$ and $z' = z''$. [The symbol $\|y\|$ denotes the norm (length) of the vector y.]

It may be verified that the contour sets of ρ_0 are convex and that if $x' > x''$, then $\alpha x' + (1 - \alpha)x'' > x''$ for $0 < \alpha < 1$ (with the preference inequality in the sense of ρ_0).

Clearly, $d_0 > d'$ for all $d' \in D'$, since $\lambda d_0 \notin D'$ for all $\lambda \geq 0$. Now take $x_0 = (0_y, \frac{1}{2}\delta_0)$. Then $x_0 < d_0$, since both have zero as the norm of the first component; on the other hand, $x_0 > d_1'$ for all $d_1 = (Q_y, \delta) \in D'$, since it must be that $\delta < 0$; also, $x_0 > d_2' = (y, z)$ for $y \neq 0_y$, since then $\|y\| > 0$. This completes the proof.

REFERENCES

1. ARROW, K. J., "An Extension of the Basic Theorems of Classical Welfare Economics," in J. Neyman, ed., *Proceedings of the Second Berkeley Symposium on Mathematical Statistics and Probability*, Berkeley and Los Angeles: University of California Press, 1951, pp. 507–32.

2. ARROW, K. J., and G. DEBREU, "Existence of an Equilibrium for a Competitive Economy," *Econometrica*, 22 (1954), 265–90.

3. DEBREU, G., "Valuation Equilibrium and Pareto-Optimum," *Proceedings of the National Academy of Sciences*, 40 (1954), 588–92.

4. HAYEK, F. A., "The Use of Knowledge in Society," *American Economic Review*, 35 (1945), 519–30.

5. HURWICZ, L., "Decentralized Resource Allocation," *Cowles Commission Discussion Paper: Economics No. 2112*, May, 1955.

6. MARSCHAK, J., "Elements for a Theory of Teams," *Management Science*, 1 (1955), 127–37.

7. MARSCHAK, T., "Centralization and Decentralization in Economic Organizations," Technical Report No. 42, Office of Naval Research Contract N6onr-25133, April, 1957, Department of Economics, Stanford University.

8. MCKENZIE, L., "On the Existence of General Equilibrium for a Competitive Market," *Econometrica*, 27 (1959), 54–71.

9. RADNER, R., "The Application of Linear Programming to Team Decision Problems," *Management Science*, 5 (1959), 143–50.

Welfare economics and economic policy*

A. RADOMYSLER

When, some time ago, socialist economists were presented with the challenge that, without private ownership in the means of production, no rational economic calculation would be possible, they fell back on what came to be known as "the competitive solution". It was, it will be remembered, a simple device. Private ownership in the means of production would be abolished, but money, markets, and prices would be retained; consumers would spend their incomes as they liked; and the managers of all socialised enterprises would be instructed to meet the demand for all goods until costs and prices were equal. An exact reproduction, in fact, of the conditions of perfect competition.

Since then, the discussion of socialism has moved to another plane. The practicability of a socialist economy is no longer denied. But other issues have come to the fore. Will socialism produce better results than capitalism or worse? What will happen to political freedom? The setting, as a consequence, has become broader than before; economic, psychological, social, and political considerations are all linked together.

Alongside this development, however, there has also been another. The one-time juxtaposition of only *laissez faire* and socialism is no longer true. There is now a third scheme which differs from both. It is generally referred to as a planned economy. Its most important target is full employment.

Seen against this triple background, Mr. Lerner's recent book[1] is difficult to place. The views held by others, unfortunately, are not related to his; the term "planning", for example, in the modern sense, is never used. This rugged individualism makes it difficult at first, to find one's way. The scheme that emerges appears to be closest to the third; but the reasons that he advances in its favour are unusual and the picture as a whole is not clear.

The author opens with a brief autobiographical statement. When this book was begun, about twelve years before publication, he believed in the completely

* *Economica*, N. S. 13(1946): 190–204. Reprinted by courtesy of *Economica*.

[1] Abba P. Lerner, *The Economics of Control. Principles of Welfare Economics* (New York: Macmillan Company, 1944).

collectivist economy. Since then, however, his views have changed. The history of Russia and Germany have convinced him that the maintenance and extension of democracy require more urgent attention than collectivisation; and that collectivisation, moreover, represents a danger to democracy. The completely collectivist economy, therefore, is no longer his ideal; collectivisation, on the other hand, is not ruled out. His present ideal, the controlled economy, "suggests the deliberate application of whatever policy will best serve the social interest, without prejudging the issue between collective ownership and administration or some form of private enterprise".

This book is thus different from what it was meant to be when it was begun. The earlier plan had been to solve each economic problem for the completely collectivist economy first, and then to compare it to a capitalist economy. This procedure, nevertheless, despite the change of view, is retained; and this, as will be shown, has several unfortunate consequences. But let us first summarise part of the argument.

The most important means to maximise welfare, to Mr. Lerner, is the equality of price and marginal cost. This could have been easily realised everywhere in the completely collectivist economy and this, apparently, would have been its chief merit. The equality of price and marginal cost then becomes the decisive test for the controlled economy too. But as public ownership threatens democracy, we must prefer to see it realised, wherever possible, under private enterprise. Where perfect competition rules, nothing need be done; it is realised automatically. We must only see to it that competition survives. Where competition is imperfect or where there is monopoly, we must either re-establish perfect competition under private enterprise, or, where this cannot be done, collectivise. Where marginal costs are below average costs, perfect competition is clearly impossible; hence we must nationalise industries where this is the case. Nationalisation may further be necessary, though of only some firms in an industry, to maintain perfect competition; public and private enterprise would then compete with each other. The government agents operating the nationalised industries or firms would be instructed to follow "the rule"; i.e., they would equate price and marginal cost. Where marginal costs are below average costs, this will lead to losses, but for public enterprise this is irrelevant. Thus, the economy is no longer completely collectivist; but though some private enterprise is retained, the equality of price and marginal cost nevertheless rules everywhere. Private firms establish it by maximising profits; public managers by obeying the rule. In taxation also, and other fields, wherever this can be avoided, the equality between price and marginal cost must not be disturbed. This sums up the argument of the greater part of the book.

Leaving the merits of this for the present on one side, in approach and exposition, one can see, this bears all the marks of the author's original intentions. The completely collectivist economy is still treated first in the book and still occupies more space than anything else. The actual capitalist economy, on the other hand, is treated only incidentally, and so is the controlled economy. For his present intentions, however, this does not make sense. The level of his exposition, moreover, varies. A great part of it is very elementary; much of it, in fact, is written as if it were for the beginner. Barter exchange, we are told, for example, would be extremely inconvenient but can be avoided by the use of money. There are most painstaking explanations of things like the elasticity of demand. Other parts, on the other hand, are very advanced and compressed, and obviously inaccessible to anyone who is not thoroughly familiar with the issues. In some parts, this is also difficult to understand, the usual diagrams are avoided, whilst in other parts they are used.

The discussion is subdivided according to the conditions of costs. The author examines, for example, the problems that arise with one scarce factor under collectivism, under perfect competition, under capitalism, and in the controlled economy. Political observations, on the other hand, and some statements about reality, are made throughout. We thus get all these different elements in very rapid and ever-recurring succession, and this is one of the most striking features of the book.

These are, unfortunately, not simply faults of exposition, for his central theme becomes submerged. The different elements, for one thing, of the ideal that he recommends are torn apart, and as one tries to put them together, they do not fit. Sometimes there are contradictions, as in his statements about consumers' choice. At one extreme, freedom from government interference is all-important because only then will satisfactions be maximised; at the other, many people are said to spend their incomes unwisely, and guardianship, in the form of rationing, may legitimately be applied. The optimum division of incomes is discussed rigidly apart from all else and the problem is not discussed again in relation to other matters. Who is to pay for the losses incurred by public enterprise? The answer is missing. When he comes to the maintenance of employment, there is, as was to be expected, only a faint echo of his earlier conclusions.

This last point is important. Unemployment is reached only after we are three-quarters through the book. Thus, what was in reality the most important single factor that brought *laissez faire* to an end, comes here near the end. The maintenance of employment, moreover, is now by many economists considered to be the most important objective of economic policy. Mr. Lerner, on the other hand, comes to his controlled economy, not from *laissez faire*, but from the completely collectivist economy. To him, the decisive reason for controlling the economy, it appears, is the establishment of equality between price and marginal cost.

With the question of practicability he is not concerned. " We shall assume a government that wishes to run society in the general interest and is strong enough to override the opposition afforded by any sectional interest." This attitude, too, one feels, is now inappropriate. Now that Mr. Lerner has returned from his completely collectivist world, he should, one feels, also concern himself with what it is practicable to do. However, he merely wants to show "what is socially desirable". "We must leave to the politicians the political problems of compromise."

All these, however, are comparatively minor matters.

How much perfect competition do we find in the real world? And how much perfect competition could be restored under private enterprise? These are, evidently, important questions. We need an answer, for example, to know how large, in the controlled economy, the private and public sectors would be. The author's observations about reality are said to refer to "the actual world and the United States in particular." How much perfect competition does Mr. Lerner believe to exist in the actual world? This we cannot find out.

The author is aware, of course, of the existence of imperfect competition, but his references to it are scattered and few. He writes, for example, whilst discussing a one-scarce factor world: "The infrequency of perfect competition is shown by the importance of salesmanship" (p. 78). Later, under indivisibilities: "Small indivisibilities in the actual world are perhaps more important than big ones of the public utility type...." (p. 182); and this is followed by some observations on product differentiation and similar causes of imperfect competition. The problem of excessive varieties is discussed at length. He well recognises, in some places, that even where there are many small firms, they may yet act in combination.

Nevertheless, of perfect competition, he evidently believes that it exists somewhere; for he often writes that in certain conditions it would be "maintained" or would "survive", quite distinct from other statements where he writes it could be "restored". What he apparently relies on to support these statements, is limitation of size; and the factor that prevents firms from growing, at least in the short run, is the single nonaugmentable entrepreneur. This is followed by a statement that must be quoted in full:

... in important parts of the economy the optimum size of the firm is still small compared to the size of the market. There is then no danger that perfect competition will be destroyed by the growth of firms or by combination of firms. There is still the danger that quasi-monopolistic institutions will be developed by trade associations, by political measures such as tariffs to prevent competition from abroad, and by licensing or other legal restrictions to hinder domestic competition. But if these are kept in check, perfect competition can be maintained in such industries. If the rule is kept in operation in the other parts of the economy where perfect competition is not stable or possible, the optimum use of resources can be obtained without any interference with private enterprise in these particular industries (p. 211).

Now, product differentiation, in the first place, is here ignored. On the preceding page the author had, once, used the words "something approaching perfect competition", but both before and after, it is "perfect competition" again. Where, in reality, the conditions here described do apply is not stated.

The "if" of this paragraph, "if these are kept in check", is here left obscure so that one does not know which of several measures he thinks could here be applied "without any interference with private enterprise". The cost-conditions upon which this argument is based are those of steeply rising marginal costs and these are due to the fixed factor of the nonaugmentable entrepreneur. Empirical cost studies that show marginal costs to be, not steeply rising, but fairly constant over a wide range of output, are ignored. After all this, the paragraph leads to the conclusion that "the optimum use of resources can be obtained without any interference with private enterprise in these particular industries". Such is the basis upon which Mr. Lerner rests his case.

All this, to my mind, can be explained in only one way. The equality between marginal cost and price the author believes to be all-important. Private enterprise, on the other hand, is needed for the maintenance of political freedom, and the less interference there is, the safer democracy will be. These two things, he feels, one can see this in many places, are not easily combined. But he is not prepared to give up either. He is resolutely determined to have both. And, in the end, he does find them together. "There are many branches," he quite simply asserts, where private enterprise and perfect competition coexist.

A simple assertion of this kind, of course, will not do. The whole attempt, furthermore, shows a lack of a sense of proportion. Mr. Lerner believes, it will be remembered, that state control of economic affairs endangers political freedom. This view, of course, can, in this simple form, hardly be true. If, with regard to Germany for example, Mr. Lerner had asked himself why Brüning failed and the Nazis came to power, he might have found that the opposite may be the case. It was not economic planning that killed German democracy, but failure to plan; a vigorous economic policy in, say, 1930 might have saved us much. It was not economic planning that killed political freedom, nor was it planning that prevented its return. For after he had arrived Hitler consolidated his power by a few rapid political blows long before any economic measures had been put into effect. And it was Himmler and his S.S. that kept him secure. All this, however, is not my present point. If Mr. Lerner believed that, under state control, democracy would be in danger whilst under private enterprise, democracy would be safe, he should, one feels, have put this objective first. Political freedom, after all, is very important. The equality between price and marginal cost, on the other hand, even if it mattered much, would surely matter less.

Mr. Lerner, of course, believes this too: "The controlled economy may consider that even some sacrifice of efficiency in the allocation of resources is worthwhile as a contribution to the safeguard of democracy...." (p. 85, discussing a one-scarce-factor controlled economy). Well, if this is so, why this relentless pursuit?

We must now, however, get on to more important matters.

II

The pure theory of value, as everyone knows, is a highly abstract thing. Many consider it simply as an exercise in the logic of choice. It is often considered as a mere tool of thought. Many, perhaps, never ask how much it contains of reality. Some, it is true, take it as a first approximation. Mr. Lerner takes pure theory as reality itself.

It is difficult, it must be stressed, to know when, in this book, reality is discussed. There is the discussion, first of all, of the completely collectivist economy; this, clearly, is not our world. There are, furthermore, many simple illustrations; these, of course, are also not our world. Nevertheless, with some care, what is meant to be actual and real can be found. And what thus emerges is the theory of value.

Take, for example, the following statement:

> Perfect competition has advantages over the attainment of the optimum by the Rule: the incentive to the managers is of the ideal intensity ... because the entrepreneur will apply his efforts up to the point where a dollar's worth of effort can be expected to bring a dollar's worth of results. He will not stop short of this ideal point, as he would if the incentive were too weak, or wastefully go beyond this point, as would happen if too strong an incentive were applied (pp. 83–84).

Under state enterprise

> the incentive to apply it [the rule] accurately is not so clear or so great ... Some incentives in the form of rewards (and punishments too perhaps) will have to be developed for the manager who is subjected to the Rule, and there will be a delicate problem of making them neither too weak nor too strong. In private enterprise under conditions of perfect competition, all these problems are solved (p. 84).

Look at this, quite apart from everything else, as a statement on incentives. The only thing, in the first place, for which the author allows is personal reward; no one, apparently, whether private manager or public servant, ever does anything for any other reason. The adjustment, moreover, is perfectly mechanical, there has to be a delicate balance between what is too strong and too weak. Such are Mr. Lerner's observations on human behavior.

We are all familiar, of course, with statements of this kind; but where we usually find them is in theoretical discussions that stand far apart from practical affairs. And the question whether they are meant to apply to reality is usually left open or not raised at all. But here, in this discussion, we are left in no doubt; what the author thinks he is describing is the actual world. The above statement on incentives, for example, is to him one of the decisive points; it is one of the reasons why private enterprise, if there is perfect competition, is to be preferred to nationalisation.

Or take the following statement on consumers' behavior: "If there is a free market in consumption goods and consequently no discrimination between different consumers, the price will measure the marginal substitutability for each consumer" (p. 78). This, too, is a statement about the actual world.

Statements like these, unfortunately, will not even cause surprise; we usually accept them as well-established propositions. They are the core of our text-books and lectures and classes. This, after all, is the stuff of which economic theory is made. And economic theory is an impressive structure; it is mathematical, orderly, complete, and precise. Economics, we often feel, is the queen of the social sciences. Our propositions, unlike those of others, are not fumbling and vague; unlike others, we have discovered laws. Are these propositions and laws true in the actual world? This is usually, apparently, an unimportant point.

Mr. Lerner, however, leaves no doubt; he evidently believes these propositions to be true in the actual world. And this may well turn out to be the great value of this book. For to find these propositions accepted as representing the real world produces an unusually startling effect. And it is a wholesome reminder, and one that is overdue, of what sort of statements we are content to use.

Mr. Lerner thinks these propositions represent the whole of the truth. Others would probably say that this is not so. Propositions like these, it is usually believed, are only part of the truth; there are in reality, it is usually argued, many disturbing factors. This qualification, however, does not make these propositions any more true than they were before; for what is wrong with statements like these is that they contain no truth at all.

Their defect, however, is not that they are general and abstract; abstract and general is not the same as incorrect. The opposite of this statement, in fact, is true; these propositions are incorrect because they are not abstractions at all.

The problem of abstraction has given rise to a good many misunderstandings, and we must turn aside for a moment to examine it again. Abstraction, it is well to stress, is the characteristic of every science; all sciences are concerned with abstraction and generalisation. Laments, in economics, about abstraction as such are therefore not to the point. There are, however, two different kinds of "abstractness", and only one of them does what the word abstraction implies. Only one of them does in fact ab-stract certain elements from reality; the other, however, does nothing of the kind. It is a pity that for these two kinds we use one and the same term, for the two are entirely different things.

Take, for example, Keynes's *General Theory* and compare it with *Value and Capital* by Professor Hicks. In level of abstractness both books are alike; both alike deal with abstractions and generalisations. On this simple view, there is no difference between the two. But there is, nevertheless, an important distinction. What we find, in Keynes, are abstractions from experience; what we find in Hicks are not. The assumptions of the former are derived from observation of reality; the assumptions of the latter are got in a different way. The former, accordingly, contains some abstract generalisations that are yet applicable to the real world; for the generalisations of the latter this is not the case.

Look, to confirm this, at *Value and Capital*. "We need," writes Professor Hicks, "the principle of diminishing marginal rate of substitution.... Unless, at the point of equilibrium, the marginal rate of substitution is diminishing, equilibrium will not be stable" (p. 21). So far, of course, there is no reference to experience. Listen, however, to the argument of the following page. "Since we know from experience that some points of possible equilibrium do exist on the indifference map of nearly everyone (that is to say, they do decide to buy such-and-such quantities of commodities, and do not stay hesitating indefinitely like Buridan's ass), it follows that the principle of diminishing marginal rate of substitution must sometimes be true" (p. 22). He admits that this could not be established by introspection, but he nevertheless believes that it can be justified in this way; he is appealing, he believes, to experience and finds his assumption confirmed.

Mr. Lerner's argument, to quote another example, is simpler, and no appeal to experience comes in at all. "Certain assumptions have to be made about human satisfactions.... including the principle of diminishing marginal substitutability between goods" (p. 8). "We must assume that in general consumers try to obtain that which gives them more satisfaction rather than that which affords them less satisfaction..." (p. 9). And after this his consumers proceed to their familiar equilibrium positions. Why we "must" make these assumptions, the author does not say, but his reasons are presumably similar to those of Professor Hicks.

Now it will be clear from these quotations that these are not empirical statements. With Mr. Lerner they are not empirical even in form. With Professor Hicks they appear to be empirical, but on closer inspection this turns out to be incorrect. What his argument amounts to is simply this. Many housewives, for example, step into a shop; but they do not indefinitely stay undecided inside; and when they leave, their baskets are filled with a precise collection of goods. This is proof, to Professor Hicks, that they have equated marginal utilities and prices, or rather that they have moved to a point where the price-line and an indifference curve are tangential. He does not say explicitly that this is what they do; what he says is that this is the simplest assumption possible. Mr. Lerner, on the other hand, is less cautious than this; at first he simply states that we "must" assume this, but later, as was shown above, he believes that this actually happens.

These and similar propositions, of course, we often use. They are not, as is clear, empirical propositions. They are not, as is sometimes argued, first approximations to reality; it is not true that they take from reality what is essential and leave disturbing factors out. It is not true that they represent reality "expurgated" and "sterilised"; even Veblen's criticisms do not go far enough. What is contained in these propositions is not even a part of reality. The truth is quite simply that human beings do not behave like that.

The defect of these propositions, therefore, is not that they are abstractions; some very valuable parts of economic theory consist of abstractions too. It is not that some parts of reality have been left out, for this must inevitably be done in theoretical analysis. This, in fact, is the difference between the theoretical and the applied. But there is, nevertheless, an important distinction: between theory that does apply to reality and theory that does not.

Mr Lerner's theory evidently does not. Professor Hicks's theory also does not apply. Our theory of value is not true to fact. It is not that our views contain only part of the truth. Our views about human behavior, here as elsewhere, are not simplifications; they are incorrect. They do not represent anything that happens in the real world.

In macro-economic generalisations, the harm done by this is small. And it was here, after all, that the abstract method and deduction were first applied. The advantages, moreover, of the abstract method and deduction are here immense; it is clear, in the work of Ricardo for example, what powerful instruments they can be. Keynes's *General Theory*, too, contains for the most part macro-economic generalisations; no one would deny that, in essentials, they are both important and true. Mr. Lerner's statements on the principles of "Functional Finance" (Ch. 24) for example, are as "abstract" as the rest of the book; but here, he is concerned with macro-economic issues, and the chapter, accordingly, is, though abstract, correct. (This chapter, incidentally, is an admirable piece of work, and it shows what Mr. Lerner can do when his tools are adequate for the job.)

When we turn, on the other hand, to individual behavior, all this ceases to hold. It is useless, in the first place, to say that we *must* make certain assumptions. And this is true of consumers' behavior, of the behavior of entrepreneurs, or that of trade unions, or of anyone else. An empirical science can find its material in only one way: by looking at the real world. And this is no less true of technical conditions; they cannot be inferred from mathematical propositions. It is useless, furthermore, to say that everyone must maximise something, whether it be satisfactions, or the wage-bill,[2] or anything else. This degree of precision is not found in the world. Men and women, in cafes and shops, do not behave like calculating machines. Even if they would, they could not do this, for psychical magnitudes are not precise. These are not problems that can be solved by differential equations. In business, on the other hand, conditions are neither fixed nor certain; and even where the desire for profit is decisive, our usual degree of precision is out of place.

In economic theory, these are serious defects. We shall here make no progress until we get rid of *a priori* construction. In the other branch of economics, however, things are even more seriously wrong than this, and we must now return to welfare economics.

III

Economic theory, it is sometimes argued, is concerned with the explanation of what is; welfare economics, on the other hand, it is said, examines what

---

[2] See, for a recent example, J. T. Dunlop, *Wage Determination under Trade Unions*, p. 4: "An economic theory of a trade union requires that the organisation be assumed to maximise (or minimise) something."

ought to be done. This view, however, is not universally held; it is not, for example, the view of Professor Pigou. Professor Pigou in his *Economics of Welfare* does not prescribe; he examines what would increase economic welfare and leaves it at that. This is important. As *The Economics of Welfare* is concerned with the *causes* of welfare, it follows that it is a *positive* study. Though the causes which Professor Pigou examines may not all be correct and though they may not be those that are most important in the real world, in approach and in method, at any rate, his book is objective. It is a positive study of causes, not a normative study of what ought to be done.

The study of the causes of welfare, of course, and prescription are not far apart; the former, to most people, is only a preparation for the latter. Nevertheless, they are two different things.

In recent contributions to welfare economics,[3] this has been obscured. It was overlooked, in the first place, that all prescription is normative; prescription says what ought to be, it does not say what is. And prescription would yet be normative even if it were universally agreed. Mr. Kaldor and Professor Hicks apparently believe the opposite to be true; if some people welcomed a certain measure and no one was opposed, prescription, they believe, would then be objective. This, however, is a sense in which the word objective is not used elsewhere.

But, though this meaning of objectivity is inappropriate, another one is not. The sense in which *The Economics of Welfare* is objective, in fact, is the central point. This book, to repeat, is not concerned with prescription; it asks what is welfare and what would happen to it if certain things were done. Any study that does this and no more is an objective study.

It is a study, it is true, of sensations and feelings. And these are often referred to as "subjective". But a study of subjective feelings is not the same thing as a subjective study. We study valuations, as we all know, in economic theory too; and yet we are all agreed that it is nevertheless an objective study. What is true of valuations there, is true of feelings here. Both economic theory and welfare economics are positive studies. But though, if welfare economists would be content to study causes and not to prescribe, there would not be a distinction between "science" and "art"; there would nevertheless be an important difference.

Economic theory would be concerned, in the main, with external matters like prices, incomes, employment, and output. Welfare economics, on the other hand, would be concerned with internal sensations and feelings. The terms "price economics" and "welfare economics" have sometimes been suggested, and this may well be an appropriate choice. This division would not, however, imply a rigid keeping apart of external magnitudes, like prices, and

---

[3] See N. Kaldor, "Welfare Propositions in Economics," *Economic Journal*, September 1939, and J. R. Hicks, "The Foundations of Welfare Economics," *Economic Journal*, December, 1939; and further references given in these two.

subjective feelings. We need valuations, for example, for the explanation of prices. And we need the conclusions of "price economics" to examine the causes of welfare. There would, however, be a difference in objective. In "price economics", it is prices and similar things that matter; valuations are brought in only where they are needed for explanation. In "welfare economics", on the other hand, feelings are not instrumental, but the object of our study; everything else is considered only insofar as they influence these.

If all this is granted, one difficulty remains. Though the causes of welfare may be a positive study, what happens if we turn from the individual to all? Is it possible to make any statement about social welfare? Can we compare, in other words, the satisfaction between one individual and another? This is the question, it will be remembered, that has been the centre of the discussion on whether objectivity is possible or not. If we are looking for an accurate measure, the answer, of course, is no; we have no direct measure for internal states of feeling. We may guess, of course, and surmise, and clear evidence is usually there; and most of us are quite prepared to act on the strength of this evidence in practical affairs. But there is no need, even though this is so, to call an hypothesis a fact.

Mr. Kaldor some time ago suggested[4] that we might overcome this difficulty by the payment of compensation; and his suggestion has since been taken up, among others, by Professor Hicks. If a given measure of economic policy leads to a change in the distribution of income, nothing, it had been maintained before, could be said about welfare as a whole. For whilst some people gain, others may lose, and we have no way of saying that the gain exceeds the loss. This difficulty, it was suggested, could be overcome by the device of compensation. If all that lose are, or can be, compensated so that they are no worse off than before, whilst others, though they may have to pay this compensation, are yet better off than before, then, it was argued, social welfare has increased. We can then say that total satisfaction has increased without comparing the satisfaction of one individual with that of another.

This device, however, will not do. For the relation between incomes, also, is a component of welfare, and the payment of compensation may be considered unfair. Or, if the rich become richer, though everyone else's income remains the same, the increase in inequality may yet be resented and total welfare may thus be less than before. To measure the satisfaction derived from all incomes together, this cannot be done; some incomes rise, some fall, that is all we can say.

That is all we can say, and that is all that need be said. To attempt to say more would be saying less. There is no need to get a single measure for "general welfare" or "total satisfaction". It is not this that counts in practical affairs. And so long as we use this as a single measure, however we may get it,

----

4 *Loc. cit.*

the essence of the matter would drop out; the problem of conflict would be assumed away.[5]

Even if we assume that the division of income is all that matters between one individual and another, even then it is clear that conflict is the essence of the problem. In reality, however, it is a matter far wider than this. There are many other conflicts as well. Between individuals and groups and classes and nations. There are also, for society as a whole, conflicts between objectives. Efficiency and security, progress, stability, fairness, freedom from control—to achieve each by itself is an easy matter; if we try to achieve more, we find that each clashes with all.

What, then, would it mean, to say that "aggregate welfare" has increased? What meaning would there be if all these things were lumped together into one single measure of "social welfare"? To search for a single answer, here, is beside the point; as conflict is the essence of the problem, we must not assume it away.

In current writings of welfare economists, it is true, the matter is simpler than this. However, they are hardly concerned with the problem of welfare. They believe they are discussing welfare; in fact they are not. They claim to be objective, but this claim is untrue.

They cannot, in the first place, resist the temptation to prescribe. Though what they consider may be irrelevant, unimportant, impracticable, or untrue, they nevertheless insist on telling us what ought to be done. What ought to be done, everyone can say. And whilst we want, of course, to say this too, this is not our primary task. Our primary task is to show what it is that can be done and what particular measures would lead to an increase in welfare. If we want to be objective, we must not prescribe. If we want to be objective, moreover, we must consider everything that matters; we must consider the things that matter to the people concerned. And we must consider these matters whether we like them or not; our own views of what is important are mere prejudice and opinion. To say that everyone will be happier is neither possible nor required; if we can show that some will gain and some lose, that will be enough. What ought to be done will easily follow from this, but we should not expect science to tell us all. Science can show us who would gain and who would lose; no one can escape the obligation then to choose for himself.

To achieve objectivity, in this real sense, is, of course, as we all know, no easy matter; and no one ever entirely succeeds. But unless we try, and succeed at least in part, welfare economics will remain a sham.

The task of welfare economics is to study the causes of welfare—what would make men happier, and what would not. What people's needs are and how far they can be fulfilled; which needs remain unsatisfied and how far this can be reduced. Before we can study the causes of welfare, however, we must

---

[5] See Gunnar Myrdal: *Das Politische Element in der National-Ökonomischen Doktrinbildung*, Ch. VIII. I owe much of this article to this book. Myrdal's suggestions on how to achieve objectivity in welfare economics are not, it should be noted, the same as the concept of "Wertfreiheit" in Max Weber.

first know what welfare is. Welfare, or happiness, however, is no simple thing. What our welfare economists consider is only one part; and what they see in this, moreover, is quite simply not there. All the things that matter, on the other hand, are left out.

We want to show, welfare economists usually begin, how we can best satisfy people's wants. The one want which most of them then consider is the demand for consumption. Even the division of income, where it is considered, is treated as no more than a subproblem of this; and so, quite often, is the problem of employment. This one want, for consumption, is then considered with infinite care. But not, as one might expect, to show how we could produce more with our current resources. No, welfare economists are concerned with the problem of allocation.

This, it appears, is of immense importance. Consumers, in the first place, choose with the utmost of wisdom and care; in restaurants and shops and pubs and stores, they equate marginal utilities with the maximum of precision. Our duty, then, is to see that all this is not done in vain. In the first place, we must make sure that this optimum is not disturbed. We must ensure, then, that what they allocate are not simply goods but resources. All the weapons of economics are then brought to bear on this problem—the calculus, geometry, in two and three dimensions. In Mr. Lerner's book the problem is examined for simple cases first. Two goods that have already been produced. Two goods and one scarce factor. Two goods and two scarce factors. First in fixed and then in variable proportions. Diminishing marginal transformability and the elasticity of substitution. Indivisibilities. Fixed factors. Short periods and long. In the end there emerges the triumphant conclusion: prices and marginal costs have been made equal throughout. Unemployment has been reduced. Total satisfactions have been maximised.

Lockouts and strikes? Industrial relations? The control of wages and the control of prices? The vicious spiral? The problem of incentives? The motive of profit and the motive of service? The training of workers and the choice of a job? The problem of discipline? The guaranteed week? The location of industry and the planning of towns? Private ownership or nationalisation? The problem of justice in distribution? Government regulation or freedom from control?

Equate prices and marginal costs everywhere, writes Mr. Lerner. If you can do this under private enterprise, keep it; if you cannot, nationalise. Counterbalance cyclical fluctuations. This is Mr. Lerner's advice. "We must leave to the politicians the political problems of compromise."

IV

The idea of "economic welfare" as a part of "general welfare" is a misleading conception; welfare is one harmonious whole.[6] It is both possible

---

[6] See Graham Wallas, *The Great Society*, p. 351; J. A. Hobson, *Free Thought in the Social Sciences*, pp. 170–71; L. T. Hobhouse, *The Elements of Social Justice*, p. 27.

and convenient, on the other hand, to study the economic causes of welfare by themselves. But to study the economic causes of welfare, we must first find out what all the causes of welfare are. Only thus shall we be able to know whether what we usually consider is enough. To take only consumption and consider that alone cannot yield conclusions of any value. Warnings against this, after all, abound. "But his conclusions... do not authorise him [the economist] in adding a single syllable of advice. That privilege belongs to the writer or the statesman who has considered all the causes which may promote or impede the general welfare of those whom he addresses, not to the theorist who has considered only one, though among the most important, of those causes."[7] "Pleasurable sensations of consumption are not," Veblen urged, "the sole end of economic endeavour."

The economic problem, it may be, is the problem of choice; but the choice between food and clothes and entertainment and travel is of only minor importance. In the welfare of everyone, the satisfactions of consumption form only a part. Welfare is a thing made of more elements than this. If we wish to know what they are we can only look and see; one glance at reality will show us how much we leave out. But if we want to do this well, we should not rely on personal observation, but turn to science. The study of sensations and feelings, after all, is another science's task; if we turn first to psychology we shall be better equipped for the job.

In many countries, the central economic problem is no longer poverty but conflict. Everyone wants more, no one wants less. Many want more leisure more income, and less work. Some want no interference, others want control. Some want control of others, but not of themselves. Some want to keep private enterprise, others want nationalisation. Some want to see justice, but what justice is is not agreed. Some want stability, others want change. It is a problem of conflict, for all wants of all cannot be satisfied. What we need, both for each individual and for society as a whole, is some sort of balance between many conflicting desires. Once this is seen, the search for the maximum, whatever Bentham may have thought, will be at an end. We would be content to see all happy; and if not happy, at least happier than now. The difficulty is not only that the means to do this conflict, but conflict itself is its greatest foe. And this, perhaps, is the welfare economist's chief task; to show how conflict arises and how it can be reduced.

---

[7] Nassau Senior, *An Outline of the Science of Political Economy*, 1836, 1938 reprint, p. 3.

Preface—and a manifesto*

JOHN R. HICKS

Author's Note. The following is an extract from the preface to a volume of essays on practical topics. In relation to such topics I would by no means hold to the theoretical purism which I have defended in some other writings. "It is inevitable (I said) that in forming an opinion about contemporary events one should be making *value judgments*—that one should have some idea, at the bottom of one's mind, about the things, the conditions or the arrangements, which one thinks to be good or to be bad." So much, no doubt, is nowadays noncontroversial; but " I had come to be conscious that the position to which I had been coming is different from that which seems to be occupied by many economists "—as I proceeded to explain.

The view which, now, I do *not* hold I propose (with every apology) to call 'Economic Welfarism'; for it is one of the tendencies which has taken its origin from that great and immensely influential work, the *Economics of Welfare* of Pigou. But the distinction which I am about to make has little to do with the multifarious theoretical disputes to which the notion of Welfare Economics has given rise. One can take any view one likes about measurability, or addibility, or comparability of utilities; and yet it remains undetermined whether one is to come down on one side or other of the Welfarist fence. The line between Economic Welfarism and its opposite is not concerned with what economists call utilities; it is concerned with the transition from Utility to the more general good, Welfare (if we like) itself.

The general concept of Welfare from which Pigou begins is so all-embracing that it includes everything which any reasonable person might think to be of value; no one (simply as a matter of definition) can want to go outside that. It is, however, Pigou's contention that the concern of the economist does not lie with Welfare in general, but with that *part* of general Welfare which he calls economic welfare; and this is the point where the trouble arises. Of course it is well known that there is trouble at this point. Of course the philosopher has told us that the social good is not a thing which can be divided into parts, of which one can be taken and another left; all of us have accepted that reproof, and all of us are careful to avoid the phrase which has become

---

* *Essays in World Economics* (Oxford: Clarendon Press, 1959): pp. viii-xiv. Corrected by the author. Reprinted by courtesy of the author and Clarendon Press.

so suspect. Yet I maintain that in substance the division has sunk in, and has sunk in very deeply. Welfarists, even those who limit their concept of economic welfare to the Production and Distribution of the Social Dividend, have become, almost unconsciously and unintentionally, something like the dominant school of economic thought.

It is indeed true that economic welfare can be conceived (and was conceived by Pigou) as something much wider than that. It can be defined so as to include subjective elements—" surpluses " which are not fully expressed in the money value of goods and services, as well as the "efforts and sacrifices" which are involved in labour and perhaps in saving also. But that is only to say that it may be extended so as to include elements that are more "indirectly" brought "into relation with the measuring-rod of money." Even with these extensions, the characteristic feature of Economic Welfarism—that it finds the *ends* of economic life *within* economics—is preserved.

Differently stated, this characteristic feature can be described as a belief that these ends can be adequately expressed in terms of " utility functions " or "indifference maps" that are "revealed on the market," or could be so revealed under suitable conditions. That we need some such constructions as these I do not at all deny. Our basic concepts. Production and Distribution themselves, make no adequate sense without them; I have indeed devoted a good deal of attention to investigating the connexion, and I hope that it has been somewhat clarified as a result of my own work.[1] But, even in the course of these investigations, I have become more and more conscious of the artificiality of these assumptions. They are simplifications by which we beat reality into a form which makes it tractable to economic analysis; they are not more than that. In our role as economic technicians, we cannot do without them; but as soon as we aspire to be something more than technicians, we must see them for the shaky supports that they are.

I cannot therefore now feel that it is enough to admit, with that very moderate Welfarist Sir Dennis Robertson, that "the economist must be prepared to see some suggested course of action which he thinks would promote economic welfare turned down—his own judgement perhaps consenting, perhaps not—for overriding reasons."[2] This is still no more than an admission that there are " parts " of welfare which are not included in Economic Welfare, and that the two sorts of ends may conflict. The economist, as such, is still allowed, and even encouraged, to keep within his " own " frontiers; if he has shown that a particular course of action is to be recommended, *for economic reasons*, he has done his job. I would now say that if he limits his function in that manner, he does not rise to his responsibilities. It is impossible to make " economic " proposals that do not have " noneconomic aspects," as the Welfarist would call them; when the economist makes a recommenda-

---

[1] See, for instance, "The Measurement of Real Income," *Oxford Economic Papers*, June 1958.

[2] *Lectures on Economic Principles*, i, p. 29.

tion, he is responsible for it in the round; all aspects of that recommendation, whether he chooses to label them economic or not, are his concern.

Several examples of the kind of thing which I am meaning will be found among these essays; for the present it will be sufficient to take one strong example, from a different field from those that are represented here. One of the issues that can be dealt with most elaborately by Welfarist methods is that of Monopoly and Competition: the theory of the social optimum which would be reached in a (practically unattainable) condition of all-round perfect competition, and of the departures from the optimum which must occur under any form in which a system of free enterprise can in practice be organized, is one of the chief ways in which the Welfarist approach has left its mark. I do not question that we have learned a great deal from these discussions; but they leave me with an obstinate feeling that they have failed to penetrate to the centre of the problem with which they are concerned. I did indeed, at one time, suppose that the unacceptability (to me) of the practical conclusions which seem to follow from such a work as Mrs. Robinson's *Economics of Imperfect Competition* was due to the narrowness of the " production and distribution " or cost-minimization standards that were being applied; if one widened it out, in a more faithfully Pigouvian manner, so as to take account of gains and losses in consumers' surplus, the conclusions which followed would be less paradoxical. I still think that this extension is a help; the more Robertsonian conclusions, which then emerge, are easier to swallow; but I do not now feel that this extension goes far enough. It does not, even yet, carry the discussion fully over into the territory where it largely belongs.

Why is it, for instance, that antimonopoly legislation (and litigation) get so little help, as they evidently do, from the textbook theory? Surely the answer is that the main issues of principle—security on the one side, freedom and equity on the other, the issues that lawyers, and lawmakers, can understand—have got left right out. They cannot be adequately translated, even into terms of surpluses. (One crucial example of this inadequacy is the Welfarist incomprehension of the role of advertisement. To the Welfarist, advertisement appears as sheer waste; but from the other side, although the abuses to which it is liable would of course be admitted, freedom of advertisements is the opposite number to freedom of the press. It is the hall mark of economic freedom, just as the other is of political.)

To put the same point another way. The liberal, or noninterference, principles of the classical (Smithian or Ricardian) economists were not, in the first place, economic principles; they were an application to economics of principles that were thought to apply over a much wider field. The contention that economic freedom made for economic efficiency was no more than a secondary support. As the nineteenth century wore on, the increasing specialization of economists led to an increasing emphasis on the economic argument. Then it was discovered—it was rightly discovered—that the economic case for noninterference is riddled with exceptions; exceptions which may well have become more important in fact in the course of technological progress, and which certainly became of greater importance as the demands which were made on the economic system, in the direction of stability as well as of growth, became more exacting. Accordingly, since the other side of the case, which had at one time been the more important side, had been so largely forgotten, what had begun as an economic argument for noninterference became an economic argument for the opposite. I do not question that on its own assumptions that argument, in its latter form, was very largely right.

What I do question is whether we are justified in forgetting, as completely as most of us have done, the other side of the argument. Not that I wish to regard that "noneconomic" side as overriding; all that I claim for it is a place, and a regular place. I do not suppose that if we gave it this due attention, we should find ourselves subscribing, on that side, to all of the liberal principles of a century ago. We have not been helped to maintain our balance by the exaggerations to which the surviving adherents of those principles—for whom all controls are a " Road to Serfdom "—have been prone. It is useless to close one's eyes to the defects of competition, because one is so much in love with an ideal competitive system, set up in heaven. Neither side should give way to the other; but there is no reason why there should not be scope for marginal adjustments, in great things as well as small.

If there is room for marginal adjustments, there is also room for a "law of diminishing marginal significance" (or whatever we like to call it) that transcends the economic field. As wealth increases, wealth itself becomes (or should become) less important. At low levels of income, it is right to concentrate on economics; the first need of man is to fill his belly; politics are at best a distraction, at worst no better than communal drug-taking. But as wealth increases, there is room for other (and better) standards. It is no accident that the principles of liberal democracy were the work of those classes, first aristocratic, then bourgeois, who were the first to rise clean above subsistence so that they had opportunity to turn round and time to think. That is no reason to be ashamed of those principles. The same opportunities—they are in large measure the same opportunities—are now being spread, in the more fortunate countries of the world, far and wide throughout society. We are not so "affluent" that the need for more wealth has disappeared; but it has become *relatively* less urgent. The problems of combining security with freedom, equity with responsibility, come thereby more strongly to the fore.

But though there is a general presumption, when we look at things in this way, that the attainment of the liberal goods is facilitated by increases in wealth (that is as much as I would now retain of the harmony between economic and noneconomic welfare that was assumed by Pigou), it would be too much to maintain that *all* increases in wealth must have so favourable an effect. It is possible, by policy, to increase wealth but to diminish freedom; it is possible, again, that the growth of knowledge, though it must in some sense increase wealth or the possibility of wealth (with some kind of a surplus of economic gains over losses), may diminish the opportunities for freedom. Technological progress is ethically neutral; what is gives with one hand, it can take with the other. The opportunities for freedom have, without doubt, not been enhanced by progress in the military arts; I see no reason why we should count upon progress in other techniques to be uniformly beneficent. Much of the concentration of power in the hands of large organizations, which is the major threat to freedom within Western societies, is technological, not sociological, in its origin.

I have accordingly no intention, in abandoning Economic Welfarism, of falling into the "fiat libertas, ruat caelum" which some latter-day liberals seem to see as the only alternative. What I do maintain is that the liberal goods are goods—that they are values which, however, must be weighed up against other values. The freedom and the justice that are possible of attainment are not the same in all societies, at all times, and in all places; they are themselves conditioned by external environment, and (in the short period at least) by what has occurred in the past. Yet we can recognize these limitations and still feel that these ends are worthier ends that those which are represented in a production index. It is better to think of economic activity as means to these ends than as means to different ends, which are entirely its own.

Efficiency and amenity*

BERTRAND DE JOUVENEL

Men have ever desired to improve their material lot. But the idea that year after year the material lot of all or most members of a nation can and should be increased is new. Medieval radicals called for the rejection of the burdens laid upon the workers for the benefit of the privileged classes, but looked no further than the once-for-all improvement procured thereby. The thought that practically everybody can get somewhat richer continuously could not have arisen but for the gradual progress achieved over time and the awareness that it was due to successive gains in the productivity of labour. Awareness of the process has fostered a demand that it be accelerated. Accountancy has become a major criterion of our judgments.

We find nothing strange in the grading of nations according to their National Product per inhabitant, estimated in dollars, never mind how imperfectly. Those which lie in the lower ranges we call "underdeveloped": they are to be pitied, spurred, and helped up. Those which stand on the higher rungs we call "advanced." Such classification is common ground for leaders of opinion in both "Capitalist" and "Communist" countries. Indeed for more than thirty years, the avowed objective of Soviet planning has been "to overtake the American standard of life." Further, the vast increase in the worldwide prestige of Communism is due to the very high rates of growth achieved, and paradoxically enough the poorer countries are tempted to follow the Communist path as that which leads fastest to the way of life of the Capitalist countries.

In the advanced countries themselves the yearly rate of growth is a subject of great interest: if high it redounds to the credit of the Government, if low it affords an argument to the Opposition. Such focusing of attention upon economic growth should lead to the acceleration of the process.

May I quote just a few figures? The United States have amazed the world by multiplying real product per inhabitant almost sevenfold since 1839, according to the estimate of Raymond W. Goldsmith; that is a pace of 1.64 percent per year; in France during the last decade (i.e. 1949–1959), real product per

---

* Earl Grey Memorial Lecture, King's College, Newcastle upon Tyne, 1960. Reprinted by courtesy of the author and The Academic Board of King's College.

inhabitant has increased by more than one half, growing at a rate of 3.5 percent a year. If such a rate were sustained, it would *treble* the flow of goods and services per inhabitant in 32 years. This would imply a metamorphosis of life in the course of a generation. The British rate of increase has been a good deal lower, about 2.1 percent yearly (1948–1958), which if sustained would imply *doubling* the flow of goods and services per inhabitant within a generation. May I be so indiscreet as to say that I hope to see the British rate of growth increased by British entry into the faster growing Common Market? I must stress that the figures quoted all refer to progress of Gross National Product per inhabitant, not to the progress of production per man-hour, which is higher.

My figures serve no other purpose than to indicate the magnitude or speed of change. Surely if all the children now being born can, when reaching the age of 32, find themselves two or three times better off than their parents are now, it is worth thinking what to make of this opportunity. This is the problem I wish to raise. As we shall find, it is by no means an easy one to discuss.

II

The statement of the problem contains by implication two value judgments which should be made explicit. Firstly, I have assumed that people could obtain more and more goods and services and implied that it is a good thing; I so believe. Secondly, I have said that we should think of increasing riches as an increasing opportunity and implied that we can make thereof a better or worse use. These two assumptions may well pass unchallenged because they agree with current common sense. But however trivial the position taken, it has to be noted that it contradicts two strongly entrenched schools of thought, one ancient the other modern. The ancient moralists have all held that Man should limit his desires, that the pursuit of ever more goods and services is folly, bound to make men wicked and miserable. By reason of our first premise therefore we run foul of their venerable wisdom, and indeed we shall find that our wealth-mindedness brings us into conflict with many values which deserve respect. The second premise clashes with the relativist school, so powerful nowadays, which holds that there are no values other than subjective. If every man be the only judge of his own interest, if we can ascertain what makes him better off *solely* by observation of the *preferences* his actions *reveal*, then however Society develops under free individual choices, we must assume that whatever is, is the best possible world at the moment.

The position sketched out therefore is *modern* in opposition to the ancient moralists, and if you will it is progressive. It is however *classical* in opposition to the relativists, in its assumption that the judgments we pass upon the quality of life are not mere expressions of individual fancy but tend to objective value, however approximately attained.

III

To approach our problem, let us firstly ask ourselves how much good has come out of the economic progress already achieved and how near it has brought us to a Golden Age. A great deal of good has come out of economic progress up to date. Among these goods some figure in our statistics and some do not—housing does, and so does the labour-saving equipment provided to housewives; in the case of the latter however, mere statistics fail to do justice to a major boon, which has transformed the life of the better part of Mankind. The shortening of the workweek figures in our statistics as well as the holidays, but what cannot figure is the great lessening of the physical labour involved in work. Indeed if we could draw two curves, one of them describing the shortening of the work-time and the other the lessening of the intensity of muscular effort per hour, we would find the second falling far more than the first.[1] Some changes such as Full Employment which spares men the anxiety and indignity of being unwanted do not arise directly out of the progress of Productivity but are closely linked with it, and so are the social measures for the relief of misery which we could not have afforded but for our enrichment. Some effects figure in statistics but have connotations which do not so figure; for instance the great transformation of workers' clothing has erased a visible distinction. If I may add a light note, when I see two drivers locked in conflict, I reflect that but for the automobile, one of them might be on horseback the other on foot, while now they are on the same footing.

It is idle to say that all have benefited from economic progress. Obviously the class which had servants cannot afford them any more due to the up-pricing of labour; and this by itself involves for the class mentioned a great decline in the ease of life; but also it makes for greater similarity of situations, and presumably for readier understanding.

We could of course say more about the benefits of progress but some shall be stressed in due time. On the other hand can we say that our progress has brought us anywhere near the Golden Age? I fear not.

In writing and image, many glimpses of the Golden Age have been vouchsafed to us, they concur quite remarkably. *Homo Felix* moves against a background of beauty, delights in his workmanship, is benefited by the company he keeps, and his song of joy praises his Creator. Most often he is shown in a landscape mellowed by the human hand, with a nice balance of trees, meadows and stream; a graceful temple however testifies to urbanity. Contrariwise, if *Homo Felix* happens to be painted in a public place, then the greenery of the surroundings shows through the monuments of the town. The latter is no more than a meeting place for worship and conviviality. *Homo Felix* is not idle, but the enjoyment of doing things so overcomes the awareness that they must be done as to exclude any sense of drudgery. His associates move his heart and quicken his wit, expecting the best of him, they help him to achieve it. He opens his eyes at dawn, eager for the activities of the day, and closes them at dusk; free from worry, he exerts no pressure on any other man nor does he endure any.

Such, in brief, is the picture of *Homo Felix*. As against it the man of our day

---

[1] Note that I speak of muscular effort, nervous fatigue is quite a different business.

lives steeped in ugliness, injured, whether he be aware of it or not, by ugly sights, ugly sounds, ugly smells. His labours, in the great majority of cases, give little scope for his talents, and he can seldom forget that they are done solely for the sake of the reward. He is exceptionally fortunate if the company he keeps induces him to reach the excellence of which he is inherently capable.

It is a long way indeed to the Golden Age. Maybe the picture drawn thereof was a fanciful one. But surely there is some way of life which would be an improvement upon that which we find.

IV

An opinion which enjoys great currency is that the productivity gains we may look to, will for the greater part, translate themselves into a very rapid shortening of the time of work, so that we may expect in a few years the thirty-hour week or even the twenty-eight-hour week, i.e. three days and a half. Minds which start with this assumption then find themselves faced with the " problem of leisure "; what shall the people do, with all that spare time? They will be half workers, half gentlemen of leisure. Now it is no easy thing to be a gentleman of leisure, and not so many gentlemen have made a good showing at it. So runs the argument.

I happen to doubt very strongly that the working-week shall be shortened as much or as fast as people imagine. A lot of things can be reckoned out on paper which can not happen in reality. For instance, we may picture, say a 3.5 percent increase in production per man-hour, of which 2 percent would be taken out in the shortening of the time of work and 1.5 percent in the increase of production per worker. Under such conditions a thirty-hour week could easily be achieved within twenty years, while presumably production per inhabitant would be stable or declining, due to the reduction in the proportion of workers relatively to population, of which more anon.

This can be worked out with closer arithmetic than mine, but it simply would not work out in life. It is inconceivable that a 3.5 percent increase in productivity per year could occur with a slow expansion of production. High rates of productivity gain are linked to high rates of expansion. High overall rates of expansion are themselves linked with the introduction of new products in the production of which, or thanks to the production of which, the great productivity gains are achieved.

Some people reason as if we could nicely immobilize needs and then take out all our productivity gains in leisure. Let us follow this fancy. Suppose that our needs in lighting had been assessed in 1760, and that the candle industry had been asked to work down the time necessary for the provision of that much amount of lighting. Under such circumstances, the electricity industry could never have appeared as it required a rapidly expanding market. That example has been chosen because lighting is of all goods and services that in which labour-saving has been greatest, but it has also been that for which the expansion of the market has been greatest.

The nature of productivity gains is best grasped if one traces over time the cost in minutes of labour of the several goods and services. Nearly all these costs decline but at very different rates. What makes for a great gain in the collection of goods and services obtained per average hour is the presence, in the "mix," of an increasing variety of products intervening with increasing weights; such presence will be felt the more, the greater the overall expansion. Therefore, if, counting upon a high rate of productivity gains, we proposed to apply them mostly to shortening the time of work, and only to a lesser degree to the increase of production, we might find that the expected productivity gains withered away.

According to Moses Abramovitz, over the last seventy-five years, the productivity increase obtained in the U.S. has been cashed-in to the proportion of three-fourths in the increase of production per man, to the proportion of one-fourth in the decrease of work-time per man. Should we assume that progress continued at just the same rate and was allocated according to the same proportions, it would take another seventy years to bring the U.S. to the thirty-hour week. Now of course one should shun such extrapolations. On the one hand productivity gains can be stepped up considerably. On the other hand we should take into account that cutting down the workweek from very high levels certainly does not cut down pro rata the effective input of labour, because the effective input per hour then rises; it is very doubtful whether this same phenomenon would remain operative when cutting down the work-time from lower levels.

I do not pretend to know at what rate through the years the workweek can be shortened. But it seems very necessary to point to the demographic phenomena which shall militate against any very great and rapid shortening of the workweek. We can easily perceive that the workweek of the adult shall have to support an increasing proportion of weeks of existence of nonlabouring population.

We tend to live longer, and every year more that we live beyond working age is an added charge upon the worker. To an increasing degree the poor of an advanced society are its aged, and if we wish, as I feel we should, to pursue our effort for the relief of poverty, we must give to the aged a greater share of the proceeds of our work because of their increasing proportion and in order to raise their relative status. In the same manner, every year more which an adolescent spends at school is an added charge upon the adult workers. And surely nothing is more desirable than the successive prolongation of education. This can endow youths both with a better capacity for production and, what seems to me more important, with a better capacity for the right use of life and leisure, of which more anon.

Indeed I strongly feel that we should think of giving less time to productive work, not in terms of less hours per week but in terms of coming later to gainful employment and remaining longer in existence after retirement. Speaking very roughly, delaying entry into the labour market by one year is the arithmetic equivalent of shortening the workweek by two hours for a period of twenty years.[2] Shown that the change in labour input arising from the one or the other change is the same, and given the choice, what father would hesitate to prefer longer schooling for his child to shorter hours for himself? Whatever the choice of the individual, the choice to be made in the name of Society can give rise to no hesitation. Our opportunities for labour-saving should be applied by preference to the longer and more elaborate formation of our citizens.

This is not to say that the normal workweek shall not be shortened, but the effective workweek need not evolve in the same manner except for those who are the least employable. There exists already a clearly marked tendency for the duration of work to be longest for the most able—which is a quite natural feature of an expansive economy, which presses harder upon its most scarce resources, human as well as material.

V

People are apt to confuse the two notions of " time not spent at work " and of " free time," this is a mistake; it neglects the time spent in getting to the work place and back home. While such time is not spent in productive processes, it is not available to the individual. Such transport time was nil in the case of the artisan, negligible in the case of a factory hand of a nineteenth century mill-town. Nowadays it is very seldom less than five hours a week, frequently ten, sometimes fifteen. This is a subject which our passion for surveys has left untouched. Yet it would be very interesting to have a distribution of the working population according to the number of hours spent on transport to and from work, and the evolution of this distribution over time. It would not be at all astonishing if we found that in recent times average transport time has risen a good deal more than the average workweek has shrunk. Indeed in some countries, such as Britain and France, there has been of late no visible trend towards the reduction of the effective workweek while there has been a clear trend towards the rise of transport time. I know quite a few workers to whom it costs twelve hours a day to do an eight hour spell. This great waste of time, attended by nervous fatigue, does not figure in our statistics. We say that John Smith makes so much for say 44 hours of presence; in fact he gets so much less fares for 44 hours of presence involving n hours of transport.

National Accounting constitutes a great intellectual advance but its best experts are least prone to believe that it offers a comprehensive picture of the human situation. We know that rapid progress in National Income involves a ceaseless process of shifting men from A positions to B positions where they contribute more to overall product and are better rewarded. Talking of such Labour Mobility, we stress the increase in market power which it brings to the subject, and we are apt to forget the psychological costs which may be incurred in the process. The very fact that Labour Mobility has to be preached testifies

---

[2] Assuming a typical year of 48 weeks of 44 hours, it shall take 22 years at a rate of two hours per week to retrieve one year of delay in entry.

that men are often reluctant to break off their links with a given place, a given job, given work associates. Instances of such reluctance are often enough noted in our newspapers, and testify to psychological costs. Economists will say that when people do move, thereby they reveal a preference for the *B* position—the gain in market power is subjectively superior to the cost of uprooting. True enough if the man has the choice of remaining in the *A* position or of moving to the *B* position; but such is not always the case; it may well be that the *A* position folds up and that he is left no choice. If a professor of Greek becomes an employee of an advertising firm, it may be by reason of the superior reward offered, and then he has indeed revealed a subjective preference; not so if the teaching of Greek is being discontinued in the institution which employed him.

While taking into account the increase in a man's real earnings we fail to take into account the unpleasantness of his uprooting. Nor is this only a subjective cost. It has ever been accepted that there is value in attachment to a place, a skill, and a fellowship. Indeed the Good Society as it was traditionally pictured was one in which such loyalties were strong; but they must be weak for the proper working of our Progressive Society. The point deserves to be pondered.

The bias of our accounting is most strikingly reflected in our assessment of what occurs when a tannery or paper factory is set up. Its product—in terms of value added—is registered as a positive increment to National Product. But the discharge from the factory pollutes the river. Nobody would deny that this is to be deplored; but such an incidental effect is regarded as alien to the realm which we agree to consider in earnest. Nobody says that on the one hand the factory produces *goods*, but that on the other, quite as concretely, it produces *bads*. I would argue that this is what we should state: there are two forms of production, one of positive value, the other of negative value. Most economists are very unwilling to speak in this manner; they would say that the positive values produced are proved and measured by the prices paid for them in the open market, while what I call negative values cannot be so proved and measured. True enough, because people can buy leather or paper by the yard, while they can not buy a yard of unpolluted river. The factory produces its *goods* in divisible form; it produces its *bads* as indivisible nuisances. There are no economic means of stating their negative value, yet this exists, and it is proved by the fact that we become increasingly disposed to vast public expenditures to remove such nuisances. Incidentally the champions of free private enterprise would be well inspired to force upon firms measures for the prevention of nuisances, for want of which the removal of nuisances must inevitably lead to the development of a great new field of public activities. Indeed in any case, important " Utilities " of the future will be the industries designed to remove nuisances.

Looking upon our rivers today one thinks of the times when they were personified into semideities. Such Pagan fancies can only be allegories to

Christians, but not useless allegories. The Renaissance made much of the river figures in poetry and scultpure; what poor bedraggled figures we should paint today if we returned to such allegories! With this suggestion we touch upon the *Amousia* of modern civilization.

VI

In an economic policy-making committee I recently happened to suggest that the Parthenon was an addition to the wealth of Athenians, and its enjoyment an element of their standard of life. This statement was regarded as whimsical. When I had made it clear that it was seriously meant, I was told that the standard of life is expressed by per capita Private Consumption of goods and services acquired on the market. Meekly accepting this correction, I asked my colleague whether when he drove out to the country on weekends, his satisfaction was derived from the costly consumption of gasoline, or from the free sight of trees and possibly the free visit of some cathedral. At this point people are wont to make a distinction between the useful and the pleasant. I would certainly not deny that there is a stark utility in being so clad as to be protected against the cold, but I fail to see any difference in kind between enjoying a variety of clothes and enjoying a variety of flowers, and happen to prefer the latter.

Until quite recently the labourer meant the agricultural labourer. Throughout the millennia, Production would be equated with Agriculture. The business of procuring food undoubtedly has a prior claim upon our attention, and I feel no doubt that growing food is more important business than Art. Strangely enough, while Production had this vital character, it was looked down upon. In all the civilizations of the past the producer was a mean person and his concerns mean concerns. Paradoxically Production has acquired an unprecedented moral status while less and less of it caters to indispensable needs, to whit the precipitous fall in the agricultural labour force. I have no quarrel with the enhanced status of Production; indeed I feel certain that modern Society's great success in Production is mainly due to our thinking better and thinking more of Production. It is not a matter I propose to discuss here but in my view the great contrast offered by our civilization with the civilizations of the past lies in that *their* social leaders would have deemed it *improper* to think of Production, a concern of underlings, while *our* social leaders are recruited on the basis of their *interest* in and contribution to the heightening of *efficiency* in Production, a change which occurred in our own Society within a small number of generations.

But if I do not at all object to the much enhanced status of Production, I may point out that Production has come to embrace so much that it would be foolish to grant any and every productive activity the moral benefit of an earnestness not to be found in so called "nonproductive activities." When popular newspapers propose to bring out their comic strips in colour, I find it hard to regard such "progress in production" as something more earnest than planting flowering shrubs along the highways. I am quite willing to regard poetry as a frivolous occupation as against the tilling of the soil but not as against the composing of advertisements.

When organizers of production have to relieve a situation of hunger, efficiency is the one and only virtue. But when this virtue has been thoroughly developed and comes to be applied to less and less vital objects, the question surely arises of the right choice of objects.

VII

Most economists, among whom the masters of the science, would deny that there is any real problem here. They would stress that individuals, in the handling of their family budgets, display their preferences, and that therefore the allocation of total consumer expenditures, subject to the existing distribution of incomes, reveals the preferences of the public as a whole; that therefore also the collection of goods and services obtained at present is presently the best possible, the right one. They would go on to say: "You personally may think that a different collection would be better, but in so stating all you do is to pit your single subjective preference against the aggregate of individual subjective preferences."

However powerful this argument, it is not decisive. We can point out, firstly, that current choices are made between currently available goods and services, secondly, that they are a function of the consumer's own past.

Speaking to the first point, it is not true that the buyer is the sole author of his choices. These of course depend upon what is offered. Let us turn our minds, not without shame, to the goods which were first offered by colonial traders to American Indians and African Negroes. What where they? Trinkets and liquor, objects useless or harmful, the market for which could be rapidly expanded because emulation fostered the demand for baubles and habit the demand for liquor. In the case of our own labouring populations the initial exploitation of the popular market was little better. The first industries which really benefited the people were the cotton and glass industries, both conducive to neatness and hygiene.

As our working classes got richer, a great obstacle stood in the way of selling them anything worthwhile. There was a fatter weekly pay envelope, but accumulating out of this weekly pay the wherewithal to acquire, say, a house required an inordinate strength of character. In my own country the point was made *ad nauseam* that people would rather spend on drink, the movies, and other evanescent goods and services than upon getting a proper home. This was a most unfair judgment; the situation altered radically as soon as housing could be made available, to be paid consecutively out of incoming pay.

The order in which goods come to be offered is also important. The American economy was characterized after World War I by the great upsurge of the motor car and the movie, after World War II by the comparable upsurge of household equipment and television. It is at least plausible that if the second set of goods had become available before the first, their home-binding influence would have coloured the American way of life.

The second point is of course that consumer choices are a function of the consumer's own past. For instance, in my library there is not a single book in Russian; this of course is because I cannot read the Russian language. Now suppose that there were no books left or published in any other language than Russian. Then I would have no books at all, which, by the reasoning which is now current, would establish that I do not like reading. Presumably I would take pains to learn Russian, but, starting at my time of life, I would not become proficient at it; it would take me a great deal of time to work through a book; possibly I would then turn to comic strips; this would triumphantly reinforce the proof that " people prefer " comic strips. Revealed preferences in fact reveal *ignorances*, the lack of intellectual and aesthetic formation.

VIII

I suspect that our Society is the most deficient in Culture which has ever been seen. It is a natural need of man to express himself in oratory, poetry, song, dance, music, sketching, sculpture, and painting. If Culture has any meaning, it means that the aptitudes which all children have, in diverse degrees, for some or other of these pleasurable activities should be cultivated. This can not harm the development of another and more scarce aptitude, that for understanding and conveying such understanding in the language either of philosophy or of mathematics. But the aesthetic pleasures should naturally be the most common. Their lack makes us properly Barbarians, if the Barbarian be the man without powers of appreciation or expression.

Strangely enough anything which lies in the realm of aesthetic enjoyment is regarded in our wealthy Society as nonessential. Nonessential and " distinguished "; no doubt we think highly of " works of art " which the rich may possess and which the poor are invited to admire in a museum. But this treatment of works of art by itself displays their " eccentricity " in the literal sense of the word, with regard to our Civilization.

In my opinion, it is the very definition of Philistinism to think of Art with a capital A, no matter indeed whether this way of thinking is that of the much-blamed bourgeois or of the artist himself. In the epochs of Culture, the term " the arts " corresponded to our present notion of " the industries." Thus in Florence the " arte di la lana " meant the industry of woollens. One did not think that turning out woollens was one thing, concerning oneself with beauty another. One did not think that building edifices of worship, or public edifices, or private houses was one thing entirely distinct from any preoccupation for beauty. The nineteenth century, which was basically Philistine, developed the notion of the " objet d'art," the small thing of beauty which the rich, having turned out goods without beauty, could thus afford to lodge in their houses built without beauty.

The dizzy height of prestige to which painting has risen in the last two generations is, I feel, the true index to the Philistinism of our Society. In an age of Culture, painting is not a thing in itself, it is an element of decoration fitting into a general pattern of beauty.

The fact that there are objects of beauty in the museums of London and Paris does not acquit us of the fact that London and Paris are not beautiful; within them any combination of buildings we can point to with pride is at least a century and a half old. Since then we have done nothing to improve; everything which has been done has tended to degrade.

It is claimed that people do not care. It seems to me that their behaviour testifies to the contrary. How do people spend their holidays? In escaping from the setting in which they are forced to live; they go to the country to see what the world was meant to look like, and they go to ancient cities whose inhabitants were concerned, however poor, to achieve a beauty which in our wealth we neglect. Indeed when on weekends one sees people teeming out of London one is tempted to think that the word *Sunday* has been restored to its primitive meaning; it is now the day without smog.

From people's behaviour it seems apparent that as individuals we attach far more importance to beauty than we do collectively as a Society. Why do we, as a Society, set so little importance upon it? My own feeling is that the pre-occupation with Beauty is always associated with the feeling that life centres upon singing the glory of God; were I to discuss how Puritanism has divorced the Good from the Beautiful, and how the secularist concern for man alone has become a concern for the "functional." I would be treading upon ground which would be controversial and moreover using big words in an elliptic manner which is apt not only to mislead the audience but to muddle the speaker. Such investigation of causes is indeed not relevant at this time and for the purpose on hand.

IX

I find it hard to agree that the man of our Society has a high standard of life. The life of modern man seems to me unstructured; it flexes to embrace the new good which is offered; possession thereof alters the shape of life which is therefore a function of what happens to be put on the market. This is an invertebrate, amoeba-like progress of the way of life. If anyone were to furnish a house by accumulating "good buys" wherever and whenever encountered, that house would be a meaningless clutter, without style or personality. This is to me the aspect offered by our life.

Imagine that an eighteenth century philanthropist, say the Marquis de Mirabeau or Thomas Jefferson, were resurrected and briefed as to the increase in labour productivity and wealth which has occurred since his day. He would certainly imagine a world where beauty and culture prevailed, where the setting of life would immediately manifest the social wealth; in poorer societies the edifices of God, the palaces of rulers, and the mansions of the rich had been made beautiful. An epoch of general wealth would surely be one where the houses of the people and their work places would be built with the same loving care, that we were on the threshold of such an age was assumed already by Ledoux (1736–1806) in the last third of the eighteenth century[3]. Also it had previously been the good fortune of the artisans serving a rich market that they could work with delight. When the mass market had become a rich market this would seem destined to be the lot of all workers; finally it had been the privilege of the well-to-do that they could enjoy good company, with pleasant manners and interesting topics. Presumably, with a society wealthy throughout, this sort of company would be that of everyman.

Now of these three goals relating to the setting, the work, and the company, which seemed natural outcomes of growing wealth, the first—setting—and the last—good company—have not been achieved merely, as it seems to me, through an inexplicable lack of attention to them; the second, which is possibly the most important, deserves special attention.

It does seem true, up to date, that we have had to pay a price for the increasing productivity of labour in the sense that the Industrial Revolution from its very beginning has created a new phenomenon which I would call " pure labour ". In order to live, men have ever needed to perform certain activities, be it hunting, fishing, tilling, building, weaving, etc. It seems to me however that in the case of those folk we call " primitive " the activities devoted to the material sustenance of life have been admixed with play, sport, devotion, as we can still see it in the case of vine harvesting, which is all suffused with joking, laughing, its brief spells of matching speeds interspersed with episodes of bantering and courting. As against this, modern work has become an altogether bleaker thing, purely a task to be performed for the result, under the sign of efficiency alone. It is by no means different in the so-called Socialist countries where " norms " of work are successively raised. I have noted that work has become in the last generations very much less exacting in a physical sense, but as against this we must set, I think, the bleakness of work. The lessening of the physical strain of work is a recent phenomenon, its bleakness is an altogether more ancient phenomenon. It is probably as old as the regimentation of work, which has existed for a long time (think of the galley slaves) but which has become a far more extensive phenomenon.

It is, I think, the bleakness of work which has led to our current dichotomy of man, of whom it is expected that he be purely efficient in his hours of work, while he is allowed, nay, encouraged, to satisfy his wants in his hours of leisure. From which it naturally follows that nothing seems more important than to successively whittle down the hours of work. But work is so essential that the psychological deprivation experienced by man at work colours, I believe, his whole life. It can be observed that the men who in fact seem to have a good life are not those who work few hours (in which case the good life would have been that of the rentier who had no hours of work at all) but those who can take pleasure in their work. And therefore I believe that we should regard the amenity of work as a much more interesting goal than the shortening of work hours.

---

[3] The industrial city of Chaux, then designed and built by Ledoux, testifies to the preoccupation.

X

There are many other points I would like to touch upon, one of them is the following. Those out of work on a pension by reason of age shall form an increasing proportion of our population. This shall constitute a very large " leisure class " of a very different complexion from the " leisure class " of the nineteenth century; much more numerous on the one hand, and on the other, distinguished from the working class to which all adults now belong, not by *greater* incomes but by *smaller* incomes. Our society now comprises no " leisure class " at the top of the income ladder, but a large " leisure class " at the bottom of the income ladder: the aged.

This phenomenon of a very large population combining a great deal of leisure with very little money poses the problem of its way of life. I think it is very miserable in the present day. Surely it deserves to be given some thought, and the problem is not insoluble since the combination new to us of a great deal of leisure with scant material means is the very condition under which Greek culture flourished. The aged may be the Greek among us, if we attack the problem in that way.

This is but one of the points I wished to raise. I would deem myself fortunate indeed if I had found it possible to contribute towards the crystallization of a concern to induct our increasing wealth in the service of a greater amenity of life.

I am grateful to Rector Bosanquet and the Academic Board of King's College for allowing me to discuss what I am sure is very much in all our minds.

Part II
POLITICAL ASPECTS OF WELFARE ECONOMICS

The political system is one important mechanism for the allocation of resources (dominant in a socialist system) of major importance in virtually all modern systems. The participants in the political system, the voters, are after all the same individuals as the participants in the market system, and it is at least an interesting hypothesis that their choices as voters are governed by the same preference systems as those which determine market choice. The implications of this assumption are examined in different ways in the papers in this part.

In theory, at least, political decisions are made by majority voting. But Condorcet[1] in 1785 had already observed the following problem (restated in modern terminology): If social welfare or social preference is rational in any of its usual meanings, it must lead to transitive choices. But in general, majority voting need not have this property. It is perfectly possible that a majority prefers alternative A to alternative B, a majority prefers B to C, and a majority prefers C to A, even though each voter has perfectly transitive preferences. Bowen, however, has examined the particular problem of allocation of resources between public and private uses by voting and shown that when the distribution of the tax burden is assumed given, then there will be one resource allocation which is preferred to any other by a majority. Black in effect generalized Bowen's result by exhibiting a wide class of cases (single-peaked preferences) for which majority voting led to transitivity of social choice. Arrow, on the other hand, showed that if the voting method had to work for a wider variety of individual preferences than those satisfying Black's conditions, then not merely majority voting but any other conceivable voting

---

[1] Marquis de Condorcet, *Essai sur l'application de l'analyse à la probabilité des decisions rendues à la pluralité des voix*. Paris, 1785.

method of a democratic nature could yield intransitivity for certain sets of individual preferences.

Tullock examined the resource allocation implications of majority voting and showed the possible inefficiencies resulting. Samuelson characterized collective goods as those which enter everyone's utility function, and derived a characterization of all possible Pareto optimal allocations as between public and private uses. He also stressed the incentive on the part of individuals to misrepresent their true preferences for collective goods.

The interpretation of voting in the allocation of economic resources[*]

HOWARD R. BOWEN

Economic goods are of two types: individual goods and social goods. The two types are similar in that each serves the needs of human beings and each is produced only through the use of scarce resources. They differ, however, in the character of their demand. Individual goods are characterized by *divisibility*. They can be divided into small units over which particular persons can be given exclusive possession (e.g. carrots, sewing machines, barber services). Such goods are amenable to individual demand and to free consumer choice. The amount consumed by any individual can be adjusted to his particular tastes. Social goods, on the other hand, are not divisible into units that can be the unique possession of individuals. Rather, they tend to become part of the general environment (e.g. education, protection against foreign enemies, beautification of the landscape, flood control). Consequently, these goods cannot easily be sold to individual consumers and the quantities available to different individuals cannot be adjusted according to their respective tastes. The amount of the good must be set by a single decision applicable jointly to all persons. Social goods, therefore, are subject to collective or political rather than individual demand.

Economists have, on the whole, been preoccupied with the portion of economic activity relating to the production of individual goods. They have developed an impressive body of theory describing the enterprise economy under various conditions, and have formulated a set of principles for determining the most economical outputs of individual goods. But no comparable body of theory exists for social goods, despite the fact that the production of the latter—even in peacetime—uses up no less than a fifth of all available resources and that the relative importance of social goods is steadily growing. The purpose of the present paper is to show how certain portions of conventional economic theory may be adapted to problems relating to the production of social goods.

---

[*] *The Quarterly Journal of Economics*, 58(1943); pp. 27–48. Reprinted by courtesy of the author and *The Quarterly Journal of Economics*.

According to accepted theory, a maximum of human satisfactions will be attained, through the use of a given supply of factors, if: (1) production is carried on in response to the free choices of individual consumers (providing the consumers make the "right" choices and income is distributed "correctly"),[1] (2) all units of each good and of each factor are priced uniformly, (3) the output of each constant—or increasing-cost industry is adjusted so that the price of the product is equal to average cost, and the output of each decreasing-cost industry is adjusted so that the price of the product is equal to marginal cost, (4) production is carried on with the least costly known methods, and (5) the price of each factor is set so that the demand for it is equal to the supply.[2]

The first three of these principles are not entirely relevant to the production of social goods, because such goods are not suitable for individual consumer demand. It will be shown, however, that these principles can be modified for use in determining the ideal output of social goods. The argument will proceed in three steps: (1) formulation of the basic principles to guide the production of social goods, (2) practical application of these principles, and (3) examination of problems in the distribution of costs.

QUANTITATIVE MEASUREMENT OF SOCIAL GOODS

In discussing the ideal output of social goods, it is necessary at the outset to establish meaningful units in which quantities of social goods may be measured. This raises certain difficulties, because most of the things ordinarily regarded as social goods are highly complex. Each comprises whole congeries of particular goods which can be provided in many different ways and in different combinations. For example, an increase in the "quantity" of education available in a given community may take the form of additional buildings, changes in curricula, inclusion of a greater number of students, addition of new educational units such as kindergartens or junior colleges, raising of minimum teacher requirements, etc. Thus, quantities of "education" cannot be measured in simple physical units of volume, time, or weight. There are, however, other practicable quantitative measures of education and other such similar complex social goods.

One approach is to treat separately each component element of the complex social good. Thus, instead of dealing with quantities of "education" taken as a whole, attention would be centered on buildings, equipment, number of teachers, training and grade of teachers, hours devoted to particu-

---

[1] By "right" consumer choices I mean simply those choices which make for proportionality between prices and marginal rates of substitution; by "correct" distribution of income, a distribution such that marginal satisfactions from income are equal, in terms of socially accepted valuations, for all persons.

[2] See A. C. Pigou, *Economics of Welfare*, 4th ed., London, 1933; Oskar Lange *et al.*, *On the Economic Theory of Socialism*, Minneapolis, 1938; Harold Hotelling, "The General Welfare in Relation to Problems of Taxation and of Railway Rates and Utility Rates," *Econometrica*, July, 1938, pp. 242–69; J. R. Hicks, "The Foundations of Welfare Economics," *Economic Journal*, December, 1939, pp. 696–712.

lar subjects, number of students participating, hours of instruction per day, days of instruction per year, etc. Reasonably satisfactory quantitative measures could be assigned to each of these components. This solution is essentially similar to that which is ordinarily applied in measuring quantities of individual goods. Here the good is defined, not in terms of complexes such as food, but in terms of particular components such as cane sugar or No. 2 red wheat. Another possible approach is to measure the quantity of complex social goods simply in terms of their money cost. This solution is based on the principle that any decision to change the quantity of a complex social good may be resolved into two distinguishable parts: (1) a decision as to the relative priorities of various particular component services, and (2) a decision as to the amount of the overall increase or decrease. If the scale of priorities is established so that it is known what particular services are to be added with increasing expenditure and what services are to be dropped with decreasing expenditure, then the quantity of the complex social good can be usefully measured in terms of the amount of money expended.

Each of the two approaches is useful and each is applicable to certain practical situations. Whenever the scale of priorities is not definitely established or agreed upon, the separate treatment of each component in terms of physical units would be preferred. On the other hand, whenever the scale of priorities is clearly established or whenever the determination of the scale is to be referred to experts or representatives, the second approach of measuring quantities in terms of cost would be preferred.

The following analysis is arranged so that either of the two measures may be employed alternatively. If physical units are used, increasing, constant, or decreasing cost may apply, whereas if cost units are used, only constant cost may apply. It should be emphasized that the quantity of a social good, whatever measure is used, refers to the quantity available in the community as a whole, not necessarily to the amount available to any particular person or consumption unit.

IDEAL OUTPUT OF SOCIAL GOODS

Suppose that the citizens of a given community are faced with the task of deciding how much public education should be made available. It is inevitable that the citizens will differ regarding this question. Some, perhaps, will wish to have no education under any circumstances, some will want no more than the three R's, and others will desire a highly developed system of schools. Assuming a "correct" distribution of income, each person's taste can be expressed by a curve indicating the amount of money he would be willing to give up in order to have successive additional quantities made available in the community. Such a curve would be analogous to an individual demand curve. It would express, for different possible quantities of education, the individual's marginal rate of substitution between education and other goods (money). A series of such curves of individual marginal substitution is shown in Figure 1 for a community which is assumed to contain three persons

(MS_a, MS_b, MS_c). The marginal rates of substitution of the three individuals, for each quantity of education, can be added to give the total marginal rate of substitution of the entire population. In this way a " curve of total marginal substitution" (TMS in Figure 1) can be constructed, expressing the amount

Figure 1

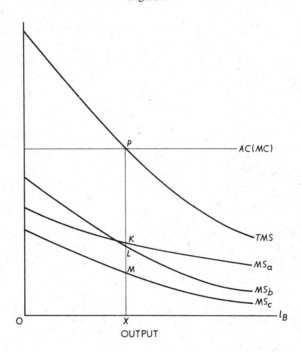

of money the members of the group collectively would be willing to give up in order to obtain successive units of education. This curve corresponds, as closely as is possible under the conditions, to the familiar curve of total demand.[3]

One of the cardinal principles in determining the output of an individual good is that price should equal cost, i.e. average cost or marginal cost, whichever is lower. This implies that the ideal output is indicated by the point of intersection between the demand curve and the appropriate cost curve. Through the use of the curve of total marginal substitution, this principle

---

[3] It must be noted that this curve differs from the familiar curve of total demand, which denotes the amount of a good that individuals are willing to buy at each of several prices. The demand curve is obtained by adding the number of units of the good that would be purchased by the various individuals at each possible price (horizontal addition); whereas the curve of total marginal substitution is obtained by adding the marginal rates of substitution (expressed in money) of the various individuals at each possible quantity of the social good (vertical addition).

can be adapted to the problem of determining the ideal output of a social good. Thus, to continue with our illustration, the ideal output of education is indicated by the point of intersection between the curve of total marginal substitution and the appropriate cost curve—which one depending upon whether increasing or decreasing cost prevails at relevant outputs. This is shown in Figure 1 (assuming constant cost) by the point of intersection (P) between the curve of total marginal substitution (TMS) and the curve of average cost (AC). OX is the ideal output.[4]

Ideal output can also be indicated in another way, which will prove more useful for subsequent analysis. For this, three new curves are required: (1) a curve expressing the average marginal rate of substitution per person (TMS/N), (2) a curve expressing average cost per person (AC/N), and (3) a curve expressing marginal cost per person (MC/N). These curves are derived by dividing the total marginal rate of substitution, average cost, and marginal cost, respectively, by the number of people (N). Ideal output, originally defined as the output at which the total marginal rate of substitution is equal to average (or marginal) cost, can also be designated as the output at which the average marginal rate of substitution is equal to average cost per person (or marginal cost per person.) This follows since, at the output where AC (or MC) equals TMS, AC/N (or MC/N) must equal TMS/N. See Figure 2.

INDIVIDUAL VOTING ON OUTPUTS

It has been shown that the optimum output of social goods is indicated by the intersection of the curve of average marginal substitution (TMS/N) and the appropriate curve of cost per person $(AC/N$ or $MC/N)$. If this formulation is to be practically useful, something must be known—directly or by inference—about marginal rates of substitution and costs. It is, of course, no more difficult to obtain information on the cost of producing social goods than to get similar data on individual goods; but to estimate marginal rates of substitution presents serious problems, since it requires the measurement of the preferences for goods which, by their very nature, cannot be subjected to individual consumer choice.

The closest substitute for consumer choice is *voting*. Consequently, it may be worthwhile to explore the possible use of voting as a means of measuring or inferring marginal rates of substitution and hence of determining ideal output. Suppose that our community, faced with the problem of determining the precise quantity of education to provide, allows each individual to indicate, by means of voting, the amount of education that he prefers. Each individual's preference will depend upon two factors: (1) the relative amount of satisfaction *he* expects to derive from different amounts of education—as indicated by his curve of marginal substitution, and (2) the cost to *him* of different amounts of education. The latter will depend partly on the total

---

[4] If there were no point of intersection between the two curves, i.e. if average cost were at all outputs greater than total marginal substitution, the service should not be offered at all.

Figure 2

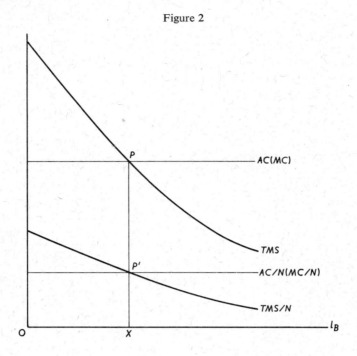

cost to the community of different amounts and partly on the contemplated distribution of that cost among different individuals. Each individual will, of course, vote for that quantity at which *his* marginal rate of substitution is equal to *his* marginal cost. This would be indicated by the point of intersection between his curve of marginal substitution and his curve of marginal cost.

At this point it is necessary to digress briefly in order to introduce four assumptions:

First, it is assumed that all individuals in the community actually vote and that each expresses a preference which is appropriate to his individual interests.

Second, it is assumed that the cost to the community of providing various possible quantities of education is known. Curves AC, AC/N, M/C, and MC/N can then be constructed.

Third, it is assumed that the cost of whatever amount of education is to be "produced" will be divided equally among all the citizens. Thus the curve of average cost for each citizen will be equal to AC/N and the curve of marginal cost for each citizen equal to MC/N. The implications of this assumption will be analyzed in a later section on the distribution of the cost of social goods.

Fourth, it is assumed that the several curves of individual marginal substitution are distributed according to the normal law of error. This implies that there is a large number of such curves—one for each person—and that these curves are arranged so that at *each quantity of education* the marginal rates of substitution of the several persons are distributed symmetrically about a mode (see Figure 3). Thus, if a vertical line, cutting the several curves, is

Figure 3

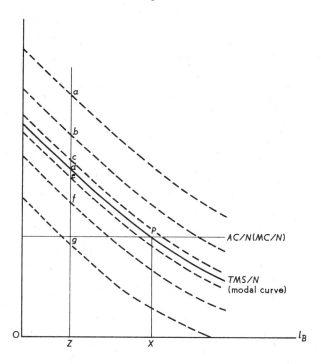

erected at any point Z along the horizontal axis, the points of intersection (a, b, c, d, e, f, g) between this line and the several curves of marginal substitution will tend to be distributed along the line according to the normal law of error. Most of the intersections will occur near the mode (d), but some will occur at varying distances above and below the mode. Indeed, a modal curve can be drawn indicating the position of the mode at each quantity of output, and this modal curve will, still assuming a symmetrical distribution of the curves, coincide with the curve of average marginal substitution (TMS/N).[5]

---

[5] In a symmetrical distribution the mode and the arithmetic mean are identical. It is to be noted, however, that the symmetry of a frequency distribution may be disturbed by the fact that zero is the lower limit of the data. In terms of the present problem, zero represents the lowest possible marginal rate of substitution (except in cases where the commodity is so abundant as to be a nuisance). At relatively large outputs, therefore, the marginal rate of substitution of some individuals would be zero, and the modal marginal rate of substitution would be less than the average per capita.

This assumption can conform to the facts of individual preference only if two conditions are met. (*a*) The tastes or desires of individuals must actually be distributed according to the normal law of error. Whether this condition is realized in practice is not known definitely, but available information suggests that it is not an unreasonable hypothesis. For example, the data in the Consumer Purchases Study of the United States Department of Agriculture indicate that consumer tastes for individual goods are distributed normally. Three series from this study, selected from hundreds of similar series, are shown in Table 1. (*b*) All individuals must be potentially in an equal position

Table 1

PERCENTAGE DISTRIBUTION OF FAMILIES BY EXPENDITURES
FOR VARIOUS PURPOSES: WHITE, NONRELIEF, NATIVE-BORN
FAMILIES, 1935–36*

Annual Expenditures for Food: farm families with three or more children, and with incomes from $1,000 to $1,499 per year, Middle Atlantic and North Central States.†		Annual Expenditures for Clothing: village families with two young children and with incomes from $1,500 to $1,999, Pennsylvania and Ohio‡		Total Annual Expenditure for Family Living: small city families with incomes from $2,000 to $2,249, North Central States§	
Expenditure	*Percentage of Families*	*Expenditure*	*Percentage of Families*	*Expenditure*	*Percentage of Families*
$50–$99	4%	Under $50	4%	$750–$999	2%
100–149	16			1,000–1,249	8
150–199	25	$50–$99	15	1,250–1,499	13
200–249	17	100–149	28	1,500–1,749	21
250–299	19	150–199	33	1,750–1,999	29
300–349	9	200–249	16	2,000–2,249	17
350–399	5	250–299	4	2,250–2,499	5
400–449	3			2,500–2,999	4
450 or over	2			3,000–3,499	1
Total	100	Total	100	Total	100

* Data based on Consumer Purchases Study made by the United States Department of Agriculture in co-operation with the Work Projects Administration.
† U.S.D.A., Miscellaneous Publication, No. 405, 1941, p. 14.
‡ U.S.D.A., Miscellaneous Publication, No. 422, 1941, p. 17.
§ U.S.D.A., Miscellaneous Publication, No. 396, 1940, p. 33.

to benefit from the social good. This condition is not always realized in practice. For example, childless persons may be less interested in education than families with children. Thus, even though the curves of marginal substitution of either class of persons might be arranged symmetrically, the distribution of the curves for the two classes together might be significantly skewed or multimodal. However, most social goods are or can be made available on relatively equal terms to all persons, e.g. health services, protection from foreign enemies, maintenance of law and order, etc. For the moment, therefore, we shall postulate that all individuals are equally able to benefit from the social good under consideration. In this way, we may continue with the assumption that individual marginal substitutions are distributed according to the normal law of error. Later we shall take up the problem of social goods which are not equally available to all.

Under the conditions assumed, if the citizens are allowed to vote on the quantity of education to be provided, each person will vote for the quantity indicated by the intersection between his individual curve of marginal substitution and his curve of marginal cost (MC/N). Since the various individuals will presumably be interested in education to varying degrees, as indicated by the dispersion of the individual curves of marginal substitution, a wide variety of preferences will be indicated. Referring to Figure 3, those whose curves of marginal substitution lie in the lower left part of the diagram will favor a relatively small amount; those whose curves of marginal substitution lie in the upper right will favor a relatively large amount. But, assuming that the curves of marginal substitution are distributed according to the normal law of error, one intermediate amount (OX) will be voted for by more individuals than any other single amount. The individuals voting for this quantity are those whose marginal rates of substitution are modal, and the amount voted for by this modal group may be presumed to indicate the point of intersection (P) between the curve of marginal cost per person (MC/N) and the modal or average curve of marginal substitution (TMS/N). Thus voting makes possible the location of one point (P) on the curve of average marginal substitution (TMS/N), namely, the point at which the curve of individual marginal cost (MC/N) intersects with (TMS/N).[6] See Figure 3.

If education is "produced" under conditions of constant cost, as shown in Figure 3, marginal and average cost will be identical. Hence the modal vote will indicate not only the point of intersection between TMS/N and MC/N but also the point of intersection between TMS/N and AC/N. This latter point, as stated above, occurs at the optimum output. Hence the modal vote provides direct information as to the most economical amount of education to provide.

If education is "produced" under decreasing cost, the modal vote will also give the desired information directly. In this case the marginal cost curve (MC/N) lies below the average cost curve (AC/N). However, the most economical output is that at which the marginal rate of substitution and marginal (rather than average) cost are equal. Thus the modal vote directly indicates the most economical output.

If, however, education is produced under conditions of increasing cost, the modal vote cannot directly denote optimum output. It can indicate only

---

[6] In order to designate this point of intersection, it is not necessary that the majority of *all* the voters should prefer this amount. It is only necessary that more persons vote for this amount than for any other.

the point of intersection between MC/N and TMS/N, not the point of intersection between AC/N and TMS/N which is required. A further elaboration of our technique is therefore necessary.

This case requires a different procedure of taxation. The cost must be raised by means of a tax levied upon each individual in the form of a "price" per unit of the social good, it being understood (1) that the price is to remain constant regardless of output, and (2) that the price is to be uniform for all individuals. From the point of view of any one individual, this "price" represents his marginal cost. His marginal cost curve would appear, therefore, as a horizontal line, the height of which would be determined by the "price." Moreover, since the same "price" would be charged all individuals, the marginal cost curve would be the same for all. This curve is shown in Figure 4 as IMC (individual marginal cost).

Figure 4

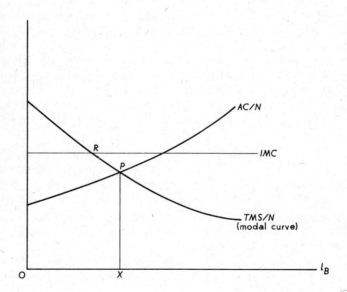

Let us now suppose that the "price" of education is set, and that the citizens are asked to vote on the quantity of education they prefer. Each person will, of course, vote for the quantity indicated by the intersection between his curve of marginal substitution and the curve of marginal cost (IMC), and the modal vote will locate the point of intersection (R) between TMS/N and IMC. The optimum output, however, is determined by the intersection of TMS/N and AC/N; the modal vote does not locate this point. From the position of point R relative to curve AC/N, it can be ascertained, however, whether the intersection of TMS/N and AC/N lies to the right or to the left of point R.

If R is above curve AC/N, then the point of intersection lies to the right of R,[7] and the output should be increased beyond the amount voted for by the modal group. And if R lies below curve AC/N, the point of intersection is to the left of R and output should be reduced to less than the amount voted for by the modal group. This relationship is to be explained by the fact that if R lies above curve AC/N, the price announced to the voters is so high that (at this price) the modal group prefer less than the optimum amount of the good; and if R is below curve AC/N, the price is so low that the modal group prefer more than the optimum amount. Only when R lies on curve AC/N (i.e., when curves AC/N, IMC, and TMS/N all intersect at the same time) will the vote of the modal group indicate the optimum output.

The result of the voting depends entirely on the price announced. The question arises, then, whether there is any rule by which the correct price could be ascertained in advance of the voting. The answer is in the negative. However, as a result of successive trials and errors over a period of time the correct price could be closely approached, especially since (1) the direction of the error is known after each trial, and (2) more than one point on the TMS/N curve would be known after several trials.[8] It is conceivable, moreover, that the voters might be asked to indicate their preferences at each of several possible prices so that the position of TMS/N could be ascertained along several points and the intersection of TMS/N and AC/N could be located immediately.[9]

INDIVIDUAL VOTING ON INCREMENTS TO EXISTING OUTPUTS

Let us now assume that the individuals of a community are permitted to vote, not on how much of the good they prefer, but rather on whether or not they wish a given increment or decrement to the quantity already provided. This situation is illustrated by school elections, common in the United States, in which citizens are asked to vote "yes" or "no" on a proposed bond issue for the purpose of constructing a new school building.

Suppose the community is composed of seven persons whose marginal substitution curves are distributed symmetrically, as shown in Figure 5, and that the cost of education (or any increment in the quantity) is to be divided equally among them. Assume that quantity OX (Figure 5) is actually being provided and that the people are asked to vote on the question whether or

---

[7] Assuming that curve TMS/N slopes negatively.

[8] This raises a problem similar to that of deducing a demand curve from a time series.

[9] It is tempting to assume that the average of the amounts voted for by the several individuals represents the optimum output. In fact, it does not. The average amount voted for will be greater or less than the optimum output, depending upon the slope, shape, and position of the individual curves of marginal substitution. Similarly, the assumption that the curves of marginal substitution are distributed according to the normal law of error in no way implies that the results of the *voting* will also be distributed in the same way. The distribution of the vote may be skewed in either direction—depending on the shape of the curves—without violating the assumption that the curves are distributed according to the normal law of error.

Figure 5

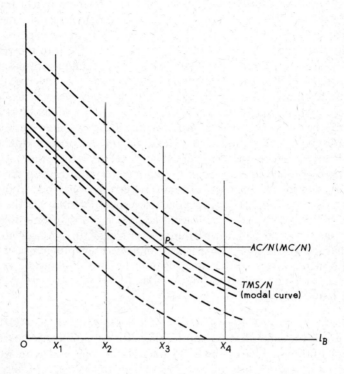

not they wish a small increase in the quantity up to OX_2. All those persons whose marginal rates of substitution at quantity OX_2 are greater than the marginal cost (MC/N) at that quantity will vote "yes," and those whose marginal rates of substitution are less than marginal cost will vote "no." In this case, as shown in Figure 5, the vote will be six in favor of the increment and one against. Suppose, then, that the citizens are asked to vote on another increment which will raise the quantity to OX_3, the point at which MC/N and TMS/N are equal. On this question, one-half the citizens will vote "yes" and one-half "no." Finally, suppose the citizens are asked to vote on still another increment which will increase the quantity to OX_4. This time, six persons will vote against and one will be in favor.

From these illustrations it may be seen that as the quantity of education is increased, bit by bit, a majority of the voters will favor each additional increment until a quantity is reached such that the average marginal rate of substitution (TMS/N) is equal to marginal cost (MC/N). At this point the vote is equally divided. Beyond this point, the majority of the voters are opposed to additional increments. Thus it is possible to locate the point of intersection between curves TMS/N and MC/N by finding an increment (or decrement), through trial and error, which is favored by one-half of the voters and opposed by the other half.

This procedure makes possible the direct determination of optimum output for "industries" subject to constant cost and decreasing cost. In these cases, the intersection of TMS/N and MC/N determines the most economical quantity of the social good. This procedure does not, however, directly give the answer for "industries" of increasing cost. For them, it is the point of intersection between curves TMS/N and AC/N (not between TMS/N and MC/N) which must be located. This can be done, but only by a procedure so awkward as to be virtually useless.[10]

On the whole, the procedure of voting on increments does not lend itself well to the determination of optimum output. For constant and decreasing cost of "industries" it is somewhat more complicated than the method of asking voters to indicate the quantities they prefer, and for increasing cost "industries" is it hopeless.

ALTERNATIVES TO VOTING

In a society which has outgrown the town-meeting stage, it is seldom practicable to decide on the output of specific social goods by means of popular voting. More commonly, public officials (legislators, elected or appointed administrators, dictators, etc.) are endowed with the power to make such decisions and are expected to act in the "general interest." This means that such officials, if they are to carry out their duties, must have methods of finding out what the people want, i.e. how much of each social good should be produced.

The people can be consulted by letting them vote on particular questions, or perhaps letting them vote for candidates who identify themselves with particular policies. In this case, if the issues are clearly understood, the results of the election can be interpreted as suggested in the preceding sections. In practice, however, the issues are seldom clear-cut. The result of an election can seldom be regarded as an unequivocal indication of public desires. Hence there is a real need for other techniques of gauging public opinion, i.e. finding the points of intersection between the curves of total marginal substitution and average (or marginal) cost. It is for this reason that a number of writers have recently suggested the possibility of using polls, questionnaires, interviews, budget investigations, and other devices involving samples to study

---

[10] Several separate trial-and-error procedures would be involved. First an arbitrary fixed "price" per unit of education would be set so that the curve of marginal cost for the individuals (IMC) would be a horizontal line. Then each individual would be asked to vote "yes" or "no" on successive increments or decrements, until the point of intersection between IMC and TMS/N could be determined. It would be located at the increment for which one-half the voters are in favor and one-half opposed. After that, in order to find the intersection of AC/N and TMS/N, it would be necessary to adjust the price and again ask voters to express preferences on increments (or decrements) so that other points on the curve TMS/N could be located. By a wearisome process, it might ultimately be possible to find enough points on curve TSM/N so that the intersection between that curve and AC/N could be located.

the desires of the individuals who compose the public. Indeed, with the increasing emphasis upon economic planning, it is imperative that these and other techniques for discovering individual tastes and preferences be developed and employed.[11]

If a poll is based on a representative sample of the population, and if the questions are put in the same way as if the entire citizenry were voting, the results can of course be interpreted in exactly the same way. For such a poll to be as reliable as the results of actual voting, however, several conditions would have to be met.[12] First, it would be necessary that the issue had been discussed sufficiently to enable the pollees to become informed. Second, in order to be sure that the individual pollees would use thought and discretion in reaching their decisions, it would be necessary for them to have a sense of responsibility, i.e. to feel that their choices would actually influence policy.

It is conceivable that techniques involving polls and questionnaires would yield information in greater detail than could be obtained through large-scale voting. It might be possible in this way to carry on minute studies of individual preferences so that actual curves showing marginal rates of substitution, instead of merely a few isolated points on curves, could be obtained.[13]

DISTRIBUTING THE COST OF SOCIAL GOODS

In the discussion of voting it has been consistently assumed that the cost of providing social goods is to be divided equally among all individuals. This assumption requires further examination. If income were distributed "correctly," so that apportionment of the cost of social goods would not be designed for the purpose of redistributing income, the benefit principle would provide the ideal basis for assessing the costs of social goods. Each person would contribute according to the benefit received by him, and the distribution of real income would be unaffected. In applying the benefit principle, each individual would be charged *as if* he were paying a price per unit for the social good, the price being equal to his marginal rate of substitution at the particular amount of the good being produced. Thus, instead of applying a uniform price to all individuals and allowing each to adjust his consumption according to that price, as with individual goods, a uniform amount of the social good would be provided, and the "price" charged individuals would vary according to their marginal rates of substitution. Referring to Figure 1,

---

[11] See Maurice Dobb, *Review of Economic Studies*, February, 1935, pp. 137–48; and Barbara Wootton, *Lament for Economics*, London, 1938, chap. 5 and 6, especially pp. 289–91.

[12] The polling of a "scientifically" selected sample might produce more accurate results than general voting, unless arrangements were made to insure that every person would actually vote. If voting is voluntary, it is possible that the results may represent the preference of a biased sample of the population, including a relatively large proportion of, perhaps, the "politically minded," the well-to-do, or the better educated.

[13] The work of Professor L. L. Thurstone in deriving the indifference schedules of actual individuals is suggestive. See his article "The Indifference Function," *Journal of Social Psychology*, 1931, pp. 139–67. The difficulty with this approach is that individuals must be asked what they would do under various hypothetical conditions. There is always the possibility that verbal preferences would differ significantly from actual choices in a real situation.

if quantity OX were being provided, Individual A would pay a "price" equal to XK, and his contribution would be equal to this price multiplied by the number of units of the good provided (OX). The "price" charged Individual A under this arrangement would be such that, if free individual consumer choice were possible, he would choose the particular quantity of the social good that is actually available.[14] In this way his marginal contribution to the cost of the social good would correspond to his marginal rate of substitution, and his real income would remain unchanged. Any other arrangement would result in his being made worse or better off. Similarly, the "price" charged Individual B would be XL, and the "price" charged Individual C would be XM (Figure. 1). Thus the total amount paid by the three individuals would be equal to the total cost of the service.[15]

The application of the benefit principle is difficult, however, because of problems involved in the measurement of benefit. To determine the cost that should be assessed against an individual, if the benefit principle is to apply, requires that something be known about his marginal rates of substitution. At first thought it might be supposed that this information could be obtained from his vote (or other expression of preference). But the individual could not vote intelligently, unless he knew *in advance* the cost to him of various amounts of the social good, and in any case the results of the voting would be unreliable if the individual suspected that his expression of preference would influence the amont of cost to be assessed against him. Moreover, the practical administrative problem of making nice adjustments between individual benefit and cost would be insuperable.

On the whole, the possibility of distributing costs according to benefit is not very promising. It seems clear that some more or less arbitrary alternative method must be adopted. The problem is to find that arbitrary method which will involve the least error and the fewest practical problems. With an initially "correct" distribution of income, an *equal* distribution of cost seems most practicable. This means, of course, that the provision of social goods may involve the redistribution of income. Those individuals who are forced to pay more in taxes than they get back in benefits will find their real incomes diminished, whereas those who pay out less than they receive in return will enjoy an addition to their real incomes. The seriousness of this redistribution is greatly lessened, however, by the fact that many social goods are ordinarily produced simultaneously. Thus the gain to any one individual from the

---

[14] If the social good were financed in this way, all individuals would vote for the same output, namely, the most economical quantity.

[15] An exception to this solution for the problem of distributing the burden of costs must be made in the case of a social good provided under conditions of decreasing cost. Here economy requires that output be increased to the point where total marginal substitution is equal to marginal cost. At this output, however, if each individual beneficiary were to contribute an amount equal to his marginal rate of substitution times the number of units of the good produced, total revenue would be insufficient to defray total cost. In this case, therefore, it would be necessary to devise an alternative method that would raise sufficient revenue and yet leave the distribution of incomes unaffected.

provision of a particular social good may be counterbalanced by a loss to him resulting from the provision of another social good, and on balance the redistribution of income may be slight.

The great advantage of the equal distribution of cost is that it involves only random errors, whereas any other arbitrary distribution introduces a constant bias in favor of some particular group or class. It also has the advantage that it helps to clarify the desires of the public regarding the distribution of social goods. If costs are not distributed equally, variations in amounts voted for by different individuals would depend quite as much upon differences in individual marginal costs as upon differences in individual marginal rates of substitution, and the modal vote would not necessarily indicate the point of intersection between the curve of marginal (or average) cost per capita and the curve of average marginal substitution. Indeed, if the output of social goods is to be determined by the preferences of individuals it must be possible to obtain expressions of individual preferences unalloyed by differences in individual marginal costs. In other words, a necessary condition to the use of individual preferences in determining the ideal output of social goods is that the cost of social goods be distributed equally. Since equal distribution of cost is desirable on other grounds, as pointed out, this condition does not necessarily render the technique of voting impracticable or objectionable.

It must also be recognized that the condition of equal distribution of cost does not in any way preclude the use of taxation for purposes of redistributing income. It is required only that redistributive taxes be levied independently of taxes for the purpose of financing the production of social goods. This is, of course, at variance with present practice. Commonly the functions of redistributing income and of providing funds for public services are merged into a single tax system. Under these conditions, any expressions of preference on the part of individual citizens are ambiguous in that they reflect not only marginal rates of substitution but also (different) marginal costs.

Neither does the condition of equal distribution of cost require that incomes be distributed equally. The only assumption is that the distribution of income is "correct" in the sense that it is socially accepted. Thus, if some individuals have more income than others, they may well vote for more of a particular social good than others, with less income—if the cost of the social good is uniformly distributed. This corresponds exactly to the fact that the individuals with larger incomes buy more individual goods than persons with smaller incomes. The fact that such differences in income are socially sanctioned implies that the preferences of richer persons ought to count for more than that of the poorer persons in determining the allocation of the society's resources.

SOCIAL GOODS NOT EQUALLY AVAILABLE TO ALL VOTERS

Up to this point it has been assumed that any social good voted upon is accessible to all voters upon equal terms, and that differences in individual preferences are to be accounted for solely by differences in taste. This postulate, however, does not always conform to practical reality. When it does not, recourse to the benefit principle becomes more necessary and at the same time more practicable. It would then be desirable to classify the voters according to the amount of potential benefit that they would be expected to derive from the social good, and to tabulate the voting separately for each class. The intersection of the modal curve of marginal substitution and the curve of marginal cost per person (MC/N) could then be located for each class. For example, in Figure 6, the curves of marginal substitution for a group of citizens (Class I) who are in a position to benefit greatly from a social

Figure 6

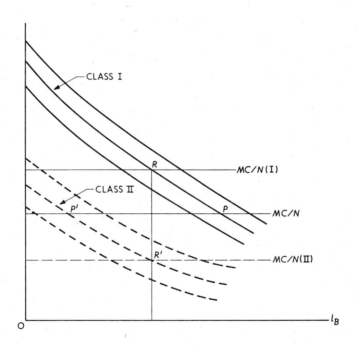

good are shown in solid lines, and the curves of marginal substitution for those able to benefit to a much smaller degree (Class II) are shown in dotted lines. The modal vote of the first group is indicated by P and of the second group by P'. In such a situation, application of the benefit principle would require that the cost assessed against citizens of Class I should be increased and that levied against citizens of Class II decreased, until two conditions are satisfied: (1) the modal output voted for by persons of Class I (indicated by point R) is equal to that voted for by persons of Class II (point R'), and (2) the entire cost of providing the social good is covered. The difficulty with this solution is that if the citizens realize that their voting affects the amount of cost they will be expected to bear, individually or as a class, the results of the voting will tend to be unreliable. Hence the cost to be levied on the several groups must be determined (apparently or in fact) without reference to the voting. Hence other methods of estimating potential benefit—drawing heavily upon common sense—are undoubtedly necessary. Such techniques are illustrated by the methods used in many American cities of distributing special assessments for street improvements. By such methods only very rough adjustments, for obvious and clear-cut differences in potential benefit, can be made.

On the rationale of group decision making*

DUNCAN BLACK

When a decision is reached by voting or is arrived at by a group all of whose members are not in complete accord, there is no part of economic theory which applies. This paper is intended to help fill this gap; to provide a type of reasoning which will contribute to the development of the theory of trade unions, the firm, and the cartel, and to provide the basis for a theory of the equilibrium distribution of taxation or of public expenditure. Still other uses of the theory might be not less important. For reasons of space we avoid discussion of many points that demand fuller treatment and only attempt to indicate the course of the argument.[1]

I. GENERAL ASSUMPTIONS

Let us suppose that a decision is to be determined by vote of a committee. The members of the committee may meet in a single room, or they may be scattered over an area of the country as are the electors in a parliamentary constituency. Proposals are advanced, we assume, in the form of motions on a particular topic or in favor of one of a number of candidates. We do not inquire into the genesis of the motions but simply assume that given motions have been put forward. In the case of the selection of candidates, we assume that determinate candidates have offered themselves for election and that one is to be chosen by means of voting. For convenience we shall speak as if one of a number of alternative motions, and not candidates, was being selected.

To develop our theory, we must make some further assumptions. Our major assumption will be that each member of the committee ranks the motions in a definite order of preference, whatever that order may be. To take a simple illustration, if there are four motions denoted by a_1, a_2, a_3, a_4, say, before a committee, the member A may prefer a_2 to any of the others, may be indifferent between a_3 and a_4, and may prefer either of them to a_1.

* *The Journal of Political Economy*, 56(1948): pp. 23–34. Corrected by the author. Reprinted by courtesy of the author and *The Journal of Political Economy*.

[1] The theory will be set out at greater length in a forthcoming book.

If so, A's valuation of the motions could be represented by the schedule of preferences on the left-hand side of Figure 1, in which a_2 stands highest; a_3 and a_4 next highest, each at the same level; and a_1 lowest. And similar scales could be drawn for other members of the committee with $a_1 \ldots a_4$ appearing in some definite order on each scale, though the ordering of the motions might be different on the scale of each member.

We are here using the theory of relative valuation of orthodox Economic Science, whether the theory of relative utility or the theory of indifference curves. The only points which have significance on the directed straight line representing a member's schedule of preferences are those at which motions are marked, and his scale really consists of a number of points placed in a certain order in relation to each other. No significance attaches to the distance between the points on the scale, and any two scales would be equivalent on which the motions occurred in the same order.

Figure 1

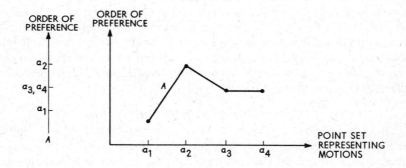

When a member values the motions before a committee in a definite order, it is reasonable to assume that, when these motions are put against each other, he votes in accordance with his valuation, i.e., in accordance with his schedule of preferences. Thus the member A would be assumed to vote for a_2 when it was put in a vote against a_1 or if a_3 were put against a_4 (since he is indifferent between the two and it would be irrational for him to support either against the other) he would be assumed to abstain from voting.

A member's level of preference between the different motions may also be shown by denoting the motions put forward by particular points on a horizontal axis, while we mark level of preference along the vertical axis. For instance, the same set of valuations of the individual A is shown in the right and left parts of Figure 1. The only points in the diagram having significance would be those for the values a_1, a_2, a_3, a_4 on the horizontal axis, corresponding to the motions actually put forward. We have joined these points standing at various levels of preference by straight-line segments, but this is done merely to assist the eye, since the curve would be imaginary except at the four points. In this diagram, as in the case of the preference schedule, it it is only the relative heights of different points which have meaning, not their absolute heights.[2]

While a member's preference curve may be of any shape whatever, there is reason to expect that, in some important practical problems, the valuations actually carried out will tend to take the form of isolated points on single-peaked curves. This would be particularly likely to happen were the committee considering different possible sizes of a numerical quantity and choosing one size in preference to the others. It might be reaching a decision, say, with regard to the price of a product to be marketed by a firm, or the output for a future period, or the wage rate of labor, or the height of a particular tax, or the legal school-leaving age, and so on.

In such cases the committee member, in arriving at an opinion on the matter, would often try initially to judge which size is for him the optimum. Once he had arrived at his view of the optimum size, the farther any proposal departed from it on the one side or the other, the less he would favor it. The valuations carried out by the member would then take the form of points on a single-peaked or ∩-shaped curve.

In working out our theory we shall devote considerable attention to this class of curves which slope continuously upward to a peak and slope continuously downward from that peak. We shall refer to the motion corresponding to the peak of any curve—the most-preferred motion for the member concerned—as his optimum.

Another case likely to be of frequent occurrence in practice—especially, again, where the committee is selecting a particular size of a numerical quantity—is that in which the valuations carried out by a member take the form of points on a single-peaked curve with a truncated top. Such a case would arise when the individual feels uncertain as to which of two or more numerical quantities proposed represents his optimum choice. He cannot discriminate in choice between (say) two of these numerical quantities; but the farther the proposal made falls below the lower of these values, or the higher it rises above the larger of them, the less he esteems the motion concerned.

We shall work out the theory first for the case in which the members' preference curves are single-peaked, and after that, we shall show how the answer to any problem can be obtained no matter what the shape of the members' curves may be. When any matter is being considered in a committee, only a finite number of motions will be put forward and only a finite number of valuations will be carried out by each member. If three motions or six motions were put forward, each member would be assumed to value each of them in relation to the others. When we are drawing our preference curves, however, we will draw continuous curves and—since there are an infinite number of points on any continuous curve—we imply that the person for

---

[2] Cf. F. H. Knight, *Risk, Uncertainty and Profit*, pp. 68–70.

whom the curve is drawn has carried out an evaluation of each of an infinite number of motions in regard to each of the others. This is unrealistic, it is true, but when the theory is worked out for this case, we can easily get the answer for any case in which only a finite number of motions is put forward and valued by the members.

We assume that the committee with which we are concerned makes use of a simple majority in its voting. In practice, voting would be so conducted that, after discussion, one motion would be made and, after further discussion, another motion (an "amendment," that is) might be moved. If so, the original motion and amendment would be placed against each other in a vote. One of the two motions having been disposed of, leaving a single motion in the the field, a further amendment to it might be moved; then a further vote would be taken between the survivor of the first vote and the new motion; and so on. If two motions were put forward, one vote would be taken; if three motions, two votes; and, in general, if m motions were put forward, there would be $(m - 1)$ votes.[3]

Now it will be found to simplify the development of the theory if, in the first instance, we suppose that the voting procedure is different from this. We wish to make the assumption that when m motions $a_1, a_2, \ldots, a_m$ (say) have been put forward, the committee places each of these motions against every other in a vote and picks out that motion, if any, which is able to get a simple majority against *every* other motion. The motion a_1 is to be envisaged as being put against all the other motions $a_2 \ldots a_m$; a_2 will already have been put against a_1, and we assume that it will then be put against $a_3 \ldots a_m$; and so on, a_{m-1} finally being pitted against a_m. On this assumption the number of votes taken will be the number of ways of choosing two things out of m, i.e., $m(m - 1)/2$ votes, instead of the $(m - 1)$ votes which would be taken in practice.

This assumption enables the theory to proceed more smoothly and quickly than the assumption that only $(m - 1)$ votes are held. When we have worked out the theory on this basis, we can go on to prove that—in the class of cases in which we are mainly interested—the same answer would be given whether $m(m - 1)/2$ votes were held, as we assume, or only the $(m - 1)$ votes of reality. The assumption is a kind of theoretical scaffolding which can be discarded once it has served its turn .

These, then, are our assumptions: that in a committee m motions are put forward, that each member carries out an evaluation of each motion in regard to every other, that in the voting each motion is put against every other, and that the committee adopts as its decision ("resolution") that motion, if any, which is able to get a simple majority over every other.

---

[3] In addition, the motion which is selected by this process is usually put to the meeting for final acceptance or rejection. This is equivalent to putting it against the motion "that there be no change in the existing state of affairs." The step in theory to correspond to this stage in the procedure could easily be supplied.

It can be shown that, at most, only one motion will be able to get a simple majority over every other. To prove this, let us assume that a_h is such a motion, i.e., that a_h can get a simple majority over every other. And let us assume that this is also true of some other motion, a_k. By our first assumption, however, a_h can get a simple majority over every other motion, including a_k. Therefore a_k cannot get a simple majority over a_h. Hence, at most, only one motion can get a simple majority over every other.

II. MEMBERS' PREFERENCE CURVES ALL SINGLE-PEAKED

The method of reasoning which we employ can be seen most easily from a particular example. Figure 2 shows the preference curves of the five members of a committee. Only part of each curve has been drawn, and the curves are supposed to extend over a common range of the horizontal axis.

Figure 2

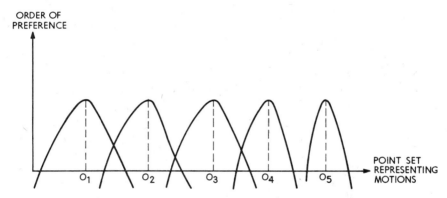

Then if a_h is put against a_k (where $a_h < a_k \leq O_1$), the preference curve of each member—irrespective of what its precise shape may be—is upsloping from a_h to a_k; and a_k, standing at a higher level of preference on the curve of each member, will get a 5:5 (5 out of 5) majority against a_h. If a_h is put against a_k, (where $a_h < a_k \leq O_2$), at least four members—viz., those with optimums at or above O_2—will have preference curves which are upsloping from a_h to a_k; and a_k will get at least a 4:5 majority against a_h. If $a_h < a_k \leq O_3$, a_k will get at least a 3:5 majority against a_h. And similar relations hold for motions corresponding to values above O_3. If two values above O_3 are placed against each other in a vote, the nearer of the two values to O_3 will get a majority of at least 3:5 against the other.

If a value a_h (where $a_h < O_3$) is put against a value a_k (where $a_k > O_3$), before we could find which of the values would win in a vote, we would have to draw the complete preference curve for each member, find whether a_h or a_k stood higher on the preference curve of each member and count up the votes cast for a_h and a_k. But even though a value below the median optimum O_3 should defeat all values to the left of itself, and should defeat some of the values above O_3, this would be without significance. What we are looking for is that motion which can defeat every other by at least a simple majority. And we notice that the preference curves of at least three members are downsloping from O_3 leftward, and the preference curves of at least three members are downsloping from O_3 rightward. Therefore O_3 can defeat any other value in the entire range by at least a simple majority. And, as we have already seen (end of Sec. I), this can be true of only a single value. The resolution adopted by the committee must be the motion corresponding to the value O_3.

To give the general proof, two cases must be worked out—that in which the number of members in the committee is odd and that in which it is even. We will consider each in turn.

Let there be n members in the committee, where n is odd. We suppose that an ordering of the points on the horizontal axis representing motions exists, rendering the preference curves of all members single-peaked. The points on the horizontal axis corresponding to the members' optimums are named O_1, O_2, O_3, ..., in the order of their occurrence. The middle or median optimum will be the $(n + 1)/2$th, and, in Figure 3, only this median optimum, the one immediately above it, and the one immediately below it are shown.

Then $O_{(n+1)/2}$ will be the motion adopted by the committee. Suppose $O_{(n+1)/2}$ were placed against any lower value, say, a_h. Since $(n + 1)/2$ members have optimums at or above $O_{(n+1)/2}$, as we move from left to right from a_h to $O_{(n+1)/2}$, at least $(n + 1)/2$ curves are upsloping, viz., those of members with optimums at or to the right of $O_{(n+1)/2}$. At least $(n + 1)/2$ members prefer $O_{(n+1)/2}$ to a_h and, in a vote against a_h, $O_{(n+1)/2}$ will get a majority of at least $(n + 1)/2 : n$, and this is sufficient to give it at least a simple majority. Therefore $O_{(n+1)/2}$ can get at least a simple majority against any lower value

Figure 3

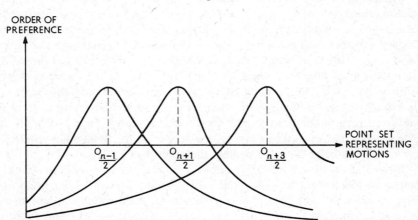

ORDER OF
PREFERENCE

$O_{\frac{n-1}{2}}$ $O_{\frac{n+1}{2}}$ $O_{\frac{n+3}{2}}$

POINT SET
REPRESENTING
MOTIONS

which is put against it. Similarly it can get at least a simple majority against any higher value. Thus it can get a simple majority against any other value which can be proposed. And by previous argument, it is the only value which can do so.

When the number of members, n, in the committee, is even, there may be a tie in the voting. We will suppose that in the event of a tie one of the members, acting as chairman, has the right to casting a vote.

Let us suppose, first, that this member who acts as chairman has his optimum at $O_{n/2}$ or at one of the lower optimums. It can be shown that the motion corresponding to the value $O_{n/2}$ will be able to defeat any lower value (Figure 4). Let a_h be such a value, that is, $a_h < O_{n/2}$. Then $(n/2 + 1)$ members

Figure 4

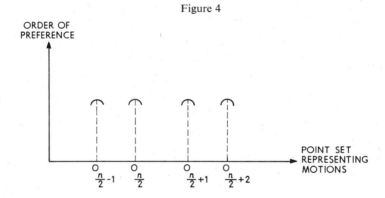

ORDER OF
PREFERENCE

POINT SET
REPRESENTING
MOTIONS

$O_{\frac{n}{2}-1}$ $O_{\frac{n}{2}}$ $O_{\frac{n}{2}+1}$ $O_{\frac{n}{2}+2}$

have optimums at or above $O_{n/2}$; and at least $(n/2 + 1)$ preference curves will be upsloping as we move from left to right from a_h to $O_{n/2}$. At least $(n/2 + 1)$ members will vote for $O_{n/2}$ against a_h, and this is sufficient to give $O_{n/2}$ a simple majority.

If $O_{n/2}$ is put against any value a_k (where $a_k > O_{n/2}$)—since there are $n/2$ optimums at or below $O_{n/2}$—the preference curves of at least $n/2$ members will be downsloping from $O_{n/2}$ to a_k, and $O_{n/2}$ will get at least $n/2$ votes against a_k, i.e., will at least tie with a_k. In the event of a tie, $O_{n/2}$ will defeat a_k with the aid of the chairman's casting vote because, by hypothesis, his optimum is situated at or below $O_{n/2}$ and his preference curve must be downsloping from $O_{n/2}$ to a_k.

Thus, when the chairman's optimum is situated at or below $O_{n/2}$, $O_{n/2}$ will be able to get at least a simple majority against any other value which may be proposed.

Similarly when n, the number of members in the committee, is even, and the chairman's optimum is at or above $O_{(n/2)+1}$, it can be shown that $O_{(n/2)+1}$ will be able to get at least a simple majority against every other value.

One cannot leave the theorem of the preceding paragraphs without pointing out its analogy with the central principle of economics—that showing how price is fixed by demand and supply. The theorem we have proved shows that the decision adopted by the committee becomes determinate as soon as the position of one optimum—which we can refer to conveniently enough as the median optimum—is given. No matter in what manner the preference curves or optimums of the other members alter or move about, if it is given that one optimum remains the median optimum, the decision of the committee must remain fixed. The analogy with economic science is that, in the determination of price in a market, price remains unchanged so long as the point of intersection of the demand and supply curves is fixed and given, irrespective of how these curves may alter their shapes above and below that point. Or, in the version of the theory due to Böhm-Bawerk, which brings out the point very clearly, price remains unaltered so long as the "marginal pairs" of buyers and sellers and their price attitudes remain unchanged.

But the analogy exists only between the two theories; there is a marked difference in the materials to which they relate. In the case of market price, when the price of a commodity is being determined, a series of adjustments on the part of the consumers will bring into existence a state of affairs in which this commodity, and all others which they purchase, will have the same significance at the margin for each consumer. This is one of the several grand harmonies running through the material of economic life, a harmony by which no one who understands it can fail to be impressed—and by which the economists of the last generation were perhaps over-impressed. In the material of committee decisions (or of political phenomena in general), on the other hand, no such grand harmony exists. The possibility of the persistence of disharmony and discord is as striking in the one case as is the certainty of harmony in the other.

In reaching the foregoing conclusions, we have assumed that a member of the committee voted on the various motions put forward in accordance with their order in his schedule of preferences. It can be shown that, when a motion exists which would defeat every other if the members voted in this way, it is not open to any member, or any number of members acting in concert, to alter their voting so that some other motion which is more preferred by them can be adopted as the resolution of the committee.[4] It is open to them, however, to vote in such a way that no motion will be able to get a majority over all the others.

If all members voted as we have supposed, the motion adopted by the committee would be that corresponding to the median optimum, O_{med}, say. Let us suppose now that one or more members with optimums above O_{med}— by voting otherwise than directly in accordance with their schedule of preferences—attempt to give some other value, say a_h, a majority over all the others, where $a_h > O_{med}$.

But when the members vote directly in accordance with their preference scales, those who have a_h higher on their scales than O_{med} would already be

---

[4] If only $(m - 1)$ votes are held, this conclusion no longer holds.

supporting a_h against O_{med} and, even so, a_h would be defeated by O_{med}. Before it could defeat O_{med}, a_h would require the support of members whose optimums lie below O_{med}. The only members who—by voting otherwise than in accordance with their scales of preferences—could make a_h the resolution of the committee, are those with optimums below O_{med}, i.e., those against whose interest it is to do so.

It would be possible, of course, for a number of members to vote so that no motion would get a majority over every other. If, for example, a sufficient number of voters with optimums above O_{med} were to vote against O_{med} when it was placed against some value which stood lower on their scales of preferences, O_{med} might be defeated. At most, therefore, a group of voters would have it in their power to prevent any resolution at all being adopted by the committee.

When the members' preference curves are single-peaked, as we suppose, it can be shown that voting between the different motions obeys the transitive property[5] and that if—of any three values a_1, a_2, a_3—a_1 can defeat a_2 in a vote and a_2 can defeat a_3, then, of necessity, a_1 can defeat a_3.

This can be proved by consideration of the orderings of the points a_1, a_2, a_3, in relation to the median optimum. It can be shown that each ordering of the four points a_1, a_2, a_3, and the median optimum either renders the assumption impossible that a_1 defeats a_2 and a_2 defeats a_3 or else satisfies the assumption and, at the same time, necessitates that a_1 defeats a_3.

The transitive property can easily be extended to show that, if a_1 can defeat a_2, a_2 can defeat a_3, ... and a_{l-1} can defeat a_l, then a_1 can defeat a_l.

It follows from the transitive property that a_1 can defeat a_3. By hypothesis, a_3 can defeat a_4. Hence a_1 can defeat a_4. Proceeding by successive applications we can see that a_1 can defeat a_l.

In arriving at the above-mentioned results, we assumed that every motion was placed against every other and that in all $m(m - 1)/2$ votes were held. We can now remove this assumption and show that the same motion will be adopted by a committee when only $(m - 1)$ votes are taken as in the committee practice of real life.

For the case when n is odd, $O_{(n+1)/2}$ is one of the motions put forward and it must enter into the series of votes at some point. When it does, it will defeat the first motion which it meets. It will likewise defeat the second and every other motion which is put against it. That is, $O_{(n+1)/2}$ must enter the voting process at some stage, and when it does, it will defeat the other motions put against it and become the decision of the committee. The conclusion we reached holds good not only for the imaginary procedure of placing every motion against every other but also for the actual committee procedure of real life. The same is true of the conclusions we reached for the case in which the number of members in the committee was even. In the committee procedure of real life $O_{n/2}$ or $O_{(n/2)+1}$ will be the motion actually adopted.

---

[5] The transitive property is defined in L. S. Stebbing, *A Modern Introduction to Logic*. pp. 112 and 168.

The assumption, that $m(m-1)/2$ votes were held, enabled us to give a mathematical proof which was both definite and short. But our conclusions are true independently of this assumption.

As an example of the use of this technique, we may suppose that the three directors of a monopolistic firm are fixing the price of their product for a forthcoming period. Let us further assume that neither future sales nor future costs can be calculated with certainty and that there is no possibility of a choice of price being made purely by means of cost accounting. Subjective factors enter, and varying estimates of the future position are formed by the different directors. If, on their different views of the situation, the directors' scales of preference are as shown (Figure 5), the price fixed will be that corresponding to the motion a_3.

III. WHEN THE MEMBERS' PREFERENCE CURVES ARE SUBJECT TO NO RESTRICTION

When the members' preference curves are not of the single-peaked variety, a solution to any problem can always be arrived at arithmetically, provided the number of motions put forward is finite.

Figure 5

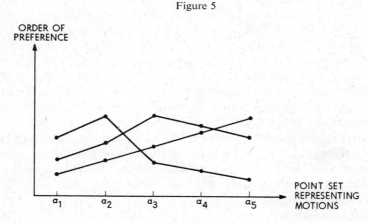

To begin with, we return to the assumption that every motion is placed in a vote against every other. The results of the series of votes can be shown very readily by the construction of a voting matrix.[6]

The construction of a matrix is illustrated in Figure 6, which gives the matrix corresponding to the schedule of preferences of the single member A who is voting in a committee in which the four motions $a_1 \ldots a_4$ have been put forward. Along the top row and down the left-hand column are shown the motions $a_1 \ldots a_4$. In each cell of the matrix, we record the individual's vote for one motion when it is placed against another. Looking to the top-

---

[6] I am indebted to Dr. R. A. Newing for suggesting the use of a matrix notation.

Figure 6

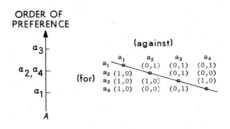

most row of figures, when a_1 is placed against a_2, A votes for a_2, and we enter in the cell (a_1, a_2) the figures $(0, 1)$. When a_1 is placed against a_3, he votes for a_3 and, in the cell (a_1, a_3), we enter the figures $(0, 1)$ standing for 0 votes for and 1 against. The other cells are filled in the same way. Since A is indifferent in choice between a_2 and a_4, he will abstain from voting when a_2 is placed against a_4, and the cell (a_2, a_4) will show $(0, 0)$. The figures in the cell (a_4, a_2) will also be $(0, 0)$.

Along the main diagonal of the matrix, instead of having cells of the usual type, we have simply placed a series of zeros and joined them by a straight line. This is to indicate that the cells $(a_1, a_1), (a_2, a_2), \ldots$, which would denote that a_1 was placed against a_1, a_2 against a_2, $\ldots$, have no meaning. In constructing the matrix in practice, it is usually easiest to enter these zeros along the main diagonal first and join them by a straight line.

Each row to the right of the main diagonal is a reflection in the diagonal of the column immediately beneath, with the figures in the cells reversed. Thus the cell (a_2, a_3) immediately to the right of the diagonal shows $(0, 1)$, the reflection in the diagonal of the figure $(1, 0)$ immediately below the diagonal. The cell (a_2, a_4), two places to the right of the diagonal, is the reflection of the cell (a_4, a_2) two places below the diagonal. The reason for this is that the cells (a_h, a_k) and (a_k, a_h), on opposite sides of the diagonal, present the same information in the reverse order. This feature roughly halves the work of constructing a matrix: we can fill in the figures on one side of the diagonal and then complete the matrix by reflection of these figures in the diagonal.

The construction of an individual matrix would be gratuitous labor since it merely gives, in a clumsier form, information which is shown clearly enough in the members' schedule of preference. When, however, we have a group of individuals voting on a particular topic and the preference schedule of each is known, the matrix for the group presents in very convenient form the information that we need. For instance, for the group of schedules shown in Figure 7, the accompanying matrix has been constructed precisely as described above. Along the main diagonal, as before, we enter zeros and join them by a straight line. In the cell (a_1, a_2) we enter the figure $(2, 3)$ because

Figure 7

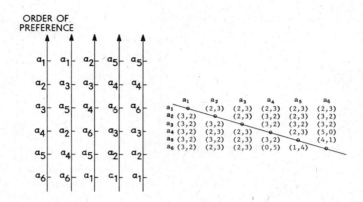

on the scales of two members a_1 stands higher than a_2, and on the scales of the remaining three members a_2 stands higher. The other cells are filled in the same way and, as before, the half of the matrix on one side of the diagonal can be obtained by reversal of the frequencies in the corresponding cells on the other side.

From the group matrix we can read off immediately that—when the motions $a_1 \ldots a_6$ are placed each against every other, as we suppose—a_3 will be able to get a simple majority over each of the other motions put forward. For this committee a_3 would be the resolution adopted.

If a motion exists which would be able to get a simple majority over all the others when the members voted directly in accordance with their schedules of preferences, it would not be open to any member or group of members—by voting in some other fashion—to bring into existence as the resolution of the committee a motion which stood higher on the scales of all of them. Proof of this proposition is almost identical with that of our earlier analysis (see above, p. 137).

If, when $m(m-1)/2$ votes are held, a motion exists which is able to get at least a simple majority over each of the other motions put forward, it can be proved, as before, that when the members vote directly in accordance with their schedules of preferences, this would be bound to be the motion adopted even though only $(m-1)$ votes had been held.

But when the members' preference curves are not single-peaked, no motion need exist which is able to get at least a simple majority over every other. This can be seen very quickly from the accompanying group of schedules (Figure 8) in which the arrangement of the motions a_1, a_2, a_3, on the members' scales is symmetrical. When a_1 is put forward, it is defeated by a_3, which gets the votes of B and C; when a_2 is put forward, it is defeated by a_1; when a_3 is put forward, it is defeated by a_2.

Figure 8

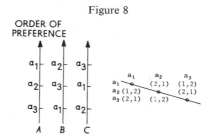

That is, no one of the three motions is able to get a simple majority over the other two.

By writing down groups of schedules in which six or seven motions are arranged in various ways and by constructing the group matrices, the reader can quickly satisfy himself that such cases—in which no motion exists which can get a simple majority over each of the others—are by no means exceptional. The greater the number of motions put forward in a committee of any given size, the greater will be the percentage of the total number of possible cases in which there exists no motion which is able to get a simple majority over each of the others.

In this state of affairs, when no one motion can obtain a simple majority over each of the others, the procedure of a committee which holds only $(m - 1)$ votes will arrive at the adoption of a particular motion, whereas if the requirement were that a motion should be able to get a simple majority over every other, no motion would be adopted. The particular motion which is adopted by the committee using the procedure of practice will depend on chance—the chance of particular motions coming earlier or later into the voting process. For Figure 8, if only $(m - 1 = 2)$ votes were taken, that motion, a_1 or a_2, or a_3, would be adopted which was introduced last into the voting process. If, for example, a_1 were first put against a_2, a_2 would be eliminated; and, with the field thus cleared, a_3 would defeat a_1.

If, then, only $(m - 1)$ votes are held and if no motion exists which is able to get a simple majority over every other, we cannot read off directly from the matrix the decision adopted by the committee. But when, in addition to the matrix, we know the order in which the motions are put against one another in a vote, again we can deduce what the decision of the committee must be.

Reference to Figure 8 will show that, when the shapes of the preference curves are subject to no restriction, the transitive property does not necessarily hold good.

IV. CONCLUSION

The technique of this paper applies irrespective of the topic to which the motions may relate. They may refer to price, quantity, or other economic phenomena; they may relate to motions put forward in regard to colonial government, to the structure of a college curriculum, and so on. The theory applies to a decision taken on any topic by means of voting—so far, of course, as the assumptions which are made correspond to reality. And it is possible to widen the assumptions, for example, to include cases of complementary valuation; to make allowance for the time element; and to cover the cases of committees making use of special majorities of any stipulated size. With these extensions in the assumptions there would be a widening of the field of phenomena to which the theory aplies.

The theory, indeed, would appear to present the basis for the development of a pure science of politics. This would employ the same theory of relative valuation as economic science. It would employ a different definition of equilibrium. Equilibrium would now be defined in terms of voting, in place of the type of definition employed in economic science. We could move from the one science to the other with the alteration of a single definition. This, in in the view of the writer, would be the main function of the theory. It fairly obviously, too, enables some parts of economics—those which relate to decisions taken by groups—to be carried a stage beyond their present development.

A difficulty in the concept of social welfare*

KENNETH J. ARROW[1]

I. INTRODUCTION

In a capitalist democracy there are essentially two methods by which social choices can be made: voting, typically used to make "political" decisions, and the market mechanism, typically used to make "economic" decisions. In the emerging democracies with mixed economic systems, Great Britain, France, and Scandinavia, the same two modes of making social choices prevail, though more scope is given to the method of voting and to decisions based directly or indirectly on it and less to the rule of the price mechanism. Elsewhere in the world, and even in smaller social units within the democracies, the social decisions are sometimes made by single individuals or small groups and sometimes (more and more rarely in this modern world) by a widely encompassing set of traditional rules for making the social choice in any given situation, e.g., a religious code.

The last two methods of social choice, dictatorship and convention, have in their formal structure a certain definiteness absent from voting or the market mechanism. In an ideal dictatorship, there is but one will involved in choice; in an ideal society ruled by convention, there is but the divine will or perhaps, by assumption, a common will of all individuals concerning social decisions, so that in either case no conflict of individual wills is involved. The methods of voting and of the market, on the other hand, are methods of amalgamating the tastes of many individuals in the making of social choices.

* The Journal of Political Economy, 58(1950): pp. 328–46. Reprinted by courtesy of the author and The Journal of Politcal Economy.

[1] This paper is based on research carried on at the RAND Corporation, a project of the United States Air Force, and at the Cowles Commission for Research in Economics and is part of a longer study, "Social Choice and Individual Values," to be published by John Wiley & Sons as a Cowles Commission monograph. A version was read at the December, 1948, meeting of the Econometric Society. I am indebted to A. Kaplan, University of California at Los Angeles, and J. W. T. Youngs, University of Indiana, for guidance in formulating the problem, and to A. Bergson and A. G. Hart, Columbia University, and T. C. Koopmans, Cowles Commission and the University of Chicago, who have read the manuscript and made valuable comments on both the presentation and the meaning. Needless to say, any error or opacity remaining is the responsibility of the author.

The methods of dictatorship and convention are, or can be, rational in the sense that any individual can be rational in his choice. Can such consistency be attributed to collective modes of choice, where the wills of many people are involved?

It should be emphasized here that the present study is concerned only with the formal aspects of the foregoing question. That is, we ask if it is formally possible to construct a procedure for passing from a set of known individual tastes to a pattern of social decision making, the procedure in question being required to satisfy certain natural conditions. An illustration of the problem is the following well-known "paradox of voting." Suppose there is a community consisting of three voters and this community must choose among three alternative modes of social action (e.g., disarmament, cold war, or hot war). It is expected that choices of this type have to be made repeatedly, but sometimes not all of the three alternatives will be available. In analogy with the usual utility analysis of the individual consumer under conditions of constant wants and variable price-income situations, rational behavior on the part of the community would mean that the community orders the three alternatives according to its collective preferences once for all and then chooses in any given case that alternative among those actually available which stands highest on this list. A natural way of arriving at the collective preference scale would be to say that one alternative is preferred to another if a majority of the community prefer the first alternative to the second, i.e., would choose the first over the second if those were the only two alternatives. Let A, B, and C be the three alternatives, and 1, 2, and 3 the three individuals. Suppose individual 1 prefers A to B and B to C (and there- fore A to C), individual 2 prefers B to C and C to A (and therefore B to A), and individual 3 prefers C to A and A to B (and therefore C to B). Then a majority prefers A to B, and a majority prefers B to C. We may therefore say that the community prefers A to B and B to C. If the community is to be regarded as behaving rationally, we are forced to say that A is preferred to C. But, in fact, a majority of the community prefers C to A.[2] So the method just outlined for passing from individual to collective tastes fails to satisfy the condition of rationality as we ordinarily understand it. Can we find other methods of aggregating individual tastes which imply rational behavior on the part of the community and which will be satisfactory in other ways?[3]

---

[2] It may be added that the method of decision sketched above is essentially that used in deliberative bodies, where a whole range of alternatives usually comes up for decision in the form of successive pairwise comparisons. The phenomenon described in the text can be seen in a pure form in the disposition of the proposals before recent Congresses for federal aid to state education, the three alternatives being no federal aid, federal aid to public schools only, and federal aid to both public and parochial schools.

[3] The problem of collective rationality has been discussed by Professor Frank H. Knight, but chiefly in terms of the sociopsychological prerequisites; see "The Planful Act: The Possibilities and Limitations of Collective Rationality," in *Freedom and Reform* (New York: Harper & Bros., 1947), pp. 335–69, esp. pp. 346–65).

If we adopt the traditional identification of rationality with maximization of some sort, then the problem of achieving a social maximum derived from individual desires is precisely the problem which has been central to the field of welfare economics.[4] However, the search for a clear definition of optimum social welfare has been plagued by the difficulties of interpersonal comparisons. The emphasis, as is well known, has shifted to a weaker definition of optimum, namely, the determination of all social states such that no individual can be made better off without making someone worse off. As Professors Bergson, Lange, and Samuelson have argued, though, the weaker definition cannot be used as a guide to social policy; the second type of welfare economics is only important as a preliminary to the determination of a genuine social maximum in the full sense. E.g., under the usual assumptions, if there is an excise tax imposed on one commodity in the initial situation, it can be argued that the removal of the tax accompanied by a suitable redistribution of income and direct tax burdens will improve the position of all individuals in the society. But there are, in general, many redistributions which will accomplish this end, and society must have some criterion for choosing among them before it can make any change at all. Further, there is no reason for confining the range of possible social actions to those which will injure no one as compared with the initial situation, unless the status quo is to be sanctified on ethical grounds. All we can really say is that society ought to abolish the excise tax and make some redistribution of income and tax burdens; but this is no prescription for action unless there is some principle by which society can make its choice among attainable income distributions, i.e., a social indifference map.

Voting can be regarded as a method of arriving at social choices derived from the preferences of individuals. Another such method of more specifically economic content is the compensation principle, as proposed by Mr. Kaldor:[5] in a choice between two alternative economic states x and y, if there is a method of paying compensations under state x such that everybody can be made better off in the state resulting from making the compensations under x than they are in state y, then x should be chosen in preference to y, *even if the compensation is not actually paid.* Apart from the ethical difficulties in the acceptance of this principle,[6] there is a formal difficulty which was pointed out by Professor Scitovszky:[7] it is possible that simultaneously x

---

[4] See P. A. Samuelson, *Foundations of Economic Analysis* (Cambridge, Mass.: Harvard University Press, 1947], chap. viii; A. Bergson (Burk), *"A Reformulation of Certain Aspects of Welfare Economics," *Quarterly Journal of Economics*, LII (1938), 310–34; O. Lange, *"The Foundations of Welfare Economics," *Econometrica*, X (1942), 215–28; M. W. Reder, *Studies in the Theory of Welfare Economics* (New York, 1947), chaps. i–v.

[5] N. Kaldor, *"Welfare Propositions of Economics and Interpersonal Comparisons of Utility," *Economic Journal*, XLIX (1939), 549–652; see also J. R. Hicks, "The Foundations of Welfare Economics," *Economic Journal*, XLIX (1939), 698–701 and 711–12.

[6] See W. J. Baumol, "Community Indifference," *Review of Economic Studies*, XIV (1946–67), 44–48.

[7] T. Scitovszky, *"A Note on Welfare Propositions in Economics," *Review of Economic Studies*, IX (1942), 77–88.

should be preferred to y and y be preferred to x. Just as in the case of majority voting, this method of aggregating individual preferences may lead to a pattern of social choice which is not a linear ordering of the social alternatives. Note that in both cases the paradox need not occur; all that is said is that there are preference patterns which, if held by the individual members of the society, will give rise to an inconsistent pattern of social choice. Unless the trouble-breeding individual preference patterns can be ruled out by a priori assumption, both majority voting and the compensation principle must be regarded as unsatisfactory techniques for the determination of social preferences.

The aim of the present paper is to show that these difficulties are general. For *any* method of deriving social choices by aggregating individual preference patterns which satisfies certain natural conditions, it is possible to find individual preference patterns which give rise to a social choice pattern which is not a linear ordering, In particular, this is very likely to be the case if, as is frequently assumed, each individual's preferences among social states are derived purely from his personal consumption-leisure-saving situation in each.[8] It is assumed that individuals act rationally, in the sense that their behavior in alternative situations can be described by an indifference map. It is further assumed that utility is not measurable in any sense relevant to welfare economics, so that the tastes of an individual are completely described by a suitable preference pattern or indifference map.

II. DEFINITIONS AND NOTATION

1. A Notation for preferences and choice

In this paper I shall be interested in the description of preference patterns both for the individual and for society. It will be found convenient to represent preference by a notation not customarily employed in economics, though familiar in mathematics and particularly in symbolic logic. We assume that there is a basic set of alternatives which could conceivably be presented to the chooser. In the theory of consumers' choice, each alternative would be a commodity bundle; in the theory of the firm, each alternative would be a complete decision on all inputs and outputs; in welfare economics, each alternative would be a distribution of commodities and labor requirements. These alternatives are mutually exclusive; they are denoted by small letters, x, y, z. ... On any given occasion the chooser has available to him a subset S of all possible alternatives, and he is required to choose one out of this set. The set S is a generalization of the well-known opportunity curve; thus, in the theory of consumer's choice under perfect competition, it would be the budget plane. It is assumed further that the choice is made in this way: Before knowing the set S, the chooser considers in turn all possible pairs of alternatives, say x and y, and for each pair he makes one and only one of three

---

[8] See, e.g., Samuelson, *op. cit.*, pp. 222–24; Bergson,* *op. cit.*, pp. 318–20; Lange,* *op. cit.*, p. 216.

decisions: x is preferred to y, x is indifferent to y, or y is preferred to x. The decisions made for different pairs are assumed to be consistent with one another, so that, for example, if x is preferred to y and y to z, then x is preferred to z; similarly, if x is indifferent to y and y to z, then x is indifferent to z. Having this ordering of all possible alternatives, the chooser is now confronted with a particular opportunity set S. If there is one alternative in S which is preferred to all others in S, then the chooser selects that one alternative.[9]

Preference and indifference are relations between alternatives. Instead of working with two relations, it will be slightly more convenient to use a single relation, "preferred or indifferent." The statement, "x is preferred or indifferent to y," will be symbolized by xRy. The letter R, by itself, will be the name of the relation and will stand for a knowledge of all pairs such that xRy. From our previous discussion, we have, for any pair of alternatives x and y, either that x is preferred to y or y to x or that the two are indifferent. That is, we have assumed that any two alternatives are comparable. But this assumption may be written symbolically,

Axiom I: For all x and y, either xRy or yRx.

Note that Axiom I is presumed to hold when $x = y$, as well as when x is distinct from y, for we ordinarily say that x is indifferent to itself for any x, and this implies xRx. Note also that the word "or" in the statement of Axiom I does not exclude the possibility of both xRy and yRx. That word merely asserts that at least one of the two events must occur; both may.

The property mentioned above, of consistency in the preferences as between different pairs of alternatives, may be stated more precisely as follows: if x is preferred or indifferent to y and y is preferred or indifferent to z, then x must be either preferred or indifferent to z. In symbols,

Axiom II: For all x, y, and z, xRy and yRz imply xRz.

A relation satisfying both Axiom I and Axiom II is termed a weak ordering or sometimes simply an ordering. It is clear that a relation having these two properties taken together does create a ranking of the various alternatives. The adjective "weak" refers to the fact that the ordering does not exclude indifference; i.e., Axioms I and II do not exclude the possibility that for some distinct x and y, both xRy and yRx.

It might be held that the two axioms in question do not completely characterize the concept of a preference pattern. For example, we ordinarily feel

---

[9] It may be that there is a subset of alternatives in S such that the alternatives in the subset are each preferred to every alternative not in the subset, while the alternatives in the subset are indifferent to one another. This case would be one in which the highest indifference curve which has a point in common with a given opportunity curve has at least two points in common with it (the well-known case of multiple maxima). In this case, the best thing to say is that the choice made in S is the whole subset; the first case discussed is one in which the subset in question, the choice, contains a single element.

that not only the relation R but also the relations of (strict) preference and of indifference satisfy Axiom II. It can be shown that, by defining preference and indifference suitably in terms of R, it will follow that all the usually desired properties of preference patterns obtain.

Definition 1: xPy is defined to mean not yRx.

The statement "xPy" is read "x is preferred to y."

Definition 2: xIy means xRy and yRx.

The statement "xIy" is read "x is indifferent to y." It is clear that P and I, so defined, correspond to the ordinary notions of preference and indifference, respectively.

Lemma: (a) For all x, xRx.
　　　　(b) If xPy, then xRy.
　　　　(c) If xPy and yPz, then xPz.
　　　　(d) If xIy and yIz, then xIz.
　　　　(e) For all x and y, either xRy or yPx.
　　　　(f) If xPy and yRz, then xPz.

All these statements are intuitively self-evident from the interpretations placed on the symbols.

For clarity, we shall avoid the use of the terms "preference scale" or "preference pattern" when referring to R, since we wish to avoid confusion with the concept of preference proper, denoted by P. We shall refer to R as an "ordering relation" or "weak ordering relation" or, more simply, as an "ordering" or "weak ordering." The term "preference relation" will refer to the relation P.

Suppose that we know the choice which would be made from any given pair of alternatives; i.e., given two alternatives x and y from which the chooser must select, we know whether he would take x or y or remain indifferent between them. Since choosing x from the pair x, y implies that x is preferred to y, and similarly with a choice of y, a knowledge of the choice which would be made from any two given alternatives implies a knowledge of the full preference scale; from earlier remarks this, in turn, implies a knowledge of the choice which would be made from any set of alternatives actually available. Hence, one of the consequences of the assumption of rational behavior is that the choice from any collection of alternatives can be determined by a knowledge of the choices which would be made from pairs of alternatives.

2. The ordering of social states

In the present study the objects of choice are social states. The most precise definition of a social state would be a complete description of the amount of each type of commodity in the hands of each individual, the amount of labor to be applied by each individual, the amount of each productive resource invested in each type of productive activity, and the amounts of various types of collective activity such as municipal services, diplomacy, and its continuation by other means, and the erection of statues to famous men. It is assumed that each individual in the community has a definite ordering of all conceivable social states in terms of their desirability to him. It need not be assumed here that an individual's attitude toward different social states is determined exclusively by the commodity bundles which accrue to his lot under each. The individual may order all social states by whatever standards he deems relevant. A member of Veblen's leisure class might order the states solely on the criterion of his relative income standing in each; a believer in the equality of man might order them in accordance with some measure of income equality. Indeed, since, as mentioned above, some of the components of the social state, considered as a vector, are collective activities, purely individualistic assumptions are useless in analyzing such problems as the division of the national income between public and private expenditure. The present notation permits perfect generality in this respect. Needless to say, this generality is not without its price. More information would be available for analysis if the generality were restricted by a prior knowledge of the nature of individual orderings of social states. This problem will be touched on again.

In general, then, there will be a difference between the ordering of social states according to the direct consumption of the individual and the ordering when the individual adds his general standards of equity (or perhaps his standards of pecuniary emulation).[10] We may refer to the former ordering as reflecting the *tastes* of the individual and the latter as reflecting his *values*. The distinction between the two is by no means clear-cut. An individual with aesthetic feelings certainly derives pleasure from his neighbor's having a well-tended lawn. Under the system of a free market, such feelings play no direct part in social choice; yet, psychologically, they differ only slightly from the pleasure in one's own lawn. Intuitively, of course, we feel that not all the possible preferences which an individual might have ought to count; his preferences for matters which are "none of his business" should be irrelevant. Without challenging this view, I should like to emphasize that the decision as to which preferences are relevant and which are not is itself a value judgment and cannot be settled on an a priori basis. From a formal point of view, one cannot distinguish between an individual's dislike of having his grounds ruined by factory smoke and his extreme distaste for the existence of heathenism in Central Africa. There are probably not a few individuals in this country who would regard the former feeling as irrelevant for social policy and the latter as relevant, though the majority would probably reverse the judgment. I merely wish to emphasize here that we must look at the entire system of values, including values about values, in seeking for a truly general theory of social welfare.

---

[10] This distinction has been stressed to the author by M. Friedman, University of Chicago.

It is the ordering according to values which takes into account all the desires of the individual, including the highly important socializing desires, and which is primarily relevant for the achievement of a social maximum. The market mechanism, however, takes into account only the ordering according to tastes. This distinction is the analogue, on the side of consumption, of the divergence between social and private costs in production which has been developed by Professor Pigou.[11]

As for notation, let R_i be the ordering relation for alternative social states from the standpoint of individual i. Sometimes, when several different ordering relations are being considered for the same individual, the symbols will be distinguished by adding a superscript. Corresponding to the ordering relation R_i, we have the (strict) preference relation P_i and the indifference relation I_i. If the symbol for the ordering has a prime or second attached (thus, R_i', R_i''), then the corresponding symbols for preference and indifference will have the prime or second attached, respectively.

Similarly, society as a whole will be considered provisionally to have a social ordering relation for alternative social states, which will be designated by R, sometimes with a prime or second. Social preference and indifference will be denoted by P and I, respectively, primes or seconds being attached when they are attached to the relation R, respectively.

Throughout this analysis, it will be assumed that individuals are rational, by which is meant that the ordering relations R_i satisfy Axioms I and II. The problem will be to construct an ordering relation for society as a whole which is also to reflect rational choice making, so that R also will be assumed to satisfy Axioms I and II.

III. THE SOCIAL WELFARE FUNCTION

1. Formal statement of the problem of social choice

I shall largely restate Bergson's formulation of the problem of making welfare judgments[12] in the terminology here adopted. The various arguments of his social welfare function are the components of what I have here termed the " social state," so that essentially he is describing the process of assigning a numerical social utility to each social state, the aim of society then being described by saying it seeks to maximize the social utility or social welfare subject to whatever technological or resource constraints are relevant, or, put otherwise, it chooses the social state yielding the highest possible social welfare within the environment. As with any type of behavior described by maximization, the measurability of social welfare need not be assumed; all that matters is the existence of a social ordering satisfying Axioms I and II. As before, all that is needed to define such an ordering is to know the relative ranking of each pair of alternatives.

---

[11] A. C. Pigou, *The Economics of Welfare* (London: Macmillan & Co., 1920), Part II, chap. vi. For the analogy see Samuelson, *op. cit.*, p. 224; Reder, *op. cit.*, pp. 64–67; G. Tintner, "A Note on Welfare Economics," *Econometrica*, XIV (1946), 69–78.

[12] Bergson,* *op. cit.*

The relative ranking of a fixed pair of alternative social states will vary, in general, with changes in the values of at least some individuals; to assume that the ranking does not change with any changes in individual values is to assume, with traditional social philosophy of the Platonic realist variety, that there exists an objective social good defined independently of individual desires. This social good, it was frequently held, could be best apprehended by the methods of philosophic inquiry. Such a philosophy could be and was used to justify government by elite, secular or religious, although the connection is not a necessary one.

To the nominalist temperament of the modern period the assumption of the existence of the social ideal in some Platonic realm of being was meaningless. The utilitarian philosophy of Jeremy Bentham and his followers sought instead to ground the social good on the good of individuals. The hedonist psychology associated with utilitarian philosophy was further used to imply that each individual's good was identical with his desires. Hence, the social good was in some sense to be a composite of the desires of individuals. A viewpoint of this type serves as a justification of both political democracy and laissez-faire economics or at least an economic system involving free choice of goods by consumers and of occupations by workers.

The hedonist psychology finds its expression here in the assumption that individuals' behavior is expressed by individual ordering relations R_i. Utilitarian philosopy is expressed by saying for each pair of social states that the choice depends on the ordering relations of all individuals, i.e., depends on $R_1, \ldots, R_n$, where n is the number of individuals in the community. Put otherwise, the whole social ordering relation R is to be determined by the individual ordering relations for social states, $R_1, \ldots, R_n$. We do not exclude here the possibility that some or all of the choices between pairs of social states made by society might be independent of the preferences of certain particular individuals, just as a function of several variables might be independent of some of them.

Definition 3: By a "social welfare function" will be meant a process or rule which, for each set of individual orderings $R_1, \ldots, R_n$ for alternative social states (one ordering for each individual), states a corresponding social ordering of alternative social states, R.

As a matter of notation, we shall let R be the social ordering corresponding to the set of individual orderings $R_1, \ldots, R_n$, the correspondence being that established by a given social welfare function; if primes or seconds are added to the symbols for the individual orderings, primes or seconds will be added to the symbol for the corresponding social ordering.

There is some difference between the concept of social welfare function used here and that employed by Bergson. The individual orderings which enter as arguments into the social welfare function as defined here refer to the values of individuals rather than to their tastes. Bergson supposes individual values to be such as to yield a social value judgment leading to a particular

rule for determining the allocation of productive resources and the distribution of leisure and final products in accordance with individual tastes. In
effect, the social welfare function described here is a method of choosing
which social welfare function of the Bergson type will be applicable, though
of course I do not exclude the possibility that the social choice actually
arrived at will not be consistent with the particular value judgments formulated by Bergson. But in the formal aspect the difference between the two
definitions of social welfare function is not too important. In Bergson's
treatment the tastes of individuals (each for his own consumption) are represented by utility functions, i.e., essentially by ordering relations; hence, the
Bergson social welfare function is also a rule for assigning to each set of
individual orderings a social ordering of social states. Further, as already
indicated, no sharp line can be drawn between tastes and values.

A special type of social welfare function would be one which assigns the
same social ordering for every set of individual orderings. In this case, of
course, social choices are completely independent of individual tastes, and
we are back in the Platonic case.

For simplicity of exposition, it will be assumed that the society under
study contains only two individuals and that the total number of alternatives which are conceivable is three. Since the results to be obtained are
negative, the latter restriction is not a real one; if it turns out to be impossible
to construct a social welfare function which will define a social ordering of
three alternatives, it will a fortiori be impossible to define one which will
order more alternatives. The restriction to two individuals may be more
serious; it is conceivable that there may be suitable social welfare functions
which can be defined for three individuals but not for two, for example.
In fact, this is not so, and the results stated in this paper hold for any number
of individuals. However, the proof will be considerably simplified by considering only two.

We shall not ask, in general, that the social welfare function be defined for
every logically possible set of individual orderings. On a priori grounds we
may suppose it known that preferences for alternative social states are formed
only in a limited set of ways, and the social welfare function need only be
defined for individual orderings formed in those ways. For example, we may
suppose (and will later on) that each individual orders social alternatives
according to his own personal consumption under each (the purely individualistic case). Then the social welfare function need be defined only for those
sets of individual orderings which are admissible, in the sense of being consistent with our a priori assumptions about the empirical possibilities.

Condition 1: The social welfare function is defined for every admissible pair of
individual orderings, R_1, R_2.

Condition 1, it should be emphasized, is a restriction on the form of the
social welfare function, since we are requiring that for some sufficiently wide

range of sets of individual orderings, the social welfare function gives rise to a true social ordering.

2. Positive association of social and individual values

Since we are trying to describe social "welfare" and not some sort of "illfare," we must assume that the social welfare function is such that the social ordering responds positively to alterations in individual values or at least not negatively. Hence, we may state the following condition:

Condition 2: If an alternative social state x rises or does not fall in the ordering of each individual without any other change in those orderings and if x was preferred to another alternative y before the change in individual orderings, then x is still preferred to y.

3. The independence of irrelevant alternatives

Just as for a single individual, the choice made by society from any given set of alternatives should be independent of the very existence of alternatives outside the given set. For example, suppose an election system has been devised whereby each individual lists all the candidates in order of his preference, and then, by a preassigned procedure, the winning candidate is derived from these lists. (All actual election procedures are of this type, although in most the entire list is not required for the choice.) Suppose an election is held, with a certain number of candidates in the field, each individual filing his list of preferences, and then one of the candidates dies. Surely, the social choice should be made by taking each of the individual's preference lists, blotting out completely the dead candidate's name, and considering only the orderings of the remaining names in going through the procedure of determining the winner. That is, the choice to be made among the set of surviving candidates should be independent of the preferences of individuals for the nonsurviving candidates. To assume otherwise would be to make the result of the election dependent on the obviously accidental circumstances of whether a candidate died before or after the date of polling. Therefore, we may require of our social welfare function that the choice made by society from a given set of alternatives depend only on the orderings of individuals among those alternatives. Alternatively stated, if we consider two sets of individual orderings such that, for each individual, his ordering of those particular alternatives under consideration is the same each time, then we require that the choice made by society be the same if individual values are given by the first set of orderings as if they are given by the second.

Condition 3: Let R_1, R_2, and R'_1, R'_2 be two sets of individual orderings. If, for both individuals i and for all x and y in a given set of alternatives S, $xR_i y$ if and only if $xR'_i y$, then the social choice made from S is the same whether the individual orderings are R_1, R_2, or R'_1, R'_2. (Independence of irrelevant alternatives.)

The reasonableness of this condition can be seen by consideration of the possible results in a method of choice which does not satisfy Condition 3, the rank-order method of voting frequently used in clubs.[13] With a finite number of candidates, let each individual rank all his candidates, i.e., designate his first-choice candidate, second-choice candidate, etc. Let preassigned weights be given first, second, etc., choices, the higher weight to the higher choice, and then let the candidate with the highest weighted sum of votes be elected. In particular, suppose there are three voters and four candidates, x, y, z, and w. Let the weights for first, second, third, and fourth choices be 4, 3, 2, and 1, respectively. Suppose that individuals 1 and 2 rank the candidates in the order x, y, z, and w, while individual 3 ranks them in the order z, w, x, and y. Under the given electoral system, x is chosen. Then, certainly, if y is deleted from the ranks of the candidates, the system applied to the remaining candidates should yield the same result, especially since, in this case, y is inferior to x according to the tastes of every individual; but, if y is in fact deleted, the indicated electoral system would yield a tie between x and z.

The condition of the independence of irrelevant alternatives implies that in a generalized sense all methods of social choice are of the type of voting. If S is the set consisting of the two alternatives x and y, Condition 3 tells us that the choice between x and y is determined solely by the preferences of the members of the community as between x and y. That is, if we know which members of the community prefer x to y, which are indifferent, and which prefer y to x, then we know that choice the community makes. Knowing the social choices made in pairwise comparisons in turn determines the entire social ordering and therewith the social choice made from any set of alternatives. Condition 2 guarantees that voting for a certain alternative has the usual effect of making surer that that alternative will be adopted.

Condition 1 says, in effect, that, as the set of alternatives varies and individual orderings remain fixed, the different choices made shall bear a certain type of consistent relation to one another. Conditions 2 and 3, on the other hand, suppose a fixed set of alternatives and say that for certain particular types of variation in individual values, the various choices made have a certain type of consistency.

4. The condition of citizens' sovereignty

We certainly wish to assume that the individuals in our society be free to choose, by varying their values, among the alternatives available. That is, we do not wish our social welfare function to be such as to prevent us, by its very definition, from expressing a preference for some given alternative over another.

Definition 4: A social welfare function will be said to be *imposed* if for some pair of distinct alternatives x and y, xRy for any set of individual orderings R_1, R_2, where R is the social ordering corresponding to R_1, R_2.

---

[13] This example was suggested by a discussion with G. E. Forsythe, National Bureau of Standards.

In other words, when the social welfare function is imposed, there is some pair of alternatives x and y such that the community can never express a preference for y over x no matter what the tastes of both individuals are, indeed even if both individuals prefer y to x; some preferences are taboo. (Note that, by Definition 1, asserting that xRy holds for all sets of individual orderings is equivalent to asserting that yPx never holds.) We certainly wish to require of our social welfare function the condition that it not be imposed in the sense of Definition 4; we certainly wish all choices to be possible if unanimously desired by the group.

Condition 4: The social welfare function is not to be imposed.

Condition 4 is stronger than need be for the present argument. Some decisions, as between given pairs of alternatives, may be assumed to be imposed. All that is required really is that there be a set S of three alternatives such that the choice between any pair is not constrained in advance by the social welfare function.

It should also be noted that Condition 4 excludes the Platonic case discussed in section 1 of Part III above. It expresses fully the idea that all social choices are determined by individual desires. In conjunction with Condition 2 (which insures that the determination is in the direction of agreeing with individual desires), Condition 4 expresses the same idea as Professor Bergson's Fundamental Value Propositions of Individual Preference, which state that of two alternatives between which all individuals but one are indifferent, the community will prefer one over the other or be indifferent between the two according as the one individual prefers one over the other or is indifferent between the two.[14] Conditions 2 and 4 together correspond to the usual concept of consumer's sovereignty; since we are here referring to values rather than to tastes, we might refer to them as expressing the idea of citizens' sovereignty.

5. The condition of nondictatorship

A second form of social choice not of a collective character is the choice by dictatorship. In its pure form this means that social choices are to be based solely on the preferences of one man. That is, whenever the dictator prefers x to y, so does society. If the dictator is indifferent between x and y, presumably he will then leave the choice up to some or all of the other members of society.

Definition 5: A social welfare function is said to be "dictatorial" if there exists an individual i such that for all x and y, $xP_i y$ implies xPy regardless of the orderings of all individuals other than i, where P is the social preference relation corresponding to those orderings.

---

[14] Bergson,* *op. cit.*, pp. 318–20. The Fundamental Value Propositions of Individual Preference are not, strictly speaking, implied by Conditions 2 and 4 (in conjunction with Conditions 1 and 2), although something very similar to them is so implied; see Consequence 1 in Part IV, section 2 below. A slightly stronger form of Condition 2 than that stated here would suffice to yield the desired implication.

Since we are interested in the construction of collective methods of social choice, we wish to exclude dictatorial social welfare functions.

Condition 5: The social welfare function is not to be dictatorial (nondictatorship).

We have now imposed five apparently reasonable conditions on the construction of a social welfare function. These conditions are of course value judgments and could be called into question; taken together, they express the doctrines of citizens' sovereignty and rationality in a very general form, with the citizens being allowed to have a wide range of values. The question is that of constructing a social ordering of all conceivable alternative social states from any given set of individual orderings of those social states, the method of construction being in accordance with the value judgments of citizens' sovereignty and rationality as expressed in Conditions 1–5.

IV. THE POSSIBILITY THEOREM FOR SOCIAL WELFARE FUNCTIONS

1. The range of possible individual orderings

For simplicity we shall impose on the individual preference scales two conditions which in fact have almost invariably been assumed in works on welfare economics: (1) Each individual's comparison of two alternative social states depends only on the commodities that he receives (and labor that he expends) in the two states, i.e., he is indifferent as between any two social states in which his own consumption-leisure-saving situations are the same or at least indifferent to him; (2) in comparing two personal situations in one of which he receives at least as much of each commodity (including leisure and saving as commodities) and more of at least one commodity than in the other, the individual will prefer the first situation. Suppose that among the possible alternatives there were three, none of which gave any individual at least as much of both commodities as any other. For example, suppose that there are two individuals and a total of ten units of each of two commodities. Consider three alternative distributions described by the accompanying tabulation. The individualistic restrictions imposed do not tell us anything about

Alternative	Individual 1		Individual 2	
	Commodity 1	Commodity 2	Commodity 1	Commodity 2
1..........	5	1	5	9
2..........	4	2	6	8
3..........	3	3	7	7

the way either individual orders these alternatives. Under the individualistic assumptions there is no a priori reason to suppose that the two individuals will not order the alternatives in any given way. In the sense of Part III, section 1, above, all individual orderings of the three alternatives are admissible. Condition 1 therefore requires that the social welfare function be defined for all pairs of individual orderings, R_1, R_2.

2. The possibility theorem

Some consequences will be drawn from Conditions 1–5 for the present case of a social welfare function for two individuals and three alternatives. It will be shown that the supposition that there is a social welfare function satisfying those conditions leads to a contradiction.

Let x, y, and z be the three alternatives among which choice is to be made, e.g., three possible distributions of commodities. Let x' and y' be variable symbols which represent possible alternatives, i.e., range over the values x, y, z. Let the individuals be designated as 1 and 2, and let R_1 and R_2 be the orderings by 1 and 2, respectively, of the alternatives x, y, z. Let P_1 and P_2 be the corresponding preference relations; e.g., $x'P_1y'$ means that individual 1 strictly prefers x' to y'.

Consequence 1: If $x'P_1y'$ and $x'P_2y'$, then $x'Py'$.

I.e., if both prefer x' to y', then society must prefer x' to y'.
Proof. By Condition 4 there are orderings R_1' and R_2', for individuals 1 and 2, respectively, such that, in the corresponding social preference, $x'P'y'$. Form R_1'' from R_1' by raising x', if need be, to the top, while leaving the relative positions of the other two alternatives alone; form R_2'' from R_2' in the same way. Since all we have done is raise alternative x' in everyone's esteem, while leaving the others alone, x' should still be preferred to y' by society in accordance with Condition 2, so that $x'P''y'$. But, by construction, both individuals prefer x' to y' in the orderings R_1'', R_2'', and society prefers x' to y'. Since, by Condition 3, the social choice between x' and y' depends only on the individual orderings of those two alternatives, it follows that whenever both individuals prefer x' to y', regardless of the rank of the third alternative, society will prefer x' to y', which is the statement to be proved.

Consequence 2: Suppose that for some x' and y', whenever $x'P_1y'$ and $y'P_2x'$, $x'Py'$. Then, for that x' and y', whenever $x'P_1y'$, $x'Py'$.

I.e., if in a given choice, the will of individual 1 prevails against the opposition of 2, then individual 1's views will certainly prevail if 2 is indifferent or if he agrees with 1.
Proof. Let R_1 be an ordering in which $x'P_1y'$, R_2 be any ordering. Let R_1' be the same ordering as R_1, while R_2' is derived from R_2 by depressing x' to the bottom while leaving the relative positions of the other two alternatives unchanged. By construction, $x'P_1y'$, $y'P_2x'$. By hypothesis, $x'P'y'$, where P' is the social preference relation derived from the individual orderings R_1', R_2'. Now the only difference between R_1', R_2' and R_1, R_2 is that x' is raised in the scale of individual 2 in the latter as compared with the former. Hence,

by Condition 2 (interchanging the R's and the R_i's) it follows from $x'P'y'$ that $x'Py'$. I.e., whenever R_1, R_2 are such that $x'P_iy'$, then $x'Py'$.

Consequence 3: If $x'P_1y'$ and $y'P_2x'$, then $x'Iy'$.

I.e., if the two individuals have exactly opposing interests on the choice between two given alternatives, then society will be indifferent between the alternatives.

Proof. Suppose the consequence is false. Then, for some orderings R_1 and R_2 and for some pair of alternatives x' and y', we would have $x'P_1y'$, $y'P_2x'$, but not $x'Iy'$. In that case, either $x'Py'$ or $y'Px'$. We will suppose $x'Py'$ and show that this supposition leads to a contradiction; the same reasoning would show that the assumption $y'Px'$ also leads to a contradiction.

Without loss of generality it can be assumed that x' is the alternative x, $y' = y$. Then we have, for the particular orderings in question, xP_1y, yP_2x, and xPy. Since the social choice between x and y depends, by Condition 3, only on the individual choices as between x and y, we must have

$$\text{Whenever } xP_1y \text{ and } yP_2x, xPy. \tag{1}$$

It will be shown that (1) leads to a contradiction.

Suppose individual 1 prefers x to y and y to z, while individual 2 prefers y to z and z to x. Individual 2 then prefers y to x. By (1) society prefers x to y. Also, both prefer y to z; by Consequence 1, society prefers y to z. Since society prefers x to y and y to z, it must prefer x to z. Therefore, we have exhibited orderings R_1, R_2 such that xP_1z, zP_2x, but xPz. Since the social choice between x and z depends only on the individual preferences for x and z,

$$\text{Whenever } xP_1z \text{ and } zP_2x, xPz. \tag{2}$$

Now suppose R_1 is the ordering y, x, z, and R_2 the ordering z, y, x. By Consequence 1, yPx; by (2) xPz, so that yPz. By the same reasoning as before,

$$\text{Whenever } yP_1z \text{ and } zP_2y, yPz. \tag{3}$$

If R_1 is the ordering y, z, x, and R_2 the ordering z, x, y, it follows from Consequence 1 and (3) that zPx and yPz, so that yPx. Hence,

$$\text{Whenever } yP_1x \text{ and } xP_2y, yPx. \tag{4}$$

If R_1 is the ordering z, y, x, and R_2 the ordering x, z, y, then from Consequence 1 and (4), zPy and yPx, so that zPx.

$$\text{Whenever } zP_1x \text{ and } xP_2z, zPx. \tag{5}$$

If R_1 is the ordering z, x, y, and R_2 x, y, z, then, using (5), zPx and xPy, so that zPy.

$$\text{Whenever } zP_1y \text{ and } yP_2z, zPy. \tag{6}$$

From (1) it follows from Consequence 2 that whenever xP_1y, xPy. Similarly, from (1) to (6) it follows that for any pair of alternatives x', y', whenever $x'P_1y'$, then $x'Py'$. That is, by Definition 5, individual 1 would be a dictator. This is prohibited by Condition 5, so (1) must be false. Therefore, Consequence 3 is proved.

Now suppose individual 1 has the ordering x, y, z, while individual 2 has the ordering z, x, y. By Consequence 1,

$$xPy. \tag{7}$$

Since yP_1z, zP_2y, it follows from Consequence 3 that

$$yIz. \tag{8}$$

From (7) and (8), xPz. But, also xP_1z, zP_2x, which implies xIz by Consequence 3. It cannot be that x is both preferred and indifferent to z. Hence the assumption that there is a social welfare function compatible with Conditions 1–5 has led to a contradiction.

Put another way, if we assume that our social welfare function, satisfies Conditions 2–3 and we further suppose that Condition 1 holds, then either Condition 4 or Condition 5 must be violated. Condition 4 states that the social welfare function is not imposed; Condition 5 states that it is not dictatorial.

Possibility theorem. If there are at least three alternatives among which the members of the society are free to order in any way, then every social welfare function satisfying Conditions 2 and 3 and yielding a social ordering satisfying Axioms I and II must be either imposed or dictatorial.[15] The Possibility Theorem shows that, if no prior assumptions are made about the nature of individual orderings, there is no method of voting which will remove the paradox of voting discussed in Part I, neither plurality voting nor any scheme of proportional representation, no matter how complicated. Similarly, the market mechanism does not create a rational social choice.

V. SOME IMPLICATIONS FOR THE FORMATION OF SOCIAL WELFARE JUDGMENTS

1. Interpretation of the possibility theorem

The interpretation of the Possibility Theorem is given by examination of the meaning of Conditions 1–5. In particular, it is required that the social ordering be formed from individual orderings and that the social decision between two alternatives be independent of the desires of individuals involving any alternatives other than the given two (Conditions 1 and 3). These conditions taken together serve to exclude interpersonal comparison of social utility either by some form of direct measurement or by comparison with other alternative social states. Therefore, the Possibility Theorem can be restated as follows:

---

[15] The negative outcome expressed in this theorem is strongly reminiscent of the intransivity of the concept of domination in the theory of multiperson games; see John von Neumann and Oskar Morgenstern, *Theory of Games and Economic Behavior* (2d ed.; Princeton University Press, 1947), pp. 38–39.

If we exclude the possibility of interpersonal comparisons of utility, then the only methods of passing from individual tastes to social preferences which will be satisfactory and which will be defined for a wide range of sets of individual orderings are either imposed or dictatorial.

The word "satisfactory" in the foregoing statement means that the social welfare function does not reflect individuals' desires negatively (Condition 2) and that the resultant social tastes shall be represented by an ordering having the usual properties of rationality ascribed to individual orderings (Condition 1 and Axioms I and II).

In view of the interpretations placed on the conditions for a social welfare function in Part III above, we can also phrase the result this way: If consumers' values can be represented by a wide range of individual orderings, the doctrine of voters' sovereignty is incompatible with that of collective rationality.

If we wish to make social welfare judgments which depend on all individual values, i.e., are not imposed or dictatorial, then we must relax some of the conditions imposed. It will continue to be maintained that there is no meaningful interpersonal comparison of utilities and that the conditions wrapped up in the word "satisfactory" are to be accepted.[16]. The only condition that remains to be eliminated is the one stating that the method of forming a social ordering would work properly for a wide range of sets of individual orderings. That is, it must be supposed that it is known in advance that the individual orderings $R_1, \ldots, R_n$ for social actions satisfy certain conditions more restrictive than those hitherto introduced.

2. A reflection on the new welfare economics

As noted in Part I, the so-called new welfare economics has concentrated on the determination of the totality of social states which have the property that any change which benefits one individual injures another, "maximal states" in Lange's terminology. In particular, this problem has usually been analyzed under the assumption that individual desires for social alternatives are formed in the individualistic way described above in Part IV, Section 1. But if the only restrictions that we wish to impose on individual tastes are those implied by the individualistic assumptions, then, as we have seen, there is no satisfactory social welfare function possible when there is more than one commodity. Since, as we have seen, the only purpose of the determination of the maximal states is as a preliminary to the study of social welfare functions, the customary study of maximal states under individualistic assumptions is pointless. There is, however, a qualification which should be added. It is conceivable that, if further restrictions are added to the individualistic ones, a social welfare function will be possible. Any state which is maximal under

---

[16] The only part of the last-named conditions that seems to me to be at all in dispute is the assumption of rationality. The consequences of dropping this assumption are so radical that it seems worth while to explore the consequences of maintaining it.

the combination of individualistic and other restrictions will certainly be maximal if only individualistic restrictions are imposed on the individual orderings. Hence, if the proper handling of the social welfare problem is deemed to be the imposition of further restrictions in addition to the individualistic ones, then the social maximum in any given situation will be of one the maximal elements under the combined restrictions and hence one of the maximal elements under individualistic conditions. It is therefore not excluded that the current new welfare economics will be of some use in restricting the range in which we must look for the social maximum.

The failure of purely individualistic assumptions to lead to a well-defined social welfare function means, in effect, that there must be a divergence between social and private benefits if we are to be able to discuss a social optimum. Part of each individual's value system must be a scheme of socio-ethical norms, the realization of which cannot, by their nature, be achieved through atomistic market behavior. These norms, further, must be sufficiently similar among the members of the society to avoid the difficulties outlined above.

3. A one-commodity world

The insufficiency of the individualistic hypotheses to permit the formation of a social welfare function, as developed in the previous sections, hinged on the assumption that there was more than one commodity involved. An investigation of the one-commodity case may be of interest to bring out more clearly the issues involved.

In a one-commodity world, if we make assumptions 1 and 2 of Part IV, Section 1, there is for any given individual only one possible ordering of the social states. He orders various social states solely according to the amount of the one commodity he gets under each. In such a situation the individual orderings are not variables; Conditions 2, 3, and 4 become irrelevant since they relate to the variation in the social ordering corresponding to certain specified types of changes in the individual orderings. Condition 5 (nondictatorship) becomes a much weaker restriction, though not completely irrelevant. Any specification of a social ordering which does not coincide completely with the ordering of any one individual will be a social welfare function compatible with all the conditions. For example, for each fixed total output, we might set up arbitrarily an ordering of the various distributions, then order any two social states with different total outputs in accordance with the total output, any two social states with the same total output according to the arbitrary ordering. This sets up a genuine weak ordering which does not coincide with the ordering of any one individual. For let x and y be two states with total outputs s and t, respectively, and apportionments s' snd t', respectively, to the given individual. If $s > t$, but $s' < t'$, then society prefers x to y, while the individual prefers y to x.

The qualitative nature of the difference between the single- and multi-commodity cases makes any welfare arguments based on an implicit assumption of a single commodity dubious in its applicability to real situations. The fundamental difficulty is that, in a world of more than one commodity, there is no unequivocal meaning to comparing total production in any two social states save in terms of some standard of value to make the different commodities commensurable; and usually such a standard of value must depend on the distribution of income. In other words, there is no meaning to total output independent of distribution, i.e., of ethical judgments.

4. Distributional ethics combined with individualism

We may examine briefly a set of assumptions about individual values which seem to be common to those who feel that the new welfare economics is applicable in a fairly direct way to the solution of specific economic problems. It is assumed that there are (1) an accepted (let us say, unanimously accepted) value judgment that if everybody is better off (more precisely, if everybody is at least as well off and one person better off) in one social state than another *according to his tastes*, then the first social state is preferred to the second; and (2) a universally accepted ordering of different possible welfare distributions in any given situation. The latter value judgment usually takes an egalitarian form.

This ethical schema is quite explicit in the work of Bergson; the second value judgment is contained in his Propositions of Relative Shares.[17] The same set of ethics underlies the compensation principle of Professors Kaldor and Hicks. More recently, some proposals made by Professors Johnson and Modigliani for meeting the problem of the increased cost of food due to European demand seem to have been based on value judgments 1 and 2 above.[18] To prevent the inequitable shift in real income to farmers, it was proposed that there should be imposed an excise tax on food, accompanied by a per capita subsidy to consumers. Under the assumption that the supply of agricultural goods is completely inelastic, the tax would be absorbed by the farmers while the subsidy would have no substitution effects at the margin, so the marginal rate of substitution for any pair of commodities would be the same for all consumers and hence the first value judgment would be fulfilled. The taxes and subsidies perform a purely distributive function and can be so arranged as to restore the status quo ante as near as may be, though actually the payment of a per capita subsidy implies a certain equalizing effect.

The value judgments are assumed here to hold for any individual. Note that even to state these judgments we must distinguish sharply between values and tastes (see Part II, Section 2). All individuals are assumed to have the same values at any given instant of time, but the values held by any one individual will vary with variations in the tastes of all. Our previous argu-

---

[17] Bergson, *op. cit.*

[18] D. G. Johnson, "The High Cost of Food—a Suggested Solution," *Journal of Political Economy*, LVI (1948), 54–57; Modigliani's proposals are contained in a press release of the Institute of World Affairs, New York, October, 1948.

ments as to the nonexistence of social welfare functions were based on the diversity of values; do they carry over to this particular kind of unanimity?

The actual distribution of welfare dictated by the second value judgment cannot be stated simply in money terms. As Professor Samuelson points out, such a value judgment is not consistent with any well-defined social ordering of alternative social states.[19] The distribution of real income, for a given environment, must vary with individual tastes. Thus, for a given set of individual tastes (as represented by the ordering relations of all individuals, each for his own consumption) and a given environment, there is a given distribution of purchasing power (somehow defined); then exchange under perfectly competitive conditions proceeds until an optimum distribution is reached. The given distribution of real income and the individual tastes uniquely determine the final outcome, which is a social state. Therefore, the given ethical system is a rule which selects a social state as the choice from a given collection of alternative distributions of goods as a function of the tastes of all individuals. If, for a given set of tastes, the range of social alternatives varies, we expect that the choices will be consistent in the sense that the choice function is derivable from a social weak ordering of all social states. Thus, the ethical scheme discussed in this section, which we may term the "Bergson social welfare function," has the form of a rule assigning a social ordering to each possible set of individual orderings representing tastes. Mathematically, the Bergson social welfare function has, then, the same form as the social welfare function we have already discussed; though, of course, the interpretation is somewhat different, in that the individual orderings represent tastes rather than values and that the whole function is the end product of certain values assumed to be unanimously held rather than a method of reconciling divergent value systems. If the range of tastes is not restricted by a priori considerations (except that they must be truly tastes, i.e., refer only to an individual's own consumption, however that may be defined), then, indeed, the Bergson social welfare function is mathematically ismorphic to the social welfare function under individualistic assumptions. Hence the Possibility Theorem is applicable here; we cannot construct a Bergson social welfare function, i.e., cannot satisfy value judgments 1 and 2, which will satisfy Conditions 2–5 and which will yield a true social ordering for every set of individual tastes. Essentially, the two value judgments amount to erecting individualistic behavior into a value judgment. It is not surprising, then, that such ethics can be no more successful than the actual practice of individualism in permitting the formation of social welfare judgments.

It must of course be recognized that the meaning of Conditions 2–5 has changed. The previous arguments for their validity assumed that the individual orderings represented values rather than tastes. It seems obvious that Conditions 2, 4, and 5 have the same intrinsic desirability under either interpretation. Condition 3 is perhaps more doubtful. Suppose there are just two

---

[19] Samuelson, *op. cit.*, p. 225.

commodities, bread and wine. A distribution, deemed equitable by all, is arranged, with the wine lovers getting more wine and less bread than the abstainers get. Suppose now that all the wine is destroyed. Are the wine lovers entitled, because of that fact, to more than an equal share of bread? The answer is, of course, a value judgment. My own feeling is that tastes for unattainable alternatives should have nothing to do with the decision among the attainable ones; desires in conflict with reality are not entitled to consideration, so Condition 3, reinterpreted in terms of tastes rather than of values, is a valid value judgment, to me at least.

Problems of majority voting*

GORDON TULLOCK

Economists have devoted a great deal of thought to problems of governmental policy and, in particular, to the question of proper allocation of resources between the public and private sectors.[1] On the other hand, little attention has been given to the actual process of decision-making or to the type of policy likely to come out of the process.[2] It is the purpose of this article to discuss one particular method of making governmental decisions—majority voting—and to attempt to derive conclusions about it implications for resource allocation and government policy. It is hoped that the conclusions will be more realistic than current doctrine, which is based on an essentially economic view of what " ought " to happen.

Since it is impossible to talk about everything at once, the demonstration will be confined to certain features of the majority process. A number of other serious problems raised by the voting system will be disregarded. The most important of these concerns a series of difficulties and paradoxes in the voting process itself.[3] I will also disregard the fact that voters are frequently very poorly informed or even deceived in voting, the great oversimplification of issues necessary in order to reduce them to a form such that they can be determined by vote, and innumerable other possible limitations on the functional efficiency of the democratic process.

I shall consider the operation of majority rule under two different restrictions: logrolling (i.e., vote-trading) permitted and logrolling not permitted, starting with the latter. Since logrolling is the norm, discussion of the non-logrolling case must start with consideration of the institutional structure which eliminates logrolling. The standard referendum on a simple issue is the

---

* *The Journal of Political Economy*, 67(1959): pp. 571–79. Reprinted by courtesy of the author and *The Journal of Political Economy*.
[1] See Julius Margolis, "The Economic Evaluation of Federal Water Resource Development," *American Economic Review*, XLIX (March, 1959), 69–111, for a review of some of the recent literature on the subject.

[2] Pioneers have begun to appear. See Anthony Downs, *An Economic Theory of Democracy* (New York: Harper & Bros, 1957), and Duncan Black, *The Theory of Committees and Elections* (Cambridge: Cambridge University Press, 1958).

[3] See Black (*op. cit.*) for a comprehensive view of the difficulties discovered to date.

best example. The voter cannot trade his vote on one issue for votes on others because he and his acquaintances represent too small a part of the total electorate for this to be worth the effort involved. Further, the use of the secret ballot makes it impossible to tell whether voting promises are carried out. In these circumstances the voter will simply vote in accord with his preferences on each individual issue.

The contrary case, logrolling permitted, occurs under two circumstances. First, it occurs where a rather small body of voters vote openly on each measure; this is normally to be found in representative assemblies, but it may also be found in very small "direct democracy" units. Under these circumstances, trades of votes are easy to arrange and observe and significantly affect the outcome. It is probable that this fact is one of the major reasons for the widespread use of representative democracy. The second type of logrolling, which may be called implicit logrolling, occurs when large bodies of voters are called on to decide complex issues, such as which party shall rule, or a complex set of issues presented as a unit for a referendum vote. Here there is no formal trading of votes, but an analogous process goes on. The "entrepreneurs" who offer candidates or programs to the voter make up a complex mix of policies to attract support.[4] In doing so, they keep firmly in mind the fact that the voter may be so interested in the outcome of some issue that he will vote for the party which supports it, although the party opposes him on other issues. This implicit logrolling will not be discussed further.

In the system in which logrolling is not permitted every voter simply indicates his preference, and the preference of the majority of the voters is carried out. The defect, and it is a serious one, of this procedure is that it ignores the various intensities of the desires of the voters. A man who is passionately opposed to a given measure and a man who does not much care but is slightly in favor of it are weighted equally. Obviously, both could very easily be made better off if the man who felt strongly were permitted to give a present to the man who had little preference in return for a reversal of his decision. The satisfaction of both would be improved, and the resulting situation would, on strictly Paretian grounds, be superior to the outcome of voting that weighed their votes equally. By way of illustration it is conceivable that a proposal to send all Negroes to Africa (or all Jews to Israel) would be passed by referendum. It would have not the slightest chance of passing Congress because the supporters of these two minorities would be willing to promise to support almost any other measure in return for votes against such a bill. In the absence of vote-trading, the support for it might reach 51 percent, but it would not be intense, at least in the marginal cases, and hence the trading process would insure its defeat.

Even voters who are more or less indifferent to a given issue may find their votes on it counting as much as those of the most highly concerned indivi-

---

[4] This problem is discussed in a paper presented by Julius Margolis before the Conference on Public Finances: Needs, Sources, and Utilization, of the Universities–National Bureau of Economic Research Committee, held April 10 and 11, 1959, at Charlottesville, Virginia.

duals. The fact that a voter votes normally proves that he is not completely indifferent, but many voters are motivated to vote on referendum issues more by a sense of duty to vote than by any real concern with the matter at hand. Under these circumstances even the tiniest preference for one side or the other may determine the issue. Permitting the citizens who feel very strongly about an issue to compensate those whose opinion is only feebly held can result in a great increase of the well-being of both groups, and prohibiting such transactions is to prohibit a movement toward the optimum surface.

Note that the result under logrolling and under nonlogrolling differs only if the minority feels more intensely about the issue than the majority; if the feeling of the majority is equal to or more intense than the minority, then the majority would prevail both with and without logrolling. It is only when the intensity of feeling of the minority is enough greater than that of the majority so that they are willing to make sacrifices in other areas sufficient to detach the marginal voters from the majority (intense members of the majority might make counteroffers if they wished) that the logrolling process will change the outcome.

As an introduction to logrolling, let us consider a simple model. A township inhabited by one hundred farmers who have more or less similar farms is cut by a number of main roads maintained by the state. However, these roads are limited-access roads, and the farmers are permitted to enter the primary network only at points where local roads intersect it. The local roads are built and maintained by the township. Maintenance is simple. Any farmer who wishes to have a specific road repaired puts the issue up to vote. If the repairing is approved, the cost is assessed to the farmers as part of the real property tax. The principal use of the local roads by the farmers is to get to and from the major state roads. Since these major roads cut through the district, generally there are only four or five farmers dependent on any particular bit of local road to reach the major roads.

Under these circumstances the referendum system would result in no local roads being repaired, since an overwhelming majority would vote against repairing any given road. The logrolling system, however, permits the roads to be kept in repair through bargains among voters. The bargaining might take a number of forms, but most of these would be unstable, and the "equilibrium" involves overinvestment of resources.

One form that the implicit bargain among the farmers might take is this: each individual might decide, in his own mind, the general standard that should be maintained. That is, he would balance, according to his own schedule of preferences, the costs of maintaining his own road at various levels of repair with the benefits to be received from it and reach a decision as to the point where the margins were equal. He could then generalize this decision: he could vote on each proposal to repair a given road in the same way as he would vote for repairs on his own road. If every voter followed this rule, we would find a schedule of voting behavior such as that illustrated in Figure 1. Each mark on the horizontal line represents the standard of one voter for maintenance of all roads. If a proposal for repairing a given road falls to the left of his position, he would vote for it; if it falls to his right, against. If each road has at least one farmer whose preference for road repairs falls to the right of the median (*A* in Figure 1) then a proposal for repairs would be made

Figure 1

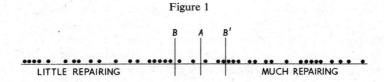

as soon as a given road fell below his preferred degree of repair and successive further such proposals as the road gradually deteriorated. When it reached the median level, a repair proposal would pass; hence all roads would be repaired at the median preference.

Although this result would not be a Paretian optimum, it would be possible to argue for it in ethical terms. In fact, I believe that this is the result that most proponents of democracy in such situations have in the back of their minds. In any event, I intend to use this result, which I shall call "Kantian" as the "correct" result with which I shall contrast what actually happens. Since my Kantian result differs from the "equal marginal cost and marginal benefit" system used by most economists in this field, it is incumbent on me to explain why I use it. The reason is simple—it is the best I can do. I have been unable to find any system of voting which would lead to a social matching of costs and benefits at the margin.

If the farmers generally followed this policy in voting, then any individual farmer could benefit himself simply by voting against all proposals to repair roads other than his own and voting for proposals to repair his road at every opportunity. This would shift the median of the schedules slightly so that his taxes would be reduced or his road kept in better-than-average repair. If the other farmers on his road followed his example (we shall call farmers who follow this rule "maximizers"), they would be able to shift the standards of repair so that the roads on which they lived would be repaired at level *B'* while reducing the standard of repair on other roads to *B*. Since the largest share of the cost of keeping their road up falls on other taxpayers, while the largest share of their taxes goes for the repair of other roads, this change would be greatly to the advantage of the maximizers and greatly to the disadvantage of the Kantians.

If the farmers along another road also switched to a maximizing pattern, this would bring the level of road-repairing on the two maximizing roads down toward about that which would prevail under the Kantian system, while still further lowering the standards on the Kantian roads. However, it is likely that the two groups of maximizers could benefit by forming a coalition in order to raise the standards of road maintenance on their own roads. Let us consider the situation of an individual maximizer debating whether or not to enter such a coalition. Since he will pay only about 1/100th of the cost, practically any proposal to repair his own road is to his benefit. If, however, in order to obtain support for some repair project on his own road, he must also vote for the repair of another road, then he must also count the cost to him of this other repair project as part of the cost of his own road. In weighing the costs and benefits, he must consider not only the tax cost to himself of the repair of his own road but the tax cost of the other repair job which he must vote for in order to get his road done. In the particular case we are now discussing, when the farmers on all the roads except two are still Kantian, this would put few restraints on feasible projects, but it would still have to be considered. However, as more and more Kantians become tired of being exploited by the maximizers and switch to a maximizing pattern of behavior, this consideration would become more and more important.

Let us now examine a rather unlikely, but theoretically important, special case. Suppose that exactly 51 of our 100 farmers were maximizers, while 49 were Kantians. Further suppose that all the maximizers lived on some roads while all the Kantians lived on others. Under these circumstances the Kantians clearly would never get their roads repaired, but the level of repair on the maximizers' roads presents a more difficult problem. In order to simplify it, let us assume (plausibly) that they are maintained on a high enough level so that all the Kantians vote against any project for further repair. Under these circumstances it would be necessary to obtain the votes of all the maximizers for each repair project. A farmer considering when he wants to have his road repaired must consider the whole cost, including the taxes he must pay in order to repair the roads of the other parties to the bargain. He can, however, simply compare his own marginal benefits and costs, and this requires no knowledge of anyone else's utility. He need only decide whether the total bargain is to his advantage or not.[5]

Note, however, that, while no roads leading to the Kantian farmers' houses will be repaired, they are required to contribute to the repair of the roads leading to the houses of the maximizers. Thus part of the cost of the road-repair projects will be paid by persons not party to the bargain, and, since the maximizers only count the costs to themselves of their votes, the general standard of road maintenance on the roads on which they live should be higher than if they had to count also the cost of maintaining the roads on which the Kantians lived. Under such conditions, where virtue so conspicuously is not paying, it seems likely that at least some of the Kantian farmers would decide to switch to a minimizing policy. For simplicity, let us assume that all of them do this at once. Since they would still be in a minority, their change of policy would not immediately benefit them, but surely they could

---

[5] In practice the problem of getting the unanimous agreement of 51 persons might be insoluble. Since we are now only discussing a rather unlikely special case, we can ignore the point. Alternatively, the reader can assume that there are 53 or 54 maximizers, and those who set their terms too high can simply be left out.

find two of the original maximizers who would, in return for very good maintenance, desert their former colleagues. It is again obvious that the new majority would be susceptible to similar desertions; a permanent coalition of 51 farmers for the purpose of exploiting the remaining 49 could thus not be maintained. In terms of game theory any combination of 51 voters dominates any other size of combination, but no combination of 51 dominates all other combinations of 51.[6]

The outcome is clear. Each farmer would enter into bilateral agreements with enough farmers on other roads to insure that his own was repaired. He would then be forced to count as part of the cost of getting his road repaired the cost (to him) of repairing the roads of the other 50 farmers. These bilateral agreements, however, would overlap. Farmer A (more precisely the farmers on road A) would bargain with Farmers B, ..., M. Farmer M, on the other hand, might make up his majority from Farmer A and Farmers N, ..., Z.

Counting the cost to himself of the maintenance of his road in terms of support for other road-repair projects, each farmer would consider only those projects for which he voted. Thus his expenditure pattern would count the tax payments of 49 voters as a free gift. The natural result would be that each road would be maintained at a level considerably higher and at greater expense than is rational from the standpoint of the farmers living along it. Each individual behaves rationally, but the outcome is irrational. This apparent paradox may be explained as follows: each voter pays enough in support for repair of other roads to equalize the benefit he receives from the repair of his own road. But his payments counted under this system include only part of the road repair jobs undertaken.[7] There are others which are the result of bargains to which he is not a party. Taken as a group, the road-repair projects for which he votes represent a good bargain for him, but other *ad hoc* bargains to repair other roads will also take place. He will vote against these, but, as he will be in the minority, he will have to pay for them. The result is a sizable loss to him.

Any farmer following any other course of action will be even worse off. A Kantian farmer, for example, would never have his own road repaired but would pay heavy taxes for the support of repair jobs on other roads. The whole process will proceed through elaborate negotiations; the man who is the most effective bargainer will have a considerable advantage, but the general pattern will be less than optimal for all parties.

This seems a rather unsatisfactory result, and we should consider whether they are not ways of improving it. First, however, I should like to discuss

---

[6] In the "Theory of the Reluctant Duelist" (*American Economic Review*, XLVI [December, 1956], 909–23) Daniel Ellsberg contends that game theory really only applies to "reluctant" players. Our case is a particularly pure example. The voter must "play the game" by entering into bargains with 50 of his fellows, even though this leads to rather unsatisfactory results, simply because any other course of action is even worse.

[7] The fact that he is taxed for other roads not part of his bargain reduces his real income and hence, to some extent, reduces the amount of road repairing he would wish to consume.

certain possible objections to my reasoning.[8] It may be said that the maximizers are behaving wickedly and that ethical considerations will prevent the majority of the population from following such a course. Ethical systems vary greatly from culture to culture, and I do not wish to rule out the possible existence somewhere of an ethical system which could bar logrolling, but surely the American system does not. Under our system logrolling is normally publicly characterized as "bad," but no real stigma attaches to those who practice it. The press describes such deals without any apparent disapproval, and, in fact, all our political organizations bargain in this fashion.

A second argument asserts that each farmer in our community would realize that, if he adopted a maximizing policy, this would lead all other farmers to do the same. Since the "maximizing equilibrium" is worse for all[9] the farmers than the "Kantian median," each farmer would, on the basis of cold selfish calculation, follow the Kantian system. This argument is similar to the view that no union will force its wage rate up because each union realizes that such action will lead other unions to do the same, the eventual outcome being higher prices and wage rates but no increase in real income. There seems to be overwhelming empirical evidence that men do not act this way; in addition, the argument contains a logical flaw. This is the observation that, in any series of actions by a number of men, there must be a first one. If this can be prevented, then the whole series can be prevented. This is true, of course, but there also must be a second, a third, etc. If any one of these is prevented, then the whole series cannot be carried out. If all our 100 farmers would refrain from a maximizing course of action because each one felt that his personal adoption of such a course would lead to a switch to the "maximizing equilibrium," then, if one of them had done so, we could construct an exactly similar argument "proving" that no 1 of the 99 remaining farmers would follow his example. But if this second argument is true, then the first is false; and hence the chain of reasoning contains an inconsistency.

I turn now to possible methods of improving the results. Could the members of a community somehow enter into an enforceable bargain under which they act according to the Kantian model? In the very narrow special case of our model, it is at least conceivable that they could. It is possible that a clear, unambiguous formula for telling when a road needed repair might be agreed upon, and then the exact figures to be inserted in the formula determined by general voting. Probably even in our case this would not be practical, but the theoretical possibility must be admitted.

In the more general and realistic case where governmental units deal with a continuing stream of radically different projects, no such agreed formula

---

[8] James Buchanan kindly permitted me to present this paper before his graduate seminar in public finance, and the objections made by some of the students tended to follow these lines.

[9] Not necessarily for all. There might well be one or more farmers whose personal preference schedules called for a large enough investment in roads so that the "maximizing equilibrium" was preferable to the "Kantian median."

would be possible. A formula which would permit weighing such diverse programs as building giant irrigation projects in the West to increase farm production, paying large sums of money to farmers in the Midwest to reduce farm production, giving increased aid to Israel, and dredging Baltimore's harbor is inconceivable. There could not, therefore, be any agreement on an automatic system of allocating resources, and this throws us back to making individual decisions with the use of logrolling.

This is by no means a tragedy. If it were possible to set up some system by present voting to determine future resource allocation, it is more likely that this determination would take a form favored by a simple majority of the voters than a form favored by the whole group unanimously. This is likely to result in a worse decision than that resulting from logrolling. The problem of intensity must also be considered. The Kantian system makes no allowance for the differential intensities of the voters' preferences. If the voters who wanted more resources spent on road-repairing felt more intensely about it than the voters who wanted less, then the Kantian system would not result in an optimum distribution of resources. Permitting logrolling would take care of this problem.

Requiring more than a simple majority would reduce the resources spent on roads, since more people would have to be included in each bargain, and the cost to each voter of repair to this road would consequently be increased. The larger the majority required, the more closely would the result approach a Pareto optimum. Practically, however, the difficulty of negotiating a bargain would increase exponentially as the number of required parties increased, and this might make such a solution impossible. The provision in so many constitutions for a two-house legislature, each house elected according to a different system, raises much the same issues.

Our next problem is to inquire to what extent the results obtained in our simple model can be generalized. It would appear that any governmental activity which benefits a given individual or group of voters and which is paid for from general taxation could be fitted into our model. It is not necessary that the revenues used to pay for the projects be collected equally from all voters. All that is necessary is that the benefits be significantly more concentrated than the costs. This is a very weak restraint, and a very large number of budgetary patterns would fit it. If the taxes were collected by some indirect method so that individuals could not tell just how much they were paying for any given project, then this fact would accentuate the process. In the marginal case the individual might be indifferent about projects benefiting other people whose cost to him was slight and difficult to calculate.

One requirement of the process has not yet been emphasized. It is necessary that the voting on the various projects be a continuing process. A number of different projects or groups of projects must be voted on at different times. If all projects were inserted in a single bill to be accepted or rejected for all time, then 51 percent of the voters could fix the bill permanently to exploit the remainder. In fact, of course, since government is a continuing process, our condition is fulfilled.

The process which we have been discussing can be generalized to cover other types of government activity. We shall start by generalizing it to cover other types of taxation-expenditure problems and then turn to other types of governmental problems. First, let us suppose that we have some governmental activity of general benefit, police work, for example, which is paid for by some general type of taxation. By reasoning paralleling that which we have done so far, we can demonstrate that special tax exemptions to special groups at the expense of the general efficiency of the police force would be carried on to a degree which would far exceed the Kantian median. Similarly, if a given sum of money is to be spent on two different types of governmental activity, one of which is of general benefit and one of which benefits a series of special groups, too much will be spent on the latter. Defense, for example, will be slighted in favor of river and harbor work.

The same reasoning can be applied to the tax structure. If a given amount of money had to be raised, we would expect it to be raised by general taxes that were "too heavy" but riddled by special exemptions for all sorts of groups. This would greatly reduce the effect of any general tax policy, such as progression, that had been adopted. This pattern appears to be very realistic. On the basis of our theory, we would predict general and diffuse taxes, riddled with special exceptions, and governmental functions of general benefit sacrificed in favor of the interests of particular groups. I see no great conflict between the prediction and reality.

To apply our theory generally to all types of governmental activity, however, we must radically generalize it. For any individual voter all possible measures can be arranged according to the intensity of his feeling. His welfare can be improved if he accepts a decision against his desire in an area where his feelings are comparatively weak in return for a decision in his favor in an area where his feelings are strong. Bargains between voters, therefore, can be mutually beneficial. Logically, the voter should enter into such bargains until the marginal "cost" of voting for something he disapproves of but about which his feelings are weak exactly matches the marginal benefit of the vote on something else which he receives in return. Thus he will benefit from the total complex of issues which enter into the set of bargains which he makes with other people. In making these bargains, however, he must gain the assent of a majority of the voters only, not all of them. On any given issue he can safely ignore the desires of 49 percent. This means that he can afford to "pay" more to people for voting for his measures because part of the inconvenience imposed by the measure will fall on parties not members of the bargains.

Unfortunately, the converse also applies. Bargains will be entered into in which our voter does not participate but part of the cost of which he will have to bear. As a result, the whole effect of the measures which result from his bargains and on which he votes on the winning side will be beneficial to him. But this will be only slightly more than half of all the " bargained " measures passed, and the remainder will be definitely contrary to his interest. The same would be true for the *average* voter under a pure referendum system. In fact, the whole problem discussed in this paper arises from the system of compelling the minority to accept the will of the majority.

Although this paper so far has been an exercise in " positive politics," the analysis does raise important policy problems, and at least some comment on them seems desirable. It seems clear that the system of majority voting is not by any means an optimal method of allocating resources. This fact should be taken into account in considering whether some aspect of our economy would be better handled by governmental or market techniques. On the other hand, these problems and difficulties do not materially reduce the advantage which voting procedures have over despotism as a system of government. The primary lesson would appear to be the need for further research. Majority voting plays the major role in the governments of all the nations in which the social sciences are comparatively advanced. It seems likely that careful analysis of the process would lead to the discovery of improved techniques and a possible increase in governmental efficiency.

The pure theory of public expenditure*

PAUL A. SAMUELSON

1. ASSUMPTIONS

Except for Sax, Wicksell, Lindahl, Musgrave, and Bowen, economists have rather neglected the theory of optimal public expenditure, spending most of their energy on the theory of taxation. Therefore, I explicitly assume two categories of goods: ordinary *private consumption goods* $(X_1, \ldots, X_n)$, which can be parcelled out among different individuals $(1, 2, \ldots, i, \ldots, s)$ according to the relations

$$\overline{X}_j = \sum_{i=1}^{s} X_j^i;$$

and *collective consumption goods* $(X_{n+1}, \ldots, X_{n+m})$, which all enjoy in common in the sense that each individual's consumption of such a good leads to no subtraction from any other individual's consumption of that good, so $X_{n+j} = X_{n+j}^i$ simultaneously for each and every ith individual and each collective consumptive good. I assume no mystical collective mind that enjoys collective consumption goods; instead I assume each individual has a consistent set of *ordinal preferences* with respect to his consumption of all goods (collective as well as private), which can be summarized by a regularly smooth and convex utility index $u^i = u^i(X_1^i, \ldots, X_{n+m}^i)$ (any monotonic stretching of the utility index is of course also an admissible cardinal index of preference). I shall throughout follow the convention of writing the partial derivative of any function with respect to its jth argument by a j subscript, so $u_j^i = \partial u^i / \partial X_j^i$, etc. Provided economic quantities can be divided into two groups, (1) *outputs* or goods which everyone always wants to maximize and (2) inputs or factors which everyone always wants to minimize, we are free to change the algebraic signs of the latter category and from then on to work only with "goods," knowing that the case of factor inputs is covered as well. Hence by this convention we are sure that $u_j^i > 0$ always.

---

* *The Review of Economics and Statistics*, 36(1954): pp. 387–89. Reprinted by courtesy of the author and *The Review of Economics and Statistics*.

To keep production assumptions at the minimum level of simplicity, I assume a regularly convex and smooth production-possibility schedule relating totals of all outputs, private and collective; or $F(X_1, \ldots, X_{n+m}) = 0$, with $F_j > 0$ and ratios F_j/F_n determinate and subject to the generalized laws of diminishing returns.

Feasibility considerations disregarded, there is a *maximal* (ordinal) *utility frontier* representing the Pareto-optimal points—of which there are an $(s - 1)$-fold infinity—with the property that from such a frontier point you can make one person better off only by making some other person worse off. If we wish to make normative judgments concerning the relative ethical desirability of different configurations involving some individuals being on a higher level of indifference and some on a lower, we must be presented with a set of ordinal interpersonal norms or with a *social welfare function* representing a consistent set of ethical preferences among all the possible states of the system. It is not a "scientific" task of the economist to "deduce" the form of this function; this can have as many forms as there are possible ethical views; for the present purpose, the only restriction placed on the social welfare function is that it shall always increase or decrease when any one person's ordinal preference increases or decreases, all others staying on their same indifference levels: mathematically, we narrow it to the class that any one of its indexes can be written $U = U(u^1, \ldots, u^s)$ with $U_j > 0$.

2. OPTIMAL CONDITIONS

In terms of these norms, there is a "best state of the world" which is defined mathematically in simple regular cases by the marginal conditions

$$\frac{u^i_j}{u^i_r} = \frac{F_j}{F_r} \qquad \begin{matrix} (i = 1, 2, \ldots, s; r, j = 1, \ldots, n) \text{ or} \\ (i = 1, 2, \ldots, s; r = 1; j = 2, \ldots, n), \end{matrix} \tag{1}$$

$$\sum_{i=1}^{s} \frac{u^i_{n+j}}{u^i_r} = \frac{F_{n+j}}{F_r} \qquad \begin{matrix} (j = 1, \ldots, m; r = 1, \ldots, n) \text{ or} \\ (j = 1, \ldots, m; r = 1), \end{matrix} \tag{2}$$

$$\frac{U_i u^i_k}{U_q u^q_k} = 1 \qquad \begin{matrix} (i, q = 1, \ldots, s; k = 1, \ldots, n) \text{ or} \\ (q = 1; i = 2, \ldots, s; k = 1). \end{matrix} \tag{3}$$

Equations (1) and (3) are essentially those given in the chapter on welfare economics in my *Foundations of Economic Analysis*. They constitute my version of the "new welfare economics." Alone (1) represents that subset of relations which defines the Pareto-optimal utility frontier and which by itself represents what I regard as the unnecessarily narrow version of what once was called the "new welfare economics."

The new element added here is the set (2), which constitutes a pure theory of government expenditure on collective consumption goods. By themselves (1) and (2) define the $(s - 1)$fold infinity of utility frontier points; only when a set of interpersonal normative conditions equivalent to (3) is supplied are we able to define an unambiguously "best" state.

Since formulating the conditions (2) some years ago, I have learned from the published and unpublished writings of Richard Musgrave that their essential logic is contained in the " voluntary-exchange " theories of public finance of the Sax-Wicksell-Lindahl-Musgrave type, and I have also noted Howard Bowen's independent discovery of them in Bowen's writings of a decade ago. A graphical interpretation of these conditions in terms of *vertical* rather than *horizontal* addition of different individuals' marginal-rate-of-substitution schedules can be given; but what I must emphasize is that there is a different such schedule for each individual at each of the $(s-1)$fold infinity of different distributions of relative welfare along the utility frontier.

3. IMPOSSIBILITY OF DECENTRALIZED SPONTANEOUS SOLUTION

So much for the involved optimizing equations that an omniscient calculating machine could theoretically solve if fed the postulated functions. No such machine now exists. But it is well known that an " analogue calculating machine " can be provided by competitive market pricing, (*a*) so long as the production functions satisfy the neoclassical assumptions of constant returns to scale and generalized diminishing returns and (*b*) so long as the individuals' indifference contours have regular convexity and, we may add, (*c*) so long as all goods are private. We can then insert between the right- and left-hand sides of (1) the equality with uniform market prices p_j/p_r and adjoin the budget equations for each individual

$$p_1 X_1^i + p_2 X_2^i + \cdots + p_n X_n^i = L^i \qquad (i = 1, 2, \ldots, s), \qquad (1')$$

where L^i is a lump-sum tax for each individual so selected in algebraic value as to lead to the " best " state of the world. Now note, if there were no collective consumption goods, then (1) and (1') can have their solution enormously simplified. Why? Because on the one hand perfect competition among productive enterprises would ensure that goods are produced at minimum costs and are sold at proper marginal costs, with all factors receiving their proper marginal productivities; and on the other hand, each individual, in seeking as a competitive buyer to get to the highest level of indifference subject to given prices and tax, would be led as if by an Invisible Hand to the grand solution of the social maximum position. Of course the institutional framework of competition would have to be maintained, and political decision making would still be necessary, but of a computationally minimum type: namely, algebraic taxes and transfers $(L^1, \ldots, L^s)$ would have to be varied until society is swung to the ethical observer's optimum. The servant of the ethical observer would not have to make explicit decisions about each person's detailed consumption and work; he need only decide about generalized purchasing power, knowing that each person can be counted on to allocate it optimally. In terms of communication theory and game terminology, each person is motivated to do the signalling of his tastes needed to define and reach the attainable-bliss point.

Now all of the above remains valid even if collective consumption is not zero but is instead *explicitly set* at its optimum values as determined by (1), (2), and (3). *However no decentralized pricing system can serve to determine optimally these levels of collective consumption.* Other kinds of "voting" or "signalling" would have to be tried. But, and this is the point sensed by Wicksell but perhaps not fully appreciated by Lindahl, now it is in the selfish interest of each person to give *false* signals, to pretend to have less interest in a given collective consumption activity than he really has, etc. I must emphasize this: taxing according to a benefit theory of taxation can not at all solve the computational problem in the decentralized manner possible for the first category of "private" goods to which the ordinary market pricing applies and which do not have the "external effects" basic to the very notion of collective consumption goods. Of course, utopian voting and signalling schemes can be imagined. ("Scandinavian consensus," Kant's "categorical imperative," and other devices meaningful only under conditions of "symmetry," etc.) The failure of market catallactics in no way denies the following truth: given sufficient knowledge the optimal decisions can always be found by scanning over all the attainable states of the world and selecting the one which according to the postulated ethical welfare function is best. The solution "exists"; the problem is how to "find" it.

One could imagine every person in the community being indoctrinated to behave like a "parametric decentralized bureaucrat" who *reveals* his preferences by signalling in response to price parameters or Lagrangean multipliers, to questionnaires, or to other devices. But there is still this fundamental technical difference going to the heart of the whole problem of *social* economy: by departing from his indoctrinated rules, any one person can hope to snatch some selfish benefit in a way not possible under the self-policing competitive pricing of private goods; and the "external economies" or "jointness of demand" intrinsic to the very concept of collective goods and governmental activities makes it impossible for the grand ensemble of optimizing equations to have that special pattern of zeros which makes *laissez-faire* competition even *theoretically* possible as an analogue computer.

4. CONCLUSION

To explore further the problem raised by public expenditure would take us into the mathematical domain of "sociology" or "welfare politics," which Arrow, Duncan Black, and others have just begun to investigate. Political economy can be regarded as one special sector of this general domain, and it may turn out to be pure luck that within the general domain there happened to be a subsector with the "simple" properties of traditional economics.

Part III
SOCIAL VERSUS PRIVATE COSTS AND BENEFITS

The beginings of welfare economics had much to do with the realization that increasing returns, owing to internal and external economies, can lead to faulty resource allocation even in the most perfectly competitive economic system. The subject was as obscure as it was intriguing, and matters were not helped by the apparent symmetry between increasing and decreasing returns and between internal and external economies. The former gave rise to the famous controversy of the 1920's over the "empty economic boxes";[1] the latter is still a source of confusion. In our view, the main distinction between different causes of market failure is that between nonmarket interdependence on the one hand and increasing returns due to indivisibilities or peculiarities of the production function on the other hand.

Nonmarket interdependence is better known as externalities or external economies and diseconomies, and it is responsible for divergence between social and private costs, and social and private benefits. Its first modern definition and discussion is contained in Meade's paper reprinted here; its earliest full exposition is to be found, together with much other welfare economics besides, in A. C. Pigou's *The Economics of Welfare*.[2] The Buchanan-Stubblebine paper carries Meade's analysis further and probably represents the most rigorous and complete analysis of the subject to date, with some important distinctions between relevant and irrelevant, operational and nonoperational externalities, and the clearing up of an error Pigou made concerning the removal of or payment for externalities. This error was first exposed and

---

[1] Cf. the papers of J. H. Clapham, A. C. Pigou, and D. H. Robertson, reprinted in *A. E. A. Readings in Price Theory* (Homewood, Ill.: Irwin, 1952).

[2] *Loc. cit.*, General Introduction, footnote 2.

corrected in R. H. Coase's "The Problem of Social Costs";[3] unfortunately, his paper, with its many legal examples, was too long for inclusion here.

The other papers in this part deal more generally with the causes of the competitive market's failure to lead to efficient resorce allocation. Allyn Young's and Frank Knight's papers are among the early classics in the field; the former, together with a paper by P. N. Rosenstein-Rodan (not reprinted here),[4] provided the starting point and inspiration for much of the writing on the problems of developing countries. Scitovsky's paper distinguishes the (technological) externalities created by nonmarket interdependence from what he calls "pecuniary externalities," which cause market failure owing primarily to economies of scale (increasing returns) and the long lag with which market prices transmit information about investment decisions. Since Scitovsky's paper attempts a not quite satisfactory classification of the causes of market failure, it is worth mentioning the existence of a competing system of classification in F. M. Bator's "The Anatomy of Market Failure."[5]

---

[3] *Journal of Law and Economics*, 3(1960): 1–44.
[4] "Problems of Industrialization of Eastern and South-Eastern Europe," *Economic Journal*, 53(1945): 202–11.
[5] *Quarterly Journal of Economics*, 72(1958): 351–78.

External economies and diseconomies in a competitive situation*†

JAMES E. MEADE

I. THE SCOPE OF THE PAPER

The purpose of this note is to distinguish between certain types of external economies and diseconomies which are connected with marginal adjustments in purely competitive situations. We shall not be dealing with divergences between private and social interests due to monopolistic or monopsonistic situations, nor with any of the problems which arise from indivisibilities such as the lumpiness of investment in particular forms, nor with any questions about large structural changes such as whether a particular industry should exist at all or not. We shall be concerned only with small adjustments to existing competitive situations.

II. THE COMPETITIVE SITUATION WITH NO EXTERNAL ECONOMIES OR DISECONOMIES

Let us consider two industries. These "industries" may or may not in fact produce identically the same product and so in reality constitute a single industry. That is immaterial to our general theory. But we assume that within each "industry" there are a large number of independent competing firms so that to each individual entrepreneur the price of the product and of the factors is given. In the absence of any external economies or diseconomies, each entrepreneur will hire each factor up to the point at which the additional product of the factor multiplied by its price is equal to the price of the factor. Moreover, there will be constant returns to scale. If every factor in either of our two industries were increased by 10 percent, including the number of entrepreneurs, then the product also would be increased by 10 percent.

* *The Economic Journal*, 62(1952): pp. 54–67. Reprinted by courtesy of the author and *The Economic Journal*.

† This note has arisen, out of a consideration of the problems of the economic development of under developed territories, in the preparation of Volume II of my *Theory of International Economic Policy* for the Royal Institute of International Affairs.

Let us write x_1 and x_2 for the products of industry 1 and industry 2, respectively. We assume that there are two factors, l and c, or labor and capital, employed in both industries, so that $l_1 + l_2 = l$ and $c_1 + c_2 = c$. We will write $\bar{x}_1$, l_1, $\bar{c}_1$, etc., for the market prices of the products and factors; and $X_1 = x_1\bar{x}_1$, $L_1 = l_1 l_1$, $C_1 = c_1\bar{c}_1$, etc., for the total value of the output of x_1 or for the total income earned by l_1, etc. Finally, we shall write $\bar{L}_1$, $\bar{C}_1$, etc., for the amounts which the factors would have to be paid if they received the value of their marginal social net products. In our model, capital is always the hiring factor, and its reward is, therefore, always equal in each industry to the total output of that industry minus the wages paid to labour in that industry, so that $C_1 = X_1 - L_1$ and $C_2 = X_2 - L_2$.

In the case in which there are no divergences between private and social net products we can write

$$x_1 = H_1(l_1, c_1) \\ x_2 = H_2(l_2, c_2) \Big\rbrace, \qquad (1)$$

where H_1 and H_2 are homogeneous functions of the first degree, expressing the fact that there are constant returns to scale in both industries. Now

$$x_1 = \frac{\partial x_1}{\partial l_1} l_1 + \frac{\partial x_1}{\partial c_1} c_1,$$

Euler's equation

or

$$1 = \frac{l_1}{x_1} \frac{\partial x_1}{\partial l_1} + \frac{c_1}{x_1} \cdot \frac{\partial x_1}{\partial c_1}.$$

sum of derivatives

We shall write $\epsilon_{l_1}^{x_1}$ for $(l_1/x_1) \cdot (\partial x_1/\partial l_1)$ and so on, so that we have

$$\epsilon_{l_1}^{x_1} + \epsilon_{c_1}^{x_1} = \epsilon_{l_2}^{x_2} + \epsilon_{c_2}^{x_2} = 1. \qquad (2)$$

These expressions describe the fact that if, for example, a 10 percent increase in labour alone causes a 3 percent increase in output, then a 10 percent increase in capital alone must cause a 7 percent increase in output, because a 10 percent increase in both factors will cause a 10 percent increase in output.

In this situation l_1 will be paid a money wage (L_1) equal to $(\partial x_1/\partial l_1)l_1\bar{x}_1$ or $\epsilon_{l_1}^{x_1} X_1$, and this will also be equal to the value of its marginal social net product. Capital in industry 1 will receive $X_1 - L_1$, which from equation (2) equals $\epsilon_{c_1}^{x_1} X_1$, which is also equal to the value of capital's marginal social net product, so in this case we have

$$L_1 = \bar{L}_1 = \epsilon_{l_1}^{x_1} X_1, \qquad L_2 = \bar{L}_2 = \epsilon_{l_2}^{x_2} X_2,$$
$$C_1 = \bar{C}_1 = \epsilon_{c_1}^{x_1} X_1, \qquad C_2 = \bar{C}_2 = \epsilon_{l_2}^{x_2} X_2.$$

Moreover, since $\epsilon_{l_1}^{x_1} = (L_1/X_1)$, we can measure $\epsilon_{l_1}^{x_1}$ from the proportion of the total product in industry, which goes to labour. And similarly for the measurement of $\epsilon_{c_1}^{x_1}$, $\epsilon_{l_2}^{x_2}$, and $\epsilon_{c_2}^{x_2}$.

elasticity = labour & share

III. TWO TYPES OF EXTERNAL ECONOMY AND DISECONOMY

Such is the simplest competitive model. We intend now to consider cases where what is done in one industry reacts upon the conditions of production in the other industry in some way other than through the possible effect upon the prices of the product or of the factors in that other industry. All such reactions we shall describe as constituting external economies or diseconomies because the individual entrepreneur in the first industry will take account of the effect of his actions only upon what happens inside the first industry (the internal effect), but will leave out of account the effect of his actions upon the output of the second industry, in which it may improve production (an external economy) or diminish production (an external diseconomy).

But the purpose of this note is to distinguish between two types of such external economies or diseconomies. The first type we shall call "unpaid factors of production," and the second the "creation of atmosphere." The essential difference between these two types of external economy or diseconomy is that in the first case there are still constant returns to scale for society as a whole, though not for the individual industry, whereas in the second case there are still constant returns to scale for each individual industry but not for society as a whole.

IV. UNPAID FACTORS

Suppose that in a given region there is a certain amount of apple-growing and a certain amount of bee-keeping and that the bees feed on the apple-blossom. If the apple-farmers apply 10 percent more labour, land, and capital to apple-farming they will increase the output of apples by 10 percent; but they will also provide more food for the bees. On the other hand, the bee-keepers will not increase the output of honey by 10 percent by increasing the amount of land, labour, and capital applied to bee-keeping by 10 percent unless at the same time the apple-farmers also increase their output and so the food of the bees by 10 percent. Thus there are constant returns to scale for both industries taken together: if the amount of labour and of capital employed both in apple-farming and bee-keeping are doubled, the output of both apple and honey will be doubled. But if the amount of labour and capital are doubled in bee-keeping alone, the output of honey will be less than doubled; whereas, if the amounts of labour and capital in apple-farming are doubled, the output of apples will be doubled, and in addition, some contribution will be made to the output of honey.

We call this a case of an unpaid factor because the situation is due simply and solely to the fact that the apple-farmer cannot charge the bee-keeper for the bees' food, which the former produces for the latter. If social-accounting institutions were such that this charge could be made, then every factor would, as in other competitive situations, earn the value of its marginal social net product. But as it is, the apple-farmer provides to the bee-keeper some of his factors free of charge. The apple-farmer is paid less than the value of his marginal social net product, and the bee-keeper receives more than the value of his marginal social net product.

This situation is shown if industry 1 represents bee-keeping and industry 2 apple-farming and if we replace equations (1) and (2) with

$$\left.\begin{array}{c} x_1 = H_1(l_1, c_1, x_2) \\ x_2 = H_2(l_2, c_2) \end{array}\right\} . \tag{4}$$

so that

$$\epsilon_{l_1}^{x_1} + \epsilon_{c_1}^{x_1} + \epsilon_{x_2}^{x_1} = \epsilon_{l_2}^{x_2} + \epsilon_{c_2}^{x_2} = 1$$

In this case, l_1 will be paid the value of its marginal social net product, and we have $L_1 = \bar{L}_1 = \epsilon_{l_1}^{x_1} X_1$. c_1 will be paid $X_1 - L_1$ or $\epsilon_{c_1}^{x_1} X_1 + \epsilon_{x_2}^{x_1} X_2$; but $\epsilon_{c_1}^{x_1} X_1$ is the value of c_1's marginal social net product, so that we have $C_1 = \bar{C}_1 + \epsilon_{c_1}^{x_1} X_1$. In other words, c_1 will have to have its earnings taxed at an *ad valorem* rate of $(X_1/C_1)\epsilon_{x_2}^{x_1}$ in order to be paid a net reward equal to the value of its marginal social net product.

But, on the other hand, l_2 and c_2 will be paid just so much less than the value of their marginal social net products.

$$\bar{L}_2 = l_2\left(\bar{x}_2 \frac{\partial x_2}{\partial l_2} + \bar{x}_1 \frac{\partial x_1}{\partial x_2} \cdot \frac{\partial x_2}{\partial l_2}\right)$$

$$= \epsilon_{l_2}^{x_2} X_2\left(1 + \frac{X_1}{X_2} \epsilon_{x_2}^{x_1}\right).$$

But l_2 will receive only $\epsilon_{l_2}^{x_2} X_2$, so that

$$\bar{L}_2 = L_2\left(1 + \frac{X_1}{X_2} \epsilon_{x_2}^{x_1}\right)$$

and the wages of labour in apple-farming will need to be subsidised at an *ad valorem* rate of $(X_1/X_2)\epsilon_{x_2}^{x_1}$ in order to equate rewards to the value of the factor's marginal social net product. Similarly,

$$\bar{C}_2 = C_2\left(1 + \frac{X_1}{X_2} \epsilon_{x_2}^{x_1}\right),$$

and the same *ad valorem* rate of subsidy should be paid to the earnings of capital in apple-farming. Since $C_2 + L_2 = X_2$, the total tax revenue of $X_1 \epsilon_{x_2}^{x_1}$ raised on C_1 will be equal to the two subsidies of

$$C_2 \frac{X_1}{X_2} \epsilon_{x_2}^{x_1}$$

and

$$L_2 \frac{X_1}{X_2} \epsilon_{x_2}^{x_1}.[1]$$

___

[1] In this case it would, of course, have exactly the same effect if the subsidy were paid not on the wages of labour and profits of capital in apple-farming but at the same *ad valorem* rate on the value of the apple-output, X_2.

In order to discover the appropriate rates of tax and subsidy the essential factor which will need to be estimated is $\epsilon_{x_2}^{x_1}$, the percentage effect on the output of honey which a 1 percent increase in the output of apples would exercise.

Now the relationship which we have just examined might be a reciprocal one. While the apples may provide the food of the bees, the bees may fertilise the apples.[2] Once again we may have constant returns to scale for society as a whole; a 10 percent increase in all factors in both industries would cause a 10 percent increase in the output of both products. In this case, instead of equations (4) we should have

$$x_1 = H_1(l_1, c_1, x_2)$$
$$x_2 = H_2(l_2, c_2, x_1)$$
$$\epsilon_{l_1}^{x_1} + \epsilon_{c_1}^{x_1} + \epsilon_{x_2}^{x_1} = \epsilon_{l_2}^{x_2} + \epsilon_{c_2}^{x_2} + \epsilon_{x_1}^{x_2} = 1$$

$$(5)$$

By a process similar to that adopted in the previous case we can obtain formulae to show what subsidies and taxes must be imposed in order to equate each factor's income in each industry to the value of its marginal social net product.

We can obtain the actual rewards of the factors in exactly the same way as in the previous example. Labour in industry 1 will obtain a wage equal to the value of its marginal private net product or $\bar{x}_1(\partial x_1/\partial l_1)$, so that $L_1 = \epsilon_{l_1}^{x_1} X_1$. Capital in industry 1 will receive the remainder, or $X_1 - L_1$, so that from equations (5) $C_1 = X_1(\epsilon_{c_1}^{x_1} + \epsilon_{x_2}^{x_1})$. Similarly, $L_2 = \epsilon_{l_2}^{x_2} X_2$ and $C_2 = X_2(\epsilon_{c_2}^{x_2} + \epsilon_{x_1}^{x_2})$.

To obtain expressions for the value of each factor's marginal social net product we have now to allow for the repercussions of each industry upon the other. Thus the value of the marginal social net product of labour in apple-farming includes not only the increased output of apples directly produced but also the increased output of honey caused by this increase in apple-output plus the further increase in apple-output due to this increase in honey-output plus the still further increase in honey-output due to this increase in apple-output and so on in an infinite progression. The final result can be obtained in the following manner. Differentiating the main equations in equations (5), we have

$$dx_1 = \frac{\partial x_1}{\partial l_1} dl_1 + \frac{\partial x_1}{\partial c_1} dc_1 + \frac{\partial x_1}{\partial x_2} dx_2,$$

$$dx_2 = \frac{\partial x_2}{\partial l_2} dl_2 + \frac{\partial x_2}{\partial c_2} dc_2 + \frac{\partial x_2}{\partial x_1} dx_1.$$

---

[2] If the bees had a bad effect upon the apples, then we should have an external dis-economy, which may be regarded as an unpaid negative factor of production. The bee-keepers, in addition to getting the bee-food free of charge, are also not charged for some damage which they do to the apple-farmers. In what follows $\epsilon_{x_1}^{x_2}$ would be <0, so that $\epsilon_{l_2}^{x_2} + \epsilon_{c_2}^{x_2} c_2 > 1$.

If we keep c_1, l_2, and c_2 constant ($dc_1 = dl_2 = dc_2 = 0$) but allow l_1 to vary ($dl_1 \neq 0$), dx_1 and dx_2 will give the marginal social net products of l_1 in the two commodities. We obtain

$$\frac{dx_1}{dl_1} = \frac{\dfrac{\partial x_1}{\partial l_1}}{1 - \dfrac{\partial x_1}{\partial x_2} \cdot \dfrac{\partial x_2}{\partial x_1}} \quad \text{and} \quad \frac{dx_2}{dl_1} = \frac{\dfrac{\partial x_2}{\partial x_1} \cdot \dfrac{\partial x_1}{\partial l_1}}{1 - \dfrac{\partial x_1}{\partial x_2} \cdot \dfrac{\partial x_2}{\partial x_1}}.$$

But

$$\bar{L}_1 = l_2 \bar{x}_1 \frac{dx_1}{dl_1} + l_1 \bar{x}_2 \frac{dx_2}{dl_1}$$

$$= l_1 \frac{\partial x_1}{\partial l_1} \frac{\bar{x}_1 + \bar{x}_2 \dfrac{\partial x_2}{\partial x_1}}{1 - \dfrac{\partial x_1}{\partial x_2} \cdot \dfrac{\partial x_2}{\partial x_1}}$$

$$= L_1 \frac{1 + \dfrac{X_2}{X_1} \cdot \epsilon_{x_1}^{x_2}}{1 - \epsilon_{x_2}^{x_1} \epsilon_{x_1}^{x_2}}.$$

Similarly, we get the following expressions for the value of the marginal social net products of the other factors.

$$\bar{L}_2 = L_2 \frac{1 + \dfrac{X_1}{X_2} \epsilon_{x_2}^{x_1}}{1 - \epsilon_{x_2}^{x_1} \epsilon_{x_1}^{x_2}},$$

$$\bar{C}_1 = \epsilon_{x_1}^{x_1} X_1 \frac{1 + \dfrac{X_2}{X_1} \epsilon_{x_1}^{x_2}}{1 - \epsilon_{x_2}^{x_1} \epsilon_{x_1}^{x_2}} = (C_1 - \epsilon_{x_2}^{x_1} X_1) \frac{1 + \dfrac{X_2}{X_1} \epsilon_{x_1}^{x_2}}{1 - \epsilon_{x_2}^{x_1} \epsilon_{x_1}^{x_2}},$$

$$\bar{C}_2 = (C_2 - \epsilon_{x_1}^{x_2} X_2) \frac{1 + \dfrac{X_1}{X_2} \epsilon_{x_2}^{x_1}}{1 - \epsilon_{x_2}^{x_1} \epsilon_{x_1}^{x_2}}.$$

On these expressions we can make the following three comments:

First, remembering that $L_1 + C_1 = X_1$ and $L_2 + C_2 = X_2$, we can see from the above expressions that $\bar{L}_1 + \bar{L}_2 + \bar{C}_1 + \bar{C}_2 = X_1 + X_2$. In other words, if the factors were all paid rewards equal to the value of their marginal social net products, this would absorb the whole of the product, neither more nor less. This is due, of course, to the essential constant-returns nature of the production functions at equations (5), from which it can be seen that if l_1, l_2, c_1, and c_2 were to increase by 10 percent, then the production conditions would be satisfied if both outputs also increased by 10 percent. In other words, we are still dealing with a pure unpaid-factor case; there is no adding-up problem for society; every factor can be given a reward equal to the value of its marginal social net product if the revenue from the taxes levied on those which ought to be taxed is used to subsidise the earnings of those which ought to be subsidised.

Secondly, $\bar{L}_1$, $\bar{L}_2$, $\bar{C}_1$, and $\bar{C}_2$ are all seen to be positive finite quantities provided that $\epsilon_{x_2}^{x_1} \epsilon_{x_1}^{x_2} < 1$. From the last of equations (5) it can be seen that $\epsilon_{x_2}^{x_1}$ and $\epsilon_{x_1}^{x_2}$ are both <1; it requires a 10 percent increase of land, labor and apple-blossoms to increase the output of honey by 10 percent, so that a 10 percent increase in the supply of apple-blossoms alone will increase the output of honey by less than 10 percent. But $\epsilon_{x_2}^{x_1}$ and $\epsilon_{x_1}^{x_2}$ are both positive since we are dealing with external economies and not diseconomies. It follows, therefore, that $0 < \epsilon_{x_2}^{x_1} \epsilon_{x_1}^{x_2} < 1$, so $\bar{L}_1$, $\bar{L}_2$, $\bar{C}_1$, and $\bar{C}_2$ are all positive finite quantities. It is because $\epsilon_{x_2}^{x_1}$ and $\epsilon_{x_1}^{x_2}$ are both positive fractions that the infinite progression of an increase in apple-output causing an increase in honey-output, causing an increase in apple-output, and so on, adds up only to a finite sum. For example, if both $\epsilon_{x_2}^{x_1}$ and $\epsilon_{x_1}^{x_2}$ are one-half, a 10 percent increase in apple-output causes a 5 percent increase in honey-output, but this 5 percent increase in honey-output causes only a $2\frac{1}{2}$ percent increase in apple-output; which causes only a $1\frac{1}{4}$ percent increase in honey-output and so on in a diminishing geometric progression.

Thirdly, from the above expressions for L_1 and $\bar{L}_1$, we obtain

$$\frac{\bar{L}_1 - L_1}{L_1} = \frac{\dfrac{X_2}{X_1} \epsilon_{x_1}^{x_2} + \epsilon_{x_2}^{x_1} \epsilon_{x_1}^{x_2}}{1 - \epsilon_{x_1}^{x_2} \epsilon_{x_2}^{x_1}},$$

which shows the *ad valorem* rate of subsidy which must be paid to l_1 to bring its earnings up to the value of its marginal social net product. We can obtain a similar expression for the rates of tax levyable upon C_1.

$$\frac{C_1 - \bar{C}_1}{C_1} = \frac{\epsilon_{x_2}^{x_1} \dfrac{X_1}{C_1} - \dfrac{X_2}{X_1} \epsilon_{x_1}^{x_2} + \dfrac{X_2 - C_1}{C_1} \epsilon_{x_2}^{x_1} \epsilon_{x_1}^{x_2}}{1 - \epsilon_{x_2}^{x_1} \epsilon_{x_1}^{x_2}}$$

Corresponding expressions for $(\bar{L}_2 - L_2)/L_2$ and $(C_2 - \bar{C}_2)/C_2$ can be obtained by interchanging the subscripts 1 and 2. It can be seen from adding $C_1 - \bar{C}_1$ and $C_2 - \bar{C}_2$ that there will be a positive tax revenue raised from capital as a whole. But either $C_1 - \bar{C}_1$ or $C_2 - \bar{C}_2$ might be negative, *i.e.*, a subsidy might be payable on the earnings of capital in one of the two industries as well as upon the earnings of labour in both of the industries. For example, $C_2 - \bar{C}_2$ would be <0 if $\epsilon_{x_2}^{x_1}$ were very large relative to $\epsilon_{x_1}^{x_2}$. This would mean, for example, that the production of honey (industry 1) did very little to help the production of apples (industry 2), while the production of apples did much to help the production of bees. Capitalists in apple-farming should be subsidised because the unpaid benefits which they confer upon the bee-keepers more than outweigh the unpaid benefits which they receive from labour and capital employed in bee-keeping. Indeed, all the results obtained from equations (4) can be obtained from the expressions derived from equations (5) by writing $\epsilon_{x_1}^{x_2} = 0$.

V. THE CREATION OF ATMOSPHERE

A distinction must be drawn between a "factor of production" and a physical or social "atmosphere" affecting production. We may take the rainfall in a district as a typical example of atmosphere. The rainfall may be deficient in the sense that a higher rainfall would increase the farmers' output, but nevertheless what rainfall there is will be available to all farms in the district regardless of their number. Thus if in the district in question the amount of land, labour, and capital devoted to, say, wheat-farming were to be increased by 10 percent, the output of wheat would also be increased by 10 percent, even if the rainfall were to remain constant. This is quite different from the case of a factor of production for which no payment is made; in our previous example, a 10 percent increase in the output of apples (and so in the supply of apple-blossoms) would be necessary, in addition to a 10 percent increase in the amount of land, labour, and capital devoted to bee-keeping, if the output of honey is to be increased by 10 percent. In these examples, rainfall is an "atmosphere" for wheat-farming; but the output of apples is an "unpaid factor of production" for bee-keeping.

The distinction should now be clear. Both a factor of production and an atmosphere are conditions which affect the output of a certain industry. But the atmosphere is a fixed condition of production which remains unchanged for all producers in the industry in question without anyone else doing anything about it, however large or small—within limits—is the scale of operations of the industry. On the other hand, the factor of production is an aid to production which is fixed in amount, and which is therefore available on a smaller scale to each producer in the industry if the number of producers increases, unless someone does something to increase the total supply of the factor.

The external economies which we have examined in the last section are concerned with factors of production for which the individual producer pays nothing. We must turn now to external economies and diseconomies which are due to the fact that the activities of one group of producers may provide an atmosphere which is favourable or unfavourable to the activities of another group of producers. For example, suppose that afforestation schemes in one locality increase the rainfall in that district and that this is favourable to the production of wheat in that district. In this case the production of timber creates an atmosphere favourable to the production of wheat.

In these cases there is an adding-up problem for society as a whole. There may be constant returns to the factors of production employed in either industry alone. That is to say, a 10 percent increase in the amount of land, labour, and capital employed in producing wheat might, in any given atmosphere, result in a 10 percent increase in the output of wheat. And a 10 percent increase in the amount of land, labour, and capital employed in producing timber might, apart from its effect in changing the atmosphere for wheat-farmers, cause a 10 percent increase in the output of timber. It follows that a 10 percent increase in the amount of land, labour, and capital employed both in the timber industry and in wheat-farming will increase the output of timber by 10 percent and the output of wheat by more than 10 percent (because of the improvement in the atmosphere for wheat producers). To society as a whole there are now increasing returns to scale; to pay every factor a reward equal to the value of its marginal social net product will account for more than the total output of the two industries; revenue will have to be raised from outside sources by general taxation if subsidies are to be paid on a scale to bring every factor's reward up to the value of its marginal social net product.

We can express this sort of situation by the following equations:

$$\left.\begin{array}{l} x_1 = H_1(l_1, c_1)A_1(x_2) \\ x_2 = H_2(l_2, c_2) \end{array}\right\} . \tag{6}$$

where once more $\qquad \epsilon_{l_1}^{x_1} + \epsilon_{c_1}^{x_1} = \epsilon_{l_2}^{x_2} + \epsilon_{c_2}^{x_2} = 1.$ [1]

$x_2 = H_2(l_2, c_2)$ is the ordinary competitive constant-returns production function for the timber industry. There is the same type of production function for the wheat industry; but in this case the output due to the use of labour and land $[H_1(c_1, l_1)]$ is subject to an atmosphere (A_1). If the atmosphere is favorable, then $H_1(l_1, c_1)$ is multiplied up by a large factor to give the actual output (x_1). In the case which we are examining the atmosphere for the wheat industry (A_1) is made to depend upon the output of the timber industry $[A_1 = A_1(x_2)]$.

The atmosphere factor (A_1) is thus subject to the following conditions: $A_1(0) = 1$; i.e., we define our terms in such a way that $H_1(l_1, c_1)$ is equal to what the output of wheat would be if there were no timber output. A_1 is always > 0; i.e., there cannot be so powerful an external diseconomy that the output of the industry affected becomes negative. When $A_1(x_2) > 1$, then there is an average external economy; i.e., the output of wheat is greater than it would have been had there been a zero output of timber instead of a positive output (x_2); and similarly, when $A_1(x_2) < 1$, there is an average external diseconomy. When $A_1'(x_2)$ is > 0, then there is a marginal external economy i.e., the output of wheat would be improved by a further increase in the output of timber; and when $A_1'(x_2)$ is < 0, there is a marginal external diseconomy.

The actual rewards of the factors of production are easily seen to be $L_1 = \epsilon_{l_1}^{x_1} X_1$, $C_1 = X_1 - L_1 = \epsilon_{c_1}^{x_1} X_1$, $L_2 = \epsilon_{l_2}^{x_2} X_2$, and $C_2 = X_2 - L_2 = \epsilon_{c_2}^{x_2} X_2$. In the case of the factors employed in wheat-farming (industry 1) there will be

---

[3] Since

$$l_1 \frac{\partial H_1}{\partial l_1} = \frac{l_1}{H_1 A_1} \cdot \frac{A_1 \partial H_1}{\partial l_1} H_1 = \frac{l_1}{x_1} \frac{\partial x_1}{\partial l_1} H_1 = \epsilon_{l_1}^{x_1} H_1,$$

we have $H_1 = \epsilon_{l_1}^{x_1} H_1 + \epsilon_{c_1}^{x_1} H_1$, so $1 = \epsilon_{c_1}^{x_1} + \epsilon_{c^1}^{x_1}$.

no divergence between the reward paid and the value of the marginal social net product; and $L_1 = \bar{L}_1$ and $C_1 = \bar{C}_1$.

But the rewards actually paid to the factors of production in the timber industry (industry 2) will be lower than the value of their marginal social net products because they will not be paid for the favourable atmosphere which they create for wheat farmers. Thus

$$\bar{L}_2 = \epsilon_{l_2}^{x_2} X_2 + l_2 \bar{x}_1 \frac{\partial x_1}{\partial x_2} \cdot \frac{\partial x_2}{\partial l_2}$$

$$= L_2 \left(1 + \frac{X_1}{X_2} \cdot \epsilon_{x_2}^{x_1} \right),$$

where

$$\epsilon_{x_2}^{x_1} = \frac{x_2}{x_1} \cdot \frac{\partial x_1}{\partial x_2} \quad \text{or} \quad \frac{x_2}{A_1} \cdot \frac{\partial A_1}{\partial x_2},$$

the percentage increase in the output of wheat which would be brought about by a 1 percent increase in the output of timber through the improvement in the atmosphere for wheat production. And similarly, it can be shown that

$$\bar{C}_2 = C \left(1 + \frac{X_1}{X_2} \epsilon_{x_2}^{x_1} \right).$$

In other words, the earnings of both l_2 and c_2 or, alternatively, the price of the product x_2 must be subsidised from general revenue at the *ad valorem* rate of $(X_1/X_2)\epsilon_{x_2}^{x_1}$ if all factors are to receive rewards equal to the value of their marginal social net products.

As in the case of unpaid factors, these reactions of one industry upon the other may be reciprocal. Industry 2 may create a favourable or unfavourable atmosphere for industry 2, as well as industry 2 for industry 1. In this case we have

$$\left.\begin{array}{l} x_1 = H_1(l_1, c_1)A_1(x_2) \\[4pt] x_2 = H_2(l_2, c_2)A_2(x_1) \end{array}\right\} \tag{7}$$

where

$$\epsilon_{l_1}^{x_1} - \epsilon_{c_1}^{x_1} = \epsilon_{l_1}^{x_2} + \epsilon_{c_2}^{x_2} = 1$$

Here again $L_1 = \epsilon_{l_1}^{x_1} X_1$, $C_1 = X_1 - L_1 = \epsilon_{c_1}^{x_1} X_1$, $L_2 = \epsilon_{l_2}^{x_2} X_2$, and $C_2 = X_2 - L_2 = \epsilon_{c_2}^{x_2} X_2$.

But when we come to consider the marginal social net product, we have to take into account the infinite chain of action and reaction of the one industry upon the other, as in the case of apple-growing and bee-keeping examined above. The marginal social net product of l_1, for example, is obtained by differentiating the first two of equations (7), keeping l_2, c_1, and c_2 all constant. We obtain

$$\frac{dx_1}{dl_1} = \frac{\epsilon_{l_1}^{x_1} \cdot \frac{x_1}{l_1}}{1 - \epsilon_{x_2}^{x_1} \epsilon_{x_1}^{x_2}} \quad \text{and} \quad \frac{dx_2}{dl_1} = \frac{\epsilon_{l_1}^{x_1} \epsilon_{x_1}^{x_2} \cdot \frac{x_2}{l_1}}{1 - \epsilon_{x_2}^{x_1} \epsilon_{x_1}^{x_2}}.$$

Now

$$\bar{L}_1 = l_1 \bar{x}_1 \frac{dx_1}{dl_1} + l_1 \bar{x}_2 \frac{dx_2}{dl_1},$$

so

$$\frac{\bar{L}_1}{L_1} = \frac{1 + \frac{X_2}{X_1} \epsilon_{x_1}^{x_2}}{1 - \epsilon_{x_2}^{x_1} \epsilon_{x_1}^{x_2}}.$$

Similarly, we can show that

$$\frac{\bar{C}_1}{C_1} = \frac{\bar{L}_1}{L}$$

and that

$$\frac{\bar{L}_2}{L_2} = \frac{\bar{C}_2}{C_2} = \frac{1 + \frac{X_1}{X_2} \epsilon_{x_2}^{x_1}}{1 - \epsilon_{x_2}^{x_1} \epsilon_{x_1}^{x_2}}.$$

In other words, in order that each factor should obtain a reward equal to the value of its marginal social net product both labour and capital in industry 1 or, alternatively, the price of the product of industry 1, should be subsidised at the *ad valorem* rate of

$$\epsilon_{x_1}^{x_2} \frac{\frac{X_2}{X_1} + \epsilon_{x_2}^{x_1}}{1 - \epsilon_{x_2}^{x_1} \epsilon_{x_1}^{x_2}};$$

and similarly, in industry 2 a rate of subsidy of

$$\epsilon_{x_2}^{x_1} \frac{\frac{X_1}{X_2} + \epsilon_{x_1}^{x_2}}{1 - \epsilon_{x_2}^{x_1} \epsilon_{x_1}^{x_2}}.$$

should be paid.

So far throughout this note we have assumed that in all external economies or diseconomies, whether of the unpaid-factor or of the atmosphere-creating kind, it is the *output* of one industry which affects production in the other. But this is, of course, not necessarily the case. It may be the employment of one *factor* in one industry which confers an indirect benefit or the reverse upon producers in the other industry.[4] Moreover, in the case in which atmosphere is created, the output of industry 2 may create an atmosphere for industry 1 which increases the efficiency of a particular *factor* in industry 1 rather than the general level of *output*.[5] Or the employment of a particular *factor* in industry 2 might create conditions which improved the efficiency of a particular factor in industry 1.[6] And any combination of these indirect effects of industry 2 upon industry 1 might be combined with any other combination of such effects of industry 1 on industry 2. Clearly, we cannot consider in detail all the very many possibilities.

But consider the following particular case:

$$\left.\begin{aligned}
x_1 &= H_1(\lambda_1, c_1) \\
x_2 &= H_2(\lambda_2, c_2) \\
\lambda_1 &= l_1 A(l) \\
\lambda_2 &= l_2 A(l) \\
l &= l_1 + l_2
\end{aligned}\right\}, \tag{8}$$

where l_1 = the number of workers employed in industry 1 and λ_1 = the equivalent number of workers of an efficiency which an individual worker would have if the total labour force were very small ($l \to 0$, so that $A \to 1$.)

This is the case where the total labour force in the two industries (l) affects the general efficiency of labour. We may suppose that, up to a certain point, a growth in the absolute size of the labour force employed in these two industries causes a general atmosphere favourable to the efficiency of labour by enabling workers to communicate to each other a certain know-how about, and interest in, the mechanical processes which are common to the two industries.

Now the individual employer in any one firm in either industry will regard A as being unaffected by his own actions, because the indirect effect which an increase in the number of workers employed by him alone will have upon the general efficiency of his own labour will be a negligible quantity. He will go on taking on labour of any given level of efficiency until the wage paid to a unit of labour is equal to the price paid for its marginal product at that level of efficiency. In other words,

$$L_1 = \lambda_1 \bar{x}_1 \frac{\partial x_1}{\partial \lambda_1} = \epsilon_{\lambda_1}^{x_1} X_1.$$

The reward paid to c_1 will be $C_1 = X_1 - L_1 = \epsilon_{c_1}^{x_1} X_1$.
Similarly, $L_2 = \epsilon_{\lambda_2}^{x_2} X_2$ and $C_2 = \epsilon_{c_2}^{x_2} X_2$.

In this case $\bar{C}_1 = \epsilon_{c_1}^{x_1} X_1$ and $\bar{C}_2 = \epsilon_{c_2}^{x_2} X_2$ because there are no external economies or diseconomies involved in decisions to apply more capital in either industry, so that $C_1 = \bar{C}_1$ and $C_2 = \bar{C}_2$.

---

[4] In this case we should have equations of the type of $x_1 = H_1(l_1, c_1, l_2)$ in the case of unpaid factors, and of the type of $x_1 = H_1(l_1, c_1)A_1(l_2)$ in the case of atmosphere-creation.
[5] In this case the equations would be of the type $x_1 = H_1\{l_1 A_1(x_2), c_1\}$.
[6] For example, $x_1 = H_1\{l_1 A(c_2), c_1\}$.

But in evaluating the value of the marginal social net product of labour we have to take into account the effect which the employment of more labour by one particular employer may have upon the efficiency of labour for all other employers in industry 1 and for all other employers in industry 2. The value of the marginal social net product exceeds the wage which will be offered for it by these two sums, so that

$$\bar{L}_1 = L_1 + l_1 \bar{x}_1 \frac{\partial x_1}{\partial \lambda_1} \cdot \frac{\partial \lambda_1}{\partial l} \cdot \frac{\partial l}{\partial l_1} + l_1 \bar{x}_2 \frac{\partial x_2}{\partial \lambda_2} \cdot \frac{\partial \lambda_2}{\partial l} \cdot \frac{\partial l}{\partial l_1}.$$

Since

$$\frac{\partial l}{\partial l_1} = 1, \frac{\partial \lambda_1}{\partial l} = \frac{\lambda_1}{A} \cdot \frac{\partial A}{\partial l},$$

and

$$\frac{\partial \lambda_2}{\partial l} = \frac{\lambda_2}{A} \cdot \frac{\partial A}{\partial l},$$

we have

$$\bar{L}_1 = L_1 + (L_1 + L_2) \frac{l_1}{l} \epsilon_l^A,$$

where

$$\epsilon_l^A = \frac{l}{A} \cdot \frac{dA}{dl}.$$

Similarly,

$$\bar{L}_2 = L_2 + (L_1 + L_2) \frac{l_2}{l} \epsilon_l^A.$$

Now if the wage rate is the same in both industries so that $l_1/l = L_1/(L_1+L_2)$ and $l_2/l = L_2/(L_1 + L_2)$, we have $\bar{L}_1/L_1 = \bar{L}_2/L_2 = 1 + \epsilon_l^A$. The employment of labour in both industries must be subsidised at the *ad valorem* rate of ϵ_l^A, if rewards are to be raised to the value of marginal social net products.

VI. CONCLUSION

It is not claimed that this division of external economies and diseconomies into unpaid factors and the creation of atmosphere is logically complete. External economies exist whenever we have production functions of the form

$$x_1 = F_1(l_1, c_1, l_2, c_2, x_2)$$

$$x_2 = F_2(l_2, c_2, l_1, c_1, x_1),$$

where F_1 and F_2 are not necessarily homogeneous of the first degree. But it is claimed that it may clarify thought on different types of external economy and diseconomy to distinguish thus between: (1) those cases in which there are constant returns for society, but not necessarily constant returns in each industry to the factors which each industry employs and pays for, and (2) those cases in which there are constant returns in each industry to those factors which it controls and pays for, but in which there are not constant returns for the two industries taken together, the scale of operations being important in the one industry because of the atmosphere which it creates for the other. One of the most important conclusions to be drawn is that in the case of type (1)—the unpaid-factor case—there is no adding-up problem for society as a whole; in order to pay every factor a reward equal to the value of its marginal social net product some factors must be taxed and others subsidised, and the revenue from the appropriate taxes will just finance the expenditure upon the appropriate subsidies. But in the case of the creation of atmosphere [type (2)] the subsidies (or taxes) required to promote (or discourage) the creation of favourable (or unfavourable) atmosphere are net additions to (or subtractions from) society's general fiscal burden. But, in fact, of course, external economies or diseconomies may not fall into either of these precise divisions and may contain features of both of them.

Externality[*]

JAMES M. BUCHANAN AND WM. CRAIG STUBBLEBINE

Externality has been, and is, central to the neo-classical critique of market organisation. In its various forms—external economies and diseconomies, divergencies between marginal social and marginal private cost or product, spillover and neighbourhood effects, collective or public goods—externality dominates theoretical welfare economics, and, in one sense, the theory of economic policy generally. Despite this importance and emphasis, rigorous definitions of the concept itself are not readily available in the literature. As Scitovosky has noted, " definitions of external economies are few and unsatisfactory ".[1] The following seems typical:

> External effects exist in consumption whenever the shape or position of a man's indifference curve depends on the consumption of other men.
>
> [External effects] are present whenever a firm's production function depends in some way on the amounts of the inputs or outputs of another firm.[2]

It seems clear that operational and usable definitions are required.

In this paper, we propose to clarify the notion of externality by defining it rigorously and precisely. When this is done, several important, and often overlooked, conceptual distinctions follow more or less automatically, Specifically, we shall distinguish marginal and inframarginal externalities, potentially relevant and irrelevant externalities, and Pareto-relevant and Pareto-irrelevant externalities. These distinctions are formally developed in Section I. As we shall demonstrate, the term, " externality ", as generally used by economists, corresponds only to our definition of Pareto-releveant externality. There follows, in Section II, an illustration of the basic points described in terms of a simple descriptive example. In Section III, some of the implications of our approach are discussed.

It is useful to limit the scope of the analysis at the outset. Much of the discussion in the literature has been concerned with the distinction between

---

[*] *Economica*, N. S., 29(1962): pp. 371–84. Reprinted by courtesy of the authors and *Economica*.
[1] Tibor Scitovsky,**" Two Concepts of External Economies,"*Journal of Political Economy*, vol. LXII (1954), p. 143.
[2] J. de V. Graaf, *Theoretical Welfare Economics*, Cambridge, 1957, p. 43 and p. 18.

technological and *pecuniary* external effects. We do not propose to enter this discussion since it is not relevant for our purposes. We note only that, if desired, the whole analysis can be taken to apply only to technological externalities. Secondly, we shall find no cause for discussing production and consumption externalities separately, Essentially the same analysis applies in either case. In what follows, "firms" may be substituted for "individuals" and "production functions" for "utility functions" without modifying the central conclusions. For expositional simplicity only, we limit the explicit discussion to consumption externalities.

I

We define an external effect, *an externality*, to be present when,

$$u^A = u^A(X_1, X_2, \ldots, X_m, Y_1). \tag{1}$$

This states that the utility of an individual, A, is dependent upon the "activities", $(X_1, X_2, \ldots, X_m)$, that are exclusively under his own control or authority, but also upon another single activity, Y_1, which is, by definition, under the control of a second individual, B, who is presumed to be a member of the same social group. We define an *activity* here as any distinguishable human action that may be measured, such as eating bread, drinking milk, spewing smoke into the air, dumping litter on the highways, giving to the poor, etc. Note that A's utility may, and will in the normal case, depend on other activities of B in addition to Y_1, and also upon the activities of other parties. That is, A's utility function may, in more general terms, include such variables as $(Y_2, Y_3, \ldots, Y_m; Z_1, Z_2, \ldots, Z_m)$. For analytical simplicity, however, we shall confine our attention to the effects of one particular activity, Y_1, as it affects the utility of A.

We assume that A will behave so as to maximise utility in the ordinary way, subject to the externally determined values for Y_1, and that he will modify the values for the X's, as Y_1 changes, so as to maintain a state of "equilibrium".

A marginal externality exists when,

$$u^A_{Y_1} \neq 0. \tag{2}$$

Here, small u's are employed to represent the "partial derivatives" of the utility function of the individual designated by the superscript with respect to the variables designated by the subscript. Hence, $u^A_{Y_1} = \partial u^A / \partial Y_1$, assuming that the variation in Y_1 is evaluated with respect to a set of "equilibrium" values for the X's, adjusted to the given value for Y_1.

An inframarginal externality holds at those points where,

$$u^A_{Y_1} = 0, \tag{3}$$

and (1) holds.

These classifications can be broken down into economies and diseconomies: a marginal external economy existing when

$$u^A_{Y_1} > 0; \tag{2A}$$

that is, a small change in the activity undertaken by B will change the utility of A in the same direction; a marginal external diseconomy existing when

$$u_{Y_1}^A < 0. \tag{2B}$$

An inframarginal external economy exists when for any given set of values for $(X_1, X_2, \ldots, X_m)$, say, $(C_1, C_2, \ldots, C_m)$,

$$u_{Y_1}^A = 0, \quad \text{and} \quad \int_0^{Y_1} u_{Y_1}^A \, dY_1 > 0. \tag{3A}$$

This condition states that, while incremental changes in the extent of B's activity, Y_1, have no affect on A's utility, the total effect of B's action has increased A's utility. An inframarginal diseconomy exists when (1) holds, and, for any given set of values for $(X_1, X_2, \ldots, X_m)$, say, $(C_1, C_2, \ldots, C_m)$, then,

$$u_{Y_1}^A = 0, \quad \text{and} \quad \int_0^{Y_1} u_{Y_1}^A \, dY_1 < 0. \tag{3B}$$

Thus, small changes in B's activity do not change A's level of satisfaction, but the total effect of B's undertaking the activity in question is harmful to A.

We are able to classify the effects of B's action, or potential action, on A's utility by evaluating the "partial derivative" of A's utility function with respect to Y_1 over all possible values for Y_1. In order to introduce the further distinctions between *relevant* and *irrelevant* externalities, however, it is necessary to go beyond consideration of A's utility function. Whether or not a relevant externality exists depends upon the extent to which the activity involving the externality is carried out by the person empowered to take action to make decisions. Since we wish to consider a single externality in isolation, we shall assume that B's utility function includes only variables (activities) that are within his control, including Y_1. Hence, B's utility function takes the form

$$u^B = u^B(Y_1, Y_2, \ldots, Y_m). \tag{4}$$

Necessary conditions for utility maximisation by B are

$$u_{Y_1}^B / u_{Yj}^B = f_{Y_1}^B / f_{Yj}^B, \tag{5}$$

where Y_j is used to designate the activity of B in consuming or utilising some numeraire commodity or service which is, by hypothesis, available on equal terms to A. The right-hand term represents the marginal rate of substitution in "production" or "exchange" confronted by B, the party taking action on Y_1, his production function being defined as

$$f^B = f^B(Y_1, Y_2, \ldots, Y_m), \tag{6}$$

where inputs are included as activities along with outputs. In other words, the right-hand term represents the marginal cost of the activity, Y_1, to B. The equilibrium values for the Y_i's will be designated as $\bar{Y}_i$'s.

An externality is defined as *potentially relevant* when the activity, to the extent that it is actually performed, generates *any* desire on the part of the externally benefited (damaged) party (A) to modify the behaviour of the party empowered to take action (B) through trade, persuasion, compromise, agreement, convention, collective action, etc. An externality which, to the extent that it is performed, exerts no such influence is defined as *irrelevant*. Note that, so long as (1) holds, an externality remains; utility functions remain interdependent.

A potentially relevant marginal externality exists when

$$u_{Y_1}^A \Big|_{Y_1 = \overline{Y}_1} \neq 0. \tag{7}$$

This is a potentially relevant marginal external economy when (7) is greater than zero, a diseconomy when (7) is less than zero. In either case, A is motivated, by B's performance of the activity, to make some effort to modify this performance, to increase the resources devoted to the activity when (7) is positive, to decrease the quantity of resources devoted to the activity when (7) is negative.

Inframarginal externalities are, by definition, irrelevant for small changes in the scope of B's activity, Y_1. However, when large or discrete changes are considered, A is motivated to change B's behaviour with respect to Y_1 in all cases *except* that for which

$$u_{Y_1}^A \Big|_{Y_1 = \overline{Y}_1} = 0, \tag{8}$$

and

$$u^A(C_1, C_2, \ldots, C_m, \overline{Y}_1) \geqq u^A(C_1, C_2, \ldots, C_m, Y_1), \text{ for all } Y_1 \neq \overline{Y}_1.$$

When (8) holds, A has achieved an absolute maximum of utility with respect to changes over Y_1, given any set of values for the X's. In more prosaic terms, A is satiated with respect to Y_1.[3] In all other cases, where inframarginal external economies or diseconomies exist, A will have some desire to modify B's performance; the externality is potentially relevant. Whether or not this motivation will lead A to seek an expansion or contraction in the extent of B's performance of the activity will depend on the location of the inframarginal region relative to the absolute maximum for any given values of the X's.[4]

Pareto-relevance and Pareto-irrelevance may now be introduced. The existence of a simple desire to modify the behaviour of another, defined as potential relevance, need not imply the ability to implement this desire. An externality is defined to be Pareto-relevant when the extent of the activity may be modified in such a way that the externally affected party, A, can be made better off without the acting party, B, being made worse off. That is to say,

---

[3] Note that $u_{Y_1}^A \Big|_{Y_1 = \overline{Y}_1} = 0$ is a necessary, but not a sufficient, condition for irrelevance.

[4] In this analysis of the relevance of externalities, we have assumed that B will act in such a manner as to maximise his own utility subject to the constraints within which he must operate. If, for any reason, B does not attain the equilibrium position defined in (5) above, the classification of his activity for A may, of course, be modified. A potentially relevant externality may become irrelevant and *vice versa*.

"gains from trade" characterise the Pareto-relevant externality, trade that takes the form of some change in the activity of B as his part of the bargain.

A marginal externality is Pareto-relevant when[5]

$$(-)\, u^A_{Y_1}/u^A_{X_j} > [u^B_{Y_1}/u^B_{Y_j} - f^B_{Y_1}/f^B_{Y_j}]_{Y_1 = \bar{Y}_1} \quad \text{and when} \quad u^A_{Y_1}/u^A_{X_j} < 0, \quad \text{and}$$

$$u^A_{Y_1}/u^A_{X_j} > (-)[u^B_{Y_1}/u^B_{Y_j} - f^B_{Y_1}/f^B_{Y_j}]_{Y_1 = \bar{Y}_1} \quad \text{when} \quad u^A_{Y_1}/u^A_{X_j} > 0. \tag{9}$$

In (9), X_j and Y_j are used to designate, respectively, the activities of A and B in consuming or in utilising some numeraire commodity or service that, by hypothesis, is available on identical terms to each of them. As is indicated by the transposition of signs in (9), the conditions for Pareto-relevance differ as between external diseconomies and economies. This is because the "direction" of change desired by A on the part of B is different in the two cases. In stating the conditions for Pareto-relevance under ordinary two-person trade, this point is of no significance since trade in one good flows only in one direction. Hence, absolute values can be used.

The condition (9) states that A's marginal rate of substitution between the activity, Y_1, and the numeraire activity must be greater than the "net" marginal rate of substitution between the activity and the numeraire activity for B. Otherwise, "gains from trade" would not exist between A and B.

Note, however, that when B has achieved utility-maximising equilibrium,

$$u^B_{Y_1}/u^B_{Y_j} = f^B_{Y_1}/f^B_{Y_j}. \tag{10}$$

That is to say, the marginal rate of substitution in consumption or utilisation is equated to the marginal rate of substitution in production or exchange, i.e., to marginal cost. When (10) holds, the terms in the brackets in (9) mutually cancel. Thus, potentially relevant marginal externalities are also Pareto-relevant when B is in utility-maximising equilibrium. Some trade is possible.

Pareto-equilibrium is defined to be present when

$$(-)u^A_{Y_1}/u^A_{X_j} = [u^B_{Y_1}/u^B_{Y_j} - f^B_{Y_1}/f^B_{Y_j}], \quad \text{and when} \quad u^A_{Y_1}/u^A_{X_j} < 0, \quad \text{and}$$

$$u^A_{Y_1}/u^A_{X_j} = (-)[u^B_{Y_1}/u^B_{Y_j} - f^B_{Y_1}/f^B_{Y_j}] \quad \text{when} \quad u^A_{Y_1}/u^A_{X_j} > 0. \tag{11}$$

Condition (11) demonstrates that marginal externalities may continue to exist, even in Pareto-equilibrium, as here defined. This point may be shown by reference to the special case in which the activity in question may be undertaken at zero costs. Here Pareto-equilibrium is attained when the marginal rates of substitution in consumption or utilisation for the two persons are precisely offsetting, that is, where their interests are strictly opposed, and *not* where the left-hand term vanishes.

What vanishes in Pareto-equilibrium are the Pareto-relevant externalities. It seems clear that, normally, economists have been referring only to what we have here called Pareto-relevant externalities when they have, implicitly or

---

[5] We are indebted to Mr. M. McManus of the University of Birmingham for pointing out to us an error in an earlier formulation of this and the following similar conditions.

explicitly, stated that external effects are not present when a position on the Pareto-optimality surface is attained.[6]

For completeness, we must also consider those potentially relevant infra-marginal externalities. Refer to the discussion of these as summarised in (8) above. The question is now to determine whether or not, A, the externally affected party, can reach some mutually satisfactory agreement with B, the acting party, that will involve some discrete (nonmarginal) change in the scope of the activity, Y_1. If, over some range, any range, of the activity, which we shall designate by ΔY_1 the rate of substitution between Y_1 and X_j for A exceeds the "net" rate of substitution for B, the externality is Pareto-relevant. The associated changes in the utilisation of the numeraire commodity must be equal for the two parties. Thus, for external economies, we have

$$\frac{\Delta u^A}{\Delta Y_1} \bigg/ \frac{\Delta u^A}{\Delta X_j} > (-)\left[\frac{\Delta u^B}{\Delta Y_1} \bigg/ \frac{\Delta u^B}{\Delta Y_j} - \frac{\Delta f^B}{\Delta Y_1} \bigg/ \frac{\Delta f^B}{\Delta Y_j}\right]_{Y_1 = \bar{Y}_1}, \tag{12}$$

and the same with the sign in parenthesis transposed for external diseconomies. The difference to be noted between (12) and (9) is that, with infra-marginal externalities, potential relevance need not imply Pareto-relevance. The bracketed terms in (12) need not sum to zero when B is in his private utility-maximising equilibrium.

We have remained in a two-person world, with one person affected by the single activity of a second. However, the analysis can readily be modified to incorporate the effects of this activity on a multiperson group. That is to say, B's activity, Y_1, may be allowed to affect several parties simultaneously, several A's, so to speak. In each case, the activity can then be evaluated in terms of its effects on the utility of each person. Nothing in the construction need by changed. The only stage in the analysis requiring modification explicitly to take account of the possibilities of multiperson groups being externally affected is that which involves the condition for Pareto-relevance and Pareto-equilibrium.

For a multiperson group $(A_1, A_2, \ldots, A_n)$, any one or all of whom may be externally affected by the activity, Y_1, of the single person, B, the condition for Pareto-relevance is

$$(-)\sum_{i=1}^{n} u_{Y_1}^{A^i}/u_{X_j}^{A^i} > [u_{Y_1}^{B}/u_{Y_j}^{B} - f_{Y_1}^{B}/f_{Y_j}^{B}]_{Y_1 = \bar{Y}_1} \quad \text{when} \quad u_{Y_1}^{A^i}/u_{X_j}^{A^i} < 0, \text{ and}$$

$$\sum_{i=1}^{n} u_{Y_1}^{A^i}/u_{X_j}^{A^i} > (-)[u_{Y}^{B}/u_{Y_j}^{B} - f_{Y_1}^{B}/f_{Y_j}^{B}]_{Y_1 = \bar{Y}_1} \quad \text{when} \quad u_{Y_1}^{A^i}/u_{X_j}^{A^i} > 0. \tag{9A}$$

---

[6] This applies to the authors of this paper. For recent discussion of external effects when we have clearly intended only what we here designate as Pareto-relevant, see James M. Buchanan, "Politics, Policy, and the Pigovian Margins," *Economica*, vol. xxvix (1962), pp. 17–28, and also James M. Buchanan and Gordon Tullock, *The Calculus of Consent*, Ann Arbor, 1962.

That is, the summed marginal rates of substitution over the members of the externally affected group exceed the offsetting " net " marginal evaluation of the activity by B. Again, in private equilibrium for B, marginal externalities are Pareto-relevant, provided that we neglect the important element involved in the costs of organising group decisions. In the real world, these costs of organising group decisions (together with uncertainty and ignorance) will prevent realisation of some " gains from trade "—just as they do in organised markets. This is as true for two-person groups as it is for larger groups. But this does not invalidate the point that potential " gains from trade " are available. The condition for Pareto-equilibrium and for the inframarginal case summarised in (11) and (12) for the two-person model can readily be modified to allow for the externally affected multiperson group.

II

The distinctions developed formally in Section I may be illustrated diagrammatically and discussed in terms of a simple descriptive example. Consider two persons, A and B, who own adjoining units of residential property. Within limits to be noted, each person values privacy, which may be measured quantitatively in terms of a single criterion, the height of a fence that can be constructed along the common boundary line. We shall assume that B's desire for privacy holds over rather wide limits. His utility increases with the height of the fence up to a reasonably high level. Up to a certain minimum height, A's utility also is increased as the fence is made higher. Once this minimum height is attained, however, A's desire for privacy is assumed to be fully satiated. Thus, over a second range, A's total utility does not change with a change in the height of the fence. However, beyond a certain limit, A's view of a mountain behind B's property is progressively obscured as the fence goes higher. Over this third range, threrefore, A's utility is reduced as the fence is constructed to higher levels. Finally, A will once again become wholly indifferent to marginal changes in the fence's height when his view is totally blocked out.

We specify that B possesses the sole authority, the only legal right, to construct the fence between the two properties.

The preference patterns for A and for B are shown in Figure 1, which is drawn in the form of an Edgeworth-like box diagram. Note, however, that the origin for B is shown at the upper left rather than the upper right corner of the diagram as in the more normal usage. This modification is necessary here because only the numeraire good, measured along the ordinate, is strictly divisible between A and B. Both must adjust to the same height of fence, that is, to the same level of the activity creating the externality.

As described above, the indifference contours for A take the general shape shown by the curves aa, $a'a'$, while those for B assume the shapes bb, $b'b'$. Note that these contours reflect the relative evaluations, for A and B, between money and the activity, Y_1. Since the costs of undertaking the activity, for B, are not incorporated in the diagram, the " contract locus " that might be

Figure 1

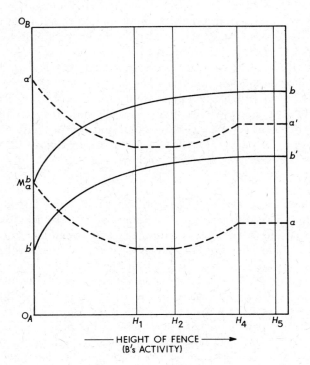

HEIGHT OF FENCE
(B's ACTIVITY)

derived from tangency points will have little relevance, except in the special case where the activity can be undertaken at zero costs.

Figure 2 depicts the marginal evaluation curves for A and B, as derived from the preference fields shown in Figure 1, along with some incorporation of costs. These curves are derived as follows: Assume an initial distribution of "money" between A and B, say that shown at M on Figure 1. The marginal evaluation of the activity for A is then derived by plotting the negatives (i.e., the mirror image) of the slopes of successive indifference curves attained by A as B is assumed to increase the height of the fence from zero. These values remain positive for a range, become zero over a second range, become negative for a third, and, finally, return to zero again.[7]

B's curves of marginal evaluation are measured downward from the upper horizontal axis or base line, for reasons that will become apparent. The derivation of B's marginal evaluation curve is somewhat more complex than that for A. This is because B, who is the person authorised to undertake the action, in this case the building of the fence, must also bear the full costs. Thus,

---

[7] For an early use of marginal evaluation curves, see J. R. Hicks, "The Four Consumer's Surpluses," *Review of Economic Studies*, vol. XI (1943), pp. 31–41.

Figure 2

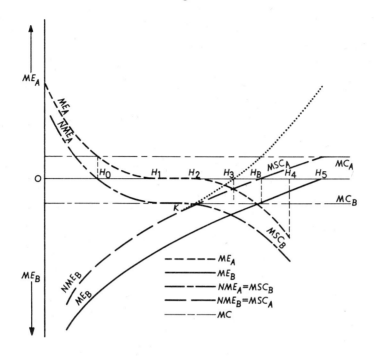

as B increases the scope of the activity, his real income, measured in terms of his remaining goods and services, is reduced. This change in the amount of remaining goods and services will, of course, affect his marginal evaluation of the activity in question. Thus, the marginal cost of building the fence will determine, to some degree, the marginal evaluation of the fence. This necessary interdependence between marginal evaluation and marginal cost complicates the use of simple diagrammatic models in finding or locating a solution. It need not, however, deter us from presenting the solution diagrammatically, if we postulate that the marginal evaluation curve, as drawn, is based on a single presumed cost relationship. This done, we may plot B's marginal evaluation of the activity from the negatives of the slopes of his indifference contours attained as he constructs the fence to higher and higher levels. B's marginal evaluation, shown in Figure 2, remains positive throughout the range to the point H_5, where it becomes zero.

The distinctions noted in Section 1 are easily related to the construction in Figure 2. To A, the party externally affected, B's potential activity in constructing the fence can be assessed independently of any prediction of B's actual behaviour. Thus, the activity of B would:

1) exert marginal external economies which are potentially relevant over the range OH_1;

2) exert inframarginal external economies over the range H_1H_2, which are clearly irrelevant since no change in B's behaviour with respect to the extent of the activity would increase A's utility;

3) exert marginal external diseconomies over the range $H_2 H_4$ which are potentially relevant to A; and,

4) exert inframarginal external economies or diseconomies beyond H_4, the direction of the effect being dependent on the ratio between the total utility derived from privacy and the total reduction in utility derived from the obstructed view. In any case, the externality is potentially relevant.

To determine Pareto-relevance, the extent of B's predicted performance must be determined. The necessary condition for B's attainment of "private" utility-maximising equilibrium is that marginal costs, which he must incur, be equal to his own marginal evaluation. For simplicity in Figure 2, we assume that marginal costs are constant, as shown by the curve, MC. Thus, B's position of equilibrium is shown at H_B, within the range of marginal external diseconomies for A. Here the externality imposed by B's behaviour is clearly Pareto-relevant: A can surely work out some means of compensating B in exchange for B's agreement to reduce the scope of the activity—in this example, to reduce the height of the fence between the two properties. Diagrammatically, the position of Pareto-equilibrium is shown at H_3, where the marginal evaluation of A is equal in absolute value, but negatively, to the "net" marginal evaluation of B, drawn as the curve NME_B. Only in this position are the conditions specified in (11), above, satisfied.[8]

III

Aside from the general classification of externalities that is developed, the approach here allows certain implications to be drawn–implications that have not, perhaps, been sufficiently recognised by some welfare economists.

The analysis makes it quite clear that externalities, external effects, may remain even in full Pareto-equilibrium. That is to say, a position may be classified as Pareto-optimal or efficient despite the fact that, at the marginal, the activity of one individual externally affects the utility of another individual. Figure 2 demonstrates this point clearly. Pareto-equilibrium is attained at H_3, yet B is imposing marginal external diseconomies on A.

This point has significant policy implications for it suggests that the observation of external effects, taken alone, cannot provide a basis for judgment concerning the desirability of some modification in an existing state of affairs. There is not a *prima facie* case for intervention in all cases where an

---

[8] This diagrammatic analysis is necessarily oversimplified in the sense that the Pareto-equilibrium position is represented as a unique point. Over the range between the "private" equilibrium for B and the point of Pareto-equilibrium, the sort of bargains struck between A and B will affect the marginal evaluation curves of both individuals within this range. Thus, the more accurate analysis would suggest a "contract locus" of equilibrium points. At Pareto-equilibrium, however, the condition shown in the diagrammatic presentation holds, and the demonstration of this fact rather than the location of the solution is the aim of this diagrammatics.

externality is observed to exist.[9] The internal benefits from carrying out the activity, net of costs, may be greater than the external damage that is imposed on other parties.

In full Pareto-equilibrium, of course, these internal benefits, measured in terms of some numeraire good, net of costs, must be just equal, at the margin, to the external damage that is imposed on other parties. This equilibrium will always be characterised by the strict opposition of interests of the two parties, one of which may be a multiperson group.

In the general case, we may say that, at full Pareto-equilibrium, the presence of a marginal external diseconomy implies an offsetting marginal *internal* economy, whereas the presence of a marginal external economy implies an offsetting marginal *internal* diseconomy. In " private " equilibrium, as opposed to Pareto-equilibrium, these net internal economies and diseconomies would, of course, be eliminated by the utility-maximising acting party. In Pareto-equilibrium, these remain because the acting party is being compensated for " suffering " internal economies and diseconomies, that is, divergencies between " private " marginal costs and benefits, *measured in the absence of compensation.*

As a second point, it is useful to relate the whole analysis here to the more familiar Pigouvian discussion concerning the divergence between marginal social cost (product) and marginal private cost (product). By saying that such a divergence exists, we are, in the terms of this paper, saying that a marginal externality exists. The Pigouvian terminology tends to be misleading, however, in that it deals with the acting party to the exclusion of the externally affected party. It fails to take into account the fact that there are always two parties involved in a single externality relationship.[10] As we have suggested, a marginal externality is Pareto-relevant except in the position of Pareto-equilibrium: gains from trade can arise. But there must be two parties to any trading arrangement. The externally affected party must compensate the acting party for modifying his behaviour. The Pigouvian terminology, through its concentration on the decision-making of the acting party alone, tends to obscure the two-sidedness of the bargain that must be made.

To illustrate this point, assume that A, the externally affected party in our model, successfully secures, through the auspices of the " state ", the levy of a marginal tax on B's performance of the activity, Y_1. Assume further that A is able to secure this change without cost to himself. The tax will increase the marginal cost of performing the activity for B and, hence, will reduce the extent of the activity attained in B's " private " equilibrium. Let us now presume that this marginal tax is levied " correctly " on the basis of a Pigouvian calculus; the rate of tax at the margin is made equal to the negative marginal

---

[9] Cf. Paul A. Samuelson, *Foundations of Economic Analysis*, Cambridge, Mass., 1948, p. 208, for a discussion of the views of various writers.

[10] This criticism of the Pigouvian analysis has recently been developed by R. H. Coase; see his " The Problem of Social Cost," *Journal of Law and Economics*, vol. III (1960), pp. 1–44.

evaluation of the activity to A. Under these modified conditions, the effective marginal cost, as confronted by B, may be shown by the curve designated as MSC_B in Figure 2. A new "private" equilibrium for B is shown at the quantity, H_3, the same level designated as Pareto-equilibrium in our earlier discussion, if we neglect the disturbing interdependence between marginal evaluation and marginal costs. Attention solely to the decision calculus of B here would suggest, perhaps, that this position remains Pareto-optimal under these revised circumstances, and that it continues to qualify as a position of Pareto-equilibrium. There is no divergence between marginal private cost and marginal social cost in the usual sense. However, the position, if attained in this manner, is clearly neither one of Pareto-optimality, nor one that may be classified as Pareto-equilibrium.

In this new "private" equilibrium for B,

$$u^B_{Y_1}/u^B_{Y_j} = f^B_{Y_1}/f^B_{Y_j} - u^A_{Y_1}/u^A_{X_j}, \tag{13}$$

where $u^A_{Y_1}/u^A_{X_j}$ represents the marginal tax imposed on B as he performs the activity, Y_1. Recall the necessary condition for Pareto-relevance defined in (9) above, which can now be modified to read,

$$(-)u^A_{Y_1}/u^A_{X_j} > [u^B_{Y_1}/u^B_{Y_j} - f^B_{Y_1}/f^B_{Y_j} + u^A_{Y_1}/u^A_{X_j}]_{Y_1 = \overline{Y}_1}, \quad \text{when} \quad u^A_{Y_1}/u^A_{X_j} < 0,$$

$$\text{and} \quad u^A_{Y_1}/u^A_{X_j} > (-)[u^B_{Y_1}/u^B_{Y_j} - f^B_{Y_1}/f^B_{Y_j} + u^A_{Y_1}/u^A_{X_j}]_{Y_1 = \overline{Y}_1}, \quad \text{when} \quad u^A_{Y_1}/u^A_{X_j} > 0. \tag{9B}$$

In (9B), $\overline{Y}_1$ represents the "private" equilibrium value for Y_1, determined by B, after the ideal Pigouvian tax is imposed. As before, the bracketed terms represent the "net" marginal evaluation of the activity for the acting party, B, and these sum to zero when equilibrium is reached. So long as the left-hand term in the inequality remains nonzero, a Pareto-relevant marginal externality remains, despite the fact that the full "Pigouvian solution" is attained.

The apparent paradox here is not difficult to explain. Since, as postulated, A is not incurring any cost in securing the change in B's behaviour, and since there remains, by hypothesis, a marginal diseconomy, further "trade" can be worked out between the two parties. Specifically, Pareto-equilibrium is reached when,

$$(-)u^A_{Y_1}/u^A_{X_j} = [u^B_{Y_1}/u^B_{Y_j} - f^B_{Y_1}/f^B_{Y_j} + u^A_{Y_1}/u^A_{X_j}] \quad \text{when} \quad u^A_{Y_1}/u^A_{X_j} < 0, \quad \text{and}$$

$$u^A_{Y_1}/u^A_{X_j} = (-)[u^B_{Y_1}/u^B_{Y_j} - f^B_{Y_1}/f^B_{Y_j} + u^A_{Y_1}/u^A_{X_j}] \quad \text{when} \quad u^A_{Y_1}/u^A_{X_j} > 0. \tag{11A}$$

Diagrammatically, this point may be made with reference to Figure 2. If a unilaterally imposed tax, corresponding to the marginal evaluation of A, is placed on B's performance of the activity ,the new position of Pareto-equilibrium may be shown by first subtracting the new marginal cost curve, drawn as MSC_B, from B's marginal evaluation curve. Where this new "net" marginal evaluation curve, shown as the dotted curve between points H_3 and K, cuts the marginal evaluation curve for A, a new position of Pareto-equilibrium falling between H_2 and H_3 is located, neglecting the qualifying point discussed in Footnote 8, page 208.

The important implication to be drawn is that full Pareto-equilibrium can never be attained via the imposition of unilaterally imposed taxes and subsidies until all marginal externalities are eliminated. If a tax-subsidy method, rather than "trade", is to be introduced, it should involve bilateral taxes (subsidies). Not only must B's behaviour be modified so as to insure that he will take the costs externally imposed on A into account, but A's behaviour must be modified so as to insure that he will take the costs "internally" imposed on B into account. In such a double tax-subsidy scheme, the necessary Pareto-conditions would be readily satisfied.[11]

In summary, Pareto-equilibrium in the case of marginal externalities cannot be attained so long as marginal externalities remain, until and unless those benefitting from changes are required to pay some "price" for securing the benefits.

A third point worthy of brief note is that our analysis allows the whole treatment of externalities to encompass the consideration of purely collective goods. As students of public finance theory will have recognised, the Pareto-equilibrium solution discussed in this paper is similar, indeed is identical, with that which was presented by Paul Samuelson in his theory of public expenditures.[12] The summed marginal rates of substitution (marginal evaluation) must be equal to marginal costs. Note, however, that marginal costs may include the negative marginal evaluation of other parties, if viewed in one way. Note, also, that there is nothing in the analysis which suggests its limitations to purely collective goods or even to goods that are characterised by significant externalities in their use.

Our analysis also lends itself to the more explicit point developed in Coase's recent paper.[13] He argues that the same "solution" will tend to emerge out of any externality relationship, regardless of the structure of property rights, provided only that the market process works smoothly. Strictly speaking, Coase's analysis is applicable only to interfirm externality relationships, and the identical solution emerges only because firms adjust to prices that are competitively determined. In our terms of reference, this identity of solution cannot apply because of the incomparability of utility functions. It remains true, however, that the basic characteristics of the Pareto-equilibrium position remain unchanged regardless of the authority undertaking the action. This point can be readily demonstrated, again with reference to Figure 2. Let us assume that Figure 2 is now redrawn on the basis of a different legal relationship in which A now possesses full authority to construct the fence, whereas B can no longer take any action in this respect. A will,

---

[11] Although developed in rather different terminology, this seems to be closely in accord with Coase's analysis. Cf. R. H. Coase, *loc. cit.*

[12] Paul A. Samuelson, *"The Pure Theory of Public Expenditure," Review of Economics and Statistics*, vol. xxxvi (1954), pp. 386–89.

[13] R. H. Coase, *loc. cit.*

under these conditions, "privately" construct a fence only to the height H_0, where the activity clearly exerts a Pareto-relevant marginal external economy on B. Pareto-equilibrium will be reached, as before, at H_3, determined in this case, by the intersection of the "net" marginal evaluation curve for A (which is identical to the previously defined marginal social cost curve, MSC, when B is the acting party) and the marginal evaluation curve for B.[14] Note that, in this model, A will allow himself to suffer an internal marginal diseconomy, at equilibrium, provided that he is compensated by B, who continues, in Pareto-equilibrium, to enjoy a marginal *external* economy.

Throughout this paper, we have deliberately chosen to introduce and to discuss only a single externality. Much of the confusion in the literature seems to have arisen because two or more externalities have been handled simultaneously. The standard example is that in which the output of one firm affects the production function of the second firm while, at the same time, the output of the second firm affects the production function of the first. Clearly, there are two externalities to be analysed in such cases. In many instances, these can be treated as separate and handled independently. In other situations, this step cannot be taken and additional tools become necessary.[15]

---

[14] The H_3 position, in this presumably redrawn figure, should not be precisely compared with the same position in the other model. We are using here the same diagram for two models, and especially over wide ranges, the dependence of the marginal evaluation curves on income effects cannot be left out of account.

[15] For a treatment of the dual externality problem that clearly shows the important difference between the separable and the nonseparable cases, see Otto Davis and Andrew Whinston, "Externalities, Welfare and the Theory of Games," *Journal of Political Economy*, vol. LXX (1962), pp. 241–62. As the title suggests, Davis and Whinston utilise the tools of game theory for the inseparable case.

Some fallacies in the interpretation of social cost*

FRANK H. KNIGHT

In two recent articles in this journal,[1] Professor F. D. Graham of Princeton University has developed an ingenious argument to prove that the classical theory of comparative cost as a demonstration of the economic advantage of trade between nations is "all wrong." He contends that a protective tariff may, after all, be a wise national policy in that it may enable the nation which adopts it to secure a larger product from its resources than would be secured if free trade were permitted. It is the opinion of the present writer, and the contention of this paper, that it is Professor Graham's argument which is fallacious, though the way in which the classical theory has been formulated in many instances leaves much to be desired. The matter is of the greater importance because the most important argument, from the standpoint of general theory, in Professor A. C. Pigou's monumental work on *The Economics of Welfare*[2] is, as I shall also try to show, marred by the same, or a very similar, fallacy.

If economic theory is interpreted as a critique of the competitive system of organization, its first and most general problem is that of determining whether the fundamental tendencies of free contractual relations under competitive control lead to the maximum production of value as measured in price terms. The problems of the validity of the price measure of "real value" and of the distribution of the value produced are larger but subsequent problems,

---

* *The Quarterly Journal of Economics*, 38(1924): pp. 582–606. Reprinted by courtesy of the author and *The Quarterly Journal of Economics*.

[1] February 1923, November, 1923.

[2] The Macmillan Co., 1918. This paper was written and submitted to the editor of the *Quarterly Journal* before the appearance of the March number of the *Economic Journal*. In that number, Professor D. H. Robertson has an article covering some of the same ground and treating it with his usual analytic penetration and stylistic brilliancy. Moreover, in a rejoinder appended to that article, Professor Pigou admits the particular error in his analysis and states that it is to be eradicated in a forthcoming revised edition of his book. It seems inadvisable to recast and enlarge the present paper so as to include a discussion of Professor Robertson's argument, which is notably divergent from that presented herewith. I trust it will not be thought presumptuous to print without change the few pages which in some sense cover ground already covered by Professor Robertson.

and belong to ethics as much as to economics, while the detailed comparison of the theoretical tendencies of perfect competition with the facts of any actual competitive society lie in the field of applied economics rather than that of theory. The theory of international or interregional trade is a special case under the more general problem, whether "society" can increase the production of exchange value by interfering with free bargaining relations: the case, namely, of bargains between its own members and members of some other society possessing a distinct body of productive resources. The peculiarity of international trade as compared with domestic lies in the immobility of population viewed as labor power. Natural resources are immobile even within a country, and capital goods enter into international commerce in the same way as goods ready for consumption.

Both Professor Graham and Professor Pigou reason to the conclusion that freedom of trade between regions may reduce the production of wealth in one or even both; and Professor Pigou extends essentially the same logic to cover the relations between different industries, irrespective of regional separation. The contention is that individual profit-seeking leads to an excessive investment of resources in industries of increasing cost (decreasing returns), part of which would yield more product if transferred by social action in some form to industries of constant or decreasing cost. The fallacy to be exposed is a misinterpretation of the relation between social cost and *entrepreneur's* cost. It will be convenient to take up first Professor Pigou's argument, which presents the more general problem.

I

In Professor Pigou's study the argument that free enterprise leads to excessive investment in industries having relatively upward-sloping cost curves is developed with the aid of a concrete example, the case of two roads.[3] Suppose that between two points there are two highways, one of which is broad enough to accommodate without crowding all the traffic which may care to use it, but is poorly graded and surfaced, while the other is a much better road but narrow and quite limited in capacity.[4] If a large number of trucks operate between the two termini and are free to chose either of the two routes, they will tend to distribute themselves between the roads in such proportions that the cost per unit of transportation, or effective result per unit of investment, will be the same for every truck on both routes. As more trucks use the narrower and better road, congestion develops, until at a certain point it becomes equally profitable to use the broader but poorer

---

[3] *Economics of Welfare*, p. 194.

[4] For simplicity, no account is taken of costs involved in *constructing* the two roads. The aim is to study the effects of the two types of "cost"—that which represents a consumption of productive power which might have been put to some other use, and pure rent or the payment for situation and opportunity. The assumption adopted is the simplest way of making the separation. The conclusion will not be changed if various types of cost are taken into account, so long as one of the roads has a definite situation advantage while the investment in the other can be repeated to any desirable extent with equivalent results in other locations.

highway. The congestion and interference resulting from the addition of any particular truck to the stream of traffic on the narrow but good road affects in the same way the cost and output of all the trucks using that road. It is evident that if, after equilibrium is established, a few trucks should be arbitrarily transferred to the broad road, the reduction in cost, or increase in output, to those remaining on the narrow road would be a clear gain to the traffic as a whole. The trucks so transferred would incur no loss, for any one of them on the narrow road is a marginal truck, subject to the same relation between cost and output as any truck using the broad road. Yet whenever there is a difference in the cost, to an additional truck, of using the two roads, the driver of any truck has an incentive to use the narrow road, until the advantage is reduced to zero for all the trucks. Thus, as the author contends, individual freedom results in a bad distribution of investment between industries of constant and industries of increasing cost.

In such a case social interference seems to be clearly justified. If the government should levy a small tax on each truck using the narrow road, the tax would be considered by the trucker as an element in his cost, and would cause the number of trucks on the narrow road to be reduced to the point where the *ordinary cost, plus the tax*, became equal to the cost on the broad road, assumed to be left tax free. The tax could be so adjusted that the number of trucks on the narrow road would be such as to secure the maximum efficiency in the use of the two roads taken together. The revenue obtained from such a tax would be a clear gain to the society, since no individual truck would incur higher costs than if no tax had been levied.

It is implied that the same argument holds good over the whole field of investment wherever investment is free to choose between uses subject to cost curves of different slope. Take, for example, two farms, one of superior quality, the other marginal or free land. Would not labor and capital go to the better farm, until the product per man became equal to the product to be obtained from the marginal land? If so, it is clear that the total product of all the labor and capital could be increased, as in the case of the roads, by transferring some of it from the superior to the inferior farm. This application of the reasoning will probably suggest the fallacy to any one familiar with conventional economic theory. The statement does in fact indicate what would happen *if no one owned the superior farm*. But under private appropriation and self-seeking exploitation of the land the course of events is very different. It is in fact the social function of ownership to prevent this excessive investment in superior situations.

Professor Pigou's logic in regard to the roads is, as logic, quite unexceptionable. Its weakness is one frequently met with in economic theorizing, namely that the assumptions diverge in essential respects from the facts of real economic situations.[5] The most essential feature of competitive conditions

---

[5] For the edification of the advocates of "inductive economics" it may be observed that the "facts" are not in dispute: that what is needed in the case is not more refined observation or the gathering of "statistics," but simply correct theorizing. There is, of course, also a large field in which the crucial facts are *not* obvious.

is reversed, the feature, namely, of the private ownership of the factors practically significant for production. If the roads are assumed to be subject to private appropriation and exploitation, precisely the ideal situation which would be established by the imaginary tax will be brought about through the operation of ordinary economic motives. The owner of the broad road could not under effective competition charge anything for its use. If an agency of production is not subject to diminishing returns, and cannot be monopolized, there is, in fact, no incentive to its appropriation, and it will remain a free good. But the owner of the narrow road can charge for its use a toll representing its "superiority" over the free road, in accordance with the theory of rent, which is as old as Ricardian economics. An application of the familiar reasoning to this case will show that the toll will exactly equal the ideal tax above considered—though the application may need to be more careful and complete than that made by many of the expositors of the classical theory.

The owner of a superior opportunity for investment can set the charge for its use at any amount not greater than the excess of the product of the first unit of investment above what that unit could produce on the free opportunity. Under this charge investment will flow into the superior road up to the point where congestion and diminishing returns set in. (It is better in such a simple case to use the notion of diminishing returns than to use that of diminishing costs, since in the large the practical objective is to maximize the product of given resources and not to minimize the expenditure of resources in producing a given product.) By reducing the charge, the owner will increase the amount of traffic using his road (or in general the amount of investment of labor and capital in any opportunity). But obviously the owner of the road will not set the charge so low that the last truck which uses the road secures a return in excess of the amount which it adds to the total product of the road (that is, of all the trucks which use it). This is clearer if we think of the owner of the road hiring the trucks instead of their hiring the use of the road. The effect is the same either way; it is still the same if some third party hires the use of both. The toll or rent will be so adjusted that *added* product of the last truck which uses the narrow road is just equal to what it could produce on the broad road. No truck will pay a higher charge, and it is not to the interest of the owner of the road to accept a lower fee. And this adjustment is exactly that which maximizes the total product of both roads.

The argument may be made clearer by the use of simple diagrams.[6]

Chart A and B represents the case of constant cost or constant returns, the cost of successive units of output or the return from successive units of investment on the broad road. In Chart C, the curve $DD'D_u$ is a *cost* curve for the narrow road, showing the cost of successive units of output. It starts at a lower level than the cost on the broad road, but at a certain point D', congestion sets in and increasing cost appears. Curve $DD'D_m$ is a curve of *marginal* costs on the narrow road, as Professor Pigou uses the term marginal

[6] Cf. Pigou, *op. cit.*, Appendix iii, pp. 931–38.

Chart A and B   Chart C   Chart D

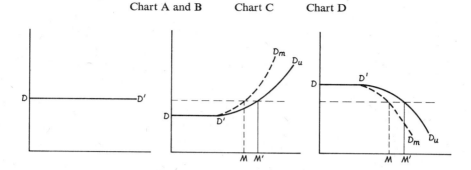

cost; the marginal cost of the nth unit of product is the difference between the total cost of producing n units and the total cost of producing $n + 1$ units. When costs being to increase, the marginal cost will increase more rapidly than the cost of the added unit, since the production of each additional unit raises the cost of the earlier units to a level with that of the new unit. It must be observed that the cost of the additional unit is always the same as the cost per unit of the whole supply produced; much economic analysis is vitiated by a spurious separation of these two conceptions of cost.

Chart D represents the same facts as Chart C, but in terms of the product of successive units of investment instead of the cost of successive units of output, that is, as curves of "diminishing returns" instead of "increasing costs." The output begins at a higher level than on the broad road, but at the point D', which corresponds to the point of the same designation on Chart C, the return from investment begins to fall off. The curve $D'D_u$ shows the actual product of the added unit of investment, and the curve $D'D_m$ its marginal product, its addition to the total. The latter decreases more rapidly because the application of the additional unit reduces the yield of the earlier ones to equality with its own. The argument is the same, but stated in inverse or reciprocal form. As indicated, the viewpoint of Chart D is to be preferred, and it may be surmised that, if Professor Pigou had put his argument in this form, he would probably have avoided the error into which he was very likely misled by measuring efficiency in terms of cost of output instead of output of resources.[7]

The owner of the road will adjust his toll so that the traffic will take his road out to the point M in Chart C or D. It will *not*, under conditions of profit-seeking exploitation, be continued to M', as argued by Professor Pigou. The actual output is the same as the "ideal" ouput which is wrongly defined in Pigou's treatment (p. 937). Evidently, the adjustment is correct

---

[7] It may be noted that Robertson makes the opposite contention, that the concepts of increasing and decreasing costs are to be preferred to those of decreasing and increasing returns. *Loc. cit.*, p. 17. He gives no argument for this position. It seems to me that this is the entrepreneur's point of view, while that of either the investor or society is the inverse one advocated in the text above and is distinctly to be preferred for general analysis.

when the *marginal* product of the last unit of investment on the superior road is equal to the product of a similar unit on the free road. Confusion arises in translating this condition into terms of cost and selling price of product. Selling price will be determined by cost on the free road, or at least these two will be equal, however the causal relation is conceived. That is, the *money* cost of any unit of product is the value of the investment which is necessary to produce it on the free opportunity, where cost is constant, or, in general, at an opportunity margin where rent does not enter. Comparison of the two viewpoints shown by our Charts C and D above shows that under competitive conditions the application of investment to the superior opportunity will be stopped at the point where *marginal real cost* (cost in terms of the transferable investment) is equal to real cost on the free opportunity. When equal additions to investment make equal additions to output, equal units of output have the same cost. But the condition of equilibrium cannot be stated in terms of money cost and money selling price of product on the superior opportunity, *because these would be equal however the investment might be distributed*, whatever rent were charged, or whether the opportunity were appropriated and exploited at all. The condition of equilibrium is that the rent on the superior opportunity is maximized as an aggregate. The rent per unit of output is a variable portion of a total unit cost which is fixed.

Extension of the foregoing argument to the general case of land rent involves no difficulties and will not be carried out in detail. The point is that any opportunity, whether or not it represents a previous investment of any sort, is a productive factor if there is sufficient demand for its use to carry into the stage of diminishing returns the application to it of transferable investment. The charge made by a private owner for the use of such an opportunity serves the socially useful purpose of limiting the application of investment to the point where *marginal* product instead of product per unit is equal to the product of investment in free (rentless) opportunities; and under competitive conditions this charge will be fixed at the level which does make marginal products equal, and thus maximizes productivity on the whole.[8]

---

[8] It is a theoretically interesting fact that the rent on an opportunity which maximizes the return to its owner and brings about the socially correct investment in it is its "marginal product" in the same sense as used to describe the competitive remuneration of other productive factors transferable from one use to another or ultimately derived from labor and waiting. It is exactly the amount by which the product of the whole competitive system would be reduced if the opportunity were held out of use or destroyed and the investment which would be combined with it were put to the next best possible use. This point is brought out in Professor Young's chapter on "Rent in Ely's Outlines of Economics" (pp. 409, 410 in the fourth edition). Professor Young also pointed out the essential fallacy in Professor Pigou's argument, in a review of the latter's earlier work on "Wealth and Welfare" *Quarterly Journal of Economics*, August, 1913.

The relation between "investment" and "opportunity" is an interesting question; by no means so simple as it is commonly assumed to be. In the writer's view there is little basis for the common distinction in this regard between "natural resources" and labor or capital. The qualities of real significance for economic theory are the conditions of supply and the degree of fluidity or its opposite, specialization to a particular use. In a critical examination neither attribute forms a basis for erecting natural agents into a separate class.

It is pertinent to add that in real life the original "appropriation" of such opportunities by private owners involves investment in exploration, in detailed investigation and appraisal by trial and error of the findings, in development work of many kinds necessary to secure and market a product—besides the cost of buying off or killing or driving off previous claimants. Under competitive conditions, again, investment in such activities of "appropriation" would not yield a greater return than investment in any other field. These activities are indeed subject to a large "aleatory element"; they are much affected by luck. But there is no evidence proving either that the luck element is greater than in other activities relating to economic progress, or that in fact the average reward has been greater than that which might have been had from conservative investments.

II

While Professor Pigou constantly refers to industries of decreasing cost, or increasing returns, the principles at issue do not necessarily imply more than a *difference* in the way in which efficiency varies with size from one industry to another. Some of Professor Graham's reasoning in regard to international trade and international value depends upon decreasing cost as such. It seems advisable, before taking up his argument concretely, to devote a few paragraphs to this conception, which the writer believes to involve serious fallacies, and to the meaning of cost and its variation.

Valuation is an aspect of conscious choice. Apart from a necessity of choosing, values have no meaning or existence. Valuation *is* a comparison of values. A single value, existing in isolation, can no more be imagined than can a single force without some other force opposed to it as a "reaction" to its "action." Value is in fact the complete analogue of force in the interpretation of human activity, and in a behavioristic formulation is identical with force—which is to say, it is an instrumental idea, metaphysically nonexistent. Fundamentally, then, the cost of any value is simply the value that is given up when it is chosen; it is just the reaction or resistance to choice which makes it choice. Ordinarily we speak of cost as a consumption of "resources" of some kind, but everyone recognizes that resources have no value in themselves; that they simply represent the products which could have been had by their use in some other direction than the one chosen.

The notion of cost suffers greatly in logical clearness from confusion with the vague and ambiguous term "pain." In the broad true sense every cost is a pain, and the two are identical. Little or nothing can be made of the distinction between pain and the sacrifice of pleasure, or between pleasure and escape from pain. The subject cannot be gone into here from the point of view of psychology; it is enough to point out that the way in which a particular person regards a particular sacrifice depends mainly upon the direction of *change* in the affective tone of his consciousness or upon the established level of expectations. The essential thing is that the pleasure-pain character of a value is irrelevant, that the universal meaning of cost is the sacrifice of a value alternative. This is just as true of the "irksomeness" of labor, as of a payment of money. The irksomeness of digging a ditch reflects the value of the loafing or playing which might be done instead. And there is no significant difference between this irksomeness or pain and that of using the proceeds of the sale of a liberty bond to pay a doctor's bill when it might have been used to procure a fortnight's vacation.[9]

The natural and common rule in choice is necessarily that of increasing cost. In the exchange of one good for another at a fixed ratio, the further the exchange is carried, the more "utility" is given up and the less is secured. This is merely the law of diminishing utility. It is only when one commodity is given up in order that another may be produced by the use of the common and divertible productive energy that we ordinarily think of the variation of cost. If two commodities are produced by a single homogeneous productive factor, there is no variation of cost as successive portions of one are given up to procure more of the other by shifting that factor—except in the sense of increasing utility cost as met within the case of exchange. Ordinarily, however, new considerations enter, as a matter of fact. If we wish to produce more wheat by producing less corn, we find that the further the shift of production is carried, the more *bushels* of corn (as well as corn value) have to be given up to produce a *bushel* of wheat (and still more for a given amount of wheat value). This is the economic principle of increasing cost (decreasing returns) as generally understood, reduced to its lowest terms and freed from ambiguity.

When costs are measured in value terms and product in physical units there are two sorts of reasons for increasing cost, one reflecting value changes and the other technological changes. The first would be operative if all productive resources were perfectly homogeneous and perfectly fluid. But this is not, in general, the case, and technological changes supervene which work in the same direction and add to the increase which would otherwise take place in the cost of a unit of the product which is being produced in larger volume. Principal among these technological changes is the fact that some of the resources used to produce the commodity being sacrificed are not useful in the production of that whose output is being increased, and in consequence the resources which are transferred are used in progressively larger proportions in the second industry and in smaller proportions in the first, in combination with certain other resources which are specialized to the two industries respectively. The consequent reduction in the physical productive effect of the transferred factors is what is meant by diminishing returns in one of the

---

[9] Besides confusion with the notion of pain, which has at last obtained in psychology a definite meaning independent of unpleasantness, the notion of cost encounters in economics another source of obscurity. This is in the relation between those values which do not pass through the market and receive prices and those which do. The "loafing" which underlies the irksomeness of labor is such a value, and there is a tendency to associate the notion of cost with these nonpecuniary values. In this connection it should be noted that not merely labor but all types of productive service are subject to the competition of uses which yield their satisfactions directly and not through the channel of a marketable product. Thus land is used for lawns as well as for fields, and examples could be multiplied at will.

many narrower uses of that highly ambiguous expression. Another techno-logical cause still further aggravating the tendency to increasing costs arises from the fact that productive factors are not really homogeneous or uniform in quality. As productive power is transferred from corn to wheat, it will be found that the concrete men, acres, and implements transferred are those progressively more suitable for corn-growing and less suitable for wheat. Thus each unit suffers a progressively greater reduction in its value in terms of units of either commodity, or it takes more units to represent in the wheat industry the value of a single unit in the corn industry, and value costs of wheat mount still higher for this third reason.

All three changes so far noted clearly involve increasing cost in the real sense, the amount of value[10] outlay or sacrifice necessary to produce an additional physical unit of the commodity whose production is increased. In addition to these we have to consider two further possible sources of in-creased cost. The first is that, when an additional unit of, say, wheat is pro-duced, and the factors transferable from other industries to wheat are raised in price, the quantities of these factors already used to produce wheat will rise in price along with those added to the industry. Should all this increase in cost be charged up to the production of the last unit of wheat produced, which causes it to appear? In a sense, this is in truth a social cost of this last unit. Yet the transfer of productive energy will not take place unless there has been a shift in the market estimate of wheat in comparison with competing commodities such as to justify it. That is, as the exchange system measures values, making all units of the same good equal in value, the increase in the total value of the wheat must be greater than the decrease in the value of the output of competing commodities. (A discrepancy—*in either direction*—may result from considering the potential significances of inframarginal units commonly designated as consumers' surplus.) The second additional possible source of increased cost is the increased payments which will be made for the specialized factors used in producing wheat,[11] the cost elements which are of the nature of rent or surplus. These payments evidently do not represent social costs at all, but redistributions of product merely. Such redistributions may be " good " or " bad," depending on the moral position, according to some standard, of the owners of the two classes of factors respectively.

Decreasing cost (or increasing returns) is alleged to result in several ways, which can be dealt with but briefly. The most important is the technological economy of large-scale production. When the output of a commodity is increased, the cost of the productive services used to produce it will be higher; but this increase in their cost per unit may, it is held, be more than offset by economies in utilization, made possible by larger-scale operations, which

---

[10] Value as used in this discussion means "real" value, relative significance, or utility. No assertion as to exchange value or price is implied.

[11] The fallacy of identifying specialized factors with natural agents and transferable factors with labor and capital has been referred to above. It will not be elaborated in this paper.

increase the amount of product obtained from given quantities of materials and resources consumed.[12] But technological economies arise from increasing the size of the productive unit, not from increasing the total output of the industry as a whole. The possibility of realizing such economies—by the distribution of "overhead," or more elaborate division of labor, or use of machinery—tends to bring about an increase in the *scale* of production, but this may happen independently of any change in the output of the industry. If competition is effective, the size of the productive unit will tend to grow until *either* no further economies are obtainable, *or* there is only one establishment left and the industry is a monopoly. When all establishments have been brought to the most efficient size, variation in total output is a matter of changing their *number*, in which no technical economies are involved.

The rejoinder to the above argument is the doctrine of "external economies," which surely rests upon a misconception. Economies may be "external" to a particular establishment or technical production unit, but they are not external to the industry if they affect its efficiency. The portion of the productive process carried on in a particular unit is an accidental consideration. External economies in one business unit are internal economies in some other, within the industry. Any branch or stage in the creation of a product which offers continuously a chance for technical economies with increase in the scale of operations must eventuate either in monopoly or in leaving the tendency behind and establishing the normal relation of increasing cost with increasing size. If the organization unit is not small in comparison with the industry as a whole, a totally different law must be applied to the relation between output, cost, and price.

Two other alleged sources of decreasing cost are the stimulation of demand and the stimulation of invention. Neither can properly be regarded as an effect of increasing output, other things being equal. Producing a commodity and distributing it at a loss might result in developing a taste for it, but would be no different in principle from any other method of spending money to produce this result. Inventions tend to enlarge the scale of production rather than large-scale production to cause inventions. It is true that an increase in demand from some outside cause may stimulate invention, but the action takes place through first making the industry highly profitable. The result is not uniform or dependable, nor is it due to increased production as such.

These brief statements form a mere summary of the argument that, with reference to long-run tendencies under given general conditions, increasing the output of a commodity must increase its cost of production unless the industry is, or becomes, a monopoly. They also indicate the nature of the

---

[12] Professor Graham says (p. 203, note) that decreasing cost is an "aspect of the law of proportionality." This is a form of statement frequently met with, but rests on a misconception sufficiently refuted in the text. It is true only accidentally, if it is true in any general sense at all, that a more elaborate technology is associated with a change in the proportions of the factors.

relation between social cost and entrepreneur's money cost. Under competition, transferable resources are distributed among alternative uses in such a way as to yield equal marginal[13] value product everywhere, which is the arrangement that maximizes production, as measured by value, on the whole. Nontransferable resources secure "rents" which equalize money costs to all producers and for all units of product under the foregoing condition; or, better, the rents bring about that allocation of resources which maximizes production, under the condition that money costs are equalized.

A further major fallacy in value theory which suffuses Professor Graham's argument will be pointed out in general terms before proceeding with detailed criticism. The reference is to the notorious "law of reciprocal demand." This so-called law, that the prices of commodities exchanged internationally are so adjusted that a country's exports pay for its imports, is at best a truism. To say that what one gives in exchange pays for what one gets is merely a statement of the fact that one is exchanged for the other. What calls for explanation in the case is the process which fixes *how much* of one thing will be parted with, and *how much* of the other received in return.

III

We are now ready to take up concretely the proposed refutation of the law of comparative advantage. Professor Graham begins by assuming two countries, which he calls A and B, but which it appears simpler to designate as England and America, respectively. Suppose then that in England 10 days' labor produces 40 units of wheat and 10 days' labor produces 40 watches; in America 10 days' labor produces 40 units of wheat and 10 days' labor produces 30 watches. America has a comparative advantage in wheat, England in watches.[14] According to the accepted theory, trade at any ratio intermediate between the two cost ratios will be of advantage to both countries. Our author assumes it to begin at the ration of 35 watches for 40 units of wheat. Then, for each ten days' labor devoted to producing wheat and exchanging for watches, America can get 35 watches instead of the 30 which could be produced by using the same labor in producing the watches. England, for each ten days' labor devoted to producing watches and exchanging for wheat can secure $(40/35) \times 40$ ($= 45\frac{5}{7}$) units of wheat, instead of the 40 units which could be directly produced with the same labor.

So far, well and good for the theory. But at this point Professor Graham's blows begin to fall. Assuming that wheat-growing is an industry of increasing, and watch-making one of decreasing costs, it will come to pass, as the two

---

[13] "Differential" is the term in use in other sciences for the idea commonly referred to as a marginal unit in economics.

[14] The use of labor as equivalent to productive power, or the treatment of labor as the only factor which may be transferred from one industry to the other, is a simplification likely to mislead the unwary, but it will not be criticized here. It is of interest to note, however, that historically the whole doctrine of comparative cost was a prop for a labor cost theory of value.

countries progressively specialize, that the cost of both commodities is decreased for England and increased for America. It clearly follows, first, that if the process goes on long enough, America will begin to lose, and just as clearly, from the assumptions of the article, that the process will go on forever! For the further it is carried, the greater becomes England's comparative advantage in the production of watches and the greater becomes America's comparative advantage in the production of wheat. Yet this conclusion must arouse a suspicion that there is something wrong in Denmark.

First, in accordance with the argument above, drop the assumption of decreasing cost as a permanent condition in the watch-making industry; then the two cost ratios in the two countries must come together instead of separating as the specialization of productive efforts progresses. Under any assumption whatever, *either* this must happen, *or else* one country must entirely cease to produce one of the commodities. In the first event, the exchange ratio will be the common cost ratio of the two countries (transportation costs being neglected, as usual in these discussions). If the second result ensues—that one country abandons one of the industries—*the exchange ratio will be the cost ratio in the country which still produces both commodities* (assuming, always, that monopoly is absent). Professor Graham "assumes" that the comparative advantage has become progressively greater as the result of specialization and then "assumes" (page 210) that, with the cost ratio in one country half what it is in the other, the market price may be established at any ratio between the two. In reality the only possible result under the cost conditions he states would be that America would stop producing watches at once and would exchange wheat for watches at the ratio of 40 for 40 (the cost ratio in England), thus making a *gain* of 20 watches on each ten days' labor so employed as compared with using it to produce the watches in America.

Next, the author proposes to consider the effect of interpreting his cost figures as representing marginal cost instead of cost per unit. He gets no further, however, than to average up the marginal with assumed inframarginal costs, which amounts merely to a slight change in the numbers assumed for cost per unit. He nowhere gives an explicit statement of what he means by cost, and must be suspected of not having clearly faced the difficulties and ambiguities in the notion, as brought out in the argument of the first and second parts of this paper. Certainly it will not do to recognize a possible permanent difference under competition in the money cost of different units of a supply, or in their marginal real cost. The money costs which represent real costs differ in different situations, but the rent element always equalizes them, or produces *coincidence* between equality of money cost, which would result in any case, and equality of marginal real cost, which is the social desideratum. Value and cost are like action and reaction, axiomatically equal, and as in an exchange system the value of all similar units must be equal, so must their costs.

In the writer's opinion this also is socially and morally correct. We do not, and should not, value the first slice of bread more highly than the last, nor systematically value anything at more or less than its necessary cost. As between units of supply consumed by different persons, the case is different, because different persons do not come into the market with equal exchange power in the form of productive capacity. But the question is one of ethics, entirely outside the field of exchange as a mechanical problem. The famous surpluses have the same kind of significance as potential energy in physics. They relate to possible changes in fundamental conditions, but have nothing to do with the conditions of equilibrium in any particular situation. With reference to relations among actual magnitudes, cost curves and utility curves should always be interpreted to mean that, as supply varies, the cost, or utility, of every unit changes in the manner shown by the curve.

Marginal money cost, in the sense in which it is used by Professor Pigou, is meaningless with relation to competitive conditions. It is true that under monopoly the supply is so adjusted that the contribution of the last unit to total selling price (marginal demand price) is equal to the addition to total cost incurred in consequence of producing it (marginal supply price); but this is a mere equivalent of the statement that the difference between total cost and total selling price is made a maximum. Professor Graham seems to use the expression marginal cost to mean the particular money expense of producing the last unit of supply; but, as already stated, there cannot in the long run under competitive conditions be a difference between the cost of this unit and that of any other, or the cost per unit of producing the whole supply.

Professor Graham's article makes use at several points of the effects of different elasticities of demand for different goods, especially as between agricultural products and manufactures. He fails to recognize that, with reference to large and inclusive groups of commodities, demand, which is an exchange *ratio*, is merely a different view of a production ratio, and hence of a cost ratio. In discussing the sale of a single commodity in a complicated economic society and with reference to small changes, it is permissible to treat money as an absolute; but in reducing all exchange to barter between two classes of goods, this procedure is quite inadmissible.

Moreover, consideration of the actual course of events when trade is opened up will show that elasticity of demand has little to do with the special theory of international trade or international value. Each country continues to specialize in the commodities in which it has a comparative advantage, until there is no gain to be secured from further specialization, that is, until it will cost as much to secure the next unit of the imported good by exchange as it will to produce it within the country. Now at a certain point, a country will obtain as much of the imported good as it would have produced for itself under an equilibrium adjustment within itself if foreign trade had been prohibited; and in consequence of the saving of productive power effected by the trade, a part of the resources which in its absence would be used to produce that commodity will be left to be disposed of. *Beyond this point*, that is, in the disposition of the saved productive power, elasticities of demand come into operation. This fund of saved productive power will not all be used to produce either of the commodities concerned in the exchange with the foreign nation, but will be distributed over the whole field of production in accordance with the ordinary laws of supply and demand.

The foregoing paragraphs are believed to cover the main points in the writings criticized which involve fallacies in the interpretation of cost and so come under the title of this paper. The entire argument of Professor Graham's second article falls to the ground, as he has stated it, as soon as the principles of cost are applied to the determination of international values instead of "assuming" the latter. Many further points in his first article are especially inviting to criticism, but fall outside the scope of the present paper. It suffices for the solution of the essential problem of international trade to recognize that the production of one good to exchange for another is an *alternative method of producing* the second commodity. Under competitive conditions, productive resources will not be used in this indirect process of production unless the yield is greater than that obtained by the use of the direct method. The task of economic analysis is to show why the profit-seeking motive impels the private producer to put resources to the use which brings the largest yield. Now to the entrepreneur producers of wheat and watches, in a case like that used in the illustration, the choice is not a question of comparative advantage, but of absolute profit or loss. If ten days' labor will produce a quantity of wheat which can be exchanged for more than 40 watches, then that amount of labor will be *worth more* than 40 watches, and the business enterprise which uses it to produce the watches will simply lose money. It is an example of the common fallacy of thinking in terms of physical efficiency, whereas efficiency is, in the nature of the case, a relation between value magnitudes.

That free enterprise is not a perfectly ideal system of social organization is a proposition not to be gainsaid, and nothing is further from the aims of the present writer than to set up the contention that it is. But in his opinion the weaknesses and failures of the system lie outside the field of the mechanics of exchange under the theoretical conditions of perfect competition. It is probable that *all* efforts to prove a continued bias in the workings of competition as such, along the lines followed by Professors Pigou and Graham, are doomed to failure. Under certain theoretical conditions, more or less consciously and definitely assumed in general by economic theorists, the system would be ideal. The correct form of the problem of general criticism referred to at the outset of this paper is, therefore, that of bringing these lurking assumptions above the threshold into the realm of the explicit and of contrasting them with the facts of life—the conditions under which competitive dealings are actually carried on.[15]

When the problem is attacked from this point of view, the critic finds

---

[15] The great bulk of the critical material in Professor Pigou's "Wealth and Welfare" is of this character.

himself moving among considerations very different from the logical quantitative relations of such discussions as the foregoing. Human beings are not
"individuals," to begin with; a large majority of them are not even legally
competent to contract. The values of life are not, in the main, reducible to
satisfactions obtained from the consumption of exchangeable goods and
services. Such desires as people have for goods and services are not their own
in any original sense, but are the product of social influence of innumerable
kinds and of every moral grade, largely manufactured by the competitive
system itself. The productive capacities in their own persons and in owned
external things which form the ultimate stock in trade of the human being
are derived from an uncertain mixture of conscientious effort, inheritance,
pure luck, and outright force and fraud. He cannot be well or truly informed
regarding the markets for the productive power he possesses, and the information which he gets has a way of coming to him after the time when it would
be of use. The business organizations which are the directing divinities of the
system are but groups of ignorant and frail beings like the individuals with
whom they deal. (In the perfectly ideal order of theory the problem of
management would be nonexistent!) The system as a whole is dependent
upon an outside organization, an authoritarian state, made up also of
ignorant and frail human beings, to provide a setting in which it can operate
at all. Besides watching over the dependent and noncontracting, the state
must define and protect property rights, enforce contract and prevent non-
contractual (compulsory) transactions, maintain a circulating medium, and
most especially prevent that collusion and monopoly, the antithesis of competition, into which competitive relations constantly tend to gravitate. It is in
the field indicated by this summary list of postulates, rather than in that of the
mechanics of exchange relations, that we must work out the ultimate critique
of free enterprise.

Increasing returns and economic progress*†

ALLYN A. YOUNG

My subject may appear alarmingly formidable, but I did not intend it to be so. The words economic progress, taken by themselves, would suggest the pursuit of some philosophy of history, of some way of appraising the results of past and possible future changes in forms of economic organisation and modes of economic activities. But as I have used them, joined to the other half of my title, they are meant merely to dispel apprehensions, by suggesting that I do not propose to discuss any of those alluring but highly technical questions relating to the precise way in which some sort of equilibrium of supply and demand is achieved in the market for the products of industries which can increase their output without increasing their costs proportionately, or to the possible advantages of fostering the development of such industries while putting a handicap upon industries whose output can be increased only at the expense of a more than proportionate increase of costs. I suspect, indeed, that the apparatus which economists have built up for dealing effectively with the range of questions to which I have just referred may stand in the way of a clear view of the more general or elementary aspects of the phenomena of increasing returns such as I wish to comment upon in this paper.

Consider, for example, Alfred Marshall's fruitful distinction between the internal productive economies which a particular firm is able to secure as the growth of the market permits it to enlarge the scale of its operations and the economies external to the individual firm which show themselves only in changes of the organisation of the industry as a whole. This distinction has been useful in at least two different ways. In the first place it is, or ought to be, a safeguard against the common error of assuming that wherever increasing returns operate there is necessarily an effective tendency towards monopoly. In the second place it simplifies the analysis of the manner in which the prices

* *The Economic Journal*, 38(1928): pp. 527–42. Reprinted by courtesy of *The Economic Journal*.

† Presidential Address before Section F (Economic Science and Statistics) of the British Association for the Advancement of Science, Glasgow, September 10, 1928.

of commodities produced under conditions of increasing returns are determined. A representative firm within the industry, maintaining its own identity and devoting itself to a given range of activities, is made to be the vehicle or medium through which the economies achieved by the industry as a whole are transmitted to the market and have their effect upon the price of the product.

The view of the nature of the processes of industrial progress which is implied in the distinction between internal and external economies is necessarily a partial view. Certain aspects of those processes are illuminated, while, for that very reason, certain other aspects, important in relation to other problems, are obscured. This will be clear, I think, if we observe that, although the internal economies of some firms producing, let us say, materials or appliances may figure as the external economies of other firms, not all of the economies which are properly to be called external can be accounted for by adding up the internal economies of all the separate firms. When we look at the internal economies of a particular firm we envisage a condition of comparative stability. Year after year the firm, like its competitors, is manufacturing a particular product or group of products, or is confining itself to certain definite stages in the work of forwarding the products towards their final form. Its operations change in the sense that they are progressively adapted to an increasing output, but they are kept within definitely circumscribed bounds. Out beyond, in that obscurer field from which it derives its external economies, changes of another order are occurring. New products are appearing, firms are assuming new tasks, and new industries are coming into being. In short, change in this external field is qualitative as well as quantitative. No analysis of the forces making for economic equilibrium, forces which we might say are tangential at any moment of time, will serve to illumine this field, for movements away from equilibrium, departures from previous trends, are characteristic of it. Not much is to be gained by probing into it to see how increasing returns show themselves in the costs of individual firms and in the prices at which they offer their products.

Instead, we have to go back to a simpler and more inclusive view, such as some of the older economists took when they contrasted the increasing returns which they thought were characteristic of manufacturing industry taken as a whole with the diminishing returns which they thought were dominant in agriculture because of an increasingly unfavourable proportioning of labour and land. Most of them were disappointingly vague with respect to the origins and the precise nature of the "improvements" which they counted upon to retard somewhat the operation of the tendency towards diminishing returns in agriculture and to secure a progressively more effective use of labour in manufactures. Their opinions appear to have rested partly upon an empirical generalisation. Improvements had been made, they were still being made, and it might be assumed that they could continue to be made. If they had looked back they would have seen that there were centuries during which there were few significant changes in either agricultural or industrial methods. But they were living in an age when men had turned their faces in a new direction and when economic progress was not only consciously sought but seemed in some way to grow out of the nature of things. Improvements, then, were not something to be explained. They were natural phenomena, like the precession of the equinoxes.

There were certain important exceptions, however, to this incurious attitude towards what might seem to be one of the most important of all economic problems. Senior's positive doctrine is well known, and there were others who made note of the circumstance that with the growth of population and of markets new opportunities for the division of labour appear and new advantages attach to it. In this way, and in this way only, were the generally commonplace things which they said about "improvements" related to anything which could properly be called a doctrine of increasing returns. They added nothing to Adam Smith's famous theorem that the division of labour depends upon the extent of the market. That theorem, I have always thought, is one of the most illuminating and fruitful generalisations which can be found anywhere in the whole literature of economics. In fact, as I am bound to confess, I am taking it as the text of this paper, in much the way that some minor composer borrows a theme from one of the masters and adds certain developments or variations of his own. Today, of course, we mean by the division of labour something much broader in scope than that splitting up of occupations and development of specialised crafts which Adam Smith mostly had in mind. No one, so far as I know, has tried to enumerate all of the different aspects of the division of labour, and I do not propose to under-take that task. I shall deal with two related aspects only: the growth of indirect or roundabout methods of production and the division of labour among industries.

It is generally agreed that Adam Smith, when he suggested that the division of labour leads to inventions because workmen engaged in specialised routine operations come to see better ways of accomplishing the same results, missed the main point. The important thing, of course, is that with the division of labour a group of complex processes is transformed into a succession of simpler processes, some of which, at least, lend themselves to the use of machinery. In the use of machinery and the adoption of indirect processes there is a further division of labour, the economies of which are again limited by the extent of the market. It would be wasteful to make a hammer to drive a single nail; it would be better to use whatever awkward implement lies conveniently at hand. It would be wasteful to furnish a factory with an elaborate equipment of specially constructed jigs, gauges, lathes, drills, presses, and conveyors to build a hundred automobiles; it would be better to rely mostly upon tools and machines of standard types, so as to make a relatively larger use of directly applied and a relatively smaller use of indirectly applied labour. Mr. Ford's methods would be absurdly uneconomical if his output were very small, and would be unprofitable even if his output were what many other manufacturers of automobiles would call large.

Then, of course, there are economies of what might be called a secondary order. How far it pays to go in equipping factories with special appliances for making hammers or for constructing specialised machinery for use in making different parts of automobiles depends again upon how many nails are to be driven and how many automobiles can be sold. In some instances, I suppose, these secondary economies, though real, have only a secondary importance. The derived demands for many types of specialised production appliances are inelastic over a fairly large range. If the benefits and the costs of using such appliances are spread over a relatively large volume of final products, their technical effectiveness is a larger factor in determining whether it is profitable to use them than any difference which producing them on a large or small scale would commonly make in their costs. In other instances the demand for productive appliances is more elastic, and beyond a certain level of costs demand may fail completely. In such circumstances secondary economies may become highly important.

Doubtless, much of what I have said has been familiar and even elementary. I shall venture, nevertheless, to put further stress upon two points, which may be among those which have a familiar ring, but which appear sometimes to be in danger of being forgotten. (Otherwise, economists of standing could not have suggested that increasing returns may be altogether illusory, or have maintained that where they are present they must lead to monopoly.) The first point is that the principal economies which manifest themselves in increasing returns are the economies of capitalistic or roundabout methods of production. These economies, again, are largely identical with the economies of the division of labour in its most important modern forms. In fact, these economies lie under our eyes, but we may miss them if we try to make of *large-scale* production (in the sense of production by large firms or large industries), as contrasted with *large* production, any more than an incident in the general process by which increasing returns are secured and if accordingly we look too much at the individual firm or even, as I shall suggest presently, at the individual industry.

The second point is that the economies of roundabout methods, even more than the economies of other forms of the division of labour, depend upon the extent of the market—and that, of course, is why we discuss them under the head of increasing returns. It would hardly be necessary to stress this point, if it were not that the economies of large-scale operations and of "mass-production" are often referred to as though they could be had for the taking, by means of a "rational" reorganisation of industry. Now I grant that at any given time routine and inertia play a very large part in the organisation and conduct of industrial operations. Real leadership is no more common in industrial than in other pursuits. New catchwords or slogans like mass production and rationalisation may operate as stimuli; they may rouse men from routine and lead them to scrutinise again the organisation and processes of industry and to try to discover particular ways in which they can be bettered. For example, no one can doubt that there are genuine economies to be achieved in the way of "simplification and standardisation," or that the securing of these economies requires that certain deeply rooted competitive wastes be extirpated. This last requires a definite concerted effort—precisely the kind of thing which ordinary competitive motives are often powerless to effect, but which might come more easily as the response to the dissemination of a new idea.

There is a danger, however, that we shall expect too much from these "rational" industrial reforms. Pressed beyond a certain point they become the reverse of rational. I have naturally been interested in British opinions respecting the reasons for the relatively high productivity (per labourer or per hour of labour) of representative American industries. The error of those who suggest that the explanation is to be found in the relatively high wages which prevail in America is not that they confuse cause and effect, but that they hold that what are really only two aspects of a single situation are, the one cause, and the other effect. Those who hold that American industry is managed better, that its leaders study its problems more intelligently and plan more courageously and more wisely can cite no facts in support of their opinion save the differences in the results achieved. Allowing for the circumstance that British industry, as a whole, has proved to be rather badly adjusted to the new post-war economic situation, I know of no facts which prove or even indicate that British industry, seen against the background of its own problems and its own possibilities, is less efficiently organised or less ably directed than American industry or the industry of any other country.

Sometimes the fact that the average American labourer works with the help of a larger supply of power-driven labour-saving machinery than the labourer of other countries is cited as evidence of the superior intelligence of the average American employer. But this will not do, for, as every economist knows, the greater the degree in which labour is productive or scarce—the words have the same meaning—the greater is the relative economy of using it in such indirect or roundabout ways as are technically advantageous, even though such procedure calls for larger advances of capital than simpler methods do.

It is encouraging to find that a fairly large number of commentators upon the volume of the American industrial product and the scale of American industrial organisation have come to surmise that the extent of the American domestic market, unimpeded by tariff barriers, may have something to do with the matter. This opinion seems even to be forced upon thoughtful observers by the general character of the facts, whether or no the observers think in terms of the economists' conception of increasing returns. In certain industries, although by no means in all, productive methods are economical and profitable in America which would not be profitable elsewhere. The importance of coal and iron and other natural resources needs no comment. Taking a country's economic endowment as given, however, the most important single factor in determining the effectiveness of its industry appears to be the size of the market. But just what constitutes a large market? Not area or population alone, but buying power, the capacity to absorb a large annual output of goods. This trite observation, however, at once suggests another equally trite, namely, that capacity to buy depends upon capacity to produce. In an inclusive view, considering the market not as an outlet for the products of a particular industry, and therefore external to that industry, but as the outlet for goods in general, the size of the market is determined and defined by the volume of production. If this statement needs any quali-fication, it is that the conception of a market in this inclusive sense—an aggregate of productive activities, tied together by trade—carries with it the notion that there must be some sort of balance, that different productive activities must be proportioned one to another.

Modified, then, in the light of this broader conception of the market, Adam Smith's dictum amounts to the theorem that the division of labour depends in large part upon the division of labour. This is more than mere tautology. It means, if I read its significance rightly, that the counterforces which are continually defeating the forces which make for economic equilibrium are more pervasive and more deeply rooted in the consitution of the modern economic system than we commonly realise. Not only new or adventitious elements, coming in from the outside, but elements which are permanent characteristics of the ways in which goods are produced make continuously for change. Every important advance in the organisation of production, re-gardless of whether it is based upon anything which, in a narrow or technical sense, would be called a new "invention," or involves a fresh application of the fruits of scientific progress to industry, alters the conditions of industrial activity and initiates responses elsewhere in the industrial structure which in turn have a further unsettling effect. Thus change becomes progressive and propagates itself in a cumulative way.

The apparatus which economists have built up for the analysis of supply and demand in their relations to prices does not seem to be particularly helpful for the purposes of an inquiry into these broader aspects of increasing returns. In fact, as I have already suggested, reliance upon it may divert attention to incidental or partial aspects of a process which ought to be seen as a whole. If, nevertheless, one insists upon seeing just how far one can get into the problem by using the formulas of supply and demand, the simplest way, I suppose, is to begin by inquiring into the operations of reciprocal demand when the commodities exchanged are produced competitively under conditions of increasing returns and when the demand for each commodity is elastic, in the special sense that a small increase in its supply will be attended by an increase in the amounts of other commodities which can be had in exchange for it.[1] Under such conditions an increase in the supply of one commodity *is* an increase in the demand for other commodities, and it must

---

[1] If the circumstance that commodity *a* is produced under conditions of increasing returns is taken into account as a factor in the elasticity of demand for *b* in terms of *a*, elasticity of demand and elasticity of supply may be looked upon as different ways of expressing a single functional relation.

be supposed that every increase in demand will evoke an increase in supply. The rate at which any one industry grows is conditioned by the rate at which other industries grow, but since the elasticities of demand and of supply will differ for different products, some industries will grow faster than others. Even with a stationary population and in the absence of new discoveries[2] in pure or applied science there are no limits to the process of expansion except the limits beyond which demand is not elastic and returns do not increase.

If, under these hypothetical conditions, progress were unimpeded and frictionless, if it were not dependent in part upon a process of trial and error, if the organisation of industry were always such as, in relation to the immediate situation, is most economical, the realising of increasing returns might be progressive and continuous, although, for technical reasons, it could not always proceed at an even rate. But it would remain a process requiring time. An industrial dictator, with foresight and knowledge, could hasten the pace somewhat, but he could not achieve an Aladdin-like transformation of a country's industry so as to reap the fruits of a half-century's ordinary progress in a few years. The obstacles are of two sorts. First, the human material which has to be used is resistant to change. New trades have to be learnt and new habits have to be acquired. There has to be a new geographical distribution of the population and established communal groups have to be broken up. Second, the accumulation of the necessary capital takes time, even though the process of accumulation is largely one of turning part of an increasing product into forms which will serve in securing a further increase of product. An acceleration of the rate of accumulation encounters increasing costs, into which both technical and psychological elements enter. One who likes to conceive of all economic processes in terms of tendencies towards an equilibrium might even maintain that increasing returns, so far as they depend upon the economies of indirect methods of production and the size of the market, are offset and negated by their costs, and that under such simplified conditions as I have dealt with the realizing of increasing returns would be spread through time in such a way as to secure an equilibrium of costs and advantages. This would amount to saying that no real economic progress could come through the operation of forces engendered *within* the economic system—a conclusion repugnant to common sense. To deal with this point thoroughly would take us too far afield. I shall merely observe, first, that the appropriate conception is that of a *moving* equilibrium, and second, that the costs which (under increasing returns) grow less rapidly than the product are not the " costs " which figure in an " equilibrium of costs and advantages."

Moving away from these abstract considerations, so as to get closer to the complications of the real situation, account has to be taken, first, of various kinds of obstacles. The demand for some products is inelastic, or, with an

---

[2] As contrasted with such new ways of organising production and such new " inventions " as are merely adaptations of known ways of doing things, made practicable and economical by an enlarged scale of production.

increasing supply, soon becomes so. The producers of such commodities, however, often share in the advantages of the increase of the general scale of production in related industries, and so far as they do productive resources are released for other uses. Then there are natural scarcities, limitations, or inelasticities of supply, such as effectively block the way to the securing of any important economies in the production of some commodities and which impair the effectiveness of the economies secured in the production of other commodities. In most fields, moreover, progress is not and cannot be continuous. The next important step forward is often initially costly, and cannot be taken until a certain quantum of prospective advantages has accumulated.

On the other side of the account are various factors which reinforce the influences which make for increasing returns. The discovery of new natural resources and of new uses for them and the growth of scientific knowledge are probably the most potent of such factors. The causal connections between the growth of industry and the progress of science run in both directions, but on which side the preponderant influence lies no one can say. At any rate, out of better knowledge of the materials and forces upon which men can lay their hands there come both new ways of producing familiar commodities and new products, and these last have a presumptive claim to be regarded as embodying more economical uses of productive resources than the uses which they displace. Some weight has to be given also to the way in which, with the advance of the scientific spirit, a new kind of interest—which might be described as a scientific interest conditioned by an economic interest—is beginning to infiltrate into industry. It is a point of controversy, but I venture to maintain that under most circumstances, though not in all, the growth of population still has to be counted a factor making for a larger *per capita* product—although even that cautious statement needs to be interpreted and qualified. But just as there may be population growth with no increase of the average *per capita* product, so also, as I have tried to suggest, markets may grow and increasing returns may be secured while the population remains stationary.

It is dangerous to assign to any single factor the leading role in that continuing economic revolution which has taken the modern world so far away from the world of a few hundred years ago. But is there any other factor which has a better claim to that role than the persisting search for markets? No other hypothesis so well unites economic history and economic theory. The Industrial Revolution of the eighteenth century has come to be generally regarded, not as a cataclysm brought about by certain inspired improvements in industrial technique, but as a series of changes related in an orderly way to prior changes in industrial organisation and to the enlargement of markets. It is sometimes said, however, that while in the Middle Ages and in the early modern period industry was the servant of commerce, since the rise of "industrial capitalism" the relation has been reversed, commerce being now merely an agent of industry. If this means that the finding of markets is one of the tasks of modern industry, it is true. If it means that industry imposes its will upon the market, that whereas formerly the things which were produced were the things which could be sold, now the things which have to be sold are the things that are produced, it is not true.

The great change, I imagine, is in the new importance which the *potential market* has in the planning and management of large industries. The difference between the cost per unit of output in an industry or in an individual plant properly adapted to a given volume of output and in an industry or plant equally well adapted to an output five times as large is often much greater than one would infer from looking merely at the economies which may accrue as an existing establishment gradually extends the scale of its operations. Potential demand, then, in the planning of industrial undertakings, has to be balanced against potential economies, elasticity of demand against decreasing costs. The search for markets is not a matter of disposing of a "surplus product," in the Marxian sense, but of finding an outlet for a potential product. Nor is it wholly a matter of multiplying profits by multiplying sales; it is partly a matter of augmenting profits by reducing costs.

Although the initial displacement may be considerable and the repercussions upon particular industries unfavourable, the enlarging of the market for any one commodity, produced under conditions of increasing returns, generally has the net effect, as I have tried to show, of enlarging the market for other commodities. The business man's mercantilistic emphasis upon markets may have a sounder basis than the economist who thinks mostly in terms of economic statics is prone to admit. How far "selling expenses," for example, are to be counted sheer economic waste depends upon their effects upon the aggregate product of industry, as distinguished from their effects upon the fortunes of particular undertakings.

Increasing returns are often spoken of as though they were attached always to the growth of "industries," and I have not tried to avoid that way of speaking of them, although I think that it may be a misleading way. The point which I have in mind is something more than a quibble about the proper definition of an industry, for it involves a particular thesis with respect to the way in which increasing returns are reflected in changes in the organisation of industrial activities. Much has been said about industrial integration as a concomitant or a natural result of an increasing industrial output. It obviously is, under particular conditions, though I know of no satisfactory statement of just what those particular conditions are. But the opposed process, industrial differentiation, has been and remains the type of change characteristically associated with the growth of production. Notable as has been the increase in the complexity of the apparatus of living, as shown by the increase in the variety of goods offered in consumers' markets, the increase in the diversification of intermediate products and of industries manufacturing special products or groups of products has gone even further.

The successors of the early printers, it has often been observed, are not only the printers of today, with their own specialised establishments, but also the producers of wood pulp, of various kinds of paper, of inks and their different ingredients, of type-metal and of type, the group of industries concerned with the technical parts of the producing of illustrations, and the manufacturers of specialised tools and machines for use in printing and in these various auxiliary industries. The list could be extended, both by enumerating other industries which are directly ancillary to the present printing trades and by going back to industries which, while supplying the industries which supply the printing trades, also supply other industries, concerned with preliminary stages in the making of final products other than printed books and newspapers. I do not think that the printing trades are an exceptional instance, but I shall not give other examples, for I do not want this paper to be too much like a primer of descriptive economics or an index to the reports of a census of production. It is sufficiently obvious, anyhow, that over a large part of the field of industry an increasingly intricate nexus of specialised undertakings has inserted itself between the producer of raw materials and the consumer of the final product.

With the extension of the division of labour among industries the representative firm, like the industry of which it is a part, loses its identity. Its internal economies dissolve into the internal and external economies of the more highly specialised undertakings which are its successors, and are supplemented by new economies. Insofar as it is an adjustment to a new situation created by the growth of the market for the final products of industry the division of labour among industries is a vehicle of increasing returns. It is more than a change of form incidental to the full securing of the advantages of capitalistic methods of production—although it is largely that—for it has some advantages of its own which are independent of changes in productive technique. For example, it permits of a higher degree of specialisation in management, and the advantages of such specialisation are doubtless often real, though they may easily be given too much weight. Again, it lends itself to a better geographical distribution of industrial operations, and this advantage is unquestionably both real and important. Nearness to the source of supply of a particular raw material or to cheap power counts for most in one part of a series of industrial processes, nearness to other industries or to cheap transport in another part, and nearness to a larger centre of population in yet another. A better *combination* of advantages of location, with a smaller element of compromise, can be had by the more specialised industries. But the largest advantage secured by the division of labour among industries is the fuller realising of the economies of capitalistic or roundabout methods of production. This should be sufficiently obvious if we assume, as we must, that in most industries there are effective, though elastic, limits to the economical size of the individual firm. The output of the individual firm is generally a relatively small proportion of the aggregate output of an industry. The degree in which it can secure economies by making its own operations more roundabout is limited. But certain roundabout methods are fairly sure to become feasible and economical when their advantages can be spread over the output of the whole industry. These potential economies, then, are segregated and achieved by the operations of specialised undertakings which, taken together, constitute a new industry. It might conceivably be maintained that the *scale* upon which the firms in the new industry are able to operate is the secret of their ability to realise economies for industry as a whole, while presumably making profits for themselves. This is true in a way, but misleading. The scale of their operations (which is only incidentally or under special conditions a matter of the size of the individual firm) merely reflects the size of the market for the final products of the industry or industries to whose operations their own are ancillary. And the principal advantage of large-scale operation at this stage is that it again makes methods economical which would be uneconomical if their benefits could not be diffused over a large final product.

In recapitulation of these variations on a theme from Adam Smith there are three points to be stressed. First, the mechanism of increasing returns is not to be discerned adequately by observing the effects of variations in the size of an individual firm or of a particular industry, for the progressive division and specialisation of industries is an essential part of the process by which increasing returns are realised. What is required is that industrial operations be seen as an interrelated whole. Second, the securing of increasing returns depends upon the progressive division of labour, and the principal economies of the division of labour, in its modern forms, are the economies which are to be had by using labour in roundabout or indirect ways. Third, the division of labour depends upon the extent of the market, but the extent of the market also depends upon the division of labour. In this circumstance lies the possibility of economic progress, apart from the progress which comes as a result of the new knowledge which men are able to gain, whether in the pursuit of their economic or of their noneconomic interests.

NOTE

In the accompanying construction (which owes much to Pareto), a collective indifference curve, I, is defined by the condition that, at equal cost, there would be no sufficient inducement for the community to alter an annual production of x units of one commodity and y units of another in order to secure the alternative combination of the two commodities indicated by any other point on the curve.[1] Each commodity might be taken as representative of a special class of commodities, produced under generally similar conditions. Or one commodity might be made to represent " other goods in general," the annual outlay of productive exertions being regarded as constant. Alternatively, one commodity might represent " leisure " (as a collective name for all

---

[1] The collective indifference is to be taken as an expository device, not as a rigorous conception. The relative weights to be assigned to the individual indifference curves of which it is compounded will depend upon how the aggregate product is distributed, and this will not be the same for all positions of P.

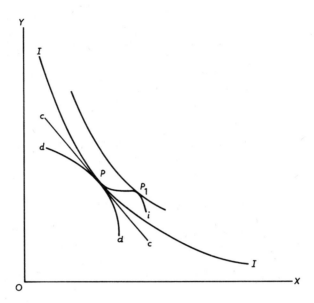

nonproductive uses of time). The other would then represent the aggregate economic product.

There will be equilibrium (subject to instability of a kind which will be described presently) at a point P, if at that point a curve of equal costs, such as d, is tangent to the indifference curve. The curve of equal costs defines the terms upon which the community can exchange one commodity for the other by merely producing less of the one and more of the other (abstraction being made of any incidental costs of change). Negative curvature, as in d, reflects a condition of decreasing returns, in the sense that more of either commodity can be had only by sacrificing progressively larger amounts of the other. Although a sufficient condition, the presence of decreasing returns is not a necessary condition of equilibrium. There would be a loss in moving away from P if equal costs were defined by the straight line c, which represents constant returns. Increasing returns, even, are consistent with equilibrium, provided that the degree of curvature of their graph is less than that of the indifference curve. It might happen, of course, that returns would decrease in one direction and increase in the other. Curve d, for example, might have a point of inflexion at or near P.

Consider now the conditions of departure from equilibrium. The curve i is drawn so as to represent *potential* increasing returns between P and P_1, which lies on a preferred indifference curve. If these increasing returns were to be had merely for the taking, if i were, for example, merely a continuation of the upper segment of d or c, P would not be a point even of unstable equilibrium. The advance from P to P_1 would be made by merely altering the proportions of the two commodities produced annually. To isolate the *problem* of increasing returns it is necessary to assume that P is a true point of equilibrium in the sense that it is determined by a curve of equal costs, such as d or c. The problem, then, has to do with the way in which the lower segment of d or c can be transformed into or replaced by such a curve as i. This requires, of course, that *additional* costs be incurred, of a kind which have not yet been taken into account. To diminish the amount of the one commodity which must be sacrificed for a given increment of the other, some of the labour hitherto devoted to its production must be used indirectly, so that the increase of the annual output of the one lags behind the curtailing of the output of the other.

This new element of cost might be taken into account by utilising a third dimension, but it is simpler to regard it as operating upon Δx, the increment in x accompanying the movement from P to P_1, so as to move the indifference curve upon which P_1 lies towards the left. It would be an error, however, to think that the combinations of x with y and $x + (\Delta x)$ with $y - \Delta y$ (where (Δx) is the contracted form of Δx) are themselves indifferent, so that P_1 is, in effect, brought over on to the original indifference curve, I, and no advantage is reaped. The path from P to P_1 is a *preferred* route, not merely a segment of an indifference curve. The cost of moving along that route is a function of the *rate* (in time) of the movement. An equilibrium rate (which need not be constant), such as would keep the movement from P to P_1 continuous and undeviating, would be determined by the condition, not that (Δx) and $-\Delta y$ should negate one another, but that either an acceleration or a retarding of the rate would be costly or disadvantageous. Because a mountain climber adjusts his pace to his physical powers and to the conditions of the ascent, it does not follow that he might as well have stayed at the foot. Or, alternatively but not inconsistently, the movement from P to P_1 may be conceived as made up of a series of small steps, each apparently yielding no more than a barely perceptible advantage, but only because the scale of reference for both costs and advantages depends at each step upon the position which has then been reached.

Several sets of circumstances will affect the amount and direction of the movement. (1) Even if i has no point of inflexion, such as has been indicated at P_1 (merely to simplify the first stages of this analysis), it will sooner or later (taking into account the "contraction" of Δx) become tangent to an indifference curve. In the absence of any other factor making for change, progress would then come to an end. (2) There may be another possible alternative path of increasing returns extending upwards from P and curving away from I. The most advantageous route will then be a compromise between (or a resultant of) the two limiting alternatives. In such circumstances the only effective limitation imposed upon the extent of the movement may come from the failure of elasticity of demand on one side or the other. (3) Successive indifference curves cannot be supposed to be symmetrical, in the sense that dy/dx remains the same function of y/x. If, for example, the slope of successive indifference curves at points corresponding to given values of y/x decreases (indicating that the demand for the commodity measured in units of y is relatively inelastic), freedom of movement in the direction of P_1 is reduced, while it becomes advantageous to move a little way in the opposite direction along even such a path as c or d. Under inverse conditions (with $-dy/dx$ increasing relatively to y/x for successive indifference curves) the extent of the possible movement in the direction of P_1 is increased. This conclusion amounts to no more than the obvious theorem that the degree in which the decreasing returns encountered in certain fields of economic activity operate as a drag upon the securing of increasing returns in other fields depends upon the relative elasticities of demand for the two types of products. But this consideration, like the others of which note has been made, serves to make clear the general nature of the reciprocal relation between increasing returns and the "extent of the market." (4) Discoveries of new supplies of natural resources or of *new* productive methods may have either or both of two kinds of effects. They may tilt the curves of equal cost and they may modify their curvature favourably. In either event a point such as P is moved to a higher indifference curve, and the paths along with further progress can be made are altered advantageously.

Two concepts of external economies*†

TIBOR SCITOVSKY

The concept of external economies is one of the most elusive in economic literature. Our understanding of it has been greatly enhanced by the active controversy of the twenties over the nature of the "empty economic boxes"; but full clarity has never been achieved. Definitions of external economies are few and unsatisfactory. It is agreed that they mean services (and disservices) rendered free (without compensation) by one producer to another; but there is no agreement on the nature and form of these services or on the reasons for their being free. It is also agreed that external economies are a cause for divergence between private profit and social benefit and thus for the failure of perfect competition to lead to an optimum situation; but for this there are many reasons, and it is nowhere made clear how many and which of these reasons are subsumed under the heading of "external economies." Nor do examples help to clarify the concept. The literature contains many examples of external economies; but they are as varied and dissimilar as are discussions of the subject. Some give the impression that external economies are exceptional and unimportant; others suggest that they are important and ubiquitous. Indeed, one might be tempted to explain this strange dichotomy by ideological differences between the different authors; but such an explanation would be both unwarranted and unnecessary. For, with the increasing rigor of economic thinking and separation of the different branches of economic theory, it is becoming increasingly clear that the concept of external economies does duty in two entirely different contexts. One of these is equilibrium theory, the other is the theory of industrialization in underdeveloped countries. It is customary to discuss these two subjects at different levels of abstraction and on the basis of very different sets of assumptions: no wonder that "external economies" stand for very different things in the two contexts. Indeed, I shall argue that there are two entirely different definitions of ex-

* *The Journal of Political Economy*, 17(1954): pp. 143–51. Reprinted by courtesy of the author and *The Journal of Political Economy*.

† I am indebted to Professor Bernard Haley and Mr. Ralph Turvey for many helpful suggestions. The responsibility for errors, however, is entirely mine.

ternal economies, one much wider than the other; and that external economies as defined in the theory of industrialization include, but go far beyond,
the external economies of equilibrium theory. The latter have been discussed
and rigorously defined in Professor Meade's * " External Economies and Diseconomies in a Competitive Situation ",[1]; but since they form part of external
economies as defined in the theory of industrialization, we shall deal with
them briefly here.

I

Equilibrium theory, in both its general and its partial form, is a static
theory, concerned with the characteristics of the economic system when it is
in equilibrium. Most of its conclusions are based on the assumptions of
(1) perfect competition on both sides of every market and (2) perfect divisibility of all resources and products. These assumptions underlie the main
conclusion of general equilibrium theory, viz., that the market economy leads
to a situation of economic optimum (in Pareto's sense), provided that every
economic influence of one person's (or firm's) behavior on another person's
well-being (or firm's profit) is transmitted through its impact on market
prices. Expressed differently, equilibrium in a perfectly competitive economy
is a situation of Paretian optimum, except when there is interdependence
among the members of the economy that is direct, in the sense that it does
not operate through the market mechanism. In general equilibrium theory,
then, direct interdependence is the villain of the piece and the cause for conflict between private profit and social benefit.

One can distinguish four types of direct (i.e., nonmarket) interdependence
(and one of these—the last one in the following enumeration—is known as
" external economies "); (1) The individual person's satisfaction may depend
not only on the quantities of products he consumes and services he renders
but also on the satisfaction of other persons. In particular, the high income
or consumption of others may give a person pain or pleasure; and so may his
knowledge that some others are less well off than he is. This is known as the
" interdependence of consumers' satisfaction." (2) A person's satisfaction may
be influenced by the activities of producers not only through their demand
for his services and supply of the products he buys but also in ways that do
not operate through the market mechanism. These may be called the producer's " direct " (i.e., nonmarket) influence on personal satisfaction and are
best known by the example of the factory that inconveniences the neighborhood with the fumes or noise that emanate from it. (3) The producer's output
may be influenced by the action of persons more directly and in other ways
than through their offer of services used and demand for products produced by
the firm. This is a counterpart of the previous case, and its main instance is
inventions that facilitate production and become available to producers without charge. (4) The output of the individual producer may depend not only

---

[1] *Economic Journal*, LXII (1952), 54–67.

on his input of productive resources but also on the activities of other firms. This is a counterpart of case 1 and may be called "direct interdependence among producers" but is better known under the name of "external economies and diseconomies."[2]

Of these four cases of direct interdependence, the first, interdependence among consumers, is undoubtedly important. It is (together with the case mentioned in n. 2) among the main reasons for the current controversy in welfare economics and the reluctance of economists to make any welfare statements concerning the consumer. Nowadays, welfare statements are usually confined to the field of production, where the main conclusion of general equilibrium theory seems to stand on firmer ground, primarily because the remaining three cases of direct interdependence (all of which involve the producer) seem exceptional and unimportant. The second case seems exceptional, because most instances of it can be and usually are eliminated by zoning ordinances and industrial regulation concerned with public health and safety. The third case is unimportant, because patent laws have eliminated the main instance of this form of direct interdependence and transformed it into a case of interdependence through the market mechanism.[3] The fourth case seems unimportant, simply because examples of it seem to be few and exceptional.

The last statement appears at first to be contradicted by the many examples of external economies and diseconomies quoted in the literature; but most of these are *not* examples of direct interdependence among producers, which is the only meaning that can be attributed to the term "external economies" within the context of equilibrium theory. It will be useful in this connection to have a rigorous definition of direct interdependence among producers. Meade gave such a definition when he defined external economies; and I can do no better than to reproduce it. According to him, external economies exist whenever the output (x_1) of a firm depends not only on the factors of production $(l_1, c_1, \ldots)$ utilized by this firm but also on the output (x_2) and factor utilization $(l_2, c_2, \ldots)$ of another firm or group of firms.[4] In symbols,

$$x_1 = F(l_1, c_1, \ldots; \quad x_2, l_2, \ldots),$$

where the existence of external economies is indicated by the presence of the variables to the right of the semicolon. Since F is a production function, external economies as here defined are a peculiarity of the production function. For this reason it is convenient to call them "technological external

---

[2] A fifth and important case, which, however, does not quite fit into the above classification, is that where society provides social services through communal action and makes them available free of charge to all persons and firms.

[3] I.e., patent laws have created a market and a market price for the inventor's services, which in the absence of such laws would often be free goods. The case where the results of government-sponsored research into industrial and agricultural methods are made gratuitously available to industrialists and farmers belongs in the category mentioned in n.2 above.

[4] *Op. cit.*

economies."[5] While this will distinguish them from another category of external economies to be introduced presently, we must bear in mind that technological external economies are the only external economies that can arise because of direct interdependence among producers and within the framework of general equilibrium theory.

The examples of external economies given by Meade are somewhat bucolic in nature, having to do with bees, orchards, and woods. This, however, is no accident: it is not easy to find examples from industry. Going through the many examples of external economies quoted in the literature, I found only two that fit the above definition: the case in which a firm benefits from the labor market created by the establishment of other firms and that in which several firms use a resource which is free but limited in supply.[6] For a more detailed discussion the reader is referred to Meade's article, which will, I think, convince him of the scarcity of technological external economies.

II

The other field in which the concept of external economies occurs frequently is the theory of industrialization of underdeveloped countries, where the concept is used in connection with the special problem of allocating savings among alternative investment opportunities. This last is one of the many practical problems to which economists are wont to apply the conclusions of general equilibrium theory. Most of them realize, of course, that general equilibrium theory is limited in its assumptions and applicability; but the only limitation taken seriously by most economists is that imposed by the assumption of perfect competition; and this—as is well known—is not always a necessary condition for the conclusions of equilibrium theory to hold good. In particular, many economists regard a uniform degree of monopoly as all that is necessary for market forces to bring about an optimum allocation of investment funds; and this weaker condition is held to be more nearly fulfilled in our society. Whether for this reason or for some other, the private profitability of investment is usually considered a good index of its social desirability, at least as a general rule.

To this rule, however, the exceptions are too great and obvious to be ignored, especially in underdeveloped countries; and it is customary to impute most of them to external economies. While the nature of these external economies is often discussed, I have been unable to find a definition of the concept in the literature dealing with underdeveloped countries. It is possible, however, to infer a definition from the many examples, discussions, and obiter dicta. It seems that external economies are invoked whenever the profits of

---

[5] The term is used in Jacob Viner's "Cost Curves and Supply Curves," *Zeitschrift für Nationalökonomie*, III (1931), 23–46

[6] Instances of this are the oil well whose output depends on the number and operation of other wells on the same oil field; the fisherman whose catch depends on the operations of other fishermen in the same waters; and the firm that uses a public road (or other publicly owned utility) and is partly crowded out of it by other firms using the same road.

one producer are affected by the actions of other producers. To facilitate comparison with Meade's definition, we can express this in symbols by the function

$$P_1 = G(x_1, l_1, c_1, \ldots ; x_2, l_2, c_2, \ldots),$$

which shows that the *profits* of the firm depend not only on its own output and factor inputs but also on the output and factor inputs of other firms; and we shall say that in the context of underdeveloped countries external economies are said to exist whenever the variables to the right of the semi-colon are present.

This definition of external economies obviously includes direct or non-market interdependence among producers, as discussed above and defined by Meade. It is much broader, however, than his definition, because, in addition to direct interdependence among producers, it also includes interdependence among producers through the market mechanism. This latter type of interdependence may be called "pecuniary external economies" to distinguish it from the technological external economies of direct interdependence.[7]

Interdependence through the market mechanism is all-pervading, and this explains the contrast between the exceptional and often awkward examples of external economies cited in discussions of equilibrium theory and the impression one gains from the literature on underdeveloped countries that the entrepreneur creates external economies and diseconomies with his every move.

What is puzzling, however, is that interdependence through the market mechanism should be held to account for the failure of the market economy to lead to the socially desirable optimum, when equilibrium theory comes to the opposite conclusion and *relies* on market interdependence to bring about an optimum situation. Pecuniary external economies clearly have no place in equilibrium theory. The question is whether the concept is meaningful elsewhere. To answer this question we must first investigate the nature of the pecuniary external economies, to which interdependence through the market mechanism gives rise.

Investment in an industry leads to an expansion of its capacity and may thus lower the prices of its products and raise the prices of the factors used by it. The lowering of product prices benefits the users of these products; the raising of factor prices benefits the suppliers of the factors. When these benefits accrue to firms, in the form of profits, they are pecuniary external economies —Marshall called, or would have called, them (together with the benefits accruing to persons) consumers' and producers' surplus, respectively. According to the theory of industrialization, these benefits, being genuine benefits, should be explicitly taken into account when investment decisions are made; and it is usually suggested that this should be done by taking as the maximand

---

[7] Cf. Viner, *op. cit.*

not profits alone but the sum of the profits yielded and the pecuniary external economies created by the investment.

This prescription seems to be in direct conflict with the results of equilibrium theory. For, according to the latter and subject to its usual assumptions and limitations, market interdependence in the competitive system insures that the maximization of profit by each firm and of satisfaction by each person brings about an optimum situation, which, as is well known, is sometimes described as a situation in which consumers' and producers' surpluses are maximized. In other words, equilibrium theory tells us that in equilibrium the sum of consumers' and producers' surpluses will be maximized, although they do not enter explicitly, as part of the maximand, the economic decisions of any producer.[8] Assuming that these conflicting views are both right, the conflict can be resolved only if we should find that the limitations of general equilibrium theory render it inapplicable to the problems of investment. This indeed, must often be so, but in the following we shall single out three special cases which seem especially important and in which the above conflict is resolved.

a) One reason why the conclusions of general equilibrium theory may be inapplicable to the practical problem of investment is that the former's assumption of perfect divisibility is not always fulfilled. Perfect competition leads to a position of economic optimum, because under perfect competition the marginal conditions of economic optimum are contained (in the absence of direct interdependence) in the marginal conditions of profit maximization by producers and satisfaction maximization by householders. Indivisibilities, however, may prevent the producer from fulfilling these marginal conditions. For example, he may find himself unable to equate marginal costs to price and, instead, face the choice of producing either less or more than the output that would equate these two quantities. In such a case, one of the available alternatives will still yield him a higher profit than all others; but this need no longer be the one that is also the best from society's point of view. Hence the need, in such cases, to take society's point of view explicitly into consideration.

This fact was recognized as early as 1844 by Dupuit.[9] He was looking for a criterion of the social desirability of investment in such public utilities as canals, roads, bridges, and railways—the typical examples of indivisibilities in economics—and he found this criterion not in the actual profitability of such investments but in what their profitability would be in the hypothetical case in which the operator of the utility practiced price discrimination and

---

[8] Cf. J. R. Hicks, "The Rehabilitation of Consumers' Surplus," *Review of Economic Studies*, VIII (1941), 108–16. We need not enter here the debate on the usefulness of this terminology. Nor is it necessary to stress that this way of stating the results of perfect competition is characteristic of partial equilibrium analysis.

[9] Cf. Jules Dupuit, "De la mesure de l'utilité des travaux publics," *Annales des ponts et chaussées*, 2d ser., Vol. VIII (1844); reprinted in *International Economic Papers*, No. 2 (1952), pp. 83–110.

thus appropriated to himself the consumers' surplus that would normally (i.e., in the absence of price discrimination) accrue to the users of the public utility. In other words, Dupuit's test of social desirability is whether the sum of profit and consumers' surplus is positive.[10] Dupuit's test and his use of the consumers' surplus concept underlying it were vindicated by Professor Hicks;[11] but neither Hicks nor Dupuit makes clear the role of indivisibilities in rendering the above test necessary. For this last point, as well as for an excellent statement of the entire argument, the reader should consult chapter xvi of Professor Lerner's *Economics of Control*.[12]

b) The second reason for the inapplicability of general equilibrium theory to the problems of investment is that the former is a static or equilibrium theory, whereas the allocation of investment funds is not a static problem at all. According to equilibrium theory, the producers' profit-maximizing behavior brings about a socially desirable situation *when the situation is in equilibrium*; or, to give this result a more dynamic, if not entirely correct, interpretation, profit-maximizing behavior brings closer the socially desirable optimum if it also brings closer equilibrium. Investment, however, need not bring the system closer to equilibrium; and, when it does not, the results of equilibrium theory may not apply.

Profits are a sign of disequilibrium; and the magnitude of profits, under free competition, may be regarded as a rough index of the degree of disequilibrium.[13] Profits in a freely competitive industry lead to investment in that industry; and the investment, in turn, tends to eliminate the profits that have called it forth. This far, then, investment tends to bring equilibrium nearer. The same investment, however, may raise or give rise to profits in other industries; and to this extent it leads away from equilibrium. For example, investment in industry A will cheapen its product; and if this is used as a factor in industry B, the latter's profits will rise. This, then, is a case where the price reduction creates, not a consumers' surplus proper, accruing to persons, but pecuniary external economies, benefiting firms. Is this difference sufficient to render the conclusions of general equilibrium theory inapplicable?

To answer this question, we must pursue the argument a little further. The profits of industry B, created by the lower price of factor A, call for investment and expansion in industry B, one result of which will be an increase in

---

[10] This is so whether the consumers' surplus accrues to persons or represents external economies accruing to firms.

[11] Cf. J. R. Hicks, "L'Économie de bien-être et la théorie des surplus du consómmateur," and "Quelques applications de la théorie des surplus du consommateur," both in *Économie appliquée*, No. 4 (1948), pp. 432–57.

[12] A. P. Lerner, *Economics of Control* (New York: Macmillan Co., 1944). Lerners' solution is slightly different and, I believe, more correct than Dupuit's, in that he takes account also of producers' surplus. It might be added in passing that the type of indivisibility considered by Dupuit establishes a relation among the users of the public utility that is similar in all essentials to direct interdependence among consumers.

[13] However, the absence of profits is not a sufficient condition of equilibrium.

industry B's demand for industry A's product. This in its turn will give rise to profits and call for further investment and expansion in industry A; and equilibrium is reached only when successive doses of investment and expansion in the two industries have led to the simultaneous elimination of profits in both. It is only at this stage, where equilibrium has been established, that the conclusions of equilibrium theory become applicable and we can say (on the usual assumptions and in the absence of direct interdependence) that the amount of investment profitable in industry A is also the socially desirable amount. This amount is clearly greater than that which is profitable at the first stage, before industry B has made adjustment. We can conclude, therefore, that when an investment gives rise to pecuniary external economies its private profitability understates its social desirability.

Unfortunately, however, the test of social desirability applicable in the previous case is not applicable here, although it would probably give a better result than a simple calculation of profitability. This can easily be seen by comparing the situation under consideration with that which would obtain if industries A and B were integrated (although in such a way as to preserve the free competition assumed so far). In this case the pecuniary external economies created by investment in industry A would become "internal" and part of the profits of the investors themselves. Investment in A would be more profitable and pushed further than in the absence of integration; but, *without investment and expansion also in industry B*, it would not be pushed far enough. For what inhibits investment in A is the limitation on the demand for industry A's product imposed by the limited capacity of industry B, the consumer of this product; just as investment in industry B is inhibited by the limited capacity of industry A, the supplier of one of industry B's factors of production. These limitations can be fully removed only by a simultaneous expansion of both industries. We conclude, therefore, that only if expansion in the two industries were integrated and planned together would the profitability of investment in each one of them be a reliable index of its social desirability.

It hardly needs adding that the relation between industries A and B discussed above illustrates only one of the many possible instances of pecuniary external economies that belong in this category. Expansion in industry A may also give rise to profits (i) in an industry that produces a factor used in industry A, (ii) in an industry whose product is complementary in use to the product of industry A, (iii) in an industry whose product is a substitute for a factor used in industry A, or (iv) in an industry whose product is consumed by persons whose incomes are raised by the expansion of industry A—and this list does not include the cases in which the expansion causes external *dis*economies. It is apparent from this list that vertical integration alone would not be enough and that complete integration of all industries would be necessary to eliminate all divergence between private profit and public benefit. This was fully realized by Dr. Rosenstein-Rodan, who, in dealing with the "Problems of Industrialisation of Eastern and South-Eastern Europe,"[14] considered most instances of pecuniary external economies listed above and advocated that "the whole of the industry to be created is to be treated and planned like one huge firm or trust."[15] To put this conclusion differently, profits in a market economy are a bad guide to economic optimum as far as investment and industrial expansion are concerned; and they are worse, the more decentralized and differentiated the economy.

This entire argument can be restated in somewhat different terms. In an economy in which economic decisions are decentralized, a system of communications is needed to enable each person who makes economic decisions to learn about the economic decisions of others and coordinate his decisions with theirs. In the market economy, prices are the signaling device that informs each person of other people's economic decisions; and the merit of perfect competition is that it would cause prices to transmit information reliably and people to respond to this information properly. Market prices, however, reflect the economic situation as it is and not as it will be. For this reason, they are more useful for coordinating current production decisions, which are immediately effective and guided by short-run considerations, than they are for coordinating investment decisions, which have a delayed effect and—looking ahead to a long future period—should be governed not by what the present economic situation is but by what the future economic situation is expected to be. The proper coordination of investment decisions, therefore, would require a signaling device to transmit information about present plans and future conditions as they are determined by present plans; and the pricing system fails to provide this.[16] Hence the belief that there is need either for centralized investment planning or for some additional communication system to supplement the pricing system as a signaling device.

It must be added that the argument of this section applies with especial force to underdeveloped countries. The plant capacity most economical to build and operate is not very different in different countries; but, as a percentage of an industry's total capacity, it is very much greater in underdeveloped than in fully industrialized economies. In underdeveloped countries, therefore, investment is likely to have a greater impact on prices, give rise to greater pecuniary external economies, and thus cause a greater divergence between private profit and social benefit.

c) I propose to consider yet another reason for divergence between the profitability of an investment and its desirability from the community's point of view; but this is very different from those discussed in the last two sections and has to do with the difference between the national and international

---

[14] *Economic Journal*, LIII (1943), 202–11.

[15] *Ibid.*, p. 204.

[16] Professor Kenneth Arrow pointed out to me, however, that, in a formal sense, futures markets and futures prices could provide exactly such a signalling device.

points of view. In appraising the social desirability of an economic action from the international point of view, all repercussions of that action must be fully taken into account, whereas, from the national point of view, the welfare of domestic nationals alone is relevant and the losses suffered and benefits gained by foreigners are ignored. The two points of view need not necessarily lead to different appraisals; but they usually do when the economic action considered is the allocation of investment funds among purely domestic, import-competing, and export industries. From the international point of view, all external economies and diseconomies must be taken into consideration; from the national point of view, one must count only the external economies and diseconomies that accrue to domestic nationals and leave out of account the pecuniary external economies accruing to foreign buyers from the expansion of export industries and the diseconomies inflicted on foreign competitors by the expansion of import-competing industries. Accordingly, investment in export industries is always less, and that in import-competing industries is always more desirable from the national, than from the international point of view.

In discussions on investment policy this difference between the national and international points of view usually appears in the guise of a difference between the criteria of social benefit and private profit. For social benefit, when considered explicitly, is usually identified with national benefit in our society, whereas private profit, although an imperfect index of social desirability, accounts or fails to account for external economies and diseconomies without national bias and therefore probably comes closer to registering the social welfare of the world as a whole than that of a single nation. Hence investment tends to be more profitable in export industries and less profitable in import-competing industries than would be desirable from a narrow nationalistic point of view.

It is worth noting that this argument is in some respects the reverse of the argument of Section II*b* above. There it was the failure of profit calculations to take into account pecuniary external economies that caused the divergence between private profit and social benefit; here the divergence is caused by the entry into the profit criterion of pecuniary external economies and diseconomies that accrue to foreigners and should therefore be excluded from social accounting concerned with national, rather than world welfare. The argument is well known as the "terms-of-trade argument" and has been used to explain the failure of foreign investments in colonial areas to benefit fully the borrowing countries.[17] The divergence between national welfare and private profit depends on the foreigners' import-demand and export-supply elasticities; and it can be offset by an appropriate set of import and export duties. This has been shown by Mr. J. de V. Graaff, in his " Optimum Tariff

---

[17] Cf. H. W. Singer, "The Distribution of Gains between Investing and Borrowing Countries," *American Economic Review* (*Proceedings*), XL (1950), 473–85.

Structures."[18] De Graaff presents his optimum tariff structure as one that will bring about that flow of goods and services which optimizes[19] the nation's welfare; but the same tariff structure will also bring about the allocation of investment funds that is optimal from the national point of view.

[18] *Review of Economic Studies*, XVII (1949–50), 47–59.
[19] In Pareto's sense.

Part IV
INCREASING RETURNS

The papers in this section discuss in different ways the appraisal of public policies in industries producing under increasing returns. It is of course obvious that perfectly competitive equilibrium is precluded by the existence of increasing returns; under those circumstances, whatever equilibrium configuration is assumed by the free play of the market will have monopolistic elements, and hence welfare losses. Ideally, state intervention by public ownership or regulation may reduce or eliminate welfare losses but to do so requires appropriate knowledge of both the criteria for engaging in the activity and the pricing policy to be adopted.

These issues were all developed in the extraordinary 1844 paper of Dupuit, an inspector of bridges and highways who was seeking an economic criterion for the construction of the public works in his jurisdiction. Both the welfare implications of marginal-cost pricing and the use of consumer's surplus as a measure of benefits were introduced by Dupuit, who even went on to measure the benefits of one activity for complementary activities.

Dupuit's work was sometimes ignored, sometimes repeated during the next 90 years; only in the past quarter-century has there been some genuine development. In 1938, Hotelling, in his presidential address to the Econometric Society, stated with great vigor and generality the welfare case for marginal-cost pricing and sketched some of its practical implications. He also developed a generalized form of consumers' and producer's surpluses to take account of all interrelations in supply and demand.

The problems of optimal pricing and investment policy for state enterprises were examined in greater detail by Meade and Fleming. The conceptual problems in the theory of consumer's surplus were examined with great care by Hicks; he showed how, under suitable assumptions, its use could be justified.

Chenery studied in detail the problem of market failure in the case of increasing returns. With the aid of a numerical example he appraised the importance of the welfare losses and the effects on investment decisions.

In any specific public investment project, elements of both externalities and increasing returns are likely to be present; this is certainly true of the irrigation projects which have been so important in the United States. Margolis has subjected the investment criteria of the U.S. Bureau of Reclamation to close scrutiny with regard to the appropriate measurement of benefits and costs and, in the process, clarified considerably the concrete implications of the abstract economic principles.

On the measurement of the utility
of public works*

JULES DUPUIT†

Legislators have prescribed the formalities necessary for certain works to be declared of public utility; political economy has not yet defined in any precise manner the conditions which these works must fulfil in order to be really useful; at least, the ideas which have been put about on this subject appear to us to be vague, incomplete, and often inaccurate. Yet the latter question is more important than the former; enquiries—be they ever so numerous—laws and ordinances will not make a road, a railway, or a canal useful if it is not so already. The law ought merely to confirm the facts demonstrated by political economy. How is such demonstration to be made? Upon what principles, upon what formula, does it rest? How, in a word, is public utility to be measured? Such is the object of our enquiry in this chapter.[1]

* Translated in *International Economic Papers*, 2(1952): pp. 83–110. English translation by R. H. Barback from "De la Mesure de l'Utilité des Travaux Publics," *Annales des Ponts et Chaussées*, 2d series, Vol. 8, 1844. Reprinted by courtesy of *International Economic Papers*.

† Editors' note: As the forerunners of Jevons and Menger in respect of utility analysis, Cournot and Dupuit were both singled out for special mention by Marshall. While Cournot's *Recherches sur les Principes Mathématiques de la Théorie des Richesses* was translated in Marshall's lifetime, Dupuit's essay, *De la Mesure de l'Utilité des Travaux Publics*, had, so far, found no translator. Edgeworth, in his article "Application of Probabilities to Economics" (*Economic Journal*, 1904), gives a free translation of isolated passages and regards Dupuit as "the earliest, and still, I think, the highest authority on the theory of discrimination."

Twice in his paper Dupuit mentions that his article is part of a larger work entitled *Economie Politique Appliquée aux Travaux Publics*. This work was never published.

Dupuit does not give the source of his quotations from Say and McCulloch. The editors of this volume have thought it useful to include precise references, which are printed in *italic* footnotes; in so doing they are indebted to Mario de Bernardi's annotations to his edition of Dupuit's writings (Turin and Paris, 1934), and to the assistance rendered by the translator of this essay, R. H. Barnack, Lecturer in Economics, Canberra University College.

The passages Dupuit, somewhat inaccurately, quoted from Say, would appear to have been extracted from the 5th edition (1826) of *Traité d'Economie Politique*; they differ very slightly, and not in substance, from the 4th edition, which C. R. Prinsep has translated into English (Boston, 1821). One of the passages quoted comes from the Annex to Say's *Traité*, which Prinsep did not translate; the translation of the others, for convenience' sake, leans on Prinsep so far as strict accuracy permits.

[1] This article is taken from a work entitled *Political Economy Applied to Public Works*, which the author intends to publish in the near future. See editors' note, above.

Utility and its measurement lie at the foundation of political economy; they have, therefore, been the objects of rigorous definitions. Let us see whether these definitions can serve as a basis for one of public utility.

J. B. Say says:

UTILITY. In political economy, utility is the power possessed by things of being able to serve man in some manner or other.

The most useless and even the most uncomfortable thing, like a Court cloak, has what is here called its utility if the use to which it is put, no matter what that use may be, is enough for a *price* to be attached to it.

This price is the measure of the utility which men judge the thing to have, of the satisfaction which they derive from its *consumption*; for they will not seek to consume this utility if, for the same price, they could acquire another which would yield them greater satisfaction.

Utility, thus understood, is the basis of the *demand* for products and consequently of their *value*. But this value does not exceed the *costs of production,* for beyond this amount it will pay anyone who needs a *product* to make it himself; or rather, he will never be reduced to the necessity of making it himself, because at that price it pays any *entrepreneur* to take it upon himself to produce the thing.[2] (Epitome.)

If one accepts these definitions without qualification and generalizes them, one may be led into grave errors in the measurement of the utility of many things which call for a different treatment. Let us give an example:

Some very capable engineers wanted to know what was the utility of the French roads, and starting from the datum that the prices paid by society for their use amounted to 500 million *per annum,* and applying J. B. Say's principles, they said that since society consents to pay 500 million for these transport facilities, their utility is 500 million; society would not give up this sum if it did not receive an equivalent satisfaction; 500 million, therefore, is the measure of this utility. A moment's reflection will suffice to show up the error in this reasoning. Let us suppose the introduction of some improvement in the means of transport—roads or carriages—and that it results in a fall in costs by one half, so that the same services for which society paid 500 million, will now be rendered for 250. Is it to be concluded that the roads are now only half as useful, as the principles set out above would require us to do? Is it not evident, on the contrary, that the utility of the roads, far from having diminished, would have increased by 250 million?

If society is paying 500 million for the services rendered by the road, that only proves one thing—that their utility is *at least* 500 million. But it may be a hundred times or a thousand times greater; we are left in ignorance of this. If you take the above figure as the measure—and not as the lower limit—of a quantity the exact magnitude of which you do not know, you are acting like a man who, wishing to measure the height of a wall in the dark and finding that he cannot reach the top with his arm raised, says: "This wall is two

---

[2] J. B. Say, *Traité d'Economie Politique*, article on Utility in the annexed *Epitome des Principes Fondamentaux de l'Economie Politique.*

meters high, for if it were not, my hand would reach above it". Now, if you say that the wall is at least two meters in height, then we are agreed; but if you go so far as to say that this is the actual measurement, then we are no longer agreed. In daylight, and equipped with a ladder, you will perceive that our alleged two-meter wall is fifty meters high.

As the distinction which we are trying to establish rests upon considerations of some refinement, we must stress these preliminary notions and elucidate them by somewhat numerous quotations and examples:

J. B. Say says:

Although price is the measure of the value of things, and their value the measure of the utility imputed to them, it would be absurd to draw the inference that, by forcibly raising their price, their utility can be augmented. Exchange value, or price, is an index of the utility men recognize a thing to have only so long as human dealings are subject to no influence alien to that same utility.

In fact, when one man sells any product to another, he sells him the utility vested in that product: the buyer buys it only for the sake of its utility, for the sake of the use he can make of it. If, for any reason whatever, the buyer is obliged to pay more than this utility is worth to him, he pays for value which does not exist and which, consequently, he does not receive.

This is precisely the case when the government grants to a particular group of merchants the exclusive privilege of engaging in a certain trade, the India trade for instance; the price of the merchandise concerned is thereby raised, without any accession to its utility or intrinsic value. This excess of price is money transferred from the pockets of the consumers into those of the privileged traders, whereby the latter are enriched by exactly as much as the former are impoverished.

In like manner, when the government imposes a tax on wine, which causes to be sold for 15 sous a bottle which would otherwise have been sold for 10 sous, what does it else but transfer 5 sous per bottle from the hands of the producers or the consumers of wine to those of the tax collector? The merchandise is here only a more or less convenient means of reaching the taxpayer, and its current value is composed of two elements, *viz.* its real value based on its utility, and the value of the tax which the government thinks fit to levy upon its manufacture, transport, or consumption.[3]

It is beyond doubt that a tax can add nothing to the utility of a product; but when we look at it from the consumer's point of view we can say that its existence brings to light undeniably that the product has a utility greater than the cost of production. Why is the bottle of wine purchased at 15 sous? It is because the buyer finds at least an equivalent utility in it; for, in spite of the tax, he is at perfect liberty to but it or not to buy it. It is not within the power of the state to make him pay, by means of the tax, anything more than the utility which he derives from this purchase.

This is how we see the situation: several individuals want to buy wine; but the need of each to acquire this good is different. Thus some of them, the rich,

---

[3] J. B. Say, *Traité d'Economie Politique*, 5th edition, Vol. 1, pp. 7–9; Prinsep translation pp. 5–7.

attach such a utility to it that they would be willing to buy even at 30 sous a bottle if that were the current market price; others, less rich, would not go above 15 sous; the less well-off would not pay more than 10 sous; others, in narrow circumstances, would only buy at 6 sous, and the poor only at 4 sous. On entering the market, they find that the price of the wine itself is 10 sous but, the government having imposed a tax of 5 sous, the commodity can only be supplied at a price of 15 sous.[4] What happens? All those who attach to the purchase of wine a value greater than 15 sous will buy, and will derive a kind of profit which will vary according to the significance which they put upon their acquisition; all those who would have bought wine at 10, 12, 13, or 14 sous will go without on account of the tax; and lastly those to whom the significance of such a purchase was less than 10 sous will not buy and would not have bought in any case. There is, then, only one single class of individuals to whom we can be certain that the utility is just 10 sous and that is the producers or sellers of the wine: they cannot derive a greater utility from it, no matter what the tax; for those who buy, it is greater than 15 sous, and for those who do not buy, it is less.

Thus, on examining the facts more closely, we have come to see that the utility of everything which is consumed varies according to the person consuming it. Nor is this all: each consumer himself attaches a different utility to the same thing according to the quantity which he can consume. Thus, a purchaser who would have bought 100 bottles at 10 sous might only buy 50 at 15 sous, and 30 bottles at 20 sous. Let us show this by an entirely different example, in order to demonstrate that it is a general phenomenon and one which, therefore, arises in the case of public works and must be taken into account when measuring their utility.

Consider the establishment of a water system in a town which, being situated at a high altitude, could previously procure water only at considerable trouble. Water then was so valuable that the supply of 1 hectoliter per day cost 50 francs, by annual subscription. It is obvious that each hectoliter consumed in these circumstances has a utility of 50 francs. With the installation of pumps this same quantity of water costs only 30 francs. What will happen? The inhabitant who was consuming 1 hectoliter will at first continue to do so and will derive a profit of 20 francs on this first hectoliter; but it is highly probable that the fall in price will induce him to increase his consumption; instead of using the water sparingly for personal purposes he will employ it also for less urgent and less essential needs, the satisfaction of which is worth more than 30 francs to him—since that is the sacrifice he makes to obtain the water—but less than 50 francs, since at that price this consumption was foregone. Thus, of these two hectoliters supplied to the same individual by the public pumps, one has a utility greater than 50 francs, while the other has a utility of between 30 and 50 francs. Suppose that by virtue of a technical

---

[4] For this to be the effect of the tax, it would have to have been in existence long enough to have diminished the quantity of wine produced.

improvement in the pumps, or by the very fact of increased consumption, the price is now reduced to 20 francs; it may well be that the same individual would take 4 hectoliters in order to be able to scrub his house every day. Let him have them at 10 francs each, and he will demand ten to water his garden; at 5 francs he will demand 20 to keep up the level of his pond; at 1 franc he will want 100 to keep a fountain going, and so on. If you look at this situation and ask what is the utility of the water supplied by the public pumps to this consumer, you must not say that it is 50 francs per hectoliter, because that is the price of the one he formerly consumed, before the installation of the pumps. There is only one hectoliter for which this figure is the measure of utility. That of the second hectoliter is between 30 and 50 francs; of the next two, between 20 and 30 francs; of the next six, between 10 and 20 francs; of the next ten, between 5 and 10 francs; and of eighty more, between 1 and 5 francs.

If you want to verify this, raise the price of the water. A tax of 4 francs per hectoliter, when the price is 1 franc, will immediately reduce consumption from 100 hectoliters to 20; a tax of 9 francs, from 20 hectoliters to 10; a tax of 19 francs, from 10 hectoliters to 4; and so on, until the price is brought up to 50 francs and only 1 hectoliter is consumed. By going further, you would eventually discover the utility of this last hectoliter, which you do not at the moment know.

Thus every product has a different utility not only for each consumer but for each of the wants for the satisfaction of which he uses it: we shall see this at every turn when we come to deal with the measurement of public utility. But first we must lay stress once again on those general notions, which are fundamental to the method which we shall presently expound.

At the outset, too, we feel it needful to deal with the objection which might be raised about our use of the word utility; it might be said that we have deviated from its scientific meaning and used it in a completely new sense in order to unfold a method of mensuration which, at first sight, is rather complicated. We shall merely recall that the distinction which we are expounding is to be found in Doctor Smith, who recognizes two values in an object—its *value-in-use,* which is its utility as we understand it, the value to him who has a need to consume the product; and its *value-in-exchange,* which is the value of the same product to him who has a need to sell it. McCulloch, who has annotated Smith, sets out this important distinction in a note:

"The word *value*", he says, "has been frequently employed to express, not only the exchangeable worth of an article, or its capacity of exchanging for other things obtainable only by means of labour, but also its utility, or its fitness for satisfying our wants, and contributing to our comforts and enjoyments. But it is obvious that the utility of commodities—that the capacity of bread, for example, to appease hunger, or of water to quench thirst—is a totally different quality from their capacity of exchanging for other commodities. Dr. Smith perceived this difference, and showed the importance of distinguishing between the utility, or, as he expressed it, the *value-in-use* of commodities, and their value in exchange. To confound such essentially different qualities must evidently lead to the most absurd conclusions. And hence, to avoid mistaking the sense of so important a word as value, it would be better not to use it except to signify exchangeable worth or value in exchange; and to use the word utility to express the power or capacity of an article to satisfy our wants or gratify our desires."[5]

We are therefore not the first to point out the importance of this distinction; and the example we quoted, of the manner in which the utility of the roads was evalued, shows that McCulloch was not mistaken in saying that without this distinction one could be led into the gravest errors.

As for the more or less complicated measure of utility which follows from this new definition, we need only point out in its defence that political economy is not a science of expediency but of positive facts, to the statement of which it confines itself. The facts must be accepted just as society supplies them. We cannot adopt one idea which is simple but inaccurate, and reject another which is complex but true. Besides, is J. B. Say's formula really so simple? If we are to say that the utility of a bottle of wine being sold at 15 sous is only 10 sous, on the grounds that costs of production are 10 sous and 5 sous are tax, how are we to measure the utility of a kilogram of tea sold in Paris for 50 francs? How are we to deduct all the taxes which have hit this product in the course of being picked in China, sold over so many different counters, carried under three or four flags, until finally it arrives at the merchant's shop? And would not justice require us, after having made such deduction—which would need a lengthy study of this branch of business—to add on the benefit afforded to tea production by the distribution of the tax? After all, if the state keeps up a naval squadron, if it has agents, consuls, and ambassadors to represent it in these distant countries, in order to protect the purchase and carriage of tea—why then, here are real expenses to be added to those of tea production. The pay of the army of the *Compagnie des Indes* must of necessity be added to the cost of production of the sugar which it brings to market. In like manner, state expenditure which favours certain lines of production in some special manner forms part of their net cost; that is patently obvious in cases where bounties are granted. It can be seen, then, that although this method of calculation appears to be simple, yet it too has its difficulties.

The variable, yea mobile, nature of the value of utility is indeed well known to business men and has long been exploited by them. That is what lies behind all transactions which are sheltered from competition, either by dint of secret manufacturing processes, or by any other means which secures a monopoly profit to the seller. If some very useful object only costs a monopolist 1 franc to produce, will the manufacturer fix its value at 100 francs,

---

[5] Adam Smith, *An Inquiry into the Nature and Causes of the Wealth of Nations*, edited by J. R. McCulloch, Edinburgh, 1853, p. 438, in *Supplemental Notes and Dissertations*, by J. R. McCulloch.

knowing full well that there will be buyers at that price? Not in the least, for he also knows full well that there would not be very many of them—say a hundred perhaps, which will only yield him 9,900 francs profit; and that by reducing the price to 20 francs he might have a thousand buyers, which would give him a profit of $1,000 \times 19$ francs = 19,000 francs. Nor is that all. He knows, too, that of these thousand purchasers many would have been willing to pay a higher price—some would have been willing to pay 25 francs, others 30, 50, 80, or 100 francs—and that these buyers thereby derive a kind of gain of 5, 10, 30, 60, and 80 francs, respectively; and therefore he has recourse to a great variety of devices to secure the payment to him by each one of the buyers of as large a part as possible of this gain, which he considers is made at his expense. The same commodity in various guises is very often sold in different shops at quite different prices to the rich, the moderately well-off, and the poor. The fine, the very fine, the superfine, and the extra fine, although drawn from the same barrel and although alike in all real respects other than the superlative on the label, sell at widely different prices. Why? Because the same thing has a widely differing utility depending on the consumer. If there were only one medium price, there would be a loss to those who did without the product because its utility to them was less than that price, and a loss to the seller who, from many buyers, would be receiving payment for only a fraction of the utility of the service rendered. God forbid that we should try to justify all the frauds that go on in business; but it is well to study them because they are founded on a close knowledge of human nature, and are often found to be more equitable and fairer than one might expect at first sight and, indeed, they might be good examples to follow. We shall return later to this subject in the article on "Tolls", because this same consideration of a varying utility for the same object is the basis of pricing for all things the production costs of which are composed of two parts—one, a large outlay, made once for all or at least for a good many times; and the other, a small outlay, incurred for each object produced. Thus when a bridge is built and the state establishes a tariff, the latter is not related to cost of production: the heavy cart is charged less than the sprung carriage even though it causes more wear to the timber of the carriageway. Why are there two different prices for the same service? Because the poor man does not attach the same value to crossing the bridge as the rich man does, and raising the charge would only prevent him from crossing. Canal and railway tariffs differentiate between various classes of goods and passengers, and lay down markedly different rates for them although the costs are more or less the same. In drawing up these tariffs in advance the legislator merely defines certain features and characteristics which seem to him to indicate a greater or lesser degree of utility in the same service rendered to different people. In business, the merchant—who is in direct contact with the purchaser—goes further, he sets traps for the buyer's vanity and his credulity; but the aim is always the same, and that is to make the payment for the service rendered equal not the cost but what the buyer thinks it is worth. If, therefore, this variable utility for each object were unknown, none of these devices for taking in dupes would exist—if dupes there be; for no one is ever a dupe except in relation to the cost of production. The purchaser never pays more for the product than the value he places on its utility.

To sum up, political economy has to take as the measure of the utility of an object the maximum sacrifice which each consumer would be willing to make in order to acquire the object. We say political economy, because this is not, in the last analysis, a rigorous measure of the quality which things have *of being able to satisfy men's needs*;[6] it would be difficult to say whose hunger was the greater—the rich man's, who would be willing to give a million for a kilogram of bread, or the poor man's, who, having nothing else to give, would risk his life for it. But political economy, being concerned only with wealth, can take account of the intensity of a wish only through its monetary expression. Political economy only bakes bread for those who can buy it, and leaves to social economy the care of supplying it to those with nothing of value to give in exchange.

The utility which we have just been considering and measuring is the absolute utility of all things that satisfy our desires—of those which nature supplies free as well as of those which can only be bought at the cost of the most arduous labour. If, in consuming a product, someone says: "It would take 30 francs to make me give it up," then that product really has 30 francs' worth of utility for him, no matter whether he only had the trouble of picking it up from the ground, or whether he paid 20 francs for it. But the relative utility to the consumer will be very different in the two cases. In the first case it will be all of the 30 francs of absolute utility, but in the second case it will be no more than 10 francs, the difference between the absolute utility and the purchase price. In effect, to satisfy a want which seems to him to be worth 30 francs, he is obliged to sacrifice another want to the extent of 20 francs. Thus he benefits only from the difference between these two sums. For the consumer who valued the satisfaction of the same want at only 29, 28, or 21 francs, the utility would only be 9, 8, or 1 franc. It would be zero to him, who, valuing it at only 20 francs, would be undecided whether to acquire it. There would be a loss of utility to anyone forced to pay 20 francs for a satisfaction which he valued at only 19, 18, or 17. Lastly, no utility would be produced if no one were willing to give more than 15 francs for an object which cost 20; there would be a loss of utility to the seller, and production would cease. Hence the saying which we shall often repeat because it is often forgotten: the only real utility is that which people are willing to pay for. We see that in general the relative or definitive utility of a product is expressed by the difference between the sacrifice which the purchaser would be willing to make in order to get it, and the purchase price he has to pay in

---

[6] See above, Note 2. This is not a textual quotation.

exchange.[7] It follows that anything which raises the purchase price diminishes the utility to the same extent, and anything which depresses the price increases the utility in the same manner.

Suppose, for example, that the market price of an article is 20 francs, which is more or less equivalent to the costs of production. According to the circumstances in which it is consumed, the (absolute) utility of this article may have any one of the following values:

30, 29, 28, 27, 26, 25, 24, 23, 22, 21, 20 francs;

and in corresponding circumstances, its utility will be

10, 9, 8, 7, 6, 5, 4, 3, 2, 1, 0.

If a tax of 5 francs is imposed, the utility of the product will diminish by 5 francs in the case of all those who were deriving a utility of 10, 9, 8, 7, 6, or 5 francs from it, and they will now only derive 5, 4, 3, 2, 1, or 0 francs of utility; the loss is the same in each case. As for those who only derived 4, 3, 2, 1, 0 francs of utility and who, because of the tax, cease to consume the article, they lose precisely that utility which they would have derived from the consumption of the article; their loss will therefore be different in each case and will equal 4, 3, 2, 1, 0 francs, respectively. Thus the tax affects not only those who pay it, but all those who would have been consumers but for the tax. We shall return to this consideration later.

Let us now make the opposite assumption—that the costs of production, and consequently the expense of purchase, fall by 5 francs; so that what cost 20 francs now only costs 15. It is clear that those who, at 20 francs, had a utility of

10, 9, 8, 7, 6, 5, 4, 3, 2, 1 franc

will in the same circumstances now have a utility of

15, 14, 13, 12, 11, 10, 9, 8, 7, 6 francs.

The effect of this fall in price is obviously to leave them 5 francs more with which to satisfy other wants. Nor is this all. The price having fallen, the

---

[7] The error of the physiocrats, who claimed that industrialists and farmers produced no utility because the consumption represented by the cost of production cancelled the utility produced by them, was founded on nothing other than the false measurement of utility based on production costs. If the carriage of a hogshead of Burgundy to Paris has no utility other than the 15 francs which it has cost and which you pay to the carrier, then it is right to conclude that the carrier has produced no utility because those 15 francs represent his consumption and that of his horses; but if it be recognized that among the purchasers of this Burgundy wine there are some who would have paid much more than 15 francs over and above its price in order to obtain it if that had been necessary, then it follows that the carrier, his cart, and the road which he used have been able to produce a much greater utility.

article is now within reach of those who formerly only estimated the utility of the article at

20, 19, 18, 17, 16, 15 francs

and did not buy because this utility was less than the market price: thus there will now be some new consumers. What will the utility of the product be for them? Still the difference between the absolute utility and the purchase price,

5, 4, 3, 2, 1, 0 francs.

The fall in price therefore yields a different amount of utility to each new consumer.

In general every rise or fall in price decreases or increases utility by an amount equal to this variation for those who are consumers in both situations; for those who disappear or who appear, the utility lost or acquired is equal to the old or to the new relative utility yielded to them by the product.

This formula comprises, implicitly, the measurement of all kinds of utility, including public utility, which is no different from any other. It is the latter with which we shall now be concerned, but we feel we ought to pause for a moment to see where we are in agreement with, and where we differ from, those who have preceded us in this line of inquiry.

J. B. Say has said:

Roads and canals are costly public amenities, even in countries where they are set up judiciously and economically. Yet probably, the benefits which they afford to the community, in most cases, far exceed the annual cost to the latter. Of this, the reader may be convinced on reference to what I have said of the creation of value, due alone to the commercial operation of transfer from one place to another, and of the principle that every saving in the cost of production is a gain to the consumer. Were we to calculate what would be the cost of carriage of all the goods and merchandise now passing annually along this road, if the road did not exist, and to compare that enormous cost with the cost under present circumstances, then the difference would show the gain to the consumers of all those goods—a real and net gain to the nation.

It would be wrong to say that, if the road did not exist, the costs of transport would not be so enormous as here suggested, because the transportation would not take place at all and people would do without the goods now transported. It is not to be rich, to do without things because one cannot meet their cost. Each consumer is infinitely poor in respect to any good which is too dear for him to consume; and he becomes richer in respect to it in the measure in which its value diminishes.[8]

This method of evaluating public utility is the one which has been most widely adopted. Note that it turns aside completely from the measurement of utility based on cost of production. Here, on the contrary, utility is measured by means of a reduction in these expenses, as it should in fact be. There is thus a kind of contradiction between these two definitions which does not exist in

---

[8] J. B. Say, *Traité d'Economie Politique*, 5th edition, Vol. 3, pp. 136–37; Prinsep translation p. 334.

the manner in which we have looked upon utility. Moreover, if the general principle which we have just quoted is basically true, it is so incomplete in formulation and in detail that it cannot but lead to entirely erroneous results.

To show this we shall take an example from an article in *Annales des Ponts et Chaussées* (1832, 1st half year), in which M. Navier has treated the same question with literal application of J. B. Say's formula. This method of calculation has, incidentally, been widely used, and if we needed other examples they would not be lacking.

"The government", he says, "by using funds raised from the taxpayers, has spent money on a construction and, further, it will have to take from these same funds whatever is necessary to provide for the costs of maintenance. It imposes a toll with a view to reimbursing itself for the costs which it has met and the new expenses to which it is committed. It is not difficult to perceive that, in order for this operation not to be a burden on the taxpayer, the annual economy effected by the transport must be at least equal to the interest on the capital expended together with the costs of maintenance. This fact establishes a limit to the tonnage of traffic below which the enterprise could not be conducted without loss.

"To give them greater precision, we shall try to apply these notions to the building of canals, and we shall assume the following data:

Cost of constructing one league of navigable canal, 590,000 francs; which becomes 700,000 when costs of management and loss of value to property are added; the annual interest on this is 35,000 francs.

Annual upkeep, costs of management and administration for one league of the same canal, 10,000 francs.

Charges paid by merchants for the transportation of one ton of merchandise per league: by road 1 franc, by canal 0 fr.13 (excluding the toll). Saving effected by latter mode of transport 0 fr.87.

According to these data it is possible to work a canal without loss to the state wherever the quantity of goods carried annually by the canal could be equal to 45,000/0.87, or 52,000 tons: if the tonnage is greater than that, the state will earn annually a sum equal to the product of 0 fr.87 and the number of tons exceeding 52,000."

The error in this calculation, following as it does the terms of J. B. Say's formulation, is to attribute to all the tons carried by the canal a value of utility which is true of only a very small number of them so that the utility of the canal is vastly exaggerated. Thus one is led to completely false results which could have the most serious consequences for the public wealth.

In the first instance, there is no very clear reason why, in this measurement of utility, it should be the road which is the standard of comparison: if a canal is built alongside a river where navigation is laborious and therefore costly, is it not clear that in the case of some goods it is with the river charges that the canal charges ought to be compared in order to get to know the utility of the canal? When a railroad is built, will it be the canal which is to serve as the standard of comparison or the road? And in the case of a road, what is to be done?

Our method provides an answer to all these difficulties. We shall illustrate it by a series of examples, comparing it with the preceding one.

A town uses 10,000 tons of stone each year for the construction and repair of its houses. Twenty francs are paid for each ton. That is the total of the costs of production, the components of which we shall set out in detail presently. A new means of communication is established, which may be a canal, if you like, or anything else;[9] as a result, the costs of production of a ton of stone are reduced from 20 to 15 francs. In this case we say that the measure of the utility of the canal is the product of 5 francs—by which the price of a ton has fallen—by 10,000, the number of tons formerly consumed; *i.e.* 50,000 francs. It will be seen that here we are no longer comparing the costs of transport by the new and the old routes, but the costs of production. Herein lies a capital difference between the two methods. Thus, in this example, it could happen that the actual cost of transporting the stone was higher by the new route than by the old, on account of the new route being longer, and that this extra cost could be compensated by other circumstances. Suppose that the components of the old price of 20 francs are as follows:

Extraction from the quarry	16 francs
Transport over a short distance (say 4 leagues)	4 francs
Total of former costs of production	20 francs

As against this the canal, passing by an easily worked quarry which had not formerly been exploited, or the product of which had not been brought to this particular town because of the great distance involved, now brings about the following costs:

Extraction	2 francs
Transport over long distance (100 leagues)	13 francs
Total present costs of production	15 francs

We see then that the transportation cost of the old stone was only 4 francs, whilst that of the new is 13 francs; so that if we were to stick to the letter of J. B. Say's words[10] on the matter and compare the costs of transport only, we should find that the canal causes a loss of 9 francs of utility; whilst if we were to use M. Navier's method we should say that a ton of stone carried 100 leagues costs 13 francs by canal and would have cost 100 francs by road, and that therefore the utility of the canal is 87 francs per ton. But actually it is only 5 francs, that is to say more than 17 times smaller.

---

[9] It could even be a piece of equipment, some machine or other.

[10] We say 'letter', because on going back to the principles developed elsewhere by J. B. Say it is seen that it is the costs of production and not the costs of transport that this economist is comparing.

We could assume that the stone comes a greater distance still, and so long as the canal delivers it at less than 20 francs the new stone will replace the old. Thus, when the stone is worth 19 francs, the cost of transport being 17 francs, the utility of the canal will only be 1 franc; yet M. Navier's method would make it more than 113 (0 fr.87 multiplied by the number of leagues travelled by the stone).

The foregoing is not an exceptional case which could be neglected: things almost always happen in that way. Indeed, if one considers how a centre of consumption is supplied, one finds that it is provisioned by a series of radiating routes which form a certain pattern around it. When a new and more economical route of communication is established in one direction, not only does it substitute entirely in the supply of goods carried by the parallel route but it enters into competition with the routes running in other directions because its lower charges allow it to push back the sources of supply to a much greater distance. Thus, when the canal appears after the roads, it can, the other costs of production being the same, go six or seven times as far away; it will go twenty times and a hundred times further if certain circumstances allow it to take advantage of cheaper production. It is seen, then, that in general the result of the establishment of a much more economical means of communication is to alter the sources of supply, so that a comparison of the cost of transport by the canal and by the parallel road is necessarily wrong for the vast majority of products. This will be seen also from other considerations which we shall put forward.

The ultimate aim of a means of communication must be to reduce not the costs of transport, but the costs of production.[11] It may be quite rational to build a road of 40 kilometers in order to fetch, at its far end, goods which are to be had only 10 kilometers away by another road. The utility produced for the new objects, which replace the old, is equal to the difference in price multiplied by the quantity formerly consumed.

We say formerly consumed because that is an essential qualification; if we did not make it we should be led into grave errors.

The effect of the canal in having reduced the cost of production of the stone by 5 francs and consequently in having yielded a utility of 50,000 francs on the 10,000 tons used will not stop there. This fall in price will necessarily render the stone suitable for new uses; in many buildings it will replace brick and timber; streets will now be paved which were not so before, and so on; so that consumption, instead of being 10,000 tons will become perhaps 30,000. Thus before the canal was built, 10,000 tons were consumed at 20 francs; after the canal is built, 30,000 tons will be consumed at 15 francs. Is the utility produced for these 20,000 extra tons measured by 5 francs, as it is for the first 10,000? The considerations we have expounded on utility in general show that this cannot be so. Since the new purchasers did not buy

---

[11] By cost of production we mean what it costs to make an article available for consumption.

at the price of 20 francs it is apparent that they did not attribute that much utility to the consumption of stone; they do not, therefore, benefit by the kind of gain which constitutes relative utility. True, they buy at 15 francs; but amongst them there are some who attach so little value to the consumption of this material that they would give it up if the price were to rise by as little as 1 franc. For them the relative utility, the gain, is therefore less than 1 franc. Others would cease to buy only after a rise of 2 francs: for these latter the utility is between 1 and 2 francs. In short, in order to know the utility of each ton consumed it would be necessary for each consumer to make known the strength of his desire in terms of the price which would make him cease consuming. Then the calculation would become very easy. Suppose that a tax of 1 franc imposed on this stone, the production costs of which are 15 francs, deprives the canal of the carriage of 7,000 tons, then we will not be far wrong in saying that the utility of this transport is 1 franc. A new tax of 2 francs reduces traffic by another 5,000 tons, for which, therefore, the utility may be estimated at 2 francs at the most. By thus relating taxes with the amounts of traffic which they cause to disappear, we can arrive at the following result for the 20,000 new tons carried by the canal:[12]

7,000 tons at 1 franc	....	7,000 francs	
5,000 " 2 francs	....	10,000 "	
4,000 " 3 "	....	12,000 "	
3,000 " 4 "	....	12,000 "	
1,000 " 5 "	....	5,000 "	
20,000 tons	....	46,000 "	

That is to say an average utility of 2 fr.30 instead of 5 francs, which we would get from a calculation based only on the fall in the cost of production.

If to these 46,000 francs of utility we add the 50,000 francs corresponding to the 10,000 tons of initial consumption—which we could have included in the same calculation since they disappear with a tax of 5 francs—we arrive at a figure of 96,000 francs for the total utility of this type of transport. M. Navier's formula would give $30,000 \times 87 = 2,610,000$. Is it not necessary before starting a canal to know whether its utility is one or the other of these quantities?

So far we have been concerned with products which are already being consumed. But at the stage of civilization which European nations have now reached, there has arisen, besides the essential needs which men have felt at all times, an infinite number of new needs which vary with different lands, climates, and customs; at the same time, human industry has varied the products with which to satisfy the same needs. Because of all this the opening of a new means of communication, if it be cheap as canals are, and speedy

---

[12] For convenience of exposition we have used calculated differences instead of using the differential calculus. Those who are familiar with the elements of the calculus will see later how precision may be substituted for approximation. See the end of the chapter for the exact formula.

as railways are, causes altogether new products to make their appearance in the areas which it serves. Tiles come to replace thatch on all houses of some village: elsewhere slate, in its turn, comes to replace tiles; the rich will have excellent wine where the surrounding countryside only yields poor wine; the poor, who used to drink water, now find that beer is within their reach; where sea fish was salted it now comes fresh; there will be plaster instead of lime; stone instead of brick, or *vice versa,* and so on. How are we to measure the utility of these new commodities which were not in use before the new means of communication?

We have seen above how J. B. Say answered this objection. "Each consumer", he says, "is infinitely poor in respect to any good which is too dear for him to consume; and he becomes richer in respect to it in the measure in which its value diminishes".[13] And this famous economist would have us take account of the utility of these commodities in the same manner as for the others, by estimating the difference between the cost of transport in the supposed absence of the road, and the actual transport cost since it is open, no matter how large this difference might be.

Here, the exaggerated character of this method of evaluation seems to hit the eye. Slate, unknown previous to the new road or the new canal, will be worth 20 francs per thousand, whereas it might be worth perhaps 200, 300, or even 1,000 francs without the canal. The slate quarries, which the canal now skirts, may not previously have had any means of exploitation, and if one had insisted on extracting the slate, it would have had to be taken away on muleback. Are we to say that because slate would have cost 1,000 francs when everybody did without it, and because it is worth 20 francs now that everybody uses it, that therefore the utility of the service rendered by the canal is 980 francs per thousand slates? We can easily convince ourselves that it is not so, because it might well happen that a tax of 10 francs per thousand would reduce consumption by half; half of the consumers would go back to the tile which they had abandoned; this being so we can say that one half of the transported slate has a utility not greater than 10 francs per ton. Further, if a tax of 20 francs would cause slate to disappear from the market altogether, we should say that the utility of this second half was less than 20 francs. The figure of 980 francs, based on what would have been its cost, is therefore imaginary; there is no utility other than that people are willing to pay for. That is the dictum of political economy which we must always keep in mind when dealing with all these questions. If you have put 1,000 francs' worth of work into a product, and yet can only find a buyer at 100 francs, you have lost 900 francs' worth of utility.

In the case of new commodities being transported, as in the case of those now transported in excess of the former consumption, the measure of utility is not the fall in the costs of production, but the lowest tax which it would be necessary to impose on them in order to prevent their being carried by the

---

[13] See above, Note 11.

new route. This latter measure could even be applied to the amounts of commodities which were formerly being carried, because the tax which they can sustain is obviously equal to the fall in the cost of production. Moreover, this method is not peculiar to means of communication, but can be applied to everything, to any working tools whatever and to their products; so that we can say in general that the measure of the utility of a product is the tax which would prevent it being consumed. In order to discover the utility of a large number of products, or of a machine which turns out a large number of products, it would be sufficient to add up the utilities of each of them. The simplest method of doing this is the following.

Suppose that all those similar commodities of which we want to discover the utilities are all subjected to a tax which rises by small steps. Each successive increase will cause a certain quantity of the commodity to disappear from consumption. This quantity, multiplied by the rate of tax, will give its utility expressed in money. By thus letting the tax go up until there are no more consumers, and by adding together all the products of this multiplication process, we will arrive at the total utility of the goods.

Let us illustrate this formula by an example. We want to know the utility of a footbridge which is being used free of charge at the rate of 2,080,000 crossings annually. Suppose that a toll of 0 fr.01 would reduce the number by 330,000, that a tax of 0 fr.02 reduces it by 294,000, and so on. We then say that for 330,000 crossings the utility is about 0 fr.01 and that for the next 294,000 crossings the utility is about 0 fr.02 and we can then draw up the following table.

330,000 crossings at	0 fr.01	produce a utility of	3,300	francs
294,000	"	.02	"	"	5,880	"
260,000	"	.03	"	"	7,800	"
228,000	"	.04	"	"	9,120	"
198,000	"	.05	"	"	9,900	"
170,000	"	.06	"	"	10,200	"
144,000	"	.07	"	"	10,080	"
120,000	"	.08	"	"	9,600	"
98,000	"	.09	"	"	8,820	"
78,000	"	.10	"	"	7,800	"
60,000	"	.11	"	"	6,600	"
44,000	"	.12	"	"	5,280	"
30,000	"	.13	"	"	3,900	"
18,000	"	.14	"	"	2,520	"
8,000	"	.15	"	"	1,200	"
2,080,000					102,000	"

Thus 102,000 francs would be the absolute utility to society of the bridge. We can find the relative utility by deducting the costs of maintenance and the interest on the capital expended in construction. If this latter sum were to reach or exceed 102,000 francs, the construction would have produced no utility, the difference expressing the loss which would have been made. Such is the calculation to be made in the case where crossing is free of charge. If there is a toll, we must take only the figures below that of the charge. Thus for a toll of 0 fr.05, for example, the absolute utility of the bridge is expressed by the sum of the ten last figures or 66,000 francs; the utility lost, by the sum of the first five, or 36,000 francs; the product of the toll would be 770,000 crossings at 0 fr.05 or 38,500 francs. With this toll, then, the possible utility of the bridge would be distributed in the following manner:

To the toll collector..................................	38,500 francs
Derived by those crossing the bridge (66,000–38,500).......	27,500 "
Loss of utility arising from the 1,310,000 crossings which would have been made but for the toll.......................	36,000 "
Total	102,000 "

As the toll increases, so does the utility of the bridge diminish in proportion; it becomes zero when the toll equals 0 fr.15, at which price noone crosses the bridge; it is therefore possible for the loss of utility to rise to as much as 102,000 francs. Does this mean that there should only be very low tolls or even that there should be none at all? That will not be our conclusion when we come to speak of tariffs; but we hope to show that their height needs to be studied and operated according to rational principles, in order to produce the greatest possible utility and at the same time a revenue sufficient to cover the cost of upkeep and interest on capital.

If instead of a footbridge you have a bridge for carriages, all you need do is to apply an analogous calculation to each article on the tariff—to horsemen, to sprung carriages, to carts, *etc.,* and to add the utilities together.

The type of calculation that we have just described is a general one; instead of crossings of a bridge you could write in the table pairs of stockings and so discover the utility of the stocking frame. If you assume that the tax is only applied to stockings made by this process, you will obtain a figure which will cause this machine to disappear completely from use so that there will be a return to handknit stockings. The sum of the amounts below this figure will give you the utility of the stocking frame. Go further, assume that the tax falls upon stockings without distinction as to their process of manufacture, and when you have caused the last pair of stockings to disappear, the sum will represent the utility of this garment.

If it were a question of discovering the utility of transportation on the royal and departmental roads, it would be necessary in the same way to assume a traffic tax increasing little by little, which would cause the successive disappearance of several of the tons together comprising the 50 million tons being carried on these roads. Each ton multiplied by the tax which would prevent it from moving would give this utility. It is seen that the total figure would not have the slightest relation to the 500 million costs of production.

It remains for us now to show that our formula is complete, that it expresses the whole of the utility of the objects we are considering and that there is nothing to be added to it. It often happens, in effect, that when the cost of production of an article falls, competition causes the price of the same commodity produced by a different method to fall to the same level, as it does also for similar commodities. Thus, coal is carried by canal; and the utility of the coal is given exactly by our formula. But the presence of this coal on the market might, through the effect of competition, result in a fall in the price of wood, which the canal does not carry. If there is a fall of 2 francs per cubic meter of wood and people continue to consume 100,000 cubic meters, are we not entitled to say that there are 200,000 francs of utility which are owed to the canal? At another place the opposite may happen; the presence of the canal may cause large quantities of wood to be carried away so that the local price of wood rises. Complaints against the canal will follow: "It may be very useful to some places", it will be said, "but as for us, who have to pay 2 francs more for our wood, it really costs us 200,000 francs a year". Those are 200,000 francs which should be deducted from its utility. Lastly, it is often said that means of communication increase the income from and the value of the properties which they traverse, as well as the revenue from certain taxes, and so on. Without entering into the details of these effects, it can readily be shown either that their measurement is included in the above formula or else that they are merely changes in the distribution of wealth which it is not for us to take into account, because the losses and gains counterbalance each other. When we say that we are not to take them into account, we are speaking only with respect to the calculation of utility. The state, on the contrary, must concern itself very seriously with them. A new means of communication is opened; whilst it has a utility of 10 million for society as whole, yet it causes one million to pass from Peter's pocket into Paul's. Although this may at first be merely an individual misfortune, it will have repercussions on the wealth of society which the state has an interest in preventing, redressing, or mitigating.

For an increase or decrease of utility to take place, there must be, provided there is no change in quality, a decrease or increase in the *costs of production*. When there is merely a change in the *market price*, the consumer gains what the producer loses, or *vice versa*. Thus, when an object costing 20 francs to produce is sold at 50 francs because of a monopoly or concession, the producer exacts 30 francs' worth of utility from each purchaser. If for some reason or another he is forced to cut his price by 10 francs, his profit falls by 10 francs per article and each purchaser gains by that amount. It is a question of compensation, but no utility has been produced. There would have been an increase of utility if the drop in the market price had been due to a fall in the costs of production, because the gain to consumers would not have been offset by any loss to the producer. When, therefore, coal brought by canal brings about a fall in the price of wood at the place of destination, the income of the wood owners falls by as much as that of the consumers rises. If, on the other hand, the canal, by taking wood away, causes the price of the remaining wood to rise, then the income of the wood owners rises by as much as that of the consumers falls. However, it often happens that the compensation is not as precise as we have just described it. The fall in the market price indeed brings about an increase in consumption and thereby secures for new consumers a utility which the product did not previously possess. But if we look more closely at how things actually happen, we see that although this increase of utility is very real, it cannot be attributed to the public undertaking, which in this case has merely caused the market price to fall—a result which might equally well have been obtained by a simple legislative measure. It is possible to conceive of a canal carrying neither wood, nor stone, nor iron, and yet causing a fall in the prices of those commodities because of the possibility it prevents to buyers of procuring these things more cheaply; for this possibility forces the existing producers to lower their prices in order to retain their market. Now it is evident that the utility due to this fall of price, and thereby enlarged consumption, cannot be attributed to the canal, which, carrying nothing, is but a fiction, so to speak, and the course of which could be replaced by a line of stakes. That is the situation whenever utility is produced by competition: a bridge yields large profits to the company which collects the toll; a rival company builds another bridge alongside and forces the first to cut its tariff by half; the number of people crossing the first bridge doubles and its utility increases enormously. Is this increase due to the second bridge, which no one in fact crosses? Obviously not; it is merely a result of the cut in the tariff of the first, which could have been brought about by some other means; on the contrary, since the construction of the second bridge required a considerable amount of capital it actually diminishes the public utility. Therefore when measuring the utility of public undertakings only those commodities must be included, to the production of which the undertaking contributes directly. When the method of evaluation outlined above is applied to those commodities, one may be sure not only of omitting nothing which should be included, but also of counting in nothing which should be left out.

We have shown that the methods we refuted are fallacious in several respects. First of all we saw that it is not costs of transport which have to be compared in order to arrive at the measure of utility, but costs of production; this was the first error. Then we saw that to apply this measure to the quantity by which the consumption of some commodities increases, was a second error; and that to do so for new products was a third. It remains to be shown that the unqualified application of this measure to the rare products where the substitution of one machine for another leads to no change in the quantity consumed, is nearly always a fourth error. In fact, it does not often happen that a modification of the productive process which reduces costs does not also modify the quality of the product; the latter becomes better or worse, larger or smaller, lighter or heavier, quicker or slower, and so on. Now all these qualities have a value which must be taken into account in the calculation of utility. Thus in the example borrowed from M. Navier in which comparison is made between a canal and a road, the advantage being valued at 0 fr.87 per league in favour of the former, it would not even be correct to apply this calculation to the goods which now come by canal in the same quantities in which they formerly came by the parallel road. The fact is that carriage by road being quicker, more reliable, and less subject to loss or damage, it possesses advantages to which business men often attach a considerable value. However, it may well be that the saving of 0 fr. 87 induces the merchant to use the canal; he can buy warehouses and increase his floating capital in order to have a sufficient supply of goods on hand to protect himself against the slowness and irregularity of the canal, and if all told the saving of 0 fr.87 in transport gives him an advantage of a few centimes, he will decide in favour of the new route. But the advantages of the new route to him will only be precisely these few centimes, and if a toll of the same amount is established on the canal, then goods will no longer be moved by this route; and there we have the true measure of the utility of the canal so far as these goods are concerned. For there is no utility other than that people are willing to pay for; thus, although there is a saving of 0 fr.87 in the cost of production, there may well be two or three centimes' worth of utility, because the method of production has changed. This method of measurement by comparing costs of production would deny any degree of utility to a railway which was built after a road and which, although it charged higher fares, was able to take passengers from the latter because of its sole advantage of speed. What is its utility? Only the toll which would dissuade passengers from stepping out of the stagecoach and into the railway carriage can give us the exact measurement.

It will be seen that this method takes account of the previous situation whatever it may have been. The measure of the utility of a machine or of a public enterprise is not an absolute measure, but a measure of progress; it is the distance between the point of departure and the point of arrival. Here we have a tun of wine which has been brought 100 leagues by a new canal, and you say that 87 francs' worth of utility has been produced because the cost of transport is only 13 francs as against 100 francs for a similar distance by road. That is a grave mistake; before the advent of the canal this wine may have gone by road from the vintner's caves to a seaport, whence a coaster took it to the mouth of a river, up which it was taken to the beginning of another canal, and after travelling a certain distance along that canal it may have been brought by goods cart to its destination: now the opening of the new canal has led to the use of a new route, which in turn involves several means of transport. A mere difference of 1 franc in total costs will suffice for the adoption of this new route. The amount of 87 francs' worth of utility for a journey of 100 leagues claimed for the canal may then be reduced to as little as 1 franc, provided there has been no change in the length or circumstances of the journey.

This shows that there may be an enormous difference between the utility of two means of communication which are used with equal frequency and which cost the same to use; this difference arises from the nature of the route previously used. Thus two railways may be equally patronized and produce the same receipts with the same tariff, yet one of them may be very useful and the other practically useless. What has happened is that the first railway has replaced a longer and badly laid out road on which transportation was costly and slow. Each of its passengers therefore derives a great advantage in going by rail, whilst the second railway runs parallel to a steamboat service and only saves its passengers a few minutes on an already short trip. The least rise in its fares would cause the loss of all its custom and show that its utility was really very small, whilst a similar step would not lose the other railway a single passenger. And so it may happen that of two railways the one that is used less, was more costly to build, and has the more defective layout and the higher fares, may be the one with the greater utility. In order to measure the latter, in fact, it is not sufficient to count the services rendered: they must also be weighed; many small services may give a smaller result than a few large services.

So far we have been concerned solely with acquired utility, because to increase utility is the purpose of all instruments of production including public undertakings; however, it will be well to say a word about the measurement of lost utility, because a loss of utility results from anything which raises the price of commodities, and because in the management of public enterprises recourse often has to be had either to tolls—which raise the market price of those commodities using the service supplied by the public undertaking—or to taxes, which have the same effect on those not using the service. It is therefore necessary to know how to calculate the loss of utility in these circumstances. We shall need but a few words, for it is merely a case of making a calculation exactly similar to that which has been put forward for the measurement of acquired utility.

We have assumed that in a town where 10,000 tons of stone had been consumed at 20 francs, the appearance of a canal or any other piece of equipment causing costs of production to fall to 15 francs had brought about a rise in consumption to 30,000 tons. And we have calculated the utility due to this fall in costs as follows:

Utility yielded on 10,000 tons formerly consumed, at 5 francs
per ton .... 50,000 francs
Utility yielded on 20,000 tons of new consumption at a rate
varying between the limits 0 and 5 francs, found to average
2 fr.30... 46,000

Total utility produced........................ 96,000

Now suppose that for some reason or another a tax of 5 francs a ton is imposed on this stone. It is quite obvious that its effect will be to reduce consumption of the stone to 10,000 tons, since it will bring the price to purchasers back to 20 francs. Only the uses for which the stone has a utility greater than that price will be satisfied. The yield of the tax will therefore only be 50,000 francs; but is that alone the utility lost by the taxpayers? Evidently not. It might even be said that for the nation as a whole the yield of the tax is not a loss, since it must be supposed that it is put to some good use. It is merely a change in the distribution of wealth; there is no loss to society as a whole, as if an extra amount of work had been required which would have raised the costs of production to 20 francs; the 5 francs per ton would then have represented something which had been consumed. But there is a real loss to those who would have bought the stone at 16 francs and who, when buying it at 15 francs, benefited to the extent of 1 franc, of which they are now deprived by the tax of 5 francs even though they do not pay the latter; similarly there is a loss of 2 francs to those who would have been willing to pay 17 francs, and so on. In order to estimate the total amount of this loss the only data required are the quantities by which consumption falls with each increase in the tax; we find ourselves back at the table we drew up earlier, now showing 46,000 francs' worth of utility lost for the 20,000 tons of stone which are not consumed because of the tax; here, then, is a tax which yields but 50,000 francs, and which, besides, causes a loss to society of 46,000 francs of utility. We have chosen an example where the rate of the tax is fairly moderate relative to the cost of production—one third, in fact (5 francs in 15); there are some taxes on articles of consumption which double, treble, or quadruple the price of the commodities concerned, with the result that their consumption drops off enormously and there is a loss of utility to society incomparably larger than the yield of the tax. One can gain an idea of this effect by supposing that the government is so ill-advised as to treble, quadruple, quintuple . . ., indeed to raise the postal rate for letters to such a level that the public, which is at present paying 50 million for postal services, will expend no more than 25 million. A moment's reflection will show that this result is quite possible; in the measure in which the charge increases, the number of letters falls, eventually becoming zero when the postage is such that no one thinks the carriage of a letter worth that price. At a slightly lower charge there will be some letters and a very small yield. Therefore there actually is some charge higher than the present one which would reduce the yield to 25 million. Let us look at this state of affairs: is it not obvious that although the public is in some sense relieved of a burden, since it is paying 25 million less than before, yet it is losing a very considerable amount of utility in respect of the letters which are not carried because of the impost? From this may be seen how false are the comparisons which are sometimes made between the budgets of different countries; the people of one country say: we are paying 25 million, you are paying 50 million—therefore our government is twice as good as yours. Now, it may well be that the contrary is true, quite apart from the question of how the 25 and the 50 million are employed; it may well be that the harm done in levying the 25 is a hundred times more considerable than that done in levying the 50 million. The fallacy lies in taking account of only one class of citizens— those who pay the charge: account must also be taken of the much greater number who do not pay it because they cannot afford to, and who therefore are no longer consumers. In many cases, therefore, the rate or basis of a tax has a greater effect on the general well-being than does the amount which it raises.

Let us indicate some of the general properties of taxes which it is well to bear in mind in questions concerning public undertakings, since the latter always and necessarily give rise to a tax or a toll.

Suppose that we have two columns of figures showing the number of articles consumed corresponding to each market price from zero, at which consumption is largest, right up to the price which causes all consumption to cease. This series of relationships is not known for any commodity, and it can even be said that it will never be known since it depends on the volatile will of human beings; it is today no longer what it was yesterday. It is thus of no avail to try to determine this relationship exactly by experience or groping experiment, but there do exist certain general laws to which the relationship, in its very mobility, remains constantly subject, and out of these general laws there arise certain immutable general principles. One of these laws is that consumption expands when price falls; another, that the increase in consumption due to a price fall will be the greater, the lower the initial price. If a fall in the price of an article from 100 to 95 francs brings in another thousand consumers, a further fall from 95 to 90 will bring in more than a thousand. This property reflects the structure of society which, if it is divided into groups according to income, and these groups are placed one on top of the other starting with the poorest, has a shape similar to one of those pyramids of cannonballs which are to be seen in parks of artillery—the lower the layer, the more balls it contains. Thus, as the price of an article falls, its use spreads to more and more consumers, quite apart from the fact that existing consumers purchase it in greater quantities, as we have seen. All this is a fact of experience which has been verified statistically too often to need labouring here.

It follows that when the change in consumption brought about by a tax is known, it is possible to find an upper limit to the amount of utility lost by multiplying the change in consumption by half the tax. The same holds for the utility produced by a piece of equipment. Thus in the example of the consumption of stone which we took as the basis for our calculations, we found that a fall of 5 francs in the price only gave an average utility of 2 fr.30 per ton. The figures we worked on are fictitious, it is true: but no matter what they might be, so long as they obey the laws which we have just invoked, they would always give a result less than 2 fr.50; to arrive at that figure we would have to assume that the 20,000 tons by which consumption has increased have arisen in a uniform manner, that is to say 2,000 by the drop from 20 francs to 19, 2,000 by that from 19 to 18, and so on down to the drop from 16 to 15 francs. Now that is not possible, since each successive fall in price brings in more and more numerous consumers. Thus it is possible to lay down the principle that the utility lost or gained through a change in price has for its upper limit the amount by which the quantity consumed changes, multiplied by half the change in price. If a tax of 5 francs reduces the number of consumers from 30,000 to 10,000, the utility lost by the community is below $20,000 \times \frac{1}{2} 5 = 50,000$ francs. Further, it is easily seen that the smaller the tax the nearer does this limit approach the actual figure.

Although consumption diminishes less and less rapidly as the tax rises, it is permissible, where a tax is small relative to the cost of manufacture, to suppose a uniform rate of decrease. Thus a tax of 1 franc on a thing worth 100 francs will cause the number of consumers to fall to an extent not markedly different from a tax of 2, 3, 4, 5, or 6 francs; for the relations between the numbers 100, 101, 102, 103, 104, 105, and 106 are little different. Now, the utility lost as a result of a tax of 1 franc is this unknown number multiplied by $\frac{1}{2}$ of 1; the utility lost through a tax of 2 francs will be twice this number multiplied by $\frac{1}{2}$ of 2; for 3 francs, $\frac{1}{2}$ 3 × 3. It may thus be said that the loss of utility is proportional to the square of the tax; so that a tax of 10 francs will lead to the loss of 100 times more utility than a tax of 1 franc. The enormous advantage of spreading taxes out is apparent; instead of putting a tax of 10 francs on one article, taxing 10 articles at 1 franc each may reduce the loss of utility by 90 per cent. Let us note further that the product of a tax is not proportional to its rate. A tax of 10 francs will not yield ten times as much as one of 1 franc.

If a tax is gradually increased from zero up to the point where it becomes prohibitive, its yield is at first nil, then increases by small stages until it reaches a maximum, after which it gradually declines until it becomes zero again. It follows that when the state requires to raise a given sum by means of taxation, there are always two rates of tax which will fulfil the requirement, one above and one below that which would yield the maximum. There may be a very great difference between the amounts of utility lost through these two taxes which yield the same revenue. This even applies in the case of a tax which yields the maximum revenue, for appreciably different rates of tax may yield more or less the same revenue while bringing about quite considerably different losses of utility; even in this situation there is much to choose.

Loss of utility resulting from a rise in price is not peculiar to tolls and taxes; it applies to the very price, representing costs of production, which could be considered as a kind of tax upon natural resources. Thus the price of a thing is not only a burden to him who pays it, but also to him who cannot acquire the thing because of its price. The effect of mechanical equipment in reducing prices, and of taxes in raising them, is thus merely to increase or diminish an already existing disadvantage; which latter may be calculated by the same method, for it is but the utility of a machine which would reduce the costs of production to nothing. This calculation only requires the measurement of the utility between a price of zero and the actual price, and is one which we have already performed above for the case of a bridge which it cost nothing to cross. Instead of a charge for crossing a bridge we can consider the price of some object or other and arrive at exactly the same result. This loss of utility due to a price which is not a payment for labour expended plays in political economy the part which friction plays in mechanics. No doubt the Pont des Arts does take 5 centimes' worth of utility from all those who cross over it, but insofar as this is merely a repayment of capital advanced, it is a law of human nature and of the present state of progress of the human mind to which we must needs resign ourselves; insofar as it is a profit for him who has built the bridge, it is but a change in the distribution of public wealth which does not appreciably affect its total. But this is not all: this toll of 5 centimes greatly detracts from the utility of the bridge (we could say that this price of 5 centimes greatly detracts from the utility of such and such a commodity), because it forces many people who only attach a utility of 4, 3, 2 centimes, or 1 centime to the crossing, to go round by the Pont Neuf. Here the loss is complete and uncompensated: it is the useless friction of mechanics. You want to raise a weight of two kilogrammes to a height of one meter: don't complain that you must make an effort of one kilogramme, so long as you need not sustain it for more than two meters—this must be so unless the laws of nature were changed; but if your one-kilogramme effort has to hold out for three or four meters, then there is useless friction which mechanics will teach you how to reduce or avoid. In the same way political economy can show how to reduce those losses of utility which result from changes in price. We have, here, only inquired into the principles which can be used to measure them, and the following chapters will seek to apply those principles.

It may perhaps be objected that our formula depends upon certain data which no statistical method can furnish and that therefore we shall never be able to express by an exact figure the utility yielded by a machine, a road, or any undertaking, nor the utility lost as the result of a tax or a toll.

We might content ourselves with replying that when something cannot be known, it is a great deal, already, to realize that one knows nothing. If those who first occupied themselves in the attempt at measuring the wealth of nations had limited themselves to declaring that the question was beyond their powers, instead of putting forward the doctrine of the balance of trade, they would perhaps have rendered a greater service than those who came later and demonstrated their error. In fact, the barriers to international trade which have been erected under the influence of this doctrine have resisted, and in all likelihood will continue to resist for several generations yet, all the arguments of the true principle. This question of the measurement of utility is in like case with all other problems in political economy in that a rigorous solution is impossible in practice; yet this science alone can furnish the means to approach such a solution. It may be impossible to say that the utility of a canal would be more than five million, yet possible to say that it would be less than six, which is sufficient information upon which to base a decision not to build; it may be impossible to say that the utility of a bridge would be as much as 120 thousand francs, yet possible to say that it would be more than 80 thousand, which is sufficient to show that the bridge is worthwhile. In political economy the data for reaching a complete solution are often lacking; but this disadvantage makes a knowledge of the basic laws and general principles all the more necessary. They alone can show how to turn to account what is known so as to discover what is not known, point out what is lacking and thereby provide the means of seeking it, of finding it if that is possible, and if it is not, provide a substitute. Political economy is like geometry which, although stating its principles in terms of squares, triangles, circles, and other regular figures, yet shows how to measure the area of a field bordered by the sinuous course of a stream and a lane of which only a few points are known. Are the known points sufficient? What are the missing ones? How find them? What will be the margin of error if we have to do without them? Those are questions which require a closer and deeper knowledge of geometry than those where all the elements of the calculation are given exactly. In like manner, the less complete and accurate are the available data in problems of political economy, the more needful is it that the rigor of fundamental scientific principles be applied to them if they are to be handled skilfully and effectively in practice.

NOTE

The various points about utility which have been developed above may be presented geometrically in a very simple manner.

If it be supposed, as in Figure 1, that along a line OP the lengths Op, Op', Op'' . . . represent various prices for an article, and that the verticals pn, $p'n'$, $p''n''$ . . . represent the number of articles consumed corresponding to these prices, then it is possible to construct a curve $Nnn'n''P$ which we shall call the curve of consumption. ON represents the quantity consumed when the price is zero, and OP the price at which consumption falls to zero.

Since pn represents the number of articles consumed at price Op, the area of the rectangle $Ornp$ expresses the cost of production of the np articles, and, according to J. B. Say, also their utility. We trust we have demonstrated that the utility of each of these np articles is at least Op and that for almost all of them the utility is greater than Op. Indeed, by raising a perpendicular from p' it can be seen that for each of $n'p'$ articles the utility is at least Op', since they are bought at that price. Of the np articles there are therefore only $np - n'p' = nq$ for which utility is really only Op (or rather the average between Op and Op'); for the others it is at least Op'. We are thus led to the conclusion that for nq articles the utility is represented by the area $rnn'r'$, and that for the remainder, qp or $n'p'$, it is greater than the rectangle $r'n'p'O$; by supposing a further rise in price $p'p''$ we could show that for $n'p' - n''p'' = n'q'$ articles the utility is an average between Op' and Op'', and is measured by the area $r'n'n''r''$ and so on. By continuing this process it can be shown that the

Figure 1

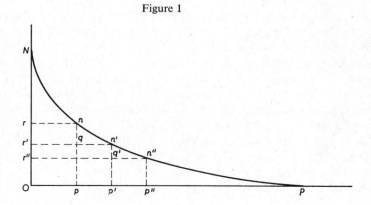

absolute utility of the *np* articles to the consumer is the mixtilinear trapezium *OrnP*. The relative utility is arrived at by subtracting the costs of production, shown as the rectangle *rnpO*, which leaves the triangle *npP*; this, according to our view, is the utility remaining to the consumers of the *np* articles after they have paid for them. It is seen that the area of this triangle on one side of the line *np* has no relation to that of the rectangle on the other side.

The utility of a natural product the acquisition of which requires no expense, is expressed by the large triangle *NOP*.

It may be noticed that as the price of an article rises, the utility diminishes, but less and less rapidly: and that, on the other hand, as the price falls, the utility increases more and more rapidly; for it is expressed by a triangle which shortens or stretches as the case may be.

Figure 2 shows the effect of an improvement in the methods of manufacture which reduces the costs of production from *Op* to *Op'* without any change in quality; utility is increased by the difference between the two triangles *n'p'P* and *npP*, or the mixtilinear trapezium *n'p'pn*. The error of which we have accused M. Navier was to take, instead of this area, the rectangle *n'p'pq*. If a change in quality occurred, say for the worse, the utility would only be the difference between the triangles *mp'S* and *npP*, which could be quite small and even zero, according to the shape of the new curve of consumption.

Let *Op*, in Figure 3, be the price of an article which is cheap and consumed in large quantities. A small tax of *pp'* will yield the rectangle *pp'n'q* and the utility lost both to the taxpayers and the fisc is the small triangle *nqn'*. If the tax is doubled, its yield of *pp''n''q'* is not double the rectangle *pp'n'q*; yet the loss of utility *nq'n''* is four times the loss represented by the triangle *nqn'*, since both its base and its height have doubled. Similarly, if the tax is trebled, the loss of utility increases ninefold, and so on. From this may be derived the following propositions developed in the text: *The heavier the tax, the less it yields relatively. The loss of utility increases as the square of the tax.*

By thus gradually increasing the tax it will reach a level *pM* at which the yield is at a maximum, *pMTQ*, and the utility lost is fairly considerable, being represented by the triangle *TQn*. Beyond *pM* the yield of the tax diminishes

Figure 2

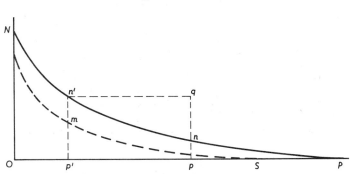

Figure 3

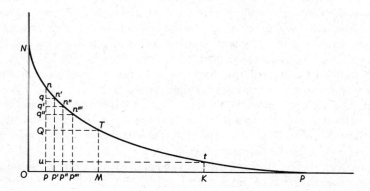

and equals that given by a lower rate of tax. For example the high tax pK would only yield $pKtu$ which is equal to or even smaller than the yield of the tax pp'. In the former instance the loss of utility is the large triangle tun, which may be ten times as large as the yield of the tax. Thus a tax of pM which yields 10 million will do less harm than a tax of pK which only yields 2 or 3 million. Lastly, a tax of pP will yield nothing; it is the one which does society the greatest harm, though it brings nothing into the treasury. Therefore it must be recognized that the yield of a tax is no measure of the loss which it causes society to suffer. It all depends on the way in which taxes are combined.

Tolls lead to similar results, for they are either taxes or increases in price. If it is wished by means of a toll on a bridge to raise a sum A representing the interest on capital expended, then, given the curve of consumption $y = f(x)$, we must solve the equation $xy = A$. If it is wished to raise the greatest revenue, we must solve the equation $dyx/dx = 0$. If, in Figure 4, Op is the value of x derived from the first equation, the product of the toll will be $Ornp$, the utility of the bridge to those who use it will be the triangle npP, and the loss of utility the triangle Nrn. If OM is the value which will raise the greatest product $ORTM$, the utility of the bridge to those who use it is no greater than the triangle TMP, and the loss of utility becomes the triangle RTN. When the consumers can be placed in several categories each of which attributes a different utility to the same service, it is possible by a certain combination of taxes, to increase the product of the toll and to diminish the loss of utility. If from among the pn consumers at price Op you can distinguish the number pq who would consume at the price OM, and from among these latter the number Mq' who would consume at price Op', and can oblige them by various combinations to pay those prices, then the yield of the tax will be the sum of the three rectangles $Ornp + pqTM + Mq'n'p'$; the utility to consumers will be the three triangles $nqT + Tq'n' + n'p'P$; while the loss of utility is merely that due to the lowest tax, the triangle Nrn.

We shall not pursue the application of geometry to political economy any

Figure 4

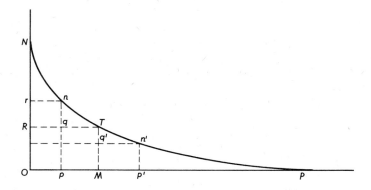

further here, for that would need developments which will be found in the following chapters.

In presenting, in this note, some of the principles of our science in this particular form it was our wish to try and make clear how great would be the advantages of an alliance with mathematics, despite the anathema which economists of all times have pronounced against the latter. So soon as it is realized, with J. B. Say, that political economy is concerned with quantities susceptible of a more or a less, it must also be recognized that it is in the realm of mathematics. If one has gone astray in political economy every time one has relied on mathematical calculations, it is because there are mathematicians who make false calculations, just as there are logicians who produce false arguments: the former no more invalidate mathematics than the latter invalidate logic, which alone is sometimes regarded as a science. Not only do the symbols and drawings of mathematics give body and form to abstract ideas and thereby call the senses to the aid of man's intellectual power, but its formulae take hold of these ideas, modify them, and transform them, and bring to light everything that is true, right, and precise in them, without forcing the mind to follow all the motions of a wheelwork the course of which has been established once for all. They are machines which, at a certain stage, can think for us, and there is as much advantage in using them as there is in using those which, in industry, labour for us.

The general welfare in relation to problems of taxation and of railway and utility rates*†

HAROLD HOTELLING

In this paper we shall bring down to date in revised form an argument due essentially to the engineer Jules Dupuit, to the effect that the optimum of the general welfare corresponds to the sale of everything at marginal cost. This means that toll bridges, which have recently been reintroduced around New York, are inefficient reversions; that all taxes on commodities, including sales taxes, are more objectionable than taxes on incomes, inheritances, and the site value of land; and that the latter taxes might well be applied to cover the fixed costs of electric power plants, waterworks, railroads, and other industries in which the fixed costs are large, so as to reduce to the level of marginal cost the prices charged for the services and products of these industries. The common assumption, so often accepted uncritically as a basis of arguments on important public questions, that "every tub must stand on its own bottom," and that therefore the products of every industry must be sold at prices so high as to cover not only marginal costs but also all the fixed costs, including interest on irrevocable and often hypothetical investments, will thus be seen to be inconsistent with the maximum of social efficiency. A method of measuring the loss of satisfactions resulting from the current scheme of pricing, a loss which appears to be extremely large, will emerge from the analysis. It will appear also that the inefficient plan of requiring that all costs, including fixed overhead, of an industry shall be paid out of the prices of its products is responsible for an important part of the instability which leads to cyclical fluctuations and unemployment of labor and other resources.

A railway rate is of essentially the same nature as a tax. Authorized and enforced by the government, it shares with taxes a considerable degree of

* *Econometrica*, 6(1938): pp. 242–69. Reprinted by courtesy of the author and *Econometrica*.

† Presented at the meeting of the Econometric Society at Atlantic City, December 28, 1937, by the retiring president.

arbitrariness. Rate differentials have, like protective tariffs and other taxes, been used for purposes other than to raise revenue. Indeed, the difference between rail freight rates between the same points, according as the commodity is or is not moving in international transport, has been used in effect to nullify the protective tariff. While it has not generally been perceived that the problems of taxation and those of railway rate making are closely connected, so that two independent bodies of economic literature have grown up, nevertheless the underlying unity is such that the considerations applicable to taxation are very nearly identical with those involved in proper rate making. This essential unity extends itself also to other rates, such as those charged by electric, gas, and water concerns, and to the prices of the products of all industries having large fixed costs independent of the volume of output.

I. THE CLASSICAL ARGUMENT

Dupuit's work of 1844 and the following years[1] laid the foundation for the use of the diagram of Figure 1 by Marshall and other economists. A rising supply curve SB is used, and is sometimes regarded as coinciding with the marginal-cost curve. Such a coincidence would arise if there were free competition among producers, in the sense that each would regard the price

Figure 1

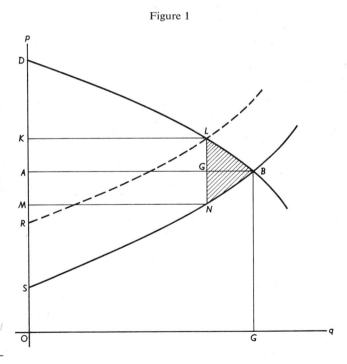

---

[1] Collected and reprinted with comments by Mario di Bernardi and Luigi Einaudi. *"De l'Utilité et de sa Mesure," La Riforma Soziale, Turin, 1932.

as fixed beyond his control, and adjust his production so as to obtain maximum net profits. This condition is approximated, for example, in most agriculture. *DB* is a declining demand curve. The buyers are presumed to compete freely with each other. The actual quantity and price are the coordinates of the intersection *B*. Then it is supposed that a tax *t* per unit is imposed upon the sellers. Since this is a uniform increment to marginal cost, the marginal-cost curve *SB* is lifted bodily to the new position *RL*, at height $t = SR = NL$ above its former position.

Three conclusions have been derived with the help of this figure, all of which must be reviewed to take account of the interrelations of the particular commodity in question with others. One of these arguments has almost universally been accepted, but must be rejected when account is taken of related commodities. A second has been accepted, and is actually true. The third has been condemned and attacked by a long line of prominent economists, but in the light of more thorough analysis made possible by modern mathematical methods must now in its essence be accepted. The first is the proposition that since the point *L* of intersection of the demand curve with the supply curve *RL* is higher by *GL*, a fraction of the tax rate *NL*, than the intersection *B* with the tax-free curve *SB*, therefore the price is increased as a result of the tax, by an amount less than the tax. That this conclusion is not necessarily true when account is taken of related commodities I have shown in an earlier paper.[2] The second proposition—whose conclusion remains valid under certain plausible assumptions[3]—is that, since *L* is to the left of *B*, the quantity of the taxed commodity will diminish. With this diminution is associated an approximately measurable net social loss.

The third argument is based on Dupuit's, and is of primary concern here. Dupuit sought a criterion of the value of society of roads, canals, bridges, and waterworks. He pointed out the weakness of calling the value of a thing only what is paid for it, since many users would if necessary pay more than they actually do pay. The total benefit he measured by the aggregate of the maximum prices that would be paid for the individual small units of the commodity (a term used here to include services, e.g., of canals) corresponding to the costs of alternatives to the various uses. If $p = f(q)$ is the cost of

---

[2] "Edgeworth's Taxation Paradox and the Nature of Demand and Supply Functions," *Journal of Political Economy*, Vol. 40, 1932, pp. 577–616. Edgeworth had discovered, and maintained against the opposition of leading economists, that a monopolist controlling two products may after the imposition of a tax on one of them find it profitable to reduce both prices, besides paying the tax. However he regarded this as a "mere curiosum," unlikely in fact to occur, and peculiar to monopoly. But it is shown in the paper cited that the phenomenon is also possible with free competition, and is quite likely to occur in many cases, either under monopoly or under competition.

[3] On p. 600 of the paper just cited the conclusion is reached that it is reasonable to regard the matrix of the quantities h_{ij} as negative definitive. From this and equation (19) of that page it follows that a positive increment in the tax t_j on the *j*th commodity causes a negative increment in the quantity of this commodity.

the best alternative to the use of an additional small unit of the commodity when q units are already used, then, if q_0 units are used altogether,

$$\int_0^{q_0} f(q)\, dq \tag{1}$$

is the total benefit, which Dupuit called *utilité*, resulting from the existence of the canal or other such facility making possible the commodity (service) in question. Since $p = f(q)$ is the ordinate of the demand curve DB in Figure 1, this total benefit is the total area under the arc DB. To obtain what is now called the *consumers' surplus* we must subtract the amount paid by consumers, namely the product of the price by the quantity, represented by the rectangle $OCBA$. Thus the consumers' surplus is represented by the curvilinear triangle ABD. There is also a *producers' surplus* represented by the lower curvilinear triangle SBA; this is the excess of the money received by producers (the area of the rectangle $OCBA$) over the aggregate of the marginal costs, which is represented by the curvilinear figure $OCBS$. The total net benefit, representing the value to society of the commodity, and therefore the maximum worth spending from the public funds to obtain it, is the sum of consumers' and producers' surpluses, and is represented by the large curvilinear triangle SBD. It is the difference between the integral (1) of the demand function and the integral between the same limits of the marginal-cost function.

Imposition of the tax, by raising the price to the level of KL, appears to reduce the consumers' surplus to the curvilinear area KLD. The new producers' surplus is the area RLK, which equals SNM. There is also a benefit on account of the government revenue, which is the product of the new quantity MN by the tax rate NL, and is therefore measured by the area of the rectangle $MNLK$. The sum of these three benefits is $SNLD$. It falls short of the original sum of producers' and consumers' surpluses by the shaded triangular area NBL.

This shaded area represents the net social loss due to the tax, and was discovered by Dupuit. If the tax is small enough, the arcs BL and NB may be treated as straight lines, and the area of the triangle is, to a sufficient approximation, half the product of the base NL by the altitude GB. Since GB is the decrement in the quantity produced and consumed because of the tax, and NL is the tax rate, we may say that the net loss resulting from the tax is half the product of the tax rate by the decrement in quantity. But since the decrement in quantity is, for small taxes, proportional to the tax rate, it then follows that the net loss is proportional to the *square* of the tax rate. This fact also was remarked upon by Dupuit.

This remarkable conclusion has frequently been ignored in discussions in which it should, if correct, be the controlling consideration. The open attacks upon it seem all to be based on an excessive emphasis on the shortcomings of consumers' and producers' surpluses as measures of benefits. These objections are four in number: (1) Since the demand curve for a necessity might for very small quantities rise to infinity, the integral under the curve might also be infinite. This difficulty can be avoided by measuring from some selected value of q greater than zero. Since in the foregoing argument it is only *differences* in the values of the surpluses that are essentially involved, it is not necessary to assign exact values. The situation is the same as in the physical theory of the potential, which involves an arbitrary additive constant and so may be measured from any convenient point, since only its differences are important. (2) Pleasure is essentially nonmeasurable and so, it is said, cannot be represented by consumers' surplus or any other numerical magnitude. We shall meet this objection by establishing a generalized form of Dupuit's conclusion on the basis of a ranking only, without measurement, of satisfactions, in the way represented graphically by indifference curves. The same analysis will dispose also of the objections (3) that the consumers' surpluses arising from different commodities are not independent and cannot be added to each other, and (4) that the surpluses of different persons cannot be added.

In connection with the last two points, it will be observed that if we have a set of n related commodities whose demand functions are

$$p_i = f_i(q_1, q_2, \ldots, q_n), \qquad (i = 1, 2, \ldots, n),$$

then the natural generalization of the integral representing total benefit, of which consumers' surplus is a part, is the line integral

$$\int (f_1 \, dq_1 + f_2 \, dq_2 + \cdots + f_n \, dq_n), \qquad (2)$$

taken from an arbitrary set of values of the q's to a set corresponding to the actual quantities consumed. The net benefit is obtained by subtracting from (2) a similar line integral in which the demand functions $f_1, f_2, \ldots, f_n$ are replaced by the marginal-cost functions

$$g_i(q_1, q_2, \ldots, q_n), \qquad (i = 1, 2, \ldots, n).$$

If we put

$$h_i = f_i - g_i,$$

the total net benefit is then measured by the line integral

$$w = \int \sum h_i \, dq_i. \qquad (3)$$

Such indeterminacy as exists in this measure of benefit is only that which arises with variation of the value of the integral when the path of integration between the same end points is varied. The condition that all these paths of integration shall give the same value is that the integrability conditions

$$\frac{\partial h_i}{\partial q_j} = \frac{\partial h_j}{\partial q_i}$$

be satisfied. In the paper on "Edgeworth's Taxation Paradox" already referred to, and more explicitly in a later note,[4] I have shown that there is a good reason to expect these integrability conditions to be satisfied, at least to a close approximation, in an extensive class of cases. If they are satisfied, the surpluses arising from different commodities, and also the surpluses belonging to different persons, may be added to give a meaningful measure of social value. This breaks down if the variations under consideration are too large a part of the total economy of the person or the society in question; but for moderately small variations, with a stable price level and stable conditions associated with commodities not in the group, the line integral w seems to be a very satisfactory measure of benefits. It is invariant under changes in units of measure of the various commodities, and also under a more general type of change of our way of specifying the commodities, such as replacing "bread" and "beef" by two different kinds of "sandwiches." For these reasons the total of all values of w seems to be the best measure of welfare that can be obtained without considering the proportions in which the total of purchasing power is subdivided among individuals, or the general level of money incomes. The change in w that will result from a proposed new public enterprise, such as building a bridge, may fairly be set against the cost of the bridge to decide whether the enterprise should be undertaken. It is certainly a better criterion of social value than the aggregate $\sum p_i q_i$ of tolls that can be collected on various classes of traffic, as Dupuit pointed out for the case of a single commodity or service. The actual calculation of w in such a case would be a matter of estimation of vehicular and pedestrian traffic originating and terminating in particular zones, with a comparison of distances by alternative routes in each case, and an evaluation of the savings in each class of movement. Determination whether to build the bridge by calculation merely of the revenue $\sum p_i q_i$ obtainable from tolls is always too conservative a criterion. Such public works will frequently be of great social value even though there is no possible system of charging for their services that will meet the cost.

II. THE FUNDAMENTAL THEOREM

But without depending in any way on consumers' or producers' surpluses, even in the form of these line integrals, we shall establish a generalization of Dupuit's result. We take our stand on the firm ground of a system of preferences expressible by a function

$$\Phi = \Phi(q_1, q_2, \ldots, q_n)$$

of the quantities $q_i, q_j, \ldots, q_n$ of goods or services consumed by an individual per unit of time. If the function Φ, Pareto's ophélimité, has the same value for one set of q's as for another, then the one combination of quantities is as

---

[4] "Demand Functions with Limited Budgets," *Econometrica*, Vol. 3, 1935, pp. 66–78. A different proof is given by Henry Schultz in the *Journal of Political Economy*, Vol. 41, 1933, p. 478.

satisfactory to the individual in question as the other. For two commodities, Φ is constant along each of a set of "indifference curves"; and likewise for n commodities, we may think of a system of hypersurfaces of which one passes through each point of a space of n dimensions, whose Cartesian coordinates are the quantities of the various goods. These hypersurfaces we shall refer to as *indifference loci*.

It is to be emphasized that the indifference loci, unlike measures of pleasure are objective and capable of empirical determination. One interesting experimental attack on this problem was made by L. L. Thurstone, who by means of questionnaires succeeded in mapping out in a tentative manner the indifference loci of a group of girls for hats, shoes, and coats.[5] Quite a different method, involving the study of actual family budgets, also appears promising.[6] The function Φ, on the other hand, is not completely determinable from observations alone, unless we are prepared to make some additional postulate about independence of commodities, as was done by Irving Fisher in defining utility,[7] and by Ragnar Frisch.[8] The present argument does not depend on any such assumption, and therefore allows the replacement of Φ by an arbitrary increasing function Ψ of Φ, such as sinh Φ, or $\Phi + \Phi^3$. The statements we shall make about Φ will apply equally to every such function Ψ. Negative values of the q's are the quantities of labor, or of goods or services, produced by the individual. It is with the understanding that this kind of indeterminacy exists that we shall sometimes refer to Φ and Ψ as utility functions.

Consider now a state in which income and inheritance taxes are used to pay for the construction of bridges, roads, railroads, waterworks, electric power plants, and like facilities, together with other fixed costs of industry; and in which the facilities may be used, or the products of industry consumed, by anyone upon payment of the additional net cost occasioned by the particular use or consumption involved in each case. This additional net cost, or marginal cost, will include the cost of the additional labor and other resources required for the particular item of service or product involved, beyond what would be required without the production of that particular item. Where facilities are not adequate to meet all demands, they are made so either by enlargement, or by checking the demand through inclusion in the price of a rental charge for the facilities, adjusted so as to equate demand to supply. Such a rental cost, of which the site rental of land is an example, is an additional source of revenue to the state; it must not be confused with carrying charges on invested capital, or with overhead cost. Some such

---

[5] "The Indifference Function," *Journal of Social Psychology* Vol. 2, 1931, pp. 139–167, esp. pp. 151 ff.

[6] R. G. D. Allen and A. L. Bowley, *Family Expenditure*, London, 1935.

[7] *Mathematical Investigations in the Theory of Value and Prices*, New Haven, 1892.

[8] *New Methods of Measuring Marginal Utility*, Tübingen, 1932. Dr. Frisch also considered the possibility of substitute commodities in his *Confluence Analysis*, and in collaboration with Dr. F. V. Waugh made an attempt to handle this situation statistically.

charge is necessary to discriminate economically among would-be users of the facilities. Another example is that of water in a dry country; if demand exceeds supply, and no enlargement of supply is possible, a charge must be made for the water sufficient to reduce the demand to the supply. Such a charge is an element of marginal cost as here defined.

The individual retains, after payment of taxes, a money income m. At prices $p_1, p_2, \ldots, p_n$ determined in the foregoing manner, he can buy or sell such quantities $q_1, q_2, \ldots, q_n$ as he pleases, subject to the condition that

$$\sum p_i q_i = m. \tag{4}$$

The combination he chooses will be such as to make his indifference function Φ a maximum, subject to the condition (4). We may put aside as infinitely improbable—having probability zero, though not impossible—the contingency that two different sets of values of the q's satisfying (4) will give the same degree of satisfaction. We therefore have that, if $q_1, \ldots, q_n$ are the quantities chosen under these conditions, and if $q'_1, \ldots, q'_n$ are any other set of quantities satisfying (4), so that

$$\sum p_i q'_i = m, \tag{5}$$

then

$$\Phi = \Phi(q_1, \ldots, q_n) > \Phi(q'_1, \ldots, q'_n) = \Phi + \delta\Phi,$$

say. Hence, putting $q'_i = q_i + \delta q_i$ in (5) and subtracting (4), we find that any set of values of $\delta q_1, \ldots, \delta q_n$ satisfying

$$\sum p_i \, \delta q_i = 0, \tag{6}$$

and not all zero, must have the property that

$$\delta\Phi = \Phi(q_1 + \delta q_1, \ldots, q_n + \delta q_n) - \Phi(q_1, \ldots, q_n) < 0 \tag{7}$$

Let us now consider an alteration of the system by the imposition of excise taxes and reduction of income taxes. Some of the taxes may be negative; that is, they may be bounties or subsidies to particular industries; or, instead of being called taxes, they may be called tolls, or charges for services or the use of facilities over and above marginal cost. There ensues a redistribution of production and consumption. Let p_i, q_i, and m be replaced respectively by

$$p'_i = p_i + \delta p_i, \qquad q'_i = q_i + \delta q_i, \qquad m' = m + \delta m, \tag{8}$$

where the various increments $\delta p_i, \delta q_i$ are not constrained to be either positive or negative; some may have one sign and some the other. The yield of the new excise taxes will be the sum, over all individuals, of the quantity which for the particular individual we are considering is $\sum q'_i \delta p_i$. (We use the sign $\sum$ to denote summation over all commodities, including services.) Since this person's income tax is reduced by δm, the net increment of government revenue

$$\delta r = \sum q'_i \, \delta p_i - \delta m \tag{9}$$

may be imputed to him, in the sense that summation of δr over all persons gives the total increment of government revenue.[9] We neglect changes in administrative costs and the like.

The individual's budgetary limitation now takes the form $\sum p_i' q_i' = m'$, which may also be written

$$\sum (p_i + \delta p_i)(q_i + \delta q_i) = m + \delta m. \tag{10}$$

Subtracting the budget equation (4) corresponding to the former system and using (8) we find that

$$\delta m = \sum q_i' \, \delta p_i + \sum p_i \delta q_i. \tag{11}$$

Substituting this in (9) we find that

$$\delta r = -\sum p_i \, \delta q_i. \tag{12}$$

Suppose that, to avoid disturbing the existing distribution of wealth, the excise taxes paid by each individual (in the sense of incidence just defined; not in the sense of handing over the money to the government in person) are exactly offset by the decrement in his income tax. Then $\delta r = 0$. From (12) it then follows that (6) is satisfied. Except in the highly improbable case of all the δq's coming out exactly zero, it would then follow from (7) that this man's new state is worse than his old. The change from income to excise taxes has resulted in a net loss of satisfactions. Conversely, if we start from a system of excise taxes, or any system in which sales are not at marginal cost, this argument shows that there is a possible distribution of personal income taxes such that everyone will be better satisfied to change to the system of income taxes with sales at marginal cost. The problem of the distribution of wealth and income among persons or classes is not involved in this proposition.

This argument may be expressed in geometrical language as follows: Let $q_i, \ldots, q_n$ be Cartesian coordinates in a space of n dimensions. Through each point of this space passes a hypersurface whose equation may be written $\Phi(q_i, \ldots, q_n) = $ constant. The individual's satisfaction is enhanced by moving from one to another of these hypersurfaces if the value of the constant on the right side of the equation is thereby increased; this will usually correspond to moving in a direction along which some or all of the q's increase. The point representing the individual's combination of goods is however constrained in the first instance to lie in the hyperplane whose equation is (4).

---

[9] A friendly critic writes. "It is not clear to me why δp_i should be the exact per-unit revenue of the state from an excise tax which raises the price by δp_i from its old level. . . . I should expect (referring to Figure 1) an increase in price of GL, and a revenue to the state of NL." The answer to this is that the summation of δr over all persons includes the sellers as well as they buyers, and that the government revenue per unit of the commodity is derived in part from each—though it must be understood that the contribution of either or both may be negative. In the classical case represented by Figure 1, the buyers' δp is the height GL, while the sellers' is NG in magnitude and is negative. Since q' is positive for the buyer and negative for the seller, the product $q'\delta p$ is in each case positive. The aggregate of these positive terms is the total tax revenue from the commodity.

In this equation the p's and m are to be regarded as constant coefficients, while the q's vary over the hyperplane. A certain point Q on this hyperplane will be selected, corresponding to the maximum taken by the function Φ, subject to the limitation (4). If the functions involved are analytic, Q will be the point of tangency of the hyperplane with one of the "indifference loci." The change in the tax system means that the individual must find a point Q' in the new hyperplane whose equation is $\sum p_i' q_i = m'$. If we denote the coordinates of Q' by $q_1', \ldots, q_n'$, we have upon substituting them in the equation of this new hyperplane, $\sum p_i' q_i' = m'$. If the changes in prices and m are such as to leave the government revenue unchanged, (12) must vanish; that is,

$$\sum p_i q_i' = \sum p_i q_i.$$

Since $\sum p_i q_i = m$, this shows that $\sum p_i q_i' = m$; that is, that Q' lies on the same hyperplane to which Q was confined in the first place. But since Q was chosen among all the points on this hyperplane as the one lying on the outermost possible indifference locus, for which Φ is a maximum, and since we are putting aside the infinitely improbable case of there being other points on the hyperplane having this maximizing property, it follows that Q' must lie on some other indifference locus, and that this will correspond to a lesser degree of satisfaction.

The fundamental theorem thus established is that *if a person must pay a certain sum of money in taxes, his satisfaction will be greater if the levy is made directly on him as a fixed amount than if it is made through a system of excise taxes which he can to some extent avoid by rearranging his production and consumption.* In the latter case, the excise taxes must be at rates sufficiently high to yield the required revenue *after* the person's rearrangement of his budget. The redistribution of his production and consumption then represents a loss to him without any corresponding gain to the treasury. This conclusion is not new. What we have done is to establish it in a rigorous manner free from the fallacious methods of reasoning about one commodity at a time which has led to false conclusions in other associated discussions.

The conclusion that a fixed levy such as an income or land tax is better for an individual than a system of excise taxes may be extended to the whole aggregate of individuals. In making this extension it is necessary to neglect certain interactions among the individuals that may be called "social" in character, and are separate and distinct from the interactions through the economic mechanisms of price and exchange. An example of such "social" interactions is the case of the drunkard who, after adjusting his consumption of whisky to what he considers his own maximum of satisfaction, beats his wife, and makes his automobile a public menace on the highway. The restrictive taxation and regulation of alcoholic liquors and certain other commodities do not fall under the purview of our theorems because of these social interactions which are not economic in the strict sense. With this qualification, and neglecting also certain possibilities whose total probability is zero, we have:

If government revenue is produced by any system of excise taxes, there exists a possible distribution of personal levies among the individuals of the community such that the abolition of the excise taxes and their replacement by these levies will yield the same revenue while leaving each person in a state more satisfactory to himself than before.

It is in the sense of this theorem that we shall in later sections speak of "the maximum of total satisfactions" or "the maximum of general welfare" or "the maximum national dividend" requiring as a necessary, though not sufficient, condition that the sale of goods shall be without additions to price in the nature of excise taxes. These looser expressions are in common use, and are convenient; when used in this paper, they refer to the proposition above, which depends only on rank ordering of satisfactions; there is no connotation of adding utility functions of different persons.

The inefficiency of an economic system in which there are excise taxes or bounties, or in which overhead or other charges are paid by excesses of price over marginal cost, admits of an approximate measure when the deviations from the optimum system described above are not great, if, as is customary in this and other kinds of applied mathematics, we assume continuity of the indifference function and its derivatives. Putting for brevity

$$\Phi_i = \frac{\partial \Phi}{\partial q_i}, \qquad \Phi_{ij} = \frac{\partial^2 \Phi}{\partial q_i \, \partial q_j},$$

we observe that the maximum of Φ, subject to the budget equation (4), requires that

$$\Phi_i = \lambda p_i, \qquad (i = 1, 2, \ldots, n), \tag{13}$$

where the Lagrange multiplier λ is the marginal utility of money. Differentiating this equation gives

$$\Phi_{ij} = \lambda \frac{\partial p_i}{\partial q_j} + p_i \frac{\partial \lambda}{\partial q_j}. \tag{14}$$

Expanding the change in the utility or indifference function we obtain, with the help of (13), (12), and (14),

$$\delta \Phi = \sum \Phi_i \delta q_i + \tfrac{1}{2} \sum \sum \Phi_{ij} \delta q_i \, \delta q_j + \cdots$$

$$= -\lambda \, \delta r + \tfrac{1}{2}\lambda \sum \sum \frac{\partial p_i}{\partial q_j} \delta q_i \, \delta q_j - \tfrac{1}{2} \delta r \sum \frac{\partial \lambda}{\partial q_j} \delta q_j + \cdots \tag{15}$$

where the terms omitted are of third and higher order, and are therefore on our assumptions negligible. Their omission corresponds to Dupuit's deliberate neglect of curvilinearity of the sides of the shaded triangle in Figure 1. With accuracy of this order we have further,

$$\delta p_i = \sum_j \frac{\partial p_i}{\partial q_j} \delta q_j, \qquad \delta \lambda = \sum_j \frac{\partial \lambda}{\partial q_j} \delta q_j.$$

Upon substituting for these expressions, (15) reduces to

$$\delta\Phi = -\lambda\,\delta r + \tfrac{1}{2}\lambda \sum \delta p_i\,\delta q_i - \tfrac{1}{2}\,\delta r\,\delta\lambda + \dots \tag{16}$$

If the readjustment from the original state of selling only at marginal cost, with income taxes to pay overhead, is such as to leave $\delta r = 0$ as above, (16) reduces to

$$\delta\Phi = \tfrac{1}{2}\lambda \sum \delta p_i\,\delta q_i + \dots, \tag{17}$$

where the terms omitted are of higher order.

As another possibility we may consider a substitution of excise for income tax so arranged as to leave this person's degree of satisfaction unchanged. Upon putting $\delta\Phi = 0$ in (16) and solving for δr we have, apart from terms of higher order,

$$\delta r = \tfrac{1}{2} \sum \delta p_i\,\delta q_i + \dots . \tag{18}$$

This is the net loss to the state in terms of money, so far as this one individual is concerned. The net loss in terms of satisfactions is merely the product of (18) by the marginal utility of money λ, that is, (17), if we neglect terms of higher order than those written. The total net loss of state revenue resulting from abandonment of the system of charging only marginal costs, and uncompensated by any gain to any individual, is the sum of (18) over all individuals. If the prices are the same for all, this sum is of exactly the same form as the right-hand member of (18), with δq_i now denoting the increment (positive or negative) of the total quantity of the ith commodity.

The approximate net loss

$$\tfrac{1}{2} \sum \delta p_i\,\delta q_i \tag{19}$$

may be regarded as the sum of the areas of the shaded triangles in the older graphic demonstration. It should however be remembered that the readjustment of prices caused by excise taxes is not necessarily in the direction formerly supposed, that some of the quantities and some of the prices may increase and some decrease, and that some of the terms of the foregoing sum may be positive and some negative. But the aggregate of all these varying terms is seen by the foregoing argument to represent a dead loss, and never a gain, as a result of a change from income to excise taxes, or away from a system of sales at marginal cost. Any inaccuracy of the measure (19) is of only the same order as the error involved in replacing the short arcs LB and NB in Figure 1 by straight segments, and can never affect the sign.

It is remarkable, and may appear paradoxical, that without assuming any particular measure of utility or any means of comparison of one person's utility with another's, we have been able to arrive at (19) as a valid approximation measuring in money a total loss of satisfactions to many persons. That the result depends only on the conception of ranking, without measurement, of satisfactions by each person is readily apparent from the foregoing demonstration; or we may for any person replace Φ by another function Ψ as an index of the same system of ranks among satisfactions. If we do this in such a way that the derivatives are continuous, we shall have $\Psi = F(\Phi)$, where F is an increasing function with continuous derivatives. Upon writing the expressions for the first and second derivatives of Ψ in terms of those of F and Φ it may be seen that the foregoing formulae involving Φ are necessary and sufficient conditions for the truth of the same equations with Ψ written in place of Φ. The result (18) is independent of which system of indicating ranks is used. The fundamental fact here is that *arbitrary* analytic transformations, even of very complicated functional forms, always induce *homogeneous linear* transformations of differentials.

Not only the approximation (19) but also the whole expression indicated by (18) are absolutely invariant under all analytic transformations of the utility functions of all the persons involved. These expressions depend only on the demand and supply functions, which are capable of operational determination. They represent simply the money cost to the state of the inefficiency of the system of excise taxation, when this is arranged in such a way as to leave unchanged the satisfactions derived from his private income by each person.

The arguments based on Figure 1 have been repeated with various degrees of hesitation, or rediscovered independently, by numerous writers including Jevons, Fisher, Colson, Marshall, and Taussig. Marshall considered variation of the figure involving downward-sloping cost curves and multiple solutions, and was led to the proposal (less definite than that embodied in the criterion established by our theorm) that incomes and increasing-cost industries be taxed to subsidize decreasing-cost ones. He observed the difficulty of defining demand curves and consumers' surplus in view of the interdependence of demand for various commodities. These difficulties are indeed such that it now seems better to stop talking about demand *curves*, and to substitute demand *functions*, which will in general involve many variables, and are not susceptible of graphic representation in two or three dimensions. Marshall was one of those misled by Figure 1 into thinking that a tax of so much per unit imposed on producers of a commodity leads necessarily to an increase of price by something less than the tax.

Though the marginal-cost curve in Figure 1 slopes upward, no such assumption is involved in the present argument. It is perfectly possible that an industry may be operated by the state under conditions of diminishing marginal cost. The criterion for a small increase in production is still that its cost shall not exceed what buyers are willing to pay for it; that is, the general welfare is promoted by offering it for sale at its marginal cost. It may be that demand will grow as prices decline until marginal cost is pushed to a very low level, far below the average cost of all the units produced. In such a case the higher cost of the first units produced is of the same character as fixed costs, and is best carried by the public treasury without attempting to assess it against the users of the particular commodity as such. Our argument likewise makes no exception of cases in which more than one equilibrium is possible.

Where there are multiple solutions we have that sales at marginal cost are a necessary, though not a sufficient, condition for the optimum of general welfare.

The confusion between marginal and average cost must be avoided. This confusion enters into many of the arguments for laissez-faire policies. It is frequently associated with the calm assumption, as a self-evident axiom, that the whole costs of every enterprise must be paid out of the prices of its products. This fallacious assumption appears, for example, in recent writings on government ownership of railroads. It has become so ingrained by endless repetition that it is not even stated in connection with many of the arguments it underlies.

III. TAX SYSTEMS MINIMIZING DEAD LOSS

The magnitude of the dead loss varies greatly according to the objects taxed. While graphic arguments are of suggestive value only, it may be observed from Figure 1 that the ratio of the dead loss NBL to the revenue $MNLK$ depends greatly on the slopes of the demand and supply curves in the neighborhood of the equilibrium point B. It appears that if either the demand or the supply curve is very steep in this neighborhood, the dead loss will be slight. For a tax on the site rental value of land, whose supply curve is vertical, the dead loss drops to zero. A tax on site values is therefore one of the very best of all possible taxes from the standpoint of the maximum of the total national dividend. It is not difficult to substantiate this argument in dealing with related commodities; for the δq_i's corresponding to such a tax are zero. Since the incidence is on the owner of the land and cannot be shifted by any readjustment of production, it has the same advantages as an income tax from the standpoint of maximizing the national dividend. The fact that such a land tax cannot be shifted seems to account for the bitterness of the opposition to it. The proposition that there is no ethical objection to the confiscation of the site value of land by taxation, if and when the non-landowning classes can get the power to do so, has been ably defended by H. G. Brown.[10]

Land is the most obviously important, but not by any means the only good, whose quantity is nearly or quite unresponsive to changes in price, and which is not available in such quantities as to satisfy all demands. Holiday travel sometimes leads to such a demand for the use of railroad cars as to bring about excessive and uncomfortable crowding. If the total demand the year around is not sufficiently great to lead to the construction of enough more cars to relieve the crowding, the limited space in the existing cars acquires a rental value similar to that of land. Instead of selling tickets to the first in a queue, or selling so many as to bring an excessive crowding that would neutralize the pleasure of the holiday, the economic way to handle this situation would be to charge a sufficiently high price to limit the demand.

---

[10] *The Theory of Earned and Unearned Incomes*, Columbia, Missouri, 1918.

The revenue thus obtained, like the site value of land, may properly be taken by the state. The fact that it helps to fill the treasury from which funds are drawn to pay for replacement of the cars when they wear out, and to cover interest on their cost in the meantime, does not at all mean that any attempt should be made to equate the revenue from carspace rental to the cost of having the cars in existence.

Another thing of limited quantity for which the demand exceeds the supply is the attention of people. Attention is desired for a variety of commercial, political, and other purposes, and is obtained with the help of billboards, newspaper, radio, and other advertising. Expropriation of the attention of the general public and its commercial sale and exploitation constitute a lucrative business. From some aspects this business appears to be of a similar character to that of the medieval robber barons, and therefore to be an appropriate subject for prohibition by a state democratically controlled by those from whom their attention is stolen. But attention of some kinds and in some degree is bound to persist; and where it does, it may appropriately be taxed as a utilization of a limited resource. Taxation of advertising on this basis would be in addition to any taxation imposed for the purpose of diminishing its quantity with a view to restoring the property of attention to its rightful owners.

If for some reason of political expediency or civil disorders it is impossible to raise sufficient revenue by income and inheritance taxes, taxes on site values, and similar taxes which do not entail a dead loss of the kind just demonstrated, excise taxes may have to be resorted to. The problem then arises of so arranging the rates on the various commodities as to raise the required sum while making the total dead loss a minimum. A solution of this theoretical question, taking account of the interrelations among commodities, is given on p. 607 of the study of Edgeworth's taxation paradox previously referred to.

IV. EFFECT ON DISTRIBUTION OF WEALTH

We have seen that, if society should put into effect a system of sales at marginal cost, with overhead paid out of taxes on incomes, inheritances, and the site value of land, there would exist a possible system of compensations and collections such that everyone would be better off than before. As a practical matter, however, it can be argued in particular cases that such adjustments would not in fact be made; that the general well-being would be purchased at the expense of sacrifices by some; and that it is unjust that some should gain at the expense of others, even when the gain is great and the cost small. For example, it appears that the United States Government can by introducing cheap hydroelectric power into the Tennessee Valley raise the whole level of economic existence, and so of culture and intelligence, in that region, and that the benefits enjoyed by the local population will be such as to exceed greatly in money value the cost of the development, taking account of interest. But if the government demands for the electricity generated a price sufficiently high to repay the investment, or even the interest on it, the benefits will be reduced to an extent far exceeding the revenue thus obtained by the government. It is even possible that no system of rates can be found that will pay the interest on the investment; yet the benefits may at the same time greatly exceed this interest in value. It appears to be good public policy to make the investment, and to sell the electric energy at marginal cost, which is extremely small. But this will mean that the cost will have to be paid in part by residents of other parts of the country, in the form of higher income and inheritance taxes. Those who are insistent on avoiding a change in the distribution of wealth at all costs will object.

One answer to this objection is that the benefits from such a development are not by any means confined to the persons and the region most immediately affected. Cheap power leads for example to production of cheap nitrates, which cut down the farmers' costs even in distant regions, and may benefit city dwellers in other distant regions. A host of other industries brought into being by cheap hydroelectric power have similar effects in diffusing general well-being. There is also the benefit to persons who on account of the new industrial development find that they can better themselves by moving into the Tennessee Valley, or by investing their funds there. Furthermore, the nation at large has a stake in eradicating poverty, with its accompaniments of contagious diseases, crime, and political corruption, wherever these may occur.

A further answer to the objection that benefits may be paid for by those who do not receive them when such a development as that of the Tennessee Valley is undertaken is that no such enterprise stands alone. A government willing to undertake such an enterprise is, for the same reasons, ready to build other dams in other and widely scattered places, and to construct a great variety of public works. Each of these entails benefits which are diffused widely among all classes. A rough randomness in distribution should be ample to ensure such a distribution of benefits that most persons in every part of the country would be better off by reason of the program as a whole.

If new electric-power, railroad, highway, bridge, and other developments are widely undertaken at public expense, always on the basis of the criterion of maximizing total benefits, the geographical distribution of the benefits, and also the distribution among different occupational, racial, age, and sex groups, would seem pretty clearly to be such that every such large group would on the whole be benefited by the program. There are, however, two groups that might with some reason expect not to benefit. One of these consists of the very wealthy. Income and inheritance taxes are likely to be graduated in such a way that increases in government spending will be paid for, both directly and ultimately, by those possessed of great wealth, more than in the proportion that the number of such persons bears to the whole population. It would not be surprising if the benefits received by such persons as a result of the program of maximum total benefit should fall short of the cost to them.

The other class that might expect not to benefit from such a program consists of land speculators. If we consider for example a bridge, it is evident that the public as a whole must pay a certain cost of construction, whether the bridge be paid for by tolls or by taxes on the site value of land in the vicinity. There will be much more use of the bridge if there are no tolls, so that the public as a whole will get more for its money if it pays in the form of land taxes. But it will not in general be possible to devise a system of land taxes that will leave everyone, without exception, in a position as good as or better than as if the bridge had not been built and the taxes had not been levied. Landowners argue that the benefits of the bridge go to others, not to them; and even in cases in which land values have been heightened materially as a result of a new bridge, the landowners have been known to be vociferous in favor of a toll system. Payment for the bridge by tolls (when this is possible) has the advantage that no one seems to be injured, since each one who pays to cross the bridge has the option of not using it, and is in that case as well off as if the bridge did not exist. This reasoning is not strictly sound, since the bridge may have put out of business a ferry which for some users was more convenient and economical. Nevertheless, it retains enough cogency to stiffen the resistance of real-estate interests to the more economical system of paying for the bridge by land taxes.

Attempts at excessive accuracy in assessing costs of public enterprises according to benefits received tend strongly to reduce the total of those benefits, as in the case of the bridge. The welfare of all is promoted rather by a generous support of projects for communal spending in ways beneficial to the public at large, without attempting to recover from each enterprise its cost by charges for services rendered by that enterprise. The notion that public projects should be "self-liquidating," on which President Hoover based his inadequate program for combating the oncoming depression, while attractive to the wealthier taxpayers, is not consistent with the nation's getting the maximum of satisfactions for its expenditure.

V. DISTINCTION OF OPTIMUM FROM COMPETITIVE CONDITIONS

The idea that all will be for the best if only competition exists is a heritage from the economic theory of Adam Smith, built up at a time when agriculture was still the dominant economic activity. The typical agricultural situation is one of rising marginal costs. Free competition, of the type that has usually existed in agriculture, leads to sales at marginal cost, if we now abstract the effects of weather and other uncertainty, which are irrelevant to our problem. Since we have seen that sales at marginal cost are a condition of maximum general welfare, this situation is a satisfactory one so far as it goes. But the free competition associated with agriculture, or with unorganized labor, is not characteristic of enterprises such as railroads, electricpower plants, bridges, and heavy industry. It is true that a toll bridge may be in competition with other bridges and ferries; but it is a very different kind of competition, more in the nature of duopoly. To rely on such competition for the efficient conduct of an economic system is to use a theorem without observing that its premises do not apply. Free competition among toll-bridge owners, of the kind necessary to make the conclusion applicable, would require that each bridge be parallelled by an infinite number of others immediately adjacent to it, all the owners being permanently engaged in cutthroat competition. If the marginal cost of letting a vehicle go over a bridge is neglected, it is clear that under such conditions the tolls would quickly drop to zero and the owners would retire in disgust to allow anyone who pleased to cross free.

The efficient way to operate a bridge—and the same applies to a railroad or a factory, if we neglect the small cost of an additional unit of product or of transportation—is to make it free to the public, so long at least as the use of it does not increase to a state of overcrowding. A free bridge costs no more to construct than a toll bridge, and costs less to operate; but society, which must pay the cost in some way or other, gets far more benefit from the bridge if it is free, since in this case it will be more used. Charging a toll, however small, causes some people to waste time and money in going around by longer but cheaper ways, and prevents others from crossing. The higher the toll, the greater is the damage done in this way; to a first approximation, for small tolls, the damage is proportional to the square of the toll rate, as Dupuit showed. There is no such damage if the bridge is paid for by income, inheritance, and land taxes, or for example by a tax on the real estate benefited, with exemption of new improvements from taxation, so as not to interfere with the use of the land. The *distribution* of wealth among members of the community is affected by the mode of payment adopted for the bridge, but not the total wealth, except that it is diminished by bridge tolls and other similar forms of excise. This is such plain common sense that toll bridges

Figure 2

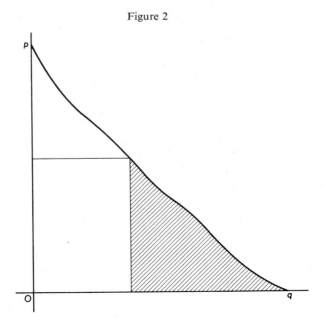

have now largely disappeared from civilized communities. But New York City's bridge and tunnels across the Hudson are still operated on a toll basis, because of the pressure of real estate interests anxious to shift the tax burden to wayfarers, and the possibility of collecting considerable sums from persons who do not vote in the city.

If we ignore the interrelations of the services of a bridge with other goods, and also the slight wear and tear on the bridge due to its use, we may with Dupuit represent the demand for these services by a curve such as that in Figure 2. The total benefit from the bridge is then represented by the whole area enclosed between the demand curve and the axes, provided the bridge is free. All this benefit goes to users of the bridge. But if a toll is charged, of magnitude corresponding to the height of the horizontal line, the recipients of the toll are benefited to an extent represented by the area of the rectangle, whose base is the number of crossings and whose height is the charge for each crossing. But the number of crossings has diminished, the benefit to bridge users has shrunk to the small triangular area at the top, and the total benefit has decreased by the area of the shaded triangle at the right. This triangle represents the net loss to society due to the faulty method of paying for the bridge. If, for example, the demand curve is a straight line, and if the owners set the toll so as to bring them a maximum return, the net loss of benefit is 25 percent of the total.

These are the pertinent considerations if the bridge is already in existence, or its construction definitely decided. But if we examine the general question of the circumstances in which bridges ought to be built, a further inefficiency is disclosed in the scheme of paying for bridges out of tolls. For society, it is beneficial to build the bridge if the total area in the figure exceeds the interest, amortization, and maintenance costs. But if the bridge must be paid for by tolls, it will not be built unless it is expected that these costs will be exceeded by the rectangular area alone. This area cannot, for our example of a linear demand function, be greater than half the total. We may in this case say that the toll system has 75 percent efficiency in use, but only 50 percent efficiency in providing new bridges. In each case the efficiency will be further diminished by reason of the cost of collecting and accounting for the tolls.

The argument about bridges applies equally to railroads, except that in the latter case there is some slight additional cost resulting from an extra passenger or an extra shipment of freight. My weight is such that when I ride on the train, more coal has to be burned in the locomotive, and I wear down the station platform by walking across it. What is more serious, I may help to overcrowd the train, diminishing the comfort of other travelers and helping to create a situation in which additional trains should be run, but often are not. The trivial nature of the extra costs of marginal use of the railroads has from the first been realized by the railroad managements themselves; indeed, it is implied in the amazingly complex rate structures they build up in the attempt to squeeze the last possible bit of revenue from freight and passenger traffic. If in a rational economic system the railroads were operated for the benefit of the people as a whole, it is plain that if people were to be induced by low rates to travel in one season rather than another, the season selected should be one in which travel would otherwise be light, leaving the cars nearly empty, and not a season in which they are normally overcrowded. Actually, our railroads run trains about the country in winter with few passengers, while crowding multitudes of travelers into their cars in summer. The rates are made high in winter, lower in summer, on the ground that the summer demand is more elastic than that of the winter travelers, who are usually on business rather than pleasure, and thus decide the question of a trip with less sensitiveness to the cost.

VI. COMPLEXITY OF ACTUAL RAILWAY RATES AND REMOTENESS FROM MARGINAL COST

The extreme and uneconomic complexity of railway freight and passenger rate structures is seldom realized by those not closely in touch with them. A few random examples will illustrate the remoteness of actual rates from what may be presumed to be marginal costs, which railway managements will find it profitable to cover even by the lowest rates. Prior to the last enforced reduction of American passenger rates the regular round-trip fare between New York City and Wilkesbarre, Pa. was $11.04. But at various times between 1932 and 1935 round-trip tickets good for limited periods were sold at $2.50, $6.00, $6.10, and $6.15. Between New York and Chicago the round-trip fare in the same period varied between $33 and $65 for identical accommodations. Between New York and Washington the ordinary round-trip fare was $18.00, but an "excursion rate" of $3.50 was applied spasmodically.

The lumber and logging activities of the country, which have been at a standstill for several years, are suffering from freight rates which in many important cases nearly equal, and even exceed, the mill price of the lumber. Thus from the large sawmills at and near Baker, Oregon, which produce lumber for the New York market, the freight amounts to $16.50 per thousand board feet. For No. 3 Common Ponderosa Pine, the grade shipped in largest quantities, the price of one-by-four inch boards ranged in the autumn of 1933 from $14.50 to $15.50 at the mill. Thus the New York wholesale buyer must pay more than double the mill price, solely on account of freight. The freight even to Chicago approximated the mill price. For No. 4 Common, also an important grade, the price was $12.50 per thousand board feet at the mill, but the New York buyer had to pay $29.00. A few months earlier, the prices were about $8 per thousand board feet less than those just given, so that the railroads received far more than the mill operators. It is hard to escape the conclusion that these high freight rates interfered seriously with the sale of lumber.

One advantage of the system of charging only marginal cost would be a great simplification of the rate structure. This is a great desideratum. It must not be assumed too readily that every purchaser distributes his budget accurately to obtain the maximum of satisfactions, or the most efficient methods of production, when the determination of the optimum requires the study of an encyclopedic railroad tariff, together with complicated trial-and-error calculations. Neither, from the standpoint of a railroad, can it be assumed that the enormously complex rate differentials have been determined at all accurately for the purposes for which they were designed. These complicated rate structures further contravene the public interest in that they enhance artificially the advantages of large over small concerns. When immense calculations are required to determine the optimum combinations of transportation with other factors of production, the large concerns are in a distinctly better position to carry out the calculations and obtain the needed information.

VII. MARGINAL COST DEPENDS ON EXTENT OF UNUSED CAPACITY

In the determination of marginal cost there are, to be sure, certain complications. When a train is completely filled, and has all the cars it can haul, the marginal cost of carrying an extra passenger is the cost of running another train. On the other hand, in the more normal situation in which the equipment does not carry more than a small part of its capacity load, the marginal cost is virtually nothing. To avoid a sharp increase in rates at the time the train is filled, an averaging process is needed in the computation of rates, based on the probability of having to run an extra train. Further, in cases in which the available equipment is actually used to capacity, and it is not feasible or is of doubtful wisdom to increase the amount of equipment, something in the nature of a rental charge for the use of the facilities should, as indicated above, be levied to discriminate among different users in such a way that those willing to pay the most, and therefore in accordance with the usual assumptions deriving the most benefit, would be the ones obtaining the limited facilities which many desire. This rental charge for equipment, which for passenger travel would largely take the place of fares, should never be so high as to limit travel to fewer persons than can comfortably be accommodated, except for unpredictable fluctuations. The proceeds from the charge could be added to the funds derived from income, inheritance, and land taxes, and used to pay a part of the overhead costs. But there should be no attempt to pay all the overhead from such rental charges alone.

Except in the most congested regions, there would, however, be no such charge for the use of track and stations until the volume of traffic comes to exceed enormously the current levels. An example is the great underutilization of the expensive Pennsylvania Station, in New York City, whose capacity was demonstrated during the war by bringing into the city the trains of the Erie and the Baltimore and Ohio railroads. These trains are now required to stop on the New Jersey shore, constituting a wasteful nuisance which had existed before government operation, which was replaced by the more efficient procedure by the government, but which was resumed when the lines were handed back to their private owners.

VIII. THE ATTEMPT TO PAY FIXED COSTS FROM RATES AND PRICES CONTRIBUTES TO RIGIDITY AND SO TO INSTABILITY

One of the evil consequences of the attempt to pay overhead out of operating revenue is the instability which it contributes to the economic system as a whole. This is illustrated by the events leading to the drepression. The immense and accelerating progress of science and technology led to the creation of new industries and the introduction of wonderfully efficient new methods. The savings from the new methods were so great that corporate profits and real incomes surged upward. So large were the profits and so satisfactory the dividends that the operating officials of great industries did not feel under compulsion to push up the selling prices of their products to the levels corresponding to maximum monopoly profit. Because they kept their prices low, while paying relatively high wages, the physical volume of goods produced and transferred became enormous. The impulse to produce, with possibly some altruistic motives besides, tempered the desire for profits in many concerns. But under a profit system this could not last. As the prices of corporate shares rose, pressure developed to pay dividends equivalent to interest on the higher prices. This pressure would probably have led presently to gradual increases in the money prices of manufactured products, if the general level of prices had remained stationary. Such however was not the case. The general level of prices was declining.

And decline it must, according to the equation of exchange, when there was such a great new flood of goods to be sold. The vast increase in physical volume of goods, created by the new technology, called for a greater use of money, if the price level was to be maintained. This need was met for a time by increases in bank loans and deposits, and in the velocity of circulation. But neither bank loans nor velocities could continue to increase as fast as goods, and prices had to fall. The fall was not uniform. Corporations under increasing pressure to cover their overhead and pay high dividends out of earnings were strongly averse to reducing the selling prices of their products, when these selling prices were already below the points which would yield maximum profit. For several years prior to the crash, the prices of manufactured products stuck fast, while the proportion of national expenditure paid for these products continued to increase. This left a shrinking volume of money payments to be made for the remaining commodities, and these, including particularly the agricultural, had to come down in price. If, as the general price level fell, railroad, utility, and manufacturing concerns had reduced their selling prices proportionately, the prosperity of the years 1922 to 1928 might have continued. But such reductions in selling prices were not possible when an increasing volume of overhead charges had to be paid out of earnings. The intensified efforts to do this resulted in a pushing up of "real" prices of manufactured products—that is, of the ratios of their prices to the general price level—and of "real" transportation rates. Indeed, with a rapidly falling general price level, railroad freight rates, measured in money, were actually increased in 1931. This increase of 15 percent on a large range of commodities, like the subsequent increases in suburban commuters' passenger rates, was obtained on the ground that the railroads needed the money to cover their overhead costs, though their operating costs had declined. Of course the effect was to make the depression worse, by stopping traffic which would have flowed at the lower rates. On the theory that bond interest and other such items must be paid out of operating revenues, the railroads were "entitled" to the higher rates, for their business had fallen off. But economic equilibrium calls for a rising rather than a declining supply curve; if demand falls off, the offer price must be reduced in order to have the offered services taken. This antithesis of rising railway rates, when general prices and the ability to pay are falling, well illustrates the disequilibrating consequences of the idea that overhead costs must be paid from operating revenues. There now seems to be a possibility of a repetition of the disastrous 15 percent freight-rate increase in a time of decline.[11]

This explanation of the contrast of the prosperity of 1928 with the cessation of production in the following years rests upon the contrast of the system of prices which results from the whole-hearted devotion of different concerns to their own respective profits, with the system of prices best for the economic organism as a whole. Under free competition, with no overhead, these two systems of prices tend to become identical. Where there are overhead costs, competition of the ideally free type is not permanently possible. Monopoly prices develop; and a system of monopoly is not a system which can serve human needs with maximum advantage.

IX. CRITERION AS TO WHAT INVESTMENTS ARE SOCIALLY WORTH WHILE

When a decision whether or not to construct a railway is left to the profit motive of private investors, the criterion used is that the total revenue $\sum p_i q_i$, being the sum of the products of the rates for the various services by the quantities sold, shall exceed the sum of operating costs and carrying charges on the cost of the enterprise. If no one thinks that there will be a positive excess of revenue, the construction will not be undertaken. We have seen in Section V that this rule is, from the standpoint of the general welfare, excessively conservative. What, then, should society adopt to replace it?

A less conservative criterion than that of a sufficient revenue for total costs is that *if some distribution of the burden is possible such that everyone concerned is better off than without the new investment, then there is a prima facie case for making the investment.* This leaves aside the question whether such a distribution is *practicable*. It may often be good social policy to undertake new enterprises even though some persons are put in a worse position than before, provided that the benefits to others are sufficiently great and widespread. It is on this ground that new inventions are permitted to crowd out

---

[11] Since this was written the Interstate Commerce Commission has allowed a part of this proposed increase and postponed consideration of a request for a passenger fare rise.

less efficient industries. To hold otherwise would be to take the side of the hand weavers who tried to wreck the power looms that threatened their employment. But the rule must not be applied too harshly. Where losses involve serious hardship to individuals, there must be compensation, or at least relief to cover subsistence. Where there are many improvements, the law of averages may be trusted to equalize the benefits to some extent, but never completely. It will always be necessary to provide for those individuals upon whom progress inflicts special hardship; if it were not possible to do this, we should have to reconcile ourselves to greater delays in the progress of industrial efficiency.

Subject to this qualification of avoiding excessive hardship to individuals, we may adopt the criterion stated. In applying it there will be the problem of selecting a limited number of proposed investments, corresponding to the available capital, from among a larger number of possibilities. The optimum solution corresponds to application of our criterion to discriminate between each pair of combinations. This total amount of calculation and exercise of judgment required will not, however, be so great as might be suggested by the number of pairs of combinations, which is immense. Numerous means are available to shorten this labor. One of these is by the application of the line integral (3), namely

$$w = \int \sum h_i dq_i,$$

which provides a measure of value corresponding to the sum of consumers' and producers' surpluses. The part of w constituting the generalized consumers' surplus is (2); the validity of this line integral as a measure of an individual's increment of satisfaction corresponding to sufficiently small changes in the q's may be seen merely by replacing p_i in (13) by f_i, and noticing that for small changes the marginal utility of money λ changes little so that f_i is very nearly proportional to the derivative of the utility function Φ. Hence the increment in Φ is proportional to the sum of the integrals of the f's, apart from terms of higher order; and the factor of proportionality λ is such as to measure this increment in money so as to be comparable to an increase in income. Similar considerations apply to the part of w corresponding to producers' surplus.

Defenders of the current theory that the overhead costs of an industry must be met out of the scale of its products or services hold that this is necessary in order to find out whether the creation of the industry was a wise social policy. Nothing could be more absurd. Whether it was wise for the government to subsidize and its backers to construct the Union Pacific Railroad after the Civil War is an interesting historical question which would make a good subject for a dissertation, but it would be better, if necessary, to leave it unsolved than to ruin the country the Union Pacific was designed to serve by charging enormous freight rates and claiming that their sum constitutes a measure of the value to the country of the investment.

Such an experimental solution of a historical question is too costly. In addition, it is as likely as not to give the wrong answer. The sum of the freight and passenger rates received, minus operating costs, is not the line integral $w = \int \sum h_i \, dq_i$, which with some accuracy measures the value to society of the investment, but is more closely related to the misleading measure of value $\sum p_i q_i$. In other words, the revenue resembles the area of the rectangle in Figure 2, while the possible benefit corresponds to the much larger triangular area. The revenue is the thing that appeals to an investor bent on his own profit, but as a criterion of whether construction ought in the public interest to be undertaken, it is biased in the direction of being too conservative.

Regardless of their own history, the fact is that we now have the railroads, and in the main are likely to have them with us for a considerable time in the future. It will be better to operate the railroads for the benefit of living human beings, while letting dead men and dead investments rest quietly in their graves, and to establish a system of rates and services calculated to assure the most efficient operation. When the question arises of building new railroads, or new major industries of any kind, or of scrapping the old, we shall face, not a historical, but a mathematical and economic problem. The question then will be whether the aggregate of the generalized surpluses of the form (3) is likely to be great enough to cover the anticipated cost of the new investment. This will call for a study of demand and cost functions by economists, statisticians, and engineers, and perhaps for a certain amount of large-scale experimentation for the sake of gaining information about these functions. The amount of such experiment and research which could easily be paid out of the savings resulting from operation of industry in the public interest is very large indeed. Perhaps this is the way in which we shall ultimately get the materials for a scientific economics.

Price and output policy of state enterprise: a symposium

JAMES E. MEADE AND J. MARCUS FLEMING

I

1. In order to achieve that use of the community's resources which is both the most efficient and the most in conformity with consumers' wishes, they should be distributed among the various uses in such a way that the value of the marginal product of a given factor is the same in every occupation. Insofar as the reward paid to any factor is the same in every occupation, this rule means that the value of the marginal product of a factor should, in every occupation, bear a constant ratio to the price of that factor.

2. The principle that the value of the marginal product of a factor should be equal to the price of that factor is a special case of this general rule; but it is a special case which, for labour at least, has a great deal to commend it. If labour is paid everywhere a reward which is not merely in a constant ratio to, but actually equal to, the value of its marginal product, two additional advantages may be achieved:

i) A larger proportion of the total national income will accrue to labour than if labour is paid everywhere a wage lower, by a constant proportion, than the value of its marginal product. This will probably serve to improve the distribution of the national income.

ii) Labour has the choice between earning more income or enjoying more leisure. The more nearly the reward for an additional unit of work approaches the value of the marginal product of labour, the greater—it may be presumed—will be the welfare achieved by means of a proper balance between work and leisure.[1]

3. How can the principle of equality between the value of the marginal product of a factor and its price best be achieved? Where competition is technically possible, by vigorous and unimpeded competition.[2] Much might

---

* *The Economic Journal*, 54(1944): pp. 321–39. Reprinted by courtesy of the authors and *The Economic Journal*.

[1] See chapter II of Part IV of the American edition (edited by C. J. Hitch) of my *Introduction to Economic Analysis and Policy*.

[2] With, of course, certain measures of State regulation to deal with divergences between private and social net products of a kind that are compatible with perfect competition.

be done by the State to promote such competition by removing legal enact-
ments which positively promote monopolisation, by reform of the patent law
and of company law with this end in view, and by the outlawing of certain
forms of business practices which are primarily designed to restrict competition. But there are many cases where monopoly is inevitable. When the
scale of production necessary to take advantage of technical economies is
large in relation to the market to be served, "trust-busting" must either be
ineffective or lead to technical inefficiency. The outstanding examples of such
cases are, of course, the public utilities. Where a community needs only one
gasworks, or electricity station, or railway network, monopoly must obviously
exist. In these cases, socialisation in one form or another, of the industries
concerned, is the only radical cure to ensure that they are run in such a way as
to equate marginal costs to prices of the product produced (or the prices of
the factors of production to the value of their marginal products) rather than
to make a profit.

II

4. Recent work by economists[3] has served to make it clear on what
principles the output and use of factors by the managers of a socialised plant
should be determined:

i) Output should be increased so long as the price of the product exceeds the
marginal (not the average) cost of production.

ii) One factor should be substituted for another so long as that quantity of the
factor taken on, which is required to replace the production of a unit of the factor
released, has a lower market price than the unit price of the factor released.

iii) Rules (i) and (ii) can sometimes most conveniently be stated as above, and
sometimes most conveniently combined into the single rule that each factor should
be taken on in greater quantity so long as the value of its marginal product is
greater than its market price.

iv) Thus, as a practical set of rules for the operation of a particular firm, it may
be best often to state (a) that more should be produced with a given plant and
equipment, so long as the price of the product exceeds the marginal prime cost of
production, and (b) that a greater amount of fixed capital should be invested so
long as the annual interest on the capital plus the annual cost of repair, depreciation,
etc., is less than the price of any additional output expected from the investment
plus the price of any existing prime factors which it is expected to save, minus the
price of any additional prime factor which it is expected to take on as a result of the
investment.

v) It is taken for granted, of course, that maximum efficiency will be an objective
throughout, in the sense that the maximum amount technically possible will always
be produced from any given collection of factors of production.

5. The fundamental difficulty of supervising State production is to determine whether managers of State plants are behaving efficiently, (a) technically
in getting the maximum output from any given collection of factors of pro-

---

[3] See, in particular, Oskar Lange *On the Economic Theory of Socialism.*

duction, and (*b*) economically in combining factors in such proportions and producing output in such amount that the value of the marginal product is in each case brought as near as possible to the market price of the factor. *Ex hypothesi*—since the aim is equality between prices and marginal costs, and not between prices and average costs—the amount of profit or loss made is irrelevant.

6. In those cases in which there are a large number of plants under different managers, producing the same product,[4] it may be possible, by collecting data from every plant for every period, to construct production functions expressing output as a function of the collection of factors used. Any manager who was exceptionally inefficient or exceptionally efficient technically would then probably stand out, since his output would not correspond to that derived from the production function based on average experience. Moreover, by working out from the production function partial derivatives of output in respect of each factor for different amounts and combinations of factors employed, some basis might be obtained for checking the marginal product of different factors in different plants. It is difficult to suggest any comparable procedure where only one or two plants exist; but, in such cases, it is doubtful whether the profit motive under private monopoly deals adequately with the problem.

7. It is, however, worth pointing out one advantage which State production will have over private production in this respect. The task of the manager of a State plant is in two respects simpler than that of a manager of a private plant; for the object of the former is to equate the price of the product to the cost of the marginal factors involved in its production, while that of the latter is to equate the marginal revenue derived from the product with the marginal cost of its production. The State manager need not consider the market questions —how much his extra sales will depress the price of his product and how much his extra purchase of factors will raise their prices; the private manager has to consider both these market questions in addition to all the other questions which the State manager must take into account. Thus:

i) both managers must consider their technical efficiency, *i.e.,* methods of producing the maximum amount from any given collection of factors;

ii) both managers must consider the marginal productivity of the various factors, *i.e.,* the additional output to be obtained from the use of an additional unit of the factor;

iii) the State manager's job is then done, since he has now only to compare the market price of this additional output with the market price of the additional factors; but

---

[4] It might, at first sight, appear inconsistent with the argument to assume that there could be a large number of socialised plants producing the same product, since the argument for socialisation rests upon the necessity of monopoly for technical reasons. There is, however, no contradiction. Because of the costs of transport of the product, there may need to be local monopolies; but the conditions of production in the various localities may be sufficiently similar to make comparisons of costs, etc., useful. Thus, for example, cost and output data might be compared for a large number of local gasworks.

iv) the private manager must proceed next to consider the marginal revenue to be derived from the sale of the additional product, which depends upon the effect which his additional sales will have in depressing the market; and

v) he must also consider the effect which his additional purchase of the factor may have in hardening the market against him, before he is ready to compare marginal revenue with marginal cost.

III

8. The rules mentioned in the preceding paragraphs would probably serve adequately to cover all the main problems except that of a large new investment either for the production of a completely new product, or for the production of an old product in a new area (*e.g.,* a new electrical generating plant), or—possibly—for a very large new investment increasing very substantially the total output of an existing product. In such cases, however, we cannot make the "atomistic" assumption that we have to deal only with changes at the margin where (i) the effect upon the total output of the product in question is not appreciable, and (ii) the effect upon the total amount of factors left for employment in any other particular alternative occupation is not appreciable. The former condition would justify the assumption that the price of the product measures the addition to utility due to its production, and the latter the assumption that the price of the factor concerned measures the loss of utility due to the contraction of output in the industries from which it is withdrawn.

9. In the exceptional cases, however, one cannot afford to neglect the consumers' surplus involved in the additional product. In order to evaluate the gain to consumers of the additional product, one needs to integrate the area under the relevant range of the demand curve for the product in question. This needs to be compared with the value to consumers of the output which is sacrificed in the alternative occupations open to the factors involved. If these factors can be abstracted at the margin from a number of different alternative uses, it will be sufficient to compare the area under the demand curve in the new industry with the price of the factors involved. If, however, it involves the abstraction of factors in a lump, on a substantial scale, from some other particular industry, it becomes necessary to compare the area under the demand curve in the new industry with the area under the relevant range of the demand curve in the industry or industries from which the factors are to be abstracted.

10. Unfortunately, all this must remain a matter of considerable numerical imprecision. While the rules for determining relatively small variations in output may be made sufficiently precise to use as actual working rules, the decision whether or not to make a large new investment must be based upon rules which, though logically watertight, are of extreme difficulty to apply accurately in practice. One thing, however, is clear. The issue does not depend upon whether the new plant has a prospect of making a profit or avoiding a loss. In other words, it has nothing to do with the question whether at any

output of the new plant the consumers will offer a price which covers the average cost of production. It depends, on the contrary, upon whether the total area under the consumers' demand curve in the new plant does or does not exceed the total areas under the relevant portions of the demand curves for the various goods, from the production of which the necessary factors of production are to be abstracted.

IV

11. These rules for the operation of socialised industries are by now more or less generally accepted by technical economists. But certain results of these rules are less familiar. Their budgetary implications are most striking. The principle is to socialise just those industries in which considerable economies of large-scale production may be enjoyed (*i.e.*, precisely those industries in which the marginal cost is below the average cost) and to operate these industries in such a way that the price charged for the product is equal to its marginal cost (*i.e.*, in such a way that a loss is made). This involves doing away with the principle of "charging what the traffic will bear" in the operation of the railways or in the sale of electric current, and charging only the marginal cost of the provision of these services. The previous owners having presumably been fully compensated will receive interest on capital now operated in such a way that a considerable loss is made upon it.

12. Nor is it possible to take comfort in the belief that these losses will necessarily be exceptional. I have argued at length elsewhere[5] that if a community's population is of the size which maximises income per head, the value of the marginal product of labour over the whole range of industries and occupations will be equal to the average product of labour, and in this case the payment of a wage equal to the marginal product of labour would absorb the whole of the national income. In terms of our present problem, this would mean that the actual losses made in the socialised "increasing returns" industries, due to charging a price for the product no greater than its marginal cost of production, would just be covered by what profits were still made in socialised industries where "increasing returns" were less marked or in competitive industries in which "increasing returns" did not play an appreciable part and in which a full return on land and capital was accordingly still being earned.

13. The rules for operating socialised industries *may* thus involve losses commensurate with the total income earned on property in other sectors of the economy.[6] To raise taxation on a scale which will cover defence, social

---

[5] See Chapter II of Part IV of my *Introduction to Economic Analysis and Policy*.

[6] This has not always been fully realised by writers on this subject. Thus, Lange (*op. cit.*, pp. 74–75, 84) discusses the way in which the income earned in socialised industries may be distributed among consumers or used for corporate savings without recognising that, far from any net profit being realised, the net losses made in socialised industries might even absorb all the profits made in competitive industries, where he allows (*op. cit.*, pp. 120 and 125) private enterprise and private property to continue.

security, and the normal expenses of government as well as the losses to be contemplated in socialised industries would involve "announcement" effects which even the most sanguine might hesitate to neglect. Even if the necessary funds could be raised by, for example, a proportionate income tax, the rate of tax might well be high enough seriously to interfere with the achievement of the best balance between work and leisure, to which reference has been made in paragraph 2 (ii) above.

14. The socialisation of "increasing returns" industries is, for these reasons, best accompanied by some measure of public ownership of property. A capital levy, or similar measure, which transfers property to State owner-ship, permits either the cancellation of debt (whether or not it has occurred in the past purchase of socialised industries) or State investment of funds in privately operated concerns. In the former case, it removes a current interest charge from the State's expenditure, and in the latter it provides for the State a current income without the unfavourable announcement effects of high rates of taxation. In a community which starts with a large national debt, such a principle can, in fact, be carried a long way before it raises any problems associated with State ownership of privately operated capital. But in such a community *State operation* of "increasing returns" industries may, through the excessive charge which it would impose on the tax revenue, do more harm than good unless it is accompanied by some extension of the principle of *State ownership* of property.

V

15. There are two incidental advantages to be derived from the socialisa-tion of "increasing returns" industries and their operation on the above-mentioned principles.

16. First, it would open up a large new range for capital investment, and this, in an economy otherwise threatened with large-scale unemployment, might appreciably aid in the maintenance of economic activity. In a socialised plant new investment will be undertaken so long as the price of the additional output (and not the marginal revenue derived from it) represents a return on the cost of the investment greater than the ruling rate of interest. Moreover, in determining whether an entirely new plant should be set up, criteria should be observed (as is argued in paragraphs 8–10 above) which, in many cases, will justify the investment, although a loss is bound to be realised on it. For both these reasons, the application of the current principles of pricing to socialised industries should justify much economically productive capital investment which private enterprise could never undertake.

17. Secondly, these principles of pricing in socialised industries involve a shift of income from profits to wages—a shift which, in the case of an optimum population, would involve the distribution of the whole national income in wages. Such a shift will be brought about by bringing down to the marginal cost of production the prices charged for the products of the socialised in-

dustries, without reducing money wages at the same time. Such a shift of income from profits to wages would probably lead to a more equal distribution as between persons.

COMMENT BY J. M. FLEMING

I

1. Mr. Meade's statement of the principles which should govern the price and output policy of a state-controlled enterprise, though possibly a little oversimplified, is not, I think, open to serious objection. Indeed, one only wishes that they commanded a wider measure of understanding and acceptance outside the narrow ranks of the economists. Where I differ from him, however, is in attaching greater importance to the administrative and less to the financial difficulties involved in applying these principles.

2. In paragraph 4 of his article, Mr. Meade formulates acceptably the conditions for "optimising" inputs and outputs where the associated variations of input and/or output can be made very small by comparison with the total turnover in the factor- and product-markets concerned.[1] Where, however, by reason of the indivisibility of the units of input or output, relatively large associated variations of input and/or output have to be considered, one can no longer determine optimal behaviour by simply comparing marginal rates of substitution with relative prices.

3. For example, if the problem is to determine whether or not a public undertaking should expand output by an amount which is significantly large in relation either to product- or to factor-markets, it will be impossible to apply the criterion that the marginal cost must not exceed product price, *i.e.*, that the factor cost per unit of additional output must not exceed the unit price of the product relative to the unit price of the factors. If the managers of the undertaking apply this criterion in terms of the prices existing prior to the contemplated expansion of output, they will be unduly predisposed to expand output. If they calculate in terms of the less favourable prices expected to exist after the contemplated change, they will be unduly biased against expansion. The right course is to value the increment of output at the price expected to prevail after the change *plus* the surplus accruing from the fall in product prices to consumers of the increment of output; and to value the

---

[1] Even in these cases the principles have to be applied with certain commonsense modifications to maintain a measure of price stability. A strict application would lead to an intolerable fluctuation of prices. For example, unless one were a season-ticket holder, one might not know how much one had to pay for one's ticket in a train or tram until one got to the station! It is worthwhile, in order to facilitate the planning of expenditure by one's customers, to introduce some stability into selling prices, even at the cost of maintaining them a little above the optimal level, and even at the cost of a little surplus capacity. Similarly, it is better to pay wages which are slightly too low than wages which fluctuate like a fever chart.

increment of factor cost at the factor prices prevailing after the change *less* the surplus accruing from the rise in factor prices to the owners of the additional factors required to produce the increment of output.

4. In paragraphs 8–10, Mr. Meade gives some attention to this case, but he neglects the producers' surpluses (which may often be more important than the consumers' surpluses), and he greatly exaggerates the exceptional character of the circumstances in which such surpluses would have to be taken into account. He says that the ordinary "marginal" rules would "probably serve adequately to cover all the main problems except that of a large new investment either for the production of a completely new product, or for the production of an old product in a new area (*e.g.,* a new electric generator plant) or—possibly—for a very large new investment increasing very substantially the total output of an existing product." This is surely wrong. Almost every enterprise socialised on the grounds advocated by Mr. Meade will find the ordinary rules inapplicable to certain of its large inputs. The question of socialisation in order to secure proper pricing and output policy will only arise in cases where the size of the optimal plant in relation to markets is such that there is a significant difference between profit at optimal output and that same profit *plus all consumers and producers surpluses.* It is only because there is such a significant difference that there is an opportunity of making monopoly profits by restricting output, and that the enterprise or industry cannot be left in private hands. Therefore, in all such cases, the question of setting up a new plant, or even of substantially extending an old plant, will necessitate taking account of such surpluses.

II

5. Having agreed—for Mr. Meade would probably not dispute the foregoing propositions—on the abstract criteria of price- and output-policy appropriate to a public enterprise, let us consider some of the practical difficulties and implications, beginning with those to which Mr. Meade attaches the greatest importance—viz., the budgetary implications. It is clear that if enterprises which have previously been run on monopolistic lines, with a view to making the maximal profit, are taken over by public authorities and run on the lines advocated by Mr. Meade, the profit earned will diminish, and, if full compensation has been paid to the previous owners, the difference will have to be met from the public purse. This will happen whether increasing, constant, or diminishing returns prevail in the undertaking in question.

6. Mr. Meade, however, seems to regard it as a circumstance particularly unpropitious from the financial point of view that undertakings socialised in order to secure optimal behaviour will, as he asserts, operate under conditions of increasing returns (in the sense of diminishing factor cost per unit of output). I doubt whether this assertion is either true or relevant.

7. Socialisation, of the type Mr. Meade is considering, comes into question only when it is impossible to secure genuine competition between units

of optimal size. This will occur when the production units are so large, relative to the product and factor markets concerned, that it would be impossible, by trust-busting, etc., to create a sufficient number of firms to secure competition without making production units too small. Under such conditions it will probably be the case that to set up and operate in optimal fashion a single additional plant will so depress product prices and enhance factor prices as substantially to reduce the profit earned by the additional plant below the level which it would have attained if prices had been unaffected. We saw, in paragraphs 3 and 4, that in such circumstances it may be right to build an additional plant if the profit at "previous" prices is substantially in excess of the capital cost, even if profit at "subsequent" prices fails to cover the cost. In this case, the additional plant (and all similar plants in the same industry) will work under conditions of increasing returns or diminishing average cost.[2] But is not another outcome equally possible? It may be right to *refrain* from building an additional plant if the prospective profit at "subsequent" prices is substantially below the capital cost, even though prospective profit at "previous" prices somewhat exceeds the capital cost. In this case the remaining plants in the industry, of a type similar to the additional plant which is just not worthwhile building, will work under conditions of diminishing returns, and will therefore make large profits. *Prima facie,* therefore, in the absence of precise knowledge regarding the demand and cost conditions in the actual industries and undertakings ripe for socialisation, it appears just as likely that socialised undertakings will work under diminishing as under increasing returns. On the average, therefore, they will probably make much the same rate of profits (abstracting from considerations of risk, etc.) as prevails in the competitive sector of private industry, where, of course, constant returns is the rule.

8. Even if Mr. Meade were justified in assuming that his socialised undertakings would operate under increasing returns, the bearing of this on the financial problem of socialisation would be at best very indirect. It is true that in such circumstances the undertakings would have to be run at a loss (in the sense of failing to cover their capital cost, failing to make a normal profit). What matters, however, in the present context is not the level of profits after socialisation, but the decline in profits as compared with the previous level. This, however, is affected not by the slope of the *average* cost curve, but by the slope of the *marginal* cost curve over the range of output extending between monopoly output and optimal output. It can be shown that the more negatively inclined the marginal cost curve over this range of output the

---

[2]   Profit $<$ capital cost
∴   revenue $<$ total cost
∴   product price $<$ average cost
∴   marginal cost $<$ average cost
∴   average cost is declining.

greater will be the disparity between monopoly profits and optimal profits.[3] I would not, of course, deny that there is a certain correlation between the slope of the *marginal* cost curve between monopoly and optimal output and the slope of the *average* cost curve at optimal output, and that if one were assured that, in socialised undertakings, average cost at optimal output was always declining, one would expect the disparity between monopoly profit and optimal profit to be greater than if increasing average cost had been the rule. But the connection is indirect and uncertain. In any event, there is, as we have seen, no particular reason to expect the average cost curve in socialised undertakings to be falling rather than rising, nor is there any particular reason why the slope of the marginal cost curve in such undertakings should as a rule be less positive than in other undertakings.

9. Whatever bearing the shape of the cost curves may have on the magnitude of the disparity between monopoly profits and optimum profits, it is indisputable that some disparity will exist, and will constitute a burden on the Exchequer. The seriousness of a financial burden of this sort consists in the adverse effects on productive incentives and on the distribution of income to which it may give rise. What these effects are will depend on how the money to meet the deficit is raised. In the present case it appears likely that if the most appropriate method of financing the loss arising out of socialisation is followed, the effect will be to annul some, but not all, of the benefits which, as

---

[3] Take the case where the demand curve is linear, and the supply curve of the factors is infinitely elastic.

Then, if R = revenue,
$\qquad O$ = output,
$\qquad C$ = cost (at constant factor prices),
$\qquad X$ = the loss involved in moving from the maximal profit position to the optimal position,
$\qquad a, b, \alpha, \beta, S$, are constants,

and if the values of the variables at the maximal profit position, and the optimal position, are indicated by suffixes m and o, respectively;
Let

$$R = aO - bO^2.$$

Then marginal revenue $= \dfrac{dR}{dO} = a - 2bO$ and product price $= \dfrac{R}{O} = a - bO$.

Let

$$C = S + \alpha(O - O_m) + \beta(O - O_m)^2$$

where O is not $< O_m$.

Then marginal cost $= \dfrac{dC}{dO} = \alpha + 2\beta(O - O_m)$.

At the maximal profit position,

$$\frac{dR_m}{dO_m} = \frac{dC_m}{dO_m}$$

$$\therefore \quad O_m = \frac{a - \alpha}{2b}$$

Mr. Meade explains in paragraphs 1 to 4 of his article, would otherwise result from the policy of socialisation.

10. Suppose, first, that the loss is financed out of a tax levied on the product of the socialised undertakings. The effect in this case is entirely to annul the benefits of socialisation. The undertaking on being socialised will be run at the same output as formerly; what was previously a disparity between price and marginal cost will now be called a tax, and what was formerly monopoly profit will accrue to the Exchequer as the proceeds of the tax and will be used to pay compensation to the former owners for the loss of their monopoly revenue.

11. Suppose next, that the tax, instead of being levied on the produce of the socialised undertakings, is levied *ad valorem* on output generally. The effect of this change will be to restore one of the most important—in fact *the* most important—of the benefits for which the socialisation was undertaken, in that it will correct the mal-distribution of resources as between the different branches of industry which resulted from the inequality in the ratio of marginal cost to price in the different branches. The other benefits, however, which it was expected that socialisation would bring—the increase in the proportion of national income accruing to labour, the raising of the incentive to work to its appropriate level—will be annulled, for the reason that, on the

---

At the optimal position,

$$\frac{R_0}{O_0} = \frac{dC_0}{dO_0}$$

$$\therefore \quad O_0 = \frac{a - \alpha + 2\beta O_m}{b + 2\beta}.$$

Substituting for $a - \alpha$

$$O_0 = \frac{2O_m(b + \beta)}{b + 2\beta}.$$

(Since $O_0 - O_m = \dfrac{bO_m}{b + 2\beta} = $ a quantity which is positive for positive values of O_m it is legitimate to determine optimal output with the aid of a cost equation applicable only to outputs in excess of O_m.)

Now the loss involved in moving from the maximal profit position to the optimal position $= X$

$$= R_m - R_0 - C_m + C_0$$
$$= aO_m - bO_m^2 - aO_0 + bO_0^2 + \alpha(O_0 - O_m) + \beta(O_0 - O_m)^2$$
$$= \frac{(a - \alpha)^2 (b + \beta)}{4(b + 2\beta)^2}.$$

Now, suppose that β varies (O_m of course remaining constant). When $\beta = \infty$, $X =$ zero. As β falls, X rises, until, as $\beta \longrightarrow -\frac{1}{2}b$, $X \longrightarrow \infty$. (β can never fall below $-\frac{1}{2}b$.) In words, the loss involved in moving from the maximal profit position to the optimal position varies inversely with the slope of the marginal cost curve for outputs exceeding monopoly output.

Similarly, it can be shown that, when the supply curve of a factor is linear, the demand curve of the product infinitely elastic, and the supply curves of any other factors also infinitely elastic, the loss involved in moving from the maximal profit position to the optimal position varies directly with the slope of the marginal product curve for inputs exceeding monopsony input.

average of all industries, the gap between marginal cost and price will remain as great as ever.

12. There are many other ways in which the loss could be financed, by an increased income tax, or death duty, by a tax on capital, by a reduction in public expenditure, etc. This is not the place to enquire into their relative merits or demerits in respect of effect on income distribution, on incentive to invest, on propensity to consume, on incentive to work, etc. One general observation can, however, be made on each and every one of them regarded as an alternative to a general indirect tax. If it is right, after the socialisation, to finance the losses resulting from the socialisation by method x rather than by a general indirect tax, it would have been right before the socialisation to raise money by method x in order to finance a general subsidy on output. The only benefit, therefore, which is properly attributable to the socialisation is that of an improved interindustrial distribution of resources. Any other benefits which may accrue from the fact that the socialisation is financed by some other way than by a general indirect tax, could have been obtained by appropriate fiscal measures, without the socialisation.

13. It might perhaps be surmised that a similar objection could be advanced against the sole remaining virtue which, in paragraph 11 above, is still attributed to socialisation—viz., that it enables the mal-distribution of resources between different industries to be corrected. Could not the same result be equally well achieved without socialisation by a combination of a subsidy on goods produced under monopolistic conditions and a tax on goods produced under competitive conditions? The answer is that once the monopolistic industries have been socialised and are being managed according to correct principles, it becomes possible to reduce the "tax" formerly imposed on their products by the monopolist owners and increase the tax on products produced by private enterprise under competitive conditions, without untoward effects on the distribution of income, whereas a policy of subsidising goods produced by private monopolies and taxing other goods would have the effect of expanding the share of monopoly profits in the national income. In addition, of course, it would provide a very undesirable incentive to adopt monopolistic practices.

14. It follows from what has been said in the foregoing paragraphs that Mr. Meade is mistaken in believing that socialisation, with its concomitant increase in taxation, provides any additional argument for the State's taking heroic steps to reduce its indebtedness or acquire property. No doubt it would be very gratifying if the State could painlessly acquire a property income which could then be used to relieve taxation. But this cannot be done except by achieving a budget surplus, which is never a painless procedure. If a large surplus is aimed at, such as would probably be required in order to offset the capitalised value of the losses involved in socialising a substantial sector of industry, it could probably only be achieved by resort to a capital tax or levy. But such a levy, particularly if it is expected to be repeated at

irregular intervals, has many unfortunate effects on incentive and the distribution of income. In order to decide whether it is worthwhile, it is necessary to balance the marginal disadvantages of a levy on capital now against the marginal advantages of the permanent reduction in general taxation which would thereby be made possible. Now, a combination of socialisation of the type under discussion *plus* a general indirect tax on output has, as we have seen, no net effects on incentive or income distribution, favourable or unfavourable, except that of removing barriers to an optimum interindustrial distribution of resources. The marginal disadvantages of a capital levy are in no wise diminished, nor are the marginal disadvantages of current taxation in any way increased. The desirability of socialisation to eliminate monopoly has therefore no bearing on the case for or against a capital levy, or (more generally) for or against budgeting for a surplus.

III

15. While I am less impressed than Mr. Meade by the financial difficulties involved in the application of criteria of optimal production and pricing by public undertakings, I am more impressed than he is by the difficulty of securing efficient management under these conditions. In the first place, I do not agree that, given good-will, the task of a manager of a State plant run on the optimal principles is significantly simpler than that of the manager of a private plant or of a State plant run on the lines of a private monopoly. Mr. Meade says that the State manager, unlike the private manager, is dispensed from considering how much extra output would depress the price of his product and raise the price of his factors. But this is only true if the State manager sets out to find his optimal position by a process of random trial and error. If he tries to cut short this process—and since, in reality, the optimal position is always changing, he ought to try to cut it short—he must guess how much a given expansion of output will affect product and factor prices, since he has to equate marginal factor cost with the ratio of product to factor prices. Much the same is true of the private manager. He can find the output corresponding to maximum profit by trial and error, but if he wishes to cut short the process, he must guess at the relationship between output and prices. Whatever may be the relative difficulty of the problems confronting State and private managers in deciding on the scale of operation of existing plants, it is clear, from what has been said in paragraph 4 above, that when it comes to deciding whether or not to set up an additional plant there is nothing to choose between the difficulties confronting State and private enterprise respectively.

16. Secondly, and more important, the application of the principles of optimisation will make it more difficult to weed out the inefficient managers than it is when the enterprises are run for profit. Admittedly, it is just as difficult for an outsider to estimate the precise efficiency of the management in the one case as in the other. But in the latter case the level of profits is at any rate a rough-and-ready index of managerial efficiency, whereas in the former

case it is no guide at all. This for two reasons. A lowering of the cost curve, reflecting technical efficiency of management, will raise monopoly profits by much more than profits at optimal output. The latter, indeed, may not be affected at all. In the second place, the manager of a plant which purports to be run on optimal lines can easily cover up any shortfall of profits due to his technical inefficiency by slightly restricting output.

17. Mr. Meade suggests that it would be possible for someone at the centre to obtain, by means of comparative statistics, an accurate and up-to-date idea of the technical production functions of the various plants in a socialised industry. If this were possible, it would certainly facilitate the task of weeding out inefficient managers. But, of course, the same methods of control would be applicable to a socialised industry run for profit, so that the relative advantage of running such an industry on the maximal profit principle rather than the optimal principle, in respect of the elimination of inefficient managers, though it would be reduced to vanishing point, would, at any rate, not be reversed.[4] In most cases, however, these methods of central control by statistics would prove themselves to be unsatisfactory. It is just because different plants have different production functions ("special circumstances") which cannot be fully comprehended at the centre, that it is necessary for private combines (and will probably be necessary for socialised industries) to devolve a good deal of initiative on the managers of individual plants.

18. More serious than the difficulty of weeding out inefficient managers is that of providing managers, so long as they are maintained in their functions with an adequate incentive to effort and efficiency. Where the enterprise is run for profit, such an incentive can be provided partly by the fear of being replaced and partly by making managerial remuneration vary with profits of the firm. Now the first incentive will, as we have seen, apply somewhat less effectively to the manager of an enterprise run on the optimal principles than to the manager of one run for profit. In any case, dismissal is a drastic and exceptional remedy for inefficiency. The lack of a gentler but more persistent and finely modulated pressure in the direction of efficient management is, therefore, a serious drawback.

19. What is the upshot of the argument? We have found that the socialisation of monopolistic or oligopolistic undertakings, accompanied by compensation, and followed by the application of the accepted criteria of optimal output and price policy, will result in an improvement in the interindustrial distribution of resources, but it is also likely to result in a lower technical efficiency of production in the industries directly affected than could have been attained had the undertakings been run for profit. From this two consequences follow: (1) Where there is a choice between securing the application of the desired criteria by direct instructions to the managers or by the

---

[4] Mr. Meade's point may count as an argument for the superior efficiency of public over private enterprise as such, when both are conducted according to the same principles. But this is a question with which we are (happily) not concerned here.

restoration of competitive conditions, the latter policy should have a measure of preference even at the cost of *some* reduction in the unit of management below the optimal size. This implies giving a measure of preference to "trust-busting" and other antirestrictionist measures over socialisation as a means of coping with monopoly, unless there is reason to believe public enterprise more efficient than private, even where an industry is competitive. (Incidentally, if antimonopoly measures of the trust-busting type can be carried through without the payment of compensation to the monopolists additional advantages arise, particularly an improvement in the incentive to work.) (2) Even where the restoration of competition is impossible industries should be managed in accordance with the principles of optimal production only in cases where the avoidance of monopolistic restriction of output with a given technique is more important than the preservation of the maximum incentive to maintain technical efficiency and progress.

REJOINDER BY J. M. MEADE

1. Mr. Fleming doubts whether the assertion that financial losses will be made in socialised industries is either true or relevant. As to its truth, he argues that the average cost in socialised industries is just as likely to be rising as falling. His argument is based upon considerations of the discontinuity of cost curves of which I had failed to take account. There is, however, still, in my opinion, a presumption that decreasing costs will be more frequent than rising costs. A large number of cases probably exist (*e.g.* transport, public utilities, and industries where the cost of transport of the product from one local market to another is high) where there is room only for a single plant in a local market. In these cases, decreasing costs alone will operate up to the optimum output of such a single plant. Between this output and the output of many plants of optimum size—in spite of intermediate ups and downs at the points at which new plant is introduced—there will be no net change in average cost, unless there are economies of large-scale production external to the individual plant. Over this range, there is no net rise or fall in average cost, while up to this point there will be only falling costs. As Mr. Fleming has pointed out to me, this is not conclusive proof that falling costs (and losses) are more probable than rising costs (and profits) at the points of intersection of the demand curve and the marginal cost curve. But to me, at least, it suggests a strong probability that on further examination this will be found to be the case.

2. The probability of decreasing costs is reinforced if allowance is made—as it should be made—for economies of large-scale production external to the individual plant. In this case, the average cost of the optimum output from a plant of optimum size will be lower when there is a large number of such plants than when there is only one. This is a second reason for expecting socialised industries to be operating under decreasing rather than increasing costs.

3. As Mr. Fleming himself points out, even when plants are operating under increasing average cost, optimal profits will be less than monopoly profits, so that even in these cases the financial problem exists if full compensation has been paid to the owners when the industry was socialised.

4. As to the relevance of the financial consideration, Mr. Fleming points out that my argument for the State ownership of property was not properly grounded. Without the further extension of State ownership of property, the financing of losses in socialised industries will not necessarily worsen the distribution of income and the incentive to work, since such losses could be financed by indirect taxation without any net adverse effects in these respects. State ownership of property should rather be regarded as a means (which could be adopted independently of the socialisation of "increasing returns" industries) for positively improving the distribution of income and the incentive to work. Mr. Fleming's criticism is correct; but I remain unrepentant in my conclusion, since I am prepared to kill more than one bird with a single stone. The socialisation of "increasing returns" industries can improve the interindustrial distribution of resources without further State ownership of property; but the full improvements which it might also bring to the distribution of income and the incentive to work cannot, I still maintain, be enjoyed without such extension of State ownership.

5. Finally, in paragraph 15 of his comment, Mr. Fleming has overlooked the central point which it was my intention to make. Given that State managers and private enterprise managers both know (i) the prices of the factors, (ii) the prices of the products, and (iii) the marginal physical products of the factors, then the State manager will, and the private enterprise manager will not, know whether more or less of any factor should be employed. True, the State manager will not yet know how much more or less to employ, but—unlike the private enterprise manager—he will at least know in which direction he should move.

The rehabilitation of consumers' surplus*

JOHN R. HICKS

When Marshall's *Principles* was first published in 1890, his theory of Consumers' Surplus was immediately recognised as the most striking novelty in the book. As such, it led to the usual controversy; some people were convinced of its validity, some not; but a sufficient number remained convinced for the theory to achieve an established place in the Marshallian tradition. Perhaps the place was even too well-established, for Marshall's adherents and followers were too much inclined to take the theory for granted and draw deductions from it, without paying sufficient attention to the limitations of the field within which alone its use can be justified; in doing so they merely encouraged the opposition. Gradually the opposition gathered strength; to the older generation of Walras and Pareto, Nicholson and Cannan, were added Cassel and the *Neue Wiener Schule,* Knight and Robbins; under the impetus of this attack even Cambridge began to lose faith. The "Digression on the Buyer" in Mrs. Robinson's *Economics of Imperfect Competition* represents the furthest point of retreat; today there are plenty of signs that the tide is beginning to turn. The discovery is being made that Consumers' Surplus is an analytical tool of great power, whose use is perfectly legitimate if proper precautions are taken; one or two of us are even beginning to suspect that some of the newer developments in economic theory have been made much poorer and less significant than they might have been made, as a result of the fashion of avoiding "surpluses." In these circumstances, there is something to be said for trying to state in simple language how the objections to Consumers' Surplus can be overcome, and how the important conclusions which the older generation reached with its aid can be restated so as to find their due place in modern theory. That is what I shall try to do in this paper.

Let us turn back to the *locus classicus,* Marshall, Book III, chapter 6. Marshall begins by defining the consumer's surplus as "the excess of the price which he would be willing to pay rather than go without the thing, over

* *The Review of Economic Studies*, 9(1941): pp. 108–16. Corrected by the author. Reprinted by courtesy of the author and *The Review of Economic Studies*.

that which he actually does pay" (p. 124). This definition, it should be observed, is quite concrete; it involves nothing more introspective or subjective than the demand curve itself. The demand curve purports to show how far the price of the commodity would have to be raised in order to reduce purchases to any given extent. A precise answer to this question can only be given "other things being equal"; thus in strictness only one point on a demand curve can ever be observed, the remainder being hypothetical—though possibly capable of estimation by suitable statistical methods. The consumer's surplus is just the same sort of hypothetical magnitude; it involves the question "what is the maximum amount which the consumer would be willing to pay for the particular quantity of the particular commodity if he were given the choice between having this quantity on such terms or not at all?" The consumer's surplus is the difference between the amount so defined and the amount of money actually paid. The critical question is just the same sort of question as that implied in the demand curve. It is limited by the same *ceteris paribus* clause as the demand curve is limited; this needs to be borne in mind very carefully, for it can be very important.

It is only at the second stage of his argument that Marshall develops the famous association of Consumer's Surplus with the curvilinear triangle under the demand curve. This, it should be noted, is not a definition; it is a theorem, true under certain restrictive assumptions, but only true if these assumptions are granted. The assumptions were expressed by Marshall in the form of saying that the "marginal utility of money" must be constant; by this formulation he gave an opportunity to his critics. Superficially the "marginal utility of money" is not an objective concept; it seems to imply a whole utilitarian background which is not always acceptable. The first step towards the rehabilitation of Consumers' Surplus was therefore taken when it was shown[1] that *constancy* of the marginal utility of money is an objective criterion, even though the marginal utility of money is not objective itself. If the marginal utility of money is constant, it implies that the consumer's demand schedules are unaffected by changes in his real income; all it need imply for this purpose is that the demand schedule *for this commodity* is unaffected (or substantially unaffected) by the changes in real income which arise as a result of changes from one to another of the various hypothetical situations we may want to consider.[2] Stated in this form, the condition does not involve any specifically utilitarian background; it belongs to the same plane of discourse as the original definition, being reduced to the kind of assumption we are ordinarily accus-

---

[1] Hicks and Allen, "A Reconsideration of the Theory of Value," *Economica*, 1934, p. 64.
[2] It is not to be denied that for Marshall the constancy of the marginal utility of money meant more than this. It was the bridge by which he passed from quantities of money to quantities of satisfaction, for it makes quantities of money and quantities of satisfaction proportionate; but we need not follow him across that bridge unless we choose. No doubt it was also associated in his mind with the assumption of a constant value of money (constant prices of other consumers' goods than the one, or sometimes ones, in question) which underlies the whole argument; that is an assumption which we certainly do have to take over.

tomed to make when dealing with demand curves.[3] It is in fact a very reasonable simplification, which is likely to be valid in most applications, though probably not in all. Whenever the commodity in question is one on which the consumer is likely to be spending a small proportion only of his total income, the assumption of "constant marginal utility of money" can usually be granted; and it can still be granted, even if this condition is not fulfilled, provided the particular change under discussion does not involve a large *net* change in real incomes. These conditions will cover a large proportion of the cases we shall be wanting to consider; but even in cases where neither of these conditions is realised, it is still not true that there is no such thing as consumer's surplus. What ceases to hold is the equivalance between the consumer's surplus and the area of the Marshallian triangle; a correction has to be introduced to overcome the discrepancy. Probably the most convenient way of making the correction is to adjust the ordinary demand curve so as to allow for the effects of the changes in real income as we pass along the curve. There is no theoretical objection to this sort of adjustment, but it is a fiddling business, fortunately not likely to be of much importance.

If variations in the "marginal utility of money" can be neglected, the consumer's surplus derived from the purchase of so many units of a commodity at such and such a price can be represented by the Marshallian triangle. I need not repeat the familiar proof of this theorem, since Marshall's version is absolutely valid when it is taken with the above qualifications. It is best to take the proof as establishing that the triangle is a close approximation to the true consumer's surplus.

So far we can follow Marshall exactly, merely reinterpreting him a little. At the next step there is much to be said for taking a slightly different direction. After establishing that the triangle under the individual demand curve is equal to the individual *consumer's* surplus (under the appropriate assumptions), Marshall proceeds to equate the triangle under the collective demand curve of the market with the collective *consumers'* surplus. He gives as his defence of the addition the statement that "by far the greater part of the events with which economics deals, affect in about equal proportions all the different classes of society" (p. 131)—a statement obviously open to dispute. As a matter of fact, it is altogether unnecessary to invoke such a principle. By definition, the individual consumer's surplus, derived from the purchase of a certain amount of a particular commodity, is the amount of money which that individual would have to lose in order to leave him as badly off as he would be left if he lost the opportunity to purchase the commodity altogether.[4]

---

[3] In the terminology of my *Value and Capital*, income effects are to be neglected.

[4] This is what I meant when I stated, in *Value and Capital* (p. 40) that consumer's surplus could be thought of as the *compensating variation* in income. But I am advised by Mr. Henderson, in the useful note printed elsewhere in this issue, that consumer's surplus (the compensating variation when the price rises so high as effectively to cut out the opportunity of purchase altogether) will not be equal to the sum of the compensating variations got by raising the price in steps, unless the marginal utility of money is constant. (At least I think that is what it comes to, and if so, I willingly accept the correction.) In the present paper I am assuming constancy of the marginal utility of money, and so I shall not worry about this refinement.

The collective consumers' surplus is the amount of money which the consumers as a body would have to lose in order to make each of them as badly off as he would be if the commodity disappeared. The amount of the collective surplus does of course tell us nothing about the way in which this loss would be distributed among the individual consumers; yet in spite of that the collective surplus has a perfectly clear meaning. How significant that meaning can be we shall see as we proceed.

II

So much for the meaning of Consumers' Surplus; let us now turn to its uses. There is one whole branch of economic theory which is absolutely dependent upon the idea of Consumers' Surplus; a very important branch it is too, though naturally enough it has been far too much neglected in recent years. It is the branch which may be called Partial Welfare Analysis, since it occupies the same place in General Welfare Analysis as the study of Partial Equilibrium does in positive economics. There are few branches of economic theory which have greater practical use.

I have explained in another place[5] the attitude I take up towards the problems of welfare economics in general; the possibility of a scientific economics of welfare has been criticised just as Consumers' Surplus has been criticised, but again I believe that these criticisms can be answered. If we accept Professor Robbins's definition of the scope of economics, *the study of human behaviour as the disposal of scarce means to achieve given ends,*[6] then the comparative study of different institutions, from the point of view of their efficiency in furthering this disposal, must fall within the scope of the science. If it neglects this study, it has simply not finished its job. In the case of a Robinson Crusoe economy, probably no one would deny this. The only thing which is interesting about the economic activities of Robinson Crusoe is the cleverness which he exhibits in the attainment of a respectable standard of living when deprived of the advantages of the division of labour. Man in society raises additional difficulties, because he is sometimes able to achieve his own individual ends more fully, not by increasing the efficiency of production, but at the expense of his neighbours. How are we to say whether a reorganisation of production, which makes A better off, but B worse off, marks an improvement in efficiency? The sceptics declare that it is impossible to do so in an objective manner. The satisfactions of one person cannot be added to those of another, so that all we can say is that there is an improvement from the point of view of A, but not from that of B. In fact there is a simple way of overcoming this defeatism, a perfectly objective test which enables us to discriminate between those reorganisations which improve productive efficiency, and those which do not. If A is made so much better off by the change that he could compensate B for his loss, and still have something

---

[5] See my article, " The Foundations of Welfare Economics," *Economic Journal*, December, 1939.

[6] *The Nature and Significance of Economic Science*, p. 15.

left over, then the reorganisation is an unequivocal improvement. As we shall see, it is precisely this criterion whose consequences are capable of being worked out by the Consumers' Surplus apparatus. Further, this criterion is more useful than any other as a basis on which to establish maxims of sound economic policy.

If the economic activities of a community were organised on the principle of making no alterations in the organisation of production which were not improvements in this sense, and making all alterations which were improvements that it could possibly find, then, although we could not say, that all the inhabitants of that community would be necessarily better off than they would have been if the community had been organised on some different principle, nevertheless there would be a strong probability that almost all of them would be better off after the lapse of a sufficient length of time. Substantially, this is the creed of classical economics; if the "improvements" are properly defined, it would appear to be a creed that is soundly based. But it is a creed which asks a great deal of human patience, more patience than is characteristic of the twentieth century, even of the economists of the twentieth century; more patience, perhaps, then we ought to ask. Yet even if we cannot wait for this long run, our criterion still has something to offer. When any considerable improvement, in our sense, is made, it ought to be possible actually to give compensation, out of the gains of the gainers, to cover the losses of the losers. It is true that some of the institutions which would be necessary to effect such compensation would themselves have a harmful effect upon production, so that reluctance to wait for the slow operation of the law of averages may have a less favourable effect in the long run than the first policy would do; but even so there will be much to be gained from due attention to the criteria of productive improvement. These criteria stand, whether distributional considerations are being given much or little weight.

I define an *optimum* organisation of production as one in which there is no further opportunity for *improvements*; no reorganisation is possible which will leave any individuals so much better off that they can compensate the losers and still be left with a net gain. The first task of welfare economics is the formal study of the conditions of optimum organisation in this sense; this study is exactly parallel to the study of equilibrium conditions in positive economics, yet it is most important for the two sets of conditions to be carefully distinguished.[7] In the article previously referred to[8] I have set out these optimum conditions systematically—the basic condition of proportionality between marginal utilities and marginal costs is the only one which we shall need to invoke directly here. The second task of welfare economics is the study of deviations from this optimum, and it is here that consumers' surplus has

---

[7] Some of the most serious fallacies of traditional economics have been due to confusion between optimum and equilibrium conditions; the apparent influence of Dr. Pangloss upon the development of economic thought is for the most part nothing but pure intellectual error.

[8] *Economic Journal*, December, 1939, p. 704.

its part to play. The idea of consumers' surplus enables us to study in detail the effects of deviations from the optimum in a particular market. It is not merely a convenient way of showing when there will be a deviation (consumers' surplus is not necessary for that purpose, since the basic optimum conditions, just referred to, show us at once when there will be a deviation); it also offers us a way of measuring the size of the deviation. This, if we are right in our general viewpoint, is a most important service. It will clearly not be worthwhile to take measures, which may have awkward repercussions on distribution, if they offer no more than a small improvement in productive efficiency. If the improvement is a large one, the case may well be altered.

III

The study of deviations from the optimum within a particular market falls into two parts: (1) that in which we assume the previous establishment of optimum conditions in other related markets; (2) that in which we do not. The second part may well be the more important in practice, but the first is simpler, so we shall begin with the first.

Apart from certain dynamic complications, not discussed here,[9] there is an obvious general rule that the establishment of perfect competition throughout an economy will automatically result in the achievement of optimum conditions. Consequently our first problem is to study the effect of deviations from the optimum in a particular market when the related markets are perfectly competitive. This is the case which is directly illustrated by Marshall's famous diagram (*Principles,* p. 811, substantially reproduced as Figure 1 below.

Figure 1

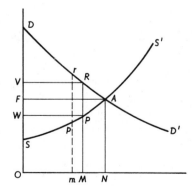

---

[9] *Economic Journal,* December, 1939, pp. 707–8.

DD' is the demand curve for the particular commodity; SS' is the marginal cost curve for the industry.[10] Their intersection, A, is the optimum point; under the assumption of perfect competition in this industry it is also the equilibrium position. DAF is the consumers' surplus, that is to say, it is the compensation which would have to be paid to consumers if they were prevented from spending their money in this particular way, and yet were to be enabled, by increasing their expenditure in other directions, to make themselves as well off as before. FAS is the producers' surplus, the compensation which would have to be given to the owners of factors of production used in the industry, if they were to lose the opportunity of employment in this industry, and though compelled to transfer themselves to other less advantageous occupations, were yet to be made as well off as before. Then, if we look solely at the position of these consumers and these producers, it is obvious that the combined surplus—the sum of the consumers' and producers' surpluses—is maximised at the optimum point. And we do not need to consider the position of anyone else, since we are assuming that related industries are perfectly competitive; consequently if resources transferred from this industry were applied at the margin in the other industries, there would be no appreciable gain or loss to any third parties which would need compensation.

If, as a result of monopolistic action on the part of the producers, output were restricted from ON to OM on our diagram, and the price therefore raised from OF to OV, consumers' surplus would be diminished from DAF to DRV, and producers' surplus increased from SAF to $SPRV$; but the combined surplus would be diminished from DAS to $DRPS$. If output were diminished in this way, the extra gain to producers might be transferred to consumers by some special levy, and yet the consumers would still be worse off than before—by a sum of money approximately represented by the triangle RAP.

This loss will be incurred in whatever way output is reduced; if the reduction is due, not to monopoly action by the producers, but to a tax per unit of output, the only difference is that a part of the producers' surplus is taken away in tax. DRV is the new consumers' surplus, WPS the new producers' surplus, $VRPW$ is taken in tax; but if the receipts of this tax were directly distributed in an endeavour to restore the producers and consumers respectively to the same levels of satisfaction as they would have attained if the tax had not been imposed, there would be a deficiency. The size of the deficiency is measured, once again, by the area of the triangle RAP.

Remembering that this triangle RAP is only an approximate measure of the loss on combined surplus (since it assumes a constant marginal utility of money), we do no serious violence to the position if we treat the triangle as

---

[10] Marshall calls it the Particular Expenses curve, and distinguishes it from the marginal cost curve. But so far as I can see, the distinction is only necessary because of the possibility of external economies, which are ruled out if we assume that related markets are optimally organised.

rectilinear. Consequently the loss on combined surplus = the area of the $\triangle RAP = \frac{1}{2}RP \times MN = \frac{1}{2}$ (reduction of actual output below optimum output) times (difference between price and marginal cost). The social loss depends partly upon the gap between price and marginal cost, partly upon the effect of that gap upon output. A large gap between price and marginal cost is not important unless it affects output seriously.

The formula thus arrived at is one of the neatest in economics, but it has to be treated carefully. It measures the social loss involved in producing a nonoptimum output instead of an optimum output; if it is used for measuring the effect of a change from one nonoptimum output to another nonoptimum output, it needs an important adjustment. For example, suppose that output has been reduced to OM by monopoly action, and that a tax is then imposed, which causes a further reduction to Om. The social loss involved in this change is not a triangle but a trapezium $pPRr$; the area of this trapezium is $\frac{1}{2}mN.(RP + rp)$. Starting from an optimum position, the social loss resulting from a tax is $\frac{1}{2}$(tax per unit) × (reduction in output); starting from a non-optimum position, it is greater than this by an amount equal to (reduction in output × average gap between marginal cost and price ex tax) the latter expression not being halved. When output has already been contracted below the optimum, a further contraction is very damaging.

IV

When related industries are not perfectly competitive, there is a further complication to be taken into account. For if there is a contraction in the output of the original industry, and the excluded factors are transferred elsewhere, the extra units produced in the other industries will be worth more than their marginal cost; thus they will generate an additional surplus, accruing to someone or other. This additional surplus means that the social cost (the *opportunity cost*) of employing factors in the first industry is greater than it appears at first sight. The surplus, accruing not merely to the producers and consumers in the original industry, but to society in general, is less than appears at first.[11]

This additional social cost is best allowed for on the diagram by moving the cost curve SS' upwards (Figure 2). The true optimum point is then not the equilibrium point of perfect competition in this industry (A) but a point to the left of it (A'). A tax which has the result of reducing output from A to A' is a social improvement, involving a gain, not a loss, in total surplus. The measure of the gain is the triangle AQA'; but it is more useful to think of it as the difference between the quadrilateral $A'QAP$ and the triangle APA'; that is, the gain due to extra profits and lower prices in the other industries, *minus* the loss of consumers' and producers' surpluses in the first industry.

---

[11] It is possible, on the other hand, that expansion of the original industry may lead to an expansion in complementary industries, which were such that in them price was initially in excess of marginal cost. In this case the social cost would be lower than that shown by the original cost curve. This is what Marshall called External Economies.

Figure 2

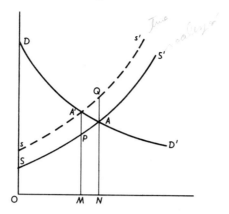

This is the difference which has to be estimated in order to see whether a contraction of the original industry is desirable.

The proposition thus established is of course the basis of Marshall's celebrated doctrine about the desirability of subsidising industries working under increasing returns and taxing those working under diminishing returns.[12] Since increasing returns industries (where price must be greater than marginal cost if there is to be a positive profit) will always work at less than optimum output unless special measures are taken, an approach to the optimum will always involve some expansion of these industries and consequent contraction of other industries. The adjacent needed can be induced, either by a combination of subsidies to increasing returns industries and taxes on diminishing returns industries (as Marshall proposed); or by subsidies to the increasing returns industries, financed out of direct taxation; or by taxes on the diminishing returns industries, whose proceeds are used to finance general expenditure. Of course there are other methods also; the choice between the various methods can be left to be governed by distributional or dynamic considerations.

V

The apparatus of consumers' and producers' surpluses can also be used (and this is one of its most important uses) to determine whether the introduction of any new commodity, or the suppression of any existing commodity, would be an *improvement* or not. This is a question which is very refractory to ordinary marginal analysis, yet it is certainly of vital importance—more so perhaps than many of the "marginal" problems.

If we assume that related industries are perfectly competitive, then it is clear that the introduction of any new commodity, whose production is

---

[12] *Principles*, p. 473.

profitable, must be an improvement. For profitability ensures a positive producers' surplus, and consumers' surplus cannot be negative. There is therefore of necessity a positive combined surplus.

The reverse, however, does not hold. A commodity produced under diminishing (average) cost may be such that it would yield a negative producers' surplus at all selling prices, so that its production would be unprofitable at any of these prices; yet it may generate a consumers' surplus which more than compensates for this negative producers' surplus, so that the combined surplus would be positive. This is the special case of "lumpy" investment, discussed in detail in Professor Pigou's famous chapter on Discrimination[13]; ordinary discrimination, however, is only one way of overcoming the difficulty, and not necessarily the best way. The "two-part tariff," commonly practised by public utilities, is in some ways a better solution; there are cases when a direct subsidy may be the best way out.

When we start from a position of perfect competition in related industries, the only problem which arises is whether new commodities ought to be introduced which were not being produced in the initial position. Each existing commodity is given its right to exist by the mere fact of its being profitable to produce it. But when we start from a position where there is an excess of price over marginal cost in the related industries, the social cost of producing a particular article is no longer represented by its marginal cost curve. We have to mark up the marginal cost curve, in the manner described in the last section; so that it becomes possible for production to be profitable when the social surplus accruing from production of the article is negative. The social surplus = consumers' surplus + producers' surplus − loss of potential surplus on other commodities; this may well be negative, when producers' surplus is positive.

This is the possibility which has been uncovered by the modern theories of Imperfect Competition; it is in fact the correct and general statement of the possibility of loss due to Imperfect Competition. In order to compress it into the marginal analysis, all the writers on the subject have made simplifications which are unwarrantable, and to some extent misleading. The different products of the different firms in an imperfectly competitive industry do generate consumers' surpluses, by the mere fact that they are different. To emphasise the differences between the products for the purpose of getting a downward sloping demand curve for the individual firm, and then to neglect the differences between the products (irrational preferences!) for the purpose of neglecting the consumers' surplus, is both inconsistent and practically dangerous. To neglect the producers' surplus for the purpose of equating price with average cost imports quite unnecessary difficulties into the theory. These two simplifications together have been responsible for the quite incorrect idea that the number of firms in an industry ought always to be reduced when an industry is imperfectly competitive—an idea which we should at once

---

[13] *Economics of Welfare*, Book II, ch. 17.

recognise as absurd if we were not bemused by diagrams, and whose practical realisation could only lead to universal monopoly. One may remark, in parenthesis, that it is particularly absurd when it is applied (as it often is) to the problems of retail trade; in retail trade both the consumers' surpluses (due to economy of shopping time) and the producers' surpluses (economy of living at one's work) which are derived from multiplicity of shops are abnormally large, so that the technical advantages of a concentration policy have to be abnormally large if there is to be a case for it.

And so one might go on. But enough has perhaps been said to show that Consumers' Surplus is not a mere economic plaything, a *curiosum*. It is the foundation of an important branch of economics, a branch cultivated with superb success by Marshall, Edgeworth, and Pigou, shockingly neglected in the last twenty years, but urgently needing reconstruction on a broader basis. Beyond all doubt it is still capable of much further development; if economists are to play their part in shaping the canons of economic policy fit for a new age, they will have to build on the foundation of Consumers' Surplus.

The interdependence of investment decisions*†

HOLLIS B. CHENERY

It is now widely recognized that the classical theory of resource allocation must be modified to take account of existing conditions in underdeveloped countries, particularly as regards investment decisions. In his celebrated article on the "Problems of Industrialization of Eastern and Southeastern Europe" (1) Professor Rosenstein-Rodan suggested that a group of investments which would be profitable if considered together may separately appear unprofitable and may not be undertaken by an individual investor who does not take advantage of external economies. Rosenstein-Rodan concluded that government coordination of investment would be necessary to make the best use of available resources and that the calculation of the profitability of a given investment should include the resulting increase in profitability of investment in other sectors.

A number of writers have followed Rosenstein-Rodan in suggesting limitations to the applicability of general equilibrium theory for the analysis of resource use in underdeveloped economies: Nurkse (2), Lewis (3), Singer (4), and Myrdal (5), to mention only a few. Although concerned with a variety of problems, they agree in doubting the existence of an automatic tendency toward equilibrium with optimal resource allocation in such economies.

In contrast to the general equilibrium system, which has been elaborated with increasing precision over a long period, the postulates of a model which would permit the analysis of the conditions thought to be characteristic of underdeveloped countries have not been stated with any accuracy. It is customary to list a number of ways in which the competitive mechanism does not

* In M. Abramovitz and others, *The Allocation of Economic Resources* (Stanford: Stanford University Press, 1959): pp. 82–120. Corrected by the author. Reprinted by courtesy of the author and Stanford University Press.

† I am indebted to Tibor Scitovsky, Kenneth Arrow, Robert Dorfman, John Haldi, and Louis Lefeber for helpful discussions of the theoretical problems analyzed here, and to the staff of the U.N. Economic Commission for Latin America for much useful background material on the steel-metalworking complex in Latin America, which provides the empirical core of the paper. My research in this field has been supported by a grant from the Ford Foundation to the Stanford Project for Quantitative Research in Economic Development.

function properly and then to draw general conclusions from them without concretely specifying the model which is being used.[1] The efforts of more orthodox theorists to demolish these conclusions are generally unconvincing, however, because they stick too closely to the classical assumptions.

One theoretical aspect of the problem has been clarified in recent articles by Scitovsky (6), Fleming (7), Arndt (8), and Bator (9): the difference between the Marshallian concept of "external economies" and the meaning given to this term by Rosenstein-Rodan and other growth theorists. In earlier usage it pertains to costs and benefits of production not adequately reflected in the price mechanism; in growth theory it refers to the effect of one investment on the profitability of another. The former uses the assumptions of competitive equilibrium, while the latter acquires its significance from the assumptions of dynamic disequilibrium.

In the present paper, I will take up one of the arguments advanced by Rosenstein-Rodan for the coordination of investment decisions, which accounts for part of his "external economies." My aim is to present a model which will permit measurement of the importance of interdependence in production for investment decisions, and to work out a concrete example in which they are thought to be significant. When this has been done, I will return to the theoretical formulation of the phenomenon of external economies and its practical implications.

THE PROBLEM

The problem may be stated as follows: To what extent and under what circumstances do coordinated investment decisions lead to more efficient resource use than do individual decisions based on existing market information? It has been shown that, if conditions of competitive equilibrium are continuously maintained and economies of scale are excluded, then external economies are limited to rather exceptional cases of nonmarket (or technological) interdependence whose quantitative significance is slight.[2]

The maintenance of competitive equilibrium over time requires that present prices must accurately reflect future as well as present demand and supply conditions and that investors should react in such a way that their price expectations are continuously realized.[3] These are very strong conditions. Under these assumptions, the "pecuniary" or market effects of one investment on the profitability calculations of other investors are part of the mechanism by which the market coordinates action among investors and eliminates the difference between private and social profitability of the initial investment.

When the continuous adjustments needed to maintain competitive equilibrium are not assumed to take place, these market effects have quite a

---

[1] There are a number of exceptions to this generalization, such as Lewis' brilliant article (3) on the implications of surplus labor for development, but they have not been concerned with the problem to be discussed here.

[2] See Scitovsky (6), Bator (9). The static case is analyzed most completely by the latter.

[3] The conditions under which competitive equilibrium is maintained over time are stated more precisely in Dorfman, Samuelson, and Solow (10), pp. 318 ff.

different significance. The resulting situation has been most precisely formulated by Scitovsky:[4]

Investment in industry A will cheapen its product; and if this is used as a factor in industry B, the latter's profits will rise . . . The profits of industry B, created by the lower price of factor A, call for investment and expansion in industry B, one result of which will be an increase in industry B's demand for industry A's product . . . equilibrium is reached only when successive doses of investment and expansion in the two industries have led to the simultaneous elimination of profits in both. It is only at this stage, where equilibrium has been established, that the conclusions of equilibrium theory become applicable . . . We can conclude, therefore, that when an investment gives rise to pecuniary external economies, its private profitability understates its social desirability.

Furthermore, if the system does not start from a position of competitive equilibrium, it cannot be assumed that the investment that takes place will necessarily lead toward such an equilibrium.

The mechanism I propose to study is essentially that outlined by Scitovsky. Although included in the concept of external economies used by Rosenstein-Rodan and Nurkse, it is subordinate in their analysis to the effects of investment that are transmitted via the increase in consumers' income. This extension of the concept, however, seems undesirable to me because it combines production phenomena which are specific to individual investments with income effects that are produced by any investment. I will therefore adopt the following definitions of external economies as applied to the effects of investment:

i) *For the whole economy*, external economies may be said to exist when the real cost of supplying a given set of demands is less with coordinated investment decisions than with individual decisions based on existing market information.

ii) *With reference to particular industries*, it can be said that industries A, B, C, . . . , provide external economies to industries K, L, M, . . . , if investment in industries A, B, C, . . . , causes a decrease in the cost of supplying the demands for the products of K, L, M, ...[5]

The following example suggests some of the situations in which external economies may be important for investment decisions. Consider two related industries, steel and metalworking. There are demands of 1000 units for the products of each industry, which are currently supplied by imports in each case. The domestic production of metal products would require an input of 0.2 units of steel per unit of output but would not be profitable at existing prices. Steel production also has not been profitable heretofore.

---

[4] Reference (6), p. 148.
[5] The earlier distinction between cost reduction via price changes (pecuniary) and cost reduction via a change in input requirements (technological) can also be made, but the second case is not of great significance for the analysis of investment decisions.

Assume now, as Scitovsky does, an innovation leading to investment in steel production which "will cheapen its product." If the existing market demand for steel is taken as a guide to the scale of the investment, a capacity of 1000 units will be installed. But if the price of steel is lowered in accordance with its lower cost, investment in metalworking will now become profitable. Investment in capacity to produce 1000 units of metal products will lead to an additional demand for 200 units of steel, so that further investment in the steel industry will be needed.

In this case, external economies exist on the above definitions because coordinated investment decisions would result in simultaneous investment in steel and metalworking and a lower-cost supply of metal products. The difference in total cost between the coordinated and uncoordinated result is due to the timing of investment and will be wiped out by the working of market forces in the long run if (i) the price of steel is reduced and (ii) the demand for steel does not increase further in the meantime.

Under other assumptions, the external economies produced by coordinated investment may not be eliminated over time by market reactions. If there are internal economies of scale in the steel industry, it may be profitable to invest at a demand of 1200 units but not at 1000. In this event, the investments must be made in both sectors together if either is to be profitable.

Innovation is only one of a number of initiating factors which can lead to external economies of this type. The discovery of a new source of iron ore, the building of a railway, a rise in the cost of securing imports, or any other change which makes the initial investment in steel profitable may have similar repercussions. These examples all involve additional sectors of the economy, and to analyze them in any detail requires some sort of interindustry model. Such a model is suggested in the next section.

Since the significance of external economies depends largely on the magnitudes involved, I will work with a concrete example based on the present conditions in the steel and metalworking industries in Latin America. The number of sectors included is the minimum which appears necessary to take account of the more directly related investments. This example has been chosen because it contains practically all of the elements that have been suggested in the discussion of dynamic external economies. My procedure will be to compare the resource allocation resulting under the two extreme assumptions of perfect coordination and complete lack of coordination of investment decisions. Alternative assumptions will then be made with regard to the factor costs, size of the market, and degree of coordination in order to measure the importance of these several factors.

THE MODEL

The interdependence of investment decisions will be discussed in the context of conditions prevailing in the less developed countries, for which it has greater significance than for more advanced countries. Interdependence is also more important for products sold to producers, and hence it occurs

340 READINGS IN WELFARE ECONOMICS

typically in sectors related to manufacturing. In the underdeveloped countries, manufacturing is initiated originally as a substitute for either handicraft production or imports. Either assumption could be made in the general case, but the latter is clearly more appropriate for the commodities discussed here.

The model to be proposed is intended to provide an explicit analysis of production and investment in a group of related sectors[6] within a simplified general-equilibrium framework. For the sectors in which the levels of production and investment are important to the result, it specifies a production function in the form of an "activity" or column of Leontief-type input coefficients. Demands for the outputs of these sectors in the rest of the economy are taken as given. Supplies of inputs from other sectors in the economy, of imports, and of labor and capital, are assumed to be available at fixed prices. The effects of relaxing these assumptions are considered later.

The model provides for the analysis of the following characteristics of underdeveloped countries, which may affect either the source of the initial incentive to invest or the extent of coordination which should be assumed:

i) *Failure to use known lower-cost techniques of production* because of ignorance, scarcity of innovators, or lack of capital in large blocks.

ii) *Small markets for manufactured goods* in relation to the size of a minimum-cost plant. The explanation may be found in relatively high transport costs and tariff barriers combined with low levels of income. Demands for these commodities are largely supplied from imports.

iii) *Imperfection in factor markets* with a wide range of prices for labor, capital, and foreign exchange, caused by institutional and cultural obstacles to the movement of these factors between uses. The opportunity cost of labor is frequently lower than its cost to industry, while capital and foreign exchange are frequently rationed in various ways.

iv) *The absence of adequate overhead facilities*—transport, power, etc.

It is this set of factors, rather than the level of *per capita* income *per se*, that is important to the discussion of the effects of interdependence of investments.

The analysis of production

To take account of the structural factors listed above, the description of production in terms of activities has important advantages. The formulation used in mathematical programming permits the determination of the optimal allocation of resources when there are limitations on the quantities demanded and on factor supplies. Such a solution corresponds to the case of perfect coordination. In addition, it will be necessary to work out solutions to represent the results of uncoordinated individual decisions.

---

[6] Market interrelations can be classified in various ways, but the most important distinction is between *interdependence in production* (supplier-user, users of a common input, etc.) and *interdependence via increased consumer incomes*. I will be concerned mainly with the first type and will therefore take consumer demands as given for most of the analysis. Fleming [(7), p. 250] distinguishes between "vertical" and "horizontal" economies in approximately the same way.

The model to be used is summarized in Table 1 as a set of 10 equations in activity analysis form. It has the following features:

i) *Each equation corresponds to a commodity* or primary factor input. The first seven equations apply to the commodities produced within the part of the economy covered in detail by the model. The first six are the outputs of sectors most directly affected by the level of production in the steel industry, either as suppliers or users. Foreign exchange (equation 7) is also treated as a commodity, and exports are included within the model to show the resources used in obtaining imports. Equation 8 applies to commodities produced elsewhere in the economy and is included in the system to account for all production costs.

ii) *The activities in the model* describe the alternative ways of supplying each commodity. The output of each activity is shown by a positive coefficient, 1.0. The activity level therefore indicates the net amount produced by the activity, there being no joint products. The use of a commodity in production is shown by a negative coefficient, a_{ij}, the amount of commodity i used in sector j being $a_{ij}X_j$. Production activities (X_j) require inputs from other sectors in the model and also from outside the system (inputs 8–10). Import activities (M_j) require an input of foreign exchange in the amount indicated by the coefficient in line 7 per unit of product supplied. Imports are possible for commodities 1, 2, 3, and 5. (For all activities, the commodity supplied is indicated by the subscript.)

iii) *The first eight equations* in the model constitute a set of restrictions on the possible levels of production, imports, and exports. Each equation is formed by multiplying each coefficient in the row by the corresponding activity level $(X_j, M_j, \text{or } E_j)$ and setting the total equal to the demand outside the system. For example, the equation for iron and steel reads:

$$-0.22X_1 + M_2 + X_2 - 0.05X_3 - 0.01X_4 - 0.01X_5 - 0.02X_6 = 1000. \quad (2)$$

The total supply is given by $(M_2 + X_2)$; the total use of iron and steel in the sectors within the system is $\sum_j a_{2j}X_j$; and the "outside" use in the rest of the economy is 1000. Outside demands are assumed only for the first two commodities, since the existence of outside demands for the remainder does not affect the nature of the solution.[7]

The equation for foreign exchange supplied and demanded has a similar form:

$$-0.85M_1 - 1.2M_2 - 1.1M_3 - 1.0M_5 + 1.0E_7 = 0. \quad (7a)$$

(For reasons explained below, alternative assumptions a and b will be made as to the magnitude of the coefficients specifying the cost of imports of commodities 1 and 2.)

---

[7] Production or import levels calculated for the remaining commodities can be considered as increases above a given level, which is not affected by the investment choices in the sectors being analyzed.

Table 1

THE MODEL OF PRODUCTION

Equation	Commodity	Activities*												Outside Demand	Given Prices
		M_1	M_2	X_1	X_2	M_3	X_3	X_4	M_5	X_5	X_6	E_7	X_8		
(1)	Metal products†	1.0		1.0										1000	
(2)	Iron and steel		1.0	−.22	1.0									1000	
(3)	Iron ore					1.0	1.0							0	
(4)	Electric power			−.01	−.08		−.02	1.0		−.05	−.01		−.02	0	
(5)	Coal			−.02	−.10		−.02	−.25	1.0	1.0	−.03		−.07	0	
(6)	Transport			−.01	−.02		−.10	−.50		−.20	1.0			0	
(7a)	Foreign exchange (a)	−.85	−1.2			−1.1			−1.0			1.0		0	
(7b)	(b)	−.815	−1.05												
(8)	Other inputs			−.17	−.09		−.10	−.08		−.17	−.10	−.10	1.0	0	
(9)	Labor			−.7	−.2		−.3	−.4		−.7	−.7	−1.0	−1.0	—	1.5
(10)	Capital			−.7	−2.7		−.5	−2.5		−.7	−2.2	−2.2	−1.5	—	1.0

* All input coefficients are measured in value per unit of output except labor, which is in man-years. The value units for outside demand (and hence for labor) are arbitrary.

† "Metal products" refers to machinery, vehicles, and other products in the 36, 37, and 38 categories of the International Standard Industrial Classification.

iv) *The use of primary factors*, capital and labor, is shown in equations 9 and 10. For these unproduced inputs, no restriction is placed on supply since only a small range of variation will be considered. Instead, prices are assumed to be given by conditions in the rest of the economy, with the price of capital arbitrarily set at 1.0. At a later stage, economies of scale will be introduced by making average capital and labor coefficients a declining function of the level of output. (The activity analysis model can readily handle supply limitations in a more general case.)

A solution to a programming model such as this consists of a set of non-negative activity levels which satisfy equations 1–8. In linear programming, it is necessary to consider only "basic" solutions—those which have only as many positive activity levels as there are equations. A similar rule holds when there are economies of scale, so that almost all of the solutions with which I will be concerned are basic solutions. In the present model, a basic solution will contain one activity having a positive output for each commodity restriction. The total number of such combinations is 2^4, or 16, in the present example, since there are alternative sources for four commodities.[8] There are only six different solutions arising from these possible combinations, however; they are given in Table 2.

The coefficients used in Table 1 are intended to be realistic, but in order to avoid local peculiarities I have not used the actual data of any one country. The selection of sectors and of the input-output data (apart from steel) was based on a comparison of interindustry structure in four countries.[9] Latin America data (13) were used for the steel industry, and Japanese labor and capital coefficients for the remaining sectors.[10] Import prices and export costs are hypothetical. The proportions of external demand for steel and metal products are initially fixed at arbitrary levels, but the effect of varying them is considered explicitly in a later section.

Prices and external economies

Since I wish to isolate the effects of interdependence in production, I assume that income is increasing and investment is taking place at a given rate in the economy as a whole. The level of income at any time determines the specified demands for steel and metal products, while the investment opportunities in the remainder of the economy fix the marginal productivity of investment and the opportunity cost of labor. Prices of "other inputs" are determined by labor and capital costs, since the internal structures of the industries producing them are omitted from the model.

---

[8] Although it would be quite simple to include alternative techniques of production in each sector, this was not necessary in the present case because exports and imports provide an alternative to local production. Since the more important choice in these sectors is between imports and the most efficient production technique, I have limited the possibilities to these two.

[9] Chenery and Watanabe (11).

[10] From unpublished studies by T. Watanabe of the Stanford Project for Quantitative Research in Economic Development.

Table 2

BASIC SOLUTIONS TO THE MODEL*

| | Activity Level | | | | | | | | | | | | Factor Use | | |
Solution	M_1	X_1	M_2	X_2	M_3	X_3	X_4	M_5	X_5	X_6	E_7†	X_8	Labor‡	Capital‡	Total
0......	1000		1000		0	0	0	0		0	1865	187	2052	4383	7461
1......		1000	1220		0		10	3		10	1285	301	2296	4035	7479
2......	1000			1001	80		20	106		20	1009	196	1425	5332	7470
3......	1000			1007		80	25		113	83	815	206	1357	5231	7267
4......		1000		1221	98		35	133		34	241	313	1532	5195	7493
5......		1000		1229		98	41		141	112		324	1446	5065	7234

* The total of 16 possible combinations of imports and production in sectors 1, 2, 3, 5 is reduced to six because (i) when steel is imported, demands for ore and coal are zero and solutions 0 and 1 each represent four possible bases; and (ii) I have omitted the possibility of importing ore and producing coal or vice versa because it does not arise under my assumptions as to the extent of coordination.
† Exports under import assumption b.
‡ Labor and capital in case I.

Except as specified, prices will be assumed to satisfy the conditions of marginal cost pricing.[11] An initial position is assumed in which each commodity is either produced or imported, which is a basic solution. I also assume a price of labor of 1.5, which is its opportunity cost. The commodity prices and the price of foreign exchange can then be calculated from the condition that price equals marginal cost. (In case I, with no economies of scale, marginal cost is also average cost.) This calculation involves solving eight simultaneous equations, one for each activity, of the following form:

$$a_{1j}P_1 + a_{2j}P_2 + a_{3j}P_3 + \ldots + a_{10j}P_{10} = 0 \; (j = 1 \ldots 8) \qquad (11)$$

where a_{ij} is the (marginal) input coefficient for input 1 in activity j. Prices as thus defined are the same as the "shadow" or equilibrium prices of a programming system for the linear case except for the exogenous labor input, whose price is given.[12]

The relative prices with which the economy starts are determined by the source of supply—from domestic production or imports—of each commodity and the cost of securing foreign exchange. I will assume that initially all of the commodities that can be imported—metal products, steel, iron ore, and coal —are imported.[13] Once the price of foreign exchange is determined, their prices will be given.

The price of "other inputs," P_8, is readily computed from the price of labor and capital to be 3.0. By substituting $P_8 - P_{10}$ into equation 11 for the export acitivity, the price of foreign exchange is determined to be 4.0. The price of each imported commodity is then found by multiplying its cost in foreign exchange by the price (opportunity cost) of foreign exchange. The same procedure is followed in later solutions.

The prices of the domestically produced commodities in this and subsequent solutions must be determined simultaneously, since each sector (except the first) sells to one or more of the others. To facilitate this solution, the matrix of coefficients has been arranged in order of maximum triangularity —i.e., the elements above the diagonal in the solution are reduced to a minimum.[14] The set of initial prices is shown in line (1) of Table 3.

Starting from this initial position, in which demands for commodities 1 and 2 are supplied through imports, I will measure the effects of various factors which would render investment in one or both sectors profitable. In each case, a calculation will be made of the amount of investment that will

---

[11] For simplicity, I ignore differences in the durability of capital and risk among sectors and assume that the gross rate of return required by investors in each sector is the same. Variations in these factors could readily be introduced but would serve no useful purpose in the present context.

[12] The general formulation used in activity analysis and the economic interpretation of shadow prices are discussed in Dorfman, Samuelson, and Solow (10), especially Chaps 6–8.

[13] Except for iron ore, for which there is no demand if steel is not produced.

[14] The solutions for both prices and quantities were made with the Gauss-Seidel method of iteration. The method as applied to input-output systems is explained in Evans (12).

Table 3

EFFECTS OF COORDINATION ON PROFITS AND PRICES: CASE I

Investment Assumptions*	Import Assumption†	Solution N	Profitability of Investment‡				Prices							Total Cost§
			1	2	3	5	1	2	3	4	5	6	7	
Example A:														
(1) Initial position	a	0					3.40	4.80	4.40	5.04	4.00	4.43	4.00	8200
(2) Individual investment in 2	a	2	−.01	+.58	—	—	3.40	4.22	4.40	5.04	4.00	4.43	4.00	7620
(3) Coordination of 1 and 2	a	4	+.12	+.59	—	—	3.28	4.21	4.40	5.03	4.00	4.42	4.00	7490
Example B:														
(4) Initial position	b	0					3.26	4.20	4.40	5.04	4.00	4.43	4.00	7460
(5) Individual investment in exports	b	0	−.01	−.01	+.70	+1.42	3.26	4.20	4.40	5.04	4.00	4.43	4.00	7460
(6) Coordination of 2, 3, 5	b	3	−.01	+.20	+.70	+1.42	3.26	4.00	3.70	4.68	2.58	4.32	4.00	7260
Example C:														
(7) Coordination of 1, 2, 3, 5	a	5	+.17	+.79	+.70	+1.42	3.23	4.00	3.70	4.68	2.58	4.32	4.00	7230
	b	5	+.03	+.20	+.70	+1.42								

* The necessary expansion in sectors 4 and 6 is assumed in all cases.
† Import assumptions: (a) $m_1 = .85$, $m_2 = 1.2$,
(b) $m_1 = .815$, $m_2 = 1.05$.

‡ Profitability per unit of output at input prices indicated, with output price that of the initial position.
§ Total cost equals $(1000\ P_1 + 1000\ P_2)$.

take place under alternative assumptions as to investors' reactions.[15] The social efficiency of these reactions will be measured by the reduction in the total cost of supplying the given demands. Total cost in turn equals capital plus labor used, with labor valued at its opportunity cost of 1.5.

The two assumptions about investors' behavior can be stated as follows:

i) *Individual reactions*: Investment will take place in sectors which yield profits greater than or equal to the existing marginal productivity of capital (taken as 1.0) at *present prices* and in amounts determined by *present demands* for the commodity.

ii) *Coordinated reactions*: Investment will take place in sectors and in amounts which together will supply the outside demands at the minimum total cost. (For the linear case I, this assumption can be stated in terms of individual profitability at *future prices*.)

These assumptions represent the extreme range between no foresight and socially optimum decisions on investment. They are not intended as descriptions of the actual behavior of unplanned and planned economies, but as a basis for estimates of the maximum difference in performance.

The second part of the assumption as to individual reactions will not be applied to sectors in which domestic production is already established, because no investment could take place in a power-using industry, for example, without an expansion of power production. The amount of induced investment required in sectors where production is already established will therefore be assumed to take place even with individual reactions. This assumption is necessary in order that a given set of alternatives be feasible— i.e., satisfy all the restrictions.

The cost of each set of alternatives can be measured in one of two ways. The first is to calculate the production required in each sector and from this result to determine the amount of labor and capital needed throughout the economy. This has been done for the six basic solutions in Table 2. In the initial situation (solution 0) the outside demands are supplied from imports, and production takes place only in sectors 7 and 8, exports and "other inputs." The total cost of this production is 2052 units of labor and 4383 units of capital. Using the assumed opportunity cost of 1.5 labor, the total cost of this alternative is 7461. The total cost of the other alternatives is calculated in the same way.

The use of prices provides a second method of calculating the total cost of each set of alternatives, which is more interesting from an economic point of view. Each price represents the total capital used directly and indirectly to produce a unit of net output. In the initial situation of example B in Table 3 below, the prices of commodities 1 and 2 are shown as 3.26 and 4.20. Multiplying the outside demands by these prices and adding gives 7460 as the total

---

[15] The maintenance of the original pattern of supply also requires investment in exports, but it will keep the original prices unchanged.

cost as before (except for rounding). This result corresponds to the "dual" solution of a linear programming system.[16]

Under the assumptions made, any profitable investment will necessarily reduce the total cost of factors required to supply the given final demands. The difference between the amounts required under the two assumptions about investors' reactions provides a measure of the quantitative importance of the interdependence of investment decisions. In considering some types of policy, it is desirable to allocate this difference to individual sectors. When this is done, we will have a partial measure of the type of external economies which Rosenstein-Rodan had in mind: the difference between social and private profitability resulting from the recognition of interdependence.

MEASUREMENT OF THE EFFECTS OF INTERDEPENDENCE

Investment will take place in an industry[17] only if its marginal productivity is greater than or equal to that assumed for the rest of the economy. Assuming that investments which were profitable in the past have already been made, one of the following conditions must obtain if investment in steel or metalworking is now to become profitable:

i) *The availability of technology* which is more efficient at existing prices of inputs and outputs than that already in use;

ii) *A change in cost* of one of the exogenous inputs, such as a fall in the price of labour or capital;

iii) *A rise in the cost* of obtaining foreign exchange (i.e., a change affecting activity E_7 in Table 1);

iv) *Coordinated planning,* provided unused resources exist in one of the supplying sectors;

v) *The expansion of demand.*

These factors may produce investment in one or several sectors, and the results may or may not be different as between individual investment decisions and coordinated decisions. In this section I will try to identify the more important types of external effects—cases in which the results of the two assumptions are different—and to measure their quantitative significance in the example I have chosen.

It will be useful to separate the case in which there are internal economies of scale from that with constant costs throughout, since it is often asserted that external economies are merely the result of internal economies elsewhere in the economy. I will take up the constant cost assumption first as case I, since it is analytically simpler although empirically less important.

In order to make the analysis easier to follow, I will use the same set of interindustry data (equations 1–6) throughout. This permits the use of the basic solutions given for sectors 1–8 of Table 2 for both cases. Economies of

---

[16] The calculation of the price solution is explained further in the Appendix.

[17] I assume no difference among plants in an industry except for the scale effects discussed under case II below.

scale are assumed to affect only the labor and capital coefficients, which are outside of the interindustry system.

For each case, the same three examples, illustrating some of the initiating factors listed above, will be worked out and the magnitude of the external effects measured.

Case I: External effects with constant costs

The principal effects of interdependence in production can be classified as *effects on users* and *effects on suppliers*.[18] Each type will first be illustrated separately by assuming only partial coordination among investment decisions, and then their combined effect will be shown by assuming complete co-ordination.

Example A: Effects on users. External effects of investment in industry Y on users of commody Y can be illustrated by Scitovsky's example of the effects of an innovation in Y. Assume that it is now profitable to invest in the production of steel, which had previously been imported. In example A of Table 3, the import price of steel has been taken as 1.2 to illustrate this possibility. The initial prices, as calculated above, are given in line (1) for all commodities. The import price of metal products has been set just under the cost of production with current prices, however, so that without coordination investment will take place only in steel. The effect on steel cost and the total cost are shown in line (2). If coordination takes place, however, investment in sector 1 will also be profitable because of the lower cost of steel, and a larger investment in sector 2 will be needed to supply the increased demand. (This is the situation envisaged by Scitovsky in the example previously cited.) No change in the source of supply of other inputs is assumed, so the reduction in the total cost of supplying the given demands—from 7620 to 7490—can be attributed entirely to the coordination of investment in steel and the steel-using industries. Others of the initiating factors listed above—a fall in the cost of labor or capital, or a rise in the cost of securing imports—can produce the same effect.

It should be emphasized that, under the assumption of constant costs, the difference between uncoordinated and coordinated investment in this case is only one of time. Once the investment in steel has been made, it will be profitable to invest in metalworking unless the price of steel is kept above its cost. Furthermore, if *both* sectors are unprofitable at the initial prices of imports, coordination will not make them profitable. Both of these conclusions will be changed in succeeding examples.

Example B: Effects on suppliers. When expansion in one sector increases demands for inputs, no external economies are created if the price of the inputs reflects the opportunity costs of the factors used to produce them.

---

[18] I have abstracted from less direct effects, such as the use of common factors of production, by assuming an elastic supply of exogenous inputs at constant costs over the relevant range of demand. All produced inputs are therefore available at constant cost.

When increased demand in one sector leads to a demand for immobile factors which have no alternative uses, or for commodities produced from immobile factors, however, the situation may be different.

In the present example iron ore and coal illustrate this possibility. The market for them is limited by transport costs, particularly in areas where transport facilities are not well developed.[19] If an industry which can use them locally is established, however, they may be much cheaper than would the imported material, as has been assumed here.

Example B in Table 3 illustrates the effect of investment in the steel industry on the profitability of investment in coal and ore supplies. If it is assumed that there is no market for these commodities outside the region because of high transport costs,[20] additional investment in these sectors will not take place unless steel production (or some other use) is established locally. On the other hand, steel production on the basis of imported materials is unprofitable. In this case, there will be no investment in any sector without coordination of all three. With coordination, the cost of supplying the existing demand for steel is reduced from 4200 to 4000.

A similar external effect on suppliers may be produced by a reduction in the cost of a factor which affects profits in all sectors. Assume that the opportunity cost of labor is reduced (e.g., by using its calculated value instead of market cost) from 1.5 units of capital to 1.0. (A reduction in the supply cost of capital or a rise in the cost of foreign exchange would have a similar effect.) Investment in both sectors 1 and 2 will then become profitable to individual investors, but the amount of investment undertaken in sector 2 will be 18 percent less than if there is coordination, since the demand from sector 1 will not be taken into account initially. The difference in the cost of supplying the given demands is 130 in this case.[21] As in example A, coordination will affect only the timing of investment because it will be profitable to expand investment in sector 2 when the demand for steel from sector 1 becomes apparent.

Example C: Effects on both suppliers and users. Example C in Table 3 shows the effects of complete coordination of both the suppliers and the users of the steel industry. In this case, all commodities are produced locally and nothing is imported. As compared to partial coordination in example A, prices drop in both sectors 1 and 2, and there is a reduction of 260 in the total cost of supplying the given demands. As compared to partial coordination in example B, only the price of metal products drops and the saving is much smaller.

A comparison of example C with the initial assumption of example B shows the maximum external economies that can be attributed to coordination

---

[19] The case becomes more significant when we make the more realistic assumption of economies of scale in transportation.

[20] An example is provided by the coal and iron ore deposits in Colombia, which cannot be economically transported to the coast.

[21] The calculation is not shown because the mechanism is similar to that in example A.

alone in the present example when there are no economies of scale. In the initial position, no investment is profitable by itself, and demand would continue to be supplied from imports at a cost of 7460. Coordinated investment in all sectors reduces the cost of supplying the same demands to 7230. The saving is attributable to the existence of local resources of coal and iron ore which can be economically exploited with coordination but not otherwise.

Case II: external effects with economies of scale

The introduction of economies of scale not only makes external effects more important in the examples given previously, but it makes possible some types which do not exist in the case of constant costs. These will be taken up after the empirical basis for introducing economies of scale has been discussed.

The nature of economies of scale.   Despite the theoretical importance of economies of scale, their quantitative significance has been investigated only in a limited number of industries. The available evidence suggests that the economies of producing a larger volume of output occur mainly in the direct use of capital and labor and in inputs (maintenance, overhead costs of various kinds) related to them. The quantities of materials needed to produce a given commodity seem to vary little with output unless the increase in scale makes possible the use of a different type of process. The value of such materials may fall with increases in the amount purchased, due to internal economies in other sectors, but this results from the working of the model itself.

Most studies of scale effects apply to plants or processes rather than to whole industries. The determination of cost variation for a whole industry must take into account location factors and market structure—e.g., whether the increase will come from one plant or several, from new plants or the expansion of old, etc. In the present example, these problems are important mainly in the metalworking sector because in steel and its suppliers it can be assumed that the increase in output will come from a single source.

Steel is the sector in which economies of scale are of greatest importance in the present case. Fortunately, the Economic Commission for Latin America has made a detailed study (13) of economies of scale in the steel industry based on design data for plants of various sizes; some of the results are summarized in Table 4. Production cost in the smallest plant considered is 65 percent higher than in the largest, and this does not exhaust the economies which are possible with a smaller range of products.[22]

To use these data in the interindustry analysis, I have based the input coefficients of Table 1 on a plant of 250,000 tons, which is typical of Latin American steel production. Economies of scale will be assumed only in the use of capital and labor, which account for perhaps 90 percent of the cost

---

[22] The plants are designed to produce 80 percent of the range of steel products typically demanded in Latin American countries. The remainder would not normally be economical and would be imported. See Table 8.

Table 4

ECONOMIES OF SCALE IN STEEL PRODUCTION*

Cost per Ton‡	Capacity of Plant†				Decrease from 50 to 1000
	50	250	500	1000	
Raw materials............	33.84	31.26	31.26	25.68	8.16
Maintenance and misc.....	20.59	11.11	10.57	9.83	10.76
Capital charges	122.93	101.20	87.10	85.05	37.88
Labor cost	32.00	15.20	8.57	6.60	25.40
Total cost	209.36	158.77	137.50	127.16	82.20
Total investment per ton ..	492	405	348	340	152

* Adapted from data in *A Study of the Iron and Steel Industry in Latin America* (13), pp. 112–16.
† Capacity in 1000 tons of finished steel per year.
‡ The costs (in dollars) are taken from engineering calculations for hypothetical integrated plants of different sizes located in the eastern United States. Labor costs are taken here at 50 percent of U.S. costs and charges for depreciation and profit at 25 percent of capital invested to reflect Latin American conditions. (These are not the capital charges used in the original study, which are unrealistically low.) Data for iron, steel, and finishing stages have been consolidated.

reduction shown in Table 4 if the price of inputs is kept constant.[23] For this and the other sectors of the model, capital and labor will be treated as a single input, which is represented by a linear equation[24]

$$f_i = \bar{f}_i + \gamma_i X_i \qquad (12)$$

where f_i is total use cost of capital and labor at the prices assumed, $\bar{f}_i$ is a constant, and γ_i is the long-run marginal cost of labor and capital.

A linear function fits the data for steel production costs quite well above 250,000 tons. At the representative size of plant chosen, the ratio of marginal to average cost of labor and capital inputs is about two-thirds. This ratio has been used to determine the input function for sector 2 in Table 5, with the constant term fixed so as to equate total cost in cases I and II at the initial demand of 1000.

The input functions for the remaining sectors were established on the same principles but on a hypothetical basis.[25] It would be hard to specify a typical situation for mining, transport, and power production without assuming a specific location.

---

[23] All of the reduction shown in the cost of raw materials is due to economies of scale in the transport sector.

[24] Capital and labor inputs in chemical process industries (which include metallurgy) have been found to conform quite well to a relation of the following form:

$$f = f_0 (X/X_0)^\psi.$$

Wessel and Chilton (14) give engineering data for chemical plants in which the value of ψ averages about 0.6 for capital and 0.2 for labor. ψ is the ratio of marginal to average cost. Equation 12 may be regarded as a linear approximation to this function which holds over a specified range.

[25] The greatest economy of scale is assumed in transportation, the least in mining.

Table 5

INPUT FUNCTIONS FOR LABOR AND CAPITAL: CASE II

Sector	Input Function for Combined Input*	Total Cost Equal to Case I at†	MC/AC‡
1.........	$f_1 = 500 + 1.25\ X_1$	$X_1 = 1000$	0.71
2.........	$f_2 = 1000 + 2.00\ X_2$	$X_2 = 1000$	0.67
3.........	$f_3 = 0.80\ X_3$	$X_3 = 0$	0.84
4.........	$f_4 = 2.5\ X_4$	$X_4 = 0$	0.66
5.........	$f_5 = 1.1\ X_5$	$X_5 = 0$	0.85
6.........	$f_6 = 1.75\ X_6$	$X_6 = 0$	0.49
7.........	$f_7 = 3.7\ X_7$	All values	1.00

* Expressing labor in capital units at the ratio of 1.5 : 1.0.
† I.e., output at which total cost for labor and capital are the same in both case I and case II.
‡ Marginal cost in case II divided by average cost in case I.

No economies or diseconomies of scale have been assumed in exports. Total cost has been assumed to be equal for each sector in cases I and II as the values of exogenous demand for each commodity, which are those that the individual investor takes into account.[26]

The form of the analysis is such that it can readily be adapted to utilize cost studies of the kind usually prepared in connection with investment programs.

A comparison of cases I and II. When economies of scale exist in supplying sectors, external economies will be larger because the increase in demand from the using sector will make possible cheaper production by the supplier. I will now analyze the same examples as before with the assumptions just made as to input functions for capital and labor in order to show the significance of introducing economies of scale.

Table 6 has been constructed by applying the alternative input functions of cases I and II to the basic quantity solutions given in Table 2.[27] Unlike case I, a coordinated investment will be profitable with the given economies of scale without any innovation, and so I have assumed the import prices of example B throughout. The use of factors in each sector shows that in example A most of the difference between the two cases comes from the larger output in sector 2, but in example B the difference is almost entirely due to the other supplying sectors. The difference is most pronounced in example C, where

[26] This assumption results in a constant term of 500 in sector 1 and of zero in the other sectors. It might have been more realistic to assume a constant term in sectors 3 and 5, where no production exists in the initial position, but the difference in result would be small.

[27] For case I, this calculation serves as a check on the results of the price solution given in Table 3. For case II, marginal cost prices can also be used to determine total factor use, but the quantity solution is the more convenient. The price solution for this case is given in the Appendix. With economies of scale, the optimal solution will be a basic solution, as it was in the linear case.

Table 6

DIRECT FACTOR USE BY SECTOR AND EXTERNAL ECONOMIES: CASES I AND II

Sectors Coordinated*	Economies of Scale	Solution N	Direct Factor Use in Sector†							Total Factor Use‡	Difference from Initial Position		External Economies in Sector 2
			1	2	3	4	5	6	7		Case I	Case II	
(1) Initial Position		0	0	0	0	0	0	0	7460	7460			
Example A:													
(2) 2	I	2	0	3272	0	80	0	81	4038	7471	+11		
(3) 1, 2	I	4	2260	3992	0	138	0	140	961	7491	+31		
(4) 1, 2	II	4	2260	3772	0	95	0	78	961	7166		−294	0.030
Example B:													
(5) 2, 3, 5	I	3	0	3295	100	100	174	337	3260	7266	−194		.020
(6) 2, 3, 5	II	3	0	3287	88	69	151	188	3260	7043		−417	.046
Example C:													
(7) 1, 2, 3, 5	I	5	2260	4019	123	162	217	453	0	7234	−226		.023
	II	5	2260	3790	108	111	189	252	0	6710		−750	.097

* Import assumption b is used for all 3 examples.
† Direct factor use in the sector includes the use of "other inputs."
‡ Figures vary slightly from those given in Tables 2 and 3 because of rounding.

investment in all sectors is coordinated, because in this case the economies of scale in the supplying sectors (particularly transportation) reach substantial proportions.

The allocation of external economies by sector

The savings in factor use which result from coordination pertain to the whole set of investments, rather than to any one of them, because all are necessary to the result. If all investments in the economy were centrally planned, there would be no need to try to allocate this type of external economies because the determination of the optimum integrated plan would be sufficient. In economies, however, in which not all investment is under government control, the question arises as to how external economies can be taken into account in policies designed to improve the efficiency of individual investment decisions. This problem arises concretely in the less well-developed countries in the attempt to establish investment priorities for the economy as a whole or within certain areas, such as manufacturing. These priorities are intended to guide the allocation of loan funds or foreign exchange, or to be used as a basis for other measures by which the government influences investment.

The rationale for allocating the benefits of coordination to one sector or another must derive from the institutional setting. In the extreme case, it may be assumed that if one investment is made and its output sold at the price of the optimal solution, then investment in supplying industries and using industries will follow if the return on these investments is equal to the marginal productivity of capital elsewhere in the economy. In the present example, investment in the steel industry may have this effect, and, in fact, many governments undertake direct investment in the steel industry partly to stimulate investment in related industries. Let us calculate, therefore, the effect that taking account of external economies has on the profitability of investment in steel.

External economies may be thought of either as an addition to the value produced by a plant or as a reduction in its cost. Since I have assumed given demands in this paper, it is more convenient to take the latter approach.[28] The savings due to the coordination of investment shown in Table 6 can be taken therefore as being equivalent to a reduction in the investment required in the steel industry. The profitability of investment is increased thereby, and the difference provides a measure of external economies in sector 2. In example I B the calculation would be as follows:[29]

---

[28] In an earlier discussion (15), I suggested that external economies be treated as an addition to the value added in production, although I did not indicate how they might be measured. If this approach were adopted, the additional value would be the additional production achievable with the factors saved.

[29] In each case I have used the scale of investment without coordination (1000) as the basis of comparison. Input costs are derived by taking the price of capital equal to its marginal productivity (0.25) in exports.

	Market Prices	Shadow Prices
Price of output	1.050	4.20
Cost of inputs	.379	1.517
Profit margin	.671	2.683
Capital per unit of output..........	2.700	
Capital saved per unit of output (194/1000)....................	−.194	
Adjusted capital per unit of output..	2.506	
Profitability: Original.............	.248	
Adjusted	.268	
External economy..............	0.020	

The concept is somewhat more complicated when there are economies of scale in steel production because the average productivity of investment in the plant is less than the marginal productivity of additional increments of capacity. This phenomenon will lead to some overbuilding of capacity for the given demand at any moment in time, a factor which I ignore. Here I have calculated the average productivity of investment in the same way for case II as for case I, with the results shown in the last column of Table 6.

The external economies measured in this way add some 8 to 10 percent to the productivity of investment in the steel industry in case I, and up to 40 percent with coordination of all sectors in case II. If possible economies in the supply of exogenous inputs of goods and services (which account for about 15 percent of all costs) were taken into account, the figure would be somewhat higher. The inclusion of external economies of this magnitude might make the difference between an unpromising steel project and one which should be included in a development program.

The size of the market

The effect of small markets combined with economies of scale in production is one of the main explanations given for the lack of growth of poor countries.[30] In analyzing external economies, I have so far taken the size of the market as given. In case II, the demand for each commodity was taken to be just below the size which would make investment attractive to an individual entrepreneur. Let us now abandon this assumption and determine the difference that coordination makes in the minimum scale at which investment becomes profitable. I will consider first sectors 1 and 2 separately and then the optimum pattern of investment for the whole complex.

Investment in individual sectors. The analysis of investment in individual sectors will compare the effect of variation in exogenous demand on the cost of supply under four assumptions:

   i) *Imports*;
   ii) *Uncoordinated investment* in one sector;

---

[30] See Nurkse (2).

iii) *Coordinated investment* in supplying sectors 3–6;
iv) *Coordinated investment* in all sectors.

The cost of supplying demands of any size in each sector under these assumptions is given by the equations in Table 7.

Table 7

COST OF SUPPLY IN EACH SECTOR UNDER VARIOUS ASSUMPTIONS*

Assumption	Sector 1	Sector 2
(i) Imports	$S_1 = 3.26 Y_1$	$S_2 = 4.2 Y_2$
(ii) Uncoordinated investment	$S_1 = 500 + 2.78 Y_1$	$S_2 = 1000 + 3.22 Y_2$
(iii) Coordination of sectors 3–6	$S_1 = 500 + 2.739 Y_1$	$S_2 = 1000 + 2.782 Y_2$
(iv) Coordination of all sectors	$S_1 = 500 + 2.429 Y_1$ $+ (1000 - 1.418 Y_2)$ where $Y_2 < 1040$	$S_2 = 1000 + 2.782 Y_2$ $+ (500 - 0.831 Y_1)$ where $Y_1 < 1040$ $Y_1 > 600$

* Source: Appendix.

The differences among the last three equations arise as follows:

ii) Uncoordinated investment takes account of economies of scale in the given sector but assumes average cost of inputs as given by the initial prices of Table 3 (line 4);

iii) Coordination of sectors 3–6 takes the cost of these inputs as determined from the input functions of Table 5;

iv) Complete coordination makes the same assumptions as (iii) and, in addition, determines the net cost of supplying the given sector—i.e., 1 or 2—when the demand in the other is held constant. If uncoordinated investment in sector 1 is unprofitable but investment in sector 2 makes it profitable, the investment in sector 2 is credited with the difference between the cost of supplying commodity 1 from domestic production and from imports. These functions, therefore, are valid only over the range in which uncoordinated investment in the other sector is not profitable.[31]

A comparison of the several alternatives is given for each sector in Figures 1*a* and *b*.[32] In each case, I have assumed a single value of production in the other sector (the general case is taken up in the next section). In sector 1, imports are profitable up to a demand of 1040 at the assumed value of Y_2, and investment in sector 1 alone gives the lowest cost supply from this point to a demand of 1640. Thereafter, investment in both sectors is profitable with

---

[31] In sector 2 there is no saving over assumption (iii) and no justification for investment in 1 unless Y_1 is greater than 600—i.e., unless the second term is negative. In sector 1, the last term can be either positive or negative.

[32] In sector 1 curve (iii) is omitted because it is only slightly below curve (ii).

Figure 1a

MINIMUM SCALE OF INVESTMENT IN SECTOR 1.
METAL PRODUCTS ($Y_2 = 300$)

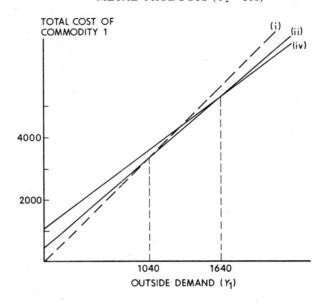

Figure 1b

MINIMUM SCALE OF INVESTMENT IN SECTOR 2.
STEEL PRODUCTION ($Y_1 = 1000$)

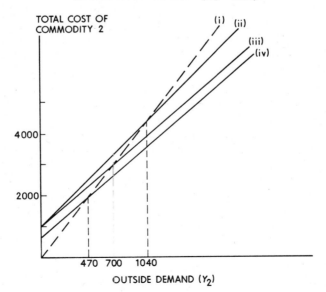

coordination. In sector 2, coordination of the supplying sectors lowers the minimum scale at which investment becomes profitable from 1040 to 700. Coordination of investment in the using sector lowers it still further at the assumed demand in sector 1.

The pattern of investment over time. The preceding analysis can be generalized to shed some light on the optimal pattern of investment over time. When investment is completely coordinated, there are four alternative combinations of production and imports that may be most efficient at different combinations of demand:

A) Imports of both 1 and 2
B) Production of 1, imports of 2
C) Imports of 1, production of 2
D) Production of both 1 and 2

In the analysis of sector 1 above, it was shown that it would be efficient to proceed from A to B to D as demand for metal products expands. I now wish to find all possible efficient expansion paths for this set of production functions.

The four alternatives can be expressed as combinations of the supply functions in Table 7, as follows:[33]

Alternative	Sector 1	Sector 2
A	i	i
B	iii	i
C	i	iii
D	iv	iv

The areas in which each alternative is most efficient can be delineated by solving each pair of equations simultaneously to find the boundary at which the two alternatives have equal cost. The results of this analysis are given in Figure 2.

Figure 2 shows that any one of the three sequences from A to D may be the most efficient, depending on the proportions of demand for the two commodities. The possibilities are illustrated by the three expansion paths shown. Path α represents the ratio $Y_1/Y_2 = 3.0$ and gives the sequence A-B-D as in the example in Figure 1. Path β has the ratio 1.0 and leads directly from A to D, while path γ has the ratio 0.5 and leads to A-C-D.

Although this model is much too simplified to permit a direct application of the results, it indicates at least that industrial development may take different paths. To take only Latin American examples, it may be suggested that, roughly speaking, Peru and Venezuela recently have been in area A, Argentina in area B, Chile in area C, and Brazil and Mexico in area D, as

---

[33] The combined cost function for alternative D is shown in the Appendix to be $S = (500 + 2.429\,Y_1) + (1000 + 2.782\,Y_2)$.

Figure 2

EFFECTS OF DEMAND ON OPTIMAL INVESTMENT

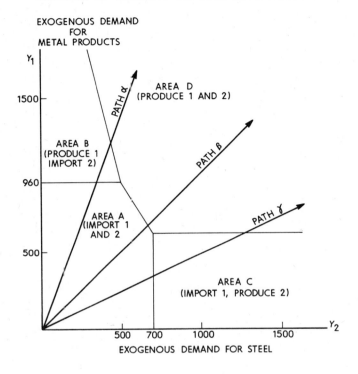

Table 8

A. PRODUCTION AND IMPORTS OF CRUDE STEEL*
(*1000 metric tons per year*)

	Production			Imports			1955 Imports as % of Total
	1946	*1950*	*1955*	*1946*	*1950*	*1955*	
Argentina	170	250	250	440	870	1450	85
Brazil	230	820	1160	430	400	400	26
Chile..........	30	70	340	100	80	90	14
Colombia......	0	10	40	120	190	300	88
Mexico........	270	390	730	270	370	340	32
Peru	0	0	0	—	—	190	100
Venezuela	—	—	50	340	700	860	93

* Source: ECLA. (All steel-producing countries in Latin America are included.)

B. RELATIVE COSTS OF PRODUCTION OF HYPOTHETICAL PLANTS†

	Capacity	Relative Cost‡	Import Prices§
Argentina	850	92	115
Brazil	716	85	110
Chile	230	82	111
Colombia	250	76	108
Mexico	430	83	108
Peru.	150	90	110
Venezuela	300	94	106
U.S.A.	1000	72	—

† Source: ECLA (13), p. 51. Capacity is based on domestic market in 1950.
‡ Based on a 250,000 ton plant in U.S. as 100. The figures do not include profit on the investment.
§ Based on Pittsburgh price plus freight in 1948.

indicated by the data in Table 8 on production and imports. All of the countries mentioned have local sources of iron ore, but the scale at which steel production becomes profitable varies with costs of production and imports.[34]

EVALUATION

The main purpose of this analysis has been to develop a model which could measure some of the principal effects of interdependence on investment decisions. In evaluating the results, it is necessary to see first whether the simplifications made in setting up the model change the nature of the conclusions. I will then try to point out some of the theoretical and practical implications of the results achieved.

The theoretical formulation

Effect of the simplifying assumptions. The most important simplifications made in the analysis appear to be the following:

i) *The omission of income effects.* In taking as given the final demands for the commodities studied, I have calculated the saving in factor use resulting from the coordination of investment rather than the increase in income generated. Factor use is measured in investment units, and so the increase in income achievable with the factors saved can be determined by multiplying the total by the marginal productivity of capital (0.25 in export prices). In example II C, an increase in output of 188 (9.9 percent of the outside demands) could be produced with the factors saved.

The argument for including additional income effects as part of external

---

[34] Steel production has now been established with government help in all these countries, but the timing may or may not have been optimal.

economies has not been stated very clearly. If market prices of labor or other resources exceed their opportunity costs, this fact is a source of difference between private and social benefit, but it is not necessarily a result of the interdependence of productive activities. If opportunity costs rather than market prices are used for labor and other resources, the method used here will include this effect in the calculated return to capital.[35]

The income effects which have not been included are those stemming from economies of scale in sectors outside the model. An increase in total demand will lower the average cost of production in each sector where scale economies are significant and will give rise to a real saving for the economy. These effects can be measured only in a model covering the whole economy in which resources rather than demands would be taken as given.

ii) *Agglomeration effects.* Agglomeration effects derive from the physical propinquity of different types of production. In part they consist of the Marshallian type of external economies—creation of a pool of skilled labor, common services, etc.—which can result from the expansion of one or several industries in one place. In part they are due to a reduction in the physical quantities of certain inputs required—particularly transport and storage. To take account of these factors adequately would require a regional model, but some of them can be included in the prices at which imports are assumed to be a substitute for domestic (or local) production. For example, it is estimated that a metalworking plant in Latin America which relies on imported steel has to keep a stock equal to six to nine months of consumption to allow for longer delivery times, while a plant using local supplies needs only a three-month supply.[36] The cost of carrying the larger stock should be charged to the import activity. (In the present example, an extra six-month supply of steel increases the capital coefficient by 0.1 and lowers profits in metalworking by 12 percent.)

iii) *Partial vs. general equilibrium.* The model used here is a truncated interindustry system in which the exogenous inputs used in the sectors studied were assumed to be available at constant prices. As the total inputs employed in the omitted sectors represent only about 15 percent of the total factor requirement, the use of a more complete model is not likely to change the calculation of labor and capital requirements significantly. Since I have assumed a given outside demand, the use of labor is changed only to the extent that production in the sectors analyzed is more or less labor-intensive in the aggregate than production in the export sectors for which it substitutes. It has been assumed here that the industrial complex would use less labor and

---

[35] This difference may, of course, prevent individual investors from reaching the socially desirable decisions.

[36] One suggestion of the importance of having a local supply of steel is the spurt in metalworking production which has accompanied the establishment of steel production in each Latin American country. (See ECLA (13), pp. 59–67.) It is hard to evaluate this experience, however, because the countries concerned suffer from balance of payments difficulties and imports are periodically restricted.

more capital than the primary production for export which it replaces. In a complete model, the accuracy of the initial assumption as to the relative value of labor and capital could be tested in a complete solution, but it cannot be said a priori whether the external economies calculated with equilibrium prices would be greater or smaller.

iv) *Substitution*. Substitution in production and consumption is omitted from the present model, although substitution in production could be allowed for by using alternative activities with varying input coefficients. Any substitution effects resulting from the price changes produced by investment coordination would add to the total economies achieved.

v) *Changes over time*. The preceding analysis has concentrated on one future period and ignored the fact that both demands and the expected efficiency of production with new techniques will change over time. In a more complete model, the discounted sum of values and costs in each alternative would have to be compared in order to determine the optimum timing for investment in each. Economies of scale cause plants to be built in advance of the growth of demand,[37] and hence the more complete analysis would lower the break-even point between domestic production and imports in both the individual and coordinated cases. It would probably be lowered more in the coordinated case, particularly if coordination justifies the use of a lower discount rate.

A second dynamic phenomenon, the fact that the efficiency of new plants which must train their labor force may be expected to increase over a considerable period, is usually allowed for in static analysis by assuming "normal" operating conditions at some time in the future. This simplification would not lead to a difference between the individual and coordinated decisions unless different discount rates are used.

Each of these simplifying assumptions is thus seen to be either neutral or to have the effect of understating the magnitude of the external economies resulting from coordination. Of the factors mentioned, agglomeration effects are probably the most important, as well as the hardest to measure. The other four could be included in the present type of model if it were desirable to do so.

Dynamic and static external economies. The analysis of the effects of investment necessarily assumes that a certain amount of net investment takes place in a growing economy. The cases studied have traced the difference between the response of individual investors to various factors that might make investment profitable—innovation, a change in relative factor prices, unused resources, or the growth of demand—and the optimal response of the whole economy. Since these differences are due mainly to the fact that present prices do not provide accurate guides to the optimal allocation of investment resources, it seems appropriate to call them dynamic external economies. If the further adjustments envisioned by static equilibrium theory take place, some (but not all) of these differences will disappear.

---

[37] This phenomenon has been investigated in Chenery (16).

In the examples of case I, the external economies resulting from innovation or from a fall in the price of one of the inputs are purely dynamic phenomena. If there is no further increase in demand, individual investors will eventually arrive at the same result as coordinated investment, since it is assumed that they are not barred by indivisibilities, ignorance, or other market imperfections. This does not mean that the economies of coordination are illusory even in this case, however. If a certain amount of investment is being made each year, the increase in output will be higher with coordination than without it, and the rate of growth will be greater.[38] The adjustment to a condition of static equilibrium may therefore never be made.

In the remaining example of case I, in which coordinated investment is profitable because of unused resources, the elimination of growth does not produce any tendency for individual investors to arrive at the same result as coordination because the reason for the existence of unused resources is the absence of complementary investment in several interrelated sectors. Neither is there any tendency for the difference to be eliminated in the examples of case II, where there are economies of scale.

The difference between the effects of the initial assumptions of growth (increasing factor supplies) and stationary equilibrium (given factor supplies) is shown in Fleming's criticism (7) of the use made of external economies by Rosenstein-Rodan and Nurkse. On static equilibrium assumptions, potential external economies from a given investment are largely offset by rising factor costs. When there is positive net investment and a growing labor force, the question is one of alternative uses of these additional factors, and there is no a priori assumption that a coordinated program which realizes external economies will utilize more of any factor than the alternative investments that would take place without coordination. In fact, it is quite possible that coordination will use less of both capital and labor to obtain the same result as uncoordinated investment.

Although I have been analyzing an essentially dynamic phenomenon, the method used has been that of comparative statics—comparing the results of alternative behavioral assumptions at a given moment in the future. The method is adequate for the assumption of perfect coordination, and also for the case where there is no tendency to depart from the existing pattern of production and prices, since in both cases the expectations of investors are fulfilled. An explicitly dynamic model would be needed to trace out intermediate cases when the expectations of investors are not fulfilled. I am, therefore, not able to estimate the extent to which uncoordinated investment falls short of the ideal, except in the case where it leads to a perpetuation of the existing sources of supply. All of my comparisons (except I A) were made with this limiting case of an unchanging production pattern.

---

[38] This case is studied in the context of a programming model for the whole economy in Chenery (17), where a difference in growth rates of 10 to 20 percent is suggested by the difference in marginal productivity of investment.

Importance of external economies

If my assumptions as to the economies of scale in the principal sectors are at all realistic, it can be concluded from the analysis (p. 354) that the economies of coordination are likely to be substantial in the case studied; furthermore, the external economies may be significantly greater if account is taken of the factors omitted from the analysis. I can only speculate as to the probable importance of external economies in other parts of the economy. Irrigation, for example, is similar to the steel-metalworking case in several respects: the existence of large economies of scale in the supply of inputs (dam building, etc.), the significance of the cost of the commodity produced (water) to agricultural processes using it, and the existence of immobile resources (dam sites, arid land) without alternative uses.

Other overhead facilities—transportation, power—resemble the steel mill in having large economies of scale, although the cost of their product is usually a smaller fraction of the cost of production of users. The most distinguishing feature of overhead facilities, however, is that their services must be supplied locally, and imports do not provide an alternative source. The case for planned investment in such facilities is, therefore, particularly strong, but the variety of uses which they can serve may make it less important to influence the decisions of individual investors in using industries.

Among manufacturing industries, the example studied is perhaps the most important case. Interrelated chemical process industries, such as petroleum refining and petrochemicals, may provide examples in which the economies of coordination are comparable, particularly when the intermediate products are not readily salable.

One may perhaps conclude from this kind of observation that dynamic external economies are sufficiently important to affect the optimal pattern of development throughout the transitional period from a primary-producing economy to one with well-developed overhead facilities and diversified industry. The effect of recognizing external economies is to make it more desirable to undertake interrelated activities together on an adequate scale than to increase production on all fronts simultaneously.

The existence of dynamic external economies has sometimes been used as an argument for the necessity of a large spurt in investment to get a process of cumulative growth underway. In a closed economy with economies of scale this might be true, but when a large proportion of manufactured goods is imported, emphasis can be placed first on one group of investments and then on another. In any case, it is doubtful that democratic governments have much leeway in picking the level of investment, and the more realistic problem is to make the best use of what is available.

Implications for development policy

The most important policy question raised by the preceding analysis is the extent to which the government has to intervene in order to secure the benefits of coordination. This is a very large subject, on which I have only a few scattered comments to offer. I will take up three types of mechanism for coordination: (i) integration under private control; (ii) the Lange-Lerner system of centrally administered prices; and (iii) direct control of investment.

Private integration. The main form of private coordination is the integration of several investments under a single ownership or control. It is likely to take place where the external economies are substantial and the sectors involved are not too numerous. The exploitation of natural resources provides a common example; mining, specialized transport, and primary processing are often developed together in order to produce a salable commodity when the domestic processing industry does not already exist.

From the public point of view, the drawback to private coordination is the large amount of capital required for an integrated investment, which is often not available to a single firm in an underdeveloped country, and which, if made, leads to a monopolistic position because of the difficulties of entry. These arguments do not apply so strongly to foreign investment for export, where such integration is very common.

With private integration of investment, some of the benefits of coordination are likely to be lost because the capacity of the auxiliary facilities (machine shops, power, transport, etc.) will usually be designed to satisfy the needs of the integrated firm only rather than to serve other potential users. The investment which might be profitable in other sectors, therefore, may not take place.

Private coordination is likely to occur only when it is institutionally feasible to capture a substantial part of the external economies through integration, price discrimination, or otherwise. In the steel complex, the integration of the sectors supplying the steel mill is quite common in underdeveloped countries (although limited in the U.S. by the antitrust laws), but the integration of steel production and metalworking is less common because of the diversity of products; it is also less desirable socially because the monopoly problem would be made much worse.

Indirect coordination through administered prices. The discussion of the Lange-Lerner system of administratively controlled prices and decentralized production decisions has been concerned with the ability of such a system to maintain an efficient level of production in each industry.[39] Here the question is whether or not a correct calculation of future equilibrium prices would lead individual investors to the optimal investment decisions.

In my case I, with constant returns to scale, the shadow prices of the optimal solution would lead to the right choice of investments, but not necessarily to the right magnitudes.[40] In order to determine the proper prices, the government would also have to calculate the corresponding quantities, however, and publication of these estimates might furnish adequate guides to the probable demand for various products. This is one of the main functions

---

[39] The argument and the exceptions to it are summarized in Bator (9).
[40] See Dorfman, Samuelson, and Solow (10), pp. 61–63.

of a development program. The actual path by which the economy would move from its initial position to a future equilibrium would have to be explored in a dynamic model, but it would appear that, where economies of scale are not too great, prices could serve as the main instrument of coordination, unless the lags in private responses in critical sectors were too long. (The administrative problems raised by this procedure are serious but will not be explored here.)

Direct coordination of investment. Although marginal cost pricing (combined with a subsidy or other method of covering total cost) leads to the optimum scale of use of an existing capital good when there are economies of scale—as in the classical railroad examples—it is not adequate to produce the optimum amount of investment in new facilities. To secure the optimal choice of investments in the examples of case II, the total cost of various alternatives must be compared. As in the short-run analysis, the marginal conditions determine the optimal scale of output, but the total cost calculation determines whether the investment is desirable at all.[41]

The policy implication of this result is that the magnitude of the initial investment as well as the price of output may have to be controlled in order to secure all the external economies.[42] If the optimum plant could be built by successive expansions, there would be less argument for determining the optimum scale in advance, but in the range of output where economies of scale are most important—whether in dam construction, power plants, or steel mills—this is unlikely to be the case.

Given, then, that some control of the magnitude of investment may be needed, it may be possible to limit it to a few key sectors in an industrial complex. In my example, the construction of the optimum size steel mill, power plant, and transport facilities would make profitable to private investors the optimal investment in coal, ore production, and metalworking. Of course, if any of these products is monopolized, the price will be higher and the quantity of output lower than the optimum. It is particularly important to prevent monopoly pricing of inputs to other industries because, unless the effects of decreasing costs are externalized, the investment in other sectors may not take place.

The sectors in which correct initial investments are critical to securing the optimal results are those having the most significant economies of scale and those for which imports do not provide a substitute. These properties are combined in most overhead facilities, and the case for government ownership or control has long been recognized. As between steel and metalworking in the present example, establishment of either one might make the other

---

[41] The situation is no better at the level of mathematical programming, where no systematic procedure exists for distinguishing a local maximum from the optimum solution other than the comparison of all possibilities. See Arrow and Hurwicz (18).

[42] The question of the optimal scale of output and the feasibility of various forms of marginal-cost pricing are discussed for the case of irrigation by Margolis (19).

profitable, but the greater economy of scale[43] and monopoly position of steel argue for its selection.

The preceding discussion should not be taken as an endorsement of indiscriminate building of steel mills or other basic industries through government intervention. What has been shown is that the benefits to the economy of such investments may be understated by their expected profitability to an individual investor, and that coordinated planning may tip the balance in their favor. In the absence of any measure of the quantitative significance of external economies, however, the benefits of such investments may easily be overestimated by the governments of underdeveloped countries. The main purpose of this paper has been to present a framework for objective comparison of the alternatives. Given elastic demand and supply and a somewhat lower capital coefficient in the export sector of the example used here, the rational policy would be to increase exports, notwithstanding the existence of unused mineral resources and potential external economies.

APPENDIX

THE CALCULATION OF PRICES AND TOTAL COSTS

Case I: No economies of scale

Two types of prices are used in the solutions given in Table 3. *Present prices* are those to which the individual investor responds in deciding whether to invest. *Future prices* are those which satisfy the conditions of marginal-cost pricing given by equation 11 after a given set of investments has been made. Present prices are also assumed to satisfy equation 11 for the sectors included in the model, although the exogenous inputs may or may not have prices representing their opportunity costs. Future prices are therefore equal to present prices if the source of supply is unchanged, as in example B, line (5).

The determination of the optimum pattern of investment with coordination of all sectors is (in case I) a problem in linear programming. It can be stated as follows: to minimize total cost of production, as measured by the prices of the exogenous inputs, subject to the restrictions in equations 1–8 of Table 1. The dual variables (u_j) or shadow prices of this solution are identical with the future prices and may be defined as:[44]

$$u_j = \sum_i^{(i \neq j)} a_{ij} u_i + c_j \qquad (j = 1 \dots 7) \tag{13}$$

where c_j is the cost of the exogenous inputs (8–10) in each activity.

---

[43] The economy of scale in some sectors of metalworking (e.g., automobile production) may be equally great and justify government action.

[44] See Dorfman, Samuelson, and Solow (10), Chapter 7. The equation is the same as eq. 1 with c_j substituted for the cost of exogenous imports, since $a_{jj} = 1.0$ by assumption.

The solution to equation 13 can be determined in a number of ways, including the iterative procedure suggested above and the use of the inverse of the basis. The second method is given by the following equation:

$$u_j = \sum_i r_{ij} c_i \qquad (14)$$

where r_{ij} is the element in row i and column j of the inverse matrix. For the optimum solution, in which all commodities are domestically produced, the first two columns in the inverse and the calculation of the corresponding shadow prices are shown in Table 9.

As indicated earlier, the total cost of supplying the exogenous demand is given by:

$$S = u_1 Y_1 + u_2 Y_2. \qquad (15)$$

Case II: Economies of scale

With decreasing average costs, the dual variables can still be defined by equation 13 with c_j taken as marginal cost, since I have assumed constant marginal cost over the relevant range of output. The total cost of production must include all constant terms in the input functions (12) of Table 5, however. The equation for total cost of supply then becomes:

$$S = \sum_i \bar{f}_i + u_1 Y_1 + u_2 Y_2 \qquad (16)$$

where the constant terms $\bar{f}_i$ apply to all sectors supplied from domestic production. The values of u_1 and u_2 for case II are also computed in Table 9. Substituting them in equation 16 gives the total cost with coordination as

$$S = 1500 + 2.429\, Y_1 + 2.782\, Y_2. \qquad (16a)$$

To derive the equations in Table 7 above, I assume the outside demands in one sector to be constant and determine the cost of supplying various levels of demand in the other sector. The overhead costs are allocated by holding

Table 9

CALCULATION OF DUAL VARIABLES IN CASES I AND II

Rows	Columns in Inverse Matrix		c_i	Case I Sector 1	Case I Sector 2	c_i	Case II Sector 1	Case II Sector 2
(i)	r_{i1}	r_{i2}	c_i	$c_i r_{i1}$	$c_i r_{i2}$	c_i	$c_i r_{i1}$	$c_i r_{i2}$
1	1.000	0	2.26	2.260	0	1.76	1.760	0
2	.222	1.007	3.27	.726	3.293	2.27	.504	2.286
3	.018	.080	1.25	.022	.100	1.10	.020	.088
4	.016	.025	3.99	.062	.101	2.74	.043	.069
5	.028	.113	1.54	.043	.174	1.34	.038	.151
6	.029	.083	4.06	.117	.337	2.26	.065	.188
Dual variables (u_j)			—	3.231	4.005	—	2.429	2.782

Table 10

CALCULATION OF DUAL VARIABLES FOR EQUATION 17*

Inputs	Sector 1 Input Cost			Sector 2 Input Cost	
	Case (ii)	(iii)	(iv)	Case (ii)	(iii) + (iv)
2	.92	.92	.61	—	—
3–6	.10	.06	.06	.95	.51
7	.51	5.1	.51	.27	.27
c_j	1.25	1.25	1.25	2.00	2.00
u_j	$\overline{2.78}$	$\overline{2.74}$	$\overline{2.43}$	$\overline{3.22}$	$\overline{2.78}$

* Each entry is the corresponding $(a_{ij}u_i)$ from equation 13.

the cost of supplying the other (fixed) demand constant at the cost of imports, which is subtracted from the total supply cost. The equations in Table 7 can therefore be derived from equations 16 as follows:

$$S_1 = S - 4.2\ Y_2, \qquad S_2 = S - 3.26\ Y_1. \qquad (17)$$

The calculation of the dual variables u_j from equation 13 for each assumption is shown in Table 10.

Assumptions.

i) *Imports.* The supply functions are merely the cost of imports.

ii) *Uncoordinated investment.* The values u_i are taken from Table 3, line 4; c_j is the marginal direct cost from Table 5.

iii) *Coordination of sectors 3–6.* The u_i are those of the coordinated solution for sectors 3–6 and the same as (ii) for sector 2.

iv) *Coordination of all sectors.* The values of u_j for each sector are those computed in Table 9. In this case, where there is domestic production in both sectors 1 and 2, equations 17 become:

$$S_1 = S - 4.2\ \ Y_2 = 1500 + 2.429\ Y_1 - 1.428\ Y_2,$$
$$S_2 = S - 3.26\ Y_1 = 1500 + 2.782\ Y_2 - .831\ Y_1. \qquad (17a)$$

(These equations apply only over the range for which imports are the economical alternative without coordination and in which domestic production in the other sector would be profitable with coordination.)

REFERENCES

1. P. N. ROSENSTEIN-RODAN, "Problems of Industrialization in Eastern and South-Eastern Europe," *Economic Journal,* June–September, 1943.
2. R. NURKSE, *Problems of Capital Formation in Underdeveloped Countries.* Blackwell, Oxford, 1953.

3. W. A. Lewis, "Economic Development with Unlimited Supplies of Labor," *Manchester School,* May 1954.

4. H. W. Singer, "Economic Progress in Underdeveloped Countries," *Social Research*, March 1949.

5. G. Myrdal, *Economic Theory and Underdeveloped Regions*. Duckworth, London, 1957.

6. T. Scitovsky, *"Two Concepts of External Economies," *Journal of Political Economy,* April 1954.

7. M. Fleming, "External Economies and the Doctrine of Balanced Growth," *Economic Journal*, June 1955.

8. H. W. Arndt, "External Economies in Economic Growth," *Economic Record*, November 1955.

9. F. Bator, "The Anatomy of Market Failure," *Quarterly Journal of Economics*, August 1958.

10. R. Dorfman, P. A. Samuelson, and R. M. Solow, *Linear Programming and Economic Analysis*. McGraw-Hill, New York, 1958.

11. H. B. Chenery and T. Watanabe, "International Comparisons of the Structure of Production," *Econometrica*, January 1959.

12. W. D. Evans, "Input-Output Computations," in T. Barna (ed.), *The Structural Interdependence of the Economy*. Wiley, New York, 1956.

13. United Nations, Economic Commission for Latin America, A Study of the Iron and Steel Industry in Latin America, II. G. 3, Vol. 1, 1954.

14. H. E. Wessel, "New Graph Correlates Operating Labor Data for Chemical Processes," and C. H. Chilton, "'Six-Tenths Factor' Applies to Complete Plant Costs," in *Data and Methods of Cost Estimation*, a collection of reprints from *Chemical Engineering*, 1953, 1952.

15. H. B. Chenery, "The Application of Investment Criteria," *Quarterly Journal of Economics*, February 1953.

16. H. B. Chenery, "Overcapacity and the Acceleration Principle," *Econometrica*, January 1952.

17. H. B. Chenery, "The Role of Industrialization in Development Programs," *American Economic Association Proceedings*, May 1955.

18. K. J. Arrow and L. Hurwicz, "Decentralization and Computation in Resource Allocation," in R. W. Pfouts (ed.), *Essays in Economics and Econometrics*. University of North Carolina Press, Chapel Hill, n.d.

19. J. Margolis, "Welfare Criteria, Pricing and Decentralization of a Public Service," *Quarterly Journal of Economics*, August 1957.

Secondary benefits, external economies, and the justification of public investment[*][†]

JULIUS MARGOLIS

One argument often used to justify public services is that the benefits of the activity cannot be limited to the direct recipients of the services—those who would purchase the product if it were privately produced. These benefits, which are presumed to accrue to a large sector of the nation, are referred to as secondary or indirect benefits. There are many formulations of these secondary benefits. This paper will focus on the use of this concept and its measurement by the Bureau of Reclamation. In the case of the Bureau of Reclamation the development of this concept and its measurement is more than an argument for an extension of the public sector. The measurement is claimed to be part of the planning process, since it is supposed to enter into the determination of the scale of investment in water projects and the allocation of public funds among projects.

There are several other formulations of the appropriate concept of secondary benefits in use in federal agencies, but these will receive only passing attention.[1] As background it should be mentioned that those who advocate the use of the secondary benefits concept in project justification are today on the defensive. The current position of several staff coordinating

* *The Review of Economics and Statistics*, 39(1957): pp. 284–91. Corrected by the author. Reprinted by courtesy of the author and *The Review of Economics and Statistics*.

† This work was supported by the Office of Naval Research under contract N6 onr-25133.

[1] For a sample of different viewpoints see: Bureau of Reclamation, *Draft of Revision of Reclamation Manual, Vol. XIII, Benefits and Costs*, June 27, 1951; Federal Inter-Agency River Basin Committee, Subcommittee on Benefits and Costs, *Revised Statement on Secondary Benefits*, January 1952; J. M. Clark, M. M. Kelso, and E. Grant, *Secondary or Indirect Benefits of Water-Use Projects*, Report of Panel of Consultants to the Bureau of Reclamation; S. V. Ciriacy-Wantrup, "Benefit-Cost Analysis and Public Resource Development," *Journal of Farm Economics*, xxxvii (November 1955); House Committee on Public Works, Subcommittee to Study Civil Works, *Economic Evaluation of Federal Water Resources Development Projects*, 82d Cong., 2d Sess., House Committee Print No. 24, 1952.

agencies in Washington is to minimize the importance of secondary benefits. In this paper we shall restrict our attention to one type of public investment— dams and distribution systems for irrigation projects. The conclusions of this paper are that the procedures followed by the government agencies are confusing and incorrect, but that secondary benefits can be significant. The proper framework within which to discuss the secondary benefits is the theory of external economies.

I

1.1 Projects in the area of water resources development are expected to justify themselves by the computation of a benefits/costs ratio. In general the benefits assigned to a project are the difference in the national income with and without the project. The increase in the national income is then broken into two groups, primary and secondary benefits. The primary benefits are the increases in the net incomes of the project farmers, after a full allowance has been taken for their costs including an imputed return on their own capital, land, and labor. No one challenges this increase in productivity as a benefit though there persist unresolved problems of how to measure the income, how to forecast the increase, and how to compare the income of different time periods. The secondary benefits are quite different.[2]

1.2 At a general level there is little disagreement about the meaning to be attached to the concept of secondary benefits. This is surprising since there does not exist a clear theoretical or statistically operational definition. "Secondary benefits . . . are the values added by incurring secondary costs in activities stemming from or induced by the project."[3] Almost all parties to the discussion of the role of secondary benefits accept this two-way classification of "stemming from and induced by," though there is no defense of the meaningfulness of the classification. Essentially the "stemming from" benefits are the net incomes in the secondary activities which transport, process, or sell the products of the project area. Benefits "induced by" the project are less clearly stated. Their major characteristic is that they are the net incomes in activities which sell to the project area, though in some formulations they include the incomes of the activities whose products or services are utilized by those who derive income from the activities involved in producing, transporting, processing, or selling the products of the project.[4]

1.3 The Manual of the Bureau of Reclamation presents the secondary benefits in the following detail:

---

[2] The secondary benefits discussed in this paper refer to national benefits. There is another formulation of secondary benefits which refer to local benefits, the growth in economic activities in the area of the project. For an example of the analysis of local secondary benefits see: H. V. Holje, R. E. Huffman, and C. F. Kraenzel, *Indirect Benefits of Irrigation Development, Methodology and Measurement* (Montana State College, Agricultural Experiment Station, Technical Bulletin No. 517, March 1956).

[3] Federal Inter-Agency River Basin Committee, *Proposed Practices for Economic Analysis of River Basin Projects* (Washington, D.C., May 1950), 10.

[4] F.I.A.R.B.C., *Revised Statement on Secondary Benefits*, 2–3.

.5 Indirect irrigation benefits comprise the increase in:

    A. Profits of local wholesalers and retailers from handling increased sales of farm products consumed locally off the project without processing.

    B. Profits of all other enterprises between the farm and the final consumer, from handling, processing, and marketing increased sales of farm products locally and elsewhere.

    C. Profits of all enterprises from supplying goods and services for increased farm purchases for family living and production expenses.

    D. Land value of local residential property.

.6 Like direct farm benefits, indirect irrigation benefits will be calculated from summaries of farm budget data representing future conditions with and without the project. Indirect benefit factors will be applied to increases or decreases in the value of individual commodities listed in the budget summaries. The indirect benefit from increased land value of local residential property will be calculated separately.

.7 The following factors will be used to derive indirect irrigation benefits from summaries of farm budget data:

Indirect Benefit A	5 percent	
Indirect Benefit B		
Cotton	83	"
Wool	78	"
Grain (wheat, oats, corn, barley)	48	"
Oil crops (flax, cottonseed,		
soybeans)	30	"
Sugar beets	26	"
Fruits and vegetables	24	"
Dry beans	23	"
Rice	13	"
Livestock (meat)	11	"
Seed crops	10	"
Dairy products	7	"
Poultry products	6	"
Indirect Benefit C	18	"

A factor of 4 percent will be applied to the increase in land value of local residential property to derive an annual value for Indirect Benefit D.

.8 Improvement in noncommercial land value of property in towns on or near irrigated areas will create an indirect benefit to persons other than project farmers. For example, twenty acres of unimproved land worth $100 an acre might be subdivided for residential purposes and sell for $800 an acre. Higher-grade use of the land would then have increased its value from $2,000 to $16,000. The indirect benefit would be 4 percent of the $14,000 increase, or $560 per year.[5]

---

[5] U.S. Bureau of Reclamation, *Draft of Revision of Reclamation Manual Vol. XIII, Benefits and Cost*, June 27, 1951, ch. 2.2. In addition to these indirect benefits they also claim intangible public benefits as: increased farming opportunities—$1,000 for each new family farm; employment of seasonal or otherwise unemployed labor; the increase in property tax payments as a community service benefit, ...

1.4 It is difficult to characterize in analytical terms the above-listed benefits. The first confusion surrounds the word "profits" which is used in the Manual. Other statements indicate that the incremental incomes are not restricted to profits but include "wages, and salaries, rents, interest and profits before income taxes."[6] Explanations of an earlier version of the Manual clearly state that the increments to be included in indirect benefits are to include all factor incomes.[7] But the secondary benefit factors to be applied to gross value of farm products used in the earlier Bureau reports are uniformly greater than the factors in the Manual. This would indicate that only profits are used in the Manual.[8] But in some cases the differences are too small to support the belief that there has been a change in definition The cotton and wool factors fell from 124 and 91 to 83 and 78 percent, respectively. Clearly this is not a change from all income payments to profits. But compare the changes in livestock and dairy products, which fell from 55 and 71 to 11 and 6 percent, respectively. Whichever definition is used in practice, the restriction of the benefits to the profits of the supplying and processing industries is more consistent with the rationale of the concept than the use of all factor incomes.

1.5 If all factor incomes were included in benefits, and this was certainly done prior to 1951, the secondary benefits could be best characterized as the value of the incremental product on the project farms, valued as a final product in the national income sense, less the increased income on the farm attributable to the incremental project waters. With the inclusion of the primary direct benefits, the total benefits would be the increases in project farms' product valued as a final product. The Bureau procedure would value the final product at factor costs rather than at market prices. To see the applicability of this characterization, consider the product produced on the farm and valued at the price it brings when it enters into the final product as inventory accumulation, exports, or in the pantries or closets of households. This price is equal to the sum of all incomes paid out to the productive factors plus the indirect taxes paid. If we summed all the incomes associated with bringing a physical product to the point where it reaches final consumption, it would be equivalent to valuing it at factor costs. This involved method is used by the Bureau if "profits" refer to factor incomes.

1.6 If "profits" refer to the net income of the firms processing the farm output or supplying the farm input, then implicitly the Bureau has valued (primary plus secondary benefits) the incremental product as final product

[6] House Committee on Public Works, *op. cit.*, 15. The description of the Bureau of Reclamation's methods in this report was published a year and a half after the Manual was published.

[7] F.I.A.R.B.C., *Measurement Aspects of Benefit-Cost Practices* (Washington, D.C., November 1948).

[8] Mr. Alfred R. Golzé, Chief of the Division of Program Coordination and Finance of the Bureau of Reclamation says that, "*In general*, the Bureau has not used wages and interest in computing indirect benefits." Private letter of June 25, 1956. Italics added.

at business (including farm) net income costs. This may seem a stranger measure than factor costs, but it is more defensible, though it is rejected in this article. It is more defensible since it assumes that there is an opportunity cost to most of the complementary resources in either further processing the farm product or preparing the farm inputs. These factors are paid according to their productivity in producing the agricultural final product, and their productivity in these activities approximates their productivity elsewhere. Therefore the payments these factors receive cannot be claimed as incomes created because of the incremental project output. The logic of this argument should extend to the factor payment, profits, since there is no reason to assume that there will be anything other than normal profits in the complementary industries.

1.7 The substitution of profits for factor incomes goes a long way toward surrendering the secondary benefits as a major contribution of the project. The Federal Inter-Agency River Basin Committee has gone even further in reducing secondary benefits. They retain the same structure of "stemming from" and "induced by" benefits. They expand the concept of induced benefits to include quasi-Keynesian effects.

1.8 Induced benefits in the case of the Bureau are the profits of the suppliers of the project area, while the induced benefits of the F.I.A.R.B.C. include the incomes to the suppliers of the materials and services used in producing, processing, transporting, and marketing the materials grown on the farms. Though the F.I.A.R.B.C.'s stream of benefits exceeds the Bureau's they quickly reduce them by saying that the alternative investment undertaken by the government other than the irrigation project in question would have given rise to a similar stream of benefits. The secondary benefits without the project are subtracted from those with the project to derive the net secondary benefits attributable to the project. The net secondary benefits are linked to the project's primary benefits. The proportion of the secondary benefits which they credit to a project is determined by the ratio of net primary project benefits (farm net income) to the government's project costs. Why this ratio has any meaning in terms of secondary benefits is not given. It would seem irrelevant since the secondary benefits are presumed to be a function of gross farm production rather than the rate of return on public investment in the project. Therefore the secondary benefits with the project as against the secondary benefits without the project have no relationships to the amount of primary benefits or the ratio of primary benefits to project costs.

1.9 Though the F.I.A.R.B.C. reduces the amount of secondary benefits by this peculiar linkage to the rate of return on the project, they are in agreement with the Bureau of Reclamation in claiming that secondary benefits develop because of expansion in complementary industries. How legitimate is this claim? Three types of arguments can be used in defense. First is the crude argument, implicit in the measurement procedures adopted, which state that supply creates its own demand. A second level of argument is that there exists a large volume of unemployed resources for which the opportunity costs are zero. A final level of argument, which is implicitly used though more frequently implicitly rejected, is the existence of external economies. The latter argument, we would hold, is the only valid defense of the inclusion of secondary benefits, but unfortunately economic analysis is still too primitive to allow for an accounting of these external economies.

II

2.1 The first argument, supply creating its own demand, is on the surface absurd. The Bureau of Reclamation assumes that there will be an increase in production on the farms in the project area and that this increment will be a net increase of production of all similar goods. Further they assume that the increment of goods will be processed and will require for processing complementary inputs used under conditions of constant costs so that the same incomes per unit of commodity will be generated. These assumptions violate the basic axioms of economic behavior. If we ignore the reality of agricultural price supports and surpluses which make a mockery of using current market prices as a basis to evaluate agricultural products, any expansion of production must lead to the competitive reduction of agricultural incomes and production elsewhere. Therefore no more goods would be processed and no further complementary inputs would be required. In the short run, if we accept the common assumptions of inelasticity in the demand for most agricultural goods and the immobility of farmers, we can expect a reduction of both farm and market prices with reductions in incomes for both farms and processing industries.

2.2 Price and income reduction may not be necessary consequences if the economy is expanding and demand curves are generally shifting upward so that the additional project products would not force a reduction in prices. But what would happen if the project had not been initiated? Agricultural prices would have risen and there would have been an expansion of agricultural production thus giving rise to all of the indirect benefits credited to the irrigation project.

2.3 There is one possible defense of the above argument. It could be claimed that the irrigation project is more efficient and that for the same investment more production is forthcoming, thus restraining the rise in price, allowing more sales, and thereby more employment in the secondary industries. In this case secondary benefits are dependent upon the existence of an economically justified primary investment in the project works and upon a further assumption that the additional employment of resources to be used had no alternatives. Both are probably unwarranted. The large public investment in irrigation systems in the West if valued solely in terms of the returns to the project farmers is probably inefficient.[9] The assumption of no

---

[9] We cannot hope to document this point in this brief article. One striking evidence of the inefficient investment is the poor repayment histories of the projects. See Bureau of Reclamation, *Repayment Histories and Payout Schedules*, 2d ed. (Washington, D.C., 1953).

alternatives to the resources used in secondary activities would similarly be improper, given the argument of the government that the projects are based upon assumptions of general expansion and growth in the economy.

2.4 The second defense of indirect benefits is closely related to the above. It is argued that there exists a large body of unemployed resources. Therefore there exist no opportunity costs for the use of these resources. Therefore the costs assigned to factor inputs in industries servicing the project area, as well as the "stemming from" activities, should not be so considered but are instead benefits. In national income terms, the project product is being valued at market prices, and since the inputs complementary to the project product have no alternatives the full market value could be assigned to the project product. This argument violates in general the assumption underlying the irrigation program—that there is a general growth of the economy requiring further agricultural goods.

2.5 Further one might question the basic assumption underlying this argument—that employment effects should be considered in choosing irrigation projects. Irrigation projects are very inefficient countercyclical measures. They take a long period in planning and in construction so that they have none of the flexibility necessary for countercyclical programming. Further, it is certainly not obvious that one should encourage certain projects just because they give employment to otherwise unemployed resources. It might be more in line with social policy that the resources be made more mobile and move to more efficient locations or occupations. Further, even if the irrigation projects could be used in an effective countercyclical program there is no reason to assume that the unemployed resources which would be employed would be any greater than in many other forms of public or private investment.

III

3.1 The final argument, the stress on possible external economies, is defensible but it cannot be used to defend the measurements used by the Bureau of Reclamation or the F.I.A.R.B.C. The conventional formulation of Marshallian external economies and diseconomies is to restrict them to the changes in the supply price of factor inputs to a firm as the industry expands. It is common to extend the frame of reference beyond firm-industry relationships and discuss firm-local-area or industry-national economy relationships. In these cases the expansion of an industry may not lead to a reduction in factor costs to that industry, but external economies are said to exist if there are reductions in factor costs to other industries. Beyond this simple statement of external economies and diseconomies the discussion becomes very confused.[10]

---

[10] There are repeated references to external economies in economic writing but Ellis and Fellner were being overcautious when they "confessed that the theoretical treatment of this subject still leaves much to be desired." H. Ellis and W. Fellner, "External Economies and Diseconomies," *American Economic Review*, xxxiii (1943), reprinted in G. Stigler and K. Boulding, *Readings in Price Theory* (New York, 1952), 255.

3.2 It is usual to distinguish between technological and pecuniary external economies. When the discussion centers around the problems of the divergence between social and private costs and benefits the writers point out that they are

interested in what have been referred to as technological economies or diseconomies of scale, i.e. economies or diseconomies in the use of resources by other firms (usually taken to be in the same industry) resulting from an increase in the output of one particular firm. There are also what have been called pecuniary diseconomies of scale (which caused the main difficulties in the early discussion of Marshall and Pigou), and which refer to increases in money costs of production resulting from increases in the remuneration of those factors already employed as their scarcity value increases with increasing output of the firm in which they are employed. These costs are not directly relevant to the question of the technical efficiency with which the goods are produced and hence they do not enter into the discussion of social cost.[11]

The pecuniary external economies are not social benefits since they are transfers of rent among specialized factors. The gains to one group are offset by the losses of another group—there is no net increase in the efficiency of the economy.[12] In the case of technological external economies we do have a set of benefits to the nation which extend beyond the product of the firm or the industry.

3.3 The sources of external economies as stressed in the literature are manifold. The "balanced growth" literature relies on an assumption of a growth of productivity as the size of the market increases. Allyn Young elaborated on a theme of Adam Smith—the division of labor. The division of labor is necessary for increasing returns. The degree of specialization is a function of the extent of the market. Young was explaining some of the causes of historical growth and thereby correctly assumed that the economy was never at an equilibrium. This theme has been continued by the more recent writers, though they have added the moral for planners that induced growth along many lines would be self-justifying. Rosenstein-Rodan in addition to the Marshallian external economies adds the reduction in risk attendant on the planned creation of a complementary industrial system.[13] This argument has provided much of the basis for the espousal of balanced growth which sometimes is urged independently of considerations of economies of scale.

3.4 The usual assumption made in the balanced growth and development

---

[11] W. J. Baumol, *Welfare Economics and the Theory of the State* (Cambridge, 1952), 32.

[12] See Roland McKean, *Efficiency in Government Through Systems Analysis* (New York: John Wiley, 1958), pp. 136–43, for many illustrations of transfers involved in "pecuniary spillovers." There are many cases of mixed pecuniary and technological economies where, due to market imperfections, prices would be an imperfect indicator of social costs and benefits. Tibor Scitovsky analyzes the cases of indivisibilities and incomplete information in "Two Concepts of External Economies," *Journal of Political Economy*, April 1954.

[13] P. N. Rosenstein-Rodan, "Problems of Industrialization of Eastern and South-Eastern Europe," *Economic Journal*, LIII (1943), 206)

literature is that there exists a large volume of underemployed resources, both human and natural. At the same time there exists a storehouse of technology which is not being applied. The problem, as seen in this literature, is one of social engineering to program the installation of the technology in order to convert the underutilized resources to optimal employment. The possibilities of external economies in this case are tremendous. Rather than marginal effects, any new investment bringing new industrial techniques is a school of industrial, financial, and marketing techniques for labor, managers, and entrepreneurs. The costs of the plant are markets for utilized factors. These "external economies" are also present in the alternative model offered to underdeveloped areas—the development of services to facilitate the basic export industries. Government will often undertake this form of "social overhead" capital on the assumption that this will improve the competitive position of their export-oriented industries and the presence of a large volume of underutilized resources will enable the expanded export base to generate investment in many allied fields. Care must be taken that the claimed external economies do not degenerate into an equivalance with some sort of "snowballing" effect. If the "snowball" effects do involve opportunity costs, if they use factors which have alternative uses, the benefits of the external economies are likely to be overstated.

3.5 Though one might establish grounds for the presumption of external economies in the case of underdeveloped areas, is it reasonable to assume that the same type of reasoning would be applicable in the United States? First let us recall that there are no special "economic laws" dealing with external economies for underdeveloped areas. In every case it must be established that we are not dealing with transfers but with a reorganization of the economy which makes better use of resources. Therefore, the question cannot be answered by a statement that the United States is developed and therefore the analysis is not applicable, but we must look at the specific circumstances and see whether the investment creates external economies.

3.6 The secondary benefits listed by the Bureau of Reclamation are instances of complementarities, but complementarities can result in both simple transfers as well as more efficient organizations. We must assume that the alternative to irrigated agriculture would be an expansion of production of similar agricultural products in other regions of the country. The case for secondary benefits would then depend upon the presumption of special conditions in the West giving rise to external economies, or the existence of a supply of underutilized resources in the West. The "stemming from" benefits extending to processing and marketing at distant points would be indefensible since the alternative production would bring the same volume of materials to the market.

3.7 The question therefore is reduced to one of spreading fertilizer in the Mid-West or water in the arid West. On a primary benefits basis the choice probably would be for the Mid-West. The return to the Mid-Western farm would be greater than the return to a Western irrigated farm. A study which compared returns in Mecklenburg County, Virginia, with those on the Columbia Basin Project of central Washington estimated that 7.5 acres of land could be cleared and developed in Mecklenburg County for the cost of each acre brought into production on the Columbia Basin Project.[14] The defense of the irrigation project in terms of the goal of economic efficiency would have to rely on secondary benefits arising from the use of unused resources, or external economies enabling a more efficient organization of the resources.

3.8 In general it would seem plausible to argue that regional redistributions of income through direct transfers or government expenditures would have positive efficiency effects. The highly unequal per capita incomes among the states imply that a reshuffling of resources would bring the economy closer to a Paretian optimum. The inequality indicates a distance from equilibrium which is a necessary condition for the developmental types of external economies. The underdeveloped regions usually have a much lower capital to labor or capital to land ratio. The usual proposal is that the mobile factors shift. Irrigation by the federal government is essentially a capital subsidy to an underdeveloped region and therefore a shift of capital. Commonly these regions lack capital, entrepreneurial talents, highly skilled workers, and similar necessary ingredients for an expanding economy.[15] The irrigation expenditures have induced effects not only by the employment of labor on construction and operations but also in bringing capital funds in the area. The farmers selected for the project are expected to be capable of managing the difficult tasks of the more intensive irrigated farming. Labor skill will be improved and capital will become more accessible in an area which lacked them. The more dense settlements characteristic of irrigated farming will permit improvements in transportation, reductions in public costs, and population growth extending the market. All of these are conditions of economies of scale.

3.9 An additional consideration might be the pattern of growth of the Western states where the projects are located. Their population has grown rapidly relative to the United States, but their manufacturing industries have lagged. They export lumber and agricultural products and import manufactured goods. They are sparsely settled so that the distances between urban

---

[14] R. Ulrich, "Relative Costs and Benefits of Land Reclamation in the Humid Southeast and the Semiarid West," *Journal of Farm Economics*, xxxv (February 1953), 72.

[15] In a study of comparative returns to farming in Montana, Iowa, and Alabama it was concluded: "Our estimates are for farmers in Alabama with capital in a form representing 'poor techniques.' The same amount of capital in 'improved techniques' might give much higher returns. While Alabama is near the 'tail end' in capital productivity, returns on this resource could actually be very great if more capital were also invested in educational resources for farmers; more capital also would allow livestock production on a commercial basis rather than as a semihousehold enterprise. A reorganization of agriculture to give larger farms would also bring about a higher productivity of capital" E. O. Heady and R. Shaw, "Resource Returns and Productivity Coefficient in Selected Farming Areas," *Journal of Farm Economics*, xxxvi (May 1954), 253.

places are large. How do irrigation projects fit into this picture? The increased crops provide an expansion of the export base of the area, but this one may claim is only a regional benefit—a transfer—and can only be used to justify national investment if it leads to such external economies as increased capital funds, transport economies, enhanced labor and entrepreneurial skills, and so on. The projects result in a shift to an intensive agriculture with more dense settlement patterns. New urban places develop and older urban places grow. This development has two consequences. The urbanization is an extension of the market which permits economies of scale for the development of manu- facturing in the West, and it also enables efficiencies in transportation to be realized. These are less likely to occur in the settled areas of the East.

3.10 The existence of these economies is dependent on an assumed shift of population to the West—an areal preference function which is not that of the government but implied in the large migration of recent decades. The population will be underequipped with capital, public facilities, supplying industries, or jobs. Irrigated agriculture will provide some external economies under these conditions, especially when one considers that the alternative would be importing food, thereby creating a very heavy leakage to any invest- ment undertaken in the area. But the extent of the economies that could be justified under this sort of argument is small compared to the actual practices of the Bureau. Labor resources are not free in spite of their possible willing- ness to take a smaller wage in order to live in the West. The labor moving to the West is mobile and could return. The full opportunity costs should be assessed against labor as well as the interest on the entrepreneurial capital. In this case the only "induced by" or "stemming from" effects which can be considered legitimate are those which create external economies—the major part of the indirect benefits being transfers. Unfortunately no one has devised a general method by which these economies could be measured.

3.11 Though theory has not progressed to the point where the statistical counterparts of theoretical concepts can be constructed, the discussions of external economies can provide some insights into what the analyst should investigate when looking for economically justifiable secondary benefits. One major source of external economies is the growth of the market. The local market will grow both because of the project farmers and the service industries associated with them. The question for the analyst is: Has the market grown to the point where it is sufficiently large to support an optimum- sized plant, instead of requiring local imports and high transport costs from the production centers of the dense Eastern market areas?[16] The argument that the new firm is an "economy" for the nation is dependent upon the assumption of a continued existence of population in the underpopulated West.

---

[16] See Joe S. Bain, *Barriers to New Competition* (Cambridge, 1956), for a discussion of minimum-sized efficient plants in twenty industries. An extension of the number of industries and an estimate of the regional markets for the industries would enable the analyst to judge the possibilities of introducing efficient firms in the area rather than importing.

3.12 A second source of external economies is use or expansion of social overhead capital. In some cases, roads, schools, urban centers, and so on may have excess capacity. They are in the nature of a decreasing-cost industry. An expansion may be provided without an increase in these social costs.[17] This is probably not an important case since the irrigation investment and associated expansion is usually large relative to the local economy, so that an expansion of overhead capital is usually required. This growth of overhead capital and its implications for the establishment of efficient plants instead of importing should be investigated.

3.13 These studies of external economies involve an analysis of the local area, but the results will bear little relationship to the local secondary benefits estimated by the Bureau of Reclamation.[18] The major technique of the Bureau is to compare the trends of many economic indexes in counties with irrigation as against nearby comparable counties without the projects. It is possible that the difference in the levels may be attributed to the project, but this difference is not a national benefit since a large part of this enhanced income would have arisen wherever the project had been located.

3.14 To gain insight into the incidence of external economies, rather than comparing nearby counties with and without irrigation, the Bureau should compare the economic growth of Western areas with irrigation against Eastern areas with soil-treatment programs. It is the speculation of this paper that the Western investment will show larger external economies than the Eastern.

---

[17] See W. C. Wheaton and M. J. Schussheim, *The Costs of Municipal Services in Residential Areas*, Housing and Home Finance Agency (Washington, 1955), for the differences in public marginal costs to service population growth in established cities as against unpopulated peripheral suburbs.

[18] Holje, Huffman, and Kraenzel, *op. cit.*; M. E. Marts, *An Experiment in the Measurement of the Indirect Benefits of Irrigation, Payette, Idaho*, Bureau of Reclamation (Boise, Idaho, June 1950); M. K. Strantz, *Reclamation Accomplishments, 1905–53, Klamath Project, California*, Bureau of Reclamation, 1953; and M. S. Bentson and R. E. Struthers, *Accomplishments of Irrigation, Weld County, Colorado,* Bureau of Reclamation (Denver, February, 1952).

Part V
THE MEASUREMENT OF WELFARE

To measure the degree of human satisfaction seems too alluring an idea to be easily abandoned, despite the many reverses it has suffered. Measurable utility, once thought safely dead and buried, has had a new incarnation (see footnotes to introduction, Part I), and Marshall's "money measure" of utility, of which consumers' surplus is the best-known part, has had an equally tenacious hold on life (see Hicks's and Hotelling's papers in Part IV). The treacherous, many-faced nature of consumers' surplus has often been exposed, but the need for its services seems great enough to overcome scruples about its unreliability. Samuelson's funeral oration over the concept notwithstanding,[1] several papers in this part and many others elsewhere continue to utilize it. An example is the compensation test for choosing between alternative states or policies proposed in Kaldor's paper, used partly for its simplicity and partly because the conditions of Pareto optimality are usable only for choosing between an optimal and a nonoptimal alternative, while most practical choices in our imperfect world arise between nonoptimal alternatives. Scitovsky's criticism of Kaldor may be regarded as one more exposure of the unreliability of the money measure of welfare gains and losses, but the compensation test he proposed was in turn criticized by Samuelson, though the latter's purist approach was not fully accepted by the profession.[2] There followed a lengthy controversy on the proper compensation test; the one most generally accepted is that proposed by I. M. D. Little in his *A Critique of Welfare Economics*.[3] Samuelson's paper also marks the end of another

---

[1] *Foundations of Economic Analysis* (Cambridge, Mass.: Harvard University Press, 1947).

[2] His insistence on nonintersecting utility possibility curves as the only basis for welfare judgments.

[3] (2d ed.; Oxford: Clarendon, 1957.)

controversy that started between Hicks and Kuznets[4] and bore on the economic meaning of real national income and product.

Bailey's paper is an especially interesting example of the numerous attempts to measure the areas of Marshallian consumers' surplus triangles and so express in money terms losses due to economic inefficiency—in this case the loss inflicted by inflation as an inefficient means of levying taxes. Other examples of this kind of measurement are A. C. Harberger's papers on the welfare loss created by monopoly and the corporation tax,[5] and the work of international trade economists on the gain to be had from economic integration, tariff reduction, etc.[6]

Vickrey's paper, an excerpt from a longer article, deals with the question of how a practical means of measuring utility could be evolved. In some respects this paper is a pragmatic counterpart to Harsanyi's paper in Part I, which deals with much the same problem in an abstract theoretical way. The paper by Foster and Beesley is a careful and detailed estimate of the monetary and nonmonetary costs and benefits of an investment project; it may be looked upon as a practical carrying out of what Dupuit advocated 120 years earlier in the paper reprinted in Part IV. The four-generation-long distance between the two papers makes one pause to think about the pace at which economics is progressing.

---

[4] Cf. J. R. Hicks, "The Valuation of the Social Income," *Economica* N.S., 7 (1940): 105–24; Simon Kuznets, "On the Valuation of Social Income: Reflections on Professor Hicks's Article," *Economica* N.S., 15 (1948): 1–16 and 116–31; and J. R. Hicks, "The Valuation of the Social Income: A Comment on Professor Kuznets' Reflections," *Economica* N.S. 15 (1948): 163–72.

[5] Cf. A. C. Harberger, "Monopoly Resource Allocation," *American Economic Review Papers and Proceedings*, 44 (1954): 77–87; "The Corporation Income Tax: An Empirical Appraisal," U.S. House of Representatives, Ways and Means Committee, Tax Revision Compendium, Nov., 1959: 231–50.

[6] Cf. H. G. Johnson, "The Gains from Freer Trade with Europe: An Estimate," Manchester School, 26 (1958): 237–55; B. Balassa and M. E. Kreinin, "Trade Liberalization under Kennedy Round: The Static Effects," *Review of Economics and Statistics*, 49 (1967): 125–37.

Welfare propositions of economics and interpersonal comparisons of utility*

NICHOLAS KALDOR

In the December, 1938, issue of the *Economic Journal* Professor Robbins returns to the question of the status of interpersonal comparisons of utility.[1] It is not the purpose of this note to question Professor Robbins' view regarding the scientific status of such comparisons; with this the present writer is in entire agreement. Its purpose is rather to examine the relevance of this whole question to what is commonly called "welfare economics." In previous discussions of this problem it has been rather too readily assumed, on both sides, that the scientific justification of such comparisons determines whether "economics as a science can say anything by way of prescription." The disputants have been concerned only with the status of the comparisons; they were—apparently—agreed that the status of prescriptions necessarily depends on the status of the comparisons.

This is clearly Mr. Harrod's view. He says:

Consider the Repeal of the Corn Laws. This tended to reduce the value of a specific factor of production—land. It can no doubt be shown that the gain to the community as a whole exceeded the loss to the landlords—*but only if individuals are treated in some sense as equal.* Otherwise how can the loss to some—and that there was a loss can hardly be denied—be compared with the general gain? If the incomparability of utility to different individuals is strictly pressed, not only are the prescriptions of the welfare school ruled out, but all prescriptions whatever. The economist as an adviser is completely stultified, and unless his speculations be regarded as of paramount aesthetic value, he had better be suppressed completely.[2]

---

* *The Economic Journal*, 49 (1939): pp. 549–52. Reprinted by courtesy of the author and *The Economic Journal*.
[1] "Interpersonal Comparisons of Utility: A Comment," *Economic Journal*, December 1938, pp. 635–91.
[2] "Scope and Method of Economics," *ibid.*, September 1938, pp. 396–97. (Italics mine.)

This view is endorsed by Professor Robbins:

All that I proposed to do was to make clear that the statement that social wealth was increased [by free trade] itself involved an arbitrary element—that the proposition should run, *if* equal capacity for satisfaction on the part of the economic subjects be assumed, *then* social wealth can be said to be increased. Objective analysis of the effects of the repeal of duties only showed that consumers gained and landlords lost. That such an arbitrary element was involved was plain. It seemed no less plain, therefore, that, here as elsewhere, it should be explicitly recognised.[3]

It can be demonstrated, however, that in the classical argument for free trade no such arbitrary element is involved at all. The effects of the repeal of the Corn Laws could be summarised as follows: (i) it results in a reduction in the price of corn, so that the *same* money income will now represent a higher real income; (ii) it leads to a shift in the distribution of income, so that some people's (*i.e.*, the landlord's) incomes (at any rate in money terms) will be lower than before, and other people's incomes (presumably those of other producers) will be higher. Since aggregate money income can be assumed to be unchanged, if the landlord's income is reduced, the income of other people must be correspondingly increased. It is only as a result of this consequential change in the distribution of income that there can be any loss of satisfactions to certain individuals, and hence any need to compare the gains of some with the losses of others. But it is always possible for the Government to ensure that the previous income distribution should be maintained intact: by compensating the "landlords" for any loss of income and by providing the funds for such compensation by an extra tax on those whose incomes have been augmented. In this way, everybody is left as well off as before in his capacity as an income recipient; while everybody is better off than before in his capacity as a consumer. For there still remains the benefit of lower corn prices as a result of the repeal of the duty.

In all cases, therefore, where a certain policy leads to an increase in physical productivity, and thus of aggregate real income, the economist's case for the policy is quite unaffected by the question of the comparability of individual satisfactions; since in all such cases it is *possible* to make everybody better off than before, or at any rate to make some people better off without making anybody worse off. There is no need for the economist to prove— as indeed he never could prove—that as a result of the adoption of a certain measure nobody in the community is going to suffer. In order to establish his case, it is quite sufficient for him to show that even if all those who suffer as a result are fully compensated for their loss, the rest of the community will still be better off than before. Whether the landlords, in the free-trade case, should in fact be given compensation or not, is a political question on which the economist, *qua* economist, could hardly pronounce an opinion.

---

[3] *Loc. cit.*, p. 638.

The important fact is that, in the argument in favour of free trade, the fate of the landlords is wholly irrelevant: since the benefits of free trade are by no means destroyed even if the landlords are fully reimbursed for their losses.[4]

This argument lends justification to the procedure, adopted by Professor Pigou in *The Economics of Welfare*, of dividing "welfare economics" into two parts: the first relating to production, and the second to distribution. The first, and far the more important part, should include all those propositions for increasing social welfare which relate to the increase in aggregate production; all questions concerning the stimulation of employment, the equalisation of social net products, and the equalisation of prices with marginal costs, would fall under this heading. Here the economist is on sure ground; the scientific status of his prescriptions is unquestionable, provided that the basic postulate of economics, that each individual prefers more to less, a greater satisfaction to a lesser one, is granted. In the second part, concerning distribution, the economist should not be concerned with "prescriptions" at all, but with the relative advantages of different ways of carrying out certain political ends. For it is quite impossible to decide on economic grounds what particular pattern of income distribution maximises social welfare. If the postulate of equal capacity for satisfaction is employed as a criterion, the conclusion inescapably follows that welfare is necessarily greatest when there is complete equality; yet one certainly cannot exclude the possibility of everybody being happier when there is some degree of inequality than under a regime of necessary and complete equality. (Here I am not thinking so much of differences in the capacity for satisfactions between different individuals, but of the satisfactions that are derived from the prospect of improving one's income by one's own efforts—a prospect which is necessarily excluded when a regime of complete equality prevails.) And short of complete equality, how can the economist decide precisely how much inequality is desirable—*i.e.*, how much secures the maximum total satisfaction? All that economics can, and should, do in this field, is to show, given the pattern of income distribution desired, which is the most convenient way of bringing it about.

---

[4] This principle, as the reader will observe, simply amounts to saying that there is no interpersonal comparison of satisfactions involved in judging any policy designed to increase the sum total of wealth just because any such policy *could* be carried out in a way as to secure unanimous consent. An increase in the money value of the national income (given prices) is not, however, necessarily a sufficient indication of this condition being fulfilled: for individuals might, as a result of a certain political action, sustain losses of a non-pecuniary kind—*e.g.*, if workers derive satisfaction from their particular kind of work, and are obliged to change their employment, something more than their previous level of money income will be necessary to secure their previous level of enjoyment; and the same applies in cases where individuals feel that the carrying out of the policy involves an interference with their individual freedom. Only if the increase in total income is sufficient to compensate for such losses, and still leaves something over to the rest of the community, can it be said to be "justified" without resort to interpersonal comparisons.

A note on welfare propositions in economics[*]

TIBOR SCITOVSKY

Modern economic theory draws a sharp distinction between positive economics, which explains the working of the economic system, and welfare economics, which prescribes policy. In the domain of welfare economics the impossibility of interpersonal utility comparisons has for a long time been believed to impose strict limitations on the economist, which kept this branch of economic theory in the background. Recently, however, there has been a reawakening of interest in welfare problems, following assertions that these limitations are less restrictive than they were hitherto supposed to be.[1] The present note attempts to analyse the problem in detail.

I

The aim of welfare economics is to test the efficiency of economic institutions in making use of the productive resources of a community. For analytical and historical reasons it is useful to distinguish between welfare propositions based on the assumption of a fixed quantity of employed resources and those that regard that quantity as a variable.

The former are concerned with the allocating efficiency of the system;[2] i.e. with its ability of best allocating a given quantity of utilised resources among their various uses in consumption and production. They can be conceived of as criteria for judging institutions and policy in a closed community

---

[*] *The Review of Economic Studies*, 9 (1941): pp. 77–88. Reprinted by courtesy of the author and *The Review of Economic Studies*.

[1] Cf. N. Kaldor: **"Welfare Propositions of Economics and Interpersonal Comparisons of Utility," *Economic Journal*, vol. 49 (1939), p. 549; J. R. Hicks: "Foundations of Welfare Economics," *Economic Journal*, vol. 49 (1939), p. 696. See also N. Kaldor "A Note on Tariffs and the Terms of Trade," *Economica* (N.S.), vol. 7 (1940), p. 377; and J. R. Hicks: "The Rehabilitation of Consumers' Surplus," *Review of Economic Studies*, vol. 8 (1941), p. 108. The present note is a criticism of the principle enunciated in Mr. Kaldor's first-quoted article and underlying the argument of the others. It is not presented in polemic form, in order to enable the reader not acquainted with the articles here quoted to follow its argument.

[2] This expression was suggested to me by Mr. George Jaszi to whom I am indebted for reading the manuscript and making valuable suggestions.

whose potential resources are fixed and can be trusted to be fully employed, either because of the automatism of the system or because of the existence of a governmental policy aiming at full employment.

The latter, which may be called welfare propositions in the wider sense, are in addition to the above problems concerned also with the total quantity of resources available to an open group and the degree of utilisation of those resources. They are therefore relevant, first of all, to problems of international trade from the point of view of a single country; and secondly, to the general problem of employment.

II

All the welfare propositions of the classical economists—viz., perfect competition, free trade, and direct taxation—belong in the first category; a fact which has not always been realised. They are all based on the principle that given the total quantity of utilised resources, they will be best distributed among different uses if their rates of substitution are everywhere and for every person equal; for only in such a situation will each person's satisfaction be carried to that maximum beyond which it cannot be increased without diminishing someone else's. Perfect competition, free trade, and direct taxation are one (probably the simplest) among the many ways of achieving this aim.

By limiting our universe of discourse to two commodities and two persons, we can illustrate this principle on a simple diagram. Let us draw the indifference maps of the two individuals superposed on each other, one of them reversed, with the axes parallel and in such a position that their intersection gives the quantities of the two goods jointly possessed by the two people. Every point of the rectangle enclosed by the axes corresponds to a given distribution of the two goods between the two persons, and the two indifference curves going through that point show their respective welfare positions. At some points, indifference curves do not cut but are tangential one to another. At these points the rate of substitution of the two goods is equal for the two persons, and they represent optimum situations, because once such a point has been reached no redistribution of the two goods can increase the welfare of either person without diminishing that of the other. The locus of all optimum points gives the contract curve.

We judge the allocating efficiency of economic institutions by the criterion whether or not they enable people so to redistribute goods and services among themselves (irrespective of their initial position) as to arrive on the contract curve. That perfect competition or, from the point of view of the universe, free trade are efficient in the above sense can be proved by showing that all pairs of offer (reciprocal demand) curves drawn from any point within the rectangle intersect on the contract curve. Similarly, excise taxes and, from the point of view of the universe, import and export duties are inefficient, because they can be represented as distortions of offer curves that make them intersect outside the contract curve. The arguments based on this diagram can be generalised for any number of persons and commodities.[3] It implies only one limitation: the quantities of goods available to the community as a whole must be fixed; for they determine the points of intersection of the axes and the position of the contract curve. This shows that the propositions illustrated by the diagram are allocative welfare propositions; and it also appears to limit their applicability to the problem of the exchange of goods whose quantities coming onto the market are given. It can be proved, however, that our arguments are equally valid when instead of these quantities those of the factors utilised in their production are considered to be fixed. For the formal proof of the geometrical arguments and their generalisations the reader is referred to the original sources and to textbooks dealing with the subject.[4]

III

We have seen above that allocative welfare propositions are based on the criterion of economic efficiency. They state that of alternative situations, brought about by different institutions or courses of policy, one is superior to the other in the sense that it would make everybody better off for every distribution of welfare, *if* that were the same in the two situations. This is different from saying that one situation is actually better than the other from everybody's point of view, because a change in institutions or policy almost always redistributes welfare sufficiently not to have a uniform effect on everybody but to favour some people and prejudice others. It follows from this that economic welfare propositions cannot as a rule be made independently of interpersonal comparisons of utility.

It would hardly be satisfactory, however, to confine the economist's value judgments to cases where one situation is superior to the other from the point of view of everybody affected. It is doubtful if in practice any choice comes within this category; besides, there would not be much point in soliciting the economist's expert opinion when everybody is unanimous, except in order to enlighten people as to their true interest.

Favouring an improvement in the organisation of production and exchange *only* when it is accompanied by a corrective redistribution of income fully compensating those prejudiced by it might seem to be a way out of the difficulty, because such a change would make some people better off without making anyone worse off. For instance, it might be argued that the abolition of the Corn Laws should not have been advocated by economists in their capacity of pure economists without advocating at the same time the full compensation of landowners out of taxes levied on those favoured by the cheapening of corn.

---

[3] This also holds good for all arguments based on other diagrams in this note.

[4] Cf. F. Y. Edgeworth: *Mathematical Psychics*, London, 1881, and "The Pure Theory of International Trade," *Economic Journal*, vol. 4 (1894); Alfred Marshall: *The Pure Theory of Foreign Trade* (1879), London School reprint, 1930; and his *Principles of Economics*, Bk. V, Chap. II. Note on Barter and Mathematical Note XII; A. P. Lerner; "The Symmetry between Export and Import Taxes," *Economica* (N.S.), vol. 3 (1936); J. R. Hicks: *Value and Capital*, Oxford, 1939, etc. For the best analysis of the nature of this kind of diagram see A. L. Bowley; *The Mathematical Groundwork of Economics*, Oxford, 1924.

Yet, in a sense, and regarded from a long-run point of view, such propositions are not independent of value judgments between alternative income distributions either. For, going out of their way to preserve the existing distribution of income, they imply a preference for the *status quo*.

There seem to be two solutions of the problem. First of all, in addition to admitting his inability to compare different people's satisfaction, the economist may postulate that such comparisons are impossible, and that therefore there is nothing to choose between one distribution of income and another. He may then make value judgments on the sole criterion of efficiency without bothering about concomitant shifts in the distribution of income, since he considers one income distribution as good as any other.[5] In this case, however, he cannot claim that his value judgments are independent of interpersonal utility comparisons, because they depend on the assumption of their impossibility.

Secondly, the economist may put forward his welfare propositions with due emphasis on their limitations, as being based on the sole criterion of efficiency. He may then point out the nature of eventual redistributions of income likely to accompany a given change, and stress the necessity of basing economic policy on considerations both of economic efficiency and of social justice.[6] Such an attitude, which I think is the only correct one, may diminish the force of the economist's welfare propositions but does not make them less useful. The above considerations qualify also the welfare propositions to be discussed below.

IV

When we come to the problem of welfare propositions in the wider sense, we can no longer illustrate a change in economic institutions or policy on a single diagram. For such a change will no longer mean a mere redistribution of income and alteration of the rules of production and exchange; but may also involve a change both in the total quantity of resources available to the community, and in their degree of utilisation. The former may be due to the imposition of a duty on international trade, which from the point of view of an individual country alters the quantities of imports and retained exports available for home consumption; while the latter may be caused by this or any other change, if it affects the propensity to save or the inducement to invest and thereby changes employment. Analytically there is no difference

---

[5] This, I think, was the attitude of the classical economists; at least of those who did not, like Bastiat, impute ethical values to the distribution of income under perfect competition. It seems to be the correct interpretation of that fairly representative statement of Cairnes': "... standards of abstract justice ... are inefficacious as means of solving the actual problems of ... distribution. ... If our present system of industry (perfect competition) is to be justified, it must ... find its justification ... in the fact that it secures for the mass of mankind a greater amount of material and moral well-being, and provides more effectively for its progress in civilisation than any other plan."

[6] Or, of course, he may also renounce his claim to purity and base his own recommendations on both criteria.

between the two cases. In both, the quantities of resources available for consumption are changed, hence the relative position of the indifference maps is altered; whence it follows that welfare propositions in the wider sense must involve the comparison of two diagrams. Since these are constructed from the identical two indifference maps and differ only in the latter's relative position to each other, such comparisons are not the hopeless task they might seem at first sight. For we can represent some (not all) welfare positions on both diagrams; and it is possible to represent on one diagram the welfare positions corresponding to all those points of the other diagram's contract curve that are inferior to its " own " contract curve. This follows from the fact that our diagrams admit the representation of all welfare situations that are inferior (worse from the point of view of at least one of the two persons) to their contract curve, while welfare positions superior to the contract curve cannot be represented on them.

Our welfare propositions may necessitate the comparison of points on the contract curves of the two diagrams, or of points suboptimal to them, or of a point on one contract curve with a point suboptimal to the other contract curve. The first case is that where the system's allocating efficiency is at an optimum both before and after the given change; the second, where it is suboptimal both before and after the change; the third, where the change affects allocating efficiency. Taking an example from the theory of international trade, the first case may be illustrated by the imposition of an import duty by a country in which taxation is direct and domestic markets are perfectly competitive;[7] the second case can be represented by a duty imposed in a monopolistic world; and the third by a duty which favours the formation of monopolies or is linked with an excise tax on the home production of import substitutes.

V

Let us draw two diagrams (Figure 1), both consisting of the superposed indifference maps of individuals A and B, but with the difference that in the second, B's map has been shifted by $0_B 0'_B$; so that the joint possessions of A and B have increased by $x_0 x_1$ of X and $y_0 y_1$ of Y compared with what they were in the first. This shift will bring into a position of tangency indifference curves that in the first diagram have neither touched nor intersected, and will thus make the second diagram's contract curve superior to that of the first diagram throughout its range. This follows from that fundamental postulate of economic theory that indifference curves can never have a positive slope, and it will be the case whenever the shift in the relative position of the indif-

---

[7] A tariff on foreign trade is not incompatible with the tariff imposing country's domestic trade and production being of optimum allocating efficiency. The reader must not let himself be confused by the fact that similar diagrams have been used for illustrating the waste caused by tariffs from the point of view of the universe as a whole. We are here solely concerned with the effects of a tariff on the welfare of a single country; consequently the indifference maps that constitute our diagrams belong to inhabitants of the same country.

Figure 1

DIAGRAM 1

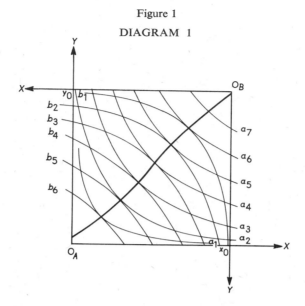

ference maps represents an increase in the quantity of at least one of the two commodities without a diminution in that of the other. From the fact that the second diagram's contract curve is superior to that of the first, it follows that the latter can be represented on the second diagram by tracing the locus of the points of intersection of all the indifference curves that in the first diagram are tangential to each other. This will give us a curve on each side

Figure 1

DIAGRAM 2

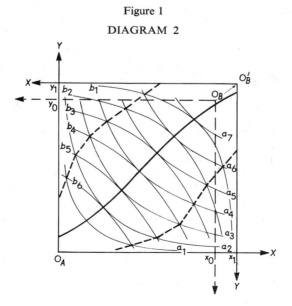

of the second diagram's contract curve, and the area between them represents welfare positions that are superior to the first diagram's contract curve. Hence, a change that brings the welfare of our group from a point of the first diagram's contract curve onto a point of the second diagram's contract curve (or at least within the area between the broken lines) can be said to be desirable with the same generality and significance with which perfect competition or direct taxation are said to be desirable on the ground of their allocating efficiency. In other words, while it need not actually improve everybody's position, it would do so for every possible distribution of welfare if the change were to leave that distribution unaffected.

The above argument is an explicit formulation of the statement that getting more of some (or all) commodities at no cost of foregoing others is a good thing. This may be considered as overpedantic, since that statement seems to be obvious; on the other hand, it is subject to the same limitations that qualify allocative welfare propositions (cf. Section 3 above); and besides, it is not even always true. Increased plenty is a good thing only if it is not linked with a redistribution of welfare too retrogressive from the point of view of social justice; and if it does not lead to a serious deterioration of the allocating efficiency of the economic system. For the former there exists no objective criterion, but there is a simple test for the latter. To test whether a diminution in allocating efficiency has not obviated the advantages of increased plenty, we must see if after the change, it is possible fully to compensate people prejudiced by it out of funds levied on those favoured by the change, without thereby completely eliminating the latter's gain. From the geometrical argument above it follows that if this test is fulfilled for one initial income distribution, it will be fulfilled for all possible initial income distributions, and *vice versa*. Our test is completely general also in the sense that it is applicable whether or not the initial situation is of optimum allocating efficiency (i.e., whether or not it lies on the contract curve).

VI

The kind of change contemplated above, where the quantity of some or all goods is increased without a diminution in others, is likely to occur as a result of increased employment, capital accumulation, technical progress, better utilisation of strategic advantages in international trade (by putting a duty on the export of goods for which foreign demand is inelastic), and the like. Another kind of change, especially important in international trade, is that where the quantity of some resources is increased and that of others diminished.[8] In Figure 2, this is represented by a parallel displacement of one of the two indifference maps in the negative direction; so that the quantity of X is diminished by $x_0 x_1$ and that of Y increased by $y_0 y_1$. Nothing general can be said about the relationship of the two contract curves in this case without detailed knowledge of the shape of the indifference maps. It is possible

---

[8] This is the effect of import and export duties whenever the foreigners' reciprocal demand for exports is not inelastic and employment is given.

Figure 2

DIAGRAM 1

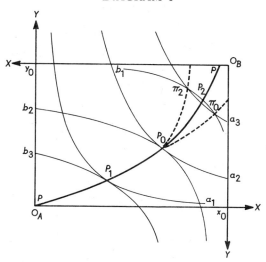

that the change will result in superior welfare positions throughout the whole range of the contract curve, in the same way as was depicted in Figure 1. This is especially likely to happen when the increase is large and the diminution small. When on the other hand, the diminution is large and the increase small, the change may result in inferior positions throughout the contract curve; a situation which can be visualised by thinking of diagram 2 (Figure 1)

Figure 2

DIAGRAM 2

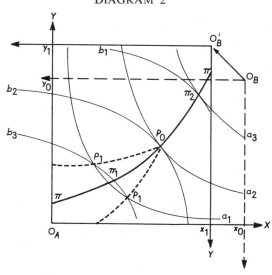

as showing the initial, and diagram 1 the new, position. Between these two extremes lies the more general case in which some sectors of the new contract curve are superior to the old one, while others are inferior to it. Its simplest example is illustrated in Figure 2, where P_0 is a common point of the two contract curves, to the left of which the new contract curve, $\pi\pi$, represents welfare positions superior to the corresponding welfare positions of the old contract curve, PP; while to the right of P_0, the old contract curve is superior to the new one. In each diagram the broken lines show the welfare positions corresponding to the other diagram's contract curve wherever that is inferior to the diagram's own contract curve.

The economic meaning of this is that the identical change in the composition of the national income would improve general welfare for some hypothetical welfare distributions and worsen it for others. Imagine members of a community divided into two groups according to their preference for goods Y and X respectively.[9] Then assume a change that increases the quantity of Y and diminishes that of X, but leaves the distribution of money income between our two groups unaffected. From the point of view of individuals, the change will appear as a shift in relative prices which, given the distribution of income, will be likely to make those with a special preference for Y better off, and those with a liking for X worse off, than they were before. Assume next that the members of our first group are rich and those of the second poor. Then the gain of the first group expressed in money (or in terms of any single commodity) will be greater than the money equivalent of the loss suffered by the second group. Therefore, if we so redistributed income as to restore approximately the initial distribution of welfare, there would be a net gain, making members of both groups better off than they were before. Conversely, if the people favoured by the change were poor, and those prejudiced by it were rich, the money equivalent of the former's gain would be insufficient fully to compensate the latter's loss, so that a redistribution of income tending to restore the initial distribution of welfare would result in a net loss of satisfaction for everybody.

What significance are we to attach to this case? To refrain altogether, as the classical economists did, from making welfare propositions relating to it, seems unduly restrictive. It is true that, as we have seen, such a change would improve general welfare for some welfare distributions and worsen it for others; on the other hand, we are not interested in all possible welfare distributions. There are only two distributions of welfare that really matter— those actually obtaining immediately before and after the change contemplated.[10] It seems therefore sufficient to concentrate on these and to investigate

---

[9] The term "preference" is used in a loose sense. It denotes the whole shape of indifference surfaces and not only their slope at the relevant point, which in equilibrium conditions is the same for everybody.

[10] The reader's attention is called to the fact that in reality the distribution of income is not *given* as we have assumed in the argument above. As a rule, the change will affect the distribution of welfare not only by shifting relative prices but also by boosting some industries and depressing others, and thereby redistributing money income.

how the change would affect general welfare if it were to leave the distribution of welfare unaffected and if that were both before and after it, first what it actually is before, secondly what it actually is after, the change. Whenever these two comparisons yield identical results, we can make welfare propositions of almost the same generality and significance as the allocative welfare propositions of the classical economists; especially since the identical results for the two welfare distributions imply a strong presumption in favour of the same result holding for all intermediate welfare distributions as well.

We propose, therefore, to make welfare propositions on the following principle. We must first see whether it is possible in the new situation so to redistribute income as to make everybody better off than he was in the initial situation; secondly, we must see whether starting from the initial situation it is not possible by a mere redistribution of income to reach a position superior to the new situation, again from everybody's point of view. If the first is possible and the second impossible, we shall say that the new situation is better than the old was. If the first is impossible but the second possible, we shall say that the new situation is worse; whereas if both are possible or both are impossible, we shall refrain from making a welfare proposition.[11]

We can illustrate this procedure in Figure 2 for the special case when allocating efficiency is at its optimum both before and after the change. Each situation can then be represented by a point on its respective contract curve and compared with the corresponding point on the other contract curve. If both points lie to the left of P_0 on their respective contract curves the change will increase general welfare, because starting from the new situation on the second diagram's contract curve it is always possible to travel along that curve by redistributing income and arrive at a point which is superior to the initial situation from everybody's point of view; whereas starting from the initial situation on the first diagram's contract curve, it is impossible by travelling along that curve to reach a position superior to the new situation. If on the other hand, both points lie to the right of the common point P_0, the change can be said to diminish general welfare on the same reasoning; while if one point lies to the left and the other to the right, we can make no welfare propositions relative to our group.

VII

Our two criteria for making welfare propositions bear a close resemblance to Paasche's and Laspeyre's formulae in the theory of cost of living index numbers. There, just as here, the difficulty lies in comparing averages whose weighting is different;[12] and the solution is sought in comparing the two real situations not one with another, but each with a hypothetical situation, which

---

[11] It need hardly be recalled that in the situation discussed in Section 5—that is, when the quantities of goods and services all change in the same direction—this last case can never occur, and we can always make welfare propositions.

[12] Because the general welfare can be conceived of as average welfare.

resembles it in weighting but is otherwise identical with the other real situation. In the theory of index numbers, budgets of different dates or places are compared each with the cost of the identical bundle of commodities at the prices of the other date or place; and these two comparisons, expressed as ratios (Paasche's and Laspeyre's formulae), are the limits within which the true difference in the cost of living must lie.[13] In welfare problems, of course, we can aim neither at a "true" answer nor at its quantitative expression without measuring satisfaction and comparing different people's. But our two criteria are exactly analogous to Paasche's and Laspeyre's formulae. For we compare the first welfare situation with what general welfare would be if the satisfaction yielded by the physical income of the second situation were distributed as it was in the first; and contrast the second situation with the welfare that the first situation's physical income would yield to each person if it were so distributed as to make the distribution of welfare similar to that of the second situation.[14]

VIII

Mr. Kaldor and Professor Hicks have asserted that it is *always* possible to tell whether a given change improves general welfare, even if not all people gain by it and some lose. The test suggested by them, to see whether it is possible after the change fully to compensate the losers at a cost to those favoured that falls short of their total gain, is fundamentally identical with the first of our two criteria. The objection to using this criterion by itself is that it is asymmetrical because it attributes undue importance to the particular distribution of welfare obtaining before the contemplated change. If the government had a special attachment to the *status quo* before the change and would actually undertake to reproduce that welfare distribution by differential taxation after the change, then Mr. Kaldor's test would be sufficient. For then, the economist could regard that particular welfare distribution as the only relevant one and would be entitled to use it as his sole standard of reference. But in the absence of such a governmental policy there can be no justification in attaching greater importance to the welfare distribution as it was before than as it is after the change.

To illustrate the pitfalls of this one-sided criterion, imagine a change, say the imposition of a duty on imports, that brings the welfare of A and B from P_1 (Figure 2) on the contract curve of diagram 1 onto π_2 on the contract curve of diagram 2. According to Mr. Kaldor's test this change is desirable, because by redistributing income we could travel from π_2 along the $\pi\pi$ curve to π_1, which is superior to P_1. But once the tariff has been imposed and

---

[13] Cf. Henry Schultz: "A Misunderstanding in Index Number Theory," *Econometrica*, vol. 7 (1939), p. 1; and A. A. Konüs: "The Problem of the True Index of the Cost of Living," *Econometrica*, vol. 7 (1939), p. 10.

[14] We say that the distribution of welfare is similar in two situations if every member of the community prefers the same situation. A more exact definition would be unnecessary for our purposes; besides, it is also impossible, since welfare cannot be measured.

situation π_2 established, it will be free trade and the resulting (original) situation P_1 that will appear preferable *by the same test*, because starting from P_1, income could be so redistributed (travelling along the PP curve in the first diagram this time) as to reach P_2, which is superior to π_2. So the two situations can be shown each to be preferable to the other by the identical criterion: an absurd result, which can only be avoided by using our double criterion.

Evaluation of real national income*

PAUL A. SAMUELSON

INTRODUCTION

1. Improved measurement of national income has been one of the out-standing features of recent progress in economics. But the theoretical inter-pretation of such aggregate data has been sadly neglected, so that we hardly know how to define real income even in simple cases where statistical data are perfect and where problems of capital formation and government expenditure do not arise.

In 1940 J. R. Hicks made an important advance over the earlier work of Professor Pigou. This has given rise to recent discussions between Kuznets, Hicks, and Little, but the last word on the subject will not be uttered for a long time. I have tried to treat the problem somewhat exhaustively in this paper, relating it to the modern theories of welfare economics of Pareto–Lerner–Bergson type. The result is not easy reading even to the author—but without such a careful survey I doubt that even the classical writings of Pigou can be adequately gauged.[1]

2. In Figure 1, the point *A* represents observed consumption data for a single consumer in equilibrium at the indicated price-slope line through *A*. All the other points are each to be regarded as alternative to *A* and have nothing to do with each other. The following statements are immediate consequences of the modern theory of a single consumer's behaviour and

---

* *The Oxford Economic Papers*, N. S., 2 (1950): pp. 1–29. Reprinted by courtesy of the author and *The Oxford Economic Papers*.
[1] The principal references are to J. R. Hicks, "The Valuation of the Social Income," *Economica*, 1940, pp. 105–24; Simon Kuznets, "On the Valuation of Social Income—Reflections on Professor Hicks' Article," *Economica*, Feb. 1948, pp. 1–16, and May 1948, pp. 116–31; J. R. Hicks, "The Valuation of the Social Income—A Comment on Professor Kuznets' Reflections," *Economica*, Aug. 1948, pp. 163–72; I. M. D. Little, "The Valuation of the Social Income," *Economica*, Feb. 1949, pp. 11–26; A. C. Pigou, *Economics of Welfare*. 4th ed. (1932), Part I, especially chaps. ii, iii, v, vi; P. A. Samuelson, *Foundations of Economic Analysis* (1948), chap. viii. Since writing this article I have benefited from reading two further papers by Little and from corresponding with him. See I. M. D. Little, "The Foundations of Welfare Economics," *O.E.P.*, June 1949, and an addendum to his *Economica* article "A Note on the Significance of Index Numbers."

Figure 1

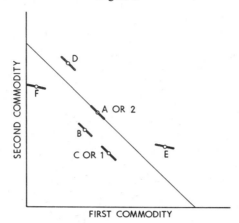

FIRST COMMODITY

are based on $\sum pq$ data such as the national income statistician might be able to measure:

  a) We can immediately infer that B is on a lower indifference curve than A.
  b) Less directly, but with equal certainty, C reveals itself to be inferior to A.
  c) The point D reveals itself to be superior to A.
  d) The points E and A reveal nothing about their order in the consumer's taste-pattern.
  e) The point F is inconsistent with A. The consumer has changed his tastes, or he is not in equilibrium at the indicated points.

PROBLEMS OF INFERENCE FROM GROUP MARKET DATA

  3. Let us now regard Figure 1 as applying to market data for two or more individuals, so that each quantity, q, represents the total of two or more individuals' consumption $q' + q'' +, \ldots$, etc. The slope through A or any other point represents the market-price ratio of the first and second goods, the only commodities in our simplified world.

What can we now say about our points? Advances in the theory of welfare economics since 1940—many of them growing out of Hicks's own researches —suggest that certain of the definitions and propositions then laid down need to be modified. I resurrect these matters only because most people who have seen the recent discussion between Kuznets, Hicks, and Little must find their heads swimming, and must be in considerable doubt as to what the proper status of this vital matter is.

  4. First we may clear up one misunderstanding, in itself unimportant, but giving an initial clue that we cannot make any very sweeping inferences from aggregate price-quantity data. In 1940 it was held that a situation like that of A and F is quite impossible on the assumption that individuals preserve the

same well-defined tastes and are in true equilibrium in competitive markets.[2] It was held that, for national totals,

$$\sum p_2 q_2 > \sum p_2 q_1 \quad \text{implies} \quad \sum p_1 q_1 < \sum p_1 q_2.$$

As stated earlier, for a single individual this would be a correct assertion; but it is definitely false for group data involving two or more individuals. Examples to show this can be given *ad lib.* No recourse need be made to the Kuznets case of necessaries and luxuries (understanding by the latter, goods which some individuals do not choose to buy at all)—but, of course, there is no reason why such examples should not also be used. Perhaps the very simplest example to illustrate the possibility of a contradiction would be one in which we keep the exact national totals of the point *A*, but reallocate goods between the individuals so that they come into final equilibrium with a new and different price ratio. Then already we are on the borderline of a contradiction, and by making a slight change in the totals we can obviously get a strong outright contradiction.

Already we are warned that $\sum p_2 q_2 > \sum p_2 q_1$ cannot imply that the second situation represents an "increase in social real income" over that of the first—since this implication would leave us with the real possibility that each situation is better than the other!

This should also warn us against thinking that we can save such a definition by applying it only where there is no such outright contradiction. For suppose that we consider a case which just escapes *revealing* itself to be contradictory; being so close to a nonsense situation, such a case can in no wise escape being subject to the same *fundamental* (as yet undiagnosed) difficulty, even though it may not be advertising the fact to us.

INADMISSIBILITY OF THE 1940 DEFINITION OF INCREASED REAL INCOME

5. This tells us already that either there is something inadequate about the 1940 definition of an "increase in society's real income" or else there is something faulty about the logical proof that the index-number criterion $\sum p_2 q_2 > \sum p_2 q_1$ implies such a defined increase in real income.

The 1940 passage in question is so compact that one must be careful in interpreting it. In my judgement the root of the trouble lies more in the inadequacy of the definition enunciated than in the logic of the demonstration that the stated index-number criterion does imply an increase in defined real income. Although it has already been extensively requoted, the relevant 1940 passage is so brief that it can be given completely here.

... What does it signify if $\sum p_2 q_2 > \sum p_2 q_1$?

It should first of all be noticed that since this condition refers only to the total quantities acquired, it can tell us nothing about the distribution of wealth among the members of the group. There may be a drastic redistribution of wealth among the members and the aggregates will remain exactly the same. Thus what the condi-

---

[2] See *Economica*, May 1940, pp. 112–13.

tion $\sum p_2 q_2 > \sum p_2 q_1$ tells us is that there is *some* distribution of the q_1's which would make every member of the group less well off than he actually is in the II situation. For if the corresponding inequality were to hold for every individual separately, it would hold for the group as a whole.

As compared with this particular distribution, every other distribution of the q_1's would make some people better off and some worse off. Consequently, if there is one distribution of the q_1's in which every member of the group is worse off than he actually is in the II situation, there can be no distribution in which everyone is better off, or even as well off. Thus if we start from any actual distribution of wealth in the I situation, what the condition $\sum p_2 q_2 > \sum p_2 q_1$ tells us is that it is impossible to reach, by redistribution, a position in which everyone is as well off as he is in the II situation.

This would seem to be quite acceptable as a definition of increase in real social income. Let us say that the real income of society is higher in Situation II than in Situation I, if it is impossible to make everyone as well off as he is in Situation II by any redistribution of the actual quantities acquired in Situation I. If this definition is accepted, our criteria can be applied to it without change.[3]

6. A diagram that we shall place major reliance on in the later discussion can be used to illustrate exactly what is involved in this definition of an " increase in social real income." On the axes in Figure 2 there is laid out the ordinal utility of each of two individuals: the exact scale of U'' or U' is of no consequence, only the north-south and east-west orderings being important. Corresponding to the point A or 2 in Figure 1, there will actually be some allocation of the total of goods between our individuals, and hence some determined level of well-being for each. Let the point labelled 2 in Figure 2 represent that actual level of ordinal well-being. Now consider the other situation that was labelled C or 1 in our earlier figure. Behind the scenes, unknown to us from the totals, there is again an actual allocation of the goods to the individuals and again a new point in Figure 2. If we knew where it was, we could write it in and label it 1. We do not know where this

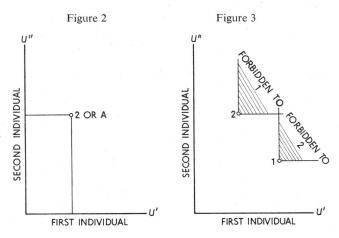

Figure 2   Figure 3

[3] J. R. Hicks, "The Valuation of the Social Income," *Economica*, May 1940, p. 111.

new point will fall: it may be southwest of point 2 so that all individuals are worse off, or southeast so that one individual is better off and the other worse off, and so forth.

Hicks's 1940 definition cf an increase in real income from the point 1 to 2 consists of this: if we can be sure that neither point 1 nor any reallocation of its quantities among individuals lies northeast of point 2 (with both individuals better off in 1 than in 2), then point 2 is defined to represent an increase in real income over point 1.

How acceptable is this definition, leaving aside for the moment the question of whether the index-number criteria does permit us to place such a restriction on the admissible position of point 1? Upon reflection, we will all agree, I think, that such a definition is not very satisfactory. By means of it a point 1 may be both better and worse than another point 2. This is shown in Figure 3. Also the definition has small claims on our affections in terms of our common-sense intuitions. Its last disadvantage is a subtle but important one: correctly stated, the new welfare economics is a body of doctrines which attempts to go as far as possible in preparing the way for the final a-scientific step involving ethical judgements; it should never, therefore, prejudice the final step, but only make statements which are uniformly valid for a wide class of ethical systems. Suppose now that we have given to us in Figure 2 a set of social indifference curves (the contours of a Bergson social welfare function). It is more than possible that a "point" or "situation" (they are not quite the same thing) judged by the 1940 criterion to be the superior one may actually be the "inferior" one in terms of the wider ethical judgements.

7. Instinctively Hicks was reaching out, I believe, for a rather different definition than the one he actually enunciated. The simpler problem of comparing A and B in Figure 1 will bring this out and at the same time require no intricate index-number reasoning. As before, corresponding to the point A in Figure 1 there is in Figure 2 a point 2 representing the ordinal well-being of all individuals. Now with less of *all* goods available to society as shown by B, there will be a new point of individuals' well-being in Figure 2. Where will the new point lie with respect to the former point 2?

We would have to give the unsatisfactory answer "anywhere" were it not for one important assumption. We have assumed that behind the scenes of A all individuals are in competitive equilibrium facing the same price ratio. This assures us that all marginal rates of substitution are equal and that there exists no reallocation of the goods of A between them which will permit them both to be better off. (In technical parlance the competitive solution lies somewhere on the *Edgeworth contract locus*.) *A fortiori*, for a point like B, which involves smaller totals for *every* commodity, there is *no* reallocation of goods that could possibly make all individuals better off than they were in A. Without introducing price or index numbers, we know therefore that the point B is forbidden to be northeast of the point A—and we know that B corresponds to a decrease in real income over A according to the old 1940 definition.

But that is not really saying much. It is possible that one individual may be worse off even though the other individual is better off. And we must still entertain the darkest suspicions of a possible contradiction. But this simple case turns out to have at least one surprising feature: if we try to reallocate goods in either of the two situations—always letting the individuals come ultimately into competitive equilibrium—it turns out that we shall *never* find a case where on the 1940 definition the situation *B* turns out to be " better " (as well as " worse ") than *A*. I have not yet proved this in my discussion; but, accepting this fact as true, we find ourselves on the trail of a better way of defining an increase in real income—or more accurately, an increase in *potential* real income.

THE CRUCIALLY IMPORTANT 'UTILITY-POSSIBILITY FUNCTION'

8. Let us consider all possible reallocations between individuals of the consumption totals corresponding to *A* or 2. For each way of allocating the goods there will be a given level of well-being for each and every individual —as can be indicated by a point on the $U' - U''$ diagram. The totality of all such possible points obviously cannot go indefinitely far in the northeast direction; equally obviously there is a frontier curve or envelope giving, for each amount of one person's utility, the maximum possible amount of the other person's utility. This frontier is the important "utility-possibility function" corresponding to *A*.

The point 2 happens to lie on the frontier because at 2 all individuals are known to be in competitive equilibrium. Corresponding to the smaller totals of point *B*, there is also a utility-possibility function. We can now state the sense in which *A* or 2 is *potentially* better than *B*.

The total of all goods being greater in *A* than in *B*, the utility-possibility function of *A* is uniformly outside and beyond the utility-possibility function of *B*. (This is shown in Figure 4.) The reason for this statement is intuitively

Figure 4

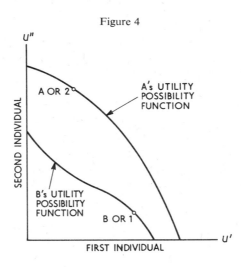

FIRST INDIVIDUAL

obvious and can be expressed in the language of a currently popular song: *A* can do everything *B* can do—(and) better.

9. This, then, is the sense in which we can, without introducing detailed ethical assumptions, define an "increase in society's potential real income in going from point *B* to point *A*." Such an increase means a uniform outward shift in society's utility-possibility function.

Let us now return to the index-number problem. Can we infer that *A* is superior to *C* in terms of our new definition of potential real income? If we can, then with minor modifications the 1940 analysis can be accepted. But, unfortunately for economic theory, we cannot make any such inference about potential superiority from the index-number analysis of aggregate price-quantity data.[4]

Any single counterexample will prove the falsity of the index-number criteria as applied to more than one individual. Perhaps the simplest such example would be one in which the first individual cares only for so-called necessaries. If less of total necessaries are available in *A*, then *A*'s utility-possibility curve must cut inside of *B*'s when we get in the region of the U''–U' quadrant favouring the necessary-loving individual; and hence *A* cannot represent an unequivocal increase in potential real income. Simple as this example is, it is open to the objection that it seems to involve the case where the individuals consume nothing of some commodity. Actually this is an irrelevant feature of the example.

But, in any case, greater insight into the nature of the problem can be had if we examine the steps in the reasoning linking up the index-number criterion and the 1940 definition of an increase in real income.

10. If we have between the points *A* and *C*, or 2 and 1,

$$\sum p_2(q_2' + q_2'' + \ldots) > \sum p_2(q_1' + q_1'' + \ldots),$$

then according to the 1940 argument we can find some redistribution of the quantities in *C* or 1, so that the new quantities of every good going to each individual, which we may call

$$q_3' + q_3'' + \ldots = q_1' + q_1'' + \ldots,$$

are such as to make the crucial index-number criteria hold for each and every individual; namely,

$$\sum p_2 q_2' > \sum p_2 q_3', \qquad \sum p_2 q_2'' > \sum p_2 q_3'', \ldots.$$

Hence there exists a new situation resulting from the reallocation of the q_1's which is worse for *every* individual than is situation 2.

A missing step in the 1940 logic must be filled in at this point. The fact that we can reallocate the q_1's to get a new point q_3 which makes both individuals worse off than they are in 2 is taken to mean that the utility-possibility curve of 1 must be southwest of the point 2. But nothing has been said to

---

[4] Simple logic tells us that this negative answer must be forthcoming in a comparison of *A* and *F* since each of two curves cannot both lie uniformly outside of each other; and already we have seen reason to believe that the *A* and *F* comparison does not differ materially from that of *A* and *C*.

show that q_3 is a frontier point on the utility-possibility function of point 1. Fortunately, it can be easily proved that there does exist at least one (and actually an infinite number) reallocation of the q_2's that (*a*) lies on the utility-possibility function of 1, and (*b*) causes our index-number criteria to hold for each and every individual.[5]

---

[5] Figure 5 shows all this. An Edgeworth-Bowley box has been drawn up with the dimensions of the quantities in the q_1 situation. From the southwest corner of the box we measure off the consumption of the first individual, U'. From the northeast corner we measure downward and to the left the consumption of the U'' individual. Any point in the box represents a possible allocation of the total q_1 quantities, with the point marked q_1 being the one actually observed.

Figure 5

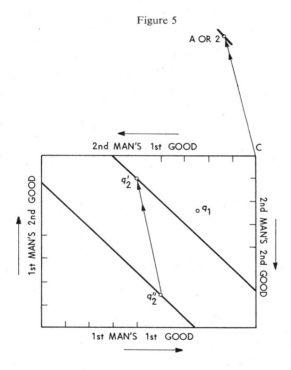

On this same diagram we may also show the actual quantities consumed by the individuals in the q_2 situation. But now it takes two points in the box, as far apart from each other as C is from A. They are marked q_2' and q_2'', respectively, and the price-lines through their points are drawn in with the slope of the p_2 situation.

As the picture stands q_1 does *not* satisfy the index-number criteria for the U' individual since q_1 does *not* lie inside the crucial triangle of the point q_2'. Hicks's statement is that there is some reallocation which will move the point q_1 to a new point q_3 which lies between the two parallel lines. For any such point our index-number criteria are satisfied for both individuals. The missing step is to show that there exist points in this strip which are also on the Edgeworth contract curve. Since the contract curve must go from one corner of the box to the other and pass through all levels of U' and U'', it must obviously somewhere pass through the intervening strip between the parallel lines. This supplies the missing step. Readers of Kuznets should note that it is the totals of q_1, not of q_2, that are reallocated so as to lead to Hicks's conclusion.

With the above provision, we may accept the 1940 demonstration that when aggregate data satisfy the index-number criterion, the 1940 definition of superiority is definitely realized.[6] But there is nothing in this demonstration that tells us whether the utility-possibility function of 2 lies above (or below) the point 1;[7] all we know is that 1's utility-possibility function lies somewhere southwest of the point 2.

11. Our final conclusions may be summarized briefly. The index-number criterion,

$$\sum p_2(q_2' + q_2'' + \ldots) > \sum p_2(q_1' + q_1'' + \ldots),$$

tells us that the utility-possibility function of 2 does lie outside of that of 1 *in the neighbourhood* of the actual observed point 2—but that is all it tells us. The curve may intersect and cross elsewhere—as shown in the later Figure 6.

THE HICKS-KALDOR-SCITOVSKY VERSION OF NEW WELFARE ECONOMICS

12. Having failed to relate the stronger definition of potential superiority to index-number criteria, we must reconsider whether, after all, the 1940 definition of superiority may not be tolerably acceptable. If we examine this definition, we find that it is in all essentials the same one as that earlier suggested by N. Kaldor and by Hicks in his earlier article on the "Foundations of Welfare Economics."[8] It will be recalled that these two writers had ruled that situation X is better than situation Y if there exists a reallocation of the goods in X which makes everybody better off than he was in Y. Except that the 1940 definition applied to a *decrease* in well-being between 2 and 1, this is identical with the earlier 1939 definition.

Dissatisfaction early developed over the 1939 definition. In particular T. Scitovsky[9] came forward with the objection that it seemed to assume that there was something right (ethically) about the distribution of income in the *status quo ante* of the Y situation. To get around this he suggested (in effect) that a *double* test be applied.

To say that "X is better than Y" we must be sure that (*a*) there exists a reallocation of the X goods that could make everybody better off than he actually was in Y; and (*b*) we must make sure there exists a reallocation of the goods in Y that could make everybody worse off than he actually was in X.

Or, in our terminology, the Scitovsky definition of superiority requires the

---

[6] This is apparently what Little means when he concludes that the 1940 definition is "immune from Professor Kuznets conditions" (*loc. cit.*, p. 13).

[7] In any case, no one should think that the condition $\sum p_1q_2 > \sum p_1q_1$ which is satisfied in C (but not in F) helps to rule out a contradiction.

[8] N. Kaldor, *"Welfare Propositions in Economics," Economic Journal*, xlix, 1939, pp. 549–52; J. R. Hicks, "Foundations of Welfare Economics," *Economic Journal*, xlix, 1939, pp. 696–712.

[9] T. Scitovsky, *"A Note on Welfare Propositions in Economics," Review of Economic Studies*, 1941, pp. 77–88, and "A Reconsideration of the Theory of Tariffs," *Review of Economic Studies*, 1942, pp. 89–110. To be precise Hicks is in 1940 riding the Scitovsky and Kuznets the Kaldor horse.

utility-possibility curve of one situation to be beyond that of the other in the neighbourhood of *both* actual observed points.

13. In his criticism of the 1940 definition Kuznets can be generously interpreted to be trying (presumably independently) in effect to reiterate the Scitovsky double criterion. Kuznets says at one point that we must supplement the Hicks condition [that there must be a reallocation of the q_1's that makes everyone worse off than he actually was in the q_2 situation] by the further condition that "[it must be] impossible to make *everyone* as well off as he is in situation I by any redistribution of the actual quantities acquired in situation II" (*Economica*, 1948., p. 4).

Kaldor has explicitly accepted the Scitovsky correction, and as far as I know so has Hicks. Therefore they would both presumably have no quarrel with this Kuznets reversibility condition.[10] But both Kuznets and Hicks do not seem to realize that the difficulty is basic and has nothing to do with the question of substitutability of necessaries or luxuries. On the Scitovsky-amended definition, the whole demonstration of superiority of one position over another by aggregate index-number criteria breaks down completely.[11]

14. Our whole theory of arriving at a measure of real income by aggregative price-quantity data has broken down. But the worst is still to come. The Scitovsky conditions are themselves very definitely unsatisfactory. It is not enough to double the 1939 conditions—we must increase them infinitely. Instead of a two-point test we need an infinitely large number of tests—that is to say, we must be sure that one of the utility-possibility functions *everywhere* lies outside the other. Without this test at an infinite number of points, no acceptable definition of an increase in potential real income can be devised at the nonethical level of the new welfare economics.

Just as Scitovsky has criticized Kaldor and "compensationists" for assuming the correctness of the *status quo ante*, so we must criticize him for assuming in some sense the correctness of the *status quo ante* and/or the *status quo post*.

Suppose, for example, we have *everybody actually* better off in situation 2 than in 1. Kaldor and Hicks will be satisfied to call 2 better than 1. So will Scitovsky. But the utility-possibility curves might very well cross as in Figure 6, so that according to many ethical welfare functions both Scitovsky and the others would be rendering false statements.

What Scitovsky should have done was to free all of his comparisons from any dependence upon either *actually observed U"–U'* situation. He should,

---

[10] Little has argued (*Economica*, 1949, pp. 12–16) that there is a confusion in Kuznets on the point of reversibility. Perhaps I am setting down what Kuznets should have meant rather than what he meant to say.

[11] The best that we can say is the following. Imagine the change from point 2 to point 1 to be a continuous one. So long as the two points are sufficiently (!) close together, then the condition $\Sigma p_2 q_2 > \Sigma p_2 q_1$ assures us that 2 is better than 1 in the Scitovsky sense. For changes of any size $\Sigma p_2 q_2 > \Sigma p_2 q_1$ tells us that 1 *cannot* be superior to 2 in Scitovsky or in my sense. and that is all it tells.

Figure 6

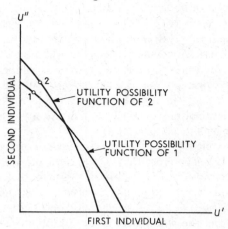

FIRST INDIVIDUAL

instead, have made the comparison depend upon the totality of all *possible* positions in each situation. This would have led to the definition of potential real income earlier proposed, which seems to be the only satisfactory, self-consistent definition within the sphere of the "new" (relatively *wert-frei*) welfare economics. Aggregate index numbers can tell us little about this except in a negative way. Even this definition is not—by itself—worth very much of anything for policy purposes, as will be shown.

INADEQUACIES FOR POLICY OF THE NEW WELFARE ECONOMICS

15. We have seen that the new welfare economics is able to define an increase in potential real income which is unambiguous, consistent, and which will not turn out to contradict a wide class of ethical social welfare functions that must later be introduced into any problem. The new welfare economics does not go all the way in settling the problems of normative policy: taken by itself, and without supplementation, it goes virtually none of the way; but taken in conjunction with later ethical assumptions, it attempts to clear the way of all issues that can be disposed of in a noncontroversial (relatively) ethical-free fashion. This is the solid kernel of usefulness in the new approach begun by Pareto, and this should not be lost sight of in the welter of exaggerated claims for the new welfare economics.

The inadequacy for actual policy decisions—even in the most idealized, simplified world—of all of the discussed measures of "real income" can be illustrated by numerous examples. Consider the very best case where we can establish the fact that situation 2 is *potentially* better than 1 (in the sense of having a uniformly farther-out utility-possibility function). Would a good fairy given the chance to throw a switch from 1 to 2 be able to justify doing so? Upon reflection we must, I am afraid, answer *no*. Potentialities are not actualities—and unless she can give a justification of her act that will satisfy all reasonably defined social welfare functions, she cannot know whether or not to pull the switch.

A few negative remarks are possible: for any ethical system with the property that an increase in one individual's well-being is, others' being equal, a good thing[12]—for all such systems a final optimum position must necessarily be on 2 and not on 1. That we can certainly say. But without going into the realm of (modern, streamlined) " old " welfare economics, we cannot say more or get conclusive advice on this problem of policy. The attempt to divide the problem into two parts so that one can say " a change from 1 to 2 is *economically* desirable in the sense of objectively increasing production or wealth, whether or not the actual resulting situation will be ethically superior," only gets one into a semantic snarl and glosses over the intrinsic difficulties of the problem.

How much more severe are the policy limitations of some of the modern even weaker " compensationist " definitions! Following them, the good fairy might do perpetual and irremediable harm. Suppose, for example, that our two *actually observed* points, 1 and 2, both lie above the intersection of the two schedules in Figure 6, but with the point 1 being southeast of point 2, so as to represent an increase in well-being of one individual and a decrease for the other. The Kaldor condition would be satisfied and so would the Scitovsky condition. Suppose that once the angel has thrown the switch, she can never again reverse it (e.g. capital sunk into a mine may be irrecoverable). Let her now follow the counsel of the compensationists and throw the switch from 1 to 2. According to any ethical view that considers individual U' to be of the elect (or relatively so) and U'' to be relatively undeserving of consideration, the good life lies in a rather easterly direction. For ever and ever " society " is condemned to " unhappiness " because of the premature decision based on the Kaldor–Hicks–Scitovsky rules.[13]

PRODUCTION POSSIBILITIES AND GROUP INFERENCES

16. This completes the problem of making group inferences from simple index-number comparisons. At the nonphilosophical level there are still two more grave difficulties to be faced. Up till now I have always spoken of the utility-possibility function of *point A*, not of situation A. But the totals of goods at A or 2 do not fall from heaven in fixed amounts. Obviously other

---

[12] i.e. for all social welfare propositions W, with the property $W = F(u', u'', \ldots)$ and
$$\frac{\partial W}{\partial u'} > 0 < \frac{\partial W}{\partial u''}, \ldots$$

[13] If both individuals are better off in the observed 2 point than in the observed 1 point, how reasonable it seems to counsel that the switch be pulled. And if the only alternative were these two situations, almost all old welfare economists might agree. But this need not be our choice of alternatives at all. Realistically, the choice may be between these two points and a third ethically superior point that lies on 1's locus. As a matter of tactics and *realpolitik*, one will sometimes want to follow such simple criteria *and* actually give compensation, or perhaps fail to compensate. But tactics aside, these rules are in principle incomplete.

total quantities might instead have been produced. Therefore, the true utility-possibility function corresponding to situation A is really wider and out farther than the one defined for point A. At best, if all markets are perfect and there are no external effects or government distortions, the utility-possibility function for point A may just touch that of situation A at the actual observed point, elsewhere being inside it. The wider schedule is the envelope of a family of schedules corresponding to each *possible* point of total consumption goods. (See Figure 8.)

Obviously it is the wider possibility function of a " situation " rather than of a " point " with which we should be concerned, and before we go throwing any switches or making policy decisions we must make sure how alternative production possibilities affect the problem. A few truths continue to remain self-evident, but, generally speaking, this new element makes the problem of definite inference even more difficult—an important but sad fact.

Let us consider an example. Up till now the one unshaken truth that remained was this: If more of every good is observed in point A than in point B, then A represents an increase in potential real national income over B. Even this is no longer necessarily valid! Suppose we draw up production-possibility curves showing how much of each good can be produced in total when the total of the other good is specified. Such a chart might look like Figure 6 except that now the two outputs rather than utilities are on the axes. In Figure 7 our observed point A lies northeast of the observed point B, and yet it is obvious that the production-possibility curves can still cross; and it is also obvious, upon reflection, that depending upon how much people like one good as compared to another, the *corresponding utility-possibility curves can most definitely cross*—making no unambiguous inference about an increase in potential real income possible.

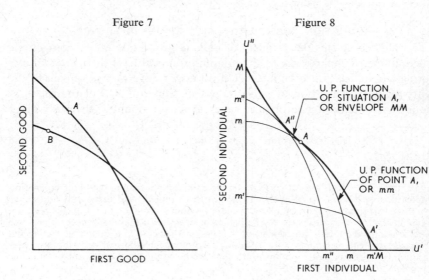

Figure 7   Figure 8

17. So long as commodities are really economic rather than free goods, this much can be said: *If the production-possibility function of one situation lies uniformly outside that of a second situation, then the utility-possibility function of the one will also be outside that of the other.* In the limiting case where one or both individuals do not care at all for one of the goods, the schedules might just be touching at one or more points. Also it is to be understood that if the total of resources (land, labour, etc.) is not the same in the two situations, these resources are to be treated just like negative commodities, and it is in this sense that one production-possibility function must lie uniformly outside the other.

Hicks attempted in 1940 to explore the relationship between index-number criteria based on price-quantity data and productivity as measured by the position of the production-possibility function of society. His treatment was brief and much of it he had abandoned prior to Kuznets' 1948 criticisms. But even after the recent exchange of views I do not feel the subject is left in its proper state. To analyse the problem in its entirety would be too lengthy a task, but a number of observations are relevant to our discussion. In all that follows I shall assume that there are no excise taxes, so that the irrelevant distinction between income-at-factor-prices and income-at-market-prices can be disregarded.

Under this last assumption, would the same $\sum pq$ tests relevant to indicating a (1940-defined) increase in welfare also serve to indicate a shift in productivity? One is almost tempted to read such a belief into the following passage:

> If competition were perfect, and if state activities were so designed as not to disturb the *optimum* organization of production, marginal utilities and prices and marginal costs would all be proportional, so that the same valuation which would give us the social income as a measure of economic welfare would also give us the social income as a measure of productivity.[14]

Kuznets objected to all this on the grounds that production-possibility curves, unlike indifference curves, can intersect and can be of variable curvature. His instinct that something is rotten in Denmark may be a sound one, but the precise trouble has not really been isolated, nor a worse difficulty brought to light.

In the first place, there is no need for an individual's indifference curves always to be concave: he need only be assumed to be in equilibrium at the

----

[14] *Economica*, 1940, p. 122. Hicks goes on to say, parenthetically: "It would not be very reliable as a measure of productivity, but it might usually satisfy the productivity tests for small displacements, over which the substitution curves might not differ very much from straight lines." To make the only comparison between different situations that are valid, this last linearity assumption can be shown to be unnecessary; but it foreshadows Hicks's later desire for an approximate representation of the production-possibility function in the neighbourhood of an observed optimal point. A straight line gives, under the assumed conditions, an upper (rather than a conservative, lower) bound as to what is producible.

observed points. In the second place, it is untrue that collectively defined indifference curves (*à la* Scitovsky or otherwise) are forbidden to intersect and cross. Our earlier discussion of the points A and F may be referred to in this connexion. Neither of these two reasons can serve to isolate the basic difficulties of making production inferences.[15]

In the production or firm field we have an institutional difficulty absent from the household markets: few families act like monopsonists, but many, if not most, firms sell in markets which are less than perfectly competitive. Let us waive this difficulty for the moment and assume that technological and market conditions are most suitable to perfect competition: namely, constant-returns-to-scale prevails and there is "free entry." In this case, any observed point of total output—such as A or 2 in Figure 1—would represent a *maximum* of $\sum p_2 q$ subject to all the production possibilities of the situation. Geometrically the straight line running through A can never be inside the true production-possibility schedule.

Does this mean that the criterion $\sum p_2 q_2 > \sum p_1 q_1$ in Figure 1 assures us of *both* of the following: that 2 is better than 1 *in welfare*, and 2 is better *in a production-possibility sense* than 1? It must *not* be so interpreted. The production problem involves a certain *maximum* condition, the consumption case a related *minimum* condition. The same index-number calculation can never serve as a crucial indicator for the two problems: if it is a reliable criterion for welfare, it tells us nothing about production; if it has unambiguous production implications, then welfare inferences are impossible.

There are essentially only four possible cases that have to be considered: a comparison of A and C in Figure 1, of A and D, of A and F, and the almost trivial case of A and B. In this last case, where the A situation has more of every good than the B, we know immediately that the production-possibility function of A lies outside that of B in the neighbourhood of both observed points, and we also know that A's utility-possibility function (defined narrowly for the points rather than broadly for the situations) lies everywhere outside of that of B. All this is obvious, so we can concentrate our attention on the three other possible comparisons. To keep the notation simple we can always give the point A the number 2 and give all other compared points the number 1. Our cases, then, are as follows:

---

[15] Kuznets has a third objection which has little or nothing to do with the problem here discussed. Working by analogy with the consumption problem, he makes the strange and unnecessary assumption that a perfect price system is in some sense maximizing "producers' surpluses," and he raises the question whether specificity of some resources may not make it impossible for every producer to be as well off as previously. Both Hicks and I would consider producers and consumers to be the same units, who buy goods and also sell services; all such services can be treated as negative goods and all ordinal disutilities treated along with ordinal utilities. Firms (corporations) provide the place where producers work but themselves have no welfare feelings, although their owners' welfare is important. The problem at hand is what we can or cannot say about the production-possibility functions *of society* in two situations.

	Concerning 1940 def. of welfare	Concerning position of production-possibility function (p.p.f)
Case A (or 2) and C (or 1):		
$\Sigma p_2 q_2 > \Sigma p_2 q_1$ tells us	2 better than 1	nothing
$\Sigma p_1 q_2 > \Sigma p_1 q_1$ tells us	nothing	p.p.f. of 1 outside of p.p.f. of 2 near point 2
Case A (or 2) and D (or 1):		
$\Sigma p_2 q_2 < \Sigma p_2 q_1$ tells us	nothing	p.p.f. of 1 outside of p.p.f. of 2 near point 1
$\Sigma p_1 q_2 > \Sigma p_1 q_1$ tells us	nothing	p.p.f. of 2 outside of p.p.f. of 1 near point 2
Case A (or 2) and F (or 1):		
$\Sigma p_2 q_2 > \Sigma p_2 q_1$ tells us	2 better than 1	nothing
$\Sigma p_1 q_1 > \Sigma p_1 q_2$ tells us	1 better than 2	nothing

Under the present assumptions we can make inferences about the shifting of production-possibility functions that are no less strong than those about welfare. We can never hope to infer from index-number tests that one production-possibility curve has shifted *uniformly* with respect to another —but then we have earlier seen that we can never hope to make such welfare inferences either. It will be noted from the table that where light is thrown on productivity it is withheld from welfare, and vice versa. This might almost seem to offer comfort: we seem always to be able to say *something* about any situation. But, alas, this is an illusion.

THE IMPOSSIBILITY OF UNEQUIVOCAL INFERENCES

18. Even that which we have in the field of welfare indicators is to be taken away from us now that we have enlarged our alternatives to all the production possibilities of each situation rather than to the single observed points. *We shall never be able to infer a genuine change in potential real income as I have earlier defined the term*—no, not even in the simplest comparison of A which shows more of every good than the point B. (This was already shown in Figure 7.) Unsatisfactory as the 1940 definitions of welfare were, we are tempted to beat a hasty retreat back to them. But to no good purpose: even these fragile reeds are blown down by the new winds.

Specifically, the observation $\Sigma p_2 q_2 > \Sigma p_2 q_1$ no longer implies that the utility-possibility function of *situation* 1 lies inside that of A even in the neighbourhood of the point 2, or anywhere at all for that matter! The whole 1940 proof by Hicks—as supplemented in my earlier lengthy footnote concerning the box-diagram—breaks down completely. The demonstration fails, the argument no longer leads logically to the desired conclusion. By itself this does not show that there may not be found some different proof. However, the theorem can be proved to be false, so that no valid alternative proof exists.

A single example provides a decisive exception to the theorem (that we can infer a local shift in the utility-possibility function). The point F in Figure 1 has a utility-possibility curve which may be almost anywhere with respect to that of A, as far as anything we know. There is no reason why it could not always lie outside of A's; there is also no reason why the point F should not lie on C's production-possibility curve; there is also no reason why the utility-possibility function of the general situation C should not be close to or identical with the utility-possibility function of the point F (except possibly at the observed point C itself). It follows that we can easily imagine the utility-possibility function of the situation C to lie *above and beyond* the observed point A—which contradicts the Hicks-like theorem that situation C's curve must lie somewhere southwest of the A point. This example shows that the Hicks proof remains no longer valid when it ceases to be simply a question of reallocating a given fixed total in the 1 situation.

THE INTERRELATION BETWEEN PRODUCTION AND UTILITY-POSSIBILITY FUNCTIONS

19. Production possibilities as such have no normative connotations. We are interested in them for the light they throw on utility possibilities. This is why economists have wanted to include such wasteful output as war goods in their calculations of national product; presumably they serve as some kind of an index of the useful things that might be produced in better times. Our last hope to make welfare statements lies in spelling out the welfare implications of any recognizable shifts in production possibilities.

A uniform outward shift in the production-possibility function—such as can never be revealed by index-number comparisons—must certainly shift the utility-possibility schedule outward. The converse is not true. An outward shift in the utility-possibility function may have occurred as the result of a *twist* of the production-possibility curve. This is because people's tastes for different goods may be such that the points on the new production schedule that lie inward may be points that would never be observed in any optimal competitive market. An "observable" point is one which, as the result of some allocation of initial resources or so-called "distribution of income," would lead to one of the points on the utility-possibility frontier.

In the typical case where $\sum p_1 q_1 < \sum p_1 q_2$, so that we know that the production-possibility function of 2 is outside of that of 1 somewhere near the observed point 2, we should like to be able to say that 2's utility-possibility function lies outside that of 1 in the neighbourhood of the observed point 2. But we cannot. The utility-possibility functions of situation 2 and of point 2 both lie outside the utility-possibility function of the points which are known to lie southwest of the observed point 2 on the production-possibilities diagram. But all such points might turn out to be nonobservable ones. Only if an observable point 2 is known to give more of all goods than an *observable* point of the situation 1 can we even infer that situation 2 is superior to 1 in the weak 1940 sense. Index-number data are never enough to provide us with knowledge of two such observable points except in the trivial case (like A and B) where one point is better in respect to every good, and where index-number calculations are unnecessary to establish the only fact that can be established: namely, the production-possibility function of A must lie outside that of B near the observed points and the same must be true about the related utility-possibility function.

Under the best conditions of the purest of competition very little indeed of welfare significance can ever be revealed by price-quantity data alone. Needless to say, with the actual statistical problems in a world of imperfect competition and decreasing costs, observed prices have even less significance as indicators of the shape of society's true production-possibility curve.

POLITICAL FEASIBILITY AS A CRUCIAL CONDITION IN WELFARE ECONOMICS

20. The last limitation on the applicability to policy of the new welfare economics concepts is in practice one of the most important of all. It hinges around the practical unattainability of the production-possibility and utility-possibility function earlier discussed. It is not simply that imperfections of competition are so widespread as to keep society from reaching its optimal production frontier; or that government interferences inevitably cause distortions; or that external diseconomies and economies can never be recognized and computed. All these are true enough.[16]

The essential point now to be stressed is that we could move people to different points on the utility-possibility function only *by an ideally perfect and unattainable system of absolutely lump-sum taxes or subsidies.* In point of fact, suppose that, in the simplest case, competitive *laissez-faire* puts us at one point on the utility-possibility function. Then we can only seek to change the distribution of income by a system of *feasible* legislation: e.g. progressive income tax, rationing, etc. All such policies involve a distortion of marginal decisions, some involving great distortions but in every case some distortion. They move us then *inside* the utility-possibility curve. We can pick policies which strive to minimize the harmful effects of redistribution, but in practice we cannot reduce such effects to zero. A "feasible utility function" can conceptually be drawn up which lies more or less far inside the utility-possibility function, depending upon how Utopian were our assumptions about legislation, public opinion, etc.

---

[16] They can be thought of as forces keeping us from reaching the true possibility frontier; or if we are in a nonperfectionist mood and willing to compromise with evil, they may be thought of as defining a not-so-far-out but pragmatically obtainable frontier. If the latter interpretation is made, we must be careful to realize that the slopes of the defined frontiers need have little correspondence with market prices, marginal costs of production, etc. As I have earlier pointed out (*Foundations*, p. 221), the constraints under which society is conceived as working are arbitrary and must be given by noneconomic assumptions. England's production possibilities would be different if the laws of physics could be disregarded or if we could assume that all workers would do their "best," or ... or.

All this is shown in Figure 9. The point L represents the imputation resulting from a situation of relatively *laissez-faire*. It is made to lie on the heavy-line utility-possibility function—which it would only do in a very perfect competitive world.

Let us suppose that the tastes and abilities of the two individuals are identical so that we can use similar indicators of their ordinal preferences. But let them differ in their ownership of resources (say land) so that the income of U'' is much greater than that of U', as indicated by the position of L relative to the 45°-line of "equal income." In a Utopia there might be some way of redistributing wealth or income that would move us along the outside curve from L to the point of complete equality, E, or even beyond. But in practice the only feasible path that Congress or Parliament could follow would be along the light-line utility-feasibility curve.[17]

Space does not permit me to work out the far-reaching implications of this point of view. It is enough to point out here that situation A may have a uniformly better production-possibility function than B, and also a uniformly better utility-possibility function. But a change from B to A might so alter the distribution of market-imputed income away from the "worthy" and towards the "unworthy" as to make it an undesirable move from many ethical viewpoints. The *utility-feasibility function* of A may very well cross that of B, so that no statement about potentialities, much less about actualities, can be validly made.

By all means let us pray that feasibilities and possibilities be brought

Figure 9

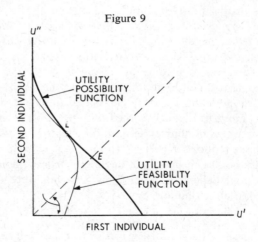

SECOND INDIVIDUAL

UTILITY POSSIBILITY FUNCTION

UTILITY FEASIBILITY FUNCTION

FIRST INDIVIDUAL

U'

U''

---

[17] A strong ethical equalitarian would have to reckon with this fact; and unless his social welfare functions had complete L-shaped corners along the 45° line, or even bent back *à la* Veblen and like the dog-in-the-manger, he would find his feasible optimum at some distance from equality of incomes. All this has a bearing, I believe, on the debate between Meade and Kahn as to whether rationing and food subsidies ought necessarily to be rejected by rational equalitarians in favour of greater reliance on income taxes or other more orthodox devices.

closer and closer. But let us not indulge in the illusion that our prayers have been answered and that we can issue new-welfare-economics prescriptions accordingly.[18]

FINAL SUMMARY

21. This has been a long and closely reasoned essay. A brief summary may pull the threads together.

1. Certain $\sum pq$ calculations tell us when a single individual has improved himself.

2. The only consistent and ethics-free definition of an increase in potential real income of a group is that based upon a uniform shift of the utility-possibility function for the group. $\sum pq$ calculations based on aggregate data never permit us to make such inferences about uniform shifts.

3. The condition $\sum p_2 q_2 > \sum p_2 q_1$ does tell us that the utility-possibility function of the *point* 2 is outside the utility-possibility function of the *point* 1 somewhere near 2. It is not acceptable to define this as an increase in real income for a number of reasons, not the least being that we may end up with 2 defined to be both "better" and "worse" than 1.

4. Scitovsky and later Kuznets have suggested a partial strengthening of the earlier definitions of superiority so as to rule out certain revealed inconsistencies. But even these two-sided requirements are not stringent enough; when made infinite-sided, as they must be to avoid inconsistency or implicit ethics, they become equivalent to the definition based upon a uniform shift of the utility-possibility schedule. And even when this rigid definition is realized, we cannot properly prescribe complete policy prescriptions without bringing in ethics.

5. When we come to make inferences about two *situations*, each of which involves a whole *set* of production possibilities rather than about just the observed *points*, even the limited welfare inferences of point 3 break down completely. Under the most perfect conditions suitable for pure competition (where the production-possibility curve can never be concave) a few inferences concerning the local shifts of the production-possibility schedules are possible; e.g., $\sum p_2 q_2 < \sum p_2 q_1$ implies that 1's production-possibility function is outside 2's in the neighbourhood of the observed 2 point.

6. The inferred shifts of production-possibility functions are not enough to permit similar inferences about the utility-possibility functions. This is

---

[18] A few comments on the cited Little article on "Foundations" are perhaps in order. There is much I agree with in this paper, and much I do not yet understand. His semantic jousts with the post-Kaldor school falls under the first heading; his analysis of the meaning of a *social or economic welfare function* under the second. The part of his paper that is most relevant to the present technical discussion is his proposed "foundations" for a "system" of welfare economics. In my present understanding of it—still admittedly vague—Little has stated a few theorems of one type. These are understandable in terms of the language of a welfare function, and are more in the nature of one arch or wing of a structure than its foundations. The technical content of the theorems is discussed in the last footnote of the appended Pigou note.

because that portion of a production-possibility curve which has clearly been revealed to be inside another or "inferior" may (for all we know) consist entirely of "unobservable points" that have no correspondence with the truly observable points along the related utility-possibility frontier.

7. The utility-possibility functions defined above are not really possible or available to society; they would be so only in a Utopian world of "perfect" lump-sum taxes and other ideal conditions. Depending upon how optimistic our assumptions are, we must think of society as being contained within a *utility-feasibility function* which lies inside the *utility-possibility function*. At best these are close together in the neighbourhood of the "points of relative *laissez-faire*." Other things being equal, redistribution of income will usually involve "costs," which have to be weighed against the ethically defined "advantages" of such policies.

8. All this being true, we come to the paradoxical conclusion that a policy which seems to make possible greater production of all goods and a uniformly better utility-possibility function for society may result in so great (and ethically undesirable) a change in the imputation of different individuals' incomes, that we may have to judge such a policy "bad." Such a judgement sounds as if it necessarily involves ethics, but it may be reworded so as to be relatively free of value judgements by being given the following interpretation: A policy that shifts society's utility-possibility function uniformly outward may not at the same time shift the utility-feasibility function uniformly outward, instead causing it to twist inward in some places. One last warning is in order: to define what is feasible involves many arbitrary assumptions, some of them of an ethical nature.

The above analysis enables us to appraise critically Pigou's important definitions of real income; this has been reserved for a separate appendix, which—except for a few cross-references—is self-contained.

A NOTE ON PIGOU'S TREATMENT OF INCOME

1. Despite the vast efforts of government agencies and bureaux in the last 20 years, Pigou's *Economics of Welfare* remains the classic discussion of the definition of real national income. Our previous analysis permits us to make a rapid critique of his masterly analysis. Even if I am right that certain of his formulations need minor amendation, his conclusions for welfare economics remain untouched. Pigou's principal theorem—that each resource should have equal marginal (social) productivity in every use, with price everywhere equal to marginal (social) cost—does not depend for its demonstration upon the elaborate discussion of the national dividend in Part I. In the days, when the national income approach is all the rage as a pedagogic device for coating the pill of elementary economics, it is worth noting that Pigou had seized upon this method of exposition more than a quarter of a century ago. Whether it would have been possible for him to have side-stepped completely the introductory discussion of real national income is irrelevant, since by choosing not to do so Pigou was led to make substantial contributions to the modern theory of economic index numbers (of the Könus, Bowley, Haberler, Staehle type).

2. According to Pigou, economic welfare is "that part of social welfare that can be brought directly or indirectly into relation with the measuring-rod of money." The national dividend or real national income is "the objective counterpart of economic welfare." Pigou would like to adopt the intuitive position that the dividend should be a function of objective quantities of goods alone, and not depend on "the state of people's tastes." But since (a) there is not a single commodity, and (b) all commodities do not move in the same proportion, or (c) even all in the same general direction, Pigou reluctantly considers such an objective definition not feasible, and settles for a more subjective definition according to which *the real income of any person is said to be higher for batch of goods II than for I if II is higher up on his indifference or preference map.*

These are not his words but my interpretation of them, expressed so as to be theoretically independent of any relationship with money or market-price behaviour. Pigou's exact statement for the case of a single individual is as follows:

Considering a single individual whose tastes are taken as fixed, we say that his dividend in period II is greater than in period I if the items that are added to it in period II are items that he wants more than the items that are taken away from it in period II. (*Economics of Welfare*, 4th ed., p. 51.)

The wording is cast in a comparative form to pave the way for consideration of the more complex case of many individuals where it may be especially difficult to ask people about their wants and desires and theoretically difficult to define what is meant by the *wants* of the *group*. Pigou extends his definition further:

Passing to a group of persons (of given numbers), whose tastes are taken as fixed and among whom the distribution of purchasing power is also taken as fixed, we say that the dividend in period II is greater than in period I if the items that are added to it in period II are items *to conserve which they would be willing to give more money than they would be willing to give to conserve the items that are taken away from it in period II.* (Ibid., pp. 51–52.)

For the moment let us accept the assumption of constant tastes and "distribution of purchasing power" and the assumption that people know their own minds and correctly identify *ex ante* desire with *ex post* satisfaction. Pigou then gives another verbal reformulation of his definition, saying that the dividend is higher in period II than in I if "the economic satisfaction (as measured in money) due to the items added in period II is greater than the economic satisfaction (as measured in money) due to the items taken away in period II" (p. 54). Under the assumptions stated, Pigou believes this method of definition to be "the natural and obvious one to adopt" (p. 52).

3. I wonder. One can sympathize with the attempt to introduce into the definition something that a statistician might sink his punch-cards into, but

has the introduction of money left the problem unambiguous? I have repeated the definition to myself aloud again and again; and yet even in the case of a single consistent individual about whom unlimited data were available, I would still not be sure how to proceed.

Pigou himself, according to my interpretation of his various writings, is also put in an ambivalent mood by his definition. In the next chapter he proceeds to work with index-number expressions of the form $\sum pq$ where the p's and q's are observed market data. To my mind this is a perfectly valid procedure in the case of a single individual (and it can be given a measure of validity for the case of a group along the lines indicated in my present article). But it is not at all clear that Pigou regards his own procedure as really valid. Again and again he states that the proper procedure is to measure the monetary strength of people's desires not by the marginal price data observed but rather by some kind of consumers-surplus type of construction indicating how much they could be made to pay rather than do without the thing altogether.[1]

Pigou's definition has for the moment betrayed him, and I am willing to defend his practice against his precept. I suspect that what happened is something like the following: instead of continuing to look for an ordinal indicator of utility, Pigou suddenly caught a glimpse of the butterfly of cardinal utility and set out in hot pursuit. But he realized that the difficulties of this approach were more than statistical, necessarily involving all the familiar difficulties of Marshallian consumers' surplus. Whether or not the butterfly is obtainable or of any use once caught, we must take care not to belittle the solid fruits of index-number theory that are in our grasp.

4. What Pigou does establish—on pp. 62–63—is that

$$\sum p_2 q_2 > \sum p_2 q_1$$

means that II is better than I for any consistent individual. The reasoning is exactly that of the A and C comparison in my Figure 1. Likewise

$$\sum p_1 q_1 > \sum p_1 q_2$$

---

[1] *Ibid.*, pp. 57, 59. In his 1945 introductory work, *Income*, p. 13, Pigou still shows a desire to use some measure of consumers' surplus (or total utility) rather than market values. In the 1949 *Veil of Money* he is even more explicit in insisting that the relative weight of goods should in principle depend upon "how much of their money income people *would have been willing* to spend ... [rather than on] how much money they *actually do spend*. ... Weighting by reference to this entails, other things being equal, giving a smaller weight to changes in items of inelastic and a larger weight to changes in items of elastic demand than "ought" to be assigned to them if our object is, as I have suggested it might be, to measure importance by reference to impact on economic satisfaction, given that tastes are constant. Thus at the very basis of any structure we may erect there is an incorrigible flaw. At the best, we shall have to content ourselves with a makeshift measure, what exactly in the last resort it is measuring being ill-defined and blurred" (pp. 60–61). Cf. J. R. Hicks, "Foundation of Welfare Economics," *Economic Journal*, xlix, 1939, p. 697, for a related criticism of Pigou's treatment of marginal and intramarginal concepts.

would have meant that I was better than II. Pigou prefers to make the comparisons in the more usual Laspeyre and Paasche index-number ratios[2]

$$P = \frac{\sum p_2 q_2}{\sum p_2 q_1} \gtreqless 1 \quad \text{and} \quad L = \frac{\sum p_1 q_2}{\sum p_1 q_1} \gtreqless 1.$$

If we treat work and other efforts as negative commodities, our analysis becomes slightly more general.[3] But our $\sum pq$ expressions may then be zero or negative, so that the method of ratios may be inapplicable even though the proper comparisons can be made in nonratio form. As we shall see, the use of such ratios has the further disadvantage that it tempts people to attach *cardinal* significance, in an exact or probalistic sense, to the numerical value of the $\sum pq$ ratios.

5. If both P and L are greater than unity, II is clearly better than I. If both are less than unity, then I is better than II. If they are numerically almost equal—and Pigou seems to think they often will be—then the measurement of welfare is thought to be fairly definite. When they differ numerically, Pigou would often measure welfare by some kind of intermediate mean between them: because the geometric mean—which is the Irving Fisher so-called " Ideal-Index "—has certain convenient properties, Pigou accepts it " as the measure of change most satisfactory for our purpose " (p. 69).

I cannot persuade myself to follow Pigou's use of the numerical value of the P and L ratios. In the first place, he—along with Kuznets and many others —treats the measures much too symmetrically. When $P > 1$, we already know that II is better than I. If we learn in addition that $L > 1$, we cannot regard this as further corroboration that II is superior to I; at best it serves as corroboration of the fact that we are dealing with a consistent individual.

The case is much different when you tell us that $L > 1$, and nothing else. We have no right to presume that II is definitely better than I. If now you volunteer to us the second bit of information that $P > 1$ also, we cannot regard this as corroboration of an earlier presumption or certainty yielded by the first bit of information. *In its own right* the second fact, that $P > 1$, tells us all we want to know.

With respect to the opposite case, of recognizing when I is better than II, we must attach crucial importance to $L < 1$; and once again the behaviour of P is corroboration of nothing, except of the presence of inconsistency and changed tastes.

---

[2] Pigou lets $x, y, z, \ldots$ stand for q's and $a, b, c, \ldots$ for p's and writes these expressions in the form

$$P = \frac{I_2}{I_1} \frac{x_1 a_1 + y_1 b_1 + \ldots}{x_1 a_2 + y_1 b_2 + \ldots} \text{ or } \frac{\sum p_2 q_2}{\sum p_1 q_1} \frac{\sum p_1 q_1}{\sum p_2 q_1} = \frac{\sum p_2 q_2}{\sum p_2 q_1},$$

$$L = \frac{I_2}{I_1} \frac{x_2 a_1 + y_2 b_1 + \ldots}{x_2 a_2 + y_2 b_2 + \ldots} \text{ or } \frac{\sum p_2 q_2}{\sum p_1 q_1} \frac{\sum p_1 q_2}{\sum p_2 q_2} = \frac{\sum p_1 q_2}{\sum p_1 q_1}.$$

[3] Pigou's difficulty concerning an increase in the dividend at the expense of leisure, p. 87, n. 1, could then have been avoided.

6. Looking into Pigou's probability argument, we will find one difficulty that stems from his treating of P and L as symmetrical indicators of welfare. Suppose $P = 3 > 1$ and $L = 0.99 < 1$, and these measurements are known to be perfectly accurate, statistically speaking. Then the testimony of the two measures is contradictory, one being greater and the other less than unity. But P exceeds unity by a greater ratio than L falls short of unity, so that $\sqrt{PL}$, the ideal-index, is much greater than unity. Pigou would conclude—according to my interpretation of pp. 65–66—that II is *probably* greater than I.

My conclusion would be different. I would say that either the individual's tastes have definitely changed between the periods or that he was not in equilibrium in both situations. This is because $P > 1$ tells me that II is higher on his indifference curves than is I, and $L < 1$ tells me the exact opposite, and that is the end of it. There is no sense that I can see in believing that, because P is much greater than 1, its testimony is in a loud enough voice to shout down the whisper of $L < 1$.

7. Actually all is not lost as far as exact inference from such a case is concerned. We can validly state: $P > 1$ implies that the batch of goods II is higher *on the indifference curves that prevailed in period II* than *is* the batch of goods I; and $L < 1$ implies that the first batch of goods is higher than batch II *on the indifference curves that prevailed in period I.*

It would be tempting to argue that P always measures welfare from the II period's tastes and L always measures welfare from the I period's tastes. This would be quite wrong, as Pigou is clearly aware. If $P = 0.99$ and $L = 3.0$, we most certainly cannot state the reverse of the previous paragraph's conclusions. We cannot even infer anything about inconsistency. By its nature P can only give definite evidence concerning batch II's superiority over I, and L can only give definite evidence concerning batch I's superiority over II.[4]

8. The case where $P < 1$ and $L > 1$ is the only one to which Pigou explicitly applies his probability reasoning. As in Figure 1's comparison of A and E, no certain inference is possible. The unknown indifference curve through A could pass above or below the point E. Now the closer is E to the budget-line through A, or what is the same thing the closer is P to 1, then, "other things being equal," we should expect that the chance of A's indifference curve's passing above E would be increased. The same chance would be increased, the more L is reduced towards unity, "other things being equal." This is the basis for Pigou's common-sense view that the degree to which

---

[4] In § 5, chap. vi, p. 58, Pigou leans over backward too far on the issue of the inferences possible when tastes have changed. He believes that the best we can hope for is to devise measures giving the correct results *when tastes have not changed.* This is because he thinks that to make the inference that the batch II is better than the batch I on the basis of the indifference curves of II, we must know what the batch I *would have been* if the indifference curves of II (rather than the actual indifference curves of I) had then prevailed. This is incorrect, as can be noted from the above discussion and from the fact that in my earlier Figure 1 the inference about A and C was independent of the actual indifference-ratio slope *through C.*

$\sqrt{(PL)} \gtrless 1$ determines the likelihood of II's being better or worse than I. Between 1928 and 1932 Pigou felt compelled to abandon an argument based upon "the principle of sufficient reason" that attempted to establish this common-sense conclusion. His reason for abandoning it was not because of any impregnation with the modern tendency among statisticians and philosophers to question arguments based on ignorance or on the "equal-probability of the unknown," but because of technical difficulties previously unnoticed. I think that some of these difficulties could be side-stepped, but since Pigou is content to abandon his old view, and since I am not enamoured of the principle of sufficient reason, I shall confine my attention to the exact inferences possible.

Consider a point A on an individual's indifference map. Consider the region of all alternative points in comparison with A, A being regarded as II and each of these points as I. Consider the contour lines of any symmetric mean of P and L, such as $\sqrt{(PL)}$ = constants. Also consider the contour lines of P = constants and L = constants.

Then this much is true: the contour lines $P = 1$, $L = 1$, and $\sqrt{(PL)} = 1$ all go through A and are tangent to the indifference curve through A. Suppose we use any of the three measures $P \lessgtr 1$, $L \gtrless 1$, or $\sqrt{(PL)} \gtrless 1$ to decide whether A is better or worse than the other point tested. Then the "percentage of points" for which we get wrong answers by these methods goes to zero as we confine ourselves to smaller and smaller regions around A. Also the probability will approach one, as we confine ourselves to ever closer regions around A, that all three methods will give the same testimony. In the limit as the region around A shrinks, the use of the P criterion in those rare cases when it disagrees with the L criterion will lead to a biased estimate—in that all points under such conditions of contradiction will in the limit be declared to be worse than A, including those points which are really better than A. Exclusive reliance on L in case of contradiction will result in an opposite bias towards declaring all doubtful points better than A. In the limit as the second point is constrained to lie in ever closer regions to A, the use of $\sqrt{(PL)} \gtrless 1$ criterion will lead to a percentage of wrong decisions that approaches ever closer to zero.[5] These are exact statements about limits.

9. Besides Pigou, other writers such as Kuznets and Little have seen fit to attach significance to the numerical values of the P and L ratios. (Readers not interested in technicalities can skip this section.) Kuznets argues as follows:

Suppose as we go from I to II, both P and L are greater than they are when we go from I to III. Then II is "generally" better than III, provided that the shift in prices from II to III has effects on the ratios of certain identical quantity aggregates of an [allegedly] usual sort.[6]

---

[5] Mathematically, the indifference curve through A is tangential to the $P = 1$ and $L = 1$ contours, lying "half-way" between them. The contour $\sqrt{(PL)} = 1$ also has their mean curvature and is an osculating tangent to the indifference curve, differing only in its third and higher derivatives. See my *Foundations* p. 148.

[6] This is my brief transcription of Kuznets's Appendix, *Economica*, 1949, pp. 124–31 and his remarks on p. 5.

It will be noted that Kuznets is attempting to use certain numerical or cardinal comparisons for the sole purpose of arriving at a purely *ordinal* comparison. There is nothing methodologically objectionable about this; but nonetheless the Kuznets result is a self-contained truism that does not permit us to make any general inferences of certain validity in any empirical situation.

First an example may illustrate the loopholes in Kuznets's results. Back in my Figure 1, let us consider the three points *A, B, C*. Kuznets will find that *P* and *L* computed for *A* and *B* are *exactly* the same as for *A* and *C*. According to his theorem, *C* and *B* should be equally satisfactory or approximately so. Actually the indifference curve through *C* passes above that of *B*, and if there were any sense in speaking of " well above " we might use this stronger expression. More than that, by moving *C* southwest a little or *B* northeast a little, we could arrive at the even falser presumption that *B* is better than *C*.

There is nothing faulty about Kuznets's arithmetic or the truism he derives from his substitution. He would have to say in this connexion: " My proviso about price-quantity correlation has been violated in the example." And why should it not be? When Kuznets says that *P* is " in general " less than *L*, he does not mean by the words " in general " what a mathematician means when he says that the two sides of a triangle are " generally " greater than the third. Kuznets means, I think it is clear, that *usually* the price-quantity correlation will be such as to make *P* less than *L*. (Actually a long line of writers in index-number theory fell into the actual error of thinking that $P \leqslant L$ and between them lies some " true " value; an almost equally long line of writers have pointed out the falsity of this relation.) I venture the conjecture that Kuznets formed his belief concerning the usual or normal numerical dominance of *L* over *P* from considering the special case where there are no real income changes and where any increase in the price of a good (or set of goods) is followed by a necessary decrease in its quantity. But it is precisely when we are trying to arrive at an estimate of whether II is better or worse than III that we must not beg the question by assuming that they are on the same indifference locus.

Even in a loose probability sense, it would be dangerous to say that *P* is usually less than *L*. If all goods had an income elasticity of exactly one— so that a pure income change resulted in proportionate changes in every item of consumption—then this would be a certainty. But so long as the well-attested Engel's laws and observed budgetary patterns hold, we must *certainly* have a reversal of the *P–L* relations throughout the area between the income-expenditure curve through *A* and the straight line joining *A* to the origin. This shows that my *ABC* example is not an isolated case, but is typical of what will always be true in some region.[7]

---

[7] Little gives a probability interpretation of the significance of the cardinal size of *P* on pp. 46–47, *Economica*, 1949. He has in mind a closely related, but distinct, group inference from that discussed in this paper. He also relies on our rough empirical knowledge of preference patterns in evaluating his probabilities.

10. So far I have discussed only the single-individual aspects of Pigou's treatment of real income. All these pages of the Appendix were necessary to cover what took scarcely more than a page of my main text. But now I must consider Pigou's analysis of national income in its group-welfare aspects. Because this problem was treated so fully in the main text, my treatment here may be rather brief.

It will be recalled that Pigou regards his inferences as being valid if the members of the group always have " a fixed distribution of income " (and, of course, unchanging tastes). When we subject his book to microscopic examination, two questions immediately come to mind. (1) Exactly what is meant by " a fixed distribution of income " between two situations? And (2) even after this by-no-means-simple question has been adequately disposed of, what is it that Pigou thinks is true of the group or of the individuals in the group as we go from one situation to another? Is there a group-mind that registers more utility? Or is it the algebraic sum of utility that has gone up for the group? Or is it that every single member of the group is now better off than before?

11. One must read between the lines to answer these questions—at least, I have not been able to find their explicit answers. I suspect that Pigou does not have any place in his philosophy for any group-mind. But his technical argument seems to come very close to the following Wieser construction:

> The theory of the "simple economy" ... begins with the idealizing assumption that the subject is a single person. However, we do not have in mind here the meagre economy of an isolated Robinson Crusoe ... [but] the activities of an entire nation. At the same time millions of people are regarded as a massed unit.[8]

We may read elements of this general line of reasoning in Pigou's concern with the question of whether market prices can be considered as given to society in the way that they can be assumed to be prescribed for a single small competitive individual. If Figure 10 applied to a single individual, he could legitimately regard the straight line NN through A as being open to him. But if the chart holds for society, there could be shown on it the true (but possibly unknown) production-possibility or opportunity-cost curve of type MM or of some other shape.

Pigou is uneasy about applying the argument to the group as a whole. " But, when it is the whole of a group, or, if we prefer it, a representative man who shifts his consumption in this way, it is no longer certain that prices would be unaffected " (p. 61). For a moment, Pigou seems to lapse into the assumption that the representative man knows that he is an image of the group and therefore acts collusively as if a group decision were being made. The group-mind knows that the only choice really open to it is along MM; therefore in the initial A situation it does not think that C is obtainable; consequently we cannot infer that A has been revealed to be better than C

---

[8] F. v. Wieser, *Social Economics* (1927), pp. 9–10.

Figure 10

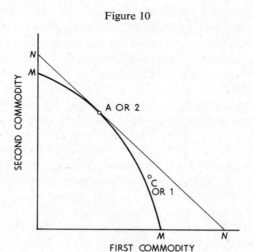

by a deliberate act of choosing A over C. Something like this Pigou must have believed for the moment, else he would not have felt the need to add a "certain assumption" of paragraph 8, ruling out the possibility that the production-possibility curve of society is like MM, but instead requiring it to show constant slope like NN. It is fortunate that Pigou's argument can be salvaged without making this extraneous assumption—fortunate because I cannot agree with his appraisal of the *a priori* probabilities: "In real life, with a large number of commodities, it is reasonable to suppose that the upward price movements caused by shifts of consumption would roughly balance the downward movements" (p. 62). That is to say, concave or convex curves are equally likely, so we may assume the curve to be a straight line. Rather, I would think that in the conditions most suited to healthy competition—where external economies either balance external diseconomies or both are negligible and where tendencies towards increasing or decreasing returns *to scale* are absent or just balancing—we would still be left with the good old law of diminishing returns in the classical (qualitative and quantitative) senses, so that convex production-possibility schedules are the "normal" case.

Actually, if Pigou is concerned to make normative statements about points like A and C that hold valid for groups, it does not matter that the true production-possibility curve is something other than NN.[9] We have seen in Hicks's paper and in the text what these valid inferences are. Another way of

---

[9] Pigou does not stand alone. "Unless the groups considered are small in relation to the whole, market prices cannot be considered as constant, and therefore the condition $\Sigma p_2 q_2 > \Sigma p_2 q_1$ would no longer indicate that goods of situation I were rejected in favour of those of situation II" (*Economica*, 1949, p. 17).

looking at the problem is by means of the "collective indifference curves" that Professor Scitovsky has taught us to use in the second of his cited papers.

12. But first we must settle what is meant by Pigou's "fixed distribution of income." How tempting to think of money as being concrete and the distribution of income to be fixed if everybody's money income changes proportionately. But money itself means nothing. If two men each have the same money income and if one likes meat and the other cheese and the terms of trade between meat and cheese change, then would Pigou consider the distribution of income to have remained fixed? Probably not. Moreover, if we follow the convenient practice of treating the services of labour and property that people supply as negative commodities, then in the absence of government taxes we might say that everybody has a zero (net) income *always.*

Probably in the beginning Pigou had in mind the simple case of identical individuals, any one of whom is representative, and where they all fare alike. Then when situation II is better than I, it is also true that both individuals are better off. When we leave the case of perfect symmetry, it becomes difficult to say that the extra welfare of one man is always to be some fixed multiple of the increment of welfare of another since this involves ethical interpersonal comparisons that Pigou is trying to avoid in these chapters dealing with the relatively objective aspects of welfare and the national dividend. But for his purposes Pigou needs only to assume that the ordinal well-being of all individuals are required to move always *in the same direction* according to some prescribed relationship. [Some complicated monetary shifts must be assumed to take place to bring this about.]

If I am right in this interpretation, then the comparison of *A* or 2 and *C* or 1 in terms of

$$\sum p_2 q_2 > \sum p_2 q_1$$

is immediately obvious and independent of the shape of *MM* or of any assumptions of group-consciousness. The fortunes of all being linked, any one person reflects the fate of all. Now, obviously, for some one person we must have

$$\sum p_2 q_2 > \sum p_2 q_1,$$

because if the opposite were true for each and every person, how could the totals show this relation? But if at least one has been made worse off in I than in II, then the "fixed distribution of income assumption" means that they must all have been made worse off. Q.E.D.

In terms of Scitovsky indifference curves, the story runs as follows: For a prescribed amount of both people's ordinal utility, U' and U'', we can draw up a collective indifference curve. For any prescribed distribution linking U' and U'' in a monotonic fashion we can draw up a family of collective indifference curves. If each person has concave indifference curves, the collective curves will also be concave. But regardless of concavity, the collective curve through A is never permitted to cross below the NN line. This will be obvious to every reader in the case of concave curves; and the same can be shown to be true in general by simple mathematical argument. It follows that C lies on a lower collective indifference curve than A—*regardless of the true shape of Society's production-possibility curve MM.*

13. Pigou's argument has been removed from any dependence on constant (opportunity) cost assumptions. But a worse restriction remains. For him to make any inference, *everybody* in the community must have been made better or worse off. The wind scarcely ever blows that brings good to absolutely everyone. Lucky it is that the remaining fifty-odd chapters of the *Economics of Welfare* do not depend in an essential way upon the results of the early chapters of Part I dealing with the national dividend. Fortunately, too—just as was seen to be true when tastes change—we can make some valid inferences when the distribution of income is known *not* to remain fixed. From our earlier analysis we know that $\sum p_2 q_2 > \sum p_2 q_1$ implies that the II's utility-possibility curve lies outside of I's at least in the neighbourhood of the actual observed situation II.

14. One last case not yet considered by any of the writers. Suppose we have given to us certain well-defined ethical notions concerning interpersonal well-being. In the simplest case they can be summarized in a Bergson social welfare function, $W = W(U', U'', \ldots)$, with the usual property that anything that helps one man without hurting anyone else will mean in increase in W.

As before, let us observe prices, p, and total quantities for all society, q. And finally, suppose that *the distribution of income is ethically optimal both in situation 1 or C and 2 or A.* What can we now infer from the condition $\sum p_2 q_2 > \sum p_2 q_1$? The answer is that situation A lies higher on the ethical social welfare function than does C.[10]

The logical proof of this result is not so easy as I at first thought it would be. This is because our move from C to the better position A need not represent an improvement for all individuals. U' may go down provided U'' goes up relatively more, as measured, of course, by the W function. Hence, when cost conditions change in such a way as to make it optimal to alter the relative "distribution of income," our earlier argument cannot apply.

To prove that $W(A) > W(C)$, we can use "social indifference curves." But they are not the arbitrary ones of the Scitovsky new-welfare-economics type. They are a unique old-welfare-economics set of curves showing the combinations of total goods capable of giving (when all optimal arrangements have been made) equal levels of W. In the "normal" case, where playing the game of competition can be depended to follow the invisible hand to bliss, these social indifference curves will be concave. It follows that whenever C

---

[10] This is related to Bergson's interesting interpretation of Pigou in infinitesimal terms. Bergson, *"Reformulation of Certain Aspects of Welfare Economics," *Q.J.E.*, lii (1938), p. 331.

lies inside the straight line NN going through A, it must also lie inside the social indifference curve (of equal W) going through A. This proves our result.[11]

---

[11] In the last two of his cited papers Little has stated theorems a little bit like the one above. There are two or three different versions, but the typical Little theorem shows that a certain point A is better than another point C because we can imagine going from C to A in two steps: one of these involves an improved distribution of real income (somehow defined) and the other an improvement in each and every person's well-being. I give an abbreviated interpretation of one of the variants discussed in *O.E.P.*, pp. 235–37.

1. Suppose we have a W function as defined above, with $\partial W/\partial U' > 0$, etc., and start at a point C and end up at a point A.
2. The point A is assumed to lie out and beyond the utility-possibility locus of the point C; e.g., there is a point C' on the latter locus that is southwest of the point A in the U'–U'' plane. Thus the Scitovsky test is satisfied.
3. Now make the assumption that in terms of W "the distribution of real income is better" at C' than in C. (Thus, ideally, we should not have been in C in the first place.)
4. Then it follows that A is higher on the assumed welfare function than is C. (This conclusion does not depend upon whether the Hicks–Kaldor test is satisfied.)
5. It does not follow that a little angel, given the choice of throwing a switch that moves society from C to A, ought to throw that switch. There may be an infinity of points on C's locus still better than A. Little's policy conclusion is to be qualified, therefore, by the following statement that he has been kind enough to send to me in private correspondence: "The shift from C to A ought to be made if the shift does not prejudice any other move which might result in a position still more favourable than A."

The chain of reasoning involved in 1–4 is simple once we pin down what is meant by "the distribution of real income being better." This means $W(C') > W(C)$. Since the Scitovsky test implies $W(A) > W(C')$, the Little result $W(A) > W(C)$ immediately follows. Just as Little talks prose, he can be said to be using a *welfare* function whenever he talks welfare economics. But like the new welfare economists, he wants to see what results he can get with an *incompletely* defined welfare function—a commendable effort, perhaps useful for an important class of policy decisions, but necessarily not complete for all policy situations.

The welfare cost of inflationary finance*†

MARTIN J. BAILEY

I. INTRODUCTION AND PRELIMINARY ANALYSIS

In recent years several governments have been tempted to resort to open inflation as a method of financing a desired diversion of resources to the government sector of the economy, because of the apparently painless character of this method of diversion. This temptation has not always been resisted in spite of the evidence from the past that this process is not so painless as it appears at first glance. On the other hand, most economists in this country have virtually taken it for granted that this method of finance is not desirable. In many cases the governments of other countries which desired to divert a substantial fraction of their countries' economic resources to postwar reconstruction and development have been advised against inflationary finance by at least some of the economists whose opinions were requested.

In general, however, the reasons why open inflation is not an advisable method of government finance have not been worked out with theoretical precision; the arguments against it have concentrated on the redistributive and disruptive aspects of inflation—the hardship involved for people whose income and wealth are fixed in money terms and the misallocations of resources that may result from the heightened uncertainties concerning future relative and absolute prices. Such arguments have, by and large, overlooked another aspect of the effects of inflationary finance, an aspect which in a certain sense is more fundamental because it cannot be avoided by sliding-scale arrangements or by precise foreknowledge of the courses of individual

* *The Journal of Political Economy*, 64(1956): pp. 93–110. Corrected by the author. Reprinted by courtesy of the author and *The Journal of Political Economy*.

† An earlier version of this article was delivered as a paper, under the same title, at the December, 1955, meeting of the Econometric Society in New York. I am much indebted to Phillip D. Cagan for his patience with my persistent delving into his data and work sheets and to Milton Friedman for suggestions for greater logical and terminological rigor. I am also indebted to Professor Richard A. Musgrave, whose sweeping criticisms of my New York paper impelled me to restate and illustrate my argument for greater clarity. Such flaws as this article still possesses are, of course, my own responsibility.

prices. This aspect is a welfare cost of open inflation, which, in effect, is a tax on the holding of cash balances, a cost which is fully analogous to the welfare cost (or "excess burden") of an excise tax on a commodity or productive service.

The theoretical analysis of the welfare cost of open inflation is, in fact, a reasonably straightforward extension of the theory of the welfare cost of an excise tax and, indeed, is in some respects much simpler. For the time being, I shall take it for granted that this welfare cost is measured by the area under an appropriately defined liquidity preference curve, but in Section III, I shall discuss the logic of this assumption in detail.

In order to keep separate the redistributive-disruptive effects of open inflation, on the one hand, and the welfare cost associated with the cash-balance effect, on the other, it is useful to think in terms of a model with the following characteristics: (a) A given, unchanged rate of inflation is expected by everyone (after initial adjustments), because, say, of the announcement by the government of the rate at which it expects to increase the money supply. (b) All appropriate adjustments are made by everyone in the face of this expectation; in particular, all contracts are rewritten in such a way that their real values remain constant, all old and new money loans have a raised nominal interest rate, and all salaries, wages, pensions, and so on have regular "cost-of-living" adjustments or the like. (c) Bank deposits are not used as money or are negligible in amount. In such a model incidental redistribution of real income is avoided (other than that directly involved in the acquiring of resources by the government), as is the incidental maldistribution of resources in the private economy which might arise from heightened uncertainty. The effect on the affairs of the private economy would not be any different from that of a direct tax on the holding of cash balances.[1]

Suppose that in such an economy the "liquidity preference function," showing the demand for real balances of currency at a full-employment level of real income as a function of the money rate of interest, is that shown by the curve LL in Figure 1. If the money rate of interest, say that consistent with a stable price level, is r_0, the amount of real cash balances people will wish to hold is $(M/p)_0$; if the money rate of interest should rise to r_1 because of a rate of inflation $r_1 - r_0$,[2] the amount of real cash balances people will wish to hold is $(M/p)_1$. This implies that as soon as the government announces that the rate of inflation will be, say, $r_1 - r_0$, everyone, desiring to reduce his real cash balances, will at once try to purchase physical assets, including stocks of consumer goods and some other things, and the price level will at once rise in the proportion $(M/p)_0/(M/p)_1$. After this, prices will rise steadily at the

[1] For a discussion of this proposition and of the dynamics of inflation see Milton Friedman, "Discussion of the Inflationary Gap" (revised version), in his *Essays in Positive Economics* (Chicago, 1953), pp. 253–57.

[2] If interest is compounded continuously, these rates are simply additive; for simplicity of exposition and analysis, therefore, I shall assume continuous compounding.

same proportionate rate as that at which the government is adding to the supply of currency, so that real cash balances will remain constant at $(M/p)_1$.[3] The proceeds of the tax in real terms (that is, the resources obtained by the government by printing money) will be equal to the area of the rectangle $r_1 P Q r_0$.

Now the curve LL may be interpreted as showing the marginal productivity of cash balances (or, if one prefers to express it in utility terms, the subjective marginal rate of substitution of real goods for cash balances for everyone holding the latter). For example, if the rate of inflation is 30 percent per month, the marginal productivity of a dollar at $(M/p)_1$ would be equal to 30¢ per month (or its marginal utility would be equal to the marginal utility of 30¢ worth of real income per month). Otherwise, people would not be willing to hold the indicated quantity of real cash balances in the face of the sacrifice which this involves. If the price index used has a value of 1 at $(M/p)_0$, the unit of measurement along the horizontal axis is dollars of the real value a dollar would have if there were no inflation (at the pre-existing quantity of money). The height of LL at any point measures a fraction of such a dollar per unit of time, and the area under LL over a given segment of the horizontal axis measures the flow of productivity from the indicated quantity of real balances. In particular, the shaded area in Figure 1 measures the aggregate loss of productivity (utility) resulting from the destruction of real cash balances which occurs when prices rise initially at the announcement that there will be an inflation. The further rise of prices representing the inflation itself is merely sufficient to keep real balances at their new low level and so to guarantee that this loss of productivity (utility) will continue as long as the inflation does.

Figure 1

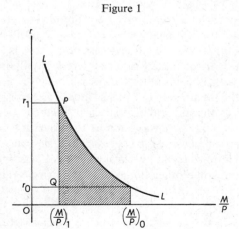

---

[3] Friedman, *op. cit.*, p. 255.

II. REAL CASH BALANCES AT HIGH RATES OF INFLATION

Although no very precise conclusions can be drawn from the available evidence about the real cash balances that people would desire to hold at fully anticipated, but relatively low, rates of inflation, a great deal of precise and useful information about desired cash balances at very high rates of inflation is given in Cagan's study of seven European hyperinflations.[4] The present section of this study is primarily a summary and interpretation of those parts of Cagan's results which have a bearing on the present inquiry.

Some salient information is presented in Table 1 about the movement of prices and of real cash balances (or velocity) during the hyperinflations studied by Cagan; in some cases the figures are his, in other cases they are derived directly from his data. Column 1 gives for each of these countries the dates approximately delimiting the periods during which high rates of inflation were experienced or were evidently expected by the public; column 2 gives the lengths of these periods in months. Column 3 gives the monthly

Table 1

SELECTED DATA ON SEVEN HYPERINFLATIONS

Country	Approximate Dates of Inflation (1)	No. of Months (2)	$\delta p/p_{-1}$ in Month before First Date of Col. 1 (Percent) (3)	Maximum Monthly Price Rise (First Day of Month $p = 100$) (4)	Col. 4 Expressed as Average Daily Percentage Price Rise (5)
Austria	Jan., 1921, to Aug., 1922	20	70.3	234	2.78
Germany	Sept., 1920, to Nov., 1923	39	6.1	32.5×10^5	39.8
Greece	Jan., 1943, to Nov., 1944	23	48.9†	85.5×10^8	83.8
Hungary I	July, 1922, to Feb., 1924	20	17.2	198	2.23
Hungary II ..	July, 1945, to July, 1946	13	36.5‡	41.9×10^{17}	244.
Poland	Apr., 1922, to Jan., 1924	22	15.8	375	4.36
Russia........	Dec., 1921, to Jan., 1924	26	44.5	313	3.75

† October, 1942.
‡ July, 1945.

---

[4] Phillip Cagan, "The Monetary Dynamics of Hyperinflations," a paper delivered at the Washington meeting (December, 1953) of the Econometric Society, the abstract of which appeared in *Econometrica*, October, 1954, p. 518. Cagan's results in complete form are presented in his unpublished doctoral dissertation for the University of Chicago, with the same title as the paper just cited; this dissertation will appear in revised form in *Studies in the Quantity Theory of Money*, ed. Milton Friedman (in press).

Table 1 (*continued*)

SELECTED DATA ON SEVEN HYPERINFLATIONS*

Country	Month of Cols. 4 and 5 (6)	Minimum M/p (Base Yr. M/p = 1) (7)	Max. Rise of "Velocity" of Currency (1/Col. 7) (8)	Minimum (M + D)/p (Base Yr. M + D/p = 1) (9)	Max. Rise of "Velocity" of All Money (1/Col. 9) (10)	Base Year for Cols. 7–10 (11)
Austria	Aug., 1922	0.252	3.97	0.0556	18.0	1914
Germany	Oct., 1923	0.00741	135	0.00239	418.	1913
Greece	Nov., 1944	0.00277	361	§	§	1941
Hungary I	July, 1923	0.185	5.40	0.105	9.54	1921
Hungary II ..	July, 1946	§	§	0.000259	3,860	1939
Poland	Oct., 1923	0.0357	28.0	0.0429	23.3	1921
Russia........	Jan., 1924	0.00775	129	0.00388	258	1914

§ Not available.
* *Source:* Cagan, "The Monetary Dynamics of Hyperinflations," and Cagan's data sheets and work sheets.

percentage rate of price rise that had been experienced in the month immediately preceding the beginning of hyperinflation, except as otherwise indicated; these figures give a rough notion of the prevailing inflationary atmosphere at about the time when really rapid rises in prices commenced. Column 4 gives the ratio of the price level at the end of the month to that at the beginning of the month (col. 6) in which prices rose the most rapidly, while this same information is expressed in column 5 as an average daily percentage price rise. Column 7 gives the minimum level of real balances of currency held by the public attained during the hyperinflation, relative to the real balances held in a base year (col. 11); the inverse of this figure, representing the relative rise in income velocity of currency circulation without any correction for possible changes in income, is given in column 8. Columns 9 and 10 give the corresponding information (changes in real balances and in "velocity") for currency plus deposits.

The figures in column 5 give a rough idea of the day-to-day situation at the peak of hyperinflation (although these figures, since they are monthly averages, understate the maximum daily rates of inflation that must have been achieved). The two extremes are the figures for Hungary after the first and second World Wars, respectively; in the first case the maximum average daily price rise was 2.23 percent, while in the second case prices more than tripled daily, on the average, throughout the peak month. The inflations in Austria, Poland, and Russia were not markedly more severe than the first Hungarian inflation; while Germany after the first World War and Greece after the second had peak rates of inflation which approached that of the second Hungarian inflation.

The ratios in which real cash balances fell relative to a base year (or in which "velocity" rose), as indicated in columns 7–10, rank the countries in almost the same order as their peak average daily rates of price rise. However, as will be seen shortly, this by no means carries with it the presumption that all these countries had precisely the same demand curve for real cash balances. These figures have a very wide range and, among other things, cast considerable doubt on the hypothesis that there is some (fairly low) limit on the extent to which the velocity of circulation of an actually used currency can rise. In Hungary after the second World War, the proportionate rise in the price level was almost four thousand times as great as the proportionate rise in the quantity of money, and the corresponding rises in some of the other countries shown were also very substantial.[5]

Cagan's data show, in addition, a great deal of month-to-month fluctuation (and in the case of Germany, where weekly figures are available, even wider week-to-week fluctuation) in the public's holdings of real cash balances or in velocity. In other words, the ratio of the price index to an index of the quantity of money was anything but constant; since people's demand for cash balances must be presumed to have been one of the determinants of the price level, along with the quantity of money, it follows that this demand itself was by no means constant, even in the face of price rises so substantial that any "speculative" demand for cash must have long since disappeared. That is, the evidence is not consistent with the notion of a constant "transactions" demand for real cash balances.

Cagan's principal conclusion, indeed, is that the demand for real cash balances is a function of the expected rate of price rise and that this demand has a higher and higher elasticity at higher and higher rates of inflation. Using an expectations model which implies that the currently expected rate of price change is a weighted average of past rates of price change, with monotonically decreasing weights as one goes back into the past,[6] Cagan obtained very high correlations (the r^2 was never less than 0.94) for all seven hyperinflations with a demand function of the form

$$\frac{M}{p} = e^{\alpha E + \gamma}, \tag{1}$$

where E is the expected rate of price rise and where α and γ are constants (Cagan's notation). That is, he found that the logarithm of real cash balances is a linear function of the expected rate of inflation, with a close fit over a wide range of variation in each case. His results very convincingly suggest the

---

[5] Cagan's figures for Germany differ sharply from those presented by Frank Graham in *Exchange, Prices, and Production in Hyper-inflation: Germany, 1920–1923* (Princeton, 1930), pp. 106–7, and by Bresciani-Turroni in *The Economics of Inflation* (London: Allen & Unwin, 1937), pp. 166–74; both these investigators failed to avail themselves of the weekly data and used instead once-a-month data which happened to miss the peaks of velocity.

[6] Cagan assumed that the expected rate of inflation, E, equals the expected rate of a month previous plus a constant times the difference between that expectation and the experienced rate of price rise. With a suitable transformation, using what amounts to a difference equation, this assumption becomes equivalent to the statement in the text.

Table 2

PARAMETERS OF DEMAND FOR REAL CASH BALANCES IN SEVEN HYPERINFLATIONS*

Country	Dates of Regression (1)	$-\alpha$ (2)	c $[=M/(M+D)]$ (3)	k_0^* $(=e^{\gamma}/R)$ (4)	k_0 $[=(1/R)(M/p)^0]$ (5)	Date k_0 Observed (6)	$-k_0^*/\alpha$ $(=\text{Col. 4}/\text{Col. 2})$ (7)	Max. g $(=-ck_0^*/\alpha e)$ (8)	Max. g for $c=1$ $(=-k_0^*/\alpha e)$ (9)
Austria	Jan., 1921, to Aug., 1922	8.55	0.30	2.92	8.48	1929	0.342	0.0377	0.126
Germany	Sept., 1920, to July, 1923	5.46	0.50	2.09	5.03	1927	0.383	0.0704	0.141
Greece	Jan., 1943, to Aug., 1944	4.09	(0.50)†	1.27	2.04	1949–52	0.311	(0.0572)	0.114
Hungary I	July, 1922, to Feb., 1924	8.70	0.90	4.18	4.70	1936	0.480	0.159	0.177
Hungary II	July, 1945, to Feb., 1946	3.63	0.90	(0.521)	(4.0)	....	(0.139)	(0.0460)	(0.0511)
Poland	Apr., 1922, to Nov., 1923	2.30	0.75	0.289	1.62	1929	0.126	0.0346	0.0461
Russia	Dec., 1921, to Jan., 1924	3.06	1.00	0.0746	0.90	1926–29	0.0244	0.00885	0.00885

* *Sources*: For cols. 1-3: Cagan, *op. cit.* Col. 4 involves a transformation of Cagan's data using col. 5.

For col. 5: For Austria, income figures are from *Statistisches Jahrbuch für das deutsche Reich* (1938), and money figures are from *Wirtschafts-statistisches Jahrbuch* (Vienna) (1920/30). For Germany, all figures are from *Statistisches Jahrbuch* (1929, 1938). For Greece, the basic figures are from *International Financial Statistics*; the observed ratio M/pR for each year was corrected for the continuing mildly inflationary conditions by assuming that each year's rise in prices over the previous year was fully anticipated and by using Cagan's α to obtain a figure for M/pR that would have obtained, had there been no inflation; these "adjusted" figures for M/pR were then averaged for the indicated years to give the figure in col. 5. For Hungary after the first World War, the income figures are from M. Matolcsy and Stephen Varga, *The National Income of Hungary* (London, 1938); the money figures are from the *Hungarian Economic Yearbook* (Budapest, 1939). For Hungary after the second World War, the figure for M/pR is an arbitrary guess; it is assumed to be somewhat smaller than the 1936 figure because it was observed that real cash balances in the beginning months of inflation were very small relative to the previous experience. For Poland, the income figures are from *The National Income of Poland* (Birmingham Information Service on Slavonic Countries, July, 1937); the money figures are from the *Polish Economist* (1930). For Russia, all figures come from *Histoire économique de l'U.R.S.S*, by S. N. Prokopovicz (Paris, 1952); an average of M/pR was taken for the indicated years.

† Parentheses indicate weak estimates and figures derived from them.

hypothesis that this form of demand equation for real cash balances is generally representative of the form of such demand equations for most or all economically interesting countries; insofar as this is true, the welfare cost of openly pursued inflationary finance, among other things, can be calculated in a straightforward fashion as a function of the parameters of expression (1).

A summary of the results of Cagan's regressions is given in Table 2. Column 2 gives the value of the parameter α, a parameter whose variation among all the countries studied is statistically significant. Column 3 shows the approximate ratio of currency (government money) to the total money supply during hyperinflation; and column 4 shows the value of real cash balances predicted by the demand function when extrapolated to a zero rate of inflation, expressed as a ratio to the real income per month in the base year given in column 11 of Table 1. This ratio was calculated by using the cash balances observed in the base year, on the one hand, and the observed ratio of cash balances to monthly income in a postinflationary year, shown in columns 5 and 6, on the other (it was assumed that the cash balances held in the base year represented the same fraction of income as in the later year for which this fraction could be observed). Since the intercept of the demand curve on the cash-balance axis is at a smaller value than the observed cash balances in a noninflationary year, it may be inferred that the actual demand for real cash balances at low rates of inflation must be much more elastic than is implied by extrapolating the demand curve observed at high rates of inflation. Columns 7, 8, and 9 of Table 2 will be discussed in Section IV.

III. THE WELFARE COST, OR "EXCESS BURDEN," OF INFLATIONARY FINANCE

We are now in a position to consider the welfare cost aspect of inflation for an economic model of the type outlined in Section I. The demand function for real cash balances obtained by Cagan enables me to state this cost in very precise terms, if I may assume, as seems reasonable, that the demand for real cash balances will be substantially the same if an economy succeeds in making all the arrangements necessary to prevent the inflation from causing any incidental redistribution of wealth or income.

Before going on to numerical results, however, I shall consider some aspects of the supposed welfare cost as people experienced it. This will make my results more concrete and therefore possibly more plausible. The cost arises from the changes in payment procedures and habits which take place during hyperinflations, which, in general, involve the adoption of barter or involve people's rushing to make purchases as soon as they receive payment for anything.[7] As rates of price rise became really high, it was typically true that

---

[7] These observations, on matters on which no published data are available, are based primarily on impressions gained from people with firsthand experience of hyperinflation. It should be noted that their function in the argument is purely illustrative.

firms began to pay their workers more and more frequently:[8] first weekly, then daily, and then sometimes twice a day or more. Having received payment, the workers or their wives rushed to purchase consumer goods, foreign currencies, or other assets. Shopkeepers tended to close early or even to close after making a few sales, in order to exchange their newly acquired cash at once for more inventories. Outside the cities, where it was especially inconvenient to scurry around trying to make cash payments, trade quickly went on a barter basis; such cash trading as farmers did generally occurred only when they visited the cities to exchange farm products for manufactured goods.

It was also observed that some firms paid their workers in kind rather than with cash; that is, barter arrangements were made even in the cities. As long as they hold the goods in which they are paid, such workers do not, in general, suffer any loss from the rise in prices; they can then hunt at their leisure for advantageous opportunities to barter further. Let us consider how a hypothetical person might behave under these circumstances. Suppose that A, B, C, and D are different persons being paid in kind, each with a different commodity, and suppose that A is acquainted with each of the others, can conveniently trade with each of them, and wants some of each of their commodities. Suppose, on the other hand, that B, C, and D do not know each other, but that (as A knows) B wants A's product, C wants B's product but not A's, and D wants C's product but not A's or B's. Suppose further that any good can be sold for cash at certain locations at a certain inconvenience and that the goods held by B, C, and D can also be bought for cash at certain separate, but reasonably convenient, locations.

In this situation A can follow one of several possible plans: he can sell his entire " wage " for cash and buy the other goods at the specified locations; he can arrange to barter with B to some mutually agreed amount but obtain all other commodities through cash transactions; he can (if B is willing) barter in excess of his needs with B and exchange some of B's commodity with C but otherwise deal in cash; or he can first barter in excess of his needs with B, then with the excess he can barter in excess of his needs with C in order to exchange some of C's commodity with D. At a low rate of inflation it may be more convenient for him to sell all his wage goods for cash (here he at least avoids any loss while he is traveling from his place of employment to the place where he sells his commodity); at a somewhat higher rate of inflation it becomes worthwhile for him to engage in direct barter with B, who wants some of his commodity but who may be less conveniently located (apart from the incentive of inflation) than the cash markets; at a still higher rate of inflation the more roundabout barter arrangement with C via B becomes worthwhile; and so on.

All these changes in payment procedures that took place necessarily involved a cost for the persons concerned. Had it not been inconvenient for firms to pay their workers more and more frequently, they would, at the first sign of steady inflation, have commenced making the most frequent

---

[8] See Graham, *op. cit.*, pp. 111–16.

payments ever observed; the costs involved probably included both extra accounting costs and the loss of working capital, which previously had been supplied them by workers willing to accept delayed wage payments. The daily rush to buy goods both by the workers or their wives and by traders must also have involved loss of convenience, additional time spent in trading because trading was done in smaller lots than before, and other additional costs of making transactions. The same is true of the wider and wider adoption of barter; having to seek out more and more people willing to engage in barter, both direct and roundabout, would evidently involve inconvenience, additional time spent in transactions, and other costs.

Each of the devices mentioned makes it possible for a given volume of transactions to be carried out with smaller average real cash balances for all parties concerned. When everyone simultaneously adopts these means of reducing his holdings of cash balances, the effect is a price rise over and above any rise directly implied by an increase in the nominal quantity of money, which brings about the desired reduction in real cash balances for the community as a whole. Hence when everyone tries to reduce his average real cash balances in order to avoid the losses imposed by inflation, this action has the effect of driving the price level upward even faster and thereby of wiping out that part of the real value of his cash balances of which everyone desired to be rid. However, a given structure of payments carries with it the automatic presumption that the average nominal balances held by everyone will rise proportionately with the quantity of money and the price level and hence that real balances will remain constant. If each day a person is paid with X percent more (nominal) cash than the day before and if he makes exactly the same haste as the day before to be rid of it, his average nominal holding of cash will have gone up by X percent also; if everyone is doing this, the price level will have risen by only X percent, and everyone's average real holdings will have remained constant.

When each individual acts so as to maintain a given payments structure, therefore, he is adding to his nominal cash balances just sufficiently to maintain their real value. Since he suffers a "capital loss" each day equal to the daily rate of price rise multiplied by his average real cash balance, he is in effect sacrificing part of his apparent income to maintain the real value of his cash balances; the additional pieces of paper he holds each day may be regarded as certificates or receipts indicating that he has paid the tax on his cash balances implied by the government's policy of inflation.[9]

At any given rate of inflation, people will settle down to some structure of payments, including barter arrangements, for which at the margin the cost of holding cash balances just equals the cost of altering the payments structure so as to reduce these balances. At a somewhat higher rate of inflation, equality between these costs will be found at a somewhat tighter payments structure implying lower real balances. (That the adoption of a tighter structure imposes

---

[9] Friedman, *op. cit.*

an additional capital loss on everyone is irrelevant, since each person makes his decision independently and has no reason to consider the negligible effect of his own action on the price level.) Since this equalizing of alternative costs goes on at every level of inflation, the rate of inflation (that is, the rate of real capital loss from holding cash) at which people regard a given level of real balances as just appropriate measures the marginal convenience yield of real balances at that level; if the last unit of average real cash balance is just worth holding to a person when the rate of inflation is X percent per day but is not worth holding when the rate of inflation rises to $(X + dX)$ percent per day, the marginal convenience yield of that last unit must have been just X percent per day. Hence it follows that the area under the demand curve for real cash balances, over the range of that part of real cash balances which is relinquished because of a given rate of inflation, measures the costs in loss of convenience, increasingly awkward barter arrangements, and so on, involved in relinquishing those real balances.

This conclusion, that the area under the observed demand curve for real cash balances during an inflation measures the welfare costs of the reduction of these balances, applies regardless of the particular manner in which these costs affect real income and leisure. In the German hyperinflation, the only one for which real income figures are available, it was found that real income did not fall until the last, most rapid stages of the hyperinflation.[10] Before real income fell, it may be presumed that the costs were absorbed entirely in leisure (except insofar as some costs, such as increased travel in connection with barter arrangements, might erroneously be included in real national product); then, as the costs mounted at higher rates of inflation, it evidently became necessary to devote less time to productive activity in order to have more time for making transactions. Regardless of the distribution of costs between real income and leisure, however, the welfare implications of the demand curve for cash balances remain the same; this consideration merely requires that, in strict rigor, the real value of cash balances should be evaluated with a price index that includes the "price" of leisure (weighted by its net amount after the deduction of time absorbed in transactions).

IV. SOME NUMERICAL CONCLUSIONS AND THEIR INTERPRETATION

We may now proceed to the consideration of quantitative results. The revenues G (real product per month) derived by the government at any constant rate of inflation of, say, E percent per month, to which the public has accommodated itself, will be equal to the rate of inflation times the real cash balances then held by the public:

$$G = E\left(\frac{M}{p}\right)_E . \tag{2}$$

If we divide both sides by some level, R, of real national income that is considered relevant, say income per month in some base year preceding the

---

[10] Cagan, *op. cit.*

adoption of inflationary finance, we obtain the government budget as a fraction of that income, g. Furthermore, if Cagan's demand curve for cash balances can be considered as relevant all the way down to a zero rate of inflation and if k_0^* is the number of months of income held in real balances when there is no inflation, we have

$$g = \frac{G}{R} = \frac{E}{R} \left(\frac{M}{p}\right)_E = k_0^* E e^{\alpha E}. \tag{3}$$

Now, if we integrate the demand curve (1) over the relevant range and if we let $(1/R)(M/p)_E$ be denoted by k_E^* (where R is constant), we have

$$\frac{D}{R} = \int_{k_0^*}^{k_E^*} E(k)\, dk = \int_0^E (k_E^* - k_x^*)\, dx$$
$$= k_0^* \int_0^E (e^{\alpha x} - e^{\alpha E})\, dx \tag{4}$$
$$= -\frac{k_0^*}{\alpha} [1 - e^{\alpha E}(1 - \alpha E)].$$

Dividing this result by equation (3) then produces

$$\frac{D}{gR} = \frac{(1 - \alpha E) - e^{-\alpha E}}{\alpha E}, \tag{5}$$

where D is the welfare cost expressed in real terms. This last expression is the proportion by which the burden on the private economy exceeds the government budget financed by inflation and may be interpreted as a "cost of collection" of the government budget, expressed as a fraction of the amount collected.

A modification of these results may be called for if we relax the assumption that there is no bank money in the economy under study; that is, we may consider a more generally applicable model in which bank deposits as well as currency are used for cash payments. In the course of an inflation that everyone anticipates perfectly, it would become extremely profitable for banks to create the maximum possible quantities of bank deposits, if they were interest-free, while making loans at the high nominal rates of interest which the competitive bidding of would-be borrowers would necessarily create in the loan markets. For any individual bank it would be profitable, if banking were competitive, to attempt to attract deposits from other banks in order to expand its loans. An individual bank could do so by offering interest on its deposits, and the effect of all banks competing with one another for deposits would be that they would all offer a nominal interest rate on deposits approaching, but not equal to, the rate of inflation.

In this case the public would no doubt be tempted to hold no currency at all, since it pays no interest, and to hold cash only in the form of bank deposits; at high rates of inflation the incentive to substitute bank deposits for currency would be very great. The fact that banks may have legal or traditional minimum reserve ratios, however, sets a lower limit on the ratio of currency (including bank reserves) to deposits: the most extreme possibility is that all newly issued currency (along with all old currency) flows immediately into the reserves of the banking system, which then issues new bank money in whatever ratio is permitted by its reserve ratio. In this case the ratio of currency to deposits becomes constant, after the inflation gets underway, at a level below that which obtained in noninflationary conditions.

On the other hand, it is often observed in practice that banks ration their loans to customers and do not charge the maximum rate of interest they could get on the volume of loans they issue, or even the maximum they could get from the particular customers who borrow from them on the actual amounts borrowed. At the opposite extreme from the case just considered, banks might from pure force of habit or for other reasons, such as the existence of usury laws, continue to charge the preinflationary nominal rate of interest on their loans, rationing their loans to their regular customers in the customary amounts and paying no interest on deposits. (In this case the real income extracted from the holders of bank balances through the inflationary process would be transferred to those lucky enough to get bank loans.) If this happened, the ratio of currency to deposits might remain at its preinflationary value. Something rather nearer to this latter extreme than to the former was what in fact happened in the European hyperinflations studied by Cagan.

Now consider the effect on the social cost of inflation and on people's behavior of the introduction of bank deposits in the first of the two cases, in which everyone behaves absolutely rationally. Virtually the only money used for payments would be bank deposits; newly created currency would have to be paid by the government directly to the banks in exchange for deposits with which to pay for the resources bought by the government (since otherwise the government could not get resources at the same prices as those paid in the private economy). Since an individual bank, when it obtains a new deposit either from direct currency inflow or from an interbank transfer, can expand its loans only by the amount of the new deposit times the quantity 1 minus the reserve ratio, the rate of interest it can offer to bid deposits away from other banks will be, at most, the rate of inflation times the quantity 1 minus the reserve ratio (if the equilibrium interest on deposits when there is no inflation is zero); the net cost of holding cash balances will therefore be the reserve ratio times the rate of inflation. People's holdings of bank balances will be adjusted to this net cost, and the real effect will be the same as if the government had issued the entire money supply and was inflating at only the rate of the bank reserve ratio times the actual rate of inflation. In other words, the presence of the banks in this completely rational economy implies that the government must inflate at a much higher rate (than it would have to if currency were the only money) in order to command the same share of national income; but a given share of the national income taken by the government will involve the same social cost and the same change in aggregate real cash balances in either case. The presence of the banking system has no real effect whatever but merely alters the nominal rate of inflation necessary to achieve a given real size of the government budget.

However, if the banks do not, in fact, charge the economic rate of interest on their loans and pay no interest on deposits, the situation is quite different. In this case it is a good first approximation to say that the fraction of currency in the total money supply will be the same with inflation as without it, since there is no reason to expect this fraction to change. Here the welfare cost of inflation will be the same for a given rate of inflation (and for a given demand curve for the total money supply), regardless of what fraction of the money supply is currency; however, the government's share of the total "tax" on cash balances is only the share of currency in the total money supply. The balance of the tax is appropriated by people who are fortunate enough to get bank loans. For a given welfare cost, the size of the government budget is less, and the ratio of the welfare cost to the size of the government budget is multiplied by the inverse of the ratio of currency to total money supply. For this case, then, equations (3) and (5) must be rewritten to read

$$g = ck_0^* E e^{\alpha E} \tag{3*}$$

and

$$\frac{D}{gR} = \frac{1 - \alpha E - e^{-\alpha E}}{c\alpha E}, \tag{5*}$$

where c is the ratio of currency to the total money supply. Equations (3*) and (5*) may be considered the relevant ones for all cases, since for those cases where either the entire money supply is currency or where bank deposits pay the full rate of interest dictated by the inflation and by reserve ratios we may set $c = 1$.

The government's share of income has a maximum at the rate of inflation

$$E = -\frac{1}{\alpha}; \tag{6}$$

and, since the elasticity of the money demand curve is

$$\eta_E = \alpha E, \tag{7}$$

equation (6) states that the government maximizes its real revenue from inflation at that rate of inflation at which the elasticity of the money demand function is -1.[11]

The interpretation of these results is aided by Figures 2, 3, and 4, which represent equations (3*), (4), and (5*). Figure 2 shows that g rises to a maximum as the rate of inflation E rises to $-1/\alpha$; the maximum value

$$g_{max} = -\frac{ck_0^*}{\alpha e}$$

---

[11] *Ibid.*

Figure 2

THE GOVERNMENT'S SHARE OF NAT-
IONAL INCOME AS A FUNCTION OF THE
RATE OF INFLATION

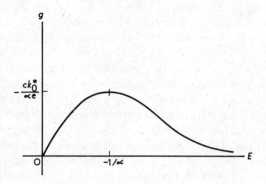

is obtained directly from equation (3*). At higher rates of inflation the government's real revenue falls away again and approaches zero as the rate of inflation approaches infinity. Figure 3 shows that the welfare cost of inflation rises monotonically as the rate of inflation increases, approaching an upper limit $-k_0^*/\alpha$ times real income as the rate of inflation approaches infinity. Since real cash balances approach zero as the rate of inflation rises without limit, this upper limit of the welfare cost measures the cost to society of abandoning money entirely.

Figure 4 combines equations (3*) and (5*) into an implicit function showing the "cost of collection" of the government budget, expressed as a fraction of that budget, as a function of the share of the base-year income

Figure 3

THE RATIO OF WELFARE COST TO INCOME AS
A FUNCTION OF THE RATE OF INFLATION

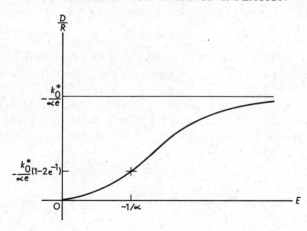

Figure 4

THE RATIO OF THE WELFARE
COST TO THE GOVERNMENT BUD-
GET AS A FUNCTION OF THE
GOVERNMENT'S SHARE OF IN-
COME

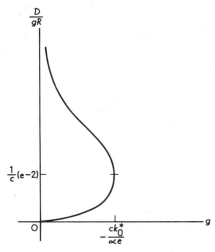

taken by the government. Since D/gR rises without limit as the rate of inflation increases, while g has a maximum and then approaches zero, this
implicit function is double-valued and approaches infinity on the upper wing
as g approaches zero (E approaches infinity). When the government maximizes its budget by setting $E = -1/\alpha$, the value of D/gR is $(1/c)(e-2)$; that
is, it is independent of all parameters except c, the fraction of the money
supply represented by currency. The minimum value of this constant, attained
when $c = 1$, is 0.72; that is, if the government tries to obtain the maximum
possible revenue by steady, openly announced inflation, the welfare cost (the
"excess burden") of doing so will be at least 72 percent of the amount of
revenue.

Other numerical results may now be obtained with the data in Table 2.
Column 7 gives the values of the maximum welfare costs of inflation, for
total abandonment through inflation of the use of money; none of these
values is above 0.5 of real income, and the median value is 0.311 (Greece).
Column 8 gives the maximum fraction of income that the government could
obtain by inflation, where c has the value indicated in column 3 and where
inflation is openly pursued at a steady rate. As indicated by my discussion
of bank money, these real revenues could be increased in inverse proportion
to c if the banks paid the appropriate rate of interest on deposits; the maximum value of g for each country, for $c = 1$, is given in column 9.

If one compares columns 2 and 9 of Table 2, an interesting point emerges:
although maximum g when $c = 1$ varies inversely with $-\alpha$, when other
things are equal, it turns out that from country to country this quantity varies

directly with $-\alpha$, because of more than offsetting variation in k_0^*; if one ranks the seven countries in all possible pairs by the figures in columns 2 and 9, these rankings will disagree as between the two columns in only two cases (Austria-Germany and Poland-Russia). The generalization to be drawn from this is that in those countries in which the demand curve for real cash balances is relatively elastic ($-\alpha$ is large), the quantity of real cash balances demanded at low rates of inflation [near zero but where the extrapolation of eq. (1) toward k_0^* is still approximately correct] is relatively large. From the standpoint of the possibility of obtaining government revenue at a low collection cost (including welfare cost), these two parameters are about mutually offsetting, the balance of advantage being on the side of the country with a large, though sensitive, demand for real cash balances at moderate rates of inflation.

For the purpose of drawing the most charitable possible conclusion about the advantages of inflationary finance, let us consider a hypothetical country, "Sylvania," which is so situated that it would lose less from inflation than any of the countries observed. The values of its relevant parameters, corresponding to those given in Table 2 for the observed countries, are given in Table 3.

The implications for low rates of inflation of the information in Tables 2 and 3 and of equations (3*) and (5*) are shown in Figures 5 and 6. In each of these figures D/gR is plotted against g (the function shown in Figure 4) over the interesting range for the observed hyperinflations and for "Sylvania." In Figure 5, D/gR is plotted against the value of g implied by the value of c given in column 3 of Table 2, whereas in Figure 6, D/gR is plotted against the value of g implied by $c = 1$. The corresponding curve for "Sylvania" ($c = 1$ in both cases) is shown in both figures for comparison.

We can now see the costs of various rates of inflation, on the basis of any reasonable factual assumptions we wish to make consistent with a demand equation for real cash balances of the form of equation (1). In "Sylvania," a country with the most favorable situation likely to occur anywhere, the government can obtain up to 18.4 percent of the national income by inflation. If it is content with taking 10 percent of the national income by this means, the "collection cost" will be almost 15 percent of the amount collected; if it takes only 6 percent of the national income, the "collection cost" may be as low as 7 percent of the amount collected. (Preliminary analysis of the total costs of collection of other forms of taxes, including welfare costs, compliance

Table 3

PARAMETERS OF DEMAND FOR REAL CASH BALANCES IN "SYLVANIA"*

	$-\alpha$ (2)	c (3)	k_0^* (4)	k_0 (5)	$-k_0^*/\alpha$ (7)	Max. g (8)
"Sylvania"	9.0	1.0	4.5	4.5	0.50	0.184

* *Source:* Text; compare Table 2.

Figure 5

ORDERS OF MAGNITUDE OF D/gR AS A FUNCTION OF g
FOR OBSERVED VALUES OF c

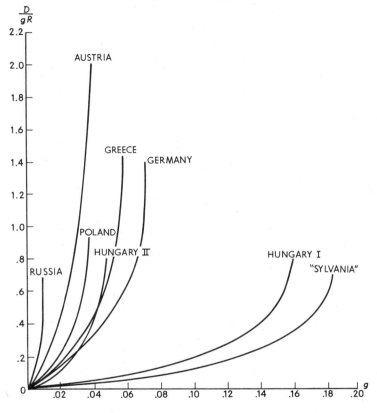

Figure 6

ORDERS OF MAGNITUDE OF D/gR AS A FUNCTION OF g
FOR $c = 1$

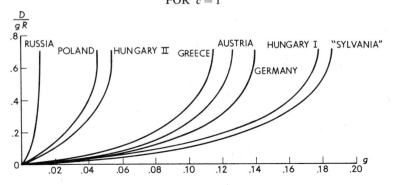

costs, and direct administrative costs, by Professor Arnold C. Harberger and me suggests that the figure of 7 percent may not be unreasonable, at least for countries with relatively poor tax administrations and tax morality.) Assuming that 7 percent is the maximum collection cost that is economical for "Sylvania" and assuming that the figures in Table 3 are appropriate in every respect, equation (3*) can be shown to imply that the maximum desirable rate of inflation is 18 percent a year, at which rate the government will secure about 6 percent of national income. For the other countries studied, if they propose to inflate openly and make $c = 1$, the maximum share of income to be obtained economically in this way (again using 7 percent as the maximum economical collection cost) can be found from Figure 6. These percentages of income range from about 6 percent for Hungary I to an almost infinitesimal amount (say 0.2 percent) for Russia. The corresponding rates of inflation range from 9 percent per year for Hungary I to 42 percent per year for Russia, with the others falling within this range.

V. SOME QUALIFYING CONSIDERATIONS

Several qualifying observations are now in order. The first concerns a possible lag in the adaptation of the public to inflationary conditions. As time and inflation go on, it may be expected that people will become more expert at making arrangements to reduce their average holdings of real cash balances; that is, they may find ways to reduce the cost to themselves, in loss of convenience and so on, of a given reduction in such balances. If this is true, the real cash balances the public would hold would tend to fall over time, even at a constant proportionate rate of nominal money-creation, and the share of national income going to the government would fall in proportion to real cash balances (because of the "independent" price rise implied by the fall in real cash balances, which would reduce the amount of real resources commanded by the given flow of new money). If the leftward drift of the demand curve for money followed the pattern we observed in comparing one country with the next (see the discussion of cols. 2 and 9 of Table 2, p. 450), which would imply that, as time went on, the government could get a given share on the national income only at an ever-increasing welfare cost.

Some support is lent to this conclusion by the comparison of Hungary after the second World War with Hungary after the first: the share of national income that the government could get at a given welfare cost (see Figures 5 and 6) was far smaller in the second hyperinflation than in the first. One possible explanation for this is that a second hyperinflation within a single generation found people far better prepared to reduce their real cash balances than they had been when they had had no such previous experience. Most of the reduction in real cash balances in the second case occurred *immediately* at the beginning of serious inflation (compare k_0^* for the two cases).

A second, much less significant, qualification has to do with the fact that the observed preinflationary value of real cash balances was much larger than would be predicted by extrapolating equation (1) to a zero rate of inflation. [This is indicated by the difference between cols. 4 and 5 in Table 2. The ratio of these two figures does, in fact, measure the ratio of *pre*inflationary real cash balances to the intercept of the demand function (1), because of the way in which k_0^* is calculated, even though k_0 is reported as a *post*inflationary ratio of real cash balances to income.] That is, the demand function for real cash balances is much more elastic at rates of inflation near zero than is indicated by equation (1). It is not possible to say a priori how large the error from this factor is, and it could be quite small. All we can say is that some error, perhaps small, on the side of charity toward inflation is introduced by failing to consider this elastic section of the demand curve; the welfare cost associated with a given rate of inflation (a given size of government budget) is greater than that indicated in Figures 5 and 6 by the amount that the area under the more elastic section of the demand curve exceeds the area under the corresponding section of curve (1). A similar small error on the side of charity is introduced by making all calculations in terms of E, the rate of inflation, rather than in terms of the money rate of interest, which includes E plus the real rate of return on capital.

A third possible qualification, of a statistical nature, cuts the other way. All but one (Hungary II) of Cagan's regressions showed a high degree of serial correlation in the residuals (with respect to time); this suggests the possibility of inappropriate specification of the estimating system, which might be due to any of a number of causes. One such possible cause, the detailed discussion of which will have to be omitted, is that it was inapropriate for Cagan to assume that the weights people assigned to various past prices, in forming their current expectations, remained constant over time in a given country. If, as is plausible, increasing rates of inflation over time were accompanied by a shift of these weights in the direction of attaching more and more importance to the most recently experienced rate of price change, then the effect on the affected regressions would be to bias the estimate of $-\alpha$ in an upward direction. That is, on this consideration the true demand curve for real cash balances in each country in response to known rates of inflation might be *less* elastic than it appears to be from Cagan's results. If true, this consideration implies that the curves in Figures 5 and 6 for all countries except Hungary II are too uncharitable to inflationary finance and should be shifted to the right.

It should be mentioned, however, that this conclusion is purely hypothetical, being based on only one of several possible explanations of the observed serial correlation in Cagan's regressions. Again the case of Hungary II comes to our aid in evaluating the possible importance of this conclusion, since there was no evidence of serial correlation in the residuals around the demand function for Hungary II and, in particular, since the public's reaction to the first signs of inflation was prompt and extreme, after which the curve was relatively inelastic. What we see is that the shift to the left of Hungary's demand function, possibly because of the previous experience, was far more than enough to offset the apparent reduction in the curve's elasticity. If the correct factors have been taken into account here, then the conclusion still stands that the curve for "Sylvania" definitely errs on the side of understating the cost of a long-sustained steady inflation.

VI. CONCLUDING OBSERVATIONS

The idea discussed here of a deliberate, openly announced inflation has little to do, of course, with inflation as it is customarily experienced; and it has particularly little to do with what happened in the seven cases studied by Cagan. Governments typically do not admit that they have in any way contributed to an existing inflation, whether rapid or moderate; in their view they are helpless pawns forced to issue increasing quantities of money in response to price rises generated by forces beyond their control. In practice this has meant, on the one hand, that it was possible for governments to get far more resources, by increasingly rapid money-creation constantly outrunning the public's expectation, than is implied by our results and, on the other hand, that the redistributive and disruptive effects of inflation were considerable. In the very severe cases that Cagan studied, this policy led to the progressive abandonment of the currency, the disappearance of any further possibility of obtaining substantial revenues by the inflationary means, and consequently to reform of the "currency" (that is, of government fiscal policy!), with all the disruption and complete impoverishment of some sections of the population which this whole process implies.

While there is no evident numerical way to compare the costs of these disruptive and redistributive effects with those of the destruction of real cash balances, on mature consideration most economists would probably agree that even for a short period (two or three years, say) the harmful effects of a severe inflation pursued in a covert fashion are more serious than would be the effects of an openly announced inflation in which all redistributive and disruptive effects were avoided; for a longer period the obtaining of very substantial resources by the traditional covert method is impossible. It may then be agreed that the approach taken here, in assuming an openly announced inflation of relatively moderate proportions, makes the best possible case for inflationary finance. When allowance is made for the difficulty, if not the impossibility, of avoiding serious disruptive and redistributive effects even when inflationary finance is openly pursued, the case for inflationary finance as a means of obtaining substantial resources for the government is very bad indeed.

Why, then, has inflationary finance been employed at such tremendous cost in some cases and at definitely excessive cost in most others? The reason appears to be that the costs are at first largely hidden, whereas the costs of other forms of taxation—the costs of administration and compliance—are obvious. Where a country has a serious problem of reconstruction (or reparations, as in the case of Germany) and therefore wishes to channel a large share of the national income through the government budget and where, on the other hand, the costs of administration are especially high because of war damage and other factors, the temptation to use the apparently almost costless method of printing money has evidently been irresistible. Most such countries might very well agree in retrospect that the temptation should have been resisted. The analysis here provides new concrete grounds, in addition to those already well known, for believing that such temptation should be resisted in every case.

Utility, strategy, and social decision rules[*]

WILLIAM S. VICKREY

SOCIAL WELFARE FUNCTIONS BASED ON CARDINAL UTILITY

Once we decide to accept some susceptibility of social welfare functions to strategy, there seems to be no reason to limit the argument of the function to rankings, and we naturally turn to the Benthamite social welfare function consisting of a summation of individual utilities. If each individual is to report his own utility evaluations for each of the alternative social states, however, it is necessary to specify a little more closely just how these evaluations are to be made, whether because it may not be clear a priori what the standards of measurement are, or because in the absence of any constraint a strategy of exaggeration might be so obviously and generally attractive as to result in the complete demoralization of the process. Moreover, while Bentham and his followers often seemed to assume as a matter of course that eventually some methods of assigning quantitative values to pleasures and pains would be developed that would be interpersonally valid, more modern writers have been increasingly skeptical of this possibility.

CALIBRATION BY THRESHOLD OF DISCRIMINATION

Indeed, the only method thus far suggested for actually measuring cardinal utility that gives rise naturally to a unique basis for interpersonal comparisons is that of Armstrong, who uses just noticeable differences of satisfaction as a unit.[1] But there seem to be many serious objections to the acceptance of such a unit. The ability of an individual to distinguish levels of satisfaction may vary rather systematically with the temperament, training, and occupation of the individual: does one really want to weight more heavily the preferences of an introvert than an extrovert, of a sybarite than an anchorite, of a professor of

---

[*] *The Quarterly Journal of Economics*, 74(1960): pp. 507–35; pp. 519–26 reprinted here. Reprinted by courtesy of the author and *The Quarterly Journal of Economics*.
[1] W. E. Armstrong, "Utility and the Theory of Welfare," *Oxford Economic Papers*, Vol. 3 (Oct. 1951), pp. 259–71. J. Rothenberg, "Marginal Preference and the Theory of Welfare," *Oxford Economic Papers*, Vol. 5 (Oct. 1953), pp. 248–63, with "Reply" by Armstrong. J. Rothenberg, "Reconsideration of a Group Welfare Index," *Oxford Economic Papers*, Vol. 6 (June 1954), pp. 164–80.

economics or psychology than a professor of chemistry or German literature? An affirmative answer might be maintained in some of these cases, but surely not in all.

Moreover, the difficulties involved in actually performing such a measurement appear more and more formidable as one seeks to make the definition more nearly operational. In the psychophysical experiment to which this proposed determination of utility is analogous, the conditions of the experiment must be carefully specified and the objects to be ranked must differ, so far as possible, only in the quality to be ranked and not in other irrelevant dimensions, if consistent results are to be obtained. For example, in comparing weights, different results are to be expected if the two weights are close together and can be hefted several times in alternate sequence, than if they are placed at opposite ends of the campus; or if the objects to be compared as to weight are all, say, books, the results may be expected to be different from those where the objects are books, pillows, lampshades, and lead ingots. Moreover, the experiment must usually be repeated a sufficient number of times to reduce to a reasonable level the effects of differences in the degree to which subjects would be willing to guess where they are not sure.

In the measurement of utility, however, the circumstances under which the comparison is to take place are so far removed from those of the psychophysical experiment as to lead to doubt as to whether the analogy has any validity at all. The experiment consisting of having the subject actually experience the various social states to be evaluated is certainly out of the question as a practical matter, and may not even be conceivable, in any fully consistent sense, as a *gedankenexperiment*, since a social state includes a complete set of anticipations regarding the future. The alternative social states must therefore be presented to the subject, not through direct experience but by description. Now if the descriptions of the states being compared differ in more than one parameter, we will have the difficulty that the accuracy with which the difference in utility is perceived will depend on the degree of qualitative difference in directions roughly orthogonal to utility. For example, even though a subject would probably assert with considerable certainty that he would prefer a trip to Paris plus 1,000 francs spending money to the same trip with only 950 francs to spend, he might at the same time find it quite difficult to decide between, say a trip to Honolulu plus x dollars of spending money and either Paris plus 1,000 francs, on the one hand, or Paris plus 800 francs, on the other.[2] Or more generally, a subject might be quite willing to assert that he would be better off with an income of $5,001 than with an income of $5,000, prices being the same; but if we consider another set of prices p_2 and ask how much money income must be obtained to make a person definitely and perceptibly better off than with $5,000 at prices p_1, and on the other hand (and independently), how much money income could be obtained at prices p_2 and still leave the individual definitely

---

[2] This illustration is adapted from one given by Howard Raiffa.

and perceptibly worse off than with \$5,000 at prices p_1, the difference between the two p_2 incomes thus determined, which should be equivalent to two "*jnd*'s" will in general be much larger than twice the \$1 difference in incomes that was perceptible when prices were held the same at p_1. Moreover, this difference will in general depend on the degree of divergence between the prices p_1 and the prices p_2. Thus there seems to be no suitably unique and uniform measure of utility to be obtained by this method.

It might be thought that something could be salvaged by sharpening the question that is being asked of the subjects. Thus it may be felt that when a respondent states that at constant prices a \$5,001 income is better than \$5,000, he is saying, in effect, not that he could actually "feel" the difference, but that he can tell in which direction the change for the better lies, so that if a sequence of differences of the same kind were combined he would be able to tell the difference, just as an assertion that a weight of 1,000 grams is heavier than one of 999 grams is not the same thing as stating that if asked to select the heavier of two such weights he could do it infallibly, under specified conditions. Thus the respondent must be asked to report, not whether he is able to tell reliably that one state is preferable to another, but rather that if allowed to experience the two states (in "sequence"?) he would "feel" significantly different, and moreover, he must be required to suppress any temptation he might have for strategic reasons to shade his reports in the direction of distinguishing smaller differences than would "really" be significant.

Even if these difficulties could be overcome, there would be undoubtedly a considerable bias introduced in such a measure of utility arising from the fact that for most respondents differences in the neighborhood of their current level of income would appear to be relatively more vivid and significant than differences between incomes both of which are remote from their current state. Thus one might expect a person with a small income to minimize the importance of differences between high incomes, and vice versa, and this natural bias would reinforce any tendency there might be to give consciously biased reports for strategic reasons. Thus for a number of widely differing reasons, measuring utility by minimum sensible increments seems to offer little promise for purposes of constructing social welfare functions.

INDEPENDENCE OF MARGINAL UTILITIES AS A CRITERION OF CARDINALITY

Another approach to the measurement of utility is the Fisher-Frisch construction[3] based on the assumption that classes of commodities can be defined in such a way that the marginal utility derived from a given increment in one class of commodities consumed will be independent of the amount of

---

[3] Irving Fisher, "A Statistical Method for Measuring Marginal Utility," in *Economic Essays in Honor of J. B. Clark* (New York: Macmillan, 1927), pp. 157–93. Ragnar Frisch, "New Methods of Measuring Marginal Utility" (Tubingen: J. C. B. Mohr, 1932).

consumption in the other class.[4] If this assumption can be accepted, a utility function is defined up to a linear transformation, and can be determined from observations on the choices of an individual under a suitable variety of circumstances. This still leaves no basis for interpersonal comparisons; Fisher and Frisch hurdled this barrier by in effect assuming that the average behavior of consumers within each income stratum could be taken as the behavior of a "typical" consumer in the various income and price situations, and that all deviations of individuals in either behavior or utility from that of this typical or average individual could be neglected insofar as the construction of a social welfare function that considers only the distribution of incomes is concerned. This was done in the first instance in order to permit the construction of a utility function from consumer studies by income classes, but this assumption also has the effect of hurdling the interpersonal chasm.

Given the assumption that independence exists as between two commodity classes, a utility function could be determined, to within linear transformations, for each individual separately, in principle at least. This would leave the interpersonal chasm unbridged, but would require less heroic assumptions. But the assumption that independence exists is in itself no mean hurdle to take. It involves first that the behavior of the individual be compatible with this assumption: as a counterexample, the utility function $U = \log (x^2 + xy)$ satisfies all of the usual requirements, but there is no monotonic transformation of this U that will make x and y independent. It also involves the assumption that if behavior is capable of being so explained, the utility function so determined will be relevant to the construction of a social welfare function. This is by no means assured, and indeed it is possible to exhibit cases where absurd results would be obtained. For example, $U = \log[\log(x + 3) + 2y + y^2]$ is a utility function that produces indifference curves convex to the origin throughout, with declining marginal utility for an adequately wide range of values, which range can be extended at will by suitable transformations of the function. If we decide to select for welfare purposes that transformation that produces independence, we have as the selected function $V = \log(x + 3) + 2y + y^2$, and the marginal utility of y is everywhere an increasing function of y, which in many cases would be completely unacceptable. Considering the many points at which doubts are raised, it does not appear that a utility determined by reference to independence has any special virtue as a basis for a social welfare function.

RISK, UTILITY, AND INCOME DISTRIBUTION

There seems to be much more promise, for social welfare function purposes, in the Bernoullian utility function, which has been given such a modern

---

[4] This is not quite the same thing as saying that the total utility must be expressible as the sum of separate utilities produced by the two commodity classes considered in isolation, since a third class of commodities may enter the picture, as in the utility function $U = \log(x + z) + \log(y + z^2)$.

vogue by Von Neumann and Morgenstern.[5] This function rests on the hypothesis, of course, that human behavior in the face of risk can be explained in terms of maximizing the mathematical expectation of a utility function; if the facts do conform to such a hypothesis, then the relevant utility function is determined uniquely to within linear transformations. Thus like the independence utility function, the Bernoullian utility function provides no immediate basis for interpersonal comparisons.

There is a sense, however, in which the Bernoullian utility function appears to have a logical connection with the selection of a social state that is somewhat closer than any possessed by the utility functions discussed previously. For example, if for the moment we make the heroic assumption that, abstracting from differences in age, sex, or family status, each individual has preference patterns exactly similar to those of every other individual, then we can take any two income-price situations as calibrating points for the setting up of a utility function, and interpersonal comparisons will be independent of the choice of calibrating points. The analogy in thermometry is the selection of two temperatures as calibrating points for gas thermometers using different gases as the thermometric medium: if we assume that all gases are "perfect" in that they follow the same law of expansion, it makes no essential difference what temperatures we select for calibration. Let us now further imagine a series of communities, each with the same resources, with individuals all having the same tastes, but differing within each community as to talents (but each community enjoying the same distribution of talents). Unequal degrees of talent among individuals would tend to produce corresponding differences in individual incomes; we can imagine that each of the communities adopts some form of redistributive policy, which, however, can be pushed beyond a certain point only at the expense of reducing total output through the effects on incentives. Suppose that different policies are adopted in the different communities, and then consider the choice of a potential immigrant who is making up his mind as to which of the various communities to migrate to. If he knows his own talents exactly and is able therefore to predict the net income he will enjoy in each of the communities, he can, of course, make his choice accordingly on the basis of these net incomes without recourse to the imputation of utility. If on the other hand he is quite uncertain as to the role that his talents will enable him to fill in the various communities, he may, if his tastes are the same as those of everyone else, make his decision on the basis of maximizing his expected utility, the alternative utilities in question being those of the various members of a given community, and the probabilities attached to each being the immigrant's appraisal of the probability of his being able to attain a comparable role if he chooses in favor of that community. If we identify the social welfare with the attractiveness of the

[5] Daniel Bernoulli, "Exposition of a New Theory on the Measurement of Risk," (1738), trans. Louise Sommer, *Econometrica*, Vol. 22 (Jan. 1954), pp. 23–36. J. Von Neumann and O. Morgenstern, *Theory of Games and Economic Behavior* (2d ed.; Princeton University Press, 1947). W. Vickrey, "Measuring Marginal Utility by Reactions to Risk," *Econometrica*, Vol. 13 (Oct. 1945), pp. 319–33.

various communities to this prospective immigrant, we see that the social welfare function takes the form of a weighted summation of individual utilities. If the immigrant is completely ignorant as to what role he will fill in the new community and weights the roles of all individuals equally, we get the Benthamite summation of individual utilities with the utilities being Bernoullian.

INTERPERSONAL COMPARISONS AND DIFFERENCES IN TASTES

It is possible to relax somewhat the rather drastic assumptions as to similarity of tastes and still retain some interesting properties. Assume for example, that tastes vary only in such a way that for each individual the ratio of the income necessary to achieve a given level of satisfaction at one set of prices to the income necessary at another set of prices is independent of the level of satisfaction specified (i.e., that the "true" index of the cost of living between two price situations is independent of the level of income); this will be true in particular when there is "expenditure proportionality," i.e., when for any given set of prices expenditure on any given commodity varies in direct proportion to income. A change in prices will then change the scale, but not the shape, of the relation between utility and money income. If in addition we assume that the utility function is such that for some set of prices utility is proportional to the logarithm of income, then any given change in prices changes the utility of all incomes by a constant amount, and leaves the marginal utility of money unaffected. There is then no inconsistency in postulating that the marginal utility of money at a given level of money income is the same for all individuals, whereas under more general assumptions, making interpersonal comparisons on the basis of equating the marginal utility of money at given income levels at one set of prices would give results that would in general differ from those obtained if the same procedure were adopted using another set of prices as a basis. Thus differences in taste do not make consistent interpersonal comparisons impossible, but the differences must be confined to very special kinds of difference. The fact that the logarithmic function turns out to have such special properties in this connection may perhaps be scored as a minor triumph for Bernoulli's intuition, for this was the function that he picked out to use in resolving the Petersburg paradox. His intuition may have been somewhat stronger than his logic at this point, however, for while this function resolves the particular paradox that was presented to him, it does not resolve all paradoxes of this type. Indeed, only if a utility function has an upper bound is it impossible to construct a gamble of the Petersburg type that will yield an infinite expectation of utility. However, the fact that a Petersburg-type paradox can be constructed giving an infinite expectation of utility for the logarithmic utility function is probably not a serious objection to its use, especially if we note that the infinite sequence of tosses of coins or the equivalent required for such a paradox could never be carried out in a finite period of time with the aid of a finite amount of equipment.

Estimating the social benefit of constructing an underground railway in London*†

C. D. FOSTER AND M. E. BEESLEY

I. INTRODUCTION

1.1. This paper gives the findings and method of a study estimating the gains and losses expected to result from building the Victoria Line—whoever gains, or suffers the losses, i.e., the social benefits and social costs of the Line (Pigou, 1920, Part II, Chap. 6 ff.). The ambition and method are essentially the same as in earlier water resource and transport studies where the aim was also to measure the surplus of social benefits over social costs expected to result from an investment; or, as it is sometimes called, the consumers' surplus return on investment (McKean, 1958, Part 3; Hirshleifer *et al.*, 1960, Chaps. 10, 11; Coburn *et al.*, 1960). In effect, the purpose of the study is to measure the effect on the community of the investment, so far as practicable. (For discussion of the relation between different surplus criteria see Foster, 1960).

The Victoria Line (V.L) will be a London Transport Underground railway from Victoria at its southern end to Walthamstow in northeast London. First proposed as part of the London Plan Working Party's Route C (B.T.C. 1949), its construction was authorized by the Treasury in August 1962. It will be the first underground railway built in central London since before 1914.

1.2. Difference from a financial calculation

The difference between this and an ordinary financial calculation of the profitability of an investment is that the latter normally considers only the private costs and benefits of the investment: changes in the outlays and receipts of the parent enterprise, in this instance London Transport, because of it. On a financial calculation it is almost certain not to earn enough at

* *Journal of the Royal Statistical Society*, Series A, 126(1963): pp. 46–92. Reprinted by courtesy of the authors and the *Journal of the Royal Statistical Society*.

† This paper was read before the Royal Statistical Society, on Wednesday, December 12th, 1962, the president, Dr. J. O. Irwin, in the Chair.

present fare levels to meet its interest charges after covering operating costs and providing for depreciation. Re-calculated for an interest rate of 6 percent, the most recent, April 1962, prediction is an annual loss of £2.14 million on the V.L., and of £3.12 million to London Transport overall because of the fall in net revenues on London Transport's other services from traffic diverting to the V.L. (If calculated at a 5 percent rate, the loss on the V.L. would be £1.59 million, to London Transport £2.58 million.) Though it seems possible that the standard rate of fare on the whole of London Transport will be raised to avoid a loss from the V.L., this does not, of course, mean the V.L. will pay; only that fares can be raised so that London Transport can continue to break even, or make a small profit.

1.3. Reasons for a social benefit–social cost calculation

Those reasons often given (e.g., by Hirshleifer *et al.*, 1960, pp. 125ff.) for preferring a social to a financial calculation are: (i) that the investment is large and indivisible (e.g. a large dam will have a low marginal value when built, which if made equal to the price would not yield enough revenue to cover costs, but it has a high aggregate value and therefore should be built); (ii) that there are secondary costs which a private firm can avoid (e.g. the cost on the neighbourhood of smoke from a factory chimney), or benefits which it is not paid because of imperfections of the market mechanism; (iii) that there are specially desirable social consequences such as the relief of unemployment. None of these is an important reason for wanting a social calculation in this case. The two overwhelming reasons why the financial and social returns diverge are (i) the pricing policy of the Underground system and (ii) relative prices on road and rail in London.

i) Implicit in the idea of using a financial rate of return on investment is the assumption that prices are determined by the market and that business men set out, broadly, to maximize profits. But London Transport set fares so as to cover costs currently attributed to all their operations only. This is a consequence of the policy of the Government and the Transport Tribunal, regulating fares, which have, in practice, required public enterprise to earn enough to cover costs, taking one year with another. Such average-cost pricing implies that the value to intramarginal users of the railway system is greater than the fares they pay, and these are less than would be set by a commercial enterprise. This implies that the fares paid by users of the V.L. are less than the value to them of the fares which would be asked by a private firm.

ii) But the money which people would be prepared to pay for the services and indirect effects of the V.L. does not fully represent the value of the V.L., because the price that vehicle-users pay in London does not reflect the real costs of their travel (Pigou, 1920, p. 194; Walters, 1954; Beesley *et al.*, 1962). If the road-user paid an economic price there would, depending on the elasticity of substitution between urban road and rail transport, be a shift to public rail transport. There is no reliable evidence on this elasticity, but given evidence (Smeed, 1961, pp. 22ff.) that the change in the relative prices would be considerable we believe it would be sufficient to increase markedly the financial profitability of investing in the V.L. if a profit-maximizing fares policy were to be adopted. (Once a vehicle is bought and licensed, only fuel tax, among vehicle taxes, is relevant to the decision to use it. Purchase taxes and licence duties which are more than 40 percent of the total burden of vehicle taxation are not. Our argument here refers to the incidence of taxation. Whether the total burden of taxation on vehicle-users is too high is irrelevant. Even should it be judged so, a smaller total burden of vehicle taxation would mean more vehicles and vehicle usage, but this would mean more congestion unless the incidence of the taxation were related to congestion.)

These arguments would indicate raising the price of public and private urban road transport until each covered its real costs, when there could hardly be any doubt that it would pay to build the V.L. But if we accept that such a correction of prices is politically undesirable or impossible, we should not forget that benefits accruing to transport-users from investment in improving urban transport are greater than are indicated by purely financial calculations; and that the relative benefits of investing in urban road and underground railway improvements are not those given by measurements based on the existing relative prices to transport-users of travel by road and underground. It is generally recognized to be absurd to try to decide where to build and improve roads by a financial calculation. Indeed the effect of a road improvement may be to reduce the financial returns to the Exchequer since these, by and large, depend on the quantity of petrol consumed, which declines when congestion is relieved (rather as building a new underground line reduces the receipts of London Transport since these depend on the distance traveled). Road investment is beginning to be decided by calculation of consumers' rates of return by estimating the social benefits and costs incurred by building a new road. It seems sensible to treat urban rail investment similarly: which is what we have done for a particular investment in this paper.

2. RESULTS

2.1. Overall results

The costs and benefits which we have measured are set out in Table 2 and described in detail in later sections; the methods of reaching them are described in the Appendix. Broadly, costs are the initial capital invested and the operating expenses of the V.L.; the measured benefits are of three main kinds: time savings to those affected by the investment; savings involving cash transactions, e.g. cost reductions to motorists in less-congested running conditions or savings in bus-operating costs; and the value of increased comfort and convenience.

One conventional but crude way of describing the relationship of total costs and benefits is to compute the yearly return on the capital outlay when it is completed and at intervals thereafter. Deducting the current costs of operation from benefits and applying this to the capital outlay attributable to the V.L. gives the crude yearly rate of return as shown in Table 1.

Table 1

CRUDE YEARLY RATE OF RETURN ON THE VICTORIA LINE

1st year of operation 11.2%
20th year of operation..........12.6%
50th year of operation..........15.3%

The later years have the higher rates of return because, while costs remain practically constant, some benefits are predicted to rise over the years.

The crude rate fails to take time into account: benefits will only accrue when the V.L. is open; meanwhile investment is proceeding without return. Moreover, since the net benefits vary over time, we need a measure to take account of this variation. Similarly, the distinction between capital and other outlays is conventional, for the costs are simply those occurring at different dates. A procedure of discounting is used to give them a common denominator in time. Because decisions have to be made now, the present (discounted) value of benefits and costs is relevant. The rationale of discounting is that benefits or costs experienced in the future have less value than those of today because of the possibility of reinvestment. If, other things being equal, one is given the choice of £100 now or in a year's time, one would be foolish if one did not plump for the £100 now since one could, if one wished, invest it and, at 6 percent, for example, it would be worth £106 in a year's time. Similarly, if given the choice of paying a bill now or in a year's time it would be foolish, other things being equal, not to postpone payment. If various rates of interest are used for discounting, various results will be found. (Fuller disquisitions on discounting can be found in McKean, 1958, pp. 74ff.; Hirshleifer *et al.*, 1960, pp. 115ff.; Ashton, 1962.) The difficulties of deciding on a particular interest rate are discussed below in Section 4.2: here we present results for a variety: 4 percent, 6 percent, 8 percent.

Table 2 presents both the undiscounted annual amounts of costs and benefits (with trend assumed) and their discounted or present value equivalents. Discounted at 6 percent the present value of benefits is £86 million; of all costs £55 million; of net benefits £31 million. Net benefit is the predicted quantified addition to national wealth of the investment. The ratio of discounted benefits to costs is 1.57. To express the results as a rate of return which allows for the effect of time, we calculate the surplus of benefits over current costs of the V.L. for each year of its life separately; discount these back to the present; and express the total as a level annual rate of return over the period of construction and operation on the present value of the capital invested. This return is shown in Table 2: at 4 percent discount, 11.6 percent; at 6 percent discount, 11.3 percent; at 8 percent discount, 10.9 percent.[1] Yet

---

[1] Rankings of investments by this rate of return will be invariant to those produced by net present values except for investments of varying lives.

Table 2

SOCIAL BENEFIT AND LOSS TABLE—VICTORIA LINE

(5½ years' construction plus 50 years' operation)

	Trend Assumed	Rate of Interest 6 Percent		Rate of Interest 4 Percent		Rate of Interest 8 Percent	
		Annual Amount	P.D.V.†	Annual Amount	P.D.V.†	Annual Amount	P.D.V.†
A) *Costs* (other than interest charges)		£m	£m	£m	£m	£m	£m
Annual working expenses . . .	0	1.413	16.16	1.448	25.07	1.391	11.14
B) *Traffic Diverted to V.L.*							
Benefits							
1) Underground: Time savings . .	0	0.378	4.32				
Comfort and convenience .	φ	0.347	3.96				
2) British Railways: Time savings . .	1½%C	0.205	2.93				
3) Buses: Time savings . . .	0	0.575	6.58				
4) Motorists: Time savings . .	‡	0.153	3.25				
Saving in vehicle operating costs	‡	0.377	8.02				
5) Pedestrians: Time savings . .	1½%C	0.020	0.28				
B) Sub-total		2.055	29.34	2.055	45.30	2.055	20.35

C) *Traffic not diverted to V.L.*							
1) Underground: Cost savings	0	0.150	1.72				
Comfort and convenience	φ	0.457	5.22				
3) Buses: Cost savings	0	0.645	7.38				
4) Road users: Time savings	0	1.883	21.54				
Savings in vehicle operating costs	0	0.781	8.93				
C) Sub-total		3.916	44.79	3.916	66.41	3.916	32.03
D) *Generated traffic*							
Outer areas: Time savings	1½%C	0.096	1.37				
Fare savings	1½%C	0.063	0.90				
Other benefits	1½%C	0.375	5.36				
Central area: Time savings	1½%C	0.056	0.80				
Fare savings	1½%C	0.029	0.41				
Other benefits	1½%C	0.203	2.90				
D) Sub-total		0.822	11.74	0.822	18.65	0.822	7.91
E) *Terminal scrap value*			0.29		0.82		0.10
F) Total benefits (B+C+D+E)			86.16		131.18		60.39
G) Net current benefit (F−A)			70.00		106.11		49.25
H) Value of capital expenditure			38.81		41.14		36.68
I) Net benefit (G−H)			31.19		64.97		12.57
J) Social surplus rate of return§			11.3%		11.6%		10.9%

Notes: † P.D.V.'s are present or year 1 values discounted at the relevant rate of interest set out in the column heading.

‡ The assumption is made that the trend will be 5 percent for 15 years and 2 percent thereafter.

§ Total benefits less costs other than interest charges (G) as a return on the capital invested (H), averaged over the whole period of operation and construction.

C compound

φ Assumed to fall to 0 at the end of 50 years of operation of V.L.

another way of expressing the return is to calculate the rate of interest equating the present values of benefits and costs. This, usually called the internal rate of return, is approximately 10.5 percent (see Section 5.2 for mention of its use.)

2.2. Life of the Victoria Line

For this paper it is assumed to be 50 years' operation. This does not imply a prediction that all capital invested will need replacement by then. The tunnels and other earthworks should never need it. But it is rash to assume in this kind of calculation that a capital asset, though it last forever, will have value forever: it is always possible that scientific progress or changes in the location of population or industry, etc., will make the V.L. obsolete. To guard against obsolescence, it is necessary to limit the period of time over which benefits (and costs) are counted. The choice of period was arbitrary within limits of what seemed sensible. However, though 50 years was used in the principal calculations, separate estimates were made, using a discount rate of 6 percent, of the discounted rates of return assuming 90 years, and perpetual life. (The trends were as set out in Table 2 except that traffic diverting from private cars was assumed to be constant after 90 years; and all trends were assumed constant after 200 years. At lower discount rates, the rates of return and the differences between them would be greater (however, see Section 4.3).) Table 3 shows the effect of varying " lives ":

Table 3

EFFECT ON THE AVERAGE DISCOUNTED RATE OF RETURN OF VARYING THE ASSUMED LIFE OF THE VICTORIA LINE.

Discounted at 6 percent, $5\frac{1}{2}$ years' construction

50 years' operation 11.3%
90 years' operation 11.7%
Perpetual 11.8%

2.3. Construction period

From information given by London Transport it is assumed that it will take $5\frac{1}{2}$ years to build the V.L. But a calculation has also been made assuming a 4-year construction period—assuming the capital expenditure would be incurred in the same proportions over time. Discounted at 6 percent this raises the average discounted rate of return from 11.3 percent to 11.6 percent, for a 50-year operating life.

This means that it would pay the community to incur anything up to approximately £4 million additional capital expenditure if it would reduce the period of construction by $1\frac{1}{2}$ years. Quicker construction costs more (in terms of present discounted value of outlays) but is more than offset by the earlier realization of revenues. While there may be other particular difficulties the chief problem seems to be that the rebuilding of Oxford Circus is expected to take $5\frac{1}{2}$ years. If it should not be possible to speed up its excavation and construction, a possibility might be to use the Line before Oxford Circus was open. Although benefits would be less than if Oxford Circus were open, they would be positive and therefore, if the additional capital expenditure were not too great, the return would be better than if no trains were run until Oxford Circus were ready. But whatever the practical expedients which might or might not be feasible, it would be desirable if London Transport, within limits, could shorten the construction period by incurring extra capital expenditure.

2.4. Particular categories of costs and benefits

Costs in Table 2 are the private costs—financial outgoings—of London Transport (see Appendix, Section A). Other—social—costs are concealed in the categories of benefits, which are mostly net benefits, that is, social benefits minus social costs. Categories of benefits are organized generally as they accrue to various classes of beneficiaries. Diverted traffic comprises all those who will use the V.L. for at least part of its length, substituting, in part at least, for other means of travel. Undiverted traffic means traffic elsewhere on the Underground or on other means of travel which will not divert to the V.L. but will benefit indirectly—through a faster, better, more comfortable transit. Generated traffic is new traffic which will result from the fall in costs of transport, not only on the V.L. but because of the V.L.

It will be seen that, discounting at 6 percent, benefits to undiverted traffic are about 52 percent of the whole; to diverted traffic about 34 percent of the whole. The benefits to all traffic predicted to use the V.L.—diverted and generated traffic—are approximately 48 percent.

The most important single category, amounting to 25 percent of the total, is time savings of vehicle-users from reducing congestion in London streets. If the other effect of decongestion—savings in vehicle-operating costs—is added, the two make 35 percent of total benefits. Other important categories are: savings in bus costs (9 percent); time savings of V.L. traffic diverting from buses (8 percent); savings in vehicle-operating costs to motorists diverting to the V.L. (9 percent); and the value to undiverted passengers on the Underground of the increased probability of getting a seat (6 percent), which as explained in the Appendix (B2) is given in Table 2 as "comfort and convenience".

The items distinguishing this from earlier calculations concerned with public investment (e.g. Coburn et al., 1960) are the direct measurement of comfort and convenience, and of savings accruing to people not directly connected with, using, or operating, the Underground system—here road-users benefiting from decongestion. These two categories account for 46 percent of all benefits.

3. BENEFITS AND COSTS OF THE VICTORIA LINE

3.1. General nature of the benefits quantified

Time savings. People will save time travelling if the V.L. is built. Time has a value to most people. The two problems are to measure the time saved (less any time lost) and to value it. The basis of the valuation of time is explained in the Appendix (especially Section B1).

Fare and cost savings. Because London Transport fares are based on standard rates for distance travelled and passengers transferring to the V.L. usually save distance, at present levels aggregate fares from existing traffic will be less. This would be a reduction in gross revenues to London Transport, but a gain to the passengers themselves who must be presumed willing to pay at least as much for the new and faster method of getting where they want to go involving the V.L. as they did for the old inferior journey. It is partly because of this that London Transport expected to lose money from operating the V.L. If it were decided to raise fares throughout the system to meet any such loss, the position would be slightly different. Compared with the assumption made in this study the result would be a transfer of benefit from users of the V.L. and of the rest of the London Transport system. In addition London Transport, British Railways, and road vehicle-users will save operating costs as a result of the V.L. The railways and bus services will save through withdrawal of some trains and buses: partly because of reduced traffic, partly because of better scheduling.

Comfort and convenience. In principle this is a residual category, meaning every other benefit or cost which would result from the V.L. except those mentioned above or in the last category below. In practice we cannot hope to get at everything which should be included in this category. The factor chosen is measured because it seemed possible to have a shot at measuring it: it is the value of the increased probability of getting a seat due to the building of the V.L. Another benefit which one would very much like to measure, apart from time and vehicle-operating costs savings, is the pleasure people get from decongested streets. The V.L. should also lead to a fall in the accident rate as people transfer from more to less accident-prone forms of transport.

After a section (A) on costs, benefits are estimated for: (B) Traffic diverted to the V.L.; (C) Traffic not diverted to the V.L., and (D) Generated Traffic.

The category Generated Traffic perhaps needs comment at this stage.

There are two problems: (1) to explain what one is attempting to measure as generated traffic; (2) to explain why it is that once one has measured all benefits to diverted and undiverted traffic, all other benefits can be measured (with a few trivial exceptions) as benefits (or losses) accruing to generated traffic.

1) The effects of the V.L. in generating new traffic can be distinguished in various ways: the effect in generating traffic on the V.L. itself and elsewhere because of reduced traffic flows due to diversion to the V.L. It is also possible to distinguish short- and long-run effects. We may define short-run effects as effects which do not involve workers changing their homes, or shops, factories, etc., changing their location. Long-run effects are those that do so. In the short run one would expect, for example, office-workers in Walthamstow to travel to work in the centre of London, whereas before the V.L. was built they did not. There would be changes of jobs, but not of residences.

Similarly more shoppers would find it worth while to travel to centres served by the V.L. These short-run effects will be reflected by changes in land values. Office buildings in the West End and City will become somewhat more valuable because of the new labour market now tapped. Shops in certain centres will become more valuable because of the new source of customers.

In the long run people will move their homes, businesses and location. For example, one would expect easier and cheaper travel to the West End from the north-east to mean that more commuters would want to move to live in Waltham Holy Cross, Edmonton, Enfield, and Cheshunt, and that houses would be built for them there. Shifts like these will generate traffic for the V.L. and for other forms of transport connected with the V.L.—e.g., central bus services, coaches, suburban surface and underground rail connections with V.L.

2) If we could estimate all the traffic likely to be generated over the life of the V.L. the only important costs and benefits omitted from our calculation would be those caused by the V.L. other than as a means of transport. Traffic on a new road or surface railway imposes a cost of noise, dirt, fumes, etc., on those in its neighbourhood. This one would expect to be negligible for an underground railway, but at present the effect is unquantifiable.

We must demonstrate that, with this exception, no increase in value due to the V.L. is excluded if we are able to estimate generated traffic. Since this is a complicated matter requiring somewhat extended discussion it is postponed to Section 4.3.

3.2. Magnitudes of the costs and benefits

The discounted figures given in this subsection are those using a 6 percent rate. Other figures are given in Table 2.

A) *Total annual outgoings* over the life of the V.L. are predicted for the purposes of our calculation to be £1,413,000 working expenses and maintenance including all expenditure needed to keep the line in operation. (Two other items appear as outgoings in the financial accounts: interest charges and provision for redemption of capital. Neither is relevant here: redemption because it would be double-counting to take into account both capital outlays and their redemption; interest charges because here we are interested in the net benefit of a project, not in whether it can serve a particular fixed interest charge. If the interest charge were 6 percent, this project with an average discounted rate of return of 11.3 percent at the 6 percent level could certainly meet it.

B), (C) *Benefits to diverted and undiverted traffic.* These are time savings, net receipts and fare savings, and the value of increased comfort and convenience.

Time savings. The principle is that people choosing to travel on the V.L., or on other forms of transport speeded up by the V.L., will save time which has a value to them. A profit-maximizing business man would be able to expropriate some of this benefit by charging accordingly. Because of public policy L.T.E. does not. Therefore these are benefits to users of the V.L. in the first place. But other transport-users save time because V.L. lessens congestion and speeds up traffic on the rest of the Underground (where fewer passengers means shorter station stops and so more trains can be run per hour), British Railways, and the roads. We have estimated that time saved by Underground traffic diverting to the V.L. is worth £378,000 p.a., remaining constant over the V.L.'s life; by British Railways traffic diverting to the V.L.—£205,000 p.a., increasing at $1\frac{1}{2}$ percent p.a. compound over the life of the V.L.; by bus traffic diverting to the V.L.—£575,000 p.a. constant over the life of the V.L.; by motorists—£153,000 at 5 percent p.a. compound for the first 15 years and 2 percent p.a. compound thereafter; pedestrians diverting—£20,000 p.a. at $1\frac{1}{2}$ percent compound. No estimate has been made of time savings on the rest of the Underground or to traffic remaining on British Railways (together they are unlikely to be less than £10,000 or more than £30,000). Time savings to remaining road-users, including bus traffic, have been estimated at £1,883,000, all constant over the life of the V.L. The assumptions on which these figures are based are explained in the Appendix.

L.T. receipts from existing traffic will fall, other things being equal, when the V.L. is opened since they are, approximately, related to mileage travelled. The V.L. will mean that most passengers who profit from it will travel a shorter distance and so pay less. The resulting net fall in receipts rightly appears as a negative item in an ordinary commercial calculation of the return on the V.L.

It is cancelled out in our type of calculation by the value of fares saved by passengers. This must be so as L.T.E's loss is the passengers' gain. If a passenger paid, say, 9d. for the old and necessarily slower journey, then he should be at least prepared to pay 9d. for the new, quicker journey made possible by the V.L. Since he pays less, he has made a gain which should be attributed to the V.L. as a benefit cancelling out L.T.E's loss of revenue.

Although these cancel out for L.T.E. and British Railways traffic which diverts to the V.L., elsewhere there are net gains. Motorists in general save money by diverting to the V.L. The estimate is £278,000, increasing at 5 percent p.a. compound for the first 15 years of the V.L. and thereafter at 2 percent compound. L.T.E. saves £150,000 p.a. on remaining Underground services and £645,000 on bus services, both assumed to be constant over the life of the V.L. British Railways cost savings will be negligible.

Road-users will save in vehicle-operating costs because of reduced congestion. These savings have been estimated at £781,000 p.a. constant; the reason for this assumption is given in the Appendix.

Comfort and convenience.   One effect of building the V.L. will be to increase the comfort or convenience of many journeys. There will be less standing at peak hours. Motorists may value less congested roads by more than what they save in time and vehicle-operating costs. Driving along less congested roads may give them a positive pleasure, though this is less likely when the effects of the improvement, the V.L., are diffused over a wide area. The only element in comfort and convenience which has been quantified in this study is the increased probability of getting a seat for Underground passengers diverting to the V.L. and to those remaining on the existing Underground. This may be a more considerable benefit than the figures suggest: £347,000 p.a. for diverted traffic; £457,000 p.a. for undiverted traffic. These have been assumed to fall exponentially to zero over 50 years.

It has not been possible to make any reasonable calculation of accident savings.

D) *Benefits to generated traffic.* Estimates have been made of the likely generation of journeys to the centre from the major part of the Greater London area. These are both work and nonwork journeys. It is estimated that journeys from outer areas will be worth £96,000 in time savings to passengers using the line; £63,000 in fare savings; and £375,000 in other net benefits. The meaning of these benefits is explained in the Appendix.

To these have been added figures to cover other generated journeys: £56,000 time savings, £29,000 fare savings and £203,000 other net benefits. Generated traffic has been assumed to increase at $1\frac{1}{2}$ percent p.a. compound.

4. SPECIAL PROBLEMS

4.1. Capacity of the Victoria Line

Our estimates of benefit would be exaggerated if the V.L. were unable to carry all the traffic predicted. London Transport have commented that the theoretical capacity of the Line should not be exceeded even on the bottleneck section between Oxford Circus and Warren Street—until the forty-ninth year of operation. This means we have not overestimated the value of this particular version of the V.L.; though it may mean that some form of the Line could have been designed which would have shown a higher return.

4.2. Choice of discount rates

Recently the tendency has been to require nationalized industries to use higher discount rates in assessing the desirability of investment. One reason has been the general increase in the Government's cost of borrowing. Another is the opinion that nationalized industries should provide for a risk premium over the cost of borrowing. The third is a feeling of some kind that investment in the public sector should yield more or less as high a return as in the private sector.

If there were a perfect capital market and no uncertainty there would be a unique rate of interest which would be the rate of time preference expressed by the capital market given the investment opportunities available and predicted. The only possible difference of opinion over the interest rate would be if the Government, or some other body, had a different opinion on what the rate of social preference—the weight to be given to consumption at different periods in time—should be. If there is uncertainty, as indeed there always is, interest rates will diverge in so far as the discount rates are used to allow for risk, and these risks vary between projects. It is also possible that various people will have different opinions of the risk of a particular investment and will wish to use different interest rates accordingly. The treatment of risk in this study is discussed in the next subsection.

If there is an imperfect capital market, as again there always is, the relevant rates of interest or discount will vary because the cost of borrowing or any other method of finance will vary between firms. A firm which for some reason of market imperfection can borrow at 8 percent, should discount at that rate— or at some higher rate allowing for risk. It may also be the case that the borrowing and lending rates of a commercial firm are different. When considering investment the relevant rates are the interest rate at which it can borrow money if it is thinking of borrowing, the rate at which it can lend, if it is thinking of lending money. Whichever is relevant, it is the opportunity cost of the capital measured as a straightforward financial rate of return.

But financial rates of discount would seem irrelevant to the kind of social surplus calculation done here. One would expect discounting to be done by such a social surplus rate of discount. If all investment in the economy were judged by this, then the relevant discount rate would be the marginal social rate of return. The analogy with the choice of the ordinary financial discount rate in a perfect capital market is exact. The right rate is determined by the (social surplus) opportunity cost of capital. But there is not in this sense a perfect market. First of all there is a sector where social surplus calculations hold and the remainder of the economy where other criteria, principally financial, hold. If the use of funds in the social surplus sector were determined solely by social considerations, then the relevant discount rate would be the opportunity costs of capital in that sector—the marginal social surplus rate of return. Apart from any practical difficulty of measuring this, there is a fundamental problem in that we do not know just how large the social surplus sector is. This is a political decision which the Government has not taken. Or, in other words, we do not know what kinds of investments (made by which enterprises) are to be ranked in order of priority by this criterion; and therefore we do not know what rate of return to use, even if we could determine it. Even if we should treat the sector as coterminous with London Transport, we would be in a quandary because we do not know what London Transport's marginal social surplus rate of return is. To find this it would be necessary to do a large number of calculations of the kind we have done. However, even if some such rate of return were known and agreed on, there is a problem unsettled: the criterion by which to allocate funds between the social surplus sector and sectors where other rates of discount hold. This cannot be decided except by a higher order criterion; and this has not been formulated.

But in fact it would seem that the Government solves the problem of what rate of discount to use in the public sector (not necessarily coterminous with the social surplus sector in our sense) by relating it to the rate of discount held to operate in the private sector. Government projects are usually required to earn at least as much as their opportunity cost in the private sector measured by the cost of borrowing to the Government (plus a risk premium). It would be possible to modify this principle for unremunerative investment by requiring projects to lead to at least as much in terms of (unearned) net benefits as a remunerative investment would in terms of earned net revenue. This would imply a 1 : 1 weighting of the social surplus and financial discount rates—which would mean that the same percentage discount rate would operate in both sectors, though the beneficiaries, by and large, would in one case be internal to the enterprise, in the other external. Therefore marginal funds would be used in the social surplus sector in as much as the social surplus rate of return there was higher than the marginal rate of return in the private sector, and vice versa. This is roughly the value judgement that seems implicit in the proposal that the Government should require the same discount rate (with any allowance made for difference in risk) for remunerative as for unremunerative investment. (But if the Government should wish, it could, of course, adopt any weighting it chose. If the relative weighting were, say, 2 : 1 this would mean that an investment in the social surplus sector would have to be discounted at twice the rate for an investment judged by ordinary financial estimates of profitability.)

4.3. Treatment of risk

Broadly there are three methods of allowing for risk; in calculating the figures chosen for each category of costs and benefits; in choosing the notional life of the Line; in the discount rate. We have allowed for the risk of obsolescence of the V.L. by the second method, and for other risks, so far as we have been able, by the first, estimating the most probable value in each category. Where calculations have been most susceptible to uncertainty—e.g. comfort and convenience—we have been conservative. If the Government should also wish to allow for risk in its choice of discount rate, that of course is its choice.

4.4. Land value

It is often said that one should take into account the effect on land values of a transport investment. Many of the highest "returns" estimated are high because of very large changes in land values. But these are often a false measure of benefits for two reasons. They do not distinguish appreciation of land values caused by the improvement from appreciation which would have occurred anyway; and they do not take into account falls in land values elsewhere (or declines in the prospective rate of increase of land values) because of the transport improvement. The second reason why these arguments are often false is because they involve double-counting. Land values only rise as a result of a transport improvement because of some realized or prospective reduction in transport costs. The value of land in a residential area rises because it is now nearer the workplace of some of its inhabitants, and because people wish to move into it to be nearer their workplace. The value of industrial land only rises for a passenger railway because it is easier to tap labour or because there is some value to the firm in having people move more quickly in working time. Any change in the value of land, residential, industrial, commercial, etc., must be related to the actual movement of people, unless it anticipates a prospective change in movement. In this study we have made predictions of the new journeys which will arise because of the V.L. and have set a value on these. If we were also to allow for changes in land values because of the V.L. we should be double-counting, measuring the same benefits at two points: as they reach passengers and as they may be reflected in land values.

5. USES OF THE CALCULATIONS

Given these findings, to what use can they be put, and what are the limitations on their usefulness?

5.1. Present worth positive

Since there have been no other investments for which similar calculations have been made, the decision-making value of the calculation is small. Its value is as a precursor of other calculations. However, the calculations do give some indications of the magnitude and distribution of the net benefits to be expected from the V.L. The categories enumerated in Table 2 were not exhaustive. Some categories of benefit and cost are excluded because we could think of no way of valuing them at present. Nevertheless, what is included is substantial. It is virtually certain that if it were possible to complete the calculation, the returns would be somewhat higher than shown, since in all cases where categories are omitted we can be reasonably certain that the benefits arising from the V.L. will be greater than its costs: accident savings, amenity measured by fumes, noise, etc. The calculation also indicates that, at the rates of discount considered, there would be some net increase in national wealth as a result of the investment. In other words the benefit is positive.

But this calculation on its own cannot answer the question whether there would not be a greater gain from investing somewhere else.

5.2. Comparison with other urban rail projects

If calculations were done for other surface and underground railway investment possibilities in London and other large cities, it would be possible to use them to decide priority of investment. Since by and large the fares charged in such facilities bear the same relation to costs, direct comparison of social desirability on this basis should be straightforward. In these calculations, the estimated internal rates of return might play a useful role (compare Beesley et al., 1962).

5.3. Comparison with urban road projects

It is of the greatest importance that these should be made (see Beesley et al., 1962). But there are difficulties, already mentioned, of fact and value judgement. The difficulty of fact is that it would be necessary to estimate the elasticity of substitution over a sufficient range to allow for the difference in the relative prices of urban road and rail transport mentioned in Section 1.2. The difficulty of judgement is to decide just how to allow for the difference in relative prices. This must be a political decision. We have in Section 1.3 given the reasons why we regard them as distorted, giving a relative encouragement to road transport with unfortunate consequences; but if the Government should decide notwithstanding that these are the " right " relative prices, then it would be logical if it wanted them reflected in investment policy. This would imply that investment would be biased towards heavy urban road investment even if it should be cheaper to build or improve railways. However, the Government might take up an intermediate position, declaring that the prices were " right " because a change would be politically undesirable or impossible, but that investment should be made as if the prices were corrected so that both reflected the real costs involved. (It would be possible to proceed either on the assumption that pricing policy was the same on the road as on the Underground, which would imply assuming a lower demand for transport, or that pricing policy on the Underground were the same as on the road which would imply assuming a higher overall demand for transport. To decide which of these would also be a political decision.) The last possibility is that the Government acts to correct the present relative prices, in which case investment would proceed on the assumption of the corrected prices.

5.4. Comparison with other investment in the public sector

If such calculations became widespread they could be used to decide the allocation of funds among various enterprises in the public sector as well as among investments within each enterprise.

APPENDIX: METHODS OF REACHING FIGURES SHOWN IN SOCIAL BENEFIT AND LOSS TABLE—TABLE 2

The 1962 prices and costs are used. Traffic estimates are based on 1970 predictions. Figures given are for calculation at 6 percent.

(A) COSTS

The capital cost given in the April 1962 memorandum was £56.1 million; £8 million of this, L.T.E. assert, would have had to have been incurred anyway in rebuilding Victoria, Oxford Circus, Euston, and King's Cross stations. (Additional expenditure will have to be incurred at these stations when the V.L. is built.) On this assumption the capital cost of the V.L. is reduced to £48.1 million. This appears as item H in the table, in terms of present value. Some assets would have unexpired lives at the end of 50 years' operation (by assumption, assets which have been replaced previously, e.g. rolling-stock replaced at the end of 40 years). Their scrap value (item E of the table) is assumed to be equal to the value of their unexpired lives. This implies an assumption either that (1) they will be used elsewhere equally valuably if the

V.L. is discontinued, or (2) they will continue to be used on the V.L. which will yield at least enough revenue to cover their depreciation.

Annual working expenses have been esimated by L.T.E. (£1,413,000). The only way in which this could be improved would be by converting maintenance cost from average annual expenditure to show the actual pattern of maintenance cost over time. Some maintenance costs, e.g. on way and structures and rolling-stock, would not be incurred for several years. A correction, were it possible, would slightly reduce annual working expenses. No allowance has been made for any divergence between average and marginal costs of train operation.

(B) BENEFITS TO TRAFFIC DIVERTED TO V.L.

(1) Traffic diverted from underground

a) *Time savings.* It was assumed all passengers given the choice of their present route and a new one via the V.L. would choose the quicker, and that if both took the same time half would use one, half the other. (Since this assumption is used again, we will call it Assumption A.) Separate estimates were made by L.T.E. of potential time savings for peak and off-peak traffic. Time savings were estimated for all journeys which would be affected by the V.L. except for journeys beginning and ending at stations outside the central area not on the V.L. L.T.E. believe these are quantitatively unimportant and do not justify the extra work needed to identify them. The value of this item is therefore a slight underestimate. The central area means, broadly, the area bounded by the Circle Underground line, including the main British Railways termini.

Time saved has been valued at different rates for time travelled in working and nonworking time. The proportion of journeys in working time has been taken from Dawson (1962, p. 14). This is based on the London Travel Survey (1954). It has been assumed that the proportion of journeys in working time is slightly higher on the Underground than on buses and coaches: 5 percent on the Underground as against 3 percent on buses. Time savings on other journeys have been valued at 5s. an hour. The choice of 5s. here and elsewhere in this report is arbitrary but not perhaps unreasonable. Time savings on journeys in working time have been valued at 7s. 3d. an hour. Dawson (1962, p. 15) gives the average hourly income of travellers by bus in working time (between 8 A.M. and 6 P.M. on weekdays) at 6s. 6d. in 1958. This was converted to 1962 figures by using the Index of Wage Rates published in the *Ministry of Labour Gazette* (March 1962).

Average time saved per diverted journey on the Underground is 4.5 minutes. Total time savings on the Underground are predicted to be 1.48 million hours per annum.

$$5 \text{ percent of } 1.48 \text{ m.} = 0.07 \text{ m.}: \quad 0.07 \text{ m.} \times £0.363 = £0.0254 \text{ m.}$$
$$95 \text{ percent of } 1.48 \text{ m.} = 1.41 \text{ m.}: \quad 1.41 \text{ m.} \times £0.25 \quad = £0.3525 \text{ m.}$$

$$£0.3779 \text{ m.}$$
$$\text{or } £378,000 \text{ approximately.}$$

Trend. In recent years passenger-journeys have remained constant on the Underground, but passenger-mileage has fallen as very long journeys from the extremities of the system to the centre have fallen off in recent years. It would be easier to make a better estimate if we knew rates of growth or decline of traffic on different parts of the Underground. Although the material for this exists, the calculation, which would be laborious, has not been made. We have assumed no trend on the grounds that a high proportion of journeys on the V.L. will be middle-distance journeys which have not, measured in passenger-miles, fallen off in recent years. Since this trend assumption is made again we will call it Assumption B.

b) Comfort and convenience. The problems here are (i) to estimate and (ii) to value the increased probability of getting a seat.

i) L.T.E. have data giving the ratios of standing to sitting passengers in the maximum unidirectional peak of 20 minutes between each pair of adjacent stations in most of the area to be affected by the V.L. It has also predicted the effect of the V.L. on these ratios and what the equivalent ratios would be between adjacent stations on the V.L. From them can be deduced the average probability of getting a seat for travel between each pair of adjacent stations before and after the V.L. is built. (The average probability at a station will not be the same as the actual probability confronting the passenger entering at any one station, which will normally of course be less; but this does not affect this calculation. If assumptions C and D *infra* were altered, it could.) The percentage change in the probability of getting a seat (e.g. 80 percent − 60 percent = 20 percent change, where 100 percent is the certainty of a seat) multiplied by the density of traffic can be used as a measure of the change in comfort and convenience (e.g. an 8 percent change in probability experienced by a density of 3,400 passengers between two adjacent stations can be expressed as 27,200 percentage changes). Adjusting for the time-interval between stations to convert the measure to percentage changes per minute of journey-time, the change in the probability of getting a seat multiplied by the densities of traffic was estimated for each pair of adjacent stations and summed for the undrground system: for traffic diverting to the V.L. and benefiting from the greater probability there and for traffic remaining on the rest of the Underground system. These totals for diverted and undiverted traffic referred only to the maximum peak of 20 minutes, one direction only. Calculations suggested it was reasonable to multiply them by 1.92 to arrive at differences in the percentage probability of getting a seat one way during the whole of the peak hour. Between some stations traffic is almost as heavy in the reverse direction. Between others it is not. Without elaborate calculation it was decided it would be reasonable to multiply the first figures by 2.5 (1.92 + 0.58) to allow for the change in the percentage probability for the other direction of traffic. These were then multiplied by 520—2 peaks Monday to Friday × 260 working days—to convert to annual totals: 2,360 million percent changes in the probability of getting a seat per minute of journey-time to diverted traffic; 3,010 million to undiverted traffic.

ii) The second problem was to value these. It was assumed: C—the passengers' valuation of comfort and convenience is proportional to a percentage change in the probability of getting a seat, yet it is plausible that it is a decreasing function of this; D—it is proportional to distance travelled, yet it is plausible that it is an increasing function of this. A survey would be needed to improve on our assumptions. From ignorance they were retained.

The principle of valuation was to find a way of measuring the probability in terms of time, and to value the increased probability of valuing a seat indirectly through the value set on time. This could be estimated because there are situations where passengers have a choice between time saving and an increased probability of a seat: where express and stopping trains use the same track. The advantage of the slow trains to those who have the choice is the greater probability of getting a seat at the peak.

For any such journey let $V(t_s - t_f)$ be the value of the time saved by the faster train, the value being known independently. (The actual values of variables are given later in this subsection.) Let $V(P_s - P_f)$ be the value of the difference in the probability of getting a seat on the two trains. Then $V(P_s - P_f) > V(t_s - t_f)$ for the passenger at the margin who is just persuaded to opt for the slow train. If we define Vms_{pt} as the value to the marginal passenger on the slow train of a single percent difference lasting one minute then

$$Vms_{pt} > V\frac{(t_s - t_f)}{t_s(P_s - P_f)}.$$

This is an inequality because adjustment must be made as passengers using the slow train endure the probability they experience longer.

Therefore, let us assume that the disutility of travelling is inversely proportional to the probability of getting a seat so that if P_s is x, D_s is $100 - x$ (the certainty of a seat implying zero disutility). The benefit from a percent per minute of journey-time gain in the probability of getting a seat is the disutility on the fast train multiplied by the time spent on the fast train minus the disutility on the slow train multiplied by the time spent on the slow train, all divided by the time spent on the slow train:

$$\frac{(D_f t_f - D_s t_s)}{t_s}.$$

Therefore

$$Vms_{pt} = \frac{V(t_s - t_f)t_s}{(D_f t_f - D_s t_s)t_s}$$

$$= \frac{V(t_s - t_f)}{(D_f t_f - D_s t_s)}.$$

This is the valuation of the marginal passenger who chooses the slow train rather than the fast. There will be passengers who value the higher probability of getting a seat by more than this: there can be none who, taking the slow rather than the fast train, can value it less. The valuation placed by the average user of the slow train will therefore be more than Vms_{pt}. Pending a survey we do not know it. The conservative assumption is made that 25 percent should be added to Vms_{pt} to get Vas_{pt}. In subsequent equations this scaling factor will be called α.

So far we have considered only the valuation of those passengers who actually go by the slow train, but it is reasonable to suppose those passengers who do not value comfort relatively to time enough to choose the slow train would yet be ready to pay something for the increased probability of getting a seat. *A priori* there is no reason to suppose that the average passenger who chooses the fast train has a lower valuation of comfort and convenience than those who choose the slow. They may have a relatively higher valuation of time. But since we are to use an average value of time to value the total increase in the probability of getting a seat, and it is probable that some users of the fast train have a lower valuation of the probability than the marginal user of the slow train, it has been assumed arbitrarily that the valuation of the average passenger who goes by the fast train (Vaf_{pt}) is half that or the average passenger by the slow (Vas_{pt}). Therefore the average valuation of all passengers is assumed to be

$$Va(s + f)_{pt} = \frac{V(t_s - t_f)}{(D_s t_s - D_f t_f)} \times \frac{[(z/2) + 50]}{100} \alpha.$$

This average valuation, based on some observations of choices made, is used to impute the value of comfort and convenience to all those using the Underground system. The values used were : V, the value of time, 5s. 2d. an hour as for B1 *supra*; t_s, 3 minutes; t_f, 2 minutes. The only data available to estimate $P_s - P_f$ showed 7 percent, but on reflection it was felt that this must be too small a difference to be representative so 20 percent was chosen. The values of 40 and 20 were selected for D_f and D_s. It was assumed that z was 12 percent. These were chosen on the basis of the intuition and experience of several members of L.T.E. staff with great experience of passenger behaviour. In our opinion it would be valuable to L.T.E. to acquire more accurate knowledge of these variables by survey. There is no way now of estimating the benefit of investment to improve the probability of getting a seat and it seems to us reasonable that it gets therefore a lower priority than it deserves. As given above, α is 1.25.

On these values the value of the total change in the probability of getting a seat was estimated to be

$$= 2{,}360 \text{ m.} \times £0{\cdot}00423 \times \frac{(3 - 2)}{(40 \times 2 - 20 \times 3)} \times \frac{[(12/2) + 50]}{100} \times \frac{5}{4}$$

$= £347{,}000$ for diverted traffic; similarly, $£457{,}000$ for undiverted traffic.

Trend. Since, taking all the effects noted in this paper into account, traffic on the Underground will grow in the future, and the limit of capacity on parts of the V.L. at least will be reached in the future, we have assume that comfort and convenience savings will decumulate to zero in the fiftieth year of operation of the V.L.

c) *Accident savings.* Nil.

(2) British Railways

a) *Time savings.* Provisional calculation. L.T.E. have estimated the number of passenger miles assumed to be diverted from B.R. to the V.L. (London Travel Committee, 1959). The average time saved is assumed to be greater than that saved on the Underground: 6 minutes compared with $4\frac{1}{2}$ minutes. No exact calculation of time savings has yet been done, but this is unlikely to be an overestimate. Assumption A has been used in assigning traffic to the V.L.

The valuation of time is on the same basis as described for (1*a*). Five percent is assumed to be in working time—valued at 7*s*. 3*d*. per hour: 95 percent not in working time—valued at 5*s*. an hour. Total time savings are predicted at 0.8 million hours.

$$5 \text{ percent of } 0.8 \text{ m.} = 0.04 \text{ m.}: \quad 0.04 \text{ m.} \times £0.363 = £0.0145 \text{ m.}$$
$$95 \text{ percent of } 0.8 \text{ m.} = 0.76 \text{ m.}: \quad 0.76 \text{ m.} \times £0.25 \ \ = £0.1900 \text{ m.}$$

$$£0.2045 \text{ m.}$$
$$\text{or } £205{,}000 \text{ approximately.}$$

Trend. It has been estimated that B.R. traffic will rise by 12 percent from 1962 to 1970. This rate of increase has been projected over the life of the V.L. Although the particular rate of growth to 1970 is influenced by modernization programmes which are unlikely to occur as frequently during the life of the V.L. B.R. traffic will certainly grow as London grows and more people come to work at the centre. Therefore it does not seem an unreasonable rate of growth to assume: $1\frac{1}{2}$ percent compound.

b) *Comfort and convenience.* This has not been calculated. The procedure would be the same as described for (1*b*) above.

c) *Accident savings.* Nil.

(3) L.T. buses

a) *Time savings.* L.T.E. have estimated the passenger-miles which will be diverted to the V.L. (London Travel Committee, 1959). Assignment has been made by Assumption A. Assignment was made by L.T.E. officials experienced in bus operation using their judgment, but it would seem that their leading principle in practice was time saving. Allowance was made for the incidence of queueing, the accessibility of stations and bus stops, and other factors such as the difference in fares per mile on road and rail due to season tickets on the latter. There are people who would not transfer from bus to Underground merely because of time savings. They have a definite preference for bus travel which for different people has to be overcome by varying, but considerable, time savings to induce them to change. This is offset: (i) by the omission of passengers on certain bus routes who might be expected to transfer (the bus routes have been omitted because the numbers expected to transfer are very small); (ii) the omission of people who now make journeys by Underground and bus—changing from one to the other—who might save time by diverting to the V.L. (L.T.E. believe that these will be few also); (iii) the omission of people who will divert to the V.L. from buses even though they lose time by doing so—either from ignorance or because they prefer the Underground.

Average time saved is assumed to be slightly more than on the Underground: 5 minutes per journey diverted. Although time savings should be more for long bus journeys diverting to Underground, time savings would be slight on many short bus journeys because bus stops are more frequent than Underground stations. On this basis total time savings are predicted to be 2.27 million hours per annum. The valuation of time is on the same basis as described for (1a). From Dawson (1962), 3 percent bus journeys are assumed to be in working time—valued at 7s. 3d. an hour; 97 percent not in working time—valued at 5s. an hour.

3 percent of 2.27 m. = 0.068 m.:   0.068 m. × £0.363 = £0.0247 m.
97 percent of 2.27 m. = 2.202 m.:   2.202 m. × £0.25 = £0.5505 m.

£0.5752 m.
or £575,000 approximately.

Trend. The rationale behind the choice of trend rates for Underground and British Railways was that traffic diverting from these sources might be expected to increase at the same rates as the traffic from which the original diversion took place. In as much as the V.L. is a substitute for British Railways suburban services, one would expect traffic on it to increase at the same rate as predicted for B.R. suburban services. On this basis we would have to predict a decline for bus diverted traffic. This would seem unrealistic. Bus traffic is falling in the central area principally because congestion makes buses less attractive. Hence we assume that this item will remain constant over the life of the V.L.

b) Comfort and convenience. Because a reduction in bus services will match the fall in bus traffic caused by the V.L. this is probably negligible.

c) Accident savings. The relevant facts would seem to be—considering accident savings from the V.L. as a whole—that although the accident-rate on the Underground is much lower than on the roads and though the increase in mean speeds on the roads caused by the V.L. is insufficient to make an appreciable difference to the accident-rate on the roads, many people transferring to the V.L. will run more risk of an accident as a pedestrian. It is likely that accident savings will be positive but not as considerable as one might think at first: they have not been calculated.

(4) Motorists

a) Time savings. London Transport have estimated the number of private car passenger-miles which might be expected to divert to the V.L. This has not been done for journeys in the central area or wholly outside the central area—only for journeys (presumably mostly by commuters) from the N.E. and South catchment areas to the central area. The South is relevant on the supposition that there are motorists who are deterred from taking a train to Victoria because there is no direct Underground connection with the West End. The data used were parking and similar traffic offence statistics for the West End Central subdivision of the Metroplitan Police Force. This includes the Mayfair area. From these were calculated the proportions of offences committed by motorists with cars registered outside the London area and in the various local authority areas within it. The total figures of traffic entering the central area by road are known. The parking offence proportions were used to estimate the proportion of that traffic originating in the N.E. and South catchment areas of the V.L. The data were collected in July 1956. There are three drawbacks to this use of them. (i) Although the sample was large enough to establish the main flows of traffic entering the central area, it was not large enough to be used with confidence to fix the proportions coming from individual boroughs. (ii) It is possible that parking offence data are not a good reflection of traffic flows. One might argue that less familiar traffic (from further out) would commit more offences proportionately than traffic familiar with the central area. But it might be argued that though this might be true of traffic domiciled outside the London area, it should not affect vehicles domiciled inside it—especially since the traffic domiciled in the central area itself is excluded from the calculation. (iii) It is possible that the choice of the West End central area biases the results. But as the V.L. will benefit mainly the West End traffic, this bias is desirable.

It was assumed that roughly one-third of the central area could be regarded as being served by the V.L. Using the parking offence data it was assumed that 1.2 percent of cars in this part of the central area relevant to the V.L. came from Area A; 2.2 percent from Area B; and 3.3 percent from Area C. Area A is Walthamstow, Chingford, Waltham Holy Cross, Edmonton and Tottenham. Area B is Stoke Newington, Islington, and part of Hornsey. Area C is Croydon, Mitcham, Sutton, Carshalton, Wallington, Coulsdon, Banstead, and Reigate. The number of vehicles assumed to enter the central area during the day in 1960 was adjusted to 1970 by allowing for an increase of 25 per cent. The prediction for 1970 is that 85,000 cars and 15,000 motor cycles and scooters per day will enter the relevant third of the central area.

A notional journey time was calculated for each of the three areas—by road and by the quickest alternative using the V.L. These were intended to be *average* journey times. Not more than one journey time per area could be calculated, partly because of insufficient data but more significantly because the smallness of the sample made pointless the calculation of separate traffic volumes and therefore separate journey times for areas smaller than these three. In areas A and B it was estimated it would take roughly as long by the new (V.L.) facility as by car. Using the Washington, D.C. traffic assignment curve—Washington (1958)—it was predicted that 40 percent of this traffic should divert: 480 trips per day from Area A, 880 trips per day from Area B.

It was estimated that the new facility from Area C would be 9 minutes faster on average than by car. It was predicted from the same curve that 55 percent would divert: 1,810 trips, or 3,170 vehicle trips in all. A further allowance was made for motorists living in areas indirectly benefiting from the V.L., e.g. in the Cockfosters area, where the Piccadilly line acts as a convenient feeder to the V.L. The final figure, 5,000 vehicle trips per day, was predicted to be some 5 percent of all private passenger vehicles with destinations in the in-town area served by the V.L. This was converted to passenger trips per year as follows:

$$\begin{aligned} \text{ex-car trips: } 2 \times 4,000 \times 330 \times 1.5 \text{ passengers} &= 3.96 \text{ m. p.a.} \\ \text{ex-motor cycle trips: } 2 \times 1,000 \times 330 \quad\quad\quad &= 0.66 \text{ m. p.a.} \\ \hline & 4.62 \text{ m. p.a.} \end{aligned}$$

The weighted average of road trips from Areas A, B, and C to the central area was 9.6 miles (based on Oxford Circus). Thus car mileage diverted is 25.4 million, and motor cycle mileage 2.4 million.

The valuation of time has been on the same basis as described in (1a). Average time saved is assumed—arbitrarily by comparison with the average time of 4.5 minutes saved on the Underground—to be 5 minutes per passenger journey. Total time savings are assumed to be 0.38 million hours: made up of 0.054 million motor cycle and 0.326 million car hours. From Dawson (1962, pp. 14 and 15) the percentage travel by cars in working time, when travelling between central and outer zones, is assumed to be 13 percent:[1] the percentage of motor cycle travel in working time is 6 percent. From the same source the average hourly income of motor cycle riders is assumed to be the same as that of travellers by bus: 7s. 3d. The average hourly income of those who travel by car in working time is, adjusted to 1962 values, 11s. 9d.

(I) 6 percent of 0.054 m. = 0.0032 m.:   0.0032 m. × £0.363 = £0.0012 m.
    94 percent of 0.054 m. = 0.0508 m.:   0.0508 m. × £0.25 = £0.0127 m.
(II) 13 percent of 0.326 m. = 0.0424 m.:   0.0424 m. × £0.586 = £0.0248 m.
    87 percent of 0.326 m. = 0.2836 m.:   0.2836 m. × £0.25 = £0.0709 m.

$$\begin{aligned} &£0.1096 \text{ m.} \\ \text{or } &£110,000 \text{ approximately.} \end{aligned}$$

This calculation could be improved—before the publication of the *London Traffic Survey* which would supersede it—by increasing the size of the sample, making a more exact estimate of journey times, replacing parking offence statistics by a sample survey based on parking lots, and, most important, by a detailed survey of central area traffic. Except for the last, it would not be

---

[1] There is no figure for percentage car travel in working hours between zones for all days of the week.

Since the proportions of overall car travel in working time is 14 percent on all days of the week (all hours) and 28 percent on weekdays between 8 A.M. and 6 P.M., it has been assumed that for travel between zones the proportion in working time on all days of the week (all hours) is half the figure of 25 percent shown for weekdays 8 A.M. to 6 P.M.

worth troubling to improve data for this item alone, since the amount involved, even if we were to assume 100 percent error, is relatively small. But since a change in motorists assumed to divert would have important consequences for savings for undiverted traffic we do attempt, in C4 below, to make a general estimate for the extra traffic diverted on to the tubes for the central area. The estimate is that a further 8.2 million car miles will divert to tubes. Assuming a similar shift for motor cycles and allowing for an average time saving of 2 minutes per vehicle, the extra time savings would amount to 39 percent of £110,000, or £43,000. Thus total time savings are £153,000 per annum.

Trend. It has been assumed that the trend is 5 percent compound for the first 15 years—the rate at which motor traffic entering the central area has been increasing—and 2 percent compound thereafter.

b) Savings in vehicle-operating costs. Diverted vehicles will save money. In general, the cost of the V.L. journey will be less. It is assumed that no motorist will sell his car or potential motorist refrain from buying a car because he uses the V.L. Therefore, the only relevant costs are of fuel, lubricants, tyres, maintenance, and depreciation, so far as these are caused by use and not age. Cost figures have been taken from Roth (1959). The 8.2 million miles of diverted car traffic will, we assume, be split up as between central area running 2 miles (out of 9.6 per journey) where the average speed is 10 m.p.h., 4 miles in which the average speed is 15 m.p.h., and 3.6 miles at 20 m.p.h. At these speeds, the cost savings per mile are:

		d.
10 m.p.h.	small car 1,000 (c.c.)	3.32
	large car 2,250 (c.c.)	4.81
15 m.p.h.	small car	2.60
	large car	3.80
20 m.p.h.	small car	2.23
	large car	3.37

We assume that half the mileage is performed by small and half by large cars. Applying these cost savings to the car mileage, and allowing for motor cycle savings at one-third the rate for small cars, we arrive at £364,200 a year. The mileage by V.L. will, however, be generally greater than by road, hence we take 75 percent of cost savings under this head, or £274,000. There remains to be added a figure for the extra diverted traffic in the central area. With similar assumptions it amounts to £103,000. The total under this head is thus £377,000.

Trend. As for (4a) above.

c) Comfort and convenience. No calculation, but it should not be assumed negligible since motorists get benefit from decongestion besides time and vehicle-operating costs savings.

d) Accident savings. No calculation. See (3c), above.

(5) Pedestrians

a) Time savings. £20,000. During the morning peak 16,500 leave Victoria Mainline station on foot. L.T.E. have estimated that of these 1,350 cross the parks to the Green Park area. It is assumed that only half of these will divert because of the positive pleasure, on a fine day, of walking across the parks. It is assumed that they value their time at 5s., that it takes them on average 20 minutes to cross the parks and that they save 15 minutes on average by diverting.

No other calculations have been made of pedestrians who might use the V.L.

Trend.   As for British Railways. See (2a) above.

(C) BENEFITS TO UNDIVERTED TRAFFIC

(1) Underground

   a) *Time savings.*   Not calculated.

   b) *Savings in Underground costs.*   This is not directly a benefit to traffic on the Underground but it is indirectly since it accrues to L.T.E. Although one could decide to include it under another or a separate head in the Table (Benefits to L.T.E.) wherever put, it is a benefit. The figure was supplied by L.T.E.

   c) *Comfort and convenience.*   Calculated as described in (B: 1*b*).

   d) *Accident savings.*   Negligible.

(2) British Railways

   a) *Time savings.*   Not calculated. Probably negligible.

   b) *Savings in B.R. costs.*   Reported negligible.

   c) *Comfort and convenience* and

   d) *Accident savings.*   Not calculated. Both probably negligible.

(3) L.T. buses

   a) *Time savings.*   Not calculated separately. See (4) below.

   b) *Savings in bus costs.*   Figure supplied by L.T.E. These are savings due to reduction and rescheduling of services only.

   c) *Comfort and convenience.*   Nil.

   d) *Accident savings.*   Probably negligible.

(4) Road users

Road-users benefit from decongestion caused by diversion to the V.L. The first problem was to estimate total annual vehicle mileage run by private cars, public service vehicles, taxis, and commercial vehicles in the London area. It was assumed that motor and pedal cycles had a negligible effect on traffic speeds, and that increase in speeds had a negligible effect on their speeds. The proportions of vehicles of each type in total traffic flow were taken from the Metropolitan Police census. This source has two defects. (i) The census points are located on crowded important streets where public service vehicles and taxis are likely to be a higher proportion of the total flow. (There are only two census points where there are not bus routes.) Dawson (1962) used the 1954 *London Travel Survey* to estimate the proportions of passenger-mileage travelled by different means. It was assumed that the Metropolitan

Police census undervalued the proportion of commercial vehicles in the total to the same extent it undervalued private car mileage. Making this assumption, Dawson's findings were used to correct the census data. (ii) The second shortcoming was that it was difficult to adjust for average journey lengths. Although average journey lengths are known, the census points are sufficiently close together to make it certain that vehicles going longer journeys will pass more census points than those going short journeys, but it is not clear whether they are sufficiently close together to make it unnecessary to correct for average journey length. Since Dawson's data do not need to be corrected for this reason, some allowance for average journey length has indeed been made. From ignorance no further correction has been made. The error is unlikely to be significant.

The Metropolitan Police census gives the following percentages of total flow of private cars, public service vehicles, taxis and commercial vehicles (whole London area, 1958).

Car	50.0%
Public service vehicle....	9.1%
Taxi	8.7%
Commercial vehicle	32.2%

These are vehicle-miles. Dawson (1962) gives the following percentages of total passenger-miles travelled by private cars, public service vehicles, and taxis.

Car	40.7%
Public service vehicle....	58.1%
Taxi	1.2%

If we adjust these by average number of persons carried—private cars, 1.5; public service vehicles, 18; taxis, 1.5—we get the following percentages in vehicle-miles:

Car	87.1%
Public service vehicle....	10.4%
Taxi	2.5%

Making the assumption given in the last paragraph to include commercial vehicles, and adjusting the Metropolitan Police data by Dawson's data, we get the following percentages:

	1958	1970
Private car	55.8%	64.1%
Public service vehicle....	6.7%	4.0%
Taxi	1.6%	1.5%
Commercial vehicle	35.9%	30.4%

Road Research Laboratory experiments have shown that a bus causes 3 times as much, and a commercial vehicle on average 1·65 times as much, congestion as the average private car. Adjusting for this, we get the following percentages of equivalent private car mileage (1970):

Private car	50.2%
Public service vehicle....	9.4%
Taxi	1.2%
Commercial vehicle	39.2%

These calculations are then inflated to total annual equivalent private car mileage by using as a base the predicted annual car mileage run by L.T.E. public service vehicles in the London area in 1970: 240 million vehicle-miles, or 720 million equivalent private car-miles. On this basis, total annual equivalent private car mileage in the whole London area is 7,700 million.

   a) *and* (b) *Time savings* and *Savings in vehicle-operating costs.* It is easy to see that an inconsiderable change in traffic estimates here could have a considerable effect on the total value of time savings under this head. To estimate the savings to other vehicles when vehicle mileage is removed from roads, we use somewhat different approaches for traffic in the central area and the area outside. The average saving of 9.6 miles per trip is assumed to be divided as follows: 2 miles in the central area, 4 miles in a bordering area subject to some town congestion, and 3.6 miles, the remainder, in a zone subject to freer suburban running conditions. We assume that relief in the last area would be negligible. We must first estimate the total vehicle mileage run in each of the areas. The only firm datum we have is that 15.4 percent of public service mileage is run in the central area, i.e. the area bounded by the main line stations but including an area south of the river incorporating the Elephant and Castle. (This conforms closely to the area distinguished in road data on the central area to be used later.) Bus mileage tends to be higher in the central area than outside: hence we assume that 12 percent of total vehicle mileage is performed there. If we suppose that the volume of traffic in zones decreases according to the *linear* distance from the centre, the other zones have some 30 percent and 58 percent, respectively, of the total traffic. This division gives 930 million car-miles for the central area, 2,310 million for the bordering area, and 4,460 million in the outer area.

   It is estimated by L.T.E. that 5.0 million public service car-miles per annum will be saved if the V.L. is built. In terms of private car equivalents, this equals 15.0 million miles. The car trips diverted to the V.L. total 25.4 million per annum. This counts 4,000 car trips × 2 × 330 × 9.6. The latter is the weighted average distance of diverted car journeys from areas A, B, and C. Motor cycles are excluded as they have a negligible effect on congestion. The total is thus 40.4 million equivalent car-miles; of this 8.4 million will be diverted from the central area (40.4 × 2.0/9.6).

   i) The savings from removing the central area equivalent private car-miles (8.4) million may be estimated directly from data on the central road network giving speed, flows, and journey times.[2] Using the speed/flow and road width data,[3] we may associate each link in the network of some 35 miles (there are 87 in total) with an equation giving the speed as a function of flow.[4] To use the data it is necessary to convert the 8.4 million passenger car-miles

---

[2] The data refer to 1960. Road Research Laboratory, D.S.I.R., RN/3695. These data have been supplemented for other roads in the network by data from London County Council.

[3] Road Research Laboratory, D.S.I.R., RN/3679.

[4] More detail and work with these data are referred to in M. E. Beesley *et al.*, 1962.

to the equivalent vehicle mileage for central area flows (i.e. for the average of all vehicles). The figure is 5.91 million. It is convenient to work with a random sample of the links, one-third of the total. Our problem in estimating the savings by vehicles remaining on the network is twofold: to estimate time saved, and to estimate other cost savings, for which an estimate of speed of traffic after removing the vehicle-miles is necessary. On time saving, two alternative assumptions may be made, reflecting the possibility that the vehicle mileage saved will be concentrated or wider spread on the network. For one bound of the estimate, we assume that vehicle-mile savings are concentrated on one-third of the links: for the other bound, that they are spread over two-thirds of the links. The latter is the upper bound for the reason that the greater the spread of a given vehicle mileage saving, the greater the saving in time (benefit is a decreasing function of increasing mean speed).

First, we need to correct the 5.91 million vehicle-miles to an hourly basis to use the R.R.L. data. It has been estimated that the factor to bring the R.R.L. data to a daily figure lies between 14.1 and 16.1.[5] Multiplying these by 330 to convert days to a yearly basis, we get factors of between 4,650 and 5,310: hence the per hour equivalent of 5.91 million lies between 1,270 and 1,110 vehicle-miles an hour. We take 1,250 vehicle-miles an hour as the basis here. (For the reason previously given, this will be a conservative estimate: whatever factors we use we are bound to come back to 5.91 million a year; the smaller the per hour figure the greater will its proportionate effects on time savings be.) Now we distribute the vehicle mileage over the random sample of links, according to the mileage of each link. If we suppose the effect to be spread over two-thirds of the network links we may distribute 625 (of 1,250) vehicle-miles to the links and multiply the resulting savings by 2 (Assumption F). Supposing the effect to be confined to one-third of the links, we may distribute the 1,250 to the sample (Assumption E). For each link is calculated the resulting speed when vehicle miles are removed; a new link time for journey speed is calculated, and the difference between it and the old times multiplied by the remaining quantity of vehicles. The results, in terms of vehicle-minutes/hours saved, and consequent vehicle-hours per year, are:

Assumption E	Assumption F
16,200 vehicle-minutes/hr	13,400 vehicle-minutes/hr
=1,255,000 vehicle-hours/year	=1,040,000 vehicle-hours/year

Since there is probably a general tendency to underestimate, because the rather freer flowing main network only is sampled, a reasonable conclusion would be that 1,200,000 vehicle-hours a year may be saved.

The new speed to be expected is obtained by summing the vehicle-hours and vehicle-miles after removal and comparing with a similar calculation before removal.

---

[5] The basis for these is described in detail on pp. 19ff., *op. cit.*

For both assumptions, the old speed is 10.34 m.p.h. On assumption E, the new speed is 10.75 m.p.h., for F it is 10.95. Thus we have differences of 0.41 m.p.h. and 0.61 m.p.h., respectively. The lower of these two will be used.

Within the central area, 1,200,000 vehicle-hours (in terms of average central area vehicles) are saved. Allowing for the proportions of public service vehicles, cars and taxis in the total flow, and multiplying the public service vehicle hours by 18 and cars and taxis by 1.5 to get the person hours saved, we find, for public service vehicles, 1,940,000 hours, and for cars and taxis 951,000 hours. Valuing these at 5s. 1d. and 5s. 10d. an hour,[6] respectively, time savings total £770,000. (Savings in crew time on buses, drivers' time in taxis, and drivers' and mates' time in commercial vehicles are excluded here: they are included in the next item.)

For vehicle-operating costs savings, data from Roth (1959) are used. The following decreases in vehicle-operating costs per mile are deduced to be associated with that increase in speed. It is assumed that all costs, including all depreciation, licence duties, insurance, etc., are relevant for commercial vehicles, taxis, and public service vehicles, since a reduction in time spent travelling a given mileage should make possible the realization of economies somewhere in the purchase of, or rate of increase of, vehicles. Contrarily, it was assumed that no private motorist gave up his car, or did not buy a car he otherwise would have, because of use of the V.L. This is a strong assumption. The fall in vehicle-operating costs per mile for each type of vehicle considered by Roth is:

	d.
Small cars	0.0705
Large cars	0.0881
Taxis	0.3083
Commercial vans	0.3083
5-ton petrol lorries	0.5287
5-ton diesel lorries	0.6166
Public service vehicles	1.949

It was assumed that public service vehicles had three times the savings in costs per mile of 5-ton diesel lorries; that taxi mileage was one-quarter of car mileage, and that they had the same costs as vans; that half the car mileage was run by small (1,000 c.c.) and half by large (2,250 c.c) cars; that half the commercial vehicles were vans, one-quarter 5-ton diesel lorries, and one-quarter 5-ton petrol lorries; and that public service vehicles had three times the cost of 5-ton diesel lorries. The total vehicle mileage left on the roads affected by the removal of mileage was estimated to be 194 million per annum, divided between public service vehicles 17.5 million, cars and taxis 104.5

---

[6] The percentage and hourly incomes of those travelling in working and nonworking time were based on figures given in Dawson (1962, pp. 7ff.). These corrections also apply to the hourly valuations used later.

million, and commercial vehicles 72 million. Applying these to the data just given, savings in vehicle costs are:

	£
Cars	26,400
Taxis	25,700
Commercial vehicles	123,400
Public service vehicles	128,700
	304,200

ii) In the area adjacent to the central area, 16.8 million equivalent miles are saved. The average speed of traffic in this area was assumed to be 15 m.p.h. Here we may use data from Dr. Smeed (Feb. 1961). The 16.8 million miles represent a reduction of 0.73 percent in traffic flow (2,310 million). This is associated (from Dr. Smeed's data) with an increase in speed from 15 m.p.h. to 15.12 m.p.h. Over the wide area concerned, it is reasonable to suppose that savings can be valued at the same constant rate, because the effects would be widely distributed in time and space. The increase of speed yields a time saving of 0.03 minute per vehicle, or 1,146,500 vehicle-hours a year $[0.03/60 \times (2310 - 16.8)]$. To value these it is necessary to perform two operations: (1) multiply the figures for each class of vehicle by the average number of persons carried, as before, and (2) recorrect from equivalent private car mileage to vehicle mileage by dividing public service vehicles by 3. These operations yield 862,000 person hours a year saved in cars, 639,000 person hours in public service vehicles, and 20,400 person hours in taxis. The basis of valuations (as in B: *a*) was: cars 5*s*. 10*d*. an hour, public service vehicles 5*s*. 1*d*. and taxis 5*s*. 11*d*. Thus time savings per annum are worth:

	£
Private cars	252,000
Public service vehicles	162,500
Taxis	6,050
	420,550

The increase in speed leads also to vehicle cost savings. Based on Roth (1959), the savings for each type of vehicle are:

	d.
Small cars	0.12
Large cars	0.22
Taxis	0.383
Commercial vans	0.383
5-ton petrol and diesel lorries	0.48
Public service vehicles	0.144

These figures imply the following savings in costs per annum:

	£
Cars	72,200
Taxis	3,900
Public service vehicles	38,000
Commercial vehicles	88,400
	202,500

The estimates in this section do not, so far, include the relief to roads that would be associated with the diversion of short distance, mainly central area traffic, to the tube system. The traffic concerned would be mainly off-peak traffic which could be carried on the tubes at negligible extra cost. No direct estimate of savings is possible, yet such is its potential importance that the attempt to allow for it must be made, as follows.

The implied elasticity of substitution, in terms of journey time, of rail for car journeys in the longer distance journeys of areas A, B, and C is 1.21. The average central area saving in time off peak, consequent on the V.L., is 2·7 percent. In estimating the latter, tube stations of main-line termini have been excluded, in order to exclude the strong influence on the data of commuting traffic entering the tube system through them. This reduces the average substantially. The 2.7 percent measures the change in all other station to station movements.

If we suppose the elasticity to be much lower for central area journeys, say $\frac{1}{2}$ or 0.605, we arrive at an estimate of 1.78 percent diversion of car journeys in the central area. As approximately 465 million car-miles are performed in the central area, less 8.4 million already transferred, we may estimate a further shift to tubes of some 8.2 million car-miles. This we must suppose to be diffused quite widely in the area. Thus the central area savings are increased by about 90 percent, allowing for some decrease in the rate of benefit.

To summarize the time and cost savings in both areas, the final totals are:

Time savings	£
Central area	1,462,000
Other...........	420,550
	1,882,550

Other vehicle costs	
Central	578,000
Other	202,500
	780,500

Trend. It might seem that this benefit would disappear very quickly, on the theory that traffic abhors a vacuum. But this is to confuse the problem of measuring a gain to road users from a road improvement with that from an improvement on a competitive facility. With a road improvement, it may be true that a part of measured gains to road users is lost when new traffic emerges in response to the fall in cost: but this cannot be true of an improvement of a competitive facility such as rail, for its effect is that the demand falls on roads; cost savings are measured straightaway at the new demand and cost equilibrium. The argument so far ignores trend; however, we may assume that in both types of cases there is an exogenously determined trend which shifts demand outwards and to the right. At any one time the benefits in terms of cost savings to road users are the difference in the position the demand curve would have taken up in the absence of the V.L. with the position it does take up with it. As traffic grows so does the implied V.L. cost saving, both because speeds fall on roads and because a greater quantity of traffic is enjoying saving. The precise amount is impossible to predict with present information. On the other hand, it is true that not only costs but the whole area under the demand curves is relevant in an estimate of benefits. The shift induced by the V.L., which would, one supposes, in general increase the elasticity of the demand curve, means that there may be a tendency to over-estimate, by measuring cost savings, the true benefit. We cannot measure these opposing effects, and we have taken the arbitrary course of assuming the measured cost savings will be constant over the life of the V.L.

(D) BENEFITS TO GENERATED TRAFFIC

(1) Outer areas

To estimate this, we need some measurement which will give expected percentage increase in rail and Underground traffic due to the shortening of time on the V.L. The estimator must, therefore, include travelling time; and we need procedures to test the hypothesis that travelling time as we are able to measure it is a significant factor. The data that we have been able to bring to bear are divided into two parts—(a) those useful for an estimate of journey to work, to the centre of London from outlying boroughs, for which the data are very good, and (b) data for other journeys, which are used in conjunction with (a) because insufficient information exists for a separate estimate.

For time, we have good data only for journeys on rail and Underground combined. It seemed likely a priori that time thus measured would be the more important the further away the borough concerned; also, since population change is a very important element in any prediction, boroughs of very different demographic characteristics should be separated. Thus estimates for three groups of boroughs, forming bands at different distances from the centre, were built up. The boroughs were made the units because Census of Population data were available for them.

The first group (I) consisted of 21 outer boroughs; the second (II) of 19 middle-ring boroughs; and the third (III) of 28 inner boroughs.

The constituents were:

I	II	III
Potters Bar	Harrow	Tottenham
Barnet	Ruislip	Wood Green
Elstree	Hayes	Finchley
Bushey	Southall	Friern Barnet
Uxbridge	Heston	Hendon
Yiewsley	Twickenham	Wembley
Feltham	Surbiton	Ealing
Sunbury	Epsom	Brentford
Walton	Sutton	Barnes
Esher	Carshalton	Richmond
Banstead	Beddington	Wimbledon
Coulsdon	Bromley	Merton

I	*II*	*III*
Caterham	Chislehurst	Mitcham
Orpington	Bexley	Croydon
Dartford	Erith	Penge
Crayford	Barking	Beckenham
Romford	Dagenham	Lewisham
East Barnet	Ilford	Woolwich
Chigwell	Enfield	Greenwich
Hoddesdon		West Ham
Waltham Holy Cross		East Ham
and Cheshunt		Leyton
		Wanstead
		Chingford
		Walthamstow
		Edmonton
		Southgate
		Harrow*

* II and III overlap in one case—Harrow. Cheshunt and Waltham Holy Cross were combined.

The outer limit of I was selected as the likely limit, for practical purposes, of the V.L.'s catchment area, and of its effects elsewhere. The inner limit of III was determined by the consideration that time, as measured on rail and Underground, was likely to be very misleading for boroughs closer to the centre. I and II are distinguished, apart from distance, principally by their difference in the intercensal (1951–61) changes in total population: all the boroughs of I experienced an increase of over 10 percent whilst none in II exceeded 7 percent and some decreased slightly.

The Census (1951) gives us a full listing of workplace, by borough, for people resident in a given borough. Our hypothesis was that the numbers going from a borough to the centre to work would be a function of the following factors: (1) the total resident population in the borough; (2) the social class of the borough, as measured by the residents per 1,000 population found in the top two social classes distinguished in the Census; and (3) the time to the centre measured by the time taken in 1951 on railways and/or tubes.

Thus we argued, in effect, that the journey to work from a borough to the centre may be determined by the size of the total population from which workers originate, an income factor (for that is what the use of a social class variable will largely reflect), and a cost factor, for, by and large, time is an indication of costs of travel. This, we believe, is a useful framework of analysis, but it could be improved by developing new data. At this stage, this three-part explanation has the merit of being rooted in the best data yet to appear on workplace. (The publication of comparable 1961 census results will be useful here.)

Since social class is determined in particular by the occupation of the male head of the household, it seemed wise to estimate separately for men and women. Also it seemed quite possible that the tendency of women to go out to work might be positively associated with social class at both ends of the class spectrum—i.e. upper-class women have a professional interest in working, and lower-class women *have* to work.

It was also thought that there might well be sharp differences between different parts of the centre in their relative attraction for workers in the boroughs. Accordingly, the centre was divided into two—on the one hand the City and Holborn, and on the other Westminster and St. Marylebone. The time from the outlying boroughs was computed for the first by selecting as representative stations Liverpool Street and Holborn; Victoria and Oxford Circus were selected for the second. The times were estimated by finding the quickest time from each station in a given borough to the relevant two centre stations (some boroughs, of course, have many stations), and averaging these times for each borough.[7]

Thus the data provided material for twelve partial regression equations—four for each ring of boroughs—where

U_1 = central area workers in 00's,
U_2 = total resident population in 000's,
U_3 = social class, nos. per 000 population in social classes I and II,
U_4 = time.

These results show the expected worsening of predictions as the centre is approached, and indicate poorer results for women, area for area, than for men. Further analysis is clearly indicated for women in all rings, and for men in the Inner ring. However, the results for men in rings I and II give a good enough result, it seems, to be used. They were:

	City/Holborn	Westminster/St. Marylebone
Outer ring	$U_1 = -0.367 + 0.035U_2 + 0.005U_3$ $-0.025U_4$ $R^2 = 0.901$	$U_1 = -0.071 + 0.019U_2 + 0.004U_3$ $-0.021U_4$ $R^2 = 0.916$
Middle ring	$U_1 = 2.98 + 0.059U_2 + 0.008U_3$ $-0.125U_4$ $R^2 = 0.908$	$U_1 = -0.0671 + 0.072U_2 + 0.009U_3$ $-0.056U_4$ $R^2 = 0.848$

The t-test of the parts of the regressions shows that for these four regressions all parts are significant at the 5 percent level, except for U_4 in II, Westminster, which just fails. These, then, are the basic equations used for men in I and II. The equations are used to predict for 1961 total population and time data. Social class is held constant (unlike total population, census data are not available for this at 1961). Then a prediction is made substituting the time as modified by the V.L. The difference between the two predictions is expressed as a percentage of the first prediction. This then becomes our measure of generation for work journeys in rings I and II, for men: the assumption is thus that rail (plus tube) journeys are unaffected by the opportunities to travel by bus and car. Since these are quite distant journeys, and in view of the known

---

[7] A. Each station in a borough, so long as it was in use, had equal weighting with another. To have weighted, say, by estimated number of passengers, would, of course, have reduced the independence of time as an explanation of the numbers of people travelling to the centre.

B. Another measure of time was tried—viz. the average time for all services during the day. The quickest time measure gave the better predicting equations.

dominance of public transport, this seems reasonable.[8] The estimate has to be modified for nonwork journeys, for which data from the 1954 London Travel Survey are used.

To estimate a factor for women in rings I and II we may make use of the differences each borough shows in the numbers working at the two central areas. This procedure is clearly less systematic than the previous one in that it lacks the explanatory framework; it does not permit of specific reestimation for census data later than 1951. However, if we pool the data for rings I and II, and compare the differences per thousand resident (female) population going from a given borough to the two central areas to work with the relevant times to the areas, we find that in 30 of the 40 boroughs, a difference in times is associated with a difference (with an opposite sign) in numbers going to each centre. In 10 cases, one finds either that signs are the same, or that one variable has no difference. We may arrive at least at a conservative estimate by the following procedure:

We sum the time difference over the 30 cases and add the sum of the 10 cases; and for differences in population per thousand going to the centres we sum the 30 cases and deduct the 10 cases. Dividing the second sum by the first, we get a figure of 0.00116 per thousand population per minute time difference. In essence, what we have done, having failed a fuller explanation with partial regressions, is to fall back on a simpler, but cruder hypothesis that time alone is the determining factor explaining differences within each borough's central area workers figures, corrected again, for 1961 population. Clearly, further work could usefully explore the probabilities of combining the two approaches. A similar exercise for ring III men, yet more speculative, yields 21 nonperverse, 7 perverse cases, and an estimate of 0.0021 per thousand population per minute. For ring III women no plausible estimates along these lines are possible: the reason seems to be the disproportionately large number who work in Westminster and St. Marylebone. A prediction here would probably have to run in terms of specific job opportunities. We have not included any generation for ring III women.

The total daily number of journeys thus predicted is 30,000. This includes all journeys, and is composed of work journeys, estimated directly, plus other journeys which were based on data derived from the London Travel Survey, 1954. The latter gave, by groups of boroughs, an estimate of work journeys and other journeys. We found a correlation of 0.98 between the work journeys and the census data. Hence it seemed reasonable to increase the estimate of census work journeys by the ratio of nonwork to work journeys shown in the London Travel Survey data. Nonwork journeys were reduced by 10 percent to allow for the swing towards car travel experience in the last decade, as estimated from independent L.T.E. data.

Multiplied by 300 to an annual figure, this became 9,000,000 journeys per

---

[8] Until the London Traffic (O and D) Survey is completed, this point cannot be checked in the necessary detail.

annum. The average time saving per journey was found to be 5.0 minutes. Therefore, 45,000,000 minutes are saved by the building of the V.L.

a) Time savings. On first thought it may seem absurd to talk of the value of time savings to generated traffic: the journeys were not made; now they are. How can anyone save time by making a journey he did not make before? The point is this. At present there are some journeys which are just not made. A slight decrease in their time and distance and they would be made. Then there are other journeys which would be made, given a somewhat larger decrease in their time and distance. And so on. If the V.L. is built, the time and distance of many journeys will be reduced. Some of the new journeys made will be only just worthwhile to those who make them. Others would have been made even if the V.L. had not cut journey time as much as it has. These last are the journeys where, in effect, time is saved. This "time saving" is the difference between the most time the traveller would have to spend and still make the journey and the time he actually takes. There is an upper limit to the amount of time which can be saved in this sense—the difference the V.L. makes to the length of the journey—for if the time saved were longer than this the passenger would have been irrational if he did not make the journey before the V.L. were built. His would be a diverted not a generated journey. It is for this reason that the average value of time saving in this sense has been assumed to be half the value of time saving to generated traffic. The value of time savings, at £0.256 per hour, is £96,000 per annum.

b) Fare savings. The fares faced by prospective passengers are also reduced as a result of building the V.L. The average reduction is necessarily calculated roughly. It has been assumed that, for prospective passengers as a whole, half the time saved would have had to be travelled by bus and half by rail. Valuing fares at $2\frac{1}{2}d$. a mile, and dividing the total by two—by analogy with the procedure for time savings—the total benefit is estimated at £63,000.

c) Other benefits. £375,000. L.T.E. will also gain £750,000 in fares from generated traffic, but this cannot be assumed to be pure gain since there must be a fall in producers' surpluses elsewhere. On certain assumptions these would cancel. We have not assumed this but have taken half £750,000 as a social gain. This gain is assumed to be distributed between: employers of the new labour moving to the centre, the labour itself, shopkeepers who benefit from the new trade, the shoppers who gain from access to the central area, and all other similar beneficiaries.

(2) Central areas

This represents generated traffic over a part only of the area affected by the V.L. It was not possible to measure the remainder directly. However, we felt it wise to hazard a calculation. The average elasticity of demand implied by traffic generation in the *part* was estimated at 1.25. If this elasticity obtained over the whole, the resulting additional benefit of traffic generation would, on the same basis, be:

	£
Time savings	55,500
Fare savings	29,000
Other benefits....	203,000
	287,500

This is calculated for the estimated rail passenger mileage run in the central area, and the average time savings from station to station in that area, due to the V.L. (5 percent). Generated traffic already accounted for is, of course, deducted. Extra L.T.E. receipts are estimated at approximately £400,000 per annum.

ACKNOWLEDGMENTS

The authors are indebted to Mr. J. D. C. Churchill, Mr. P. E. Garbutt, Mr. C. R. Grant, Miss J. McLaren, Mr. H. Newman, Mr. E. Rockwell, and Mr. M. Webster of London Transport, without whose collaboration this study would have been impossible; to Mr. Colin Clark and Mr. G. H. Peters of the Agricultural Economics Research Institute of the University of Oxford for permission to use their analysis of the 1954 *London Travel Survey*; to Professor A. A. Walters, Professor W. M. Gorman, Mr. D. L. Munby, and Mr. C. B. Winsten for comment and advice; and to Miss M. Shah of the London School of Economics and Mr. C. Xenos of University College, London, for performing calculations. None of these shares responsibility for any findings or recommendations.

REFERENCES

ASHTON, A. S. (1962). "Investment planning by private enterprise," *Lloyds Bank Rev.* Oct. 1962.

BEESLEY, M. E. (1961). "Mr. Glassborow on investment criteria," *Bull. Oxf. Univ. Inst. Stat.* 23, No. 2.

———— (1962). "Financial criteria for investment in railways," *Bull. Oxf. Univ. Inst. Stat.* 24, No. 1.

BEESLEY, M. E., BLACKBURN, A. J. and FOSTER, C. D. (1962). "Investment in urban motorways," Paper presented to a *Conference on the Economics of Urban Congestion.* London School of Economics, September 13–16th, 1962.

B.T.C. (1949). "British Transport Commission: London Plan Working Party," *Report to the Minister of Transport.* London, H.M.S.O.

COBURN, T. M., BEESLEY, M. E. and REYNOLDS, D. J. (1960). "The London–Birmingham motorway," *Tech. Paper*, 46. Road Research Laboratory, D.S.I.R.

DAWSON, R. F. F. and WARDROP, J. G. (1962). "Passenger mileage in Greater London," *Tech. Paper*, 59. Road Research Laboratory, D.S.I.R.

FOSTER, C. D. (1960). "Surplus criteria for investment," *Bull. Oxf. Univ. Inst. Stat.* 22, No. 4.

FOSTER, C. D. (1963). *The Transport Problem.* London, Blackie.

GENERAL REGISTER OFFICE (1951). *England and Wales: Report on Usual Residence and Workplace.* Table 5. London, H.M.S.O.

GLASSBOROW, D. F. (1960). "The Road Research Laboratory's investment criteria examined," *Bull. Oxf. Univ. Inst. Stat.* 22, No. 4.

———— (1961). "Mr. Glassborow on investment criteria: a reply," *Bull. Oxf. Univ. Inst. Stat.* 23, No. 4.

HIRSHLEIFER, J., DE HAVEN, J. C. and MILLIMAN, J. V. (1960). *Water Supply: Economics Technology and Policy.* University of Chicago Press.

LONDON TRANSPORT EXECUTIVE (1954). *London Travel Survey.*

LONDON TRAVEL COMMITTEE (1959). "The Victoria Line," *Report to the Minister of Transport.* London, H.M.S.O.

MCKEAN, R. N. (1958). *Efficiency in Government through Systems Analysis.* New York, Wiley.

METROPOLITAN POLICE PARKING and TRAFFIC OFFENCES STATISTICS (1958). Census.

MINISTRY OF LABOUR (1962). "Index of wage rates," *Min. of Lab. Gazette*, Mar. 1962.

PIGOU, A. C. (1920). *Economics of Welfare.* London, Macmillan.

ROAD RESEARCH LABORATORY D.S.I.R. (1961). "Report on London Traffic Survey No. 9," J. E. Eaton and June J. Bryant. *R.N.* 3695.

———— (1961). "Traffic capacity," J. G. Wardrop. *L.N.* 3679.

ROTH, G. J. (1959). "The economic benefits to be obtained by road improvement, with special reference to vehicle operating costs," *Report to the Rees Jeffreys Road Fund, R.N.* 3426/*GJR*, Road Research Laboratory, D.S.I.R.

SMEED, Dr. R. J. (1961). "The traffic problem in towns," *Manchester Stat. Soc.*, Feb. 1961.

WALTERS, A. A. (1954). "Track costs and motor taxation," *J. Indust. Econ.*

WASHINGTON (D.C.) (1958). *Mass Transportation Survey, National Capital Region,* Wilbur Smith and Associates.

DISCUSSION

MR. C. B. WINSTEN: The paper we have just heard deals with a subject that raises several different problems: the economics of road and rail, the economics of towns and problems of town planning. It can also be interpreted as an attempt to develop a tool of management for service industries such as London Transport. Because of this width one can pick up subjects to discuss at almost every point. I will pick just a few at random.

The authors' main emphasis is on the economics of road and rail. They made the point that because (especially in towns) these are closely competing forms, investment should be assessed by computing a return in terms of benefit to the consumer in both cases. The repercussions of such investments are far wider than those on the users of the particular transport system, and these wider effects must also be taken into account.

This is a point of view with which I and many who have thought about the problem will thoroughly agree. The agreement owes something to the persuasive advocacy of Mr. Foster and Dr. Beesley. The usefulness of the point depends on how possible it is to make the calculations, on how far one can follow the ripples that are set up by the building of the line, and whether it is possible to give to them a valuation that most people will think is fair. The authors are to be congratulated on plunging in and making the attempt.

Have the authors counted and valued all the important ripples? One of these which might follow the investment, in fact a sizeable wave, might be a consequence of the way the line is financed. If fares are raised to cover the costs over the whole underground system, then passengers may be deterred from using the system both on the Victoria Line and elsewhere, and thus not gain the benefits of it. These journeys lost to the system might go back to the roads. The loss of benefit might well cancel much of the gain from building the line. In this sense it is a pity that the authors did not do two calculations: one for the case where fares are raised, and one for the case in which they are not. They do not explicitly say with which case they are dealing, but one supposes that they assume fares will not be raised.

We are here traversing familiar ground. In the nineteenth century the French engineer Dupuis made the point that if you have once built a bridge, it is better not to charge people to cross it, for then some will not do so, and society will have lost some of the benefit of the bridge. The argument was given a new impetus by Harold Hotelling in the thirties, and it has always been used, and successfully used, by road engineers to fight against the imposition of tolls on uncongested roads, sometimes on congested roads too, but that is another story; the argument is available to railwaymen too, if they want it. It is, in fact, an argument for marginal-cost pricing. If marginal variable costs do not suggest a price which covers the total costs of the investment, then the investment may make a financial loss but has to be assessed for the benefits it would bring. This seems identical with the case 1.3 (i) on p. 463 of the paper, the example of the dam, and I do not understand why the authors dismiss that analogy. Of course the argument depends very much on the fact that the price has a quite substantial deterrent effect.

If the argument is accepted, one has then to think of a way of raising the money for the investment. It is interesting to see some developments in the United States on this. For example, in New York the city authorities finance capital equipment of the transit system: the track, the stations, and rolling stock, but the running costs are paid by the transit authority out of its revenue. In New Jersey some rail developments were financed by the road authority with the probable implication that they are assessed on a roughly similar basis. It would be interesting to study in detail how these schemes work out in practice.

Some other costs to consumers may occur when those savings of buses mentioned on Table 2 leave passengers waiting longer in the cold, especially if they are to be saved in " off peak " hours. These are costs to the passengers which should occur in the calculation. So are delays caused by the thinning of services on other railway lines if they happen to occur, though I doubt if they will in this case.

It is in this way, too, that calculations of this sort might be considered as a tool of management. The benefits and costs of running a service can be calculated to determine, for instance, the best frequency of bus or train services. The aim should be to get as much excess of customer benefit over long-term cost as possible. The only peculiarity of the Victoria Line calculation in this respect is the heavy investment which is entailed.

The authors rightly admit that the figures given to the benefits are fairly arbitrary, though they agree it would be nice to relate them to people's own valuations of the benefits involved. In this respect, one can learn a lot from talking with people about the services—a thing that is difficult to avoid on occasion. That very traditional variable " time " certainly comes in to some extent, particularly for journeys in working time. The figure the authors use for the cost of time " in working time " is very low: quick communication has a value quite apart from the wages of the person making the trip. It opens up extra possibilities of organizing and adapting work. Getting a seat, which has been dealt with so interestingly in the appendix, also occurs often in such conversations. So does sheer crushing, which is a real nuisance on the lines to be relieved by the Victoria Line—perhaps the most important discomfort of all. Another great nuisance very much commented on is the weariness of long changes between lines—with walks up and down stairs and along long corridors. Changing trains is itself a tiring business. Many people do not mind a long journey to work provided they can sit relaxed and read. The Victoria Line cuts down the number of changes for many people. Its designers, realizing the nuisance of an awkward change, have spent much care on making changes that have to be made easy ones. All are very real benefits, which should be acknowledged in the calculations. The subject is one for detailed market research. Incidentally the worst places for changes are often at the linking points of two systems; catching a bus at a railway terminus, for example. There is a great field for beneficial investment here.

The Victoria Line is designed to go to the centre of the town: here is one of the points where town planning comes in. Will it not cause more crowding elsewhere on the system when its passengers change trains? More crowding on the pavements of Oxford Street? Pedestrians are still unlucky in this sort of analysis. Though there are figures for car costs and benefits there are none for pedestrians, for congestion on pavements and the increasing unpleasantness that the quick cornering and acceleration of the modern car give to the simple act of crossing a road. If a figure were given to these it might bring closer the work of town planners, on the one hand, and engineers and economists, on the other—at the moment rather far apart.

Many of the trends in the paper must depend on town planning considerations, and eventual goals. One cannot hope to do well by step-by-step planning in this field. Does the line help in building up and serving new " town centres" further out of London? Then the trends will be quite sharply upwards. But of such a comprehensive plan I have not heard. Does the line form part of an enlarged and thriving public transport system? Then the trends will be upwards. Or will the attempt be made to rebuild London as a motor-car town? Then the trends may be lower than the ones suggested.

Concealed in this weighty paper on p. 496 is a statistical exercise which surely must be a leg-pull. The authors study the numbers travelling to town from various boroughs. Most statisticians would work in terms of the *proportions* of people of working age living in these boroughs who commute. But the authors related the total number of people who travel up to London with the total population of the borough. The correlations they get are large: from big boroughs like Harrow (with 200,000 people) the total number of people going up to town is larger than from small boroughs like Penge or Barnes (with 20,000 people). The authors proudly exhibit their large correlations, then solemnly test this profound relationship with a t-test, to see if it could have happened by chance. The particular attitude of scepticism expressed by significance tests can rarely have been carried further. The exercise as it stands just will not do, but the subject is fascinating, and we must look forward to a more convincing treatment. Incidentally I am not quite sure that "social class" should be treated as an independent variable. People who travel to the centre are much more likely to be in groups 1 and 2.

Finally the authors distinguish between benefit rates of return and financial rates of return. Would it not help towards finding a common standard for these to assess the benefit returns of some investments in private industry carried out for profit, but which produce benefits in terms of increased productivity, etc.? This type of calculation would surely help the Government decide what relative weight to give to the financial and benefit types of calculation.

The authors have given us a paper which has tackled an important subject with resource and ingenuity. I have much pleasure in moving the vote of thanks.

PROFESSOR A. A. WALTERS: Quite a lot of the wind has been taken out of my sails by Mr. Winsten's remarks but I should like to join him in congratulating the authors on a very good paper. The authors have followed the lead of economists such as Lord Stamp, Sir Arthur Bowley, and Colin Clark who have fearlesssly tried to quantify, while theorists have still been carping about nice points of principle.

This paper is, I believe, the first application of a benefit–consumer surplus calculation to the underground railways of London, and probably the first to be read to the Society about the consumer-surplus criterion in practice. One learns a great deal about criteria when one tries to apply them and our knowledge of the consumer-surplus criteria is severely limited by the fact that they have been rarely applied. The consumer-surplus criterion was proposed by Alfred Marshall towards the end of the nineteenth century: and theorists have been busy finding faults with the concept ever since. Some theorists, Samuelson for example, think that the concept ought to be dropped altogether and that it is both redundant and misleading. This is too sweeping a judgment. With proper precautions it can provide a most useful framework for approaching the data. One of the main reasons is that in advanced countries most of the gains from transport works accrue to existing traffic. On the Victoria Line, for example, the reductions in cost of existing traffic account for about 88 percent of the estimated total return. Only 12 percent is due to the generated traffic. We should have much more difficulty in measuring the benefits accruing to roads such as the proposed Asian highway, which, in certain stretches, has virtually no existing traffic. Almost all traffic is generated —and the main difficulties occur in estimating the gains from new traffic. A second reason is that, in spite of theoretical objections, it does no harm to the calculations to assume, as the authors (and Marshall) have done, that the marginal utility of income is constant. But the third reason is simply that no one has suggested a criterion to replace the consumer-surplus criterion. (The only one I can recall is the "coefficient of resource utilization", suggested by Professor Debreu; but it seems to be impossibly difficult to apply in practice.)

The practical importance of studies of this kind lies in their value for decision making, that is, to examine whether or not the M1 and the Victoria Line were good investments. It is unfortunate that these studies always seem to be done after the decision to build has been taken. This is in fact understandable because many of the statistics do not come to light until after the money has been committed. Clearly an *ex-ante* survey of the Hyde Park–Marble Arch project might have prevented so much money from being sunk in so futile a scheme. It is something of a relief to know that the Victoria Line is, at least, not a disaster.

Although I broadly agree with the approach and analysis in the paper, at times I find some difficulty in understanding the authors' treatment. One of the problems—discussed earlier by Mr. Winsten—is to find the best investment policy when prices are out of line with costs. Consider the existing situation where prices by road are much lower than costs during peak periods, and prices by rail are only a little below costs. Now, even though one agrees with the authors that it may be politically impossible to change these prices (and I must record here that I do not), it would be disastrous to invest in roads and rail as if the prices were nicely adjusted to costs. (This is the authors' "intermediate position" in Section 5.3.) Following such a policy one would have few or no new roads, together with substantial investment in underground railways. Roads would be jammed while the tubes would be relatively empty. Any inefficiency in the price system would be compounded by the inefficient investment programme. If one agrees that prices by road cannot be raised, that is to say we cannot impose tolls or increase taxes on congested roads, then the best procedure is surely to make the investment policy conditional upon the price policy actually pursued or expected to be pursued in the future. One hopes that a more rational price policy will soon be introduced, but one prepares for the worst. This pricing-investment problem crops up a number of times in the practical computation in the paper. I do not always agree with the authors' treatment. For example, in Section 3.1 on fares and cost saving, they suggest that fares over the whole system may be raised to cover the expected financial loss on the Victoria Line. They then argue that it is reasonable to assume that this will make no net difference to the calculated rate of return. They suggest that it will simply result in a transfer (of income) from users of the underground system. Is this really so? Surely the increase in fares will drive people from tube to bus and private car; and most studies suggest that this reallocation would be bad. Costs of carrying the existing volume of passengers would be increased by the additional road congestion, and this would clearly offset some of the savings of the Victoria Line. Increasing fares in this way is no doubt a bad policy, but of course this merely underlines the bad price policy into which we have drifted. If the authors agree with this point, I wonder whether they could provide an estimate of the costs of the increase in tube fares.

In the detailed calculations I found some trouble in understanding the treatment of the movement of jobs and homes. It is curious to read that changing jobs is a short-run effect whereas changing houses is a long-run reaction. In Appendix D, a cross-section study across boroughs is used to predict the number of new journeys when the time of a journey is reduced by about five minutes. The result is some 30,000 new journeys (or about 25,000 new journeys to work). The authors clearly imply that these are new jobs (journeys) which did not exist before; somehow the Victoria Line increased employment (?), or are these new journeys merely due to people changing their homes and keeping the same jobs? or does this reflect an increase in the volume of employment in Central London at the expense of employment elsewhere? Whichever definition one takes, one has a large number of questions to answer. Take the last interpretation, for example; this suggests that the only factor determining the distribution of employment between Central London and other areas is the willingness of people to travel the extra five minutes or so. This is, I believe, the interpretation of the cross-section result which is used for this prediction. Surely the supply of jobs in central areas will have a role to play. If the elasticity of employment in central areas is low relative to wages, it is conceivable that notwithstanding the cross-section results, no new traffic is generated. There is simply a transfer around to the Victoria Line—and perhaps not even a lengthening in the average length of journey. Some of these difficulties arise from using a cross-section analysis of existing conditions to predict what is going to happen when those conditions are changed. This technique has been used in other branches of econometrics and the results have not been very encouraging. But I agree with the authors that this seems the only thing to do in the circumstances—though there is the possibility of more detailed analysis of changes with the 1961 data. At this stage I should like to ask the authors for an interpretation of their results.

I believe that there are some fallacies in the discussion of the effects of trends on elasticities. Shifts in demand due to the Victoria Line will not normally result in a reduction in the elasticity of demand for travel—and this is the concept relevant for their calculations. The demand for road services becomes more elastic, but, to counteract this, the demand for tube journeys becomes rather more inelastic. I believe that it is incorrect to distinguish, as the authors do at the end of Appendix C, between the little improvement due to a new road and the great improvement due to a competitive facility. Road works bring benefits although they become congested.

I found the paper very stimulating and most provocative. I have had time to touch on only a few of the points at which I disagree with the authors, but this is the sort of paper where one tends to disagree at every comma, and certainly at every full stop. I do feel, however, when we have got to the end, when we have arrived at the 11 percent, the result is somehow about right! It is a great pleasure warmly to second the vote of thanks.

The vote of thanks was put to the meeting and carried unaminously.

MR. P. SHEAF: There are two points I should like to refer to. First, I would like to go back to Dr. Beesley's summing up of the main points of the paper, and to a question which Professor Walters referred to when seconding the vote of thanks. This is the question of the value of "benefit" calculations of this kind. Dr. Beesley suggested various uses of the calculations, and various factors which might effect their validity—for example, investment policy or charging policy. As somebody who will have to make practical use of such calculations in the course of his work, I would suggest that the calculation will nearly always be a valuable help to decision making, even if there are all sorts of difficulties and reservations about it. The seconder of the motion (I may be doing him an injustice) seemed to suggest that if there were inequalities in pricing policy this kind of calculation might be of very little value. My own feeling is that, on any of the bases Dr. Beesley mentioned in his summing up of the paper, the calculation would help decision making. On a related point, I would not feel so strongly as Mr. Foster, I think, suggested in his own re-marks, that the main value of the thing would be in deciding between individual projects, particularly those within the same undertaking. In making Govern-ment decisions, calculations, of this kind may be at least as useful for more general judgements as for particular judgements. It is in any case very difficult to find projects that are reasonably comparable when you are thinking in these terms; one advantage of a calculation of this sort is that you can evaluate, and thus compare, types of investment which are not obviously comparable in more ordinary ways.

My second point is the method of presenting calculations of this kind to a decision-making body. You have to present them so that a layman can make reasonable sense of them. Now one of the points made in the "popular" version of this evening's paper which appeared in *The Times* is that you do not need to know all the ins and outs of the case in order to produce a helpful calculation. Mr. Winsten, in proposing the motion, demonstrated the difficulty of following all the "ripples"—the side-effects and consequences—of a particular element in the calculation. There are all sorts of ripples I should like to follow up in the Victoria Line one. But you must stop somewhere. I would emphasize that when you are presenting your findings it is a tremendous help, if you say why you have made your stand where you did; why, for example, some of the "ripples" have been taken account of and some have not.

PROFESSOR WALTERS: There is clearly some misunderstanding of what I said. All the calculations are conditional upon the prices: the prices are of overwhelming importance in estimating the rate of return. By charging the wrong prices you could make the rate of return dwindle to zero and even below.

MR. E. G. WHITAKER: I should like to say straightaway that I am not a statistician. One point on which I should like to seek information is the statement that "the most important single category, a matter of 25 percent of the total, is time saving to vehicle users in reducing congestion in London streets". I wonder whether the authors have made sufficient allowances for motorists such as myself, who use public transport at the present time, but will get back on to the streets again as soon as there is less congestion. This is pretty well exemplified in Los Angeles where they have provided a magnificent network of roads with the hope of accommodating all the traffic, but find that motorists are just as "cussed" in that country as here and they still have serious congestion.

MR. R. W. THOMAS: I should like to ask the authors if they could give us an estimate of the proportion of the social benefit of the Victoria Line which arises from changes in peak journeys to and from Central London. This would give us a useful indication as to what extent the Victoria Line is an attempt to solve part of the peak problem, and to what extent it will be a general improvement in London's transport system.

I anticipate that this proportion is very high, and I think this helps to illustrate the magnitude of the peak problem. The average journey to work in Central London probably takes between 50 and 60 minutes, many railway passengers are overcrowded, and virtually all road travellers are delayed by congestion. The potential social benefit of reducing the time, and increasing the comfort, of only a small proportion of these journeys must be measured, on the valuations suggested in this paper, in terms of tens of millions of pounds per year.

This indicates that the section of the paper on " Uses of the Calculation " is far too modest. It mentions only comparisons with other transport projects and public investments. Comparisons should also be made with the social benefits of possible policies which relate to the private sector. This ought to be done because it seems likely that improvements in transport may not be the best solution to the peak problem. It may be better to change locations— to encourage people to live nearer to their work. It would be proper, for example, to calculate the social benefit of subsidizing housing in Central London, and to compare this benefit with those arising from such projects as the Victoria Line.

Considerations of this kind make me disagree with the calculations made for the social benefits of time savings and reduced fares for generated journeys. The time spent on existing journeys is treated as a social cost, but the time spent on new journeys is only partly treated in this way. This seems inconsistent and I think it reveals some unstated assumptions. The comparison with how much time people would be willing to spend on travel seems inappropriate to me. The comparison ought to be made with the time that would have been spent had the Victoria Line not been built.

Let me give some examples. Suppose I live and work in Walthamstow but because of the existence of the Victoria Line I change my job to one in Central London. (This is not a new journey but a changed journey, not included in diverted traffic because the destination has changed.) The total time I spend travelling will be increased and this will be a social loss. There may of course be benefits to myself and my employer but it would require further investigation or assumptions to establish their value.

Suppose, to take another example, an organization establishes a new office in Central London because the Victoria Line is built. The journeys to work of their employees may be genuinely new in that they are related to an increase in the level of employment. But there will be a social benefit so far as travel time is concerned only if these journeys are shorter than they would otherwise have been. This is very unlikely. Journeys to work in Central London are longer than other journeys and the employees will almost certainly spend a longer time travelling than they would if the office had been established elsewhere. The result of the construction of the Victoria Line, so far as these journey times are concerned, will be a social loss not a benefit.

Finally, I should like to ask another question. There are eight references in this paper to material produced by L.T.E., but only two are published documents. It is gratifying to learn that L.T.E. collect some of these data, but lack of familiarity with them made the paper much more difficult to follow. Need this light be hidden under a bushel?

MR. J. M. THOMSON: I would make three points: (1) It may be of interest to know that we at the Road Research Laboratory have made a similar social calculation with reference to the M1. The basic data were provided by the London–Birmingham Motorway Study published two years ago. The published paper did not attempt to look into the distant future and produce a true rate of return, but this has since been done. We considered a period of 40 years and arrived at a social rate of return of about 18 percent. This figure should be more or less comparable with the rate of return used in this Victoria Line study but I cannot be sure of this because I cannot follow the method used. And this brings me to my second point.

2) I have worked through the explanation on p. 468 in order to find out how these returns of 11.3 percent, 11.6 percent and 10.9 percent are derived. I have completely failed to understand this and I should be obliged if the authors could elucidate. It seems to me very odd that these three percentage figures should be so very similar. The initial capital required is much the same in all three cases, but the net benefits at present values are nearly five times as large when the rate of interest is 4 percent as when it is 8 percent. I realize that there is probably a simple answer to this and I should be grateful to be told what it is.

3) My third point is one of disagreement. The most important benefits of the Victoria Line are said to come from improved conditions on the roads. Much trouble has been taken to assess the value of the time savings and the savings of operating costs to different types of vehicles. The basic premise is that the transfer of traffic from the roads to the railways would cause a 4 percent improvement in traffic speeds in the centre of London. Is this so? Surely all the evidence is to the contrary. It was estimated in 1955 that 57 percent of car-owners travelling into Central London did not use their cars. This proportion must be nearly 70 percent now. This represents a huge reserve of potential motorists who it may be supposed would begin to use their cars as soon as there was some relaxation in congestion and in the shortage of parking space. In five years time this reserve of potential motorists will be bigger still. Surely the greater part of any improvement in congestion will be taken up by these people and the situation on the roads will soon sink back almost to where it would have been.

PROFESSOR G. A. BARNARD: I should like to protest against the assumptions of some of the earlier speakers in the discussion that in the event of a relief of traffic congestion more motorists will take to the road. There is at least one motorist standing here who in the event of a reduction in congestion sincerely hopes to be able to travel by bus, and conversation with friends of mine indicates that I am not alone in this. I do not think it is true that people take to cars whenever congestion is reduced. It may well be that the opposite happens, with at least as great frequency. The number of "frustrated bus passengers", in the technical sense, may well exceed the number of "frustrated motorists" —and in the nontechnical sense this is certainly so. And if any forms of priority are given to buses over private cars, as they obviously should be, the effect will become more marked.

The other point I should like to make was stimulated by this very useful concept of social benefits and costs and the fascinating idea that the time those of us who have no particular fixed working hours spend doing nothing is worth 5s. an hour. In connection with another project involving large capital expenditure, the supersonic transport, we are told that this will cut three hours off the time of the journey from London to New York. Assuming that the value of the time of perhaps a hundred or so passengers on that journey is valued at this rate, this comes out at £75 a journey. One can set this alongside the fact that the noise and so on which will be created by these jets will affect, one might guess, 100,000 people who would be perhaps prepared to pay a penny a day to be rid of it. In this event it seems that unless one has more than six journeys a day by supersonic transport from London to New York the people who want to lead a quiet life will win. This of course is not the whole of the balance of social advantage and cost relevant to that particular issue but it does seem to offer food for thought.

MR. G. N. RUBRA: Reference was made in this paper to the possibility of applying this type of calculation to other examples and to proposals whereby railways or other services might be closed down. Instances of this are being considered in a very rough-and-ready fashion, not so much to give definitive results with the refined detail and complexity displayed in the Victoria Line calculation, but rather to indicate briefly the sort of thing that might come out of it if you did this work properly. I would refer to the North London Line, the railway that runs in obscurity from Broad Street to Richmond. There have been rumours that British Railways intended to close this line to passenger traffic and while these were hotly denied, it is true that a serious cut in the service has been made this autumn by withdrawing the evening service after 9 P.M. on Mondays to Fridays. This is totally unprecedented for any rail service carrying the volume of passenger traffic carried by the line or operating the density of service operated on it during the rest of the day. The cut renders the route completely useless for anyone wishing to use it for off-peak visiting of friends and relations or for going to the theatre, the cinema, or entertainments of this kind. It is surprising, too, because the line is one on which a larger proportion than average, for British Railways, are off-peak journeys and not work journeys: the average on British Railways London lines is about 80 percent work journeys whereas on this particular line it is only about 50 percent. In estimates that have been made some very crude figures of loadings have been used (because none has been published) from a rather scanty ratio delay or activity sampling study, and some very arbitrary assumptions have been made about lengths of journey and about whether, roughly speaking, the loadings that were observed are approximately stable throughout the length of the line. These are not strictly proper, but the results are so astonishing that the reservations one must make about how the results were collected seem to become comparatively unimportant. The present cuts have resulted in a net saving of only about £13,000 p.a. out of a total expenditure which we have estimated from B.T.C. reports—again this figure is subject to considerable reservations and corrections from anyone who knows the right answer—of about £475,000 p.a.

The consumer surplus, or rather consumer deficit, which is incurred by the removal of the evening service on the passengers using the line immediately before its withdrawal amounts to £56,000 p.a. or four times as much, based on the type of savings that can be made in journey times only, regardless of road congestion (which does not affect this route in the evenings in any case). For this purpose it has been supposed that 80 percent of those travellers would have to go by other forms of public transport or stay at home and that 20 percent would go by private cars and not be any worse off in terms of time. If the service were withdrawn completely the net saving would be about £50,000 a year, that is to say, the actual cost of running the service of £475,000 is paid for to a substantial extent by the fares collected, which are believed to amount to about £420,000. Capital investment does not need to be considered because this could not be reduced by removing the passenger service. The social cost to those users of the service at present going by other routes would on the above basis be £1,148,000 according to the calculations, and if all the people who could profitably use the line and are unaware of its existence were included (shall we say because it does not appear on the tube map?) it would be £2,947,000. This means that to retain the line in service would give a net yield each year of 440 percent over the expenditure in running it, or that the social cost from time saved alone is more than sufficient to pay the total cost of maintaining the line, and it would therefore be worth while to maintain it even if no fares were charged or collected at all.

MR. P. W. GLASSBOROW: I am very pleased to see this kind of analysis attempted and even more so that the authors have been brave enough to place their report before us; therefore any of my comments which appear critical should not be taken as a criticism of the paper as a whole. This method of accounting is a good one and should be used to test out the national financial justification for capital investment in those places where it is considered desirable that investment should be made to achieve social ends. I believe that the Government and many of us are worried about the increasing size of London and the continual addition to the London conurbation. One of the reasons for the growth of London is that so many things are provided in London at under cost. Further it is my belief, which I think can be substantiated by an examination of the past, that motorists, pedestrians, railway travellers, and in fact everybody have a limit of discomfort and a limit of wasted time which they will tolerate in any particular length and type of journey. Therefore, however many facilities are provided within London at however little direct cost to the persons concerned, the existing facilities and the new facilities will all reach the previous state of congestion after a comparatively limited period of time. The only effect of building new roads or new railways in London is to increase the size of the London conurbation. This brings me to a serious omission in the social account set out in this paper —the appalling social cost of increasing the London conurbation. I would suggest that this social cost far exceeds any of the savings which the authors have placed to the credit of the Victoria Line.

Now I should like to mention two very small points which I think might be corrected. The first concerns the time taken to cross the parks by the new

Victoria Line. I should like to see the passenger who can get down on to the new platforms at Victoria station and up from the platforms on the other side of the parks after waiting for a train for an average of perhaps a minute and a half and still succeed in doing this journey in 5 minutes. I suggest the journey would take far more like 10 or 12 minutes. My second point is that the authors have gone for information to two sources. London Transport thinks that the Victoria Line at the eastern end will attract a large number of passengers from British Railways. This may or may not be true. British Railways were asked what savings would be made on British Railways as a result of the building of the Victoria Line and replied that it was negligible. This, however, was not because they expected to make no savings if there was a marked reduction in travel but because British Railways did not believe London Transport's views about the transfer of passengers. Time will prove which view is correct.

Mr. R. M. Robbins: I want to contribute two points to this discussion because as well as being a Fellow of the Society I am the officer at London Transport in whose department the basic figures upon which the authors have made their calculations have been produced, and also because, by a freak of administration, I am also responsible for the public relations of the Executive and their publicity. My points relate hardly at all to what the authors said in the paper, but to one or two of the remarks in the discussion. The first one is the regret expressed that certain of the figures referred to have remained unpublished until now. London Transport published so many things about the Victoria Line in the long period leading to the decision that it should be built, that it seemed to us, knowing that the kind of decision-makers we have to deal with are very sensitive of having their elbows jogged at critical moments, that it would be better to stick to what we were putting out and to compile figures—some on a pretty sophisticated basis—to have ready for the next lot of questions that came in. It is a tribute to those of my own staff who were looking after this that they were very nearly always ready with a lot of figures for the questions when they came. We attempted to avoid blinding people with arithmetic. The other point was the remark by one of the speakers that it was a pity this sort of thing was done after the event and not before it. It gives me great satisfaction to hear that criticism, because when the exercise was undertaken, it was by no means after the event of the decision to build the line but before it. We thought it might come in very handy indeed in hastening that decision. That it has in fact been published and laid before you a few months after the decision to build was taken is to us a matter of satisfaction rather than the reverse.

Mr. N. Seymer: I want to tie together the remarks made by Mr. Rubra about the North London Line with a point made by one of the first speakers on fares and distances. The present fares are based on the distances travelled. There was a letter in *The Guardian* this morning by a gentleman who lives somewhere in Kilburn. He does not use the North London Line to get to the City because his season ticket by that line would cost him 30s. more than it does by the Bakerloo Line and Central Line, using the most congested sections of those lines. Surely it is in the public interest that people who are in a position to use a more circuitous but less congested route should be encouraged to do so. It is high time that fares were put on a basis of point-to-point distances. That could be done quite rapidly and easily, and must certainly encourage use of the North London Line.

Value judgements of road works were mentioned. I hope that this sort of study will be done in future on road works in London. We have for instance the Hyde Park underpass—there was a value judgement of that in a cartoon in the *Daily Express* showing a woman saying to her daugther, "An underpass, my dear, is the shortest distance between two bottlenecks." That is the kind of comment that is going about.

On the general question of whether you should spend money on road works or on railways, the answer largely depends on the nature of the road works. It is noteworthy that other big cities are planning to spend vast sums on enterprises like the Victoria Line. Paris, for instance, plans to build a Résau Exprès Régional, which will include main-line gauge tunnels criss-crossing the central area, and Los Angeles—biggest surprise of all—is now planning a 75-mile network of rail routes costing about £200,000,000 because they have found that relying solely on private car transport cannot move the millions in an efficient way despite all the money they have spent on expressways.

I should have thought that the basic principle to adopt is quite a simple one: that whether you are building roads or railways, both are channels for public movement and such channels should be paid for out of the public purse. The operating costs of public transport ought to be covered by the operating authority. Having accepted that basic principle, you can then decide in a particular case which is the most efficient type of movement channel to build.

In Central London it will obviously be routes like the Victoria Line. Farther out, it becomes a little less obvious; for instance, North London is the sort of area where you could contemplate building a tangential motorway skirting the northern edge of Central London. Would it be more advantageous to build that motorway, or to improve the interchange facilities on the North London Line so as to encourage more people to make use of that facility? I hope that many more studies of this kind will be done on that type of question.

The following contribution was received in writing after the meeting:

Mr. D. L. Munby: The authors of this study have made a notable contribution to a kind of analysis which has been lamentably rare in this country, but without which rational decisions can hardly be made about public sector investment. Its value is the greater in that it can be compared with the M1 study and the formulae devised by the Road Research Laboratory. On the other hand, perhaps its main virtue lies " as a precursor of other calculations ". This is not to belittle the solid hard work behind this pioneering study, and the imaginative way in which novel attempts have been made to measure what might at first sight be thought unquantifiable. It is to be hoped that others will follow in the footsteps of those who have pioneered this work.

The following four points are relevant to this aspect of the work rather than in criticism of the paper itself:

1) Time savings are, as in the M1 study, one of the most important items of benefit. 25 percent of the total are time savings of vehicle-users, 8 percent are time savings of the Victoria Line traffic which diverts from buses. Some figure has to be put in for these savings, but they are bound to be largely arbitrary, even for those travelling in working time, until we know more about the actual benefits which travellers of all sorts gain from saving time. This requires further research into the actual purposes of journeys, and into the possibilities, in practice, of making use of vehicles and time saved. In addition, as is noted in the paper, only some of these benefits would accrue as revenue to a profit-maximizing business-man; this is important when comparisons are made between profit making and public enterprises. Meantime, if these savings are taken into account in estimating the benefits of road improvements, they must be taken into account in the same way in dealing with similar competing investments.

2) Major questions may be raised about the assessment of generated traffic as a benefit to the community. The estimates are interesting for their own sake, and as forecasts of what might happen within a more *laissez-faire* framework than is in fact likely to exist with the present planning powers and targets of the town-planning authorities. If it is desired (as is roughly the case) to discourage further employment in the centre of London, and to encourage migration of employment from the centre to the outskirts and less travel to work within London, then it can hardly be counted as a benefit that the Victoria Line will encourage the reverse process. There are good economic as well as social reasons for this policy, and if it is more effectively enforced in the future, the benefits from generated traffic may not be so great as envisaged in the paper. Though a sizeable fraction of total benefits (15 percent), they are not, however, among the more important items.

3) One would like to know what difference would be made to the results with different assignment assumptions for diverting traffic. The paper uses three different assignment assumptions in different places, neither of which is the same as that used for the M1 study. (Assumption A for traffic diverted from the Underground to the Victoria Line is that all take the quicker route, and, if two routes take the same time, half take one route and half the other. The assignment from buses was made by L.T.E. officials on the basis of commercial judgement, though mainly relying on time saving. For road traffic, the Washington, D.C., traffic assignment curve was used.) All these four assign-

ments relate to different circumstances, so that they cannot be directly compared, but one would like to know how they affect the results.

4) It is not at all clear what is the significance of the discounted rate of return. There is something odd in putting in one rate of discount (6 percent) and coming out with another (11.3 percent). If 6 percent, say, is the proper rate of discount to use, then, if the present value of the stream of benefits less costs is positive, it implies that the scheme should be undertaken; any positive present value when discounted at a chosen rate of discount proclaims a benefit. If two different projects have to be compared, the two present value sums can be directly compared. If one wants to study the effects of different rates of discount, the only significant use of these calculations for one given project is to know at what rates of discount the present values become negative. This is given by the internal rate of return, which, from many points of view, may be a more useful tool. It is difficult to see what is the purpose of expressing a present value calculation in terms of a rate of return.

The AUTHORS subsequently replied in writing as follows:

We feel it would be irrelevant to comment here on any of the suggestions, though interesting, that our methods have application, or our results implication, elsewhere. Otherwise the comments made fell principally under five heads.

1. Data and methods

a) Mr. Winsten and Mr. Munby notice the arbitrariness of the values assumed for time saving which we have not disguised. We agree on the great importance of more research here. Meanwhile we have made sensitivity calculations: for the 6 percent discount rate valuing time savings at 3*s*. an hour would produce a Net Current Benefit (G of Table 2) of £52 million instead of £70; for 10*s*. an hour the figure would be £115 million. It is difficult to choose where there is little relevant evidence. Most writers would consider our values are low in the circumstances and with this by and large, we agree.

b) Mr. Glassborow argued that it would take longer by Underground from Victoria to Green Park than we have allowed. The estimate was made by London Transport, which stands by it.

c) On the regression analysis: R^2 is useful as an indication of the proportion of the variance in the dependent variable explained by the variation in the independent variables. Of course, in our analysis, a large part was, we agree due to the size of boroughs. We wished to predict the consequences of a change in the independent variable, time. The measured sampling variance is not a good indicator of the true sampling variance, and perhaps for a large variety of reasons, for each of the boroughs has unique characteristics. When we varied the independent variable, we did not expect these unique characteristics to change appreciably. Consequently all these characteristics are reflected in the sampling variance in cross-section studies such as ours were. We did not attach much importance to the high correlations as such, but used their relative magnitude as between the various regressions as an aid to judging which to reject; over the full analysis, only one R^2 fell below 0.7, at 0.66. In this connection it is interesting to note that the coefficient of variation for the variable size of boroughs is higher in the (rejected) Inner boroughs than in the (accepted) Middle and Outer boroughs—by about 17 percent in each case. We have calculated what would approximately have been the effect on the predicted generated traffic had we adopted a regression of the type percentage of a borough's population employed in the centre, social class, and time. The tentative answer is that generated traffic would have been about 11 percent less. The further analyses for which both Mr. Winsten and we have argued will be needed to settle the question of which has made the better prediction. This analysis might well incorporate a quadratic term to allow for the differential effects of borough size.

d) We are sorry that, without much further work, we cannot tell Mr. Thomas what proportion of the benefits accrue to peak traffic, but it is undoubtedly a very high one.

2. Definitions

a) Mr. Winsten, Mr. Sheaf, and Mr. Thomas have noticed that our definitions of social costs and benefits are incomplete. We agree. We measured what we could and there are many items we would have liked to quantify. We look forward to research which will make this possible. Although noise is probably unimportant for this investment, Professor Barnard's example of its social cost represents the kind of calculation which needs to be made. Mr. Sheaf asked why we limited our enquiries as we did. Our stand was a result of available research resources, data, and judgment. We went as far as we could, given that we wished to say something in good time; our judgment was that the important effects to investigate would be users' gains and the gains and costs on closely competitive investments, e.g. roads. Hence the distribution of our effort.

b) Our results have also been challenged by Mr. Glassborow and Mr. Munby because we have not considered the social costs of metropolitan growth induced by the Victoria Line. We could reply again that we do not know how to measure these social costs, but that is not the whole difficulty. It is quite conceivable that, if the Government were to adopt a marginal social cost pricing policy, there might be no lessening of metropolitan growth. Principally that would depend on the elasticities of substitution between public and private transport, and the attractiveness of public road transport as congestion diminished. It is possible that a considered fall in the demand for road space might be associated with no fall, or even an increase, in travel. Because there are so many unknowns—of fact, in Government pricing and other policies—we did not attempt to allow for this in our calculations. But we would be surprised if, for most pricing policies the Government is likely to adopt, the V.L. would not be justified.

c) Mr. Thomas has criticized our definition of the social benefits of time savings and reduced fares for urban journeys. We think he has misunderstood our argument in Appendix, Section D, and has reversed it. Our contention is that the benefits to generated traffic will be less for a given reduction in journey-time than it will be for diverted traffic, but not that the benefit will be negative —for if the people who made these new journeys will be worse off than they were before, why do they make them? To try to establish a net *social* cost, Mr. Thomas would have to bring in other categories of costs than we have.

3. Elasticities

a) Mr. Munby has asked for the sensitivity of the calculations to the use of different assignment curves (elasticities of substitution). The reason for not using the M1 elasticities of substitution is that there is no reason to suppose them relevant to urban conditions. The bases for assignment for buses and Underground seemed to us to be the most plausible in the circumstances. We were less happy about the assumed elasticity of substitution between Underground and car travel, but its use, we feel, does not overestimate the benefit. There may be something to be gained by testing the sensitivity of the valuations to various elasticities of substitution used in this and in other cost-benefit studies. Unfortunately, this would have been a large task in itself, for which we had not the time.

b) Professor Walters has asked us to justify the elasticities of demand for, and supply of, employment, in the central area we have assumed relevant to generated traffic. The basis of the distinction between short- and long-run effects was simply that, in the short run, it was felt that some people domiciled in the V.L. catchment area would change to work in the central area, while, in the long run, some people would change their homes to take advantage of the V.L. whether they had been working in the central area or not. We have no theory of the journey to work in Central London which would allow us to discuss in detail the determinants of the elasticities we assume. On the supply side, we had in mind, as an explanation of the regression, the net nonpecuniary and possibly pecuniary advantages of working in the centre of London for many classes of labour. We also believed that a short saving in journey-time could make a difference at the margin (everywhere) to the choice of workplace. This was our interpretation of the regression relationships found. On the demand side, we are convinced that, with the increase in office building already authorized and the generally high level of employment in the London area, there will be no shortage of jobs. It is for this kind of reason that we believe that the elasticity of employment in central areas is high relative to transport costs.

c) Several critics have questioned the benefits to road users from decongestion. We should first point out that the improvement in traffic speed was *not* assumed to apply to all central London traffic, as Mr. Thomson implied, but only to some of it [see Appendix, B.4(*a*) (i), (*b*)]. Professor Barnard has pointed out that there may be more frustrated bus passengers than motorists.

If so, we may have underestimated the benefits from decongestion. The argument can only be resolved by observation. Even if motorists were to pour onto the roads, returning the speeds of traffic to their present levels, it would not be true to say there would be no benefits to road-users. The benefits to generated traffic would have to be considered; though, of course, the total benefit would be much reduced. We believe that the experience of the last few years, when traffic engineering has increased the mean speed of traffic in Central London, does not support the view that there is a reserve army of frustrated motorists waiting to annul improvement. Although the view that traffic generation from traffic engineering in London has been negligible is not incontrovertible, it is plausible. *A fortiori* it is more plausible where the "announcement effect" of higher mean speeds is smaller, as it would be when the improvement (from V.L.) is more widely diffused over the Central London area. It was these thoughts that led us to the assumption made.

4. Average discounted rate of return

a) Mr. Munby has questioned the significance of this rate of return. It does not present any different ranking of projects from that yielded by the discounted present net benefit. We felt it conceivable that some people, more familiar with rates of return than with discounted present values, might prefer to use it, although they would have to understand its peculiarities not to be led astray. Perhaps no one will want to use it. However, for what it is worth, it does provide a correct ordering of projects on our assumptions of what constitutes social costs and benefits, given the rate of discount.

b) Mr. Thomson has asked how it is calculated. There are two alternative forms of the rate. The first is found by deducting all costs, except capital costs from benefits for each year of the life of the investment. These are then discounted back to year 1, at the given rate of discount. The capital stream is discounted back to year 1 at the same rate. It is then calculated what would be the annuity over the life of the investment equivalent to the discounted net benefit which could be bought for the value of the discounted capital. The rate of interest is calculated which would be implied by buying an annuity for the life of the investment equivalent in value to the discounted present value of the net benefit stream at the purchase price of the present discounted value of the capital stream. The second method proceeds as the first except that the present value of net benefit stream, as defined above, is divided through by the expected life of the investment, and this average annual discounted sum is expressed as a rate of return on the present value of the capital stream. Both must give the same ranking of projects. The second will yield lower rates of return than the former. The intuitive rationalization of the two are, of course, different. This is a complicated subject and we propose to write more on it elsewhere.

5. Pricing policy

a) As Mr. Winsten supposes, our calculations assumed that fare levels would be unchanged by V.L. Thus, for example, the estimates of diverted passenger miles assume that normal fares would be charged. This, we are aware, leaves open the question of how V.L.'s finance, which these fares will not cover, will affect fares and therefore benefits (and probably costs). We are preparing a paper on the effects of various possible ways of financing the Line, which will be published in due course. In this, the present calculations will provide something of a bench-mark against which the modes of finance can be judged, in terms of their effect upon benefits and costs. To have proceeded otherwise in the present paper, we would either have had to know what the fares policy *would* be, or else to have had a definite notion, or notions, about what it *should* be. But when doing the work, we did not know, in detail, what the Government would decide upon V.L.'s finance; and we had then no outright opinion on how it ought to be financed. Certainly, we could not ask L.T.E. to commit themselves to a view on the effects of various methods of finance that could be adopted. The preliminary results of our new calculations, indeed, do indicate some support for Mr. Winsten's and Professor Walters's points about the effects of an average fare increase over the L.T. system; but there are other modes of finance to be considered.

b) Professor Walters, dealing with our Section 5, in which we discuss the problems of comparison with urban road projects, criticized our " intermediate " position as " disastrous ". However, we in our turn fail to see why, if the Government invested *as if* prices were adjusted to costs on road and rail, we should have " few or no " new roads. In such a case, the (notional) price of road space would reflect congestion costs; on many urban roads there would be high (notional) rents to roads, and the Government would invest, presumably, to reduce these " rents " to some (notional) return on capital. Of course, roads would then still be over-used, and losses of benefit occur, because no actual price would be charged; but investment would certainly be positive, and perhaps quite substantial.

Part VI
TAXES AND PRICES

This part represents only a small sample from the vast literature on the welfare effects of taxes and of prices to the extent that they are regulated by government action. Much of this literature has been only implicitly related to welfare criteria; for a survey, see the papers of Nancy Ruggles.[1]

The general implications of welfare arguments for prices and taxes in a closed economy were set forth in Hotelling's paper in Part IV. In a large, open economy, the possibility of improving welfare by turning the terms of trade against the rest of the world was early noted by Bickerdike and Edgeworth[2] and is given rigorous and general treatment by Graaff. The particular application of general pricing principles to public utilities has been extensively developed in recent years. In addition to the paper of Henderson following, there are observations in the paper of Meade and Fleming in Part IV, the deep and ramified work of the French economists associated with Electricité de France (P. Massé, M. Boiteux, G. Dessus, and others),[3] and H. S. Houthakkers' study of electricity pricing.[4]

In situations where it may be technically difficult to charge prices in the strict sense of the word, it is nevertheless frequently possible to impose taxes (thereby using the coercive power of the state to substitute for a possibly impractical free market) which have the same allocative effect. Vickrey has explored a variety of such possibilities in the field of municipal services.

The situation which is fully optimal in the usual sense of welfare economics

---

[1] "The Welfare Basis of the Marginal Cost Pricing Principle," and "Recent Developments in the Theory of Marginal Cost Pricing," *Review of Economic Studies*, 17(1949–50): 29–46 and 107–26.

[2] C. F. Bickerdike, "The Theory of Incipient Taxes," *Economic Journal*, 16(1906): 529–35; F. Y. Edgeworth, "On Some Curiosities of Mathematical Theory: Bickerdike's Theory of Incipient Taxes," in *Papers Relating to Political Economy* (London: Macmillan, 1925), Vol. II, pp. 240–66 (originally published in 1908).

[3] Translated in J. R. Nelson, *Marginal Cost Pricing in Practice* (*loc. cit.*, General Introduction, footnote 1).

[4] "Electricity Tariffs in Theory and Practice," *Economic Journal*, 61(1951): 1–25.

may not always be achievable because the government in effect lacks sufficient instruments to influence the economy. J. E. Meade[5] and, following him, R. G. Lipsey and K. Lancaster[6] have studied cases where the problem was to achieve an optimum within the limited range of instruments available. Two examples of this kind of analysis are presented here. Fleming assumes that both exchange rates and factor prices in different countries are unalterable and exhibits the optimal restrictions needed to assure balance of payments equilibrium. Little observes that the welfare case against indirect taxes—that they distort choices by making marginal rates of substitution between a given pair of commodities different in different activities—also holds against the income tax, which is in effect an excise tax on labor.

---

[5] *The Theory of International Economic Policy*. Volume 2. *Trade and Welfare* (London, New York, and Toronto: Oxford, 1955); Chapter VII.

[6] "The General Theory of Second Best," *Review of Economic Studies*, 24(1956–57): 11–32.

On optimum tariff structures[*]

JAN DE V. GRAAFF

This is an essay in welfare statics—in the strictest sense of the term. It seeks to apply to a classic problem in tariff theory a tool of considerable power and generality forged by Professor Paul A. Samuelson in his *Foundations of Economic Analysis*.[1] The tool to which I refer is a community's "possibility locus." Some of its salient properties are indicated in the first of the sections that follow. In the second I introduce a closely related concept, the community's "efficiency locus." The third is concerned with their application to the problem of determining optimum tariff structures, and discusses the argument—due essentially to Bickerdike[2] and Edgeworth,[3] writing at the turn of the century, but recently revived by a distinguished band of contemporary economists: Professor Lerner,[4] Mr. Kaldor,[5] Professor Scitovsky,[6] Mrs. Robinson,[7] and Mr. Kahn[8]—that it is, in the absence of retaliation, *always* possible for a full-employment country to turn the terms of trade in its favour by imposing a "small" protective tariff on imports, and to benefit itself thereby. In the fourth section I examine rather critically Mr. Kahn's revival of Bickerdike's theory that the "small" tariff may, in fact, be quite a "large" one. A mathematical note concludes the paper. The treatment throughout differs essentially from that of Mr. Little's article on "Welfare

---

[*] *The Review of Economic Studies*, 17(1949): pp. 47–59. Corrected by the author. Reprinted by courtesy of the author and *The Review of Economic Studies*.
[1] P. A. Samuelson: *Foundations of Economic Analysis* (Cambridge, Mass. 1947), Chapter VIII.
[2] C. F. Bickerdike: "The Theory of Incipient Taxes," *Economic Journal*, December, 1906, pp. 529ff; and his review of A. C. Pigou's *Protective and Preferential Import Duties*, *Economic Journal*, March, 1907, pp. 98ff.
[3] F. Y. Edgeworth: *Papers Relating to Political Economy*, Vol. II, pp. 340ff. (Reprinted from the 1908 *Economic Journal*.)
[4] A. P. Lerner: *The Economics of Control* (New York, 1944), pp. 382–85.
[5] N. Kaldor: "A Note on Tariffs and the Terms of Trade," *Economica*, November, 1940.
[6] T. de Scitovszky: "A Reconsideration of the Theory of Tariffs," *Review of Economic Studies*, IX (2), (1941–42), pp. 89–110. (Reprinted in *Readings in the Theory of International Trade*, Philadelphia, 1949).
[7] Joan Robinson: "The Pure Theory of International Trade," *Review of Economic Studies*, XIV (2), (1946–47), pp. 107–8.
[8] R. F. Kahn: "Tariffs and the Terms of Trade," *Review of Economic Studies*, XV (1), (1947–48), pp. 14–19.

and Tariffs"[9] in that the existence of no criterion is assumed on the basis of which interpersonal comparisons of well-being can be made.

I. THE POSSIBILITY LOCUS

Consider—for geometrical simplicity: the general case is treated in the mathematical note—a community consisting of but two citizens, Alpha and Beta. They are assumed to have definite preference scales, which can be represented by ordinal utility indexes, α and β. These indicate the disutility of effort as well as the utility of leisure and consumption. No special significance attaches to the particular indexes selected, but—once adopted—they must be adhered to without change. We shall maintain the convention that α rises whenever Alpha is able to satisfy his preferences more fully; and we shall then say that his welfare has increased. A similar remark applies to β and Beta.

We do not assume the absence of external economies in consumption: when Alpha installs a telephone the utility of Beta's will probably grow.[10] Nor do we assume the absence of external diseconomies: when Beta buys ostentatious diamonds Alpha may well discard his in disgust.[11]

Now fix β at some arbitrary level, β_0, and make Alpha as well off as is possible under the circumstances. Just how great a value α will be able to attain will depend upon (*i*) the value β_0; (*ii*) the supply of goods and services available to the community; and (*iii*) the possibility of transforming goods and services of one kind into goods of another kind. This transformation can be performed in factories at home, or by trade with communities abroad. Its maximum extent cannot be unambiguously determined until we know how much provision is to be made for capital accumulation, and how much foreign indebtedness is to be incurred. It is not generally recognized that this knowledge can be obtained from nowhere but a *dynamic* welfare theory. Here, however, we are concerned solely with welfare statics. We must take the dynamic theory for granted, and derive our transformation possibilities from it.

A word of justification for this procedure might, however, be added. We are going to abide very firmly by the rule that interpersonal comparisons of well-being are inadmissible. We shall never say that the community's welfare has increased unless both Alpha and Beta are better off—or, more strictly, unless at least one is better off, the other being no worse off than before. But if we cannot make interpersonal comparisons among the living, still less can we make them among the unborn and the dead. That is why we confine ourselves to statics. In a dynamic world the composition of our community necessarily changes in the course of time. To be able to say something of its welfare, we must have a concept of welfare that is independent of the earthly existence

---

[9] I. M. D. Little: "Welfare and Tariffs," *Review of Economic Studies*, XVI (2), (1948–49).
[10] R. W. Souter: *Prolegomena to Relativity Economics* (New York, 1933), pp. 50ff.
[11] A. C. Pigou: "Some Remarks on Utility," *Economic Journal*, March, 1903, p. 62.

of particular citizens. Into this problem it is inappropriate to enter at the moment. It is sufficient to note that we must have a dynamic theory before we can pursue our statics—perhaps this is an application to welfare theory of Professor Samuelson's well-known Correspondence Principle. But *any* dynamic theory will do—we do not have to have a particular one closely specified.

Once we have arrived at an unambiguous statement of the possibilities of transformation, the problem of making Alpha as well off as possible, subject to $\beta = \beta_0$, resolves itself into the problem of establishing the conditions for the Paretean General Optimum of Production and Exchange. The solution involving the equality of marginal rates of transformation and substitution, is well known for a closed economy—in recent years it has penetrated to the level of the elementary texts. These, it is true, do not generally deal with external economies or diseconomies in consumption—but they too have been exhaustively handled.[12] Section III of this paper extends the analysis to open communities. For the moment it is sufficient to assume the solution, which will give us a particular value of α, say α_0, corresponding to β_0.

If we fix β at some other level (by means of a lump-sum tax or bounty, which is assumed to cost nothing to collect or distribute), we shall obtain another value of α. Proceeding in this way, we can map out a locus in the (α, β)-plane. This is Professor Samuelson's "possibility locus," and is illustrated by $P_0 P_0$ in Figure 1. Its shape and position (for convenience, it has been drawn in the northeast quadrant) depend upon our particular choice of the indexes α and β. But the direction of slope is invariant.[13] It will normally slope downwards: Alpha can be made better off only at Beta's expense. In rare cases, however, it may slope upwards. Two examples deserve especial notice. The first is the one treated more fully in the mathematical note:

Figure 1

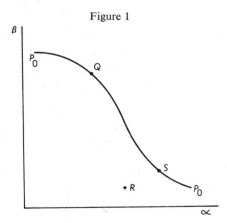

---

[12] G. Tintner: "A Note on Welfare Economics," *Econometrica*, January 1946, pp. 69–78.
[13] Mathematical Note, equation (15).

external economies in consumption may be so marked and asymmetrical that a transfer of wealth from Alpha to Beta increases the welfare of each. One might expect this situation to be unstable, Alpha simply making Beta a gift. The second, and more important, example is where the community's productive power depends in an essential way on the distribution of wealth: where workers are underfed, a redistribution of wealth in their favour may so increase their efficiency that everybody benefits. It is an open question whether or not considerations of this kind belong to welfare statics or dynamics. I propose to interpret " statics " very strictly indeed, and to exclude these considerations from our analysis. Thus, in formal language, the transformation functions are assumed to be independent of the distribution of wealth.[14]

We are left then, with a downward-sloping possibility locus.[15] Some of its salient properties may conveniently be summarised at this stage. (This and the next paragraph lean very heavily indeed on Professor Samuelson's treatment): Movements towards the locus are secured by establishing the conditions necessary for the Paretean General Optimum; movements along the locus by lump-sum taxes and bounties—assumed to cost nothing to collect and distribute. No point to the northeast of it can be attained with the given state of technique, etc. To any point to the southwest of it there corresponds

---

[14] By "a distribution of wealth (or welfare)" is meant no more than "a point in the (α, β)-plane."

[15] It should perhaps be emphasised that, when we leave a two-person community, slightly stronger assumptions are required to insure that the possibility locus should slope downwards. For instance, in a three-person community it may slope upwards because of external *dis*economies in consumption. Consider the community consisting of Alpha, Beta, and Gamma. For simplicity, let us say that there is but one commodity, "riches," the supply of which is fixed. Assume that Alpha's utility is uninfluenced by the riches possessed by either Beta or Gamma, and that these in turn are uninfluenced by Alpha's possessions. But assume, too, that marked external diseconomies in consumption exist between Beta and Gamma. Then, if we are interested in the slope of the possibility locus in the (α, β)-plane, we must examine the rate of change of β when α is diminished slightly by a transfer of riches from Alpha to Beta, when γ (Gamma's index of utility) is kept constant. But the increase in Beta's riches makes Gamma worse off, so to keep γ constant it is necessary to transfer some riches to Gamma. This, however, makes Beta worse off on two scores: firstly, because the riches are taken from him; and secondly, because Gamma's possession of them increases. It is easy to construct examples along these lines in which the original small decrease in α causes β to decrease too, γ being kept constant, i.e., where the possibility locus slopes upwards in the (α, β)-plane. The marked external diseconomies we assumed to exist between Beta and Gamma can secure this result in spite of the fact that after the decrease in α both Beta and Gamma possess more riches than before. The matter is discussed more thoroughly in the mathematical note.

It should also be noted that when the possibility locus slopes upwards over a certain range there is not perfect symmetry between α and β in its definition—even in a two-person community. We get one result when we choose to hold β constant, and another when we hold α constant. The first will give α as a single-valued function of β; the second β as a single-valued function of α. The complete locus is obtained by combining the two (i.e. by holding each constant in turn) to obtain what will in general be a multivalued function of α, β, or both. The reader will have no difficulty in constructing a simple diagram to illustrate this, or in verifying that there is perfect symmetry between α and β when the locus slopes downwards throughout the entire range.

a better point on the locus itself—"better" because both Alpha and Beta are better off. Between points actually on the locus we cannot judge without a criterion for making interpersonal comparisons of well-being. We cannot say that a point on the locus, like Q, is better than a point off it, like R—for in Q Alpha is worse off than in R. But we can (and shall) say that Q is *potentially* better than R—for there necessarily exists a point S in which both Alpha and Beta are better off than in R, and to which a mere redistribution of wealth can lead us. Whether or not such a redistribution should actually be made is, of course, another matter altogether, and cannot be decided without a criterion for interpersonal comparisons of well-being.[16]

Let us now confine ourselves to positions actually on the possibility locus —the more general situation is discussed in the next section—and consider a change such as might be caused by, for example, technological "progress." There are two distinct possibilities. On the one hand, the new locus may lie either wholly inside, or wholly outside, the old one. Such a movement we shall refer to as a *shift*. It is illustrated by $P_1 P_1$ in Figure 2, which lies wholly outside $P_0' P_0''$. In this case a position on the new locus is clearly at least potentially superior to any position on the old one. Thus the technological "progress" can be said to be at least potentially beneficial. On the other hand, the new locus may intersect the old one. This is represented by $P_2' P_2''$ in Figure 2, where the intersection is in X. We shall refer to this as a *twist*. Now all that can be said is that the situations on $P_2' X$ are at least potentially superior to those on $P_0' X$; and that those on $P_0'' X$ are at least potentially superior to those on $P_2'' X$. We cannot say that the technological "progress" is even potentially beneficial unless we have some criterion on the basis of

Figure 2

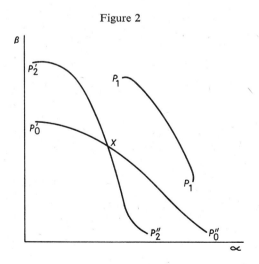

[16] Cf. W. J. Baumol: "Community Indifference," and N. Kaldor: "A Comment," *Review of Economic Studies*, XIV (1), (1946–47), pp. 44–49.

which we can judge between the situations on $P_2' X$ and those on $P_0'' X$—some criterion for making interpersonal comparisons of well-being.

It might be thought that this indeterminacy, which arises whenever the loci cross, makes the whole possibility concept rather a clumsy one for welfare theory. To a certain extent this is true. But in a number of cases we can establish quite unambiguously that the locus shifts, and does not twist to intersect the old one. Thus we shall see that the erection of an optimum tariff structure can never twist the locus, but must always shift it outwards.

II. THE EFFICIENCY LOCUS

In any actual situation our community is unlikely to be on the possibility locus: it is likely to be well inside it. A redistribution of wealth by lump-sum taxes and bounties (which are assumed to cost nothing to collect and distribute) will normally move it to another position inside the locus. Any such redistribution will normally also affect the allocative efficiency of the system, increasing the degree of monopoly in some parts and diminishing it in others. The locus of all points in the (α, β)-plane traced out by redistributions of this kind we shall call the *efficiency locus*, because it indicates the allocative efficiency of the system for various distributions of welfare. Optimum allocative efficiency, for a particular distribution of welfare, is not attained unless the possibility and efficiency loci coincide in the point corresponding to that distribution. But optimum allocative efficiency is seldom achieved, and the efficiency locus will usually lie beneath the possibility one.

Those steeped in the traditional surplus analysis may find it helpful to think of a point on the efficiency locus as indicating the total consumer's and producer's surplus enjoyed by each of Alpha and Beta in any actual situation. A point on the possibility locus, on the other hand, represents the maximum either could enjoy, given the amount enjoyed by the other, if the economic system were to be organised in an optimum manner—i.e., if the Paretean General Optimum were to obtain.

Technological progress, or a change of some other kind, is likely to affect both the possibility and the efficiency loci. It may shift one and twist the other, or affect both in the same way. There are, in fact, nine different combinations to consider: any one of the three different types of movement of the possibility locus can be associated with any one of the three different types of movement of the efficiency locus. For instance, an invention which shifts the possibility locus outwards may confer on the innovator monopoly power so that the efficiency locus is given a twist, or even shifted inwards.

The question therefore arises: to which locus should we refer in judging the potential desirability of a particular change? The answer, I think, depends upon the context. There is little point in bothering about possibility loci if there is no chance of the community ever attaining them. A change will lead us from a point on one efficiency locus to a point on another. Its potential desirability should normally be judged on this basis. Then we can consider the further question of improving the allocative efficiency of the system so as to make the efficiency locus approach closer to its possibility boundary. Such an improvement is always at least potentially beneficial. But it cannot be taken for granted. Its achievement is a matter quite distinct from the potential desirability of the change. Thus an invention which shifts the efficiency locus inwards should normally be regarded as potentially harmful, even if it shifts the possibility locus outwards. But it may well be that the same invention *plus* a vigorous trust-busting campaign would shift the efficiency locus outwards. In that case the invention *plus* the trust-busting, as opposed to the invention alone, is to be judged at least potentially beneficial. This would be true even if the invention were to involve an inward shift of the possibility locus—although, in the latter eventuality, it might be thought that the trust-busting without the invention might be potentially even more beneficial. This would not necessarily be correct, however, for the success of a given trust-busting campaign might not be altogether independent of the invention.

The question to which the various exponents[17] of "compensation tests" in welfare theory have addressed themselves is essentially a part of the wider problem of determining just what a particular change will do to the efficiency locus. But even the most powerful of these tests—Professor Scitovsky's well-known double one—cannot always detect a twist in the locus. This the reader can verify by glancing at Figure 3. There we consider a move from R on the first locus to S on the second. It benefits Alpha, but Beta suffers.

Figure 3

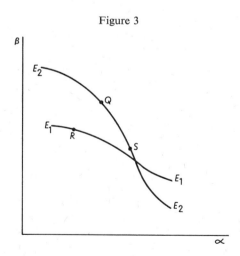

[17] N. Kaldor: *"Welfare Propositions and Interpersonal Comparisons of Utility, *Economic Journal*, 1939, pp. 549–52. J. R. Hicks: "The Foundations of Welfare Economics," *Economic Journal*, 1939, pp. 696–712; and *"The Rehabilitation of Consumer's Surplus," *Review of Economic Studies*, VIII (1940–41), pp. 111–12. T. de Scitovszky: *"A Note on Welfare Propositions in Economics," *Review of Economic Studies*, IX (1), (1941–42), pp. 77–88 and *loc. cit.*, M. W. Reder: *Studies in the Theory of Welfare Economics* (New York, 1947).

Alpha can, however, profitably bribe Beta into accepting the change (cf. Q), and Beta cannot profitably bribe Alpha into rejecting it. Yet the loci cross. Professor Scitovsky's test is not quite strong enough for our purposes. (It is, of course, perfectly correct to say that Q represents a point of greater welfare than R, for both Alpha and Beta are better off in Q than in R. But this is not to say that the change is even potentially beneficial. For there is no reason whatsoever why we should judge the old situation with reference to the single point R. Nor is there any reason for judging the new situation with reference to Q alone.)

The problem of determining the behaviour of the efficiency locus in any actual situation is a very difficult one, and does not lend itself at all readily to theoretical treatment. In discussing optimum tariff structures in the next section, therefore, we shall concern ourselves chiefly with the possibility locus. But we should bear in mind that this is very much a second best, and that what we are really after is the efficiency locus.

III. TARIFFS AND THE TERMS OF TRADE

In the first part of this section we shall simplify to the extent of considering a community where external economies and diseconomies are absent from both production and consumption. Let us adopt the following notation:

π_i = the domestic price of the ith good.

p_i = the foreign price of the ith good.

z_i = the net import of the ith good into the country under consideration. (When z_i is negative it means that the ith good is exported.)

$F = \sum p_i z_i + K = 0$. We shall call F the *foreign trade transformation function*. It means that, correct provision being made for foreign lending (K),[18] trade must balance. Note that:

$$0 = dF = \sum_i \frac{\partial F}{\partial z_i} dz_i$$

$$\sum_i \left\{ p_i + \sum_s \frac{\partial p_s}{\partial z_i} z_s \right\} dz_i$$

$$= \sum_i \left\{ p_i + a_i \right\} dz_i$$

So the *marginal rate of transformation through foreign trade* is:

$$-\frac{\partial F}{\partial z_i} \bigg/ \frac{\partial F}{\partial z_j} = \frac{p_i + a_i}{p_j + a_j}$$

$$a_i = \sum_s \frac{\partial p_s}{\partial z_i} z_s.$$

---

[18] For simplicity it is assumed that K is a constant, given independently of the level of prices. The details, but not the substance, of the argument is affected if this assumption is relaxed.

This indicates the total rate of change of world prices, weighted by quantities imported, as imports of the ith good are increased. Note that when "cross-elasticities" vanish identically, a_i/p_i reduces to the reciprocal of the ordinary elasticity; and that, whether they vanish identically or not, $p_i(1 + a_i/p_i)$ represents the marginal cost to the country of importing the ith good (or, if it is an export, the marginal revenue derived from its sale).

It is well known that the establishment of the General Optimum in a closed economy requires that consumers' marginal rates of substitution between any two goods should equal the marginal rate of transformation of these goods into each other in home factories. It is usually suggested that this is to be effected through the price mechanism: consumers equate their marginal rates of substitution, and producers their marginal rates of transformation, to given domestic price ratios. In an open economy, however, the establishment of the General Optimum requires too that marginal rates of transformation in home factories should be equal to marginal rates of transformation through foreign trade. Therefore, these must also be equal to the domestic price ratios. That is to say:

$$\frac{p_i + a_i}{p_j + a_j} = \frac{\pi_i}{\pi_j} \qquad (i, j = 1, 2, \ldots, n). \tag{1}$$

The reader who doubts that the establishment of the General Optimum requires this equality of marginal rates of transformation is referred to equations (7) and (8) of the mathematical note; but the matter is, after a little thought, rather obvious.

In the exceptional case where a_i/a_j is fortuitously proportional to p_i/p_j, equation (1) holds whenever domestic prices are proportional to foreign prices—as they always are under universal free trade, whatever the exchange rate. In this exceptional case, therefore, free trade establishes the General Optimum—i.e. lands us on the possibility locus.

In the more usual case, however, it will be necessary to adjust domestic prices (since foreign prices are not within our control) to secure the satisfaction of equation (1). The simplest method of adjustment is to put an *ad valorem* tax of a_i/p_i on the ith good whenever it crosses the frontier—the tax being calculated on the foreign price. Then we would have:

$$\frac{\pi_i}{\pi_j} = \frac{p_i(1 + a_i/p_i)}{p_j(1 + a_j/p_j)} \qquad (i, j = 1, 2, \ldots, n),$$

which is what is required. In the welfare terminology of previous sections, these taxes lead us to the possibility locus, and are therefore at least potentially beneficial: once they have been imposed wealth can be so redistributed that every citizen of our country is better off than he was under free trade. Stated in another way: compared with the free trade situation, the imposition of the optimum taxes shifts the possibility locus outwards.

This scheme of taxing both imports and exports is essentially the same as the one Professor Lerner suggests in *The Economics of Control*.[19] The only difference results from the fact that he implicitly assumes that all "cross-elasticities" of demand and supply vanish identically. It will readily be seen that whenever this procedure is legitimate our tax on imports reduces to the reciprocal of the foreign elasticity of supply, and our tax on exports to the reciprocal of the foreign elasticity of demand. This is Professor Lerner's elegant result. When the "cross-elasticities" cannot be neglected, however, it is likely to be a little misleading. For, in general, we cannot even say what the *signs* of the a_i will be; and, as we shall see, cases can arise where the attainment of the General Optimum requires *subsidies* (or negative taxes) on both imports and exports. Yet this phenomenon is in no way related to changes in the signs of Professor Lerner's elasticities.

Our formula is also very closely related to the Bickerdike-Edgeworth-Kahn-Little formula for the optimum tariff. In fact, ours reduces to it in a world in which but two commodities are traded internationally,[20] and where all the "cross-elasticities" vanish identically. We are then left with one export and one import. Denote them by e and m, respectively. Our General Optimum conditions (1) reduce to:

$$\frac{p_m + a_m}{p_e + a_e} = \frac{\pi_m}{\pi_e}.$$

We have here but one international price ratio. To adjust the domestic import-export price ratio to it we need not tax both imports and exports: a single tax will do the trick. Thus if an *ad valorem* tariff, t, is imposed on imports (the tariff being reckoned on the foreign price), we must have:

$$\frac{p_m(1 + t)}{p_e} = \frac{p_m + a_m}{p_e + a_e}$$

or

$$t = \frac{a_m/p_m - a_e/p_e}{1 + a_e/p_e}. \tag{2}$$

When all the "cross-elasticities" vanish identically, and we write η_d for the elasticity of foreign demand for exports (taken with a *minus* sign to make it positive) and η_s for the elasticity of the foreign supply of imports, (2) reduces still further to:

$$t = \frac{1/\eta_s + 1/\eta_d}{1 - 1/\eta_d}. \tag{3}$$

---

[19] *Loc. cit.*, pp. 382–85.

[20] Since we employ two prices in the argument that follows, we must have at least one domestic good (in addition to the two international ones) to play the role of *numéraire*. It is, therefore, not quite correct for Mr. Little to say that formula (3) gives the optimum tariff "for the two-good case."

This is substantially the Kahn-Little formula. The assumptions which have to be made to derive it are rather restrictive. In particular, it is, of course, extremely unlikely that all "cross-elasticities" will ever vanish identically.[21] Even when all goods are independent in production (i.e. when all productive factors are completely specific), they still compete for the consumer's income. Indeed, only when all consumer demand schedules have unit elasticity is it possible for a change in the price of any one good to have no effect at all on the demand for one or more of the others. When there is some degree of substitutability in production, and demand schedules are not thus circumscribed, the "cross-elasticities" must be taken into account. To neglect them is to commit the unjustifiable act of carrying over into general equilibrium analysis assumptions appropriate to partial equilibrium analysis only.

The objection to the use of formula (3) rather than formula (2) is twofold. Firstly, it may give an exaggerated idea of the height of the optimum tariff. And, secondly, it obscures the interesting fact that the optimum "tariff" is sometimes a subsidy. This fact is interesting because it throws light on the usual discussion on Tariffs and the Terms of Trade, in which the possibility of a subsidy on imports being required to turn the terms of trade in one's favour is seldom considered.

Economists have been aware of the possibility of a country turning the terms of trade in its favour by protection ever since the time of John Stuart Mill[22]—if not Torrens and Ricardo.[23] But the actual effect of a tariff on the terms of trade is a rather complicated matter, and has seldom been analysed in detail. The fullest theoretical treatment available is probably that provided by Dr. Mosak, to whose monograph on *General Equilibrium Theory in International Trade*[24] the reader may find it helpful to refer. Briefly, the position is that if we make the simplifying assumption that the government spends the proceeds of the tariff on exports only, the terms of trade must, in a two-country, two-commodity model, move in favour of the protecting country—unless the imported good is markedly inferior, so that the demand for it increases as its price rises. In a multicommodity world, on the other hand, it does not seem to be possible to generalise about the direction of the movement in the terms of trade—even when we abstract from the inevitable index number problem involved in saying what the tems of trade are when more than two commodities are traded internationally. The crucial factors turn out to be the relations of complementarity and substitution existing between the traded goods. They can turn the terms of trade in either direction.

---

[21] Mr. Kahn is aware of this when he warns that his elasticities are not true elasticities at all, but what might be called "elasticities in the Pigou sense." Cf. *loc. cit.*, p. 17 and A. C. Pigou: *Public Finance*, third edition (London, 1947), pp. 199–200.

[22] *Essays on Some Unsettled Questions of Political Economy* (London, 1844), pp. 26–30, of L.S.E. reprint.

[23] Cf. J. Viner: *Studies in the Theory of International Trade* (New York, 1937), pp. 298–99 and 320.

[24] Bloomington (1944), especially pp. 65–66 and 103–5.

The two-commodity case, however, is the one most theoretical economists have in mind when discussing problems of international trade. It is the easiest to handle geometrically; and by talking of "two bales of commodities" rather than "two commodities" it can be invested with a fictitious air of generality. It is not altogether surprising, therefore, that they should have tended to ignore the rather odd case where imports are markedly inferior and the Giffen Paradox operates, and to have acquired the habit of stating, without qualification, that the terms of trade will move in favour of the protecting country. Marshall, it is interesting to recall, did not do this. In his *Memorandum on Fiscal Policy*[25] he suggested that the Giffen Paradox might operate in respect of imports of wheat into England, and pointed out that if it did the effect of a tariff on wheat would be to turn the terms of trade against her. But the Giffen Paradox is not an everyday market phenomenon; and if it were it alone that could cause this perverse movement in the terms of trade, economists would be justified in dismissing the whole matter as a mere *curiosum*.

We do not live in a two-commodity world, however, and so it is not necessarily a *curiosum*. Our treatment has the advantage that it evades the difficult matter of what happens to the terms of trade and tackles the problem of the optimum taxes quite directly. It does seem, moreover, that when some of our optimum taxes turn out to be negative, those of us who are accustomed to think the matter through with reference to the terms of trade need not feel too suspicious. We need simply remind ourselves that in a multicommodity world the terms of trade is a rather elusive concept, and that—however useful —it may occasionally play us tricks.

Leaving the matter of the terms of trade, we might—before concluding this section—pause for a moment to consider the modifications that would have to be introduced into our earlier analysis if we were to relax the assumption that external economies and diseconomies are absent from both production and consumption. If they are present in production, our formula for the optimum taxes remains the same, but domestic prices must be corrected by the imposition of proportionate taxes to bring marginal private rates of transformation in domestic factories into line with the marginal social rates— otherwise the General Optimum will not be attained, even in the closed economy. If they are present in consumption, our simple formula is no longer correct, but it remains true that free trade will land us on the possibility locus in quite exceptional (one might almost say "degenerate") circumstances only. It is, therefore, in general, always possible to approach the locus more closely by imposing a suitable tariff structure. But the formula defining it is complicated, and little purpose would be served in deriving it here. It is worth noting, however, that it is still true that the attainment of the possibility locus requires that the marginal rates of transformation through foreign trade should equal the marginal social rates of transformation at home.[26]

---

[25] *Official Papers* (London, 1926), pp. 382–83.
[26] Cf. Mathematical Note, equation (7).

Finally, it hardly requires emphasis that throughout the preceding analysis we have stuck rigidly to statics, and ignored completely such important dynamic considerations as the probability of retaliation and the chance of protection in an important country precipitating a world slump.

IV. TWO PROBLEMS OF CONSISTENCY

There remain for consideration two problems of consistency. Both are related to the matter of estimating the probable height of an optimum tariff. The first is concerned with the extent to which protection is consistent with the maintenance of a high degree of allocative efficiency in an economy. In the welfare jargon of earlier sections, the problem might be phrased: Granted that the imposition of an optimum tariff structure will shift the possibility locus outwards, may it not twist, or even shift inwards, the efficiency locus—for may not protection give birth to monopoly, and so disrupt the allocative efficiency of an economy? This is one of those questions we cannot answer theoretically. But it does seem probable that considerations of this nature might require an appreciable *lowering* of the optimum taxes. They constitute an important qualification we should bear in mind when discussing the probable height of the taxes.

The point just made is closely akin to the classical distinction between revenue duties and protecting duties.[27] The burden of the former can be thrown on the foreigner, through the movement in the terms of trade; whereas the latter "are purely mischievous," to use Mill's phrase. The distinction should not be pressed too far, however, for any actual duty cannot but be a compound of the two: it will affect the possibility and efficiency loci to different degrees.

The second problem of consistency is concerned with Mr. Kahn's revival of Bickerdike's argument that the optimum tariff is likely to be "large" rather than "small." Bickerdike, it will be recalled, maintained that "rather strong assumptions have to be made . . . if the rate of tax affording maximum advantage is to come below 10 percent."[28] We are not here concerned with the fact that the formula on which this conclusion is based is itself dependent upon "rather strong assumptions" about "cross-elasticities" vanishing identically. The point is rather this: whatever the elasticities may be, there can be no escaping the fact that their magnitudes will depend upon the height of the tariff—they are functionally related. One relation which must exist between them at the optimum point has been produced, but there are undoubtedly others. Thus, consider the case where the foreign elasticity of demand is unity. This does not mean, as a simple substitution in Mr. Kahn's formula might seem to suggest, that the optimum tariff is infinitely high—for an infinite tariff is not consistent with a demand elasticity of unity. As the tariff grew one would expect the elasticity to change. Speaking very generally,

---

[27] Cf. Mill, *loc. cit.*, pp. 26–28; and *Political Economy*, Book V, Chapter IV, 6.
[28] *Loc. cit.*, (*Economic Journal*, 1907), p. 101.

there is perhaps a presumption that it will increase as the tariff grows; and there is perhaps a further presumption that the foreign supply of imports will become more elastic too. Both these changes would tend to *reduce* the height of the optimum tariff. It is not quite legitimate, therefore, to make deductions about its probable height from so simple a formula as Mr. Kahn's—one can never be sure that the values one attributes to the elasticities are, in fact, consistent with the tariff the formula indicates.

Once it is recognized that the elasticities depend on the height of the tariff, it is natural to ask if it is possible to establish rather more precisely the nature of the dependence. Into this matter I do not propose to enter. But it is probably worth pointing out that one of the obvious factors influencing the final result is the way in which the tariff affects the prices of imports and exports. This in turn depends in part upon *domestic* elasticities of demand and supply, and so upon the domestic distribution of income.

We have here the resolution of two paradoxes. The first is Mr. Kahn's[29]: that the optimum tariff formula should depend upon the foreign elasticities only. The second is one which may have troubled the careful reader: We have been making no interpersonal comparisons of well-being; we have merely been seeking a position on the possibility locus. There are an infinity of such positions, each corresponding to a different distribution of welfare. How is it that we have been able to derive a unique formula for the optimum tariff structure? The answer is that, while the formula is unique, the actual tariff structure it indicates depends very intimately indeed upon the initial distribution of wealth—for this is one of the factors determining the consistency of the elements in the formula. *Thus we have an infinity of optimum tariff structures, each corresponding to a different initial distribution of wealth, but all determined by the same rule.* We cannot judge between them without making interpersonal comparisons; and their existence makes it rather difficult to attach significance to attempts at discovering the "probable height" of an optimum tariff.

The situation is precisely analogous to that encountered in a closed economy. There we can formulate a rule such as "equate marginal cost to price" which is quite general. But this rule will not tell us how high prices must be until we know something about the pattern of demand, and therefore the distribution of wealth. Without a criterion for judging between different distributions we cannot say at what level prices and marginal costs are to be equated; and so we can say but little of the "probable height" of the prices.

This does not, of course, mean that we can never obtain any idea at all of the "probable height" of prices or tariffs, for it is at least conceivable that the infinity of possible heights will occasionally lie within a reasonably narrow range. But it does make the task of determining the range rather difficult. For this reason it may be thought that the preceding analysis has yielded few positive results. To a certain extent that is true. What has emerged very

---

[29] *Loc. cit.*, p. 16, bottom.

clearly, however, is that what I take to be Professor Scitovsky's main conclusion is even more firmly based than his treatment might lead one to suspect. His conclusion, the reader will recall, was that it is, generally speaking, the *rational* thing for each country, acting separately, to try to turn the terms of trade in its favour by protection—that there is nothing *natural* about free trade, and that if we want it to obtain we must see that it is *imposed and enforced*.[30] The analysis of this paper has refined the argument somewhat. It has shown that its validity depends in no way upon the possibility of making interpersonal comparisons of well-being,[31] or upon the absence of external economies and diseconomies in production and consumption. It has unearthed the rather odd case where the optimum tariffs are, in fact, subsidies, and it has established that (whether tariffs or subsidies) their imposition is *always* at least potentially beneficial, unless it impairs the allocative efficiency of the economy.[32]

Thus the force of Professor Scitovsky's conclusion is considerably strengthened. The moral to be drawn from it is too obvious to require emphasis.

V. MATHEMATICAL NOTE

Consider a community of N people. We adopt the convention that the services of productive factors are negative commodities, inputs negative outputs, and exports negative imports. Denote by x_i^α the quantity of the ith commodity consumed by the αth citizen. Then the utility indexes take the form:

$$u^\theta = u^\theta(x) \qquad (\theta = 1, 2, \ldots, N), \qquad (1)$$

where x is the row vector of x_i^α ($\alpha = 1, 2, \ldots, N$; $i = 1, 2, \ldots, n$). In a community where external economies and diseconomies in consumption are

---

[30] *Loc. cit.*, especially pp. 100–101 and 109–10. Cf. also Kahn, *loc. cit.*, pp. 18–19.

[31] Professor Scitovsky's treatment does not make this quite clear, since he bases his welfare judgments upon but two of the infinity of possible distributions of wealth—viz. that obtaining in the free trade situation, and that obtaining once the tariff has been imposed.

[32] The reader familiar with Professor Scitovsky's analysis of the optimum tariff problem will recall that he employs Marshallian offer curves superimposed on a set of community indifference loci; and that he is careful to distinguish cases where the community indifference loci intersect between the points representing free trade and the optimum degree of protection from those in which they do not intersect. In the former event we can, on his welfare criteria, make no statement about the desirability of the tariff; in the latter event we can say that it is desirable. What our analysis (which runs along lines rather different from Professor Scitovsky's) has shown is, in effect, that the community indifference loci can *never* intersect in the relevant range, unless the allocative efficiency of the system is impaired. I say "in effect" because it is rather difficult to translate our results into Professor Scitovsky's language, because he considers an exchange- rather than a production-economy, and because I am by no means clear on just what his community indifference curves mean. (Author's note, 1966: For a subsequent clarification of this matter, see R. E. Baldwin, "A Comparison of Welfare Criteria," *Review of Economic Studies*, XXI (2), No. 55, pp. 154ff.

unknown, we have u^θ independent of x_i^α for $\alpha \neq \theta$. For the moment, however, it is unnecessary to make this simplification.

We maintain the notation of Section III, and so have:

$$\sum_a x_i^\alpha = X_i + z_i, \tag{2}$$

where X_i is the home production, and z_i the net import, of the ith commodity. Our dynamic welfare theory is held to provide us with a domestic transformation function of the form:

$$T(X) = 0. \tag{3}$$

This tells us the maximum amount of any output we can obtain with given amounts of the other outputs, if our dynamic conditions are to be fulfilled— i.e. if correct provision is to be made for capital accumulation. Our dynamic welfare theory is also held to provide us with a foreign trade transformation function of the form:

$$F(z) = 0, \tag{4}$$

which tells us that, correct provision being made for foreign lending, trade must balance. The function F is specified more completely at the beginning of Section III.

Our problem is now to maximise, subject to (3) and (4), each in turn of the u^θ of (1), holding on each occasion all the other constant. The first order conditions can be written:

$$\sum_\theta \lambda^\theta \frac{\partial u^\theta}{\partial x_i^\alpha} + \mu \frac{\partial T}{\partial X_i} = 0 \qquad \begin{array}{l} (\alpha = 1, 2, \ldots, N). \\ (i = 1, 2, \ldots, n) \end{array} \tag{5}$$

and:

$$\sum_\theta \lambda^\theta \frac{\partial u^\theta}{\partial x_i^\alpha} + \mu' \frac{\partial F}{\partial z_i} = 0, \tag{6}$$

where μ, μ' and the λ^θ are Lagrange multipliers. It follows immediately that:

$$\frac{\partial T/\partial X_i}{\partial T/\partial X_j} = \frac{\partial F/\partial z_i}{\partial F/\partial z_j} \qquad (i, j = 1, 2, \ldots, n) \tag{7}$$

—i.e. that the marginal rates of transformation through foreign trade must equal those in domestic factories.

When there are no external economies or diseconomies in consumption, equations (5) and (6) reduce to:

$$\frac{\partial u^\alpha/\partial x_i^\alpha}{\partial u^\alpha/\partial x_j^\alpha} = \frac{\partial T/\partial X_i}{\partial T/\partial X_j} = \frac{\partial F/\partial z_i}{\partial F/\partial z_j} \qquad \begin{array}{l} (a = 1, 2, \ldots, N) \\ (i, j = 1, 2, \ldots, n) \end{array}. \tag{8}$$

This is the situation primarily considered in the first part of Section III.

Our final problem is to derive an expression for the slope of the possibility locus. Multiplying equations (5) and (6) by dx_i^α, summing over the i and the a, and taking account of equations (2), (3), (4) and (7), we obtain without difficulty:

$$\sum_\theta \sum_\alpha \sum_i \lambda^\theta \frac{du^\theta}{dx_i^\alpha} dx_i^\alpha = 0. \tag{9}$$

But, taking the total differentials of (1), we have:

$$du^\theta = \sum_\alpha \sum_i \frac{\partial u^\theta}{\partial x_i^\alpha} dx_i^\alpha \qquad (\theta = 1, 2, \dots, N). \tag{10}$$

Therefore, from (9):

$$\sum_\theta \lambda^\theta du^\theta = 0 \tag{11}$$

and so the slope of the possibility locus is given by:

$$\frac{\partial u^\alpha}{\partial u^\beta} = -\frac{\lambda^\beta}{\lambda^\alpha} \qquad (\alpha, \beta = 1, 2, \dots, N). \tag{12}$$

Now we have but to derive an expression for $\lambda^\beta / \lambda^\alpha$ $(\alpha, \beta = 1, 2, \dots, N)$. This may be done by selecting a subset of N of the $2Nn$ equations (5), (6), which are linear in the λ's. Thus, if we define the Nth order determinant, A_s, by:

$$A_s = \left| \frac{\partial u}{\partial x_s^\beta} \right| \qquad (s = 1, 2, \dots, n) \tag{13}$$

(α indicating the columns, and β the rows), and denote by A_s^θ the determinant obtained by replacing each element in the θth column of A_s by unity, it is completely straightforward to show that:

$$\frac{\lambda^\beta}{\lambda^\alpha} = \frac{A_s^\beta}{A_s^\alpha} \qquad (\alpha, \beta = 1, 2, \dots, N). \tag{14}$$

Thus:

$$\frac{\partial u^\alpha}{\partial u^\beta} = -\frac{A_s^\beta}{A_s^\alpha} \qquad (s = 1, 2, \dots, n), \tag{15}$$

which is seen to be independent of the particular choice of s; and the sign of which is invariant under any arbitrary transformations of the utility indexes of the form $\Phi(u)$, where $\Phi'(u) > 0$.

In a two-person community, (15) reduces to:

$$\frac{\partial u^\alpha}{\partial u^\beta} = -\frac{\dfrac{\partial u^\alpha}{\partial x_s^\alpha} - \dfrac{\partial u^\alpha}{\partial x_s^\beta}}{\dfrac{\partial u^\beta}{\partial x_s^\beta} - \dfrac{\partial u^\beta}{\partial x_s^\alpha}}, \tag{16}$$

which shows that the possibility locus can slope upwards only when external economies in consumption are marked and asymmetrical. That is to say: in a two-person community, the absence of external economies in consumption is sufficient for a downward sloping locus.

In the general N-person community in which there are no external economies or diseconomies in consumption, all the off-diagonal elements of A_s vanish, and so the slope of the locus reduces to:

$$\frac{\partial u^\alpha}{\partial u^\beta} = -\frac{\partial u^\alpha/\partial x_s^\alpha}{\partial u^\beta/\partial x_s^\beta} \qquad (\alpha, \beta = 1, 2, \ldots, N), \tag{17}$$

which is necessarily negative. But when external economies and diseconomies are present the slope can be either positive or negative. Indeed, even when there are no external economies in consumption—i.e. when none of the off-diagonal elements of A_s are positive—the locus can acquire a positive slope in a community consisting of more than two people. On most definitions of social welfare, however, this would not correspond to positions of maximum welfare: when the possibility locus slopes positively we can make everybody better off.

The pricing of public utility undertakings*

ALEXANDER M. HENDERSON

I

A controversy has developed as to the most desirable pricing policy of public utility undertakings.[1] The controversy arises from a desire to find a policy which can be applied universally and from the natural discovery that any policy which has been put forward produces nonsensical results in some cases. The solution here offered is simply an attempt to provide a framework which can be applied in concrete cases and will give rise to different pricing policies in different circumstances. But first two question-begging terms must be considered.

The term public utility is one applied over the nineteenth century to those services, especially water, some forms of transport, gas, and later electricity, in which it was seen that the normal regulating force of competition could not operate. It could not operate because legal or technical conditions imposed a local monopoly. Thus even if two rival water mains could be laid down in a street, there were serious objections to the double disturbance of the roads. In addition, so long as one water main could carry all the water required to the road, the first supplier would always be able to offer more favourable terms to consumers than a rival who was proposing to lay a second main. This is because laying of the main involves a large outlay compared with the marginal cost of supply additional water. The supplier who has made that outlay will reduce his price to marginal cost rather than allow a competitor to establish himself, while the new entrant will only lay mains if he expects his receipts to cover both the marginal cost and a return on the capital expenditure involved.

* *Manchester School of Economics and Social Studies*, 15(1947): pp. 223–50. Reprinted by courtesy of *Manchester School of Economics and Social Studies*.
[1] H. Hotelling, **"The General Welfare in relation to problems of Taxation and of Railway and Utility Rates,"** *Econometrica*, July, 1938; J. E. Meade & J. M. Fleming, **"Price and Output Policy of State Enterprise,"** *Economic Journal*, December 1944; A. P. Lerner, *The Economics of Control*, R. H. Coase, "Price and Output Policy of State Enterprise: A comment," *Economic Journal*, April 1945; T. Wilson, "Price and Output Policy of State Enterprise," *Economic Journal*, December 1945; R. H. Coase, "The Marginal Cost Controversy," *Economica*, August 1946 and subsequent controversy in *Economica*.

Only when the existing main is fully used, so that a new main must be laid whoever supplies the water, is competition possible. But then there is likely to be duplication involved at some other stage of distribution which will enable the existing supplier to underbid his rival. Competition would then work only through one firm expanding into the area of a neighbouring supplier or through the competition of suppliers trying to attract consumers to their area. But both forms of competition are too indirect and uncertain to be relied on, and, even at the height of *laisser-faire* opinion in this country, these industries were subjected to various measures of price regulation.

The reason then for regulation was that competition was impossible; and it was impossible because the average cost of production of each producer was falling. It is then convenient to use the term public utility to cover all cases where the market is too small to allow of more than one firm of optimum size. In all such cases competition is excluded and the same problems arise. This covers the traditional field of public utilities because they all involve large fixed equipment and are necessarily restricted to a local market. It may also cover additional cases. Imperfect competition presents very similar problems which are referred to in the final section.

The second preliminary difficulty is connected with the word "desirable." What is the criterion of desirability? It must be conceived in terms of the satisfaction of consumers' preference, since otherwise, no criteria of policy are available.[2] Two criteria are needed, that of efficiency and that of distribution. The efficiency criterion is that the marginal rates of consumers' substitution between different goods shall be the same for all consumers (since otherwise they can gain by interchange among themselves) and shall be equal to the marginal rates of producers' substitution. When this condition is satisfied, output of every commodity is said to be "ideal" relative to the distribution of income. This criterion can, in same cases, be satisfied by a number of different distributions of incomes as between persons.

When this is so, we need a further criterion to decide which distribution is to be preferred. This is an ethical or political choice which we must take as given by the preferences accepted in the community we are considering, and as interpreted, more or less imperfectly, by the political apparatus.

II

Consider first the simplest possible case. A bridge costs a certain sum to build and the cost is not thereafter affected by the number of times it is used. The marginal cost is nothing and the average cost simply represents the spread-

---

[2] It is not maintained that consumers' preferences as expressed in the market are the sole criterion of social desirability. But if consumers' preferences are accepted as constituting a criterion then it is of importance to examine how they are best satisfied, although the principles arrived at will have to be modified by the preferences of individuals as expressed through the ballot box (or it may be, in some formulations, by some general social purposes known only by revelations vouchsafed to some leader). See A. P. Lerner, "Statistics and Dynamics in Socialist Economics," *Economic Journal*, June 1937, p. 256.

ing of the fixed costs over a variable number of users.[3] There are then three problems to be solved:

i) if a bridge is built, what toll should it charge to users—what should be the price for its services?

ii) what is the criterion for deciding when a bridge should be built?

iii) If the answers to the first two questions involve a loss on the construction of the bridge, how should this loss be financed?

The first question is easy enough. Any toll charged will prevent the bridge being used on some occasions. But the cost of using a bridge, once it is built, is nothing and the loss of those people who are prevented from crossing it is a loss which is not compensated by a gain to anyone else. The best use of resources available is then obtained if everyone who wants to cross the bridge does so, and a toll prevents this. We can express this by saying that ideal output is reached with zero price.

The second question is more complicated. If the decision to build the bridge is taken by a private firm and financed by a toll, then the bridge will be built, provided the most advantageous rate of toll just covers the cost. This means that the receipts must cover the value of the factors employed in producing it, which is equal to the value of their product elsewhere (providing that in the alternative industries competition is perfect). But consider the case of a bridge which, on this criterion, is just not worth while building. If it is not built there will be losses under two heads which the investor does not take into account. First, those consumers who are willing to pay the rate of toll which the firm would fix include some who would be ready to pay more than that rate rather than dispense with the bridge. Thus if the bridge is built they receive a net gain above the toll they pay; if the bridge is not built that gain is lost. Secondly, there is the loss of the people who are unwilling to pay the toll which the private bridgebuilder will fix. They will only benefit providing the bridge is built and no toll is charged. Thus the criterion of profitability is not adequate for deciding whether the bridge is a gain for the community as a whole.

Suppose however that the owner of the bridge were in a position to charge different prices for each user so that each user paid the maximum amount he would be willing to pay for the use of the bridge on each occasion. That is, we suppose perfect discrimination to be possible. Then, since the cost to the owner of allowing someone to cross the bridge is nothing, every potential user who is willing to pay anything at all will use the bridge; the use of the bridge will be optimum. But the users gain nothing from the bridge since each time they use it they pay for the full value of that use. All the advantages accrues to the owner and none to the consumers. If the owner finds that, with perfect discrimination, his receipts exceed expenses, then its construction is a net gain

---

[3] This is the case considered by Dupuit, *Annales des ponts et Chaussées*, 1844, in the first treatment of the problem.

to the community—no one is worse off and the owner is better off than if it were not built.[4]

The criterion, therefore, for deciding whether the bridge should be built is whether it would meet its costs if it could charge on the basis of perfect discrimination.

These points can be made in terms of the Marshallian theory of consumers' surplus. In Figure 1, DD' is the demand curve, and AP the rate of toll which

Figure 1

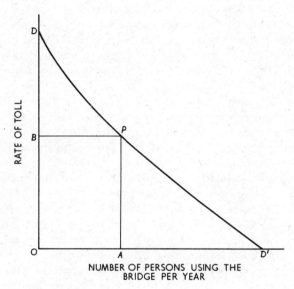

NUMBER OF PERSONS USING THE
BRIDGE PER YEAR

will maximize the bridge owner's receipts (the rectangle $OAPB$). The bridge will be built by a private *entrepreneur* providing these receipts exceed the annual cost of the bridge, but not otherwise. If it is built and a toll of AP

---

[4] This involves neglecting the producers' surplus accruing to the factors employed (see J. M. Fleming, *"Price and Output Policy of State Enterprise," Economic Journal*, December 1945, who considers that the producers' surplus may well be more important than the consumers' surplus). This can be covered by supposing that the bridge-builder can also discriminate perfectly in his purchases, so that both surpluses accrue to the bridge owners. In this article, however, the problems connected with producers' surplus have been neglected. This can be justified on the ground that they are of considerable complexity and that it is proposed to examine them in detail elsewhere. Thus it is assumed that the factors of production are in perfectly elastic supply to any given public utility. Where this is not justified it is easy, once we know what the producers' surplus is, to adjust the wording to allow for it. The difficulty is to know what it is. The recognition of producers' surplus as a relevant factor covers the point emphasised by Mr. Lerner (*The Economics of Control*), that, where the supply of factors to a firm is imperfect, marginal cost to the firm is higher than marginal cost to the community. The difference is the marginal producers' surplus.

charged, the consumers' surplus is represented by the area BDP.[5] The fact that a toll is charged means that all consumers for whom the use of the bridge is worth less than AP, lose a consumers' surplus represented by APD' although, *ex hypothesi*, no expenditure would be required to satisfy them. The discriminating monopolist would then have receipts represented by the whole area ODD' and every consumer to whom the bridge was worth anything would use it.

If the demand curve is a straight line, then if a private *entrepreneur* builds the bridge only half the potential users of the bridge will in fact use it and it will be built only if the total potential gain is twice the cost of the bridge.[6] This is some measure of the inefficiency of a system of providing public utilities on the basis of the revenue which can be obtained from them.

It now appears that for two reasons the bridge will fail to finance itself if the optimum supply of its service is to be obtained. Firstly, any toll will cause a maldistribution of resources and secondly bridges should be built which, on any practicable method of fixing tolls, would not be able to pay for themselves. The third question then arises as to how this loss is to be met.

The obvious answer appears to be that it should be borne out of the general Exchequer Funds—that is by taxpayers as an addition to the taxes which they are already paying. This is the solution maintained by Professor Hotelling[7] and Mr. Lerner,[8] but it is not wholly satisfactory. It neglects the fact that taxation is not a painless process and also that the beneficiaries from the bridge may be different from the people who have to pay the extra taxation.

Professor Hotelling relies on the fact that there will always be taxes which involve no cost to society. But in fact, though there may be some taxes which it would be desirable to impose even though there were no need for revenue (alcoholic drinks or possibly taxes on the very rich) all these taxes will already have been imposed. Nor are there available any neutral taxes in any modern state. If further outlays have to be met from the Exchequer, the additional taxes will themselves cause a maldistribution of resources. Professor Hotelling recognises this with respect to income tax, which causes a diversion from paid to unpaid activity (from work to leisure and also from earning to working for oneself), from risky to safe investment and from improving efficiency to

---

[5] This consumers' surplus is a sum of money and not (as Marshall sometimes implies) a quantum of utility. For present purposes the relevant consumers' surplus is that loss of income which exactly offsets the gain to consumers from the existence of a bridge charging a toll of AP. This is not exactly measured by the area under the demand curve, but in most cases the difference is of secondary importance (see J. R. Hicks, "The Four Consumers' Surpluses," *Review of Economic Studies* (Winter 1943)). The importance of the discussion of the complexities of the consumers' surplus is not that it proves Marshall wrong, but, on the contrary, that it shows how nearly right he was and how simply the adjustments can be made whenever it may be found necessary.

[6] Since if DD' is a straight line, $OA = AD'$ and $BPD = APD' = \frac{1}{2}OBPA$ (Figure 1).

[7] *Op. cit.*

[8] *Op. cit.*

avoiding taxation. He, therefore, argues that the deficit should be met from taxes on land rents.[9] But if the taxation of rents at a higher rate than other incomes is legitimate (and most of us probably feel that it is not) then they should be taxed 100 percent whether or not public utilities are to be financed out of general taxation.[10] Thus once again the additional expenditure incurred must be met from the normal sources of revenue: principally income taxes or indirect taxation.

Mr. Lerner is less explicit, but he seems to visualize the state distributing a social dividend which would be independent of other income.[11] Then if losses on public utilities had to be met this dividend could be appropriately reduced without causing a maldistribution of resources.[12] However a positive social dividend (except in a fully collectivised society where all income from property went to the state) is hardly conceivable unless state expenditure is financed from other taxes. Mr. Lerner considers the possibility of a negative social dividend—that is a poll tax. This would indeed be a solution; a poll tax, is from one point of view, the ideal tax, since it causes no maldistribution of resources. Unfortunately it is the most regressive tax, so that as a practical solution to the problem of obtaining revenue it is only available in very exceptional societies.

The position then remains that a full solution of the pricing policy of public utilities must consider both the advantage from operating them under conditions which must give rise to losses and at the same time the taxes which will have to be imposed to meet this loss. A bridge might produce a small net gain over its cost but if the collection of the additional taxation required to finance it involved a greater loss of consumers' surplus then it should not be built. The two sides to the problem must be treated together.

The other objection to making use of general taxation is that those who pay the taxes may not reap the benefit. To this, the answer, which runs through all economic reasoning since Adam Smith, is that if every change is made which benefits some more than it harms others,[13] then in the end everyone will

---

[9] H. Hotelling, *op. cit.*, pp. 256–57 also his " Prices and Marginal Costs in an Optimum System," *Econometrica*, April 1939; pp. 154–55.

[10] Providing that the revenue is required by the Exchequer. In fact income from rents is far below the tax requirements of public authorities in nearly all countries, and only a small proportion of these rents are payments for the indestructible powers of the soil.

[11] *Economics of Control*, p. 259.

[12] A change in the social dividend would affect the supply of labour, but it would not, as a change in the rate of income tax would, alter the rate at which income can be substituted for leisure. There is no economic criterion for deciding whether the supply of labour forthcoming with a social dividend of £1 a week is more desirable than that forthcoming with a social dividend of 5/-. But presumably there is some social criterion for deciding between them and if the finance of deficits from public utilities involves reducing the social dividend below the optimum, then a loss is incurred, even though no economic measure can be found for it.

[13] The comparison must be in terms of the money value of the gains and losses, since this is the only measure which admits comparison of one man's gain with another's loss. The merit of consumers' surplus analysis is that it shows that the comparison is always conceivable.

benefit more than he loses.[14] This is likely to be so, providing that the changes are numerous and the benefits and losses distributed at random among the population. But it need not be so. If we took bridges alone, then there would be a presumption that people living near rivers would be likely to gain more than the average. If we took the whole range of public utilities it might well seem that all would gain. But Mr. Coase has shown[15] that there is a presumption that the inhabitants of small towns would be more likely to gain than either city dwellers or countrymen. And in fact in most countries we find complaints that state help in this field has benefitted some areas or some classes at the expense of extra taxation borne by the whole community. Such charges are almost incapable of disproof and, whether they are justified or not, there is some objection to a policy which is almost certain to provoke them. There is, therefore, a presumption in favour of some form of financing which ensures that the people who gain from the bridge pay the whole cost as against making the deficit a charge on the national exchequer.

When a bridge is built, for which no toll is charged, for each user there is some reduction of his income which would leave him just as well off as before. This is his consumers' surplus.[16] The criterion as to whether the bridge should be built is whether the sum of all the consumers' surpluses which it produces exceeds the cost of the bridge. If then a method can be devised for charging a fixed annual sum to each user, adjusted so that no one has to pay more than his consumers' surplus, this will be the ideal method of charging.[17] As the sum is fixed it cannot be avoided by any change in consumption or the supply of factors, so it does not produce any maldistribution of resources. It does not cause any redistribution of income between taxpayers and bridge-users. Finally, and probably most important, it provides a check on the amount of investment.

This is a matter of the greatest difficulty. We can supply a formal criterion of the cases when a bridge should be built: when it would pay with perfect discrimination or, which is the same thing, when the consumers' surplus exceeds the cost. But how can we discover whether this condition is met in any particular case? Professor Hotelling considers that this is "not a historical but a mathematical and economic problem."[18] But it is not as simple as this. How do we proceed to discover the consumers' surplus obtained from the service of a bridge? If there has been a ferry it will be greater than the gross revenue from the ferry, but how can we attempt to guess how much greater? The only solution possible (and that is only possible in some cases) is to assess each user for a lump sum specifically attributable to the bridge and to allow

---

[14] Hotelling, *"The General Welfare" and Hicks, *"Rehabilitation of Consumers Surplus," *Review of Economic Studies*, February 1941. p. 111. (P. 328 above.)

[15] "The Marginal Cost Controversy," pp. 177–78.

[16] Strictly, the price-compensating variation.

[17] Subject to the exception that it may be desired to redistribute income in favour of the users of this bridge. Thus subsidising public utilities in depressed or isolated areas might properly be used as a means of equalising incomes in different parts of a country.

[18] "The General Welfare," p. 269.

them to refuse to pay—at the cost of never using the bridge—if the charge seems too high. The only person who can attempt to make an estimate of his consumer's surplus is the consumer himself.[19] Unless there exists some check which enables the consumer to compare the cost with the advantage, there is the serious risk of guesses being made which are wholly unrelated to the facts and which are never revealed as such. Once it is admitted that investments which are unprofitable may be justified, and that no practicable calculation will show whether they are or not, the way is open for any investment which is favoured by any public authority. In most cases it will be found that no complete check is possible, but some methods of financing are better than others at providing a partial check.

It is worth describing a case which occurs occasionally in practice and does achieve the ideal pricing system. Suppose a bridge to be contemplated by a small group of farmers who will have to bear the whole cost. Each will make up his mind as to what it would be worth paying to prevent the scheme falling through, that is, he estimates his consumers' surplus. If the cost is less than the aggregate consumers' surplus it will be built, if not, not. The farmers will meet and bargain, so that if the gain is considerable, the division of the costs will depend largely on ability at bluffing, while if the gain is small the costs will be distributed nearly in proportion to each farmer's consumers' surplus from the bridge. In this way a bridge may be built which no practicable system of tolls would finance and no user is prevented from using it because of a toll. But such a method is only practicable where the community is small. Where it is large, the individual contribution cannot be fixed by negotiation but must be determined by some authority on the basis of objective criteria. Even then, provided that the consumer knows how much he is paying for each form of public utility, some check is possible, since the consumer can protest through the ballot box if he thinks there is too much or too little investment.[20] But if he does not know he cannot protest.

III

It is simplest to judge various pricing policies by considering the ideal as charging a price equal to marginal cost (in the case of the bridge this is nothing). This will cause a loss which must be met by a tax, which may take various forms—income tax, local rates, a toll on users, or the sale of season tickets. Some of these "taxes" are ones that can only be levied by a taxing authority, while others can be levied by private *entrepreneurs*. The principle, however, is

---

[19] As Mr. Coase puts it: "If it is to be discovered whether consumers are willing to pay an amount equal to total cost, this can be done, under a pricing system, only by asking them to pay this amount."
"The Marginal Cost Controversy: Some Further Comments," *Economica*, May 1947, p. 151.
[20] It will be noted that this is the theory of neutral finance (see di Viti di Marco, "First Principles of Public Finance"). It must, however, be supplemented by the redistribution theory, which is based not on economic reasoning but on generally accepted social aims. Despite their different origin, the two theories can be combined.

the same. Some tax must be imposed and the problem is to find the best. Naturally there will not be *one* answer; the best tax will be different according to the detailed nature of any particular case.

First we must lay down the criteria for deciding which taxes are good:

1) ideal output from a given investment. A tax is good if it ensures that once investment has taken place it is used by all who are willing to pay the marginal cost.

2) ideal investment. A tax is good if it ensures that a bridge which cannot be made to pay with any rate of toll can still be built. It is also good to the extent that it ensures that bridges are not built where the cost exceeds the consumers' surplus. There is the double problem; the financing system must neither be too niggardly nor must it be too spendthrift.

3) distribution of the burden. A good tax is one which places the burden where political preferences wish it to be put. If the distribution of incomes was ideal before the bridge was built this involves putting it on the users of the bridge.

4) autonomous financing. Most recent discussions of this problem have ignored the influence of the method of financing on the organisation of the industry.[21] It is clear that if public authorities are to bear the losses they will have to control the operation of the enterprise. In a world where the future cannot be fully foreseen the loss to be made good will vary from year to year and depend on the efficiency of the managers. So whoever has to bear the loss must nominate and check the managers. This means not only nationalisation but nationalisation with political control of detailed operations. It is usually held that a private enterprise will have more incentives to efficiency than a state owned enterprise (though this may be more than offset by the fact that the state enterprise can aim to forward the interests of consumers, whereas a private firm will only do so under special conditions which are never present in the public utility field). Further, it is usually held that a public enterprise is likely to be more efficient, the greater the degree of autonomy it enjoys. But it can only enjoy autonomy if its financing is autonomous. Thus a pricing system that enables the enterprise to meet the loss involved by marginal cost pricing directly and without recourse to political authorities is, to that extent, preferable to one that does not. How important this consideration is depends on an estimate of the administrative advantage of autonomy.[22]

It will be noted that the question of the incentives to efficiency of operation of the enterprise, as opposed to the efficiency of investment decisions has not

---

[21] A notable exception is Mr. Wilson.

[22] The L.N.E.R. has proposed a system by which a large part of the fixed costs of the railways would be financed by the State, thus making marginal cost pricing possible, but the operation of the railways would remain in the hands of the railway companies. It would, however, be impossible for the Exchequer to agree to a system which might enable large dividends to be paid without strict control over the operation and dividends of the railway companies. Further a division of control between operation and permanent investment is impracticable.

been included as a criterion. Short of allowing full monopolistic exploitation (which is nowhere allowed) all systems of pricing of public utilities abandon the automatic incentive to efficiency which is supplied by the profit motive. How well any system will work depends then on detailed administrative methods of control and appointment. In general all that one can say is that autonomy of decisions makes efficiency possible, while the division of responsibility for decisions makes it very difficult.

Applying the four criteria of a good tax we can consider the following methods of financing the deficit:

a) subsidy from national funds; this is equivalent to an increase of national taxation, of which we need only consider an increase of income tax or of indirect taxes on consumption.[23]

b) the two-part tariff; this is a tax on real property as a condition of supply by the public utility.

c) subsidy from local funds; in the United Kingdom this is equivalent to a tax on real property.

d) average cost pricing; this is equivalent to marginal cost pricing plus a tax on the consumption of the service of the public utility (levied directly by the public utility).

e) discriminating pricing; this is equivalent to marginal cost pricing plus a tax on consumption at different rates for different classes of consumers.

All these methods of financing can be considered simply as different methods of raising the taxation necessary to cover the deficit resulting from the ideal method of pricing the services of the bridge. The advantages of these methods are discussed in detail, with reference to a wider range of public utilities than the bridge which has been used as an example. This involves anticipating some of the arguments of the following section and ignoring some of the complications which arise with other public utility pricing. It will be seen that each of these methods of taxation may be justified in particular cases and that there can be no *a priori* judgment that any one is always right.

(A) National funds

The advantage of this solution is that it makes pricing at marginal cost possible and that it enables investment to be undertaken which would not be possible if any of the last three methods were used. Where the advantage is local (as it is with so many public utilities) it has no advantage not shared with the use of local rates, but where the advantage is spread over a wider range it is the only method which can prevent the supply from the public utility being curtailed below what it should be. Railways, trunk roads, or (for the principle is the same) the defence services must be directed for the country as a whole

---

[23] An increase of the burden on the national exchequer should lead to an increase of all taxes already imposed, and possibly the addition of new ones. These are the main sources of revenue in most countries and can be taken as those which will be raised to meet additional outgoings.

and, therefore, financed on a national basis. This advantage has seemed conclusive to Professor Hotelling. But, as Mr. Coase has pointed out, it suffers from major disadvantages. It does not prevent the investment in public utilities from being expanded to the ideal level, but it does nothing to prevent it from being expanded beyond that level. It is liable to tax some for the benefit of others and it ensures the loss of financial autonomy.

If national finances relied on a poll tax, this would be the main objection. But in fact we must consider other taxes. An income tax, as already stated, leads to a maldistribution of resources and there is no reason why that maldistribution should not be as important as the gain from marginal cost pricing in a particular public utility. If the tax is an indirect tax on consumption, it means that marginal cost pricing is obtained in one industry at the cost of a departure from marginal cost pricing in some other direction.[24] There should be some gain, because the indirect tax could be placed on the product of the public utility (in which case we revert to average cost pricing); if it is not it is because some other indirect tax is thought to produce a smaller loss of consumers' surplus. But the gain may well be less than the loss of financial autonomy and of a check on over-investment.

To argue, therefore, that the use of general taxation must be the right answer in all cases of public utilities is wrong. It is equally wrong to maintain that it can never be. In the case of the use of roads and bridges by pedestrians, any other form of finance would be intolerably inconvenient. For railways the only alternatives are average cost or discriminating pricing, and a subsidy from state funds may well be justified. Most important of all, the general services of the state (for example, the defence services) are public utility services whose beneficiaries are the citizens of the country. The only method of financing them is through general taxation arranged so that the taxpayer pays no more than the consumers' surplus which he derives from them.

---

[24] It used to be held that all forms of indirect taxation (except those specifically required to equalise private and social net product) were always undesirable, and that all taxes should be on income or capital. If this were true we could ignore indirect taxation in a discussion of an ideal pricing system. But experience of very high marginal rates of income tax has caused a change of opinion in this country. It is now widely held that there is some theoretical reason for believing that indirect taxation has a smaller effect on the supply of the factors of production than income taxes. This is a mistake. The main advantage of a switch from direct to indirect taxation is that it can be used to reduce the degree of progression of the tax system. But the same change in the rate of progression can be obtained by altering the income tax formula and will have the same effect on the supply of the factors. However, there are important reasons for preferring some use of indirect taxation. Politically, the use of indirect taxation is an easier way of reducing the degree of progression; administratively, it may well be cheaper, and indirect taxation is less subject to certain kinds of evasion which arise with high marginal rates of tax. Finally, it is often maintained that the psychological reaction (and hence the effect on the supply of the factors) is different if the same progression is obtained by direct or indirect taxation. It is for these reasons (reinforced by the fact that all countries in fact make use of indirect taxation) that we must consider the possibility that, if public utilities are financed from general funds, this will mean an increase of indirect taxation.

(B) Two-part tariff

The principle of this method is that the consumer pays a fixed sum per year if he wishes to consume the product of the public utility at all and in addition he pays the marginal cost for each unit supplied. If the fixed sum were fixed separately for each consumer, so that no consumer was asked to pay more than the surplus he would derive from consumption, this method would be ideal. It would indeed be identical with the case of the farmers who have to decide whether to build a bridge. In fact, individual assessment is impossible and the fixed charge has to be related to some objective criterion. This means that it can be viewed as a tax on something other than the consumption of the services of the public utility. The usual method is to base the charge on the rateable value of premises.

This provides a check on excessive investment, since as investment increases the fixed charge has to be raised, and consumers have the opportunity of withdrawing. It does not indeed ensure that investment shall not exceed the ideal but it does ensure that it shall not exceed the ideal by so much as to exceed the consumers' surplus.[25] Further this method preserves autonomous financing by the public utility and ensures that the cost is borne by the beneficiaries. Finally it enables those who do decide to incur the fixed charge to consume the ideal quantity of the service supplied.

These reasons convince Mr. Coase that this is *the* right method of financing. There are, however, objections both theoretical and practical. It is true that the method allows those who are willing to pay the fixed charge to consume the ideal amount, but it also excludes completely those who consider the charge too high. The method is, therefore, only efficient for services where there exists some criterion which enables the charge to be related closely to individual surpluses. Whatever basis is used implies a tax on some form of outlay and, therefore, a corresponding diversion of resources. If the fixed charge is based on rateable value it is equivalent, for consumers, to an increase of rates and constitutes a discouragement to the construction of houses of high rateable value.

The value of this system in any given case depends wholly on the basis on which the fixed charge can be assessed; it depends on the tax it involves. For electricity it works well because the discouraging effect of the tax is small[26]

---

[25] Suppose there to be three sizes of bridges available for which the annual cost and annual consumers' surplus are as follows:

Size of bridge	Cost	Consumers' surplus
A	£100	£200
B	£200	£250
C	£300	£280

Then if consumers have to pay a fixed charge covering the cost of the bridge, bridge C will be eliminated, whereas it might well be built by a public authority financed out of general taxation. But bridge B will not be eliminated, although bridge A is the ideal (because an extra £100 spent only raises the consumers' surplus by £50).

[26] In Manchester the fixed charge is equivalent to a rate of 2/6d in the pound.

and because the tax corresponds fairly well to the surplus derived from the use of electricity at marginal cost, but even so it must exclude some consumers who would be willing to buy electricity at marginal cost. For gas this system of charging is restricted because of objections of this kind. For railways individuals differ widely in the use they make of service supplied and no basis for assessing the fixed charge can be found. In the limited sphere where the two-part tariff is easily applied, a strong case can be made for it, but it must not be forgotten that this sphere is very limited.[27]

(C) Local rates

A subsidy from local funds financed by rates appears to be quite different from the two-part tariff. But, except for the fact that it involves a loss of financial autonomy, it is exactly equivalent to the use of a two-part tariff in the case of any service which all ratepayers will consume. This is the case for the supply of water. The difference then arises solely from the loss of financial autonomy and the loss of the right to contract out if the fixed charge (or the appropriate element in the general rate) exceeds the consumers' surplus. The latter is an advantage where contracting out would involve costs to other people (for example, the refuse disposal) and is inevitable when consumers cannot be identified (the use of local roads or buses). Thus, this again is the proper method of financing for some kinds of public utility.

(D) Average cost pricing

This can be viewed as marginal cost pricing combined with an indirect tax on the service supplied. Once it is admitted that the loss arising from marginal cost pricing may be financed by indirect taxes, we cannot exclude the possibility that the best tax may prove to be one on the particular public utility which gives rise to it. Were it not for other factors this could be treated as a possible case, but one which could only occur rarely and by accident.

The method has the obvious disadvantages that it reduces the exploitation of existing investment below the ideal and reduces the amount of investment undertaken below the ideal. On the other hand it ensures financial autonomy and ensures that there is no redistribution of income from one section of the community to another. Finally it ensures, as none of the previous methods do, that investment is not excessive. Thus where financial autonomy is important, where the disadvantages of excessive investment are greater than of insufficient investment and where no suitable basis is available for a two-part tariff, the best available method of financing may well be to allow the enterprise to charge a price equal to its average costs.

---

[27] The case is strengthened because the two-part tariff is easy to apply where the requirement of a fixed installation for each customer makes it possible to identify customers. Where this is the case part of the costs are dependent on the number of consumers and not on the amount supplied. A fixed charge per customer to cover marginal consumer cost is, therefore, required as a component of marginal cost pricing.

(E) Price discrimination

This is a variant of the previous method, whereby the tax to finance the loss involved in marginal cost pricing is imposed on the consumers but at different rates for different classes of consumers. Where discrimination is practicable, differential rates can always be found which will increase output and investment above the level reached by single-pricing but which can never exceed (or, as perfect discrimination is never practicable, can never reach) ideal.[28] It is, therefore, preferable to a single price policy whenever it is practicable. In practice the scope for discrimination may be limited by the fact that maximising output might involve discriminating against classes of consumers whom it is desired, on social grounds, to favour. Discrimination by the railways has been handicapped in this way.

The standard examples of discrimination are railway rates and (as an alternative to the two-part tariff) electricity charges. Before the development of road transport railway rates were not unsatisfactory. The only alternative would have been finance through general taxation, and it is reasonable to believe that the nationalisation, which this would have involved, would have rendered railway development much less active—that it would have reduced rather than increased investment. In the climate of opinion of the nineteenth century, there was indeed no alternative and it may well be that the deviation from ideal output was negligible as compared with those caused by other factors. The complication has arisen from the competition of road haulage where pricing is on a wholly different system, and charges are much closer to marginal costs (despite the taxation of road hauliers). The result has been that while the underdevelopment of transport as a whole may not have been serious, the maldistribution of resources between road and rail did become serious. This had led to a system of controls by licensing road hauliers, and attempts to force up road transport rates. The latest attempt to find a solution, since these methods are likely to be insufficient, is the proposal to nationalize all transport both by road and rail. It is clear that the restrictive policy of the Road Traffic Act was highly inefficient, and it is likely that the Transport Commission, as long as it is bound to cover its costs both for rail and road separately, will be no less so. The inefficiency arises from attempts to force traffic to go by rail when the marginal cost is lower than for road transport, although the pricing system is such that the road charge is the lower. The system of financing is at fault and some modification involving finance of the railway losses either through general taxation or taxation on all forms of transport is necessary.[29] This illustrates the contention that there is no

---

[28] See J. V. Robinson, "Economics of Imperfect Competition," Chap. 15.

[29] The reason why the maldistribution of resources becomes more serious when average cost pricing is applied to close substitutes is that the maldistribution between any two industries is greater (for any given disparity between the ratio of the price to marginal cost in the two industries), the greater the elasticity of consumers' substitution for their products. In the extreme case where the elasticity of substitution is zero, no maldistribution occurs. A similar case is that of the competition of gas and electricity. Gas is largely supplied at average cost and electricity by a two-part tariff or discriminating rates and there is, therefore, a tendency to eliminate gas even though the marginal cost may be lower than that of electricity.

unique right method of finance for public utilities. The appropriate method depends on the detailed conditions of each case, and these may change from time to time.

IV

The argument has so far developed in terms of a public utility for which the marginal cost is zero. There are several cases of public utilities of which this is true, broadcasting being the most striking example.[30] But for most public utilities the marginal cost will be positive. Then, if in all other industries, price is equal to marginal cost, ideal output will be obtained if price is equal to marginal cost. But if average cost is falling, fixing price equal to marginal cost involves a loss. This loss must be financed by some tax, with the alternatives discussed in the last section.

Certain complications, however, arise. Where, in other industries, competition is not perfect and hence prices exceed marginal cost, pricing of one product at marginal cost will produce an output in excess of the ideal.[31] The ideal distribution of resources between industries will be obtained if the ratio of prices to marginal cost is the same in all industries. But if prices are above marginal cost the supply of factors of production will not be ideal.[32] This suggests that, if we are concerned with price fixing for a particular public utility and must take as given the fact that for all other products price equals marginal cost multiplied by some factor $a(>1)$, then ideal output will be achieved if in this public utility price is fixed between marginal cost and $a \times$ marginal cost. Where the ideal price will lie in this range depends on the effect of this price on the supply of the factors, and on their distribution. A similar problem arises when one industry provides a close substitute for the product of one where the ratio of price to marginal cost is very different from that in the mass of industries. Thus, if prices are twice marginal costs on the railways, and equal to marginal costs in all other industries, then to reduce road charges to marginal costs would involve expanding the resources available to the transport industry towards the ideal, at the cost of reducing the output of the railways further below the ideal. An intermediate price would then be appropriate.

The second complication concerns the control of investment policy. It has been maintained that if prices are fixed equal (or proportional) to marginal cost there is an automatic criterion as to the amount of investment which should be undertaken.[33] This is only true if we are concerned with the amount of investment undertaken by an enterprise which already exists, and if the amount of investment can be treated as a continuous variable (that is, if there

[30] Another example is the exploitation of inventions considered by Professor Polanyi in "Patent Reform," *Review of Economic Studies*, Summer 1944.

[31] See A. F. Kahn "Notes on Ideal Output," *Economic Journal*, January 1935: and J. R. Hicks, *"The Rehabilitation of Consumers' Surplus," *Review of Economic Studies*, February 1941 pp. 114–15.

[32] See Lerner, "The Economics of Control," pp. 102–4.

[33] See J. A. Nordin, "The Marginal Cost Controversy, A Reply," *Economica*, May 1947, p. 143.

are no significant indivisibilities of plant). In this case, long period average and marginal cost curves can be drawn up, and ideal output is obtained when price is equal to both short and long period marginal cost.[34] The former ensures that ideal output is obtained from given capital equipment, the latter that the ideal amount of capital equipment is available. But this criterion does not help to decide whether or not the enterprise should be established at all. For this exactly the same problem is involved as with the bridge; it is necessary to compare the consumers' surplus with the loss involved in marginal cost pricing. The problem is to this extent easier: if there is some scale at which an enterprise can meet its costs by any method of charging, then there must be a gain from establishing it. That gain will be maximised if price is equal to long and short period marginal cost.[35] If investment is only possible in discontinuous lumps a long period marginal cost curve cannot be drawn up. The problem of estimating consumers' surplus arises again, but in a less intractable form, so that if the lumps are small relative to the size of the enterprise a moderately accurate criterion of investment policy is possible.[36] The problem of investment is, therefore, only to a minor extent the problem of the amount of investment by existing enterprise; it is rather the problem of when an enterprise should be established.

The major complication of public utility pricing arises from the fact that costs do not depend uniquely on output. They depend also on the number of consumers and the time and place of supply. The principle involved in marginal cost charging is simple, though its application may not be. Each consumer must pay the total costs of the enterprise if he does consume its products, less the costs the enterprise would incur if he did not consume at all. In many cases this will involve multipart pricing to ensure that this principle is applied to the consumer's consumption in the aggregate and also to each component of that consumption. Thus the telephone subscriber must pay the installation cost, a rent for his telephone, and a charge for each call dependent on the

---

[34] See J. Viner, "Cost Curves and Supply Curves ,"*Zeitschrift für Nazionalökonomic*, September 1931, and Lerner, "Statics and Dynamics in Socialist Economics," *Economic Journal*, June 1937.

[35] Professor Nordin (*loc. cit*). is wrong in maintaining the contrary. He overlooks (in his chart III) that, if there are two products A and B, the production of a negligible amount of B may involve the use of resources which could have produced a concrete quantity of A. The transformation curve might be $ACDB$ in Figure 2. Both should be produced if the indifference curve tangential to CD cuts Oy above A and Ox beyond B. It is not possible to discover whether this is so by fixing prices proportional to marginal cost.

[36] Suppose, in Figure 3, DD' is the demand curve, MC_1 the existing marginal cost curve, and MC_2 the marginal cost curve if an additional investment costing £A is carried out. Then the consumers' gain from this investment if price is reduced from CG to FH is $BCED$ in respect of the gain to consumers who would have bought at the higher price, plus CEF for the units which are only sold owing to the reduction of price. The investment should be undertaken if the gain $BCFD$ is greater than £A and not otherwise. $BCED$ can be estimated before the investment is carried out with as much accuracy as any other forecast of the results of investment. CEF can only be estimated by making assumptions as to the shape of the demand curve. But the smaller the indivisible lumps, the smaller CEF relative to the total gain.

Figure 2

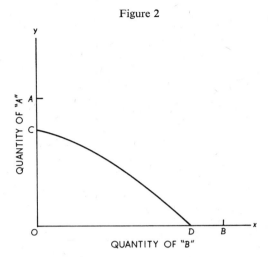

QUANTITY OF "B"

distance. Multipart pricing which arises from this factor may (but need not) be combined with the two-part tariff discussed in the last section as a method of financing the loss incurred by marginal cost pricing. In the sense relevant here, multipart pricing is a component of a system of charging marginal cost.

Finally a complication arises from the fact that marginal costs may fluctuate widely over short periods. If the ten o'clock train to Liverpool has vacant seats one Monday morning, the marginal cost of carrying an extra passenger may be negligible. On Tuesday, however, there may be a rush and a

Figure 3

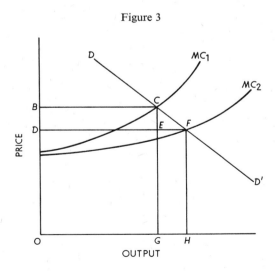

OUTPUT

"special" be required, so that the marginal cost is high. But such variation in charges would be inconvenient to the extreme.[37] If it is decided that, to enable consumers to plan in advance, the same charge must be made on both Monday and Tuesday and that the rate shall only be changed once a year, what then is the marginal cost? The only solution is to average the marginal cost over the range for which uniform prices are decided.[38] This solution is a compromise between exact equality of marginal cost and price and the gains of convenience both to consumers and the enterprise from some degree of stability. Since it involves charging more than marginal cost to some consumers and less to others[39] it produces some maldistribution of resources which can be reduced only by increasing the number and flexibility of different rates.

V

Finally reference must be made to the application of this analysis to an imperfect market. In an imperfect market price exceeds marginal cost for each firm. Therefore firms are not producing their ideal output.

Suppose that all firms are compelled to equate price to marginal cost. Then each firm must try to expand output. But all firms cannot do so simultaneously. If all firms are affected equally they will all be producing the same output as before and their marginal costs will have risen to equal price. But the profits of each firm will be reduced and some will go out of business.[40] Therefore resources are set free, which enables the remaining firms to expand, and at the same time raises the demand curve for all firms still in business. This reduction of the number of firms will continue until such time as the demand curve is sufficiently raised, and the cost curves sufficiently lowered for the demand curve to cut the average cost curve at its intersection with the marginal cost curve.[41]

---

[37] Mr. Lerner points out: "price changes should not be made more rapidly than the adjustments to them are made by the producers or consumers who determine how much will be bought or sold," "The Economies of Control," p. 216.

[38] Thus, if the fare must be 20/- or 20/6d. (or some multiple of sixpence) and the number of passengers will be P_1 or P_2, respectively, and the total cost of the railway C_1 if the lower price and C_2 if the higher price is fixed, then we can define this "averaged" marginal cost as $(C_1 - C_2)/(P_1 - P_2)$ then if this is greater than 20/3d. the fare should be 20/6d. or higher; if it is less than 20/3d. the fare should be 20/- or lower.

[39] See R. H. Coase, "The Economics of Uniform Pricing Systems," *Manchester School,* May 1947.

[40] This can be illustrated by a diagram. (See Figure 4.) Let AC_1 and MC_1 be the average and marginal cost curves when firms are maximising profits, and DD' and MR be the demand and marginal revenue curves. The competition for factors resulting from the attempt to expand output from OA to OB leads to a rise in the marginal cost curve until it passes through P. This must also raise the average cost curve which therefore no longer passes through P.

[41] See R. F. Kahn, *op. cit.,* p. 24.

Figure 4

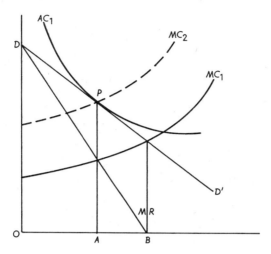

If we treat consumers' preferences as wholly irrational,[42] this method of regulating imperfect markets is satisfactory and is superior to Mr. Kahn's method of making all markets equally imperfect. It is superior because it ensures the optimum supply of the factors in addition to their optimum distribution between industries.

It is, however, unrealistic to consider all, or even most, consumer preferences as irrational.[43] But if we do not make this assumption, the enforcement of marginal cost pricing involves the elimination of firms and with it a loss of consumers' surplus. As Mr. Kahn has shown, the gain from the elimination of a firm may, or may not, exceed the loss of surplus from the reduced choice available to the consumer. No practicable test is available to discover whether a particular source of supply should be eliminated or not. This is so because the consumers' surplus derived from the existence of firm *A* depends on whether firms *B* and *C* continue to exist. Thus even if we know the complete

---

[42] Such a position is reached only if there is an optimum size for every type of industry. Mr. Norris obviously assumes that there is not for retail trading ("State Enterprise Price and Output Policy," *Economica*, February 1947, pp. 57–58). If in any type of business the optimum size turns out to be so large that one optimum firm would be too large for its market it has to be treated as a public utility (section II and III). There is the related problem that in many firms it is impossible to discover marginal costs with any degree of accuracy. Even so, marginal costs can be used as a criterion of policy, to the extent that they can be estimated.

[43] See J. R. Hicks, *"The Rehabilitation of Consumers' Surplus," p. 116.

preference scales of every individual the condition as to which firms should remain could only be expressed in an insoluble system of inequalities.[44]

We revert, therefore, to the problem of section III. There is a justification for maintaining some sources of supply which would fail to cover their costs with marginal cost pricing, and if they are maintained their ideal output will be achieved with marginal cost pricing. The cost must be borne in some way and, since the two-part tariff is not available,[45] the alternatives open are nationalising and finance through state funds, or average cost pricing. But the government, if it bears the loss and has no criterion of the firms it should retain, must feel a strong incentive to the concentration of production in the interest of efficiency and the elimination of losses. The alternatives seem to be between the operation of Mr. Lerner's rule, with the reduction of the scale of consumer's choice, and the retention of the present system of average cost pricing in imperfect markets. The latter system maintains consumers' choice (and will indeed probably provide more than the ideal variety of choice) at the cost of productive inefficiency and a distorted supply of the factors.

The choice between these methods is, therefore, not dictated by the logic of economic reasoning. It can only be based on a personal estimate of the relative importance of maintaining variety of choice, or of eliminating the wastes of imperfect competition.

---

[44] Professor Meade has raised a similar problem, "suppose that industries X and Y produce close substitutes (gas and electricity) and that each involves the employment of an individual factor. Should the community produce (a) no gas and no electricity, (b) some gas but no electricity, (c) some electricity but no gas, or (d) some electricity and some gas" ("Mr. Lerner on 'The Economics of Control,'" *Economic Journal*, April 1945, p. 60). With only two industries, the solution is simple, providing we assume more measure of the consumers' surplus derived from a single commodity. For then, if one of the two products shows an excess of consumers' surplus over loss in operation (assuming the other is not supplied), the product which gives the larger net gain should be supplied. Once it is supplied, it is possible, *ex hypothesi*, to decide whether the other also provides a net gain. But with three this is no longer true. Suppose them to be gas, electricity, and district heating, we can know the consumers' surplus for each on the assumption that the others are not supplied. But it does not follow that the one which gives the largest net gain should be supplied. So we must then take the surplus from each pair, assuming the third not to be supplied. If there are n products, we need to consider the consumers' surplus from $2n - 1$ products or combinations of products. That combination should be supplied which gives the largest net gain. This can only be done by knowing all transformation and all indifference curves. As a criterion of policy this can be ruled out.

[45] See W. A. Lewis, "The Two-Part Tariff," *Economica*, August 1941, pp. 262–63.

General and specific financing of urban services*

WILLIAM S. VICKREY

The purpose of this paper is to reexamine the degree to which municipal services are properly financed from (1) general purpose taxes, levied without close attention to the way in which the taxpayers benefit from public services or affect the costs of rendering them, and (2) specific taxes, fees, and prices that attempt to reflect these costs and effects more closely. To some extent the concern with bringing payments more closely into line with costs and benefits is related to concepts of equity, in that it is conceived to be in some sense proper that those who enjoy benefits or give rise to costs should, in the absence of countervailing considerations, pay accordingly. But more weight, on the whole, is given in the current investigation to the possibility that such correlation of charges with costs and benefits can be made to increase the efficiency with which services are utilized, prevent waste, and in general improve the patterns along which our mushrooming metropolitan areas will grow. Indeed, it is this latter consideration that leads to a dissatisfaction with a mere statistical or average balance or proportionality between benefits and contributions and an insistence on a greater precision of detail: situations can easily arise in which groups of more or less similarly situated individuals share a cost equally and hence no individual is in fact treated unfairly, yet if the institutions are such that no one person can reduce his share in the cost by suitably economizing or restraining himself, the amount of the service demanded and supplied may be grossly excessive.

GENERAL CRITERIA

In determining whether an attempt should be made to pay for a municipal service by means of a specific charge, a number of general principles or criteria can be referred to; their specific impact varies, of course, from case to case. One of these concerns the distributional impact of the charge relative to that of the general tax that it might displace. In many cases this differential

* In H. G. Schaller (ed.), *Public Expenditure Decision in the Urban Community* (Washington, D.C.: Resources for the Future, 1963). Chapter 4, pp. 62–90. Corrected and abridged by the author. Reprinted by courtesy of the author and Resources for the Future.

will be small enough or uncertain enough in its direction to be considered a wholly secondary matter, but in particular cases it is important and even paramount. In New York, for example, a straight increase in transit fares can be considered almost tantamount to a poll tax in its incidence, and certainly far more regressive in its distributional impact than even the sales tax. The distributional impact of an attempt to finance educational, hospital, or welfare services entirely by direct charges would obviously be so unacceptable as to preclude such a solution, at least in its simple and direct form.

Another general principle that can be appealed to is the extent to which the proposed charge can be related to benefits derived from the service in a way which will appeal to concepts of equity. This immediately raises the question of how to measure the benefit: should it be in terms of the cost of providing the service to the individual concerned or in proportion to the amount that the individual would pay rather than go without the service altogether? To what extent, for example, should water charges be based on the income of the user, or be differentiated according to the cost of his obtaining water from another source? It seems fairly clear that answers given to such questions will vary widely from case to case and that the variation will have to be explained on grounds other than a general adherence either to cost or to utility as a basis.

Indeed, one factor that will often enter into the general attitude taken is the nexus, as perceived by the public, between the payment made and the benefit received. In many cases this perceived nexus will be significantly influenced by historical development. A new service accompanied by a new charge is likely to generate a vivid conception of a *quid pro quo*; a new charge made for a preexisting service is more likely to create a feeling of inequity, even if the charge is a necessary means of preserving the value of the service, as in the case of the ferry that is worthless as long as it is free (because then queues accumulate until it is just as quick or convenient to detour via a bridge or tunnel), or where transit services are subsidized in part from funds obtained from highway use charges. Another element in the perception of this nexus is the manner of payment: a toll is immediately visible as an out-of-pocket cost financing a distinctive service; a gasoline tax is slightly less so; payment for a sewer connection may evoke different attitudes, even though computed on the same base, according to whether it is merely included in a global tax bill paid to a municipality performing all of the various functions itself, or paid as a separately itemized item on a consolidated tax bill, or paid separately as an entirely distinct transaction. All of these may have a significant effect on the way in which the relation between benefit and burden is perceived by the general public and in the degree of acceptance of this relationship.

More attention is to be paid here, however, to the matter of allocational efficiency. This in effect means extending the concept of marginal cost pricing as far as possible into the realm of municipal services with the intent of attaching, to each choice by individuals that affects municipal operations or that has an impact on others in the community, a differential charge that will properly represent these impacts to the individual. Ideally, this charge would serve to coordinate decentralized decision making on the part of individuals into a harmonious whole. In many areas, however, it will be an adjunct, though an important one, to more centralized planning activities as represented by building codes and zoning ordinances.

Moreover, even in the absence of pressures arising from considerations of progressivity and of equity perceptions, it will in practice be impossible to approach even very closely to this theoretical idea. The relative social costs occasioned by alternative choices contemplated by individuals cannot be measured, in many cases, with anything like complete accuracy, and in other cases the costs of carrying out the measurements would be such as to outweigh the benefits. Even where the costs can be ascertained with adequate accuracy, the costs of assessing the corresponding charges may be great, and in some cases the terms of the assessment might tend to become so complicated as to be beyond the comprehension of the individual making the decision, and thus be ineffective in securing the improvement in the allocation of resources that was the original *raison d'être* of the more elaborate assessment. And finally due consideration must be given to the fact that in nearly all cases, even with the fullest possible utilization of specific charges, municipalities are almost always in such pressing need of funds that they must have recourse to general taxes that themselves have adverse effects on allocation. Consequently, by virtue of the general principle of "second best," if any specific charges are to be made, they should in nearly all cases be designed in part to contribute to the public treasury over and above the amount that would flow in on the basis of charges strictly reflecting marginal costs.

SPECIFIC CASES

General principles are seldom as enlightening in the abstract as in their application to specific cases, and accordingly some specific examples are discussed in the remainder of the paper which will serve to illustrate their application and explain their meaning. In considering specific cases, we will include on the one hand some items that may not ordinarily be thought of as municipal services, but which would lend themselves to financing by methods ordinarily associated with municipal finance; and on the other hand some municipal services, including some of the more important ones, will not be considered because of the inherent difficulty of applying to them the methods being considered here.

Fire protection

Fire protection accounts for some 7.6 percent of all general expenditures by cities. It serves here as a striking example of the difference between benefit and cost as a basis for charging.

Actually, fire protection is considered most appropriately paid for on the basis of property assessment, and in terms of benefit this is a fairly good basis. Benefit can be roughly measured in terms of the reduction in insurance rates on protected as against unprotected property, and in terms of the enhancement of land values in view of the provision of the protection to any structures built on the land. The value of land plus improvements would accordingly seem to be a good measure of benefit. Even here, of course, there are cases where increased property value fails to indicate increased benefit: replacing an old, obsolescent building with a modern fireproof one may lessen the amount of benefit obtained from fire protection even though the value of the property be increased.

Viewed from the cost side, however, the picture is entirely different. Providing a given grade of fire protection to an area is almost entirely a matter of providing an engine company within a suitable distance of the property, or more operationally, within a suitable number of minutes of travel time. The National Board of Fire Underwriters, in setting standards for fire protection, requires as a rough rule of thumb that in residential areas a company be stationed within about 1.5 miles for a property to be considered adequately protected; for industrial and commercial property, apartments, and the like, the distance is shortened to 0.75 mile, while for areas containing only widely scattered residences a distance up to 3 miles is tolerated. There are in addition minor differences in the cost per engine company: in business and industrial areas a complement of seven men on duty is considered normal, whereas in residential areas five men on duty may be considered sufficient; in addition the property occupied by the fire house may be more valuable in the former case. Roughly speaking, therefore, the ratio of the cost of protecting an acre of residential area and that of protecting an acre of business area may be about one to five (leaving the fringe areas out of consideration, for the moment). This is a much smaller range than the corresponding range in assessed values, in most cases.

From the point of view of resource allocation, however, it would not be sufficient to remain content with property values as the basis for paying for fire protection even if it could be shown that these costs in fact varied in proportion to assessed value. An increase in the value of the improvements in a given area, through new construction or otherwise, does not in any significant way increase the cost of furnishing a *given grade* of protection to the property already there, even though it may make it worth while to provide a higher and more costly grade of protection. Even though in principle the construction of new buildings in a given area may increase the frequency of fires within the area and thus might increase the probability that the equipment might be out on another call when fire breaks out in a given property, this is normally a very minor factor, made quite negligible in most cases where alternate protection is normally available from adjacent fire companies. The basic act that is causally related to the need for added fire protection is the occupancy of land in the protected area. It is the exclusive occupancy and not the nature of the occupancy that counts: if an acre of land is used for tennis courts or a clay products depot, involving of itself almost no fire hazard, the displacement of the occupancies that might have used this land to outlying areas where new fire protection will have to be provided is a cost that should properly be assessed against such uses. Similarly it makes no difference to the cost to be assessed against a given acreage whether it is developed with residences on half-acre lots or row houses cheek-by-jowl, even though this might make a difference to the way an insurance company might rate the hazard.

Accordingly, the appropriate way to charge for fire protection would be on the basis of area. Possibly some gradation in the charge might be made in terms of distance from the fire house, but in most cases this would be a negligible factor. An exception might be made where the protected area dependent on a given fire house includes both residential and business property: areas zoned for business and located within the 0.75 mile distance might be assessed at a higher rate based on the higher degree of protection offered and the need of business for this higher grade of protection if it is forced to locate elsewhere by inferior occupancy of the business-zoned area. In this case it would be the nature of the zoning rather than the nature of the occupancy that would be the appropriate basis for the distinction in the charge. Moreover there is in a sense a joint product problem here: a given fire house required to provide residential-grade protection for the 1.5 mile radius necessarily provides incidentally for business-grade protection within its 0.75 mile radius. On the one hand if the inner zone thus generated is greater than the demand for business sites, the business-grade protection is a by-product to be provided at no marginal cost, the residential occupancy bearing the full burden; on the other hand if the business demand increases so as to require the provision of an additional fire house, the additional residential protection, if enclosing some unoccupied but developable land, is likewise a by-product, and the full cost of such a fire house should be borne by the business protection area.

Translating the charges thus indicated into an actual tax is of course another matter. In the long run it would probably not make too much difference if the assessment were made on the basis of land value rather than land area, as any difference between the two forms of charge could readily be capitalized into the land value. In the short run transitional effects would arise, but consideration of these effects will have to be relegated to another analysis. In any event it is clear that on a cost basis, the basis for assessment is clearly land value, exclusive of improvements, in spite of the fact that at first glance the benefit basis would seem to indicate that it is improvements that should be assessed.

Another factor associated with fire could be the basis for the assessment of charges—the external economies associated with what are technically termed "exposure fires," i.e., fires not starting on the premises under the same ownership. Individuals who take precautions against fire are not only reducing their own risk, but that of their neighbors. To the extent that they are reducing their own risk in recognizable ways, they may qualify for lower insurance premiums, but since neighboring properties are insured by independent companies, and indemnities are paid regardless of the source of the fire, these rating allowances of necessity include no allowance for reductions in the likelihood of contagion or exposure losses. It would accordingly be of some merit for property tax assessments to make some small concession to structures that are fireproof or are sprinklered or are otherwise protected, over and above what building codes may make mandatory. The tax concession could even be more widely applied than building codes, since the latter are often full of grandfather exceptions; in some cases the tax concession might even motivate an improvement where otherwise the owner would be willing to hide behind an excepting clause.

Too much should not be made of this, however: over the period 1953–59 the property loss claims from exposure fires amounted to $221 millions, which is 7.2 percent of losses from known causes, which in turn was 45 percent of total losses. Since exposure fires probably constituted a relatively low percentage of the " causes unknown " category, such losses probably amounted to not more than 4 percent of the total. Though the principle may be applicable, the practical consequences are *de minimis*.

Water supply

In water supply we are faced with a wide range of situations as to source of the bulk supply, but the over-all characteristics of distribution tend to be somewhat more uniform, and we will discuss the latter first.

In some fortunate areas, reasonably pure water may be available from a nearby source in ample quantities, so that the main problem is one of distributing this supply to users. Moreover the economies of scale in water main size are so substantial that it is only a minor oversimplification to say that the cost of the mains is proportional to their length and relatively independent of the required volume of flow. Another factor tending to warrant such a simplification is that for fire protection purposes a certain minimum size main is required to provide the flows needed for fire-fighting purposes.

The problem is how to relate the total length of main required to the nature of the occupancy of the area. It is tempting to say again that area is the critical factor, but this is overruled by the observation that if we take two communities that are laid out in a similar pattern, but on different scales so that streets and mains are twice as far apart in the one community as the other, while lots are four times as large, the second community will only require twice the length of mains. The simplest rule would be to use the front foot as the unit; this however produces awkward results when applied to corner lots, but even so is perhaps the best simple rule available. One can of course expect any minor variations in the system of charges to become capitalized in the price of the lots, in this case, so that the corner problem is perhaps not a crucial one. The same is true of variations in the relative amount of frontage associated with various lots due to odd shapes, curves in the street, and the like. It would be tempting to try some more general linear measure of lot size, such as the square root of the area, or the maximum diameter, but these would produce results that make the aggregate charge for a group of lots vary according to the way the total area is subdivided in ways that bear no very close relation with the length of mains required.

In smaller communities endowed with an ample source of supply this may be all that marginal cost pricing requires; there would remain, in addition to the cost of the mains, the cost of the collection and purification system and the transmission aqueduct from the source to the edge of the community. In many cases the incremental cost of added capacity may be so low as not to warrant the cost of installing and reading water meters. These intra-marginal costs not covered by explicit charges for mains can then be covered out of general revenues, or from any other source on the basis of "least harm." One source would be surcharges on the cost of the mains; not only would this probably not be too much of a distorting influence, but it would have considerable public appeal on equity grounds. Actually, data for 1959 indicate that over-all expenditures for water supply amount to $1,423 million as against revenues of $1,201 million, indicating some support from general revenues, though since expenditures are largely on a cash rather than an accrual basis, with considerable confusion between current and capital outlays and probably a considerable understatement of real interest and amortization charges, this conclusion should be made with caution.

In many cases, however, especially in the more densely populated areas and arid regions, the incremental cost of the gross supply will be a significant factor. The problem is complicated by the large size of the lumps in which increments to supply are often available, the great durability of the facilities, and by the significant seasonal and random fluctuations in the supply furnished by given facilities. Under such circumstances charges according to the amount of water used are obviously in order, but have in the past been justified far more on grounds of equity than on grounds of controlling the use. Indeed, the idea of using water charges to ration use seems quite at variance with typical attitudes of water supply engineers, who seem to view their function as one of providing an ample supply almost regardless of the cost of meeting whatever standard they decide to set, and limiting the charges to the user to whatever minimal rates prove necessary to finance the scheme over all, regardless of what the incremental cost of the particular supply involved happens to be.

Reluctance to use water charges as a means of rationing use is illustrated in the fact that rates generally remain much the same from one season to another and from one year to another. To some extent this is the result of sheer administrative inertia, but to a considerable extent it represents the view that to raise rates at a time of shortage represents exploitative profiteering that is considered undesirable and even immoral, regardless of whether the beneficiary is a private individual or a public body. Nevertheless, to an economist, at least, the possible improvement in the allocation of resources through such variation in rates should be fairly obvious, the main question being how difficult such variation would be and how important the benefits that would result.

Variations in supply may arise either as a regular seasonal phenomenon, or irregularly as a result of variations in rainfall or large accretions of capacity. In all three cases variation in rates would improve resource allocation, but the difficulty of applying the changes varies considerably. One difficulty common to all three situations is that meters are usually read quarterly, and often on a rotating schedule, so that it would be difficult to bring the impact of the rate change to bear on all consumers simultaneously. In a system having large reserves, where a situation of shortage or abundance can be expected to persist over several quarters, or in the case of the addition of large increments of supply, it may be sufficient to continue a quarterly pattern, simply pro-rating the consumption indicated for a given quarter into the portions of the quarter falling into the low and the high rate periods. This works fairly well with utility bills at present, where rate changes occur, but in such cases the rate changes are relatively minor and the principal issue is one of equity; it would be relatively less satisfactory where rate changes are of a magnitude intended to be sufficient to affect consumption. Then the discriminations would be somewhat more severe and the dilution of the incentive to economize during the latter scarcity part of a quarter, by reason of the fact that such consumption would be prorated back to the earlier or abundance part (and vice versa in case of rate reductions), would be of significant concern. Ideally, extra meter readings should be arranged as nearly as possible to the time of the rate change, so as to minimize this prorationing effect; possibly this might be done economically by combining them with electricity and gas meter readings. Self-reporting by the consumer, such as is often practiced either for interim readings or where the regular reader was not able to gain access to the premises, would seem somewhat less feasible here than where no rate change is taking place: with constant rates there is ordinarily no significant incentive for the consumer to falsify or fudge his report of the meter reading, and even where there is, the consumer would often have to be fairly sophisticated and prescient about his future consumption to take advantage of the opportunity; where a substantial rate change is involved, both the magnitude of the incentive and the clarity to the consumer of the direction in which it is to his advantage to misreport would operate to make misreporting more of a problem.

One objection to fluctuating rates is that they make it more difficult for the consumer to budget, particularly with rates that fluctuate with unpredictable variations in rainfall. The problem would be less significant with predictable seasonal fluctuations in rates. Unlike a private utility, a municipality is in a position to offset changes in water charges with changes in the general property tax rate, so that what the average consumer would gain on a given occasion in lower water rates he would lose in higher property taxes, and vice versa; the incentive for conservation of water in times of shortage would remain. In effect, a substitution effect is generated while the income effect is minimized.

With water more than with most other utility services, the tenant who turns the tap is often insulated from the impact of water rates by their inclusion in his over-all rent, and for this reason rate variations may be less effective here than with other services. Such use is however relatively inelastic to price in any case, and control at such points is hardly worth while. There remains, in any case, the incentive for the landlord to pay special attention to leaks and other outright wastage and for economizing in large-scale industrial use, lawn watering, and the like.

One need not necessarily maintain that rate changes can entirely take the place of water conservation campaigns in times of threatened shortage, but high water charges should provide a significant reinforcement for such campaigns, if they become necessary. Certainly such charges provide a more efficient means of rationing than such methods as the prohibition of certain uses at certain times, or in extreme cases the shutting off of the supply in various areas at various times, with the attendant danger of contamination and increased fire hazard.

Variable rates should permit considerable economies to be made in scheduling expansion of supply. Given a means of efficiently controlling the demand in cases of drought of rare intensity, it will be less necessary to expand supply quite so far to take care of such contingencies. Similarly, it will be less necessary to plan new additions to supply quite so far in advance, since a faster than anticipated growth in demand or shortage due to subnormal rainfall can be adapted to more effectively. On the other hand, new additions to supply can be used more fully and more promptly upon their completion if charges are reduced or eliminated as long as the supply is ample.

However, a policy of raising charges prior to the completion of a new project and lowering them when it is brought into production means a drastic change in traditional modes of financing public works. To the extent that funds are accumulated out of the earlier high rationing charges, the project will be more nearly on a "pay-as-you-go" basis; on the other hand, after the new supply becomes available, there will be no funds flowing from water charges to pay off the balance of the cost until such time as the new addition is being fully utilized and rationing charges are again needed. Whether or not this pattern can be followed in its pure form will of course depend on the over-all fiscal and financial pattern of the municipality, but substantial changes in financial procedures are indicated in any case, even if the limiting situation is not a feasible one.

There is one further difficulty with drastic variation in rates over fairly long periods: consumers may be induced to install water-using equipment, such as nonrecirculating cooling equipment, on the basis of current low rates only to find that when rates are later raised their investment turns out to have been unprofitable. In principle, of course, consumers should be put adequately on notice of the likelihood of water rates being increased in the future. Fortunately, most decisions of this sort that involve substantial fixed capital and that would be significantly affected by water rates are of a commercial or industrial nature. In such instances the decision-maker can be presumed to be sufficiently sophisticated to take account of such a prospect.

Transportation facilities

The over-all picture of the finances of urban transportation conceals a great deal of inefficiency and distortion within an aggregate picture that seems spuriously close to being in balance. Aside from a few outstanding instances of substantial subsidy, such as the New York subways and rail commuter service, it appears superficially that the transit rider is about paying the costs of the service he uses. Likewise, for motor traffic as a whole, revenues from user charges seem to be roughly in balance with outlays on facilities: in 1957 total tax revenue from all motor vehicle related sources, including licenses, fuel taxes, manufacturer's excises, tolls, and parking meter revenues amounted to $8,162 million; expenditures directly on highways amounted to $7,931 million, not counting that part of local police expenditures of $1,290 million that could be regarded as spent for traffic control (roughly one-tenth, judging from the number of police assigned to traffic duty in New York City), or the portion of the $562 million of "other sanitation" expenditures that could be regarded as spent for snow removal and other traffic-related purposes.[1] On this basis one would be inclined to doubt whether there is any large scale misallocation of traffic between various modes, or substantial under-or-overutilization of facilities.

When looked at in more detail, however, the picture is quite different, especially when full economic costs not represented adequately in the financial accounts are added in. If we attempt to separate out the urban component of the motor vehicle revenues and expenditures, we find that in 1960 the forty-three largest cities spent $600 million on highways, exclusive of police and sanitation expenditures for traffic related purposes. Of this only $289 million was financed from vehicle user charges in terms of any explicit flow of funds: $155 million from state highway grants and $134 million from city licenses, parking fees, and user charges, leaving $311 million, or 52 percent of the total outlay to be defrayed out of general revenues.[2] In 1957, all cities spent $2,941 million on streets and highways, of which only $1,471 million, just 50 percent, was derived specifically from use-related charges.

To get closer to the allocation of resources, however, we cannot stop here for the relevant matter is not through what channels the funds flow, but whether, on balance, the charges the motorist pays, to whatever governmental agency, correspond to the costs they occasion, in whatever form and by whatever agency these costs are borne. (Indeed, one could argue that the general purpose grants from state to local governments include some highway funds.) Figures of this sort are harder to come by. However, in a recent study of the Philadelphia metropolitan area, it was found that

---

[1] U.S. Bureau of the Census, *Census of Governments, 1957* (federal excise taxes added).
[2] U.S. Bureau of the Census, *Compendium of City Government Finances in 1960*.

in 1957 total motor vehicle tax charges allocable to use of motor vehicles in the city of Philadelphia amounted to $30 million to all levels of government, but that motor vehicle expenditure by all levels of government for facilities within the city amounted to $46 million. Thirty-five million dollars of this was spent by the city itself, of which only $6.5 million was financed by grants from federal and state highway funds, and by user charges (chiefly parking meters), leaving $28.5 million to be financed from general revenue sources.[3] While this is only one instance, there is no obvious reason to suppose that the total cost of facilities being provided in Philadelphia is significantly higher relative to use than in other metropolitan areas, nor that the level of charges being paid by motorists is significantly lower. On this basis motorists in large cities appear to be paying only about two-thirds of current expenditures made for the facilities they use.

To obtain the true economic cost of urban traffic facilities, however, it is necessary to go even further than this and substitute, in place of current capital outlays, an appropriate rental charge representing interest and depreciation or amortization on the value of the facilities used. The current capital outlays to be substituted for, as representing provision for future use rather than for current use, amounted to $351 million out of a total of $600 million for the forty-three largest cities; for all cities in 1957 the figure is $754 million out of $1,753 million. But what to put in place of these figures is something of a problem. Farrell and Paterick, of the Bureau of Public Roads, put the value of the depreciated investment in urban street and highway improvements at $10.2 billion as of January 1, 1953; $11 billion would seem a reasonably rough figure for 1957.[4] A figure of $8.25 billion for the value of land in city streets was produced by the Federal Trade Commission for 1922;[5] a more recent estimate appears not to be available but by considering trends in property values, a 1957 value on this basis of $21 billion seems roughly reasonable. At 4 percent interest on the total value of $32 billion, plus 2 percent amortization on the depreciated improvements, this gives $1,500 million to be substituted for the $754 million of current capital outlays in figuring true economic cost. The full annual economic cost of city street use thus comes to $2,319 million, as compared with actual outlays of $1,573 million, exclusive in both cases of police and sanitation. Even at this, the computation includes no equivalent for property taxes or corporation income taxes that would be covered by rental payments for the use of privately constructed property requiring comparable amounts of land and construction. If property taxes were figured at 1 percent on the full value (in 1956, assessments of $280 billion were estimated to represent 30 percent of full value, or about $930 billion; property tax collections were $11.7

[3] Philadelphia Bureau of Municipal Research, *Improved Transportation for Southeastern Pennsylvania* (Mary, 1960), pp. 294, 314.

[4] Proceedings of the 32nd Annual Meeting of the Highway Research Board, January 1953.

[5] National Bureau of Economic Research, *Studies in Income and Wealth*, Vol. 12, p. 547.

billion)[6] $326 million would be added to the bill; in addition if as little as 20 percent of the investment were financed by equities, with a net return to equity holders of only 4 percent, the corresponding corporation income tax of 52 percent would add $277 million to the cost. With these elements added in, urban vehicular traffic is found to be paying $1,050 million in charges as compared to roughly $2,916 million that users of comparable resources in the private sector of the economy have to pay.

Obviously, if there is a way in which the cities can collect an additional $1,866 million from urban vehicular traffic so as to bring the charges more nearly in line with the costs, it would not only help to improve the resources allocation pattern but would ease the financial pressure on municipal governments very substantially. (Total city revenues from all sources were $13,748 million in 1959.) Unfortunately, there has hitherto been no easy way to approximately triple the charges payable by the urban motorist without excessive interference with the smooth flow of that part of the total traffic that has a legitimate and urgent need for the use of the city streets. A number of techniques for doing this have, however, been developed recently.[7] It remains to be seen, however, whether what is economically sensible can be made politically palatable.

Some demurrer to the assignment of all city street costs to vehicular traffic is often entered on the ground that in addition to carrying through traffic such streets also serve as "access" to the adjacent property, and that the cost of such an access function is properly chargeable against the property owners rather than against the users as such. To be sure, if conditions are such that the roadway is no more elaborate than that which would be required to provide a mere access, and if traffic conditions are such that there is in fact no interference with other users of the roadway during such "access," then the marginal cost of such use is effectively zero in the short run, and charging the entire cost of the access street against the property owner would be conducive to unrestrained use of the uncongested facility, so that efficiency would be served. The bulk of the cost, however, particularly in view of such factors as the use-related character of much of the outlay for renewal of pavement and the high proportion of the property values accounted for by the downtown areas, is more nearly chargeable against users than abutting property owners. Even when a vehicle is performing an access function, its impact on traffic and on costs may be substantial; the amount of these costs is a function of the movement of the vehicles performing the access function and is not related in any direct way to the value of the property accessed. While some allowance might legitimately be made for the access function of low-traffic residential streets, this allowance would be small. Moreover, even on equity grounds, one could well raise a question

---

[6] U.S. Bureau of the Census, *Statistical Abstract of the United States, 1961*, pp. 403, 418, 419.

[7] An extensive survey of these techniques is given in R. J. S. Smeed, *Road Pricing: The Economic and Technical Possibilities*, H.M. Stationery Office, No. 55–411 (1964).

as to whether the charge for the provision of common access facilities would not be more fairly allocated according to amount of use, rather than according to the value of the property accessed.

For example, even where a cul-de-sac is used almost solely for access purposes, with no traffic movement other than that destined to one of the abutting property owners, if conditions of use are such that there is interference between users, some means of bringing the cost of this interference home to them directly is needed. This can be done conveniently if the costs associated with providing the area and the pavement are assessed against users in proportion to use. It is both inequitable and inefficient to charge these costs to the abutting property owners under these circumstances, making the abutting occupant whose business requires relatively little use of the access facility pay just as much as his neighbor whose operations seriously interfere with the ease of access of the adjacent occupants. Some of the most serious congestion in New York is the result of the way in which " access " is had to firms in the garment district.

The special problem of the rush hour. The disparities in treatment between various forms of transportation are even further aggravated by the nature of rush-hour conditions. Nearly all forms of rush-hour transportation are grossly underpriced. In 1951, at a time when the fare of 10 cents on the New York subways was just about covering operating expenses, it was estimated that the marginal cost of a moderately long rush-hour ride was somewhere between 20 and 40 cents, possibly even higher in some cases. The differential between rush hour and nonrush hour or between rush-hour costs and average over-all costs varies widely as among alternative forms of service, so that even if various forms of transportation were on an equal footing over the entire week, either each paying its way or being subsidized by about the same proportion, this still would not bring about an economical allocation of traffic among the various modes during the peak hours. For one thing transit systems can handle overloads in general much more readily than highways, by putting more persons into the same vehicle, and while this causes some deterioration in the service, sometimes to a truly inhuman degree, there is no complete breakdown. On the highways, on the other hand, there is no mechanism whereby increased traffic flow results in more persons riding per car, and there is a rather strong tendency for the system to jam up once a critical flow has been reached. Another and more important factor is the distribution of traffic through the day. At one extreme, commuter railroads handle half of their total traffic during the fifteen peak hours per week; for subway traffic the figure is about one-third, while for expressway traffic on routes to and from the central city the proportion is about 18 percent. This means that when costs are averaged over the entire traffic flow, the rush-hour traveler, who should bear the bulk if not the entire amount of the cost or providing the capital facilities, is able to shift over four-fifths of this burden to nonrush riders if he is an auto rider, but only two-thirds if he is a subway rider and only half if he is a rail commuter. Differentiation of the charge between peak and off-peak use is thus not only a matter of encouraging peak use and discouraging off-peak use, but it is also a matter of inducing the selection of a suitable mode of transportation given the time and volume of travel.

. . . .

Peak-off-peak transit pricing. The problem of suitable pricing of transit service to take account of the variations in cost between peak and off-peak service is relatively simple, at least for subway and commuter lines, and need not concern us here. . . .

An interesting suggestion has been put forth in connection with subscriber fare systems for suburban service: it would be at least conceivable that the agency furnishing the service should be set up as a membership organization along cooperative lines, and if so, one might argue that the subscribers should be entitled to deduct that part of their payments representing interest on capital and taxes, somewhat as the owners of cooperative apartments do. The deduction would have at least this much rationale: commuting to relatively low rent suburban housing is a more or less direct substitute for the payment of higher rentals in close-in housing. Indeed, one could present the further case that with the commuter service the efficiency of allocation of resources is being fostered rather than otherwise by the discrimination, in that the service is one offered under conditions of decreasing costs; this much cannot be said of the deductions for interest and taxes on dwellings. But this is admittedly stretching matters pretty far.

Financing the intramarginal residue in urban transportation. While the most urgent need is to increase charges on rush-hour service of various kinds, especially motor vehicle usage, there will remain, ultimately, a fairly substantial portion of the cost of urban transportation that cannot be fully allocated on marginal cost principles. On equity grounds many would argue for allocating this residue as a charge added to marginal cost and paid by the users, and the second best principle would support this treatment at least to some extent. Thoroughness, however, requires that some attempt be made to trace out the way in which the assessment of transportation costs affects urban land use.

In this area more than most, extreme models produce paradoxical results. Land values are widely held to be created, or at least enhanced by transportation developments, particularly those that produce changes of mode or nodes in the transportation network. Indeed at times it almost seems as if it is imperfections in transportation that create land values. Where transportation has uniform costs, models seem to indicate that the better transportation is, the lower land values will be, as for example with the assertion often made that if transportation could be made instantaneous and costless, site value would disappear. Even with less extreme models, if demand for urban land as a whole is considered to be completely inelastic, and if rents are made to vary so that for all developed urban land the sum of rents and the transportation costs required by the activities carried out on the land to and from the center of the model is constant, then land rents are proportional to total transportation costs, and cutting transportation costs in half will preserve the the same geographical pattern of activity with rents likewise cut in half.

A considerably different model emerges if we admit some elasticity into the demand function for access to the urban center, the amount of access being measured by the area of land occupied and the price of access being the sum of land rent plus the cost of a uniform amount of transportation per unit of land from the site to the center. If for simplicity we assume that all land uses have the same transport-to-the-center requirement, and that the elasticity of the demand function is unity, then the total price paid in terms of rent plus transportation cost is constant, and of this total price one-third is rent and two-thirds is transportation cost. The total cost can be thought of as a cylinder of height $h = tr$, where r is the radius of the developed area, and t the transportation cost per unit distance; at the edge of the cylinder transport cost is tr and rent is zero; at the center transport cost is zero and rent is tr; total rent can be represented by the cone fitting into the cylinder, which will have one-third of its volume. As the transport cost t increases, r shrinks (as the cube root of the transport cost rate), rents at the center rise, but the developed area shrinks, so that outside the developed area rents fall to zero. With a more elastic demand curve for access to the center, total rents would increase as transportation costs fall, but rents at the center would still fall, the increase being accounted for by enlargement of the developed area.

In order to produce a model in which improvement in transportation raises rents at the center, it would be necessary to produce a demand curve for access to the center which is in a sense perverse, i.e., in which the larger the aggregate, the more a given buyer is willing to pay for access to the center, and in which this effect is so strong as to outweigh the diminishing marginal utility of access to a center of a given size to successively less eager buyers. In other words if the Nth renter is willing to pay R for access to a center of size N, then even though the $N + 1$st renter would be willing to pay only $R - \delta$ for access to a center of size N, the Nth renter is willing to pay $R + \delta + \epsilon$ for access to a center of size $N + 1$, and the $N + 1$st renter is thus willing to pay $R + \epsilon$ for access to a center of size $N + 1$. Such an upward sloping demand curve would indeed imply that a decrease in transportation costs would increase the marginal value of access to the center, and hence increase rents throughout the developed area. Thus it is possible for an improvement in uniform transportation to increase property values at the center; but whether the economies of scale in urban aggregations of the present size of most of our large cities are still significant enough to bring about this result would seem to be unlikely on an impressionistic basis.

On balance it seems likely that improvements in uniform transportation, as exemplified by travel in private automobiles over a standardized network of city streets, would benefit owners of outlying property more than owners of centrally located property, and that if intramarginal highway costs are to be charged against property values at all, they should be charged primarily against peripheral property values rather than against central property values. Indeed some of the deterioration observed in downtown areas over a period coinciding with the growth of the automobile relative to transit's decline is rather suggestive of the agreement of reality with some of the above models; this result may not be any adventitious one resulting from strangulation by inadequate development of facilities, but may be an inherent property of a nonfocusing transportation system.

Models reflecting node effects. Models which will reflect the focusing effect of a transportation system with pronounced nodes are rather hard to come by, and it seems reasonable to suspect that a number of other facts, such as the variation in the relative demand of activities for space and for transportation, the possibility of linkages that do not pass through the center, the possibility of creating space through building upward, and the effect of the aggregate magnitude of activity on the demand for space would all interact with the existence of transportation nodes in affecting the pattern. . . .

. . . One might hazard the guess that significant differences would emerge between the patterns that result when transportation costs are uniform as compared to what they are when transportation along certain channels is specially favored. If this expectation is substantiated this would be a further reason for using property tax revenues to subsidize node-creating transit rather than unfocused motor vehicle transportation.

Rationales for subsidy of one mode by another. If for one reason or another outside financing cannot be obtained to meet the intramarginal residues of transportation as a whole, there still may be sound justification for financing the intramarginal residues of mass transit by the levying of charges on urban motor traffic, even if these charges cannot be made to vary closely with the diurnal and other variations in congestion. In one sense, such a use of motor vehicle user revenues for the finance of transit would be merely the equalization of the subsidy that now is given to the urban motorist, partly in the financing of actual outlays on streets out of property taxes, and partly in the failure to account at all for the rental value of the space the motorist occupies.

In some cases a politically more acceptable rationale can be derived from adventitious historical circumstances, as when it is proposed to turn some of the San Francisco Bay Bridge toll revenues over to the Bay Area Transit Authority, on the ground that originally the bridge did carry rail transit cars of the Key System, and the tracks were later removed to make way for additional roadways. The plea is made that this diversion of tolls is in lieu of the recapture of the bridge space for rail transit use. Actually, while use of the bridge would be considerably cheaper in capital cost than the present plan to construct a new tunnel for the transit system under the bay, use of the bridge would be rather less satisfactory because of the awkward approaches that would be required and the severe speed restrictions that seem inevitably to apply to rail equipment operating over suspension bridges.

A more basic argument for subsidy of this sort can be derived from the following example, however, which illustrates how far off the "every tub on its own bottom" philosophy can get when misapplied to what seem superficially to be aggregates of similar tubs (even without an introduction of decreasing costs!). Suppose a facility of type M attracts rush-hour and nonrush-hour passengers in the ratio of 1 to 4, and costs $1 for each rush-hour passenger provided for and $0.20 for each nonrush-hour passenger. On the other hand a facility of type T costs only $0.75 for each rush-hour passenger and $0.15 for each nonrush-hour passenger, or uniformly 25 percent less; however, it attracts only one nonrush-hour passenger for each rush-hour passenger. If no differentiation between rush-hour rates and nonrush-hour rates is possible, facility M can break even with a charge of [$1 + 4($0.20)]/5 = $1.80/5 = $0.36; for facility T the break-even fare is ($0.75 + $0.15)/2 = $0.90/2 = $0.45. Thus with each facility required to be self-liquidating, the passenger is offered a 9-cent fare differential in favor of facility M, alike in the rush hour and in the nonrush hour, whereas the consequence of his choosing facility M rather than T is to increase the costs, by 25 cents in the rush hour and 5 cents in the nonrush hour.

Of course, if it were true that if five rush-hour and five nonrush-hour passengers were to shift from T to M, they would automatically convert themselves in some way into two rush-hour and eight nonrush-hour travellers, then the 9-cent reduction in fare that they would obtain would be justified. But there is no reason to expect any effect in this direction, and an effect of even a fraction of this magnitude would be a highly unlikely occurrence. Actually, if peak-off-peak differentiation in charges is impossible for one reason or another, the next best thing would be to reverse the relationship between the charges, and raise the charges on M to 45 cents and lower the charges on T to 35 cents, resulting in a subsidy of about 25 percent to T from excess revenues of M. If for the M facility we read streets and highways and for T we read suburban rail service, the correspondence with the typical facts is reasonably close. Thus if charges for peak use are ruled out, there is an even stronger case than would exist otherwise for subsidizing mass transportation at the expense of vehicular traffic.

Police and custodial service

Police expenditures amount to slightly over 10 percent of city expenditures, ranking below education and sanitation, but are perhaps less amenable than most other services to financing by means of specific charges. There is nevertheless something to be gained by an examination of the ways in which the revenue structure can be brought more closely in line with the costs of performing this service.

Unfortunately, not very much is as yet known concerning the specific factors that influence or should influence the level of police service provided. In New York City, under a "Post Hazard Plan" promulgated in 1955 and subsequently revised, an index of the relative volume of police problems in the various areas is used as an aid in allocating personnel. The index uses the following items with corresponding weights: Crimes of personal violence, 0.25; other crimes and offences, 0.20; juvenile delinquency, 0.15; accidents and aid cases, 0.10; population, 0.10; area, 0.05; business establishments, 0.05; school and recreation areas and crossings, 0.05; and radio alarms transmitted, 0.05. Obviously, at most 0.20 of the total weight is assigned to factors that could be made the basis for some form of tax, and even here the basis is impressionistic rather than based on any rigorous study.

There would seem to be a relatively close relationship between the characteristics of buildings in an area and the magnitude of the policing problem. But even if this can be substantiated, it is not clear how this relationship could be converted into a tax base and whether it would be desirable to do so if it could be done. Buildings converted to single room occupancy may appear to increase the policing problem, but it is at least possible that a tax on such occupancy would only result in the tax being passed on very largely to tenants. Indeed, to the extent that police problems are most intense in low income neighborhoods, it may be almost inevitable that any attempt to levy a tax in proportion to some factor that seems to be causally related to policing costs will result in a severely regressive levy. This can be illustrated, for example, if it is proposed to allow some sort of tax credit for the provision of doormen, full-time janitors, and the like, whose presence would tend to reduce the policing problem.

There is, indeed, a whole array of situations where the line between private and public policing is unclear. At one time it was the practice in New York for city police to be detailed as guards to accompany payrolls and other similar transfers. This had serious ill-effects: gratuities were often offered in connection with this service, to the detriment of morale; the gratuities failed in most cases to cover the full cost, so that in effect an incentive for converting to a payment-by-check basis that should have been brought to bear was held off. A further effect was the diversion of unduly large numbers of police to this duty at peak periods near weekends. In some instances police are hired to perform such duties during their off-work hours; this also may lead to abuses. Similar difficulties occur in conjunction with sporting events and other occasions where large numbers of persons are assembled. The range over which this problem of drawing the line between that for which the public police department will be responsible and that which is a private responsibility is a wide one. At one extreme, the Morningside Heights Association has recently arranged for a corps of private police to patrol the areas as a supplement to the city police. At the other there is said to be at least one case where the municipal police deliver the morning newspapers as a part of their early morning patrol. While this could obviously cause difficulty if carried too far, there are obvious complementaries between patrolling an area and performing other functions that may be worth taking advantage of, and of course if police are involved in such activities, the possibilities for obtaining revenues by appropriate charges should not be overlooked. But on the whole there is at this stage little that can be said definitely about appropriate modifications of revenue structures on the basis of their impact on police expenditures.

Recreational facilities

Expenditures on recreational facilities account for about 5 per cent of general expenditures, or about one-third as much as highways (in terms of cash outlay). In terms of the nature of the benefit, one could argue that here is an even stronger case for the levying of specific charges. However, it is rather more difficult to isolate a marginal cost that makes very much sense because in many cases the amenity provided by a park is enjoyed by occupants of abutting property, even if they impinge in no way upon the enjoyment of others. Some uses are joint rather than exclusive, in that one goes to an event in part in order to be a part of the multitude. Even where the use is definitely exclusive, as in playing golf or tennis in periods of heavy demand, and accordingly efficient allocation would definitely call for the levying of a specific charge sufficient to equate demand and supply, there is a case to be made on distributional grounds for rationing by queue rather than by price. Many groups have more time than money, and it can be argued that it is desirable to preserve a reasonably wide variety of areas in which those who possess little coin of the realm can cash in that coin of which they have relative abundance.

Thus while a professor of economics, accustomed to value time highly and to think of queuing as an essentially wasteful process may at first take a dim view of a system where people line up for hours to get on a public golf course, this may not accurately reflect the feelings of those who do the lining up. Existence of a queue, to be sure, is *prima facie* evidence of inefficiency, in that if somehow reservations could be handed out to approximately the same group of persons who eventually play, the waiting, at least, could be eliminated. The cost involved in handling the reservations, however, may be greater than that of the waiting (this is essentially the analog of the former situation with respect to vehicular traffic, where it was maintained that the cost of toll collection would be greater than the cost of the congestion it was to eliminate). Permitting nontransferable reservations to be made on a first-come, first-served basis involves an alternate waste of induced excessive precommitment to a specific plan of behavior some time in advance, on pain of forfeiting the privilege represented by the reservation. Again at first glance one might suppose that this waste could be eliminated by making the reservations transferable, to the mutual benefits of transferor and transferee, but this would only make the reservations either an attractive area for speculators to operate in, or require the application of some prior criteria for the issuing of the reservations.

Where the capacity of the facility is fairly rigid, as with tennis courts, and the demand somewhat unpredictable, because of the influence of the weather if for no other reason, it will in any case be almost impossible to clear the market with any degree of precision through pricing alone, and in such cases a combination of pricing and queuing is likely to occur. In the absence of distributional considerations, a proper balance is to be sought between the wastes of queuing and the wastes of underutilization of the facilities: the higher the price the less the queuing but the greater the underutilization in periods of unusually low demand. On the other hand the lower the price, the lower the revenues over the range of prices that is relevant here, while the greater, presumably, is the favorable effect on the distribution of income.

The outcome of the balance of these considerations is not a cut-and-dried matter, in any particular case. In considering the weight to be given to the losses of queuing, however, it is appropriate to consider the degree of compulsion involved in the queuing: if the associated service is one easily dispensed with or for which there are reasonably close substitutes available, as for example where private facilities are available at moderate fees, then the queuing losses can be assigned a relatively low value in the appraisal of alternatives, whereas if the queuing is more nearly associated with a necessity, with only relatively remote substitutes available, the costs of the queuing are likely to weigh more heavily in the decision.

The same principles apply to the case where there is a temptation to continue the same fee that is inadequate to eliminate queues in peak periods over into periods of slack demand where the facilities are lightly used. In these cases the argument seems to be that the demand is highly inelastic over the range of prices in question anyhow, and that the redistributive effect of reducing the fees is less likely to be favorable, partly because of the absence of the selective effect of the queue, and partly on the ground that possession of leisure during the off-peak period is evidence of economic prosperity. There is also the problem of whether in view of the relatively low level of demand the facility should be closed down entirely during off-peak periods, or whether, contrariwise, only the fee collecting element should be closed down. This is not an important problem, but it is one that often seems to have been resolved more in terms of administrative convenience than in terms of any serious economic appraisal of the situation.

Education

Education is by far the largest single item in local government budgets, and there is no dearth of material on its financing. This is not the place to attempt a review of the volumes that have been written, but rather to sketch out new avenues of approach that might follow from an examination of the economics of the problem.

If provision of a uniform minimum standard of educational opportunity for all were more nearly a fact, rather than the rather remote aspiration that it actually is, the problem might be considered relatively simple. In fact, communities differ widely in their ability as well as in their willingness to provide a high grade of education. While intrastate differences in ability are met to a moderate degree by state aid formulae, the degree to which interstate differences in ability are met by federal aid is as yet minimal. The desire to provide adquate or even superior educational facilities thus often is severely constrained by the lack of adequate public revenue resources.

The problem is aggravated to a certain degree by the imbalance of internal migration. Regions that are net exporters of educated personnel fail to realize the tax base that would ordinarily result from the activities of the persons they educate, a process that has certain vicious circle elements in it as areas with high educational aspirations relative to their tax base fail thereby to attract the base necessary to support the aspirations without recourse to burdensome rates. It is easy to exaggerate the importance of this, but it seems clear that some means of breaking through this situation is needed. The essence of the problem is that the opportunity for a profitable investment in education is being missed because the parents of the children involved may be unable to finance the education, either individually or collectively, while the community finds it very difficult to finance an investment from which the returns will accrue elsewhere. The problem is how to arrange for the repayment to the investing community of some of the returns generated by that investment in education.

The somewhat exotic proposal that these considerations seem to point to is as follows. Each federal income taxpayer should be required to report on his income tax form the state (or school district) in which he received his public education, if any. A portion of his tax would then be turned over to the state (or school district) so indicated. The intended effect would be primarily one of making "educational export" regions more willing to upgrade their educational standards in view of an expectation that even though the region might not benefit directly from the better education of those who leave, the region would nevertheless get a return in this form.

Such a principle is of course capable of great modification in detail. It could, for example, be applied, only prospectively, to taxpayers in the future that are now getting educated; presumably the incentive to educational export regions to upgrade their education would remain as strong, even though they might have to borrow to do it on the strength of the expectation of these revenues. They merely would not obtain an unexpected windfall from the incomes of their previous students. However, this would be subject to the perennial problem of the inability of any government to commit itself effectively to a program that would have to extend for so many years into the future if it were to be effective at all, and in the absence of some mechanism of effective commitment, the incentive effect on current expenditures on schools might not be realized. Also, it would be possible to limit the distributions in some way to those educational systems that represent a high degree of effort in relation to the revenue resources available. Another possibility would be to vary the amount of the income tax payable by the individual according to the degree to which his income might be considered to be the result of superior or inferior educational facilties, the variation in tax above the minimum level being the amount available for redistribution back to the educational agencies.

The difficulties of putting any such plan into practice are obvious and probably insurmountable, and accordingly it must be considered as being presented as an aid and stimulus to discussion rather than as a serious proposal. Possibly a more likely, but less effective, variant would be to propose that some of the federal grants in aid to the states might be calculated on the basis of their being, in effect, *ex post* compensation to the exporting states for the loss of human capital they experienced as a result of net emigration in the past, insofar as this capital export could be considered to reflect the value of the education given. Another way of doing it would be to make current and future migration patterns the basis for grants, without attempting to relate the grants to the income actually yielded by the investment in education.

Health and hospital services

The main element that is peculiar to health and hospital services is the close interrelationship between municipally financed services and services covered by insurance, and the presence of a " moral hazard " element, by which is meant the tendency to make unjustified use of the facilities because they are either free or covered by insurance. In a sense the " moral hazard " here is only an acute form of the general tendency to overuse a facility that is underpriced; if a difference exists it is mainly that here the justification for use is supposed to reside more in objective medical facts and less in individual preferences, and the moral hazard arises because the objective medical facts are never quite as objective as the concept of a welfare standard or an insurance indemnity would like them to be. The moral hazard arises from many motives, from the doctor's desire to have the patient where it is easy to visit him, or the use of the hospital as a refuge, or to the desire to take advantage of section 105(d) of the federal income tax, which allows a deduction for sick pay for the first seven days of illness only if the employee is hospitalized during that time. The problems are so diverse that about all that could be done here is to simply list the area as one in which there is the possibility of some financing by fees.

Public utility services

Although such public utility services as electricity supply, telephone service, gas distribution, mail service, parcel delivery, and even newspaper delivery are not ordinarily included among the services considered as part of the standard pattern of governmental activity at the local level, the lines between these services and those such as water supply, garbage collection, and sewage disposal, that more typically are so considered, are to a degree arbitrary. Of these, the one that is most frequently added to the list of municipal activities, electricity supply, is perhaps the one for which the special powers of the municipality are least needed.

Dissatisfaction with the results of public utility regulation of private utilities plus the attractions of the availability of relatively low cost capital and certain other tax advantages relative to federal and state taxes are among the major factors which have led to the entry of municipalities into the business of supplying electricity, but these factors are common to the other utilities as well. In some cases the establishment of a municipal electricity service is the result of such special stimuli as the TVA and other public power agencies. But to a large extent the fact that these forces were effective with respect to electricity but not to other utility services can be laid to the fact that of all the predominantly privately supplied ones, electricity is the one that is most nearly an absolute necessity for the typical urban resident. Actually, it is precisely this characteristic that would make it possible for a privately operated utility to come reasonably close to an optimum allocation of resources through the adoption of a schedule of charges that will closely reflect marginal cost and yet at the same time extract a sufficient additional revenue from the intramarginal consumption to earn a normal return on its investment. There are several ways of doing this, but the most appropriate would be to charge rates for kilowatt-hours at the appropriate marginal cost, and assess in addition a front-foot charge to cover the basic cost of the distribution system. The front-foot charge could be expressed, if need be, in the form of a higher rate per kilowatt-hour for the first x kilowatt-hours per month per front foot; since practically all consumers would be using more than this initial block, the result would be essentially marginal cost pricing. This device is available to the electric power company primarily because the use of electricity is so nearly universal that no customers to speak of would find it advantageous to refuse service because of this initial rate.

With nearly all of the other services, however, an attempt to charge for the service according to front feet, to cover the basic costs of traversing the streets so as to cover the area effectively, would result in many potential customers refusing the service in order to escape the cost, and it does not seem likely that a privately operated service would be empowered to assess charges on property owners who do not take the service. It is here that there is a definite opportunity for improvement in the efficiency of allocation of resources through the collection by the municipality of a special frontage tax to defray the basic traversal costs of these various services, and then make available to the residents these various services at rates that would be fairly close to the incremental cost of rendering the service. It would not be absolutely necessary for the municipality to render the service on its own account: this could be done by contract, though of course in this case care would have to be taken lest abuses occur, and if anything of this sort were to be done at all, many would be inclined to favor some method that would not result in the subdivision of responsibility and the introduction of opposing monopolistic interests. Including mail delivery in this list is perhaps a bit quixotic in view of the firm preemption of this field by the federal government, yet it is technologically no more unreasonable to contemplate the local handling of mail that is transmitted nationwide by a national service than it is to contemplate local distribution of electric power generated and transmitted over a wide area by a federal agency.

SPECIFIC FINANCING AND THE OVER-ALL FISCAL PICTURE

In considering the extent to which specific charges should be used in each instance, some attention must of course be given to the relation of the costs and revenues in that area to the over-all fiscal picture of the governmental unit, both as to the aggregate amount and as to the distributional impact of the costs and revenues. The first of these elements can be adequately represented for most purposes by introducing as a parameter the "marginal cost of public funds."

The marginal cost of public funds

The marginal cost of public funds is defined as the net reduction in the over-all allocational efficiency of the economy resulting from the raising of an increment of revenue from a given source, expressed as a ratio or percentage of that increment in revenue. It includes, over all, the loss in consumers' surplus, the loss in producers' surplus or economic rent, the marginal costs of administration, and the marginal costs of compliance. If we are considering an established set of taxes and charges and only the rates are under consideration, the compliance and administrative costs may be approximately constant, so that they can be neglected, and we can focus our attention on the effects of the rate changes on surplus.

The simplest case to analyze is that of a simple excise tax on a commodity produced under conditions of constant or increasing costs and where complementarity and substitution effects can be neglected. In Figure 1, AC is the supply curve, BC is the demand curve, C is the price and quantity resulting under competition with no tax, and ACB is the net social gain generated as a result of the production of the commodity in question, divided into consumers' surplus CNB and producers' surplus or rent, ANC. If a tax equal to DE is imposed, per unit of output, the supply curve inclusive of tax moves from ACS to $A'ES'$, there is a tax revenue of $EDGF$, the consumers' surplus is reduced to EFB, producers' surplus is reduced to AGD, and there is a net loss of potential surplus to the community as a whole of DEC, representing

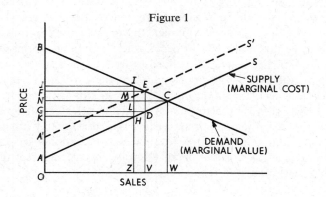

Figure 1

the excess of the value *VECW* of the output that is no longer being produced *VW*, over what it would cost to produce it, *VDCW*.

Suppose that now the tax is increased to *HI*. Consumers' surplus is now *IJB*, revenue is now *HIJK*, and producers' surplus is now *AKH*, the total loss of potential surplus now having increased to *CHI*. The net increase in this loss, *EDHI*, is what is to be compared to the increase in revenue, which is *HIJK − DEFG*. This comparison can be made in terms of the somewhat simplified Figure 2, in which we in effect regard the tax as the margin which the government acting as a monopolist adds to what it pays for the total supply to determine the price at which the total amount will be sold. *BC* is the demand curve as before, and *BQ* is the corresponding marginal revenue curve (in the case of straight line demand curves it is twice as steep as *BE*), representing the net increase in gross revenues from the sale of one more unit at the correspondingly lower price. Similarly, *AR* is the marginal cost of purchase curve, representing the cost of buying one more unit, allowing for the fact that buying one more unit will raise the price which must be paid for all units in the open market. The difference *RQ* is then the loss in net revenue resulting from the purchase of one more unit at an over-all additional cost of *VR* and its sale at an over-all additional revenue of *VQ*; this is what is to be compared to the loss of net social surplus represented by *ED*, the difference between the value *VE* the buyer would place on the additional unit and the cost of producing it, *VD*.

A third way of presenting the situation is to subtract the supply curve *AC* vertically from the demand curve *BC* to get the curve *BC* in Figure 3 which shows the relation between the tax rate and the amount sold. This can be regarded as the net demand for the government's (costless) services in transferring the product from sellers to buyers. The total surplus generated if there is no tax is *ABC*, as before, and the amount that is sacrificed if a tax of *DE* is imposed is *DEC*, the total tax revenue being *ADEF*. The marginal government revenue curve *BUT* being the marginal curve corresponding to the average revenue or tax rate curve *BEC*, represents the net revenue from arranging for the sale of an additional unit. Increasing the tax to reduce the

Figure 2

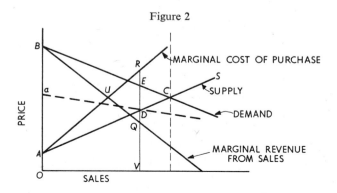

Figure 3

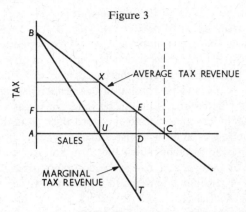

sales by one unit thus increases revenues by DT (the negative marginal revenue), and increases the net social loss by DE. It is the ratio ED to DT that is the marginal cost of public funds; this obviously begins at zero for no tax at C and increases steadily as the tax rate is increased, becoming infinite as the tax is raised to the point UX, where the revenue is a maximum.

If taxes are being raised from several such sources at once, the optimum arrangement is one in which the ratio ED/DT is the same in all cases. It can be shown that for excise taxes this relation obtains if the ratio of tax to price for each commodity taxed is proportional to the sum of the (absolute) inelasticities of demand and of supply, provided that we measure the inelasticity of demand net of the tax (i.e., as though the demand curve had been shifted downward by the amount of the tax; inelasticity is the reciprocal of the elasticity).

Another way of arriving at the same result is to require the ratio AD/AC to be the same in all cases, i.e., the tax is to be such as to result in the same proportionate reduction in sales of each commodity as compared to the no-tax situation (assuming demand and supply curves to be linear projections).

. . . .

SUMMARY

Enough has been said to indicate that even though the decision to provide a given facility or service may well require a weighing of costs and benefits, benefit may not provide a suitable basis for the assessment of charges to defray the costs. The decisions made by governments in deciding whether to offer a service and of what extent and character, and those made by individuals in availing themselves of whatever service is provided, are of a different scope and often of a different dimension, so that the comparisons that are pertinent for the one decision are not always relevant for the other. Generally speaking, the considerations adduced in considering appropriate charges lean rather more towards the taxation of land rather than improvements, not necessarily in terms of its market value, but rather in terms of such parameters as area and frontage. Even where benefits seem to be most closely measurable in terms of improvements, the causal nexus is found to be more nearly independent of actual improvements and to relate more to the fundamental site-determined characteristics. Finally, a comprehensive approach to the pricing of municipal services may lay the groundwork for a new and more fruitful approach to over-all urban planning in terms of economic costs as well as of architectural design.

On making the best of balance of payments restrictions on imports*

J. MARCUS FLEMING

PART I—THE THEORY

Introduction

1. The title of this paper very exactly describes its theme. No view is expressed or implied regarding the desirability, or otherwise, from the international standpoint, of the use of import restriction as a short- or medium-term stabiliser of the balance of payments. The fact that the principal stabilising device of the old system—variation in employment, production, and incomes —is now generally regarded with disfavour, makes it necessary to lean more heavily on such alternative techniques as remain available, *e.g.*, import restriction, flexible exchange rates, international short-term credit flows of a compensatory type and the use of substantial gold reserves. Economists will differ in the relative emphasis they lay upon the various alternatives. That issue is not examined here. Our theme is a more limited one; given that import restrictions continue to be rather widely employed as a means of meeting middle-term disequilibria in the balance of payments, how would they have to be applied in order to reduce to a minimum their admitted diseconomies?

Assumptions of the economic model

2. Assume that import restriction is the only method whereby a country can correct an adverse balance of payments. In each country full employment is maintained, and the level of factor prices is kept stable relative to the levels in other countries—thus excluding deflation and exchange depreciation as methods of restoring balance-of-payments equilibrium. Export subsidisation or restriction and any kind of manipulation of capital movements are also excluded. Currency reserves are negligible, so that any balance-of-payments disequilibrium has to be at once corrected. All currencies are convertible. Import restrictions, however, can be applied with varying degrees of severity according to commodity and country of origin.

* *The Economic Journal*, 61(1951): pp. 48–91. Reprinted by courtesy of the author and *The Economic Journal*.

Perfect competition prevails within each country, so that the severity of any import restriction is reflected in the margin between the price in the importing and that in the exporting country. Commodities exchange internationally at the prices prevailing in the country of export; any margin accrues to the importing country. The export-supply curves and the import-demand curves of the several commodities traded between the several pairs of countries are all given independently of each other and of the actual course of trade. (This assumption is later removed.) Export supply conditions are such as to ensure that any expansion in the demand for a country's exports increases the value as well as the quantity exported. Considerations of space prevent examination of the exceptional cases where these supply conditions do not obtain.

Welfare conventions

3. It is assumed that there are no external economies of production or consumption, that producers equate value of marginal factor with product price for each factor and product, that consumers secure an equimarginal return in private utility from all forms of expenditure, and that increments in the general utility or welfare are made up of the sum of the increments of the private utilities of individuals. This allows us henceforward to speak of " utility " without distinguishing whether it is private or general. Finally, it is assumed that the marginal utility of money expenditure is the same for each individual in whatever country he may live; or at least that it is, on the average, the same for those who gain by any given change in the economic situation as for those who lose. This implies that the marginal utility of any commodity to any individual can be measured by the price of that commodity within the country inhabited by the individual in question.

Criteria of " optimisation " and " improvement "

4. The problem is to define the characteristics of an optimal structure of restrictions on imports of each commodity into each country from each other country subject to the conditions of the model. In order to do this one has to be able to judge whether the change in the economic situation consequential on any alteration in an assumed initial structure of import restrictions is or is not an improvement.

5. Under the assumed conditions the net gain from any small change in the economic situation can be measured by: (*a*) any increments in output *minus*, (*b*) any increments in input *plus*, (*c*) any increments in goods, services, or claims received by an individual *minus*, (*d*) any increments in goods, services, or claims supplied by any individual, all such increments being valued at the prices prevailing in the countries inhabited by the firm or individual in question. Most of these items will cancel out. All transfers between individuals in the same country, or between individuals in countries having the same price for the commodity or claim in question (there being no trade barriers between the countries in that commodity or claim) will count equally as gains and losses. Since we are here concerned with economic changes

initiated by shifts in trade barriers, production changes are merely consequential and, since perfect competition prevails, each firm's increments of
output will equal in value its increments in input. *The net gain from the whole
operation can therefore be measured by the sum of the increments of international
trade in such items as are subject to import restriction, each increment being
valued by the margin between the inland price in the importing country and that
in the exporting country.* This margin will vary with the degree of restriction
currently applied to the imports in question and will equal the specific import
duty corresponding to that degree of restriction.[1]

6. The structure of import restrictions may be deemed optimal when no
change in international trade quantities, capable of being brought about by a
change in that structure, will yield a net gain by the above criterion. It is
possible to define the characteristics of an optimal structure by considering a
limited number of types of changes in international trade quantities or, as
we shall call them, "trade adjustments."

Types of equilibrated trade adjustment

7. Starting from an initial position in which each country is in balance-of-
payments equilibrium with the others taken as a group, but only because some
or all countries are applying restrictions on imports, consider the following
types of adjustment, each of which is so applied as to leave each country's
overall balance of payments unchanged.

a) A change in a certain country's import of a certain commodity and a
change of opposite sign in its import of a second commodity, both from the
same exporting country.

b) A change in a certain country's import of a certain commodity from a
second country and a change of the same sign in the second country's import
of a second commodity from the first country.

c) A change in a certain country's import of a certain commodity from a
second country, a change of the same sign in second country's import of a
second commodity from the third country and a change of the same sign in
the third country's import of a third commodity from the first country.

d) A change in a certain country's import of a certain commodity from a
second country, a change of the same sign in the second country's import of
a second commodity from a third country and a change of opposite sign in
the first country's import of a third commodity from the third country.

Type (a) adjustments (unilateral)

8. Suppose that B's restrictions on imports of *m* from A are relaxed, while
those on imports of *n* from A are intensified in such a way as to preserve

---

[1] This amounts to defining an improvement as any change which increases the value of
world output less the value of world input at constant market prices. An alternative definition
would have been "any change the gainers from which could (though they do not) overcompensate the losers." Where, as in the case examined here, the economic model is such
that the payment or nonpayment of compensation in itself affects real world output these
criteria diverge. I hope to discuss the relative merits of the two criteria in such cases in a
future paper.

unchanged any initial inequality of payments between A and B. The rise in the cost (at A prices) of imports of m must balance the fall in cost of imports of n. The gain, if any, from the adjustment is measured by the rise in imports of m, weighted by the margin between B prices and A prices of m, *less* the fall in imports of n, weighted by the price margin of n. There will be a net gain only if the ratio of m's price margin to n's price margin is higher than the rate at which imports of n fall as those of m rise. But the price margins of m and n depend on the severity of B's restrictions on imports of m and n, respectively, and the rate at which imports of n fall as those of m rise depends on the elasticities of supply from A to B of n and m, respectively.

9. At this point it is convenient to introduce the notion of "responsiveness of supply" by which is meant the ratio of the proportionate increase in quantity sold to the proportionate increase in the seller's money receipts. "Responsiveness of supply" as thus defined is, of course, a function of the elasticity of supply with respect to price. Now, reverting to our example, the adjustment described will yield a net gain if, but only if, the ratio of the *ad valorem* tariff-equivalent of the import restriction on m to that of the import restriction on n exceeds the ratio of the responsiveness of supply (from A to B) of n to that of m. (In what follows the expression "the 'tariff'" is used to signify "the tariff-equivalent of the import restriction.") The situation will be incapable of improvement by Type (a) adjustments when the ratio of the percentage "tariffs" on any pair of commodities imported by any country from any other country equals the reciprocal of the ratio of the corresponding export supply responsiveness.[2]

Type (b) adjustments (bilateral)

10. Suppose that A's restrictions on imports of p from B, and B's restrictions on imports of q from A are both relaxed in such a way as to leave unaffected A's balance of payments with B.

11. The mutual relaxation of import restrictions will give rise to an increase both in the value and in the volume of the exports both of p and q. So long as the price of each of these commodities in the importing country exceeds its price in the exporting country, *i.e.*, so long as import restrictions are in force in both cases, the adjustment must, according to our criterion of meliorisation, be beneficial. The mutual relaxation of import restrictions can therefore be continued with advantage up to the point at which one or other of the commodities is being imported entirely without restriction. At this point, according to the conditions of our model, the adjustment must stop (though if import subsidisation had been permitted, it could have proceeded farther with advantage).

Type (c) adjustments (trilateral)

12. Suppose that A relaxes restrictions on imports of r from C, B relaxes restrictions on imports of s from A, and C relaxes restrictions on imports of t from B in such a way as to leave unchanged the balance-of-payments surplus

---

[2] See Appendix, paragraph 1.

or deficit of each country *vis-à-vis* the other pair. There will ensue an expansion in the value and volume of exports of r, s, and t which can continue with advantage up to the point at which one of the three commodities—say t—is being imported without restriction. At this point, according to the conditions of our model, the adjustment must stop.

Type (d) adjustments (trilateral)

13. Suppose that C intensifies restrictions on imports of x from A, and relaxes restrictions on imports of y from B, while B relaxes restrictions on imports of z from A in such a way as to leave unchanged the balance-of-payments surplus or deficit of each country *vis-à-vis* the remaining pair taken together. This implies that the decline in value of C's imports of x must equal the increase in value of its imports of y, which in turn must equal the increase in value of B's imports of z. Starting from a point at which C's " tariff " on x is negligible, this type of adjustment can be carried either to a point at which it is abruptly brought to a stop by the disappearance of all import restrictions in B on z or in C on y, or to a point at which, thanks to the decline in B's " tariff " on z and C's " tariff " on y, and the increase in C's " tariff " on x, it ceases to show a net advantage. This optimal point will be attained when C's percentage " tariff " on x *times* the responsiveness of supply of x from A to C *equals* C's percentage " tariff " on y *times* the responsiveness of supply of y from B to C *plus* B's percentage " tariff " on z *times* the responsiveness of supply of z from A to B.[3]

Optimal structure of import restrictions

14. By combining advantageous adjustments of Type (a) and (b), applying them to all commodities traded between all pairs of countries, and pushing them to the point of maximum advantage, we reach a situation in which in each pair of countries one country is importing all commodities from the other without restriction, while the second country is imposing on commodities imported from the first percentage " tariffs " inversely proportional to the corresponding responsivenesses of export supply.

15. By proceeding similarly, in addition, with advantageous adjustments of Types (c) and (d), and by pursuing the practice, whenever advantageous adjustments are checked by the elimination of one country's restrictions on imports from another, of initiating a new set of adjustments involving the restriction of the second country's imports from the first, it is always possible to arrive at a situation of the following kind. *All countries are ranged in an order, which we may term an order of " strength," such that: (i) each country is importing freely from countries " weaker " than itself and restricting imports of all commodities from countries " stronger " than itself; (ii) the percentage " tariffs " imposed by any country on the various commodities imported from any " stronger " country are inversely proportional to the corresponding export supply responsive-*

---

[3] See Appendix, paragraph 2.

nesses; (iii) as between any three countries, the " weak " country will be impos-
ing on any commodity imported from the " strong " country a percentage
" tariff " which, when multiplied by the corresponding export supply responsive-
ness, will equal the sum of (a) the percentage " tariff " which it imposes on any
commodity imported from the " intermediate " country, times the corresponding
export supply responsiveness, and (b) the percentage " tariff " which the " inter-
mediate " country imposes on any commodity imported from the " strong "
country, times the corresponding export-supply responsiveness.

16. Where all export-supply responsivenesses are equal each country
should impose on all commodities imported from each " stronger " country a
uniform percentage " tariff " equal to the sum of the percentage " tariffs "
applied by itself and by each " intermediate " country on imports from the
country immediately superior in order of " strength."

17. It could probably be demonstrated mathematically, given the relevant
demand and supply conditions, that only one order of countries will satisfy
the criteria set forth in paragraph 15 above, *i.e.*, that any situation satisfying
these criteria is not merely a " local " optimum but the absolute optimum
subject to the conditions of the model. For suppose that, starting from a
position which satisfies the criteria, a country is " promoted " to a higher place
in the order over the heads of a number of other countries. The " promoted "
will have to remove any restrictions on imports from the " demoted " countries,
while the latter will impose some restrictions on imports from the " promoted " country. Moreover, all countries of lower order will intensify their
restrictions on imports from the " promoted " country relative to the restrictions on imports from the " demoted " countries. It seems impossible that
both the " promoted " and the " demoted " countries will, under these conditions, maintain their overall balance-of-payments positions unchanged. The
" promotion " will therefore not be permissible.

18. No advantage will be gained by proceeding to consider adjustments
between four or more countries. Quadrilateral and multilateral adjustments
can be resolved into a combination of notional trilateral adjustments of the
kind already described, and can yield no improvement over the position already defined.

Intertrade repercussions

19. We must now consider to what extent the results so far attained will
be affected by the removal of the simplifying assumption of paragraph 2 that
each of the relevant export-supply curves and import-demand curves is
unaffected by the volume of imports or exports in other commodities or with
other countries.

20. The most important for our purpose of the possible interrelationships
between particular trades are the following:

i) an increased export of a particular commodity from one country to
another may raise the supply curves of other commodities exported by the
first country to the second particularly in the short run;

ii) increased exports from one country to a second may raise the supply curves of exports from the first country to third countries, particularly of the same commodities, and particularly in the short run;

iii) increased imports by one country from a second country will tend to reduce the demand curves in the first country for imports from third countries, particularly imports of the same commodities.

Effect of intertrade repercussions on the optimal structure of import restrictions

21. Repercussion (i) affects the optimal relative " tariffs " imposed by any one country on the various commodities imported from another. Any commodity which is highly substitutible in the export country for other commodities exported to the same importing country should be restricted more severely by the latter than its supply responsiveness would otherwise warrant. This will tend to make optimal relative percentage " tariffs " on different commodities imported from the same country more nearly equal than on the assumption of independent supply curves.

22. Repercussions (ii) and (iii) affect the desirability of carrying mutual trade between each pair of countries to the point at which only one of the two is restricting imports from the other. Suppose there are only three countries, A, B, and C, ranged in that order, between which prevails a system of import restrictions of the type described in paragraph 15. A and B begin to restrict imports from each other without altering the initial inequality in their bilateral balance of payments. Can this be advantageous? Both A and B will tend, in accordance with (iii), to take additional imports from C in substitution for each other's products. Moreover, in accordance with (ii), the contraction in A's and B's mutual exports should tend to lower the supply prices of their exports to C. C will then be able to increase its imports from A and B without detriment to its balance of payments.

23. Up to a point the advantage of the expansion in C's imports from A and B might outweigh the disadvantage of the contraction of B's imports from A and also—though for small adjustments this is unimportant—the contraction of A's imports from B. In the longer-run, however, the effects of (ii) will become negligible, and a contraction of A's and B's mutual trade, though justifiable in the short run, might well be unjustifiable in the long run.

24. Suppose, now that starting from the position described in paragraph 15, countries B and C begin to contract their mutual imports while leaving their bilateral balance of payments unaltered. This will *not* lead automatically to any reduction in imports from A, since B's and C's imports from A are determined by their balance of payments position *vis-à-vis* A. It will, however, in the short-run at any rate, probably lead to a decline in the supply prices of B's and C's exports respectively to A. Everything now depends on the elasticity of demand in A for imports from B and C, respectively. If, as will normally be the case, this elasticity is in both cases higher than unity, A will *increase*

its expenditure on imports from B and C, which will therefore be in a position to expand their imports from A.

25. This operation will be advantageous only if the additional imports into C and B from A outweigh the fall in B's and C's mutual imports. It is clearly much less likely to be advantageous than the mutual restriction of imports between A and B previously considered. Import diversion plays no part in it. The effect of export diversion is indirect and is unlikely to be as beneficial as was export diversion in the case previously considered unless A's elasticity of demand for imports from B and C is at least 2. In the long-run, this elasticity of demand may well be substantially higher than 2, but by that time the fall in B's and C's export-supply prices, resulting from their mutual contraction of trade, may have become negligible. It, therefore, seems most unlikely that any mutual restriction of imports by B and C will prove to be advantageous. The same applies, in even greater measure, to a mutual restriction of imports between A and C.

26. Consider now the effect of intertrade repercussions on the optimum for trilateral adjustments as previously established. Start once more with countries A, B, C in that order of strength, with a structure of import restrictions as described in paragraph 15. Suppose that C imports more from A and less from B, thus forcing B to import less from A. A *small* trade adjustment of this sort, which leaves undisturbed each country's balance of payments with the other two combined, would, in the absence of the repercussions discussed below, have a negligible effect on welfare. Now the fall in B's imports from A will lead to an expansion in B's imports from C [repercussion (iii)] so that the fall of C's imports from B need no longer be so great in value as the rise of her imports from A. Moreover, the fall in B's exports to C may lead, in the short run, to a fall in the supply price of B's exports to A [repercussion (ii)] and (if A's demand is of more than unit elasticity) to an increase in B's export receipts from A, so that the fall in B's imports from A need no longer be as great in value as the fall of C's imports from B. These mitigations in the fall of C's imports from B, and of B's imports from A, constitute, for small adjustments, a net advantage. An extension of such an adjustment, however, as it got farther from the position defined in paragraph 15 would create disadvantages which would, after a point, outweigh the advantages just mentioned.

27. To sum up, the examination of intertrade repercussions alters our conception of an optimal structure of import barriers from that arrived at on the assumption of the independence of demand and supply curves,

a) by mitigating the degree of intercommodity discrimination in the restrictions to be imposed by any country on imports from a second country;

b) by indicating a possible but doubtful advantage in some degree of mutual import restriction as between relatively " strong " countries, and

c) by reducing the degree of preference to be given by " weaker " countries to imports from " intermediate " countries over imports from " stronger " countries.

PART II—THE THEORY APPLIED

28. Let us now examine to what extent various existing, projected or possible trade-and-payments arrangements satisfy the requirements of an optimal structure so set forth in Part I.

Nondiscriminatory import restriction

29. Consider, first, the system under which balance-of-payments import restrictions are applied in a nondiscriminatory manner, so as to be equivalent to a uniform tariff *vis-à-vis* all supplying countries. If, as was assumed in Part I, all currencies were fully convertible, each country, insofar as it acted unilaterally without exchanging concessions with other countries, and without taking account of their supply elasticities or other indirect repercussions, would have an incentive to apply its import restrictions in this way.

30. In a world in which exchange rates or internal money cost levels were sufficiently flexible to dispense with the necessity for balance-of-payments restrictions on imports, the principle of nondiscrimination would undoubtedly be the right one. But, under the conditions of our model, which have to a considerable extent prevailed in reality in the post-war period, any system constructed on this principle would operate in a most unsatisfactory way. Starting from the supposition that, in the absence of import restrictions, one set of countries would be in balance-of-payments surplus and another set in deficit, imagine that the deficit countries seek to restore equilibrium in their external accounts by nondiscriminatory restrictions on imports from all other countries, including each other. Not merely will these restrictions reduce the export income of the original deficit countries and force them to intensify their restrictions, but they will also transform countries originally in approximate balance into deficit countries, and force them, in turn, to apply import restrictions. If nondiscriminatory import restrictions were the only way of correcting disequilibria, this process would continue until every country but one was applying import restrictions of a greater or lesser degree of severity.

31. Clearly, such a situation is very far removed from that described in paragraph 15 as optimal. Each country, other than the "strongest" country, will be withholding from each other country goods less valuable to itself than those which it could have obtained in exchange. "Strong" countries will be restricting imports from "weak" countries, thus enforcing unnecessary hardships on the latter without benefit to themselves. "Weak" countries will be giving no preference to imports from "intermediate" countries over imports from "strong" countries, thus imposing on "intermediate" countries a sacrifice which outweighs the benefit which they themselves derive from buying in the cheapest market.

Bilateral balancing of payments

32. Compared with this the regime of trade-and-payments bilateralism, which limited currency convertibility, as practised in Europe and South America since the war, has considerable advantages. Under such a regime,

payments between a pair of countries, or "monetary areas," are canalised ultimately through the two central banks concerned and, after offsetting, eventuate in a net addition to or subtraction from the balance held by one of the control banks with the other. If one of the pair has a continuing balance-of-payments surplus with the other, it accumulates in the other's currency a balance which it can use only if it can transform its surplus with the other into a deficit.

33. Such an arrangement gives each country an incentive to expand imports from the other, and particularly the surplus country from the deficit country, and thus tends to favour a bilateral expansion of trade, of the type discussed in paragraph 11, to the point at which one of the two countries has abandoned all balance-of-payments restrictions on imports from the other.

Mitigations of bilateralism

34. The weakness of trade-and-payments bilateralism, of course, is in its failure to take advantage of trilateral adjustments, i.e., its tendency to eliminate or unduly to reduce bilateral surpluses and deficits. There are however, three channels through which a measure of trade-and-payments multilateralism is frequently achieved within the general framework of the bilateral system:

i) The existence of substantial or indefinite credit margins under bilateral agreements permits a—sometimes considerable—departure from strict bilateral balancing of payments. A country may be running a deficit with a second country and a surplus with a third, both financed out of bilateral credit. Where, however, there is a persistent imbalance in bilateral accounts, the surplus country will probably seek to impose limits on the credit which it provides.

ii) If a substantial proportion of a country's exports consist of "essentials" or "dollar-worthy" items it may succeed in maintaining bilateral surpluses without giving credit, by inducing its bilateral trading partners to settle their deficits in gold or hard currency. The second country, however, will desire, in these circumstances, to impose on imports from the first country restrictions which, if the first country is, from the "world" standpoint, relatively "weak," may be far more severe than is appropriate according to our formula. In practice, however, the second country may be deterred from applying the criterion of "dollar essentiality" to its purchases from the first country by fear that the latter may retaliate by ceasing to import freely from the former.

iii) Under an arrangement which has assumed particular importance in connection with the use of sterling a country may permit the transfer of balances in its currency from holders resident in a second country to holders resident in a third country. The first country is likely to offer this facility provided that the currency of the second country is at least as scarce to it as that of the third country; the second country is likely to make the transfer provided that the currency of the third country is at least as scarce to it as that of the first country; and the third country is likely to accept the transfer provided that the currency of the first country is at least as scarce to it as that of the second country. In this connection the "scarcity" of a country's currency may be measured by the severity of the restrictions which it is necessary, on balance-of-payments grounds, to impose on imports from that country.

35. This device of "selective transferability" if fully exploited would enable all possible trilateral adjustments of Type (c), as defined in paragraph 12, to take place. Whenever country B is restricting imports from country A, country C from country B, and country A from country C, an expansion of exports from A to B, B to C, and C to A will normally be advantageous to each of the countries concerned. The whole operation can be carried out in A-currency (with A allowing its transfer from C to B), in B-currency (with B allowing its transfer from A to C), or in C-currency (with C allowing its transfer from B to A).

36. Transferability of this kind will also enable trilateral adjustments of Type (d) to be carried to a certain point, though somewhat short of the optimum. Suppose, to start from the example in the previous paragraph, that the adjustment of Type (c) is brought to an end by the elimination of A's barriers against imports from C. Then C will probably find it worth while to start restricting imports from A if it is allowed to use its earnings of A-currency to purchase additional imports from B. B will be glad to accept A-currency, which will enable it to obtain additional imports from A. A will probably consent to the transfer of its currency from C to B, which will leave its aggregate exports and importing power unaffected; unless, indeed, it had hoped to extract from B gold or some currency scarcer than its own. If we can assume that A will not withhold its consent to the transfer for the sake of earning scarce currency from countries "weaker" than itself, the Type (d) operation just described will continue to the point at which C is restricting imports from A as severely as from B.

37. As a result of selective transferability then, we might arrive at a situation in which countries are ranged in an unambiguous order of "strength" and "weakness" in which each country will have practically eliminated restrictions against imports from all countries "weaker" than itself, and in which each country, in restricting imports from countries "stronger" than itself, will restrict imports from a relatively "strong" supplier *at least* as severely as those from an "intermediate" supplier. This not unsatisfactory result is, however, dependent on relatively "strong" countries refraining from either restricting imports from, or refusing transfers to relatively "weak" countries for the sake of earning gold or scarce currencies from them. In the post-war period countries have in fact refrained to a surprising extent from exercising their power to extract gold from bilateral debtors.

Group discrimination based on international planning

38. Dissatisfaction with the contrasted evils of nondiscriminatory restriction and of pure bilateralism has led to attempts to devise arrangements which would promote a modulated group discrimination of a desirable kind. The most intellectually audacious attempts of this sort are those by Professor

Frisch in his articles " On the Need for Forecasting a Multilateral Balance of Payments" in the *American Economic Review* of September 1947 and " The Problem of Multicompensatory Trade" in the *Review of Economics and Statistics* of November 1948.

39. In the former article Frisch proposes:

a) that information should be collected regarding the amounts of goods and services which countries would be able and willing to exchange with each other;

b) that this information should be arranged in " matrices," *i.e.*, square tables in which the columns show the amounts (in value terms) which particular importing countries would import from the various exporting countries, and the rows show the amounts which particular exporting countries would export to the various importing countries;

c) that some international authority (*e.g.*, the I.T.O.) should attempt, both by recommendatory and permissive action, to ensure that such cutting down in the various elements of this matrix of potential trade as is necessary to bring balance-of-payments surpluses and deficits within the limits permitted by international lending is carried out in such a way as to maximise the quantum of international trade.

40. This scheme is open to objection on grounds both of principle and practicability. It takes account only of the *quantum* of international trade and neglects its *quality*—as measured by the (proportionate) margin between the price of the goods in question in the importing country and their price in the exporting country. The result is that no matter how essential may be the goods which a " weak" country imports from a " strong" country, the weak country must practically always be prepared to restrict them further if there is some intermediate country from which it can then expand its imports by an equal amount, thus enabling the latter in turn to expand imports from a " strong" country.[4] It is extremely doubtful whether the results of such a maximisation process would be preferable to the results of ordinary bilateralism qualified by " selective transferability" of currencies.

41. The practical difficulties are those of:

a) arriving at a matrix of potential trade, the elements of which are: (i) agreed between the importing and the exporting country and (ii) forecast with reasonable accuracy; and

b) inducing the countries concerned to take the action deemed desirable by the international authority.

42. The problem of providing an incentive to countries to implement an " optimal" structure of import restrictions arises, of course, whatever the principles on which the structure is designed. Where, as here, the pattern of trade is planned in quantitative terms, and if countries are unwilling to regulate their every import at the behest of an international authority, consideration

---

[4] This is what is implied in the priority which Frisch gives to " first-order" over " second-order" adjustments.

might be given to a technique employed by the O.E.E.C., viz. the extension of drawing-rights on a bilateral basis. A " drawing-right " is a grant in the donor's more or less inconvertible currency and hence available for the purchase of only such imports as are normally purchasable with that currency. Since the right is liable to lapse or lose its value at the end of a stated period, the recipient has a strong incentive to develop a balance-of-payments deficit *vis-à-vis* the donor of an amount corresponding to the size of the grant. In the past this technique has been used in connection with the provision of United States aid to Europe. It could, however, be used as a method of implementing a planned pattern of bilateral surpluses and deficits without any country being on balance a donor or a recipient; *i.e.*, each country would receive as large a sum in drawing rights from some countries as it extended to others. Of course, even this technique merely shifts the problem of incentive back one stage, since countries have to be induced to accept the pattern of drawing rights assigned to them.

43. A further difficulty about any attempt to bring about an optimal structure of import restrictions by quantitative planning is that the characteristics of an optimal structure of import restrictions set forth in paragraph 15 can be translated into quantitative terms only by making very artificial assumptions about elasticities of import demand and export supply. On the assumption that all export elasticities are infinite and all import elasticities equal and starting from an estimated trade pattern corresponding to universal free imports, each country would have to cut down its imports from each country stronger than itself by a proportion equal to the sum of the proportionate reductions imposed by any intermediate country on imports from the strong country and by the weak country on imports from the intermediate country.

Frisch's multicompensatory grade system

44. In the second article referred to in paragraph 15, Frisch makes new proposals which purport to take account of the " quality " as well as of the quantity of trade. The essence of his scheme is as follows:

a) all trade to be subject to import licence;

b) all licence applications to be assigned a priority number (ranging from 9 to 0) by the exporting country and a priority number by the importing country and to be submitted for final approval to an International Bureau of Compensation;

c) the Compensation Bureau to approve or disapprove applications in such a way as to satisfy certain criteria.

45. The first criterion is that the value of each country's imports should equal the value of its exports (with a predetermined deviation). The second criterion is not very clearly formulated. After considering a number of alternatives Frisch concludes:

A plausible principle seems to be simply to put up as a goal the maximisation of the global surplus, *i.e.*, the maximisation of the priority sum for import *minus* the priority sum for exports, both taken as a total for all countries, the figures for each country being normalised, so as to let only the relative, and not the absolute, magnitudes of the priority numbers influence the result.

The " priority sum " for imports (or exports) is the sum of the products of the import (or export) priority numbers *times* the value of the imports (or exports) falling within the corresponding priority class. Frisch illustrates this principle by a mathematical formula, which, however, seems scarcely to correspond with the verbal description. According to the formula what is to be maximised is the product of two terms, one of which is the aggregate value (at given prices) of the permitted trade, and the other is the sum of each country's " surplus " (as defined in the quotation above) expressed as a proportion of its " priority sum " for imports.[5]

46. The Frischian concepts cannot be compared with the formulae developed earlier in this article unless the principles governments are to follow in assigning priority numbers to imports and exports are specifically laid down and expressed in terms of market prices. Thus a given priority number (whether on imports or exports) might represent a given proportional excess of the value of the good in question in the internal market over its value in the international market. On this interpretation the appropriate criterion would be that of maximising the " global surplus," *i.e.*, maximising the excess of the priority sum for imports over the priority sum for exports—prices and priority numbers both being treated as constants. Bearing in mind that, on the assumptions of my system, export subsidisation is not permitted and hence the priority number on exports must always be zero, this maximisation criterion is identical with the optimisation criterion employed elsewhere in this article.

47. Frisch's own verbal formulation appears to be vitiated by the " normalisation " procedure. This aims at preventing countries from gaining any advantage by manipulating the levels of their priority numbers, but could achieve this only by depriving the " weaker " countries of the benefit of the preference to which they are entitled in export competition with the " stronger " countries. Frisch's mathematical formula, on the other hand, reduces, when export priority numbers are taken as equal to zero, to the maximisation of the quantum of aggregate trade which is open, as shown in paragraph 40, to quite the opposite objection.

48. I take on trust Frisch's assurance that it is mathematically possible for the Compensation Bureau to tailor the import-licence applications originally submitted so as to satisfy both the balance-of-payments conditions and the maximisation criterion—and I assume this remains true when my criterion is substituted for his. Even so, the scheme is fraught with what are I fear overwhelming practical difficulties.

---

[5] See Appendix, paragraph 3.

The clearing union approach:
international control of national import duties

(a) *Variant one.*

49. The methods so far discussed for bringing into effect an optimal structure of import restrictions have involved the regulation of trade as a quantitative basis. But the criteria for such an optimal structure are expressed in terms of rates of import duty having equivalent effect to the import restrictions in question, and it would be possible to get a much closer approximation to the ideal if import restrictions imposed for balance-of-payments reasons took the form of actual import duties. Schemes whereby such duties would be internationally controlled in the light of ideal criteria are most naturally conceived in the institutional framework of a clearing union, of the type, for example, of the recently founded European Payments Union.

50. In such a Union all surpluses and deficits arising out of bilateral payments arrangements are submitted periodically for offsetting, and the net deficits and surpluses thus accruing are settled by adjusting the accounts which each country keeps with the Union. Persistent net creditors accumulate credit balances, and persistent net debtors accumulate debit balances on the Union's books. Suppose that all countries are members of a Union of this type and that to each country is assigned a quota, proportional to the value of its external trade. Defining a country's "normalised balance" as its balance, positive or negative, with the Union divided by its quota, it might be laid down that to each size of normalised balance should correspond a certain "basic percentage" which will be negative, zero, or positive according as the balance is negative, zero, or positive, and which should vary with the size of the "normalised balance," though not necessarily in proportion thereto. Countries would be deemed "stronger" or "weaker" according as their "basic percentages" were more or less positive. Now each country would be required:

a) to import without balance-of-payments restriction or import duty from any country "weaker" than, or equally "strong" with, itself;

b) to impose on imports from any country "stronger" than itself a percentage duty equal to the "basic percentage" of the country from which it is importing *less* its own "basic percentage."

51. In order to avoid constant fluctuation in import duties it would be expedient that basic percentages should vary with normalised balances only at discrete intervals. Thus to each basic percentage would correspond a certain "tranche" of credit which a country would have to run through before its "basic percentage" would be altered. Under this scheme a structure of import duties would be established corresponding roughly to the optimal criterion in paragraph 15, but making no allowance for differences in the responsiveness of supply of exports or for intertrade repercussions. Short-term fluctuations in the balance of payments would be covered by the use of Union credit. Somewhat longer-term disequilibria, if not covered by international capital movements outside the Union, would be corrected by alterations in the structure of import duties.

52. Nothing has been said about any limits to the extent to which a country should be allowed to incur indebtedness to the Union. To set rigid limits would make it difficult to keep extreme net debtors within the system and would deprive the Union of its principal sanction for inducing "weak" countries to apply the desired degree of discrimination in favour of intermediate countries. Unlimited credit facilities would deprive the "weak" countries of any incentive to live within their means by the imposing of import duties appropriate to their position in the scale of "strong" and "weak" countries. The best solution might be to give the Union power to withhold further credit from countries which decline to adjust their import duties to the appropriate levels.

(b) *Variant two.*

53. To deny access to the resources of the Union is, however, something of a blunt instrument, and one which it would be difficult to apply to a country in a net creditor position in the Union. A more refined incentive to apply the correct degree of discrimination might be supplied by the following variant of the scheme outlined above.

54. For each country there would be a special rate called the "rate of equivalence" between its own currency and the unit of account in terms of which members' balances with the clearing union are expressed. Each country's rate of equivalence (expressed as a proportion of its par of exchange in clearing units) would rise or fall with the state of its "normalised balance" in a way rather similar to that previously described for the "basic percentage." When neither in debt nor in credit with the Union, a country's "equivalence" would be equal to unity.

55. While payments and receipts between countries would continue to be netted bilaterally at par, the equivalences would be used for turning net bilateral surpluses and deficits into clearing units for the purpose of multilateral offsetting as follows. Surpluses and deficits incurred by a country *vis-à-vis* "weaker" or equally "strong" countries would be converted into clearing units at the first country's own rate of equivalence. Surpluses or deficits incurred *vis-à-vis* "stronger" countries would be converted into clearing units at the rate of equivalence of the "stronger" country. Each country would be required to impose a percentage duty on imports from each "stronger" country equal to the proportionate excess of the "stronger" country's equivalence over that of the importing country.[6] Countries will have some incentive to apply the degree of import-discrimination required by this system in that it corresponds to the relative exchange rates actually effective for *marginal* transactions with the countries concerned.

The clearing union approach, combined with quantitative import restrictions

56. Systems of the sort discussed in the last seven paragraphs are, of course, far from being practical politics at the present time. Import duties are frequently bound under international trade agreements and in any event govern-

---

[6] See Appendix, paragraph 4

ments are reluctant to use them in defence of the balance of payments because of (*a*) the difficulty of anticipating their precise effects on that balance, (*b*) inflexibility resulting from parliamentary control over taxation, and (*c*) their effect in raising the internal prices of imported goods. Quantitative restriction of imports by means of quotas and individual licensing is more convenient from all these standpoints, though in respect of the last point, its superiority depends on its being buttressed by internal price control and rationing.

57. An attempt might be made to use the clearing union device—for example, the system of variable " equivalence " described above—not to control import duties but merely to provide governments with an incentive to apply quantitative import restrictions with the right degree of severity and discrimination. The system, however, can provide the incentives for an appropriate discrimination only if countries are induced, by their shortage of clearing units, to apply import restrictions of an adequate overall severity; and it would be very difficult for the Union management to determine whether a country's import restrictions were in fact falling so far short of the appropriate degree of severity as to warrant the denial of further access to the Union's resources.

The question of fundamental disequilibrium

58. Any scheme for making the best of import restrictions involving as it must systematic discrimination in favour of " weak " countries is open to the objection that it reduces the incentive to such countries to remedy (*e.g.*, by the adjustment of exchange rates) what may be a fundamental disequilibrium. Recognition that this is so may well deter " stronger " countries from co-operating in building up the type of structure of import restrictions which would be optimal at current exchange rates. Yet it would be a pity if long-run adjustment could be secured only at the price of short-run frustration and waste.

59. The question therefore arises whether procedures for correcting fundamental disequilibrium could not be grafted on to the arrangements for ensuring that such import restrictions as are at any time necessary are applied with an optimal degree of discrimination. If some practicable system on clearing union lines could be devised for the latter purpose, it might also be made to serve the former. Countries which, in spite of the application of severe import restrictions, remain persistent net debtors are clearly marked out for devaluation, while persistent net creditors are equally clearly marked out for revaluation. Against the former at any rate, means of coercion lie to hand in the withdrawal both of credit facilities and of the preferential treatment hitherto accorded to their exports.

Conclusion

60. None of the arrangements examined in Part II of this paper have attempted to carry into effect *all* the features of an optimal system of import restrictions. They have in general ignored the desirability of adjusting the

severity of import restrictions to the responsiveness of export supply of the commodities in question, and they have ignored the refinements rendered desirable by intertrade repercussions. The system of bilateral agreements modified by selective currency transferability probably takes more account of these factors than the more formal multilateral arrangements subsequently examined.

61. The principal features of an optimal structure, however—the ordering of countries according to "strength" with free imports from "weaker" countries, and preference for "intermediate" over "strong" countries—are reproduced in all the schemes considered: (i) bilateralism *plus* selective transferability; (ii) international trade planning; (iii) Frisch's multicompensatory system; and (iv) the various variants of the clearing union approach. My own preference is for schemes of type (i), as the most practicable, and of type (iv), as the nearest approximation to the ideal. I have no illusions as to the immediate practicability of the various clearing union schemes suggested, culminating as they do in a streamlined I.M.F. *cum* I.T.O., but think it possible that some of the features roughly sketched in here may find a place in the international monetary and commercial system of the future—unless, indeed, that system is based on a much more continuous adjustment of exchange rates than has been assumed in the preparation of this paper.

MATHEMATICAL APPENDIX

1. Let

q_m, q_n denote the quantity of m, n respectively imported by B from A.

$p_{m,A}$, $p_{m,B}$ denote the price of m in A and in B, respectively;

$$E = \frac{dq}{dp} \frac{p}{q}$$

denote "elasticity of supply";

$$R = \frac{dq}{d(pq)} \frac{pq}{q} = \frac{1}{1 + \dfrac{1}{E}}$$

denote "responsiveness of supply"; $T_m = (p_{m,B} - p_{m,A})/p_{m,A}$ denote the *ad valorem* tariff equivalent restrictions in B on imports of m from A; and G denote the gain in welfare from the trade adjustment in question.

Then

$$G = p_{m,A} T_m \, \delta q_m + p_{n,A} T_n \, \delta q_n.$$

But the balance of payments must not be altered. Therefore

$$\delta(p_{m,A} q_m) + \delta(p_{n,A} q_n) = 0$$

and

$$G = p_{m,\text{A}}\, \delta q_m \left(T_m - \frac{R_n}{R_m}\, T_n \right)$$

at the optimal point $G = 0$ and

$$\frac{T_m}{T_n} = \frac{R_n}{R_m}.$$

2. Adopting the same notation *mutatis mutandis* as in paragraph 1.

$$G = p_{x,\text{A}}\, T_x\, \delta q_x + p_{y,\text{B}}\, T_y\, \delta q_y + p_{z,\text{A}}\, T_z\, \delta q_z.$$

The balance-of-payments conditions are:

$$- \delta(p_{x,\text{A}}\, q_x) = \delta(p_{y,\text{B}}\, q_y) = \delta(p_{z,\text{A}}\, q_\text{A}).$$

Then

$$G = p_{x,\text{A}}\, \delta q_x \left(T_x - \frac{R_y}{R_x}\, T_y - \frac{R_z}{R_x}\, T_z \right).$$

The optimal point will be attained when

$$R_x T_x = R_y T_y + R_z T_z.$$

3. Frisch (*Review of Economic Studies and Statistics*, November 1948) suggests maximising the following expression

$$(A_1 + A_2 + \cdots + A_n) \sum_{i=1}^{n} \frac{(1B_i^1 + 2B_i^2 + \cdots) - (1A_i^1 + 2A_i^2 + \cdots)}{(1B_i^1 + 2B_i^2 + \cdots)}$$

where $i = 1, 2, \ldots, n$ designate the individual countries, A_i being the total multicompensatory export from i and B_i, the total multicompensatory import into country i, the superscripts indicating the priority categories.

Using the same notation, and bearing in mind that my system admits no export subsidisation and thus no export priorities, I suggest maximising the following expression:

$$\sum_{i=1}^{n} (1B_i^1 + 2B_i^2 + \ldots nB_i^n).$$

4. C is restricting the import of x from A.
   C is restricting the import of y from B.
   B is restricting the import of z from A.
Let
   q_r denote the quantity of $r(= x, y, z)$ imported from the appropriate country to the appropriate country.

$p_{r,Q}$ denote the price of r in Q ($=$ A, B, C).

E_Q denote the rate of equivalence of Q's currency, expressed as a proportion of its par of exchange.

T_r denote the *ad valorem* tariff-equivalent of the restriction on imports of r.

$$R = \frac{\delta q_r}{\delta(P_r q_r)} \cdot \frac{P_r q_r}{q_r}$$

denote the responsiveness of supply of r from the appropriate country to the appropriate country.

The rule regarding import duties in paragraph 55 of the text is:

$$T_x = \frac{E_A - E_C}{E_C}$$

$$T_y = \frac{E_B - E_C}{E_C}$$

$$T_z = \frac{E_A - E_B}{E_B}$$

From which it follows that:

$$T_x = T_y + T_z + T_y T_z.$$

This, though it differs from the formula for an optimal tariff structure arrived at in paragraph 2 above, can be deduced from the same criterion of optimisation. The difference is due to the peculiar balance-of-payments conditions which characterise the system under consideration. The condition of optimisation is:

$$p_{x,A} T_x \delta q_x + p_{y,B} T_y \delta q_y + p_{z,A} T_z \delta q_z = 0.$$

And the balance-of-payments conditions are:

$$\delta(p_{x,A} q_x) = -\delta(p_{z,A} q_z),$$

$$\delta(p_{x,A} q_x) E_A = -\delta(p_{y,B} q_y) E_B.$$

From which it follows, if $R_x = R_y = R_z$, that

$$T_x = T_y + T_z + T_y T_z.$$

Direct *versus* indirect taxes

I. M. D. LITTLE

The first part of this article is designed to show that the usual theoretical treatment of the problem of direct and indirect taxation is based on extraordinary assumptions, and liable to be misleading. An alternative mode of analysis is suggested. In the second part, I try to show that no case against indirect taxation can be proved from the ordinary, general, purely competitive assumptions of economic theory; and, further, that the special assumption, necessary to prove the case, involves an unplausible conclusion concerning incentives.

I

The usual analysis of direct *versus* indirect taxation (or subsidisation) runs typically as follows:[1]

A single "economic man" who spends his income on two goods (one of which may be "money") is assumed. In Figure 1, Q_0 is the equilibrium tax-free position. When an income-tax equal to AB of X is imposed, Q_1 is reached. The same sum could be raised by an indirect tax on Y, which would result in a position such as Q_2. From the usual convexity assumption it follows that Q_2 is worse than Q_1. Q.E.D.

At first sight this result always looks like a conjuring trick. There is no overt reference to marginal costs. Yet it is well known that nothing can be proved without some such reference.[2] The covert reference is as follows: for the proof to be valid the government must be able to buy the same collection of goods whether the individual is at position Q_2 or at position Q_1. This it can do only if Q_2Q_1 has the same slope as the transformation curve of X and Y (the curve showing the maximum amounts of X which could be

---

* *The Economic Journal*, 61(1951): pp. 577–84. Reprinted by courtesy of the author and *The Economic Journal*.

[1] Cf. M. F. W. Joseph, "The Excess Burden of Indirect Taxation," *Review of Economic Studies*, June 1939; H. P. Wald, "The Classical Indictment of Indirect Taxation," *Quarterly Journal of Economics*, August 1945; A. M. Henderson, "The Case for Indirect Taxation," *Economic Journal*, December 1948; A. T. Peacock and D. Berry, "A Note on the Theory of Income Redistribution," *Economica*, February 1951.

[2] Cf. the original Frisch–Hotelling controversy—*Econometrica*, 1939, pp. 145–60; in particular Professor Hotelling's final note, pp. 158–60.

Figure 1

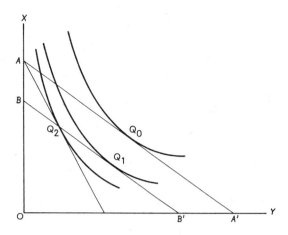

produced given varying quantities of Y, and fixed amounts of all other goods). From this it follows that the slope of BB' must equal the relative marginal costs of the two goods. Thus, in the diagram, relative marginal costs are assumed to be the same at both Q_2 and Q_1.

Although the diagram is drawn with reference to a single individual it may be presumed that it is designed to illustrate the relative effects, on each of many individuals, of two different tax systems of equal monetary incidence. Therefore, a considerable shift of production must be allowed for. This being the case, the assumption that relative marginal costs are the same at both Q_2 and Q_1 is in conflict with the normal assumption used in this connection, that of a diminishing marginal rate of transformation. The analysis is excessively

Figure 2

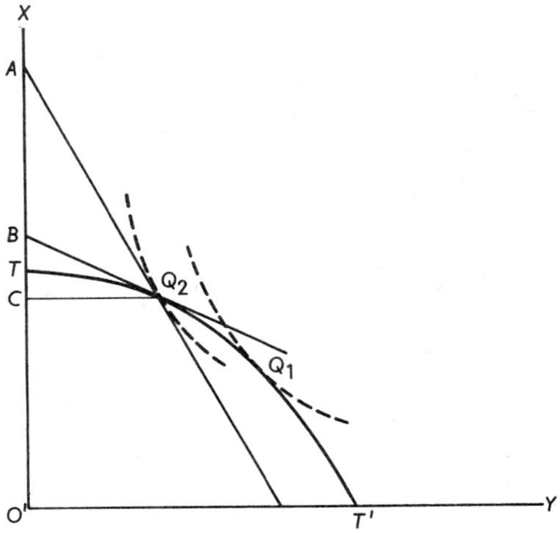

and unnecessarily partial in other ways. The prices of goods, other than those represented, may change when the indirect tax is substituted for the direct. When this is allowed for, it is even conceivable that any given individual would gain as a result of the change.

But none of this invalidates the usual conclusion (that the gainers could overcompensate the losers if direct taxes were substituted for indirect) *given that the supply of labour is not a variable*. In Figure 2 the curve TQ_2Q_1T' is the transformation curve of X and Y, given the quantities of all other goods, and also given the quantities of X and Y demanded by the government.[3] At Q_1 relative price is assumed equal to relative marginal cost (this is indicated by drawing in a "community indifference" curve tangential to the transformation curve at Q_1). Letting p_x, p_y, MC_x, and MC_y stand for the prices and marginal costs of X and Y, we have at Q_2,

$$\frac{p_y}{p_x} = \frac{AC}{CQ_2} \tag{1}$$

and

$$\frac{MC_y}{MC_x} = \frac{BC}{CQ_2} = \text{Marginal rate of transformation of } Y \text{ into } X. \tag{2}$$

Supposing X to be subsidised, otherwise perfect competition, and letting s and t stand for the rate of subsidy and tax respectively it follows from (i) and (ii) that

$$\frac{MC_y}{MC_x(1-s)} = \frac{BC}{CQ_2(1-s)} = \frac{p_y}{p_x} = \frac{AC}{CQ_2},$$

whence

$$s = \frac{AB}{AC}.$$

It is assumed above that the required revenue is raised by means of an income tax, the effects of such a tax on factor supply being ignored. Alternatively, we can suppose that Y is taxed in which case it follows that

$$\frac{MC_y(1+t)}{MC_x} = \frac{BC(1+t)}{CQ_2} = \frac{p_y}{p_x} = \frac{AC}{CQ_2},$$

whence

$$t = \frac{AB}{BC}.$$

That the position Q_2 is not "optimum" follows simply from the divergence of relative prices and relative marginal costs. No other proof is required or

---

[3] The assumption that the government's demands are absolute is made only for simplicity of exposition. We could in principle treat the government as an "economic man" with a consistent set of utility curves.

possible. A "community indifference" curve can, of course, be drawn tangential to AQ_2 at Q_2. This curve must pass below Q_1 on the given assumptions. This follows from the fact that Q_1 is an "optimum" position, while Q_2 is not.[4] So nothing is really added by drawing in the indifference curves. What matters is that at Q_2 the individual rates of substitution of X and Y are not equal to the transformation rate. This analysis is more general and requires fewer restrictive assumptions than those usually made. It also has the advantage that it shows quite clearly, for both subsidies and taxes, that the "case against indirect taxation" is merely a special case of conflict with one of the necessary conditions for the achievement of a Pareto "optimum," i.e., that relative marginal costs be equal to relative prices. At the purely theoretical level nothing more can be said; and nothing less is valid without special "partial" assumptions.

II

In Part I it was arbitrarily assumed that the supply of labour was constant; or, to put it another way, that the consumption of one good, leisure, was unaffected by changes in its own or other prices. This is clearly an indefensible assumption which must be removed. But, for the sake of simplicity, we will continue to ignore savings. The conclusion which we shall reach—that the case against indirect taxation is invalid—can only be reinforced if savings are considered, since an income tax is an indirect tax on savings, as well as on work.

It has been argued by Professor A. M. Henderson that the fact that all marginal taxation is a tax on work (it can also be regarded as a subsidy on leisure, as far as substitution effects are concerned) does not destroy the case against indirect taxation.[5] The argument is that both indirect and direct taxes sin against the necessary "optimum" condition that the rate of substitution of leisure for any other good must equal the rate of transformation between leisure and that good. But, it is argued, indirect taxes *also* prevent the rates of substitution between pairs of goods excluding leisure, being equal to their respective rates of transformation. Thus Professor Henderson writes:

> If a given revenue is required then the resources available to the consumer must be limited to the same extent by either method [i.e., direct or indirect taxation]. But the method of indirect taxation has the further disadvantage of reducing the efficiency with which these resources are used, and therefore imposes an added burden.[6]

I have previously accepted this argument.[7] But I now think I was wrong to do so. The argument is unsatisfactory because it assumes that the resources used

---

[4] Cf. J. de V. Graaff, "On Optimum Tariff Structures," *Review of Economic Studies*, 1949–50, No. 42, p. 57, n. 3.

[5] *Loc. cit.*

[6] *Loc. cit.*, p. 545.

[7] *E.g.*, in the appendix to Chapter IX of *A Critique of Welfare Economics*.

are identical in both cases. In other words, it has to be assumed that the supply of labour is the same whether the taxation is direct or indirect. This amounts to saying that, for every individual, the cross-elasticity of demand for leisure with respect to all other prices is zero; *i.e.*, leisure is not substitutable for any other good. To all intents and purposes, the assumption that the amount of labour does not vary has crept into an argument designed to show that direct taxation is better than indirect taxation, even when the supply of labour is admitted as a variable. This might not matter if it were really plausible to suppose that it would, under no conditions, vary much. I shall suggest below that this is not a plausible supposition.

Consider a perfectly competitive economy with three goods, one being leisure. Designate leisure by Z and the other two goods by X and Y. Let S and T stand respectively for the marginal rate of substitution and the marginal rate of transformation. We can now distinguish three cases as follows:

I. Direct taxation. Here we have

$$S = T \text{ for the pair } (X, Y)$$
$$S \neq T \text{ for the pair } (X, Z)$$
$$S \neq T \text{ for the pair } (Y, Z).$$

II. Indirect taxation on one good other than leisure.
Letting the taxed good be X we have

$$S = T \text{ for the pair } (Y, Z)$$
$$S \neq T \text{ for the pair } (X, Z)$$
$$S \neq T \text{ for the pair } (X, Z)$$

III. Unequal indirect taxation on both goods other than leisure. Here we have

$$S \neq T \text{ for all three pairs.}$$

A comparison of Cases I and II makes it sufficiently obvious that no argument against indirect taxation can be perfectly general. The two cases are quite symmetrical. Unless special assumptions are made, whatever can be said about one can be said about the other. But even if Case III is considered to be what is normally meant by indirect taxation, nothing appears to follow.

Let us illustrate this. In Figure 3 *ABC* is the production surface after subtraction of the government's fixed demands. It is assumed that the government succeeds in manipulating the budget surface so that the community's chosen point on that surface is also a point on the production surface *ABC*. If the chosen point were above the surface the government would not be getting the goods it required; if below it would be getting more than it required.

The points Q_0, Q_1, Q_2, Q_3, and Q_4 are points on the surface. *AA'*, *BB'*, and *CC'* are surface lines along which one of the three " optimum " conditions

Figure 3

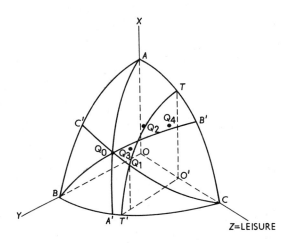

is satisfied. Thus at any point on the line CC', the partial rate of substitution (leisure constant) of Y for X equals the partial rate of transformation (leisure constant). These contract lines, if projected on to the planes BOC, AOC, and AOB, respectively, would be analogous to ordinary contract curves. The point Q_0 is the only point at which all the optimum conditions are satisfied. Case I lands us on the line CC' between C and Q_0. Case *II* lands us either on AA', between A' and Q_0, or on BB' between B' and Q_0. Case III brings us to some point which lies on none of the contract lines. Part of Figure 2 is embedded in Figure 3. The plane surface $TQ_2Q_1T'O'$ appears in both diagrams.

The advocates of direct taxation or subsidisation have to claim that every point on CC' is better than any other point on the production surface. It is intuitively obvious that there is no reason whatever for claiming that points on the line CC' are superior to those on the lines AA' and BB'. The lesser claim might, however, be made that points on a contract line are superior to points not on a contract line.

What, then, can be said about the relative superiority of points such as Q_0, Q_1, Q_2, Q_3, or Q_4? First, Q_0 is "superior" to any other point because all the "optimum" conditions are satisfied. In other words, a "community indifference" surface is tangential to the production surface at Q_0, and cannot lie below the production surface at any other point. Secondly, the "community indifference" surface appropriate to Q_1 cannot lie below the production surface in the neighbourhood of the point Q_2. This is because it is tangential to the line $T'Q_1Q_2T$ at Q_1. Thirdly, it is quite consistent, both that these two conditions should be fulfilled and that the same indifference surface should or should not lie below the production surface in the neighbourhood of a point such as Q_3. There therefore appears to be no reason whatever to support any claim that Q_1 must be "superior" to Q_3.[8] A movement from Q_1 to Q_3 would reduce the amount of leisure. But is is also conceivable, given suitable production and indifference surfaces, that the indifference surface of Q_1 should lie below the production surface in the neighbourhood of a point like Q_4, where the amount of leisure is increased. The conclusion is that nothing whatever can be said about the "superiority" of direct taxation unless it is certain that the amount of leisure will not change.

We have seen that Professor Henderson based his argument on the contention that the supply of labour would be constant. This means, in terms of Figure 3, that it is presumed that a change from direct to indirect taxes would always cause a movement from a point like Q_1 to one like Q_2, leisure remaining constant. Taken to its logical extreme, such a contention is highly paradoxical. It implies that the amount of labour supplied is a function only of the quantities of goods consumed by the government. In the limit this implies that people would work as much even if income tax was 100 percent of all incomes, consumption goods being supplied free!

But, apart from subsidies, is there any reason to suppose that the supply of labour might not be greater under a suitable indirect taxation system than under direct taxation? Surely, those who have maintained that direct taxation —quite apart from any "money illusion"— is more harmful to incentives are not necessarily wrong?

Suppose that Y, in our diagram, stands for "necessities" and X for "luxuries." Let the first situation be a direct tax equilibrium. Then the equal taxation of "necessities" and "luxuries" (equivalent to direct taxation) is replaced by a relatively large tax on "necessities," and a relatively small one on "luxuries" (Case III). Is it not then plausible to suppose that the individual, while keeping his consumption of "necessities" more or less constant, might increase his consumption of "luxuries" at the expense of leisure, i.e., move to a point like Q_3 which *may* be "superior" to Q_1? In Case II where only "necessities" are taxed the individual *must* move to a point on BB' between Q_0 and B'. Since the consumption of "necessities" is not much reduced, this may (given sets of preferences consistent with our contract lines) entail a reduction in leisure. In the extreme case, when the price-elasticity of demand for some necessity is zero, the change from an income tax to an indirect tax on the necessity would result in a movement from Q_1 to Q_0. The reason is as follows. Q_0 is the poll-tax position. But with no poll tax, and the price of Y raised to keep on the same production surface, Q_0 would still be the equilibrium position, since it is consistent with (a) zero price-elasticity of demand for Y, real income given, and (b) unchanged real

---

[8] By saying one point is "superior" to another we mean that its "community indifference" surface passes inside (further from the origin than) the other point in the neighborhood of that point; which implies that the potential losers by a move from the latter to the former would be unable profitably to bribe the potential gainers to oppose the change. Therefore no point x can be "superior" to any other chosen point y if the indifference surface of x is below the production surface in the neighbour hood of y.

income. It has often been held that a tax on such a good is the equivalent of an income tax. This is wrong: it is the equivalent of a poll tax; while an income tax is itself the equivalent of a poll tax only if the supply of labour is perfectly inelastic. If, in such a case, we were interested more in incentives than " welfare," we could increase the tax on " necessities " in order to pay a subsidy on " luxuries." This would amount to a tax on leisure. Leisure would be subsidised in relation to " necessities," but this would have no substitution effect. It would also be taxed in relation to " luxuries " which would have an incentive effect.

If any general conclusion can be risked, it is simply that the best taxes are those on goods for which the demand is least elastic. The same holds true for subsidies. Income tax, which is a subsidy on leisure, is not exceptional. Only insofar as the demand for leisure is highly inelastic is it a good tax. The purely theoretical " case against indirect taxation " is an illusion.

Part VII
INVESTMENT AND GROWTH

The analytically and conceptually most complex problems of welfare economics are to be found in the field of investment and growth. The classical analysis of stationary states, though gradually clarifying some of the issues, was inadequate to deal with choices among alternative time paths of capital accumulation. Perhaps the first paper to set forth the issues clearly was that of Ramsey, who analyzed the problem of a society choosing at any moment of time between consumption and capital accumulation and thereby affecting its future production possibilities. The mathematics used, that of the calculus of variations, was quite formidable, and only in recent years has the subject renewed interest. There is now a very rapidly growing literature on optimal growth, extending Ramsey's methods to more general models.

In 1937 von Neumann developed a completely closed dynamic model of the economy in which all inputs were themselves produced, production took time, and consumption was regarded as simply input to the production of labor. In such a model it turned out there was a maximal rate of growth which was in fact a competitive equilibrium, at which the rate of interest equalled the rate of growth.

Malinvaud's model combined elements of Ramsey's and von Neumann's. As in Ramsey's model, there were exogenous factors of production (e.g., labor) and correspondingly there was a net output not used for further production. Unlike Ramsey, who was concerned with the maximization of a social utility function, Malinvaud developed necessary and sufficient conditions for technological efficiency, i.e., situations in which it is impossible to increase the net output of any good without decreasing that of another.

A different, though related, criteron for optimal growth is presented in the paper of Allais—that of the maximum sustainable steady (i.e., exponential) growth of consumption. It turns out that this optimum occurs when the rate of interest equals the rate of growth of original factors (e.g., labor). For a stationary economy, this result had been developed earlier by Allais, although it was partly anticipated by Wicksell and Meade (see the references in Allais' paper). The fairly straightforward extension to the dynamic economy was made almost simultaneously by an extraordinary number of scholars: J. Desrousseaux,[1] E. S. Phelps,[2] J. Robinson,[3] C. C. von Weizsäcker,[4] T. Swan,[5] and very probably several others. Allais goes on to develop an empirical model of growth, using a concept of capital closer to Jevons and the Austrians than most other writers, such as Ramsey.

The paper of Massé and Gibrat illustrates the practical solution of allocation of resources among alternative investment activities. It shows the need for careful definition of the output requirements (in this case, the recognition that demand for electricity has both peak load and average load dimensions); it also shows the power of linear programming techniques.

---

[1] "Expansion stable et taux d'interêt optimal," *Annales des Mines*, 1961, 829–44.

[2] "The Golden Rule of Accumulation: A Fable for Growthmen," *American Economic Review*, 51(1961): 638–43.

[3] "A Neo-Classical Theorem," *Review of Economic Studies*, 29(1962): 219–26.

[4] *Wachstum, Zins und optimale Investitionsquote*, p. 79 [Basel: Kyklos-Verlag, and Tübingen: J. C. B. Mohr (Paul Siebeck), 1962].

[5] "Growth Models: Of Golden Ages and Production Functions," in K. Berrill (ed.), *Economic Development with Special Reference to East Asia*, pp. 3–16 (London: Macmillan, and New York: St. Martin's, 1964).

A mathematical theory of saving*

FRANK P. RAMSEY

I

The first problem I propose to tackle is this: how much of its income should a nation save? To answer this a simple rule is obtained valid under conditions of surprising generality; the rule, which will be further elucidated later, runs as follows.

The rate of saving multiplied by the marginal utility of money should always be equal to the amount by which the total net rate of enjoyment of utility falls short of the maximum possible rate of enjoyment.

In order to justify this rule it is, of course, necessary to make various simplifying assumptions: we have to suppose that our community goes on for ever without changing either in numbers or in its capacity for enjoyment or in its aversion to labour; that enjoyments and sacrifices at different times can be calculated independently and added; and that no new inventions or improvements in organisation are introduced save such as can be regarded as conditioned solely by the accumulation of wealth.[1]

One point should perhaps be emphasised more particularly; it is assumed that we do not discount later enjoyments in comparison with earlier ones, a practice which is ethically indefensible and arises merely from the weakness of the imagination; we shall, however, in Section II include such a rate of discount in some of our investigations.

We also ignore altogether distributional considerations, assuming, in fact, that the way in which consumption and labour are distributed between the members of the community depends solely on their total amounts, so that total satisfaction is a function of these total amounts only.

Besides this, we neglect the differences between different kinds of goods and different kinds of labour, and suppose them to be expressed in terms of fixed standards, so that we can speak simply of quantities of capital, consumption, and labour without discussing their particular forms.

---

* *The Economic Journal*, 38(1928): pp. 543–59. Reprinted by courtesy of *The Economic Journal*.
    [1] *I.e.* they must be such as would not occur without a certain degree of accumulation, but could be foreseen given that degree.

Foreign trade, borrowing, and lending need not be excluded, provided we assume that foreign nations are in a stable state, so that the possibilities of dealing with them can be included on the constant conditions of production. We do, however, reject the possibility of a state of progressive indebtedness to foreigners continuing for ever.

Lastly, we have to assume that the community will always be governed by the same motives as regards accumulation, so that there is no chance of our savings being selfishly consumed by a subsequent generation; and that no misfortunes will occur to sweep away accumulations at any point in the relevant future.

Let us then denote by $x(t)$ and $a(t)$ the total rates of consumption and labour of our community, and by $c(t)$ its capital at time t. Its income is taken to be a general function of the amounts of labour and capital, and will be called $f(a, c)$; we then have, since savings plus consumption must equal income,

$$\frac{dc}{dt} + x = f(a, c). \tag{1}$$

Now let us denote by $U(x)$ the total rate of utility of a rate of consumption x, and by $V(a)$ the total rate of disutility of a rate of labour a; and the corresponding marginal rates we will call $u(x)$ and $v(a)$; so that

$$u(x) = \frac{dU(x)}{dx}$$

$$v(a) = \frac{dV(a)}{da}.$$

We suppose, as usual, that $u(x)$ is never increasing and $v(a)$ never decreasing.

We have now to introduce a concept of great importance in our argument. Suppose we have a given capital c, and are going neither to increase nor decrease it. Then $U(x) - V(a)$ denotes our net enjoyment per unit of time, and we shall make this a maximum, subject to the condition that our expenditure x is equal to what we can produce with labour a and capital c. The resulting rate of enjoyment $U(x) - V(a)$ will be a function of c, and will, up to a point, increase as c increases, since with more capital we can obtain more enjoyment.

This increase of the rate of enjoyment with the amount of capital may, however, stop for either of two reasons. It might, in the first place, happen that a further increment of capital would not enable us to increase either our income or our leisure; or, secondly, we might have reached the maximum conceivable rate of enjoyment, and so have no use for more income or leisure. In either case a certain finite capital would give us the greatest rate of enjoyment economically *obtainable*, whether or not this was the greatest rate *conceivable*.

On the other hand, the rate of enjoyment may never stop increasing as capital increases. There are then two logical possibilities: either the rate of enjoyment will increase to infinity, or it will approach asymptotically to a certain finite limit. The first of these we shall dismiss on the ground that economic causes alone could never give us more than a certain finite rate of enjoyment (called above the maximum conceivable rate). There remains the second case, in which the rate of enjoyment approaches a finite limit, which may or may not be equal to the maximum conceivable rate. This limit we shall call the maximum *obtainable* rate of enjoyment, although it cannot, strictly speaking, be obtained, but only approached indefinitely.

What we have in the several cases called the maximum obtainable rate of enjoyment or utility we shall call for short *Bliss* or *B*. And in all cases we can see that the community must have enough either to reach *Bliss* after a finite time, or at least to approximate to it indefinitely. For in this way alone is it possible to make the amount by which enjoyment falls short of bliss summed throughout time a finite quantity; so that if it should be possible to reach bliss or approach it indefinitely, this will be infinitely, more desirable than any other course of action. And it is bound to be possible, since by setting aside a small sum each year we can in time increase our capital to any desired extent.[2]

Enough must therefore be saved to reach or approach bliss some time, but this does not mean that our whole income should be saved. The more we save the sooner we shall reach bliss, but the less enjoyment we shall have now and we have to set the one against the other. Mr. Keynes has shown me that the rule governing the amount to be saved can be determined at once from these considerations. But before explaining his argument it will be best to develop equations which can be used in the more general problems which we shall consider later.

The first of these comes from equating the marginal disutility of labour at any time to the product of the marginal efficiency of labour by the marginal utility of consumption at that time, *i.e.*

$$v(a) = \frac{\partial f}{\partial a} u(x). \tag{2}$$

The second equals the advantage derived from an increment Δx of consumption at time t, to that derived by postponing it for an infinitesimal period Δt, which will increase its amount to

$$\Delta x \left(1 + \frac{\cdot \partial f}{\partial c} \Delta t \right),$$

since $\partial f / \partial c$ gives the rate of interest earned by waiting. This gives

$$u\{x(t)\} = \left\{ 1 + \frac{\partial f}{\partial c} \Delta t \right\} u\{x(t + \Delta t)\}$$

[2] As it stands this argument is incomplete, since in the last case considered above bliss was the limiting value, as capital tends to infinity, of the enjoyment obtainable by spending our *whole income*, and so making no provision for increasing capital further. The lacuna can easily be filled by remarking that to save £$(1/n)$ in the nth year would be sufficient to increase capital to infinity [since $\Sigma(1/n)$ is divergent], and that the loss of income, £$(1/n)$ would then decrease to zero, so that the limiting values of income and expenditure would be the same.

or in the limit

$$\frac{d}{dt} u(x(t)) = -\frac{\partial f}{\partial c} \cdot u(x(t)). \tag{3}$$

This equation means that $u(x)$, the marginal utility of consumption, falls at a proportionate rate given by the rate of interest. Consequently x continually increases unless and until either $\partial f/\partial c$ or $u(x)$ vanishes, in which case it is easy to see that bliss must have been attained.

Equations (1), (2), and (3) are sufficient to solve our problem provided we know c_0, the given capital with which the nation starts at $t = 0$, the other "initial condition" being supplied by considerations as to the behaviour of the function as $t \to \infty$.

To solve the equations we proceed as follows: noticing that x, a, and c are all functions of one independent variable, the time, we have

$$\frac{d}{dx} \{u(x) \cdot f(a, c)\} = \frac{du}{dx} \cdot f(a, c) + u(x) \frac{\partial f}{\partial a} \frac{da}{dx} + u(x) \frac{\partial f}{\partial c} \frac{dc}{dt} \frac{dt}{dx}$$

$$= \frac{du}{dx} f(a, c) + v(a) \frac{da}{dx} - \frac{du(x)}{dt} \{f(a, c) - x\} \frac{dt}{dx}$$

$$= x \frac{du}{dx} + v(a) \frac{da}{dx}. \quad \text{(Using (2), (3), and (1).)}$$

Consequently, integrating by parts

$$u(x) \cdot f(a, c) = xu(x) - U(x) + V(a) + \text{a constant } K,$$

or

$$\frac{dc}{dt} = f(a, c) - x = \frac{K - \{U(x) - V(a)\}}{u(x)}. \tag{4}$$

We have now to identity K with what we called B, or bliss. This is most easily done by starting in a different way.

$$\int_0^\infty (B - U(x) + V(a))\, dt$$

represents the amount by which enjoyment falls short of bliss integrated throughout time; this is (or can be made) finite, and our problem is to minimise it. If we apply the calculus of variations straight away, using equation (1), we get equations (2) and (3) again; but if, instead of this, we first change the independent variable to c, we get a great simplification. Our integral becomes

$$\int_{c_0}^\infty \frac{B - U(x) + V(a)}{dc/dt}\, dc^3$$

---

[3] The upper limit will not be ∞, but the least capital with which bliss can be obtained, if this is finite. c steadily increases with t, at any rate until the integrand vanishes, so that the transformation is permissible.

or

$$\int_{c_0}^{\infty} \frac{B - U(x) + V(a)}{f(a, c) - x} \, dc. \quad \text{Using (1).}$$

Now in this x and a are entirely arbitrary functions of c, and to minimise the integral we have simply to minimise the integrand by equating to zero its partial derivatives. Taking the derivative with respect to x we obtain:

$$\frac{-u(x)}{f(a, c) - x} + \frac{B - U(x) + V(a)}{\{f(a, c) - x\}^2} = 0;$$

consequently

$$\frac{dc}{dt} = f(a, c) - x = \frac{B - (U(x) - V(a))}{u(x)}, \tag{5}$$

or as we stated at the beginning, *rate of saving multiplied by marginal utility of consumption should always equal bliss minus actual rate of utility enjoyed.*

Mr. Keynes, to whom I am indebted for several other suggestions, has shown me that this result can also be obtained by the following simple reasoning.

Suppose that in a year we ought to spend £x and save £z. Then the advantage to be gained from an extra £1 spent is $u(x)$, the marginal utility of money, and this must be equated to the sacrifice imposed by saving £1 less.

Saving £1 less in the year will mean that we shall only save £z in $1 + (1/z)$ years not as before, in one year. Consequently, we shall be in $1 + (1/z)$ year's time exactly where we should have been in one year's time, and the whole course of our approach to bliss will be postponed by $(1/z)$ of a year, so that we shall enjoy $1/z$ of a year less bliss and $1/z$ of a year more at our present rate. The sacrifice is, therefore,

$$\frac{1}{z} \{B - (U(x) - V(a))\}.$$

Equating this to $u(x)$, we get equation (5) again, if we replace z by dc/dt, its limiting value.

Unfortunately this simple reasoning cannot be applied when we take account of time-discounting, and I have therefore retained my equation (1)–(4), which can easily be extended to deal with more difficult problems.

The most remarkable feature of the rule is that it is altogether independent of the production function $f(a, c)$, except insofar as this determines bliss, the maximum rate of utility obtainable. In particular the amount we should save out of a given income is entirely independent of the present rate of interest, unless this is actually zero. The paradoxical nature of this result will to some extent be mitigated later, when we find that if the future is discounted at a constant rate ρ and the rate of interest is constant and equal to r, the proportion of income to be saved is a function of the ratio ρ/r. If $\rho = 0$ this ratio is 0 (unless r be 0 also) and the proportion to be saved is consequently independent of r.

The rate of saving which the rule requires is greatly in excess of that which anyone would normally suggest, as can be seen from the following table, which is put forward merely as an illustration.

Family Income per Annum	Total Utility
£150	2
£200	3
£300	4
£500	5
£1000	6
£2000	7
£5000	8 = Bliss

If we neglect variations in the amount of labour, the amount that should be saved out of a family income of £500 would be about £300. For then bliss minus actual rate of utility = $8 - 3 = 5$. Savings = £300 and marginal utility of consumption at £200 = about 1/£60. (From £150 to £300 $U(x) = (13x/300) - 3 - x^2/15,000$, approximating by fitting a parabola, so that $u(x) = (13/300) - x/7,500 = 1/60$ if $x = 200$.)

It is worth pausing for a moment to consider how far our conclusions are affected by considerations which our simplifying assumptions have forced us to neglect. The probable increase of population consitutes a reason for saving even more, and so does the possibility that future inventions will put the bliss level higher than at present appears. On the other hand, the probability that future inventions and improvements in organisation are likely to make income obtainable with less sacrifice than at present is a reason for saving less. The influence of inventions thus works in two opposite ways: they give us new needs which we can better satisfy if we have saved up beforehand, but they also increase our productive capacity and make preliminary saving less urgent.

The most serious factor neglected is the possibility of future wars and earthquakes destroying our accumulations. These cannot be adequately accounted for by taking a very low rate of interest over long periods, since they may make the rate of interest actually negative, destroying as they do not only interest, but principal as well.

II

I propose now to assume that returns to capital and labour are constant and independent,[4] so that

$$f(a, c) = pa + rc,$$

where p, the rate of wages, and r, the rate of interest, are constants.

---

[4] It is worth noting that in most of (a) we only require independence of returns, and not constancy, and that nowhere do we really require *wages* to be constant, but these assumptions are made throughout to simplify the statement. They are less absurd if the state is one among others which are only advancing slowly, so that the rates of interest and wages are largely independent of what out particular state saves and earns.

This assumption will enable us

a) To represent our former solution by a simple diagram;

b) To extend it to the case of an individual who only lives a finite time;

c) To extend it to include the problem in which future utilities and disutilities are discounted at a constant rate.

On our new hypothesis the income of the community falls into two clearly defined parts, pa and rc, which it will be convenient to call its *earned* and *unearned* income respectively.

a) Equation (2), which now reads

$$v(a) = pu(x),$$

determines a as a function of x only, and we can conveniently put

$$y = x - pa = \text{consumption} - \text{earned income}$$
$$w(y) = u(x) = v(a)/p$$
$$W(y) = \int w(y)\, dy = \int (u(x)\, dx - v(a)\, da) = U(x) - V(a).$$

$W(y)$ may be called the total and $w(y)$ the marginal utility of unearned income, since they are the total and marginal utilities arising from the possession of an unearned income y available for consumption.

Equation (5) now gives

$$rc - y = f(a, c) - x = \frac{B - W(y)}{w(y)} \qquad (6)$$

or

$$B - W(y) = \frac{dW}{dy}(rc - y),$$

which means that the point (rc, B) lies on the tangent at y to the curve $z = W(y)$.

Figure 1 shows the curve $z = W(y)$, which either attains the value B at a finite value y_1 (the case shown in the figure) or else approaches it asymptotically as $y \to \infty$.

In order to determine how much of a given unearned income rc should be saved, we take the point P, (rc, B), on the line $z = B$, and from it draw a tangent to the curve (not $z = B$, which will always be one tangent, but the other one). If the abscissa of Q, the point of contact, is y, an amount y of the unearned income should be consumed, and the remainder, $rc - y$, should be saved. Of course y may be negative, which would mean that not only would the whole unearned income be saved, but part of the earned income also.

It is easy to see that there must always be such a tangent, because the curve $z = W(y)$ will have a tangent or asymptote $y = -\eta$, where η is the greatest excess of earnings over consumption compatible with continued existence.

This rule determines how much of a given income should be spent, but it does not tell us what our income will amount to after a given lapse of time. This is obtained from equation (3), which now gives us

$$\frac{d}{dt} w(y) = -rw(y)$$

or

$$w(y) = Ae^{-rt}. \tag{7}$$

Here $A = w(y_0)$, where y_0 is the value of y for $t = 0$ determined as the abscissa of Q, where P is (rc_0, B).

Supposing, then, we want to find the time taken in accumulating a capital c from an initial capital c_0, we take P to be the point (rc, B) and P_0 to be

Figure 1

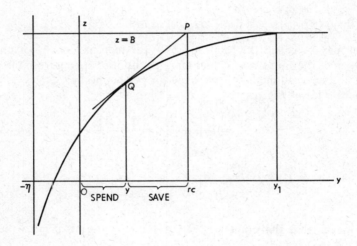

(rc_0, B). $w(y)$ is then the slope of the tangent from P, and $w(y_0)$ the slope of the tangent from P_0, so that the time in question

$$= \frac{1}{r} \log_e \frac{w(y_0)}{w(y)} = \frac{1}{r} \log_e \frac{\text{slope of tangent from } P_0}{\text{slope of tangent from } P}.$$

b) Suppose now that we are concerned with an individual who lives only for a definite time, say T years, instead of with a community which lives for ever. We still have equation (4)

$$f(a, c) - x = \frac{K - (Ux - V(a))}{u(x)}$$

or

$$rc - y = \frac{K - W(y)}{w(y)}, \tag{8}$$

but K is no longer equal to B, and has still to be determined. In order to find it we must know how much capital our man feels it necessary to leave his heirs; let us call this c_3.

Equation (S) means, as before, that y can be found as the abscissa of the point of contact Q of a tangent drawn from (rc, K) or P to the curve. P always lies on $z = K$, and its abscissa begins by being rc_0 and ends by being rc_3. K we can take as being less than B, since a man who lives only a finite time will save less than one who lives an infinite time, and the greater K is, the greater will be the rate of saving. Consequently $z = K$ will meet the curve, say, at P_4.

From both P_0 and P_3 there will be two tangents to the curve, of which either the upper or the lower can, for all we know, be taken as determining y_0 and y_3. If, however, $c_3 > c_0$ as in Figure 2, we can only take the lower

Figure 2

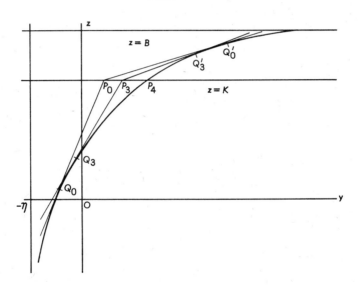

tangent from P_0, since the upper tangent gives a value of y_0 greater than either of the values of y_3, which is impossible, as y continually increases. Taking, then, Q_0 as the point of contact of the lower tangent from P_0, there are two possible cases, according as we take as giving y_3 either Q_3, the lower, or Q_3', the upper value. If we take Q_3, P_0 moves straight to P_3, and there is saving all the time; this happens when T is small. But if T is large, Q_0 moves right along to Q_3', and P_0 goes first up to P_4, and then back to P_3; to begin with there is saving, and subsequently splashing. Similarly, if $c_0 > c_3$, there are two possible cases, and in this case it is the lower tangent from P_3 that cannot be taken.

In order to determine which tangents to take and also the value of K we must use the condition derived from equation (7),

$$\frac{\text{slope of tangent taken from } P_0}{\text{slope of tangent taken from } P_3} = \frac{w(y_0)}{w(y_3)} = e^{rT}.$$

This, together with the fact that the abscissae of P_0 and P_3 are c_0, c_3, and that they have the same ordinate K, suffices to fix both K and the tangents to be taken.

c) We have now to see how our results must be modified when we no longer reckon future utilities and disutilities as equal to present ones, but discount them at a constant rate ρ.

This rate of discounting future *utilities* must, of course, be distinguished from the rate of discounting future sums of money. If I can borrow or lend at a rate r I must necessarily be equally pleased with an extra £1 now and an extra £$(1 + r)$ in a year's time, since I could always exchange the one for the other. My marginal rate of discount for money is, therefore, necessarily r, but my rate of discount for utility may be quite different, since the marginal utility of money to me may be varying by my increasing or decreasing my expenditure as time goes on.

In assuming the rate of discount constant, I do not mean that it is the same for all individuals, since we are at present only concerned with one individual or community, but that the present value of an enjoyment at any future date is to be obtained by discounting it at the rate ρ. Thus, taking it to be about $\frac{3}{4}$ percent, utility at any time would be regarded as twice as desirable as that a hundred years later, four times as valuable as that two hundred years later and so on at a compound rate. This is the only assumption we can make, without contradicting our fundamental hypothesis that successive generations are actuated by the same system of preferences. For if we had a varying rate of discount—say a higher one for the first fifty years—our preference for enjoyments in A.D. 2000 over those in A.D. 2050 would be calculated at the lower rate, but that of the people alive in A.D. 2000 would be at the higher.

Let us suppose first that the rate of discount for utility ρ is less than the rate of interest r.

Then equations (1) and (2) are unchanged, but equation (3) becomes

$$\frac{d}{dt} u(x) = -u(x)\left\{\frac{\partial f}{\partial c} - \rho\right\}$$

$$= -u(x)(r - \rho), \tag{9}$$

as we are now assuming $\partial f/\partial c$ constant and equal to r; consequently

$$w(y) = u(x) = Ae^{-(r-\rho)t} \tag{9a}$$

and

$$rc - y = \frac{dc}{dt} = \frac{dc}{dw} \cdot \frac{dw}{dt} = -(r - \rho)w\frac{dc}{dw},$$

so

$$\frac{dc}{dw} + \frac{rc}{(r - \rho)w} = \frac{y}{(r - \rho)w},$$

where

$$cw^{r/(r-\rho)} = \int \frac{yw^{\rho/(r-\rho)}}{r - \rho} \, dw + \frac{K}{r}$$

$$= \frac{1}{r} yw^{r/(r-\rho)} - \frac{1}{r} \int_b^y w^{r/(r-\rho)}(y) \, dy + \frac{K}{r}$$

(K, b constants)
and

$$\frac{dc}{dt} = rc - y = \frac{K - \int_b^y w^{r/(r-\rho)}(y) \, dy}{w^{r/(r-\rho)}(y)}. \tag{10}$$

This equation is the same as (8) except that instead of $w(y)$ and $W(y)$, which is $\int w(y) dy$, we have $w^{r/(r-\rho)}(y)$ and $\int w^{r/(r-\rho)}(y)(dy$. The method of solution both for a community and for an individual is therefore the same as before, except that instead of the real utility of unearned income we have to consider what we can call its modified utility, obtained by integrating the marginal utility to the power $r/(r - \rho)$. This has the effect of accelerating the decrease of marginal utility and lessening the relative importance of high incomes. We can in this way translate our discounting of the future into a discounting of high incomes. The rate at which this is done is governed solely by the ratio of ρ to r, so that if ρ is 0 it is independent of the value of r, provided this is not also 0. The main conclusion of section I is thus confirmed.

There is, however, a slight difficulty, because we have not really shown yet that if we are considering an infinite time, the constant K is to be interpreted as what might be called "modified bliss," *i.e.*, the maximum value of

$$\int_b^y w^{r/(r-\rho)}(y) \, dy.$$

This modified bliss would require the same income as bliss does, the modification being solely in the value set on it. This result can, however, be deduced at once from equation (9a), which shows that y increases until bliss is reached so that dc/dt can never become negative and K cannot be less than modified bliss. On the other hand, provided this condition is fulfilled, 9(a) shows that the larger y is initially, the smaller will be A, and the larger will be y throughout future time. Hence K must be as small as possible (provided it is not so small as to make dc/dt ultimately negative); so that K cannot be greater than modified bliss. Hence as it is neither less nor greater it must be equal.

As in (b), we can adapt our solution to the case of an individual with only a finite time to live, in this case drawing tangents to the modified utility curve.

An interesting special case is that of a community for which

$$w(y) = Dy^{-\alpha} \qquad (\alpha > 1).$$

We shall have

$$w^{r/(r-\rho)}(y) = Ey^{-\beta}, \; \beta = \frac{r\alpha}{r-\rho}, \; E = D^{r/(r-\rho)}$$

$$\text{savings} = \frac{K - \int w^{r/(r-\rho)}(y) \, dy}{w^{r/(r-\rho)}(y) \, dy} = \frac{K - K_1 + \dfrac{Ey^{1-\beta}}{\beta - 1}}{Ey^{-\beta}}.$$

It is clear that corresponding to $K = B$ in the case when $\rho = 0$; we have here

$$K = K_1$$

and

$$\text{savings} = \frac{y}{\beta - 1};$$

i.e., a constant proportion

$$\frac{r - \rho}{r(\alpha - 1) + \rho}$$

of unearned income should be saved, which if $\rho = 0$ is $1/(\alpha - 1)$, and independent of r.

If the rate of interest is less than the rate of discounting utility, we shall have similar equations, leading to a very different result. The marginal utility of consumption will rise at a rate $\rho - r$, and consumption will fall towards the barest subsistence level at which its marginal utility may be taken as infinite, if we disregard the possibility of suicide. During this process all capital will be exhausted and debts incurred to the extent to which credit can be obtained, the simplest assumption on this point being that it will be possible to borrow a sum such that it is just possible to keep alive after paying the interest on it.

III

Let us next consider the problem of the determination of the rate of interest.

α) In the first place we will suppose that everyone discounts future utility for himself or his heirs, at the same rate ρ.

Then in a state of *equilibrium* there will be no saving and

$$\frac{dx}{dt} = \frac{dc}{dt} = 0,$$

so that we have

$$x = f(a, c),$$

$$v(a) = \frac{\partial f}{\partial a}\, u(x),$$

$$\frac{\partial f}{\partial c} = \rho;$$

three equations to determine x, a, and c.

The last equation tells us that the rate of interest as determined by the marginal productivity of capital, $\partial f/\partial c$, must be equal to the rate of discounting ρ.[5]

But suppose that at a given time, say the present, $(\partial f/\partial c) > \rho$. Then there will not be equilibrium, but saving, and since a great deal cannot be saved in a short time, it may be centuries before equilibrium is reached, or it may never be reached, but only approached asymptotically; and the question arises as to how, in the meantime, the rate of interest is determined, since it cannot be by the ordinary equilibrium equation of supply and demand.

The difficulty is that the rate of interest functions as a demand price for a whole quantity of capital, but as a supply price, not for a quantity of capital, but for a rate of saving. The resulting state of affairs is represented in Figure 3, in which, however, variations in the amount of labour are neglected. This shows the demand curve for capital $r = (\partial f/\partial c)$, the ultimate supply curve $r = \rho$ and the temporary supply curve $c = c_0$. It is clear that the rate of interest is determined directly by the intersection of the demand curve with the temporary supply curve $c = c_0$. The ultimate supply curve $r = \rho$ only comes in as governing the rate at which c_0 approaches its ultimate value OM, a rate which depends roughly on the ratio of PM to QN. We see, therefore, that the rate of interest is governed primarily by the demand price, and may greatly exceed the reward ultimately necessary to induce abstinence.

Similarly, in the accounting of a Socialist State the function of the rate of interest would be to ensure the wisest use of existing capital, not to serve in any direct way as a guide to the proportion of income which should be saved.

β) We must now try to take some account of the fact that different people discount future utility at different rates, and, quite apart from the time factor are not so interested in their heirs as in themselves.

Let us suppose that they are not concerned with their heirs at all; that each man is charged with a share of the maintenance of such children as are necessary to maintain the population, but starts his working life without any capital and ends it without any, having spent his savings on an annuity; that within his own lifetime he has a constant utility schedule for consumption and discounts future utility at a constant rate, but that this rate may be supposed different for different people.

---

[5] Equilibrium could, however, also be obtained either at bliss with $< \rho\ (\partial f/\partial c)$, or at the subsistence level with $\rho > (\partial f/\partial c)$. Cf. ($\gamma$) below.

Figure 3

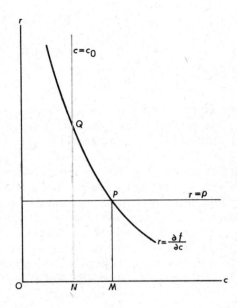

When such a community is in equilibrium, the rate of interest must, of course, equal the demand price of capital $\partial f/\partial c$. And it will also equal the "supply price," which arises in the following way. Suppose that the rate of interest is constant and equal to r, and that the rate of discount for a given individual is ρ. Then if $r > \rho$, he will save when he is young, not only to provide for loss of earning power in old age, but also because he can get more pounds to spend at a later date for those he forgoes spending now. If we neglect variations in his earning power, his action can be calculated by modifying the equations of IIc to apply to a finite life as in IIb. He will for a time accumulate capital, and then spend it before he dies. Besides this man, we must suppose there to be in our community other men, exactly like him except for being born at different times. The total capital possessed by n men of this sort whose birthdays are spread evenly through the period of a lifetime will be n times the *average* capital possessed by each in the course of his life. The class of men of this sort will, therefore, possess a constant capital depending on the rate of interest, and this will be the amount of capital supplied by them at that price. (If $\rho > r$, it may be negative, as they may borrow when young and pay back when old.) We can then obtain the total supply curve of capital by adding together the supplies provided at a given price by each class of individual.

If, then, we neglect men's interest in their heirs, we see that capital has a definite supply price to be equated to its demand price. This supply price depends on people's rates of discount for utility, and it can be equated to the rate of discount of the "marginal saver" in the sense that someone whose rate of discount is equal to the rate of interest will neither save nor borrow (except to provide for old age).

But the situation is different from the ordinary supply problem, in that those beyond this "margin" do not simply provide nothing, but provide a negative supply by borrowing when young against their future earnings, and so being on the average in debt.

γ) Let us now go back to case (α) by supposing men, or rather families, to live for ever, and discount future utility at a constant rate, but let us try this time to take account of variations in the rate of discount from family to family.

For simplicity let us suppose that the amount of labour is constant, so that the total income of the country can be regarded as a function $f(c)$ of the capital only. The rate of interest will then be $f'(c)$. Let us also suppose that every individual could attain the maximum *conceivable* utility with a finite income x_1, and that no one could support life on less than x_2.

Now suppose equilibrium[6] is obtained with capital c, income $f(c)$, and rate of interest $f'(c)$ or r. Then those families, say $m(r)$ in number, whose rate of discount is less than r must have attained bliss or they would still be increasing their expenditure according to equation (9a). Consequently they have between them an income $m(r)x_1$. The other families, $n - m(r)$ in number (where n is the total number of families), must be down to the subsistence level, or they would still be decreasing their expenditure. Consequently they have between them a total income $\{n - m(r)\}x_2$, whence

$$f(c) = m(r)x_1 + \{n - m(r)\}x_2$$
$$= n \cdot x_2 + m(r)\{x_1 - x_2\},$$

which, together with $r = f'(c)$, determines r and c. $m(r)$ being an increasing function of r, it is easy to see, by drawing graphs of r against $f(c)$, that the two equations have in general a unique solution.[7]

In such a case, therefore, equilibrium would be attained by a division of society into two classes, the thrifty enjoying bliss and the improvident at the subsistence level.

---

[6] We suppose each family in equilibrium, which is the only way in which that state could be maintained, since otherwise, although the savings of some might at any moment balance the borrowings of others, they would not continue to do so except by an extraordinary accident.

[7] We have neglected in this the negligible number of families for which ρ is exactly equal to r.

A model of general economic equilibrium*†

JOHN VON NEUMANN

The subject of this paper is the solution of a typical economic equation system. The system has the following properties:

1) Goods are produced not only from "natural factors of production," but in the first place from each other. These processes of production may be circular, i.e. good G_1 is produced with the aid of good G_2, and G_2 with the aid of G_1.

2) There may be more technically possible processes of production than goods and for this reason " counting of equations " is of no avail. The problem is rather to establish which processes will actually be used and which not (being " unprofitable ").

In order to be able to discuss (1) and (2) quite freely we shall idealise other elements of the situation (see paragraphs 1 and 2). Most of these idealisations are irrelevant, but this question will not be discussed here.

The way in which our questions are put leads of necessity to a system of inequalities (3)–(8') in paragraph 3, the possibility of a solution of which is not evident; i.e., *it cannot be proved by any qualitative argument*. The mathematical proof is possible only by means of a generalisation of Brouwer's Fix-Point Theorem, i.e. by the use of very fundamental *topological* facts. This generalised fix-point theorem (the "lemma" of paragraph 7) is also interesting in itself.

The connection with topology may be very surprising at first, but the author thinks that it is natural in problems of this kind. The immediate

---

* *The Review of Economic Studies*, 13(1945): pp. 1–9. Reprinted by courtesy of *The Review of Economic Studies*.

† The present paper was read for the first time in the winter of 1932 at the mathematical seminar of Princeton University. The reason for its publication was an invitation from Mr. K. Menger, to whom the author wishes to express his thanks. This paper was first published in German, under the title *Über ein Ökonomisches Gleichungssystem und eine Verallgemeinerung des Brouwerschen Fixpunktsatzes* in the volume entitled *Ergebnisse eines Mathematischen Seminars*, edited by K. Menger (Vienna, 1938). It was translated into English by G. Morgenstern. A commentary note on this article, by D. G. Champernowne, is printed below.

reason for this is the occurrence of a certain " minimum-maximum " problem, familiar from the calculus of variations. In our present question, the minimum-maximum problem has been formulated in paragraph 5. It is closely related to another problem occurring in the theory of games (see footnote 1 in paragraph 6).

A direct interpretation of the function $\phi(X, Y)$ would be highly desirable. Its rôle appears to be similar to that of thermodynamic potentials in phenomenlogical thermodynamics; it can be surmised that the similarity will persist in its full phenomenological generality (independently of our restrictive idealisations).

Another feature of our theory, so far without interpretation, is the remarkable duality (symmetry) of the monetary variables (prices y_j, interest factor β) and the technical variables (intensities of production x_i, coefficient of expansion of the economy α). This is brought out very clearly in paragraphs 3 (3)–(8') as well as in the minimum-maximum formulation of paragraphs 5 (7**)–(8**).

Lastly, attention is drawn to the results of paragraph 11 from which follows, among other things, that the normal price mechanism brings about— if our assumptions are valid—the technically most efficient intensities of production. This seems not unreasonable since we have eliminated all monetary complications.

1. Consider the following problem: there are n goods $G_1, \ldots, G_n$ which can be produced by m processes $P_1, \ldots, P_m$. Which processes will be used (as " profitable ") and what prices of the goods will obtain? The problem is evidently nontrivial since either of its parts can be answered only after the other one has been answered; i.e. its solution is implicit. We observe in particular:

a) Since it is possible that $m > n$, it cannot be solved through the usual counting of equations.

In order to avoid further complications we assume:

b) That there are constant returns (to scale);

c) That the natural factors of production, including labour, can be expanded in unlimited quantities.

The essential phenomenon that we wish to grasp is this: goods are produced from each other (see equation (7) below) and we want to determine (i) which processes will be used; (ii) what the relative velocity will be with which the total quantity of goods increases; (iii) what prices will obtain; (iv) what the rate of interest will be. In order to isolate this phenomenon completely we assume furthermore:

d) Consumption of goods takes place only through the processes of production which include necessities of life consumed by workers and employees.

In other words we assume that all income in excess of necessities of life will be reinvested.

It is obvious to what kind of theoretical models the above assumptions correspond.

2. In each process P_i ($i = 1, \ldots, m$) quantities a_{ij} (expressed in some units) are used up, and quantities b_{ij} are produced, of the respective goods G_j ($j = 1, \ldots, n$). The process can be symbolized in the following way:

$$P_i: \sum_{j=1}^{n} a_{ij} G_j \to \sum_{j=1}^{n} b_{ij} G_j. \tag{1}$$

It is to be noted:

e) Capital goods are to be inserted on both sides of (1); wear and tear of capital goods are to be described by introducing different stages of wear as different goods, using a spearate P_i for each of these.

f) Each process to be of unit time duration. Processes of longer duration to be broken down into single processes of unit duration introducing if necessary intermediate products as additional goods.

g) (1) can describe the special case where good G_j can be produced only jointly with certain others, viz. its permanent joint products.

In the actual economy, these processes P_i, $i = 1, \ldots, m$, will be used with certain *intensities* x_i, $i = 1, \ldots, m$. That means that for the total production the quantities of equations (1) must be multiplied by x_i. We write symbolically:

$$E = \sum_{i=1}^{m} x_i P_i. \tag{2}$$

$x_i = 0$ means that process P_i is not used.

We are interested in those states where the whole economy expands without change of structure, i.e. where the ratios of the intensities $x_1 : \ldots : x_m$ remain unchanged, although $x_1, \ldots, x_m$ themselves may change. In such a case they are multiplied by a common factor α per unit of time. This factor is the *coefficient of expansion of the whole economy.*

3. The numerical unknowns of our problem are: (*i*) the *intensities* $x_1, \ldots, x_m$ of the processes $P_1, \ldots, P_m$; (*ii*) the *coefficient of expansion* of the whole economy α; (*iii*) the *prices* $y_1, \ldots, y_n$ of goods $G_1, \ldots, G_n$; (*iv*) the *interest factor* $\beta = 1 + (z/100)$, z being the rate of interest in percent per unit of time. Obviously:

$$x_i \geqq 0, \tag{3}$$

$$y_j \geqq 0, \tag{4}$$

and since a solution with $x_1 = \cdots = x_m = 0$, or $y_1 = \cdots = y_n = 0$ would be meaningless:

$$\sum_{i=1}^{m} x_i > 0, \tag{5}$$

$$\sum_{j=1}^{n} y_j > 0. \tag{6}$$

The economic equations are now:

$$\alpha \sum_{i=1}^{m} a_{ij} x_i \leqq \sum_{i=1}^{m} b_{ij} x_i, \tag{7}$$

and if in (7) < applies, $y_j = 0$, $\qquad\qquad\qquad\qquad\qquad\qquad\qquad\qquad$ (7′)

$$\beta \sum_{j=1}^{n} a_{ij} y_j \geqq \sum_{j=1}^{n} b_{ij} y_j,$$ $\qquad\qquad\qquad$ (8)

and if in (8) > applies, $x_i = 0$. $\qquad\qquad\qquad\qquad\qquad\qquad\qquad$ (8′)

The meaning of (7), (7′) is: it is impossible to consume more of a good G_j in the total process (2) than is being produced. If, however, less is consumed, i.e. if there is excess production of G_j, G_j becomes a free good and its price $y_j = 0$.

The meaning of (8), (8′) is: in equilibrium no profit can be made on any process P_i (or else prices or the rate of interest would rise—it is clear how this abstraction is to be understood). If there is a loss, however; i.e. if P_i is unprofitable, then P_i will not be used and its intensity $x_i = 0$.

The quantities a_{ij}, b_{ij} are to be taken as given, whereas the x_i, y_j, α, β are unknown. There are, then, $m + n + 2$ unknowns, but since in the case of x_i, y_j only the ratios $x_1 : \ldots : x_m, y_1 : \ldots : y_n$ are essential, they are reduced to $m + n$. Against this, there are $m + n$ conditions (7) + (7′) and (8) + (8′). As these, however, are not equations, but rather complicated inequalities, the fact that the number of conditions is equal to the number of unknowns does not constitute a guarantee that the system can be solved.

The dual symmetry of equations (3), (5), (7), (7′) of the variables x_i, α, and of the concept "unused process" on the one hand, and of equations (4), (6), (8), (8′) of the variables y_j, β, and of the concept "free good" on the other hand seems remarkable.

4. Our task is to solve (3)–(8′). We shall proceed to show:

Solutions of (3)–(8′) *always exist*, although there may be several solutions with different $x_1 : \ldots : x_m$ or with different $y_1 : \ldots : y_n$. The first is possible since we have not even excluded the case where several P_i describe the same process or where several P_i combine to form another. The second is possible since some goods G_j may enter into each process P_i only in a fixed ratio with some others. But even apart from these trivial possibilities there may exist —for less obvious reasons—several solutions $x_1 : \ldots : x_m, y_1 : \ldots : y_m$. Against this it is of importance that α, β should have the same value for all solutions; i.e. α, β *are uniquely determined*.

We shall even find that α and β can be directly characterised in a simple manner (see paragraphs 10 and 11).

To simplify our considerations we shall assume that always:

$$a_{ij} + b_{ij} > 0 \qquad\qquad\qquad\qquad\qquad\qquad (9)$$

(a_{ij}, b_{ij} are clearly always $\geqq 0$). Since the a_{ij}, b_{ij} may be arbitrarily small this restriction is not very far-reaching, although it must be imposed in order to assure uniqueness of α, β as otherwise W might break up into disconnected parts.

Consider now a hypothetical solution x_i, α, y_j, β of (3)–(8′). If we had in

(7) always $<$, then we should have always $y_j = 0$ (because of (7′)) in contradiction to (6). If we had in (8) always $>$ we should have always $x_i = 0$ (because of (8′)) in contradiction to (5). Therefore, in (7) $\leqq$ always applies, but $=$ at least once; in (8) $\geqq$ always applies, but $=$ at least once.

In consequence:

$$\alpha = \underset{j = 1, \ldots, n}{\text{Min.}} \left[\frac{\sum\limits_{i=1}^{m} b_{ij} x_i}{\sum\limits_{i=1}^{m} a_{ij} x_i} \right] \tag{10}$$

$$\beta = \underset{i = 1, \ldots, m}{\text{Max.}} \frac{\sum\limits_{j=1}^{n} b_{ij} y_j}{\sum\limits_{j=1}^{n} a_{ij} y_j}. \tag{11}$$

Therefore the x_i, y_j determine uniquely α, β. (The right-hand side of (10), (11) can never assume the meaningless form $0/0$ because of (3)–(6) and (9)). We can therefore state (7) + (7′) and (8) + (8′) as conditions for x_i, y_j only: $y_j = 0$ for each $j = 1, \ldots, n$, for which

$$\frac{\sum\limits_{i=1}^{m} b_{ij} x_i}{\sum\limits_{i=1}^{m} a_{ij} x_i}$$

does not assume its minimum value

$$(\text{for all} \quad j = 1, \ldots, n) \tag{7*}$$

$x_i = 0$ for each $i = 1, \ldots, m$, for which:

$$\frac{\sum\limits_{j=1}^{n} b_{ij} y_i}{\sum\limits_{j=1}^{n} a_{ij} y_i}$$

does not assume its maximum value

$$(\text{for all } i = 1, \ldots, m) \tag{8*}$$

The $x_1, \ldots, x_m$ in (7*) and the $y_1, \ldots, y_n$ in (8*) are to be considered as given. We have, therefore, to solve (3)–(6), (7) and (8) for x_i, y_j.

5. Let X' be a set of variables $(x'_1, \ldots, x'_m)$ fulfilling the analoga of (3), (5):

$$x'_i \geqq 0, \tag{3′}$$

$$\sum\limits_{i=1}^{m} x'_i > 0, \tag{5′}$$

and let Y' be a series of variables $(y'_i, \ldots, y'_n)$ fulfilling the analoga of (4), (6):

$$y'_j \geqq 0, \tag{4'}$$

$$\sum_{j=1}^{n} y'_j > 0, \tag{6'}$$

Let, furthermore,

$$\phi(X'_i, Y'_i) = \frac{\sum\limits_{i=1}^{m} \sum\limits_{j=1}^{n} b_{ij} x'_i y'_j}{\sum\limits_{i=1}^{m} \sum\limits_{j=1}^{n} a_{ij} x'_i y'_j}. \tag{12}$$

Let $X = (x_1, \ldots, x_m)$, $Y = (y_1, \ldots, y_n)$ the (hypothetical) solution, $X' = (x'_i, \ldots, x'_m)$, $Y' = (y'_1, \ldots, y'_n)$ to be freely variable, but in such a way that (3)–(6) and (3')–(6') respectively are fulfilled; then it is easy to verify that (7*) and (8*) can be formulated as follows:

$\phi(X, Y')$ assumes its minimum value for Y' if $Y' = Y$, $\qquad$ (7**)

$\phi(X', Y)$ assumes its maximum value for X' if $X' = X$. $\qquad$ (8**)

The question of a solution of (3)–(8') becomes a question of a solution of (7**), (8**) and can be formulated as follows:

*) *Consider (X', Y') in the domain bounded by (3')–(6'). To find a saddle point $X' = X$, $Y' = Y$, i.e., where (X, Y') assumes its minimum value for Y', and at the same time (X', Y) its maximum value for Y'.*

From (7), (7*), (10), and (8), (*), (11) respectively, follows:

$$\alpha = \frac{\sum\limits_{j=1}^{n} \left[\sum\limits_{i=1}^{m} b_{ij} x_i \right] y_j}{\sum\limits_{j=1}^{n} \left[\sum\limits_{i=1}^{m} a_{ij} x_i \right] y_j} = \phi(x, y) \quad \text{and} \quad \beta = \frac{\sum\limits_{i=1}^{m} \left[\sum\limits_{j=1}^{n} b_{ij} y_j \right] x_i}{\sum\limits_{i=1}^{m} \left[\sum\limits_{j=1}^{n} a_{ij} y_j \right] x_i} = \phi(x, y),$$

respectively.

Therefore:

**) *If our problem can be solved, i.e. if $\phi(X', Y')$ has a saddle point $X' = X$, $Y' = Y$ (see above), then:*

$$\alpha = \beta = \phi(X, Y) = \text{the value at the saddle point.} \tag{13}$$

6. Because of the homogeneity of $\phi(X'\ Y')$ (in X', Y', i.e. in $x', \ldots, x'_m$ and $y'_1, \ldots y'_m$) our problem remains unaffected if we substitute the normalisations

$$\sum_{i=1}^{m} x_i = 1, \tag{5*}$$

$$\sum_{j=1}^{n} y_j = 1, \tag{6*}$$

for (5'), (6') and correspondingly for (5), (6). Let S be the X' set described by:

$$x'_i \geqq 0, \tag{3'}$$

$$\sum_{i=1}^{m} x'_1 = 1, \tag{5*}$$

and let T be the Y' set described by:

$$y'_j \geqq 0, \tag{4'}$$

$$\sum_{j=1}^{n} y'_j = 1, \tag{6*}$$

(S, T are simplices of, respectively, $m - 1$ and $n - 1$ dimensions).

In order to solve[1] we make use of the simpler formulation (7*), (8*) and combine these with (3), (4), 5*), (6*) expressing the fact that $X = (x_1, \ldots, x_m)$ is in S and $Y = (y_1, \ldots, y_n)$ in T.

7. We shall prove a slightly more general lemma: Let R_m be the m-dimensional space of all points $X = (x_1, \ldots, x_m)$, R_n the n-dimensional space of all points $Y = (y_1, \ldots, y_n)$, R_{m+n} the $m + n$ dimensional space of all points $(X, Y) = (x_1, \ldots, x_m, y_1, \ldots, y_n)$.

A set (in R_m or R_n or R_{m+n}) which is *not empty, convex closed and bounded* we call a set C.

Let $S°$, $T°$ be sets C in R_m and R_n respectively and let $S° \times T°$ be the set of all (X, Y) (in R_{m+n}) where the range of X is $S°$ and the range of Y is $T°$. Let V, W be two closed subsets of $S° + T°$. For every X in $S°$ let the set $Q(X)$ of all Y with (X, Y) in V be a set C; for each Y in $T°$ let the set $P(Y)$ of all X with (X, Y) in W be a set C. Then the following lemma applies.

Under the above assumptions, V, W have (at least) one point in common.

Our problem follows by putting $S° = S$, $T° = T$ and $V =$ the set of all $(X, Y) = (x_1, \ldots, x_m, y_1, \ldots, y_n)$ fulfilling (7*), $W =$ the set of all $(X, Y) = (x_1, \ldots, x_m, y_1 \ldots, y_n)$ fulfilling (8*). It can be easily seen that V, W are closed and that the sets $S° = S$, $T° = T$, $Q(X)$, $P(Y)$ are all simplices, i.e. sets C. The common points of these V, W are, of course, our required solutions $(X, Y) = (x_1, \ldots, x_m, y_1, \ldots, y_m)$.

8. To prove the above lemma let $S°$, $T°$, V, W be as described before the lemma.

---

[1] The question whether our problem has a solution is oddly connected with that of a problem occurring in the Theory of Games dealt with elsewhere. (Math. Annalen, 100, 1928, pp. 295–320, particularly pp. 305 and 307–11). The problem there is a special case of (*) and is solved here in a new way through our solution of (*) (see below). In fact, if $a_{ij} \equiv 1$, then

$$\sum_{i=1}^{m} \sum_{j=1}^{n} a_{ij} x'_i y'_j = 1$$

because of (5*), (6*). Therefore

$$\phi(X', Y') = \sum_{i=1}^{m} \sum_{j=1}^{n} b_{ij} x'_i y'_j,$$

and thus our (*) coincides with loc. cit., p. 307. [Our $\phi(X', Y')$, b_{ij}, x'_i, y'_j, m, n here correspond to $h(\xi, \eta)$, a_{pq}, ξ_p, η_q, $M + 1$, $N + 1$ there.]

It is, incidentally, remarkable that (*) does not lead—as usual—to a simple maximum or minimum problem, the possibility of a solution of which would be evident, but to a problem of the saddle point or minimum-maximum type, where the question of a possible solution is far more profound.

First, consider V. For each X of $S°$ we choose a point $Y°(X)$ out of $Q(X)$ (e.g. the centre of gravity of this set). It will not be possible, generally, to choose $Y°(X)$ as a continuous function of X. Let $\epsilon > 0$: we define:

$$w^\epsilon(X, X') = \text{Max.} \left(0, 1 - \frac{1}{\epsilon} \text{ distance } (X, X') \right). \tag{14}$$

Now let $Y^\epsilon(X)$ be the centre of gravity of the $Y°(X')$ with (relative) weight function $w^\epsilon(X, X')$ where the range of X' is $S°$. I.e. if $Y°(X) = (y_1°(x), \ldots, y_n°(x))$, $Y^\epsilon(X) = [y_1^\epsilon(x), \ldots, y_n^\epsilon(x)]$, then:

$$y_j^\epsilon(X) = \int_{S°} w^\epsilon(X, X') y_j°(X') \, dX' / \int_{S°} w^\epsilon(X, X') \, dX'. \tag{15}$$

We derive now a number of properties of $Y^\epsilon(X)$ (valid for all $\epsilon > 0$):

i) $Y^\epsilon(X)$ is in $T°$. Proof: $Y°(X')$ is in $Q(X')$ and therefore in $T°$, and since $Y^\epsilon(X)$ is a centre of gravity of points $Y°(X')$ and $T°$ is convex, $Y^\epsilon(X)$ also is in $T°$.

ii) $Y^\epsilon(X)$ is a continuous function of X (for the whole range of $S°$). Proof: it is sufficient to prove this for each $y_j^\epsilon(X)$. Now $w^\epsilon(X, X')$ is a continuous function of X, X' throughout;

$$\int_{S°} w^\epsilon(X, X') \, dX' \text{ is always } > 0,$$

and all $y_j°(X)$ are bounded (being coordinates of the bounded set $S°$). The continuity of the $y_j^\epsilon(X)$ follows, therefore, from (15).

iii) For each $\delta > 0$ there exists an $\epsilon_0 = \epsilon_0(\delta) > 0$ such that the distance of each point $[X, Y^{\epsilon_0}(X)]$ from V is $< \delta$. Proof: assume the contrary. Then there must exist a $\delta > 0$ and a sequence of

$$\epsilon_\nu > 0 \text{ with } \lim_{\nu \to \infty} \epsilon_\nu = 0$$

such that for every $\nu = 1, 2, \ldots$ there exists a X_ν in $S°$ for which the distance $[X_\nu, T^{\epsilon_\nu}(X_\nu)]$ would be $\geq \delta$. A fortiori $T^{\epsilon_\nu}(X_\nu)$ is at a distance $\geq \delta/2$ from every $Q(X')$, with a distance $(X_\nu, X') \leq \delta/2$.

All X_ν, $\nu = 1, 2, \ldots$, are in $S°$ and have therefore a point of accumulation X^* in $S°$; from which follows that there exists a subsequence of X_ν, $\nu = 1, 2 \ldots$, converging towards X^* for which distance $(X_\nu, X^*) \leq \delta/2$ always applies. Substituting this subsequence for the ϵ_ν, X_ν, we see that we are justified in assuming: $\lim X_\nu = X^*$, distance $(X_\nu, X^*) \leq \delta/2$. Therefore we may put $X' = X^*$ for every $\nu = 1, 2, \ldots$, and in consequence we have always $Y^{\epsilon_\nu}(X_\nu)$ at a distance $\geq \delta/2$ from $Q(X^*)$.

$Q(X^*)$ being convex, the set of all points with a distance $< \delta/2$ from $Q(X^*)$ is also convex. Since $Y^{\epsilon_\nu}(X_\nu)$ does not belong to this set, and since it is a centre of gravity of points $Y°(X')$ with distance $(X_\nu, X') \leq \epsilon_\nu$ [because for distance $(X_\nu, X') > \epsilon_\nu$, $w^{\epsilon_\nu}(X_\nu, X') = 0$ according to (14)], not all of these points belong to the set under discussion. Therefore: there exists a $X' = X_\nu$

for which the distance $(X_v, X'_v) \leq \epsilon_v$ and where the distance between $Y^\circ(X'_v)$ and $Q(X^*)$ is $\geq \delta/2$.

Lim $X_v = X^*$, lim distance $(X_v, X'_v) = 0$, and therefore lim $X'_v = X^*$. All $Y^\circ(Y_v)$ belong to T° and have therefore a point of accumulation Y^*. In consequence, (X^*, Y^*) is a point of accumulation of the $[X_v, Y^\circ(X_v)]$ and since they all belong to V, (X^*, Y^*) belongs to V too. Y^* is therefore in $Q(X^*)$. Now the distance of every $Y^\circ(Y_v)$ including from $Q(X^*)$ is $\geq \delta/2$. This is a contradiction, and the proof is complete.

i)–(iii) together assert: for every $\delta > 0$ there exists a continuous mapping $Y_\delta(X)$ of S° on to a subset of T° where the distance of every point $[X, Y_\delta(X)]$ from V is $< \delta$. (Put $Y_\delta(X) = Y^\epsilon(X)$ with $\epsilon = \epsilon_0 = \epsilon_0(\delta)$).

9. Interchanging S° and T°, and V and W we obtain now: for every $\delta > 0$ there exists a continuous mapping $X_\delta(Y)$ of T° on to a subset of S° where the distance of every point $(X_\delta(Y), Y)$ from W is $< \delta$.

On putting $f_\delta(X) = X_\delta(Y_\delta(X))$, $f_\delta(X)$ is a continuous mapping of S° on to a subset of S°. Since S° is a set C, and therefore topologically a simplex[2] we can use L. E. J. Brouwer's Fix-point Theorem;[3] $f_\delta(X)$ has a fix-point. I.e., there exists a X^δ in S° for which $X^\delta = f^\delta(X^\delta) = X^\delta(Y_\delta(X^\delta))$. Let $Y^\delta = Y_\delta(X^\delta)$, then we have $X^\delta = X_\delta(Y^\delta)$. Consequently, the distances of the point (X^δ, Y^δ) in R_{m+r} both from V and from W are $< \delta$. The distance of V from W is therefore $< 2\delta$. Since this is valid for every $\delta > 0$, the distance between V and W is $= 0$. Since V, W are closed and bounded, they must have at least one common point. This proves our lemma completely.

10. We have solved (7*), (8*) of paragraph 4 as well as the equivalent problem (*) of paragraph 5 and the original task of paragraph 3: the solution of (3)–(8′). If the x_i, y_j (which were called X, Y in paragraphs 7–9) are determined, α, β follow from (13) in (**) of paragraph 5. In particular, $\alpha = \beta$.

We have emphasised in paragraph 4 already that there may be several solutions x_i, y_j (i.e. X, Y); we shall proceed to show that there exists only one value of α (i.e. of β). In fact, let X_1, Y_1, α_1, β_1 and X_2, Y_2, α_2, β_2 be two solutions. From (7**), (8**) and (13) follows:

$$\alpha_1 = \beta_1 = \phi(X_1, Y_1) \leq \phi(X_1, Y_2),$$

$$\alpha_2 = \beta_2 = \phi(X_2, Y_2) \geq \phi(X_1, Y_2),$$

therefore $\alpha_1 = \beta_1 \leq \alpha_2 = \beta_2$. For reasons of symmetry $\alpha_2 = \beta_2 \leq \alpha_1 = \beta_1$; therefore $\alpha_1 = \beta_1 = \alpha_2 = \beta_2$.

We have shown:

At least one solution X, Y, α, β exists. For all solutions:

$$\alpha = \beta = \phi(X, Y) \tag{13}$$

---

[2] Regarding these as well as other properties of convex sets used in this paper, c.f., e.g. Alexandroff and H. Hopf, *Topologie*, vol. I, J. Springer, Berlin, 1935, pp. 568–609.

[3] Cf., e.g. 1c, footnote 1, p. 480.

and these have the same numerical value for all solutions, in other words: The interest factor and the coefficient of expansion of the economy are equal and uniquely determined by the technically possible processes $P_1, \ldots, P_m$.

Because of (13), $\alpha > 0$, but may be $\gtreqless 1$. One would expect $\alpha > 1$, but $\alpha \leqq 1$ cannot be excluded in view of the generality of our formulation: processes $P_1, \ldots, P_m$ may really be *unproductive*.

11. In addition, we shall characterise α in two independent ways.

Firstly, let us consider a state of the economy possibly on purely technical considerations, expanding with factor α' per unit of time. I.e., for the intensities $x_1, \ldots, x_m$ applies:

$$x_i \geqq 0, \tag{3'}$$

$$\sum_{i=1}^{m} x'_i > 0, \tag{5'}$$

$$\alpha' \sum_{i=1}^{m} a_{ij} x'_i \leqq \sum_{i=1}^{m} b_{ij} x'_i. \tag{7''}$$

We are neglecting prices here altogether. Let $x_i, y_j, \alpha = \beta$ be a solution of our original problem (3)–(8') in paragraph 3. Multiplying (7'') by y_j and adding

$$\sum_{j=1}^{n}$$

we obtain:

$$\alpha' \sum_{i=1}^{m} \sum_{j=1}^{n} a_{ij} x'_i y_j \leqq \sum_{i=1}^{m} \sum_{j=1}^{n} b_{ij} x'_i y_j,$$

and therefore $\alpha' \leqq \phi(X', Y)$. Because of (8**) and (13) in paragraphs 5, we have:

$$\alpha' \leqq \phi(X', Y) \leqq \phi(X, Y) = \alpha = \beta. \tag{15}$$

Secondly, let us consider a system of prices where the interest factor β' allows of no more profits. I.e. for prices $y'_1, \ldots, y'_n$ applies:

$$y'_j \geqq 0, \tag{4'}$$

$$\sum_{j=1}^{n} y'_j > 0, \tag{6'}$$

$$\beta' \sum_{j=1}^{n} a_{ij} y'_j \geqq \sum_{j=1}^{n} b_{ij} y'_j. \tag{8''}$$

Hereby we are neglecting intensities of production altogether. Let $x_i, y_j, \alpha = \beta$ as above. Multiplying (8'') by x_i and adding

$$\sum_{i=1}^{m}$$

we obtain:

$$\beta' \sum_{i=1}^{m} \sum_{j=1}^{n} a_{ij} x_i y'_j \leqq \sum_{i=1}^{m} \sum_{j=1}^{n} b_{ij} x_i y'_j$$

and therefore $\beta' \geqq \phi(X, Y')$. Because of (7**) and (13) paragraph 5, we have:

$$\beta' \geqq \phi(X, Y') \geqq \phi(X, Y) = \alpha = \beta. \tag{16}$$

These two results can be expressed as follows:

The greatest (purely technically possible) factor of expansion α' of the whole economy is $\alpha' = \alpha = \beta$, neglecting prices.

The lowest interest factor β' at which a profitless system of prices is possible is $\beta' = \alpha = \beta$, neglecting intensities of production.

Note that these characterisations are possible only on the basis of our knowledge that solutions of our original problem exist—without themselves directly referring to this problem. Furthermore, the equality of the maximum in the first form and the minimum in the second can be proved only on the basis of the existence of this solution.

Capital accumulation and efficient allocation of resources*†

EDMOND MALINVAUD

1. *Introduction.* Among the many questions concerning the accumulation of capital the following has been said to be the most important [31]. According to which rules should choices between direct and indirect processes of production be determined; that is, when can we say that it is efficient to save today in order to increase future consumption? The present paper is devoted to this problem, which is clearly relevant for both the theory of capital and for welfare economics. The results given below are not essentially new. The author thinks, however, that his approach is likely to show in a more vivid light a few facts which, although obscurely felt, are not yet generally accepted in economic science.

The reader acquainted with welfare economics and the theory of efficient allocation of resources knows how some appropriate price system is associated with an efficient state. Loosely speaking, such a state would be an equilibrium position for a competitive economy using the given set of prices. The model introduced to prove this result does not allow explicitly for investment and capital accumulation. Thus one may wonder whether it can be extended to the case of capitalistci production. Admittedly, this is very likely. The introduction of time does not seem to imply any new principle. Choices between commodities available at different times raise essentially the same problem as choices between different commodities available at the same time. How can

* *Econometrica*, 21(1953): pp. 233–68. The proof of Theorem 1 was then incorrect, as was pointed out to the author by several readers, notably H. Uzawa. A corrigendum was published in *Econometrica*, 30(1962), pp. 570–73. The necessary changes are inserted in the present text. Reprinted by courtesy of the author and *Econometrica*.

† Based on Cowles Commission Discussion Paper, Economics, No. 2026 (hectographed), and a paper presented at the Minneapolis meeting of the Econometric Society in September, 1951. Acknowledgment is due staff members and guests of the Cowles Commission and those attending econometrics seminars in Paris. Their interest in the subject greatly helped me to bring the study to its present formulation. I am particularly indebted to M. Allais, T. C. Koopmans, and G. Debreu. Anyone acquainted with their work will discern their influence in this paper. But the reader might not know how much I owe to their personal encouragement and friendly criticism. I am also indebted to Mrs. Jane Novick who read my manuscript carefully and made many stylistic improvements.

consumers' needs best be satisfied when the production of goods involves strong relations of interdependence?

However, one thing may not be clear: in a competitive economy there is a rate of interest that is used to discount future values both on the loan market and in business accounting. Is this rate a part of the price system associated with an efficient economic process? In particular, should prices of the same commodity available at different times stand in some definite ratio depending only on the time lag and not on the specific commodity considered?

In order to deal with this and related questions this paper is divided into four parts. In the first, the process of capitalistic production is analyzed. A general model is defined that may be given two equivalent presentations. An "extensive form" generalizes current capital-theory models, while a "reduced form" makes it possible to apply the usual welfare reasoning.

The second part is purely mathematical, the main result of the paper being proved there. It provides a somewhat straightforward generalization of what was already known for the timeless case, the only difficulty arising when the future is assumed not bounded by some given horizon. The economic meaning and implications of the main theorem are examined in Part III. As most of the previous work on the theory of capital was based on statonary economies, it is worth studying them carefully. This is attempted in Part IV.

Because this study is mainly concerned with formal results, heuristic comments are reduced as much as the subject permits. It is supposed that the reader is well acquainted with welfare economics.

2. *Notation.* The mathematical tools used here are primarily vectors and sets in finite-dimensional Euclidean spaces. A vector in m-dimensional Euclidean space is denoted by a Latin letter (x_t, for instance), with an index specifying the time considered. The components of x_t are denoted by x_{it}, the distinction between vectors and their components being shown by the placement of the index t.

The symbol $\{x_t\}$ represents a sequence of vectors $x_1, x_2, \ldots, x_t, \ldots$, where t takes all positive integral values. This sequence is also written more simply as $\mathbf{x}$, where the index is removed and the symbol is printed in boldface type.

The inequality $x_i \leqq y_t$ (as well as $\mathbf{x} \leqq \mathbf{y}$) applied to vectors x_t and y_t (or to sequences $\mathbf{x}$ and $\mathbf{y}$) means that no component x_{it} of x_t (or x_{it} of $\mathbf{x}$) is greater than the corresponding components of y_t (or of $\mathbf{y}$). The inequality $x_t \leq y_t$ (as well as $\mathbf{x} \leq \mathbf{y}$) means $x_t \leqq y_t$ and $x_t \neq y_t$ (or $\mathbf{x} \leqq \mathbf{y}$ and $\mathbf{x} \neq \mathbf{y}$).

A vector x_t (as well as a sequence $\mathbf{x}$) is said to be nonnegative if $x_t \geqq 0$ (or if $\mathbf{x} \geqq 0$).

Sets are denoted by bold faced capitals. The addition of sets is defined as follows:

$\mathbf{V} = \mathbf{U}_1 + \mathbf{U}_2$ means: v is an element of $\mathbf{V}$ if and only if it can be written as $v = u_1 + u_2$, where u_1 and u_2 are elements of $\mathbf{U}_1$ and $\mathbf{U}_2$ respectively; that is, $u_1 \in \mathbf{U}_1, u_2 \in \mathbf{U}_2$. u_0 is said to be a minimal element of $\mathbf{U}$ if there is no $u \in \mathbf{U}$ with $u \leq u_0$.

I. GENERAL MODEL OF CAPITALISTIC PRODUCTION

3. *Time, commodities, and capital goods.* Although time is usually considered as some continuous variable taking any value from minus infinity to plus infinity, it is given here as a succession of periods beginning at the present and going to infinity in the future. Indeed, since the past cannot be changed by any present economic decision, we may disregard it; moreover, there is little harm in assuming a decomposition in periods since their length may be made as short as one wishes.

Formally time appears as an index t that can take any positive integral value; $t = 1$ refers to the present moment, which is the beginning of the coming period, called period 1; $t + 1$ refers to the end of period t, or to the beginning of period $t + 1$.

The description of all economic activity proceeds in terms of commodities. Commodities, therefore, must be understood in a very general sense, and so as to cover in particular all services. The total number of commodities is supposed to be finite and equal to m.[1]

Formally, a set of given quantities of commodities is represented by a vector x_t in the m-dimensional Euclidean space. The component x_{it} of x_t defines which quantity of commodity i is included in x_t.

The concept of capital does not appear explicitly in our treatment and it is not needed. But for the interpretation of the following parts it may be better to define at least capital goods. Capital goods at time t include everything that has been made in preceding periods and is transferred to period t for further use in production. This definition is the old "produced means of production."[2] It stems from the essential character of capital. Indeed, it is made in order to make possible the use in future periods of goods or services that do not exist as natural resources or are not available in sufficient quantity.

4. *"Chronics"—extensive form.* We shall mean by a "chronic"[3] a quantitative description of the economic activity occurring during all future periods. It is one of all possible courses of events. A chronic is completely determined when the quantities produced, traded, and consumed are known, i.e., it does not require the definition of any standard of value. Two different chronics, C^1 and C^2, are distinguished by their upper indexes; any vector written with an upper index 1, x_t^1 for instance, represents the value taken by the corresponding vector, x_t, in the chronic C^1.

---

[1] This assumption is not strictly necessary. All that follows remains true as long as there is only a finite number of commodities inside each period.

[2] This might be thought of as too inclusive. Indeed, there is little in our modern world that is not the result of previous economic activity. But the origin of existing wealth does not concern us here. The distinction between natural resources and produced means of production is not important as far as past activity is concerned. The only condition we need to keep in mind is the following: the available natural resources during all future periods must be independent of any present or future economic decision.

[3] This neologism was introduced by G. Th. Guilbaud in his study on time series [11] (Added for the 1967 reprint: The word "chronic" was not used in later writings but replaced by "program," which is now the appropriate technical term.)

More precisely, a chronic C provides the following picture. At the present time certain commodities are available and are represented by a vector $\bar{b}_1$. Parts of them are devoted to consumption during period 1, the rest being kept for further consumption or used in production. Let us call x_1^+ and c_1 these two parts:

$$\bar{b}_1 = x_1^+ + c_1.$$

For production during the first period c_1 is used, together with natural resources z_1 and services x_1^- obtained from consumer (labor). If a_1 represents the aggregate vector of productive factors, then

$$a_1 = x_1^- + z_1 + c_1,$$

which is reminiscent of the familiar trilogy: labor, land, and capital.[4]

Productive activity transforms a_1 into some other vector, b_2, available at time 2.

The description of the second period will be similar to that of the first, with vectors b_2, x_2^+, c_2, x_2^-, z_2, a_2, b_3, and so on, for all periods. This defines the "extensive form" of chronics C.

The following equations hold:

$$b_t = x_t^+ + c_t \qquad \text{(for all } t\text{)}, \tag{1}$$

and

$$a_t = x_t^- + z_t + c_t \qquad \text{(for all } t\text{)}. \tag{2}$$

If we define

$$x_t = x_t^+ - x_t^-, \tag{3}$$

then, we also have

$$a_t = b_t - x_t + z_t. \tag{4}$$

C may be represented as in Figure 1.

Such a chronic is possible if and only if the transformation from a_t to b_{t+1} is technically possible and if the resources used, z_t, never exceed the resources available, given by a vector $\bar{z}_t$. The second condition is formally expressed as

$$z_t \leqq \bar{z}_t. \tag{5}$$

The condition that the transformation from a_t to b_{t+1} be technically possible may be translated into formal language by saying that the pair (a_t, b_{t+1}) must be in some set $\mathbf{T}_t$, given a priori from the state of technological knowledge at time t, or

$$(a_t, b_{t+1}) \in \mathbf{T}_t. \tag{6}$$

---

[4] The question of whether there are two or three primary factors of production has been much debated. However, the answer seems to be fairly clear. Considering any one period there are indeed three factors. But if economic development as a whole, past, present, and future, is considered, capital cannot be considered a primary factor.

Figure 1

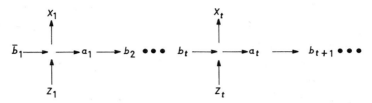

From this definition, $\mathbf{T}_t$ is clearly a set in the $2m$-dimensional Euclidean space.

5. *Assumptions concerning the sets of technological possibilities.* The theoretical results of the following sections make extensive use of some assumptions concerning the sets $\mathbf{T}_t$ of technological possibilities. The first assumption can hardly be objected to if one remembers that the limitation of resources is independently represented in the model.

ASSUMPTION 1 (additivity): *If from a_t^1 it is possible to obtain b_{t+1}^1 in period t, and from a_t^2 to obtain b_{t+1}^2 in the same period, then from $a_t^1 + a_t^2$ it is possible to obtain $b_{t+1}^1 + b_{t+1}^2$.*
Or, formally, if $(a_t^1, b_{t+1}^1) \in \mathbf{T}_t$ and $(a_t^2, b_{t+1}^2) \in \mathbf{T}_t$, then

$$(a_t^1 + a_t^2, b_{t+1}^1 + b_{t+1}^2) \in \mathbf{T}_t.$$

The second assumption is not so immediate and could be challenged by many readers. But it is taken as a crude first approximation to reality. Moreover, it is necessary in the proofs of the following sections. So it is justified in some way by its usefulness.

ASSUMPTION 2 (divisibility): *If from a_t it is possible to obtain b_{t+1}, then from αa_t it is possible to obtain αb_{t+1}, where α is any positive number less than 1.*
Or, formally, if $(a_t, b_{t+1}) \in \mathbf{T}_t$ and $0 < \alpha < 1$, then

$$(\alpha a_t, \alpha b_{t+1}) \in \mathbf{T}_t.$$

When Assumptions 1 and 2 are made, $\mathbf{T}_t$, considered as a set in the $2m$-dimensional Euclidean space, is a convex cone with vertex at the origin.

In most of the demonstrations given below, only convexity of $\mathbf{T}_t$ plays an essential role. For the sake of clarity, it is better to assume convexity alone, although in practice such an assumption is probably as restrictive as Assumptions 1 and 2 together.

ASSUMPTION 3 (convexity): *If from a_t^1 it is possible to obtain b_{t+1}^1 and from a_t^2 to obtain b_{t+1}^2, then from any combination $\alpha a_t^1 + \beta a_t^2$ it is possible to obtain the corresponding $\alpha b_{t+1}^1 + \beta b_{t+1}^2$, where α is any positive number less than 1 and $\beta = 1 - \alpha$.*

Or, formally, if $(a_t^1, b_{t+1}^1) \in \mathbf{T}_t$ and $(a_t^2, b_{t+1}^2) \in \mathbf{T}_t$, with $0 < \alpha < 1$ and $\alpha + \beta = 1$, then

$$(\alpha a_t^1 + \beta a_t^2, \alpha b_{t+1}^1 + \beta b_{t+1}^2) \in \mathbf{T}_t.$$

The next and last assumption is trivial; it amounts to saying that production is not restricted if more of each good is available.

ASSUMPTION 4 (free disposal): *If from a_t^1 it is possible to obtain b_{t+1}^1, then it is also possible to obtain it from any vector a_t such that $a_t \geqq a_t^1$.*
Or, formally, if $(a_t^1, b_{t+1}^1) \in \mathbf{T}_t$ and $a_t \geqq a_t^1$, then

$$(a_t, b_{t+1}^1) \in \mathbf{T}_t.$$

6. *Decentralization of production.* In an actual economy production is not planned by a central bureau but is accomplished by many different firms, each having its own technology. The activity of the kth production unit during period t consists in a transformation of the vector a_{tk} into the vector $b_{t+1,k}$.[5] This transformation can be performed if and only if $(a_{tk}, b_{t+1,k})$ is an element of some set of technological possibilities, $\mathbf{T}_{tk}$, or if

$$(a_{tk}, b_{t+1,k}) \in T_{tk}. \tag{7}$$

For the economy as a whole the simultaneous operation of all production units, n in number,[6] results in a transformation of a_t into b_{t+1}, with

$$a_t = \sum_{k=1}^n a_{tk}, \qquad b_t = \sum_{k=1}^n b_{tk}. \tag{8}$$

Since (a_t, b_{t+1}) is in $\mathbf{T}_t$, it is clear that in all cases

$$\sum_{k=1}^n \mathbf{T}_{tk} \subset \mathbf{T}_t,$$

which only means that, if some transformation is possible within the framework of given production units, it is also possible a priori for society as a whole. However, the decomposition into production units could be inefficient, in the sense that it would make impossible some transformations that we know to be

---

[5] The vectors a_{tk} and b_{tk} may be decomposed as follows:

$$a_{tk} = c_{tk} + q_{tk}, \qquad b_{tk} + g_{tk} = s_{tk} + c_{tk},$$

with c_{tk} representing capital equipment of firm k at time t; q_{tk}, current purchases of firm k at time t; g_{tk}, Purchases of equipment of firm k at time t; and s_{tk}, sales of firm k at time t. The following relations hold:

$$c_i = \sum_{k=1}^n c_{tk}, \qquad z_t + \sum_{k=1}^n s_{tk} = x_t + \sum_{k=1}^n q_{tk} + \sum_{k=1}^n g_{tk}.$$

[6] The reader might object that the decomposition into production units need not remain unchanged as time goes on. This is quite true. We do not want, however, to make the model too involved. From the treatment given below for consumption units the reader will see that our results hold true with little change as long as there is only a finite number of firms during each period.

possible a priori. In the following pages it is supposed that some decentralization of production has been found that is efficient, or, in other words, that

$$\sum_{k=1}^{n} \mathbf{T}_{tk} = \mathbf{T}_t. \tag{9}$$

The technological possibilities for the kth firm are given by a sequence of sets, $\{\mathbf{T}_{tk}\}$. The assumptions on each $\mathbf{T}_{tk}$ are the same as those made on $\mathbf{T}_t$.

The decomposition of $\mathbf{T}_t$ may also be used to overcome the following difficulty. The inequality $z_t \leqq \bar{z}_t$ would introduce in the following Part II some complications that can be avoided by supposing the equality sign to hold, i.e., the utilized resources to be always equal to the available resources. This can easily be done by assuming the existence of some $(n + 1)$th activity which uses $\bar{z}_t - z_t$ but does not produce anything.

Formally, there is an activity characterized by the vectors

$$\left.\begin{matrix} a_{t,n+1} = \bar{z}_t - z_t \\ b_{t,n+1} = 0 \end{matrix}\right\}. \tag{10}$$

The set associated with this activity is defined by

$$(a_{t,n+1}, b_{t+1,n+1}) \in \mathbf{T}_{t,n+1} \qquad \text{if} \quad a_{t,n+1} \geqq 0, \quad b_{t+1,\ n+1} = 0. \tag{11}$$

From Assumption 4, the following is obvious:

$$\mathbf{T}_t + \mathbf{T}_{t,n+1} = \mathbf{T}_t. \tag{12}$$

Throughout the following pages we shall write

$$z_t = \bar{z}_t \qquad \text{(for all } t\text{)}. \tag{13}$$

The fictitious activity will be removed from the picture only when the final result is reached.

7. *Chronics—reduced form.* Let us now define the "input vector" y_t for time t as

$$y_t = a_t - b_t. \tag{14}$$

From equalities (4) and (13), it follows that

$$x_t + y_t = \bar{z}_t. \tag{15}$$

The "reduced form" of the chronic C is defined when the two sequences $\mathbf{x}$ and $\mathbf{y}$ are given, with the following necessary condition:

$$\mathbf{x} + \mathbf{y} = \bar{\mathbf{z}}. \tag{16}$$

From the limitation on technological knowledge, $\mathbf{y}$ is a possible sequence of input vectors if and only if

$$\mathbf{y} \in \mathbf{Y}, \tag{17}$$

where $\mathbf{Y}$ may be defined from $\{\mathbf{T}_t\}$ in the following way:

$\mathbf{y} \in \mathbf{Y}$ *if and only if there are two sequences* $\mathbf{a}$ *and* $\mathbf{b}$ *such that*[7]

$$\left.\begin{array}{l} b_1 = \bar{b}_1 \\ y_t = a_t - b_t \\ (a_t, b_{t+1}) \in \mathbf{T}_t \end{array}\right\} \quad \text{(for all } t\text{)}. \quad (18)$$

From the convexity of $\mathbf{T}_t$, $\mathbf{Y}$ is convex. If $\mathbf{y}^1$ and $\mathbf{y}^2$ are in $\mathbf{Y}$, then there are $\mathbf{a}^1$, $\mathbf{b}^1$ and $\mathbf{a}^2$, $\mathbf{b}^2$ satisfying (18). Now, if $0 < \alpha < 1$ and $\alpha + \beta = 1$, then $\{\alpha a_t^1 + \beta a_t^2\}$, $\{\alpha b_t^1 + \beta b_t^2\}$ satisfies (18). Hence, $\alpha \mathbf{y}^1 + \beta \mathbf{y}^2$ is in $\mathbf{Y}$.

To the decomposition of $\mathbf{T}_t$ into convex sets $\mathbf{T}_{tk}$ corresponds a decomposition of $\mathbf{Y}$ into convex sets $\mathbf{Y}_k$. Each $\mathbf{y}$ in $\mathbf{Y}$ can be written as[8]

$$\mathbf{y} = \sum_{k=1}^{n+1} \mathbf{y}_k$$

with $\mathbf{y}_k \in \mathbf{Y}_k$ and $y_{tk} = a_{tk} - b_{tk}$.

8. *Social choice among chronics.* According to principles first made clear by Pareto, it is sometimes possible to say that a chronic C^2 is "better" than some other chronic C^1. The exact definition of this preference may vary, but in all cases comparison is made only on the consumption vectors x_t. Indeed, economic organization aims at satisfying consumers' needs; hence, the technical process by which this is done is irrelevant to social choice.

The simplest possible criterion is undoubtedly the following: C^2 is said to be better than C^1 if the consumption sequences $\mathbf{x}^2$ and $\mathbf{x}^1$ fulfill the condition $\mathbf{x}^2 \geq \mathbf{x}^1$.

Loosely speaking, this means that there is at least as much of everything to consume in C^2 as in C^1 and that no more labor is required. This leads us to the concept of efficiency:[9]

DEFINITION 1: *A chronic* C^1 *is efficient if there is no possible chronic* C *leading to a consumption sequence* $\mathbf{x}$ *such that* $\mathbf{x} \geq \mathbf{x}^1$.

More generally, if there are any social preferences, then, attached to any given chronic C^1, there exists a set $\mathbf{X}$ of all $\mathbf{x}$ corresponding to chronics C that are preferred to C^1. The following assumption on $\mathbf{X}$ will be made:

ASSUMPTION 5: $\mathbf{X}$ *is convex and, if it contains* $\mathbf{x}^2$, *it also contains any* $\mathbf{x}$ *such that* $\mathbf{x} \geq \mathbf{x}^2$.

---

[7] The reader might find that the constraint $b_1 = \bar{b}_1$ does not pertain to technology and should not enter the definition of $\mathbf{Y}$. Nothing is changed in the following mathematical treatment and little in the economic interpretation if $\bar{z}_1$ is defined so as to include the services of natural resources *and* all existing commodities at time 1. As was pointed out in footnote 2, the exact content of initial capital has no real significance here; thus we are free to assume $\bar{b}_1 = 0$. If this is done, the first formula in (18) must be changed accordingly and the reasoning may proceed without any alteration.

[8] Using the definitions introduced in footnote 5, we may write $y_{tk} = q_{tk} + g_{tk} - s_{tk}$, so that the input vector for firm k at time t is the difference between purchases and sales.

[9] Because of its simplicity, this definition is not fully satisfactory. In particular, it does not provide for the existence of commodities that are not wanted for consumption. However, since we shall also deal with the most general criterion for social preferences, it is advisable to choose here the simplest possible definition of efficiency so as to make the treatment of this case easily understandable.

C^1 may be said to be optimal if there is no possible C with $\mathbf{x} \in \mathbf{X}$. In the following pages we shall, however, restrict the meaning of optimality and deal only with the usual welfare criterion. According to this criterion social choices are determined from individual preferences in the following way:

There are present and future consumers,[10] each of whom is characterized by an index j (a positive number). His activity is represented by a consumption sequence $\mathbf{x}_j$, which may also be written $\mathbf{x}_j = \mathbf{x}_j^+ - \mathbf{x}_j^-$.

Since the life of any consumer j is limited,[11] then necessarily $x_{tj} = 0$, except for a finite number of values of t. More precisely, let us suppose that the indexes j are so chosen that, for a given t, $x_{tj} = 0$, except for $j_t^0 \leqq j \leqq j_t^1$. (There is only a finite number of consumers living at any time.) For a given j we also have $x_{tj} = 0$, except for $t_j^0 \leqq t \leqq t_j^1$ and, for any j, $t_j^1 - t_j^0 \leqq \theta$.

With these assumptions we may write

$$\mathbf{x} = \sum_j \mathbf{x}_j. \tag{19}$$

Now, for each consumer j, there is a set X_j of all sequences $\mathbf{x}_j$ that are at least equivalent to $\mathbf{x}_j^1$, and a set $\mathbf{X}_j$ of all sequences $\mathbf{x}_j$ that are preferred to $\mathbf{x}_j^1$. According to the Pareto principle[12] we say that $\mathbf{x}$ is preferred to $\mathbf{x}^1$ (or $\mathbf{x} \in \mathbf{X}$) if it may be written as a sum of sequences $\mathbf{x}_j$ with

$$\mathbf{x}_j \in X_j \qquad \text{for all } j, \text{ and}$$

$$\mathbf{x}_j \in \mathbf{X}_j \qquad \text{for at least one } j.$$

In the following we shall suppose that X_j and $\mathbf{X}_j$ fulfill Assumption 5. We may now give the following definition.

DEFINITION 2: *A chronic C^1 is "optimal" if there is no possible chronic C such that $\mathbf{x} \in \mathbf{X}$, where $\mathbf{X}$ is defined according to the Pareto principle.*

It is not necessary to insist here on the meaning of such concepts as efficiency and optimality for practical economic policy. This has been done elsewhere.

---

[10] It might seem strange to introduce those consumers who do not yet exist. But if we consider all the consequences of our present economic decisions, however distant they might be, we have to take account of future generations, at least in a crude fashion. If they are not taken into consideration, production of certain very durable equipment would never be profitable.

[11] It would also be possible to introduce consumption units with infinite life, such as a national army. This would not create much difficulty.

[12] One might think the Pareto principle is still too restrictive as soon as choices involving time are concerned. Old people often say they would have planned their lives differently "if they had known." Clearly, only present individual preferences are considered in this paper. Each consumer is supposed fully to appreciate the relative urgency of his present and future needs. However, should this hypothesis be rejected, it would still be possible to introduce a weaker principle for social choices. One may say C is better than C^1 if it is preferred by all consumers now, and will still be preferred by them given all their future preference patterns. The latter concept has been used extensively by M. Allais [3, Chapter VI].

II. PROPERTIES OF EFFICIENT AND OPTIMAL CHRONICS

In this part, general properties of efficient and optimal chronics are studied. Nothing is assumed regarding the rhythm of expansion in the economy. In particular, some chronics may be efficient although they include periods with low levels of consumption and high investment followed by periods of disinvestment and high consumption. As usual in welfare economics and the theory of efficient allocation of resources, the final theorem introduces a price vector and rules of decentralization very similar to those which would hold in a competitive economy.

In order to make the main proof easier to understand, it is given in full detail for efficient chronics. The generalization to optimal chronics is merely sketched in the last paragraph. The reader will probably better understand the process of deduction if we first consider the case in which there is an economic horizon.

9. *Case of a finite horizon.* A chronic C^1 is efficient if there is no chronic C fulfilling[13]

$$\left.\begin{array}{l} \mathbf{x} \geq \mathbf{x}^1, \\ \mathbf{x} + \mathbf{y} = \bar{\mathbf{z}} \text{ and} \\ \mathbf{y} \in Y \end{array}\right\} . \tag{20}$$

Suppose now that there is some finite economic horizon h; in other words suppose that the result of economic activity is no longer an infinite sequence of consumption vectors but that there are only consumption vectors x_t for the $h - 1$ coming periods and the final stock of commodities b_h for the last period. Thus, the economic output is given by the finite set

$$\mathbf{x} = \{x_1, x_2, \ldots, x_t, \ldots, x_{h-1}, b_h\}.$$

$\mathbf{x}$ is a vector in the mh-dimensional Euclidean space. In the same way,

$$\mathbf{y} = \{y_1, y_2, \ldots, y_t, \ldots, y_{h-1}, \bar{z}_h - b_h\},$$

and Y becomes a convex set in the mh-dimensional Euclidean space.

In this form the problem is mathematically the same as in the static case. From previous works it is known that an efficient state is associated with some price vector,

$$\mathbf{p} = \{p_1, p_2, \ldots, p_t, \ldots, p_h\}.$$

The reader will find, for instance, a complete treatment of this finite case in Debreu's paper [8]. The price vector $\mathbf{p}$ is introduced, and its meaning when several periods are considered is indicated. See, in particular [8, p. 282, lines 10 to 14].

---

[13] Hence, we look for minimal elements in $\mathbf{Y}$. From a mathematical viewpoint, Theorem 1 provides a characterization of a minimal element in a convex set embedded in the linear space obtained by the Cartesian product of an infinite sequence of m-dimensional Euclidean spaces.

The existence of a price sequence will also be the essential result of the next section. But, as it stands now, it is somewhat unsatisfactory because nothing implies that the final stock of commodities is economically efficient in any sense.

In order to remove this limitation the efficiency of a chronic C^1 will be determined by successive steps. First C^1 will be compared to all C that are analogous to if after some given period h. Then h will be moved farther and farther into the future. If in this process there is never found any C better than C^1, then C^1 is efficient. This is indeed, the only way in which the problem can be handled in practice; hence, one may expect that it is also the only way in which economically meaningful results can be reached.

10. *Existence of a price vector.* To justify this procedure we need, however, to establish the following lemma:

LEMMA 1: *Under Assumption 4, C^1 is efficient if and only if, for all h, there is no possible C with*

$$\begin{cases} \mathbf{x} \geq \mathbf{x}^1, \\ x_t = x_t^1 \qquad \text{(for } t > h\text{)}. \end{cases} \tag{21}$$

PROOF: If C^1 is efficient, there is clearly no C fulfilling (21). Conversely, suppose there is some possible C fulfilling $\mathbf{x} \geq \mathbf{x}^1$. Then, for at least one h, $x_h \geq x_h^1$. Given such an h, consider $\mathbf{x}^2$ defined by

$$x_t^2 = x_t \qquad \text{(for all } t \leq h\text{), and}$$

$$x_t^2 = x_t^1 \qquad \text{(for all } t > h\text{).}$$

Clearly $\mathbf{x}^2 \leq \mathbf{x}$, so that, by Assumption 4, there is associated with $\mathbf{x}^2$ some possible chronic C^2. C^2 satisfies (21), which completes the proof.

Given a chronic C^1, suppose we now restrict our attention to the possible chronic C fulfilling

$$\left. \begin{array}{c} \mathbf{y} \in \mathbf{T} \\ x_t = x_t^1 \end{array} \right\} \qquad \text{(for } t > h\text{).} \tag{22}$$

This leads to the following lemma:

LEMMA 2: *Under Assumptions 3 and 4, if C^1 is efficient among all C satisfying (22), then there are h nonnegative vectors p_t, not all zero, such that*

$$\sum_{t-1}^{h} p_t y_t$$

is minimum for C^1 among all C satisfying (22).

PROOF: For all possible C satisfying (22) the following holds:

$$\begin{cases} \mathbf{y} \in \mathbf{T} \\ y_t = \bar{z}_t - x_t^1 \qquad \text{(for all } t > h\text{).} \end{cases} \tag{23}$$

Thus, if C^1 is efficient among all C satisfying (22), $\mathbf{y}^1$ is minimal among all $\mathbf{y}$ satisfying (23).

Now, consider the following vector in the mh-dimensional Euclidean space: $\mathbf{y}_h = \{y_1, \ldots, y_t, \ldots, y_h\}$. $\mathbf{y}$ fulfills (23) only if the vector $\mathbf{y}_h$ obtained from it is in some set $\mathbf{Y}_h$ depending on C^1 and h. From the convexity of $\mathbf{Y}$ it follows that $\mathbf{Y}_h$ is convex. Thus, $\mathbf{y}_h^1$ has to be a minimal element in the convex set $\mathbf{Y}_h$. This implies the existence in $\mathbf{y}_h^1$ of a support plane to $\mathbf{Y}_h$ whose normal vector $\mathbf{p}_h$ is nonnegative;[14] or the existence of a nonnegative linear form

$$\sum_{t=1}^{h} p_t \, y_t$$

which is minimal for $\mathbf{y}_h^1$. Lemma 2 follows from this.

More precisely, if there are several support planes, the normal vectors generate a convex closed cone in the mh-dimensional Euclidean space.[15]

Going back to the extensive form of the chronics, we may write

$$\sum_{t=1}^{h} p_t \, y_t = -p_1 \bar{b}_1 + \sum_{t=1}^{h-1} (p_t a_t - p_{t+1} b_{t+1}) + p_h a_h. \tag{24}$$

Since the sets $\mathbf{T}_t$ are defined independently of the values taken by the y_t,

$$\sum_{t=1}^{h} p_t \, y_t$$

is minimal for C^1 among all C satisfying (22) if and only if:

---

[14] The following mathematical theorem is applicable here:

THEOREM: *In finite-dimensional Euclidean space, given a convex set* $\mathbf{A}$ *with a nonempty interior and a point x not interior to* $\mathbf{A}$, *there is a plane* $\mathbf{P}$ *containing x and such that* $\mathbf{A}$ *is entirely contained in one of the closed half-spaces limited by* $\mathbf{P}$.

For proof of this one may, for instance, transpose a proof by Banach [4, p. 28]. The reader may notice that $\mathbf{A}$ need not be closed.

y_h^1, being minimal, is necessarily a boundary point of $\mathbf{Y}_h$. So there is a nonzero vector p_h fulfilling the conditions of Lemma 2. The fact that $p_h \geq 0$ follows directly from Assumption 4.

[15] If

$$\sum_{t=1}^{h} p_t (y_t - y_t^1) \geq 0 \quad \text{and} \quad \sum_{t=1}^{h} p_t'(y_t - y_t^1) \geq 0,$$

then, clearly

$$\sum_{t=1}^{h} (\alpha p_t + \beta p_t')(y_t - y_t^1) \geq 0$$

for any $\alpha \geq 0$ and $\beta \geq 0$.

Also, if p_h^n is a sequence of vectors converging to p_h, and if

$$\sum_{t=1}^{h} p_t^n(y_t - y_t^1) \geq 0 \quad \text{for all } n,$$

then

$$\sum_{t=1}^{h} p_t(y_t - y_t^1) \geq 0.$$

Figure 2

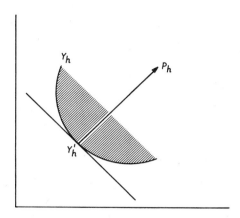

i) For all $t < h$, $p_t a_t - p_{t+1} b_{t+1}$ is minimal at (a_t^1, b_{t+1}^1) among all $(a_t, b_{t+1}) \in \mathbf{T}_t$;

ii) $p_h a_h$ is minimal at a_h^1 among all a_h that make possible $y_t = \bar{z}_t - x_t^1$ for all $t > h$.

If p_t is interpreted as a vector of discounted prices, $p_{t+1} b_{t+1} - p_t a_t$ will be the discounted profit from production during period t (see sections 14 and 15 below). Property (i) asserts that this profit should be maximized over the set of feasible productions. Property (ii) states that the value of capital at time h should be minimal over the set of chronics that permit the same consumption after time h as C^1 does.

We should now prove the existence of an infinite sequence $\mathbf{p}$ such that, for all h,

$$\sum_t p_t y_t$$

is minimal for C^1 among all C satisfying (22). But, in order to do so, we shall make a new assumption, which will be economically acceptable if we distinguish those commodities that cannot be produced or stored, essentially the various services of labor. Let us suppose they are the last n_2 commodities, and partition the vectors of inputs, outputs, and prices as follows:

$$a_t = \begin{bmatrix} d_t \\ e_t \end{bmatrix}, \qquad b_t = \begin{bmatrix} f_t \\ 0 \end{bmatrix}, \qquad p_t = \begin{bmatrix} q_t \\ s_t \end{bmatrix}, \tag{25}$$

where d_t, f_t, and q_t will be vectors of $n_1 = n - n_2$ components; e_t and s_t vectors of n_2 components, and 0 a vector of n_2 zeros.

Let us now make the following hypothesis about the optimum program C^1 and the technological sets $\mathbf{T}_t$.

ASSUMPTION 6. In any period t, it would be technically possible to produce outputs f_{t+1} larger than f_{t+1}^1 by using inputs of labor services e_t smaller than e_t^1 and some conveniently chosen inputs d_t of the other commodities.[16]

Formally, for any t, there is some $(a_t, b_{t+1}) \in \mathbf{T}_t$ such that $f_{t+1} > f_{t+1}^1$ and $e_t < e_t^1$.

Since no restriction is placed on d_t, this assumption seems to be quite acceptable. A sufficiently large increase of the inputs of nonlabor commodities should permit reducing the inputs of labor services while increasing outputs. The assumption would, however, fail to hold if no input of some particular kind of labor service appeared in the optimum program, or if technology would imply strict proportionality between total labor inputs and total outputs.

We are now able to prove the following natural generalization of the efficiency theorem:

THEOREM 1: *Under Assumptions* 3, 4, *and* 6, *associated with an efficient chronic* C^1, *there is a nonnegative nonnull sequence* $\mathbf{p}$ *such that, for all h,*

$$\sum_{t=1}^{h} p_t y_t$$

is minimal for C^1 *among all* C *satisfying* (22).

PROOF: Let us define the following norm on the nonnegative prices:

$$|q_t| = \sum_{i=1}^{n_1} q_{it}, \qquad |s_t| = \sum_{i=n_1+1}^{n_2} s_{it}. \tag{26}$$

Assumption 6 implies the existence of numbers α_t such that, in any nh-dimensional nonnegative and nonzero vector $(p_1, p_2, \ldots, p_h)$ fulfilling conditions (i) and (ii):

$$q_1 \geq 0, \qquad |q_{t+1}| \leq \alpha_t |q_t|, \qquad |s_t| \leq \alpha_t |q_t|, \qquad \text{for all } t < h. \tag{27}$$

Indeed, write condition (i) for the input-output combination whose existence is asserted by Assumption 6:

$$q_{t+1}(f_{t+1} - f_{t+1}^1) - q_t(d_t - d_t^1) - s_t(e_t - e_t^1) \leq 0 \tag{28}$$

with

$$\begin{aligned} &q_{t+1} \geq 0; \qquad q_t \geq 0; \qquad s_t \geq 0; \\ &f_{t+1} - f_{t+1}^1 > 0; \qquad e_t - e_t^1 < 0. \end{aligned} \tag{29}$$

---

[16] Assumption 6 is now known in the technical literature as the "non tightness assumption". The proof also holds if all commodities can be produced ($ne = 0$). The condition on e_t may then obviously be deleted.

Suppose now $q_t = 0$; then (28) and (29) imply $q_{t+1} = 0$ and $s_t = 0$. Since $(p_1, p_2, \ldots, p_h)$ is nonzero, q_1 must then necessarily be nonzero and the first inequality in (27) is established. [17]

Let now φ_t and δ_t be any positive numbers such that

$$f_{i,t+1} - f^1_{i,t+1} \geqq \varphi_t \qquad \text{for all } i = 1, 2, \ldots, n_1,$$
$$e_{i,t} - e^1_{i,t} \leqq -\varphi_t \qquad \text{for all } i = n_1 + 1, \ldots, n_2,$$
$$d_{it} - d^1_{it} \leqq \delta_t \qquad \text{for all } i = 1, 2, \ldots, n_1.$$

Then the left-hand side of (28) is not smaller than $|q_{t+1}|\varphi_t - |q_t|\delta_t + |s_t|\varphi_t$ which must therefore be nonpositive. Taking $\alpha_t = \delta_t/\varphi_t$, the last two inequalities in (27) follow directly.

After these preliminaries, it is possible to show how an infinite sequence of prices can be obtained. Suppose one nh-dimensional vector fulfilling condition (i) and (ii) has been found for each h ($h = 1, 2, \ldots$ ad infinitum). Let this vector be $(p^h_1, p^h_2, \ldots, p^h_t, \ldots, p^h_h)$. The first inequality in (27) shows that $q^h_1 \geqq 0$. We may therefore assume that the nh-dimensional vector has been normalized in such a way that $|q^h_1| = 1$. It then follows from the second and third inequalities in (27) that, for any t, p^h_t is bounded, uniformly in h.

The sequence $\{p^h_1\}$, for $h = 1, 2, \ldots$ ad infinitum, being bounded has a converging subsequence. Let $h^1_{\tau_1}$, with $\tau_1 = 1, 2, \ldots$ ad infinitum, be the indices of this subsequence and p_1 its limit point. Since q^h_1 has been normalized p_1 is non-null.

The sequence $\{p^h_2\}$, for $h = h^1_{\tau_1}$ with $\tau_1 = 1, 2, \ldots$ ad infinitum, is bounded and has a converging subsequence. Let $h^2_{\tau_2}$, with $\tau_2 = 1, 2, \ldots$ ad infinitum, be the indices of this subsequence and p_2 its limit point.

By induction, we can find for any t a converging subsequence $\{p^h_t\}$ with $h = h^t_{\tau_t}$ and $\tau_t = 1, 2, \ldots$ ad infinitum. We may designate by p_t the limit point of this subsequence.

The $p_1, p_2, \ldots, p_t, \ldots$ so defined provide us with the sequence whose existence is asserted by Theorem 1. Indeed, for all h and in particular for $h = h^t_{\tau_t}$, $(a_{t-1}, b_t) \in T_{t-1}$ implies:

$$p^h_{t-1}(a_{t-1} - a^1_{t-1}) - p^h_t(b_t - b^1_t) \geqq 0; \tag{30}$$

hence also, taking the limit for increasing τ_t,

$$p_{t-1}(a_{t-1} - a^1_{t-1}) - p_t(b_t - b^1_t) \geqq 0. \tag{31}$$

Similarly, as soon as a_h makes possible $y_t = \bar{z}_t - x^1_t$ for all $t > h$:

$$p^{h'}_h(a_h - a^1_h) \geqq 0 \tag{32}$$

---

[17] The reader might object that this argument does not exclude the case $p_t = 0$ for all $t < h$; $q_h = 0$, but $s_h \geqq 0$. In fact, with the partitioning of the commodities into two groups, the n_2 last components should not appear in the last period. Instead of considering the nh-dimensional vector $(p_1, p_2, \ldots, p_h)$, we should consider the $(nh - n_2)$-dimensional vector $(p_1, p_2, \ldots, p_{h-1}, q_h)$ in Lemma 2 and in all the subsequent argument. For simplicity, I preferred not to introduce this complication here.

for all h' and in particular for $h' = h^h_{\tau_h}$; hence also, taking the limit for increasing τ_h,

$$p_h(a_h - a^1_h) \geqq 0. \tag{33}$$

Therefore, the sequence $p_1, p_2, \ldots, p_t, \ldots$, in which p_1 is nonnull, fulfills the two conditions (i) and (ii), and therefore

$$\sum_t p_t y_t$$

is minimal for C^1 among all C satisfying (22), as was to be proved.

The following lemma will give the converse of Theorem 1:

LEMMA 3: *Under Assumption 4, a sufficient condition for the efficiency of a chronic C^1 is the existence of a positive* [18] *sequence* **p** *such that, for all h,*

$$\sum_{t=1}^{h} p_t y_t$$

is minimum for C^1 among all C satisfying (22).

PROOF: Suppose C^1 is not efficient. Then, by Lemma 1, there exists an h and a C satisfying (22) such that $\mathbf{x} \geq \mathbf{x}^1$; hence $\mathbf{y} \leq \mathbf{y}^1$. Since $p_t > 0$, then

$$\sum_{t=1}^{h} p_t(y_t - y^1_t) < 0,$$

contradicting the hypothesis.

11. *Decentralization rule.* The preceding section provides a generalization of the first part of the efficiency theorem which was obtained in the static case. The second part of the same theorem specifies a rule of decentralization; more explicitly, it says that **py** is minimal for the society as a whole if and only if $\mathbf{py}_k$ is minimal for each firm. This will be the subject of Lemmas 4 and 5.

LEMMA 4: *Under Assumptions 3, 4 and 6, if C^1 is efficient there is a non-negative sequence* **p** *such that, for all h and k,*

$$\sum_{t=1}^{h} p_t y_{tk}$$

is minimal at C^1 among all C satisfying

$$\left. \begin{array}{l} \mathbf{y}_k \in \mathbf{Y}_k, \text{ and} \\ y_{tk} = y^1_{tk} \end{array} \right\} \quad \text{(for } t > h\text{)}. \tag{34}$$

---

[18] The reader may notice we have $\mathbf{p} \geq 0$ in Theorem 1 and $\mathbf{p} > 0$ in Lemma 3, so that the lemma is not exactly the converse of the theorem. However, it does not seem to be worth extending our investigations here in order to reduce the gap. This would lead us into a rather long study. It was done for the static case in Koopmans' work. Moreover, in dealing with optimality we shall presently give a more satisfactory treatment of the difficulty.

PROOF: This follows directly from Theorem 1 because, if there were any C satisfying (34) such that

$$\sum_{t=1}^{h} p_t(y_{tk} - y_{tk}^1) < 0$$

for some k, then we could find a chronic C^2 identical with C^1 except for the input vectors of firm k. For the latter we would choose $y_{kt}^2 = y_{tk}$. Hence, C^2 would satisfy (22) and

$$\sum_{t=1}^{h} p_t(y_t^2 - y_t^1) < 0,$$

contradicting Theorem 1.

Let us first note as a consequence of Lemma 4 that C^1 is not efficient unless there is complete use of those resources which have a nonzero price. Indeed, for the $(n + 1)$th production unit we should have

$$\sum_{t=1}^{h} p_t(\bar{z}_t - z_t)$$

at a minimum. Since p_t and $\bar{z}_t - z_t$ are nonnegative, the minimum is reached when $p_t(\bar{z}_t - z_t) = 0$ for all t.

Even if $\mathbf{p} > 0$, the converse of Lemma 4 does not necessarily hold.[19] The difficulty lies in the possibility of having some C^2 such that

$$\begin{cases} y_t^2 = y_t^1 & \text{(for } t > h\text{), but not necessarily } y_{tk}^2 = y_{tk}^1, \\ \sum_{t=1}^{h} p_t(y_t^2 - y_t^1) < 0 \end{cases}$$

---

[19] The following counterexample illustrates the point. Suppose there are two commodities and two firms with the same technological set:

$$(a_{tk}, b_{t+1,k}) \in \mathbf{T}_{tk} \text{ if } \begin{cases} a_{itk} \geq 0, b_{i,t+1,k} \geq 0; \text{ and} \\ a_{1tk} + a_{2tk} - b_{1,t+1,k} - b_{2,t+1,k} \geq 0. \end{cases}$$

Consider C^1 defined by

$$C^1 \begin{cases} a_{1t} = 1, & a_{2t} = 2, & b_{1t} = 2, & b_{2t} = 1, & y_{1t} = -1, & y_{2t} = 1, \\ a_{1t1} = 0, & a_{2t1} = 2, & b_{1t1} = 2, & b_{2t1} = 0, & y_{1t1} = -2, & y_{2t1} = 2, \\ a_{1t2} = 1, & a_{2t2} = 0, & b_{1t2} = 0, & b_{2t2} = 1, & y_{1t2} = 1, & y_{2t2} = -1. \end{cases}$$

C^1 fulfills the condition of Lemma 4, with the price vector $p_t = (1, 1)$, but it is not efficient, as can be seen by comparison with the following

$$C \begin{cases} a_{1t} = a_{1t1} = 0, & a_{2t} = a_{2t1} = 1, & a_{it2} = b_{it2} = 0 & \text{(for all } t\text{)}, \\ b_{2t} = b_{2t1} = 0, & b_{1t} = b_{1t1} = 1, & & \text{(for all } t > 1\text{)}, \\ y_{t2} = 0, & y_{1t1} = -1, y_{2t1} = 1 & & \text{(for all } t > 1\text{)}. \end{cases}$$

Indeed, C provides us with the same net output for all periods after the first one: $x_t = x_t^1 = \bar{z}_t + (1, -1)$ for $t > 1$. And it makes possible an increase in the first consumption vector $x_1 = \bar{z}_1 + (2, 0)$, $x_1^1 = \bar{z}_1 + (1, -1)$.

although there is no C such that

$$
\begin{cases}
y_{tk} = y_{tk}^1 \\
\sum_{t=1}^{h} p_t(y_t - y_t^1) < 0 \quad \text{(for } t > h \text{, and all } k).
\end{cases}
$$

Such a case corresponds to an inadequate distribution of capital among firms, which cannot be detected when comparisons are limited to any finite horizon.

However, the possibility of this can be ruled out if $p_h a_h$ tends to zero when h tends to infinity, i.e., if the present value of capital for period h decreases to zero when h tends to infinity. This is the meaning of the following lemma.

LEMMA 5: *Under Assumption 4, a sufficient condition for the efficiency of C^1 is that there is a positive sequence $\mathbf{p}$ such that:*
i) *for all h and k,*

$$
\sum_{t=1}^{h} p_t \, y_{tk}
$$

is minimal at C^1 among all C satisfying (34);
ii) $p_t a_t^1$ *tends to zero when t tends to infinity.*

PROOF: Suppose C^1 is not efficient. There is some h and some C^2 such that

$$
\sum_{t=1}^{h} p_t(y_t^2 + y_t^1) < 0, \tag{35}
$$

$$
y_t^2 = y_t^1 \quad \text{or} \quad a_t^2 - b_t^2 = a_t^1 - b_t^1 \qquad \text{(for all } t > h). \tag{36}
$$

From Condition (i) it follows that $p_t a_{tk} - p_{t+1} b_{t+1,k}$ is minimal at $(a_{tk}^1, b_{t+1,k}^1)$ for all t and all $(a_{tk}, b_{t+1,k}) \in \mathbf{T}_{tk}$. Hence, for all t,

$$
p_t(a_t^2 - a_t^1) \geqq p_{t+1}(b_{t+1}^2 - b_{t+1}^1). \tag{37}
$$

(35) and (37) imply

$$
p_h(a_h^2 - a_h^1) < 0. \tag{38}
$$

Now, (36), (37), and (38) imply that the following is a nonincreasing sequence of negative vectors:

$$
0 > p_h(a_h^2 - a_h^1) \geqq p_{h+1}(b_{h+1}^2 - b_{h+1}^1) = p_{h+1}(a_{h+1}^2 - a_{h+1}^1) \geqq \cdots.
$$

But such a sequence cannot exist because $p_t a_t^2$ is nonnegative and, from condition (ii), $p_t a_t^1$ can be made smaller than any positive number, so that $p_h(a_h^2 - a_h^1)$ would have to be greater than any negative number.

12. *Properties of optimal chronics.* In dealing with optimal chronics the mathematical technique will be essentially the same as in the two preceding sections. Detailed demonstrations will therefore be omitted and only the main steps given.

Let us recall Definition 2: C^1 is optimal if there is no possible chronic C such that $\mathbf{x} \in \mathbf{X}$; i.e., if there is no $\mathbf{x} \in \mathbf{X}$ and $\mathbf{y} \in \mathbf{Y}$ such that $\bar{\mathbf{z}} = \mathbf{x} + \mathbf{y}$.

Let us define the set $\mathbf{Z} = \mathbf{X} + \mathbf{Y}$.

C^1 is optimal if and only if $\bar{\mathbf{z}}$ is not in $\mathbf{Z}$. From Assumptions 3, 4, and 5, $\mathbf{Z}$ is convex, and if it contains $\mathbf{z}^2$ it also contains any $\mathbf{z} \geqq \mathbf{z}^2$. Hence, the following may be proved:[20]

THEOREM 1': *Under Assumptions 3, 4, 5, and 6, if C^1 is optimal, there is a nonnegative sequence* $\mathbf{p}$ *such that*

$$\sum_{t=1}^{h} p_t(z_t - \bar{z}_t) \geqq 0$$

for all h and all $\mathbf{z}$ *satisfying*

$$\left. \begin{array}{l} \mathbf{z} \in \mathbf{Z}, \\ z_t = \bar{z}_t \end{array} \right\} \quad \text{(for } t > h). \tag{39}$$

The following trivial lemma goes in the opposite direction:

LEMMA 3': *Under the Assumptions 4 and 5, a sufficient condition for optimality of C^1 is the existence of a nonnegative sequence* $\mathbf{p}$ *such that*

$$\sum_{t=1}^{h} p_t(z_t - \bar{z}_t) > 0$$

for all h and $\mathbf{z}$ *fulfilling* (39).

Theorem 1' and Lemma 3' may be summed up into a single theorem if the following weak assumption on $\mathbf{X}$ is made:

ASSUMPTION 7: *If $\mathbf{x} \in \mathbf{X}$, then there is $\epsilon > 0$ such that if $|x_{it}^2 - x_{it}| < \epsilon$ for all i and t, it is implied that $\mathbf{x}^2 \in \mathbf{X}$.*

This says that, if $\mathbf{x}$ is preferred to $\mathbf{x}^1$, then any sequence $\mathbf{x}^2$ sufficiently close to $\mathbf{x}$ is also preferred to $\mathbf{x}^1$.[21]

We may now formulate

THEOREM 2. *Under Assumptions 3, 4, 5, 6, and 7, C^1 is optimal if and only if there is a nonnegative sequence* $\mathbf{p}$ *such that*

$$\sum_{t=1}^{h} p_t(z_t - \bar{z}_t) > 0$$

for all h and all $\mathbf{z}$ *satisfying* (39).

---

[20] As in Section 10, one would define finite sequences $\mathbf{z}_h$ and the sets $\mathbf{Z}_h$ of all $\mathbf{z}_h$ such that $\mathbf{z}^2 \in \mathbf{Z}$ if $z_t^2 = z_t$ for $t \leqq h$, and $z_t^2 = \bar{z}_t$ for $t > h$. C^1 is optimal if and only if $\bar{\mathbf{z}}_h \notin \mathbf{Z}_h$ for all h. Hence, the existence of finite nonnegative sequences $\mathbf{p}_h$ such that $\mathbf{z}_h \in \mathbf{Z}_h$ implies

$$\sum_{t=1}^{h} p_t(z_t - \bar{z}_t) \geqq 0$$

(cf. footnote 14), and hence, finally, the existence of an infinite nonnegative sequence $\mathbf{p}$.

[21] Although it is not satisfied by the efficiency concept, this assumption does not seem to be restrictive. It is clearly fulfilled if the individual preferences may be represented by continuous utility functions.

Along with the existence of a price vector, a scheme of decentralization may be introduced. This is included in Lemmas 4' and 5'.

LEMMA 4': *Under Assumptions* 3, 4, 5, *and* 6, *if* C^1 *is optimal, there is a nonnegative* $\mathbf{p}$ *such that, for all h, k, and j,*

i) $\sum_{t=1}^{h} p_t y_{tk}$ *is minimal at* C^1 *among all* C *satisfying* (34);

ii) $\sum_{t} p_t(x_{tj} - x_{tj}^1) \geqq 0$ *for all* $\mathbf{x}_j \in \mathbf{X}_j$.

Since the vectors of the sequence $\mathbf{x}_j$ are null except for a finite number, the sum in Condition (ii) does make sense. Also, Condition (ii) may be written with the strict sign if Assumption 7 holds for the individual preference sets $\mathbf{X}_j$.

For the converse of Lemma 4' one more assumption is needed:

ASSUMPTION 8: *For all t and j, there exist vectors* $\bar{u}_{tj}$ *such that* $\mathbf{x}_j \in \mathbf{X}_j$ *implies* $\mathbf{x}_{tj} \geqq \bar{u}_{tj}$.

Since $x_{tj}^+ \geqq 0$, Assumption 8 means essentially that there is some upper limit to the amount of labor x_{tj}^- that can be required from consumer j. For society as a whole we shall write

$$\bar{u}_t = \sum_j \bar{u}_{tj}.$$

Hence we have the following lemma:

LEMMA 5': *Under Assumptions* 3, 4, 5, 7, *and* 8, *a sufficient condition for the optimality of* C^1 *is the existence of a nonnegative sequence* $\mathbf{p}$ *such that, for all h, j, and k,*

i) $\sum_{t=1}^{h} p_t y_{tk}$ *is minimal for* C^1 *among all* C *satisfying* (34);

ii) $\sum_{t} p_t(x_{tj} - x_{tj}^1) \geqq 0$ *for all* $\mathbf{x}_j \in \mathbf{X}_j$;

iii) $p_t a_t^1$ *and* $p_t(x_t^1 - \bar{u}_t)$ *tend to zero when t tends to infinity.*

As in the efficiency case, Condition (iii) means that the present values of future capital and future consumption tend to zero when we consider periods that are farther and farther away in the future. Conditions (ii) in Lemmas 3' and 4' are not exactly the same. But they are equivalent if X_j is contained in the closure of $\mathbf{X}_j$, or if, for any $\mathbf{x}_j^2 \in X_j$ and any positive sequence $\mathbf{u}$, there is some $\mathbf{x}_j \in \mathbf{X}_j$ such that $\mathbf{x}_j - \mathbf{x}_j^2 \leqq \mathbf{u}$. This amounts to saying that there does not exist any complete saturation of all consumers' needs. By increasing the quantity of some conveniently chosen commodity, the consumer may be made better off, however small the increase might be.

III. EFFICIENCY AND THE RATE OF INTEREST

13. *Efficiency in actual societies.* The results of the last part were concerned mainly with the general properties of efficient and optimal chronics. They merely extended what was already known about the static case. It is, however, of paramount interest to study the extent to which these requirements are fulfilled in a real society. This is the purpose of the present part, in which we shall try to move closer to reality, introducing some institutional rules together with the general scheme of production and consumption. This inquiry aims at showing which restrictions are necessary in order to interpret the preceding formal lemmas as a justification of a competitive economic system.

We shall first rule out uncertainty in its two-fold aspect. Any firm will be supposed to know exactly which technical transformations are, and will be, possible; that is, firm k knows perfectly the sets T_{tk} for all values of t. In addition every economic unit, whether firm or consumer, also knows the present and future conditions of the market, i.e., prices and interest rates.

A second hypothesis concerns money. We shall suppose that firms and consumers do not hold money, either because they are not allowed to or because they do not want to. Once uncertainty is removed, this amounts to supposing that interest rates are positive and services of the banking system free (by which we mean only the fixed costs for any transfer from one account to another—not the normal interest discounts, which are, indeed, retained in the model). Thus, money will be a value unit only.

With these hypotheses we shall proceed to show, first, how interest rates do appear in the price system and, second, how the usual profit-maximizing principles coincide with the preceding decentralization rules. Then we shall be able to exhibit very simply some relations between private and national accounting. Finally, we shall deal with the question of why interest rates should be positive.

14. *Interest rates in actual economies.* As in Sections 11 and 12, the price system $\mathbf{p}$ apparently does not include a rate of interest. This may seem strange since, in society as we know it, interest rates are used on the loan market and in business accounting for discounting future values. The point may be made clearer by the following remark.

In the static case the efficiency theorem leads to a set of prices that are determined up to some common multiplicative scalar. Thus only a set of relative prices is given. Absolute prices may be fixed at any level in accordance with monetary conditions. Our result in the dynamic case is formally similar but entails a different interpretation: The whole set of present and future prices is still determined up to a multiplicative scalar; this, however, determines not only the relative prices for each period but also all future prices, given the present ones. If, as is usually the case, the institutional structure is such that that the absolute prices must satisfy some normalization condition within each period, then our lemmas must be modified.

A normalization rule states which multiple of p_t should be taken as the absolute price vector for period t. To avoid confusion, let us denote by p'_t the normalized price vector associated with p_t:

$$p_t = \beta_t p'_t, \tag{41}$$

where β_t is some convenient positive scalar.[22] Let us call it the discount coefficient for period t. Since the sequence $\mathbf{p}$ is determined up to a multiplicative constant, we shall suppose $\beta_1 = 1$.

In the following, the sequence $\mathbf{p}$ will be replaced by two sequences, one of nonnegative normalized price vectors $\mathbf{p}'$ and the other of the positive discount coefficients β_t. However, it should be clear that neither, taken alone, has any intrinsic meaning.

Let us define

$$1 + \rho_t = \beta_t/\beta_{t+1}. \tag{42}$$

ρ_t will appear as a rate of interest in the next section and later on in the treatment of stationary cases.

15. *Rules of behavior for consumers and firms.* As we have seen, the firm k should maximize in each period $p_{t+1}b_{t+1,k} - p_t a_{tk}$ subject to $(a_{tk}, b_{t+1,k}) \in \mathbf{T}_{tk}$. This is equivalent to maximizing

$$B_{tk} = p'_{t+1}(b_{t+1,k} - a_{tk}) + (p'_{t+1} - p'_t)a_{tk} - \rho_t p'_t a_{tk}. \tag{43}$$

B_{tk} is the usual net profit concept[23] for period t. It is computed as the sum of

$$+ \text{ value of net production,} \quad p'_{t+1}(b_{t+1,k} - a_{tk})$$

$$+ \text{ capital gains,} \quad (p'_{t+1} - p'_t)a_{tk}$$

$$- \text{ interest costs,} \quad \rho_t p'_t a_{tk}.$$

One may also note that if $a^1_{tk} = b^1_{tk} = 0$ after some horizon h, maximizing

$$\sum_{t=1}^{h} p_t y_{tk}$$

is equivalent to maximizing

$$F_{1k} - p'_1 c_{1k} = \sum_t \beta_{t+1}B_{tk}. \tag{45}$$

F_{1k}, so defined, may be interpreted as being the present value of the firm.

Formulas (42), (43), and (45) show that the theory of allocation of resources justifies the usual accounting procedures. The interest rates here introduced play the same role as they do in business accounting.

Let us also remark that, if additivity of the technical processes holds, together with divisibility, then necessarily

$$B_{tk} = 0 \quad \text{and} \quad F_{1k} = p'_1 c_{1k}. \tag{46}$$

---

[22] For the sake of simplicity, it is supposed that $p_t \neq 0$.

[23] It has not always been clear in economic literature which quantity the entrepreneur ought to maximize. (See, for instance, Boulding [7], Samuelson [28], Lutz [21], Rottier [27].) In any case, maximization of B_{tk} is a necessary but not a sufficient condition.

Indeed, if Assumptions 1 and 2 hold for firm k (i.e. if $\mathbf{T}_{tk}$ are convex cones), then Lemma 4 implies

$$-\beta_{t+1}B_{tk} = p_t a_{tk}^1 - p_{t+1}b_{t+1,k}^1 = 0.$$

Suppose for instance this quantity to be negative. Then, with

$$a_{tk} = \alpha a_{tk}^1 \quad \text{and} \quad b_{t+1,k} = \alpha b_{t+1,k}^1,$$

we would have

$$p_t a_{tk} - p_{t+1}b_{t+1,k} < p_t a_{tk}^1 - p_{t+1}b_{t+1,k}^1$$

for any α greater than 1, which would contradict the fact that $(a_{tk}^1, b_{t+1,k}^1)$ maximizes $(a_{tk}, b_{t+1,k})$ in $\mathbf{T}_{tk}$.

In interpreting the rule of behavior for consumers, suppose that they can receive or make loans. An account of their assets and liabilities is kept at some bank, and the net assets at the beginning of period t for consumer j is equal to A_{tj}. The consumer will be paid interest on it equal to

$$K_{tj} = \rho_{t-1}A_{t-1,j}. \tag{47}$$

K_{tj} may be called the consumer's capitalist income. During period t he will save

$$S_{tj} = A_{tj} - A_{t-1,j}.$$

If we write

$$C_{tj} = p_t' x_{tj}^+ \quad \text{and} \quad W_{tj} = p_t' x_{tj}^-,$$

the budget equation for j will be

$$C_{tj} + S_{tj} = Y_{tj} = W_{tj} + K_{tj}, \tag{48}$$

which may be read as *consumption + saving = income*. Formally it may be written

$$p_t x_{tj} = \beta_{t-1}A_{t-1,j} - \beta_t A_{tj}. \tag{49}$$

Minimizing

$$\sum_t p_t x_{tj}$$

subject to $\mathbf{x}_j \in \mathbf{X}_j$ amounts to maximizing the final assets $A_{tj,j}^1$ under the constraints $\mathbf{x}_j \in \mathbf{X}_j$, and $p_t x_{tj} = \beta_{t-1}A_{t-1,j} - \beta_t A_{tj}$.

Thus, roughly speaking, the rule advises us to choose C^1 if, among all chronics that are at least as good, it is associated with the greatest final assets.[24]

---

[24] This is clearly only one among many possible rules which would bring about a minimum of

$$\sum_t p_t x_{tj}$$

subject to $\mathbf{x}_j \in \mathbf{X}_j$.

The budget equation, together with this last rule, shows how the interest rates we have introduced play the usual role on the loan market.[25]

In fact, we shall introduce a somewhat different definition, which is a little more involved but makes the following section simpler. We shall suppose wages to be paid at the end of the period and to include conveniently the interest earned thereon. Thus the budget equation becomes

$$Y_{tj} = K_{tj} + (1 + \rho_{t-1})W_{t-1,j} = C_{tj} + S_{tj}. \tag{50}$$

Accordingly, formula (49) becomes

$$p_t x_{tj} = \beta_{t-1}(A_{t-1,j} + W_{t-1,j}) - \beta_t(A_{tj} + W_{tj}). \tag{51}$$

Since consumer j disposes of initial assets $A^0_{tj,j}$ but does not get any wage before the end of period t^0_j, the intuitive meaning of the behavior rule is still to maximize the final assets while enjoying a given level of utility.

16. *Real capital and assets; private and national accounting.* As was shown by Fetter [9], there are essentially two concepts of capital given in the economic literature. According to the first, capital includes all "owned sources of income"; thus, it may be defined as the totality of assets:

$$A_t = \sum_j A_{tj}.$$

According to the other definition it is a "stock of physical goods used as means of production." The latter concept is sometimes called "real capital" and could be written $p'_t c_t$.

But assets and real capital are not independent of each other. Indeed, if any net assets exist, they represent some "real" values. If, to simplify, we deal directly with aggregates and write

$$B_t = \sum_k B_{tk},$$

we may define:

$$A_t = L_t + F_t, \tag{52}$$

where L_t and F_t are the values of natural resources (land) and of firms, respectively.

$$L_t = \frac{1}{\beta_t} \sum_{\theta=t}^{\infty} \beta_\theta \, p'_\theta z_\theta, \tag{53}$$

$$F_t = p'_t c_t + \frac{1}{\beta_t} \sum_{\theta=t}^{\infty} \beta_{\theta+1} B_\theta, \tag{54}$$

supposing that the infinite sums are meaningful.

---

[25] Thus here, as in classical economics, interest rates appear in their two-fold aspect— as a marginal rate of return and as a price for loans.

From these definitions it is possible to give an expression for capitalist income:

$$K_{t+1} = \rho_t A_t = B_t + \rho_t p'_t c_t + (1 + \rho_t)p'_t z_t + G'_t, \tag{55}$$

where $G'_t = G_t - (p'_{t+1} - p'_t)c_t$, $G_t = (L_{t+1} - L_t) + (F_{t+1} - F_t)$.
Formula (55) shows that capitalist income is the sum of

+ *profits of firms* B_t

+ *interest from real capital,* $\rho_t p'_t c_t$

+ *rents from land,* $(1 + \rho_t)p'_t z_t$

+ *capital gains,* G'_t.

The capital gains on real capital, which are not included in G'_t, are part of profits.[26]

It is now possible to show very simply how national production is related to national income. Let us define the latter by

$$Y_t = \sum_j Y_{tj}, \tag{56}$$

and net national production by

$$P_t = p'_{t+1}(b_{t+1} - c_t). \tag{57}$$

Let us also define net national investment as

$$I_t = p'_{t+1}(c_{t+1} - c_t). \tag{58}$$

The reader may check that the following relations hold:

$$P_t = C_{t+1} + I_t, \tag{59}$$

$$Y_t = C_t + S_t, \tag{60}$$

$$S_{t+1} = I_t + G_t, \qquad Y_{t+1} = P_t + G_t. \tag{61}$$

These relations bear a strong resemblance to the usual national accounting equations. However, the matter of capital gains seems to introduce some

---

[26] We considered firms and consumers as different units and found some behavior rules for them separately. But actually many consumers do perform productive activities; there is no such sharp distinction in reality between production and consumption units. It is therefore important to notice here that the two behavior rules are consistent. Nobody is faced with the difficult problem of choosing between a maximum of B_t and a maximum of A_t.

difficulty.[27] Needless to say, our relations are not directly transposable to actual societies because money and international trade have been deliberately excluded.

17. *Why should interest rates be nonnegative?* Interest theory, if not capital theory, has often been thought of as dealing only with one question: Why does competition not bring the rate of interest down to zero? The emphasis on this point seems to have been a little misplaced. Once it is understood that two equal quantities of the same thing available at two different moments are not economically equivalent, there is no a priori reason for the interest rate to be zero. However, we do observe in fact that interest rates have always been positive; thus, we may wonder why this is so. The following remarks are intended to reformulate a few reasons that seem to be important in this respect.

First, in a monetary economy, consumers may always hold money, so that there would not be any loans unless the interest rate were positive. This reason, however important as it is, does not provide a complete answer. It has been argued that not only monetary but also real interest rates[28] are always positive. We also want to see if positive interest rates in a nonmonetary economy can be explained.

Note that in such an economy interest rates alone do not have any intrinsic meaning, so that the question does not make sense unless one specifies the normalization rule on the price vector p_t'. This must be kept in mind to understand the following remarks.

1. Suppose first that the prices p_t' are such that

$$p_t' \bar{z}_t = p_{t+1}' \bar{z}_{t+1} \qquad \text{(for all } t\text{)}$$

---

[27] Of course, this difficulty could be avoided by changing our definitions. But there are good reasons for our choice. If income did not include capital gains, the behavior rules could no longer be interpreted in the frame of a competitive economy. If capital gains were included in national production and investment, these aggregates would no longer be evaluated from real physical net output and investment by using a unique set of prices. Concepts like the investment schedule would also be much more difficult to define.

The above equations should not, however, lead the reader to think that the whole of the present national accounting analysis is not well founded. If one considers what would happen in times of inflation, he will find that net national production is the very concept people have in mind when they speak of national income. As we have defined the latter it would include large capital gains which should be saved and invested on the loan market if capitalists wanted to keep constant the *real* value of their assets. Thus, both income and savings might seem to be largely overrated by our definitions.

One should also notice that the equation $S = I + G$ is not an equilibrium relation on any market but rather a necessary identity as soon as net assets are supposed to equate the value of firms and natural resources.

[28] Real interest rates are defined once the effect of changes in the general level of prices is removed. Here, the real interest rate associated with chronic C^1 appears if the normalization rule is such as to make invariant the value of some representative bundle of goods. Usually this concept is defined as follows: Let r be the monetary interest rate and P the general level of prices. The real interest rate is then given by the formula: $\rho = r - (1/P) \cdot (dP/dt)$.

so that ρ_t may be computed by

$$1 + \rho_t = \frac{p_t \bar{z}_t}{p_{t+1} \bar{z}_{t+1}}.$$

If the natural resources are privately owned, they must have some value. Formula (53) defining L_t must have meaning. This implies that

$$\lim_{h \to \infty} \sum_{\theta=t+1}^{h} \beta_\theta$$

exists for all t. This cannot be so unless

$$\lim_{t \to \infty} (\beta_t/\beta_{t+1}) \geqq 1,$$

or, equivalently, unless $\lim_{t \to \infty} \rho_t \geqq 0$. Such was the idea behind Turgot's theory of fructification.

2. Suppose now that the price of some commodity i_θ is kept constant: $p'_{iot} = p'_{io't+1}$ for all t, so that ρ_t may be computed by

$$1 + \rho_t = \frac{p_{iot}}{p_{io,t+1}}.$$

If commodity i_0 may be stored without any cost, we may write $(a_t^2, b_{t+1}^2) \in$ $\mathbf{T}_t$ with $a_{it}^2 = a_{it}^1$, $b_{i,t+1}^2 = b_{i,t+1}^1$, for $i \neq i_0$; $a_{iot}^2 = a_{iot}^1 + \alpha_t$ and $b_{io,t+1}^2 = b_{io,t+1}^1 + \alpha_t$, with $\alpha_t > 0$. If $p_t a_t - p_{t+1} b_{t+1}$ is minimum for C^1, then necessarily $(p_{iot} - p_{io,t+1})\alpha_t \geqq 0$; hence $\rho_t \geqq 0$.

3. With the same normalization rule as in 2, we may suppose $\mathbf{x}^2 \in \mathbf{X}$ when $\mathbf{x}^2$ is defined by $x_t^2 = x_t^1$ for $t > 2$; $x_1^2 = x_1^1 + a$; and $x_2^2 = x_2^1 - \beta a$, with $a_i = 0$ for $i \neq i_0$ and with $a_{i_0} > 0$ and $\beta > 1$. Thus, $\mathbf{x}^2$ is analogous to $\mathbf{x}^1$ except that it allows for a greater consumption of i_0 in the first period and a smaller consumption of i_0 in the second period, the total quantity of i_0 for both periods being smaller than in $\mathbf{x}^1$. And it is supposed that C^2 is preferred to C^1.

If C^1 is optimal, then $p_1(x_1^2 - x_1^1) + p_2(x_2^2 - x_2^1) \geqq 0$. Hence

$$\rho_1 \geqq \beta - 1 > 0.$$

This is the usual theory of preference for present commodities.

4. It is sometimes said that the rate of interest is, or should be, equal to the rate of expansion of the economy. More precisely, suppose that the rate of interest is computed from nonnormalized prices by

$$1 + \rho_t = \frac{p_t c_t}{p_{t+1} c_t},$$

or, equivalently, that the normalization rule specifies $p'_{t+1} c_t = p'_t c_t$. Let us define the rate of capital accumulation δ_t as

$$1 + \delta_t = \frac{p'_{t+1} c_{t+1}}{p'_{t+1} c_t}.$$

Then $\rho_t - \delta_t$ is of the same sign as $-p'_{t+1}(c_{t+1} - c_t) + \rho_t p'_t c_t$. In particular, if the $\mathbf{T}_t$ are cones, this is also the sign of

$$p'_{t+1}x^+_{t+1} - (1 + \rho_t)p'_t(x^-_t + z_t).$$

There does not seem to be, in general, any definite sign for this expression. However, if we suppose $x^+_{t+1} = x^-_t = z_t = 0$, then, clearly, $\rho_t = \delta_t$. Such was the case in von Neumann's model of 1937 [24].

IV. STATIONARY ECONOMICS

Usually in capital theory " production is defined in relation to economic equilibrium ... in the form of a stationary economy."[29] Indeed, if such an assumption is made, the interest rate appears quite naturally in the requirements for efficiency, along with the " marginal productivity of capital." In this part we shall deal first with the properties of efficient stationary chronics,[30] second with the marginal productivity of capital, and third with the concept of the optimum amount of capital. A last section will be devoted to some historical comments.

18. *Properties of efficient stationary chronics.* We shall now assume the set of technological possibilities and the available resource vector to be identical to a set $\mathbf{T}$ and to a vector $\bar{z}$ independent of time. The chronic C^1 is said to be stationary if the vectors characterizing the economic activity remain unchanged from one period to another. Thus, C^1 is fully described by the four m-dimensional vectors, a, b, z, and x, with the conditions

$$\left.\begin{aligned} a &= b + z - x, \\ (a, b) &\in \mathbf{T}, \\ z &\leq \bar{z} \end{aligned}\right\} \qquad (62)$$

According to Theorem 1, if the stationary chronic C^1 is efficient, there is some nonnegative sequence $\mathbf{p}$ such that, for all t,

   i) $p_t a - p_{t+1}b$ is minimal at (a^1, b^1) among all $(a, b) \in \mathbf{T}$;
   ii) $p_t a$ is minimal at (a^1, b^1) among all $(a, b) \in \mathbf{T}$ such that $a - b = a^1 - b^1$.
   Conversely, if there is a positive sequence $\mathbf{p}$ such that C^1 fulfills conditions (i) and (ii), then C^1 is efficient. More precisely, we state

LEMMA 7: *Under Assumptions 3, 4, and 6, if a stationary chronic C^1 is efficient, there exists a nonnegative vector p and a scalar $\rho > -1$ such that*
   i) *$p(b - a) - \rho p a$ is maximal at (a^1, b^1) among all $(a, b) \in \mathbf{T}$;*
   ii) *$p a$ is minimal at (a^1, b^1) among all $(a, b) \in \mathbf{T}$ such that $a - b = a^1 - b^1$.*
   Conversely, if there is a positive vector p and a scalar $\rho > -1$ such that the stationary chronic C^1 fulfills conditions (i) and (ii), then C^1 is efficient.

---

[29] Knight [15].
[30] Throughout this part we shall study efficiency alone. The introduction of consumers' preferences would make the whole treatment unnecessarily involved.

PROOF: The second statement of the lemma follows directly from Lemma 3 if we define the sequence **p** by $p_t = p/(1 + \rho)^{t-1}$.

Conversely, if C^1 is efficient, there is, by Theorem 1, a nonnegative sequence **p** such that $(p_t, -p_{t+1})$ is in the closed convex cone of normals to **T** at (a^1, b^1). This implies that this cone contains some vector of the form $(p, -\beta p)$ with $\beta > 0$.[31] Lemma 7 follows, with $1 + \rho = 1/\beta$.

Thus, associated with any efficient stationary chronic, there is some set of relative prices and some rate of interest. This seems to contradict the preceding result, according to which interest rates appear only when some monetary rule is given. But this last condition is in fact implicitly included in Lemma 7.

---

[31] This is obvious if the cone of normals is just a half line. In general, the proof is somewhat more difficult. It is given here for completeness. We want to prove

LEMMA: *Given a sequence* **p** *of vectors in the m-dimensional Euclidean space, with* $p_t \geq 0$ *and the convex closed cone* $\mathbf{\Gamma}$ *generated by* $(p_t, -p_{t+1})$ *in the 2m-dimensional space, there is some vector* $p \geq 0$ *and some positive* β *such that* $(p, -\beta p) \in \mathbf{\Gamma}$.

PROOF: Define

$$p_t^{(1)} = p_t, \quad p_t^{(h)} = p_t^{(h-1)} + p_{t+1}^{(h-1)} \qquad \text{(for } h > 1\text{)}.$$

Let $\mathbf{C}^{(h)}$ be the convex closed cone generated by the $p_t^{(h)}$ in m-dimensional space $(t = 1, 2, \ldots, ad\ infinitum)$.

$$\mathbf{C}^{(h)} \subset \mathbf{C}^{(h-1)}.$$

Define

$$\mathbf{C}^\infty = \bigcap_{h=1}^{\infty} \mathbf{C}^{(h)}.$$

$\mathbf{C}^\infty$ is a nonempty closed convex cone.

By definition of $\mathbf{C}^{(h)}$, for any $u \in \mathbf{C}^{(h)}$ there is a sequence $\{u_n\}$ of vectors fulfilling the following:

$$\lim_{n \to \infty} u_n = u, \tag{a}$$

$$u_n = \sum_t \alpha_{tn} p_t^{(h)}, \tag{b}$$

with scalars $\alpha_{tn} \geq 0$, all zero except for a finite number.

Define

$$v_n = \sum_t \alpha_{tn} p_t^{(h-1)}, \qquad w_n = \sum_t \alpha_{tn} p_{t+1}^{(h-1)}.$$

Clearly, $u_n = v_n + w_n$. $\{v_n\}$ and $\{w_n\}$ are two bounded nondecreasing sequences of vectors in $\mathbf{C}^{(h-1)}$. They have limits v and w in $\mathbf{C}^{(h-1)}$, with $u = v + w$. It is trivial to note that $(v, -w) \in \mathbf{\Gamma}$.

Hence, for any $u \in \mathbf{C}^{(h)}$, there are two v and $w \in \mathbf{C}^{(h-1)}$, with

$$u = v + w, \tag{a}$$

$$(v, -w) \in \mathbf{\Gamma}. \tag{b}$$

It follows that, for any $u \in \mathbf{C}^\infty$, there are two v and $w \in \mathbf{C}^\infty$ such that (a) and (b) above are satisfied. [Indeed, for all h, $u \in \mathbf{C}^{(h+1)}$. Hence, there are $v^{(h)}$ and $w^{(h)}$ in $\mathbf{C}^{(h)}$ with $u = v^{(h)} + w^{(h)}$ and $(v^{(h)}, -w^{(h)}), \in \mathbf{\Gamma}$. $\{v^{(h)}\}$ is a sequence of positive bounded vectors; it has a limit point v which is in all $\mathbf{C}^{(h)}$. $w = u - v$ is a limit point of $\{w^{(h)}\}$; it is in all $\mathbf{C}^{(h)}$; and $(v, -w) \in \mathbf{\Gamma}$.]

Now, there is in $\mathbf{C}^\infty$ an extreme element, i.e., an element u such that $u = v + w$ with v and w in $\mathbf{C}^\infty$ implies $w = \alpha u = \beta v$ with positive scalars α and β.

Hence, for this element u, $(v, -w) = (v, -\beta v) \in \mathbf{\Gamma}$, which completes the proof.

Indeed, when prices are used in the computation of $p(b - a) - \rho pa$, it is supposed that absolute prices remain the same in all periods; or, in other words, that the normalization rule does not change.[32]

19. *Marginal productivity of capital.* It is a much debated question to know whether the interest rate is, or ought to be, equal to the marginal productivity of capital. As we shall see, the whole controversy boils down to the definition given to marginal productivity. Following Knight [15], we shall adopt here the most usual concept.

Given the efficient stationary chronic C^1, let us consider the class $\mathscr{C}$ of all possible stationary chronics for which the inputs x^- and z take the same values as in C^1. These chronics differ by their capital vector c and their consumption vector x^+. Let p^1 be an efficient price vector associated with C^1. The marginal productivity of capital for C^1 is defined as

$$\mu = \operatorname*{Sup}_{C \in \mathscr{C}} \frac{p^1(x - x^1)}{p^1(c - c^1)}. \tag{63}$$

This formula relates the gain in consumption, $p^1(x - x^1)$, to the corresponding increase of social capital, $p^1(c - c^1)$, both being evaluated from the set of prices p^1; μ is the maximum value taken by this ratio.

Now, from Lemma 7 it directly follows that

$$\rho^1 \geqq \mu, \tag{64}$$

where ρ^1 is the efficient interest rate associated with C^1. One might, moreover see that the equality holds if $\mathbf{T}$ is bounded by a differentiable surface.

On the other hand, a long line of economists[33] define marginal productivity of capital as the ratio between the increase in value of consumption, $px - p^1x^1$, to the increase in value of real capital, $pc - p^1c^1$. Or, in our present terminology,

$$\mu' = \operatorname*{Sup}_{C \in \mathscr{C}} \frac{px - p^1x^1}{pc - p^1c^1}. \tag{65}$$

Clearly, μ' is not related by any definite formula to ρ^1. Thus there is no reason why they should be equal.

There remains the question which of the two definitions should be adopted in economic theory. There seem to be at least three resaons for choosing

---

[32] Similar results may be obtained by an approach more in accordance with the usual technique in capital theory. One can say that a stationary chronic is not efficient if it is possible, without any present loss, to pass to some other stationary chronic allowing for a higher consumption.

Or, formally, C^1 is not efficient if there is some possible C such that:
i) $x \geq x^1$; and
ii) there are some b^2 and z^2 such that $(a^1, b^2) \in T$, $z^2 \leqq \bar{z}$, $a = b^2 - x^1 + z^2$.

Condition (ii) says that it is possible to go from C^1 to C in one period with a consumption vector equal to x^1.

[33] Cf., for instance, Wicksell [33]. For more detailed references the reader may consult Metzler [23].

formula (63). First, it makes the marginal productivity of capital just equal to the interest rate. Second, it is the right measure for the ratio between the permanent future increase in national consumption and the necessary present savings, as one might easily see from our model. From this viewpoint, it provides welfare economics with a concept that has a much more profound meaning than the alternative, μ'. Finally, the definition of μ coincides with the general definition of marginal productivity, while formula (65) does not. Indeed, marginal productivity is always computed with a single set of prices. This may be made clearer if we suppose that $C - C^1$ is null except for its first component γ_1, a given quantity of commodity 1, while the corresponding increase in the consumption vector $x - x^1$ is null except for commodity 2, the component then being ξ_2. Formula (63) gives $\mu p_1^1/p_2^1 \geqq \xi_2/\gamma_1$, so that the ratio on the left-hand side is directly related to physical conditions of production, like any other substitution ratio in an efficient position. A similar result does not hold with formula (65).

μ is also equal to the marginal productivity of capital such as it is sometimes defined by considering a lengthening of a production or investment period. Indeed, let us compare C^1 with a stationary chronic C absolutely similar except for a one-unit increase of the investment period of commodity 1. If the invested quantity of commodity 1 in C^1 equal to γ, $c - c^1$ is null except for its first component, which is equal to γ, then $\mu \geqq p^1(x - x^1)/p_1^1 \gamma$. Thus, μ is also at least equal to the ratio between the increase in the product from a one-unit lengthening of the investment period of some commodity to the value of the quantity annually invested of the same commodity, or equivalently, to the value which is to be saved on consumption during the present period in order to realize the given lengthening of the investment period. Such was the essential idea behind the Jevonian analysis.

20. *Optimum amount of capital.* The concept of an optimum amount of capital is given in a few places in economic literature.[34] It appears in such situations as the following. The government thinks some sacrifice should be made in order to accumulate enough capital to raise consumption above its present level. The rate of accumulation is not required to be in accordance with present consumers' preferences; these could be neglected if necessary in order to ensure a better future for the community. Is it always profitable for this purpose to increase the quantity of capital? Or is there any optimum beyond which one should rather disinvest than invest?

Indeed, as long as some increase in a_t leads to some increase in b_{t+1}, consumption may be made larger during the next period if it is reduced during the present one. However, it would not be reasonable to impose any given decrease in x_t if the corresponding increase in b_{t+1} becomes too small. This may be better formulated for stationary chronics. For these an increase of the capital vector will be said to be advantageous if it results in a permanent

---

[34] Cf., for instance, Wicksell [33, p. 209], Ramsey [25], Meade [22], Knight [16, p. 402], Allais [3].

improvement in the future or, in other words, if the stationary chronic associated with the new capital vector is preferable to that associated with the former one. It may seem likely a priori that the greater the capital vector, the higher the consumption level. This is not necessarily true because in stationary chronics provision must be made for capital replacement. The latter may become so heavy as to exceed the increase in production.

We shall adopt the following formal definition:

DEFINITION: *The efficient stationary chronic* C^1 *is associated with an optimal capital vector if there is no possible stationary chronic C such that* $x \geq x^1$, *whatever the value taken by the capital vector.*[35]

We shall show that if some optimal capital vector exists, it is associated with a zero interest rate. By comparison with Lemma 7 this is the result of the following:

LEMMA 8: *Under Assumptions 3 and 4, if* C^1 *is an efficient stationary chronic associated with an optimal capital vector, then there is a nonnegative price vector p such that* $p(b - a)$ *is maximum at* (a^1, b^1) *among all* $(a, b) \in$ T.

PROOF: If C^1 is an efficient stationary chronic associated with an optimal capital vector, there is no $(a, b) \in$ T with $b - a \geq b^1 - a^1$. Indeed, suppose there is such an (a, b); there would exist a possible stationary chronic C such that

$$x = b - a + \bar{z} \geq b^1 - a^1 + z^1 = x^1.$$

Consider now the set U of all $u = b - a$ where $(a, b) \in$ T. U is convex and has u^1 as a maximal element; hence, there is a nonnegative vector p such that pu is maximum at u^1 among all $u \in$ U.

As we noticed earlier, the rate of interest in a stationary chronic provides a measure of the marginal productivity of capital. It is therefore not surprising to find that it is equal to zero when the capital vector is optimal.

Finally, we must insist on the very restricted meaning of the concept of the optimal amount of capital and, hence, on the restricted applicability of Lemma 8.

---

[35] The objection that an optimal capital vector could not conceivably exist has frequently been raised against this concept, i.e., that a complete saturation of all capital needs can never occur, even under ideal conditions. Cf., for instance, Knight [16]. In the author's view this is not correct. It is indeed true that we shall probably never reach a state of complete saturation of all capital needs, but the reason is psychological or institutional and not technological.

The question of the existence of a stationary chronic C^1 associated with an optimal capital vector would be worth studying. Our present formulation, however, is not suitable for dealing with existence problems in a sufficiently precise way. The reader might find it interesting to consider the following example:

Suppose an economy with three commodities, the available resources vector $\bar{z} = (\bar{z}_1, \bar{z}_2, 0)$, and the technological set defined by $(a, b) \in$ T if $b_1 = 0$, $(b_2)^2 + (b_3)^2 \leq 8a_1a_2$. The following stationary chronic is associated with an optimal capital vector:

$$a = (\bar{z}_1, 2\bar{z}_1 + \bar{z}_2, 0) \qquad b = (0, 4\bar{z}_1, \sqrt{8\bar{z}_1\bar{z}_2}), \qquad x = (0, 2\bar{z}_1, \sqrt{8\bar{z}_1\bar{z}_2}).$$

Indeed, as we have seen, optimal capital vectors cannot be defined except for stationary chronics whose practical significance could be disputed.

21. *Historical note on the theory of capital.*[36] Throughout the preceding pages the traditional theory of capital has been related to welfare economics. But this attempt is now new. In economic literature, any sound approach to the analysis of capital formation stemmed from the theory of value whose connection with welfare economics is obvious. Thus, it may be worthwhile to compare the main expositions of the theory of capital and interest with the model presented here.

For this purpose we need not consider whether the authors were concerned with problems of equilibrium or with welfare, nor whether they took account consumers' preferences. Moreover, we need not consider production or distribution theories that take capital as given; indeed, from our viewpoint they miss the essential problem, which is how choices are, or should be, made between direct and indirect processes of production.

We shall examine the principal theories of capital according to two criteria: first, the descriptive scheme of the productive process and, second, the author's solution.

Broadly speaking, the models describing capitalistic production may be classified under four main headings:

First, some theories start from a law, given a priori, of substitution between present and future commodities. This is made quite clear, for instance, in Irving Fisher's theory of interest [10]. In this approach the real nature of the substitution is not explored except for some heuristic comments. Thus, the theory is bound either to consider only a particular aspect of production (as, for instance, the growing of trees) or to assume the prices for each period to be independently determined. In this way, the substitution law must be interpreted as relating present to future income. This procedure, used extensively by Fisher, will be examined below.

Second, most theories of capital describe production as the result of the simultaneous operation of numerous elementary processes,[37] each of them specialized in the production of a particular commodity from labor and natural resources. Most often, roundabout methods are introduced so that the final product may be obtained after a very long time. But, in any case, labor and natural resources are considered as the only inputs in the process. Capital goods do not exist as such; they are expressed in terms of the original services invested in them at the time of their production. These services are said to "mature" when the final product is delivered for consumption. Such is the scheme underlying the theories of John Rae [26], Jevons [14], Böhm-Bawerk [5, 6], Wicksell [33], Åkerman [1], Lindahl [19], and

---

[36] We shall not consider the theories dealing with welfare economics or efficient allocation of resources. For a short analysis of these subjects and references, see Debreu [8].

[37] Usually the models were not as general as they could have been. Many unnecessary restrictions, which were intended to simplify the theoretical exposition, in fact often resulted in making the subject more abstruse.

Hayek [12, 13]. Sometimes it is also supposed that present and future prices are determined independently, so that somewhat less care is required in setting the problem.

To these theories is often attached the concept of the production or investment period. But, although it might be very helpful from an expository viewpoint, it is not at all necessary and could be deleted altogether. Furthermore, as has been shown repeatedly, the definition of these periods raises innumerable difficulties.

In fact, the fundamental shortcoming of this approach follows from the assumption that it is possible to impute the service of capital goods to the original factors, land and labor. This is surely not the case except in some particular instances. Thus, the whole theoretical construction is dangerously weakened.

As a third alternative one may consider the services used in production as originating either from original sources or from existing equipment. Accordingly, the commodities produced include new durable equipment as well as consumption goods. This approach was used first by Walras [22] and more recently by Allais [2]. In order to arrive at manageable equations, both supposed that any capital good, once produced, provides a series of services that cannot be altered by more or less intensive utilization. Even so, this third approach seems to provide a good approximation to the conditions of the real world, as was rightly pointed out by Lindahl [19] in his penetrating essay.

It is apparent that the theory we have built throughout this paper proceeded from an attempt to give to Walras' model a more general content and to explain how a substitution law may be obtained from it.

Finally, it is also possible to give a simple and completely general description of production if the economy is assumed to be stationary. In this case there is a law relating capital equipment to the permanent consumption which it makes possible. This is the idea underlying most of Knight's writings [16]. One may wonder, however, whether his analysis can provide an answer to the question: Why should the study of stationary, and therefore artificial, economies enable us to understand the conditions of production in our changing world? Moreover, as we have seen, the efficiency of any stationary chronic cannot be determined except by comparison with other chronics that are not stationary.

It may be noted also that a stationary economy has often been assumed in theories classified under the second heading (such as those of Jevons and Wicksell), but it does not play there the essential part it does in Knight's treatment.

What sort of answers do the theories give? Here again we may group them under three headings.[38]

---

[38] To do full justice to earlier theories, we should mention that they also wanted at times to study the effects of capital increments on wages, or similar questions related to distribution theory. But this does not concern us here.

First, a few of them try to determine which relations must hold for a firm in a competitive economy. They more or less implicitly assume that these also hold for the whole economy. This is particularly clear in papers by Åkerman [1], Leontief [20], Schneider [30], and Boulding [7]. The approach is, indeed, quite successful because it provides a simple answer to a difficult problem. However, a doubt may remain as to the generality of the results. Clearly, also, it is not suitable for dealing with efficiency or welfare.

Second, most theories aim at determining the interest rates, assuming the prices for all periods given a priori.[39] Although this method may bring sound results, there are strong objections to it. In the first place, prices are determined at the same time as interest rates; it is just in the philosophy of capitalistic production that no simple dichotomy exists between the markets for present and future goods. One may wonder, moreover, whether it has always been realized that interest rates to be associated with chronics do not exist independently of the monetary conditions ruling the economy. If any misunderstanding arose on that point, it should surely be attributed to those writers who studied interest formation independently of price formation.

Finally, a few writers did show how prices and interest rates were simultaneously determined. They made quite clear the connection between interest and the general theory of value. To the author's knowledge, Böhm-Bawerk [5], Wicksell [33], Landry [18], Lindahl [19], and Allais [2] provided us with valuable theories of capital. Unfortunately, their writings were largely misunderstood, if not unknown. The diffusion of their main ideas was greatly hampered by endless discussions on details in their exposition. It was the purpose of the present paper to make the analysis more general, and it is hoped in this way to help avoid in the future such lengthy debates as have occurred on the theory of capital in the past.

REFERENCES[40]

1. ÅKERMAN, GUSTAV. *Realkapital und Kapitalzins*, Stockholm, Centraltrycheriet, 1923.

2. ALLAIS, MAURICE. *A la recherche d'une discipline économique*, Tome I, Paris: Ateliers Industria, 1943; reprinted as *Traité d'économie pure*, Paris 1953.

3. ALLAIS, MAURICE. *Economie et intérêt*, Paris, Imprimerie Nationale, 1947.

4. *BANACH, STEFAN. *Théorie des opérations linéaires*, Warsaw: Subwencju Funduszu kultury narodowej, 1932, and New York: Hafner Publishing Co., 1949.

5. BÖHM-BAWERK, EUGEN VON. *Geschichte und Kritik der Kapitalzins Theorien*, 1884.

---

[39] Here again, simplicity of exposition was often thought necessary but such misplaced simplifications were needed because all deductions had to be made on two-dimensional diagrams.

[40] This bibliography contains writings on capital theory only, except for references marked with an asterisk, which do not deal with this theory but were specifically mentioned in this paper. For references on welfare economics, see Debreu [8].

6. BÖHM-BAWERK, EUGEN VON. *Positive Theorie des Kapitales*, first published 1888, dritte Auflage, Innsbrück: Wagner'schen Universitäts-Buchhandlung, 1912.

7. BOULDING, KENNETH. "The Theory of a Single Investment," *Quarterly Journal of Economics*, Vol. 49, May, 1935, pp. 475–94.

8. *DEBREU, GÉRARD. "The Coefficient of Resource Utilization," *Econometrica*, Vol. 19, July, 1951, pp. 273–92.

9. FETTER, FRANK A. "Capital," in Seligman and Johnson, eds., *Encyclopedia of the Social Sciences*, New York: Macmillan Co., 1932, pp. 187–90.

10. FISHER, IRVING. *The Theory of Interest*, New York: Macmillan Co., 1930

11. *GUILBAUD, GEORGES TH. "L'étude statistique des oscillations économiques," *Cahiers du Séminaire d'Econométrie*, N° 1, Paris: Librairie de Médicis, 1951, pp. 5–41.

12. HAYEK, F. A. VON. "The Mythology of Capital," *Quarterly Journal of Economics*, Vol. 50, February, 1936, and *Readings in the Theory of Income Distribution*, London: Allen and Unwin, 1950, pp. 355–83.

13. HAYEK, F. A. VON. *The Pure Theory of Capital*, London: Macmillan and Co., 1941.

14. JEVONS, WILLIAM STANLEY. *The Theory of Political Economy*, London, 1871.

15. KNIGHT, FRANK H. "The Theory of Investment Once More: Mr. Boulding and the Austrians," *Quarterly Journal of Economics*, Vol. 50, November, 1935, pp. 36–67.

16. KNIGHT, FRANK H. "Capital and Interest," *Encyclopedia Brittanica*, Chicago: University of Chicago Press, 1946, pp. 799–800, and *Readings in the Theory of Income Distribution*, London: Allen and Unwin, 1950, pp. 384–417.

17. *KOOPMANS, TJALLING C., ed. *Activity Analysis of Production and Allocation*, Cowles Commission Monograph 13, New York: Wiley and Sons, 1951.

18. LANDRY, ADOLPHE. *L'intérêt du capital*, Paris: V. Giard et E. Brière, 1904.

19. LINDAHL, ERIK ROBERT. *The Place of Capital in the Theory of Prices*, 1929, reprinted in *Studies in the Theory of Money and Capital*, London: G. Allen and Unwin, 1939.

20. LEONTIEF, WASSILY. "Interest on Capital and Distribution: A Problem in the Theory of Marginal Productivity," *Quarterly Journal of Economics*, Vol. 49, November, 1934, pp. 147–61.

21. LUTZ, FRIEDRICH A. "Théorie du capital et théorie de la production," *Economie appliquée*, Janvier, 1948.

22. MEADE, JAMES EDWARD. *An Introduction to Economic Analysis and Policy*, 2d ed., London, Oxford University Press, 1937.

23. METZLER, LLOYD A. "The Rate of Interest and the Marginal Product of Capital," *Journal of Political Economy*, Vol. 58, August, 1950, pp. 289–306, and "The Rate of Interest and the Marginal Product of Capital: A Correction," *Journal of Political Economy*, Vol. 59, February, 1951, pp. 67–68.

24. NEUMANN, JOHN VON. **"A Model of General Economic Equilibrium," *Review of Economic Studies*, Vol. 13, No. 1, 1945–46.

25. RAMSEY, FRANK P. **"A Mathematical Theory of Savings," *Economic Journal*, Vol. 38, December, 1928, pp. 543–59.

26. RAE, JOHN. *Statement of Some New Principles on the Subject of Political Economy*, Boston: Hilliard, Gray and Co., 1834.

27. ROTTIER, GEORGES. "Notes sur la maximation du profit," *Economie Appliquée*, Janvier-Mars, 1951, pp. 67–84.

28. SAMUELSON, PAUL A. "Some Aspects of the Pure Theory of Capital," *Quarterly Journal of Economics*, Vol. 51, May, 1937, pp. 469–96.

29. SAMUELSON, PAUL A. "The Rate of Interest under Ideal Conditions," *Quarterly Journal of Economics*, Vol. 53. February, 1939, pp. 286–97.

30. SCHNEIDER, ERICH. "Das Zeitmoment in der Theorie der Produktion," *Jahrbücher für Nationalökonomie und Statistik*, January, 1936, pp. 45–67.

31. SCHNEIDER, ERICH. "Bemerkung zum Hauptproblem der Kapitaltheorie," *Jahrbücher für Nationalökonomie Statistik*, February, 1938, pp. 183–88.

32. WALRAS, LÉON. *Eléments d'économie pure*, Lausanne, 1877.

33. WICKSELL, KNUTT. *Lectures on Political Economy*, London: Routledge and Kegan Paul, 1934.

The influence of the capital-output ratio on real national income*†

MAURICE ALLAIS

This paper presents first a general theory of a capitalistic optimum and a model illustrating its essential features, and, secondly, the empirical justification of this model, and its principal applications.

Under very general conditions it is possible to show that we cannot expect, from an indefinite increase of available real capital, an indefinite increase of real national income consumed per inhabitant, and that there is an optimum amount of capital for which the real income per inhabitant is maximum. The conditions under which this maximum is attained are given.

The general model, which is presented, and, in particular, its exponential variety, appear quite remarkably confirmed by all presently available empirical data, with respect to both the hypotheses and the results.

A *very simple* expression of *consumed* real income is given in terms of the rate of interest i and the rate of growth ρ.

INTRODUCTION

The object of this paper is to explain the essential part of the results obtained in the research I have carried on at various times in the past twenty years[1] on the theory of a capitalistic optimum. Till now this theory has received, in my opinion, insufficient attention in the economics literature.

In the limited space available I intend to present, first, a general theory of a capitalistic optimum and a model illustrating its essential features, and, secondly, the empirical justification of this model, and its principal

* *Econometrica*, 30(1962): pp. 700–28. Corrected by the author, who added an Additional Note. Reprinted by courtesy of the author and *Econometrica*.

† This article is adapted from the Bowley-Walras Lecture delivered by Professor Allais at the American Meetings of the Econometric Society, December 28, 1961. This invited lecture was the first in a series made possible by funds provided to the Econometric Society by the U.S. National Science Foundation.—ed.

[1] In 1940, 1946, 1954, 1960, and 1961. A large part of my results have already been published in 1947 in my book *Economie et Intérêt*, and in 1960 in my communication to the Congress of the International Statistical Institute at Tokyo. Moreover, the whole of the results I have obtained will be published very soon in English as a volume in the series "Contributions to Economic Analysis," North-Holland Publishing Co. The indications that follow are naturally not sufficient by themselves and they constitute only a memorandum.

applications; for it is not a good theory if there is no verification of its results and hypotheses by facts, and if no fruitful application can be derived.

Essentially, I intend to show that we cannot expect, from an indefinite increase of available real capital, an indefinite increase of real national income consumed per capita, and that there is an optimum amount of capital for which real income per capita is a maximum.

Curiously enough, for a century now very few works have really been concerned with the influence of capital on real income, either on empirical or theoretical grounds, although such research is of the greatest importance from both the theoretical and practical points of view. *At the empirical level*, most research gives the idea that real national income can be increased indefinitely by using more and more capital. *At the theoretical level*, many works suggest the same conclusion, and though the idea of a capitalistic optimum for a zero rate of interest was positively stated by Wicksell as early as 1901, it was not until Meade's *Economic Analysis and Policy* appeared in 1937 that a more systematic, though literary statement, was given. For my part, I have met in this area two sorts of economists. For the first, the existence of a capitalistic optimum for a zero rate of interest is considered as a completely mistaken proposition; for the second, it appears as a commonplace truth, a sort of truism, that does not deserve any serious attention at all.

1. GENERAL THEORY OF THE CAPITALISTIC OPTIMUM

1.1. In this section, I intend to show, at least briefly, that in fact there is a situation of a capitalistic optimum, and that such a situation is characterized, *under stationary conditions*, by a rate of interest equal to zero, and, *in a dynamic evolution*, in which the index of labour and natural wealth increases exponentially at a rate ρ, by a rate of interest equal to ρ.

A. General production process

1.2. Definitions. I define the input and output vectors of the production processes considered as follows:

outputs
$\begin{cases} \vec{Q}_n \text{ is a representative vector of the production per unit of} \\ \quad \text{time of consumption goods.} \\ \vec{E}_n \text{ is a representative vector of the production per unit of} \\ \quad \text{time of the various forms of equipment.} \end{cases}$

inputs
$\begin{cases} \vec{X}_n \text{ is a representative vector of labour services and natural} \\ \quad \text{resources consumed per unit of time (primary produc-} \\ \quad \text{tion factors).} \\ T\vec{E}_{n-p} \text{ is a representative vector of equipment of age } p \text{ used} \\ \quad \text{during the period } T_n \text{ and produced during the period} \\ \quad T_{n-p}. \end{cases}$ (1.1)

The indexes, Q_n and X_n, of the production of consumption goods and of the consumption of primary factors, respectively, are defined by:

$$Q_n = Q[\vec{Q}_n],$$ (1.2)

$$X_n = X[\vec{X}_n].$$ (1.3)

Each of these indexes is an increasing function of each coordinate of its argument.

1.3. Hypotheses. The production process is assumed to satisfy four hypotheses (a_1)–(a_4).

HYPOTHESIS a_1: *Pareto optimality over time.* We consider a production process, P, over time, and we suppose that between two extreme situations, corresponding to any two instants, a Pareto optimum is realized in the sense that no production could be increased at any intermediate time without production being diminished at another time.[2] It is then possible to write

$$f_n(\vec{Q}_n, \vec{E}_n, \vec{X}_n, \vec{E}_{n-1}, \ldots, \vec{E}_{n-p}, \ldots) = 0. \tag{1.4}$$

HYPOTHESIS a_2: *Homogeneity of order k.*

$$f_n(\lambda^k \vec{Q}_n, \lambda \vec{E}_n, \lambda \vec{X}_n, \lambda \vec{E}_{n-1}, \ldots, \lambda \vec{E}_{n-p}, \ldots) = 0. \qquad k > 1, \tag{1.5}$$

for all λ.

HYPOTHESIS a_3:

$$|\vec{X}_n| < \epsilon \text{ implies } |\vec{Q}_n + \vec{E}_n| < \epsilon', \tag{1.6}$$

where ϵ' depends only on ϵ and tends to zero with ϵ. This says that the production of consumption and equipment goods is assumed to tend to zero when the vector of primary services of labour and natural resources tends to zero.

HYPOTHESIS a_4: *Hypothesis of advantageous growth.* Both indexes

$$Q_n^* = Q\left[\frac{\vec{Q}_n}{X_n^k}\right], \qquad X_n \tag{1.7}$$

are never decreasing.

The index Q_n^*, here defined, represents, for an order of homogeneity equal to one, the production of primary factors per unit of consumption.

1.4. We now state a general theorem about the evolution of an advantageous capitalistic process:

THEOREM I:[3] *If hypotheses (a_1) to (a_4) are satisfied then:*

a) The index Q_n^* tends, under very general conditions, to an upper limit when n increases indefinitely.

b) Under equally general conditions, the process P', given by

$$\vec{Q}'_n = \frac{\vec{Q}_n}{X_n^k}, \qquad \vec{X}'_n = \frac{\vec{X}_n}{X_n}, \qquad \vec{E}'_n = \frac{\vec{E}_n}{X_n}, \tag{1.8}$$

---

[2] Allais (1943, Chap. VII, pp. 604–82) and (1947A, Chap. VI, pp. 153–78).
[3] This theorem may be easily extended to the case in which the production function (1.4) is convex.

tends to an asymptotic process, P_a', of stationary equilibrium $[\vec{Q}', \vec{X}', \vec{E}']$ in which the rate of interest has a constant *value i'. The process P tends to an asymptotic process P_a:*

$$\vec{Q}_n^a = X_n^k \vec{Q}', \qquad \vec{X}_n^a = X_n \vec{X}', \qquad \vec{E}_n = X_n \vec{E}'. \tag{1.9}$$

c) The process P_a is characterized by a rate of interest

$$i = \rho + i' \tag{1.10}$$

with

$$\rho = \frac{1}{X} \frac{dX}{dt}, \tag{1.11}$$

ρ being the rate of growth of primary income, and i' being the rate of interest characterizing the stationary process P_a'.

In process P_a all relative prices are constant.

This theorem, *which can easily be extended to convex production functions,* has, in particular, the advantage of replacing the study of dynamic processes by the study of stationary ones.

B. General economic definitions

1.5. In this subsection, I give some general definitions and relations among them. In doing so, it has seemed better to me to keep the French notation corresponding to my previous work.

Definitions:

			In labor units[6]	In real units
Capital	Reproducible national capital[4]		C	$\bar{C}$
	Land capital[5]		C_ϕ	
	Total national capital		C_T	
Income	National income		R	$\bar{R}$
	Consumed national income		R_c	$\bar{R}_c$
	Primary income[7]		R_ω	
	from labor		R_σ	
	land		R_ϕ	

---

[4] Value of natural resources excluded.
[5] Capitalized value of natural resources.
[6] Nominal values divided by the nominal value of one hour of unskilled labor.
[7] Value of primary factors of production (wages and rents).

Relations:

$$R = R_c + \frac{dC}{dt}, \tag{1.12}$$

$$R = R_\omega + iC, \tag{1 13}$$

$$R_\omega = R_\sigma + R_\phi, \tag{1.14}$$

$$R_\phi = iC_\phi, \tag{1.15}$$

$$C_T = C + C_\phi,$$

i, the instantaneous rate of interest;

$\rho = \dfrac{1}{R_\omega} \dfrac{dR_\omega}{dt}$, the rate of growth of primary income; (1.16)

Capitalistic Characteristics

$\gamma = C/R,$ the capital-output ratio defined by reference to the income R; (1.17)

$\gamma_c = C/R_c,$ the capital-output ratio defined by reference to the consumed income R_c.

C. Characteristic functions

1.6. I now define the concept of the characteristic function, which to my knowledge was presented for the first time by Jevons in 1871, in connection with a particular model. Here is the simplest way to conceive of the characteristic curve of a production process, the curve which is represented in Figure 1. Let us suppose that we pay wages for the construction of a blast furnace. This blast furnace will produce cast iron, which will be used to produce steel. The steel will be sent to manufacturing industries, and finally

Figure 1

AVERAGE PERIOD OF PRODUCTION

$$\hat{\Theta}(t) = \int_0^\infty \theta \hat{\phi}(t, \theta)\, d\theta$$

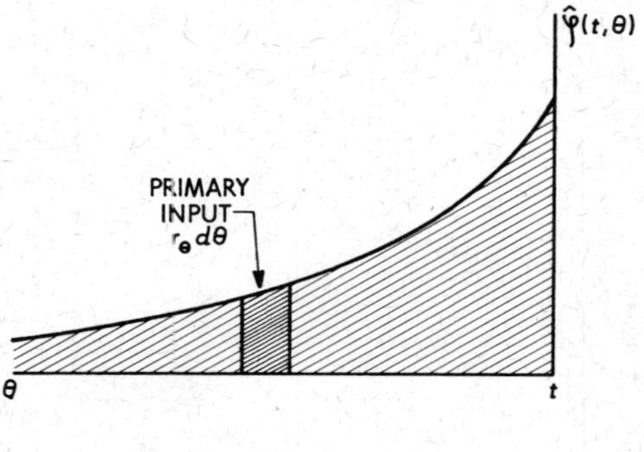

automobiles can be made out of it; and these automobiles the consumers can buy for their personal use. The expenditure on wages for the construction of the blast furnace will finally become part of the sales price of the automobiles. It will therefore appear in the national income after a certain delay.

We see then that the national income consumed at a certain time includes expenditures on wages made at an earlier time, and we can construct a curve, at least at the theoretical level, that gives the distance in time of the various previous expenditures for labour and land services which appear in the national income consumed at a given moment. This we call the "characteristic curve"[8] of the capitalistic process being studied. *By definition the primary income is imputed proportionally to the marginal productivities in physical values.*[9]

Further definitions are given in the following table:

Primary Income	Supplied at	Appearing in the income Consumed at	Primary Inputs
Elementary	t	$t + \theta$	$r_\theta \, d\theta = R_\omega(t)\phi(t, \theta) \, d\theta$
	$t - \theta$	t	$r_\theta \, d\theta = \hat{R}_\omega(t)\hat{\phi}(t, \theta) \, d\theta$
Total	t		$R_\omega = R_\omega \int_0^\infty \phi(t, \theta) \, d\theta$
		t	$\hat{R}_\omega = \hat{R}_\omega \int_0^\infty \hat{\phi}(t, \theta) \, d\theta$

In the same way, we can define an amortization curve, represented in Figure 2, which gives the distribution of the primary income of time t among the different periods that follow.

Under stationary conditions, the curves of Figures 1 and 2 are, of course, exactly symmetrical.

The average production period

$$\Theta(t) = \int_0^\infty \theta \hat{\phi}(t, \theta) \, d\theta, \qquad (1.18)$$

and the average amortization period is

$$\Theta = \int_0^\infty \theta \phi(t, \theta) \, d\theta. \qquad (1.19)$$

Consumed income is

$$R_c = \int_0^\infty r_\theta e^{i\theta} = \int_0^\infty \hat{R}_\omega(t)\hat{\phi}(t, \theta)e^{i\theta} \, d\theta = \int_0^\infty R_\omega(t - \theta)\phi(t - \theta, \theta)e^{i\theta} \, d\theta, \quad (1.20)$$

---

[8] Naturally, this concept has nothing in common with the concept of the same denomination used in statistics.

[9] See Allais, *Economie et Intérêt*, p. 118, note (2′) and *Traité d'Economie Pure*, n. 312.

Figure 2

AVERAGE PERIOD OF AMORTIZATION

$$\Theta = \int_0^\infty \theta \phi(t, \theta) \, d\theta$$

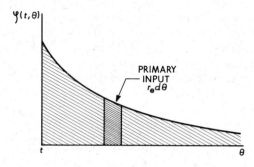

and the value of the capital stock is

$$C = \int_0^\infty dt \int_T^\infty R_\omega(t + T - \theta)\phi(\theta)e^{i(\theta - T)} \, d\theta \quad \text{for } \phi \text{ independent of } t. \quad (1.21)$$

For the particularly simple case of stationary conditions, we have

$$\hat{R}_\omega = R_\omega, \qquad \hat{\phi} = \phi, \qquad (1.22)$$

these functions being independent of t. Hence,[10]

$$R = R_c = R_\omega \int_0^\infty e^{i\theta}\phi(\theta, i) \, d\theta, \qquad (1.23)$$

$$C = R_\omega \int_0^\infty \frac{e^{i\theta} - 1}{i} \phi(\theta, i) \, d\theta. \qquad (1.24)$$

D. Capitalistic optimum in a stationary process

1.7. *Definition of a capitalistic optimum in a stationary process.* In a stationary process, equation (1.4) can be written

$$g[\vec{Q}, \vec{X}, \vec{E}] = 0. \qquad (1.25)$$

By definition, there is a capitalistic optimum if for a given vector $\vec{X}$ we have for any coordinate Q_i of vector $\vec{Q}$

$$\delta Q_i \leqq 0 \qquad \text{whatever be } \delta\vec{E}, \qquad (1.26)$$

the other coordinates of $\vec{Q}$ being maintained constant.[11] This is to define a capitalistic optimum in a stationary process by the impossibility of

---

[10] See Allais (1947A, pp. 118–31).
[11] See Allais (1947A, pp. 180–81).

Figure 3

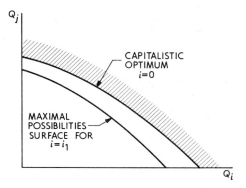

increasing the production of consumption goods by any variation of the equipment vector.

Figure 3 shows how the surface of maximal possibilities varies when the rate of interest varies.

1.8. Simplified analysis by periods. We next present the theory of a capitalistic optimum for the very simple case of a period analysis with a single kind of labour and with a given production function that determines real income as a function of the primary inputs, and that is homogeneous of degree one. (The characteristic curve is represented in Figure 4.)

Let X_p be the amount of labour of period T_p contributing to the production of the instant t.

Let

$$\bar{R} = f(X_0, X_1, \ldots, X_n, \ldots) \tag{1.27}$$

be the production function and be homogeneous of order one. The elasticities are $d\bar{R}/\bar{R} \div dX_n/X_n$.

At equilibrium the market value of production is

$$R = r\bar{R} = xX_0 + e^{iT}xX_1 + \cdots + e^{inT}xX_n + \cdots, \tag{1.28}$$

Figure 4

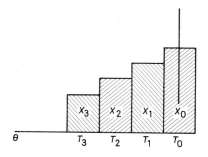

where x is the wage rate, i is the instantaneous rate of interest in wage units, and r is price per unit of output.

The functioning of the market leads to a maximization of profit subject to constraint (1.27), the prices x and i being considered as constant. Thus we have

$$\frac{1}{r} = \frac{\dfrac{\partial \bar{R}}{\partial X_0}}{x} = \frac{\dfrac{\partial \bar{R}}{\partial X_1}}{x e^{iT}} = \cdots = \frac{\dfrac{\partial \bar{R}}{\partial X_n}}{x e^{inT}} = \cdots. \tag{1.29}$$

Expressing the conditions for a maximum of $\bar{R}$ subject to the constraint

$$X_0 + X_1 + \cdots + X_n + \cdots = X \tag{1.30}$$

we obtain

$$\frac{\partial \bar{R}}{\partial X_0} = \frac{\partial \bar{R}}{\partial X_1} = \cdots = \frac{\partial \bar{R}}{\partial X_n} = \cdots. \tag{1.31}$$

From (1.29) and (1.31) we have

$$i = 0 \tag{1.32}$$

as the condition for a capitalistic optimum, *considering as given the total amount of labour available at any time*.

1.9. Analysis for the general case.[12] In this case national income is given by

$$R = R_c = R_\omega \int_0^\infty e^{i\theta} \phi(\theta, i)\, d\theta. \tag{1.33}$$

Under the assumption of homogeneity of order k, we obtain, according to the theory of the optimum allocation of resources, the index $\bar{R}$ of real income by differentiating, *at constant prices*, expression (1.33) for national income. Since the prices of the primary factors are represented here by the values of $e^{i\theta}$, this differentiation at constant prices leads to

$$\frac{1}{k}\frac{1}{\bar{R}}\delta\bar{R} = \frac{\displaystyle\int_0^\infty e^{i\theta}\,\delta\phi(\theta, i)\, d\theta}{\displaystyle\int_0^\infty e^{i\theta}\phi(\theta, i)\, d\theta}, \qquad \frac{d\Theta}{di} < 0. \tag{1.34}$$

In the vicinity of $i = 0$, we have

$$\frac{1}{k}\frac{1}{\bar{R}}\frac{\partial \bar{R}}{\partial i} \sim i\int_0^\infty \theta\,\frac{\partial\phi(\theta, i)}{\partial i}\, d\theta = i\frac{d\Theta}{di}, \tag{1.35}$$

$$\frac{1}{k}\frac{\bar{R}_M - \bar{R}}{\bar{R}_M} \sim -\frac{i^2}{2}\frac{d\Theta}{di}, \tag{1.36}$$

$$\gamma = C/R \sim \Theta, \tag{1.37}$$

$$R \sim R_\omega(1 + i\Theta). \tag{1.38}$$

---

[12] Allais (1947A, pp. 186–89 and 194–206).

Equations (1.35) and (1.37) give the expressions for the index $\bar{R}$ and the capital-output ratio, γ, in the vicinity of $i = 0$. The first one shows that real national income is stationary for a zero value of the rate of interest. The second one shows that for small values of the rate of interest, the capital-output ratio γ is, in a stationary process, approximately equal to the average production period Θ. We therefore state

THEOREM II (*Condition for a capitalistic optimum under stationary conditions*): *Real income consumed as a maximum for $i = 0$.*

E. Capitalistic optimum of a dynamic capitalistic process

1.10. The combined results of Theorems I and II lead to the following theorem concerning dynamic processes.

THEOREM III (*Condition for a capitalistic optimum in a dynamic process*): *Using the earlier notation, since we have*

$$\frac{\vec{Q}_n}{X_n^k} \to \vec{Q}'$$

and also that $Q(\vec{Q}')$ is maximum for $i' = 0$, we may infer that

$$Q_n^* = Q\left[\frac{\vec{Q}_n}{X_n^k}\right]$$

is asymptotically maximum for

$$i' = i - \rho = 0.$$

Thus, among all processes P_a that are characterized by a rate of interest $i = \rho + i'$, the one for which the consumed real income is highest, at any instant, corresponds to the rate of interest $i = \rho$.

2. THE MODEL

2.1. The general theory, the most important aspects of which I have just sketched, may be illustrated by a very simple model, which appears to have great generality. I do not claim that this model should be "the" model to illustrate in a definitive way the theory of capital. I only think that this model is very simple and highly suggestive. It has, among other advantages, the essential one of lending itself easily to numerical applications, and, in particular, of allowing an easy estimate of the influence of utilized capital on consumed real national income.

A. Hypotheses

2.2. General Model. This general model rests on the hypotheses (a_1) to (a_4) of Section 1[13] and on

HYPOTHESIS b: *Constancy of the production elasticities.* At any instant t, the elasticities of the consumed real income with respect to the primary inputs

---

[13] Here we put $Q(t) = \bar{R}_c(t), \qquad X(t) = R_\omega(t).$

may be considered as constant in a large region and independent of the instant t.

This hypothesis amounts to supposing that, in a very large region,

$$LR_c(t) = L\alpha + \int_0^\infty \beta(\theta)L\hat{r}_\theta \, d\theta; \qquad (2.1)$$

that is to say that the total production function is logarithmically linear and invariant with time.

Notation. The Laplace transform ψ of the function β, by which all results can be simply written, is

$$\psi(u) = \frac{1}{k}\int_0^\infty \beta(\theta)e^{-\mu\theta} \, du. \qquad (2.2)$$

In addition, we define the three fundamental constants of the general model, k, Θ_0, and Δ, the consideration of which is sufficient in all empirical applications, by limiting ourselves to the first three terms of the Taylor series expansion of the function ψ:

$$\left.\begin{array}{l} k = \int_0^\infty \beta(\theta) \, d\theta \\[2mm] \Theta_0 = \frac{1}{k}\int_0^\infty \theta\beta(\theta) \, d\theta \\[2mm] \Delta = \frac{1}{2k\Theta_0^2}\int_0^\infty \theta^2\beta(\theta) \, d\theta \end{array}\right\} \quad \left.\begin{array}{l} \psi(u) \sim 1 - \Theta_0 u \\[2mm] \dfrac{d\psi}{du}(u) \sim -\Theta_0[1 - 2\Delta\Theta_0 u] \\[2mm] \Delta > \tfrac{1}{2} \text{ (in any case).} \end{array}\right\} \begin{array}{l}\text{for } u \\ \text{small,}\end{array}\right\} \quad (2.3)$$

2.3. Exponential model. A particular variety of the general model, which I call the "Exponential Model" requires moreover:

HYPOTHESIS c: *Exponential decrease of the elasticities of production.*

$$\beta(\theta) = \frac{k}{\Theta_0}e^{-(\theta/\Theta_0)}. \qquad (2.4)$$

This hypothesis, which assumes an exponential decrease of production elasticities β over time, does not seem unrealistic.

B. Consequences of hypotheses

2.4. General model. Consequences of hypotheses (a) and (b). We next cite the principal consequences of hypotheses (a_1) to (a_4) and (b). The capitalistic process P tends to the asymptotic process P_a characterized by the equations shown on the next page.

Derivations of these relations are based essentially on the fact that the distribution of primary inputs must maximize consumed income, in labor terms, under the constraint of the production function. I do not reproduce the derivations here.

The main results are as follows:

I must first point out the *very simple* expression for *consumed* real income given by equation (2.12) in terms of the rates i and ρ. Relation (2.14) verifies that this real income actually reaches a maximum when the interest rate i

Equation No.	Equations of Process P_a	Taylor Expansions	Note
2.5–2.5*	$i(t) - \rho(t) = i'$ (independent of t)	$\rho(t) = \dfrac{1}{R_\omega}\dfrac{dR_\omega(t)}{dt}$	†
2.6–2.6*	$\begin{cases}\phi(t,\theta) = \dfrac{\beta(\theta)e^{-(t-\rho)\theta}}{k\psi(i-\rho)}\\[2mm]\hat\phi(t,\theta) = \beta(\theta)\dfrac{e^{-t\theta}}{k\psi(i)}\end{cases}$	$\psi(u) \sim 1 - \Theta_0 u + \Delta\Theta_0^2 u^2$ $\hat R_\omega(t) = \dfrac{\psi(i)}{\psi(i-\rho)} R_\omega(t)$	*
2.7–2.7*	$\begin{cases}\Theta(i=\rho) = \Theta_0\\ \hat\Theta(i=0) = \Theta_0\end{cases}$	$\begin{cases}\Theta \sim \Theta_0[1 - 2\Theta_0(\Delta - \tfrac12)(i-\rho)]\\ \hat\Theta \sim \Theta_0[1 - 2\Theta_0(\Delta - \tfrac12)i]\end{cases}$	†
2.8–2.8*	$\begin{cases}R_c(t)/R_\omega = 1/\psi(i-\rho)\\[2mm] R(t)/R_\omega(t) = \dfrac{i - \rho\psi(i-\rho)}{(i-\rho)\psi(i-\rho)}\end{cases}$	$R_c/R_\omega \sim 1 + \Theta_0(i-\rho)$ $R/R_\omega \sim 1 + \Theta_0 i$	†
2.9–2.9*	$C(t)/R_\omega(t) = \dfrac{1}{(i-\rho)}\left[\dfrac{1}{\psi(i-\rho)} - 1\right]$	$C/R_\omega \sim \Theta_0[1 + \Theta_0(1-\Delta)(i-\rho)]$	†
2.10–2.10*	$\begin{cases}\gamma_c = \gamma_c(i,\rho) = C(t)/R_c(t) = \dfrac{1-\psi(i-\rho)}{i-\rho}\\[2mm] \gamma_{c,0} = \gamma_c(i=\rho) = \Theta_0\end{cases}$	$\gamma_c \sim \Theta_0[1 - \Delta\Theta_0(i-\rho)]$	†
2.11–2.11*	$\begin{cases}\gamma = \gamma(i,\rho) = C(t)/R(t) = \dfrac{1-\psi(i-\rho)}{i-\rho\psi(i-\rho)}\\[2mm] \gamma_0 = \gamma(i=\rho) = \dfrac{\Theta_0}{1+\rho\Theta_0}\end{cases}$	$\gamma \sim \Theta_0[1 - \Delta\Theta_0 i + \Theta_0(\Delta - 1)\rho]$	†
2.12–2.12*	$\dfrac{\bar R_c(t)}{\bar R_{cM}(t)} = \left[\dfrac{e^{-\Theta_0(i-\rho)}}{\psi(i-\rho)}\right]^k = \left[\dfrac{1-\gamma\rho}{1-\gamma i}e^{-\Theta_0(i-\rho)}\right]^k \sim [1 - \Theta_0^2(\Delta - \tfrac12)(i-\rho)^2]^k$	$\Theta_0 \sim \sqrt{\dfrac{\gamma_c - \gamma}{\rho}}$ $\dfrac{\bar R_c}{\bar R_{cM}} = \left[\dfrac{R_c}{R_\omega}e^{-\Theta_0(i-\rho)}\right]^k$	†
2.13	$\dfrac{\bar R(t)}{K(t)} = \left[\dfrac{i-\rho\psi(i-\rho)}{(i-\rho)\psi(i-\rho)}e^{-\Theta_0 i}\right]^k = \left[\dfrac{1+\rho\gamma_c}{1-(i-\rho)\gamma_c}e^{-\Theta_0 i}\right]^k \sim [1 - \Theta_0^2(\Delta - \tfrac12)i^2 + \Theta_0^2(\Delta - 1)\rho i]^k$	$\Delta \sim \left(1 - \dfrac{2\gamma_c}{\Theta_0}\right)\Big/ \Theta_0(i-\rho)$	†‡
2.14–2.14*	$\dfrac{d\bar R_c}{di}(i=\rho) = 0$	$\bar R_{cM} = K'e^{-k\rho\Theta_0}$	*

* For ρ independent of t.   † For small ρ and i.   ‡ We suppose $\bar R/\bar R_c = [R/R_c]^k$.

is equal to the rate of growth ρ of primary income. It is also interesting to note that for a constant value of ρ *the maximum* consumed real income that can be reached at any time is represented by the relation (2.14*), which is a decreasing function of the expansion rate ρ, so that the most advantageous stationary process is better than any process of advantageous growth. All these results are of course *independent of the particular form of the function* β, which makes them quite general.

   2.5. Exponential model. Consequences of hypotheses (a), (b), and (c). Below I indicate the form that is taken by the preceding relations of the general model when the function β decreases exponentially according to Hypothesis (c) above. The capitalistic process P tends to the asymptotic process characterized by the equations:

2.15–2.15* $i(t) - \rho(t) = i'$ (independent of t) $\rho(t) = \dfrac{1}{R_\omega} \dfrac{dR_\omega(t)}{dt}$ [14]

2.16–2.16* $\begin{cases} \phi(t,\theta) \quad \dfrac{1}{\Theta} e^{-(\theta/\Theta)} \\[2mm] \hat{\phi}(t,\theta) = \dfrac{1}{\Theta} e^{-(\theta/\Theta)} \end{cases}$ $\Delta = 1, \quad \psi(\mu) = \dfrac{1}{1 + \Theta_0 u}$

$\hat{R}_\omega(t) = \left(1 - \dfrac{\Theta_0 \rho}{1 + \Theta_0 i}\right) R_\omega(t)$

2.17–2.17* $\begin{cases} \Theta = \Theta_0/[1 + \Theta_0(i - \rho)] \\ \Theta = \Theta_0/[1 + \Theta_0 i] \end{cases}$ $\dfrac{1}{\Theta} - \dfrac{1}{\Theta} = \rho$

2.18 $\begin{cases} R_c = [1 + \Theta_0(i - \rho)]R_\omega \\ R = [1 + \Theta_0 i]R_\omega \end{cases}$

2.19 $C(t) = \Theta_0 R_\omega(t)$ [14]

2.20–2.20* $\begin{cases} \gamma_c = C(t)/R_c(t) = \Theta \\ \gamma_{c,0} = \gamma_c(i = \rho) = \Theta_0 \end{cases}$ $\Theta = \dfrac{\gamma}{1 - \rho\gamma}$

2.21–2.21* $\begin{cases} \gamma = C(t)/R(t) = \Theta \\[2mm] \gamma_0 = \gamma(i = \rho) = \dfrac{\Theta_0}{1 + \rho\Theta_0} \end{cases}$ $\Theta_0 = \dfrac{\gamma}{1 - i\gamma}$

2.22–2.22* $\dfrac{\bar{R}_c}{\bar{R}_{cM}} = \left[\dfrac{\Theta_0}{\Theta} e^{1-(\Theta_0/\Theta)}\right]^k$ $\dfrac{\bar{R}_c}{\bar{R}_{cM}} = \{[1 + \Theta_0(i - \rho)]e^{-\Theta_0(i-\rho)}\}^k$

2.23–2.23* $\dfrac{\bar{R}}{\bar{R}_M} = \left[\dfrac{\Theta_0}{\Theta} e^{1-(\Theta_0/\hat{\Theta})}\right]^k$ $\dfrac{\bar{R}}{\bar{R}_M} = [(1 + \Theta_0 i)e^{-\Theta_0 i}]^k$ [15]

2.24–2.24* $\dfrac{d\bar{R}_c}{di}(i = \rho) = 0$ $\bar{R}_{cM} = K'e^{-k\rho\Theta_0}$ [14] $\dfrac{d\bar{R}}{di}(i = 0) = 0.$
−2.24**

---

[14] For ρ independent of t.
[15] We suppose $\bar{R}/\bar{R}_c = [R/R_c]^k$.

Here, all useful variables can be expressed in a remarkably simple manner; the relations obtained depend only on two constants: the time constant Θ_0, and the degree of homogeneity k. The basic constant Θ_0 is very simply expressed by relation (2.21*) in terms of two observed variables: the capital-output ratio, γ, and interest rate, i, both observable data.

It remains true, of course, that consumed real income, given by relation (2.22), reaches a maximum when the interest rate i is equal to the growth rate ρ of primary income (relation 2.24).

In this case, it is also noteworthy that real national income, given by relation (2.23), reaches a maximum when the interest rate is equal to zero [relation (2.24**)], but it is possible to show that this property is not true when the function β has not the exponential form.

Finally, let me point out the very remarkable character of relation (2.19), according to which *the capital value is independent of the rate of interest* and equal to the product of the primary income R_ω by the constant Θ_0. As we shall see, *this quite surprising result can be empirically verified.*

C. Generalisation of the model

2.6. The preceding model may be easily modified to take account of neutral technical progress on the one hand, and uncertainty about the future on the other.

If we rewrite the production function (2.1) as[16]

$$L\bar{R}_c(t) = L\alpha' + \int_0^\infty \beta_\theta L\left(\frac{\hat{r}_\theta}{e^{\pi\theta}}\right) d\theta,$$

with $\alpha' = \alpha_0 e^{\pi t}$, nothing changes, and so we can admit the possibility for α in (2.1) that it be given by

$$L\alpha = L\alpha' - \int_0^\infty \pi\theta\beta(\theta)\, d\theta.$$

Technical progress cannot therefore be considered as altering in a systematic way the production elasticities β.

We may also consider the function $\beta(\theta)$ as taking account of uncertainty about the future.

D. Estimates of model parameters

2.7. The coefficient k of homogeneity. The analysis of the statistical data of Rostas (1948), relating to the comparison of 31 American and English industries, leads to the conclusion that there is, on the whole, no substantial increasing returns to scale (the correlation coefficient between the logarithms of the ratios of productivities and number of employees is -0.43). [See Allais (1960A, Sec. 39; 1960B, pp. 36–39 and Appendix I–D, pp. 299–302);

---

[16] Since one hour of work at time $t - \theta$ is equivalent to $e^{-\pi\theta}$ hours of work at time t when the rate of technical progress is π.

Table 1

VALUES OF THE CAPITAL-OUTPUT RATIO IN THE UNITED STATES FROM 1880 TO 1956

Years	C	R'	γ'	R	γ	i_n (in %)	σ (in %)	Θ_0 $i = i_n - \sigma$	Θ_0 $i = i_n$	Θ_0 Average
1880	24.7	7.7	3.20	7.9	3.13	6.47	1.5	3.71	3.93	3.82
1890	43.3	10.9	3.97	11.2	3.87	5.68	1.5	4.62	4.96	4.79
1900	59.1	15.7	3.76	16.0	3.69	5.18	1.5	4.27	4.56	4.42
Period 1880–1900 Averages			3.64		3.56	5.78	1.5	4.20	4.48	4.34
1906	83.6	24.3	3.44	24.8	3.37	5.56	1.5	3.90	4.15	4.03
1910	99.6	28.8	3.46	29.5	3.38	5.81	1.5	3.96	4.20	4.08
1913	113.8	32.2	3.53	33.1	3.44	6.06	1.5	4.08	4.34	4.21
Period 1906–1913 Averages			3.48		3.40	5.81	1.5	3.98	4.23	4.11
Period 1880–1913 Averages			3.56		3.48	5.80	1.5	4.09	4.36	4.23
1923	253.4	73.7	3.44	75.9	3.34	6.57	1.4	4.04	4.28	4.16
1929	313.2	87.8	3.57	90.5	3.46	6.48	1.4	4.20	4.46	4.33
1937	291.8	73.6	3.96	75.2	3.88	5.15	1.4	4.54	4.85	4.70
Period 1923–1937 Averages			3.66		3.56	6.07	1.4	4.26	4.53	4.40
1950	836.9	241.9	3.46	246.1	3.40	3.86	3.95	3.39	3.91	3.65
1955	1110.6	330.2	3.36	336.3	3.30	4.25	3.95	3.33	3.84	3.59
1956	1199.6	350.8	3.42	357.8	3.35	4.57	3.95	3.42	3.96	3.69

Period 1950–1956 Averages	3.41	3.35	4.23	3.95	3.38	3.90	3.64
Period 1880–1956 Averages	3.54	3.46	5.47	2.09	3.95	4.29	4.12
Median 1880–1956	3.46	3.39	5.62	1.5	4.00	4.24	4.12
Average relative deviation	5%	5%	13%	13%	8%	7%	8%

The retained years were, as far as possible, full employment years.

I have taken $i_n = i'_n + 1\%$ where i'_n represents the rate of interest of bonds.

I have taken $R = R' + i_n C_c$ where C_c represents the value of durable consumption goods.

$\gamma' = C/R'$; $\gamma = C/R$.

We have $\Theta_0 = \gamma/(1 - i\gamma)$.

The bottom row is the average in percentage of the deviations of the 12 values from their general average.

Values of C, C_c, and C_o, : Before 1896, from Goldsmith, "The Growth of Reproducible Wealth of the U.S.A. from 1805 to 1950," *Income and Wealth of the United States, Trends and Structure*, Series II, Bowes and Bowes, 1952, p. 306; after 1896, from "National Balance Sheets and National Wealth Statements, 1896 to 1949," *A Study of Saving in the United States*, Princeton University Press, 1956, p. 14 (most of these values are given in the *Economic Almanac* of 1960, p. 389).

Values of the national income R': for 1929 and from 1950 to 1956, *Economic Almanac of 1960*, National Income, p. 392; for 1900 to 1923 and 1937, *idem*, p. 410; for 1880 and 1890 *idem*, p. 398; the values 7.227 and 10.70 for 1879 and 1889 have been multiplied by 15.647/16.158 (ratio of the values for 1900) to make them comparable with the preceding values. To obtain the values of 1880 and 1890, I have, besides, multiplied the values by 1.037 to take into account the increased trend of the real value of the national income (Allais) and by 82/77 and 78/77 to take into account the general increase of prices.

Thus we find: $7.227 \times (15.647/16.158) \times (1.057 \times 82/77) = 7.7$;

$10.701 \times (15.647/16.158) \times (1.057 \times 78/77) = 10.9$.

Values of i'_n: for 1950 to 1956, *Economic Almanac of 1960*, p. 80, Bond Yields (general average); before 1950, Macaulay, F. R., *Bond Yields, Interest Rates, Stock Prices*, National Bureau of Economic Research, 1938, Appendix A, 142, col. 5 (Adjust. Bonds). These values have been increased by 1% to make them comparable with the preceding ones (average correction for years 1925 and 1935).

and Allais (1961, Appendix II).] This result seems corroborated by those of Douglas (1948), and is not opposed to those of Verdoorn (1949, 1950, 1956). See Allais (1960A, Sec. 39) and (1960B, Appendix I–D).

All things considered, we can take the homogeneity coefficient to be slightly different from unity for the whole economy.

2.8. The coefficient Θ_0. Because of lack of space, the results obtained for the estimation of the constant Θ_0 are limited to the case of the exponential model, based on the relation (2.21*):

$$\Theta_0 = \gamma/(1 - i\gamma), \qquad \gamma = C/R.$$

In Table 1 estimates are given for the U.S. for various (full employment) years and periods from 1880 to 1956 and in Table 2 estimates of Θ_0 are provided for the U.S., France, and Great Britain for 1913.

If we take into account the fact that in a real economy a dynamic equilibrium is only imperfectly realized, the rate of interest to be considered has an intermediate value between the nominal value i_n and this value minus σ, the rate of increase of nominal wages, without there being, in the present state of things, any possibility of going further. Thus I have indicated in each case the two extreme estimates of Θ_0 to which we are led and the average.

The rate i_n is the rate of interest corresponding to a riskless loan, presenting no advantages of liquidity.

All the results, as shown in the tables, are in remarkable agreement, and show that the order of magnitude of the constant Θ_0 is 4.

In Figure 5, I indicate the shape of the curve representing consumed real income $\bar{R}_c$ as a function of the difference $(i - \rho)$, We can see that we have a quite flat maximum for every possible value of Θ_0. Figure 6 represents consumed real income as a function of the capital-output γ_c defined by reference to the consumed income R_c.

3. EMPIRICAL JUSTIFICATION OF THE MODEL

The proposed model is empirically justified with respect to both its hypotheses and its results.

A. Justification of the model with respect to its hypotheses

3.1. General model. The hypotheses (a_1) to (a_4) with respect to the structure of the capitalistic process are rather weak, except for the assumption of homogeneity of order k, but this last characteristic, as I have already pointed out, appears plausible, at least for k equal one.[17]

Hypothesis (b) simply amounts to assuming that it is possible to define production elasticities with regard to primary inputs, and that these elasticities may be considered to vary little in a large region in the vicinity of the process under consideration at a given time and to be fairly constant through time. Both these points appear justified by the results of all previous research

---

[17] In any case, Theorem I remains valid for convex production functions (see footnote 4).

Table 2

CAPITAL-OUTPUT RATIO VALUES IN 1913 IN UNITED STATES,
FRANCE AND GREAT BRITAIN

	C	R'	γ'	R	γ
United States	113.8	32.2	3.53	33.1	3.44
France	191.0	48.9	3.91	49.9	3.83
Great Britain (1914)	9138.5	2450	3.73	2490.4	3.67
Averages			3.72		3.64
Average relative deviation			3%		4%

	i_n (in %)	σ (in %)	Θ_0		
			$i = i_n - \sigma$	$i = i_n$	Average
United States	6.06	1.5	4.08	4.34	4.21
France	4.84	1	4.49	4.70	4.60
Great Britain (1914)	5.00	0	4.50	4.50	4.50
Averages	5.30		4.36	4.51	4.44
Average relative deviation	12%		4%	3%	3%

Notes: $\gamma' = C/R'$, $R = R' + iC_e$, $\gamma = C/R$, $\Theta_0 = \gamma/(1 - i\gamma)$.
Sources: Allais, 1960A, *Influence du coefficient capitalistique sur le revenu national réel par tête* (Printed Text, n. 61, presented at the Tokyo Congress), pp. 52–53.

in which no variation of the elasticities was assumed, and by the fact that technical progress in itself does not appear to have any systematic influence upon the production elasticities.

3.2. Exponential model. Finally, the hypothesis (c) of exponential decrease of the production elasticities, on which the exponential model is based, appears as rather natural, everything considered. In fact the difficulty of using roundabout processes may be considered as marginally increasing with time in an exponential way.

B. Justification of the model with respect to its consequences

3.3. General model. Consequences of its hypotheses (a) and (b). Without going into the details of the discussion, I simply state that the consequences of the general model are in agreement with the facts *on four important points*:

1) The practically undetectable variations of consumed real income $\bar{R}_c$ with the capital-output ratio $\gamma = C/R$ for various countries at a given time and for a given country through time.[18] This, a consequence of (2.12) and (2.10*), is confirmed by the available data. [See Allais (1960A, Sec. 48).]

2) The low variability of the capital-output ratio γ at a given time, for various countries. This is an implication of (2.11).[18] [See Allais (1960A, Sec. 41).]

---

[18] This result becomes particularly clear if we consider the exponential model (relations 2.22, 2.21, and 2.19 corresponding to 2.12, 2.11, and 2.9).

Figure 5 Consumed real income as a function of the difference $i - \rho$ in the case of a homogeneous production function for the exponential model.

$$\frac{\bar{R}_c}{\bar{R}_{cM}} = [1 + \gamma_{c,0}(i - \rho)]e^{-\gamma_{c,0}(i-\rho)}, \text{ equations (2.22*) and (2.20);}$$

$\bar{R}_c$ = real income consumed;
i = instantaneous rate of interest in labor units;
ρ = rate of growth of primary income;
$\gamma_c = C/R_c = \Theta$, equation (2.20);
$\gamma_{c,0} = \gamma_c (i = \rho) = \Theta_c$, equation (2.20);
$\gamma = C/R = \hat{\Theta}$, equation (2.21);

$$\gamma_c = \frac{\gamma}{1 - \rho\gamma}, \text{ equations (2.20) and (2.20*).}$$

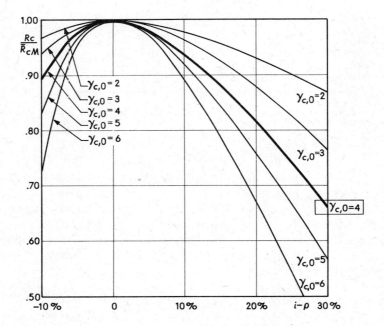

3) The low variability of the capital-output ratio γ in time for a given country. This is also an implication of (2.11) if we suppose, as is natural, that $\beta(\theta)$ changes little with time.[18] [See Allais (1960A, Sec. 41).]

4) The approximate constancy of the labor value of reproducible capital C/R_ω per unit of primary income at a given time for various countries. This, a consequence of relation (2.9), is confirmed by the available statistical data. [See Allais (1960A, Sec. 43).]

3.4. *Exponential model. Additional consequences derived from the consideration of hypothesis (c) stating the exponential decrease of $\beta(\theta)$.* Additional consequences derived from introducing the hypothesis (c) of exponential decrease of the function β also appear to be empirically verified.

Figure 6 Consumed real income as a function of the capital-output ratio in the case of a homogeneous production function for the exponential model.

$$\frac{\bar{R}_c}{\bar{R}_{cM}} = \frac{\gamma_{c,0}}{\gamma_c} e^{1 - \gamma_{c,0}/\gamma_c}, \text{ equations (2.22) and (2.20)}.$$

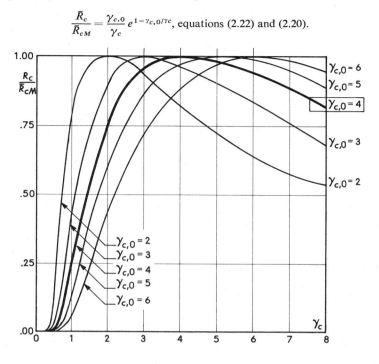

1) First, hypothesis (c) leads for the whole economy to an exponential amortization law [relation (2.16)], which appears to correspond well to the results of empirical research on durable goods depreciation whenever there is an actual market. See, e.g., the study by Boiteux (1956) on second hand cars and that by Blank and Winnick (1957) on buildings. In these cases fitting exponential curves gives average lives of 6 and 50 years, respectively [Allais (1960A, Sec. 38).]

2) Secondly, whatever the value of Douglas's results, it is interesting to compare them with the results of the model. Douglas (1948) found for manufacturing industry the empirical relation $P = KL^{\lambda}C^{\mu}$ with $\lambda + \mu$ approximately 1 and μ approximately 0.22. These are the average values for the U.S. and Australia for the period 1899–1929.[19] His production function is equivalent to

$$\frac{dP}{P} = \frac{\mu}{1-\mu}\frac{d\gamma'}{\gamma'} \quad \text{with} \quad \gamma' = \frac{C}{P}. \tag{3.1}$$

---

[19] Douglas's results have been very much discussed but, in fact, it seems that they correspond to a very real relationship.

The exponential model gives [relations (2.23), (2.21), and (2.17)]

$$\frac{d\bar{R}}{\bar{R}} = \frac{i\gamma}{1 - i\gamma} \frac{d\gamma}{\gamma}. \tag{3.2}$$

So, the product $i\gamma$ corresponds to the coefficient μ of Douglas's model.

For the period 1899–1929, we can take $\gamma = 3.5$ for i between 4 percent and 6 percent, according as we do or do not take into account the rate of growth σ of wages (Table 1). Thus we have

$$0.14 < i\gamma < 0.21. \tag{3.3}$$

The difference between the values found for μ and $i\gamma$ may be explained by the fact that Douglas's research concerns *industry only*, and *gross* production, whereas our model considers *net* production of the economy *as a whole*. [See Allais (1960A, Sec. 44).]

3) (4) Two other instances of empirical confirmation may be found [Allais (1960A, Sections 45, 47)] in the good agreement that one finds between the calculated average amortization time Θ and the labour force composition, and in the agreement between the primary income amortization law derived from the model and the percentage of primary income used in the year's national income.

5) Finally, my results lead to the conclusion that investment is approximately proportional to income, whatever its level. This conclusion appears to be in good agreement with the results found by Houthakker (1960) that, on the whole, saving is approximately proportional to income. Within the limits of the model, these results appear as consequences of the low variability of the capital-output ratio γ with time and among countries.

4. APPLICATIONS OF THE MODEL

The results I have just stated allow some rather suggestive applications, which are summarized in this section.

4.1. Possibility of increasing real national income by increasing capital intensity. On the basis of relation (2.22) and estimating $k = 1$, the relative gain of real consumed income likely to be obtained by realizing the capitalistic optimum is

$$g_c = \frac{\bar{R}_M - \bar{R}}{\bar{R}} = \frac{\Theta}{\Theta_0} e^{(\Theta_0/\Theta) - 1} - 1, \tag{4.1}$$

where, by relation (2.20*), $\Theta = \gamma/(1 - \rho\gamma)$. As an average for the years 1950, 1955, and 1956, we can take for the United States (Table 1) $\gamma = 3.35$, $\rho = 0.017$, and $\Theta_0 = 3.64$. Therefore, $\Theta = 3.55$ and $g < 0.1$ percent. Thus, the gain likely to be realized from increased capital intensity is very low, from which we can conclude that the United States is in the neighborhood of the capitalistic optimum [Allais (1960)A Sec. 55].

4.2. The optimum rate of net saving.   For countries that are in the neighbourhood of the capitalistic optimum, the optimum rate of net saving that one could try to realize is, as a consequence of relation (2.11),

$$\left[\frac{1}{R}\frac{dC}{dt}\right]_{i=\rho} = \rho\gamma_0 = \frac{\rho\Theta_0}{1 + \rho\Theta_0}. \tag{4.2}$$

For the U.S.A., we have $\Theta_0 \approx 4$ and $\rho \approx 1.7$ percent. Thus the optimum rate of net saving is about 6 percent for the American economy.

4.3. Influence of the increase of primary income on consumed real income per inhabitant.   On the basis of the general relation (2.14*) the decrease of real income per capita, due to the expansion of primary income, ranges about

$$\rho = 1 - e^{-k\Theta_0\rho}. \tag{4.3}$$

For the United States during the 1950's we may take $k = 1, \Theta_0 = 4$, and $\rho = 0.017$. Therefore, $p \approx 7$ percent, a percentage which is naturally very near the one indicated in the previous paragraph. This loss corresponds to the necessity of assigning a part of national income to maintain the capital-output ratio at a constant value.

4.4. Explanation of the differences of productivity existing among the different countries.   The present theory allows one to examine in what way differences in capitalistic intensity can explain the average difference in productivity recorded between two countries at a given time.

Thus, in 1955, the average productivity of the American economy was about 2.4 times higher than that of the French economy. One might think at first sight that the explanation of this difference must be sought in the difference in the real volume of equipment. In fact, this volume per worker was approximately 2.4 times higher in the United States than in France, in 1955. Everything indicates, however, that the capital-output ratio γ was at least as high in France as in the United States (in the U.S. it was 3.3; in France, greater). Therefore, the observed difference in productivity cannot be explained by a difference in capital intensity, since the ratios of capital to income have about the same value in the two countries.

This difference must be explained by other factors, such as the differences of natural resources per capita and, over all, the general management of the economy. [See Allais (1960A, Sec. 54) and (1960B, pp. 28–32 and 295–297).] The influence of these other factors produces the result that, for *the same value* of the capital-output ratio, equipment per worker was about 2.4 times higher in the United States than in France, a number *exactly equal* to the ratio of average productivities. Thus we see that the generally admitted explanation amounts to considering *as a cause* a difference in real capital per worker that is in fact *no more than an effect*.

4.5. The development of underdeveloped countries.   A final suggestive application of the present theory may be made to the case of the so-called underdeveloped countries.

If we accept the hypothesis that the preceding theory is valid, at least as a first approximation, Table 3 shows in percent the gain g in real income that could be obtained by increasing the capital-output ratio from the recorded value Θ to the optimum value Θ_0 (relation 4.1), which we can suppose to be equal to 4. We probably have $\Theta > 2$ for underdeveloped countries.

Then we see that, starting for instance from a situation with a capital-output ratio as low as 2, which corresponds to a difference $i - \rho$ of about 25 percent, the gain in real income likely to be obtained by attaining the capitalistic optimum is only about 36 percent. The possible gain is much lower than is usually thought. Consequently, the explanation of enormous differences in productivity recorded between the Occident and the underdeveloped countries is likely to be found much less in the possible smallness of the capital-output ratio than in differences in natural resources available per inhabitant, differences in the level of technical education, and differences in the management of the economy in general. From this we can conclude that it would not be sufficient to use American-type equipment in the so-called underdeveloped countries, if one did not at the same time improve the other factors of production, the productivity of which is so much smaller in those countries than in the Occident.

Table 3

Θ	4	3.6	3.4	3.2	3.0	2.5	2.0
$i - \rho$	0	2.8	4.4	6.3	8.3	15.0	25.0
g	0	0.6	1.4	2.7	4.7	13.9	35.9

5. STATISTICAL DATA

In this section we comment further on Tables 1 and 2 presented earlier and on further statistical materials.

5.1. Values of the capital-output ratio in the United States from 1880 to 1956. With regard to Table 1, it may be noted that the four values for γ, 3.56, 3.40, 3.56, and 3.35, for the four elementary periods considered are remarkably close to one another and show practically no systematic variation.

The four corresponding period averages for the mean value of Θ_0, 4.34, 4.11, 4.40, and 3.64, are also relatively close and fluctuate in a nonsystematic way around their general average, 4.12. The slightly lower last value, 3.64, may be imputed to the abnormally low values of the rate of interest during the period 1950–56. In fact, the rate on bonds, i_n, went from 2.86 percent in 1950 to 4.69 percent in June, 1959, tending thus to come back to its average level of previous periods.

5.2. Capital-output ratio values in 1913 in the United States, France, and Great Britain. With regard to Table 2, the concordance of values for Θ_0 for the United States, France, and Great Britain in 1913 is as good as might be hoped if we take account of the relative imprecision of the basic statistical data. The average value for Θ_0 agrees well with the four values found for the U.S.: 4.34, 4.23, 4.53, and 3.90 for the periods 1880–1900, 1906–1913, 1923–1937, and 1950–1956, as given in Table 1.

5.3. Capital-output ratios for different countries at different times. Using data of Colin Clark (1957, pp. 88 ff. and 572 ff.) we find [see Allais (1960A, pp. 54–57)] that, for the lognormal distribution of the coefficient γ' for 58 values for 21 countries considered from 1805 to 1953, the median is 3.54 and the average relative deviation is 22 percent. The median of 10 values for the U.S. is 3.46.

As far as I can judge, the recorded dispersion of the observed values of γ' may be explained *mainly* by the lack of precision of the data and the differences in calculating methods that are used. In favour of this conclusion, we notice that economically the situation in the United States corresponds to an extreme case. That the corresponding value of γ' is close to the median value of the coefficients γ' of various countries leads one to conclude that essentially the variation of the γ' has a purely statistical origin.

5.4. Comparison of the estimates of γ'. We conclude this section with the following comparison of the estimates of γ':

U.S.A. (12 Goldsmith's corrected estimates) . . . . median:[20]   3.46
Year 1913 (3 Allais' estimates) . . . . average: 3.72
World (58 Colin-Clark's estimates) . . . . median:[21]   3.54

The recorded deviations are negligible, if we take account of the lack of precision of the data.

Although Colin-Clark's values are purely illustrative, because of the great differences in the worth of the statistical materials and methods employed, one cannot be struck by the weak variations of the capital-output ratio, which are shown in §6.3, for quite different countries and periods with very different standards of living, as well as by the remarkable agreement of the median of the values found with those of both previous groups of estimates for the United States from 1880 to 1956 and for the United States, France, and Great Britain for 1913.

In fact, the three values of γ': 3.46, 3.72, and 3.54 are exactly of the same order of magnitude.

CONCLUSIONS

In this paper I have proposed a general theory of the capitalistic optimum, with a model of very general scope which illustrates it, as well as a special case of this general model corresponding to an exponential decrease of production elasticity coefficients.

This general model, and in particular, its exponential variety, appear quite remarkably confirmed by all presently available empirical data, with respect to both the hypotheses and the results.

In fact, *everything takes place* as if the proposed model could be considered

---

[20] Empirical value.
[21] Lognormal adjustment.

as correctly representing concrete reality, and explaining its essential features, very simply.

Whether the research of tomorrow confirms or contradicts this provisional conclusion, I think that in the present state of our knowledge, the proposed theory and the model certainly have the advantage of being simple, suggestive, and forcing one to think about a number of interesting circumstances. After all, this is perhaps the real service which can be rendered by any good theory at a given time.

BIBLIOGRAPHY

We here present a partially annotated bibliography restricted to works having a direct relation to concepts used in the present paper.

A. CHARACTERISTIC FUNCTION

JEVONS, S., 1871: *The Theory of Political Economy.*
In this book, in Chapter VII, the concept of the characteristic function has been used *for the first time* in the case where $\phi(\theta, i) = \phi_0$ for $0 < \theta < \lambda$ and $\phi(\theta, i) = 0$ for $\lambda < \theta$.

BÖHM-BAWERK, EUGEN VON, 1884: *Geschichte und Kritik der kapitalzins Theorien.*

BOHM-BAWERK, EUGEN VON, 1888: *Positive Theorie des Kapitales.*
In this book, the concept of the characteristic function, among others, has been studied thoroughly (see especially Exkurs I to VI).

BOUSQUET, G. H., 1936: *Institutes de science économique*, Tome III, Riviére, Chap. VI.
This book contains a very noteworthy analysis, for its time, of Jevons' concept of the characteristic function, and the point of view of Böhm-Bawerk is studied thoroughly.

STACKELBERG, VON, 1941: "Capital und Zins in der stationären Verkehrswirtschaft," *Zeitschrift für Nationalökonomie*, vol. X, Feb., 1941.
Relation (1.38) (obtained from the approximate relation $R = R_\varpi e^{i\theta}$) is applied to a particular case (p. 61).

ALLAIS, MAURICE, 1947: *Economie et intérêt.*
To my knowledge, this book gives, for the first time, a general mathematical theory of the characteristic function concept, pp. 118 to 142 and pp. 186 to 206.

B. THEORY OF THE OPTIMUM ALLOCATION OF RESOURCES OVER TIME

1. General theory of optimum management

ALLAIS, MAURICE, 1943: *Traité d'economie pure*, Imprimerie Nationale, 1952 (2d edition of the first part: "L'Economie pure" of the book *A la recherche d'une discipline économique*, Paris 1943), 5 vol. in in-4°, 1,000 pages.
This book gives in chapter VII (pp. 604–82) the first systematic and rigorous statement (to my knowledge) of the theory of the optimum allocation of resources *that takes time into account, specifies the extremal conditions, considers the distinction between divisible and indivisible activities, specifies the connection between the conditions of optimum allocation of resources and the stability conditions,* and shows clearly the arbitrary nature of the income distribution.

ALLAIS, MAURICE, 1947: *Economie et intérêt*, Imprimerie Nationale, Paris, 1947, 800 pages in two in-8° volumes (in deposit at the Librarie de Medicis).
This book gives in chapter VI, pp. 153–78, the generalization of the theory of optimum allocation of resources *when we consider the successive personalities of the same individual through time, as well as the various generations.*

MALINVAUD, EDMOND, 1953: *"Capital Accumulation and Efficient Allocation of Resources," *Econometrica*, April, 1953, pp. 233–68.
This article generalizes the application of some instruments of analysis and gives a summary statement of a certain number of previous results.

DEBREU, GÉRARD, 1959: *Theory of Value*, 114 pages, Wiley, New York.
This book gives a rigorous statement of the theory of optimum allocation of resources in the case of functions convex in the *whole* space, whereas previous works took into account only *local* conditions, at least in their general statements.

MALINVAUD, EDMOND, 1959: "Programmes d'expansion et taux d'intérêt," *Econometrica*, April, 1959.
This article studies the conditions characterizing efficient programs, and, in particular, some processes characterized by the equality $i = \rho$, but without connecting that condition to the concept of a capitalistic optimum.

MALINVAUD, EDMOND, 1961: "The Analogy Between Atemporal and Intertemporal Theories of Resource Allocation," *The Review of Economic Studies*, Vol. XXVIII, no. 3.
This article studies some relations between the rate of interest i and the expansion rate ρ.

ALLAIS, MAURICE, 1961: "L'influence des besoins sur la production des biens de consommation," Communication to the "Colloque de Grenoble," September, 1961, 107 pages.
This paper studies, in Appendix II, the problem of the convexity of production functions.

2. Theory of the capitalistic optimum for stationary processes

WICKSELL, KNUT, 1901: *Vorlesungen über Nationalökonomie*; English translation, 1934, *Lectures on Political Economy*, Volume I, "General Theory," Routledge, London, 1946.
The text is rather obscure, but the indication of a capitalistic optimum for $i = 0$ is explicitly given, in a single line (p. 209), in fact, but *for the first time* to my knowledge in the economic literature.

AKERMAN, G., 1923: *Real Kapital und Kapitalzins*, Stockholm.
In spite of a certain obscurity, this work is very penetrating. An interesting commentary is given in the English translation of the previous work, pp. 258–99.

RAMSEY, F. P., 1928: *"A Mathematical Theory of Savings," *Economic Journal*, Vol. 38, December, 1928, pp. 543–59.
This well-known paper studies optimum saving for a given generation, but not the capitalistic optimum over time as the present paper does.

KEYNES, J. M., 1936: *The General Theory of Employment, Interest and Money*.
The capitalistic optimum for $i = 0$ is mentioned in a few lines in Chapter XVI, at the beginning of the last paragraph of Section II.

MEADE, J. E., 1937: *An Introduction to Economic Analysis and Policy*, Oxford University Press.
This work gives in Chap. III *the first systematic analysis of the theory of capitalistic optimum for i = 0* (see in particular the sixth paragraph); *however, this analysis is presented in a purely literary form.*

KNIGHT, FRANK H., 1946: "Capital and Interest," *Encyclopedia Britannica*, Chicago, University of Chicago Press, 1946, pp. 799–800, and *Readings in the Theory of Income Distribution*, London, Allen and Unwin, 1950, pp. 384–417.
It is symptomatic that this paper, the purpose of which is to give a general view of the question, makes a very short allusion to the question of a capitalistic optimum, which nevertheless is so important (*Readings*, p. 402).

ALLAIS, MAURICE, 1947A: *Economie et intérêt* (see above).
In Chapter VII, pp. 179 to 228, this work gives the first rigorous statement, to my knowledge, of the theory of a capitalistic optimum as well as the formulation by which one can estimate the order of magnitude of the influence of capital intensity on real income. Among other things, this work establishes, for the case $k = 1$, formulae (1.33) to (1.38).

ALLAIS, MAURICE, 1947B: "Rendement social et productivité sociale," Paper presented at the Washington International Econometric Congress in 1947; *Proceedings of the International Statistical Conferences*, 1947, Vol. V, pp. 129 ff.
This paper summarizes some results of the book, *Economie et intérêt*.

ALLAIS, MAURICE, 1949: *Intérêt et productivité sociale*, Thesis of "Ingénieur-Docteur de l'Université de Paris," Faculté des Sciences, June, 1949.

MALINVAUD, EDMOND, 1953: *"Capital Accumulation and Efficient Allocation of Resources" (see above).
This articles gives a new demonstration of the capitalistic optimum for $i = 0$, with reference to previous works.

KOOPMANS, T. C., 1957: *The State of Economic Science*, McGraw-Hill.
This book gives some indications, although very succint, about the theory of a capitalistic optimum with only one reference to previous works: Malinvaud's article (1953).

ALLAIS, MAURICE, 1960B: *L'Europe unie, route de la prospérité*, Calmann-Lévy, Paris, 1960, 368 pp.
The theory of a capitalistic optimum is applied to a comparison of the American and French economies, pp. 28 to 32, and Appendix I C, pp. 295–97.

ALLAIS MAURICE, 1961B: *Le Tiers-Monde au carrefour*, Les Cahiers Africains, Créations de Presse, vol. 7 and 8, Bruxelles, 1962.
In one of its chapters, this book applies the theory of a capitalistic optimum to the case of underdeveloped countries (pp. 52–53).

3. Capitalistic optimum theory for dynamic processes

DESROUSSEAUX, JACQUES, 1959: "Variations sur la croissance économique," 16 pages and an Appendix of 13 typewritten pages.
For the first time, to my knowledge, this study sets forth, in a precise way, the capitalistic optimum condition $i = \rho$ for dynamic processes in the case of a particular model.

MALINVAUD, EDMOND, 1961: "On the Rate of Interest of Efficient Proportional Growth Programs," Working Paper, Berkeley.
The equality, $i = \rho$, is indicated as a general condition for a capitalistic optimum (M. Desrousseaux's priority on that proposition is stated, p. 6).

DESROUSSEAUX, JACQUES, 1961A: "Expansion stable et taux d'intérêt optimal," *Annales des Mines*, November, 1961, pp. 31 and 46.
By generalizing Allais' formulation (1947A and 1947B) to the case of a non-stationary process, and by assuming that the function $\phi(t, \theta)$ satisfies a "condition of regularity" over time, this study establishes the condition for a capitalistic optimum, $i = \rho$. Although questionable in some of its parts, this study presents original and very suggestive points of view.

ALLAIS, MAURICE, 1961C: "Théorie de l'optimum capitalistique," Notes of the 2d and the 7th of November, 1961, not published, 13 and 10 pp.
These notes demonstrate Theorems I and III, in the case of production functions homogeneous of order k or convex.

ALLAIS, MAURICE, 1962: *The Influence of the Volume of Capital on the Real National Income*, in preparation, North-Holland Publishing Co.
This work analyzes the different questions of the present paper.

C. ALLAIS' MODEL ILLUSTRATING THE GENERAL THEORY OF A CAPITALISTIC OPTIMUM

1. Stationary processes

ALLAIS, MAURICE, 1955: "Observations sur l'analyse des relations entre le capital et la production," *Works of the Congress of French-Speaking Economists, 1955*, Editions Domat-Montchrestien, 1956, pp. 188 to 223.
The "exponential" model is presented, for the first time, with some numerical applications.

ALLAIS, MAURICE, 1960A: "Influence du coefficient capitalistique sur le revenu réel par tête," Paper presented at the Congress of the International Statistical Institute of Tokyo, 1960, Document 61, 70 pages.
For reasons of copyright, only the theoretical part has been published in the *I. S. I. Bulletin*, Volume XXXVIII, 2, pp. 3–27.

2. Generalisation in the case of a dynamic process and of any function $\beta(\theta)$

DESROUSSEAUX, JACQUES, 1961B: "Caractéristiques globales des économies quelconques et taux d'intérêt optimal dans les mondes évolutifs—Généralisation du 'Modèle Allais' et confrontation avec les options de type industriel," Mimeographed paper of October 14th, 58 pp. This study is to be published in a collective book of the "Centre National de la Recherche Scientifique" grouping the lectures given at Professor Allais' Seminar during the academic year 1960–1961. This study applies the method of Desrousseaux's paper (1061A) to the case of a function $\beta(\theta)$ independent of time. It leads to results very similar to ours and which are identical if the rates i and ρ are constant. The results obtained are in general different, for M. Desrousseaux establishes his results by starting from a condition of regularity whereas ours are derived from Theorem I. This paper of M. Desrousseaux is prior to my demonstration of Theorem I.

BOITEUX, MARCEL, 1961: "Sur modèle macroéconomique de croissance—Extension du modèle de M. Allais," Mimeographed paper of 15 pages, August 28th, 1961.
This note generalizes the results of Allais' Tokyo paper (1960A) for rates i and ρ constant.

ALLAIS, MAURICE, 1961D: "Le modèle de Tokyo dans de cas l'une fonction quelconque dépendant du temps et d'un taux d'expansion du revenue originaire fonction du temps," Mimeographed paper of 26 pages, November 21, 1961.
This note generalizes the results of the Tokyo model (1960A) in the case of a rate of growth $\rho(t)$ and of any function $\beta(\theta)$.

D. EMPIRICAL RESEARCH

The reader will find in our Tokyo paper (Allais, 1960A) numerous references at the end which are not reproduced here because of the lack of space. We only mention here, and without commentary, some references explicitly cited in the preceding summary.

ROSTAS, 1948: *Comparative Productivity in British and American Industry*, Cambridge University Press.

DOUGLAS, P. H., 1948: "Are these Laws of Production?," *American Economic Review*, Vol. XXXVIII, March, 1948.

VERDOORN, P. J., 1949; "Fattori che Regolano lo Sviluppo della Produttivita del Lavoro," *L'Industria*, Milan, no. 1, 11 pp.

VERDOORN, P. J., 1950: "On an Empirical Law Governing the Productivity of Labour," Mimeographed paper, 13 pp., Econometric Society Congress, Varèse.

GOLDSMITH, R. W., 1951: "A Perpetual Inventory of National Wealth," in *Studies in Income and Wealth*, Vol. 14, National Bureau of Economic Research, New York.

GOLDSMITH, R. W., 1952: "The Growth of Reproducible Wealth of U.S.A., from 1805 to 1950," in *Income and Wealth of the United States*, Studies in Income and Wealth, Series II, Bowes and Bowes, Cambridge.

GOLDSMITH, R. W., 1955: *A Study of Saving in the United States*, 3 vols, Princeton University Press.

VERDOORN, P. J., 1956: "Complementary and Long-Range Projections," *Econometrica*, Vol. 24, No. 4.

BOITEUX, M., 1956: "L'Amortissement—Dépréciation des automobiles," *Revue de Statistique Appliquée*, Vol. IV, no. 4, 1956.

COLIN-CLARK, M. A., 1957: *The Conditions of Economic Progress*, 3d edition, Macmillan.

BLANK, D. M., and L. WINNICK, 1957: "Capital Formation in Private Nonfarm Residential Construction," in *Problems of Capital Formation*, National Bureau of Economic Research, Princeton University Press.

HOUTHAKKER, H. S., "An International Comparison of Personal Savings," I.S.I. Bulletin, vol. xxxviii, no. 2, pp. 55–69. (See also the discussion of this paper.)

ADDITIONAL NOTE

In my Bowley-Walras Lecture of December 28, 1961, reproduced as an article in *Econometrica* of October, 1962,[1,2]. I was unable to give demonstrations of all the propositions presented. The article, indeed, was too condensed to be readily intelligible.

Opportunities to remedy these shortcomings were provided by the Conference on Activity Analysis sponsored by the International Economic Association, held in Cambridge in July, 1963, and the Study Week on the Role of Econometric Analysis in the Formulation of Development Plans, organised by the Pontifical Academy of the Sciences (October 7–13, 1963). In the papers presented at these two conferences, I also presented generalizations of the propositions formulated in the *Econometrica* article.

Since that time, I have been able to undertake further investigation of a number of aspects of the subject, first in a paper, "A Theorem about the Optimum Allocation of Capital," presented in December, 1964, and again in a paper written in French, entitled "Real Gross National Product, Real National Income, and the Cobb-Douglas Function" (May, 1966).

a) In Part I of the Cambridge paper (1963A), the reader will find a rigorous and fully detailed demonstration of Theorem I of the *Econometrica* paper, together with various extensions and generalisations and detailed comments on the assumptions considered and the results obtained.

Theorem I may be extended to production functions f_n, for which there are diminishing returns (1953A, § 113 and 160) and also to functions which are of h-order of h'-order homogeneity with respect to $\vec{Q}_n$ and $\vec{E}_n$ (1953A, § 160). It may further be generalized to the case in which explicit allowance is made for the neutral component of technical progress (1953A, § 1961).

The demonstration in § 108 of the *Econometrica* article has also been extended to cover the dynamic case in which primary income R_ω grows at the rate ρ (1953A, § 151–6).

Lastly, I have shown in this section of the Cambridge Paper (§ 154) that the Von Neumann model is no more than an *extremely special* case of the asymptotic processes defined in the *Econometrica* article.

In Part II of the same paper, further arguments are presented concerning the propositions in § 4.4 of the *Econometrica* article. A particularly simple model is used to illustrate the points of veiw set forth.

The discussion of the paper at the Conference related only to Part I, and throws further light on a number of difficult points there.

b) The reader will find the detailed demonstration of the propositions of § 1.7 to § 1.10 of the *Econometrica* article, together with their generalisation

---

[1] The text above takes account of corrections published in the October, 1963, issue of *Econometrica* (p. 784).

[2] The date is not without relevance to the priority of certain propositions on the capitalistic optimum, which appear in a number of studies published *after* delivery of my lecture at New York (the full text of which was distributed), but *before* its appearance in *Econometrica*, many months later.

to the case of a rate of growth ρ of primary income R_ω, in my Rome paper (Part I, pp. 713–70). This part of the paper also contains the statement and demonstration of a number of theorems of very general scope.

Demonstrations of the propositions of § 2.4 and § 2.5 of the *Econometrica* article are given in Part II (pp. 771–809), in which further properties of the models considered are also enounced and demonstrated.

Part III (pp. 810–76) considerably extends the discussion in § 2.7 to § 3.4 of the *Econometrica* article. In § 333 to § 335, particular attention is focussed on issues relating to the determination of the characteristic amortisation function $\phi(\theta)$ on the basis of available empirical data.

An attempt is made in Part IV (pp. 870–900) to carry further, and give some details on, the applications which are very briefly discussed in § 4.1 to § 4.4 of the *Econometrica* article.

Finally, an Appendix (pp. 901–76) is developed to the case in which the function $\beta(\theta)e^{\mu\theta}$ can be expanded as a Taylor series, the expression of $\beta(\theta)$ being:

$$\beta(\theta) = \left[b_0 + b_1\theta + \cdots + \frac{b_{n-1}}{n-1!}\,\theta^{n-1} + \cdots \right]e^{-\mu\theta}.$$

Under a set of quite natural assumptions, it can be shown that in this case the coefficient Δ of the third relation (2.3) of the *Econometrica* article is generally within 0.5 on either side of unity (see pp. 875 and 926). Two special cases are given detailed study in this appendix. The first (pp. 929–40) corresponds to

$$\beta(\theta) = \frac{b\theta^{n-1}}{n-1!}\,e^{-\mu\theta} \qquad n \geqq 2,$$

the second (pp. 941–76) to

$$\beta(\theta) = \left[a + \frac{b}{n-1!}\,\theta^{n-1} \right]e^{-\mu\theta}.$$

The reader will find various points, in particular concerning the agreement of the model with observed data, treated in the report of the discussion which followed my remarks introducing the paper (pp. 979–1002).

c) Theorem I of the *Econometrica* article and its extensions as given in (1963B) are formulated as a single theorem in my 1964 paper.

Some readers of my (1963A) paper expressed doubt as to the possible existence of processes satisfying both the assumptions underlying Theorem I of the *Econometrica* article and its extensions. The (1966A) paper gives two models of such a process. In point of fact, there is an infinite number of such processes of advantageous growth.

d) My 1966 paper illustrates the general theory of the capitalistic optimum for a case which is very different from those envisaged in § 2.2 and § 2.3 of the *Econometrica* article. The model considered is structurally such that with

$\bar{P}$, X, and $\bar{C}$ representing, respectively, gross national product, labour, and real capital, the Cobb-Douglas relation

$$\bar{P} = X^\lambda C^\mu \qquad (\lambda + \mu = 1)$$

is rigourously verified. I then show that whereas $\bar{P}$ can grow indefinitely, the same is far from true for real national income, which has a maximum value for an interest rate of zero in a stationary process. This model is used to calculate the Cobb-Douglas coefficient μ from the rate of interest i, the capital output ratio $\gamma = C/R$, and the ratio of gross investment to gross national product $\alpha = I_B/P_B$.

This gives

$$\mu = \alpha e^{(1 - \alpha/\alpha)\gamma i}$$

and when calculated, μ is found as 0.36, a figure which is quite close to the average of 0.3 found by Douglas.

I show in this paper that in the general case, μ should be considered as equivalent to

$$\frac{I_B}{P_B} + i \frac{C}{P_B}$$

and not to

$$i \frac{C}{P_B},$$

as is stated by some authors such as Tinbergen and Colin Clark.

e) Finally, it may not be without value[3] to give some indications about some elements of recent extensions of the Theory of Capital for which I believe I can claim priority.

1) I believe that in 1943, in my *Treatise on Pure Economics*, I provided the first rigorous demonstration, using differential calculus, of the equivalence of situations of competitive equilibrium and situations of Paretian optimum *taking account of time* and of second-order conditions (pp. 604–82). This demonstration was the starting point of Debreu's 1959 work, *The Theory of Value*, in which the demonstration of this equivalence is based on the theory of sets.

2) I believe I was the first to give, in my book *Economie et Interet* (1947), a rigourous demonstration of the condition $i = \rho$ for the capitalistic optimum in an indefinite stationary process ($\rho = 0$).

This work underlies the subsequent research by Malinvaud, *"Capital Accumulation and Efficient Allocation of Resources" (*Econometrica*, 1953) and "Efficient Capital Accumulation" (*Econometrica*, 1962).

---

[3] See in particular, F. H. Hahn and R. C. O. Mathews, "The Theory of Economic Growth," *The Economic Journal*, Dec. 1964, pp. 780–902, especially pp. 816 and 877.

3) Credit for the condition $i = \rho$ in a dynamic optimum goes to Desrousseaux (1959) and (1961A). His demonstration, is based on use of the characteristic function $\phi(\theta)$ which I had defined for the most general case and used in my 1947 work.

Further, I believe that my December, 1961, lecture gives me priority in respect of the demonstration presented at that lecture and published in *Econometrica* in October, 1962. To my knowledge, all other demonstrations of the condition $i = \rho$ for the capitalistic optimum are subsequent thereto.

Contrary to what is thought by many authors, the condition $i = \rho$ is a necessary one whose demonstration in no way involves any condition of convexity whatsoever.

BIBLIOGRAPHY

ALLAIS, M. (1963A): "Some Analytical and Practical Aspects of the Theory of Capital," Conference on Activity Analysis, International Economic Association, Cambridge, England, July, 1963, 73 pages mimeographed.
This paper will shortly be published in the Conference Book.

ALLAIS, M. (1963B): "The Role of Capital in Economic Development," Study Week on the Role of Econometric Analysis in the Formulation of Development Plans, Oct. 7–13, 1963, Pontifical Academy of Sciences, Rome, Pontificiae Academiae Scientarum Scripta Varia, Civita Vaticana, 1965, pp. 697–1002.

ALLAIS, M. (1964: "A Theorem about the Optimum Allocation of Capital" (Mimeographed, 27 pages.) To be published shortly.

ALLAIS, M. (1966A): Models illustrating "A Theorem about the Optimum Allocation of Capital" (Mimeographed, 23 pages). To be published shortly.

ALLAIS, M. (1966B): "Real Gross National Product, Real National Income and the Cobb-Douglas Function," mimeographed, 60 pages. To be published shortly in the collective volume in honour of the late Professor Gini, Institute of Statistics, Rome.

Application of linear programming to investments in the electric power industry*†

PIERRE MASSÉ AND ROBERT GIBRAT

I

In France, the investment operations in basic industries, notably in the railroad, coal, electricity, and gas sectors, are submitted for approval of the government and the parliament.

The authors of these programs have thus to determine the most economical solution of problems and then to enlighten and persuade the authorities in charge of approving operations.

Towards the end of 1954 and the beginning of 1955, in the course of undertaking these tasks we found ourselves independently faced with remarkably similar problems.

One of us, who had worked on many studies on the economical management of resources, had to obtain official approval of the plan for a very important reservoir project in the French Alps (ROSELEND). This approval ran afoul of the objection that the cost of the investment in relation to the kilowatt hours producible in an average year was about three times higher for Roselend than for a hydroelectric plant without a reservoir. It is clear to the discerning that this difference in cost is accompanied by a difference in value—for the energy accumulated in the reservoirs can render much more service than can the fleeting energy of rivers. But this difference in value, due to the flexibility in exploitation of reservoirs, was insufficiently understood.

The other of us, who had devoted a good part of his life to the study of tidal power plants and had contributed to reducing their cost and to increasing

* *Management Science*, 3(1957): pp. 149–66. Addendum supplied by the authors. Reprinted by courtesy of the authors and *Management Science*.

† Received October 1956. Translated from the French by George B. Dantzig and edited by William W. Taylor.

Editor's note: The electric power industry in France is nationalized and operated by the "Electricité de France." Dr. Massé is the Executive Vice President. Dr. Gibrat is a private consultant.

their efficiency, sought to specify the place to be given in a national program to this characteristically new source of energy. The latter appeared endowed indeed with even more flexibility than river reservoirs, thanks to the combinations of cycles rendered possible by the ebb and flow of tides and by the utilization of a new technique of "bulbs—groups."[1]

The heart of the problem, in one case as well as the other, is that electrical investment serves to create not a unique product, the kilowatt hour, but a group of related products. The linear programming technique came to be introduced at the time in a wholly natural way in the investigations of the two authors. Indeed, they discovered one day, not without amusement, that, separately, they had come to the same conclusion; such a coincidence was not astonishing because what one planned for reservoir plants, the other had in mind for tidal plants. The details of this meeting of minds have served, as the theme for one of us in his inaugural address as the president of the "Société Française des Electriciens."[2]

II

Before starting the detailed exposition of the methods and results, we will indicate generally the lines which we have followed in our researches, considering the principal economic characteristics of the production of electricity.

A. Optimizing a given objective

It is known that optimizing problems can be viewed from two aspects:

1) Maximization of profit under assumed price factors (for production) and final products, but not the quantities to employ or to produce.

2) Minimization of cost under assumed price factors (for production) and assumed quantities to be produced but not the price of these products.

This second class coincides in principle with that adopted by Tjalling C. Koopmans in *Activity Analysis of Production and Allocation* ("The Best Allocation of Limited Means towards Desired Ends"). We ourselves have chosen it because it represents, in a more realistic manner than the first, the situation of a producer enjoying a quasi-monopoly for the sale of his services, and yet being on the other hand sufficiently small in proportion to the market for each factor required for production that unlimited quantities of each can be acquired at their corresponding given prices.[3]

These two points of view were discussed, as the point at issue in a meeting of one of us, with Mr. Allais,[4] who would have preferred to see, as the given point of departure, the price of products and not the quantities to be produced. It was replied to him that, in the context of the French economy, the given point

---

[1] Each turbine generates electricity during both the ebb and flow of the tide.

[2] R. Gibrat, "La joie de comprendre," *Bulletin de la Société Française des Electriciens,* March, 1956.

[3] P. Samuelson, Foundations of Economic Analysis, Chap. IV, p. 58.

[4] P. Massé, "Le problème des investissements à l'Electricité de France," *Nouvelle Revue d'Economie Contemporaine,* February, 1955.

of departure had been established by the requirements, but that once the solution had been found, we undertook a calculation of the break points in order to verify that the net return of the final solution would not call for a revision of the assigned requirements with regard, in particular, to the net price *arrived at* for joint products.

B. Elimination of uncertainty

In the matter of electric production, the uncertainty of the future affects at once the supply and the demand; it is necessary to take account of the joint variability of the consumption, of the water levels and of machine availability.

In the present study, as in those previously made at headquarters of the Electricité de France, the economy of uncertainty is converted into an economy of certainty by the use of safety margins over and above the probable values.

The designated demand requirement is 5 percent higher than the probable demand; it coincides with the highest quartile that would be estimated from the probability distribution of demand, according to the outline of the general goals of economic activity held by the planning commission.

The parameters representative of the production of an electric plant (which are, we shall see, its average power output for daylight hours during the middle of winter, its peak point, and its annual output) are less than their probable value. For example, the average daylight hourly output during the middle of winter of a hydroelectric plant is taken to be equal to its value at the time of a standard 1948–49 low water level estimated to happen only about three times in a century; for a steam generated electric plant it is taken at 85 percent of its net continuous output (the allowance of 15 percent is accounted for by the unavailability of material).

The probable value of the costs of investments is overestimated by a sum set up to cover the exceptional happenings.

The costs of operations, repeating themselves a great number of times, are estimated at their probable value.

C. Estimation of costs

The costs of investments considered are based on the evaluations of the " Services de Electricité de France." Similarly, the outlays for maintenance and operations conform to accepted norms.

The cost of combustibles can be treated by following a number of schemes:

The simplest scheme consists in placing in juxtaposition to the entirely new consumption C, the wholly new capacities of hydroelectric production H or steam generated production T (where C, H, T represent probable values). The probable steam generated-electric production is thus C-H, according to the conservation postulate (the dams have no overflow losses).

A scheme a little more complex consits in supposing that C is added to a pre-existent consumption and H and T are added to pre-existent production capacities. Thus the new steam plant capacity furnishes its full production T and the excess $T + H - C$ of the new product over the new consumption sets to restrict the use of older and consequently more obsolete electric groups.

This more complex scheme, moreover, can be extended in time. The 30-year life and occasionally secular duration of investments leads to the establishment of estimated operating accounts for a long period and the reducing the successive costs to a common measure by a present value calculation. During the long time span, the technical and economical data are called upon to vary under conditions which are supposedly known in advance, notably those that concern the prices, the specific consumption of combustibles and the characteristics of the steam plants. (It is this third scheme that is utilized by the Department of Equipment of Electricity of France.)

The important point is that, in all the studies made up to the present, including ours, the *linearity of costs* relative to the size of the plants and the *additivity of costs* for various plants are taken for granted even though this hypothesis is only rigorously exact in the case of infinitesimal changes in the amount of equipment or of homogenous thermal production.

D. Definition of joint products

Electricity is nonstockable—the kilowatt is a unit of energy but not an economic unit. The kilowatt hours from high water differs profoundly from kilowatt hours at the peak of winter. The producer fabricates and sells joint products which electricians call the load curve.

The question arises at this time of the choice of parameters to represent this load curve. The initial studies of the Department of Equipment, made in the period which followed the creation of the " Electricité de France " (1946), rested on the postulate which, stated a little boldly, is as follows: "A system with production convenient for the average daylight power needs of mid-winter (period of maximum consumption and minimum water levels for hydro-electric power[5]) will be superabundant from any other point of view." Otherwise stated, "With regard to service rendered, the load curve characteristic of the electricians can be represented by a unique parameter A."

Then, each hydroelectric plant with cost of investment D can be compared to a standard steam plant having the same average daylight power output in midwinter (called *guaranteed output*). One can thus calculate the increase in value, E, brought about by the substitution of the first for the second, and from this deduce its coefficient of value $V = 1 + E/D$.[6] If it were not for the limitation of total funds for investment, the programs would have been determined by taking plants in decreasing order of coefficients of value until the assigned objective A_0 for midwinter daylight power output was obtained. If, as was the case, there intervenes a limitation of total funds for authorized investment, D_0, one proceeds to a new classification of plants by a compromise between those which have the largest coefficients of value and those which carry the largest guaranteed output per franc invested.

---

[5] Because of the preponderant influence of plants in the Alps whose supply is reduced in winter by the cold.

[6] R. Giguet, "The Programming of Electric Equipment Considered from the Point of View of Applied Economics," *Economique Appliquée*, No. 1, 1951.

However, it was not long before a second criterion was imposed by the Electricité de France: *the peak output*. From that time on one hydroelectric plant became on longer substitutable in terms of equal service to a unique standard steam plant, but rather to a combination of a standard steam and a peak steam (since there must be as many elements in the characterizing combination as there are criteria in the definition of consumption).

It has thus come to us that this idea of extension could be pursued. Moreover, the possibility occurred to one of us one day that our system of production, at least theoretically, would become severely limited in summer if we fill reservoirs too much; that is to say, if we augmented too much our reserves for winter at the expense of our availabilities for summer. This concern leads to the introduction in the definition of consumption of a third criterion—for example, the annual energy. But there is no theoretical reason to limit to three the multiplication of requirements (for example, one fourth requirement can be a ceiling to the expense of investment)—from which arose the idea of a more general theory allowing *m* requirements.

It is well to see that this most general notion is contained implicitly in the preceding approaches: these consider only the limiting requirements, and admit only one differential modification of the system within existent freedom relative to other requirements. The equivalence of service rendered is evaluated relative to the limiting requirements. It is not affected by the variation within the freedom relative to the other requirements *so long as this margin of freedom exists*. But it is precisely this which one is not sure of beforehand when one works up a program which is far from being infinitesimal. (It is the essence of the objection mentioned earlier against reservoirs.)

A five-year plan which represents an increase of 40 percent in the capacity of a system is very far from being infinitesimal. The question arises of finding a guaranteed method for authors of a program which applies even when all surpluses disappear.

In this framework, it seems better to introduce at the start of the calculation *m* requirements attainable with or without a margin of freedom; doing this gives reliability to the results if the requirements have been well chosen. This new method of presentation calls for the *mathematics of inequalities* whose rapid development conveys the importance of the notions of thresholds and bottlenecks in a great number of economic processes. At the same time it is to our interests to modify our language somewhat and no longer speak of *equivalent solutions* in service rendered, but of admissible solutions relative to an objective (requirements) of *m* parameters. Among these admissible solutions, the optimal solution is that of least cost.

E. Hypothesis of groups of homogeneous plants

In order to go further, we have made for our purposes a bold hypothesis, which consists in simplifying the definition of the system of production and in supposing that the *m* requirements are to be met from *n* groups of homogeneous plants. The plants are classified into groups by distinguishing in a little vague but well-known way between plants with no reservoir, plants with a small reservoir (daily), plants with a large reservoir (seasonal), and finally tidal plants. We will criticize this hypothesis later on. Let us limit ourselves for the moment to showing its origin. Towards the end of 1954, it was held that the economical advantage of reservoir plants was at times doubtful. It was feared that they were lacking in energy in summer. It was also repeatedly said that, since we were poor in capital and were committed by this fact to making much use of steam power, we had to make the best of a bad situation, that is to say, to get all the energy we could from plants without reservoirs, whose net price per kilowatt hour was sensibly lower than that of plants with reservoirs, and to entrust their regularization to steam plants that we had been obliged to construct anyhow. This opinion was confuted by certain methods of the time, which gave to some reservoir plants a satisfactory coefficient of value. Between a vague reason and a precise calculation, there was no room for hesitation. Nevertheless, the method of coefficient of value, by its very compactness did not permit the better understanding of the underlying reason of things. It did not with sufficient clarity point up the error of considering the production of electricity from the viewpoint of only kilowatt hours and not from that of joint products. It is then from this aspect that it appears to us necessary to insist on using the technique of inequalities, that is to say, that of linear programming.

The desired purpose being to explain and to persuade, we must simplify. We would be willing to demonstrate that, if an unlimited quantity of "good" steam plants and "good" hydroelectric plants with no reservoir were possible to construct, it would nevertheless be necessary to reserve a place in our program of reservoir plants and also tidal plants. *A fortiori* must it be so if the hydroelectric plants with no reservoir become less and less good as their number increases.

III

The assumptions

At the end of 1954, the problem posed at Electricité de France consisted in determining a program of equipment performing the required service at the least cost—the requirements to be met at the end of five years were as follows:

A_0 (guaranteed power output) ......1692 MW
B_0 (peak power output)...........2307 MW
C_0 (annual power output).........7200 GWh

(1 MW = 1,000 kilowatts, 1 GWh = 1 million kilowatt hours). The ratios $B_0/A_0 = 1.36$ and $C_0 = 4.3$ are graphed on Figure 1 by the point Ω_2.

It is convenient to observe that the above requirements take into account any prior commitment for certain steam and hydroelectric plants with no reservoir. For the complete plan, the ratios B_0/A_0 and C_0/A_0 would have been 1.27 and 6.4, respectively, (Point Ω_1 of Figure 1.)

Figure 1

T = Steam plants
F = Hydroelectric with no reservoir
E = Hydroelectric with a small reservoir
R = Hydroelectric with a large reservoir
M = Tidal
Ω_1 = Consumption 1954
Ω_2 = Consumption of 2nd plan

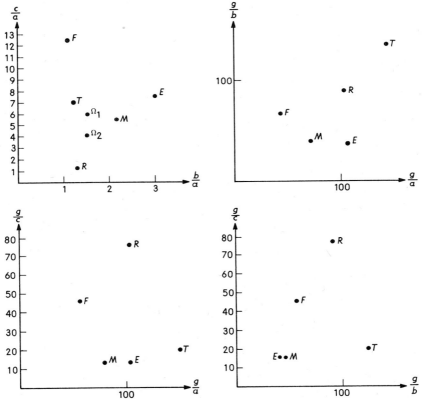

Furthermore, the authorized funds for investment had been fixed at $D_0 = 271$ Billions of Francs.

To meet these requirements, we presumed to have at our disposal five groups of homogeneous plants:

1—Steam plants (T)
2—Hydroelectric plants with no reservoir (F)
3—Hydroelectric plants with a large reservoir (R)
4—Hydroelectric plants with a small reservoir (E)
5—Tidal plants (M)

where letter in ( ) symbolizes the type.

The supplied quantities in each group will be designated by the letter x, the unit contributions to the requirements by the letters a, b, c, d, the costs of operation by the letter f, the total present value or discounted cost by the letter g, each letter having an index of the group considered.

One will find in Figure 1 the points T, F, R, E, M representing for each group the ratios for the systems of the coordinates

$$\left(\frac{b}{a}, \frac{c}{a}\right), \left(\frac{g}{a}, \frac{g}{b}\right), \left(\frac{g}{a}, \frac{g}{c}\right), \left(\frac{g}{b}, \frac{g}{c}\right).$$

The consideration of the ratios

$$\frac{b}{a}, \frac{c}{a}, \frac{d}{a}, \frac{d}{b}, \frac{d}{c}$$

makes evident, in an illuminating fashion, the diversity of the energy and economic properties of the five groups. Thus their classification by order of "merit" is very different depending on the criterion chosen.

Ranked by peak output per guaranteed output:

E, next M, then R, T, F nearly equivalent $\left(\frac{b}{a} \text{ varies from 3 to 1.15}\right)$.

Ranked by energy output per guaranteed output:

F, next E and T almost equivalent, M, then R $\left(\frac{c}{a} \text{ varies from 12.6 to 1.3}\right)$

Ranked by investment costs per guaranteed output:

T, R, M, E, F $\left(\frac{d}{a} \text{ varies from 97,000 to 420,000 fr/KW}\right)$.

Ranked by investment costs per peak power output:

T, M, E and R, F $\left(\frac{d}{b} \text{ varies from 84,500 to 381,000 fr/KW}\right)$.

Ranked by investment costs per annual energy output:

T, F, M, E, R $\left(\frac{d}{c} \text{ varies from 13.8 to 100 fr/KWh}\right)$.

The introduction of the present value of total costs (that is to say, of the capitalized costs of operations plus investment costs) again turns topsyturvy the ranking and one is not able to escape the study of the complete problem, however complicated it may appear at the outset.

According to our hypothesis the discounted total costs are a linear function of the size of different groups. This total cost consists of the initial costs of investment and the successive operating expenses converted to their present value. The method applies whatever be the law for computing the operating expenses and permits notably taking into account the improvements in efficiency of steam plants. However, in the interests of simplicity, we will limit ourselves here to the case of constant operating costs f, the total discounted cost corresponding to the unit size being then of the form

$$g = d + kf,$$

where k is a coefficient of capitalization.

Some observations on the calculation of expenses for combustibles are interesting. In the hypothesis of a plan departing from zero, the probable steam production is

$$C_0' - c_2' x_2 - c_3' x_3 - c_4' x_4 - c_5' x_5.$$

C_0' and the c_i' are probable values and are different from C_0 and the c_i defined earlier which are probable values with a safety margin. The cost of coal is proportional to the above expression.

In the case of a plan augmenting an older homogeneous production system the new steam facilities furnish $c_1' x_1$ and the reduction of the older steam production is

$$c_1' x_1 + c_2' x_2 + c_3' x_3 + c_4' x_4 + c_5' x_5 - C_0'.$$

Calling γ_0 the specific consumption of the older central steam plants and γ_1 that of the new, the cost of combustion is

$$-c_1' x_1 (\gamma_0 - \gamma_1) - \gamma_0 (c_2' x_2 + c_3' x_3 + c_4' x_4 + c_5' x_5) + C_0' \gamma_0.$$

One sees, thus, the expense of production includes a constant term, $C_0 \gamma_0$, and terms proportional to x_i with a negative coefficient (zero for x_1 if $\gamma_1 = \gamma_0$).

We give below the numerical values which we have utilized,[7] where we reduced to unity the guaranteed power output. It will be noticed that the economy of coal surpasses the costs of hydraulic plants for maintenance and operation ($f_i < 0$).

	a	b	c	d	f	g
Steam	1	1.15	7	97	+3.14	136
Hydroelectric—no reservoir	1	1.10	12.6	420	−29.10	56
Large Reservoir	1	1.20	1.3	130	−2.35	101
Small Reservoir	1	3.00	7.35	310	−16.5	104
Tidal	1	2.13	5.47	213	−10.7	79

[7] R. Gibrat, "Les plans de production d'énergie électrique et les usines marémotrices," *Flamme et Thermique*, March, 1956, No. 90.

R. Gibrat, "L'usine marémotrice de la Rance," *Revue Francaise de l'Energie*, April, 1956.

P. Massé, "Le problème des investissements à l'Electricité de France," *Nouvelle Revue d'Economie Contemporaine*, 1 February, 1955, No. 62.

Whence the following ratios used in setting up Figure 1:

	$\dfrac{d}{a}$	$\dfrac{d}{b}$	$\dfrac{d}{c}$	$\dfrac{g}{a}$	$\dfrac{g}{b}$	$\dfrac{g}{c}$
Steam	97	85.4	13.8	136	118	19.4
Hydroelectric—no reservoir	420	381	33.3	56	51	4.4
Large Reservoir	130	108	100	101	84	77.5
Small Reservoir	310	103	42.2	104	35	14.2
Tidal	213	100	38.9	79	37	14.4

(millions of francs per MW or GWh)

One should be sure to note that the assumed numbers correspond to November 1954 conditions and ought to be currently recalculated because of certain economic changes that have developed since then. The reader is thus requested to regard them only as an example.

With the rate of interest adopted by the Plan ($i = 8$ percent) the total costs of the plan, that is to say, the series of investments augmented by the capitalized value of the charges, are in the neighbourhood, when expressed in billions of francs, of

$$\sum g_i x_i + 270$$

Statement of the problem

We now precisely state the problem whose genesis and assumptions we have explained above.

a) Let there exist n groups of homogeneous plants in unlimited and continuous supply–steam plants, hydroelectric plants with no reservoir, a small reservoir, a large reservoir, tidal plants, atomic plants, etc. Associating with these plants the positive or zero quantities $(x_1, x_2, \cdots, x_n)$, one obtains by linear combinations the characteristic parameters of the system as a whole:

$$A = \sum_1^n a_i x_i, \qquad B = \sum_1^n b_i x_i, \qquad C = \sum_1^n c_i x_i,$$

$$D = \sum_1^n d_i x_i, \qquad F = \sum_1^n f_i x_i,$$

where a_i, b_i, c_i, d_i, f_i are *constants* characterizing each group of plants. The a, b, c are assumed to be positive unless otherwise indicated. It should be noted that the characteristic parameters of the system were equated above to a linear combination of the parameters of each group; *this is a postulate* whose truth should be verified in each problem (the case, for example, of a series of plants on the same river evidently merits such an examination).

b) We say that a solution $(x_1, x_2, \ldots, x_n)$, with all x positive or zero, is a feasible program if it meets the requirements A_0, B_0, C_0 exactly or in a surplus, that is to say, if

$$A \geq A_0, \qquad B \geq B_0, \qquad C \geq C_0.$$

Among the class of feasible solutions, the optimal solution will be defined by a condition of minimum cost, this cost being defined by a linear equation

$$G = D + kF$$

where

$$G = \sum g_i x_i \qquad \text{with} \qquad g_i = d_i + kf_i,$$

and where k, the coefficient of capitalization, fixes the weight given today to future expenses relative to investment expenses. This formula completes the linearization of our programming problem; but this condition of linearity of costs is less fundamental than the condition of linearity with respect to objectives, and it is true, as one knows, that rising prices can give rise to serious computational complications. The ideal formula would be $G(D, F_1, F_2, \ldots, F_i \ldots,)$, the problem remaining convex, but nonlinear. In a recent conference,[8] Ragnar Frisch has shown that one can resolve this problem by introducing gradient vectors for the cost function G and for the logarithmic potential $V = \sum \log x_i$.

In summary, our hypothesis renders our problem convex and linear; this defines the entire mathematical apparatus which we are going to use.

One is able to fix in advance other linear conditions, that is to say, to have other requirements. For example, a very interesting condition results from fixing the total investment costs at less than or equal to a given amount, $D \leq D_0$. Another interesting condition of similar type is brought about by a limitation on the size of one or several of the groups of plants, for example,

$$x_1 \leq x_1^0$$

It is known that one begins transforming the problem by introducing the surplus variables x_a, x_b, x_c, x_d corresponding to the requirements and by considering $(n + m + 1)$ vectors in total (here $m = 4$):

P_1	P_2	...	P_n	P_a	P_b	P_c	P_d	P_0
a_1	a_2	...	a_n	-1	0	0	0	A_0
b_1	b_2	...	b_n	0	-1	0	0	B_0
c_1	c_2	...	c_n	0	0	-1	0	C_0
d_1	d_2	...	d_n	0	0	0	$+1$	D_0

It is also known that the optimizing solutions involve, in general, r plant variables not zero and $m - r$ surplus variables not zero ($r \leq m$).

---

[8] Ragnar Frisch, "La résolution des problèmes de programme linéaire par la méthode du potentiel logarithmique," *C.N.R.S.*, Seminaire d'Econométrie, Séance du ler, June, 1955.

The application of the simplex method of George B. Dantzig, necessary to obtain rigorous results, is, in general, very long[9] in spite of its mechanical nature, and *it is important to be able to begin with as good an approximation as possible.* Whence the interest in a method which permits the problem to be reduced to the study of "two group structures" whatever be the parameters fixing the requirements and characterizing the plants. One of us has been able to demonstrate some very general results valid for four requirements, of which the limitation of funds D_0 varied from zero to infinity.[10] They permitted the construction of graphs which gave at a glance the optimum solution (if it exists) among the two group structures of plants for a definite value defining the limitation of authorized expenditures. Thus one combination of the two groups (hydroelectric plants with no reservoir + tidal, for example) would be strictly determined from two requirements; letting a, b, c, d denote those requirements, guarantee, peak, annual energy, or expenses, that the structure satisfies exactly, we have the six possible combinations of requirements bc, ca, ab, ad, bd, cd. In total the ten combinations of two groups furnish 60 distinct structures. We will take up their examination, being however very brief.[11]

The principle of the method is the following. A solution of the structure q, r, s, t is admissible if each of the determinants

$$\| P_0 \quad P_r \quad P_s \quad P_t \|;$$
$$\| P_q \quad P_0 \quad P_s \quad P_t \|;$$
$$\| P_q \quad P_r \quad P_0 \quad P_t \|;$$
$$\| P_q \quad P_r \quad P_s \quad P_0 \|;$$

has the same sign as the determinant $P = \| P_q, \ P_r, \ P_s, \ P_t \|$.

It is *optimum* if each of the determinants

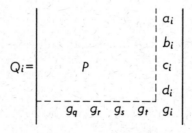

has the same sign as P.

---

[9] Translator's note: Undoubtedly the authors have in mind systems much larger than the 4-equation system considered here which could be solved with a desk calculator in under an hour.

[10] R. Gibrat, "Les plans de production d'énergie électrique et les usines marémotrices," *Flamme et Thermique*, No. 90, March, 1956.

[11] The same considerations have inspired, independent of us, Waugh and Burrows, whose article "A Short Cut to Linear Programming" (*Econometrica*, Jan., 1955), has recently come to our attention.

Figure 2

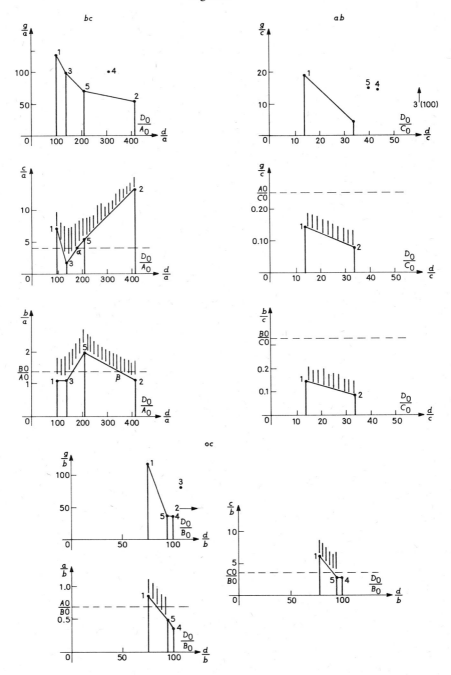

We take, for example, the structures with surpluses for b and c, with equality for expenses d and for guarantee a, and we plot three functions with (d/a) as abscissa and with g/a, b/a, c/a, respectively, as ordinates (Figure 2 on top and to the left).

Each group is characterized by a point on each of the three graphs. The application of the preceding conditions readily permits one to demonstrate that the structure comprising hydroelectric plants with no reservoir and tidal plants (points represented 2 and 5) will be optimal among all possible structures of the type bc if, in the graph g/a, the line (2,5) fulfills three conditions:

    1) It lies below all points representing other groups;

    2) Its ordinate relative to the origin is positive;

    3) Its slope is negative,

which is certainly the case in Figure 2.

Similarly, one demonstrates easily from the preceding conditions that some structures such as (2,5) will be admissible if the corresponding requirements are defined in the other two graphs by the point with abscissa D_0/A_0 and ordinates C_0/A_0, respectively, situated below the corresponding line (2,5) for the structure studies; it is this which defines the domain where the structure is admissible relative to the requirements and optimal relative to all possible structures of type bc.

Figure 2 (where are shown the values of the second plan B_0/A_0, C_0/A_0, D_0/A_0) shows that the only structures bc which can be optimal besides (2,5) are (1,3) and (3,5) because in the graph g/a the other segments such as (1,5) or (4,5) do not satisfy one of the conditions. On the other hand, (1,3) is not admissible for the second plan because B_0/A_0 is too high (graph b/a, d/a where the line of ordinate B_0/A_0 is above the line (1,3); structure (3,5) is admissible only for the ratios D_0/A_0 between 188.8 and 213 (points α and 5) because of C_0/A_0; (2,5) is admissible finally for D_0/A_0 between 213 and 367 (points 5 and β), this time because of the value B_0/A_0.

A point of interest regarding this method is that it permits at a glance the picking out of that structure which is probably optimum and fixes limits for the requirements for which it will remain feasible. The study of a new type (nuclear, for example) will be made immediately by the introduction of points which represent it in the graphs, and thus it is easy to see what values of the parameters (a, b, c, d) a new group should have in order to form part of a solution of a given structure type. The examination of the influence of variation of the energy parameters is also very easy; for example, the raising of the point 5 above the line 32 in the graph of g/a causes the disappearance of the corresponding group. (Tidal plants.)

Besides structures for two groups of the type bc, there exist analogous structures of type ca and ab. It is sufficient, in order to study them, to make a cyclic permutation of the letters a, b, c. One obtains thus the graphs ab and ac of Figure 2, whose interpretation is also easy.

Finally, the structures for three groups admits of a spatial representation which one can study in an analogous manner by descriptive geometry methods.

We shall not develop the detail of the study which can be found in a publication by one of us.[12]

Finally, when D_0 varies, one obtains the following succession of optimum structures:

Structure	D_0 (Billions)	Guaranteed Power (MW)				Total Discounted Cost (G + 270)	
		1	2	3	5	Billions	%
Impossible	0						
15 *ac*	195	2006	0	0	0	543	100
135 *c*	207	1324	0	0	368	479	88
135 *b*	227	635	0	726	331	456	84
35 *bc*	319	0	0	493	1199	415	76
25 *bc*	360	0	0	0	1692	404	74
25 *cd*	621	0	1259	0	433	375	69

Figure 3   Second plan at 8% rate of capitalization

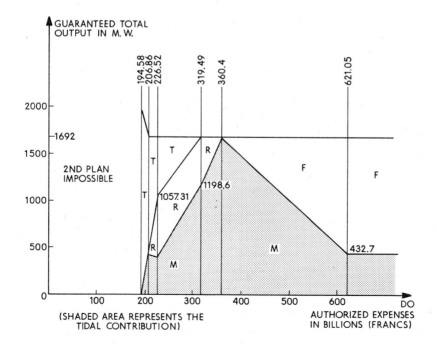

(SHADED AREA REPRESENTS THE TIDAL CONTRIBUTION)

AUTHORIZED EXPENSES IN BILLIONS (FRANCS)

[12] R. Gibrat, "Les plans de production d'énergie électrique de les usines marémortices," *Flamme et Thermique* No. 90, March, 1956.

Figure 3 shows how one can pass from one structure to another: first of all, the plan is impossible below 195 billion. If this sum is authorized, the solution is uniquely composed of steam plants and its selection is due to the peak load. After one passes this value, the tidal plants are introduced first only with steam plants, then with hydroelectric plants with a large reservoir. After the appearance of the latter ($D_0 = 207$), and for all the higher values of authorized expenses, the system becomes and remains exact for guaranteed output. The triple combination is, at the start, large in annual energy and exact in peak output; when D_0 exceeds 227, the combination becomes large in peak output and exact in annual energy. Moreover, from the start the importance of hydroelectric plants with large reservoirs is increased mainly at the expense of steam plants, but also a little at the expense of tidal plants. When the expenses reach 360, steam plants and hydroelectric plants with big reservoirs disappear, and there remain only the tidal plants. Above this expense, they yield progressively to hydroelectric plants with no reservoir. The tidal plants stabilize at 433 MW of guaranteed power output after the expenses pass 620 billions. The cost decreases when D_0 increases, passing from 543 to 375 between these two extremes. One will note in passing that for the expenses envisioned for the second plan ($D_0 = 271$ billions), the optimum is the combination 135 b. The favorable conclusion for large reservoirs, obtained by one of us in making abstractions about tidals,[13] is thus confirmed, even with the introduction of a supplementary groups.

IV

It is interesting to summarize in a few words the philosophy of the preceding study; for though it would be imprudent to place an absolute value on the numerical results stated throughout under the heading of an example, one can still regard with assurance the order of magnitude and the general tendencies that have been educed.

A first remark is that the admissible solution demanding the minimum expense of investment, the thermal, is heavier in total discounted costs than all which follow it in the table. *Poverty is costly.*

A second remarkable thing, which follows immediately from the first, is the interest to be able to formulate solutions which allow for different groups of plants. The French economy which is possessed of neither rich hydraulic resources, nor rich mine deposits like those of the United States or the Soviet Union, must remedy this relative poverty by the intelligent combination of all its resources. *One hope is variety.*

In the use of this variety there appears the phenomena of *decreasing returns.* An elementary calculation shows that the annual rent rate is in the neighbourhood of 50 percent for 12 billion of supplementary capital which permits the funds for investment to pass from the minimum of 195 billion to

---

[13] P. Massé, "Le probleme des investissements à l'Electricité de France," *Nouvelle Revue de l'Economie Contemporaine*, February, 1955.

207 billion; 20 billion in supplementary funds permits passage from 207 to 227 billion in investment and a return of 17 percent, 92 billion permits 11.5 percent return, the rate of annual rent falls after that to 10 percent and 9 percent. It is necessary to remark that above an imprecise threshold a little larger than 300 billion, the demand for power is not sufficient to balance the supply available from hydroelectric plants with no reservoir that have been built even if steam plants are shut down; hence the phenomena of loss of water over spillways appears; the steam plants and the reservoirs suffice no more to assure the adaptation of the production pattern to the consumption pattern. One concludes that above this threshold, the decrease of returns would be even more pronounced than the figures indicate.

The very important efficiency obtained at the start of the process corresponds to the fact that there are multiple techniques of production for fabricating joint products and that there exists, at the beginning, a bottleneck in the peak load with surplus annual power output and guarantee power output. The return from breaking this bottleneck, by profiting from the surpluses on the other products, is necessarily one of high annual rent (if there exists a technique, tidal or small reservoir, particularly adapted to fabricating peak output).

We note finally that the graph of G as a function of D_0 (Figure 4)is composed of break points corresponding to a discontinuity in the rent rate during the passage from one type of solution to the following. One other aspect of these sudden mutations is the fact that the optimal solution is indifferent to the choice of the rate of discount in the interior of certain intervals and undergoes a discontinuity at the extremities of the intervals. This phenomenon is accentuated by the hypothesis of groups of homogeneous plants. If each plant had its own peculiar characteristics and if besides one takes uncertainty into account in a detailed way, one would tend to more classic conclusions (i.e., continuous changes).

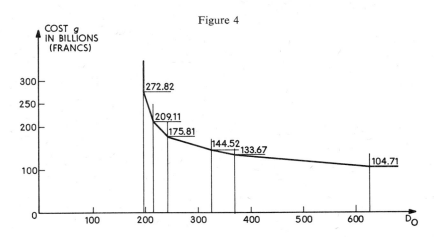

Figure 4

The preceding reflections show the richness of the linear programming method in a somewhat schematic application to investments in the production of electricity. It permits a very clear presentation of the problem of fabrication of joint products and makes understandable to nonspecialists considerations which, up to the present, have been accessible only (more or less completely) to experts. It has, thereby, a great value for education and persuasion.

Is it anything more? Does it constitute an innovation susceptible of replacing the methods of definition of an advantageous substitution and the method of composition of an optimal program, surviving to this today in the Electricité de France?

On the first point there is mainly a difference in perspective and language. We will consider here n plants of unknown size (≥ 0) and m requirements attained with unknown surpluses (≥ 0), that is to say, $m + n$ unknowns and m equations; so that, in general, taking some n independent unknowns, they ought to satisfy $m + n$ inequalities. In the n-dimensional space of these unknowns the admissible points are "on the positive side" of $m + n$ planes. Whence in the polyhedron of admissible solutions in which each vertex is the intersection of n planes, the optimum point is situated on the plane of least cost. Accordingly, let a vertex, S, be characterized by k surpluses zero and $n - k$ plants zero, that is to say, $m - k$ surpluses not zero and k plants not zero ($k \leq m$). We move along an edge (i.e., a one-dimensional variety) starting from S and chosen in such a manner that one deviates from the zero plane of a plant. One introduces by this displacement a supplementary plant which is equivalent relative to the requirements to a homogeneous linear combination of m plants and nonzero surpluses. In other terms, the new plant substitutes for a linear combination of older plants, the zero surplus remaining zero and the others remaining positive (at least as long as one is not too far away from S). The elementary operation[14] of our method is thus an admissible substitution relative to requirements (those satisfied exactly remain satisfied exactly), that is to say, in the former language, a substitution rendering equivalent service.

The uniqueness of this new point of view is not here however; it is in the hypothesis of homogenenous plants. Its strength is that it permits introduction without difficulty of a synthetic approach with general properties. That is also its weakness because it constitutes in certain cases a schematization which is realistically unacceptable. The hypothesis of plan groupings is approximately applicable for some plants in series on the Rhine or on the Rhone; it is not so for the majority of the hydraulic plants where each has an existence with its own peculiar physiognomy. It is in these, philosophically speaking, that its very profound uniqueness lies. It is this diversity of the sites which has for a long time made the equipment of waterfalls an art irreducible to the law

---

[14] Translator's note: There is undoubtedly a close relation between this elementary operation and an iteration of the simplex method which allows a new plant to substitute for a linear combination of other plants and the product surpluses.

of number and for the same reason has made it challenging. Apart from some notable exceptions, water power belongs to the realm of prototype selection rather than group selection.

The new method can, it is true, adapt itself to this situation by multiplying the number of groups and by adding in some inequalities limiting the amount of each of them.[15] It can thereby invoke an illusion of extreme precision in the definition of the energy parameters of the plants relative to the imprecision of others assumed in the calculation.

There is, however, another aspect less negative to which we would like to give consideration in terminating. It is that in France waterfall equipment has not attained its final state but is approaching it. Because of the paucity of energy, the rate of installation of new hydraulic equipment is probably going to be accelerated in the course of future years; nevertheless, one can foresee that, by 1975, it will no longer be able to occupy more than a minor part in our program because almost all the rivers will then be fully equipped. At that time the classic thermal, the gas turbine, the different categories of nuclear reactors, will have to re-enter the solution. From that time on, the linear programming, retaining its simplicity, would become more realistic. It will remain, however, in order to obtain a representation entirely adequate, to elaborate on the nonlinear cost functions, to make progress in the handling of uncertainty and finally to better insert the current (5 year) plan into those that follow or more precisely into the tree of future (5 year) plans.[16]

ADDENDUM

MARCH, 1968

This paper, published in 1957, reported on a study made about three years earlier. Since then, the application of mathematical programming to investment in the French electric power industry has been much developed. The main steps have been as follows.

In 1957, a linear programming model was solved, with about 70 constraints and 90 variables (slack variables left out). After new developments, the linear programming approach culminated in 1961 with the " Modèle des trois plans " (225 constraints and 255 variables). Its main differences from the program described in this paper concerned:

i) an extension in time (three five-year plans were considered, the horizon of the last one being 1975);

ii) a greater number of equipment (nuclear power, gas turbines ...);

iii) the operation of the plants, which was taken into account for optimization through so-called tactical variables;

---

[15] Translator's Note: Assuming data for individual hydroelectric plants (that might be constructed) is available, their injection into the model need not complicate the calculation very much when upper boundary techniques of linear programming are used.

[16] P. Massé, " L'optimum de l'entreprise dans un processus économique aléatoire," *Colloque d'Econometrie*, May, 1955.

iv) an extension of parametrization over several uncertain data (cost of nuclear power and of fuel);

v) the interpretation of dual variables as marginal costs or values.

The "modèle des trois plans" gave many useful results. That is why we wished to improve it further by introducing localization and transportation problems. It was then necessary to use nonlinear programming. But in turn this gave the possibility of new improvements, the main of which were:

i) taking into account the increasing cost of hydroelectric power plants;

ii) the computation of an expected cost of failures (instead of assuming that a *given* objective of production had to be matched).

Another advantage of nonlinear programming was that it made possible a more synthetic expression of the operation cost, with much fewer "tactical" variables. The result was that, at the first try (1963), the computation time was *lower* than for an equivalent linear model.

In 1965 we solved the "modèle investissements 85" (three five-year plans with horizon in 1985), with about 150 variables and 60 linear constraints. The cost function was made up of more than 200 terms; most of them were exponential functions, with a linear expression of the variables as an argument.

More recently we developed still larger programs with linear constraints, but with a cost function which is no longer convex, and so intricate that it can hardly be held in the fast memory of a CDC 6600 computer. The economic horizon of this model is about the end of the century.

In fact, rather than a method for solving the investment problem, this program is a synthetic model of Electricité de France used, mainly by parametrization, for testing the consistency of our main decisions (global and local investment problems; evolution of our costs, our tariffs, and of the principal difficulties which will be encountered in operating the future plants). Together with a new theory of "separability" for multilevel decisions, this model coordinates our main economic studies.